INDEX TO THE 1800 CENSUS
OF NEW YORK

INDEX TO THE
1800 CENSUS OF
NEW YORK

Compiled by
BARBRA KAY ARMSTRONG

CLEARFIELD

Reprinted for Clearfield Company, Inc.
by Genealogical Publishing Co., Inc.
Baltimore, Maryland
1996

FOREWORD

The information contained in this index was taken from microfilm copies of the Population Schedules of the Second Census of the United States (1800), rather than from the original documents. Head of household, county, and page number are indicated. Every effort has been made to reproduce names as written; however, many difficulties are encountered when working with handwriting. A small stroke of the pen changes a *T* to an *F*, an *l* to a *t*. An omission does the reverse. The letter *c* is seldom clearly written, making it indistinguishable from *i*, *e* or *r*.

All possible misinterpretations should be considered. Certain letters were so similar that it was impossible to be certain which was which. The letters *B*, *K*, and *R* were especially difficult to discern, as were *S* and *L*. *T*, *J*, and *I* were often identical in appearance. The letters *N*, *V*, and *P* also might be mistaken for one another. In some cases there was no way of knowing whether a letter was an initial or part of the surname. Therefore, *William Oliver Brian* may be found listed as *William OBrian*. *Peter Vincent Allen* may be found as *Peter V(an) Allen*. Blots, tears, folds, and unclear photography add to the problems of working with microfilm. Where a letter is missing it is indicated by a dot (.). Illegible letters are indicated by underlining (__). The number of dots or amount of underlining does not necessarily correspond to the number of missing or illegible letters.

Names were often spelled as they were heard; therefore, one will find *Warshburn* for *Washburn*, and *Goggswell* as well as *Coggswell*. Look for such "sound-alikes" as *Ph* and *F*, *Wr* and *R*, and *P* and *B*. Double letters and all vowels including *y* should be checked.

Occasionally a name may be found under two listings—*Joseph Young Cooper*, for example, where *Cooper* may refer to an occupation rather than the surname. Names which are totally illegible, or where there is an exceptionally great possibility of error due to missing first letters, partially visible letters, blurred photography, etc., are placed at the end of this index along with addenda that may be of help.

Machine stamped page numbers are used where available. In some counties, two, three, or even five handwritten numbers may be found on a page. Usually only one set of these numbers will continue through-out the entire microfilm roll, and these will be the ones applied. Care will be needed to find the appropriate numbering in these instances. Albany and Clinton Counties may be somewhat confusing as the tops of pages are numbered differently from the bottoms.

Many thanks are offered to my husband, Cedric, for his encouragement and support, and to my daughter Susan for help with alphabetizing.

BARBRA KAY ARMSTRONG

COUNTIES

NATIONAL ARCHIVES MICROPUBLICATION M32

Note
    Page 551 3/4 is list-
       ed as 551½

INDEX TO THE 1800 CENSUS OF NEW YORK

A

Name	Ref
A...e, E...	CAY 590
A__, Edward	ESS 310
A__, R	KNG 7
A....rson, Robert	MNT 4
A__, Daniel	TIO 251
Aaron, a free Negro	WST 118
Aaron, Harmen	NYK 67
Aaron, Jacob a Black	NYK 83
Ab..ett, John	MNT 84
Abail, Henry	WSH 241
Abail, Willeam	WSH 241
Abanathur, Anson	NYK 80
Abbatt, Robert	DUT 117
Abbe, Stephen	OTS 33
Abbery, William	GRN 338
Abbet, Caleb	ALB 73
Abbet, Ezra	SRA 57
Abbet, Matthias	QNS 80
Abbey, Aaron	ONT 332
Abbey, Amos	WSH 205
Abbey, David	ONT 506
Abbey, Ebenr	OTS 37
Abbey, John	OTS 8
Abbey, John	OTS 35
Abbey, John	WSH 205
Abbey, Joshua	ONT 332
Abbey, Lemuel	OTS 36
Abbey, Nathaniel	ULS 196
Abbey, Peter	DEL 281
Abbey, Samuel	ALB 30
Abbey, Shadrich	OTS 37
Abbey, William	ALB 28
Abbison, Cornelius	GRN 343
Abbison, Derrick	GRN 328
Abbison, Garret	GRN 348
Abbison, Garret	GRN 350
Abbison, Hannah	GRN 358
Abbison, John	GRN 328
Abbison, Peter	GRN 358
Ab_it, Abiel	MNT 83
Abbot, Aaron	HRK 501
Abbot, Aaron Senr	HRK 507
Abbot, Abel	COL 208
Abbot, Abel Junr	COL 208
Abbot, Adnah	WSH 189
Abbot, Anna	COL 207
Abbot, Asa	ALB 64
Abbot, Benjamin	COL 206
Abbot, Danforth	HRK 507
Abbot, Daniel	COL 206
Abbot, Joseph	ALB 74
Abbot, Nathan	OND 173
Abbot, Peter	ONN 138
Abbot, Samuel	HRK 412
Abbot, Samuel	SCH 151
Abbot, Sewall	HRK 478
Abbot, Stephen	OTS 48
Abbot, Thoda	COL 207
Abbot, William	COL 207
Abbot, William	HRK 412
Abbott, Charles	COL 184
Abbott, Danl	OTS 53
Abbott, David	OTS 23
Abbott, Ebenezer	ALB 115
Abbott, James	SUF 81
Abbott, John	CAY 678
Abbott, John	OTS 53
Abbott, John Jas	ALB 149
Abbott, Samuel	WSH 293
Abbott, Stephen	COL 202
Abbott, Timothy	SUF 88
Abbott, Wareham	COL 215
Abbott, William	OND 199
Abbott, William	OTS 9
Abby, Benj	RNS 111

Name	Ref
Abby, Daniel	CHN 874
Abby, Richard	CHN 936
Abby, Prince	CAY 688
Abeel, David	GRN 327
Abeel, Garret, B.	NYK 74
Abeel, John N.	NYK 36
Abel, Anateu	ALB 46
Abel, Azell	ESS 311
Abel, Caleb	TIO 229
Abel, Cornelius	SRA 48
Abel, David	SRA 41
Abel, David	WSH 271
Abel, Joseph	DEL 281
Abel, Seth	OTS 25
Abel, Zacheus	OND 217
Abelman, Christian	ALB 108
Aber, Abner	ORN 326
Aber, Hiram	ORN 326
Aber, Jonas	ORN 326
Aber, Mahlon	ORN 327
Abernethey, Elizabeth	NYK 104
Abertus, William	NYK 96
Abery, John	NYK 135
Abett, Squire	CHN 886
Abiel, William	DUT 149
Abigan, Faulaw	GRN 342
Abil, Jeremiah	SRA 44
Abitt, Joseph	RNS 50
Able, Jabez	CHN 934
Able, John	ALB 83
Able, William	DUT 11
Ablin, John	NYK 38
Ablos, Bruster	SRA 26
A.ott, Esek(iel?)	MNT 47
Abott, Stephen	SUF 93
Abm a Negro of W. Sha	
ier of Schoharie	ALB 90
Abraham	QNS 83
Abm a Negro	SUF 67
Abraham, Andrew	COL 262
Abraham, Hyman	NYK 24
Abraham, Joseph	QNS 72
Abraham, Oothout	MNT 81
Abrahams, Benajah	COL 246
Abrahams, Benjamin	ALB 42
Abrahams, Benjamin	QNS 76
Abrahams, Charles	QNS 72
Abrahams, Charles	QNS 73
Abrahams, Daniel	QNS 73
Abrahams, Edward	QNS 73
Abrahams, Elijah	QNS 73
Abrahams, Henry	QNS 72
Abrahams, Henry	QNS 73
Abrahams, Henry	ULS 259
Abrahams, Isaac	NYK 39
Abrahams, Isaac	NYK 71
Abrahams, Jacob	QNS 75
Abrahams, James	QNS 73
Abrahams, Jean	NYK 19
Abrahams, John	NYK 129
Abrahams, John	QNS 73
Abrahams, John	QNS 73
Abrahams, Jonas	QNS 73
Abrahams, Jonas	QNS 73
Abrahams, Joseph	QNS 73
Abrahams, Josiah	QNS 73
Abrahams, Richard	QNS 73
Abrahams, Samuel	QNS 73
Abrahams, Sarah	QNS 73
Abrahams, Silas	RCH 90
Abrahams, Thomas	QNS 73
Abrahams, Thomas	QNS 76
Abrahams, Timothy	QNS 73
Abrahams, Walter	QNS 73
Abrahams, William	QNS 73
Abrams, Azariah	RNS 84
Abrams, Christian	ALB 55

Name	Ref
Abrams, James	ONN 191
Abrams, Jesse	DUT 78
Abrams, Jesse	RNS 84
Abrams, John	DUT 78
Abrams, John	ORN 277
Abramse, Anne	WST 149
Abrason, Andrew	RCK 109
Abroil, Thomas	NYK 82
Abule, John	NYK 122
Abule, John Jun.	NYK 122
Ac_key, Elihu	MNT 43
Acerly, William	WST 113
Acher, Jacob Junr	WST 165
Acherley, Mary	NYK 115
Acherly, Jeremiah	NYK 116
Acherman, Abraham	MNT 89
Ackeler, Jacob	MNT 29
Ackeley, Learad	MNT 29
Ackens, William	NYK 132
Acker, Abraham	WST 162
Acker, Abraham	WST 165
Acker, Abraham Junr	WST 162
Acker, Benjamin	WST 165
Acker, Dirck	RCK 97
Acker, Dirck	RCK 105
Acker, George	MNT 30
Acker, Gilbert	WST 165
Acker, Isaac	WST 162
Acker, Isaac	WST 162
Acker, Jacob	NYK 100
Acker, Jacob	WST 162
Acker, Jacob	WST 165
Acker, John	ALB 65
Acker, John	COL 189
Acker, John	GRN 347
Acker, John	MNT 30
Acker, John	WSH 219
Acker, John	WST 165
Acker, Mary	WST 162
Acker, Peter	COL 260
Acker, Peter	RNS 33
Acker, Peter	WST 162
Acker, Peter	WST 165
Acker, Phillip	WST 165
Acker, Sebert	WST 165
Acker, Sibert	WST 162
Acker, Stephen	WST 165
Acker, William	NYK 100
Ackerley, Abel	SUF 85
Ackerley, Augustus	SUF 85
Ackerley, David	NYK 87
Ackerley, Nathaniel	SUF 85
Ackerley, Samuel	DUT 19
Ackerley, Samuel	SUF 85
Ackerly, Jeremiah	GRN 354
Ackerly, Jonathan	NYK 125
Ackerly, Nathaniel	ULS 210
Ackerly, Precella	NYK 136
Ackerly, Robert	ULS 210
Ackerly, Samuel	GRN 348
Ackerly, Samuel	GRN 353
Ackerly, Thomas	SUF 90
Ackerman, David	NYK 123
Ackerman, David	WST 130
Ackerman, Gilbert	ALB 125
Ackerman, Henry	NYK 105
Ackerman, Isaac	NYK 152
Ackerman, John	NYK 72
Ackerman, John	NYK 107
Ackerman, John	NYK 151
Ackerman, John D.	NYK 98
Ackerman, John P.	NYK 99
Ackerman, Morris	NYK 60
Ackerman, Peter	NYK 68
Ackerman, Samuel	NYK 142
Ackerman, William	SRA 38
Ackermon, John	NYK 93

1

Name	Ref	Name	Ref	Name	Ref
Adams, Nathan	WST 156	Adee, Daniel	WST 130	Agnes, Andrw	NYK 101
Adams, Nathan Junr	WST 156	Adee, David	NYK 35	Agnes, Henry	MNT 122
Adams, Nathaniel	CAY 716	Adee, John	ULS 252	Agnes, Jabey	MNT 122
Adams, Nathaniel	RNS 93	Adee, John	WST 131	Agnes, John	MNT 61
Adams, Noah	OTS 10	Adee, Samuel	DEL 270	Agnew, John	NYK 82
Adams, Noah	OTS 11	Adee, William	WST 131	Agnew, Wm	RNS 60
Adams, Noah	RNS 54	Ademe, Peter	MNT 26	Agnis, Sylvanus	MNT 102
Adams, Oliver	ONT 400	Aderson, Jane	NYK 97	Agur, David	SRA 53
Adams, Oliver	SRA 26	Adgar, James	NYK 69	Aiken, Alwood	OTS 53
Adams, Oliver	SRA 52	Adgate, Asa	ESS 307	Aiken, Thos	OTS 36
Adams, Park	HRK 590	Adgate, Delight	ESS 307	Aikerly, John	SUF 66
Adams, Parker	HRK 442	Adgate, Mathew	COL 210	Aikerly, John	SUF 66
Adams, Pelatiah	SCH 127	Adgate, Thomas	ULS 184	Aikins, John	OTS 22
Adams, Permeno	ONN 158	Adget, Elijah	RNS 14	Aikley, Benagah	SUF 66
Adams, Permeno Jur	ONN 158	Adget, John	RNS 106	Aikly, Elijah	SUF 67
Adams, Pinne	WSH 287	Adi ..., Phineas	MNT 101	Aikman, John	NYK 78
Adams, Reuben	DEL 270	Adie, Daniel	WST 113	Aillent, John	MNT 75
Adams, Reuben	ONT 342	Adie, Hobbe	WST 113	Ailsworth, Andrew	RNS 25
Adams, Richard	RNS 32	Adie, William	WST 114	Ailsworth, George	RNS 104
Adams, Robert	WST 132	Adjet, Nabby	OTS 41	Ailsworth, Gideon	RNS 12
Adams, Roderick	ONN 152	Adjet, Noah	OTS 41	Ailsworth, John	RNS 98
Adams, Samuel	CAY 612	Adjudant, Andrew	MNT 54	Ailsworth, Richard	RNS 104
Adams, Samuel	DEL 269	Adkins, Azor	SRA 19	Ailsworth, Rufus	RNS 73
Adams, Samuel	NYK 30	Adkins, Darius	DUT 170	Ailsworth, Rufus	RNS 76
Adams, Samuel	OND 163	Adkins, David	ULS 185	Ailsworth, Thos	RNS 25
Adams, Saml	OTS 36	Adkins, David	ULS 204	Aim, Abigail	NYK 84
Adams, Samuel	SRA 50	Adkins, Elacy	OND 173	Aimes, Benjamin	ONT 424
Adams, Samuel	ULS 267	Adkins, Richard	SRA 16	Aimes, David	ONT 426
Adams, Samuel	WST 132	Adkins, Thos	OTS 57	Aimes, Dorethy	NYK 89
Adams, Sarah	WSH 217	Adkins, Willm	OTS 57	Aimly, John	SCH 135
Adams, Seymour	DEL 268	Adkins, William	SRA 13	Aims, Whitcomb P.	RNS 18
Adams, Shubal	RNS 112	Adle, John	MNT 52	Aims, William	NYK 129
Adams, Silas	RNS 103	Adle, Joseph	MNT 52	Aimy. Thomas	SCH 160
Adams, Silas	SRA 19	Adnis, Elijah	OND 173	Aimy, Thomas	SCH 161
Adams, Simon	ALB 30	Adriance, Abraham	DUT 22	Ainsley, Joseph	CAY 586
Adams, Simon	COL 222	Adriance, Diana	DUT 22	Ainsley, William	ONT 500
Adams, Stephen	DEL 269	Adriance, Elbert	QNS 65	Ainslie, Robert	NYK 112
Adams, Stephen	DUT 52	Adriance, Garret	DUT 116	Ainsworth, Elihu	OND 183
Adams, Stephen	OND 205	Adriance, George	COL 181	Ainsworth, Nehemiah	OND 183
Adams, Thomas	DUT 139	Adriance, George	RNS 10	Ainsworth, Tracy	HRK 531
Adams, Thomas	NYK 109	Adriance, George C.	RNS 90	Aires, Elihu	NYK 152
Adams, Thomas	RNS 32	Adriance, Isaac	DUT 22	Aires, William	SUF 90
Adams, Timothy	MNT 37	Adriance, Rem	DUT 22	Airs, Camp	NYK 92
Adams, Uriah	DEL 282	Adriance, Samuel P.	NYK 29	Airs, Catherine	NYK 121
Adams, William	DUT 113	Adriance, Theodorus	COL 215	Airs, Eliakim	DEL 283
Adams, Wm	GRN 354	Adriance, Theodorus	DUT 19	Airs, Nathaniel	CLN 168
Adams, Wm	MNT 50	Adsate, Wallcut	SRA 61	Airs, Obediah	STB 205
Adams, William	NYK 48	Adsdell, Jacob	ESS 305	Airs, Peter	RNS 22
Adams, William	NYK 59	Adsdell, Joseph	ESS 305	Airs, Reuben	NYK 87
Adams, William	NYK 90	Adsdell, Phebee	ESS 305	Airs, Sarah	NYK 81
Adams, William	NYK 119	Adserlon, Roger	CHN 746	Aitken, George	QNS 83
Adams, William	ONN 162	Adset, Elisha	COL 189	Aivre, Umphree	SUF 64
Adams, William	ONT 406	Adset, Martin	COL 189	Ajudant, Bradford	STB 200
Adams, William	ORN 286	Adset, Roger	COL 205	Ake, Peter H.	CHN 942
Adams, William	ORN 370	Adsett, Stephen	COL 202	Akeley, Abijah	QNS 77
Adams, Wm	OTS 33	Adsit, Elias	DUT 127	Akeley, Amos	CHN 986
Adams, William	OTS 48	Adsit, Jesse	DUT 127	Akeley, James	QNS 77
Adams, William	RNS 89	Adsit, Joel	DUT 125	Akely, William	QNS 76
Adams, William	SRA 36	Adsit, Joseph	HRK 585	Akens, Anonias	SRA 43
Adams, William	SRA 36	Adsit, Mary	DUT 129	Akens, John	CHN 764
Adams, William	SCH 136	Adsit, Samuel	DUT 127	Akens, John Junr	CHN 764
Adams, William	WSH 192	Adue, Stephen	RNS 56	Aker, Abraham	MNT 77
Adams, William	WST 165	Aellyies, Michael	NYK 56	Aker, Abm	SCH 167
Adams, Zadock	OTS 52	Affery, Nancy	WST 114	Aker, Conrod	SCH 167
Adamy, John	SCH 166	Agar, William	NYK 39	Aker, George	MNT 124
Adancourt, William	RNS 84	Agard, Amos	WSH 213	Aker, John	MNT 38
Adcock, Joseph	RNS 53	Agard, Caleb	ESS 322	Aker, Peter	MNT 125
Addair, James	ALB 9	Agard, John	ESS 323	Aker, Thos	SCH 167
Addams, Ichabod	MNT 62	Agard, Joseph	CHN 740	Aker, William	SCH 117
Addams, Jesse	WST 118	Agate, Thomas	WST 165	Akerley, Gilbert	WST 129
Addams, Peter C.	GRN 358	Aged, Peter	SCH 132	Akerly, Annanias	DEL 272
Addison, John	NYK 32	Ager, Charles	GRN 354	Akerly, Benjamin	DEL 271
Addison, William	DUT 152	Ager, John	GRN 354	Akerly, Benjamin	WST 128
Addleton, James	TIO 230	Aggud, James	RNS 33	Akerly, Benjamin	WST 131
Addoms, John	CLN 160	Agin, James	RNS 88	Akerly, Benjamin Junr	DEL 271
Addriance, Benjamin	NYK 120	Agin, Patrick	RNS 88	Akerly, Felix	WST 128
Addy, Anthony	NYK 101	Agnell, Hynecth	NYK 37	Akerly, Felix	WST 131

Name	Co.	Pg.
Akerly, Gilbert	WST	128
Akerly, Isaac	SUF	66
Akerly, Jacob	DEL	267
Akerly, John	DEL	271
Akerly, Joseph	WST	159
Akerly, Obadiah	WST	135
Akerly, William	DEL	271
Akerly, William	DEL	273
Akerman, Andrew	ORN	373
Akerman, Jacob	ULS	255
Akerman, James	DUT	41
Akerman, John	DUT	38
Akerman, Samuel	WST	127
Akin, Abraham	ESS	304
Akin, Benaiah	DUT	50
Akin, Benjamin	DUT	51
Akin , Benjamin	DUT	104
Akin, Benjamin	RNS	48
Akin, Daniel	DUT	171
Akin, Isaac	DUT	52
Akin, Jacob	DUT	100
Akin, James	MNT	65
Akin, James Junr	DUT	51
Akin, James Senr	DUT	50
Akin, John G.	DUT	52
Akin, Jonathan	DUT	53
Akin, Joseph	RNS	48
Akin, Murray	DUT	51
Akin, Nanin	RNS	62
Akin, Peter	DUT	53
Akin, Timothy	DUT	51
Akin, William	DUT	53
Akin, William	RNS	48
Akins, Atwood	OND	191
Akins, Benjn	RNS	42
Akins, David	SRA	58
Akins, Edward	WSH	186
Akins, Gideon	WST	149
Akins, James	COL	202
Akins, John	RNS	41
Akins, Joseph H.	NYK	54
Akins, Justice	RNS	77
Akins, Lathen	WSH	185
Akins, Tartus	RNS	27
Akins, Tracy	WSH	185
Akley, Ely	CHN	864
Aksoyder, Samuel	SCH	140
Alabragh, Frederick	ALB	101
Alabragh, Jacob	ALB	101
Alba, James	RNS	6
Albat, Fredk	OTS	42
Albbet, Noah	SRA	28
Albee, Salathiel	OND	210
Alben, Jeremiah	SUF	68
Albert, David	OND	169
Albert, Willard	CHN	926
Albertson, Albert	NYK	148
Albertson, Daniel	QNS	83
Albertson, Josiah	SUF	96
Albertson, Richard	QNS	70
Albertson, Richd	SUF	71
Albertson, Samuel	NYK	148
Albertson, Stephen	ONT	502
Albertson, Wm	SUF	76
Albreadth, Henry	SCH	166
Albright, Francis	CAY	528
Albro, Benjamin	DUT	13
Albro, James	WSH	211
Albro, Samuel	DUT	10
Albro, Samuel Junr	DUT	59
Albrough, Stephen	ONT	450
Albrow, Andrew	WSH	289
Albrow, Job	WSH	289
Albrow, Lathom	SRA	52
Albrow, Latin	SRA	52
Albrow, Oliver	WSH	270
Albrow, Samuel	WSH	295
Albrow, Spencer	WSH	270
Albrow, William	SRA	34
Albut, Charles	OTS	15
Albut, Fredk	OTS	40
Albut, Henry	OTS	40
Alby, Eleazar	CAY	718
Alby, John	CAY	698
Alcock, David	GRN	331
Alcut, Araspus	WSH	187
Alcut, Havey	WSH	191
Alcut, Jacob	WSH	187
Alcut, John	WSH	183
Alcut, John	WSH	191
Alcut, Oliver	WSH	191
Alcut, Thornton	WSH	187
Alden, Andrew	TIO	237
Alden, Caleb	NYK	35
Alden, Daniel	TIO	237
Alden, Enoch	TIO	231
Alden, Isaac	OND	210
Alden, John	OND	167
Alden, Mary	ESS	308
Alden, Peggy	RNS	82
Alden, Prince	TIO	235
Alden, Seth	WSH	217
Alden, Wm M.	OTS	17
Aldenburgh, William	MNT	16
Alder, Benjamin	WSH	252
Alderman, Jonathan	ULS	184
Aldilege, Timothy	CHN	764
Aldredge, Chad	ONT	354
Aldrich, Jason	SUF	72
Aldrich, Sten Sen	SUF	72
Aldridge	RNS	41
Aldridge, Ahaz	ONT	354
Aldridge, Anthony	DUT	51
Aldridge, Benjamin	CHN	784
Aldridge, Brice	ONT	352
Aldridge, Caleb	SCH	170
Aldridge, Carmel	ULS	184
Aldridge, Daniel a Black	NYK	122
Aldridge, Daniel	ORN	273
Aldrodge, David	SCH	160
Aldridge, Eisha	SCH	170
Aldridge, Ezra	SCH	170
Aldridge, Gilbert	ONT	474
Aldridge, Jacob	HRK	408
Aldridge, James	ONT	500
Aldridge, Jethro	OND	171
Aldridge, Jonathan	ONT	328
Aldridge, Jonathan	WSH	219
Aldridge, Joseph	CHN	980
Aldridge, Leonard	ONT	342
Aldridge, Marey	ONT	458
Aldridge, Nathan	ONT	440
Aldridge, Nicholas	HRK	408
Aldridge, Peter Junr	ULS	217
Aldridge, Peter Senr	ULS	245
Aldridge, Peter W.	OND	210
Aldridge, Robert	ULS	184
Aldridge, Royal	QNS	80
Aldridge, Silas	ORN	392
Aldridge, Simeon	DUT	51
Aldridge, Solomon	DUT	49
Aldridge, Stephen	ONT	438
Aldridge, Thomas	OND	193
Aldridge, Thomas	ORN	273
Aldridge, Thos	SUF	68
Aldridge, Turner	ONT	438
Aldridge, Zadock	SUF	95
Aldridge, Zufus	CHN	874
Aldrige, Duty	SRA	5
Aldruff, Abraham	SRA	52
Aldworth, Sarah	NYK	36
Aleby, Joseph	COL	213
Alen, George	SRA	52
Alexander, Alexander	ALB	54
Alexander, Alexander	MNT	55
Alexander, Alexander	MNT	92
Alexander, Andrew	NYK	58
Alexander, Andrew	NYK	72
Alexander, Benjamin	RNS	40
Alexander, Cathrine	WSH	227
Alexander, George	SRA	24
Alexander, Gilbert	RNS	88
Alexander, Hugh	SRA	29
Alexander, James	ALB	96
Alexander, James	CAT	530
Alexander, James	ORN	277
Alexander, James	WSH	225
Alexander, James	WSH	254
Alexander, John	ALB	135
Alexander, John	ALB	140
Ale..nder, John	CAY	530
Alexander, John	CNN	140
Alexander, John mulatto	NYK	37
Alexander, John	SRA	29
Alexander, Joseph	SCH	152
Alexander, Joseph	SCH	157
Alexander, Joseph	WSH	228
Alexander, M ray	MNT	90
Alexander, Mary	NYK	138
Alexander, Robt	ALB	96
Alexander, Robert	CAY	594
Alexander, Robert	NYK	26
Alexander, Robert Junr	CAY	594
Alexander, Samuel	TIO	222
Alexander, Simon	TIO	222
Alexander, Thomas a mulatto	NYK	132
Alexander, William	HRK	452
Ale_ander, Wm	MNT	54
Alexander, William	NYK	91
Alexander, William	CNN	141
Alexander, William	ULS	250
Aley, John Battis,Black	NYK	133
Alford, Alexander	ESS	303
Alford, Asahel	HRK	481
Alford, Benedict	ESS	303
Alford, Elijah	HRK	482
Alford, Elisha	SRA	19
Alford, George	CAY	702
Alford, George	MNT	39
Algar, Abner	OTS	11
Algelt, Adam	DUT	22
Algeo, William	KNG	2
Alger, Asa	COL	177
Alger, Benajah	OTS	11
Alger, Charles	OTS	11
Alger, Ezra	COL	210
Alger, John	WSH	213
Alger, John	WSH	221
Alger, Jonathan	DUT	147
Alger, Josiah	DUT	148
Alger, Josiah	OTS	11
Alger, Mary	OTS	11
Alger, Samuel	CAY	686
Alger, Seth	DUT	7
Alger, William	OTS	11
Alger, Zebulon	SRA	42
Algie, Rosanna	NYK	57
Algor, John	ONT	392
Algor, Serrel	CHN	928
Algur, Oliver	CHN	928
Alhaer, Peter 2d	RNS	58
Alken, James	SRA	56
Alkenbrack, Adam	COL	244
Alkenbreck, Jacob	COL	245
Alkinbragh, Danl	ALB	108
All, Adam	NYK	113
All, John	NYK	127
Allaby, David	WST	160
Allair, Seaser	WST	162

Allaire, Peter	WST 121	
Allaire, Peter Alexand-		
er	NYK 36	
Allare, Nylendale	WST 162	
Allbright, Jacob F.	ORN 394	
A.lbright, John	ONN 181	
Allbro, Isaac	ALB 70	
Allcock, Asa	SRA 16	
Allcocks, Joseph	SRA 16	
Allden, James	NYK 134	
Alldridge, Catharine	NYK 132	
Alldridge, Samuel	NYK 146	
Allebey, John	SUF 68	
Allebey, Ebenezor	SUF 64	
Alleby, Samuel	SUF 81	
Alleby, William	SUF 81	
Alleger, John	ULS 217	
Alleger, Matthew	ULS 217	
Allein, Laurence	NYK 133	
Allemand, Peter	NYK 34	
Allen, Abia	WSH 303	
Allen, Abiel	DEL 276	
Allen, Abner	SRA 31	
Allen, Abraham	NYK 135	
Allen, Abrm	OTS 8	
Allen, Adam	RNS 40	
Allen, Alexander	DUT 57	
Allen, Alexander	RNS 61	
Allen, Alexander	RNS 68	
Allen, Alexander Junr	DUT 56	
Allen, Amasa	HRK 505	
Allen, Archi....	MNT 77	
Allen, Arden	SRA 30	
Allen, Aron	OND 223	
Allen, Artemas	OND 165	
Allen, Asa	DUT 130	
Allen, Asa	OTS 51	
Allen, Asa	OTS 53	
Allen, Asa	RNS112B	
Allen, Asahel	OTS 35	
Allen, Augustus	COL 205	
Allen, Barnabas	OTS 58	
Allen, Bartholomew	DUT 117	
Allen, Bela	OND 168	
Allen, Benjamin	COL 181	
Allen, Benjamin	COL 248	
Allen, Benjamin	OND 166	
Allen, Benjn	OTS 47	
Allen, Benjamin	OTS 58	
Allen, Benjamin	SRA 31	
Allen, Benjamin	SUF 99	
Allen, Benjn	OTS 47	
Allen, Bial	WSH 185	
Allen, Bodway	COL 211	
Allen, Caleb	WSH 233	
Allen, Charles	DEL 283	
Allen, Charles	DUT 56	
Allen, Charles	OND 195	
Allen, Chauncey	ONT 416	
Allen, Christopher	WSH 185	
Allen, Clark	GRN 353	
Allen, Clark	WSH 267	
Allen, Clother	MNT 110	
Allen, Comfort	OTS 35	
Allen, Comfort Junr	OTS 35	
Allen, Cyrenus	OND 169	
Allen, Dan	ESS 308	
Allen, Daniel	MNT 59	
Allen, Daniel	NYK 94	
Allen, Daniel	OND 165	
Allen, Daniel	OND 184	
Allen, Daniel	ONN 144	
Allen, Daniel	ONN 164	
Allen, Daniel	SRA 26	
Allen, Daniel	SRA 35	
Allen, Daniel	WSH 269	
Allen, Darius	QNS 78	
Allen, David	ALB 101	
Allen, David	OND 173	
Allen, David	ORN 330	
Allen, David	ORN 371	
Allen, David	QNS 70	
Allen, David	RNS 92	
Allen, David	WSH 200	
Allen, David	WSH 215	
Allen, David	WSH 237	
Allen, Dobsin	QNS 65	
Allen, Eastd	OTS 28	
Allen, Ebenezar	CAY 634	
Allen, Ebenezer	ALB 94	
Allen, Ebenezer	DUT 100	
Allen, Ebenezer	HRK 547	
Allen, Ebenezer	OND 221	
Allen, Ebenezer	WSH 186	
Allen, Ebenezer Junr	ALB 94	
Allen, Eleanor	ALB 133	
Allen, Eleazar	CAY 604	
Allen, Elihu	ULS 204	
Allen, Elijah	CLN 171	
Allen, Elijah	DUT 103	
Allen, Elijah	HRK 503	
Allen, Elijah	QNS 70	
Allen, Elijah	WSH 197	
Allen, Eliphalet	DEL 267	
Allen, Elisha	CLN 155	
Allen, Elisha	WSH 191	
Allen, Elizabeth	NYK 97	
Allen, Ephraim	ESS 294	
Allen, Ephriam	WSH 221	
Allen, Ephriam	WSH 237	
Allen, Ester	WSH 301	
Allen, Ezra	RNS112B	
Allen, Frederick	MNT 105	
Allen, Gardener	MNT 73	
Allen, George	CAY 652	
Allen, George	RNS 32	
Allen, George	RNS 96	
Allen, Gershem	WSH 198	
Allen, Gideon	CAY 650	
Allen, Gideon	DUT 51	
Allen, Gideon	ORN 333	
Allen, Gideon	SRA 36	
Allen, Gideon Junr	CAY 648	
Allen, Henry	NYK 109	
Allen, Henry	OND 203	
Allen, Henry	QNS 70	
Allen, Henry A. H.	MNT 79	
Allen, Hezekiah	ESS 294	
Allen, Holden	HRK 506	
Allen, Howard	COL 253	
Allen, Ichabod	OTS 15	
Allen, Ichabod	OTS 53	
Allen, Increase	RNS 31	
Allen, Isaac	CLN 163	
Allen, Isaac	HRK 466	
Allen, Isaac	OTS 8	
Allen, Jabez	CLN 158	
Allen, Jacob	GRN 355	
Allen, James	CLN 155	
Allen, James	CLN 167	
Allen, James	DUT 52	
Allen, James	MNT 91	
Allen, James	NYK 47	
Allen, James	OTS 53	
Allen, James	QNS 70	
Allen, James	RNS 30	
Allen, James	RNS 66	
Allen, James	SCH 145	
Allen, James	WSH 236	
Allen, James	WSH 246	
Allen, James Junr	SCH 145	
Allen, James Hervey	CAY 550	
Allen, Jarid	OTS 16	
Allen, Jedediah	DUT 120	
Allen, Jedediah		SRA 36
Allen, Jeremiah		CLN 164
Allen, Jeremiah		HRK 570
Allen, Jesse		CAY 582
Allen, John		CLN 166
Allen, John		COL 204
Allen, John		DEL 267
Allen, John		DUT 43
Allen, John		DUT 106
Allen, John		DUT 135
Allen, John		ESS 294
Allen, John		HRK 479
Allen, John		NYK 75
Allen, John		NYK 121
Allen, John		NYK 126
Allen, John		NYK 137
Allen, John		ONN 142
Allen, John		OTS 29
Allen, John		OTS 44
Allen, John		OTS 56
Allen, John		RNS 34
Allen, John		RNS 98
Allen, John		RNS 106
Allen, John		SRA 16
Allen, John		SRA 28
Allen, John		SRA 55
Allen, John		SCH 118
Allen, John		TIO 217
Allen, John		ULS 189
Allen, John		WSH 185
Allen, John		WSH 189
Allen, John		WSH 200
Allen, John		WSH 258
Allen, John		WSH 280
Allen, John Junr		MNT 104
Allen, John Junr		WSH 185
Allen, John I.		DUT 117
Allen, John W.		DUT 117
Allen, Jonas		CLN 162
Allen, Jonathan		CAY 590
Allen, Jonathan		CAY 624
Allen, Jonathan		NYK 131
Allen, Jonathan		OND 223
Allen, Jonathan		WSH 198
Allen, Jonathan		WSH 207
Allen, Joseph		DUT 121
Allen, Joseph		OND 178
Allen, Joseph		OTS 28
Allen, Joseph		OTS 44
Allen, Joseph		SRA 31
Allen, Joseph		WSH 198
Allen, Joseph Junr		COL 214
Allen, Joshua		OND 223
Allen, Joshua		ONT 452
Allen, Josiah		ONN 136
Allen, Laban		OND 179
Allen, Latin		ULS 184
Allen, Lothrop		NYK 143
Allen, Margaret		NYK 47
Allen, Mary		NYK 140
Allen, Mathew		SRA 25
Allen, Mathias		NYK 93
Allen, Milmorth		SCH 136
Allen, Moses		COL 211
Allen, Moses		HRK 542
Allen, Moses		OND 165
Allen, Moses		RNS 71
Allen, Nathan		DUT 167
Allen, Nathan		ONT 416
Allen, Nathaniel		CAY 582
Allen, Nathaniel		OND 194
Allen, Nehemiah		NYK 76
Allen, Nicholas		HRK 464
Allen, Noah		DUT 149
Allen, Obediah		CHN 758
Allen, Oliver		RNS112A
Allen, Oliver		SRA 42

5

Allen, Orlo	OTS 19	Allen, William	CAY 648	Allison, Henry	CAY 670
Allen, Othniel	SRA 36	Allen, William	COL 229	Allison, Isaac	ORN 370
Allen, Parmalee	WSH 301	Allen, William	DUT 104	Allison, Isaac	ORN 371
Allen, Patince	ONT 458	Allen, William	DUT 121	Allison, John T.	RCK 104
Allen, Paul	OTS 14	Allen, Wm	GRN 335	Allison, John W.	ORN 365
Allen, Peggy	NYK 24	Allen, William	HRK 413	Allison, Joseph	CAY 708
Allen, Peleg	CAY 672	Allen, William	HRK 589	Allison, Joseph	RCK 100
Allen, Pery	OTS 14	Allen, William	MNT 61	Allison, Michael	NYK 55
Allen, Peter	ONN 179	Allen, William	NYK 29	Allison, Parcels	RCK 103
Allen, Peter	ONT 332	Allen, William	NYK 32	Allison, Peter	RCK 103
Allen, Pheneas	OTS 34	Allen, William	NYK 103	Allison, Richard	ORN 331
Allen, Philep	WSH 197	Allen, William	NYK 138	Allison, Saml	RCK 100
Allen, Philimon	WSH 224	Allen, William	OND 194	Allison, Thos	RCK 103
Allen, Philip	CAY 628	Allen, Wm	ONN 179	Allison, Thos	RCK 106
Allen, Philip	QNS 70	Allen, Wm	OTS 51	Allison, William	
Allen, Philip	WSH 224	Allen, William	QNS 70	hospital	NYK 98
Allen, Phillip	DUT 7	Allen, Wm	RNS 31	Allison, William	ORN 359
Allen, Phillip	SRA 56	Allen, William	RNS 49	Allison, Wm	RCK 99
Allen, Phineas	OND 182	Allen, William	RNS 73	Allman, Thomas	WST 162
Allen, Prince	DUT 147	Allen, William	SRA 29	Allon, Isaac	TIO 228
Allen, Prince	WSH 200	Allen, William	SCH 145	Allridge, John	RNS 62
Allen, Rachel	NYK 29	Allen, William	ULS 210	Allsaver, Sabastian	ALB 3
Allen, Rebecca	OTS 20	Allen, William K.	QNS 70	Allsdorff, Daniel	ULS 252
Allen, Reuben	DUT 8	Allen, Wing	WSH 289	Allsdorff, Johannis	ULS 253
Allen, Reuben	OTS 58	Allen, Zachh	OTS 29	Allsdorff, Lawrence	ULS 253
Allen, Reuben	ULS 186	Allen, Zadoch	HRK 542	Allsdorff, Peter	ULS 255
Allen, Richard	QNS 70	Allen, Zebulon	CLN 155	Allsdorff, Simon	ULS 253
Allen, Richard	WSH 258	Allen, Zephaniah	CAY 620	Allsie, William	NYK 110
Allen, Richard Junr	QNS 70	Allendorph, Coenradt	COL 244	Allston, Richard	NYK 143
Allen, Robert	DEL 283	Aller, Peter	ONN 150	Ally, John	SRA 8
Allen, Robert	NYK 106	Aller, Peter	OTS 8	Almendorp, Christian	DUT 157
Allen, Rubin	CLN 163	Allerton, David	CHN 908	Almendorp, H. & Peter	
Allen, Ruth	RNS 33	Allerton, Isaac	DUT 137	Fiero	DUT 157
Allen, Samuel	NYK 74	Allerton, Reuben	DUT 133	Almery, Charles	WSH 197
Allen, Samuel	OND 169	Allery, Samuel	GRN 338	Almsbury, Abner	TIO 215
Allen, Samuel	OND 223	Alley, James	DUT 18	Almsbury, Stephen	ORN 321
Allen, Samuel	OTS 29	Alley, John	ALB 127	Almsbury, William	CAY 518
Allen, Samuel	OTS 40	Alley, John	SRA 53	Almy, Benjamin	ALB 71
Allen, Samuel	RNS 49	Alley, Peter	DUT 6	Almy, Benjamin	DUT 46
Allen, Samuel	RNS 99	Alley, Richard	COL 248	Almy, William	ALB 85
Allen, Samuel	SRA 24	Alley, Robert	SRA 57	Alner, James	NYK 82
Allen, Samuel	TIO 211	Alley, William	GRN 338	Alore see More	
Allen, Samuel	WSH 303	Alley, William	ULS 183	Alpag, .ohn	MNT 47
Allen, Samuel	WST 125	Allgelt, Catharine	DUT 24	Alsaver, Frederick	HRK 481
Allen, Samuel	WST 129	Alliby, William	QNS 76	Alsderf, Laurance	ALB 24
Allen, Samuel Junr	RNS 49	Alliger, Amos	ALB 89	Alsdorff, Simon Junr	ULS 253
Allen, Semion	WSH 253	Alligor, Joseph	ALB 131	Alsop, Abigail	QNS 62
Allen, Seth	OTS 51	Allin, Amasa	CHN 848	Alsop, John	COL 246
Allen, Seymour	ONN 177	Allin, Andrew	QNS 76	Alsop, John	ESS 302
Allen, Silas	OTS 58	Allin, Apollus	CHN 804	Alsop, Richard	QNS 84
Allen, Simion	NYK 94	Allin, Barrek	QNS 82	Alsrod, Wm	ONN 187
Allen, Solomon	DEL 280	Allin, Benjamin	QNS 69	Alstine, Abraham	NYK 41
Allen, Squire	COL 247	Allin, Caleb	MNT 104	Alston, David	RCH 92
Allen, Squire	ONN 142	Allin, Daniel	QNS 82	Alston, Isaac	NYK 96
Allen, Stepen	WSH 216	Allin, Ery	CHN 900	Alstyne, Jeronimus	WST 148
Allen, Stephen	ALB 94	Allin, Hezekeah	CHN 840	Alsworth, James	DUT 135
Allen, Stephen	MNT 106	Allin, James	MNT 104	Alsworth, Thomas	COL 242
Allen, Stephen	NYK 76	Allin, John	QNS 69	Alsworth, Wm D.	COL 209
Allen, Stephen	NYK 100	Allin, John	QNS 76	Althizer, George	DUT 153
Allen, Stephen	RNS 73	Allin, John	QNS 82	Althouse, John	QNS 74
Allen, Stephen	RNS 99	Allin, John J.	MNT 104	Althouse, Nicholas	RNS 55
Allen, Stephen	SRA 22	Allin, Jonas	ONT 394	Alton, David	CHN 914
Allen, Stephen	SRA 32	Allin, Jonathan	ONT 416	Alvard, Charles	ONN 185
Allen, Susanna	RNS 48	Allin, Noah	CHN 804	Alvard, Ebenr	ONN 185
Allen, Theophilus	CAY 632	Allin, Parley	CHN 806	Alvard, Thos G.	ONN 185
Allen, Theophilus	ONT 416	Allin, Samuel	QNS 70	Alverd, Elezer	RNS 99
Allen, Thomas	ALB 93	Allin, Silas	CHN 794	Alverd, Joseph	CHN 858
Allen, Thomas	CLN 162	Allin, Stephen	CHN 788	Alverd, Pheneus	CHN 858
Allen, Thomas	DUT 10	Allin, William	QNS 64	Alverson, Jeremiah	DEL 278
Allen, Thomas	ONT 452	Allin, Wilson	CHN 800	Alverson, John	OND 162
Allen, Thomas	WSH 240	Allinboch, John	MNT 76	Alverson, Uriah	OND 158
Allen, Timothy	ALB 102	Allinson, Richard	ALB 130	Alverson, William	OND 158
Allen, Timothy	MNT 104	Allis, Moses	CHN 746	Alvertson, Benjamin	ULS 238
Allen, Trowbridge	CAY 704	Allison, Amy	ORN 320	Alvertson, Daniel	ORN 329
Allen, Walter	DUT 120	Allison, Ben	RCK 100	Alvertson, Grant	ORN 281
Allen, Weston	RNS 34	Allison, Eliza	RCK 100	Alvertson, Isaac	DUT 118
Allen, William	ALB 103	Allison, Elsie	RCK 103	Alvertson, Japhet	ULS 260

6

Name	Loc	Name	Loc	Name	Loc
Alvertson, John	DUT 109	Amey, Anthony	WSH 198	Anderson, Jacob	COL 236
Alvertson, John	ORN 272	Amey, Jacob	SRA 18	Anderson, Jacob	ONN 133
Alvertson, Joseph	DUT 114	Amey, Philip	CAY 552	Anderson, James	ALB 60
Alvertson, Richard	ORN 281	Amiberman, Isaac	QNS 68	Anderson, James	CHN 800
Alvoord, Josiah	CHN 936	Amidon, Reuben	RNS 14	Anderson, James	NYK 45
Alvord, Aaron	OTS 40	Amidon, Walter	RNS 14	Anderson, James	NYK 47
Alvord, Alexr	OTS 42	Amigh, George	COL 230	Anderson, James	NYK 127
Alvord, Asahel	OTS 42	Amiup, John	ONT 464	Anderson, James	OTS 13
Alvord, John	CHN 758	Amla, Charles	CLN 169	Anderson, James	QNS 65
Alvord, Joseah Junr	CHN 936	Amlin, John Br	CLN 168	Anderson, James	SRA 45
Always, Hester	NYK 76	Ammerman, Derick	QNS 68	Anderson, James	SCH 125
Always, James	NYK 76	Ammerman, John	QNS 67	Anderson, James	ULS 246
Always, Obadiah	NYK 76	Ammerman, John	RCH 89	Anderson, James	WST 124
Alyea, Henry	ORN 377	Ammerman, John Junr	QNS 68	Anderson, James	WST 165
Ama, John	OTS 21	Ammerman, Peter	CAY 680	Anderson, Jeremiah	RNS 47
Amach, John	MNT 14	Ammidon, Reuben Junr	RNS 69	Anderson, John	ALB 107
Amadon, Abel	ONN 158	Amorey, James	NYK 31	Anderson, John	COL 195
Amar, Daniel	NYK 39	Amory, Robert	ULS 198	Anderson, John	DUT 84
Amar, Jane	NYK 37	Amos, David	COL 220	Anderson, John	DUT 149
Amar, John D.	NYK 31	Amos, John	NYK 151	Anderson, John	MNT 65
Amar, John J.	NYK 34	Amos, Richard	NYK 150	Anderson, John	NYK 15
Amberman, John	QNS 68	Ams en, Isaac	ONT 504	Anderson, John	NYK 16
Ambler, Abraham	COL 189	Amsby, Arnold	DEL 278	Anderson, John	NYK 33
Ambler, Benjamin	WST 142	Amsby, Ebenezer	HRK 458	Anderson, John	NYK 42
Ambler, Charles	WST 124	Amsby, Elias	HRK 587	Anderson, John	NYK 52
Ambler, Enos	DUT 168	Amsden, Simeon	ONT 506	Anderson, John	NYK 72
Ambler, Jacob	SRA 19	Amstrong, James	ONN 151	Anderson, John	NYK 86
Ambler, Jeremiah	HRK 475	Amy, a mulatto	NYK 96	Anderson, John	ORN 281
Ambler, John	COL 184	Anastase, Josep	NYK 82	Anderson, John	OTS 58
Ambler, John	DUT 168	Andariese, John	NYK 142	Anderson, John	SRA 24
Ambler, Jonothan	WST 136	Andem, William	NYK 111	Anderson, John	WST 112
Ambler, Mary	ULS 224	Anders, Stephen	NYK 41	Anderson, John	WST 165
Ambler, Peter	ALB 54	Anderson, Abraham	NYK 31	Anderson, John	WST 165
Ambler, Samuel	WST 155	Anderson, Alexander	NYK 48	Anderson, John Junr	COL 193
Ambler, Squire	ORN 281	Anderson, Andrew	ALB 145	Anderson, John B.	NYK 66
Ambrose Negro	QNS 66	Anderson, Andrew	NYK 40	Anderson, Jonathan	CHN 760
Ambrose, William	NYK 119	Anderson, Andrew	ORN 287	Anderson, Jonathan	SRA 34
Amby, Thomas a mulatto	NYK 85	Anderson, Anthony R.	NYK 70	Anderson, Josiah a	
Amerman, Albert	NYK 65	Anderson, Barnet	NYK 134	Black	NYK 41
Amerman, Daniel	DUT 31	Anderson, Bastian	COL 224	Anderson, Lambert	NYK 146
Amerman, Dirck	DUT 115	Anderson, Benjamin	ULS 264	Anderson, Lewis	ULS 224
Amerman, Dirck	ORN 279	Anderson, Bethrong	NYK 40	Anderson, Lyman	SRA 33
Amerman, John	DUT 60	Anderson, Betsey	NYK 44	Anderson, Mary	NYK 129
Amerman, John	DUT 108	Anderson, Charles	CHN 770	Anderson, Mary	OND 172
Amerman, Peter	NYK 111	Anderson, Cornelia	NYK 52	Anderson, Moses	RCK 104
Amerman, Willimpir	KNG 4	Anderson, Daniel	CHN 800	Anderson, Nathanel	WST 165
Amery, Isabella	NYK 136	Anderson, Daniel	MNT 117	Anderson, Nathaniel	WST 161
Amery, John	NYK 80	Anderson, Daniel	ONT 316	Anderson, Neil	ULS 189
Ames, Abijah	GRN 328	Anderson, Daniel	ORN 289	Anderson, Nicholas	NYK 30
Ames, Abner	OTS 51	Anderson, David	DUT 127	Anderson, Peter	NYK 140
Ames, Asahel	COL 217	Anderson, David	OND 198	Anderson, Peter	SRA 29
Ames, Benjamin	COL 178	Anderson, Davd	OTS 5	Anderson, Richard	NYK 94
Ames, Benjamine	GRN 332	Anderson, Douglas	NYK 93	Anderson, Robert	NYK 99
Ames, Brockway	COL 186	Anderson, Durham a		Anderson, Robert	NYK 119
Ames, Cyrus	OTS 23	Black	NYK 76	Anderson, Robert	SRA 3
Ames, Cyrus Junr	OTS 23	Anderson, Elbert	NYK 52	Anderson, Robert	SRA 38
Ames, David	SRA 22	Anderson, Elbert	NYK 96	Anderson, Samuel	CHN 786
Ames, Elias	ALB 88	Anderson, Elijah	OTS 57	Anderson, Samuel	DUT 54
Ames, Ezra	ALB 125	Anderson, Elijah Junr	OTS 57	Anderson, Samuel	NYK 99
Ames, Jacob	CHN 976	Anderson, Elizabeth	NYK 88	Anderson, Saml	OTS 7
Ames, James	DUT 149	Anderson, Frances	NYK 113	Anderson, Stephen	NYK 78
Ames, Jason	OTS 22	Anderson, George	CHN 800	Anderson, Stephen	WST 149
Ames, Jesse	DUT 108	Anderson, George	CLN 174	Anderson, Susan	NYK 143
Ames, John	ALB 16	Anderson, George	COL 195	Anderson, Thomas	CHN 800
Ames, John	GRN 325	Anderson, Gershom	NYK 132	Anderson, Thomas	CHN 870
Ames, Jonathan	COL 248	Anderson, Gilbert	WST 125	Anderson, Thomas	SRA 33
Ames, Joseph	SCH 147	Anderson, Hannah	NYK 33	Anderson, Thorne	NYK 132
Ames, Levi	ALB 33	Anderson, Hendrick	SRA 29	Anderson, Widow	MNT 117
Ames, Levy	COL 222	Anderson, Henry	COL 195	Anderson, William	CHN 952
Ames, Rachel	DUT 37	Anderson, Henry	NYK 57	Anderson, William	NYK 109
Ames, Robert	NYK 67	Anderson, Henry	NYK 129	Anderson, William a	
Ames, Roswell	WSH 184	Anderson, Henry Junr	COL 195	Black	NYK 132
Ames, Samuel	COL 180	Anderson, Henry J.	COL 199	Anderson, William	NYK 135
Ames, Samuel	ESS 305	Anderson, Isaac	HRK 503	Anderson, William	NYK 151
Ames, Widow	WST 146	Anderson, Isaac	NYK 103	Anderson, William	ORN 398
Ames, Zebulon	CHN 834	Anderson, Israel	NYK 90	Anderson, William	SRA 45
Amesbury, Daniel	GRN 332	Anderson, Jacob	COL 191	Anderson, William	ULS 189

Name	Ref
Anderson, William	WST 111
Anderson, William	WST 149
Anderson, William	WST 162
Anderson, William Jr	WST 111
Anderson, Wilson a mulatto	NYK 18
Andes, Peter	NYK 145
Andras, William	NYK 48
Andres, Abraham	GRN 334
Andres, Amos	NYK 117
Andres, Bartholemew	NYK 67
Andres, Elias	RNS 108
Andres, Elijah	GRN 344
Andres, Ezekiul	GRN 344
Andres, Ichabod	GRN 333
Andres, Wm	ONN 175
Andrew, David	HRK 463
Andrew, John	RNS 84
Andrew, John	WSH 295
Andrew, Peter a Black	NYK 104
Andrew, Thomas	SRA 55
Andrews, Abraham	NYK 138
Andrews, Alexander	WSH 196
Andrews, Amasa	OND 176
Andrews, Amos	SRA 35
Andrews, Amos Junr	SRA 35
Andrews, Asa	HRK 495
Andrews, Asa	NYK 135
Andrews, Asahel	HRK 536
Andrews, Ashbel	OND 177
Andrews, Ashbil	SRA 48
Andrews, Barzillai	DUT 133
Andrews, Benajah	OTS 23
Andrews, Benjamin	ESS 311
Andrews, Benjamin	ONN 182
Andrews, Benjamin	ONT 412
Andrews, Christian	NYK 117
Andrews, Christopher	RNS 47
Andrews, Christopher	WSH 211
Andrews, Daniel	ALB 75
Andrews, Daniel	COL 208
Andrews, Dennisan	SRA 47
Andrews, Ebenezer	ONT 412
Andrews, Eli	CAY 606
Andrews, Elisha	COL 184
Andrews, Elisha	OTS 53
Andrews, Elisha	SCH 132
Andrews, Ephraim	CAY 606
Andrews, Ephriam	WSH 201
Andrews, Ezekiel	OND 162
Andrews, Francis	DUT 178
Andrews, George	NYK 57
Andrews, Hezekeah	CHN 878
Andrews, Hezekiah	COL 202
Andrews, Holden	RNS 99
Andrews, Icabod	CAY 606
Andrews, Isaac	TIO 228
Andrews, Jabez	OTS 31
Andrews, James	RNS 54
Andrews, Jared	OND 188
Andrews, Jason	SRA 18
Andrews, Job	WSH 235
Andrews, Joel	CAY 726
Andrews, Joel	CLN 160
Andrews, Joel	WSH 198
Andrews, Joel	WSH 216
Andrews, John	ALB 144
Andrews, John	COL 247
Andrews, John	HRK 435
Andrews, John	HRK 546
Andrews, John	ORN 281
Andrews, John	OTS 40
Andrews, John	ULS 193
Andrews, Johnson	SRA 51
Andrews, Jonathan	SRA 16
Andrews, Jonathan	TIO 230
Andrews, Joseph	ALB 90
Andrews, Joseph	COL 183
Andrews, Joseph	COL 208
Andrews, Joseph	NYK 110
Andrews, Joseph	SRA 12
Andrews, Joshua	ONT 472
Andrews, Lebbeus	ONN 184
Andrews, Lemuel	RNS 23
Andrews, Levi	TIO 228
Andrews, Loring	ALB 129
Andrews, Loudon	OND 168
Andrews, Lowring	SRA 33
Andrews, Ludim	DUT 160
Andrews, Luther	ULS 211
Andrews, Moses	GRN 349
Andrews, Nathan	OND 204
Andrews, Nathan	SRA 16
Andrews, Nathaniel	OND 173
Andrews, Nehemiah	HRK 532
Andrews, Nehemiah Jun	HRK 536
Andrews, Obed	CAY 634
Andrews, Peleg	SRA 60
Andrews, Philander	CHN 756
Andrews, Philn	ONN 178
Andrews, Reuben	TIO 226
Andrews, Richard	COL 210
Andrews, Richard	NYK 146
Andrews, Robert	COL 215
Andrews, Robert	OTS 15
Andrews, Roger	DUT 138
Andrews, Saben	GRN 333
Andrews, Samuel	ALB 41
Andrews, Samuel	DEL 270
Andrews, Samuel	DEL 285
Andrews, Samuel	OND 174
Andrews, SAmuel	ONT 412
Andrews, Samuel	SRA 32
Andrews, Samuel	WSH 216
Andrews, Samuel Junr	DEL 285
Andrews, Seth	DEL 280
Andrews, Silas	ULS 182
Andrews, Sperry	COL 183
Andrews, Stephen	COL 216
Andrews, Stephen	COL 249
Andrews, Stephen	OTS 26
Andrews, Stephen,	SRA 16
Andrews, Thomas	COL 184
Andrews, Thomas	DEL 277
Andrews, Thomas a Black	NYK 70
Andrews, Timothy	OND 205
Andrews, Timothy	WSH 303
Andrews, Widow	DEL 285
Andrews, William	DEL 277
Andrews, William	OND 198
Andrews, William	SRA 6
Andrews, Zatu	OTS 12
Andrews, Zenus	CHN 746
Andrews, Zenus	SRA 9
Andrewson, Ashbel	OND 210
Andrewss, Simmeon	RNS 60
Andrevatte, John	RCH 88
Andrevatte, Peter	RCH 94
Andrevatte, Peter Junr	RCH 94
Andries, Barnet	NYK 69
Andries, Hezekiah Junr	COL 266
Andries, Peter	COL 218
Andrison, Isaac	GRN 340
Andrison, John	GRN 357
Andrus, Abijah	COL 187
Andrus, Amasa	COL 187
Andrus, David J.	OND 217
Andrus, Ebenezer	COL 187
Andrus, Ichobud	OND 217
Andrus, Roswell	COL 184
Andrus, Thoms	TIO 234
Andruss, Deliverance	SRA 46
Andruss, Elisha	SRA 47
Andruss, Ephraim	COL 187
Andruss, Ichabud	COL 187
Andruss, Isaac	COL 187
Andruss, John	SRA 47
Anesworth, Alcut	CHN 920
Angas, Alexander a mulatto	NYK 79
Angavine, Lewis	WST 165
Angavine, Michael	WST 165
Angel, Asa	CLN 169
Angel, Eseck	DUT 8
Angel, Ezekiel	DUT 8
Angel, Fardanand	WSH 251
Angel, John	SCH 157
Angel, Jona	OTS 39
Angel, Joseph	OTS 39
Angel, Stephen	ONN 137
Angel, Thos	OTS 49
Angelis, Gideon	NYK 54
Angell, Caleb	OTS 49
Angell, Joshua	OTS 49
Angell, Prentice	OTS 49
Angell, Wm	OTS 49
Anger, Allen	OND 219
Anger, John	OND 179
Angevine, Benjamin	DUT 173
Angevine, David	NYK 76
Angevine, Eli	DUT 116
Angevine, Gilbert	RNS 91
Angevine, Isaac	WST 165
Angevine, James	WST 119
Angevine, John	NYK 125
Angevine, John	WST 119
Angevine, Jonathan	DUT 116
Angevine, Margaret	DUT 85
Angevine, Peter	NYK 124
Angle, Asa	CHN 792
Angle, Daniel	ALB 73
Angle, Daniel	CHN 790
Angle, Daniel	SRA 57
Angle, Enos	CHN 790
Angle, Henry	WSH 286
Angle, Israel	CHN 784
Angle, Jacob	ALB 70
Angle, Jacob	SRA 28
Angle, John	SRA 15
Angle, Mathias	SCH 170
Angle, Nicholas	SRA 25
Angle, Nicholas	SRA 52
Angle, Peter	ALB 70
Angle, Stephen	CHN 798
Angle, William	SRA 14
Angll, Jahill	SRA 56
Anglos, Mary	NYK 126
Angus, Abraham	ALB 143
Angus, Benjam	MNT 88
Angus, James	ALB 46
Angus, Walter	ONT 464
Anible, Arnard	SRA 45
Anible, Ephraim	SRA 38
Anible, Ephraim	SRA 45
Anible, Isaac	SRA 45
Anible, Isaac	WSH 199
Anible, John	SRA 41
Anible, Samuel	SRA 42
Anlight, Peter	SUF 98
Ann, a free wench	ALB 8
Anna, James	MNT 111
Annable, Green	ONN 151
Ann ehan, James	NYK 123
Annes, Joseph	WSH 194
Annett, Alexander	NYK 114
Annibal, Ely	GRN 352
Annibal, Samuel	ONT 370
Annin, Butler	CAY 666
Annin, Daniel	DUT 36
Annin, Gabriel	DUT 38

Name	Ref	Name	Ref	Name	Ref
Annin, John	DUT 37	Antizle, Nathl	OTS 7	Archer, Joseph	WSH 194
Annin, Joseph	CAY 726	Antonades, Cornelius	KNG 2	Archer, Mary	WST 147
Annin, Lucretia	CAY 726	Antoney, James	QNS 77	Archer, Matthias	WST 146
Anning, Huron D.	CHN 786	Antony, George	MNT 1	Archer, Matthias Junr	WST 146
Annis, Alexander	TIO 233	Antony, John	QNS 70	Archer, Moses	NYK 98
Annis, Amanuel	TIO 233	Antony, Peter	OTS 58	Archer, Obadeah	WSH 303
Annis, Charles	CAY 700	Antwerp, Volkert	MNT 78	Archer, Reuben	WST 129
Annis, John	TIO 233	Antzberger, Daniel	ALB 45	Archer, Reuben	WST 133
Annis, Oliver	CHN 936	Antzberger, Jacob	ALB 62	Archer, Thos	SCH 167
Annor, Jacob	GRN 326	Anvile, James	MNT 76	Archer, Tobias	WST 157
Annuly, John	NYK 31	Anvill, Hugh	MNT 75	Archerl, Jacob	NYK 94
Ansing, John Junr	MNT 100	Apland, Isaac	WSH 275	Archibald	QNS 81
Ansley, Benjm	ALB 13	Aplin, James	OTS 10	Archibald	SUF 93
Ansley, Zebulon	NYK 144	Appel, Conrod	NYK 85	Arcular, Henry	SCH 117
An[sm?]isson, James	MNT 97	Appel, Henry	ALB 58	Arcularius, Christian	NYK 63
Anson, Abraham	DUT 136	Appelbe, Abraham	WST 162	Arcularius, Frederick	NYK 63
Anson, Amos	SCH 132	Appelgate, John	NYK 29	Arcularius, George	NYK 52
Anson, Ely	COL 217	Apple, Henry	MNT 33	Arcularius, Peter P.	NYK 65
Anson, Isaac	SCH 167	Apple, John	NYK 151	Arden, Catherine	NYK 67
Anson, James	RCK 107	Apple, Sophia	NYK 57	Arden, Francis	NYK 68
Anson, Job	DUT 132	Applebe, John	WST 162	Arden, Jacob	NYK 41
Anson, John	CHN 762	Applebe, Joseph	WST 162	Arden, Jacob J.	NYK 150
Anson, Jonathan	GRN 325	Applebey, Mahule	SUF 76	Arden, James	NYK 19
Anson, Lebbeus	DUT 130	Appleby, Gilbert	NYK 94	Arden, John	DUT 66
Anson, Levinus	DUT 130	Appleby, James	NYK 145	Arden, John	NYK 49
Anson, Robert	CLN 158	Appleby, Mary	NYK 125	Arden, John	NYK 119
Anson, Samuel	CLN 159	Appleby, Thomas	QNS 71	Arden, Mary	NYK 21
Anson, Silas Junr	DUT 101	Applegate, Francis	ALB 131	Arden, Susannah	NYK 71
Anspake, Frederick	NYK 146	Applegate, Wm	TIO 257	Arden, Thomas S.	NYK 30
Anteman, Christopher	NYK 144	Appleje, Martha	DUT 34	Arding, Abigal	NYK 41
Antes, John	MNT 41	Appley, Jacob	NYK 114	Ardway, Suel	ESS 309
Antgelt, Ann	NYK 93	Apply, Asa	DEL 273	Ares, Isaac	RNS 96
Anthon, George	NYK 26	Apthorp, Charles	NYK 50	Ares, Reuben	WST 158
Anthonidust, Peter	QNS 75	Ar...., Henry	MNT 54	Ares, Reuben Junr	WST 158
Anthony	SUF 92	Aramsdale, Silas	HRK 550	Areson, Stephen	QNS 64
Anthony	SUF 99	Arcambal, Louis	NYK 95	Arison, Jacob	QNS 65
Anthony, Abraham	SCH 157	Archabald, Andrew	WSH 251	Arison, James	QNS 65
Anthony, Allard	DUT 35	Archabald, James	WSH 232	Arison, William	QNS 65
Anthony, Allard	ULS 246	Archabald, John	WSH 227	Arjs, John	NYK 91
Anthony, Andrew	RNS 37	Archard, Edward	ALB 97	Arkills, Abigail	DUT 73
Anthony, Anna	NYK 45	Arche, Bazdel	SRA 56	Arkills, John	ORN 343
Anthony Asa	RNS 91	Arche, John	SRA 56	Arkills, Joshua	DUT 72
Anthony, Bartho	SCH 157	Archer, Abraham	WST 146	Arles, Cornelius	COL 212
Anthony, Benj.	RCK 108	Archer, Anna	WST 149	Arles, Samuel	GRN 350
Anthony Bob.	MNT 72	Archer, Annomus	NYK 47	Arlis, Wilber	GRN 349
Anthony, Cornelius	SRA 40	Archer, Anthony	WST 147	Arll, Peter	NYK 91
Anthony, Geo.	SCH 167	Archer, Asa	WSH 302	Arls, James	SRA 26
Anthony, Israel	ALB 49	Archer, Benjamin	WST 145	Arls, Sylvester	SRA 31
Anthony, Jacob	SCH 167	Archer, Benjamin	WST 146	Arm, Martin	NYK 37
Anthony, James	MNT 76	Archer, Caleb	WST 162	Armagh, William	ALB 32
Anthony, John	ALB 42	Archer, Earl P.	ESS 293	Armatage, Benjamin	NYK 37
Anthony, John	DUT 30	Archer, Edmond	NYK 48	Armatage, John	WSH 184
Anthony, John a Black	NYK 57	Archer, Elijah	WST 147	Armatage, John Junr	WSH 184
Anthony, John	NYK 106	Archer, Ezekiel	NYK 62	Armatage, Thomas	WSH 184
.nthony, John	RNS 94	Archer, Gabriel	WST 133	Armerman, Thomas	NYK 65
Anthony, Jonathan	HRK 413	Archer, George	ALB 139	Armes, Rufus	OND 217
Anthony, Margaret	NYK 63	Archer, George	WSH 194	Armesbury, Samuel	SRA 35
Anthony, Martin	SCH 157	Archer, Gilbert	DUT 78	Armesby, Nathaniel	GRN 333
Anthony, Michaul	MNT 62	Archer, Goodheart	WST 145	Armesby, Solomon	GRN 333
Anthony, Nicholas	NYK 63	Archer, Hezekiah	NYK 135	Armington, Russel	SRA 3
Anthony, Nicholas L.	NYK 67	Archer, Jacob	NYK 95	Armitage, John	SRA 33
Anthony, Paul	SRA 57	Archer, James	ORN 296	Armitage, Wm	OTS 7
Anthony, Rufus	HRK 413	Archer, James	WSH 194	Armor, Samuel	WST 115
Anthony, Samuel	ALB 49	Archer, James	WSH 229	Armore, David	ALB 48
Anthony, Seth	DEL 284	Archer, James	WST 147	Armore, Stephen	ALB 113
Anthony, Seth Junr	DEL 284	Archer, Job	RNS 73	Armour, John	NYK 40
Anthony, Stephen	WSH 238	Archer, John	ALB 130	Arms, Daniel	ONT 506
Anthony, Theophilus	DUT 70	Archer, John	NYK 69	Arms, David	COL 251
Anthony, Thomas	WSH 239	Archer, John	NYK 80	Arms, Samuel	COL 196
Anthony, Tillness	WSH 238	Archer, John	NYK 135	Armstrong, Abigail	DUT 82
Anthony, William	NYK 88	Archer, John	WSH 183	Armstrong, Abraham	MNT 55
Antia, Stephen	MNT 38	Archer, John	WSH 195	Armstrong, Alexander	NYK 119
Antill, John	ORN 305	Archer, John	WST 148	Armstrong, Alexander	ONT 500
Antis, Francis	ALB 58	Archer, John	WST 162	Armstrong, Alexander	WSH 286
Antis, John	OTS 28	Archer, Jonathan	NYK 94	Armstrong, Ambrose	ORN 318
Antis, William	ONT 430	Archer, Jonathan	ORN 388	Armstrong, Andrew	ALB 66
Antizle, John	OTS 7	Archer, Jonathan	WST 157	Armstrong, Andrew	CAY 616

9

Name	Loc	Name	Loc	Name	Loc
Armstrong, Andw	OTS 53	Armstrong, Samuel	WSH 226	Arnold, John	OND 172
Armstrong, Archibald	WSH 258	Armstrong, Simon	NYK 62	Arnold, John	SRA 10
Armstrong, Archibald	ONT 338	Armstrong, Solomon	ALB 31	Arnold, John	WSH 270
Armstrong, Asahel	DUT 109	Armstrong, Thomas	ORN 319	Arnold, John Junr	ALB 108
Armstrong, Ashbel	OTS 30	Armstrong, Thomas	SRA 43	Arnold, John Paptist	NYK 73
Armstrong, Asher	RNS 24	Armstrong, Thomas	WSH 226	Arnold, Jonathan	COL 181
Armstrong, Benjamine	GRN 354	Armstrong, William	DUT 79	Arnold, Joseph	CLN 159
Armstrong, Benoni	CAY 614	Armstrong, William	NYK 18	Arnold, Joseph	DUT 101
Armstrong, Charles	DUT 81	Armstrong, William	NYK 51	Arnold, Lemuel	WSH 268
Armstrong, Daniel	CAY 692	Armstrong, William	NYK 59	Arnold, Levi	ESS 323
Armstrong, Daniel	RNS 108	Armstrong, William	ORN 373	Arnold, Lydia	CLN 156
Armstrong, Daniel	SRA 45	Armstrong, William	WSH 257	Arnold, Mary	ORN 355
Armstrong, David	CAY 614	Armstrong, William Junr	ORN 373	Arnold, Moses	NYK 92
Armstrong, David	WSH 258	Arn___, David	OND 217	Arnold, Moses	NYK 146
Armstrong, David	WSH 292	Arnal, John	GRN 326	Arnold, Nathan	HRK 551
Armstrong, Ebenezer	ESS 319	Arnal, Joseph	GRN 345	A_nold, Pardon	ONT 438
Armstrong, Elias Free		Arnal, Simour	GRN 336	Arnold, Peter	CHN 380
Black	COL 253	Arnal, William	GRN 336	Arnold, Pruella	ORN 382
Armstrong, Enos	CAY 614	Arnald, Abimalick	WSH 251	Arnold, Robert	COL 257
Armstrong, Gabriel	ALB 89	Arnald, Oliver	WSH 220	Arnold, Robert	ORN 382
Armstrong, George	ONT 462	Arnand, Mary	NYK 114	Arnold, Ruth	SRA 58
Armstrong, George	ONT 504	Arnaught, George	ORN 342	Arnold, Samuel	COL 205
Armstrong, Henry	ALB 66	Arnaught, Jacob	ORN 358	Arnold, Sibbi	ONT 340
Armstrong, Henry	OND 162	Arnaught, James	ORN 291	Arnold, Silas	DUT 50
Armstrong, Henry	OND 185	Arnaught, John	ORN 291	Arnold, Smith	HRK 569
Armstrong, Isaac	SRA 17	Arnaught, Nathan	ORN 330	Arnold, Sophia	ALB 139
Armstrong, Israel	ONN 145	Arnaught, Peter	ORN 358	Arnold, Stephen	ORN 320
Armstrong, Jacob	DUT 80	Arnaught, Samuel	ORN 369	Arnold, Stephen	RNS 99
Armstrong, Jacob	MNT 83	Arnaught, Sarah	ORN 367	Arnold, Thomas	MNT 85
Armstrong, Jacob	SRA 35	Arnaught, Selah	ORN 343	Arnold, Thomas	NYK 77
Armstrong, James	ONN 151	Arneld, James	WSH 221	Arnold, Thomas	SRA 41
Armstrong, James	ORN 324	Arnet, Jonathon	NYK 17	Arnold, Valentine	NYK 129
Armstrong, James	ONT 500	Arnet, Samuel	NYK 17	Arnold, Widow	SRA 53
Armstrong, James	SRA 55	Arnet, Stephen	NYK 85	Arnold, William	DUT 50
Armstrong, James	WSH 226	Arnol, Gilbert	WST 130	Arnold, William	OND 172
Armstrong, James L.	RCK 99	Arno.d, Abraham	MNT 28	Arnold, William	ORN 279
Armstrong, Jedediah	HRK 424	Arnold, Ahab	DUT 119	Arnold, Wm	RNS 54
Armstrong, Jesse	SRA 45	Arnold, Alexander	WSH 266	Arnold, William	WSH 304
Armstrong, John	ALB 6	Arnold, Amasa	SRA 53	Arnold, Zebedee	HRK 571
Armstrong, John	ALB 31	Arnold, Anthony	SRA 20	Arnolt, Saml	RNS 104
Armstrong, John	ALB 66	Arnold, Bowley,	RNS 54	Arnot, Abraham	MNT 34
Armstrong, John	CAY 636	Arnold, Catharine	ALB 47	Arnot, George	WSH 192
Armstrong, John	DUT 68	Arnold, Christian	ALB 108	Arnot, Philip	NYK 37
Armstrong, John	DUT 155	Arnold, Daniel	RNS 104	Arnout, Jacob	ONT 310
Armstrong, John	GRN 354	Arnold, David	DUT 50	Arnspee, Isaac	SRA 57
Armstrong, John	KNG 10	Arnold, David	HRK 544	Arnst, Abigail	NYK 41
Armstrong, John	MNT 96	Arnold, David	RNS 54	Aroft, Daniel	GRN 357
Armstrong, John	NYK 119	Arnold, David Senr	HRK 570	Aro. Smith, Edmond	SRA 15
Armstrong, John	NYK 138	Arnold, David R.	ORN 346	Arrel, Powel	SRA 31
Armstrong, John	NYK 150	Arnold, Ebenezar	RNS 104	Arson, James	MNT 74
A[rmstrong?], John	ONT 462	Arnold, Ebenezer	DUT 128	Arson, Robert	SCH 167
Armstrong, John	RNS 73	Arnold, Ebenezer	RNS 24	Arter, Platt	SUF 83
Armstrong, John	WSH 226	Arnold, Edward	DUT 177	Arthur, Augustin	CLN 158
Armstrong, Joseph	CAY 616	Arnold, Edward	HRK 449	Arthur, Elephalet	SUF 84
Armstrong, Julia	ORN 394	Arnold, Edward	HRK 540	Arthur, Francis	ESS 295
Armstrong, Libbeas	SRA 6	Arnold, Eli	HRK 451	Arthur, Isaac	SUF 90
Armstrong, Martin	RNS 22	Arnold, Elisha	CLN 156	Arthur, Jessee	SUF 89
Armstrong, Martin	RCK 104	Arnold, Elizabeth	NYK 124	Arthur, John	DUT 52
Armstrong, Michael	NYK 16	Arnold, Enoch	HRK 574	Arthur, Joseph	ONT 366
Armstrong, Michael	NYK 89	Arnold, Enoch	RNS 27	Arthur, Joshua	CLN 158
Armstrong, Moses	CAY 614	Arnold, George	COL 199	Arthur, Rubin	CLN 158
Armstrong, Moses	RNS 24	Arnold, George	HRK 574	Arthur, Samuel	ORN 399
Armstrong, Nathan	MNT 92	Arnold, Hiram	WSH 306	Arthur, Thomas	CLN 158
Armstrong, Nathan	MNT 94	Arnold, Hopkins	ONT 354	Arthur, Wm	SUF 64
Armstrong, Nathan	NYK 64	Arnold, Isaac	ALB 108	Arthur, William	SUF 91
Armstrong, Nicholas	HRK 420	Arnold, Isaac	COL 236	Arthurton, Joel	STB 206
Armstrong, Patience	ORN 373	Arnold, Isaac	DUT 50	Artman, Justus	ULS 193
Armstrong, Reuben	SRA 45	Arnold, Jabez	ULS 193	Arundale, William	DUT 73
Armstrong, Richard	SRA 17	Arnold, James	ORN 349	Arven, William	NYK 152
Armstrong, Robert	CAY 578	Arnold, Jesse	SRA 40	Arvin, Peter	OND 171
Armstrong, Robert	NYK 90	Arnold, John	ALB 105	Asbill, Christopher	ORN 362
Armstrong, Robert	NYK 119	Arnold, John	ALB 108	Asbour, Joseph	STB 202
Armstrong, Robert	ORN 371	Arnold, John	ALB 127	Aschur, William	WST 162
Armstrong, Robert	RNS 82	Arnold, John	COL 264	Ascouth, John	NYK 132
Armstrong, Robert	WSH 226	Arnold, John	DUT 114	Ash, Elizabeth	SRA 8
Armstrong, Samuel	RNS 77	Arnold, John	HRK 574	Ash, Gilbert	NYK 55
Armstrong, Samuel	SRA 45	Arnold, John	MNT 85	Ash, Henry	HRK 591

10

Ash, Jacob	NYK 151	Aspinwall, Aaron	OTS 22	Atwood, Thomas	ORN 393
Ash, Jacob	SRA 8	Aspinwall, Gilbert	NYK 52	Aubineau, Mitchell	NYK 48
Ash, John	OND 217	Aspinwall, Rebecca	QNS 64	Aucer, Jonus	WST 165
Ash, John	SRA 10	Aspinwall, Rebecca	QNS 65	Aucer, Robert	WST 165
Ash, John	SRA 12	Asquitch, James	DUT 77	Aucer, Talman	WST 165
Ash, John	SCH 132	Asquith, Lister	NYK 39	Auchinvole, David	NYK 28
Ash, Peter	COL 237	Assan, John	WST 129	Auchmoty, David	ULS 233
Ash, Peter	SRA 3	Assets, Benjamin	ALB 77	Auchmoty, James	ULS 208
Ash, Peter	SRA 8	Assier, Edward	NYK 100	Auchmoty, John	ULS 233
Ash, Samuel	NYK 133	Asslin, Charles	NYK 91	Auchmoty, Peter	ULS 236
Ash, Thomas	NYK 35	Astell, Jonathan	CAY 596	Auckarman, Casps	ALB 116
Ash, William	NYK 27	Asten, John	NYK 152	Aucle, Harmanus	MNT 69
Ash, William	SRA 8	Aste[n?], Peter	WST 146	Aucute, Richard	KNG 9
Ashard, Samuel	CHN 932	Astin, Abija[el?]	WST 147	Audler, Simon	NYK 56
Ashbey, John	OND 217	Astin, Aulay	WST 147	Augan, Thomas	NYK 103
Ashby, Anthony	DUT 19	Astin, Benjamin	RNS 31	Augenbough, Jacob	ALB 58
Ashby, Asa	DUT 53	Astin, Stephen	TIO 221	Augers, Josiah	OND 204
Ashby, William	RNS 84	Astin, Wilsie	WST 147	Aughterson, Joseph	WSH 224
Ashby, Zebulon	DUT 18	Aston, Freeborn	HRK 463	Augur, James	ORN 360
Ashby, Zebulon	DUT 56	Astor, Henry	NYK 146	Auguste_, Benjamin a	
Ashcraft, Dyer	OTS 11	Astor, John Jacob	NYK 51	Black	NYK 133
Ashcraft, Joseph	OTS 11	Aswal, John	NYK 60	Augustus, George a	
Ashden, James	WSH 183	Aswell, James	NYK 136	Black	NYK 97
Ashden, James	WSH 235	Atchison, Bazaleel	ONT 318	Aukebeck, Rynart	CAY 688
Ashden, John	WSH 183	Atherly, William	COL 247	Aukerman, William	CAY 674
Ashden, Thomas G.	WSH 184	Atherton, Jonathan	ULS 268	Aul, Amisa	MNT 75
Ashdown, William	WST 165	Atherton, Theophius	ULS 238	Aul, John	MNT 75
Asher, John	NYK 141	Atkins, Abijah	CAY 648	Auld, Isaac	NYK 105
Asheton, Thomas	WSH 184	Atkins, Elisha	ALB 79	Auldrige, Joshua B.	SRA 17
Ashfield, John	NYK 64	Atkins, George	ULS 232	Auler, John	SRA 31
Ashford, Saml	CHN 930	Atkins, Hezekiah	TIO 234	Aulger, George	COL 216
Ashley, ...s	ONT 506	Atkins, Isaac	CAY 644	Aulger, Peggy	HRK 464
Ashley, Daniel	SRA 56	Atkins, Isaac	WSH 197	Aulger, Stoughton	HRK 408
Ashley, Elkanan	OTS 55	Atkins, John	ULS 232	Aulls, Ephraem	STB 197
Ashley, Horrace	DEL 274	Atkins, John	WSH 194	Aulls, Thomas	STB 197
Ashley, Jacob	NYK 20	Atkins, Levi	CAY 644	Aulls, Wm	STB 197
Ashley, James	COL 224	Atkins, Peter	ULS 232	Auly, Alexander	MNT 99
Ashley, Jonas	HRK 510	Atkins, Samuel	CAY 650	Aurman, Simon	CAY 684
Ashley, Jonas	OTS 55	Atkins, Samuel	CAY 622	Aurneman, Lawrence	CAY 608
Ashley, Leonard	WSH 286	Atkins, Samuel	CAY 670	Aurnhout, Jacob Junr	ALB 107
Ashley, Nicholas	WSH 258	Atkins, Samuel	DUT 168	Aurnhout, John	ALB 78
Ashley, Noah	COL 221	Atkins, Samuel	OND 210	Aurnult, Isaac	ALB 78
Ashley, Oliver	SRA 56	Atkinson, Aaron	SCH 141	Aurnult, James	ALB 78
Ashley, Peter	COL 224	Atkinson, Edward	NYK 18	Auronhout, Jacob	ALB 99
Ashley, Robert	NYK 129	Atkinson, John	NYK 52	Ausdoll, Nicholas	QNS 68
Ashley, Roger	WSH 305	Atorm, Lewis	NYK 71	Ause, Elizabeth	NYK 69
Ashley, Stephen	ESS 309	Atsling, John	SUF 95	Ausen, John	MNT 76
Ashley, Stephen	RNS 92	Atwater, Asa	CHN 912	Auser, Albert	RNS 50
Ashley, Thomas	OTS 49	Atwater, Benjamin	COL 180	Auser, William	NYK 86
Ashley, Thomas	SRA 30	Atwater, Caleb	CAY 582	Austen, Amos	WSH 290
Ashley, William	CHN 750	Atwater, Caleb	CAY 602	Au[s?]ten, Charles	WST 159
Ashley, William	COL 247	Atwater, Caleb	COL 184	Austen, David	WSH 267
Ashley, William	NYK 81	Atwater, Daniel	RNS 57	Au[s?]ten, David	WST 133
Ashley, William	NYK 125	Atwater, Jesse	WSH 278	Austen, Edward	WSH 297
Ashley, William	WSH 197	Atwater, John	CAY 602	Austen, Eleas	WSH 290
Ashly, Stephen	RNS 51	Atwater, John	ONT 502	Austen, Holmes	WST 161
Ashman, Adolphus	ORN 381	Atwater, Joshua	ONN 186	Austen, Isaac Jur	WSH 265
Ashman, Samuel	CLN 170	Atwater, Moses	ONT 428	Austen, Jotham	WSH 267
Ashman, William	CLN 170	Atwell, Albert	CAY 694	Austen, Levi	OTS 26
Ashmore, Ann	NYK 148	Atwell, Jehue	ALB 118	Austen, Reuben	WSH 282
Ashton, Amanda a		Atwell, Joseph	ONN 144	Auster, Edward	GRN 332
mulatto	NYK 113	Atwell, Mabell	CAY 694	Austin, Aaron	CAY 684
Ashton, John	SRA 45	Atwell, Oliver	OND 170	Austin, Abel	RNS 20
Ashur, John	DUT 166	Atwell, Paul	TIO 221	Austin, Abraham	DUT 25
Ashur, John Junr	DUT 166	Atwell, Peter	DEL 277	Austin, Abraham	ORN 312
Askins, Joseph	DEL 271	Atwick, John	ALB 96	Austin, Amos	DUT 131
Askins, Peter	ALB 42	Atwood, Benjn	TIO 259	Austin, Amos	ORN 393
Aslain, Preest Junr	CLN 169	Atwood, Isaac	ALB 74	Austin, Amos	WSH 282
Aslain, Priest	CLN 169	Atwood, Jabez	ORN 288	Austin, Anthony	WSH 282
Aslet, Thomas	RNS 15	Atwood, James	WSH 216	Austin, Asa	HRK 413
Ason, Wm	MNT 72	Atwood, Jedeiah	ALB 78	Austin, Benjamin	ALB 128
Aspell, James	ORN 373	Atwood, John	ESS 317	Austin, Benjamin	OND 209
Aspenwall, John	SRA 44	Atwood, Jonas	ONT 342	Austin, Benjn	RNS 71
Aspenwall, Matthw	OTS 33	Atwood, Joseph	OTS 13	Austin, Benjamin	WSH 291
Aspin, Samuel	SRA 50	Atwood, Noel	RNS 80	Austin, Caleb	CHN 932
Aspin, Thomas	NYK 41	Atwood, Samuel	WSH 281	Austin, Caleb	CHN 966
Aspin, William	NYK 31	Atwood, Stephen	CLN 163	Austin, Charles	RNS 31

Austin, Daniel	DUT 59	Austin, Silas	DUT 102	Avery, Enoch	DUT 178
Austin, David	DEL 267	Austin, Silas	GRN 355	Avery, Henry	COL 235
Austin, David	DEL 274	Austin, Silas	OND 191	Avery, Hezekiah	CAY 628
Austin, Deliverance	WSH 192	Austin, Smith	DUT 83	Avery, Isaac	CAY 628
Austin, Dinah	RNS 51	Austin, Solomon	CAY 626	Ave.., John	DEL 279
Austin, Ebenezer	WSH 194	Austin, Solomon	WSH 219	Avery, John	DEL 284
Austin, Edward	DUT 131	Austin, Stephen	CHN 808	Avery, John	DEL 284
Austin, Edward	RNS 110	Austin, Stephen	HRK 413	Avery, John	OTS 29
Austin, Elias	OND 212	Austin, Stephen	SUF 80	Avery, John	RNS 44
Austin, Elisha	WSH 187	Austin, Thomas	ALB 100	Avery, John Junr	OND 205
Austin, Eusebius	ORN 333	Austin, Thomas	CAY 558	Avery, John W.	NYK 79
Austin, Ezekiel	OTS 55	Austin, Thomas	COL 260	Avery, Jonathan	MNT 40
Austin, Ezra	SRA 56	Austin, Thomas	DEL 273	Avery, Joseph	OND 185
Austin, Freeborn	WSH 185	Austin, Volkert	RNS 6	Avery, Joseph	ULS 186
Austin, Freeman	DEL 272	Austin, Wilkinson	RNS 51	Avery, Joshua	DEL 285
Austin, George	SRA 30	Austin, William	CLN 157	Avery, Moses	DUT 148
Austin, George	WSH 192	Austin, William	COL 186	Avery, Nathaniel	ONT 470
Austin, George	WSH 302	Austin, William	COL 229	Avery, Nicholas	ALB 52
Austin, Grinman	DUT 47	Austin, William	DUT 130	Avery, Noel	WSH 301
Austin, Hamah	NYK 129	Austin, William	OND 168	Avery, Obediah	SCH 148
Austin, Hannah	DUT 81	Austin, William	RNS 50	Avery, Oliver	NYK 16
Austin, Henry	CAY 684	Austin, William	WSH 303	Avery, Punderson	ONN 133
Austin, Isaac	ALB 94	Austin, Zephaneah	WSH 282	Avery, Richard	DEL 284
Austin, Isaac	DUT 81	Austine, Wm	MNT 123	Avery, Richard	RNS 44
Austin, Isaac	DUT 84	Auton, Abraham	RCH 89	Avery, Richard	TIO 229
Austin, Isaac	NYK 89	Autun, Paul	CAY 556	Avery, Richardson	OND 184
Austin, Isaac	ONT 508	Auvinbaugh, Peter	ALB 57	Avery, Robert	CHN 872
Austin, Isaac	RNS 110	Avainen, Menot A.	NYK 151	Avery, Roger	SUF 64
Austin, Isaac	WSH 257	Avelin, Hulda	OND 200	Avery, Samuel	OND 177
Austin, Isaac ye 2d	DUT 85	Avens, Thomas	NYK 17	Avery, Saml	SCH 167
Austin, Isaiah	RNS 50	Aveny, Abraham	MNT 101	Avery, Sarah	NYK 33
Austin, James	DUT 131	Averel, Thos	TIO 254	Avery, Sarah	SUF 64
Austin, James	ONT 448	Averell, _____	CLN 155	Avery, Sherwood	ALB 29
Austin, Jeremiah	DUT 102	Averet, Abrm	TIO 238	Avery, Silvister	SRA 39
Austin, Job	DUT 84	Averett, William	CHN 880	Avery, Sirus	CHN 870
Austin, John	DUT 95	Averey, Peter	SRA 39	Avery, Solomon	DUT 82
Austin, John	ONN 132	Averil, Ebenezer	DEL 288	Avery, Stephen	HRK 549
Austin, John	ONT 418	Averil, Joseph	OND 223	Avery, Stephen	SRA 40
Austin, John	WSH 196	Averil, Josiah	CHN 804	Avery, Thaddeus	WST 165
Austin, John	WSH 214	Averill, Avery	OTS 9	Avery, Thomas	DEL 284
Austin, Johua	GRN 345	Averill, Isaac	COL 259	Avery, Thomas	WSH 301
Austin, Jonath	WSH 240	Averill, James	OTS 19	Avery, Timothy	WSH 281
Austin, Jonathan	DEL 273	Averill, Jesse	WSH 271	Avery, William	ALB 30
Austin, Jonathan	DUT 13	Averill, John	MNT 103	Avery, William T.	COL 202
Austin, Jonathan	DUT 21	Averill, Nathan	CLN 157	Aviat, Harriel	NYK 42
Austin, Jonathan	DUT 72	Averill, Nathan Junr	CLN 156	Avirell, Nathaniel	MNT 108
Austin, Jonathan	DUT 131	Averill, Noble	CLN 157	Avis, John	NYK 81
Austin, Joseph	WSH 269	Averill, Philo	COL 202	Avory, Solomon	WST 160
Austin, Joshua	DUT 61	Averill, Wm	OTS 14	Avry, Michael	MNT 65
Austin, Joshua	DUT 109	Averiss, Joseph	CLN 156	Awler, Abraham	ONN 150
Austin, Levi	OND 192	Averist, Isaac	MNT 18	Awney, Jesse	SRA 38
Austin, Levi	ONT 420	Averitt, George	CLN 158	Axtel, Aaron	OTS 25
Austin, Levi Junr	OND 192	Avery, Aaron	SRA 41	Axtel, Daniel	OTS 25
Austin, Mahetable	WSH 236	Avery, Abel	SRA 14	Axtel, Moses	OTS 25
Austin, Mathew	RNS 6	Avery, Abraham	CHN 784	Axtell, David	ORN 346
Austin, Matthias	HRK 459	Avery, Amos	ALB 29	Aydens, Pelilea	MNT 73
Austin, Moses	GRN 346	Avery, Amos	DUT 125	Aye, Oliver	CHN 904
Austin, Nathan	TIO 222	Avery, Asa	RNS 75	Ayers, Obadiah	NYK 131
Austin, Nathaniel	CHN 808	Avery, Bellows	MNT 124	Ayers, Salomon	TIO 230
Austin, Nathaniel	NYK 68	Avery, Benjamin	CAY 658	Ayers, Stephen	MNT 125
Austin, Pardon	DEL 273	Avery, Benjamin	SRA 42	Aykroyd, Samuel	COL 253
Austin, Pasco	WSH 267	Avery, Calven	WSH 264	Aylesbury, John	DUT 43
Austin, Peter	RNS 50	Avery, Cesor	WSH 203	Aylesworth, Daniel	HRK 525
Austin, Rebecca	DUT 84	Avery, Chauncy	ULS 194	Aylsworth, Danl	OTS 36
Austin, Reheboam	WSH 257	Avery, Constant	CHN 870	Aylsworth, Peleg	OTS 36
Austin, Reuben	OND 192	Avery, Daniel	ALB 92	Aylsworth, Stukely	OTS 9
Austin, Reuben	WSH 290	Avery, Daniel	CAY 628	Aylsworth, Wm	OTS 36
Austin, Rice	OND 189	Avery, Daniel	OTS 27	Aymar, Anna	NYK 45
Austin, Robert	DUT 84	Avery, Daniel	OND 205	Aymar, James	NYK 100
Austin, Robert	RNS 6	Avery, Dudley	CAY 628	Aymar, John	NYK 48
Austin, Robert Junr	DUT 85	Avery, Ebenezar	CAY 660	Aynsworth, Philip	OTS 4
Austin, Samuel	CAY 712	Avery, Elias	CAY 628	Ayres, Abijah	ORN 275
Austin, Samuel	DEL 273	Avery, Elias	OND 217	Ayres, Ebenezer B.	ORN 283
Austin, Samuel	WST 159	Avery, Elijah	RNS 39	Ayres, Enos	ORN 342
Austin, Seth Junr	COL 246	Avery, Eliphalet	ALB 30	Ayres, David	ORN 334
Austin, Shubel	OND 168	Avery, Elisha	ONT 498	Ayres, Jesse	ULS 259
Austin, Silas	DUT 13	Avery, Ellen	NYK 19	Ayres, Joseph	NYK 142

Name	Code	Pg
Ayres, Phillip	ULS	259
Ayres, Samuel	ULS	259
Ayres, Squier	HRK	501
Ayres, Stephen	HRK	524
Ayres, Thomas	NYK	65
Ayres, Thomas	ULS	267
Ayres, Uriah	WSH	295
Ayrs, Robert	SRA	42
Ayrs, Thomas	COL	211
Ayworth, George	CLN	158
Azel, Lewis	SUF	80

B

Name	Code	Pg
B___, __at__n	CAY	518
B_rs, Henry	CAY	528
B_er, Francis	CHN	884
B...d, Israiel	CHN	888
B_own, Jacob	CHN	946
B_ker, John	MNT	5
B...., Leona.d	MNT	11
B___, Jost	MNT	15
B.t..an	MNT	53
B___, John	MNT	82
B.tts, Richard	MNT	90
B___, Thomas	MNT	90
B___ett, Charles	ONT	476
B__er, Joseph	ORN	385
B_h_ll, ___	OTS	44
B..ne, David	TIO	244
B_rton, Benjamin	WST	148
Ba_s, John	ONT	474
Ba_, Jonathan	ORN	384
Ba_, N...	RNS	107
Ba_to_, Thomas	WST	144
Babb, Jacob	NYK	50
Babbet, Levi	OTS	12
Babbet, Nathaniel	ONT	360
Babbet, Stephen	OTS	12
Babbit, Elkaner	OTS	12
Babbit, John	DEL	271
Babbit, Stephen	HRK	552
Babbit, Warren	OTS	12
Babbit, William	OND	195
Babbot, Elijah	SCH	160
Babcock, Alexander	SRA	26
Babcock, Amas	CHN	816
Babcock, Amos	RNS	66
Babcock, Arnold	SUF	101
Babcock, Benjaman	CHN	840
Babcock, Benjamin	ORN	291
Babcock, Benjamin	RNS	66
Babcock, Benjamin	SRA	26
Babcock, Benjamin	WSH	221
Babcock, Benjamin	WSH	299
Babcock, Bennedict	CHN	824
Babcock, Caleb	WSH	232
Babcock, Charles	CAY	638
Babcock, Charles	CHN	816
Babcock, Charles Junr	CHN	816
Babcock, Christopher	ALB	121
Babcock, Clark	HRK	568
Babcock, Daniel	CAY	628
Babcock, Daniel	CHN	836
Babcock, Daniel	CHN	978
Babcock, Daniel	OND	174
Babcock, Darius	TIO	209
Babcock, Darius	TIO	225
Babcock, David	ALB	64
Babcock, David	CHN	824
Babcock, David	OND	198
Babcock, David	RCK	99
Babcock, David	WSH	299
Babcock, David Junr	ALB	64
Babcock, Easlen	WSH	185
Babcock, Edward	CHN	834
Babcock, __isha	CAY	620
Babcock, Elisha	OTS	35
Babcock, Elisha	RCK	99
Babcock, Ethan	CHN	816
Babcock, Ethan	HRK	427
Babcock, Ezekel	WSH	199
Babcock, Frederick	NYK	20
Babcock, George	ONT	448
Babcock, Geo.	OTS	16
Babcock, George	RCK	100
Babcock, George	WSH	203
Babcock, Gershom	COL	222
Babcock, Giddeon	CHN	836
Babcock, Henry	ALB	64
Babcock, Henry	WSH	207
Babcock, Isaac	DUT	148
Babcock, Isaac	RCK	100
Babcock, Isaac	WSH	224
Babcock, Isaiah	OTS	27
Babcock, Isaiah	OTS	43
Babcock, James	ALB	76
Babcock, James	OND	184
Babcock, Jason	RNS	73
Babcock, Jeremiah	CHN	844
Babcock, Jerushe	SUF	106
Babcock, Jesse	CAY	640
Babcock, Jesse	OND	204
Babcock, Jo..	RNS	105
Babcock, Job	OND	216
Babcock, Job	RCK	102
Babcock, Johial	SCH	124
Babcock, John	ALB	75
Babcock, John	ALB	113
Babcock, John	ONN	140
Babcock, John	ONN	176
Babcock, John	ONT	386
Babcock, John	RNS	74
Babcock, John	RNS	106
Babcock, John	WSH	197
Babcock, John Junr	WSH	198
Babcock, John 3d	RNS	26
Babcock, Johnson	RNS	66
Babcock, Jonas	OTS	43
Babcock, Jonathan	HRK	427
Babcock, Jonathan	HRK	455
Babcock, Jonathan	OND	195
Babcock, Jona	OTS	35
Babcock, Joseph	RCK	99
Babcock, Joshua	ALB	96
Babcock, Joshua	HRK	477
Babcock, Jothan	MNT	91
Babcock, Juda	CHN	828
Babcock, Larkins	WSH	232
Babcock, Lemuel	ONT	448
Babcock, Loadwic L.	COL	206
Babcock, Lucas	HRK	454
Babcock, Maxon	ONN	173
Babcock, Nathan	WSH	241
Babcock, Newman	OTS	14
Babcock, Oliver	DEL	282
Babcock, Ollive	CHN	816
Babcock, Paul	OND	198
Babcock, Peleg	ONN	173
Babcock, Phenius	WSH	208
Babcock, Rebecca	NYK	32
Babcock, Reynold	WSH	186
Babcock, Robert	ALB	64
Babcock, Robert	ALB	64
Babcock, Robert	WSH	250
Babcock, Robert H.	RNS	101
Babcock, Saml	OTS	43
Babcock, Seagers	OND	195
Babcock, Semion	WSH	219
Babcock, Sherman	WSH	304
Babcock, Silas	RNS	104
Babcock, Silvenus	RNS	107
Babcock, Simon Junr	WSH	220
Babcock, Solomon	ONN	173
Babcock, Thomas	RNS	99
Babcock, Thomas	RNS	105
Babcock, Thos	RCK	100
Babcock, Timo & Waldo	COL	221
Babcock, Timothy	HRK	531
Babcock, Wald & Timo	COL	221
Babcock, William	CHN	790
Babcock, Willm	COL	217
Babcock, Wm	RNS	66
Babcock, Wm	RCK	104
Babcock, Willm Junr	COL	221
Babcock, Wordon	WSH	197
Babet, Enos	CAY	666
Babry, Margaret	NYK	95
Babtest, Isaac	NYK	74
Babtest, John a Black	NYK	79
Babtis, John	NYK	74
Babtist, John a Black	NYK	113
Babtist, John a mulatto	NYK	113
Baccus, Ebenezer	NYK	128
Bache, Theophleet	NYK	30
Bacheldor, Daniel	OND	163
Bacheldor, Abram	OND	196
Bachelor, Benjamin	DEL	274
Bachelor, Perrin	CHN	798
Bachelor, William	NYK	142
Bacher, Aaron	COL	219
Bach[es?], Henry	NYK	59
Bachman, David	COL	198
Bachman, Jacob	COL	236
Bachus, Ebenezer	STB	200
Bachus, John	RNS	26
Bachus, John	RNS	30
Bachus, John Junr	RNS	58
Back, Elisha	OTS	34
Back, Simion	KNG	2
Backee, Jacob	HRK	499
Backee, John	NYK	42
Backenstose, Frederick	ONT	508
Backenstose, Jacob	ONT	508
Backer see Barker		
Backer, Aaron	COL	255
Backer, Andrew	ALB	46
Backer, Aurant	ALB	98
Backer, Cornelius	COL	253
Backer, Cornelius	COL	256
Backer, David	ALB	113
Backer, David	COL	194
Backer, Gerrit	ALB	98
Backer, Johanis	ALB	35
Backer, Johannis	ULS	224
Backer, John	COL	255
Backer, John	RNS	36
Backer, Joshua	NYK	101
Backer, Peter	ULS	221
Backer, Walter	ALB	97
Backer, Winne	ALB	106
Backhouse, Edward	NYK	62
Backman, Jacob	RNS	35
Backus, Aaron	SRA	34
Backus, Andrew	ALB	116
Backus, Benjamin	SRA	8
Backus, Delicena	GRN	332
Backus, Ebenezer	CHN	932
Backus, Electus	ALB	117
Backus, Elijah	CAY	722
Backus, Elisha Junr	ONN	170
Backus, John	SRA	57
Backus, Kalep	SRA	52
Backus, Lebbeus	SRA	30
Backus, Rufus	COL	247
Backus, Whiting	GRN	358
Bacnum, Caleb	DEL	288
Bacon, Abner	OND	195
Bacon, Asa	ONN	161
Bacon, Benjamin	COL	212

Name	Loc	No.	Name	Loc	No.	Name	Loc	No.
Bacon, Colby	OND	186	Bader, Urich	MNT	12	Bailey, Daniel	DUT	37
Ba_on, Daniel	CAY	588	Badgeley, Aaron	ONT	486	Bailey, Daniel	ORN	280
Bacon, Daniel	CAY	616	Badgely, Daniel	DUT	152	Bailey, Daniel	ORN	344
Bacon, Daniel H.	TIO	234	Badger, Abner	CHN	938	Bailey, Daniel	QNS	68
Bacon, Ebenezer	OND	192	Badger, Ebenezer	DUT	63	Bailey, David	ALB	91B
Bacon, Ebenezer	OTS	24	Badger, Edmund	TIO	215	Bailey, David	ALB	95
Bacon(?), Ephraim	RNS	105	Badger, Gideon	CAY	534	Bailey, David	CAY	562
Bacon, Frederick	CHN	774	Badger, John	OTS	16	Bailey, David	ONT	382
Bacon, Goold,	CHN	758	Badger, John	OTS	35	Bailey, David	SCH	152
Bacon, Isaac	ONT	424	Badger, Lemuel	TIO	230	Bailey, Deveaux	DUT	87
Bacon, Jacob	ONN	190	Badger, Solomon	ALB	21	Bailey, Elias	ORN	329
Bacon, James	CAY	652	Badgerd, Nathan	CHN	746	Bailey, Elias & Sarah		
Bacon, James	CHN	932	Badgerd, Samuel	CHN	746	Leverage	QNS	61
Bacon, Jesse	RNS	93	Badgers, John	CHN	804	Bailey, Elisha	RNS	68
B.con, Joel	CAY	588	Badgley, Anthony	ALB	99	Bailey, Ephraim	ORN	328
Bacon, Joel	CAY	610	Badgley, Anthony & G.	DUT	118	Bailey, Ephraim	QNS	68
Bacon, John	NYK	48	Badgley, Ford	SRA	9	Bailey, Ephraim Junr	QNS	68
Bacon, John	OND	181	Badgley, G. & Anthony	DUT	118	Bailey, Epraim	ALB	97
Bacon, John	OND	210	Badgley, Joshua	DUT	118	Bailey, Henry	OND	223
Bacon, Joseph	SRA	36	Badgley, Stephen	SRA	9	Bailey, Henry	ONT	360
Bacon, Joseph	WSH	220	Badgly, Stephen	SCH	117	Bailey, Hetty	QNS	61
Bacon, Joseph	WSH	299	Badjer, William	ONT	416	Bailey, Hugh	OTS	8
Bacon, Lemuel	WSH	299	Badjet, Wm	MNT	94	Bailey, Isaac	CAY	640
Bacon, Leonard	OND	209	Badley, Jacob	NYK	97	Bailey, Jabez	RNS	31
Bacon, Leonard	ONN	152	Badow, Elias	WST	148	Bailey, Jacob	DEL	289
Bacon, Levi	TIO	234	Badow, Erias	ALB	121	Bailey, James	CAY	534
Bacon, Moses	COL	208	Badow, John	WST	149	Bailey, James	CAY	562
Bacon, Pennywell	ONN	157	Badowe, Peter	GRN	340	Bailey, James	DUT	89
Bacon, Phinehas	RNS	29	Badowe, Widow	GRN	340	Bailey, James	QNS	83
Bacon, Pierpoint	CAY	610	Badsley, Isaac	ALB	111	Bailey, Jeremiah	CAY	654
Bacon, Rufus	ONN	161	Badsley, John	ALB	116	Bailey, Jesse	CAY	582
Bacon, Ruth	WSH	299	Badsley, Joseph	ALB	113	Bailey, Joel	OND	195
Bacon, Solomon	OND	192	Badsley, Joseph	ALB	116	Bailey, Joel	OTS	6
Bacon, Thadeus	WSH	288	Baecon, Marshael	SRA	52	Bailey, John	ALB	31
Bacon, Thomas	NYK	141	Baehr, Adam	ULS	222	Bailey, John	CLN	165
Bacon, Timothy	TIO	221	Baehr, Daniel	NYK	19	Bailey, John	DUT	123
Ba.on, William	HRK	528	Baehr, John	ULS	223	Bailey, John	ONT	406
Bacon, William	NYK	29	Baehr, Jacobus	ULS	223	Bailey, John	ORN	339
Bacon, Winthrop	WSH	299	Baets, Abraham	NYK	26	Bailey, John	OTS	6
Bacques, John	NYK	53	Bagdat, James	MNT	102	Bailey, John	ULS	264
Bad.., Melchior	MNT	17	Bagg, Dan	OTS	21	Bailey, John	WSH	265
Badcock, Amos	OTS	15	Bagg, James	OND	161	Bailey, John	WST	165
Badcock, Amos Junr	RNS	66	Bagg, Moses	OND	161	Bailey, John N.	DUT	69
Badcock, Benjamin	SUF	102	Baggs, Ebenr	OTS	56	Bailey, Jonathan	CAY	536
Badcock, Cotterill	RNS	66	Bagler, John	GRN	339	Bailey, Jonathan	CAY	644
Badcock, Daniel	RNS	66	Bagley, Barnett	GRN	342	Bailey, Jonathan	ORN	330
Badcock, Ebenezer	DUT	64	Bagley, Benjamine	GRN	338	Bailey, Jonathan	ULS	256
Badcock, Frederick	RNS	66	Bagley, David	GRN	344	Bailey, Jonathan	WSH	252
Badcock, George	OTS	15	Bagley, Edward	COL	180	Bailey, Jonathan Esqr	WST	165
Badcock, Isaac	ORN	380	Bagley, Esther	DUT	60	Bailey, Joseph	CAY	578
Badcock, Isaiah	GRN	339	Bagley, Hutten	GRN	344	Bailey, Joseph	COL	210
Badcock, James	ORN	380	Bagley, John	GRN	338	Bailey, Joseph	DUT	173
Badcock, Job	ORN	387	Bagley, John	GRN	344	Bailey, Joseph	OND	168
Badcock, John	ORN	380	Bagley, Joseph	ALB	13	Bailey, Joseph	ORN	339
Badcock, John Senr	ORN	383	Bagley, Josiah	COL	179	Bailey, Joseph	OTS	42
Badcock, Jona	OTS	39	Bagley, Patty	NYK	48	Bailey, Joseph	QNS	62
Badcock, Reuben	RNS	69	Bagley, .rudence	COL	178	Bailey, Joseph	RNS	54
Badcock, Robert	OTS	15	Bagley, Richard	ONT	494	Bailey, Lemuel	Col	248
Badcock, Roger	OTS	34	Bagley, Thomas	NYK	100	Bailey, Loring	HRK	590
Badcock, Samuel	ORN	379	Bahannan, James	NYK	138	Bailey, Mageret	SRA	10
Badcock, Thomas	RNS	77	Bahr, Christian	NYK	28	Bailey, Moses	ONN	158
Badcock, Thomas	SUF	102	Bail, George	SRA	31	Bailey, Nathan	CAY	618
Badcock, William	ORN	387	Bailes, Calvin	DUT	137	Bailey, Nathaniel	CAY	578
Badcock, Wm	OTS	39	Bailes, Elias	DUT	111	Bailey, Nathaniel	ORN	331
Badcock, William	SUF	99	Bailes, George	DUT	137	Bailey, Nathaniel	QNS	61
Baddaw, Peter	NYK	143	Bailey, Abijah	DUT	177	Bailey, Nathaniel	ULS	266
Baddeau, Elias	WST	127	Bailey, Abner	CAY	536	Bailey, Nathaniel Junr	ORN	329
Badder, Michael	ALB	15	Bailey, Abraham L.	OND	187	Bailey, Oliver	ONN	153
Badeau, Jacob	DUT	83	Bailey, Almerin	ORN	325	Bailey, Peleg	DUT	177
Badeau, John	DUT	83	Bailey, Asa	ORN	366	Bailey, Perez	ALB	92
Badeau, Isaac	DUT	83	Bailey, Barbara	ORN	325	Bailey, Dr Richard	RCH	93
Badeau, Peter	DUT	83	Bailey, Barthenia	DUT	81	Bailey, Robert	DUT	140
Bader, H....	MNT	34	Bailey, Benjamin	CAY	664	Bailey, Rowland	DUT	95
Bader, Leonard	MNT	16	Bailey, Benjam..	ONT	478	Bailey, Salmon	OND	162
Bader, Michael	MNT	10	Bailey, Caleb	SRA	56	Bailey, Samue.	CAY	538
Bader, Michael M.	MNT	7	Bailey, Charles	OTS	21	Bailey, Samuel	DUT	177
Bader, Michael W.	MNT	15	Bailey, Clark	OND	184	Bailey, Samuel	QNS	61

Name	Code	#	Name	Code	#	Name	Code	#
Bailey, Samuel	QNS	68	Baisley, Thomas	KNG	7	Baker, Ebenesar	GRN	339
Bailey, Samuel Junr	OND	167	Baisley, Thomas	WST	144	Baker, Ebeneszar	GRN	351
Bailey, Samuel Senr	OND	170	Baisley, William	KNG	8	Baker, Ebenezer	OTS	21
Bailey, Seth	OTS	49	Baisly, John	MNT	55	Baker, Edmund	COL	257
Bailey, Silas	OND	184	Baits, Caleb	OTS	46	Baker, Edward	HRK	460
Bailey, Smith	RNS	72	Baits, David	OTS	25	Baker, Edward	OTS	27
Bailey, Stanton	RNS	78	Baits, John	OTS	35	Baker, Edy	SRA	41
Bailey, Stephen	COL	248	Baits, Nathan	OTS	15	Baker, Edy Junr	SRA	41
Bailey, Stephen	OND	170	Baits, Oliver	OTS	15	Baker, Elbenezer	CHN	802
Bailey, Theodorus	DUT	64	Baits, Richard	OTS	27	Baker, Eliakim	WSH	286
Bailey, Thomas	COL	247	Baits, Wm	OTS	35	Baker, Elihu	OTS	47
Bailey, Thomas	DEL	286	Bakely, Gotlep	SCH	167	Baker, Elijah	OND	216
Bailey, Thomas	OND	184	Bakeman, Henry	NYK	79	Baker, Eliza	NYK	46
Bailey, Thos	OTS	47	Baker, Aaron	NYK	76	Baker, Elnathan	OTS	22
Bailey, Thomas	QNS	68	Baker, Abel	DUT	58	Baker, Enoch	COL	186
Bailey, Timothy	OND	167	Baker, Abraham	DUT	74	Baker, Enoch	WSH	298
Bailey, Timo	OTS	6	Baker, Abraham	RNS	81	Baker, Ephraim	DEL	272
Bailey, Vine	OND	169	Baker, Abraham	SUF	101	Baker, Erastus	ONN	138
Bailey, William	CLN	166	Baker, Abraham	SUF	108	Baker, Ezekiel	HRK	426
Bailey, Wm	MNT	47	Baker, Abraham	WST	157	Baker, Ezekiel	RNS	33
Bailey, William	NYK	86	Baker, Adam	ULS	238	Baker, Ezra	COL	209
Bailey, Wm	OTS	5	Baker, Adam	ULS	260	Baker, Ezra	OND	194
Bailey, William	QNS	61	Baker, Albert	WSH	216	Baker, Frances	NYK	119
Bailey, William	WST	120	Baker, Albert Junr	WSH	246	Baker, Frances	NYK	124
Bailie, William	NYK	31	Baker, Alderman	RNS	69	Baker, Freeland	CHN	930
Baily, Arnol	WST	124	Baker, Alpheus	WSH	274	Baker, Freelove	SRA	24
Baily, Arnol	WST	140	Baker, Amman	WSH	298	Baker, Gardner	MNT	120
Baily, Enoch	SRA	25	Baker, Amos	ALB	93	Baker, George	ALB	34
Baily, Ezra	SCH	158	Baker, Amos	QNS	80	Baker, George	HRK	460
Baily, Gilbert	WST	124	Baker, Amos	WSH	192	Baker, George	MNT	99
Baily, Hachaliah	WST	128	Baker, Amos	WSH	202	Baker, George	NYK	31
Baily, Hannah	WST	128	Baker, Andrew	WSH	237	Baker, George	ONT	400
Baily, Jam..	WST	131	Baker, Andrew	WST	165	Baker, Geo.	OTS	27
Baily, James	WST	157	Baker, Andrew Junr	WST	166	Baker, George	RCK	103
Baily, John	MNT	39	Baker, Anna	SRA	34	Baker, George	RCK	106
Baily, John	MNT	91	Baker, Annanias	SUF	108	Baker, George	WSH	270
Baily, Jonathan	WST	159	Baker, Asa	ONT	316	Baker, George	WSH	291
Baily, Joseph	MNT	106	Baker, Avery	DUT	167	Baker, Gideon	ALB	30
Baily, Joseph	NYK	69	Baker, B andel	WSH	237	Baker, Gilbert	WST	166
Baily, Joseph	TIO	260	Baker, Benajah	DUT	14	Baker, Henry	DUT	55
Baily, Joseph Jun	TIO	260	Baker, Benajah	WSH	239	Baker, Henry	NYK	73
Baily, Polly	NYK	91	Baker, Benjamin	DEL	273	Baker, Henry	OTS	11
Baily, Richard	WSH	206	Baker, Benjamin	OND	223	Baker, Henry	QNS	82
Baily, Thomas	WST	124	Baker, Benjn	OTS	11	Baker, Henry	SRA	7
Bain, Bella	NYK	116	Baker, Benjn	OTS	46	Baker, Herrington	WSH	184
Bain, Casparus	WSH	242	Baker, Benjamin	RNS	49	Baker, Honyoes	MNT	44
Bain, Catharine	WSH	242	Baker, Benjamin	SRA	30	Baker, Isaac	CLN	158
Bain, Hugh	COL	259	Baker, Benjamin	WSH	272	Baker, Isaac	SUF	76
Bain, Hugh	WSH	242	Baker, Benjamin W. T.?	CLN	162	Baker, Isaac	WSH	303
Bain, James	COL	236	Baker, Caleb	SRA	38	Baker, Israel	ONT	376
Bain, John	NYK	42	Baker, Caleb	TIO	257	Baker, Izrael	ONT	364
Bain, Peter	COL	233	Baker, Charles	DUT	66	Baker, Jacob	SUF	70
Bain, William	WSH	242	Baker, Charles	HRK	416	Baker, James	CAY	698
Bainbridge, Abner	CAY	528	Baker, Christian	COL	220	Baker, James	DUT	15
Bainbridge, Absalom	NYK	29	Baker, Clark	SCH	167	Baker, James	DUT	21
Bain[bridge?], John	CAY	528	Baker, Conrod	MNT	104	Baker, James	DUT	115
Bainbridge, Malin	CAY	532	Baker, Conrod	RCK	106	Baker, James	GRN	339
Baird, Alexander	SRA	5	Baker, Daniel	COL	229	Baker, James	GRN	342
Baird, Amos	WSH	273	Baker, Daniel	DEL	274	Baker, James	OTS	22
Baird, Charles	ORN	322	Baker, Daniel	NYK	94	Baker, James	RNS	85
Baird, David	SRA	35	Baker, Daniel	NYK	118	Baker, James	ULS	187
Baird, Gibson	ORN	313	Baker, Daniel	ONT	490	Baker, James	ULS	193
Baird, Henry	ONT	340	Baker, Danl	OTS	29	Baker, James	WSH	234
Baird, Jeremiah	ORN	322	Baker, Daniel	SUF	108	Baker, Jane	HRK	578
Baird, John	ORN	376	Baker, Daniel	WSH	270	Baker, Jeremiah	ALB	110
Baird, Joseph	ORN	341	Baker, Daniel Junr	COL	196	Baker, Jeremiah	DUT	17
Baird, Josiah	ONT	350	Baker, David	CHN	804	Baker, Jeremiah	OND	211
Baird, Nathaniel	WSH	273	Baker, David	CLN	154	Baker, Jeremiah	RNS	22
Baird, Robert	ORN	312	Baker, David	GRN	351	Baker, Jeremiah	RCH	91
Baird, Sarah	CAY	656	Baker, David	NYK	46	Baker, Jeremiah	STB	206
Baird, William	ORN	335	Baker, David	SUF	108	Baker, Jeremiah	WST	166
Baird, William	ORN	372	Baker, David	SUF	109	Baker, Jesse	HRK	421
Bairse, Hezekiah	DEL	286	Baker, David	WSH	199	Baker, Jesse	ULS	193
Baisely, James	WST	144	Baker, David	WSH	265	Baker, Jesse	WST	165
Baisley, Francis	KNG	10	Baker, David	WSH	275	Baker, Joab	ALB	120
Baisley, Fransis	KNG	7	Baker, David	WST	124	Baker, Joel	OND	163
Baisley, John	KNG	10	Baker, Demsy	RCH	94	Baker, Joel	ULS	238

Name		Name		Name	
Baker, John	ALB 141	Baker, Phillip	DUT 36	Baker, William	ONT 332
Baker, John	CAY 548	Baker, Phinehas	DUT 167	Baker, William	ONT 488
Baker, John	CLN 161	Baker, Phinehas	GRN 354	Baker, Wm	OTS 46
Baker, John	GRN 336	Baker, Reuben	ULS 187	Baker, Wm	OTS 47
Baker, John	GRN 346	Baker, Reuben	WSH 237	Baker, Wm	QNS 71
Baker, John	NYK 57	Baker, Reuben	WSH 303	Baker, Wm	RCK 103
Baker, John	NYK 84	Baker, Reynolds	RNS 78	Baker, Wm	SUF 70
Baker, John	NYK 140	Baker, Richard	DUT 21	Baker, William	WST 117
Baker, John	ONN 185	Baker, Richard	DUT 115	Baker, William	WST 125
Baker, John	ONT 390	Baker, Richard	QNS 72	Baker, William Junr	OTS 11
Baker, John	OTS 21	Baker, Robert	DEL 268	Baker, William Senr	OTS 11
Baker, John	OTS 47	Baker, Robert	NYK 118	Baker, Zachariah	MNT 104
Baker, John	RNS 10	Baker, Robert	SRA 34	Baker, Zebulen	SRA 53
Baker, John	RNS 22	Baker, Robert	WSH 266	Baker, Zebulon	ALB 110
Baker, John	RCH 92	Baker, Robert	WSH 271	Bakewell, Joseph	NYK 108
Baker, John	SUF 76	Baker, Rubin	CLN 154	Bakewell, Mathew	NYK 123
Baker, John	WSH 183	Baker, Samuel	CAY 518	Bakjorn, Jacob	ORN 396
Baker, John	WSH 186	Baker, Samuel	CAY 524	Bakhorn, Margaret	ULS 230
Baker, John	WSH 213	Baker, Samuel	CAY 590	Balance, James	SRA 7
Baker, John	WSH 293	Baker, Samuel	CAY 606	Balcom, Asa	OTS 53
Baker, John	WST 123	Baker, Samuel	CAY 662	Balcom, Constant	OTS 54
Baker, Jonathan	DEL 272	Baker, Samuel	GRN 336	Balcom, Frances	OTS 25
Baker, Jonathan	DUT 56	Baker, Samuel	GRN 342	Balcom, Henery	CHN 774
Baker, Jonathan	DUT 144	Baker, Samuel	RNS 85	Balcom, Samuel	CHN 774
Baker, Jonathan	ONT 490	Baker, Samuel	SRA 55	Balcom, Uriah	OTS 34
Baker, Jonathan	RNS 33	Baker, Samuel	WSH 293	Balcomb, John	DEL 280
Baker, Jonathan	SRA 6	Baker, Samuel	WST 115	Bald, Arcibald	NYK 126
Baker, Jonathan	STB 197	Baker, Samuel	WST 131	Balde, Henry	HRK 442
Baker, Jonathan	SUF 108	Bake, Samuel Ju	ONT 380	Balde, William	HRK 438
Baker, Joseph	CLN 163	Baker, Samul	STB 197	Balden, Enos	GRN 333
Baker, Joseph	DEL 267	Baker, Seth	SRA 3	Balden, Israel	CHN 756
Baker, Joseph	DEL 269	Baker, Sharman	RNS 22	Balden, Thomas	CHN 756
Baker, Joseph	OND 167	Baker, Silas	WSH 286	Baldin, Henry	QNS 74
Baker, Joseph	ONN 161	Baker, Simeon	ULS 215	Balding	GRN 337
Baker, Joseph	ONT 320	Baker, Solomon	OND 165	Balding	GRN 343
Baker, Joseph	RNS 81	Baker, Solomon	WSH 276	Balding,	GRN 343
Baker, Joseph	SRA 26	Baker, Stephen	COL 210	Balding, Abial	GRN 341
Baker, Joshua	DUT 16	Baker, Stephen	COL 229	Balding, Andrew	GRN 351
Baker, Joshua	GRN 336	Baker, Stephen	ESS 323	Balding, Benjamin	GRN 329
Baker, Joshua	GRN 336	Baker, Stephen	NYK 53	Balding, Courlious	GRN 341
Baker, Joshua	GRN 355	Baker, Stephen	QNS 84	Balding, Daniel	GRN 340
Baker, Joshua	WST 114	Baker, Stephen	ULS 238	Balding, Daniel	GRN 355
Baker, Josiah	COL 248	Baker, Stephen	WSH 275	Balding, David	GRN 341
Baker, Josiah	DUT 90	Baker, Stephen	WST 125	Balding, Enos	WSH 187
Baker, Jude	DUT 81	Baker, Susannah	NYK 147	Balding, George	DUT 121
Baker, Justus	ORN 277	Baker, Terry	SUF 64	Balding, Henry	GRN 325
Baker, Levi	DUT 168	Baker, Theodore	RNS 95	Balding, Isaac	DUT 112
Baker, Levy	CHN 862	Baker, Thomas	DUT 12	Balding, Ja_es	GRN 325
Baker, Lewis	SRA 13	Baker, Thomas	DUT 62	Balding, James	GRN 343
Baker, Lidia	CHN 968	Baker, Thomas	GRN 342	Balding, Jeremiah	GRN 356
Baker, Louis	DUT 17	Baker, Thomas	MNT 29	Balding, John	DUT 42
Baker, Lucy	NYK 99	Baker, Thomas	MNT 83	Balding, Johnathan	GRN 342
Baker, Lyman	WSH 244	Baker, Thomas	ORN 388	Balding, Joseph	GRN 325
Baker, Margaret	RNS 78	Baker, Thomas	OTS 27	Balding, Joseph	GRN 354
Baker, Mary	DUT 24	Baker, Thomas	RNS 10	Balding, Joseph	OTS 19
Baker, Mary	SUF 107	Baker, Thomas	RNS 47	Balding, Parmenus	GRN 338
Baker, Maurice	DUT 17	Baker, Thomas	SUF 106	Balding, Samuel	GRN 335
Baker, Morris	OND 216	Baker, Thomas	ULS 187	Balding, Warner	GRN 354
Baker, Nathan	CHN 930	Baker, Thomas	WSH 224	Balding, William	DUT 60
Baker, Nathan	ONN 135	Baker, Thomas	WST 115	Balding, William	GRN 325
Baker, Nathan	WSH 286	Baker, Thomas	WST 165	Baldridge, John	ESS 323
Baker, Nathaniel	RNS 64	Baker, Timothy	CAY 714	Baldridge, Micheal	CAY 542
Baker, Nathaniel	SRA 13	Baker, Truman	OND 216	Baldwin, Aaron	COL 206
Baker, Nathaniel	SUF 106	Baker, Valentine	DUT 64	Baldwin, Aaron	NYK 147
Baker, Nataniel	SUF 108	Baker, Widow	STB 206	Baldwin, Abel	QNS 82
Baker, Nathaniel	WSH 275	Baker, William	ALB 141	Baldwin, Abel	RNS 19
Baker, Nicholas	DUT 12	Baker, William	CHN 834	Baldwin, Abijah	KNG 2
Baker, Paul	SRA 16	Baker, William	CLN 159	Baldwin, Abraham	QNS 76
Baker, Peleg	WSH 293	Baker, William	CLN 163	Baldwin, Alexander	WSH 243
Baker, Peter	DUT 16	Baker, William	COL 210	Baldwin, Alexander	WSH 245
Baker, Peter	QNS 72	Baker, William	DUT 42	Baldwin, Allen	MNT 101
Baker, Peter	SRA 42	Baker, Wm	GRN 350	Baldwin, Amos	SUF 93
Baker, Peter	WST 123	Baker, William	NYK 39	Baldwin, Amos	WSH 210
Baker, Phebe	NYK 122	Baker, William	NYK 74	Baldwin, Aron	RNS 17
Baker, Phebe	WSH 237	Baker, William	NYK 113	Baldwin, Asa	DEL 281
Baker, Philip	WSH 202	Baker, William	NYK 145	Baldwin, Asa	MNT 12
Baker, Philip	WSH 202	Baker, William	ONN 175	Baldwin, Asa	OND 164

Name	Loc	Pg	Name	Loc	Pg	Name	Loc	Pg
Baldwin, Asa	ONT	470	Baldwin, Trueman	OTS	23	Ball, Lebeus Jur	ONN	145
Baldwin, Betsey	QNS	72	Baldwin, Uriah	QNS	74	Ball, Mathew	SCH	117
Baldwin, Charles	NYK	53	Baldwin, Waterman	TIO	255	Ball, Moses	OTS	26
Baldwin, Christion	MNT	107	Baldwin, William	SRA	6	Ball, Nathl	HRK	534
Baldwin, Corneleus	WSH	245	Baldwin, William	TIO	260	Ball, Nathl Jun	HRK	536
Balswin, Cyrus	WSH	295	Bale, Hendrick	OND	221	Ball, Nehemiah	HRK	421
Baldwin, Daniel	NYK	86	Balentine, Ebenezer	RNS	61	Ball, Noah	COL	212
Baldwin, Daniel	OND	183	Baler, Isaac	QNS	66	Ball, Noah	OND	212
Baldwin, David	ALB	13	Baler, James	NYK	133	Ball, Olliver	GRN	345
Baldwin, David	DUT	173	Baley, Amaziah	RNS	107	Ball, Peter	OTS	49
Baldwin, David	ORN	388	Baley, Augustin	QNS	83	Ball, Peter	SCH	117
Baldwin, Ebenezer	DUT	63	Baley, Benjamin	NYK	50	Ball, Phineas	MNT	50
Baldwin, Elijah	DEL	269	Baley, Benjn	SUF	76	Ball, Polly	NYK	56
Baldwin, Elisha	CAY	688	Baley, Danl	SUF	68	Ball, Reuben	NYK	136
Baldwin, Elisha	DUT	86	Baley, David	RNS	107	Ball, Ruth	SRA	13
Baldwin, Elizabeth	NYK	37	Baley, Ebenezar	SUF	67	Ball, Samuel	ALB	22
Baldwin, Elizabeth	QNS	72	Baley, Ebenezer	WSH	301	Ball, Samuel	ORN	277
Baldwin, Enoch	QNS	74	Baley, Elijah	SUF	67	Ball, Stephen	SRA	17
Baldwin, Ephraim	SUF	94	Baley, Ephraim	WSH	269	Ball, Thaddeus	CAY	702
Baldwin, Ezekiel	QNS	73	Baley, George	QNS	82	Ball, Thomas	HRK	551
Baldwin, Francis	QNS	75	Baley, James	NYK	94	Ball, Thomas	NYK	102
Baldwin, Heman	OND	180	Baley, James	OND	222	Ball, Wait	ONN	183
Baldwin, Henry	DUT	87	Baley, Jeremiah	RNS	69	Ball, William	ALB	69
Baldwin, Henry	TIO	250	Baley, John	NYK	29	Ball, William	NYK	118
Baldwin, Hezekiah	WSH	212	Baley, John	NYK	145	Ball, William	SUF	102
Baldwin, Isaac	DUT	134	Baley, John	SUF	67	Ball, Wm	TIO	247
Baldwin, Isaac	TIO	260	Baley, John	SUF	68	Ball, Zerubbabel	HRK	447
Baldwin, Jacob	QNS	76	Baley, John Junr	NYK	145	Ballad, Adam	OTS	11
Baldwin, Jacob	SRA	16	Baley, Joseph	WSH	271	Ballard, Alpheus	MNT	10
Baldwin, Jacob	SUF	82	Baley, Mary	NYK	40	Ballard, Barnabas	OND	210
Baldwin, James	DUT	87	Baley, Nehemiah	RNS	50	Ballard, Benj.	OND	210
Baldwin, James	NYK	124	Baley, Richard	NYK	20	Ballard, Benoney	SRA	48
Baldwin, James	QNS	74	Baley, Samuel	SRA	60	Ballard, Caleb	DUT	93
Baldwin, James Junr	QNS	74	Baley, Saml	SUF	66	Ballard, Daniel	CHN	892
Baldwin, Jessee	QNS	72	Baley, Stephen	RNS	101	Ballard, Ephraim	OND	209
Baldwin, John	QNS	76	Baley, Sten	SUF	76	Ballard, Icabode	WSH	233
Baldwin, Jonah	SUF	82	Baley, Thomas	RNS	83	Ballard, Isaac	DUT	176
Baldwin, Jonas C.	CAY	544	Baley, Widow	SUF	74	Ballard, Israel	OND	201
Baldwin, Jonathan	CHN	772	Baley, William	CHN	858	Ballard, Jeremiah	DUT	93
Baldwin, Joseph	DUT	128	Balhaey, James	NYK	26	Ballard, John	DUT	178
Baldwin, Levi	DUT	124	Balis, Luther	COL	258	Ballard, John	OND	165
Baldwin, Lovet	OND	184	Ball, Abner,	RNS	104	Ballard, John	ONN	181
Baldwin, Mary	DUT	87	Ball, Abner Junr	RNS	104	Ballard, Joshua	ONN	181
Baldwin, Mary	NYK	57	Ball, Adam Jr	SCH	167	Ballard, Josiah	ONT	478
Baldwin, Mathias	NYK	130	Ball, Benjamin	CHN	882	Ballard, Paul	CHN	916
Baldwin, Methusaleh	ORN	293	Ball, Christopher			Ballard, Peleg	DEL	267
Baldwin, Moses	NYK	138	Tilley	ORN	355	Ballard, Peleg	DUT	92
Baldwin, Nathan	COL	209	Ball, Daniel	TIO	247	Ballard, Rufus	MNT	11
Baldwin, Nathaniel	ONT	398	Ball, David	CHN	828	Ballard, Rufus	SRA	20
Baldwin, Noah	MNT	12	Ball, David	ORN	381	Ballard, Smithfield	HRK	466
Baldwin, Parker	QNS	76	Ball, David	SCH	118	Ballard, Thomas	MNT	11
Baldwin, Philemon	ONT	456	Ball, Eathan A.	SRA	56	Ballard, Thomas	SRA	48
Baldwin, Pierce	DUT	27	Ball, Edward	CHN	804	Ballard, Tracy	DUT	87
Baldwin, Platt	QNS	78	Ball, Edward J.	NYK	95	Ballard, Welcom	WSH	233
Baldwin, Ransford	DEL	269	Ball, Eleazer	NYK	85	Ballard, William	NYK	47
Baldwin, Richard	QNS	72	Ball, Eli	HRK	447	Ballend, David	OND	219
Baldwin, _ufus	MNT	106	Ball, Eusebus	OND	212	Ballman, Mary	NYK	110
Baldwin, S_ten	OTS	22	Ball, Fear	WSH	209	Ballmor, Jacob	NYK	134
Baldwin, Samuel	COL	266	Ball, Frederick	ALB	383	Ballord, Thomas	SRA	42
Baldwin, Samuel	NYK	69	Ball, George	ORN	345	Ballou, Benjamin	OND	161
Baldwin, Samuel	QNS	75	Ball, George	SCH	149	Ballou, Joseph	OND	161
Baldwin, Samuel	SRA	26	Ball, Gideon	ONT	496	Ballou, Silas	HRK	567
Baldwin, Samuel	ULS	254	Ball, Henry	ALB	69	Baloan, William	CHN	950
Baldwin, Samuel W.	OND	200	Ball, Isaac	NYK	88	Balown, Arnold	CHN	950
Baldwin, Sarah	QNS	77	Ball, Isabella	NYK	53	Balsh, Ebenezer	CLN	162
Baldwin, Seth	MNT	108	Ball, Jacob	DUT	30	Balsley, Andrew	ONN	166
Baldwin, Seth C.	SRA	15	Ball, James H.	RNS	109	Balsley, Jacob	ONN	166
Baldwin, Silas	COL	192	Ball, John	NYK	16	Balsley, John	ONN	166
Baldwin Silas	TIO	255	Ball, John	NYK	142	Balsley, Peter	ONN	166
Baldwin, Simeon	DEL	289	Ball, John	ORN	383	Baltz, Jams	NYK	138
Baldwin, Stephen	QNS	73	Ball, John	WSH	286	Balwin, Anna	NYK	128
Baldwin, Sylvanus	QNS	74	Ball, John P.	ALB	72	Baly, James	NYK	145
Baldwin, Sylvenus	QNS	75	Ball, John Thomas	NYK	35	Bamcon, Christopher	MNT	108
Baldwin, Thomas	DUT	173	Ball, Jonathan	COL	209	Bamford, James	CHN	778
Baldwin, Thomas	QNS	74	Ball, Jonathan	ONN	136	Bamford, Moses	CHN	778
Baldwin, Thomas	TIO	260	Ball, Josiah	TIO	247	Bamsen, Nicholas	MNT	73
Baldwin, Treat	OND	184	Ball, Lebeus	ONN	146	Bamson, John	MNT	54

Name	Loc	Pg	Name	Loc	Pg	Name	Loc	Pg
Bancher, John mulatto	NYK	65	Banta, Derick	MNT	89	Barber, John	NYK	111
Banchroft, Stephen	ONN	171	Banta, Frances	NYK	142	Barber, John	OND	210
Bancker, Abraham	NYK	86	Banta, Henry	MNT	89	Barber, John	ONN	150
Bancker, Abraham	ULS	227	Banta, Jane	NYK	69	Barber, John	ONN	152
Bancker, Adrian	RCH	93	Bant_, John	MNT	89	Barb[er], John	ONT	488
Bancker, Everit	NYK	36	Banta, John	MNT	89	Barber, John	ORN	294
Bancker, Gertrude	NYK	150	Banta, Theodosia	NYK	87	Barber, John	ULS	260
Bancker, Henry	NYK	63	Banter, John	NYK	122	Barber, John	WSH	186
Bancker, John	NYK	77	Banter, John T.	NYK	97	Barber, John	WSH	295
Bancker, John K.	NYK	51	Banter, Peter	NYK	90	Barber, Jonathan	WSH	285
Bancker, John S.	NYK	21	Banter, Peter,	NYK	122	Barber, Joseph	ORN	295
Bancker, Margaret	NYK	85	Bantues, Jacob	SCH	161	Barber, Joseph	WSH	246
Bancker, Mary	NYK	152	Banty, Henry	NYK	60	Barber, Judah	OTS	22
Bancraft, Ezekiel	CHN	788	Banull, Mary	NYK	109	Barber, Lemuel	ESS	296
Bancraft, Isaac	CHN	790	Banvard, Daniel	NYK	103	Barber, Lemuel	ONT	334
Bancraft, Joel	CHN	788	Banyer, Goldsbury	ALB	143	Barber, Martin	HRK	544
Bancroft, Caleb	OND	217	Baord, James	NYK	86	Barber, Martin	OTS	21
BAncroft, Jesse	ONN	170	Baower, Nicolas B.	NYK	36	Barber, Mathew	WSH	285
Bane, David	WST	120	Baptis, John a Black	NYK	98	Barber, Moses	COL	215
Banfield, James	CAY	574	Baptis, John a mulatto	NYK	103	Barber, Nathan	OTS	44
Bangs, Abner	DUT	87	Baptis, John a Black	NYK	112	Barber, Nathaniel	ONN	140
Bangs, Eleai__	NYK	97	Baptist, Catharine	ALB	53	Barber, Oliver	NYK	43
Bangs, Joseph	DEL	269	Baptist, John	NYK	126	Barber, Reuben	OTS	21
Bangs, Lemuel	DEL	269	Bar_ett, David	CHN	920	Barber, Robert	NYK	94
Banker, Abraham	ALB	110	Bar_er, Jeduthan	OND	224	Barber, Rowland	OND	199
Banker, Anna	NYK	140	Bar..., ...	RNS	4	Barber, Samuel	WSH	203
Banker, Daniel	DUT	84	Barager, Andries	ALB	111	Barber, Semeon	CLN	157
Banker, Daniel	WST	131	Barager, Wm	ALB	85	Barber, Silas	NYK	58
Banker, David	WST	125	Barb__, Danl	CHN	828	Barber, Smith	WSH	252
Banker, Flores	RNS	85	Barbaree, John	NYK	34	Barber, Solomon	COL	237
Banker, Frederick	DUT	107	Barbareen, Ami Joahem	KNG	9	Barber, Thomas	CAY	684
Banker, Gerrit	ALB	56	Barbarie, Adam a Black	NYK	41	Barber, Thomas A.	NYK	64
Banker, Henry	CLN	165	Barbarow, Cosporus	RCK	107	Barber, Timothy	OND	163
Banker, Henry	DUT	12	Barbarow, Fraderick	RCK	106	Barber, Uriah	OND	223
Banker, Henry	DUT	83	Barbarow, Matthias	RCK	107	Barber, Volentine	GRN	335
Banker, Isaac	SCH	143	Barber, Abram_	COL	205	Barber, William	CAY	632
Banker, Jacob	DUT	83	Barber, Albro	WSH	249	Barber, William	CHN	820
Banker, Jacobus	ALB	110	Barber, Amasa	WSH	255	Barber, William	DUT	9
Banker, James	SRA	48	Barber, Amaziah	DEL	290	Barber, William	DUT	73
Banker, John	CLN	161	Barber, Amos	ONT	414	Barber, William	ONT	372
Banker, John	NYK	39	Barber, Augustus	DEL	290	Barber, Wm	RNS	66
Banker, John	NYK	133	Barber, Benjamin	WSH	275	Barber, William	RNS	67
Banker, John	WST	132	Barber, Benjamin	RNS	103	Barber, William	WSH	255
Banker, John	WST	145	Barber, Clarck	CHN	814	Barbi__, James	MNT	94
Bankr, Joshua	RNS	41	Barber, Clark	HRK	465	Barbier, Andrw	NYK	69
Banker, Matthew	WST	132	Barber, Daniel	ONN	155	Barckhoff, Henry	NYK	150
Banker, Nathaniel	DUT	34	Barber, Daniel	WSH	255	Barckley, George	NYK	119
Banker, Nathaniel	MNT	71	Barber, David	WSH	203	Barckley, James	NYK	122
Banker, Peter	DUT	84	Barber, David	WSH	298	Barckley, Col. Thomas	QNS	63
Banker, William	RNS	85	Barber, Edward	WSH	252	Barclay, Abraham	DUT	107
Banks, Abigail	WST	141	Barber, Elijah	ALB	80	Barclay, Abm Junr	ALB	99
Banks, Al__	DEL	284	Barber, Elijah	COL	180	Barclay, Abraham Sr	ALB	99
Banks, Benjamin	WST	112	Barber, Elijah	HRK	543	Barclay, George	CAY	630
Banks, Catharine	ULS	251	Barber, Ely	ESS	322	Barclay, George	MNT	55
Banks, James	NYK	136	Barber, Freeman	ONN	179	Barclay, Henry	ORN	399
Banks, James	ULS	258	Barber, Friend	SRA	16	Barclay, Hugh	ORN	300
Banks, James	WST	112	Barber, Gardner	WSH	231	Barclay, Jacob	DUT	110
Banks, James	WST	112	Barber, Gardner	WSH	242	Barclay, James	ALB	140
Banks, James	WST	141	Barber, George	WSH	183	Barclay, James	ORN	300
Banks, John	NYK	25	Barber, George R.	WSH	237	Barclay, Joacham	ALB	67
Banks, John	WSH	194	Barber, Gideon	SRA	58	Barclay, John	KNG	4
Banks, John	WST	140	Barber, Henry	RNS	67	Barclay, John	ULS	189
Banks, Jonathan	WST	112	Barber, Herman	HRK	544	Barclay, Joseph	ORN	300
Banks, Mary	NYK	88	Barber, Isaac	WSH	275	Barclay, Mary	DUT	65
Banks, Samuel	QNS	84	Barber, Isaac Jun	GRN	352	Barclay, Samuel	ORN	300
Banks, Samuel	WST	112	Barber, James	CAY	650	Barclay, Thomas	NYK	50
Banks, amuel	WST	113	Barber, James	NYK	18	Barclay, Thomas	ORN	302
Banks, Thaddeus	DEL	268	Barber, James	WSH	184	Barclay, William	ULS	234
Banks. Thomas	DEL	268	Barber, Jane	ALB	100	Barcley, Richard	NYK	149
Bankson, Levi	OTS	27	Barber, Jane Ann	DUT	63	Barcly, James	NYK	20
Banner, Frederick	DEL	283	Barber, Jeremiah	GRN	335	Barculow, Elizabeth	KNG	6
Bannerman, Ellinor	NYK	30	Barber, Jesse	GRN	353	Barculow, Herman	KNG	6
Bannister, Christopher	SRA	16	Barber, John	ALB	72	Barculow, Jaques	KNG	6
Bannister, John	SRA	16	Barber, John	ALB	135	Barculow, John	KNG	6
Bannister, Thomas	QNS	73	Barber, John	CHN	950	Bard, Alborn	SCH	142
Bannom, John	NYK	131	Barber, John	DEL	276	Bard, Elisha	WSH	212
Banta, Aron	MNT	89	Barber, John	NYK	40	Bard, Ezra	SCH	142

Bard, Ezra	SCH 142	Barker, Caleb	RNS 20
Bard, John	NYK 54	Barker, Caleb	WST 162
Bard, John	NYK 131	Barker, Calvin	RNS 81
Bard, John	SCH 142	Barker, Daniel	OND 190
Bard, Jonathan	SUF 108	Barker, Daniel	WST 121
Bard, Luke	SCH 142	Barker, David	SRA 32
Bard, Mary	NYK 68	Barker, Ebeneze	SRA 50
Bard, Samuel	DUT 107	Barker, Ebenezer	CLN 163
Barde, Elizabeth	NYK 35	Barker, Ebenezer	OND 196
Barden, Abram	ONN 170	Barker, Ebenezer	OND 203
Barden, Elisha	RNS 41	Barker, Ebenezer D.	OND 196
Barden, Jacob	DEL 283	Barker, Elihu	OND 196
Barden, Moses	OTS 32	Barker, Frederick	ALB 125
Bardin, Azeriah	OND 183	Barker, George	NYK 109
Bardin, Edward	NYK 31	Barker, Hannah	DUT 88
Bardin, James	ONT 496	Barker, Henry	HRK 463
Bardin, Nathan	ONT 400	Barker, Hezekiah	OND 195
Bardin, Thomas	ONT 412	Barker, Ichabod	ORN 362
Bardin, T..mas, Jur	ONT 492	Barker, Ichabod	SRA 58
Bardle, Weightstill	ONT 476	Barker, Isaac	CLN 159
Bardon, John	GRN 357	Barker, James	DUT 79
Bardon, Noah	ONT 406	Barker, James	OND 197
Bardon, Otis	ONT 470	Barker, James	WSH 301
Bardsley, Beverly	CLN 154	Barker, James	WST 118
Bardsley, Emanuel	CLN 154	Barker, Jared	OND 168
Bardsley, Jehiel	CLN 154	Barker, Jesse	OND 167
Bardsley, John	CLN 154	Barker, Jesse	SRA 34
Bardsley, Thomas	ALB 11	Barker, John	CAY 586
Bardsley, William	ALB 79	Barker, John	CAY 688
Bardwell, Elias	CHN 786	Barker, John	NYK 87
Baremoore, Marshall	CLN 173	Barker, John	OND 191
Baremore, Henry	RCK 102	Barker, John	SUF 65
Baremore, John	WST 123	Barker, John	TIO 218
Baremore, Nathaniel	WST 112	Barker, John	WST 122
Bargardus, Peter	SCH 167	Barker, Jonathan	OND 193
Bargen, Gerret	QNS 68	Barker, Joseph	NYK 73
Barger, Andrew	ALB 100	Barker, Joseph	OND 185
Barger, Jacob	QNS 67	Barker, Joseph	QNS 80
Bargood, Thomas	MNT 110	Barker, Joseph	TIO 233
Bargy, Peter	HRK 455	Barker, Josephus	ONN 158
Barhight, Andrew	DUT 97	Barker, Josiah	COL 218
Barhight, John	DUT 60	Barker, Levi	OND 201
Barhight, John	DUT 116	Barker, Lora	SRA 48
Barhight, William	DUT 24	Barker, Malica	OND 191
Barhite, Peter	RNS 61	Barker, Marks	COL 255
Barhite, Walter P.	RNS 61	Barker, Mary	WST 116
Barhydt, Corns	ALB 8	Barker, Miles	OND 191
Barhydt, Hy	ALB 6	Barker, Miles	OND 201
Barhydt, Jeronomus	ALB 18	Barker, Munson	OND 167
Barhydt, Jesse	ALB 38	Barker, Nicholas	CLN 159
Barhydt, John	ALB 7	Barker, Oliver	ESS 309
Barhydt, John	ALB 27	Barker, Oliver	NYK 70
Barhydt, John C.	ALB 7	Barker, Papilon	GRN 344
Barhydt, John J.	ALB 7	Barker, Paul	HRK 414
Barhydt, Lewis	ALB 3	Barker, Peckham	OND 197
Barhydt, Matthew	ALB 19	Barker, Pellich	NYK 70
Barhydt, Peter	SCH 162	Barker, Peter	NYK 122
Barich, John	MNT 11	Barker, Pheneas	CLN 168
Barie, Daniel	KNG 5	Barker, Philo	OND 201
Barie, William	KNG 6	Barker, Phinehas	TIO 216
Baringer, Hendrick	RNS 7	Barker, Richard	DEL 289
Baringer, Jacob	RNS 64	Barker, Robt	ALB 12
Baringer, Peter	ALB 89	Barker, Rubin	CLN 165
Baringer, Zachariah	RNS 59	Barker, Russell	CHN 890
Bark see Park		Barker, Salmon	OND 199
Bark_, John-Widow	CHN 848	Barker, Samuel	DUT 39
Barkelow, Abraham	RCH 88	Barker, Samuel	QNS 77
Barkelow, Cornelius	SRA 26	Barker, Samuel	WST 121
Barkelow, John	RCH 88	Barker, Samuel	
Barker, Abijah	WST 119	Augustus	DUT 5
Barker, Abijah	WST 148	Barker, Samuel Shaw	SRA 32
Barker, Abraham	SRA 9	BArker, Silus	CHN 742
BArker, Amasa	SRA 35	Barker, Solomon	CAY 678
Barker, Benajah	SRA 56	Barker, Solomon	OND 199
Barker, Benj.	OND 209	Barker, Thomas	ALB 135
Barker, Boker	WST 150	Barker, Thomas	SRA 58
Barker, Brian B._	NYK 29	Barker, Thomas B.	ALB 10

Barker, Thomas E.	GRN 342	Barlow, Benjamin	ONT 366
Barker, Uzel	OND 191	Barlow, Daniel	DUT 110
Barker, Wardwell	OND 191	Barlow, Daniel	SRA 25
Barker, Willeam	WSH 267	Barlow, Ebenezer	OND 209
Barker, William	DUT 137	Barlow, Elisha	DUT 133
Barker, William	GRN 338	Barlow, Ensabish	GRN 337
Barker, William	GRN 343	Barlow, Jabez	SRA 24
Barker, William	HRK 416	Barlow, Jonah	CAY 632
Barker, William	ORN 355	Barlow, Jonathan	DEL 278
Barker, William	RNS 21	Barlow, Joseph	DEL 270
Barker, Wm	SUF 65	Barlow, Joseph	OTS 30
Barker, William	WST 118	Barlow, Moses	DUT 145
Barker, William	WST 120	Barlow, Nathan	ALB 30
Barker, Zebulon	RNS 74	Barlow, Nathan	OND 209
Barker, Zenas	COL 206	Barlow, Nathan	ULS 190
Barkhoof, Fredk	ALB 41	Barlow, Nathan Junr	ALB 30
Barklet, Harvey	SRA 26	Barlow, Peter	TIO 258
Barklet, Otis	SRA 26	Barlow, Peter	TIO 265
Barkman, Jacob	ALB 92	Barlow, Samuel	DEL 271
Barkwell, John	NYK 126	Barlow, Smith	DUT 145
Barky, Benjamin	NYK 34	Barlow, Thomas	CAY 578
Barlas, William	NYK 29	Barlow, Thomas	DUT 133
Barless, James	SRA 20	Barlow, Thomas ye 2d	DUT 133
Barlet, Benjamin	ALB 72	Barlow, Warren	ULS 185
Barley, Casper	NYK 134	Barlow, William	NYK 38
Barley, Edmund	DEL 269	Barlsley, Eli	SRA 21
Barley, Isaac	SRA 22	Barman, Joseph	NYK 87
Barley, Jacob	ULS 214	Barmore, Nathaniel	WSH 266
Barley, John	SUF 83	Barn, Aaron	WSH 186
Barley, Jonathan	ULS 214	Barn, Lemuel	TIO 243
Barlis, Samuel	SUF 85	Barnabe, James	SUF 69
Barllett, Joseph	NYK 115	Barnabus, Martin	MNT 114
Barlow, Abner	ONT 428	Barnaby, Thomas	CAY 548
Barlow, Benjamin	DUT 115	Barnam, Eliakim	ALB 71
		Barnard, Aaron	OND 216
		Barnard, Adonijah	OND 216
		Barnard, Ashbel	OND 187
		Barnard, Ashbel Junr	OND 187
		Barnard, David	GRN 341
		Barnard, David	OND 157
		Barnard, David	OND 164
		Barnard, David	RNS 111
		Barnard, Elihu	RNS 95

Name	Loc	Name	Loc	Name	Loc
Barnard, Foster	ONT 482	Barnes, Samuel Junr	DUT 119	Barns, Benjamin	OND 189
Barnard, Hannah	SRA 5	Barnes, Samuel Senr	DUT 125	Barns, Benjamin	QNS 70
Barnard, Jesse	GRN 341	Barnes, Seth	ONN 134	Barns, Calvin	HRK 556
Barnard, John	OND 217	Barnes, Seth	SUF 107	Barns, Chancey	WSH 270
Barnard, John	SRA 53	Barnes, Shearman	OND 207	Barns, Comfort	SRA 4
Barnard, Joseph	CLN 160	Barnes, Silas	CAY 714	Barns, Dan	COL 202
Barnard, Moses	OND 157	Barnes, Thomas	CAY 580	Barns, Dan Junr	COL 187
Barnard, Moses Junr	OND 169	Barnes, Thomas	CAY 652	Barns, Daniel	OND 196
Barnard, Pharis	OND 158	Barnes, Thomas	DUT 99	Barns, Ebenezer	CHN 924
Barnard, Reuben	OTS 9	Barnes, Titus	GRN 332	Barns, Eber	CAY 694
Barnard, Samuel	HRK 423	Barnes, Trueman	ULS 244	Barns, Elijah	MNT 55
Barnard, Samuel	OND 187	Barnes, William	DUT 39	Barns, Elisha	COL 210
Barnard, Susannah	OND 181	Barnes, William	DUT 60	Barns, Ell	ALB 115
Barnard, William	OND 187	Barnes, William	NYK 92	Barns, Gaml	OTS 14
Barnard, Wm	OTS 9	Barnes, William	ONN 133	Barns, Gilbert	RNS 18
Barne, Benajah	TIO 245	Barnes, William	OTS 24	Barns, James	OND 186
Barne, Jehu	TIO 245	Barnes, William	SUF 106	Barns, James	ONT 312
Barnes, Abraham	SUF 107	Barnes, William R.	DUT 64	Barns, James	ONT 380
Barnes, Abraham	ULS 180	Barnes, Zadock	CAY 714	Barns, James	ONT 498
Barnes, Allen	RNS 54	Barnes, Zopher	OND 207	Barns, James	WSH 304
Barnes, Aranas	GRN 346	Barnet, Dorathy	NYK 139	Barns, Jedediah	OND 172
Barnes, Asa	ONN 132	Barnet, Elbert	NYK 76	Barns, Jedediah	WSH 193
Barnes, Asa	ONN 163	Barnet, Ester	NYK 72	Barns, Jehiel	WSH 276
Barnes, Benjamin	OND 207	Barnet, Nathaniel	RNS 20	Barns, Joel	COL 210
Barnes, Bustead	NYK 122	Barnet, Robert	NYK 130	Barns, Joel	OND 177
Barnes, Charles	NYK 85	Barnet, Samuel	NYK 39	Barns, Joel	OND 221
Barnes, Cornelius	CAY 714	Barnet, Samuel a Black	NYK 106	Barns, John	OND 200
Barnes, Daniel	CAY 612	Barnet, Simon	NYK 140	Barns, John	ORN 341
Barnes, Daniel	OND 212	Barnett, Joseph	CAY 622	Barns, John	SRA 4
Barnes, David	OTS 37	Barney, Asa C.	SRA 60	Barns, John	SUF 65
Barnes, David	SUF 106	Barney, Bangs	MNT 18	Barns, John Junr	WST 111
Barnes, Edward	ORN 380	Barney, Benjamin	ONT 442	Barns, Joseph	CAY 646
Barnes, Erastus	OTS 19	Barney, Benjamin	ORN 362	Barns, Joseph	OND 196
Barnes, Ezra	OND 207	Barney, Daniel	HRK 451	Barns, Judah	OND 221
Barnes, George	NYK 36	Barney, Hauson	MNT 98	Barns, Juder	OND 218
Barnes, George	RCH 90	Barney, Henry	NYK 109	Barns, Justus	COL 248
Barnes, George	ULS 260	Barney, Luther	CAY 656	Barns, Laneda	ONT 410
Barnes, George Junr	RCH 90	Barney, Nathaniel	ALB 134	Barns, Lewis	HRK 556
Barnes, Giles	OTS 57	Barney, Samuel	WSH 282	Barns, Loan	OND 174
Barnes, Henry	DUT 106	Barney, Thomas	ONT 432	Barns, Luther	HRK 556
Barnes, Hester	NYK 96	Barney, William	CAY 532	Barns, Oliver	OND 186
Barnes, Isaac	ALB 115	Barney, Wm	STB 197	Barns, Parm rlee	ONT 458
Barnes, Isaac	OTS 9	Barney, William	WSH 254	Barns, Perigh	SCH 133
Barnes, Isaac	SUF 108	Barnham, Eliphalet	NYK 146	Barns, Philip	OND 193
Barnes, Jabez	OND 212	Barnham, Eliphalet	RNS 54	Barns, Philo	SRA 26
Barnes, James	CAY 640	Barnham, Isaac	ONN 134	Barns, Reuben	DEL 276
Barnes, James	DUT 38	Barnham, Thomas	ONN 134	Barns, Reuben	OND 164
Barnes, James	HRK 550	Barnham, Thomas	ONN 170	Barns, Reuben	SRA 51
Barnes, James	RNS 68	Barnham, Wm	RNS 55	Barns, Richard	COL 257
Barnes, John	CAY 714	Barnhard, John	OND 210	Barns, Richard	WSH 279
Barnes, John	CAY 718	Barnhardt, David	RNS 17	Barns, Robert	WSH 279
Barnes, John	ONT 318	Barnhardt, Hendrick	RNS 17	Barns, Robert Jur	WSH 279
Barnes, John	ORN 370	Barnhardt, Joseph	RNS 17	Barns, Samuel	ONT 458
Barnes, John	ORN 381	Barnhart, David	CAY 642	Barns, Samuel	WSH 224
Barnes, John	ORN 384	Barnhart, David	CAY 668	Barns, Sarah	TIO 243
Barnes, John	ULS 243	Barnhart, David	RNS 26	Barns, Shilander	MNT 49
Barnes, John	RCH 93	Barnhart, David	SRA 55	Barns, Silas	HRK 574
Barnes, John	WST 111	Barnhart, Frederick	STB 207	Barns, Solomon	OND 187
Barnes, Joseph	DUT 113	Barnhart, Henry	WSH 220	Barns, Stephen	WST 112
Barnes, Joshua	WST 147	Barnhart, Jacob	RNS 39	Barns, Thadora	WSH 252
Barnes, Joshua	WST 148	Barnhart, James	SCH 135	Barns, Theodora	WSH 223
Barnes, Levi	OND 222	Barnhart, John	DEL 271	Barns, Thomas	CAY 692
Barnes, Martha	SUF 108	Barnhart, John	NYK 153	Barns, Thomas	COL 205
Barnes, Matthias	ORN 380	Barnhart, Philip	DEL 271	Barns, Thomas	HRK 595
Barnes, Nathaniel	CAY 718	Barnhum, Abijah	OTS 6	Barns, Timothy	OND 202
Barnes, Oliver	TIO 230	Barnman, Horace	WSH 185	Barns, Warner	ALB 89
Barnes, Peter	WST 142	Barnnard, Jose	OND 222	Barns, William	OND 221
Barnes, Phinehas	ONN 132	Barns, Abel	ONT 434	Barns, William	WSH 275
Barnes, Phinehas	ONN 138	Barns, Abel	SCH 143	Barns, Ziah	SRA 50
Barnes, Pricilla	NYK 65	Barns, Abraham	ALB 115	Barnt, Aaron	RNS 30
Barnes, Richard	WST 162	Barns, Abm	RNS 101	Barnt, Jacob	RNS 86
Barnes, Robert	NYK 117	Barns, Amos	OND 194	Barnum, Aaron	OTS 32
Barnes, Roger	RCH 92	Barns, Amos	OND 221	Barnum, Azor	DUT 175
Barnes, Rozel	ONN 132	Barns, Amos Junr	OND 221	Barnum, Daniel	DUT 172
Barnes, Rufus	OND 217	Barns, Anne	ULS 207	Barnum, David	DUT 170
Barnes, Samuel	OND 210	Barns, Appleton	SRA 42	Barnum, Eliphalet	DUT 43
Barnes, Saml	RNS 64	Barns, Asal	MNT 124	Barnum, Jehiel	CLN 167

20

Name	Loc	Pg	Name	Loc	Pg	Name	Loc	Pg
Barnum, Jesse	CLN	166	Barrett, Dingy	DUT	81	Barry, Thomas T.	NYK	32
Barnum, Joshua	DUT	175	Barrett, Eleazar	ONT	406	Bars, John	MNT	77
Barnum, Joshua Junr	DUT	175	Barrett, Eliada	DEL	289	Barsh, Ludwick	HRK	475
Barnum, Levy	COL	240	Barrett, Elijah	DUT	96	Barsh, Rudolph	MNT	19
Barnum, Noah	CHN	840	Barrett, Ephraim	DEL	289	Bart, Anthony	DUT	163
Barnum, Salmon	SRA	13	Barrett, Gideon	DUT	84	Bart, Ebenezer	ONT	506
Barnum, Samuel	WSH	204	Barrett, Isaac	DUT	83	Bartas, Laurence Loura	NYK	24
Barnum, Samuel	WST	127	Barrett, Isaac	DUT	84	Bartel, John P. B.	COL	192
Barnum, Stephen	DUT	167	Barrett, Isaac	DUT	96	Bartel, Joseph	COL	259
Barnum, Thaddeus	DUT	43	Barrett, James	DUT	96	Bartell, _____	STB	203
Barnum, Thomas	NYK	70	Barrett, James Junr	DUT	87	Barteloe, Rachel	ORN	350
Barnum, William	HRK	587	Barrett, John	COL	187	Bartem, Gabriel	NYK	39
Barnum, Zar	DUT	172	Barrett, John	DUT	86	Barter, Gilbert	NYK	37
Barnum, Zebulon	CAY	716	Barrett, John	ULS	235	Barthick, Stephen	HRK	540
Barnwell, George	NYK	26	Barrett, Joseph	CHN	850	Bartholime	CHN	742
Barnyea, Wm	RCK	108	Barrett, Josephus	DUT	93	Bartholemew, John	CAY	554
Barolow, Lewis	WSH	187	Barrett, Justus	DUT	93	Bartholomew, Abigail	OTS	40
Baron see Bacon			Barrett, Marcus	DUT	17	Bartholomew, Isaac	OTS	40
Baron, Ebenezar Lee	ONT	334	Barrett, Moesman	DUT	93	Bartholomew, Jacob	OTS	40
Barow, William	ONT	378	Barrett, Reuben	DUT	95	Bartholomew, Joseph	ONN	132
Barr, Darius	WSH	290	Barrett, Roger	WSH	283	Bartholomew, Joseph	OTS	40
Barr, Frederick	NYK	94	Barrett, Samuel	DUT	21	Bartholomew, Theobalt	OTS	40
Barr, Henry	MNT	75	Barrett, Simeon	DUT	22	Bartholomew, Adam	SCH	144
Barr, Hugh	NYK	100	Barrett, Stephen	OND	185	Bartholomew, Andrew	DUT	153
Barr, James	CAY	532	Barrett, Thomas	COL	204	Bartholomew, Charles	OND	180
Barr, James	NYK	87	Barrett, Weigh	ALB	54	Bartholomew, Charles	SCH	163
Barr, John	CAY	716	Barrett, William	DUT	95	Bartholomew, Chauncey	ONN	192
Barr, Matthew	ORN	384	Barrette, Francis	NYK	92	Bartholomew, Isaac	HRK	547
Barr, Peter	KNG	8	Barretts, Francis	NYK	96	Bartholomew, Jehiel	HRK	547
Barr, Peter	NYK	123	Barrey, Daniel	SRA	28	Bartholomew, Jeptha	WSH	283
Barr, Philip	NYK	18	Barrie, William Ju.	KNG	10	Bartholomew, Jesse	HRK	547
Barrager, Abraham	QNS	68	Barrigar, Coonrod	GRN	326	Bartholomew, Jessey(?)	GRN	346
Barrager, Jacob	QNS	68	Barringer, Coenradt	COL	230	Bartholomew, Josiah	OND	166
Barrager, John	QNS	68	Barringer, David	COL	190	Bartholomew, Lemuel	WSH	283
Barrager, Luke	QNS	68	Barringer, David	RNS	7	Bartholomew, Levi	ONN	141
Barrager, Tunis	QNS	68	Barringer, George	RNS	7	Bartholomew, Oliver	OND	220
Barras, Joseph	SRA	20	Barringer, Henry C.	COL	230	Bartholomew, Philip	SCH	130
Barras, Stephen	NYK	73	Barringer, Jacob	HRK	499	Bartholomew, Squire	WSH	285
Barrass, Amos	WSH	272	Barringer, Jacob H.	COL	194	Bartholomew, William	WSH	283
Barrass, John	RNS	90	Barringer, John	COL	229	Bartholt, Henry	NYK	93
Barrat, Joshua	OTS	41	Barringer, John C.	COL	230	Barthomlus, Jedediah	SRA	50
Barratt, Asa	OTS	22	Barringer, Peter	COL	225	Barthrop, William	COL	258
Barratt, John	WST	161	Barringer, Peter	COL	230	Barthwick, James	ALB	85
Barratt, JOseph	WST	138	Barringer, Peter	COL	231	Bartine, John	NYK	93
Barratt, Nathanus	OTS	21	Barringer, Philip	RNS	4	Bartle, Andrew	MNT	97
Barratt, Samuel	OTS	21	Barringer, Zacchariah	RNS	4	Bartle, Andrew	WSH	207
Barratt, Samuel	WST	138	Barris, Ira	OTS	15	Bartle, Andrew A.	COL	223
Barratt, Samuel Junr	WST	134	Barris, Timothy	OTS	15	Bartle, Benjamin	MNT	97
Barregor, Henry	RCH	91	Barrit, Isaac P:	OND	216	Bartle, Henry	COL	198
Barrell, Colburn	WSH	268	Barrit, Thomas	ALB	127	Bartle, Jacob	COL	179
Barrell, Joseph	WSH	269	Barrit, Thos	OTS	49	Bartle, James	MNT	97
Barrell, Lazerus	WSH	268	Barron, Bethuel	CAY	686	Bartle, John	COL	235
Barret, Benjamin	OND	193	Barron, George	NYK	82	Bartle, Philip	MNT	97
Barret, Charles	OND	194	Barron, James	NYK	136	Bartle, Phillip	COL	179
Barret, David	OTS	22	Barron, William	NYK	100	Bartle, Phillip Junr	COL	179
Barret, Ebenezer	SRA	33	Barrow, Daniel	DEL	271	Bartle, Phillip H.	COL	198
Barret, Hezekiah	SRA	48	Barrow, James	OND	217	Bartle, Richard	COL	224
Barret, Israel	OND	193	Barrow, John	DEL	272	Bartleme, Justus	ESS	296
Barret, James	OND	188	Barrow, John	NYK	36	Bartles, Christopher	MNT	9
Barret, John	KNG	8	Barrow, John S.	NYK	35	Bartlet, Bartholomy	WSH	223
Barret, Joseph	NYK	52	Barrow, Samuel	NYK	17	Bartlet, Benjamin	OND	223
Barret, Marks	ALB	87	Barrow, Seth	CLN	156	Bartlet, Ebenezer	OND	191
Barret, Pearse	NYK	105	Barrow, Thomas	NYK	26	Bartlet, George	SRA	15
Barret, Philander	ONT	394	Barrow, Thomas	WSH	225	Bartlet, Gideon	HRK	534
Barret, Samuel	OND	188	Barrowe, Samuel	NYK	21	Bartlet, Hugh	SRA	16
Barret, Thos	OTS	43	Barrows, Abner	WSH	215	Bartlet, James	ESS	302
Barret, Vedam	ONT	394	Barrows, John	WSH	215	Bartlet, James	OND	217
Barret, Wm	OTS	41	Barrows, Tillson	OND	196	Bartlet, John	HRK	535
Barret, William	SRA	33	Barrs, John	ONN	148	Bartlet, Judah	DEL	280
Barret, Zalmon	OND	163	Barruk, Betsey	NYK	52	Bartlet, Levi	DEL	284
Barrett, Abraham	CAY	690	Barry see Barie			Bartlet, Moses	WSH	228
Barrett, Abraham	WST	139	Barry, Edward	NYK	44	Bartlet, Oliver	CHN	808
Barrett, Bartholemew	SRA	20	Barry, James	NYK	73	Bartlet, Phillip	SRA	10
Barrett, Bennony	CHN	966	Barry, John	ALB	43	Bartlet, Richard	DUT	127
Barrett, Bethuel	DUT	76	Barry, John	GRN	331	Bartlet, Russel	OTS	19
Barrett, David	COL	204	Barry, Thomas	ALB	136	Bartlet, Samuel	WSH	247
Barrett, David Junr	COL	204	Barry, William	NYK	62	Bartlet, Thomas	WSH	229

Bartlett, Aaron	WSH 305	Barton, Robert	OTS 33	Bass, Moses	RNS 91
Bartlett, Benjamin	NYK 129	Barton, Roger	ORN 278	Bass, Peter	CHN 978
Bartlett, Ebenezer	TIO 257	Barton, Roger	ORN 396	Bass, Rudolph	MNT 2
Bartlett, Haynes	CAY 528	Barton, Roger	ULS 255	Bass, William	OND 195
Bartlett, Henry	HRK 453	Barton, Roger	WST 148	Bass, Zanock	MNT 83
Bartlett, Isaiah	MNT 91	Barton, Ruphes	WSH 192	Bassel, Joseph	OTS 37
Bartlett, Joel	COL 212	Barton, Samuel	CHN 750	Bassel, Saml	OTS 34
Bartlett, John	RNS 75	Barton, Samuel	RNS 103	Basset, Eanoch	WSH 225
Bartlett, Joseph	COL 250	Barton, Seth	WSH 280	Basset, Ebenezer	WSH 233
Bartlett, Lewis	NYK 117	Barton, Stephen	ONN 154	Basset, Ellehu	GRN 328
Bartlett, Littlefield	DUT 126	Barton, Stephen	ONT 446	Basset, James	ALB 127
Bartlett, Michael	ALB 77	Barton, Stephen	ORN 394	Basset, John	GRN 328
Bartlett, Moses	CAY 672	Barton, Stukely	OTS 33	Basset, John	WSH 231
Bartlett, Nicholas	CHN 974	Barton, Thomas	NYK 143	Basset, Peter	SCH 158
Bartlett, Samuel	COL 212	Barton, Timothy	WSH 206	Basset, Saml	OTS 37
Bartlett, William	NYK 113	Barton, William	NYK 96	Basset, Truman	COL 218
Bartlett, William	NYK 118	Barton, William	NYK 151	Basse[tt?], ___her	OND 222
Bartlett, Wm James	MNT 51	Barton, Wm	RNS112A	Bassett, ___	ONT 492
Bartley, David	SCH 138	Bartow, Alexander	SUF 80	Bassett, Alvord	RNS 99
Bartley, David	SCH 158	Bartow, Augustus	WST 144	Bassett, David	WSH 284
Bartley, John	COL 240	Bartow, Basil T.	WST 144	Bassett, Edward	RNS 25
Barto, Jonathan L.	OND 185	Bartow, Elijah	WSH 212	Bassett, Elizabeth	NYK 99
Barto, Wm	GRN 356	Bartow, Francis	SUF 65	Bassett, Fortinatus	OND 222
Barto, Wm Jun	GRN 356	Bartow, Jesse	CHN 742	Bassett, Isaac	DUT 145
Barto_, Moses	WST 148	Bartow, John	DUT 20	Bassett, Isaac	RNS 59
Bartoff, Crynere	RCK 105	Bartow, John	QNS 69	Bassett, John	ALB 43
Bartolama, Jacobus	COL 190	Bartow, John	WST 120	Bassett, Joshua	DUT 157
Barton, Adonijah	WSH 280	Bartow, John	WST 148	Bassett, Jotham	CAY 676
Barton, Alpheus	ONN 129	Bartow, Luke	WST 150	Bassett, Maria	ALB 51
Barton, Amos	DUT 105	Bartow, Morris	SUF 80	Bassett, Nehemiah	ALB 124
Barton, Amos	ORN 395	Bartow, Nathan	SUF 65	Bassett, Rufus	ESS 322
Barton, Andrew	DUT 78	Bartow, Obediah	SUF 80	Bassett, Samuel	ALB 83
Barton, Azariah	RNS 103	Bartow, Silus	GRN 344	Bassett, Samuel	WSH 266
Barton, Benajah	WST 149	Bartow, Sten	SUF 65	Bassett, William	OND 205
Barton, Benjamin	ONN 130	Bartow, Theodorius	WST 149	Bassett, William	ONT 452
Barton, Benjamin	ONT 474	Bartow, Theophilus	WST 144	Bassinger, Sephrenus	OTS 58
Benjamin	ULS 181	Bartow, William	WST 144	Baster, George	ULS 205
Barton, Caleb	DUT 79	Bartram, Benjamin	NYK 85	Bastian, Gonsolus	MNT 88
Barton, Caleb	DUT 102	Bartram, John	NYK 143	Bastian, Sybrant	ALB 50
Barton, Caleb Junr	DUT 128	Bartrum, Anthony	ALB 131	Bastie, Jeremiah	SRA 28
Barton, David	OND 186	Bartru_, John a Black	NYK 131	Bastine, John	NYK 110
Barton, Edward	RNS 103	Barwick, John	NYK 56	Bastwick, Martin	SRA 34
Barton, Eleazer	SRA 40	Barwick, William	NYK 60	Bastwick, William W.	SRA 23
Barton, Elijah	ORN 396	Barwick, William	NYK 79	Basum, Peter	CAY 528
Barton, Elijah	QNS 75	Barwise, Thomas	KNG 8	Baswick, Everton	WSH 201
Barton, Elisha	WST 149	Barzee, Gabriel	WSH 294	Bat..in, Jacob	CAY 578
Barton, Ezra	OTS 29	Bascom, Asa	HRK 536	Batchellor, John	NYK 95
Barton, Ezra	OTS 32	Bascom, Jonathan	DEL 278	Bate, James	250
Barton, Gershom	OND 181	Bascum, Alpheus	DEL 274	Bate, Lendo_ a Black	NYK 33
Barton, Gilbert	WST 156	Base, William	SRA 21	Bateman, Eleazer	SRA 52
Barton, Isaac	ULS 238	Base, William G.	SRA 21	Bateman, Elisha	HRK 579
Barton, James	COL 256	Baseley, Jane	NYK 72	Bateman, Elisha Jun.	HRK 578
Barton, James	RCH 87	Basely, James	NYK 128	Bateman, Job	CLN 167
Barton, Jeremiah	WST 125	Bashford, Cornelius	CAY 658	Bateman, Joel	CAY 620
Barton, Jesse	ORN 345	Bashford, James	COL 228	Bateman, John J.	MNT 13
Barton, John	DUT 72	Bashford, John	COL 199	Bateman, Jonathan	CAY 536
Barton, John	ORN 395	Bashford	WST 146	Bateman, Manoah	CAY 620
Barton, John	WST 130	Bashford, Soloman	NYK 105	Bateman, Semeon	CLN 173
Barton, John	WST 155	Bashford, William	DUT 88	Bateman, Zadock	CAY 668
Barton, John Junr	DUT 76	Bashorr, Jacob	HRK 429	Bates see Baets & Baits	
Barton, Jonathan	WSH 207	Bashwick, Matthew	SRA 59	Bates, Andrew	CHN 800
Barton, Joseph	COL 255	Basinger, Andw	OTS 58	Bates, Ann	RNS 105
Barton, Joseph	RCH 90	Basinger, John	OTS 58	Bates, Anthony	NYK 117
Barton, Joseph Junr	RCH 91	Basinger, Wm	OTS 58	Bates, Archibald	OND 175
Barton, Joshua	DUT 132	Basitt, Stephen	WST 140	Bates, Benjamin	DUT 104
Barton, Joshua	OTS 21	Basle., David	TIO 251	Bates, Benjamin	ONN 133
Barton, Josiah	ONN 130	Basley, Lewis	TIO 251	Bates, Benjamin	ONT 372
Barton, Leonard	DUT 131	Bass, Abisha	RNS 103	Bates, Bnjn	TIO 243
Barton, Lewis	DUT 131	Bass, Abraham(?)	MNT 3	Bates, Bennet	ONT 352
Barton, Lewis Junr	DUT 129	Bass, Eleazer	OTS 35	Bates, Clark	CHN 910
Barton, Luke	ORN 285	Bass, George	MNT 1	Bates, Daniel	CAY 564
Barton, Mary	DUT 76	Bass, Jenny	QNS 67	Bates, Daniel	STB 200
Barton, Oster	RCH 90	Bass, Jerimiah	MNT 83	Bates, Edward	WSH 230
Barton, Peter	DUT 52	Bass, John	DUT 67	Bates, Elisha	SCH 143
Barton, Peter	SRA 29	Bass, Jonathan	OND 195	Bates, Elisha	TIO 243
Barton, Phebe	WST 114	Bass, Joseph	NYK 68	Bates, Elizabeth	DUT 139
Barton, Robert	NYK 143	Bass, Mitchell	ONN 134	Bates, Ephraim	HRK 460

22

Name	Ref	Name	Ref	Name	Ref
Bates, Ephraim	OTS 26	Bauer, Frederick	DUT 136	Bayles, John	NYK 140
Bates, George	ONT 456	Bauer, John	DUT 136	Bayley, Elias	SUF 79
Bates, Hicky	DUT 38	Bauer, Peter	DUT 136	Bayley, Elijah	ESS 296
Bates, Isacher	WSH 265	Baughman, Joseph	COL 195	Bayley, Isaac	SUF 79
Bates, Israel	MNT 12	Baughman, Solomon Junr	COL 199	Bayley, Oliver	SUF 79
Bates, Jacob	MNT 12	Bauhus, William	RNS 30	Bayley, Sarah	NYK 18
Bates, James	DUT 146	Bauky, Minto a Black	NYK 36	Bayley, Wilkee	SUF 84
Bates, James	WSH 211	Baul_er, Maulkert	MNT 33	Bayley, William	WST 148
Bates, James	WSH 293	Baum, Frederick	MNT 18	Baylis, David A.	NYK 77
Bates, John	COL 222	Baum, George	NYK 106	Baylis, Malancton	NYK 16
Bates, John	NYK 85	Baum, Henry	MNT 28	Bayner, Whitehead	QNS 77
Bates, John	OND 217	Baum, Jacob	MNT 13	Baynham, Henry	ESS 298
Bates, John	ONN 150	Baum, Philip	MNT 28	Baynton, Joseph	OND 190
Bates, John	ONT 356	Bauns, John a Black	NYK 103	Bayre, Isaac	NYK 144
Bates, John	TIO 248	Baunside, Thomas	NYK 103	Bays, Abraham	SRA 53
Bates, John	WSH 202	Baunter, John	NYK 110	Bazeley, Daniel	CAY 634
Bates, John	WST 130	Baurdin, .ichard	MNT 79	Bazella, Harman	NYK 144
Bates, John	WST 148	Bausher, Henry	NYK 64	Bazen, James	NYK 117
Bates, John B.	NYK 55	Bauton, Elijah	SRA 58	Bazen, Thomas	NYK 105
Bates, Jonathan	CHN 844	Bautwell, Abraham	ONN 143	Bazley, John	CAY 616
Bates, Jonathan	OND 210	Baux, John	NYK 63	Bazley, Joseph S.	CAY 616
Bates, Jona	OTS 33	Bavy, Elizabeth	NYK 96	Bazly, John	NYK 145
Bates, Joseph	NYK 63	Bawers, Beriah	ONN 146	Bazzill, Thomas	RNS 82
Bates, Joseph	NYK 78	Bawers, Isaac	ONN 145	Be_s, Jacob	CAY 638
Bates, Joseph	ONT 410	Bawhall, Hooper	SCH 167	Be__, Andrew	ONT 484
Bates, Luke	TIO 248	Bawman, John	SCH 168	Be__s, Daniel	WST 124
Bates, Nathen	WSH 253	Baxter, ..rael	QNS 72	Beaach, Ebenezer	GRN 325
Bates, Oliver	OND 209	Baxter, Alpheus	NYK 143	Beabon, Lidea	SRA 47
Bates, Otis	RNS 37	Baxter, Benjamin	WSH 202	Beach, Abel	DUT 138
Bates, Phineas	ONT 386	Baxter, Daniel	WST 125	Beach, Abijah H.	GRN 330
Bates, Phineas	ONT 428	Baxter, David	WST 125	Beach, Abraham	NYK 36
Bates, Reuben	RNS 81	Baxter, Elizabeth	WST 145	Beach, Adner	GRN 333
Bates, Ruphes	WSH 211	Baxter, Enoch	NYK 143	Beach, Agur	DUT 168
Bates, Saml	OTS 11	Baxter, Gideon	DUT 168	Beach, Alexander	SRA 23
Bates, Sarah	NYK 84	Baxter, James	NYK 37	Beach, Allen	ONN 145
Bates, Stephen	DUT 34	Baxter, James	WST 144	Beach, Am...	MNT 72
Bates, Stephen	TIO 244	Baxter, Jesse	DEL 274	Beach, Asa	SRA 23
Bates, Stephen	WST 148	Baxter, John	KNG 4	Beach, Asa	TIO 217
Bates, Thomas	OTS 27	Baxter, John	OND 174	Beach, Asa	WSH 217
Bates, Thomas F.	NYK 106	Baxter, John	SRA 18	Beach, Benjamin	WSH 214
Bates, Walter	WSH 211	Baxter, John	ULS 257	Beach, Bildad	ONN 155
Bates, Wm	TIO 233	Baxter, Levi	DEL 289	Beach, Cephus	DEL 281
Bates, Zadock	ESS 306	Baxter, Marcus	DUT 81	Beach, Clarke	CAY 660
Batesholt, George	SCH 124	Baxter, Michael	QNS 84	Beach, Curtis	CHN 984
Batey, Samuel	NYK 84	Baxter, Moses	WSH 306	Beach, Daniel	NYK 59
Bathalemew, Isra	MNT 122	Baxter, Nathan	DEL 274	Beach, David	DUT 13
Bathrick, Frederick	DUT 149	Baxter, Nathaniel	WST 125	Beach, Edmond	COL 206
Bathrick, Jacob	DUT 149	Baxter, Pettit	WST 126	Beach, Elnathan	COL 210
Batis, Abraham	MNT 118	Baxter, Richard	ULS 264	Beach, Elnathan	ONN 159
Batler, Nathaniel	ONT 390	Baxter, Sarah	ONT 312	Beach, Gershom	ONT 314
Batt, Silas	RNS 15	Baxter, Schuler	NYK 76	Beach, Isaac	DUT 170
Batterfield, Sherebiah	WSH 218	Baxter, Solomon	WST 144	Beach, Isaai	CAY 654
Battershell, Moses	COL 204	Baxter, Stephen	NYK 133	Beach, Jedh	OTS 58
Battershell, William	COL 204	Baxter, Stephen	OND 176	Beach, Jerard	NYK 140
Battey, James	WSH 293	Baxter, Thaddeus	DUT 86	Beach, Jesse	ONT 314
Battis, Judith a Black	NYK 110	Baxter, Thomas	WST 126	Beach, Joab	SRA 22
Battis, Peter a Black	NYK 133	Baxter, Uriah	DEL 274	Beach, Joel	SCH 141
Battison, Joseph	ESS 321	Baxter, William	OND 211	Beach, John	CAY 660
Battle, James	MNT 44	Baxtor, Henry	ONT 392	Beach, John	SCH 141
Battles, Deland	HRK 458	Baxtor, John	RNS 80	Beach, Jonathan	COL 206
Battles, James	COL 203	Bay, John	COL 191	Beach, Jonas	ORN 391
Battles, John	SCH 137	Bayard, Abijah	DEL 287	Beach, Joseph	GRN 326
Batty, Amos	WSH 240	Bayard, David	NYK 119	Beach, Joseph	ORN 363
Batty, Benjamin	WSH 239	Bayard, Hoermanus	NYK 102	Beach, Joseph	SRA 23
Batty, George	RNS 82	Bayard, Jane	KNG 3	Beach, Josiah	ALB 86
Batty, James	WSH 255	Bayard, John	NYK 133	Beach, Michael	ONT 318
Batty, John	WSH 226	Bayard, Lapie a Black	NYK 87	Beach, Philip	ONT 314
Batty, John	WSH 254	Bayard, Nicholas S.	NYK 29	Beach, Rebecca	COL 212
Bat_ty, Robert	WSH 268	Bayard, Rebecca	WST 145	Beach, Richard	DEL 280
Batty, Samuel	WSH 226	Bayard, Stephen N.	ALB 11	Beach, Roxwell	STB 206
Batty, Thomas	WSH 227	Bayard, William	NYK 150	Beach, Roze	ONN 130
Batty, William	WSH 226	Bayard, William	SCH 142	Beach, Rufus	DUT 116
Bauchford, Simeon	SRA 29	Bayeaux, Thomas	NYK 39	Beach, Samuel	NYK 85
Bauchus, Wm	OTS 6	Bayeux, Henry	RNS 93	Beach, Solomon	DUT 13
Bauder, Lodowick	MNT 21	Bayeux, Phebe	WST 149	Beach, Thadeus	RNS 110
Bauer see Bower		Bayeux, Thomas	DUT 65	Beach, Thadeus	WSH 190
Bauer, David	DUT 134	Bayle, Robert	NYK 64	Beach, Thomas	WSH 190

Name	Loc	Name	Loc	Name	Loc
Beach, Titus	WSH 217	Beale, Henry	ORN 392	Bears, Abel	SRA 34
Beach, William	DEL 280	Bealey, Samuel	ALB 132	Bears, Daniel	WST 152
Beach, William	DUT 13	Bealman, William	CHN 750	Bears, Edmond	WST 152
Beach, William	GRN 333	Beals, Abrm	OTS 49	Bears, Silas	WST 160
Beach, William	NYK 27	Beals, Barzilla	HRK 513	Bears, William	WST 151
Beach, Zera	SRA 16	Beals, Elisha	OTS 13	Bearsdlee, Elihu	DUT 137
Beachen, Joseph	ALB 84	Beals, Jacob	OTS 26	Bease, Polly	NYK 49
Beacher, Aeneas	ONT 328	Beals, Josiah	ONT 474	Beasly, Wm	RCK 103
Beacher, Lucy	WSH 286	Beam, John	COL 195	Beat, Nathaniel	SRA 4
Beacher, Willeam	WSH 278	Beam, John	NYK 98	Beatte, Adam	GRN 353
Beacher, Lyman	SUF 106	Beam, Joseph	NYK 84	Beattie, Alexander	ORN 292
Beackmon, Joseuh	CHN 838	Beam, William	COL 195	Beattie, Archibald	ORN 292
Beacon, Amos	SRA 41	Beaman, Daniel	COL 210	Beattie, Charles	ULS 200
Beacon, David	SRA 15	Beaman, Daniel	COL 217	Beattie, Francis	ORN 277
Beacin, David	SRA 41	Beaman, Elam	ALB 133	Beattie, John	ORN 290
Beacon, Harris	OTS 53	Beaman, Ezekeil	ALB 71	Beattie, John	ULS 200
Beacon, Samuel	SRA 15	Beaman, Judah	CHN 784	Beattie, Joseph	ORN 292
Beacroft, Abraham	COL 253	Beaman, Samuel Jur	WSH 287	Beattie, Martha	ORN 303
Beacroft, David	COL 256	Beamon, Freeman	ALB 83	Beattie, Robert	ORN 277
Beacroft, Jonathan	COL 253	Beamon, Simon	COL 217	Beattie, Robert	ULS 198
Beacroft, William	COL 253	Beamont, Asa	TIO 246	Beattie, Samuel	DUT 15
Beadel, Daniel	WSH 235	Beamont, Dan	COL 263	Beattie, Thomas	ORN 303
Beadle, Abraham	ULS 195	Beamont, James	ONN 165	Beattie, William	ORN 292
Beadle, Benjn	OTS 14	Beamont, James	ONT 464	Beatty, Edward	RCH 92
Beadle, Daniel	DUT 120	Beamus, Adam	ALB 21	Beatty, James	NYK 72
Beadle, David	ONT 490	Beamus, Conradt	ALB 100	Beatty, John	NYK 92
Beadle, David	OTS 14	Beamus, John	ALB 99	Beatty, John	RCH 90
Beadle, Elisha	DUT 14	Bean, Caty	NYK 37	Beatty, Robert	NYK 30
Beadle, Elisha	DUT 117	Bean, James	CLN 154	Beatty, William	ESS 294
Beadle, Ephraim	WST 126	Bean, Lewis a Black	NYK 110	Beatty, William	NYK 107
Beadle, Jacamiah	QNS 75	Bean, Richard a Black	NYK 87	Beatty, Edward	NYK 150
Beadle, James	COL 199	Beanard, Elijah	CHN 862	Beaty, Isaac	ONT 404
Beadle, Jeremiah	GRN 353	Bear, Benjn	OTS 44	Beaty, Leonard	ONT 508
Beadle, Jermiah Junr	GRN 353	Bear, George	CAY 664	Beaty, William	NYK 17
Beadle, John	DUT 121	Bear, Henry	ALB 90	Beauman, Benjamin	NYK 118
Beadle, John	OND 180	Bear, Philip	ALB 90	Beaumon, Sebastian	NYK 26
Beadle, John	OND 186	Beard, ...on	CAY 664	Beaumont, Arthur C.	NYK 18
Beadle, John Junior	OND 190	Beard, Abedi	MNT 93	Beaumont, Dan	CLN 173
Beadle, Moses	OND 180	Beard, Bearns	SRA 36	Beaumont, Hannah	NYK 50
Beadle, Silvester	GRN 354	Beard, Ezekiel	DEL 287	Beaumont, Oliver	COL 257
Beadle, Timothy	DUT 123	Beard, Jacob	ALB 58	Beaumont, Trigant	NYK 27
Beagle, David Junr	QNS 74	Beard, Jacob	SCH 158	Beaumont, William	CLN 173
Beagle, Elizabeth	QNS 73	Beard, James	ORN 284	Beaver, James	ONT 320
Beagle, Hezekiah	QNS 75	Beard, Joseph	QNS 84	Beaver, John	ULS 233
Beagle, Icabod	SUF 93	Beard, Josiah	CAY 664	Beaver, John Junr	ULS 234
Beagle, Isaac	QNS 78	Beard, Patterson	QNS 84	Beaver, Thomas	ALB 56
Beagle, John	ALB 54	Beard, Russel	ALB 33	Beavers, Phineas	TIO 250
Beagle, John	COL 220	Beard, Samuel	QNS 84	Beavins, Gabriel	DUT 160
Beagle, John	SRA 5	Beard, Volentine	ONT 500	Beazley, William	SRA 36
Beagle, Michael	COL 179	Bearde, James	CHN 788	Bebbee, Ebinr	ONN 179
Beagle, Michael	SUF 85	Beardslee see Bearsdlee		Bebber, Benjn	OTS 14
Beagle, Moses	QNS 60	Beardslee, John	DUT 109	Bebbins, Calvin	WSH 287
Beagle, Moses Junr	QNS 60	Beardslee, Squire	DUT 98	Bebbins, Luther	WSH 287
Beagle, Richard	QNS 76	Beardsley, Abel	DEL 290	Bebbins, Samuel	WSH 287
Beagle, Samuel	QNS 77	Beardsley, Benajah	DEL 286	Bebe, Abigal	WSH 215
Beagle, Samuel	QNS 78	Beardsley, Chas	OTS 53	Bebee, Abigail	HRK 588
Beagle, Silvester	QNS 73	Beardsley, Daniel	DEL 290	Bebee, Asa	RNS 98
Beagle, Stephen	QNS 77	Beardsley, David	DEL 286	Bebee, Asa Junr	RNS 98
Beagle, Sylvanus	QNS 74	Beardsley, Elijah	DEL 290	Bebee, David	CLN 158
Beagle, Sylvanus	QNS 74	Beardsley, Henry H.	OTS 13	Bebee, Elizabeth	NYK 47
Beagle, Thomas	CAY 526	Beardsley, Jabez	COL 209	Bebee, Gidion	ONN 179
Beagle, William	ONT 396	Beardsley, Jabez	OND 196	Bebee, Hopson	WSH 272
Beagle_, William	CLN 159	Beardsley, Jabez	OTS 31	Bebee, Isaac	WSH 232
Beagleston, Henry	WSH 211	Beardsley, John	OTS 53	Bebee, James	ONN 130
Beagleston, Henry Junr	WSH 211	Beardsley, Levi	OTS 3	Bebee, Joseph	ONN 185
Beagleston, Stephen	WSH 211	Beardsley, Obadiah	OTS 51	Bebee, Loster	NYK 137
Beakes, Rhoda	ORN 341	Beardsley, Partge	OTS 53	Bebee, Martin	ONN 178
Beakes, Stacy	ORN 341	Beardsley, Salmon W.	DEL 287	Bebee, Nathan	RNS 102
Beakley, Christopher	NYK 30	Beardsly, John	MNT 14	Bebee, Orlane	ONN 189
Beakmon, Elias	QNS 61	Beargaw, Isaac	DUT 69	Bebee, Peter	WSH 284
Beal, Barnard	ONT 354	Beargaw, Peter	DUT 69	Bebee, Robert	RNS 27
Beal, George	DUT 177	Bearmaker, George a		Bebee, Roderick	ONN 181
Beal, John	SRA 29	Black	NYK 22	Bebee, Samuel	DEL 277
Beal, John O.	NYK 148	Bearman, Jacob	NYK 53	Bebee, Samuel	NYK 26
Beal, Mathew	COL 217	Bearmore, Henry	ORN 393	Bebee, Samuel Junr	DEL 277
Beal, Moses	ALB 10	Bearmore, James	DUT 104	Bebee, Silas	HRK 588
Beale, Hendrick	KNG 10	Bearmore, Stephen	DUT 127	Bebee, Silas	ONN 189

24

Name	Co	Pg
Bebee, Zera	ONN	186
Bebo, John A.	NYK	95
Bebus, Heny	SUF	76
Beby, James	CHN	814
Beby, Silus	CHN	864
Beby, Silus Junr	CHN	864
Beby, Thomas	CHN	814
Beby, Zedick	CHN	814
Beby, Zedick Jur	CHN	814
Becannon, Philip	NYK	42
Becard, James	SRA	24
Beck, Asael	GRN	344
Beck, Daniel	KNG	2
Beck, John A.	MNT	8
Beck, Leopold	NYK	54
Beck, Margaret	NYK	35
Beck, Margaret	NYK	43
Beck, Peleg	KNG	9
Beck, William	NYK	50
Beck.., Dan.el	MNT	94
Beckas, Ebenezer	WSH	305
Becker, Abraham	MNT	81
Becker, Abraham	MNT	95
Becker, Abraham	SRA	11
Becker, Abraham	SCH	132
Becker, Abm Junr	SCH	132
Becke_, Adam	MNT	60
Becker, Albertus Jr	SCH	168
Becker, Aurant P.	ALB	106
Becker, Barent	SCH	127
Becker, Christian	SCH	138
Becker, David	WSH	234
Becker, David	WSH	241
Becker, Francis	NYK	23
Becker, Fret	SCH	128
Becker, Garret	OND	188
Becker, George	COL	256
Becker, George	SCH	122
Becker, Hendrick	GRN	334
Becker, Henry	HRK	449
Becker, Henry	SCH	120
Becker, Henry	SCH	122
Becker, Henry	SCH	129
Becker, Horman	GRN	347
Becker, Isaac	GRN	334
Becker, Isaac	RNS	85
Becker, Jacob	ALB	95
Becker, Jacob	GRN	326
Becker, Jacob	SCH	122
Becker, Jacob Junr	SCH	125
Becker, Jane	ALB	48
Becker, John	ALB	86
Becker, John	COL	181
Becker, John	GRN	327
Becker, John	SCH	122
Becker, John	SCH	162
Becker, John Junr	COL	198
Becker, John A.	SCH	127
Becker, John D.	WSH	221
Becker, John J.	SCH	127
Becker, John P.	SCH	127
Becker, John P.	WSH	249
Becker, John S.	SCH	127
Becker, Joseph	SCH	167
Becker, Josiah	ALB	95
Becker, Jost	SCH	122
Becker, Lawrence	COL	179
Becker, Lodowick	OTS	40
Becker, Martin	ULS	207
Becker, Nicholas	SCH	142
Becker, Nichs H.	SCH	129
Becker, Nichs J.	SCH	129
Becker, Peter	ALB	90
Becker, Peter	COL	178
Becker, Peter	GRN	334
Becker, Peter	OND	211
Becker, Peter	SCH	127
Becker, Peter	SCH	158
Becker, Peter	WSH	241
Becker, Peter Junr	COL	189
Becker, Peter Junior	SCH	158
Becker, Philip	OTS	40
Becker, Philip	SCH	131
Becker, Storm	SCH	160
Becker, Storm A.	SCH	132
Becker, Teunis	COL	229
Becker, William	COL	198
Becker, Willm	SCH	122
Becker, Willm	SCH	129
Becker, William	SCH	138
Becker, William Jr	SCH	123
Becket, Christopher	OND	170
Becket, Grant	CLN	159
Becket, Joseph	OND	184
Becket, Joseph	OND	195
Becket, Joshua	COL	187
Becket, Robins	CLN	159
Becket, Roswell	ALB	111
Becket, [Wh?]eeler	SCH	168
Beckett, Joseph	ONT	388
Beckle, John	TIO	218
Becklis, George a Black	NYK	22
Beckman, Cornelius	ULS	230
Beckman, Cornelius Junr	ULS	230
Beckman, Cornelius C.	MNT	4
Beckman, Hendricke	RNS	60
Beckman, Henry	MNT	15
Beckman, Rachel	ULS	229
Beckman, Thomas	ULS	229
Beckstead, John	ALB	68
Beckus, Benjamen	WSH	276
Beckus, John	WSH	276
Beckus, John	WSH	286
Beckus, Joseph	WSH	305
Beckus, Rufus	WSH	272
Beckwel, Elizabeth	NYK	36
Beckwell, Thomas	ALB	93
Beckwith, Abner	COL	220
Beckwith, Anderson	OTS	49
Beckwith, Asa	OND	210
Beckwith, Asa Junr	OND	210
Beckwith, Betsy	COL	220
Beckwith, Butler	WSH	302
Beckwith, Charles	OTS	4
Beckwith, Dan	COL	219
Beckwith, David	CAY	610
Beckwith, Dyre	WSH	285
Beckwith, Elisha	RNS	100
Beckwith, Henry	WSH	185
Beckwith, Joel	COL	265
Beckwith, John	DUT	61
Beckwith, Joseph	OTS	23
Beckwith, Lemuel	OND	210
Beckwith, Mathew	COL	219
Beckwith, Reuben	OND	210
Beckwith, Reuben	RNS	6
Beckwith, Rice	WSH	305
Beckwith, Silas	WSH	185
Beckwith, Sylvanus	DUT	127
Beckwith, Wait	RNS	108
Beckworth, Seth	CAY	544
Becraft, John	RCK	105
Beddence, Benjamin a Black	NYK	92
Bedel, Benajah	QNS	72
Bedele, Losee	RNS	10
Bedell, Cornelius	RCH	92
Bedell, Jacob	NYK	33
Bedell, Jacob	RCK	102
Bedell, James	RCH	90
Bedell, Jesse	RCH	95
Bedell, Jessee	RCK	102
Bedell, JOhn	RCH	90
Bedell, JOhn	RCH	92
Bedell, JOseph	RNS	57
Bedell, Joseph	RCH	92
Bedell, Nathl	HRK	449
Bedell, Silas	RCH	95
Bedell, Silvanus	NYK	33
Bedell, Walter	NYK	116
Bedell, William	RCH	91
Bedford, Andrew	ULS	245
Bedford, Cornelius	ULS	233
Bedford, David	ALB	137
Bedford, David	DUT	118
Bedford, Edward	WSH	285
Bedford, John	DUT	30
Bedford, Jonas	ULS	231
Bedford, Stephen	DUT	116
Bedient, John	NYK	64
Bedle, Abraham	QNS	73
Bedle, Abraham	WST	133
Bedle, David	WST	132
Bedle, George	RNS	10
Bedle, Isarel	NYK	17
Bedle, John	RNS	10
Bedle, William	WST	132
Bedle, William	WST	133
Bedle, William 3rd	WST	132
Bedlow, Henry	NYK	127
Bedlow, William	CLN	172
Bedwell, William	RNS	87
Bedwill, Benjamine	GRN	346
Beebe, Amon	CHN	760
Beebe, Amos	CHN	760
Beebe, Alexander	OND	177
Beebe, Ann	WSH	274
Beebe, Bezaleel	ORN	281
Beebe, Charles	OND	196
Beebe, Constant	COL	203
Beebe, David	CHN	760
Beebe, Ebenezer	WSH	274
Beebe, Ephraem	WSH	276
Beebe, Ezra	OND	196
Beebe, Gideon	OND	193
Beebe, Gideon	WSH	274
Beebe, Heman	DUT	137
Beebe, Isaac	OND	192
Beebe, James	OND	195
Beebe, John	DUT	128
Beebe, John Junr	COL	187
Beebe, Martin	WSH	276
Beebe, Philo T.	WSH	221
Beebe, Reuben	TIO	246
Beebe, Reuben	WSH	195
Beebe, Richard	ORN	321
Beebe, Roswell	COL	184
Beebe, Ruel	WSH	191
Beebe, Samuel	OND	196
Beebe, Samuel	WSH	274
Beebee, Daniel	COL	214
Beebee, David	COL	177
Beebee, David COL 216		
Beebee, David Junr	COL	178
Beebee, Hezekiah	COL	217
Beebee, Hosea	COL	216
Beebee, John	ALB	104
Beebee, John	COL	184
Beebee, Philo:	COL	215
Beebee, Roderick	COL	219
Beebee, Roswell	COL	222
Beebee, Rissel	COL	216
Beebee, Thomas	ALB	104
Beebee, Thomas	SUF	104
Beebee_, James	SUF	99
Beebey, Abogal	SUF	76
Beebey, Benjn	SUF	76
Beebey, Eliphalet	SUF	77
Beebey, Eluthan Jur	SUF	77
Beebey, Eluthan Sen	SUF	77

Name	Code	No.
Beebey, Jurdon	ALB	35
Beebey, Nathan	SUF	77
Beebey, Noah	SUF	77
Beebey, Saml	SUF	77
Beebey, Sarah	SUF	64
Beebey, Silus	SUF	76
Beebill, Elizabeth	RNS	56
Beeby, Elnathan	OTS	9
Beeby, Nethaniel	MNT	100
Beeby, Solomon	CAY	728
Beech, Abner	ONT	404
Beach, Ashbel	OND	173
Beech, Asbell	ONT	408
Beech, Benjamin	NYK	129
Beech, David	CLN	161
Beech, David	OND	192
Beech, Ezekiel	CAY	528
Beech, Gabriel	CAY	528
Beech, Israel	ONT	408
Beech, Jerusha	CLN	154
Beech, John	ONT	378
Be[ech?], Jonas	CAY	528
Beech, Rice	ALB	4
Beech, Samuel	OND	192
Beecher, Amos	ALB	86
Beecher, Salmon	ALB	86
Beeckman, Christn	ALB	149
Beeckman, Christopher	ALB	38
Beeckman, Elizth	ALB	147
Beeckman, Gradrus	RNS	62
Beeckman, Jacob	ALB	6
Beeckman, John	ALB	117
Beeckman, John	ALB	143
Beeckman, Peter D.	ALB	129
Beecraft, Moses	ORN	391
Beecraft, Wm	ALB	72
Beed, Asel	MNT	21
Beedee, Adam	GRN	351
Beedele, William	NYK	127
Beedle, Abijah	QNS	77
Beedle, Daniel	QNS	77
Beedle, Daniel	WST	129
Beedle, Eli	MNT	77
Beedle, Elijah	QNS	77
Beedle, Gilbert	QNS	77
Beedle, Jacob	WST	126
Beedle, James	QNS	73
Beedle, John	OTS	57
Beedle, Joseph	QNS	73
Beedle, Richard	WSH	297
Beedle, Wm	GRN	354
Beedy, Gilbert	ALB	55
Beegle, Benjamin	QNS	78
Beegle, Daniel	CLN	171
Beegle, Jacob	QNS	78
Beegle, John	QNS	68
Beegle, Urias	QNS	78
Beeker see Becker		
Beekley, Isaac	ORN	386
Beekman see Beckman & Bukman		
Beekman, Convas(?)	NYK	151
Beeckman, Ephraim	NYK	151
Beekman, George	NYK	95
Beekman, Gerard G.	WST	165
Beekman, John	NYK	51
Beekman, Magnus	NYK	122
Beekman, Nicholas	NYK	75
Beekman, Peter	MNT	51
Beekman, Reuben	RNS	112
Beekman, Sarah G.	NYK	145
Beekman, Theophilus	NYK	56
Beekman, William	NYK	53
Beekman, William	SCH	162
Beels, Abraham	CHN	762
Beem, John	MNT	95
Beem, John	MNT	101
Beeman, Andrew	CAY	592
Beeman, Cykes	COL	260
Beeman, Haines J.	ORN	321
Beeman, Jesse	CAY	624
Beeman, Samuel	CAY	590
Beeman, Uriah	ALB	65
Beemar, Adam	ORN	309
Beemus, James	COL	194
Been, Wm	GRN	357
Been, Wm	MNT	12
Beerens, George	SCH	132
Beers, Abija	SRA	14
Beers, Andrew	DEL	269
Beers, Conrod	MNT	96
Beers, Daniel M.	WSH	249
Beers, David	ORN	368
Beers, Elias	DUT	141
Beers, Elnathan	DEL	271
Beers, Ephraim	DEL	277
Beers, Ezra	COL	186
Beers, Holley	SUF	87
Beers, Jabez	DEL	268
Beers, Jabez	TIO	240
Beers, John	ORN	323
Beers, John	RNS	108
Beers, Joseph	SRA	19
Beers, Lewis	TIO	240
Beers, Noah	DUT	102
Beers, Silas	CAY	532
Beers, Siles	WSH	229
Beers, Stephen	DEL	268
Beers, Stephen Junr	DEL	268
Beers, Susan	SUF	70
Beers, Timothy	ORN	370
Beers, Treuman	DEL	269
Beers, William P.	ALB	136
Beeseley, Joseph	QNS	66
Beesmer, Jacobus	ALB	141
Beeve, Joseph	ALB	132
Beevens, Anthony	SCH	135
Beevens, Benjamin	SCH	123
Beevens, William	SCH	135
Beef, Adolphus	NYK	109
Begar, John	ALB	60
Begel, Joseph	WSH	217
Begelow, Arastes	WSH	233
Begelow, John	WST	156
Begels, Michael	WSH	237
Begford, Samuel	MNT	70
Beggelow, Ester	WSH	281
Beggelow, Samuel	WSH	299
Beggelow, Thomas	WSH	286
Begilow, Noah	WSH	198
Begle, Benjamin a Black	NYK	144
Begle, Daniel	QNS	77
Begle, David	QNS	75
Begle, Isaac	QNS	78
Begle, Jehaael	QNS	84
Begle, John	RNS	75
Begley, Ann	ALB	137
Beglow, Bates	RNS	21
Beglow, Jerusha	RNS	42
Begly, Thomas	ONN	145
Behm, Adam	DUT	164
Behm, George	DUT	158
Beigle, John	SCH	126
Beinhauer, Frederick	NYK	151
Beirfied, Henry	NYK	109
Beishell, Leonard	NYK	95
Bel..er, Joseph	MNT	84
Belair, Belin	OND	210
Belamy, Silas	OTS	36
Belcher, Adam	ORN	385
Belcher, David	HRK	491
Belcher, Elijah	OTS	2
Belcher, Isaac	ORN	326
Belcher, Jacob	ORN	387
Belcher, James	MNT	124
Belcher, John	ALB	112
Belcher, John	HRK	493
Belcher, John	ORN	372
Belcher, Jonathan	RNS	96
Belcher, Peter	ORN	385
Belcher, Samuel	ALB	112
Belcher, Sarah	CHN	754
Belcher, Thomas	HRK	493
Belcher, William	ORN	384
Belden, Anna	NYK	116
Belden, Ben_amin	WST	114
Belden, Ebenezer	NYK	27
Belden, Johnson	OND	202
Belden, Samuel	DUT	117
Belden, William	WST	125
Belding, Abner	WSH	207
Belding, Amos	DUT	87
Belding, Augustus	ONN	180
Belding, Chauncey	SRA	23
Belding, Chester	COL	247
Belding, Daniel	CHN	782
Belding, Ebenezer	COL	205
Belding, Ebenezer	ONN	180
Belding, Ezra	OTS	55
Belding, Joab	TIO	250
Belding, Job	COL	205
Belding, John	DUT	134
Belding, Joseph	DUT	99
Belding, Laurence	DUT	99
Belding, Nathl	ONN	180
Belding, Pawl	CHN	782
Belding, William	SRA	59
Belding, William Junr	SRA	59
Beldwing, Elisha	WSH	207
Bele_ta_, Mary	NYK	107
Belemy, Joel	GRN	328
Belfast, William a Black	NYK	93
Belinger, John 2	OND	162
Belknap, Abel	HRK	530
Belknap, Abel	ORN	283
Belknap, Abel	OTS	6
Belknap	OTS	44
Belknap, Abel Jun	HRK	423
Belknap, Asa	RNS	107
Belknap, Chauncey	ORN	277
Belknap, David	CAY	618
Belknap, David	ORN	276
Belknap, David Junr	ORN	277
Belknap, Eli	RNS	107
Belknap, Isaa	ORN	278
Belknap, Jeduthan	ORN	289
Belknap, Jesse	CAY	616
Belknap, Jesse	ORN	330
Belknap, Jesse	OND	216
Belknap, John	HRK	493
Belknap, John	ONT	480
Belknap, John	ORN	289
Belknap, John	RNS	107
Belknap, Jonas	ONT	368
Belknap, Jonathan	ORN	277
Belknap, Joseph	ORN	284
Belknap, Joseph Junr	ORN	277
Belknap, Samuel	ORN	278
Belknap, Samuel Junr	ORN	283
Belknap, Sands	ORN	277
Belknap, Sarah	ORN	288
Belknap, Stephen	SRA	30
Belknap, William	ORN	280
Bell, Abraham	ULS	214
Bell, Adam	HRK	493
Bell, Allchie	RCK	97
Bell, Amy	NYK	147
Bell, Andrew	CAY	666
Bell, Andrew	NYK	37
Bell, Anna	NYK	40

Name	Loc	Pg	Name	Loc	Pg	Name	Loc	Pg
Bell, Anna	NYK	118	Bell, William	NYK	147	Beman, Nathan	CLN	166
Bell, Bar	CLN	160	Bell, William	RNS	48	Beman, Samuel	CLN	166
Bell, Daniel	OND	188	Bell, William	RCK	97	Bement, Eben	ONT	400
Bell, David	DUT	110	Bell, William	SRA	3	Bement, George	NYK	29
Bell, David	RNS	60	Bell, William	SRA	6	Bemiss, Ephraim	COL	182
Bell, David	RNS	62	Bell, William	SRA	8	Bemiss, John	COL	177
Bell, David	RCK	98	Bell, William	SRA	39	Bemon, Solomon	GRN	338
Bell, Elizabeth	WSH	195	Bell, William	TIO	223	Bemus, John	SRA	42
Bell, Frederick	DUT	79	Bell, William	ULS	241	Bemus, Jothom	SRA	42
Bell, Frederick	HRK	474	Bell, William	WST	154	Bemus, Levy	CHN	756
Bell, George	NYK	18	Bell, William T.	ORN	340	Bemus, William	RNS	50
Bell, George H.	HRK	411	Bellamy, Jo_	ONT	494	Ben	GRN	332
Bell, Hamilton	CAY	526	Bellamy, Matthew	DEL	287	Ben	QNS	82
Bell, Hendrick	RCK	97	Bellamy, Samuel	NYK	59	Ben	QNS	82
Bell, Herman	ULS	196	Bellangere, Juliam	CLN	168	Ben	QNS	84
Bell, Hezh	OTS	2	Bellangere, Noel	CLN	169	Ben	SUF	64
Bell, Isaac	NYK	57	Bellangair, Peter	CLN	164	Ben: Jack:	SUF	108
Bell, Isaac	ORN	398	Bellard, John	MNT	101	Ben, Hugh	TIO	227
Bell, Isabella	COL	250	Bellemy, Asa	SCH	136	Ben, Peter	COL	220
Bell, Jacob	HRK	436	Bellenger, Frederick	MNT	15	Benadick, Stephen	GRN	352
Bell, Jacob	HRK	457	Bellenger, Peter	SCH	153	Benchley, David	HRK	575
Bell, Jacob	SUF	93	Beller, John	MNT	27	Benchley, Joseph	HRK	566
Bell, James	ALB	85	Belliger, Frederick J.	MNT	11	Benchly, Saml	OTS	52
Bell, James	ALB	101	Bellinger, Adam	MNT	55	Bencil, Abraham	ORN	281
Bell, James	ALB	148	Bellinger, Adam P.	MNT	24	Bencil, Elizabeth	ULS	251
Bell, James	ORN	291	Bellinger, Andrew	MNT	40	Bencoten, Egbert	COL	227
Bell, James	RCK	109	Bellinger, Christian	MNT	24	Bencroft, David	GRN	328
Bell, James	WSH	227	Bellinger, Christiphr	HRK	438	Benden, Philip	TIO	229
Bell, Jane	DUT	80	Bellinger, Christopr P.	HRK	473	Bender, Sylvanus	WST	149
Bell, Jane	NYK	39	Bellinger, Frederick	HRK	409	Bendigo, James	ALB	120
Bell, Jared	WSH	300	Bellinger, Henry	MNT	1	Benedeck, William	CHN	812
Bell, Jasper	SRA	8	Bellinger, Henry	SCH	130	Benedek, Ambrose	WSH	186
Bell, Jesse	DUT	110	Bellinger, Joel	SCH	167	Benedick, Elijah	ESS	306
Bell, Jesse Junr	DUT	109	Bellinger, John	HRK	469	Benedick, Jerred	CHN	810
Bell, Johanis	RCK	99	Bellinger, John	HRK	496	Benedick, Levi	OND	221
Bell, John	ALB	22	Bellinger, John	OND	159	Benedick, Nathan	CHN	810
Bell, John	DUT	33	Bellinger, John Jun	HRK	469	Benedick, Nathan	MNT	15
Bell, John	NYK	45	Bellinger, John Junr	MNT	19	Benedict, Aaron	CLN	156
Bell, John	NYK	74	Bellinger, John _	MNT	1	Benedict, Aaron	ONN	180
Bell, John	ORN	272	Bellinger, John N.	MNT	20	Benedict, Aaron Junr	CLN	156
Bell, John	ORN	336	Bellinger, Joseph	SCH	130	Benedict, Abrm	OTS	33
Bell, John	OTS	32	Bellinger, Jost	HRK	412	Benedict, Amos	SRA	18
Bell, John	TIO	223	Bellinger, Marcus	SCH	130	Benedict, Amos	WST	151
Bell, John	WSH	300	Bellinger, Marles	MNT	54	Benedict, Andrew	TIO	216
Bell, Jonathon	DUT	103	Bellinger, Peter	HRK	449	Benedict, Benjamin	DUT	169
Bell, Joseph	ALB	83	Bellinger, Peter	HRK	473	Benedict, Benjamin	SRA	57
Bell, Joseph	DUT	80	Bellinger, Peter F.	HRK	437	Benedict, Bushnell	SRA	16
Bell, Joseph	NYK	84	Bellinger, Peter J.	HRK	410	Benedict, Caleb	DEL	281
Bell, Lucretia a Black	NYK	24	Bellinger, Peter P.	MNT	22	Benedict, Cyrus	CLN	156
Bell, Matthew	ORN	335	Bellinger, Wm	MNT	40	Benedict, Daniel	ORN	375
Bell, Michael	ALB	67	Bellings, James	MNT	112	Benedict, David	DEL	277
Bell, Phenias	WSH	194	Bellington, John	OND	177	Benedict, Ebenezer	DUT	57
Bell, Philip	HRK	446	Bellknap, Seth	WSH	184	Benedict, Elias	HRK	475
Bell, Ralph	OTS	8	Bellowes, Jabez	SRA	19	Benedict, Elias	SRA	14
Bell, Ram	RCK	108	Bellows, Aaron	ONN	153	Benedict, Elias	SRA	18
Bell, Robert	ALB	70	Bellows, Abner	OND	166	Benedict, Elihu	SRA	22
Bell, Robert	COL	181	Bellows, Abraham	NYK	90	Benedict, Elisabeth	WST	127
Bell, Robert	NYK	103	Bellows, Ephraim	ALB	73	Benedict, Elisha	SRA	52
Bell, Robert	WSH	274	Bellows, John	SUF	96	Benedict, Elnathan	ONN	187
Bell, Samuel	ALB	140	Bellows, John S.	CHN	884	Benedict, Enock	RNS	57
Bell, Samuel	CLN	172	Bellows, .onas Jur	TIO	261	Benedict, Ezra	COL	181
Bell, Samuel	NYK	46	Bellows, Silas Sen	ONN	154	Benedict, Ezra	DEL	277
Bell, Samuel	RNS	62	Bellows, Thomas	WSH	295	Benedict, Ezra	SRA	23
Bell, Samuel	SRA	3	Bellows, William	CLN	174	Benedict, Gilbert	ONN	142
Bell, Soloman a Black	NYK	95	Bellsinger, John	DUT	164	Benedict, Isaac	WST	151
Bell, Stephen	ALB	47	Bellvue, Joseph	NYK	122	Benedict, Jacob	DUT	177
Bell, Thomas	HRK	435	Belly, Oliver	WST	121	Benedict, James	DEL	281
Bell, Thomas	NYK	83	Belnap, Jonas	ONT	334	Benedict, James	ORN	376
Bell, Thomas	NYK	117	Belnap, Jonathan	ONT	366	Benedict, James Junr	ORN	377
Bell, Thomas	NYK	122	Belote, Abel	ALB	29	Benedict, John	DUT	140
Bell, Thomas	ORN	290	Belton, Henry	NYK	117	Benedict, John	SRA	7
Bell, Thomas	SUF	91	Belton, Jonathan	NYK	44	Benedict, John	SRA	59
Bell, Truman	WSH	245	Beman, Aaron	CLN	166	Benedict, John	SRA	59
Bell, William	ALB	128	Beman, Abe_.	CAY	520	Benedict, Jonah	WST	151
Bell, William	ALB	143	Beman, Abraham	CLN	158	Benedict, Jonas	TIO	226
Bell, William	DUT	110	Beman, John	OND	210	Benedict, Joseph	ORN	373
Bell, William	DUT	132	Beman, Lyman	HRK	424	Benedict, Joseph	WST	151

Name	Code		Name	Code		Name	Code
Benedict, Joseph	WST 156		Benjamin, Christopher	OTS 39		Bennet, Agnes	NYK 26
Benedict, Joseph ye 2d	ORN 375		Benjamin, Colvin	ORN 293		Bennet, Amos	ALB 29
Benedict, Josiah	SRA 3		Benjamin, Colvin	ORN 397		Bennet, Amos	OTS 56
Benedict, Lemuel	OTS 22		Benjamin, Cyrus	DUT 20		Bennet, Andrw	NYK 85
Benedict, Levi	SRA 12		Benjamin, Daniel	COL 203		Bennet, Andrew	SRA 20
Benedict, Lewis	WST 123		Benjamin, Daniel	COL 215		Bennet, Anthony	KNG 7
Benedict, Lewis	WST 156		Benjamin, Daniel	COL 222		Bennet, Asa	DUT 55
Benedict, Martin	DUT 42		Benjamin, Daniel	ORN 373		Bennet, Asaph	OTS 14
Benedict, Mary	SRA 16		Benjamin, David	ORN 372		Bennet, Barns	NYK 137
Benedict, Matthew	ULS 263		Benjamin, David	SRA 26		Bennet, Benjm	COL 212
Benedict, Michael	DEL 277		Benjamin, David	SUF 71		Bennet, Benjamin	KNG 3
Benedict, Michael	OTS 23		Benjamin, Ebenezar	RNS 107		Bennet, Benjamin	ONN 146
Benedict, Micaijah	SRA 16		Benjamin, Ebenezer	COL 202		Bennet, Benjamin	SRA 19
Benedict, Moses	COL 207		Benjamin, Eliarkim	SRA 46		Bennet, Benjamin	SRA 38
Benedict, Obadiah	ALB 65		Benjamin, Esacar	SUF 74		Bennet, Christopher B.	OND 174
Benedict, Orison	HRK 478		Benjamin, Everit	NYK 28		Bennet, Cornelius	KNG 7
Benedict, Robert	SRA 23		Benjamin, Israel	SUF 71		Bennet, Cornelius	NYK 139
Benedict, Robert	SRA 23		Benjamin, Jacob	ORN 379		Bennet, Daniel	ONN 169
Benedict, Robert	SRA 58		Benjamin, James	ORN 350		Bennet, Dapson	COL 212
Benedict, Rubin	CLN 156		Benjamin, James	SRA 26		Bennet, David	OTS 46
Benedict, Samuel	DUT 140		Benjamin, James	SUF 96		Bennet, Ebenr	OTS 36
Benedict, Samuel	ONN 187		Benjamin, Jesse	MNT 51		Bennet, Ebenezer	ULS 188
Benedict, Samuel	WST 151		Benjamin, Jesse	ORN 320		Bennet, Elihu	ULS 188
Benedict, Samuel Junr	WST 151		Benjamin, John	DEL 267		Bennet, Elijah	ESS 319
Benedict, Silas	DEL 277		Benjamin, John	ORN 293		Bennet, Elijah	OTS 44
Benedict, Simeon	TIO 216		Benjamin, John	RNS 82		Bennet, Ephraim	CAY 562
Benedict, Solomon	WST 151		Benjamin, John	SUF 74		Bennet, Ephraim	DUT 109
Benedict, Stephen	OND 177		Benjamin, John	ULS 249		Bennet, Ephraim	OND 201
Benedict, Stephen	SRA 47		Benjamin, Joshua	HRK 549		Bennet, Fernandus	KNG 3
Benedict, Stephen	WST 143		Benjamin, Joshua	SUF 75		Bennet, Francis	OTS 55
Benedict, Thaddeus	DEL 289		Benjamin, Josiah	ONT 410		Bennet, Francis Junr	OTS 55
Benedict, Thomas	DUT 174		Benjamin, Josiah	SRA 47		Bennet, George	KNG 7
Benedict, Thomas	RNS 50		Benjamin, Judah	ONT 384		Bennet, Haynes	OND 190
Benedict, Thomas	SRA 17		Benjamin, Knuland	MNT 93		Bennet, Henry	SRA 40
Benedict, Timothy	ALB 134		Benjamin, Mary	SUF 71		Bennet, Henry	ULS 188
Benedict, Uriah	SRA 19		Benjamin, Nathan	SUF 71		Bennet, Hezekiah	DEL 278
Benedict, William	ORN 376		Benjamin, Nathan Jr	SUF 71		Bennet, Increase	COL 257
Benedict, William	ORN 378		Benjamin, Peleg	DUT 146		Bennet, Irena	OND 174
Benedict, Zar	OTS 30		Benjamin, Pheebe	COL 217		Bennet, Isaac	QNS 69
Benedit, Eliphalet	SRA 19		Benjamin, Pheneas	SUF 71		Bennet, Israel	SUF 67
Benet, James	WST 149		Benjamin, Richard	ORN 332		Bennet, Jacob	DUT 81
Benet, Lemuel	SRA 52		Benjamin, Richd	SUF 73		Bennet, Jacob	KNG 11
Be ham, A 1	TIO 256		Benjamin, Rudolphus	OTS 39		Bennet, Jacob Jur	KNG 11
Benham, Cornelius	GRN 334		Benjamin, Rufus	ULS 181		Bennet, James	DUT 66
Benham, Ebenezer	DUT 139		Benjamin, Samuel	ESS 293		Bennet, James	KNG 6
Benham, Ebenezer	GRN 325		Benjamin, Saml	OTS 39		Bennet, James	NYK 19
Benham, Eli	DUT 139		Benjamin, Silas	ORN 350		Bennet, James	NYK 53
Benham, James	OND 202		Benjamin, Solomon	OTS 39		Bennet, James	RCK 105
Benham James Junr	OND 203		Benjamin, Thomas	ORN 327		Bennet, James	SRA 21
Benham, John	DUT 101		Benjamin, Usher	SCH 134		Bennet, Jared	HRK 478
Benham, John	DUT 139		Benjamin, William	COL 202		Bennet, Jasper	DUT 139
Benham, Kenyan	TIO 256		Benjamin, Wim	SUF 73		Bennet, Jedediah	OTS 57
Benham, Olive	RNS 94		Benjamin, Zachariah	ORN 379		Bennet, Jeremiah	NYK 147
Benham, Peter	COL 227		Benjamine	GRN 343		Bennet, Jethrew	SRA 40
Benham, Peter	COL 254		Benjamine, Gamaiel	GRN 342		Bennet, John	COL 242
Benham, Thaddeus	DUT 139		Benjamon, Derrius	CHN 986		Bennet, John	COL 246
Benham, Thomas	GRN 334		Benn, Peter P.	SCH 133		Bennet, John	KNG 6
Benham, Vinson	GRN 325		Bennedick, Aaron	CHN 898		Bennet, John	KNG 6
Beniger, Isaac	WSH 230		Bennedick, Isaac	CHN 898		Bennet, John	NYK 124
Benjaman, Chester	CHN 924		Bennedict, Abm Junr	OTS 33		Bennet, John	QNS 69
Benjaman, Elisha	CHN 924		Bennedict, Isaac	OTS 33		Bennet, John	SRA 57
Benjaman, Silus	CHN 814		Bennedict, Jno T.	OTS 33		Bennet, John	ULS 188
Benjaman, Thomas	CHN 812		Benneger, John	MNT 3		Bennet, John	WSH 199
Benjamen, Elnathan	WSH 306		Bennell, John	ORN 387		Bennet, John Junr	CAY 674
Benjamin Negro	QNS 70		Bennem, Daniel	KNG 3		Bennet, Jona	OTS 8
Benjamin	QNS 74		Bennem, James	STB 201		Bennet, Jonus	KNG 8
Benjamin	QNS 81		Bennem, John	KNG 2		Bennet, Joseph	DEL 278
Benjamin	RNS 27		Bennem, Lemuel	STB 201		Bennet, Joseph	DUT 23
Benjamin	SUF 82		Bennem, Shedrick	STB 201		Bennet, Joseph	SRA 31
Benjamin, Abel	OTS 39		Benner, Henry	COL 192		Bennet, Joshua	OND 191
Benjamin, Amanuel	SUF 71		Benner, Henry	DUT 155		Bennet, Lathe	ONT 424
Benjamin, Ammeriiah	SUF 71		Benner, John	DUT 160		Bennet, Louisa mulatto	NYK 89
Benjamin, Bela E.	DUT 134		Benner, John Felter	DUT 159		Bennet, Matthw	OTS 31
Benjamin, Benjm	COL 219		Benner, Peter	DUT 160		Bennet, Matthew	OTS 36
Benjamin, Benjamin	HRK 549		Bennet, Abel Junr	WSH 201		Bennet, Micajah	OTS 37
Benjamin, Benjn Jun	HRK 549		Bennet, Abraham	KNG 7		Bennet, Miles	SRA 15
Benjamin, Caleb	RNS 91		Bennet, Abraham	KNG 7		Bennet, Nathan	DEL 278

Name	Loc	Name	Loc	Name	Loc
Bennet, Nathan	DUT 56	Bennett, James	QNS 83	Bennit, Abel	WSH 201
Bennet, Nathan	SRA 48	Bennett, James	STB 206	Bennit, Amanda	WSH 193
Bennet, Nathanl	CHN 742	Bennett, Jeremeah	WSH 241	Bennit, Asa	MNT 103
Bennet, Nathaniel	OND 202	Bennett, Jeremiah	GRN 346	Bennit, Benajah	WSH 205
Bennet, Nedebiah W.	ALB 116	Bennett, Jeremiah	ORN 327	Bennit, Benajah	WSH 251
Bennet, Philip	SRA 26	Bennett, Jeremiah	SUF 109	Bennit, Caleb	WSH 201
Bennet, Prince	DUT 103	Bennett, Jeremiah Junr	SUF 109	Bennit, Isaac	WSH 213
Bennet, Robert	ALB 122	Bennett, Jeromus	QNS 81	Bennit, James	WSH 201
Bennet, Robert	NYK 68	Bennett, Jeronimus	QNS 83	Bennit, Joseph	WSH 237
Bennet, Robinson	OTS 55	Bennett, Jerusha	ORN 371	Bennit, Joshua	WSH 215
Bennet, Samuel	DUT 8	Bennett, Jesse Junr	RNS 102	Bennit, Justice	WSH 205
Bennet, Samuel	NYK 24	Bennett, Jesse Senr	RNS 102	Bennit, Owen	ALB 134
Bennet, Samuel	ONT 340	Bennett, Job	ONT 496	Bennit, Robert	ALB 79
Bennet, Samuel	ONT 356	Bennett, Job	WSH 241	Bennit, Samuel	WSH 199
Bennet, Saml	OTS 14	Bennett, Joel	CHN 976	Bennit, Samuel	WSH 232
Bennet, Stewert	OND 203	Bennett, John	CAY 592	Bennit, Semion	WSH 232
Bennet, Thomas	NYK 144	Bennett, John	CAY 624	Bennit, Wm	MNT 123
Bennet, Thomas	SRA 40	Bennett, John	CAY 640	Bennit, William	WSH 199
Bennet, Timothy	OND 164	Bennett, John	CAY 674	Bennit, William	WSH 215
Bennet, William	KNG 3	Bennett, John	CHN 950	Benno[re?], Benoni	WST 132
Bennet, William	KNG 6	Bennett, John	DEL 269	Benns, William	ONN 137
Bennet, William	KNG 7	Bennett, John	DUT 32	Bennum, Benoni	WST 154
Bennet, Willaim	KNG 11	Bennett, John	QNS 82	Benny, John	NYK 144
Bennet, William	NYK 112	Bennett, John	QNS 83	Benord, Elias	OND 210
Bennet, William	ONT 430	Bennett, John	RNS 9	Bensen, Peter	OTS 4
Bennet, Wm	OTS 29	Bennett, John	RNS 50	Bensesty, John	NYK 121
Bennet, William	QNS 82	Bennett, John	RNS 96	Benson, Abraham	ALB 48
Bennet, William	SRA 5	Bennett, John	ULS 245	Benson, Anna	NYK 124
Bennet, Wynant	KNG 6	Bennett, John	WSH 306	Benson, Barnes	NYK 153
Bennet, Wynant	KNG 7	Bennett, Jonas	WSH 293	Benson, Benjamin	DUT 43
Bennet, Zebulon	ESS 297	Benne[tt?], Jonathan	CAY 622	Benson, Benjamin	NYK 71
Bennett see Dennett		Bennett, Jonathan	ESS 297	Benson, Biledad	WSH 204
Bennett, Aaron	QNS 62	Bennett, Jonathan	ORN 358	Benson, Charles	RCK 108
Bennett, Abijah	CAY 724	Bennett, Jonathan	STB 198	Benson, Cornelia	RCK 103
Bennett, Abraham	ORN 329	Bennett, Jonathan Junr	CAY 622	Benson, Cynthia	ULS 249
Bennett, Abraham	STB 198	Bennett, Joseph	MNT 14	Benson, Daniel	ONN 178
Bennett, Amos	CAY 696	Bennett, Joseph	TIO 254	Benson, David	DUT 43
Bennett, Barnett	QNS 67	Bennett, Josiah	STB 198	Benson, Edward	CHN 980
Bennett, Benjamin	NYK 73	Bennett, Justice	STB 204	Benson, Egbert	ALB 130
Bennett, Benjamin	ORN 384	Bennett, Justus	WSH 241	Benson, Elisha	SRA 7
Bennett, Benjamin	SUF 109	Bennett, Leister	SUF 109	Benson, Elnathan	SCH 149
Bennett, Bernard	NYK 98	Bennett, Levi	TIO 225	Benson, Garret	ULS 184
Bennett, Bernardus	QNS 68	Bennett, Maley	SUF 109	Benson, Garrit	ALB 13
Bennett, Caleb	CHN 754	Bennett, Mary	QNS 81	Benson, Gerrit	NYK 102
Bennett, Caty	QNS 83	Bennett, Matthew	ORN 374	Benson, Hudson	ONN 142
Bennett, Charles	CLN 172	Bennett, Moses	CHN 768	Benson, Jacob	WSH 240
Bennett, Charles	WSH 244	Bennett, Nathaniel	CHN 764	Benson, Jacob	WSH 272
Bennett, Cornelius	QNS 68	Bennett, Nathaniel	ORN 380	Benson, Jacob ye 1st	DUT 132
Bennett, Cromwell	CAY 720	Bennett, Poeneus	CHN 754	Benson, Jacob ye 2d	DUT 132
Bennett, Daniel	DEL 268	Bennett, Reuben	DEL 280	Benson, Jacob ye 3d	DUT 132
Bennett, Daniel	STB 197	Bennett, Reuben	ULS 245	Benson, Job	WSH 234
Bennett, David	CHN 764	Bennett, Richard	CHN 976	Benson, Joel	RNS 32
Bennett, David	CHN 766	Bennett, Samuel	CAY 640	Benson, John	ALB 45
Bennett, David	TIO 260	Bennett, Samuel	ORN 333	Benson, John	DUT 43
Bennett, Ebenezer	DUT 92	Bennett, Samuel	SUF 86	Benson, John	ULS 238
Bennett, Ebene	OTS 31	Bennett, Samuel	SUF 109	Benson, John	NYK 86
Bennett, Ebenezer	DUT 93	Bennett, Samuel	TIO 227	Benson, John	NYK 102
Bennett, Edward	SUF 109	Bennett, Sarah	SUF 86	Benson, John	ORN 356
Bennett, Ephraim	CAY 596	Bennett, Solomon	DUT 168	Benson, John	RNS 6
Bennett, Ephraim	TIO 250	Bennett, Solomon	STB 206	Benson, John	WSH 204
Bennett, Ezra	TIO 227	Bennett, Sylvanus	ESS 297	Benson, John	WSH 206
Bennett, Garret	QNS 82	Bennett, Thaddeus	TIO 261	Benson, Jonas	NYK 147
Bennett, George	CAY 520	Bennett, Thomas	STB 203	Benson, Jona	OTS 4
Bennett, George	CAY 530	Bennett, Timothy	DEL 289	Benson, Joseph	CHN 928
Bennett, George	ONT 472	Bennett, Timothy	SUF 85	Benson, Joseph	DUT 46
Bennett, Gershom	TIO 261	Bennett, Willard	RNS 107	Benson, Mathew	RCK 100
Bennett, Henery	SRA 8	Bennett, William	CAY 726	Benson, Peter	NYK 153
Bennett, Henry	QNS 83	Bennett, William	DUT 32	Benson, Peter	RCK 107
Bennett, Henry	RNS 42	Bennett, William	ESS 308	Benson, Robert	NYK 57
Bennett, Isaac	QNS 83	Bennett, William	ORN 356	Benson, Sampson	NYK 153
Bennett, Israel	RNS 102	Bennett, William	QNS 63	Benson, Samuel	DUT 132
Bennett, Jacob	QNS 63	Bennett, William	QNS 67	Benson, Samuel	ULS 184
Bennett, James	CAY 518	Bennett, Wm	RNS 25	Benson, Samuel A.	NYK 153
Bennett, James	CAY 622	Bennett, Wm	STB 198	Benson, STephen	ONT 380
Bennett, James	CHN 760	Bennett, William C.	CAY 718	Benson, Stutson	SRA 34
Bennett, James	GRN 330	Bennett, Zebulon	SUF 109	Benson, William	DUT 122
Bennett, James	NYK 80	Benninger, Abraham	NYK 47	Benson, Willaim	ONN 142

Name	Code	No.	Name	Code	No.	Name	Code	No.
Benson, William	SCH	149	Benton, Levi Ju.	ONT	472	Bernard, Enoch	COL	248
Benson, William	SRA	11	Benton, Moses	SRA	26	Bernard, John	WSH	297
Bent, Andrw	NYK	66	Benton, Moses	WST	155	Bernard, Mary	COL	247
Bent, Daniel	RNS	26	Benton, Nath. W.	COL	215	Bernard, Mary	COL	248
Bent, Peter	OND	222	Benton, Nathaniel	CHN	754	Bernard, Nathaniel	COL	201
Benten, Caleb	GRN	331	Benton, Orange	GRN	331	Bernard, Peter	COL	247
Benten, Isaac	GRN	354	Benton, Reuben	ONN	143	Bernard, Peter	ORN	334
Benthouse, William	WST	132	Benton, Seth	OND	190	Bernard, Reuben	COL	209
Bentley, Asa	WSH	211	Benton, Stephen	ULS	182	Bernard, Reuben	ULS	255
Bentley, Asel	OTS	33	Benton, Thos	OTS	42	Bernard, Valentine	COL	251
Bentley, Benjamin	TIO	261	Bents, Francis	MNT	12	Berne, David	SCH	153
Bentley, Gideon	CHN	778	Bentsley, John	TIO	253	Berner, George	SCH	153
Bentley, Gideon	ONN	152	Benum, Timothy	WSH	219	Berner, John	SCH	153
Bentley, Gold	OTS	52	Benway, James	DUT	42	Berner, Joseph	SCH	153
Bentley, Green Jur	TIO	261	Benway, Jeremiah	DUT	117	Bernhart, Herman	ULS	183
Bentley, Henry	DUT	114	Benway, John	RNS	34	Bernhart, Jeremiah	ULS	263
Bentley, John	SRA	18	Benway, Peter	DUT	117	Bernhart, John	ULS	185
Bentley, John	SRA	53	Beran, Wm	MNT	109	Bernhart, Matthew	ULS	263
Bentley, John	WSH	278	Berard, Catherine	NYK	87	Bernhart, Peter	ULS	263
Bentley, Joseph	WSH	211	Bercaw, Abraham	CAY	682	Berren, Benjamin	NYK	126
Bentley, Niles	COL	211	Berch, David	WSH	243	Berrenger, George	DUT	161
Bentley, Pardon	DUT	12	Berch, Jeremeah	WSH	243	Berrey, Charles	SUF	80
Bentley, Pardon Junr	DUT	57	Bercham, Simmons	QNS	71	Berrey, James	SUF	80
Bentley, Rufus	OTS	43	Berchell, James	QNS	72	Berrey, Sidney	SRA	50
Bentley, Samuel	CHN	778	Berd, David	WSH	240	Berrey, Simon	WSH	196
Bentley, Saml	SRA	20	Berd, Waterman	WSH	240	Berrian, Cornelius	QNS	61
Bentley, Susanna	DUT	13	Berdick, Ire	CHN	826	Berrian, Cornelius	QNS	61
Bentley, Taber	DUT	12	Berdick, Isaac	CHN	824	Berrian, Ellinor	NYK	42
Bentley, Tellinghast	SRA	19	Berdick, Oliver	CHN	830	Berrian, George	NYK	108
Bentley, Thomas	COL	213	Berdick, Samuel	CHN	828	Berrian, James	NYK	57
Bentley, William	CHN	778	Berdport, Robert	WSH	279	Berrian, James	QNS	63
Bentley, William	COL	207	Berdsall, Samuel	KNG	8	Berrian, Peter	NYK	136
Bentley, William	DUT	12	Bergain, Cornelius	KNG	2	Berrian, Richard	NYK	72
Bentley, William	DUT	136	Bergain, Jacob	KNG	8	Berrian, Samuel	QNS	61
Bentley, William	OND	204	Bergain, John	KNG	4	Berrian, William	NYK	97
Bentley, Wm	ONN	162	Bergain, John	KNG	7	Berrien, Abraham	WST	146
Bently, ...	MNT	79	Bergain, Michael	KNG	7	Berrien, Jacob	WST	145
Bently, Agustes	WSH	251	Bergain, Peter	KNG	7	Berrien, N.	WST	145
Bently, Benedick	RNS	105	Bergain, Simon	KNG	7	Berrien, Nicholas	WST	145
Bently, Benjamin	RNS	71	Bergain, Tunis	KNG	7	Berrien, Samuel	WST	145
Bently, Benjamin	WSH	219	Bergain, Tunis	KNG	7	Berringer, Henry	DUT	161
Bently, Caleb	RNS	98	Bergan, Wm	OTS	2	Berris, Wm	STB	205
Benly, Caleb	WSH	252	Berg[aw?], Andrew	QNS	63	Berry, Abraham	KNG	4
Bently, Eldrid	RNS	99	Bergaw, Isaac	QNS	63	Berry, Asael	RNS	8
Bently, Ezekiel	RNS	70	Bergaw, Ric a	QNS	63	Berry, Benjamin	MNT	10
Bently, George	SRA	53	Bergen, Asher	OTS	9	Berry, Charles	OND	167
Bently, John	RNS	99	Berger, Jacob	CAY	702	Berry, Daniel	NYK	46
Bently, John	RNS	104	Berger, John	CAY	560	Berry, David	NYK	137
Bently, Joshua	RNS	104	Bergerace, John	NYK	91	Berry, Ebenezar	RNS	107
Bently, Nathen	WSH	219	Bergert, George	COL	258	Berry, Elisabeth	GRN	358
Bently, Polly	SRA	58	Bergert, Lambert	COL	258	Berry, Elisha	RNS	98
Bently, Randall	RNS	6	Bergh, Abraham	SCH	120	Berry, Ephraim	OTS	41
Bently, Reuben	RNS	100	Bergh, Christian	NYK	140	Berry, Erastus	COL	215
Bently, Richard	ONN	162	Bergh, Christian Junr	NYK	140	Berry, Francis	DUT	23
Bently, Rowland	WSH	236	Bergh, Joachim	DUT	162	Berry, Francis	ORN	392
Bently, Sarah	WSH	253	Bergh, Philip	SCH	119	Berry, Isaac	RNS	104
Bently, Thomas	RNS	99	Bergher, Absolom	ORN	331	Berry, Jabez	DEL	275
Bently, Thomas	WSH	252	Bergher, Cornelius	DUT	80	Berry, Jacob	NYK	60
Bently, Widow	MNT	76	Bergher, Henry	DUT	159	Berry, Joab	ALB	117
Bently, Wm	RNS	105	Bergher, Jacob	DUT	158	Berry, John	CHN	178
Bently, William	WSH	279	Bergher, Jane	ORN	331	Berry, John	DUT	84
Benton, Abraham	CHN	754	Bergher, John Senr	DUT	79	Berry, John	GRN	338
Benton, Barnabas	ULS	235	Bergher, Michael	ULS	197	Berry, John	NYK	51
Benton, Benjamin	COL	264	Bergher, Paul	DUT	79	Berry, John	NYK	69
Benton, Bethel	ONT	506	Bergher, William	DUT	159	Berry, John	ONT	504
Benton, Caleb	DUT	134	Berhop, John	MNT	123	Berry, John	ORN	294
Benton, Daniel	DEL	277	Berhoper, Benjamin	MNT	124	Berry, John B.	CHN	878
Benton, Daniel	SRA	26	Berian, George	WST	119	Berry, Jonathan	SRA	52
Benton, David	OND	196	Berian, Joseph	ULS	266	Berry, Judith	NYK	44
Benton, David	ONT	328	Be[ri?]ely, David	SCH	158	Berry, Judith	RNS	98
Benton, David	ONT	498	Berkenshhoe, Robert	NYK	130	Berry, Lockwood	SRA	52
Benton, Ichabod	ULS	182	Berkley, Anthony	QNS	62	Berry, Luis	WSH	191
Benton, Isaac	CHN	754	Berman, Samuel	ONT	402	Berry, Nicholas	DUT	23
Benton, Joel	DUT	134	Bern, George	ALB	91B	Berry, Peter	DUT	20
Benton, John	CHN	808	Bernard, Aaron	COL	249	Berry, Polly	ONT	376
Benton, Lawden	OND	209	Bernard, Abisha	COL	250	Berry, Richarard	SRA	52
Benton, Levi	ONT	470	Bernard, David	CHN	946			

Berry, Richard	HRK 430	Bethell, William	NYK 73	Betts, Thomas	KNG 3
Berry, Robert	RNS 53	Beths, Peter	SRA 25	Betts, William	CHN 742
Berry, Saml	CHN 840	Bethune, David	NYK 28	Betts, William	DEL 281
Berry, Samuel	CHN 878	Bets, David	WSH 192	Betts, William	NYK 100
Berry, Samuel	RNS 98	Bets, Jonathan	WSH 191	Betts, William	NYK 151
Berry, Samuel	WSH 243	Bets, Jonathan	WSH 192	Betts, Wm	RNS 14
Berry, Seth	DEL 277	Bets, Justice	WSH 234	Betts, William	RNS 91
Berry, Thankfull	WSH 196	Betsey	SUF 91	Betts, William	RNS 94
Berry, Thomas	ULS 183	Betsley, Stephen	GRN 340	Betts, William	SRA 48
Berry, Walter	KNG 7	Bett, Peter	ALB 19	Betts, Zopha	CHN 742
Berry, William	ALB 24	Bett, Robert	NYK 86	Betty a Black	NYK 62
Bertholemew, H.	OND 223	Bett, Thomas	ALB 19	Betty	QNS 64
Bertholf, Gilliam	NYK 93	Bette Black woman	SUF 66	Betty	RNS 6
Bertholp, Gulian	ORN 377	Bette, John	NYK 22	Betty, Jacob	WSH 245
Bertholp, Henry	ORN 378	Better, John	MNT 34	Betty, John	QNS 74
Bertholp, James	ORN 381	Betteys, John	DEL 273	Beuyee(?), John	WSH 213
Bertholp, Margaret	ORN 377	Bettiger, Martin	MNT 33	Bevee, Isaac	ALB 22
Bertholp, Peter	ORN 381	Bettinger, Andrew	NYK 145	Bevee, Matthew	ALB 21
Bertholp, Samuel	ORN 377	Bettinger, John	MNT 37	Bevens, Henry S.	DEL 271
Bertholp, Stephen	ORN 381	Bettinger, Philip	ONN 165	Beveridge, Andrew	WSH 290
Berthotf, James	NYK 48	Bettinger, Philip Jur	ONN 165	Beveridge, Jane	WSH 194
Bertine, James	NYK 151	Bettis, Andrew	OND 174	Beverly, David	MNT 109
Bertine, John	WST 150	Bettis, Eli	RNS 21	Beverly, David D.	MNT 109
Bertine, Peter Junr	WST 147	Bettis, John	WST 137	Beverly, Jesse	OTS 10
Bertine, Samuel	WST 148	Bettis, John B.		Beverly, John	MNT 109
Bertine, Stephen	WST 147	Bass_ot	OND 220	Bevice, James D.	QNS 62
Bertine, William	NYK 149	Bettis, Joseph	SRA 17	Bevier, Abraham	ULS 211
Berton, Thomas	NYK 85	Bettis, William	SRA 25	Bevier, Abraham	ULS 251
Bertron, Abraham	COL 193	Bettl[in?]ger, Lewis	NYK 49	Bevier, Abraham J.	ULS 213
Beruel, John	WSH 285	Betts, Aaron	NYK 121	Bevier, Abram	TIO 225
Berup, Cramer	ALB 6	Betts, Anthony	QNS 62	Bevier, Benjamin Junr	ULS 210
Berup, John	ALB 38	Betts, Aron	GRN 353	Bevier, Catharine	ULS 242
Berup, Thomas	ALB 38	Betts, Austin	QNS 70	Bevier, Coonradt	ULS 210
Besancon, Peter	OTS 23	Betts, Bartlett	ESS 309	Bevier, Daniel	CAY 684
Besgar, Henry	ALB 82	Betts, Benjamin	QNS 61	Bevier, David	ULS 205
Besher, Frederick	NYK 146	Betts, Charles	NYK 52	Bevier, Elias	ULS 236
Besley, James	DUT 32	Betts, Daniel	NYK 118	Bevier, Jacob	ULS 241
Besley, Oliver	ULS 209	Betts, Danl	OTS 3	Bevier, Jacob J.	CAY 684
Besly, William	DUT 26	Betts, Ebenezer	ALB 138	Bevier, Jesse	ULS 210
Besonius, James	ULS 200	Betts, Widow Elizabeth	QNS 62	Bevier, Jonas	ULS 253
Beso[r?], John	MNT 51	Betts, Elizabeth	QNS 63	Bevier, Matthew	CAY 682
Besse, Ephriam	WSH 190	Betts, Gideon	RNS 94	Bevier, Phillip D.	ULS 215
Besse, Peter	WSH 190	Betts, Gideon	SRA 23	Bevier, Samuel	CAY 682
Besse, Silas	SRA 3	Betts, Gilbert	ALB 120	Bevier, Samuel	TIO 225
Besseck, Willm John	COL 248	Betts, Harris	CHN 930	Bevier, Simon	ULS 210
Bessey, Dius	WSH 212	Betts, Henry	DEL 281	Bevier, Solomon	TIO 257
Bessey, Philip	WSH 298	Betts, Hezekiah	ESS 319	Bevier, Wilhelmus	ULS 211
Bessey, Philip 2d	WSH 298	Betts, Hubbard	COL 252	Bevins, Thomas	ONT 396
Bessie, Ebenezer	WSH 188	Betts, Ire	SRA 14	Bevins, William	CAY 638
Bessie, Joseph	WSH 188	Betts, Isaiah	SRA 61	Bewel, Grove	SRA 50
Bessonstt, John P.	NYK 31	Betts, James	ALB 120	Bewel, Oliver	OTS 7
Best, Francis	NYK 71	Betts, Jared	RNS 39	Bewell, Isaac	GRN 333
Best, George	COL 223	Betts, Jared	RNS 90	Bewell, Jonathan	CHN 934
Best, George	SCH 167	Betts, Jeremiah	SRA 15	Bewell, Orange	OTS 7
Best, George J.	COL 225	Betts, Jesse	DEL 280	Bewell, Thomas	CHN 844
Best, Henry	COL 228	Betts, John	COL 243	Bewill, Murmer	GRN 333
Best, Jacob	COL 237	Betts, John	GRN 351	Bewster, Anna	NYK 136
Best, Jacob	MNT 3	Betts, John	MNT 58	Bester, Rogert	SCH 168
Best, Jacob A.	COL 235	Betts, John	NYK 122	Bexter, Thomas	SCH 167
Best, Jacob H.	COL 234	Betts, Joseph	QNS 62	Beyea, Benjamin	DUT 83
Best, Jacob J.	COL 235	Betts, Josiah	DUT 56	Beyea, John	DUT 85
Best, John	COL 236	Betts, Josiah	RNS 53	Beyea, Peter	DUT 81
Best, John Junr	COL 237	Betts, Justus	COL 222	Beyea, Peter	ULS 189
Best, John J.	COL 229	Betts, Lewis	DEL 281	Beyea, Samuel	ULS 189
Best, Peter	COL 245	Betts, Mathew	SUF 87	Biam, Joseph	OND 191
Best, Wilhelmus	COL 231	Betts, Nathan	RNS 85	Bibben, Samuel	SRA 7
Besteady, Jacob	ALB 12	Betts, Nathan & B.		Bibby, Thomas	NYK 19
Besteda, Joseph	CAY 702	Smith	RNS 90	Bice, Isaac	NYK 111
Bester, Charles	OTS 52	Betts, Nathan Junr	RNS 85	Bice, John	OND 223
Beswer, Theopholus	NYK 45	Betts, Peter	DEL 281	Bice, John Junr	OND 223
Beswick, Daniel	WSH 207	Betts, Richard	KNG 3	Bice, Peter	MNT 16
Bet a free wench	ALB 48	Betts, Richd	OTS 3	Bice, Thomas	NYK 104
Bet a free wench	ALB 131	Betts, Richard	QNS 62	Bicker, Walter	NYK 50
Bet a Negro wench	ALB 142	Betts, Robert	QNS 70	Bicknal, Joseph	CHN 756
Betcher, Andries	ALB 67	Betts, Saml	OTS 25	Bicknell, James	OND 195
Beth, Robert	ALB 20	Betts, Taylor	SRA 14	Bicknell, Japheth	ALB 80
Bethel, Alexander	WSH 226	Betts, Thaddeus	SRA 13	Bicknell, John	RNS 106

Bicknell, Parley	ALB 116	Biles, Nathl	HRK 597	Bingham, Elisha	ESS 323
Biddlcum, Daniel	OND 195	Biles, Samuel	NYK 136	Bingham, James	ULS 185
Biddlecome, Thomas	HRK 464	Bill	QNS 79	Bingham John	NYK 40
Biddlecum, Richard	ESS 319	Bill	QNS 82	Bingham, Johnson	ONN 186
Biddlecum, Thomas	OND 198	Bill free Negro	RNS 34	Bingham, Luther	ONN 172
Biddlecum, William	OND 197	Bill, Benajah	DEL 291	Bingham, Martha	NYK 42
Biddoes, John	ONT 474	Bill, Elijah	CAY 714	Bingham, Ripley L.	ORN 315
Bideman, Henry	MNT 26	Bill, Henry	SRA 40	Bingham, Royal	ONN 193
Bidlake, Asa	OTS 43	Bill, Joel	TIO 243	Bingham, Shubel	SCH 139
Bidlake, Jona	OTS 43	Bill, John	TIO 243	Bingham, Stephen	OND 168
Bidleman, Saml	TIO 254	Bill, Jonathan	ONT 426	Bingham, Thomas	ULS 265
Bidwell, Amos	TIO 227	Bill, Joshua	DEL 290	Binglegee, Christian	GRN 336
Bidwell, David	SRA 44	Bill, Oliver	OND 212	Bingley, William	NYK 97
Bidwell, Jacob	DEL 280	Billard, David	SUF 76	Binham, John	NYK 100
Bidwell, John	COL 257	Billard, Saml	SUF 76	Binham, William	NYK 101
Bidwell, Saml	OTS 27	Billeger, Michael	ULS 253	Bininger, John	ORN 385
Bigah	QNS 84	Billens, Daniel	WST 144	Bink, Philip	RNS 54
Bigaloe, Silas	ONT 482	Billens, James Jr	WST 145	Birch, Asa	RNS 102
Bigalow, Aaron	OTS 57	Billng, Ebenezer	WSH 188	Birch, Benjm	ALB 114
Bigalow, Bond	OTS 55	Billinger, Lydia	HRK 482	Birch, Benjamin	WSH 291
Bigalow, Cyrus	OTS 41	Billinghurst, Thomas	ONT 360	Birch, Ebenr	OTS 25
Bigalow, David	OTS 56	Billings, Andrew	DUT 63	Birch, Ebenezer	RNS 56
Bigalow, Eleazer	OTS 43	Billings, Benjamin	SRA 19	Birch, Edmond	CHN 762
Bigalow, Ephraim	CLN 154	Billings, Daniel	NYK 92	Birch, George	OTS 24
Bigalow, Josha Junr	OTS 43	Billings, David	CHN 964	Birch, Henry	RNS 33
Bigalow, Joshua Senr	OTS 43	Billings, David	SRA 33	Birch, Hiram	ALB 114
Bigalow, Saml	OTS 56	Billings, Ebenezer JunrWSH 188		Birch, Hiram	WSH 243
Bigalow, Zenas	ONT 318	Billings, Elihu WSH 188		Birch, Increase	RNS 33
Bigelow, Benjamin	DUT 175	Billings, Elihue	SRA 39	Birch, Isaac	QNS 78
Bigelow, Freedom	SRA 25	Billings, Ezra	SRA 22	Birch, Jerh	OTS 25
Bigelow, Gale	COL 213	Billings, Henry	NYK 102	Birch, Richard	RNS 32
Bigelow, Jabez	COL 212	Billings, Jalael	OTS 25	Birch, Richard	RNS 33
Bigelow, Jabez	OND 175	Billings, James	ALB 111	Birch, Thomas a Black	NYK 96
Begelow, Jabez Junr	COL 213	Billings, James	OTS 35	Birch, William	QNS 78
Bigelow, Joshua	COL 213	Billings, Jesse	SRA 39	Birch, William	ALB 114
Bigelow, Solomon	OND 185	Billings, John	CHN 806	Birch, William Junr	ALB 114
Bigelow, Timothy	HRK 442	Billings, John	DUT 18	Birch, Zebulan	OTS 25
Biggam, James	NYK 107	Billings, John	OTS 53	Bircham, Robbard	GRN 337
Biggar, Robert	TIO 265	Billings, John	SRA 57	Bircham, Stephen	QNS 74
Biggelow, Josiah	ONN 136	Billings, Joseph	CHN 806	Birchard, Gurdon	OND 160
Bigger, John	ORN 377	Billings, Moses	WSH 188	Birchard, Joseph	ALB 89
Biggs, Absalom	HRK 489	Billings, Nehemh	OTS 35	Birchell, James	QNS 74
Biggs, Nathaniel	SUF 83	Billings, Otis	CHN 776	Birchell, Joseph	QNS 74
Biggs, Smith	SUF 91	Billings, Perez	SRA 19	Birchell, Oliver	QNS 73
Biggs, Timothy	NYK 84	Billings, Randle	CHN 774	Bircher, James	COL 190
Biggs, William	QNS 76	Billings, Robert	HRK 419	Bircho, Samuel	MNT 91
Biggs, William	SUF 91	Billings, Samul	CHN 826	Birchum, Edward a	
Bigham, Eleazer	ALB 28	Billings, Thomas a		Black	NYK 55
Bightley, Henry	SRA 50	mulatto	NYK 87	Birchum, Squire	OTS 26
Bightley, John	SRA 48	Billings, Truman	CHN 848	Birchum, Timo	OTS 25
Bightley, Peter	SRA 50	Billings, William	ULS 181	Bird, Abraham	ALB 53
Bigilo, Isaac	SRA 4	Billington, Elias	NYK 47	Bird, Abraham	RCH 93
Bigley, Daniel	NYK 66	Billington, James	MNT 8	Bird, Anthony	RCH 93
Biglow, Joseph	RNS112A	Billington, John	MNT 8	Bird, Benj:	TIO 231
Biglow, Oliver	RNS112A	Billington, Samuel	MNT 77	Bird, Charles	NYK 143
Biglow, Samuel	WSH 207	Billord, Joshua	SUF 75	Bird, Christopher	QNS 62
Bignel, Ruliph	RNS 47	Billord, Youngs	SUF 75	Bird, Edmond	WST 130
Bignell, Jepheth	DEL 280	Billou, John	ORN 379	Bird, Henry	NYK 118
Bigs, David	SUF 66	Billou, Lucas	ULS 238	Bird, Ira W.	OND 178
Bigs, John	SUF 67	Billou, Seth	HRK 541	Bird, James	WST 115
Bigsbey, Ephraim	CHN 758	Bills, Allin	CHN 954	Bird, John	NYK 19
Bigsby, Alba	COL 177	Bills, Dan	OTS 13	Bird, John	RNS 94
Bigsby, Andrew	SRA 20	Bills, James	GRN 330	Bird, Mathew	NYK 128
Bigsby, Ebenezer	COL 177	Bills, William	CAY 550	Bird, Moore	DUT 137
Bigsby, Elias	CHN 820	Billue, Isaac	WST 129	Bird, Polly a Black	NYK 117
Bigsby, Ephrm	OTS 53	Bim, Andrew	DUT 61	Bird, Richard	DEL 284
Bigsby, George	CHN 864	Binah	SUF 109	Bird, Robert	NYK 59
Bigsby, Gr	CHN 850	Binder, Andrew	ALB 108	Bird, Saml	RCK 102
Bigsby, Hull	GRN 338	Binder, Christian	ALB 108	Bird, Thomas	NYK 35
Bigsby, Samuel	CHN 758	Binder, George	ALB 108	Bird, Thomas	NYK 119
Bigsby, Samuel Junr	CHN 758	Bindon, Joseph	NYK 47	Bird, William	NYK 66
Bigsby, William	CHN 758	Bing, Moses	NYK 121	Bird, William	WSH 232
Bijotat, Silvain	NYK 114	Bingham, Augustus	CHN 868	Bird , is	CAY 516
Bilbee, George	DEL 286	Bingham, Catharine	COL 259	Birdeck, Able	CHN 828
Bilbee, John	DEL 285	Bingham, Catherine	NYK 39	Birdeck, Thomas	CHN 830
Bilbee, Mrs M.	DEL 286	Bingham, Charles	TIO 242	Birdick, Asel	CHN 820
Biles, John	NYK 147	Bingham, Elias	ESS 323	Birdick, Elisha	CHN 836

Name	Loc		Name	Loc		Name	Loc	
Blassman, George	DEL	285	Blawvel, Daniel	WSH	190	Blivin, John	RNS	70
Blatchley, Joseph	DUT	23	Blaxton, Stephen F.	CHN	890	Blivin, Thos	RNS	15
Blatsley, Benjamin	SUF	83	Blear, Maria Louisa	NYK	36	Blizzard, Oliver	GRN	320
Blatsley, Ebenezar	SUF	82	Blecker, Garret N.	NYK	26	Blizzard, Philip	WST	144
Blatsley, Moses	SUF	83	Blecker, John	SRA	47	Bloamer, Michael	NYK	43
Blauvelt see Blanvelt			Blecker, Lewis	SRA	59	Block, Simon	NYK	45
Blauvelt, Abrm	RCK	99	Bleecker, Anthony L.	NYK	30	Blodget, David	OND	173
Blauvelt, Abrm	RCK	103	Bleecker, Barent	ALB	147	Blodget, Elijah	HRK	462
Blauvelt, Abrm A.	RCK	97	Bleecker, Catherine	ALB	149	Blodget, Ephram	CHN	878
Blauvelt, Abrm A.	RCK	103	Bleecker, Elizth	ALB	144	Blodget, Giles	ONT	358
Blauvelt, Abrm D.	RCK	101	Bleecker, Henry	ALB	144	Blodget, Jacob	SCH	135
Blauvelt, Abrm J.	RCK	105	Bleecker, Henry J.	ALB	143	Blodget, Jesse	OND	222
Blauvelt, Abrm P.	RCK	104	Bleecker, Jacob	ALB	140	Blodget, John	ALB	116
Blauvelt, Cornelius	RCK	98	Bleecker, Jacob Junr	ALB	140	Blodget, Jonathan	SCH	135
Blauvelt, Cornelius	RCK	98	Bleecker, James	ALB	125	Blodget, Joseph	OND	175
Blauvelt, Cornelius	RCK	100	Bleecker, James	NYK	31	Blodget, Ludum	OND	198
Blauvelt, Cornelius	RCK	108	Bleecker, John J.	ALB	144	Blodget, Nathan	OTS	57
Blauvelt, Cornelius	RCK	109	Bleecker, John N.	ALB	144	Blodget, Rufus	OND	198
Blauvelt, Cornelius Jos.	RCK	98	Bleecker, John R,	ALB	147	Blodget, Silas	SRA	33
Blauvelt, Danl	RCK	98	Bleecker, Nichs	ALB	149	Blodget, Solomon	OND	169
Blauvelt, Danl	RCK	100	Bleecker, Leonard	NYK	28	Blodgett, Isaac	CHN	964
Blauvelt, Danl	RCK	108	Bleecker, William	NYK	28	Blodgit, John	GRN	352
Blauvelt, Danl H.	RCK	98	Blemly, William	COL	200	Blomer, Daniel	GRN	336
Blauvelt, David	NYK	95	Blen, Solomon	SRA	26	Blood, Aaron	ONT	506
Blauvelt, David	RCK	100	Blenon, Anthony	NYK	50	Blood, David	WSH	241
Blauvelt, David D.	RCK	101	Bl_nus, Dennis	GRN	352	Blood, Ephriam	WSH	192
Blauvelt, Elenor	RCK	98	Blenus, John	GRN	352	Blood, Frederick	SRA	39
Blauvelt, Eliza	RCK	98	Bless, Henry	WSH	249	Blood, Israel	ONT	404
Blauvelt, Fraderick	RCK	98	Blessdell, Levi	ALB	121	Blood, Jeremiah	MNT	110
Blauvelt, Garret	RCK	98	Blessing, Fredk	ALB	59	Blood, John	SRA	16
Blauvelt, Garret	RCK	99	Blessing, John	ALB	59	Blood, Solomon	ONT	316
Blauvelt, Garret	RCK	100	Blessing, Martinus	MNT	36	Bloodgood, Abm	ALB	133
Blauvelt, Garret	RCK	100	Bletcher, George	ALB	138	Bloodgood, Abraham	NYK	66
Blauvelt, Hendrick	RCK	98	Blevin, Luther	WSH	218	Bloodgood, Abraham	NYK	132
Blauvelt, Hendrick	RCK	100	Blevin, Robert	NYK	120	Bloodgood, Daniel	QNS	66
Blauvelt, Hermanus	RCK	108	Blew, George	CHN	954	Bloodgood, Frs	ALB	136
Blauvelt, Hermanus	RCK	108	Blew, Jonah	CHN	946	Bloodgood, Francis A.	OND	159
Blauvelt, Isaac	RCK	98	Bliecker, John R.	MNT	47	Bloodgood, Gage	HRK	501
Blauvelt, Isaac	RCK	104	Bligh, Charles	RNS	105	Bloodgood, John	NYK	53
Blauvelt, Isaac	RCK	105	Bligh, Daniel	RNS	105	Bloodgood, John	NYK	67
Blauvelt, Isaac	RCK	107	Bligh, James	RNS	105	Bloodgood, Joshua	NYK	89
Blauvelt, Isaac	RCK	107	Bligh, Jonathan	RNS	105	Bloodgood, Lydia	ALB	149
Blauvelt, Isaac	WST	149	Bligh, Samuel	RNS	110	Bloodgood, Oliver	WST	165
Blauvelt, Isaac G.	RCK	101	Blighten, Thomas	CAY	718	Bloodgood, Robert	QNS	66
Blauvelt, Jacob	ORN	371	Bliners, John	NYK	153	Bloodgood, Sarah	QNS	66
Blauvelt, Jacob	RCK	100	Blinn, Elisha	COL	270	Bloodgood, Sarah,	QNS	66
Blauvelt, Jacob	RCK	101	Blinn, John	COL	203	Bloodgood, Thomas	NYK	67
Blauvelt, Jacob J.	RCK	105	Blinn, John Junr	COL	204	Bloodgood, Thomas	NYK	91
Blauvelt, Jacobus	ORN	371	Blinn, Samuel	COL	204	Bloodgood, William	DUT	117
Blauvelt, Jacobus	RCK	100	Blinn, Solomon Junr	COL	204	Bloodgood, William	SCH	148
Blauvelt, Jacobus	RCK	104	Blinshan, Jacob	ULS	208	Blookwell, Christion	MNT	52
Blauvelt, Jacobus	RCK	105	Blinshan, Matthew	ULS	243	Bloom see Bloore		
Blauvelt, James	NYK	106	Blinshan, Matthew Junr	ULS	209	Bloom, Abraham	CAY	582
Blauvelt, James G.	RCK	100	Blish, Aaron	DEL	270	Bloom, Barrend	KNG	7
Blauvelt, Johanis	RCK	100	Bliss, Abraham	ONT	404	Bloom, Benjamin	DUT	33
Blauvelt, Johanis	RCK	100	Bliss, Abm	RNS	55	Bloom, Benjamin	ORN	369
Blauvelt, Johanis	RCK	100	Bliss, Beza E.	NYK	48	Bloom, Bernardus	QNS	61
Blauvelt, Johanis	RCK	100	Bliss, Calvin	CHN	962	Bloom, Caleb	RNS	27
Blauvelt, Johanis	RCK	105	Bliss, Charles	OTS	18	Bloom, Ephraim	CAY	580
Blauvelt, Johanis J.	RCK	98	Bliss, Eleazer Junr	ALB	91B	Bloom, Epinetus	DUT	6
Blauvelt, John	CAY	554	Bliss, Eleazer Senr	ALB	91B	Bloom, Henry	CAY	580
Blauvelt, John	NYK	99	Bliss, Gillam	ALB	28	Bloom, Isaac	DUT	123
Blauvelt, John	RCK	103	Bliss, John	ALB	28	Bloom, Isaac B.	DUT	39
Blauvelt, John	RCK	105	Bliss, John	COL	228	Bloom, Jesse	ORN	370
Blauvelt, John	RCK	108	Bliss, John	RNS	12	Bloom, John	ORN	369
Blauvelt, John G.	RCK	100	Bliss, John	SRA	60	Bloom, Jonathan	ALB	136
Blauvelt, John J.	RCK	100	Bliss, Jonathan	OND	165	Bloom, Peter	ORN	362
Blauvelt, John J.	RCK	108	Bliss, Moses	OTS	46	Bloom, Peter	WST	148
Blauvelt, John T.	RCK	107	Bliss, Nathan	OND	166	Bloom, Richard	ORN	365
Blauvelt, Nicholas	RCK	98	Bliss, Oliver	CHN	962	Bloom, Samuel R.	DUT	103
Blauvelt, Peggy	RCK	103	Bliss, Reuben	OND	201	Bloom, Sarah Maria	NYK	68
Blauvelt, Peter	RCK	105	Bliss, Samuel	OTS	47	Bloom, Sylvester	DUT	123
Blauvelt, Peter J.	RCK	105	Bliss, Samuel	RNS	55	Bloom, Zachariah	WST	122
Blauvelt, Richard	RCK	100	Bliss, Silas	COL	234	Bloomendale, John	RNS	11
Blauvelt, Tunis	RCK	100	Bliss, Simeon	COL	207	Bloomer, Abraham	ORN	391
Blauw, John	DUT	72	Bliss, Solomon	CHN	962	Bloomer, Benjamin	DUT	31
Blaw, Cornelius	RCH	92	Bliss, William M.	RNS	93	Bloomer, David	NYK	140

Bloomer, Ebenezar,	WST 115	Blydenburgh, Isaac	SUF 90	Bodine, Vincent	RCH 93
Bloomer, George	ORN 270	Blydenburgh, James	SUF 92	Bodle, Alexander	ORN 317
Bloomer, Gilbert	ORN 390	Blydenburgh, John	SUF 90	Bodle, John	ORN 318
Bloomer, Isaac	ULS 264	Blydenburgh, Joseph	SUF 90	Bodle, Patrick	ORN 343
Bloomer, John	DUT 30	Blydenburgh, Richd	SUF 91	Bodle, Samuel	ORN 318
Bloomer, John	ORN 272	Blydenburgh, Selah	SUF 94	Bodle, William	ORN 346
Bloomer, John	WST 121	Blydenburgh, Thomas	SUF 91	Bodle, William Junr	ORN 343
Bloomer, Joseph	ALB 125	Blydenburgh, William	SUF 91	Bodley, Andries	ULS 202
Bloomer, Joseph	NYK 84	Blydenburght, Ben_ B.	SUF 91	Bodley, John	ULS 201
Bloomer, Joseph	ULS 257	Blye, Ephroditus	OND 188	Bodley, Levi	ULS 211
Bloomer, Reuben	WST 129	Blyre, Peter	NYK 78	Bodley, William	CAY 678
Bloomer, Robert	ULS 265	Bo..ham, _____	QNS 69	Body, Mary	NYK 49
Bloomer, Robert	WST 127	Boa_, John P.	NYK 146	Boen, Amos	WSH 204
Bloomer, Robert Junr	ULS 264	Boam, Frederick	MNT 4	Boen, Asa	WSH 189
Bloomer, Sarah	DUT 77	Boam, John	NYK 115	Boen, Lemuel	WSH 186
Bloomer, Stephen	WST 127	Board, Cornelius	ORN 363	Boen, William	ESS 319
Bloomer, William	DUT 75	Board, Joseph	NYK 99	Bogardas, John	NYK 146
Bloomer, William	ORN 272	Boardman, Allen	CAY 554	Bogardus see Bagardus	
Bloomer, William S.	ORN 272	Boardman, Benajah	CAY 520	Bogardus, Abraham	DUT 38
Bloomfield, Benjamin	NYK 16	Boardman, Danl	CHN 740	Bogardus, Abraham M.	DUT 35
Bloomfield, Ellus	NYK 96	Boardman, Daniel	MNT 53	Bogardus, Abraham R.	DUT 37
Bloomfield, J_ W.	OND 207	Boardman, Daniel	NYK 52	Bogardus, Adriana	DUT 162
Bloomfield, James	NYK 107	Boardman, Daniel	SRA 56	Bogardus, Annen	GRN 355
Bloomfield, Stephen	NYK 90	Boardman, Elias	HRK 490	Bogardus, Antoney	GRN 356
Bloomfield, Thomas	NYK 91	Boardman, Elijah	CAY 704	Bogardus, Benjamin	DUT 163
Bloomfield, Timothy	NYK 90	Boardman, Ephm	COL 184	Bogardus, Benjamin	ULS 227
Bloomindale, Cornelius	RNS 5	Boardman, Ephraim	COL 206	Bogardus, Cornelius	DUT 36
Bloomindale, Peter	RNS 5	Boardman, Ephraim Junr	COL 186	Bogardus, Cornelius	DUT 71
Bloomindall, Allubastus	ALB 124	Boardman, Ezra	ALB 124	Bogardus, Cornelius R.	DUT 37
Bloomindall, Jacob	ALB 126	Boardman, John	ALB 93	Bogardus, David	ALB 60
Bloomindall, John	ALB 60	Boardman, John	ALB 124	Bogardus, Egbart	GRN 330
Bloomindall, Maus	ALB 130	Boardman, John	HRK 427	Bogardus, Egbert	DUT 37
Bloomstead, Frances	NYK 107	Boardman, John	RNS 96	Bogardus, Elizabeth	DUT 37
Bloo[re?], John	SRA 3	Boardman, Joshua	CAY 712	Bogardus, Ephm	ALB 72
Bloo[re?], Joshua	SRA 10	Boardman, Levy	COL 186	Bogardus, Ephraim	GRN 335
Blon, Silas	SRA 26	Boardman, Massey	NYK 61	Bogardus, Ephraim	GRN 356
Blonck, Thomas	NYK 62	Boardman, Richard	CAY 712	Bogardus, Ephraim Jun	GRN 356
Blosome, Thomas	GRN 351	Boardman, Sabrina	OND 163	Bogardus, Everit	NYK 15
Bloss, Amice	ONT 364	Boardman, Silas	ALB 93	Bogardus, Evert	ULS 230
Bloss, John	OND 180	Boardman, Silas	DUT 148	Bogardus, Francis	DUT 33
Bloss, Josiah	OND 166	Boardman, Thaddeus	DEL 286	Bogardus, Henry	DUT 35
Bloss, Manassa	OTS 38	Boardman, Timothy	ALB 93	Bogardus, Henry	GRN 357
Blossom, Elisha	NYK 138	Boardman, William	ALB 125	Bogardus, Henry	NYK 149
Blossom, John	COL 184	Boath, Jo_	TIO 251	Bogardus, Henry	SCH 153
Blossom, John	WSH 221	Bobbison, Peter Jun.	GRN 358	Bogardus, Jacob	COL 186
Blossom, Rowland	COL 203	Bochus John Senr	RNS 58	Bogardus, Jacob	GRN 355
Blount, David	COL 193	Bocie, Miller	RNS 49	Bogardus, James	COL 182
Blour, Charles	RNS 49	Bochhorse, Harman	NYK 117	Bogardus, James	DUT 37
Blow, James	OTS 52	Bockee, Isaac	NYK 42	Bogardus, James	DUT 71
Blowee, Peter	CLN 169	Bockee, Jacob	DUT 141	Bogardus, James	GRN 330
Blower, Isaac	RNS 76	Bockhowse, William	NYK 81	Bogardus, John	GRN 328
Blower, William	OTS 22	Bocking, John	OND 161	Bogardus, John	GRN 330
Blowers, Abraham	WSH 291	Bockman, John	NYK 134	Bogardus, John	GRN 348
Blowers, Alexander	CHN 778	Bockover, Peter	NYK 148	Bogardus, John	GRN 356
Blowers, Jonas	DEL 280	Bockus, John	WSH 204	Bogardus, John	NYK 96
Blowers, Moses	ONN 142	Bockus, Joseph	WSH 204	Bogardus, Lewis	DUT 68
Bloy, John	NYK 81	Bockus, Michael	RNS 26	Bogardus, Matthew	DUT 27
Blucke, Margaret a		Bo_kus, Peter	WSH 289	Bogardus, Nicholas	ULS 227
Black	NYK 35	Bocrum, Jacob	KNG 10	Bogardus, Peter	DUT 37
Bludgood, Hazard	WST 154	Bocrum, John	DUT 61	Bogardus, Peter	DUT 129
Blumb, Samuel	MNT 107	Bocrum, Martin	KNG 9	Bogardus, Peter	GRN 330
Blumberry, Christian	NYK 59	Bocrum, Richard	DUT 25	Bogardus, Peter	GRN 356
Blumhardt, Petter	TIO 265	Bocrum, Simon	KNG 9	Bogardus, Peter	SCH 153
Blundage, Daniel	WSH 284	Bodine, Benjamin	ORN 306	Bogardus, Peter	ULS 193
Blunt, Elisha	OND 163	Bodine, Charles	ORN 306	Bogardus, Peter Junr	DUT 37
Blunt, Henry	COL 218	Bodine, David	ORN 309	Bogardus, Philip	MNT 101
Blunt, Jared	OND 188	Bodine, Francis	ORN 300	Bogardus, Robert	NYK 74
Blunt, John	OND 200	Bodine, Francis	ULS 228	Bogardus, Shibboleth	DUT 37
Blunt, Jonathan	HRK 512	Bodine, Isaac	ULS 244	Bogart, Abraham	NYK 73
Blunt, Samuel	OND 200	Bodine, Jacob	ORN 301	Bogart, Abraham	NYK 100
Blunt, William	OND 188	Bodine, Jacob	ORN 306	Bogart, Abraham O.	NYK 66
Blush, Robert	NYK 118	Bodine, Jacob	ULS 202	Bogart, Adrian	NYK 93
Bly, Asa	OND 165	Bodine, James	RCH 93	Bogart, Albert	NYK 124
Bly, Asa	OTS 36	Bodine, John	RCH 93	Bogart, Andrew	NYK 99
Bly, Joseph	HRK 597	Bodine, John	ULS 256	Bogart, Arres	NYK 100
Bly, William	HRK 597	Bodine, Lewis	ORN 309	Bogart, Barent	ALB 143
Blydenburgh, Daniel	SUF 90	Bodine, Peter	ORN 309	Bogart, Cornelius	RCK 98

Bogart, Cornelius	RCK	99	Boice, Abraham	WSH	301	Bond, Abraham	NYK	15
Bogart, Daniel	NYK	146	Boice, Abraham	WSH	301	Bond, Abraham	QNS	76
Bogart, David	NYK	102	Boice, Abraham	WSH	303	Bond, Bethuel	CAY	554
Bogart, David	RCK	101	Boice, Benjn	RNS	56	Bond, Doxey	SUF	90
Bogart, Elizabeth	NYK	67	Boice, Benjamin	WSH	196	Bond, Edward	MNT	99
Bogart, Gerrit	ALB	134	Boice, Henry	WSH	302	Bond, Elephelet	CHN	882
Bogart, Gilbert	NYK	68	Boice, John	WSH	267	Bond, Henry W.	ONN	190
Bogart, Henry	NYK	106	Boice, Peter	WSH	271	Bond, Isaac	QNS	70
Bogart, Henry, J.	ALB	134	Boice, Peter	WSH	301	Bond, Jacob	SRA	24
Bogart, Isaac	ALB	137	Boid, Elexander	GRN	333	Bond, Jacob	SUF	65
Bogart, Isaac	NYK	99	Boid, George	OTS	8	Bond, James	NYK	14
Bogart, Isaac H.	ALB	43	Boid, John	WSH	221	Bond, JAmes	NYK	134
Bogart, Jacob	ALB	46	Boid, Josep	WSH	222	Bond, John	ALB	16
Bogart, Jacobus	NYK	51	Boid, Michael	MNT	102	Bond, John	NYK	149
Bogart, Jacobus	NYK	66	Boid, Robert	WSH	225	Bond, Jonah	SRA	55
Bogart, James	NYK	66	Boid, Thomas	WSH	226	Bond, Joseph	ALB	39
Bogart, James Junr	NYK	66	Boid, Wm	RNS	36	Bond, Joseph	CAY	558
Bogart, James L.	NYK	54	Boier, William	NYK	64	Bond, Joseph	HRK	532
Bogart, John	ALB	133	Boile, James	RNS	83	Bond, Joseph Jun	HRK	532
Bogart, John	NYK	66	Boileau, Amable	CLN	169	Bond, Lawrence	QNS	76
Bogart, John	NYK	99	Boileau, Amable Junr	CLN	169	Bond, Richard	ALB	39
Bogart, John	NYK	102	Boiles, George	DEL	274	Bond, Robert	NYK	54
Bogart, John	NYK	116	Boise, John	OTS	5	Bond, Samuel	ALB	39
Bogart, John G.	COL	195	Boisseau, John	SUF	105	Bond, Seth	CLN	163
Bogart, John G.	RCK	98	Bokee, Abraham	NYK	66	Bond, Willet	QNS	75
Bogart, John V.	OND	191	Boker, Elisha	OND	217	Bond, William	WSH	204
Bogart, Joseph O.	NYK	114	Boker, Richard	NYK	124	Bond, William	WSH	220
Bogart, Leffert	NYK	93	Bokes, John	MNT	31	Bondish, Asa	OTS	32
Bogart, Leucretia	NYK	105	Boland, George	NYK	142	Boneen, Amos	CHN	794
Bogart, Margaret	NYK	66	Boland, James	NYK	96	Boner, George	NYK	108
Bogart, Myndert	ALB	97	Bold, Thomas	WSH	215	Bonestale, Frederick	RNS	87
Bogart, Myndert	COL	231	Bolden, Jahn	ORN	359	Bonestale, Jeremiah	RNS	30
Bogart, Peter	RNS	18	Boldman, James	OTS	28	Bonestale, John	RNS	87
Bogart, Vert	NYK	71	Boldman, John Junr	OTS	28	Bonestale, Peter	RNS	87
Bogatch, Frederick	NYK	42	Bolen, Mathew	OTS	5	Bonesteal, Henry	RNS	87
Bogell, William	KNG	11	Boles, Ebenezer	OND	209	Binestill, Philip	HRK	500
Bogert, Abraham	KNG	10	Boley, Nathaniel	NYK	137	Bonestill, Philip Jun	HRK	500
Bogert, Adrian	KNG	5	Bolles, John R.	COL	253	Bonet, John	WST	152
Bogert, Albert	NYK	97	Bolles, Richard	COL	247	Bonhan, Blathwait	NYK	143
Bogert, Cornelius	ULS	199	Bollmar, Peter	NYK	114	Bonington, Joseph	NYK	129
Bogert, Cornelius J.	NYK	43	Bollock, Elizabeth	NYK	65	Bonistail, DAvid	COL	192
Bogert, David	SUF	97	Bollock, Mr	GRN	349	Bonkee, Adolph	RNS	46
Bogert, Gilbert	KNG	7	Bollom, Benedick	NYK	122	Bonker, Abraham	WST	118
Bogert, Gilbert	KNG	10	Bolmer, Mathew	NYK	111	Bonker, Henry	WST	115
Bogert, George	DUT	38	Bolson, Alex	RCK	101	Bonker, John	WSH	242
Bogert, Hendrick	ULS	197	Bolson, Alex Jun	RCK	101	Bonker, Nicholas	WST	162
Bogert, Herman H.	ONT	508	Bolson, Anthony	RCK	99	Bonker, Nicholas Jr	WST	162
Bogert, Isaac	QNS	79	Bolson, Cornelius	RCK	100	Bonker, Rufus	DUT	10
Bogert, Jacob	CAY	708	Bolson, John	RCK	101	Bonker, Samuel	CAY	692
Bogert, Jacob	NYK	120	Bolster, Anna	RNS	77	Bonne, Frederick	NYK	114
Bogert, John	NYK	143	Bolster, Lot	RNS	78	Bonnel, Joseph	RCK	107
Bogert, John	ULS	204	Bolston, James	NYK	17	Bonnell, Henry	CAY	596
Bogert, Nicholas	DUT	19	Bolt, Azariah	DUT	169	Bonner, John	OND	211
Bogert, Nicholas	NYK	21	Bolt, Isaiah	SRA	25	Bonnestal, Frederick	RNS	86
Bogert, Peter	KNG	5	Bolt, John	DUT	44	Bonnet, Loduwick	RNS	69
Bogert, Peter	NYK	40	Bolt, John	DUT	166	Bonnett, John	WST	119
Bogert, Peter	NYK	50	Bolt, William	SRA	18	Bonnett, Peter	ALB	23
Bogert, Peter	QNS	62	Bolten, Robert	CHN	810	Bonnett, Peter	NYK	67
Bogert, Rulef	NYK	22	Bolter, Lemuel	ONN	190	Bonnett, Peter	NYK	122
Bogert, Simon	RCH	89	Bolton, Anthony	NYK	19	Bonney, Edward	WSH	230
Bogert, Tunis	QNS	70	Bolton, David	ALB	75	Bonney, James	QNS	62
Boget, Daniel	QNS	71	Bolton, Frederick	NYK	54	Bonney, Levi	WSH	230
Bogg, John	OTS	35	Bolton, Geo:	SCH	167	Bonney, Taires	WSH	229
Boggs, Abraham	ONN	155	Bolton, Joseph	WSH	220	Bonny, Levy	CHN	874
Boggs, James	ORN	300	Bolton, Richd	OTS	50	Bonsall, John	NYK	53
Boggs, James	RNS	82	Bolton, Thomas	ALB	76	Bonsall, John	NYK	59
Boggs, Thomas	ULS	209	Bolton, Thomas	NYK	127	Bonsall, Robert	NYK	59
Boggs, Thomas	WSH	281	Boltonhouse, Daniel	ORN	387	Bonsteel, Henry	RNS	97
Boggs, William	NYK	17	Boltonhouse, Joseph	ORN	387	Bonstell, David	RNS	84
Boggs, William	RNS	80	Boman, Thomas	CHN	812	Bonstell, Nicholas	RNS	84
Bogle, William	ULS	223	Bona, Samuel	STB	205	Bont, John	ULS	264
Bogue, Edward	OTS	9	Bonamy, Alexis	NYK	60	Bont, Joseph	ORN	275
Bogue, Elijah	OTS	16	Bonar, John	ALB	126	Bont, Peter	WST	162
Bogue, Publius Virgil s	OND	192	Bonavellt, Mary	NYK	95	Bont, Samuel	ORN	275
Bohall, James	OTS	42	Boncker see Bancker			Bonta, Aaron	SRA	4
Bohannan, Albert	OND	216	Boncker, Abraham	NYK	35	Bontecee, Samuel	RNS	81
Bohee, Frederick	NYK	57	Boncker, Abrm	RCK	104	Bonter, Cornelius	NYK	121

Bonter. Elizabeth	NYK	150	Booth, Josiah	TIO	217	Boshart, Jacob	MNT	43
Bonticou, John	NYK	70	Booth, Judson	CAY	634	Bosh..t, Jacob	MNT	45
Bonton, Mathew	GRN	340	Booth, Luther	ULS	194	Boshson, Catherine	NYK	65
Bonustille, David	ULS	192	Booth, Nathaniel	SRA	12	Bosin, Abraham	WST	115
Bonustille, Jacob	ULS	207	Booth, Peter	COL	213	Boskett, John	DUT	14
Bonustille, John	DUT	157	Booth, Phinehas	ULS	184	Boskum, Ezekel	CHN	904
Bonustille, Nicholas	DUT	158	Booth, Robert	DUT	92	Bosler, Fredk	ALB	67
Bonustille, Peter	DUT	149	Booth, Sarah	ORN	345	Bosley, Shederick	ONT	382
Bonustille, Peter	DUT	157	Booth, Seth	CAY	624	Boss, Edward	OND	167
Bonustille, Phillip	ULS	185	Booth, Stephen	COL	203	Boss, George	RNS	35
Bonustille, Phillip			Booth, Thomas	ORN	347	Boss, Isaiah	CHN	856
Junr	ULS	191	Booth, Thos	OTS	11	Boss, James	RNS	30
Bonustille, Phillip			Booth, William	DUT	96	Boss, Jeremiah	HRK	455
Ye 3d	ULS	207	Booth, William	ORN	294	Boss, John	QNS	60
Bonyon, William	SRA	25	Booth, William	ORN	372	Boss, Joseph	NYK	144
Booge, James	ORN	345	Booth, Wm	SUF	76	Boss, Mary & Eben Hicks	QNS	60
Booker, James a Black	NYK	65	Booth, William	SUF	96	Boss, Peter	SRA	28
Bookless, John	NYK	54	Booth, William	ULS	262	Bossing, Abraham	NYK	50
Bookstaver, Frederick	ORN	310	Booth, Wm A.	SUF	76	Bost, John	MNT	21
Bookstaver, Jacob	ORN	302	Booth, Whitlock	SUF	75	Bostford, Abel	ONT	464
Bookstaver, Jacob T.	ORN	302	Boothack see Brothack			Bostford, Benejah	ONT	456
Bookstaver, John	ORN	296	Boothack, Barthw	HRK	462	Bostford, Elijah	ONT	464
Bookstaver, William	ORN	309	Boothack, Jacob Jun	HRK	462	Bostford, Elnathan	ONT	456
Bool, Henry, W.	NYK	140	Boothack, John	HRK	462	Bostford, Johnathan	ONT	464
Boolmore, Elizth	ALB	19	Boothe, William	NYK	85	Bostic, Anthoney	SUF	67
Boolock, Lewis	RNS	8	Boots, Thomas	ALB	138	Bostick, Ezra	MNT	11
Boom, Andrew	GRN	337	Boovee, Tice	ALB	42	Bostick, John	GRN	351
Boom, John	OND	162	Bor, John	NYK	98	Bostick, Medad	WSH	214
Boom, John W.	GRN	357	Boran, John	MNT	108	Bostick, Robert S.	RNS	47
Boom, Samuel	ALB	62	Bordavine, Jennet	NYK	126	Bostle, Francis	ONT	356
Boome, John Junr	RNS	42	Bordeaux, Jo..	CAY	596	Boston	QNS	80
Boomer, Benjamin	OND	216	Borden, Abraham	HRK	518	Boston, Jacob	NYK	112
Boomer, Caleb	OND	210	Borden, Abraham Jun	HRK	519	Bostwic, Edward	COL	208
Boomer, Edward	OND	216	Borden, Adam a Black	NYK	108	Bostwic, Elijah	COL	208
Boomer, Isaac	WSH	219	Borden, Daniel	ORN	286	Bostwic, Elijah Junr	COL	208
Boomer, John	RNS	41	Borden, Jeremiah	HRK	518	Bostwich, James	NYK	58
Boomer, Matthew	OND	216	Borden, Joseph	HRK	519	Bostwick, Ammon	DEL	289
Boomer, Matthew Junr	OND	217	Borden, Nell	CAY	720	Bostwick, Benjamin	DUT	139
Boomhamer, Michl	ALB	82	Borden, Pelitah	SCH	168	Bostwick, Caty	OTS	12
Boomhaven, Jacob	DEL	289	Borden, Samuel	NYK	115	Bostwick, Darcus	WST	143
Boomhour, David	RNS	87	Borden, Timothy	HRK	519	Bostwick, David	DEL	289
Boomhower, Michael	GRN	344	Bordman, Israel	MNT	61	Bostwick, David	SRA	46
Boon, Benjamin	DUT	127	Bordman, J.	OND	219	Bostwick, Ebenezer	ESS	311
Boon, Frances	WSH	206	Bordman, Sherman	OTS	32	Bostwick, Ephraim	NYK	20
Boon, Samuel	WSH	185	Bordon & Deheland	QNS	66	Bostwick, George	SCH	134
Boonhor, Peter	RNS	86	Borduzat, Anthony M.	NYK	35	Bostwick, Jesse	OTS	11
Boorbeck, Barrent	NYK	35	Bordwell, Darius	OND	164	Bostwick, John	OTS	12
Boorgas, Christian	NYK	69	Bores, Jacobus	OND	223	Bostwick, John	SRA	45
Boorham, Jacob	NYK	24	Borgis, Benjamin	CAY	538	Bostwick, John	SCH	134
Boorham, John	QNS	60	Boridine, Albert	MNT	114	Bostwick, John	WST	142
Boorham, John	QNS	79	Borishton, Joseph	RNS	64	Bostwick, Joseph M.	DUT	136
Boorham, John	QNS	82	Borkus, Absalom	SRA	24	Bostwick, Levi	OTS	47
Boorham, Mary	QNS	60	Borman, Ezera	GRN	331	Bostwick, Margaret	DUT	147
Boorham, Simeon	QNS	79	Born, John	NYK	74	Bostwick, Mary	NYK	29
Boorham, Thomas	QNS	79	Borne, John R.	OND	212	Bostwick, Milo	OND	205
Boorman, Mary	NYK	20	Bornt, John	RNS	88	Bostwick, Nobel	SRA	58
Boos, Vandyle	NYK	145	Borras, John	NYK	55	Bostwick, Richard a		
Boose, Matthias	ALB	57	Borras, Laurence	NYK	58	Black	NYK	27
Boosen, John	WST	146	Borringtone, John	NYK	49	Bostwick, William	CAY	706
Booson, Peter	WST	146	Borrows, Ann	ORN	372	Boswell, Larebe	MNT	107
Booten, Henry	OND	220	Borrows, John	QNS	71	Boswick, John P.	ALB	9
Booth, Amos	ONT	408	Borrows, Joseph	NYK	129	Bosworth, Alfred	SRA	18
Booth, Benjamin	ORN	314	Borrows, Thomas	MNT	120	Bosworth, Benajh	OTS	37
Booth, Danl	SUF	76	Borsl, John J.	OTS	40	Bosworth, Benjamin	OND	193
Booth, Ebenezer	GRN	341	Borst, Josep	MNT	28	Bosworth, Dan	OND	177
Booth, Elijah	TIO	252	Bort, Andrew	RNS	11	Bosworth, Ellihu	CHN	868
Booth, Elizabeth	SUF	76	Bortel, Peter	RNS	64	Bosworth, Hezekiah	WSH	287
Booth, Erastus	DEL	278	Borth, John N.	MNT	21	Bosworth, Ichabud	CLN	172
Booth, Ezekiel	COL	221	Borth, Nicholas	MNT	21	Bosworth, Jabez	COL	251
Booth, Hezekiah	COL	203	Borthick, Jane	NYK	103	Bosworth, John	OND	177
Booth, Isaac	COL	203	Bortle, Andrew	RNS	13	Bosworth, Joshua C.	CLN	174
Booth, Isaac	DUT	92	Bortle, Peter	ONT	508	Bosworth, Marther	OND	168
Booth, Jesse	ORN	347	Borton, Israel	RNS	14	Bosworth, Nathaniel	ULS	229
Booth, John	DUT	97	Bortow, William	CHN	852	Bosworth, Samuel	OTS	31
Booth, John	NYK	35	Borttema, John	RNS	86	Bosworth, Stephen	ESS	293
Booth, John	SUF	76	Borv__, Rakael	GRN	347	Botch, Arnold	OTS	34
Booth, Joseph	DUT	51	Boscowen, John	NYK	142	Botchford, David	GRN	350

38

Botchford, Nathan	GRN 354	Bound, William	QNS 63	Bowen, Amos	OTS 54
Both, Sharon	ONT 442	Bounnel, Chester	ONT 428	Bowen, Amos	WSH 269
Bothell, James	WSH 278	Bountea_, John	NYK 66	Bowen, Amos	WSH 269
Bothier, Simon	NYK 95	Bourcaw, Nicholas	NYK 28	Bowen, Benjamin	CLN 156
Bothwell, Alexander	CAY 614	Bourdett, Peter	NYK 137	Bowen, Benjamin	HRK 587
Bothwick, John	ORN 303	Bourdett, Stephen	NYK 137	Bowen, Benj:	ONN 160
Botkings, Eleazer	CHN 944	Bouream, Francis	NYK 92	Bowen, Dan	OTS 15
Bots, Bartholemew	MNT 108	Bourk, Charles a Black	NYK 68	Bowen, Daniel	ORN 298
Botsford, Benjamin	HRK 567	Bourne, Sylvanus	DUT 153	Bowen, Darius	OTS 29
Botsford, Thomas	COL 219	Bourosan, Anthony	NYK 149	Bowen, Elijah	OTS 37
Botsford, Vine	OTS 22	Bouse, Aaron	ALB 121	Bowen, Gardner	OTS 41
Bottle, Andrew	CHN 770	Bouse, John	ALB 16	Bowen, George	WSH 186
Bottle, Henery	CHN 770	Bouse, Peter	ALB 98	Bowen, Henry	ALB 129
Bottle, John	CHN 770	Bousen, Elizabeth	ALB 52	Bowen, Henry	MNT 61
Bottle, Peter	CHN 772	Bousman, William	SRA 44	Bowen, James	WSH 264
Bpttle, Phillup	CHN 772	Boutell, John	OTS 41	Bowen, Jesse	SRA 58
Bottlefaxlk, John	QNS 60	Bouter, John	NYK 144	Bowen, John	OND 174
Bottles, John	CHN 768	Bouton, Aza	RNS112B	Bowen, Joseph	CLN 156
Bottom, Jabez	CAY 670	Bouton, Daniel	WST 161	Bowen, Joseph	WSH 290
Botty, Timothy	GRN 356	Bouton, David	DEL 267	Bowen, Michael	DUT 167
Botwich, Major	ONT 470	Bouton, David Jun	DEL 267	Bowen, Nathen	OTS 41
Bouch, Abraham	SCH 149	Bouton, Ebenezar	WST 113	Bowen, Peter	WSH 187
Boucher, Anthony	COL 193	Bouton, Elijah	RNS 111	Bowen, Richard	NYK 82
Bouchier, Silas	CAY 626	Bouton, Enoch	WST 161	Bowen, Samuel	WSH 266
Bouck, Adam	SCH 128	Bouton, Gould	WST 151	Bowen, Seth	ORN 310
Bouck, Adam	SCH 128	Bouton, Gould Junr	WST 151	Bowen, Stephen	SRA 57
Bouck, Christian	SCH 128	Bouton, Ire	WST 137	Bowen, Thos	OTS 29
Bouck, Cornelius	SCH 126	Bouton, James	DEL 268	Bowen, Timothy	ESS 319
Bouck, Frederick	SCH 167	Bouton, James	WST 159	Bower see Baower	
Bouck, Helmes	SCH 118	Bouton, Jeremiah	RNS 111	Bower, Adam	CAY 618
Bouck, Jacob	SCH 126	Bouton, Joel	WST 151	Bower, Daniel	COL 212
Bouck, Jacob	SCH 150	Bouton, Jonas	WST 137	Bower, Emma	SUF 106
Bouck, John	SCH 118	Bouton, Joseph	DUT 107	Bower, George	CAY 618
Bouck, John J.	SCH 126	Bouton, Joseph	DUT 170	Bower, Grant	ORN 277
Bouck, Lawrence	SCH 129	Bouton, Joseph	WST 158	Bower, Haun Teter	CAY 590
Bouck, Nichs	SCH 126	Bouton, Lewis	WST 160	Bower, Isaac	ORN 348
Bouck, Nichs	SCH 167	Bouton, Nehemiah	WST 159	Bower, Jacob	CAY 726
Bouck, Peter	SCH 150	Bouton, Noah	DUT 175	Bower, John	CAY 590
Bouck, Peter	SCH 167	Bouton, Roger	DEL 268	Bower, John	CAY 618
Bouck, William	SCH 128	Bouton, Samuel	DEL 267	Bower, Samuel	CAY 618
Bouck, William Jr	SCH 128	Bouton, Seth	OTS 42	Bower, Samuel	ORN 295
Boucker, Joseph	ALB 110	Bouton, Stephen	WST 161	Bower, Silas	CAY 672
Bouckir, Joseph	ESS 320	Bouton, Wm	RNS 111	Bowerman, Timothy	RNS 107
Boudar, Joseph	NYK 110	Boutwell, Jesse	RNS 91	Bowers, Abial	CHN 764
Bouden, Olma	OTS 7	Boutwell, Saml	OTS 37	Bowers, Barney	NYK 153
Boudinot, Elias	CAY 550	Bouvenhorne, Poweles	NYK 109	Bowers, Ebenezar	SUF 93
Boudish, John	RNS 26	Bouvier, Agatha	NYK 95	Bowers, Henry	MNT 44
Boughton, Abijah	OTS 6	Bovee, Jacob	SRA 25	Bowers, Jacob	ULS 182
Boughton, Abraham	ONT 410	Bovee, Mathew	ALB 53	Bowers, John	ALB 54
Boughton, David	ALB 95	Bovie, Anthony	WSH 290	Bowers, John	NYK 124
Boughton, Eleazer	ONT 402	Bovie, Cornelius	RNS 19	Bowers, Lewis S.	RNS 22
Boughton, Enoch	WST 154	Bovie, Jacob	RNS 24	Bowers, Mary	NYK 26
Boughton, Ezra	WST 151	Bovie, Jacob	RNS 27	Bowers, Michael	NYK 146
Boughton, Ira	ALB 85	Bovie, John	RNS 19	Bowers, Nicholas	RNS 18
Boughton, Jehiel	CAY 578	Bovie, Joseph	RNS 95	Bowers, Samull	GRN 341
Boughton, Jesse Junr	WST 159	Bovie, Peter	WSH 265	Bow hall, Casher	MNT 23
Boughton, John	RNS 56	Bovie, Philip	RNS 74	Bowice, Anna	NYK 53
Boughton, Levi	ONT 402	Boviee, Jacob	ALB 25	Bowie, Daniel	NYK 54
Boughton, Nathan	SRA 46	Bowan, Amos	HRK 500	Bowie, James	NYK 101
Boughton, Samuel	ALB 95	Bowan, Apoles	RNS 22	Bowin, Nathan	RNS 39
Boughton, Samuel	ONT 402	Bowcock, John	NYK 119	Bowin, William	SRA 28
Boughton, Seymour	ONT 362	Bowdeitch, John	SUF 105	Bowing, Samson	SRA 52
Boughton, Stephen	RNS112B	Bowden, Benjamin	KNG 8	Bowker, Francis B.	OND 185
Boughton, Subel	ALB 95	Bowden, Elizabeth	ALB 146	Bowker, James	WSH 223
Bouker, Joseph	CAY 610	Bowden, Samuel	KNG 10	Bowland, James	ALB 37
Bouker, John	CAY 616	Bowdine, Abraham	NYK 32	Bowlen, Samuel	KNG 10
Boukir, Daniel	DEL 274	Bowdish, Gideon	CAY 526	Bowles, Catherine	NYK 47
Boult, Jacob	OTS 25	Bowdish, John	DUT 50	Bowles, George	HRK 407
Boulton, Alexander	CAY 644	Bowdish, Luke	DUT 123	Bowles, John	RNS 78
Boulton, D'Arcy	ESS 303	Bowdish, Nathaniel	DUT 45	Bowles, Stephen	ALB 91
Boulton, Jabez	SRA 51	Bowditch, William	SUF 105	Bowles, Thomas	HRK 424
Boulton, James	CAY 722	Bowdy, Artemas	DUT 53	Bowles, Thomas	STB 198
Boulton, Jonathan	DEL 274	Bowdy, Moses	DUT 53	Bowles, Wm	RNS 78
Boulton, Samuel	CAY 650	Boweman, Thomas	RNS 101	Bowley, Joseph	OND 180
Boum, Jacob	MNT 21	Bowen see Boen		Bowline, Charles	ORN 346
Bouman, John	RNS 8	Bowen, Abel	OTS 29	Bowline, Tabitha	ORN 346
Bound, John	QNS 64	Bowen, ..ijah	ONN 160	Bowline, Thomas	ORN 346

Bowman, Abram	COL 193	Boyce, Elias	DUT 152	Boyer see Boier	
Bowman, Adam	HRK 459	Boyce, Ferdinand	DUT 160	Boyer, John	CAY 586
Bowman, Andrew	SCH 147	Boyce, Henry	DUT 62	Boyer, Joseph	NYK 39
Bowman, Benjm	ALB 108	Boyce, Isaac	CHN 766	Boyer, Nicholas	ALB 58
Bowman, Charles	ALB 61	Boyce, Isaac	DUT 102	Boyer, Richard	CLN 162
Bowman, Charles	ALB 139	Boyce, Isaac Junr	DUT 103	Boyer, Robert	MNT 54
Bowman, Christopher	HRK 459	Boyce, Jacob	CAY 530	Boyers, Anthony	NYK 64
Bowman, Elisha	HRK 529	Boyce, Jacob	DUT 19	Boyes, Benjamine	GRN 325
Bowman, Frederick	OND 162	Boyce, Jacob	NYK 111	Boyes, Thomas	COL 180
Bowman, George	HRK 460	Boyce, Jacob	WST 162	Boyes, William	CAY 584
Bowman, George	NYK 57	Boyce, Jacobus	DUT 66	Boyington, Reubin	GRN 340
Bowman, Jacob	HRK 436	Boyce, James	RCK 105	Boyl, Daniel	NYK 15
Bowman, Jacob	SCH 168	Boyce, Jane	KNG 5	Boyl, David	NYK 147
Bowman, John	ALB 35	Boyce, John	CAY 530	Boyle, Caleb	NYK 48
Bowman, John	COL 181	Boyce, John	CAY 530	Boyle, Daniel O.	NYK 79
Bowman, Joseph	DUT 66	Boyce, John	DUT 18	Boyles, Thomas	ALB 130
Bowman, Joseph	NYK 121	Boyce, John	DUT 127	Boylin, Samuel	STB 203
Bowman, Mary	ORN 280	Boyce, John	DUT 152	Boyne, Peter	CHN 850
Bowman, Moses	SRA 35	Boyce, John	WST 154	Boys, Isaac	NYK 150
Bowman, Nicholas	HRK 459	Boyce, John	WST 162	Boyse, Peter	WSH 185
Bowman, Peter	ALB 58	Boyce, John	WST 165	Bozard, John	RNS 39
Bowman, Rufus	TIO 227	Boyce, John	WST 166	Bozee, John	RNS 53
Bowman, William	RCH 91	Boyce, John I.	DUT 102	Bozley, Edmund	ONT 382
Bown, Daniel	WST 114	Boyce, Jonathan	DUT 152	Bozley, Edward	ONT 328
Bown, Jacob	WST 114	Boyce, Nicholas	WST 162	Bozley, Jacob	ONT 382
Bown, ..hn	ONN 170	Boyce, Patrick	ORN 306	Bozley, James	ONT 382
Bown, John Junr	ONN 170	Boyce, Peter	COL 240	Bozley, Shederick	ONT 328
Bown, Jonathan	NYK 140	Boyce, Peter Junr	DUT 66	Bozworth, Jabez	DUT 62
Bown, Mary	NYK 135	Boyce, Peter Senr	DUT 67	Br...., John	MNT 91
Bown, William	NYK 138	Boyce, Robert	CHN 766	Bra.., Samuel	MNT 100
Bown, Thomas	WST 114	Boyce, Samuel	DUT 102	Br__n, John	OND 212
Bown, Willett	QNS 64	Boyce, Sarah	KNG 4	Br__, Elias	OTS 27
Bowne/Bowne, Josiah	NYK 117	Boyce, Thomas	WST 162	Braat, Francis	RNS 5
Bowne, Benjamin	DUT 79	Boyce, William	WST 165	Braboy, Sarah a mulatto	NYK 85
Bowne, Betsey	NYK 87	Boyd see Boid		Brace, Abel	HRK 543
Bowne, Catherine	NYK 45	Boyd, Alexander	NYK 119	Brace, Abel Jun	HRK 543
Bowne, Conover	NYK 75	Boyd, Andrew	WST 150	Brace, Alban	SRA 20
Bowne, David	TIO 229	Boyd, David	ALB 7	Brace, Asa	COL 248
Bowne, Elisha	NYK 15	Boyd, David	ONT 476	Brace, Asahel	HRK 544
Bowne, Gershom	DUT 25	Boyd, Ebenezer	DUT 96	Brace, Banister	WSH 216
Bowne, Hannah	NYK 43	Boyd, Francis	ORN 295	Brace, Benjamin	OND 162
Bowne, Joseph	SRA 45	Boyd, Hamilton	MNT 104	Brace, Charles	HRK 543
Bowne, Margaret	NYK 69	Boyd, Hugh	ALB 128	Brace, Daniel	WSH 214
Bowne, Nancy	NYK 15	Boyd, James	ALB 132	Brace, Ebenr	ONN 168
Bowne, Obadiah	NYK 25	Boyd, James	MNT 65	Brace, Edward	HRK 544
Bowne, Rachel	WST 149	Boyd, James	NYK 16	Brace, Elijah Junr	WSH 214
Bowne, Robert	NYK 45	Boyd, James	ORN 290	Brace, Elisha	ONT 400
Bowne, Robert L.	NYK 152	Boyd, James	WSH 297	Brace, Elisha	WSH 214
Bowne, Samuel	NYK 43	Boyd, John	CAY 664	Brace, Erastus	HRK 544
Bowne, Samuel	NYK 82	Boyd, John a mulatto	NYK 83	Bra[ce?], Jeduthan	HRK 546
Bowne, Sarah	NYK 68	Boyd, John	NYK 96	Brace, Jererd	WSH 202
Bowne, Thomas	ORN 366	Boyd, John	ORN 292	Brace, Joseph	ONT 402
Bowne, William	NYK 43	Boyd, John	ORN 304	Brace, Joseph	SRA 20
Bowner, Michael	KNG 10	Boyd, John	SRA 3	Brace, Levi	WSH 183
Bowning, Thomas	NYK 125	Boyd, Joseph	CHN 814	Brace, Marvin	HRK 543
Bowrin, Ann	CLN 156	Boyd, Joseph	NYK 101	Brace, Moses	OND 167
Bowrin, Jacob	CLN 171	Boyd, Mary	OND 210	Brace, Norman	ONT 400
Bowrin, Joseph	CLN 171	Boyd, Peter	WST 121	Brace, Orange	HRK 543
Bowrin, William	WST 131	Boyd, Phillip	DUT 93	Brace, Reuben	MNT 85
Bowsh, Samuel	ORN 316	Boyd, Robert	ORN 285	Brace, Samuel	COL 186
Bowton, As__	GRN 342	Boyd, Robert	ORN 292	Brace, Stephen	WSH 216
Bowton, Enos	ONN 183	Boyd, Robert R.	ORN 296	Brace, Thomas	WSH 193
Bowton, Frances	GRN 345	Boyd, Samuel	DUT 139	Brach, William	NYK 99
Bowton, Major	GRN 342	Boyd, Samuel	MNT 67	Bracker, Peter	COL 218
Bow[us?], Isaac	TIO 252	Boyd, Samuel	NYK 26	Bracket, Chancey	CHN 976
Bow[us?], James	TIO 252	Boyd, Samuel	ORN 290	Bracket, Jared	SRA 31
Box, Nathaniel	QNS 78	Boyd, Samuel	ORN 335	Bracket, Morison	GRN 335
Box, Nathaniel	SUF 80	Boyd, Sarah	DUT 96	Bracket, Timothy	SRA 31
Boy__, ...ard	MNT 56	Boyd, Sewell	ONT 334	Bradberry, Jacob	ALB 37
Boyce, Aaron	DUT 18	Boyd, Thomas	ORN 293	Bradburry, Catherine	NYK 72
Boyce, Aaron	DUT 119	Boyd, Thomas	SRA 10	Bradbury, Amos	ULS 266
Boyce, Abraham	ALB 41	Boyd, William	NYK 17	Braddock, Nathen	WSH 205
Boyce, Abraham	DUT 8	Boyd, William	ONT 334	Braddock, Seth	WSH 209
Boyce, Abraham	NYK 147	Boyd, William	ONT 412	Braden, James	NYK 120
Boyce, Benjamin	WST 165	Boyd, William	ONT 414	Braden, John	NYK 128
Boyce, Caleb	WSH 183	Boyd, William	SRA 14	Bradey, George	NYK 118
Boyce, Ebenezer	DUT 102	Boyd, William	STB 203	Bradey, William	SRA 60

Name	Loc	Pg
Bradford, Andrew	WSH	222
Bradford, Catherine	NYK	52
Bradford, Ebenezer	DUT	105
Bradford, Esich	OTS	12
Bradford, George	SRA	55
Bradford, Henry S.	SCH	140
Bradford, James	ALB	20
Bradford, John	ALB	19
Bradford, John	ALB	25
Bradford, John S.	SCH	139
Bradford, Lirk	MNT	91
Bradford, Nathaniel	NYK	100
Bradford, Peres	OTS	12
Bradford, Richard	ULS	191
Bradford, Saml	OTS	13
Bradford, Simeon	SCH	140
Bradford, Thomas	ALB	133
Bradford, William	NYK	50
Bradict, Samuel	SRA	35
Bradin, Elizabeth	NYK	132
Bradish, Esther	ONT	356
Bradish, JOhn	ONT	352
Bradish, Josiah	ONT	336
Bradley, Abraham	COL	249
Bradley, Adad	DUT	175
Bradley, Anna	NYK	100
Bradley, Anson	ORN	282
Bradley, Asa	COL	186
Bradley, Azariah	OTS	11
Bradley, Bishop E.	TIO	213
Bradley, D___	CAY	624
Bradley, Dan	ONN	159
Bradley, Daniel	ALB	74
Bradley, Daniel	WSH	219
Bradley, Eli	CAY	600
Bradley, Eli	OND	199
Bradley, Elijah	CAY	704
Bradley, Ezekiel	SRA	21
Bradley, George	WSH	230
Bradley, Gurdon	HRK	584
Bradley, Heman	CAY	600
Bradley, Isaac	ALB	74
Bradley, Jabez	CAY	600
Bradley, James Foster	ORN	355
Bradley, John	WST	124
Bradley, Joseph	ALB	74
Bradley, Joseph Junr	ALB	74
Bradley, Julius	CHN	930
Bradley, Levi	CHN	868
Bradley, Mary	COL	251
Bradley, Medad	TIO	213
Bradley, Miles	CAY	600
Bradley, Moses	WSH	272
Bradley, Onesimus	COL	189
Bradley, Peirce	WSH	230
Bradley, Peter	DEL	268
Bradley, Roswell	DEL	275
Bradley, Roswell	ULS	194
Bradley, Sturges	OTS	24
Bradley, Susanna	DUT	135
Bradley, William	CAY	600
Bradley, William	CHN	930
Bradley, William	ORN	350
Bradley, William	RNS	80
Bradly, Elisha	CHN	932
Bradly, Thadeus	COL	181
Bradner, Andrew	ORN	373
Bradner, Benjamin	ORN	360
Bradner, Benoni	ORN	350
Bradner, Benoni	ORN	364
Bradner, Colvill	ORN	377
Bradner, James	ORN	362
Bradner, John	CAY	524
Bradner, John	ORN	330
Bradner, John	ORN	397
Bradner, Josiah	OND	190
Bradner, Moses	ORN	335
Bradner, Samuel	OND	190
Bradner, William	OND	190
Bradsham, William	NYK	127
Bradshaw, Cornelius	ULS	263
Bradshaw, Israel	WSH	189
Bradshaw, James	SRA	25
Bradshaw, James	WSH	189
Bradshaw, John	MNT	41
Bradshaw, John	SRA	7
Bradshaw, Savia	DUT	44
Bradshaw, Thomas	WSH	217
Bradshaw, William	DUT	45
Bradshaw, William	RNS	80
Bradshaw, William	SRA	10
Bradt, Andrew	RNS	85
Bradt, Daniel	RNS	32
Bradt, Daniel B.	RNS	19
Bradt, Egbart	SCH	121
Bradt, Garret	RNS	19
Bradt, Henry	OTS	58
Bradt, Jacobus	DEL	278
Bradt, John	RNS	19
Bradt, John L.	RNS	32
Bradt, Peter	OTS	58
Bradt, Samuel	DEL	278
Bradwell, John	QNS	65
Bradwell, Thomas	COL	254
Bradwick, Brice	TIO	250
Brady, Daniel	NYK	142
Brady, David	WST	154
Brady, Ezekiel	SRA	42
Brady, George	NYK	46
Brady, Hannah	NYK	144
Brady, Jesse	WST	128
Brady, John	NYK	32
Brady, John	OTS	2
Brady, Mary	NYK	150
Brady, Reuben	WST	131
Brady, Simeon	WST	154
Brady, Thomas	NYK	142
Brady, William	NYK	153
Braemen, Joseph	DUT	10
Braemen, Thomas	DUT	129
Braemer, George	ORN	373
Braemer, John	ORN	385
Brafford, Abiram	WSH	251
Brafford, Robert	WSH	251
Brag, Benjaman	CHN	740
Brag, Ebenezar	CHN	740
Bragg, Benjn	OTS	32
Bragg, Ebenezer	OND	216
Bragg, Hope Still	OTS	21
Bragg, John	WSH	234
Bragg, Julius	CLN	167
Bragg, Peleg	WSH	250
Bragg, Willard	HRK	482
Bragham, Wm	RNS	62
Braily, Gideon	ONT	408
Brainard, Ansel	OND	187
Brainard, Ichabud	COL	204
Brainard, Isaac	HRK	594
Brainard, Jeptha	OND	162
Brainard, Oliver	OTS	49
Brainard, Othniel	OND	187
Brainard, Samuel	HRK	556
Brainard, Samuel	OND	162
Brainard, Seby	ONN	164
Brainard, Timothy	HRK	592
Braine, Daniel B.	NYK	41
Braisted, John	RCH	93
Braisted, John	RCH	93
Brakart, Baltis	SCH	156
Brakart, Frederick	SCH	156
Brakeman, Christopher	DEL	287
Brakeman, John	OTS	40
Brakeman, Lodowick	OTS	40
Bral, William	NYK	140
Bram see Kram		
Braman, Cyrus	DUT	107
Braman, Jeremiah	WSH	242
Braman, Paul	RNS	99
Bramble, James	DUT	63
Bram[ble?], Moses	CAY	562
Bramer, David	WSH	295
Bramhall, Joseph	DEL	289
Bramhall, Meheteb	COL	204
Bramlee, John	DEL	290
Bramlee, William	DEL	290
Branagan, Arthur	NYK	87
Branard, Samuel	OND	221
Branch, Asahel	CAY	660
Branch, Avery	OTS	35
Branch, Daniel	CHN	910
Branch, Lemuel	ONN	140
Branch, Liberty	CLN	157
Branch, Perly	OTS	35
Branch, Samuel	CAY	650
Branch, William	CAY	660
Branch, Winter W.	CAY	660
Branch, Zaphaniah	ONT	380
Branch, Zebe	CAY	646
Branch, Zeba	OND	218
Brand, Benjamin	ALB	91
Brand, Benjamin	CLN	160
Brand, David	ALB	76
Brand, Russel	CHN	832
Brand, Thomas	NYK	111
Brando, Wilhelmus	GRN	334
Brandon, Hendri[ck?]	GRN	327
Brandow, Abraham	GRN	326
Brandow, Aron	GRN	329
Brandow, Elijah	GRN	326
Brandow, Hendrick	GRN	355
Brandow, John	GRN	332
Brandow, John	GRN	334
Brandow, John	GRN	355
Brandow, Nicholas	GRN	327
Brandow, Peter	GRN	333
Brandow, Peter	GRN	355
Brandow, William	GRN	327
Brandow, Wm	GRN	332
Brandt, Charls	WSH	248
Brandt, Christian	COL	200
Brandt, Simeon	CAY	608
Brandystill, Jacob	DEL	267
Brandystill , Michael	DEL	267
Braner, Elisha	CHN	866
Brannen, Michael	WSH	221
Brannick, Frances	WSH	216
Brannon, Patrick	CAY	708
B[r?]anshard, Joseph	WSH	199
Brant, Benjamin	SCH	148
Brant, Edward	ALB	98
Brant, George	GRN	328
Brant, Hendrick	GRN	340
Brant, Hendrick	GRN	345
Brant, Jacob	NYK	147
Brant, Jeremiah	GRN	327
Brant, Philip	WST	153
Brant, Simeon	OTS	21
Branthwit, Sarah	NYK	54
Brantingham, Joseph	NYK	85
Brantingham, Thomas	NYK	61
Brantly, James	WSH	223
Brappet, John	ORN	386
Brapren, John	NYK	79
Brard, James	NYK	56
Brardy, Lethia	NYK	43
Brasher, Gassherie	NYK	59
Brasher, James C.	NYK	17
Brasher, Low	NYK	144
Brasher, Phillip	NYK	111
Brasher, York a Black	NYK	65

Name	Place	No.
Brashford, William	NYK	79
Brashier	NYK	70
Brashier, Hellen	NYK	19
Brasier, John	NYK	92
Brass, Chris..on	MNT	90
Brass, David a mulatto	NYK	107
Brass, Gabriel	ORN	371
Brass, Henry	ORN	372
Brass, James	ORN	302
Brass, Jesse	DUT	75
Brass, John	DUT	75
Brass, John	QNS	84
Brass, Joseph	NYK	134
Brass, Josias	DUT	67
Brass, Nathaniel	QNS	70
Brass, Peter	DUT	75
Brassbridge, John	DUT	78
Brassett, Joseph	ULS	203
Brat, Derka	MNT	90
Brat, Evert	MNT	59
Brat, Frederick	MNT	95
Braton, Asa	OND	219
Braton, David	RNS	42
Braton, Thomas	OND	219
Bratt, ...us	MNT	86
Bratt, Aaron G.	ALB	21
Bratt, Abraham	ALB	18
Bratt, Adam	ALB	99
Bratt, Adrian	ALB	108
Bratt, Albert	SRA	11
Bratt, Albert A.	ALB	102
Bratt, Andrew	ALB	101
Bratt, Andrew	ALB	107
Bratt, Andries	SRA	41
Bratt, Anthy	ALB	6
Bratt, Anthony T.	ALB	47
Bratt, Aurant	ALB	141
Bratt, Aurant A.	ALB	18
Bratt, Barney	ALB	132
Bratt, Charles	MNT	85
Bratt, Coenrad	ALB	109
Bratt, Corns A.	ALB	4
Bratt, Daniel	ALB	7
Bratt, Derick	SRA	3
Bratt, Ephraim	ALB	24
Bratt, Frederick	ALB	17
Bratt, Geourt	ALB	107
Bratt, Gerrit	ALB	109
Bratt, Gerrit J,	ALB	101
Bratt, Henry	ALB	43
Bratt, Henry	ALB	47
Bratt, Henry	ALB	133
Bratt, Herms	ALB	11
Bratt, Hermanus	MNT	122
Bratt, Isaac	ALB	141
Bratt, Jacob a free Negro	ALB	62
Bratt, Jacobus	ALB	18
Bratt, Jehoicham	ALB	102
Bratt, John	ALB	15
Bratt, John	ALB	45
Bratt, John A.	ALB	17
Bratt, John B.	ALB	46
Bratt, John S.	ALB	77
Bratt, Joseph	ALB	103
Bratt, Mary	ALB	17
Bratt, Mary	ALB	21
Bratt, Myndert	ALB	18
Bratt, Ns	ALB	7
Bratt, Nicholas	SRA	34
Bratt, Nicholas A.	ALB	18
Bratt, Peter	ALB	44
Bratt, Peter	ALB	89
Bratt, Peter	ALB	99
Bratt, Peter B.	ALB	101
Bratt, Peter J.	ALB	104
Bratt, Samuel	ALB	17

Name	Place	No.
Bratt, Staats	ALB	99
Bratt, Storm	ALB	104
Bratt, Storm A.	ALB	101
Bratt, Storm D.	ALB	103
Brattlebank, Samuel	ONT	428
Brau see Brace		
Braugham, Saml	ALB	16
Braugham, Saml S.	ALB	16
Brawalibiga Las, Jacob	MNT	70
Brawbargher, Henry	RNS	35
Brawbargher, Jn	RNS	35
Brawer, Henry	SRA	44
Brawten(?), Johnson	RNS	26
Bray, Ceasar a Black	NYK	19
Bray, George	NYK	145
Bray, Sarah	NYK	27
Bray, William	ULS	198
Brayden, Robert	WST	152
Brayman, James	WSH	201
Braymen, Benjamin	CLN	155
Braymer, George	NYK	68
Braymont, James	ALB	73
Braymont, John	ALB	73
Braymont, Jonathan	ALB	73
Brayn__, Ez[era?]	CHN	866
Braynard, Amasa	HRK	535
Braynard, Benjamin	DEL	276
Braynard, Hannah	DEL	286
Braynard, Jonathan	OND	217
Braynard, Nathaniel	WSH	281
Braynard, Pheneas	WSH	286
Brayton, Benjamin	OND	189
Brayton, Caleb	WSH	266
Brayton, David	WSH	266
Brayton, Francis	HRK	453
Brayton, Henry	WSH	266
Brayton, Isaac	OND	195
Brayton, Isaac Junr	OND	195
Brayton, Jeremiah	HRK	525
Brayton, John	WSH	211
Brayton, John	WSH	266
Brayton, Matthew	CLN	170
Brayton, Thomas	WSH	218
Brayton, Thomas	WSH	266
Brazee, Andrew	DEL	283
Brazee, John C.	DEL	283
Brazee, Peter	DEL	276
Brazic, Theopelus	NYK	144
Brazier, Elizabeth	NYK	51
Brazier, Jacob	RCH	90
Brazier, John	NYK	15
Brdshaw, James	ALB	39
Breadley, James	SRA	25
Breasted, Andrew	ULS	222
Breasted, Josiah	ORN	348
Breath, James	NYK	44
Breath, John	NYK	17
Breaton, Stephen	SRA	56
Breaton, William	SRA	56
Brebner, James	COL	215
Brece, Henry	RNS	18
Breckman, Roderick	ONT	398
Bredge, George	WSH	267
Bree, John	RNS	19
Breece, Anthony	RNS	7
Breece, Garret T.	RNS	7
Breed, Allen	ONN	167
Breed, Amos	CHN	778
Breed, Gershom	ONN	167
Breed, Joseph	CHN	778
Breed, Joseph	OTS	22
Breed, Joshua	CHN	816
Breeman, Jesse	ALB	71
Breeman, Josiah	RNS	22
Breese, Arthur	OND	157
Breese, John	COL	233
Breese, John	COL	255

Name	Place	No.
Breese, John	OTS	30
Breese, John	RNS	6
Breese, Wynsandt Junr	COL	256
Breesee, Andrew F.	COL	232
Breesee, Benjamin	COL	233
Breesee, Cornelius	COL	240
Breesee, Cornelius C.	COL	228
Breesee, Cornelius F.	COL	239
Breesee, Francis	COL	239
Breesee, John N.	COL	240
Breesee, Nicholas J.	COL	240
Breesee, Pheebe	COL	240
Breesee, Teunis J.	COL	233
Breesee, Teunis T.(?)	COL	233
Breesee, Wynsandt	COL	234
Breesie, Dirck	COL	242
Breesie, Henry	COL	236
Breesie, John .	COL	242
Breesie, Nicholas	COL	239
Breevoort, Henry	NYK	150
Breeze, Chloe	COL	182
Breezee, Andrus H.	COL	185
Breezee, Gabriel	COL	185
Breezee, John H.	COL	185
Breezee, Wynandt	COL	254
Bregaw, John	OTS	57
Brenan, Laurence	NYK	73
Brenan, Martin	NYK	81
Brenard, Daniel	ONT	424
Brennan, Thomas	WST	148
Brenneyson, Charles	NYK	89
Brennon, Timothy	ULS	237
Brennon, William	ORN	305
Brennon, William Junr	ORN	305
Brentnell, Joseph	RNS	91
Brenzeghofer, Frederick	NYK	142
Brese, John	TIO	259
Bresee, Teunis	COL	236
Bresher, Philander	NYK	38
Bresze, Francis	CHN	772
Bret, Robert M.	NYK	31
Brett, Baltus	ALB	99
Brett, Elizabeth	NYK	18
Brett, George	DUT	36
Brett, John	NYK	70
Brett, Joshua H.	DEL	287
Brett, Robert	DUT	27
Brett, Theodorus	DUT	36
Brett, Uriah	ORN	280
Brett, William	ULS	207
Bretton, Robert a Black	NYK	55
Breuster, John	RNS	29
Brevee, Mathias	OND	163
Brevoort, Elias	NYK	48
Brevoort, John	MNT	10
Brevoort, John V.	ORN	306
Brewer, Abrm	RNS	74
Brewer, Adolphus	NYK	148
Brewer, Arent	MNT	9
Brewer, Charles	QNS	73
Brewer, Christian	NYK	121
Brewer, Cornelius	ALB	144
Brewer, Cornelius	DUT	70
Brewer, Daniel	WSH	232
Brewer, David	DEL	283
Brewer, David	OND	163
Brewer, Elias	DEL	283
Brewer, Elias	QNS	73
Brewer, Francis	DEL	282
Brewer, George	QNS	72
Brewer, Henry	DEL	276
Brewer, Henry	SUF	81
Brewer, Hermanus Junr	MNT	10
Brewer, Hessel	COL	260
Brewer, Israel	OTS	46
Brewer, Jacob	QNS	76
Brewer, James	QNS	76

Name	Loc	Name	Loc	Name	Loc
Brewer, Jeremiah	SRA 48	Brewster, William	ULS 189	Briggs, Elihu	ESS 306
Brewer, John	CAY 628	Breze, Sidney S.	CHN 966	Briggs, Elkanah	COL 219
Brewer, John	GRN 337	Brezee, Michael	DEL 283	Briggs, Elles	OTS 28
Brewer, John	QNS 73	Briam, Alexander	SCH 158	Briggs, Esich	OND 219
Brewer, John	WSH 190	Brian, David	RNS 35	Briggs, Ezekiel	ALB 33
Brewer, John	WST 144	Brian, John	RCK 101	Briggs, Ferdinand	ULS 267
Brewer, John Junr	DUT 77	Briant, Alexander	OTS 21	Briggs, Francis	ONT 456
Brewer, John Senr	DUT 78	Briant, David	WSH 269	Briggs, Francis	SCH 121
Brewer, Joseph	DUT 51	Briant, John	MNT 83	Briggs, Gabriel	NYK 89
Brewer, Mathew	RNS 26	Briant, Richard	RNS 31	Briggs, Gabriel	WST 161
Brewer, Nehemiah	DUT 83	Briarton, John	DUT 73	Briggs, George	CHN 802
Brewer, Oliver	QNS 72	Brice see Price		Briggs, George	DUT 163
Brewer, Peter	ALB 5	Brice, Garret	RNS 19	Briggs, George	WST 144
Brewer, Peter	ALB 32	Brice, James	ALB 107	Briggs, George	WST 153
Brewer, Peter	GRN 337	Brice, James	ORN 312	Briggs, Henry	COL 215
Brewer, Peter	WSH 241	Brice, John	ALB 62	Briggs, Henry	ORN 375
Brewer, Richard	DEL 278	Brice, Robert	ALB 107	Briggs, Henry	WSH 189
Brewer, Richard	QNS 73	Brick, Moses	COL 257	Briggs, Ichabod	SRA 35
Brewer, Richard	QNS 73	Bricker, William	NYK 67	Briggs, Isaac	ALB 33
Brewer, Samuel	DUT 19	Brickel, William	QNS 71	Briggs, Ithamer	RNS 53
Brewer, Samuel	QNS 73	Brickle, Israel	QNS 79	Briggs, Jabez	WSH 236
Brewer, Solomon	WST 162	Briddaut, John F.	NYK 143	Briggs, James	OND 209
Brewer, Teunis	DUT 77	Briddgin, Thomas	NYK 151	Briggs, James	RCK 99
Brewer, William	CLN 161	Bridenbecker, Baltus	HRK 440	Briggs, James	WST 122
Brewer, William	GRN 337	Bridenbecker, George	HRK 440	Briggs, Jeremeah	WSH 306
Brewer, William	HRK 534	Bridge, Amos	OND 164	Briggs, Jeremiah	OTS 38
Brewer, Wm	TIO 255	Bridge, Caeser a Black	NYK 66	Briggs, Jeremiah	WSH 210
Brewerton, George	NYK 100	Bridge, Joshua	ONT 350	Briggs, Joab	SRA 33
Brewerton, Henry	NYK 53	Bridgeford, Joseph	NYK 151	Briggs, Job	OND 164
Brewster see Brawten		Bridgeland, Rebecca	NYK 46	Briggs, Job	OTS 47
Brewster, Abraham	HRK 513	Bridgeman, Orlando	CHN 752	Briggs, Job	WSH 239
Brewster, Absalom	ORN 311	Bridgeman, Quartus	CHN 752	Briggs, Job Junr	ALB 36
Brewster, Alexander	CHN 814	Bridgeman, Reuben	CHN 752	Briggs, Joel	ORN 379
Brewster, Benjamin	ORN 353	Bridgen, Charles	NYK 86	Briggs, John	ALB 36
Brewster, Benjn	SUF 68	Bridges, Martin	OTS 29	Briggs, John	CAY 560
Brewster, Daniel	ORN 353	Bridges, Nathan	OTS 29	Briggs, John	COL 243
Brewster, Darius	OTS 53	Bridges, Robert	SRA 17	Briggs, John	DUT 114
Brewster, Elias	OND 210	Bridges, Thomas	NYK 75	Briggs, John	NYK 78
Brewster, Francis	ORN 281	Bridges, Thomas	NYK 124	Briggs, John	NYK 129
Brewster, Henry	ORN 350	Bridgman, Tertius	ONN 150	Briggs, John	ONT 464
Brewster, Isaac	SUF 67	Brig, Asariah	MNT 59	Briggs, John	ORN 344
Brewster, Jacob	OTS 51	Briggs, Abner	DUT 147	Briggs, John	TIO 265
Brewster, Jacob	SRA 53	Briggs, Abner	WSH 207	Briggs, John	WST 115
Brewster, James	ORN 304	Briggs, Abner	WSH 240	Briggs, John	WST 122
Brewster, James	RNS 94	Briggs, Abraham	WSH 189	Briggs, John	WST 128
Brewster, James	ULS 244	Briggs, Ama.	WSH 183	Briggs, John	WST 161
Brewster, Jeffery	SUF 65	Briggs, Anthony	COL 218	Briggs, John the 2d	DUT 119
Brewster, Jesse	CAY 532	Briggs, Anthony	DUT 144	Briggs, Jonathan	DUT 126
Brewster, John	DUT 55	Briggs, Arnold	CHN 802	Briggs, Joseph	ALB 36
Brewster, John	ORN 353	Briggs, Arnold	OND 184	Briggs, Joseph	OTS 31
Brewster, John	ORN 359	Briggs, Asahel	OND 198	Briggs, Joshua	OND 181
Brewster, John	SCH 139	Briggs, Benjamin	ALB 87	Briggs, Knight	GRN 329
Brewster, John	ULS 187	Briggs, Benjamin	DUT 113	Briggs, Lawrence	RCK 97
Brewster, John Junr	ORN 354	Briggs, Benjn	OTS 47	Briggs, Lemuel	HRK 596
Brewster, Joseph	ORN 350	Briggs, Benjn	RNS 71	Briggs, Lewis	COL 218
Brewster, Joseph	SRA 31	Briggs, Benjamine	GRN 353	Briggs, Lindall	ALB 128
Brewster, Joseph Jur	SUF 66	Briggs, Caleb	DUT 39	Briggs, Margaret	ULS 268
Brewster, Joseph Sr	SUF 66	Briggs, Caleb	DUT 126	Briggs, Matthias	RCK 99
Brewster, Mary	RCK 101	Briggs, Caleb	WST 115	Briggs, Mercy	ALB 36
Brewster, Matthew	ORN 350	Briggs, Cary	CHN 790	Briggs, Michael	OTS 38
Brewster, Nathan	MNT 59	Briggs, Charles	ONT 438	Briggs, Moses	ONT 420
Brewster, Nathan	OTS 21	Briggs, Christopher	OND 204	Briggs, Nathan	RNS 71
Brewster, Nathanl	QNS 78	Briggs, Comfort	OTS 37	Briggs, Ns a free Negro	ALB 3
Brewster, Richard	RCK 103	Briggs, Cornelius	WSH 240	Briggs, Oliver	ALB 36
Brewster, Samuel	DUT 171	Briggs, Cornell	WSH 300	Briggs, Oliver	ALB 36
Brewster, Samuel	ORN 288	Briggs, Daniel	ONN 158	Briggs, Oliver	WSH 237
Brewster, Samuel	ORN 354	Briggs, Danl	OTS 47	Briggs, Peleg	ONT 468
Brewster, Saml	RCK 103	Briggs, Darius	GRN 335	Briggs, Pelig	ONT 456
Brewster, Seth	OND 210	Briggs, David	ALB 36	Briggs, Perez	OTS 34
Brewster, Stephen	OND 166	Briggs, David	ONT 468	Briggs, Peter	ONT 330
Brewster, Stephen	OTS 16	Briggs, David	WSH 239	Briggs, Phinehas	HRK 596
Brewster, Tertullus	ORN 341	Briggs, Debby	CHN 810	Briggs, Rebecca	DUT 39
Brewster, Timy	SUF 70	Briggs, Ebenezer	HRK 449	Briggs, Reuben	HRK 539
Brewster, William	CAY 534	Briggs, Ebenezer	NYK 124	Briggs, Richard	OND 219
Brewster, William	OND 217	Briggs, Edward	DUT 51	Briggs, Robert	ONT 328
Brewster, William	ORN 338	Briggs, Edward	NYK 125	Briggs, Rowland	OND 185
Brewster, William	ORN 387	Briggs, Edward	WST 144	Briggs, Russell	OTS 35

Briggs, Samuel	OND 209	Brinck, Cornelius	ULS 248	Brisbane, James	DUT 70
Briggs, Saml	OTS 33	Brinck, Garret	ORN 318	Brisben, Crouth	SRA 48
Briggs, Samuel	SRA 35	Brinck, Jacob	ULS 197	Brisben, James	SRA 40
Briggs, Sanford	ONT 330	Brinck, Jacob	ULS 226	Brisben, James	SRA 40
Briggs, Sarah	ONT 458	Brinck, Johannis J.	ULS 219	Brisben, John	SRA 40
Briggs, Sarah	WST 124	Brinck, John	ORN 316	Brisben, William	SRA 39
Briggs, Silas	SRA 16	Brinck, John	ULS 223	Brisee, Henry	OND 223
Briggs, Spencer	OND 182	Brinck, John	ULS 248	Brislan, Partrick	NYK 20
Briggs, Spencer	OTS 32	Brinck, John Junr	ULS 220	Brissberry, Wayman	NYK 67
Briggs, Squire	OTS 33	Brinck, John C.	ULS 219	Brissonton, Samuel	ORN 320
Briggs, Stephen	OTS 28	Brinck, Peter	ULS 205	Brister, Jonathan	COL 241
Briggs, Thomas	OND 204	Brinck, Peter	ULS 224	Bristol, Abraham	CAY 690
Briggs, Thos	RNS 26	Brinck, Peter	ULS 248	Bristol, Abraham	RNS 10
Briggs, Thomas	RNS 99	Brinck, Peter C.	ULS 219	Bristol, Amos	DEL 289
Briggs, Thomas	RNS 105	Brinck, Robert	ULS 205	Bristol, Asher	COL 217
Briggs, Timothy	DUT 147	Brinck, Solomon	ORN 318	Bristol, Benjm	COL 208
Briggs, Trap	SCH 142	Brinck, Solomon	ULS 248	Bristol, Bethuel	RNS 10
Briggs, Walter	SCH 117	Brinckerhoff, Abraham	DUT 20	Bristol, Charles	DUT 102
Briggs, Walter	WSH 210	Brinckerhoff, Adrian	DUT 29	Bristol, Chester	ESS 318
Briggs, Walter	WST 146	Brinckerhoff, CorneliusNYK	45	Bristol, Cornelius	OND 217
Briggs, Walter Jr	WST 144	Brinckerhoff, Dirck A.	DUT 29	Bristol, Daniel	CAY 690
Briggs, William	ALB 36	Brinckerhoff, Dirck I.	DUT 25	Bristol, Daniel	GRN 354
Briggs, Wm	OND 210	Brinckerhoff, George	DUT 22	Bristol, Daniel	OTS 22
Briggs, William	OTS 44	Brinckerhoff, George		Bristol, Daniel	RNS 10
Briggs, Wm	RNS 27	Junr	DUT 25	Bristol, David	DUT 102
Briggs, William	WSH 189	Brinckerhoff, George G.DUT	28	Bristol, David	WSH 230
Briggs, Yelverton	OTS 33	Brincierhoff, Henry I.	DUT 38	Bristol, David Junr	DUT 102
Briggs, Zenas	ONT 416	Brinckerhoff, Isaac	WSH 292	Bristol, Eli	OND 199
Briggs, Zephaniah	TIO 211	Brinckerhoff, Jacob	DUT 26	Bristol, Elijah	CAY 720
Brigham, Abel	OND 186	Brinckerhoff, John	DUT 29	Bristol, Eliphalet	COL 212
Brigham, Abel	OTS 2	Brinckerhoff, John G.	DUT 38	Bristol, Elipht	OTS 41
Brigham, Alexr	OTS 47	Brinckerhoff, John I.	DUT 38	Bristol, Henry	CAY 690
Brigham, Asa	OND 199	Brinckerhoff, Mary	DUT 25	Bristol, Isaac	ESS 311
Brigham, Dugan	SCH 122	Brinckerhoff, Sarah	DUT 30	Bristol, Job	CAY 720
Brigham, John	CHN 890	Brinckerhoof, Abraham		Bristol, Joel	OND 199
Brigham, Jonathan	CHN 880	Junr	NYK 17	Bristol, Joel	RNS 10
Brigham, Josiah	OTS 11	Brinckerhoof, Henry	NYK 60	Bristol, John	ALB 59
Brigham, Lyman	OND 166	Brinckerhoof, Rachel	NYK 27	Bristol, John	DEL 288
Brigham, ...olas	ONT 490	Brinckerhoof, Selbe	NYK 97	Bristol, John H.	ESS 321
Brigham, Samuel	CHN 890	Brinckerhoof, George G.RCK	107	Bristol, Landon	WSH 281
Brigham, Stephen	OND 173	Brinckerhoof, Isaac	QNS 63	Bristol, Levi	CAY 720
Bright, Mary	ORN 392	Brink, ...	TIO 211	Bristol, Peter	WSH 230
Bright, Philip	CAY 580	Brink, Aaron	OTS 27	Bristol, Reuben	ALB 65
Bright, William	DUT 137	Brink, Abrm	ONN 188	Bristol, Richard	DEL 287
Brightman, Benjn	OTS 30	Brink, David	TIO 236	Bristol, Samuel	CAY 692
Brightman, Daniel	CAY 654	Brink, George	CAY 578	Bristol, Selad	WSH 245
Brightman, Isaac	OTS 29	Brink, Henry J.	CAY 684	Bristol, Simeon	MNT 82
Brightman, Johnston	WSH 236	Brink, James	TIO 238	Bristol, William	WSH 245
Brightman, Umphry	SRA 38	Brink, John	CAY 576	Bristowe, Samuel	NYK 38
Brigness, Edward	GRN 339	Brink, Nicholas	TIO 236	Britain, Benjamin	WSH 282
Brigs, Edward	MNT 119	Brink, Peter	TIO 248	Britain, Luther	OND 193
Brigs, George	MNT 119	Brinkerhoff, Abraham	NYK 24	Brite, William	ALB 99
Brigs, Jesse	MNT 112	Brinkerhoff, Abraham	QNS 61	Briton, John	ONN 168
Brigs, Joseph	MNT 119	Brinkerhoff, Abraham	QNS 72	Britt, Frederick	ALB 106
Brigs, Joshua	WST 113	Brinkerhoff, Daniel	QNS 70	Britt, Peter	GRN 326
Brigs, Mrss	GRN 326	Brinkerhoff, Daniel	QNS 71	Britt, William	WST 114
Brigs, Nathaniel	COL 262	Brinkerhoff, George	QNS 61	Brittain, Calvin	OND 193
Brigs, Weison	OND 224	Brinkerhoff, Harman	NYK 47	Brittang, Stephen	QNS 67
Brill, David	DUT 16	Brinkerhoff, Hendrick	QNS 70	Brittle, Claudius	CLN 167
Brill, Henry I.	DUT 16	Brinkerhoff, Jacob	QNS 69	Britton, Abby	NYK 28
Brill, Joel	SRA 20	Brinkerhoff, Peter	QNS 69	Britton, Daniel	CAY 592
Brill, John	DUT 16	Brinkerhoff, Tennis	QNS 60	Britton, Ebenezer	HRK 451
Brill, Joseph	DUT 58	Brinkerhoof, Abm	SUF 80	Britton, Elihu	QNS 66
Brill, Peter	DUT 13	Brinkerhoof, Derick	QNS 63	Britton, Gilbert	ALB 102
Brim, Francis	NYK 67	Brinkerhoof, George	CAY 682	Britton, James	NYK 101
Brim, Frederick	CHN 924	Brinkerhoof, George	QNS 62	Britton, James	RCH 94
Brimingstol, Michael	RNS 75	Brinkerhoof, George		Britton, John	RCH 93
Brimington, William	NYK 104	Junr	QNS 63	Britton, Lucy	ALB 102
Brimner, Betsey	NYK 90	Brinkerhoof, Jacob	CAY 682	Britton, Nathaniel	RCH 92
Brimner, John	QNS 67	Brinkerhoof, James	CAY 680	Britton, Nicholas	NYK 138
Brimstead, William	NYK 129	Brinkerhoof, Lucas	CAY 710	Britton, Otis	HRK 443
Brimstool, Abm	RNS 42	Brinkerhoof, Luke	CAY 684	Britton, Richard	CAY 548
Brimstool, Michael	RNS 42	Brinkerhoof, Rulof	CAY 682	Britton, Samuel	OND 220
Brinck, Adam	ALB 92	Brinkeroff, Cornelius	QNS 63	Britton, Samuel	RCH 90
Brinck, Anna	ULS 204	Brinkeroff, Hendrick	QNS 65	Britton, William	QNS 60
Brinck, Cornelius	ULS 204	Brinkeroff, Isaac	QNS 60	Britton, William	QNS 66
Brinck, Cornelius	ULS 224	Brintenal, Isaac	GRN 347	Briveltar, John mulatto	NYK 110

44

Name	Loc	No.	Name	Loc	No.	Name	Loc	No.
Broad, Amos	ALB	133	Brodhead, Charles C.	OND	160	Brooks, James	TIO	238
Broad, William	NYK	100	Brodie, Alexander	NYK	101	B.ooks, Jeremiah	MNT	117
Broadhead, Abraham	ULS	202	Brodie, John	NYK	111	Brooks, Jesse	CAY	666
Broadhead, Charles Junr	ULS	242	Brokins, Calvin	COL	192	Brooks, [Jesse?]	OTS	24
Broadhead, Daniel	ULS	205	Brombush, William	NYK	37	Brooks, [J?]obe	GRN	326
Broadhead, Henry	ULS	198	Bromegam, Thomas	RNS	8	Brooks, Joel	ULS	182
Broadhead, John	ULS	211	Bromegham, Isaac	RNS	56	Brooks, John	ALB	58
Broadhead, Lewis	ULS	202	Bromegham, Peter	RNS	56	Brooks, John	CAY	536
Broadhead, Mary	ULS	254	Bromgham, Richard	RNS	56	Brooks, John	NYK	86
Broadhead, Richard	ULS	204	Bromley, David	ALB	140	Brooks, John	OND	212
Broadhead, Richard	ULS	211	Bromley, James	ALB	64	Brooks, John	ONT	482
Broadhead, Samuel	ULS	182	Bromle_, John	CAY	534	Brooks, John	ORN	354
Broadhead, Thomas	COL	223	Bromley, John	ONT	376	Brooks, .ohn	RNS	64
Broadhead, Wessels	ULS	201	Bromley, Samuel	ALB	138	Brooks, John	SCH	167
Broadhurst, David	ALB	135	Bromm	QNS	77	Brooks, John	TIO	234
Broadhurst, Rachel	WST	148	Bromon, John	NYK	110	Brooks, John	ULS	186
Broadhurst, Samuel	NYK	86	Bronk, Henderick	ALB	109	Brooks, John	WSH	284
Broadshaw, Dolly	NYK	60	Bronk, Henry	ALB	106	Brooks, Jonathan	ALB	130
Broadstreet, John	NYK	150	Bronk, Jonas	ALB	121	Brooks, Jonathan	DUT	28
Broadway, Jeremy	OND	184	Bronk, Mathias	ALB	75	Brooks, Jonathan	ORN	293
Broadwell, Abigail	NYK	76	Bronson, Abijah	OND	169	Brooks, Jonathan Jr	ALB	130
Broadwell, Ezra	SRA	25	Bronson, Salmon	OND	174	Brooks, Jonethan	ALB	60
Broadwell, Noah	CLN	163	Brood, Dimius	NYK	66	Brooks, Joseph	NYK	86
Broadwell, Noah	CLN	164	Brook, Benj:	ONN	165	Brooks, Joseph	OND	184
Broadwell, William T.	DUT	157	Brook, Francis	RNS	76	Brooks, Joseph	ONT	480
Broca, David	CAY	548	Brook, Stephen	SUF	87	Brooks, Joseph Junr	OND	184
Broca, Evert	CAY	564	Brooker, Peter	ULS	183	Brooks, Joshua	SCH	167
Broca, John	CAY	680	Brooker, Sibbil	RNS	32	Brooks, Levi	WSH	204
Brock, Benoni	ULS	190	Brookes, Michael	NYK	47	Brooks, Michael	ONT	402
Brock, Caty	RNS	20	Brookes, Nathaniel	RCK	100	Brooks, Michael	ORN	388
Brock, Francis	NYK	118	Brookfield, Elizabeth	NYK	114	Brooks, Nathaniel Junr	ORN	393
Brock, John	ORN	388	Brookins, Benjamin	STB	206	Brookas, Peter	ALB	58
Brock, John	WSH	233	Brookins, Ebenezer	SCH	147	Brooks, Peter	MNT	22
Brock, Saml	OTS	4	Brookins, Ephraim	OTS	6	Brooks, Peter	SCH	129
Brock, William	ORN	294	Brookins, James	RNS	30	Brooks, Reuben	SRA	50
Brock, William	WSH	234	Brookins, ubin	MNT	69	Brooks, Rice	OTS	28
Brockaway, Elisha	ONT	368	Brookins, Thadeus	OTS	6	Brooks, Richard	NYK	68
Br__kaway, Nathan	MNT	90	Brookland, John	WST	166	Brooks, Roger	CHN	972
Brockaway, Samuel	SCH	158	Brooklyn, Artemas	NYK	78	Brooks, Samuel	OND	209
Brockaway, Samuel C.	ONT	368	Brookman, Godfrey	MNT	33	Brooks, Samuel	OND	221
Brocker, Jacob	COL	213	Brooks,	GRN	359	Brooks, Sarah	SRA	5
Brocker, Jacob Junr	COL	210	Brooks, Abner	OND	184	Brooks, Seth	DUT	131
Brockeway, Abner	WSH	226	Brooks, Abraham	OND	212	Brooks, Silas	WSH	264
Br_ckfield, Thomas	NYK	17	Brooks, Abraham Jr	OND	212	Brooks, Stephen	OND	212
Brockham, John	ALB	38	Brooks, Ananiah	ONT	362	Brooks, Stephen	WSH	288
Brockho_m, Joseph	ALB	38	Brooks, Anthony	ALB	130	Brooks, Thaddeus	TIO	217
Brockhurst, William	NYK	39	Brooks, Asa	ONN	155	Brooks, Thomas	CHN	780
Brocklin, Alexande	MNT	75	Brooks, Austin	ONT	378	Brooks, Thomas	DEL	285
Brocklin, ..errit	MNT	78	Brooks, Barnabas	OND	158	Brooks, Thomas	OND	221
Brocks, Joseph B.	OND	175	Brooks, Barney	SCH	168	Brooks, Thomas	ORN	351
Brockway	GRN	336	Brooks, Barny	OTS	22	Brooks, Thomas	OTS	49
Brockway, Abel	ALB	75	Brooks, Benjamin	ORN	351	Brooks, Thomas	TIO	259
Brockway, Beman	GRN	329	Brooks, Benjn	OTS	23	Brooks, Timothy	NYK	99
Brockway, Burben	ONT	496	Brooks, Benjn	OTS	52	Brooks, Uri	OND	203
Brockway, Consider	OTS	54	Brooks, Berne	SCH	161	Brooks, Willeam	WSH	285
Brockway, Edward	ALB	8A	Brooks, Calvin	OND	184	Brooks, Wm	GRN	359
Brockway, Eliphat	OTS	13	Brooks, Coenrod	NYK	60	Brooks, William	NYK	121
Brockway, Ezekiel	ORN	284	Brooks, Cors	OTS	28	Brooks, William	OND	175
Brockway, Ezra	COL	196	Brooks, Cornelius	TIO	237	Brooks, Wm	RCK	101
Brockway, George	ORN	398	Brooks, Cyrus	OND	212	Brooks, William	SRA	19
Brockway, Gideon	ONT	492	Brooks, Daniel	CHN	740	Brooks, William Junr	OND	175
Brockway, Jedediah	COL	217	Brooks, Daniel	CHN	760	Broom	QNS	84
Brockway, Jeremiah	RNS	64	Brooks, Daniel J.	NYK	135	Broom, John	GRN	356
Brockway, Justice	RNS	103	Brooks, David	DUT	153	Broom, John	NYK	27
Brockway, Justice Junr	RNS	103	Brooks, Eli	GRN	325	Broom, William	NYK	20
Brockway, Levi	RNS	56	Brooks, Eri	OND	205	Broombush, David	NYK	124
Brockway, Libeus	RNS	104	Brooks, Ezriel	SCH	158	Broome, John J.	NYK	50
Brockway, Luman	OTS	48	Brooks, Garret	MNT	71	Broome, William T.	NYK	28
Brockway, Moses	HRK	536	Brooks, Henry	NYK	107	Broomfield, Cuff	NYK	104
Brockway, Nathanil	RNS	64	Brooks, Henry H.	NYK	78	Broomfield, James	DUT	26
Brockway, Phillip	ORN	391	Brooks, Ichabod	ESS	293	Brosious, John	DUT	150
Brockway, Reuben	RNS	65	Brooks, Ira	OTS	22	Brost, George	RNS	89
Brockway, Richard	SRA	29	Brooks, Isaac	MNT	117	Brost, Jacob	RNS	89
Brockway, Russel	OTS	51	Brooks, Isaac	OND	173	Brost, John	RNS	89
Brockway, Sarah	COL	221	Brooks, Isaac	OND	178	Brost, Mathew	RNS	89
Brockway, Wilson	RNS	64	Brooks, Jacob	NYK	96	Broster, Benjamin	RNS	88
Brockwood, Jane	RNS	65	B[rooks?], James	CAY	518	Broster, Edward	RNS	6

45

Brot, John	WSH 198	
Brot, John	WSH 204	
Broth, Cornelius	NYK 132	
Brothack, Jacob	HRK 462	
Brother, John	TIO 213	
Brothers, Henry	ONT 504	
Brothers, William	NYK 84	
Brotherson, John	WST 160	
Brotherson, Joseph	NYK 85	
Brotherton, Daniel	SCH 160	
Brotherton, Esopher	SCH 160	
Brotherton, Jeshua	SCH 160	
Brotherton, John	ONN 145	
Brotherton, Michael	SCH 168	
Brotherton, Othaniel	SCH 160	
Brotherton, Willm	SCH 168	
Broughton, George	NYK 24	
Broughton, Nathan	SCH 148	
Broughton, Walter	SRA 47	
Broun, Aaron	RNS 75	
Broun, Alexander	NYK 90	
Broun, Alexander	RNS 102	
Broun, Caleb	RNS112A	
Broun, Christopher	RNS 97	
Broun, Daniel	RNS 100	
Broun, Elijah	RNS 68	
Broun, Elijah	RNS 100	
Broun, Isaac	RNS 5	
Broun, Jacob free Negro	RNS 12	
Broun, James	RNS 22	
Broun, James	RNS 23	
Broun, Jeptha	RNS 40	
Broun, John	RNS 101	
Broun, Jonathan	RNS 39	
Broun, Jonathan	RNS 102	
Broun, Josiah	RNS 100	
Broun, Nabath	RNS 75	
Broun, Nathaniel	RNS 26	
Broun, Noah	RNS 102	
Broun, Peter	RNS112A	
Broun, Samuel	RNS 58	
Broun, Samuel	RNS 76	
Broun, Samuel	RNS 102	
Broun, Stephen	RNS 100	
Broun, Thomas E.	RNS 58	
Broun, Wm	RNS 42	
Broun, Wm	RNS 78	
Broun, Wm Junr	RNS 42	
Broune, Robert	RNS 102	
Brounell, Benjn	RNS 15	
Brounell, Daniel	RNS 8	
Brounell, David	RNS 44	
Brounell, Simeon	RNS 44	
Brow, Christion	MNT 50	
Browd, Hesekiah	CHN 754	
Browen, John	NYK 134	
Brower see Brown		
Brower, Aaron	NYK 20	
Brower, Abraham	NYK 47	
Brower, Abraham	NYK 53	
Brower, Abraham	NYK 54	
Brower, Abraham	NYK 121	
Brower, Abraham	NYK 146	
Brower, Abrm	RCK 107	
Brower, Abraham A.	KNG 4	
Brower, Adolphus	DUT 33	
Brower, Adolphus	KNG 7	
Brower, Adolphus	KNG 10	
Brower, Benjamin	NYK 91	
Brower, Benjamin	NYK 99	
Brower, Catherine	NYK 17	
Brower, Cathranme	NYK 122	
Brower, Charles	DUT 71	
Brower, Charles	NYK 136	
Brower, Cornelius	ALB 23	
Brower, Corns	ALB 121	
Brower, Cornelius	DUT 39	

Brower, Cornelius	DUT 63	
Brower, Cornelius Senr	DUT 71	
Brower, Cornelius W.	DUT 40	
Brower, Daniel a Black	NYK 94	
Brower, Daniel	ULS 215	
Brower, David	COL 193	
Brower, David	NYK 85	
Brower, David	NYK 99	
Brower, David A.	NYK 48	
Brower, Elderd	KNG 9	
Brower, Elizabeth	NYK 15	
Brower, Garret	DUT 29	
Brower, Garret	HRK 489	
Brower, George	KNG 10	
Brower, Grant	SUF 95	
Brower, Hendrick	DUT 21	
Brower, Isaac	NYK 98	
Brower, Isaac	NYK 99	
Brower, Isaac	NYK 146	
Brower, Jacob	DUT 39	
Brower, Jacob	NYK 18	
Brower, Jacob	NYK 92	
Brower, Jacob	NYK 102	
Brower, Jacob	SCH 158	
Brower, James	NYK 53	
Brower, Jeremiah	KNG 7	
Brower, Jeremiah	KNG 10	
Brower, Jeremiah	NYK 46	
Brower, Jeremiah	SCH 158	
Brower, Job	QNS 74	
Brower, John	GRN 356	
Brower, John	KNG 10	
Brower, John	NYK 25	
Brower, John	NYK 34	
Brower, John	NYK 57	
Brower, John	NYK 57	
Brower, John	NYK 100	
Brower, John	NYK 150	
Brower, John	NYK 150	
Brower, John	RNS 68	
Brower, John Junr	DUT 41	
Brower, John Junr	ORN 306	
Brower, John P.	DUT 32	
Brower, Laurence	NYK 90	
Brower, Martha	NYK 68	
Brower, Mary	NYK 54	
Brower, Nazareth	DUT 70	
Brower, Nicholas	DUT 39	
Brower, Nicholas	NYK 15	
Brower, Nicholas	NYK 84	
Brower, Peter	COL 194	
Brower, Peter	NYK 94	
Brower, Peter	NYK 99	
Brower, Peter	NYK 112	
Brower, Poules	RCK 107	
Brower, Robert	KNG 10	
Brower, Samuel	NYK 110	
Brower, Samuel Junr	DUT 25	
Brower, Samuel Senr	DUT 27	
Brower, Theodorus	RCK 104	
Brower, Thomas	ALB 142	
Brower, Thomas P.	NYK 127	
Brower, William	ALB 125	
Brower, William	DUT 38	
Brower, William I.	DUT 39	
Browers, Jesse	NYK 49	
Browm John, Elizabeth	NYK 48	
Brown see Brower		
Brown, ___es	GRN 329	
Brown, Aaron	COL 187	
Brown, Abel	ONN 182	
Brown, Abial	NYK 36	
Brown, Abner	OTS 34	
Brown, Abraham	ALB 20	
Brown, Abraham a Mulatto	NYK 87	
Brown, Abraham	NYK 134	

Brown, Abrm	TIO 247	
Brown, Abraham	WST 128	
Brown, Abraham	WST 166	
Brown, Abraham Junr	WST 165	
Brown, Absolum	SUF 71	
Brown, Adam	DEL 281	
Brown, Adam	NYK 140	
Brown, Adam	SCH 129	
Brown, Adanijoh	WST 139	
Brown, Alexander	CAY 536	
Brown, Alexr	ONN 192	
Brown, Alexander	ORN 298	
Brown, Alexander	WSH 195	
Brown, Alexander	WSH 258	
Brown, Allen	NYK 85	
Brown, Amasa	HRK 515	
Brown, Amasa	WSH 265	
Brown, Amelia	SUF 98	
Brown, Amos	OTS 6	
Brown, Amos	ULS 260	
Brown, Andrew	ALB 68	
Brown, Andrew	ALB 134	
Brown, Andrew	CHN 824	
Brown, Andrw	NYK 100	
Brown, Andrew	SRA 61	
Brown, Andrew	WSH 267	
Brown, Andrew	WST 134	
Brown, Andrew Junr	WST 134	
Brown, Ann	QNS 73	
Brown, Anna	NYK 49	
Brown, Anna	NYK 51	
Brown, Anthony	NYK 104	
Brown, Archibald	ORN 343	
Brown, Asa	CHN 818	
Brown, Asa	OND 216	
Brown, Asa	ORN 298	
Brown, Asa	SRA 40	
Brown, Asa	WSH 206	
Brown, Asael	GRN 335	
Brown, Austen	ONT 366	
Brown, Barnabus	ONT 354	
Brown, Barry	CHN 786	
Brown, Bassilla	OTS 42	
Brown, Benjaman	CHN 818	
Brown, Benjamin	CAY 604	
Brown, Benjamin	CHN 778	
Brown, Benjamin	COL 215	
Brown, Benjamin	MNT 100	
Brown, Benjamin	MNT 126	
Brown, Benjamin	NYK 136	
Brown, Benjamin	NYK 145	
Brown, Benj:	ONN 175	
Brown, Benjamin	ONT 464	
Brown, Benjamin	ORN 313	
Brown, Benjn	OTS 50	
Brown, Benjn	TIO 245	
Brown, Benjamin	ULS 260	
Brown, Benjamin	WST 166	
Brown, Benjamin Junr	WST 166	
Brown, Bennajah	WST 159	
Brown, Bethea	WSH 273	
Brown, Billings	OTS 46	
Brown, Bostwick	ALB 22	
Brown, Brier	SUF 73	
Brown, Brockway	ULS 192	
Brown, Burnell	NYK 116	
Brown, Burrell a mulatto	NYK 92	
Brown, Caleb	ONN 136	
Brown, Caleb	OTS 48	
Brown, Caleb	WSH 234	
Brown, Caleb	WSH 264	
Brown, Calvin	OTS 5	
Brown, Catherine	NYK 127	
Brown, Charles	ALB 71	
Brown, Charles	HRK 407	
Prown, Charles	OTS 2	
Brown, Charles	OTS 34	

46

Name	Ref	Name	Ref	Name	Ref	Name	Ref
Brown, Charles	ULS 263	Brown, Elijah	ORN 290	Brown, Isaac Junr	WST 128		
Brown, Chester	WSH 302	Brown, Elijah	SUF 96	Brown, Isaac P,	OTS 37		
Brown, Christian	NYK 29	Brown, Elisabeth	WST 126	Brown, Israel	WSH 306		
Brown, Christian	SCH 150	Brown, Elisabeth	WST 145	Brown, J.	QNS 64		
Brown, Christian Jr	SCH 150	Brown, Elisha	DUT 169	Brown, Jabis	CHN 830		
Brown, Cristion	MNT 45	Brown, Elisha	ONT 474	Brown, Jacob	NYK 147		
Brown, Christiphor J.	SUF 77	Brown, Elisha	OTS 49	Brown, Jacob	ORN 333		
Brown, Conrad	SCH 167	Brown, Elisha	SRA 61	Brown, Jacob	ORN 389		
Brown, Constant	OTS 56	Brown, Eliza	NYK 44	Brown, Jacob	OTS 42		
Brown, Cornad	SCH 163	Brown, Elizabeth	SCH 168	Brown, Jacob	ULS 259		
Brown, Cornelius	DUT 94	Brown, Elizabeth	SUF 73	Brown, James	ALB 118		
Brown, Cornelius	MNT 122	Brown, Ellenor	NYK 41	Brown, James	ALB 139		
Brown, Cornelius	NYK 126	Brown, Enos	ORN 313	Brown, James	ALB 140		
Brown, Cornelius	WST 158	Brown, Ephraim	HRK 528	Brown, James	CAY 530		
Brown, Cristiper S.	SUF 77	Brown, Ephraim	ONT 418	Brown, James	CAY 582		
Brown, Cutlip	MNT 1	Brown, Ephraim	OTS 29	Brown, James	CHN 790		
Brown, Cyrus	OTS 44	Brown, Erastus	OTS 34	Brown, James	CHN 882		
Brown, Daniel	ALB 87	Brown, Evert	ALB 142	Brown, James	DEL 286		
Brown, Daniel	CAY 716	Brown, Ezekiel	WST 146	Brown, James	DUT 117		
Brown, Daniel	CHN 800	Brown, Ezra	WSH 250	Brown, James	DUT 131		
Brown, Daniel	CHN 824	Brown, Frances	WSH 305	Brown, James	NYK 61		
Brown, Daniel	CHN 902	Brown, Francis	ORN 285	Brown, James	NYK 82		
Brown, Daniel	DUT 93	Brown, Francis	ORN 294	Brown, James	NYK 101		
Brown, Daniel	HRK 424	Brown, Francis Philand	SRA 26	Brown, James	NYK 104		
Brown, Daniel	HRK 447	Brown, Franklin	NYK 128	Brown, James	NYK 112		
Brown, Daniel	OND 157	Brown, Fredereck	OTS 27	Brown, James	NYK 147		
Brown, Daniel	ONT 464	Brown, Frederick	ALB 142	Brown, James	OND 172		
Brown, Daniel	ONT 472	Brown, Frederick	ALB 142	Brown, James	OND 205		
Brown, Daniel	ONT 474	Brown, Frederick	WST 146	Brown, James	ONT 462		
Brown, Daniel	SRA 5	Brown, Garret a Black	NYK 99	Brown, James	ORN 343		
Brown, Daniel	SRA 25	Brown, George	ALB 62	Brown, James	ORN 389		
Brown, Danl	SUF 75	Brown, George	ALB 108	Brown, James	OTS 45		
Brown, Daniel	SUF 84	Brown, George	CHN 880	Brown, James	SRA 29		
Brown, Daniel	SUF 85	Brown, George	COL 205	Brown, James	SCH 120		
Brown, Daniel	SUF 91	Brown, George	NYK 141	Brown, James	SCH 131		
Brown, Daniel	ULS 180	Brown, George	NYK 145	Brown, James	SUF 83		
Brown, Daniel	WSH 206	Brown, George	NYK 145	Brown, James	TIO 264		
Brown, Daniel	WSH 257	Brown, George	NYK 149	Brown, James	ULS 186		
Brown, Daniel	WSH 264	Brown, George	OND 220	Brown, James	WST 132		
Brown, Daniel	WST 112	Brown, George	ONT 462	Brown, James	WST 160		
Brown, Daniel Jun	GRN 341	Brown, George	OTS 4	Brown, James C.	DUT 35		
Brown, Darius	OND 184	Brown, George	SCH 158	Brown, Jedediah	ALB 64		
Brown, David	ALB 88	Brown, Geradus	WST 165	Brown, Jeremiah	CAY 714		
Brown, David	COL 243	Brown, Gersham	SUF 69	Brown, Jeremiah	GRN 354		
Brown, David	HRK 517	Brown, Gilbert	NYK 153	Brown, Jeremiah	OND 184		
Brown, David	OND 212	Brown, Gilbert	ORN 343	Brown, Jeremiah	ORN 340		
Brown, David	ONT 438	Brown, Gilbert	WST 115	Brown, Jeremiah	SCH 150		
Brown, David	RCK 102	Brown, H__ea	ONT 438	Brown, Jeremiah	SUF 77		
Brown, David	SRA 15	Brown, Hachaliah	WST 128	Brown, Jeremiah	TIO 243		
Brown, David	SRA 31	Brown, Halsey	WST 112	Brown, Jeremiah	ULS 211		
Brown, David	SUF 72	Brown, Hannah	NYK 64	Brown, Jesse	CHN 784		
Brown, David	ULS 181	Brown, Hannah	QNS 66	Brown, Jesse	OND 198		
Brown, David	ULS 213	Brown, Hendrick	WST 160	Brown, Jesse	ONT 454		
Brown, David	WST 112	Brown, Henry	COL 205	Brown, Jesse	OTS 24		
Brown, David	WST 156	Brown, Henry	NYK 16	Brown, Jobe	CHN 826		
Brown, David	WST 165	Brown, Henry	ORN 325	Brown, Joel	DEL 273		
Brown, Deborah	WST 114	Brown, Henry	SCH 121	Brown, Joel	DUT 134		
Brown, Duncan	ORN 343	Brown, Henry	SCH 158	Brown, John	ALB 5		
Brown, Ebenezar	CAY 584	Brown, Henry	WST 113	Brown, John	ALB 33		
Brown, Ebenezer	DUT 93	Brown, Hezekiah	CHN 784	Brown, John	ALB 39		
Brown, Ebenezer	DUT 99	Brown, Holland	CAY 622	Brown, John	ALB 127		
Brown, Eb__zer	GRN 355	Brown, Howgel	WSH 210	Brown, John	CAY 702		
Brown, Ebenezer	GRN 351	Brown, Hubbard	OND 204	Brown, John	CHN 776		
Brown, Ebenezer	OTS 39	Brown, Icabod	CAY 622	Brown, John	CHN 802		
Brown, Ebenezer	SRA 55	Brown, Ichabod	GRN 338	Brown, John	CHN 832		
Brown, Ebenezer	ULS 187	Brown, Ichabod	HRK 436	Brown, John	CHN 888		
Brown, Eber	WST 160	Brown, Ichobud	OND 207	Brown, John	CHN 924		
Brown, Edmond	NYK 127	Brown, Isaac	HRK 476	Brown, John	CLN 160		
Brown, Edward	ALB 102	Brown, Isaac	NYK 43	Brown, John	COL 234		
Brown, Edward	ALB 135	Brown, Isaac	OND 197	Brown, John	DEL 275		
Brown, Edward	CLN 173	Brown, Isaac	ONN 152	Brown, John	DEL 287		
Brown, Edward	NYK 103	Brown, Isaac	ORN 396	Brown, John	DUT 5		
Brown, Eleazer	CHN 818	Brown, Isaac	ORN 397	Brown, John	DUT 77		
Brown, Elenor	NYK 104	Brown, Isaac	SCH 134	Brown, John	DUT 163		
Brown, Eli	SCH 149	Brown, Isaac	ULS 259	Brown, John	GRN 357		
Brown, Elijah	ONT 342	Brown, Isaac	WST 131	Brown, John	GRN 358		
Brown, Elijah	ONT 468	Brown, Isaac	WST 166	Brown, John	GRN 339		

Name	Ref	Name	Ref	Name	Ref
Brown, John	GRN 341	Brown, Joseph	ULS 186	Brown, Nehimiah	WSH 207
Brown, John	GRN 359	Brown, Joseph	ULS 235	Brown, Neil	ORN 347
Brown, John	HRK 457	Brown, Joseph	WST 115	Brown, Nicholas	HRK 413
Brown, John	MNT 58	Brown, Joshua	ONT 454	Brown, Noah	DUT 134
Brown, John	MNT 88	Brown, Joshua	ORN 355	Brown, noah	NYK 140
Brown, John	MNT 100	Brown, Josiah	ALB 100	Brown, Noah	WST 160
Brown, John	NYK 57	Brown, Josiah	NYK 141	Brown, Noah Junr	DUT 139
Brown, John	NYK 63	Brown, Josiah	ORN 303	Brown, Obadeah	WSH 194
Brown, John	NYK 106	Brown, Josiah	QNS 67	Brown, Obadiah	ULS 185
Brown, John	NYK 120	Brown, Josiah	WSH 206	Brown, Obadiah	WSH 280
Brown, John	NYK 123	Brown, Josiah	ALB 113	Brown, Obadiah Jur	WSH 280
Brown, John	NYK 139	Brown, Justice	WSH 210	Brown, Obediah	ULS 263
Brown, John	NYK 148	Brown, Justice	WST 112	Brown, Oliver	CHN 816
Brown, John	OND 181	Brown, Justus	ONT 328	Brown, Oliver	CLN 174
Brown, John	ONN 153	Brown, Justus S.	HRK 557	Brown, Oliver	MNT 88
Brown, John	ONN 190	Brown, Lear	NYK 84	Brown, Oliver	WSH 223
Brown, John	ORN 282	Brown, Leman	DUT 50	Brown, Partrick	NYK 110
Brown, John	ORN 305	Brown, Lemuel	TIO 248	Brown, Paul	NYK 134
Brown, John	ORN 359	Brown, Levi	CHN 926	Brown, Pearly	MNT 101
Brown, John	ORN 391	Brown, Levy	CHN 936	Brown, Pearsall	DUT 117
Brown, John	OTS 30	Brown, Levy	WSH 297	Brown, Peleg	OTS 46
Brown, John	QNS 62	Brown, Lively	NYK 118	Brown, Peleg	OTS 47
Brown, John	RCK 101	Brown, Loley	DUT 111	Brown, Peter	ALB 115
Brown, John	SRA 25	Brown, Lucey	WST 128	Brown, Peter	DEL 278
Brown, John	SRA 38	Brown, Lucy	ONT 458	Brown, Peter	DUT 93
Brown, John	SRA 53	Brown, Lucy	OTS 28	Brown, Peter	DUT 163
Brown, John	SCH 120	Brown, Luther	CAY 634	Brown, Peter	NYK 132
Brown, John	SCH 153	Brown, Luther	CHN 820	Brown, Peter a Black	NYK 148
Brown, John	SCH 158	Brown, Luther	OTS 46	Brown, Peter	ORN 338
Brown, John	SUF 77	Brown, Luther F.	OND 167	Brown, Peter	OTS 4
Brown, John	TIO 247	Brown, Lyman	COL 253	Brown, Peter	SUF 71
Brown, John	WSH 206	Brown, Marcus	SCH 168	Brown, Philip	MNT 17
Brown, John	WSH 259	Brown, Marian	SUF 68	Brown, Philip	SUF 68
Brown, John	WST 113	Brown, Margaret	ALB 44	Brown, Phineas	OND 205
Brown, John	WST 114	Brown, Mary	NYK 26	Brown, Phinehas	GRN 345
Brown, John	WST 124	Brown, Mary	NYK 84	Brown, Pierce	ONT 320
Brown, John	WST 129	Brown, Mary	NYK 109	Brown, Reuben	CAY 580
Brown, John	WST 131	Brown, Mary	ONT 312	Brown, Reuben	OTS 7
Brown, John	WST 154	Brown, Mary	ORN 391	Brown, Reuben	WSH 302
Brown, John	WST 166	Brown, Mary Ann	NYK 44	Brown, Rhoda	SUF 76
Brown, John H.	DEL 271	Brown, Matilda	ALB 136	Brown, Ricard	NYK 83
Brown, John H.	NYK 17	Brown, Matthew	OND 217	Brown, Richard mulatto	NYK 42 '
Brown, John M.	SCH 152	Brown, Matthew Junr	OND 217	Brown, Richd	SUF 64
Brown, John S.	ORN 333	Brown, Mehitible	SUF 76	Brown, Richd	SUF 73
Brown, John V.	DEL 271	Brown, Merrit	WST 113	Brown, Richd	SUF 77
Brown, John W.	OND 202	Brown, Micajah	ONT 464	Brown, Richd	SUF 79
Brown, Jonas	ONN 183	Brown, Michael	SCH 131	Brown, Richard	SUF 86
Brown, Jonathan	CAY 530	Brown, Mordica	ALB 112	Brown, Robert	CHN 972
Brown, Jonathan	DEL 281	Brown, Moses	CAY 544	Brown, Robert a mulatto	NYK 143
Brown, Jonathan	DUT 44	Brown, Moses	CAY 564	Brown, Robert	SCH 120
Brown, Jonathan	OND 212	Brown, Moses	TIO 233	Brown, Robert	WST 162
Brown, Jonathan	ONT 370	Brown, Nancy	NYK 55	Brown, Roger	OTS 39
Brown, Jonathan	ORN 286	Brown, Nathan	CAY 580	Brown, Roger	WST 151
Brown, Jonathan	ORN 312	Brown, Nathan	CHN 824	Brown, Roger P.	MNT 88
Brown, Jon_	OTS 34	Brown, Nathan	CHN 826	Brown, Rufus	ONT 418
Brown, Jonathan	SUF 85	Brown, Nathan	COL 215	Brown, Russel	HRK 432
Brown, Jonathan	ULS 195	Brown, Nathan	DUT 52	Brown, Russel	ONT 464
Brown, Jonathan	WSH 272	Brown, Nathan	HRK 568	Brown, Sally a Black	NYK 36
Brown, Jonathan	WST 126	Brown, Nathan	OTS 46	Brown, Samuel	ALB 88
Brown, Jonathan	WST 148	Brown, Nathan	SRA 25	Brown, Samuel	ALB 118
Brown, Jonathan Junr	ULS 263	Brown, Nathan	WST 127	Brown, Samuel	CAY 530
Brown, Jonathan 2d	WSH 271	Brown, Nathan	WST 129	Brown, Samuel	CAY 582
Brown, Jones	SUF 102	Brown, Nathan	WST 159	Brown, Samuel	CAY 622
Brown, Joseah	CHN 880	Brown, Nathaniel	CHN 806	Brown, Samuel	CLN 154
Brown, Joseph	CAY 580	Brown, Nathaniel	NYK 46	Brown, Samuel	COL 221
Brown, Joseph	COL 210	Brown, Nathaniel	OND 201	Brown, Samuel	DUT 56
Brown, Joseph	COL 216	Brown, Nathaniel	ORN 299	Brown, Samuel	GRN 339
Brown, Joseph	GRN 346	Brown, Nathaniel	ORN 395	Brown, Samuel	GRN 353
Brown, Joseph	HRK 500	Brown, Nathaniel	ORN 388	Brown, Samuel	HRK 419
Brown, Joseph a Black	NYK 109	Brown, Nathl	SUF 69	Brown, Samuel	NYK 145
Brown, Joseph	ONT 322	Brown, Nathaniel	WST 118	Brown, Samuel	OND 220
Brown, Joseph	ORN 336	Brown, Nathaniel	WST 158	Brown, Samuel	ONT 340
Brown, Joseph	ORN 355	Brown, Nathaniel B.	CHN 806	Brown, Saml	OTS 6
Brown, Joseph	QNS 74	Brown, Nehemiah	CHN 778	Brown, Saml	SCH 120
Brown, Joseph	SRA 23	Brown, Nehemiah	ORN 313	Brown, Saml	SCH 125
Brown, Joseph	TIO 246	Brown, Nehemiah	WST 113	Brown, Samuel	SCH 158
Brown, Joseph	ULS 181	Brown, Nehemiah Junr	CHN 778	Brown, Samuel	SUF 64

Name	Ref	Name	Ref	Name	Ref
Brown, Saml	SUF 73	Brown, Thomas Junr	CAY 640	Browne, Joseph	NYK 108
Brown, Saml	SUF 74	Brown, Thomas Junr	ORN 395	Browne, Mary	NYK 71
Brown, Samuel	SUF 100	Brown, Thomas E.	COL 219	Browne, Mary	NYK 129
Brown, Samll	TIO 236	Brown, Thursten	OTS 28	Browne, Richard	NYK 75
Brown, Samuel	TIO 238	Brown, Timothy	CAY 728	Browne, Robert	NYK 76
Brown, Samuel	ULS 185	Brown, Timothy	WSH 209	Browne, Samuel	NYK 58
Brown, Samuel	WSH 202	Brown, Timothy	WSH 278	Browne, Samuel	NYK 71
Brown, Samuel	WSH 209	Brown, Uriah C.	SCH 146	Browne, Silas	NYK 97
Brown, Samuel	WSH 278	Brown, Valintine	SRA 4	Brown, Squire	COL 256
Brown, Samuel	WST 113	Brown, [Vic?]ar	CHN 892	Browne, Thomas	NYK 73
Brown, Samuel	WST 127	Brown, Voluntine	WSH 210	Brownel, James	OTS 10
Brown, Samuel	WST 160	Brown, Walter	CAY 580	Brownel, John	TIO 226
Brown, Saml Junr	SUF 101	Brown, Walter	NYK 122	Brownel, Joseph	OND 211
Brown, Samuel J.	CAY 580	Brown, Weaver	MNT 123	Brownel, Samuel	DUT 17
Brown, Sarah	SUF 74	Brown, Wheeler	NYK 82	Brownell, Aaron	DUT 43
Brown, Selah	SUF 68	Brown, William	ALB 71	Brownell, Charles	OND 187
Brown, Semmeon	CHN 832	Brown, William	ALB 126	Brownell, Edward	DUT 58
Brown, Seth	WSH 221	Brown, William	CAY 622	Brownell, George	DUT 7
Brown, Siah Jun	CHN 782	Brown, William	CHN 788	Brownell, George	DUT 125
Brown, Silas	ORN 334	Brown, William	CHN 880	Brownell, Geo.	OTS 45
Brown, Silas	SRA 32	Brown, William	CLN 160	Brownell, George	SCH 148
Brown, Silas	ULS 195	Brown, William	DEL 275	Brownell, Gilbert	CAY 592
Brown, Silas	WSH 293	Brown, William	DUT 6	Brownell, Jerremiah	CHN 876
Brown, Siles	WSH 210	Brown, William	DUT 174	Brownell, John	NYK 60
Brown, Silvenus	SUF 73	Brown, William	GRN 325	Brownell, John L.	SCH 133
Brown, Silvenus Jur	SUF 73	Brown, William	GRN 344	Brownell, Jonathan	CAY 654
Brown, Simeon	HRK 477	Brown, William	HRK 419	Brownell, Joseph	OTS 21
Brown, Simeon	NYK 117	Brown, Wm	MNT 91	Brownell, Joshua	DUT 14
Brown, Simmeon	CHN 818	Brown, Wm	MNT 104	Brownell, Luthen	DUT 15
Brown, Simon	HRK 415	Brown, William	NYK 16	Brownell, P	CAY 598
Brown, Soloman	NYK 141	Brown, William	NYK 25	Brownell, Perey	CAY 592
Brown, Solomon	CAY 666	Brown, William a Black	NYK 36	Brownell, Samuel	CHN 892
Brown, Solomon	CHN 972	Brown, William	NYK 53	Brownell, Smiteing	COL 221
Brown, Solomon	ESS 322	Brown, William	NYK 62	Brownell, Thurston	CAY 592
Brown, Solomon	SRA 26	Brown, William a Black	NYK 64	Brownell, Wm	OTS 45
Brown, Solomon	WST 161	Brown, William	NYK 122	Brownell, Wm	RNS 25
Brown, Stanton	WSH 206	Brown, William	NYK 122	Brownen, Benjamin	WSH 237
Brown, Stephen	ALB 63	Brown, William	NYK 122	Brownen, Elijah	WSH 236
Brown, Stephen	DUT 143	Brown, William	OND 157	Brownen, George	WSH 236
Brown, Stephen	OND 210	Brown, William	OND 212	Brownen, Isaac	DEL 286
Brown, Stephen	OTS 12	Brown, William	ORN 326	Brownen, Jiles	WSH 219
Brown, Stephen	OTS 56	Brown, William	ORN 344	Brownen, John	WSH 238
Brown, Stephen	SUF 83	Brown, William	OTS 28	Brownen, Joshua	WSH 196
Brown, Stephen	WST 131	Brown, William	SRA 30	Brownen, Nathaniel	GRN 350
Brown, Stephen	WST 157	Brown, William	SCH 150	Brownen, Pardon	WSH 237
Brown, Stephen O.	WSH 276	Brown, William	SUF 74	Browner, Robart	GRN 346
Brown, Stephen R.	ORN 389	Brwon, William	SUF 82	Brownin, Lydia	SRA 29
Brown, Sylvanus	COL 205	Brown, William	SUF 93	Browning, George	OND 190
Brown, Sylvanus	OND 168	Brown, Wm	TIO 242	Browning, Gideon	OND 163
Brown, Sylvanus	OND 210	Brown, William	ULS 196	Browning, Jonathan	ALB 114
Brown, Thaddeus	ULS 185	Brown, William	ULS 235	Browning, Jonathan	CHN 840
Brown, Thomas	ALB 87	Brown, William	ULS 244	Browning, Oolover	OND 216
Brown, Thomas	ALB 119	Brown, William	ULS 254	Browning, Robert	ALB 30
Brown, Thomas	ALB 128	Brown, William	WSH 206	Browning, Thustin	CAY 598
Brown, Thomas	CAY 522	Brown, William	WSH 211	Brownjohn see BrownJohn	
Brown, Thomas	CAY 616	Brown, William	WSH 226	Brownjohn, Ann	KNG 2
Brown, Thomas	CHN 784	Brown, William	WSH 227	Brownlow, William	DUT 153
Brown, Thomas	CHN 924	Brown, William	WSH 298	Brownson, Corneleus	WSH 273
Brown, Thomas	DUT 147	Brown, William	WST 115	Brownson, Ebenezer	DUT 134
Brown, Thomas	ESS 319	Brown, William	WST 152	Brownson, Icabod	DEL 289
Brown, Thomas	HRK 476	Brown, William	WST 156	Brownson, Samuel	SRA 6
Brown, Thomas	HRK 528	Brown, William Junr	WSH 206	Brownson, Virtue	ONN 193
Brown, Thomas	NYK 16	Brown, William H.	ORN 312	Brownwell, Esra	MNT 112
Brown, Thomas	NYK 42	Brown, William W.	SCH 141	Bruce, Ann	NYK 106
Brown, Thomas	NYK 60	Brown, Wright	SRA 38	Bruce, Benjamin	SCH 140
Brown, Thomas	NYK 112	Brown, Zadock	ALB 86	Bruce, David	NYK 42
Brown, Thomas	NYK 128	Brown, Zebediah	DUT 177	Bruce, Eli	OTS 41
Brown, Thomas	NYK 144	Brown, Zebulon	CHN 812	Bruce, James	ALB 104
Brown, Thomas	OND 204	Brown, Zephaniah	CAY 578	Bruce, Jane	NYK 56
Brown, Thomas	ONT 410	Brown, Zera	OND 204	Bruce, Jane	NYK 91
Brown, Thomas	ORN 344	Brownall, Israel	MNT 66	Bruce, John	ONT 468
Brown, Thomas	ORN 396	Browne, Abm	SUF 71	Bruce, Judeth	NYK 19
Brown, Thomas	SRA 25	Browne, Catherine	NYK 64	Bruce, Mary	NYK 52
Brown, Thomas	SRA 42	Browne, Elizabeth	NYK 71	Bruce, Robert	RCK 110
Brown, Thos	SUF 73	Browne, Jacob	NYK 31	Bruester, Daniel	SUF 95
Brown, Thomas	WSH 279	Browne, Jacob	NYK 127	Bruin, Thomas	NYK 49
Brown, Thomas	WST 114	Browne, John	NYK 73	Brumfield, Jeremiah	WSH 232

Brumley, David	COL 203	Brunson, Asa	OND 193	Brush, Saml	SUF 89
Brumley, Levi	RNS 112	Brunson, Asa	SRA 40	Brush, Sarah	DUT 76
Brumley, Paul	RNS 73	Brunson, Ashbel	ESS 311	Brush, Smith	SUF 89
Brummode, John W.	WST 165	Brunson, Benjn	RNS 69	Brush, Thomas	NYK 76
Brumston, Ira	WST 165	Brunson, Daniel	HRK 514	Brush, Tredwell	SUF 86
Brundage, Abraham	WST 137	Brunson, Daniel	ONT 406	Brush, Tredwell	SUF 88
Brundage, Andrew	ULS 257	Brunson, David	OND 169	Brush, Zophar	DUT 173
Brundage, David	WST 137	Brunson, Ebenezer	HRK 558	Brush, Zopher	SUF 79
Brundage, David	WST 138	Brunson, Ebenezer Jun	HRK 558	Brushingham, Adren	GRN 330
Brundage, Edward	WST 156	Brunson, Elisha	CHN 808	Bruster, Isaac	SRA 60
Brundage, Gilbert	ORN 333	Brunson, Hosea	HRK 564	Bruster, Isaac	SRA 60
Brundage, Isaiah	SRA 45	Brunson, James	OND 197	Bruster, John	NYK 124
Brundage, James	DUT 129	Brunson, Jesse	GRN 337	Bruster, Samuel	NYK 74
Brundage, James	SRA 41	Brunson, John	CLN 172	Bruster, Samuel	SRA 6
Brundage, James	ULS 187	Brunson, John	ORN 359	Bruster, William	ESS 318
Brundage, Jesse	RNS 44	Brunson, Joseph	HRK 504	Bruster, William	WSH 239
Brundage, John	CAY 610	Brunson, Levi	OND 169	Brutherton, Abel	ALB 117
Brundage, Jonathan	ORN 274	Brunson, Levi Junr	OND 169	Brutherton, Isaac	ALB 109
Brundage, Jonathan Junr	WST 138	Brunson, Rubin	CLN 172	Bruvoort, Abraham	NYK 109
Brundage, Joseph	ORN 321	Brunson, Samuel	ONN 154	Bruyn, Abraham	ULS 248
Brundage, Joseph	WST 154	Brunson, Samuel	ORN 342	Bruyn, Benjamin	ULS 213
Brundage, Josiah	ULS 257	Brunson, Seth	GRN 326	Bruyn, Cornelius	ULS 251
Brundage, Lewis	WST 130	Brunson, Thomas	CAY 582	Bruyn, Jacobus	ULS 212
Brundage, Lewis	WST 134	Brunson, Thomas	ONT 464	Bruyn, Jacobus S.	ULS 227
Brundage, Nathaniel	CAY 718	Brunson, Thomas	ORN 342	Bruyn, Johannis	ULS 245
Brundage, Nathaniel	ORN 278	Brunson, Ware	NYK 27	Bruyn, Margaret	ULS 245
Brundage, Nathaniel	WST 127	Brunson, Zadock	HRK 554	Bruyn, Sufferyn	DEL 272
Brundage, Nehemiah	ORN 395	Brunt, Christian	ALB 89	Bruyn, Zachariah	ULS 250
Brundage, Oliver	SRA 41	Brunt, Michael	ALB 86	Brwer, Jacob	WST 165
Brundage, Reuben	ORN 320	Brunton, Mary	NYK 47	Bryan, Alexander	DEL 277
Brundage, Robert	WST 138	Brus.., Peter	MNT 100	Bryan, Alexander	SUF 84
Brundage, Samuel	ORN 398	Bruse, Arthur a Black	NYK 66	Bryan, Azel	SUF 85
Brundage, Sarah	DUT 91	Brush, Abel	SUF 88	Bryan, David	SUF 84
Brundage, Solomon	ORN 288	Brush, Alexander	DEL 290	Bryan, Ellen	NYK 43
Brundage, Stephen	WST 165	Brush, Alexander	OND 223	Bryan, Epinetus	SUF 84
Brundage, Thomas	DUT 18	Brush, Benjamin	SUF 79	Bryan, Gilbert	SUF 84
Brundage, Uriah	ORN 275	Brush, Caleb	NYK 93	Bryan, James	COL 178
Brundage, William	DUT 178	Brush, Corneleus	SUF 89	Bryan, James	ESS 296
Brundage, William	ORN 357	Brush, Daniel	SUF 89	Bryan, Jessee	SUF 84
Brundege, James	STB 202	Brush, David	SUF 90	Bryan, John	ALB 128
Brundge, Hachaliah	WST 137	Brush, Dolley	SUF 87	Bryan, John	ALB 135
Brundge, James	WST 137	Brush, Ebenezer	NYK 50	Bryan, John	NYK 79
Brundige, Abraham	STB 202	Brush, Ebenezer	QNS 79	Bryan, John	NYK 81
Brundige, Caleb	WST 115	Brush, Edward	COL 251	Bryan, Jonathan	DUT 149
Brundige, Charles	WST 115	Brush, Edward	NYK 124	Bryan, Lewis	RNS 33
Brundige, Ezekiel	WST 113	Brush, Eliphalet	DEL 284	Bryan, Lewis Junr	RNS 33
Brundige, Gilbert	WST 114	Brush, Elkanah	SUF 85	Bryan, Michael	NYK 60
Brundige, Jmes	WST 114	Brush, Epinetus	SUF 89	Bryan, Milancton	SUF 84
Brundige, James Jr	WST 114	Brush, Ezekiel	SUF 79	Bryan, Reuben	RNS 33
Brundige, Jonah	WST 112	Brush, Ezra	ULS 183	Bryan, Richard S.	DUT 170
Brundige, Levi	OND 177	Brush, George	WST 125	Bryan, muel	COL 178
Brundige, Mastin	WST 115	Brush, Gilbert	NYK 140	Bryant, Charles	ONT 432
Brundige, Silvanus	WST 114	Brush, Gilbert	SRA 5	Bryant, David	CHN 810
Brundridge, Caleb Ju	ONT 446	Brush, Isaac	SUF 84	Bryant, Ebenezer	SUF 84
Brundridge, Danl	RCK 104	Brush, Jacameah	SUF 79	Bryant, Elijah	DEL 282
Brundridge, George	ONT 446	Brush, Jacob	DUT 173	Bryant, Elizabet	SUF 84
Brundridge, Joseph	ONT 446	Brush, Jacob	ULS 235	Bryant, Ezra	DUT 141
Brune, Frederick Julius	NYK 56	Brush, Jacob	WST 141	Bryant, Jacob	SUF 89
Bruner, Christian	MNT 29	Brush, Jesse	WST 141	Bryant, James	ONT 340
Bruner, Felin	MNT 28	Brush, John	DUT 173	Bryant, John	CAY 566
Bruner, Jacob	MNT 28	Brush, John	NYK 105	Bryant, John	ULS 235
Brunk, Ephraim	GRN 356	Brush, John	NYK 131	Bryant, Joseph	ONT 394
Brunk, John	GRN 356	Brush, John	SUF 86	Bryant, Joseph	QNS 74
Brunk, Jonas	GRN 351	Brush, Jonas	SUF 80	Bryant, Joseph	SRA 41
Brunk, Leoynard	GRN 350	Brush, Jonathan	SUF 85	Bryant, Michael	WSH 286
Brunk, Mrss	GRN 350	Brush, Joseph	SUF 79	Bryant, Samuel	SRA 18
Brunk, Peter	GRN 356	Brush, Joseph	ULS 262	Bryant, Samuel	SRA 39
Brunk, Peter Jun	GRN 356	Brush, Joshua	RCK 97	Bryant, Samuel	SRA 41
Brunk, Peter C.	GRN 356	Brush, Lemuel	DUT 141	Bryant, Wilhelmus	COL 238
Brunk, Phillip J.	GRN 356	Brush, Molley	SUF 79	Bryant, William	COL 236
Brunk, Richard	GRN 356	Brush, Nehemiah	SUF 83	Bryar, William	NYK 30
Brunn, Andrew	NYK 72	Brush, Pearsall	SUF 80	Bryce, James	OTS 5
Brunsan, Ebenr	OTS 38	Brush, Peter	RCK 101	Bryde, Hugh	ALB 105
Brunsen, Francis	NYK 23	Brush, Platt	SUF 80	Bryden, William	NYK 107
Bruson, Abraham	ONT 434	Brush, Richard	SUF 79	Bryington, Justice	SCH 124
Brunson, Amos	HRK 564	Brush, Robert	WST 125	Brysen, William	NYK 101
Brunson, Amos	ONT 410	Brush, Samuel	CAY 628	Bryson, Archibald	NYK 27

Name	Loc	No	Name	Loc	No	Name	Loc	No
Bryson, Hugh	NYK	42	Buckbee, Gilbert	DUT	138	Budd, Gilbert	SUF	99
Bu..., Philip	CAY	538	Buckbee, Jeremiah	DUT	119	Budd, Gilbert	WSH	247
Buchan, Robert	NYK	101	Buckbee, John	ORN	316	Budd, Gilbert Junr	WST	120
Buchanan, Benjamin	ORN	285	Buckbee, John	WST	147	Budd, Griffin	WST	132
Buchanan, Georg	MNT	90	Buckbee, Palmer	KNG	8	Budd, Henry	WST	117
Buchanan, George	ORN	367	Buckbee, Richard	DUT	101	Budd, John	DUT	94
Buchanan, James	ORN	368	Buckbee, Russell	ORN	349	Budd, John	DUT	116
Buchanan, James ye 1st	ORN	292	Buckbee, Samuel	NYK	124	Budd, John	ORN	362
Buchanan, James ye 2d	ORN	291	Buckbee, Samuel	ORN	314	Budd, John	ULS	191
Buchanan, John	ALB	28	Buckbee, Susanna	WST	125	Budd, John	WST	117
Buchanan, Peter	WSH	188	Buckbee, Sylvester	WST	124	Budd, Jonathan	MNT	47
Buchanan, Robert	ALB	5	Buckell, John	NYK	47	Budd, Jonathan	WSH	247
Buchanan, Robert	ORN	293	Buckelue, John	CAY	568	Budd, Joseph	WST	117
Buchanan, Samuel	ULS	234	Buckhart, Daniel	WST	124	Budd, Joshua	SUF	99
Buchanan, Thos	ALB	5	Buckhout, Abraham	WST	122	Budd, Peggy	TIO	254
Buchanan, Thomas	NYK	28	Buckhout, Jacob	WST	162	Budd, Peter	DUT	75
Buchanan, Thomas	ULS	254	Buckhout, James	SCH	129	Budd, Saml	SUF	96
Buchanan, William	ULS	252	Buckhout, John	DUT	17	Budd, Samuel	ULS	237
Buchannan, Alexr	ALB	29	Buckhout, John	ULS	239	Budd, Selah	DUT	40
Buchannan, Alexander	NYK	112	Buckhout, John	WST	162	Budd, Underhill	DUT	30
Buchannan, Archd	ALB	29	Buckhout, John Jr	WST	162	Budd, Underhill	DUT	71
Buchannan, John	NYK	149	Buckhout, Metice	WST	122	Buddington, Asa	NYK	92
Buchannan, Mary	NYK	16	Buckingham, Benjamin	DUT	67	Buddow, Wm	GRN	357
Buchannan, Walter	NYK	51	Buckingham, George	ORN	286	Budeaux, John	CAY	600
Buchannan, Wm	ALB	29	Buckingham, Jos:	SCH	124	Budell, Joel	NYK	130
Buchannan, William	QNS	70	Buckingham, Josiahs	SUF	65	Budet, Jacques	CLN	172
Buchannen, Archibald	NYK	69	Buckingham, Reuben	OTS	39	Budlang, Willm	COL	209
Buchannon, John	HRK	448	Buckingham, Thankful	ONT	312	Budle, Mordeca	NYK	130
Buchanon, Wm	STB	199	Buckingham, Triphena	ALB	91B	Budlenson, Jeremiah	SRA	60
Buchin, James	NYK	51	Buckingham, Wm	ONN	177	Budlong, Aaron	HRK	425
Buck see Burk			Buckingham, William	ORN	280	Budlong, Benjamin	HRK	425
Buck, Aaron	WSH	299	Buckland, Joel	ONT	480	Budlong, Daniel	OND	159
Buck, Abel	WSH	282	Buckland, Widow	OTS	46	Budlong, David	OND	195
Buck, Abigal	WSH	265	Buckland, William	CAY	670	Budlong, Greene	HRK	425
Buck, Abner	DEL	288	Buckland, William	NYK	96	Budlong, John	HRK	415
Buck, Amos	SRA	53	Buckler, Peter	SRA	28	Budlong, John	OND	188
Buck, Amos	WSH	191	Buckley, Aaron	DEL	270	Budlong, Joseph	OND	188
Buck, Andries	DUT	15	Buckley, Conckling	CHN	772	Budlong, Pearse	HRK	415
Buck, Aron	SRA	44	Buckley, Daniel	NYK	124	Budona, Moses	RNS	105
Buck, Asel	SRA	60	Buckley, Danl	OTS	26	Buel, Abel	DEL	281
Buck, David	DEL	282	Buckley, Dennis	NYK	68	Buel, Azariah	HRK	599
Buck, David	WSH	209	Buckley, Ebenezer W.	DEL	270	Buel, Bela	OND	222
Buck, Ebenezer	WSH	246	Buckley, Hugh	CAY	726	Buel, Benjamin	OND	174
Buck, Elijah	CAY	700	Buckley, James	NYK	113	Buel, Catherine	NYK	27
Buck, Elijah	TIO	253	Buckley, Jason	OTS	39	Buel, Cyrus	ONT	472
Buck, Elijah	WSH	191	Buckley, Job	CHN	910	Buel, Daniel	ONT	320
Buck, Francis a Black	NYK	42	Buckley, Joel	WSH	287	Buel, David	RNS	94
Buck, George	NYK	147	Buckley, John	CHN	848	Buel, Edmond	HRK	599
Buck, Hannah	ULS	196	Buckley, John	RNS	43	Buel, Elam	RNS	17
Buck, Henry	WST	159	Buckley, Leteha	NYK	74	Buel, Ellenur a Black	NYK	84
Buck, Israel	CLN	156	Buckley, Moses	WSH	274	Buel, Grover	DUT	136
Buck, Israel	DUT	136	Buckley, Peter	OTS	26	Buel, Hezekiah	DEL	281
Buck, Israel	RNS	33	Buckley, Phineas	NYK	153	Buel, James	OND	176
Buck, James	MNT	58	Buckley, Robert	CAY	524	Buel, Jeptha	OND	158
Buck, Jared	RNS	112	Buckley, William	ESS	322	Buel, Jonathan	HRK	550
Buck, Joel	CLN	157	Buckley, Wm	ONN	154	Buel, Josiah	RNS	17
Buck, John	CLN	156	Bucklin, Abner	HRK	565	Buel, Patman	OND	222
Buck, John	WSH	212	Bucklin, Alden	HRK	575	Buel, Roswell	HRK	581
Buck, John Junr	WSH	212	Bucklin, David	HRK	453	Buel, S uel Ju	ONT	472
Buck, Jonathan	ESS	318	Bucklin, John	HRK	575	Buel, Simon	TIO	228
Buck, Josiah	CAY	642	Bucklin, William	HRK	453	Buel, Timothy	ONT	406
Buck, Justice	WSH	208	Buckly, Christopher	CHN	980	Buell, Ephraim	CAY	654
Buck, Ledeal	WSH	272	Buckman, Amasa	DUT	119	Buell, Icabud	ONT	474
Buck, Levy	WSH	266	Buckman, Caleb	RCH	87	Buell, Isreal	CAY	654
Buck, Martin	DUT	15	Buckman, Moses	GRN	339	Buell, Salmon	CAY	652
Buck, Mathias	NYK	96	Buckmaster, George	NYK	133	Buell, Samuel	ONT	474
Buck, Perrey G.	WSH	199	Buckman, Robert	HRK	418	Buell, Timothy	WSH	276
Buck, Philip	SCH	119	Bucknor, William C.	NYK	26	Buetell, Samuel	CHN	762
Buck, Solomon	WSH	247	Buckstone, Aaron	COL	203	Bufeelt, George R.	NYK	27
Buck, Thomas	DEL	282	Bud, John	TIO	242	Buffam, Moses	TIO	214
Buck, Walter	ESS	320	Bud, Mary	NYK	74	Buffet, Isaac	SUF	89
Buck, William S.	CAY	568	Budd, Daniel	DUT	116	Buffett, Elephaz	SUF	88
Buck , Levi	WST	126	Budd, Elijah	DUT	75	Buffett, Jessee	SUF	86
Buckbee, Edward	DUT	82	Budd, Elish	WSH	247	Buffett, John	SUF	88
Buckbee, Elijah	WST	141	Budd, Frederick	ONT	502	Buffett, Nathaniel	SUF	83
Buckbee, Elijah Junr	WST	141	Budd, Gilbert	DUT	34	Buffett, Zebulon	SUF	83
Buckbee, Ezekiel	WST	140	Budd, Gilbert	RNS	58	Buffington, Jerh	OTS	29

Name	Ref	Name	Ref	Name	Ref
Buffitt, Jesse W.	RNS 34	Bull, Moses Junr	ORN 344	Bulson, Gradus	HRK 473
Bugbee, Abiel	RNS 82	Bull, Nathan	TIO 263	Bulson, Henry	ALB 42
Bugbee, Daniel	CHN 920	Bull, Nathaniel	WSH 266	Bulson, Henry	RNS 87
Bugbee, John	CLN 174	Bull, Norman	CLN 154	Bulson, John	ALB 62
Bugbee, John	RNS 14	Bull, Peter	ORN 355	Bulson, Peter	ALB 42
Bugbee, Silas	RNS 91	Bull, Philip	SCH 136	Bulson, Solomon	ALB 42
Bugbey, Daniel	GRN 353	Bull, Richard	NYK 53	Bult_, Benjamin	TIO 222
Bugbey, John	QNS 61	Bull, Richard	ORN 378	Bulter, Truelove	SCH 158
Bugbey, Willeam	WSH 243	Bull, Samuel	ORN 342	Bulwinkle, Henry	NYK 144
Bugby, Edward	WST 144	Bull, Sarah	NYK 139	Buly, Benjamin	ULS 198
Bugby, Enos	WST 147	Bull, Stephen	DUT 6	Bulyea, John	WST 166
Bugby, George	DEL 272	Bull, Thomas	ORN 345	Bulyea, John Junr	WST 166
Bugby, Isaac	NYK 135	Bull, Thomas Junr	ORN 298	Bumfrees, Seth	CHN 928
Bugby, James	WSH 306	Bull, Wadsworth	WSH 275	Bump, Ansil	SRA 43
Bugby, John	RNS 93	Bull, William	NYK 73	Bump, Daniel	DUT 72
Bugby, Joseph	RNS 93	Bull, William	ORN 345	Bump, David	CHN 952
Bugby, Oliver	CHN 926	Bull, Williamson	ESS 323	Bump, Elijah	DUT 133
Bugdorf, Henry	MNT 15	Bullard, Ezekiel	HRK 517	Bump, George	DUT 72
Bugley, Daniel	GRN 338	Bullard, Jesse	CAY 564	Bump, Ithama	CHN 952
Bugley, David	GRN 334	Bullard, John	OND 223	Bump, Jacob	DUT 72
Bugley, John	GRN 338	Bullard, Nathan	HRK 523	Bump, Jedediah	DUT 133
Bugsbey, Samuel	WSH 199	Bullard, Nathan	ORN 278	Bump, Job	SRA 38
Buhman, Charles	NYK 79	Bullard, Seth	ONN 164	Bump, Laben	WSH 269
Buhman, Harman	NYK 90	Bulleard, Berack	SRA 61	Bump, Matthew	DUT 87
Buhman, John R.	NYK 50	Buller, Wm	RNS 43	Bump, Moses	OND 178
Buice, Abraham	NYK 102	Buller, Zacheus	RNS 43	Bump, Nathan	CHN 952
Bukman see Beekman &		Bulles, Charles	COL 183	Bump, Reuben	CHN 758
Beckman		Bulles, Elizabeth	COL 218	Bump, Roswell	DUT 133
Bukman, James	NYK 152	Bulles, John	COL 207	Bump, Stephen	WSH 269
Bukman, William	NYK 151	Bulles, John R.	COL 220	Bump, Wanton	WSH 269
Buknar, Samuel	NYK 95	Bulles, Peter	COL 208	Bumpbus, Benjamin	SRA 57
Bulis, John	GRN 346	Bulles, Wilmoth	COL 180	Bumpbus, Joseph	SRA 57
Bulkley, David	DUT 143	Bullet, Eleazer	SRA 28	Bumppos, Andrew	WST 147
Bulkley, Isaac	ULS 238	Bullick, Aaron	WSH 238	Bumppos, Isaac	WST 147
Bulkley, Moses	DUT 143	Bullinbe_, Wintroop	GRN 347	Bumpus, Aaron	SRA 31
Bulkley, Sturges	DUT 143	Bulling, David	OND 190	Bumpus, Abner	CHN 928
Bulkley, Thomas	NYK 82	Bulling, John	OND 191	Bumpus, Frederick	ALB 103
Bull, Abraham	OND 195	Bulling, Samuel	ONT 372	Bumpus, Gladwin	HRK 570
Bull, Abraham	RNS 80	Bullion, James	CAY 692	Bumpus, Ichabud	SRA 28
Bull, Amos	OND 211	Bullis, Charles	CLN 157	Bumpus, Isaac	HRK 547
Bull, Asher	OND 205	Bullis, Charles	CLN 159	Bumpus, James	SRA 31
Bull, Benjamin	OND 190	Bullis, Enoch	CLN 170	Bumpus, Jason	HRK 547
Bull, Cadwallader	ORN 300	Bullis, German	CLN 159	Bumpus, Jesse	CHN 928
Bull, Charles	ORN 345	Bullis, Henry G.	CLN 165	Bumpus, Nathan	HRK 544
Bull, Crissey	ORN 355	Bullis, Henry H.	CLN 165	Bumpus, Reuben	ALB 83
Bull, Daniel	COL 241	Bullis, Isaac	CLN 165	Bumpus, Simeon	HRK 547
Bull, Daniel	ORN 300	Bullis, James	CLN 170	Bumpus, Stephen	HRK 547
Bull, Daniel	ORN 349	Bullis, Jesse	CLN 170	Bumrel, Davia	NYK 40
Bull, Daniel	SRA 40	Bullis, John	DUT 147	Bumstead, Edward	NYK 142
Bull, Eliza	NYK 130	Bullis, John	SCH 157	Bumstead, Frederick	MNT 27
Bull, Elizabeth	ORN 389	Bullis, Joseph	GRN 355	Bumstead, John	NYK 125
Bull, Enos	SUF 98	Bullis, Robert J.	COL 265	Bumstead, John	QNS 79
Bull, Ephraim	COL 210	Bullis, Silas	DUT 129	Bun, Abraham	MNT 22
Bull, Francis	NYK 24	Bullis, Thomas	DUT 144	Bun, Job	OND 173
Bull, Gurdon	WSH 266	Bullmon, Edward	DUT 65	Bun, John	NYK 103
Bull, Henry	CLN 173	Bullock, Comar	DUT 127	Bunce, Daniel	RNS 10
Bull, Horace	DUT 175	Bullock, Comar Junr	DUT 127	Bunce, Ebe	NYK 78
Bull, Howel	STB 202	Bullock, Comfort	DUT 128	Bunce, Eliphalet	SUF 84
Bull, Isaac	ORN 349	Bullock, Daniel	ALB 29	Bunce, Fleet	SUF 85
Bull, Isaac	RNS 17	Bullock, Daniel	DUT 152	Bunce, Jacob	OND 212
Bull, James	COL 205	Bullock, Elijah	DUT 129	Bunce, Jeffery	NYK 126
Bull, James	OND 211	Bullock, Ellis	COL 259	Bunce, Joel	KNG 8
Bull, James	ORN 345	Bullock, Ellis Junr	COL 259	Bunce, John	CAY 654
Bull, Jeremiah	SCH 145	Bullock, Ephriam	WSH 253	Bunce, John	GRN 331
Bull, John	ALB 111	Bullock, John	ALB 105	Bunce, John	SUF 68
Bull, John	ORN 355	Bullock, Jonathan	ONT 452	Bunce, Joshua	SUF 85
Bull, John	OTS 5	Bullock, Joseph	ALB 72	Bunce, Mathew	NYK 79
Bull, John	SRA 40	Bullock, Nathan	DUT 129	Bunce, Nathan	GRN 348
Bull, John D.	COL 243	Bullock, Reuben	COL 264	Bunce, Nathan	SUF 84
Bull, Joseph	NYK 126	Bullock, Reuben	HRK 595	Bunce, Nathaniel	NYK 77
Bull, Joseph	WSH 213	Bullock, Reuben	WSH 204	Bunce, Nathaniel	NYK 83
Bull, Josias	DUT 7	Bullock, Richard	COL 264	Bunce, Richard	ONT 470
Bull, Manning	WSH 268	Bullock, Wheaton	COL 264	Bunce, Samuel	SUF 84
Bull, Mary	SUF 106	Bullock, William	DEL 272	Bunck, Zenas	COL 236
Bull, Mitchel	NYK 90	Buloid, Robert	NYK 40	Buncker, Barzilla	COL 247
Bull, Mordeca	RNS 17	Bulson, Alexander	RNS 87	Buncker, David	COL 251
Bull, Moses	ORN 345	Bulson, Cornelius	ALB 52	Buncker, Elihu	COL 249

Buncker, Elihu 2d	COL 250	Burbanck, John	RCH 89	Burchem, Benjamin	QNS 74
Buncker, Elijah	COL 246	Burbanck, Joseph	RCH 91	Burchen, Richard	NYK 37
Buncker, Francis	COL 198	Burbank, Abraham	RCH 88	Burchet, Nathaniel	WSH 212
Buncker, George	NYK 23	Burbank, Abraham	RCH 92	Burchill, George	NYK 45
Buncker, Jonathan	COL 251	Burbank, Jacob	RCH 92	Burchin, Stephen	GRN 335
Buncker, Mary	COL 255	Burbank, James	SUF 93	Burchit, Phineas	ONT 374
Buncker, Paul	COL 252	Burbank, Josiah	ORN 392	Burclue, Isaac	CAY 600
Buncker, Paul 2d	COL 249	Burbanks, Abrm	OTS 37	Burdeck, Amos	DUT 55
Buncker, Prince	COL 250	Burbanks, Daniel	COL 196	Burdeck, Caleb	DUT 91
Buncker, Reuben	COL 253	Burbanks, Daniel	ONN 162	Burdeck, Joshua	DUT 55
Buncker, Sarah	COL 255	Burbey, Nicholas	ONT 418	Burdeck, Matthew	DUT 145
Buncker, Solomon	COL 255	Burboo, Fearnot	SRA 40	Burdeck, Nathaniel	DUT 57
Buncker, Timothy	COL 255	Burch, Admarel	WSH 198	Burdeck, Samuel	DUT 54
Buncker, Tristam	COL 253	Burch, Asa	HRK 511	Burdee, Nathel	COL 217
Buncker, William	COL 246	Burch, Atha	DUT 24	Burden, Aaron	CAY 630
Bunda, Simmeon	RNS 24	Burch, Benoni	WSH 205	Burden, Benjamin	DUT 101
Bundle, Jared	DUT 152	Burch, Benoni	WSH 209	Burden, John	SRA 39
Bunduge, Jessee	SUF 80	Burch, Braemin	DUT 92	Burden, Joshua	DEL 273
Bundy, Benajah	OTS 8	Burch, Daniel	DUT 92	Burdge, Uriah	NYK 143
Bundy, Elisha	OTS 28	Burch, Daniel	DUT 171	Burdges, Samuel	NYK 145
Bundy, Ezekiel	ALB 65	Burch, Ebenezer	COL 239	Burdges, William	NYK 145
Bundy, Geo.	OTS 46	Burch, Ebenezer	DUT 143	Burdick, Alpheus	OND 194
Bundy, Lysy	ALB 81	Burch, Eliot	WSH 201	Burdick, Asa	RNS 112
Bundy, Peter	OTS 28	Burch, George	DUT 170	Burdick, Augustus	RNS 86
Bunhart, Helmus Jur	SCH 128	Burch, George Junr	DUT 52	Burdick, Caleb	WSH 235
Bunker, Betsey	NYK 71	Burch, Gidion	OTS 51	Burdick, Caleb	WSH 241
Bunker, Eunice	DUT 119	Burch, Gilbert	DUT 44	Burdick, Cary	RNS 54
Bunker, John	WSH 215	Burch, Hiram	HRK 511	Burdick, Daniel	WSH 205
Bunker, Timothy	COL 215	Burch, Isaiah	DUT 44	Burdick, David	RNS 98
Bunker, William	CLN 154	Burch, Jacob	DUT 170	Burdick, David	WSH 204
Bunker, William	NYK 81	Burch, Jacob	SRA 53	Burdick, Elisha	COL 228
Bunn, David	SUF 93	Burch, Jacob Junr	SRA 53	Burdick, Ephriam	WSH 232
Bunn, Jacob	OTS 9	Burch, James	DUT 56	Burdick, Wphriam M.	WSH 235
Bunn, James	SUF 96	Burch, James	MNT 71	Burdick, Ethan	RNS 66
Bunn, John	NYK 26	Burch, James	SUF 80	Burdick, George	CHN 924
Bunn, Nathan	DUT 72	Burch, Jasper	SRA 47	Burdick, George	WSH 189
Bunn, Reuben	NYK 29	Burch, Jeremiah	DUT 56	Burdick, Henry	ALB 113
Bunn, William	NYK 55	Burch, Jeremiah	DUT 143	Burdick, Jabez	RNS 70
Bunnel, John	TIO 238	Burch, Jerh	OTS 37	Burdick, Jesse st	RNS 76
Bunnel, Joseph	OTS 57	Burch, Jeremiah	SUF 80	Burdick, Jewit	WSH 235
Bunnel, Rufus	DEL 288	Burch, Jesse	DUT 48	Burdick, John	RNS 68
Bunnell, Abraham	ALB 88	Burch, John	DUT 170	Burdick, Joseph	RNS 76
Bunnell, Havilah	DUT 132	Burch, John Junr	DUT 55	Burdick, Joseph	RNS 76
Bunnell, Jehiel	WSH 284	Burch, Jonathan	DUT 48	Burdick, Lewis	ALB 115
Bunnell, Nathaniel	ALB 145	Burch, Jonathan	HRK 510	Burdick, Mathew	WSH 235
Bunnell, Sebah	TIO 229	Burch, Jonathan	SUF 80	Burdick, Parker	WSH 241
Bunner, Jane	NYK 28	Burch, Joshua	DUT 16	Burdick, Peleg	ALB 113
Bunscotten, Jacob	DEL 271	Burch, Joshua Junr	DUT 16	Burdick, Samuel	WSH 231
Bunt, Coenradt	ALB 119	Burch, Mary	SUF 80	Burdick, Stephen	MNT 25
Bunt, Harmon	GRN 331	Burch, Nathan	DEL 283	Burdick, Stephen R.	RNS 66
Bunt, Jacob	COL 254	Burch, Phebe	WSH 216	Burdick, Thomas	RNS 98
Bunt, James	ALB 65	Burch, Robert	HRK 462	Burdick, Thomas	RNS 98
Bunt, John	COL 254	Burch, Samuel	DUT 91	Burdick, Thomas	WSH 231
Bunt, Lodowick	CAY 706	Burch, Samuel	WSH 232	Burdick, Thompson	CHN 924
Bunt, Peter	COL 250	Burch, Silas	DUT 171	Burdick, Urbane	RNS 70
Bunt, Peter	SCH 119	Burch, Sylvanus	DUT 55	Burdick, Wels	WSH 255
Bunt, Peter	SCH 126	Burch, Thos	OTS 55	Burdick, Wilbur	RNS 70
Buntin, James	ORN 385	Burch, William	SRA 32	Burdick, William	CHN 924
Bunting, Samuel	NYK 52	Burch, Zebulon	SRA 32	Burdick, Wm	RNS 70
Bunting, Thomas	ULS 214	Burcham, Thomas	WSH 195	Burdick, Zaccheus	RNS 70
Bunting, William	NYK 84	Burchard, Amasa	OND 188	Burdick, Zebediah	WSH 235
Buntoo, John	ULS 216	Burchard, Asel	ONT 364	Burdick, Zillemus	RNS 78
Bunts, Abraham	OND 186	Burchard, Charles	RNS 41	Burdin, David	NYK 47
Bunts, Benj.	TIO 256	Burchard, Daniel	ESS 394	Burdin, Elijah	RNS 42
Bunty, Isaac	SUF 83	Burchard, Eli	ONT 230	Burdin, Nathan	RNS 42
Buntz, Edmund	SUF 89	Burchard, Elias	ONT 424	Burdine, Abraham	CAY 562
Buntz, Edward	SUF 84	Burchard, Ezra	COL 204	Burdine, Abraham	CAY 680
Buntz, Elcanor	SUF 84	Burchard, Ezra	ONT 364	Burdine, Cornelius	CAY 682
Buntz, Joseph	SUF 89	Burchard, Jesse	WST 125	Burdington, Oliver	RNS 67
Buntz, Thomas	SUF 84	Burchard, Nathan	ORN 397	Burdock, Alden	DEL 284
Bunzee, Henry Z.	ALB 67	Burchard, Phineas	ONT 372	Burd__, David	OTS 21
Bupe, Thos	RNS 20	Burchard, Phinehas	ONT 374	Burdock, John	OTS 21
Bur	GRN 334	Burchard, Zebulon	ORN 397	Burdock, Lewis	OTS 46
Bur_itt, Silas	DEL 280	Burchell, Arthur	NYK 123	Burdock, Nathan	CHN 826
Burau, Nathan	GRN 351	Burchell, Hester a Black	NYK 131	Burdock, Robert	OTS 55
Burbanck, James	RCH 90			Burdock, Rufus	DEL 290
Burbanck, James	RCH 93	Burchell, Samuel	NYK 37	Burdseye, G.	OND 221

Name	Loc		Name	Loc		Name	Loc	
Burel, John Felix	NYK	36	Burgosde_, Catherrine	SRA	11	Burlingame, Asahel	HRK	561
Burells, Nathan	GRN	353	Burgot, Lewis a			Burlingame, George	HRK	441
Burg_, Benjamin	WSH	253	mulatto	NYK	122	Burlingame, Jonathan	HRK	416
Burgalie, John P.	NYK	63	Burgum, Dezere	NYK	58	Burlingame, Russel	HRK	444
Burgar, Adam	GRN	327	Burhans, David	ALB	98	Burlingan, Freeborn	OND	192
Burgart, Lambert	SCH	129	Burhans(?), Henry	ALB	106	Burlingan, Wenton	OND	196
Burgart, Milbury	SCH	127	Burhans, Hezekiah	ALB	79	Burlinggame, Josiah	CHN	788
Burge, Lott	SRA	44	Burhans, Johannis	ALB	106	Burlinggame, Silus	CHN	788
Burgen, Chandler	DEL	290	Burhans, John	ALB	50	Burlingham, Arthur	CHN	790
Burgen, George	NYK	76	Burhans, John	ALB	91	Burlingham, Benjamin	DUT	99
Burgens, Hannah	NYK	108	Burhans, John H.(?)	ALB	108	Burlingham, Caleb	OTS	31
Burger, Alce	NYK	92	Burhant, Cornelius	ULS	231	Burlingham, Charles	OTS	35
Burger, Conradt	ALB	97	Burhant, John	SCH	119	Burlingham, Christopher	WSH	237
Burger, David	WST	114	Burhants, Abraham	ULS	226	Burlingham, Daniel	CHN	786
Burger, David Junr	NYK	34	Burhants, Abraham Junr	ULS	226	Burlingham, Job	WSH	303
Burger, Elias	NYK	60	Burhants, Cornelius	ULS	221	Burlingham, Joshua	CHN	796
Burger, Elias Junr	NYK	86	Burhants, David	DUT	42	Burlingham, Olney	OTS	49
Burger, Ezekiel	DEL	271	Burhants, Edward	ULS	208	Burlingham, Pardon	DUT	70
Burger, Gabriel	WST	111	Burhants, Elisha	DUT	43	Burlingham, Philip	SCH	123
Burger, Hannah a Black	NYK	39	Burhants, Isaac	ULS	226	Burlingham, Philip	SCH	125
Burger, Jeremiah	COL	239	Burhants, Jacob	ULS	219	Burlingham, Samuel	CHN	844
Burger, John	CHN	774	Burhants, John	DUT	98	Burlingham, Rix	CHN	772
Burger, John	NYK	77	Burhants, John	ULS	225	Burlingim, Clark	WSH	210
Burger, John	OND	219	Burhants, Mary	ULS	220	Burlingim, Ephriam	WSH	202
Burger, John	QNS	65	Burhants, Peter	DUT	42	Burlingim, Wonton	WSH	201
Burger, John Junr	NYK	64	Burhants, Peter	ULS	226	Burlington, Benjamin	MNT	15
Burger, Nicholas	WST	111	Burhants, Peter Junr	ULS	217	Burlinsing, John	OTS	38
Burger, Peter	GRN	327	Burhants, Samuel	ULS	221	Burlising, James	OTS	36
Burger, Stephen	COL	259	Burhants, Tjierck	ULS	219	Burloch, Samuel	QNS	61
Burger, Thomas	SUF	84	Buring, Conrod	MNT	4	Burlock, John	NYK	81
Burger, William	COL	244	Burk see Buck			Burlook, Thomas	NYK	141
Burger, William	DEL	272	Burk, Charles	HRK	577	Burman, Aaron	QNS	62
Burges, Abraham	NYK	89	Burk, Christian	RNS	61	Burmingham, Right	SUF	91
Burges, Benjamin	WSH	299	Burk, Davd	TIO	256	Burn, Daniel Junr	QNS	80
Burges, John	WST	165	Burk, Elizth	ALB	5	Burn, Francis	NYK	100
Burges, Richard	NYK	135	Burk, George	GRN	327	Burn, Francis	SUF	93
Burges, Thomas	CAY	534	Burk, George	GRN	328	Burn, William	OND	186
Burges, Tomothy	OND	219	Burk, James	STB	198	Burnam, Aron	GRN	337
Burges, Uriah	NYK	146	Burk, John	ALB	5	Burnam, Ashbel	WSH	216
Burgess, Archibald	DEL	270	Burk, Michael	RCK	99	Burnam, David	WSH	215
Burgess, John	ONN	157	Burk, Miles	NYK	74	Burne, Hannah	SRA	10
Burgess, John	OTS	21	Burk, Oliver	ALB	79	Burne, William	NYK	83
Burgess, Matthias	ULS	267	Burk, Richard	NYK	44	Burnes, David	OTS	15
Burgess, Michael	DUT	85	Burk, Silas	OND	193	Burnes, Dinah a Black	NYK	118
Burgess, Samuel	ALB	88	Burk, Sylvanus	OND	192	Burnes, John	NYK	32
Burgess, Samuel	DUT	48	Burk, Thomas	ORN	342	Burnes, John	OTS	15
Burget, Jacob	GRN	325	Burk, William	NYK	65	Burnet, Agnis	ORN	292
Burgett, Abraham	CHN	808	Burkdorf, John	HRK	481	Burnet, David	DUT	150
Burgett, Moses	CHN	740	Burke, James	COL	246	Burnet, Esquire	SRA	25
Burgett, Peter	CHN	772	Burkett, Robert	NYK	150	Burnet, George	NYK	85
Burghardt, Hendrick	DEL	283	Burleson, Mary	WSH	288	Burnet, Henry	QNS	62
Burghardt, Joachim	DEL	283	Burlesson, Joel	OND	180	Burnet, Isaac	DUT	68
Burghardt, William	DEL	283	Burlesson, Theodorus	OND	180	Burnet, James	NYK	150
Burghduff, Coonrod	WST	122	Burley, Ebenezer	WSH	257	Burnet, James	ORN	290
Burghduff, Philip	WST	122	Burlieu, Cornelius	CAY	674	Burnet, John	DUT	6
Burgher, Benjamin	ULS	207	Burling, ...	QNS	77	Burnet, John	DUT	109
Burgher, Daniel	NYK	64	Burling, Benjamin	ORN	281	Burnet, Joseph	NYK	145
Burgher, David	DUT	112	Burling, Ebenezer	DUT	78	Burnet, Josiah	SCH	143
Burgher, David	DUT	165	Burling, Ebenezer S.	NYK	77	Burnet, Patrick	ORN	284
Burgher, Elizabeth	ULS	212	Burling, Edward	RCK	106	Burnet, Robert	ONT	490
Burgher, Evert	ULS	231	Burling, George	QNS	63	Burnet, Robert R.	ORN	290
Burgher, George	DUT	112	Burling, Hannah	QNS	66	Burnet, Stephen	MNT	86
Burgher, Martin	ULS	195	Burling, James	QNS	64	Burnet, Thomas	DUT	6
Burgher, Peter	ULS	212	Burling, John	NYK	149	Burnet, Thomas	ORN	290
Burgher, Peter Junr	ULS	212	Burling, John	WST	111	Burnet, Thomas Junr	ORN	290
Burgher, Zachariah	ULS	218	Burling, Lancaster	NYK	81	Burnet, William	DUT	6
Burgis, Christian	WSH	206	Burling, Nancy	QNS	76	Burnet, William	DUT	31
Burgis, Eben	SCH	145	Burling, Peter	WST	111	Burnett, B stoc_	CHN	746
Burgis, Jonathan	OND	181	Burling, Pompey	DUT	171	Burnett, Benjn	CHN	746
Burgiss, Ebenezer	COL	219	Burling, Richard	WST	111	Burnett, David	SUF	98
Burgiss, Eli	COL	210	Burling, Samuel	NYK	43	Burnett, James	ONT	476
Burgiss, Jerreh	COL	216	Burling, Samuel	WST	111	Burnett, John	ONT	478
Burgiss, Joel	CAY	676	Burling, Thomas	NYK	150	Burnett, John Ju.	ONT	478
Burgiss, Jonathan	CAY	676	Burling, Thomas	WST	112	Burnett, Matthew	SCH	135
Burgiss, Samuel	COL	216	Burling, Walter	QNS	65	Burnett, Robert	ONN	167
Burgiss, Seth	CAY	676	Burling, William S.	NYK	44	Burnett, Silas	SUF	71
Burgiss, Seth Junr	CAY	628	Burlingame, Abram	RNS	32	Burnett, Thomas	CAY	710

Name	Loc	No.
Burnett, William	CHN	748
Burnett, William	ONT	478
Burney, Alexander	ONT	510
Burnham, Abel	SRA	28
Burnham, Charles	SRA	51
Burnham, Eddy	WSH	248
Burnham, Isaac	OTS	56
Burnham, Jacob	OTS	56
Burnham, James	SRA	51
Burnham, Joshua	OTS	47
Burnham, Joshua	RNS	80
Burnham, Josiah	SRA	51
Burnham, Noadiah	OND	175
Burnham, Roswell	RNS	47
Burnham, Sarah	NYK	114
Burnham, Thomas	SRA	51
Burnham, William	CAY	722
Burnham, William	SRA	44
Burnier, John	TIO	262
Burnnam, Orin	GRN	337
Burns, Aaron	OTS	28
Burns, Cobert	QNS	73
Burns, David	RCK	99
Burns, Edward	WST	160
Burns, Eleazer	ONN	160
Burns, Francis	ORN	338
Burns, Henry H.	MNT	40
Burns, Henry J.	MNT	44
Burns, James	CAY	636
Burns, James	WSH	295
Burns, James	WST	136
Burns, John	DUT	5
Burns, John	MNT	40
Burns, John	SRA	21
Burns, Jona	OTS	46
Burns, Jubeter a Black	NYK	16
Burns, Margaret	NYK	66
Burns, Mary	ORN	306
Burns, Robert	NYK	109
Burns, Samson	WSH	273
Burns, Samuel	RNS	89
Burns, Thomas	ESS	295
Burns, William	COL	265
Burns, William	NYK	104
Burns, William	ORN	307
Burnside, Andrew	NYK	32
Burnside, Saml	ALB	107
Burnside, Saml J.	ALB	107
Burnside, Thomas	ALB	107
Burnsides, Ephrm	OTS	7
Burnsides, Evert	OTS	45
Burnsides, Gloud	OTS	45
Burnsides, John	OTS	44
Burnum, Calvin	OTS	56
Burny, Anthony	NYK	127
Burpee, Nathaniel	OND	180
Burr, Aaron	NYK	56
Burr, Abraham	MNT	52
Burr, Adonijah	CHN	864
Burr, Daniel	ORN	369
Burr, Daniel	QNS	84
Burr, Daniel O.	ALB	128
Burr, Elihu	OTS	49
Burr, Elija Junr	MNT	72
Burr, Ezra	NYK	63
Burr, Gideon	COL	205
Burr, Hiram	MNT	65
Burr, Horace	MNT	65
Burr, Isaac	NYK	37
Burr, Isaac	SUF	83
Burr, Isaac Junr	NYK	34
Burr, Jacob	SUF	83
Burr, Jehu	DEL	271
Burr, John	OND	157
Burr, John	SRA	48
Burr, Jonathan	RNS	81
Burr, Joseph	RNS	81
Burr, Joseph	SUF	84
Burr, Levi	NYK	63
Burr, Morris	SUF	83
Burr, Nathan	DUT	56
Burr, Nathaniel	MNT	77
Burr, Ozias Esqr	ONN	144
Burr, Reuben	MNT	91
Burr, R ssele	MNT	69
Burr, Salem	MNT	120
Burr, Samuel	ORN	271
Burr, Samuel	QNS	81
Burr, Stephen	QNS	71
Burr, Theodore	CHN	768
Burr, Thomas	QNS	72
Burr, William	NYK	44
Burrace, James	GRN	353
Burral, Richard	ORN	270
Burrall, Jonathan	NYK	28
Burrall, Joshua	ORN	275
Burrall, Nathaniel	ULS	231
Burrall, Zachariah	ULS	231
Burras, James	KNG	10
Burras, John	RCK	101
Burregar, Nicholas	RCH	90
Burrel, Da.id	TIO	243
Burrel, Francis	TIO	243
Burrel, Job	TIO	226
Burrel, Samuel	RNS	17
Burrell, Arnold	OTS	8
Burrell, David	OTS	6
Burrell, Henry	NYK	73
Burrell, Isaac	HRK	565
Burrell, Jacob	HRK	501
Burrell, James	MNT	64
Burrell, John	OTS	45
Burrell, Jona	OTS	6
Burrell, Nathan	HRK	589
Burrell, Robard	GRN	356
Burrell, Samuel	CHN	790
Burrell, William	NYK	35
Burrens, Edward	SRA	42
Burres, Porter	SRA	30
Burret, Abel	NYK	76
Burret, Bailey	HRK	591
Burret, William	WSH	227
Burrett, Francis	DEL	267
Burrett, Josiah	COL	255
Burrett, Philip	DEL	285
Burrett, William	NYK	137
Burridge, Nathaniel	NYK	100
Burrill, James	SCH	152
Burrinn, William	NYK	71
Burris, David	ESS	293
Burris, John	QNS	60
Burris, John Junr	COL	203
Burris, Samuel	ALB	127
Burris, Thomas	QNS	60
Burris, William	ESS	294
Burriss, Benjamin	COL	203
Burriss, Daniel	COL	203
Burriss, Isaac	COL	203
Burriss, John	COL	203
Burriss, John Junr	COL	187
Burriss, Sylvester	COL	212
Burrough, James	COL	203
Burrough, William Y.	COL	247
Burroughs, Benjamin	DUT	110
Burroughs, Elizabeth	ORN	378
Burroughs, John	ORN	380
Burroughs, John	ULS	193
Burroughs, Joseph	DUT	25
Burroughs, Joseph	QNS	61
Burroughs, Thomas	QNS	61
Burroughs, Thomas Junr	DUT	26
Burroughs, Thomas	DUT	26
Burroughs, William	DUT	36
Burroughs, William	DUT	167
Burrowes, Thomas	NYK	139
Burrows, Abel	OND	217
Burrows, Amos	OND	216
Burrows, Asa	OND	216
Burrows, Benjamin	CAY	546
Burrows, Benjamin	WSH	284
Burrows, Daniel	WSH	281
Burrows, David	CAY	530
Burrows, David	WSH	197
Burrows, Eden	DEL	268
Burrows, Ephraim	DEL	269
Burrows, George a Black	NYK	151
Burrows, George G.	NYK	19
Burrows, Hubbard	DEL	279
Burrows, Jabes	WSH	270
Burrows, James	ONN	158
Burrows, Jean	NYK	21
Burrows, John	COL	212
Burrows, John	ONN	162
Burrows, John	OTS	29
Burrows, John Junr	COL	212
Burrows, John Fisher	NYK	17
Burrows, Joshua	OND	216
Burrows, Lamuel	NYK	135
Burrows, Lemuel	OND	187
Burrows, Matthew	ONN	176
Burrows, Samuel a Black	NYK	117
Burrows, William	DEL	268
Burrows, William	NYK	149
Burrows, Wm	ONN	163
Burry, Elijah	COL	218
Burry, William	COL	219
Burryman, Isaac	NYK	75
Burst, David	SCH	136
Burst, David	SCH	168
Burst, Henry	SCH	130
Burst, Henry	SCH	153
Burst, Henry	SCH	168
Burst, Henry J.	SCH	135
Burst, Jacob J.	SCH	129
Burst, Johannes	SCH	160
Burst, John	SCH	135
Burst, John J. Junr	SCH	129
Burst, Joseph Junr	SCH	127
Burst, Jost	SCH	150
Burst, Martinus	SCH	129
Burst, Martinus Jr	SCH	130
Burst, Michael	SCH	127
Burst, Michael	SCH	163
Burst, Peter	SCH	126
Burst, Philip	SCH	126
Burst, William	SCH	154
Bursted, Henry	COL	256
Burt see Birt		
Burt, Aaron	CLN	156
Burt, Aaron	WSH	301
Burt, Amos	WSH	207
Burt, Belden	ORN	374
Burt, Charles	NYK	74
Burt, Charles	OTS	47
Burt, Daniel	ONT	416
Burt, Daniel	ORN	376
Burt, David	ONT	354
Burt, Enos	HRK	448
Burt, Enos Junr	HRK	448
Burt, George	RNS	69
Burt, James	ORN	376
Burt, John	CAY	538
Burt, John	NYK	58
Burt, John	NYK	109
Burt, John	OND	217
Burt, John	SCH	121
Burt, Joseph	HRK	442
Burt, Joseph	QNS	71
Burt, Luther	DEL	278

Name	Ref		Name	Ref		Name	Ref
Burt, Moses	OND 186		Burvis, John	SUF 92		Bush, Jonas T.	ALB 100
Burt, Oliver	OTS 54		Burwell, Jonathan	TIO 237		Bush, Jonathan	OND 220
Burt, Thos	TIO 254		Burwick, John	NYK 55		Bush, Jonothan	CHN 770
Burt, Timothy	ONT 428		Bury, Elizabeth	NYK 64		Bush, Jonothan	CHN 916
Burt, Wilder	HRK 448		Busbee, William	RNS 78		Bush, Jophat	CHN 756
Burt, William	ORN 376		Busby, James	WST 144		Bush, Joseph	CHN 756
Burt, Zenus	WSH 227		Busca__, John	SUF 76		Bush, Joseph	RCH 93
Burtcher, Joseph	NYK 137		Buscark, Jacob	GRN 358		Bush, Joseph	COL 236
Burten, Amos	CHN 882		Buscark, John	GRN 358		Bush, Lambert	NYK 15
Burten, George	SUF 91		Buscea, Eneas	DUT 69		Bush, Lemuel	WSH 300
Burten, Uriah	SRA 47		Bush, Abial	CHN 770		Bush, Mary	NYK 15
Burteson, Silas	SRA 39		Bush, Abiel	HRK 506		Bush, Moses	CHN 914
Burthen, John	DUT 104		Bush, Abijah	RNS 110		Bush, Moses	RNS 111
Burtis, Abraham	QNS 75		Bush, Abraham	DUT 30		Bush, Nicholas	RCH 88
Burtis, Amelia	SUF 79		Bush, Abm	RNS 59		Bush, Oakley	ULS 202
Burtis, Arthur	NYK 146		Bush, Abraham	WST 113		Bush, Peter	CAY 524
Burtis, Asiby	QNS 75		Bush, Asel	CHN 762		Bush, Peter	COL 224
Burtis, Elias	QNS 76		Bush, Asel	SRA 42		Bush, Peter	RCK 107
Burtis, Elias Junr	QNS 76		Bush, Benj:	ONN 162		Bush, Peter	ULS 197
Burtis, Epenetus	NYK 100		Bush, Benjamin	ULS 213		Bush, Peter Junr	RCK 110
Burtis, Hendrick	QNS 75		Bush, Catherine	NYK 95		Bush, Rinardt	RCK 107
Burtis, John	QNS 71		Bush, Charles	CHN 752		Bush, Silas	CAY 690
Burtis, John	QNS 75		Bush, Coonrod	ONT 502		Bush, Simon	ULS 185
Burtis, John	QNS 75		Bush, Cornelius	ULS 196		Bush, Stephen	ULS 198
Burtis, John Junr	QNS 71		Bush, Cornelius	ULS 214		Bush, Thomas	CAY 650
Burtis, Mort B.	SUF 79		Bush, Daniel	NYK 106		Bush, Thomas	ULS 194
Burtis, Richard	SRA 7		Bush, Daniel	SRA 48		Bush, William	NYK 106
Burtis, Samuel	NYK 33		Bush, Daniel	ULS 181		Bush, William	ULS 199
Burtis, Samuel	NYK 126		Bush, David	ULS 213		Bush, Zachariah	DUT 28
Burtis, Samuel	NYK 138		Bush, Dirck	RCK 107		Bushby see Bushley	
Burtis, Simeon	QNS 77		Bush, Dirck	ULS 203		Bushby, Ireal	CAY 650
Burtis, Thomas	QNS 75		Bush, Eli	HRK 506		Bushcart, Gasnt	OND 222
Burtis, William	MNT 13		Bush, Eli	OND 209		Bushcart, Jacob	OND 222
Burtiss, Barent	DUT 14		Bush, Evert	NYK 82		Bushee, Samuel	WSH 220
Burtiss, Barent Juner	DUT 6		Bush, Frederick	ULS 198		Bushhark, Andrew	GRN 348
Burtiss, David	DUT 14		Bush, Frederick Junr	ULS 198		Bushfield, James	ORN 275
Burtiss, Fordham	DUT 113		Bush, Garret	RCH 88		Bushley see Bushby	
Burtiss, Garret	DUT 6		Bush, George	MNT 32		Bushley, Samuel C.	NYK 128
Burtiss, Gershom	DUT 6		Bush, George	RNS 61		Bushman, John	CAY 640
Burtiss, James	DUT 15		Bush, George Coonradt	ULS 191		Bushmore see Rushmore	
Burtiss, John	COL 194		Bush, Gilbert	ONT 442		Bushmore, Jacob	GRN 329
Burtiss, John	DUT 69		Bush, Gilbert	WST 116		Bushmore, Jeremiah	GRN 328
Burton see Berton			Bush, Gorge	GRN 332		Bushmore, Silas	GRN 329
Burton, Alpheus	ONN 132		Bush, Gysbert	DUT 166		Bushmore, Thomas	ALB 107
Burton, Charles	CHN 938		Bush, Heman	HRK 526		Bushnal, Aron	GRN 335
Burton, Daniel	DUT 139		Bush, Henry	CAY 704		Bushnal, Elijah	GRN 335
Burton, Daniel	HRK 458		Bush, Henry	GRN 326		Bushnal, Elijah Jun	GRN 335
Burton, Daniel	ULS 184		Bush, Henry	ORN 345		Bushnel, Amasa	HRK 525
Burton, Drusella	RNS 108		Bush, Henry	RCK 105		Bushnel, Asa	OND 216
Burton, Elijah	COL 179		Bush, Henry	STB 198		Bushnel, Daniel	HRK 531
Burton, George	NYK 122		Bush, Henry	ULS 201		Bushnel, Danl 2d	HRK 531
Burton, Hannah	ALB 91		Bush, Henry Junr	ULS 185		Bushnel, John	OTS 19
Burton, Isaac	COL 213		Bush, Isaac	DUT 28		Bushnel, Joshua	OND 209
Burton, James	ALB 112		Bush, Jacob	DUT 106		Bushnel, Josiah	OND 173
Burton, James	DUT 170		Bush, Jacob a Black	NYK 117		Bushnel, Norman	HRK 531
Burton, James	MNT 79		Bush, Jacobus	ULS 185		Bushnel, Stephen	OND 169
Burton, James	NYK 143		Bush, Jacobus	ULS 197		Bushnel, Trueman	HRK 531
Burton, James	RNS 55		Bush, Jacobus	ULS 216		Bushnell, George	COL 182
Burton, John	ALB 129		Bush, James	NYK 127		Bushnell, Joshua	HRK 585
Burton, John	HRK 566		Bush, James	ORN 397		Bushnell, Samuel	ALB 89
Burton, John	SCH 125		Bush, James	RCK 105		Bushnell, William	COL 192
Burton, John J.	CHN 882		Bush, Johannis	DUT 109		Bushner, Asa	SCH 134
Burton, Joseph	ALB 138		Bush, John	DEL 267		Buskee, Abraham	NYK 124
Burton, Josiah	ALB 124		Bush, John	DUT 28		Buskerk, Jacob	STB 197
Burton, Lewis	DUT 170		Bush, John	DUT 116		Buskerk, Joseph	WSH 265
Burton, Nathan	CHN 888		Bush, John	GRN 350		Buskerk, Lucius	NYK 94
Burton, Oliver	ONN 132		Bush, John	HRK 506		Buskerk, Selvester	NYK 53
Burton, Reuben	RNS112B		Bush, John	KNG 4		Buskirk, Andrew	NYK 89
Burton, Salisbury	OND 199		Bush, John	NYK 29		Buskirk, Andrew	RCK 104
Burton, Silas	DUT 171		Bush, John	NYK 64		Buskirk, Deborah	RCH 93
Burton, Stephen	MNT 92		Bush, John	OND 222		Buskirk, Jane	NYK 54
Bu_ton, Thomas	WST 146		Bush, John	RNS 82		Buskirk, John	OND 192
Burtons, David	OND 199		Bush, John	RCH 92		Buskirk, John	RCH 90
Burtrell, William H.	NYK 121		Bush, John	TIO 240		Buskirk, Jonathan	WSH 238
Burtsell, David	ORN 358		Bush, John	ULS 194		Buskirk, Laurence	NYK 93
Burtsell, Henry	NYK 27		Bush, John	ULS 237		Buskirk, Lawrance	OND 192
Burtsell, Peter	NYK 44		Bush, John D.	DUT 25		Buskirk, Mary	NYK 105

Name	Code	No.	Name	Code	No.	Name	Code	No.
Buys, James	SRA	3	Cabel, John	NYK	112	Cady, William	OTS	21
Buys, John Junr	ULS	196	Cabell, Denbo	NYK	118	Cady, Zadock	CAY	626
Buys, John Senr	ULS	198	Cable	GRN	355	Caerese, Peter	SRA	60
Buys, Matthew	DUT	76	Cable, Jacob	ORN	381	Caesar	QNS	80
Buys, Nicholas	DUT	69	Cable, John	SRA	16	Caesar	SUF	80
Buys, Simon	DUT	75	Cable, Jonathan	WSH	264	Caggan, Thomas	HRK	481
Byall, Abraham	QNS	79	Cable, Leman	DEL	277	Cagsdel, Crissey	WST	159
Byall, James	QNS	79	Cable, Lemuel	SRA	17	Cahie, Hugh	ALB	31
Byam, David	OND	217	Cable, Matthew	WST	126	Cahie, Thomas	ALB	28
Byam, Joseph	OND	217	Cable, Peter	COL	183	Cahill, Daniel	ORN	302
Byand, Richard	STB	207	Cabels, Zebulon	RNS	63	Cahill, Daniel Junr	ORN	301
Byass, Thomas a			Cabot, Justus	HRK	584	Cahill, William	ALB	137
mulatto	NYK	36	Cabry, John	DUT	11	Cahon, Ebenezer	WSH	250
Byce, John	COL	205	Cacham, John	NYK	65	Cahoon, Abel	WSH	231
Byce, John	NYK	143	Cackie, Andrew	MNT	109	Cahoon, Amos	WSH	238
Byce, John Junr	COL	205	Cackie, John	MNT	109	Cahoon, Andrew	DEL	280
Byers, John	WSH	297	Cada, Luthar	RNS	69	Cahoon, Benjamin	WSH	236
Byerson, Dinah a Black	NYK	88	Caddow, Lewis	NYK	126	Cahoon, Chauncey	HRK	423
Byington, Aaron	DUT	168	Caddington, Uziah	NYK	96	Cahoon, Daniel	DUT	158
Byington, Caleb	OTS	43	Cade, Samuel	GRN	338	Cahoon, Ebenezer	HRK	423
Byington, John Junr	DUT	174	Cadey, Andrew	HRK	557	Cahoon, Hanah	WSH	231
Byington, John Senr	DUT	177	Cadey, Jeremeah	SRA	42	Cahoon, James	WSH	193
Byington, Jonah	SCH	133	Cadey, John	SRA	42	Cahoon, Joseph	COL	182
Byington, Jonathan	GRN	356	Cadey, Margaret	NYK	126	Cahoon, Joseph	ORN	392
Byington, Mary	COL	211	Cadey, Warren	SRA	42	Cahoon, Mathew	WSH	233
Byington, Isaac	DUT	174	Cadle, Cornelius	NYK	25	Cahoon, Reynolds Junr	MNT	125
Byington, Solomon	DUT	177	Cadle, Thomas	NYK	36	Cahoon, Welber	MNT	125
Byram, Asa	ORN	285	Cadman, Christopher	HRK	598	Cahoon, William	SRA	35
Byram, George	WSH	196	Cadman, George	COL	212	Caimbridge, William	NYK	130
Byran, Thos	RCK	101	Cadman, John	COL	187	Cain a Negro	SUF	68
Byrd, James	NYK	45	Cadoquen, Barney	MNT	97	Cain, Barnabus	MNT	110
Byrd, Joseph	NYK	45	Cadwell, Abel	SRA	51	Cain, Isaac	WST	158
Byrn, Alexander	NYK	140	Cadwell, Daniel	RNS	41	Cain, Joseph	RNS	54
Byrn, Thomas	NYK	85	Cadwell, Horace	HRK	525	Cainer, George	MNT	35
Byrne, James	NYK	24	Cadwell, Jeduthen	HRK	547	Caird, John	ORN	306
Byrne, James	NYK	30	Cadwell, John	COL	179	Cairnes, Alexander	RCH	95
Byrne, John	NYK	30	Cadwell, Sylvia	ORN	325	Cairns, James	NYK	121
Byrne, John	NYK	62	Cady, ...es	MNT	30	Cairns, John	NYK	144
Byrne, Laurence	NYK	81	Cady, Aaron	COL	222	Cairon, Peter	NYK	44
Byrne, Patrick	RCK	102	Cady, Asahel	OTS	52	Caispen, John	NYK	122
Byrnes, Barnard	NYK	18	Cady, Benjamin	COL	246	Calchamer, Andrew	RNS	87
Byrnes, Bridget	NYK	131	Cady, Charlotte	OTS	10	Calder, Andrew	NYK	56
Byrnes, Elizabeth	NYK	87	Cady, Darius	HRK	557	Calder, James	DEL	286
Byrnes, Francis	NYK	55	Cady, David	MNT	30	Calderhouse, George	ALB	106
Byrnes, Henry	NYK	65	Cady, Ebenezer Junr	COL	214	Caldwell, Abraham	ORN	299
Byrnes, John	NYK	131	Cady, Ebenezer Junr	COL	222	Caldwell, Absalom	DUT	92
Byrnes, William	DUT	36	Cady, Eleazer	COL	208	Caldwell, Adam	WSH	253
Byrns, Devy a Black	NYK	51	Cady, Eleazer	COL	216	Caldwell, Arthur	SRA	28
Byron, William	NYK	98	Cady, Eleazer Junr	COL	219	Caldwell, Benjn	HRK	421
Byron, William	WST	165	Cady, Elias	COL	202	Caldwell, Christopher	OTS	51
Byrum, Eliab	SUF	102	Cady, Elijah	COL	214	Caldwell, Dan	OTS	51
Byse, Jacob	COL	198	Cady, Elijah	COL	218	Caldwell, Danl	OTS	52
Byshop, Jo ab	CHN	846	Cady, Elijah	DUT	122	Caldwell, George	NYK	44
Byum, David	OTS	13	Cady, Elijah Junr	COL	222	Caldwell, Harry	ORN	279
Byvanck, William	NYK	121	Cady, Ely	MNT	114	Caldwell, Isaac	DUT	92
			Cady, Ezra	COL	214	Caldwell, Isaac	OTS	51
C			Cady, George W.	ALB	22	Caldwell, Isaac	WSH	207
			Cady, Isaac	OND	168	Caldwell, Jacob	NYK	117
C_mister, David	CAY	572	Cady, Isaac	SCH	170	Caldwell, James	ALB	144
C__e, Natha.	CAY	592	Cady, James	CHN	844	Caldwell, James	DUT	178
C_eb,___ is	CAY	620	Cady, James	MNT	55	Caldwell, James	ORN	345
C__in, Nathan	CAY	666	Cady, John	ALB	30	Caldwell, James	SRA	40
C___, O	CHN	758	Cady, John	RNS	96	Caldwell, John	COL	250
C___, Joseph	CHN	830	Cady, Jonathan	HRK	520	Caldwell, John	NYK	31
C_a_, Thomas	GRN	334	Cady, Luthar	RNS	14	Caldwell, John	NYK	44
C_tter, James	MNT	66	Cady, Mary	ONT	452	Caldwell, John	NYK	76
C...tewance, Cornelius	MNT	82	Cady, Nicholas Elliot	NYK	122	Caldwell, John	QNS	64
C_bert, David	NYK	141	Cady, Oliver	COL	203	Caldwell, John	RNS	29
C__an, .illiam	OND	221	Cady, Oliver Junr	COL	203	Caldwell, John	RNS	47
C_e, John	ORN	384	Cady, Peter	MNT	114	Caldwell, Joseph	ALB	140
C___, Saml	RNS	10	Cady, Reuben	OTS	21	Caldwell, Joseph	DUT	92
Ca__ick, William	ALB	53	Cady, Roswell	COL	204	Caldwell, Joseph	HRK	420
Ca___, James	DEL	286	Cady, Ruben	CHN	980	Caldwell, Joseph	KNG	9
Ca_ell, James	MNT	59	Cady, Silas	ONN	144	Caldwell, Joseph	ORN	276
Ca_ey, Hugh	ONT	322	Cady, Skiler	OND	169	Caldwell, Joseph	OTS	51
Ca___, William	ONT	390	Cady, Uriah	HRK	421	Caldwell, Joseph	SCH	149
Caage, John	SRA	50	Cady, William	DUT	106	Caldwell, Joseph	WSH	218

Name	Ref
Caldwell, Mathew	RNS 92
Caldwell, Matthew	DUT 63
Caldwell, Moses	WSH 222
Caldwell, Robert	ORN 360
Caldwell, Robert	QNS 80
Caldwell, Samuel	DUT 168
Caldwell, Samuel	ONT 344
Caldwell, Samuel	SRA 41
Caldwell, Samuel	WSH 218
Caldwell, Stukely	OTS 52
Caldwell, Tillot	ORN 348
Caldwell, William	ALB 138
Caldwell, William	DUT 91
Caldwell, William	NYK 85
Caldwell, William	OND 191
Caldwell, William	SCH 158
Caldwell, William	ULS 191
Caldwell, William	WSH 294
Cale, Job	WSH 218
Cale, Stephen	DUT 85
Cale, Timothy	NYK 25
Caleb	QNS 84
Caleb, Sarah	NYK 128
Calendar, Daniel	CHN 808
Caler, Peter	MNT 104
Calf, Charles	RNS 26
Calf, Wm	RNS 26
Calhoon, Andrew	ONT 358
Calhoon, Joel	ONT 480
Calhoon, Nathan	ONT 462
Calhoon, Stewart	ONT 462
Calile, Samuel	MNT 125
Calkin, Elijah	ULS 185
Calkin, Enoch	GRN 330
Calkin, William	DUT 85
Calkin, William	DUT 135
Calkins, Aaron	WSH 266
Calkins, Benjn	RNS 10
Calkins, Caleb	WSH 266
Calkins, Calvin	SCH 160
Calkins, Daniel	HRK 455
Calkins, David	RNS 10
Calkins, Elijah	GRN 336
Calkins, Frederick	STB 203
Calkins, Isaac	ALB 68
Calkins, James	GRN 333
Calkins, Joel	HRK 425
Calkins, Joel	RNS 10
Calkins, John	WSH 219
Calkins, Jonathan	HRK 455
Calkins, Luther	SRA 19
Calkins, Samuel	STB 201
Calkins, Seth	SRA 53
Calkins, Stephen	GRN 331
Calkoon, Herman	ALB 65
Call, Alphaus	WSH 210
Call, Cyrus	ESS 323
Call, Ebenezer	WSH 210
Call, George	ULS 219
Call, Henry Junr	ORN 384
Call, Henry Senr	ORN 384
Call, John	ULS 219
Call, Matthias	ULS 226
Call, Nicholas	ORN 380
Call, Nicholas	RCK 101
Call, Stephen	WSH 215
Callaghan, Daniel	DUT 68
Callaner, Warren	SRA 45
Callanger, Morris	NYK 109
Callannan, John	NYK 41
Callder, Abraham	ALB 61
Calleby, Joseph	COL 180
Callegan, John	SRA 16
Callemne, Anthony	SRA 45
Callemne, Barker	SRA 45
Callender, David	ESS 318
Callender, Nathaniel	CLN 171
Callender, Samuel	ORN 341
Callender, Stephen	ALB 87
Calley, Edward	SRA 26
Calley, Thos	SUF 64
Callihan, Patrick	ALB 98
Callin, Edward	SRA 26
Callon, James	SRA 26
Caloris, Tucking	SUF 94
Calquhoon, Hugh	ALB 40
Calquhoon, John	ALB 15
Calquhoon, Thos	ALB 40
Calson, James	RCK 110
Calver, Natha..el	CLN 170
Calwell, Harvey	NYK 133
Calwell, John	GRN 353
Calwell, Simeon	CHN 982
Callwill, Joshua	RCK 102
Calwin, John	SUF 85
Camar, Jacob	COL 195
Cambell, David	NYK 135
Cambell, John	NYK 99
Cambell, John	NYK 110
Cambell, John	RNS 40
Cambell, Partrick	NYK 119
Cambell, Stephen	WST 166
Cambell, Thomas J.	NYK 100
Cambell, William	WST 166
Camber, Casper	NYK 141
Camberlin, David	NYK 138
Camble, John	CHN 756
Camble, Samuel	CHN 842
Camby, James	DUT 84
Camel, John	WST 134
Camel, Robert	STB 199
Cameli a Blackman	SRA 15
Camell, John	WST 135
Camell, William	RNS 103
Camellia, James	ALB 48
Camer, Adam	COL 232
Cameron, Alexr	ALB 134
Cameron, Angus	MNT 77
Cameron, Angus	ULS 253
Cameron, Charles	MNT 91
Cameron, Charles	ONT 338
Cameron, Daniel	NYK 55
Cameron, David	ALB 66
Cameron, Dugal	STB 198
Cameron, Hugh	MNT 76
Cameron, James	NYK 64
Cameron, John	ALB 56
Cameron, John	ALB 144
Cameron, John	MNT 77
Cameron, John	ULS 253
Cammel, Archbd	TIO 216
Cammel, David	NYK 41
Cammel, Edward	MNT 59
Cammel, James	TIO 265
Cammel, John	NYK 20
Cammel, Sarah	WST 154
Cammell, Mary	NYK 26
Cammell, William	SUF 109
Cammeron, Margaret	NYK 67
Cammeyer, William	NYK 17
Cammon, Charles L.	NYK 18
Camnrond, Peter	NYK 73
Camp, Aaron	DUT 160
Camp, Abel	OND 176
Camp, Abner	CHN 938
Camp, Abram	OND 157
Camp, Amos	HRK 425
Camp, Amos	OND 162
Camp, Asa	TIO 246
Camp, Asel	OND 219
Camp, Chester	TIO 246
Camp, Daniel	OND 201
Camp, David	ONT 434
Camp, Eder	OND 195
Camp, George	GRN 346
Camp, Isaac	CHN 938
Camp, Jacob	COL 206
Camp, James	NYK 67
Camp, John	CHN 768
Camp, John	CHN 894
Camp, John	CHN 904
Camp, John	CLN 159
Camp, John	ESS 306
Camp, Miles	CAY 664
Camp, Peter	GRN 327
Camp, Philo	ALB 88
Camp, Phineas	OND 201
Camp, Samuel	CHN 904
Camp, Samuel	GRN 335
Camp, Samuel	GRN 335
Camp, Seth	OND 201
Camp, Simeon	OTS 21
CAmp, Talcott	OND 160
Camp, Wm	MNT 51
Camp, William	NYK 100
Camp, William	OTS 11
Campbel, Samuel	SRA 52
Campbell, A. M.	NYK 37
Campbell, Aaron	NYK 139
Campbell, Abrm	RCK 103
Campbell, Adam	HRK 429
Campbell, Alexander	ALB 43
Campbell, Alexander	NYK 22
Campbell, Alexander	NYK 86
Campbell, Alexander	NYK 90
Campbell, Alexander	NYK 117
Campbell, Alexander	OTS 42
Campbell, Anna	NYK 60
Campbell, Anna	NYK 62
Campbell, Archabald	WSH 193
Campbell, Archibald	COL 210
Campbell, Archibald	DUT 54
Campbell, Archibald	RNS 82
Campbell, Archibold	SRA 46
Campbell, Barney	CAY 694
Campbell, Benjamin	CAY 598
Campbell, Benjamin	OND 223
Campbell, Catharine	DUT 78
Campbell, Catharine	ORN 292
Campbell, Charles	ALB 72
Campbell, Clove	ALB 125
Campbell, Danl	ALB 10
Campbell, Daniel	NYK 82
Campbell, Daniel	ONN 168
Campbell, David	ALB 4
Campbell, David	NYK 18
Campbell, David	NYK 104
Campbell, David	ULS 189
Campbell, Donald	RCH 89
Campbell, Dugal	NYK 59
Campbell, Duncan	NYK 58
Campbell, Duncan	NYK 102
Campbell, Duncan	WSH 251
Campbell, Edward	ORN 338
Campbell, Elizabeth	CLN 159
Campbell, Elizabeth	HRK 482
Campbell, Elizabeth	NYK 50
Campbell, Elizabeth	WSH 220
Campbell, Ezekiel	ORN 314
Campbell, George	OND 178
Campbell, George	ORN 280
Campbell, Henry	HRK 475
Campbell, Henry	NYK 15
Campbell, Henry	WSH 291
Campbell, Hermanus	ALB 52
Campbell, Hugh	CAY 596
Campbell, Hugh	OTS 4
Campbell, Jabez	OTS 46
Campbell, Jacob	COL 216
Campbell, Jacob	NYK 102
Campbell, Jacob	RNS 58

59

Name	Loc	No.
Campbell, James	CLN	161
Campbell, James	HRK	428
Campbell, James	HRK	531
Campbell, James	MNT	89
Campbell, James	NYK	118
Campbell, James	NYK	145
Campbell, James	NYK	149
Campbell, James	OND	180
Campbell, James	ORN	338
Campbell, James	OTS	5
Campbell, James	WSH	220
Campbell, Jas Senr	OTS	5
Campbell, James J.	OTS	5
Campbell, Jane	ORN	324
Campbell, Jeremiah	TIO	247
Campbell, Jesse	ULS	189
Campbell, Joel	ULS	186
Campbell, Joel Senr	ORN	314
Campbell, John	ALB	36
Campbell, John	ALB	48
Campbell, John	ALB	124
Campbell, John	ALB	140
Campbell, John	CAY	572
Campbell, John	CLN	167
Campbell, John	COL	265
Campbell, John	DEL	284
Campbell, John	DUT	144
Ca_bell, John	NYK	21
Campbell, John	NYK	67
Campbell, John	NYK	95
Campbell, John	NYK	106
Campbell, John	NYK	121
Campbell, John	NYK	140
Campbell, John	OND	190
Campbell, John	OTS	4
Campbell, John	OTS	5
Campbell, John	WSH	225
Campbell, John H.	OTS	5
Campbell, Jns Junr	OTS	3
Campbell, Jonathan	ORN	314
Campbell, Jonathan	ULS	252
Campbell, Joshua	CLN	166
Campbell, Joshua	ULS	245
Campbell, Levi	ORN	304
Campbell, Ludwick	HRK	430
Campbell, Malcom	NYK	47
Campbell, Mark	NYK	109
Campbell, Martha	WSH	220
Campbell, Mathew	NYK	119
Campbell, Matthew	OTS	5
Campbell, Michael	RNS	91
Campbell, Moses	OND	180
Campbell, Moses	OND	183
Campbell, Nathan	ORN	304
Campbell, Nathaniel	MNT	109
Campbell, Patrick	HRK	428
Campbell, Patrick	HRK	473
Campbell, Patrick	OND	183
Campbell, Peter	ONT	314
Campbell, Price	ALB	93
Campbell, Reuben	ULS	189
Campbell, Robert	COL	220
Campbell, Robert	COL	241
Campbell, Robert	ONN	134
Campbell, Robert	OTS	6
Campbell, Robt	OTS	19
Campbell, Robert	SRA	46
Campbell, Roger	WSH	250
Campbell, Roswell	OND	178
Campbell, Rufus	CLN	161
Campbell, Samuel	NYK	30
Campbell, Samuel	NYK	106
Campbell, Saml	OTS	5
Campbell, Saml	OTS	7
Campbell, Saml Junr	OTS	3
Campbell, Simeon	ORN	314
Campbell, Sollomon	SRA	47
Campbell, Stephen	OTS	55
Campbell, Stephen	RCK	104
Campbell, Sylvanus	OTS	11
Campbell, Thomas	CAY	568
Campbell, Thomas	ORN	290
Campbell, Thomas	SRA	44
Campbell, Valentine	SRA	44
Campbell, Walter	DUT	99
Campbell, Wareham	ONN	139
Campbell, William	ALB	64
Campbell, William	ALB	112
Campbell, William	NYK	78
Campbell, William	NYK	80
Campbell, William	NYK	92
Campbell, William	NYK	93
Campbell, William	NYK	135
Campbell, William	ORN	339
Campbell, Wm	OTS	7
Campbell, Wm	OTS	31
Campbell, Wm	OTS	39
Campbell, Wm	RCK	104
Campbell, Wm	RCK	109
Campbell, William	WSH	220
Campbell, William	WSH	220
Campbell, William	WSH	250
Campbell, Wm Junr	RCK	107
Campbell, Zurial	OTS	46
Campble, Alli	CHN	866
Campble, Charles	CHN	868
Campble, Charles S.	CHN	868
Campble, Danl	CHN	868
Campble, Ephram	CHN	842
Campble, Isaac	CHN	866
Campble, Jacob	CHN	948
Campble, James	CHN	926
Campble, John	CHN	758
Campble, John	CHN	868
Campble, John	CHN	946
Campble, Moses	CHN	916
Campble, Thomas	CHN	948
Campble, William	CHN	950
Campden, Daniel	NYK	89
Campfield	NYK	149
Campfield, Joseph	ONT	434
Camphield, Joseph	WSH	214
Cample, Minor	CHN	946
Camply, James	NYK	80
Campo, Mary	NYK	59
Campton, Cornelius	NYK	131
Camren, Charles	WSH	202
Camrin, Evans	TIO	230
Camrin, John	RNS	75
Camron, James	WSH	204
Camron, John	WSH	204
Camron, John Junr	WSH	204
Camron, William	WSH	204
Camron, William	WSH	204
Canada, Guy J.	GRN	351
Canada, Timothy	STB	205
Canady, John	ALB	39
Canady, Joseph	ALB	115
Canaga, John	QNS	72
Canan, Cahrles	NYK	25
Canaro, Isaac	COL	224
Cande, Medad	ALB	124
Cande, Nehemiah	SRA	29
Candee, Isaac	WST	154
Candel, David P.	DUT	126
Candy, Gidion	OTS	49
Cane, James	GRN	346
Cane, Michael	WST	145
Canept, Thomas	RNS	84
Canfield, Abraham	WST	138
Canfield, Abraham	WST	141
Canfield, Amos	WST	138
Canfield, Benajah	DUT	158
Canfield, Cornelius	WST	152
Canfield, Dan	ONT	390
Canfield, David	ESS	295
Canfield, David	ULS	181
Canfield, David	WST	152
Canfield, David	WST	153
Canfield, Ebenezer	ESS	296
Canfield, Ebenezer	ORN	319
Canfield, Elijah	DEL	270
Canfield, Elijah	ORN	326
Canfield, Eman	DUT	130
Canfield, Enos	TIO	235
Canfield, Ira	GRN	331
Canfield, Jabus	WST	152
Canfield, Jabus Junr	WST	153
Canfield, James	DUT	162
Canfield, James	ONT	444
Canfield, James	ORN	328
Canfield, James	ORN	330
Canfield, James	WST	151
Canfield, Jehiel	DUT	127
Canfield, Jesse	GRN	342
Canfield, Jesse	ORN	319
Canfield, John	SRA	45
Canfield, John M.	GRN	331
Canfield, Jonathan	ULS	195
Canfield, Joseph	ORN	330
Canfield, M....	RNS	32
Canfield, Medad	HRK	535
Canfield, Naphtali	WSH	297
Canfield, Nathan	DUT	130
Canfield, Nathan	WST	140
Canfield, Partrick	NYK	120
Canfield, Russel	WST	166
Canfield, Samuel	DUT	143
Canfield, Samuel	ORN	330
Canfield, Selah	CHN	818
C_field, Silas	CAY	564
Canfield, Silas	DUT	130
Canfield, Silas	ESS	296
Canfield, Simeon	DUT	172
Canfield, Sylvania	CLN	159
Canfield, Thaddeus	ESS	295
Canfield, Thomas	GRN	342
Canfield, Thomas	HRK	533
Canfield, Timothy	DUT	99
Canfield, William	DUT	152
Canfield, William	ESS	296
Cangeter, Nicholas	NYK	48
Caniff, Abraham	DUT	28
Caniff, Gilbert	WST	166
Caniff, James	WST	166
Caniff, Jonas	DUT	28
Caniff, Richard	WST	166
Caniff, William	DUT	118
Caniph, Levi	RNS	31
Cankrite, Francis	SRA	56
Canley, Henry	QNS	71
Cannady, James	COL	250
Cannady, James	ESS	320
Cannan, James	OTS	5
Cannedy, John	SUF	81
Canneff, Reuben	NYK	135
Cannif, James	RCK	103
Canniff, Jeremiah	ALB	114
Canniph, Levi	RNS	34
Cannohn, Mott	NYK	112
Cannon, Abraham	NYK	39
Cannon, Abraham	NYK	141
Cannon, Andw	OTS	7
Cannon, Andrew	RCH	91
Cannon, Blossom	DEL	278
Cannon, Clark	DEL	278
Cannon, David	RCH	91
Cannon, George	RNS	90
Cannon, Isaac	RCH	91
Cannon, Jacob	NYK	145

Cannon, James	DUT 76	Carde, Joseph	CHN 900	Carlisle, Ebenezer	HRK 584
Cannon, John	QNS 74	Carder, John	HRK 416	Carlisle, Joseph	ULS 184
Cannon, John	RCH 91	Cardwiner, Abel	MNT 116	Carll, Annanias	SUF 82
Cannon, Joseph	DEL 278	Careless, William	CAY 516	Carll, Elephalet	SUF 84
Cannon, Partrick	NYK 104	Careliss, Simon a		Carll, Gilbert	SUF 82
Cannon, Patrick	ALB 48	Black	NYK 41	Carll, Israel	SUF 82
Cannon, Philep	WSH 207	Cares, Nana	GRN 353	Carll, Jacob	SUF 71
Cannon, Robert	NYK 43	Carew, Samuel	CHN 774	Carll, John	SUF 88
Cannon, Thomas	CAY 664	Carey, Ann	WSH 289	Carll, Lemuel	SUF 79
Cannon, Thomas	RCH 91	Carey, David	ONT 494	Carll, Oliver	SUF 80
Cannon, Weight	DEL 278	Carey, Ebenezer	OND 207	Carll, Pheneas	SUF 82
Canny, Richard	GRN 353	Carey, Elihu	ONT 494	Carll, Platt	SUF 82
Canrass, Walter	SCH 159	Carey, John	NYK 17	Carll, Saml	SUF 87
Canselin, Samuel	SRA 44	Carey, Joseph	ONT 316	Carll, Silas	SUF 82
Cantant, Jane	NYK 142	Carey, Levi	HRK 441	Carll, Timothy	SUF 82
Canter, Jones	RNS 11	Carey, Lu__s	ONT 428	Carlock, Claus N.	RCK 106
Canter, Richard	MNT 37	Carey, Moses	WSH 244	Carlock, David	RCK 105
Cantine, Abraham	ULS 199	Carey, Nathan	STB 207	Carlock, George	RCK 106
Cantine, Elizabeth	ULS 203	Carey, Phinehas	OND 213	Carlock, Hannah	RCK 106
Cantine, John	ULS 204	Carey, Stephen	ULS 195	Carlock, John	RCK 106
Cantine, John Junr	ULS 203	Carey, Taylor	WSH 215	Carlock, William	NYK 67
Cantine, Moses	ULS 227	Carey, Thomas	WSH 185	Carlon, Silvanus	NYK 143
Cantine, Moses Junr	ULS 203	Carfield, Daniel	MNT 60	Carlos, Frances a	
Cantine, Nathaniel	ULS 204	Cargal, James	GRN 326	Black	NYK 104
Cantine, Peter	ULS 211	Cargal, Zachariah	GRN 337	Carlow, Jacob	WSH 249
Cantine, Peter Junr	DUT 153	Cargel, Nathan	SRA 58	Carlow, Stephen	WSH 249
Cantley, Jane	ALB 32	Cargeson, Hugh_	NYK 118	Carlton, Bernard	OTS 11
Cantlie, James	ALB 32	Cargil, Wm	RCK 99	Carlton, Darius	CAY 684
Canton, George	NYK 81	Cargill, Abraham	NYK 82	Carlton, Jacob	WSH 186
Canton, James	NYK 76	Cargill, Abraham	ULS 184	Carlton, John	NYK 15
Canute, Elizabeth	RNS 94	Cargill, Daniel	HRK 461	Carlton, Nathaniel	RNS 14
Canute, Josiah	OND 186	Cargill, David	NYK 24	Carlton, Rosewell	RNS 20
Canwart, James	NYK 102	Cargill, William	NYK 71	Carlton, Roswell	WSH 186
Capel, John	OTS 42	Cargin, Eliza	NYK 54	Carlton, Timothy	RNS 20
Capern, Maltire	RNS 55	Cargin, William	ALB 118	Carlwell, James	NYK 107
Capes, Elizabeth	NYK 41	Carhart, Jacob	DUT 49	Carly, Isel	SCH 147
Capes, Richard	NYK 70	Carhart, Jonathan	WST 166	Carly, James	DUT 154
Caple, Bela	OTS 42	Carick, Garrit	OND 161	Carly, Jedediah	ORN 285
Caple, Thos	OTS 42	Carihart, Joshua	WST 117	Carly, Job	COL 181
Capon, Abijah	CAY 656	Carity a free wench	ALB 131	Carly, John	ORN 285
Capon, Edmund	CAY 658	Carkren, Wm	GRN 353	Carly, Moses	SCH 135
Caporn, John	OND 209	Carl, Andrew	DUT 125	Carly, Moses	SCH 148
Capron, Gabriel	CAY 584	Carl, Jacob	DUT 28	Carly, Moses Junr	SCH 135
Capron, Oliver	ALB 119	Carl, Jacob	GRN 336	Carly, Richard	CHN 930
Capron, Welcom	WSH 235	Carl, James	DEL 273	Carly, Simon	COL 181
Capron, William	ALB 138	Carl, John	ULS 193	Carlysle, James	WSH 289
Capwell, Benaah	OTS 33	Carl, Lawrence	NYK 106	Carlysle, William	WSH 289
Capwell, Henry	OTS 33	Carl, Stephen	DUT 146	Carman, Aaron	WST 125
Car, Caleb	RNS 103	Carl, Thomas	DEL 267	Carman, Alexander	ULS 243
Car, Elvaser	MNT 125	Carl, Thomas	DUT 94	Carman, Baltus	DUT 60
Car, Joseph	RNS 56	Carl, Thomas Junr	DUT 94	Carman, Benson	QNS 76
Carahart, John	ULS 188	Carl, William	DUT 125	Carman, Caleb	GRN 353
Carberry, Daniel	NYK 49	Carle, David	COL 258	Carman, Charles	DUT 130
Carberry, John	NYK 15	Carle, Isaac	CAY 588	Carman, Coenradt	COL 244
Carbine, Zebulon	GRN 346	Carle, Isaac	COL 237	Carman, Daniel	WST 127
Carburry, Thomas	NYK 53	Carle, John	QNS 82	Carman, David	DUT 125
Carcy, Samuel	KNG 7	Carle, Richard	CHN 940	Carman, Hannah	NYK 77
Card, Abel	OTS 37	Carle, Thomas	COL 237	Carman, Henry	WST 123
Card, Benjn	OTS 38	Carles, James	SCH 144	Carman, Isaac	ALB 94
Card, Danl	OTS 38	Carley, Abraham	COL 177	Carman, Israel	DUT 23
Card, Elisha	NYK 128	Carley, Albert	MNT 19	Carman, Jacob	GRN 353
Card, Job	ONT 456	Carley, Clark	ONN 187	Carman, James	DEL 270
Card, Jonathan	DUT 139	Carley, Ebenezer	ONN 138	Carman, John	NYK 89
Card, Jona	OTS 33	Carley, Elijah	OND 224	Carman, John	NYK 133
Card, Jonathan Junr	DUT 139	Carley, Jered	MNT 106	Carman, John	TIO 236
Card, Joseph	RNS 94	Carley, Joel	COL 189	Carman, John Junr	SUF 82
Card, Lewis	MNT 48	Carley, John	DEL 282	Carman, John Senr	SUF 82
Card, Paul	RNS 72	Carley, John	SRA 46	Carman, John ye 3d	DUT 38
Card, Peleg	HRK 572	Carley, Joseph	ALB 2A	Carman, John J.	DUT 15
Card, Peleg	OTS 32	Carley, Joseph	OND 203	Carman, John R.	DUT 23
Card, Ranua	RNS 68	Carley, Peter	WSH 271	Carman, John T.	DUT 19
Card, Samuel	RNS 19	Carley, Quartus	OND 203	Carman, John T.	DUT 66
Card, Stephen	DUT 139	Carli_, John	MNT 112	Carman, Joseph	DUT 19
Card, Stephen	ONT 462	Carlile, Samuel	SRA 29	Carman, Joseph	QNS 76
Card, Thomas	RNS 19	Carlile, William	ALB 133	Carman, Joshua	DUT 63
Card, William	HRK 523	Carling, James	CAY 704	Carman, Lot	DUT 126
Card, Wm	RNS 74	Carlins, John	WSH 228	Carman, Morris	DUT 128

Carman, Peter	WST	122	Carpenter, Abraham	ONT	498	Carpenter, Jacob	NYK	133
Carman, Richard	DUT	128	Carpenter, Abraham	SRA	48	Carpenter, Jacob	ORN	282
Carman, Richard	ULS	244	Carpenter, Alsop	COL	198	Carpenter, Jacob	QNS	68
Carman, Samuel	GRN	353	Carpenter, Amas	WSH	276	Carpenter, Jacob	WST	124
Carman, Samuel	SUF	94	Carpenter, Amos	HRK	596	Carpenter, Jacob	WST	130
Carman, Sarah	NYK	64	Carpenter, Anderson	ONN	142	Carpenter, Jacob	WST	131
Carman, Sarah	NYK	66	Carpenter, Andrw	NYK	94	Carpenter, Jacob Junr	QNS	68
Carman, Silas	QNS	78	Carpenter, Anthony	ORN	293	Carpenter, James	ORN	357
Carman, Thomas	NYK	137	Carpenter, Asa	NYK	55	Carpenter, James	QNS	84
Carman, Tounsand	GRN	353	Carpenter, Asahel	HRK	595	Carpenter, James	RNS	81
Carman, William	ALB	94	Carpenter, Ashmore	ORN	364	Carpenter, James	ULS	180
Carman, William	NYK	128	Carpenter, Belovet	WSH	216	Carpenter, James	WST	111
Carmechael, Edwar	MNT	120	Carpenter, Benjamin	DUT	131	Carpenter, Jedediah	ONN	142
Carmen, Benjamin	QNS	73	Carpenter, Benjamin	NYK	113	Carpenter, Jesse	CHN	838
Carmen, Samuel	DUT	122	Carpenter, Benjamin	ORN	316	Carpenter, Jesse	OND	166
Carmer, John	SCH	145	Carpenter, Benjamin	ORN	362	Carpenter, Jesse	OND	203
Carmer, Nicholas	NYK	53	Carpenter, Benjn	OTS	31	Carpenter, Jesse	ORN	344
Carmer, Nicholas	NYK	56	Carpenter, Benjamin	RNS	100	Carpenter, Jesse	ORN	354
Carmer, Nicholas	NYK	66	Carpenter, Benjamin	SRA	55	Carpenter, Jesse	RNS	23
Carmer, Nicholas Jun	NYK	134	Carpenter, Benjn	TIO	230	Carpenter, John	ALB	85
Carmer, Nicholas G.	NYK	55	Carpenter, Benjamin	ULS	263	Carpenter, John	DUT	45
Carmer, Sally	QNS	77	Carpenter, Benjamin	WSH	277	Carpenter, John	DUT	84
Carmer, Samuel	DUT	133	Carpenter, Benjamin	WST	116	Carpenter, John	DUT	103
Carmer, Thomas	ORN	357	Carpenter, Benjamin Junr	ORN	329	Carpenter, Joyn	DUT	119
..rmichael, ...	MNT	78	Carpenter, Benjamin S.	CHN	750	Carpenter, John	DUT	153
Carmichael, Alexander	ULS	180	Carpenter, Burnardus	MNT	112	Carpenter, John	OND	193
Carmichael, Charles	MNT	72	Carpenter, Calib	WST	131	Carpenter, John	ONT	498
Carmichael, Ebenezer	ULS	188	Carpenter, Carmen	ORN	329	Carpenter, John	OTS	36
Carmichael, Ichabod	ULS	180	Carpenter, Catherine	NYK	33	Carpenter, John	OTS	49
Carmichael, John	ORN	341	Carpenter, Coleb	CHN	838	Carpenter, John	QNS	71
Carmichail, Robt	ALB	133	Carpenter, Colvill	ORN	354	Carpenter, John	RNS	14
Carmickle, John	RNS	10	Carpenter, Curtis	ONN	176	Carpenter, John	RNS	45
Carmickle, Peter	RNS	10	Carpenter, Cyrel	SRA	42	Carpenter, John	SRA	19
Carmikael, Malcomb	MNT	66	Carpenter, Cyrell	WSH	277	Carpenter, John	ULS	180
Carmon, ...	QNS	78	Carpenter, Daneil	QNS	68	Carpenter, John	ULS	262
Carmon, ...en	QNS	78	Carpenter, Daniel	CAY	626	Carpenter, John	WST	112
Carmon, Adam	QNS	77	Carpenter, Daniel	MNT	99	Carpenter, John	WST	115
Carmon, Elkanah	QNS	76	Carpenter, Daniel	ORN	325	Carpenter, John	WST	123
Carmon, Joseph	QNS	76	Carpenter, Daniel	ORN	359	Carpenter, John	WST	131
Carmon, Joseph	SUF	70	Carpenter, Daniel	ORN	368	Carpenter, John Junr	RNS	34
Carmon, Joseph	TIO	225	Carpenter, Daniel	RNS	30	Carpenter, John Junr	RNS	45
Carmon, Samuel	QNS	76	Carpenter, Dan...	RNS	93	Carpenter, John Junr	SRA	19
Carmon, Samuel	QNS	78	Carpenter, Daniel	TIO	258	Carpenter, Jonathan	WST	119
Carmon, Saml	SUF	65	Carpenter, Daniel	WST	115	Carpenter, Joseph	DUT	146
Carmon, Samuel Junr	QNS	78	Carpenter, Daniel	WST	133	Carpenter, Joseph	HRK	593
Carmon, Thomas	QNS	77	Carpenter, Daniel	WST	135	Carpenter, Joseph	ORN	369
Carn, Jacob	ULS	223	Carpenter, Daniel	WST	138	Carpenter, Joseph	RNS	101
Carn, John	ULS	193	Carpenter, David	DUT	67	Carpenter, Joseph	SRA	59
Carne, John	NYK	24	Carpenter, David	DUT	148	Carpenter, Joseph	ULS	259
Carner, Abraham	ULS	231	Carpenter, David	MNT	22	Carpenter, Joseph	WST	111
Carner, Cornelius	ULS	187	Carpenter, Deliverance	WSH	277	Carpenter, Joseph	WST	112
Carner, Philip	RNS	8	Carpenter, Ebenezer	COL	205	Carpenter, Joshua	TIO	258
Carner, Philip J.	RNS	8	Carpenter, Elijah	HRK	594	Carpenter, Josia	RNS	50
Carner, Stephen Junr	ULS	190	Carpenter, Elijah	ORN	352	Carpenter, Josiah	WST	111
Carnes, John	NYK	92	Carpenter, Elijah	ULS	243	Carpenter, Jotham	HRK	588
Carnes, Maxwell	NYK	101	Carpenter, Elisha	SRA	56	Carpenter, Jotham	WST	116
Carnes, Silina	NYK	68	Carpenter, Elisha	ULS	182	Carpenter, Latten	QNS	83
Carnet, Frasey	NYK	15	Carpenter, Elisha	WSH	274	Carpenter, Leonard	ORN	283
Carney, Ely	MNT	77	Carpenter, Ellenor	NYK	138	Carpenter, Levi	OND	203
Carney, Hugh	NYK	132	Carpenter, Frederick	DUT	45	Carpenter, Levi	WST	122
Carney, John	STB	205	Carpenter, Frederick	RNS	15	Carpenter, Levi Junr	OND	205
Carney, Sarah	WST	160	Carpenter, Gardr	OTS	31	Carpenter, Luff	ORN	270
Carney, Stephen	ORN	339	Carpenter, George	DUT	125	Carpenter, Luke	RNS	45
Carngross, Isaac	MNT	50	Carpenter, Gilbert	WST	114	Carpenter, Lydy	WST	131
Carnriet, John	OND	209	Carpenter, Gilbert	WST	130	Carpenter, Matthew	TIO	265
Carns, William	ALB	25	Carpenter, Greenman	RNS	103	Carpenter, Michael	ORN	358
Carnwell, Jacob	GRN	348	Carpenter, Henry	NYK	140	Carpenter, Morris	WST	131
Carnwright, Peter	RNS	4	Carpenter, Increase	ALB	29	Carpenter, Moses	ONN	190
Carothers, John	ONT	488	Carpenter, Increase	QNS	68	Carpenter, Nathan	CHN	772
Carpender, Benjamin	KNG	9	Carpenter, Isaac	ONN	142	Carpenter, Nathan	DEL	290
Carpen_r, J_es	KNG	8	Carpenter, Isaac	ORN	329	Carpenter, Nathl	HRK	518
Carpender, William	KNG	8	Carpenter, Isaac	SRA	55	Carpenter, Nathaniel	QNS	68
Carpenter, Abener	SRA	16	Carpenter, Isaac	SRA	56	Carpenter, Nathaniel	WST	114
Carpenter, Abiel	OND	200	Carpenter, Isaac	WST	112	Carpenter, Nehemiah	DUT	101
Carpenter, Abigail	ALB	42	Carpenter, Israel	DUT	107	Carpenter, Nehemiah	ORN	344
Carpenter, Abijah	TIO	222	Carpenter, Jacob	COL	241	Carpenter, Nehemiah	QNS	68
Carpenter, Abner	ONN	191				Carpenter, Nicholas	SRA	56

Name	Code	Page	Name	Code	Page	Name	Code	Page
Carpenter, Noah	ONN	184	Carr, Caleb	TIO	223	Carroll, Anthony	NYK	17
Carpenter, Noah	TIO	222	Carr, Charles	MNT	97	Carroll, James	COL	232
Carpenter, Peter	WST	129	Carr, Charles	RNS	104	Carroll, James	NYK	130
Carpenter, Peter Junr	WST	128	Carr, Daniel	OTS	10	Carroll, John	ALB	114
Carpenter, Phebee	WST	123	Carr, David	HRK	480	Carroll, Mary	NYK	128
Carpenter, Phoebe	WSH	265	Carr, David	OTS	19	Carrollen, Thomas	NYK	120
Carpenter, Philip	RNS	15	Carr, Ebenezar	ONN	139	Carrow, Dorothy	NYK	49
Carpenter, Powell	ONT	494	Carr, Ebenezer	OND	163	Carry, Robert	SUF	92
Carpenter, Richard	TIO	258	Carr, Edward	RNS	71	Carry, [St?]anton	WSH	248
Carpenter, Richard	TIO	260	Carr, Edward	RNS	101	Carscadden, Thomas	ORN	278
Carpenter, Richard	ULS	263	Carr, Eliza	RCK	106	Carscaddin, John	ORN	278
Carpenter, Robert	ONT	454	Carr, George	COL	266	Carsel, Asa	WSH	226
Carpenter, Robert	WST	131	Carr, George	ORN	362	Carsen, Andrew	NYK	80
Carpenter, Roger	ONN	160	Carr, Isaac	OTS	10	Carsen, James	NYK	119
Carpenter, Rowland	WSH	291	Carr, Isaac	OTS	29	Carshore, Thomas	NYK	137
Carpenter, Ruphes	WSH	239	Carr, James	COL	265	Carslyn, Michael	NYK	131
Carpenter, Samuel	ALB	112	Carr, James	MNT	99	Carson, David	ALB	66
Carpenter, Samuel	DUT	123	Carr, James	NYK	22	Carson, Elizabeth	ALB	147
Carpenter, Samuel	HRK	435	Carr, James	OTS	30	Car[son?], James	ONT	490
Carpenter, Saml	OTS	36	Carr, James	SRA	21	Carson, Johannis	ULS	214
Carpenter, Samuel	QNS	68	Carr, Jasper	ONN	177	Carson, John	ONT	326
Carpenter, Samuel	ULS	263	Carr, Jehiel	ESS	294	Carson, John	ONT	450
Carpenter, Samuel	WST	112	Carr, John	ALB	88	Carson, Patrick	WSH	227
Carpenter, Samuel	WST	117	Carr, John	ALB	112	Carson, Peter	NYK	18
Carpenter, Seth	CAY	634	Carr, John	ESS	293	Carson, Robert	ONT	496
Carpenter, Silas	OND	166	Carr, John	ORN	370	Carson, Samuel	ULS	225
Carpenter, Silas	OND	170	Carr, John	TIO	223	Carstang, Frederick	NYK	146
Carpenter, Silus	WST	112	Carr, John Junr	ORN	370	Carstang, George	NYK	133
Carpenter, Simmons	DUT	113	Carr, Jonathan	SRA	60	Carstang, Gideon	NYK	125
Carpenter, Solomon	ORN	367	Carr, Joshua	NYK	64	Carstang, Gideon	NYK	144
Carpenter, Solomon	RNS	101	Carr, Levi	SRA	21	Carstang, John	NYK	131
Carpenter, Stephen	HRK	584	Carr, Margaret	NYK	57	Carstang, John	NYK	144
Carpenter, Stephen	NYK	70	Carr, Mary	NYK	35	Carstein, John	KNG	10
Carpenter, Stephen	WST	131	Carr, Michael	WSH	191	Carswell, William	NYK	117
Carpenter, Stephen	WST	133	Carr, Peleg	OTS	30	Cartaight, Jabes	CHN	812
Carpenter, Susanah	RNS	51	Carr, Peleg	TIO	223	Cartel, William	NYK	20
Carpenter, Sylvanus	RNS	101	Carr, Percifer	OTS	39	Carter, Abel	WSH	234
Carpenter, Thomas	ALB	93	Carr, Richmund	SRA	53	Carter, Adolph	NYK	74
Carpenter, Thomas	DUT	64	Carr, Robert	OND	170	Carter, Anthony	CAY	584
Carpenter, Thomas	NYK	46	Carr, Robert	ONT	464	Carter, Asa	WSH	251
Carpenter, Thomas	ORN	395	Carr, Robert	OTS	10	Carter, Benjamin	WSH	191
Carpenter, Thomas	QNS	78	Carr, Samuel	HRK	560	Carter, Berry	CHN	846
Carpenter, Thomas	RNS	101	Carr, Samuel	ORN	366	Carter, Brodock	OND	199
Carpenter, Thomas	SRA	48	Carr, Saml	OTS	12	Carter, Charles	ORN	272
Carpenter, Thomas	WST	111	Carr, Stafford	SRA	53	Carter, Charles	ULS	266
Carpenter, Thomas	WST	128	Carr, Thomas	DUT	65	Carter, Chauncy	NYK	149
Carpenter, Timothy	RNS	44	Carr, Thurstin	RNS	103	Carter, Daniel	HRK	563
Carpenter, Timothy	WST	115	Carr, William	COL	262	Carter, David	SUF	70
Carpenter, Townsend	ORN	287	Carr, William	DEL	289	Carter, Ebenezer	DUT	134
Carpenter, Walter	NYK	100	Carr, William	HRK	453	Carter, Eber	CHN	948
Carpenter, Walter	RNS	63	Carr, William	NYK	131	Carter, Echabod	SUF	70
Carpenter, Warren	HRK	594	Carr, William	ORN	366	Carter, Edward	NYK	90
Carpenter, Warren Jun	HRK	594	Carr, William	ORN	370	Carter, Enoch	WSH	195
Carpenter, William	DEL	290	Carradean, Jane	NYK	16	Carter, Enoch	WST	144
Carpenter, William	DUT	116	Carrendeffez, Alexi			Carter, Henry	CAY	616
Carpenter, William	OND	188	Audo	NYK	123	Carter, Increase	WSH	268
Carpenter, William	ONT	370	Carrier, Andrew	DUT	108	Carter, Isaac	GRN	342
Carpenter, William	ORN	315	Car.ier, Asa	OTS	46	Carter, Jabez	OND	168
Carpenter, William	ORN	337	Carrier, David	RNS	27	Carter, Jacob	COL	253
Carpenter, Wm	RNS	70	Carrier, Ebenezer	COL	214	Carter, Jacob	SUF	70
Carpenter, William	SRA	32	Carrier, Henry	NYK	134	Carter, James	NYK	86
Carpenter, William	SRA	48	Carrier, John	OND	192	Carter, James	WSH	303
Carpenter, Wm	TIO	258	Carrier, John	OTS	55	Carter, Jared	RNS	26
Carpenter, William	WSH	218	Carrier, Jonathan	HRK	531	Carter, Jared Junr	RNS	26
Carpenter, Woodbury	WSH	294	Carrier, Marten	NYK	87	Carter, Jeddedeah	WSH	241
Carpenter, Wright	CAY	694	Carrigan, Gilbert	DUT	95	Carter, Jedediah	WSH	207
Carpenter, Wright	ULS	263	Carrigan, John	DUT	76	Carter, Jirah	ALB	27
Carpenter, Zelos	WSH	219	Carrigan, John Junr	DUT	78	Carter, John	COL	256
Carpenter, Zeno	DUT	120	Carrihart, James	QNS	81	Carter, John	MNT	85
Carpenter, Zeno Junr	ORN	395	Carrill, Phebe	NYK	113	Carter, John	NYK	39
Carr,	SRA	51	Carrington, Aaron	WSH	266	Carter, John	NYK	66
Carr, Adam	ALB	13	Carrington, Eli	WSH	266	Carter, John a Black	NYK	67
Carr, Benajah	DUT	10	Carrington, Joel	WSH	266	Carter, John	WSH	197
Carr, Benajah	OTS	35	Carrington, John	ONT	390	Carter, John	WSH	215
Carr, Benjamin Negro	QNS	71	Carrington, Samuel	OND	160	Carter, Jonathan	DUT	46
Carr, Caleb	OND	219	Carrington, Wait	WSH	273	Carter, Jonathan	ORN	283
Carr, Caleb	SRA	21	Carrol, Abraham	COL	235	Carter, Joseph	CAY	722

Carter, Lewis	ORN 282	Cary, Jesse	OTS 2	Case, Jesse	ORN 290	
Carter, Luther	GRN 346	Cary, John	WSH 289	Case, Job	COL 217	
Carter, Nathaniel	OND 170	Cary, Joseph	CHN 970	Case, Jobe	ONT 366	
Carter, Neodiah	SUF 70	Cary, Joseph	DUT 27	Case, John	ORN 355	
Carter, Polly	OND 193	Cary, Joseph	ORN 334	Case, John	RNS 110	
Carter, Robert	NYK 34	Cary, Lemuel	OTS 4	Case, John	ULS 264	
Carter, Rufus	SRA 28	Cary, Nathan Junr	DUT 54	Case, John Junr	ORN 347	
Carter, Samuel a Black	NYK 36	Cary, Nathan	DUT 54	Case, Jonathan	DUT 144	
Carter, Samuel	WSH 221	Cary, Nathaniel	DUT 49	Case, Jonathan	RNS 22	
Carter, [Sl?]eman	GRN 343	Cary, Price	DUT 49	Case, Joseph	ONT 358	
Carter, Stephen	CHN 838	Cary, Richard	OTS 56	Case, Joseph	ORN 272	
Carter, Susan a Black	NYK 99	Cary, Richard	RCH 93	Case, Joseph	ORN 337	
Carter, Vincent	NYK 22	Cary, Roger	WSH 286	Case, Joseph	SUF 105	
Carter, William	ALB 52	Cary, Samuel	ALB 80	Case, Joseph Junr	RNS 77	
Carter, William	CHN 838	Cary, Thomas	DUT 49	Case, Joshua	ORN 362	
Carter, William	ONT 312	Cary, Thomas	DUT 102	Case, Josiah	ONT 484	
Carter, William	WSH 302	Cary, William	RNS 85	Case, Lemuel	ESS 294	
Carters, Thomas	GRN 339	Caryell, Amamuel	TIO 235	Case, Levi	DUT 152	
Carthy, John	SRA 47	Caryhart, Daniel	ALB 120	Case, Luthar	SUF 75	
Cartir, Amosa	WSH 251	Caryhart, Danl Junr	ALB 120	Case, Mathias	SUF 76	
Cartright, Cyrus	WSH 301	Caryhart, John	WST 114	Case, Moses	SUF 75	
Cartright, Edward	WSH 219	Caryhart, Sarah	WST 115	Case, Nathan	DUT 124	
Cartrite, Luke	MNT 69	Caryhart, Thomas	WST 115	Case, Nathan	RNS 22	
Cartwright, Briant Junr	RNS 70	Caryhart, William	WST 114	Case, Nathl	OTS 36	
Cartwright, Bryant	RNS 70	Casaw, Averett	TIO 214	Case, Norice	ONN 147	
Cartwright, Giddion	GRN 344	Cascadden, Robert	ORN 353	Case, Oliver	OND 207	
Cartwright, Peter	GRN 344	Cascadden, William	DUT 125	Case, Pardon	COL 217	
Cartwright, Thos	OTS 29	Case, Aaron	ULS 200	Case, Phelps	ONT 506	
Cartwright, Throdate	RNS 70	Case, Aaron Junr	MNT 82	Case, Philep	WSH 294	
Cartwright, Wm	RNS 70	Case, Abner	DUT 144	Case, Phineas	DEL 278	
Carty, Timothy	NYK 44	Case, Abraham	WSH 294	Case, Phinehas	ORN 356	
Carvel, John	ONN 183	Case, Alexander	WSH 231	Case, Ralph	SRA 53	
Carver, Amaziah	RNS 111	Case, Archable	SUF 75	Case, Roger	DEL 277	
Carver, Barnabus	DUT 87	Case, Aron	MNT 82	Case, Roger	DEL 282	
Carver, Barton	OTS 54	Case, Asa	DEL 282	Case, Roger Junr	DEL 277	
Carver, Daniel	CAY 646	Case, Aseph	HRK 532	Case, Rufus	DUT 136	
Carver, Dyer	CAY 646	Case, Barnabus	SUF 76	Case, Runey	TIO 233	
Carver, Elihu	CAY 646	Case, Bela	DUT 69	Case, Saml	SUF 73	
Carver, Gardiner	ONT 314	Case, Benjamin	OND 183	Case, Sebe	ONT 424	
Carver, Henry	MNT 21	Case, Benjamin	ORN 278	Case, Thomas	SRA 59	
Carver, John	COL 199	Case, Bernard	WSH 268	Case, Timothy	WSH 291	
Carver, Joseph	OTS 54	Case, Caleb	OND 181	Case, Whitfield	ULS 265	
Carver, Joseph	WSH 285	Case, Calvin	SCH 148	Case, Willm	COL 213	
Carver, Mathias	NYK 76	Case, Charles	OND 207	Case, William	DUT 176	
Carver, Oliver	OTS 52	Case, Daniel	ONT 424	Case, Willis	ONT 506	
Carver, Salmon	WSH 286	Case, Daniel	ORN 332	Case, Zaccheus	ORN 356	
Carver, Samuel	CHN 804	Case, Danl	SUF 75	Case, Zenas	OND 216	
Carver, Samuel	ONT 314	Case, David	COL 220	Case, Zenus	DEL 283	
Carver, Timothy	DUT 86	Case, David	COL 221	Case, Zenus Jun	DEL 283	
Carver, William	NYK 50	Case, David	DUT 124	Casen, John	NYK 131	
Carverly, Elizabetn	NYK 29	Case, David	ONN 175	Caser Black	QNS 69	
Carvescart, Christion	GRN 347	Case, David	ORN 356	Casety, Robt	TIO 255	
Carvey, William	ORN 368	Case, David	SUF 75	Casey, Edmund	CLN 170	
Carvill, John	ORN 299	Case, Ebenezer	MNT 90	Casey, George	DUT 43	
Carvin, Dennis	COL 207	Case, Elihu	MNT 69	Casey, James	NYK 38	
Carwright, Nichs	OTS 29	Case, Elijah	HRK 469	Casey, Jesse	RNS 112	
Cary, Absolom	ORN 334	Case, Elijah	WSH 255	Casey, Jesse Junr	RNS 112	
Cary, Ananias	ORN 389	Case, Elijah Junr	WSH 255	Casey, John	NYK 94	
Cary, Anson	CHN 772	Case, Elkaner	OTS 41	Casey, John	ORN 308	
Cary, Arthur	MNT 99	Case, Emanuel	ALB 113	Casey, Silas	RNS 112	
Cary, Asa	CHN 970	Case, Enos	ORN 337	Casey, Thomas Junr	DUT 60	
Cary, Augustin	CHN 882	Case, Ephraim	CAY 656	Casey, Thomas Senr	DUT 60	
Cary, Bela	OND 201	Case, Ephraim	DEL 277	Casey, William	WSH 235	
Cary, Calvin	OTS 42	Case, George	COL 214	Cash, David	DUT 126	
Cary, Chapen	OND 162	Case, Gersham	SUF 75	Cash, James	SCH 148	
Cary, Danl	OTS 3	Case, Gersham Jur	SUF 75	Cash, Jonathan	RNS 44	
Cary, Darius	OTS 51	Case, Gilbert	SUF 75	Cash, Josep	GRN 351	
Cary, Ebenezer	DUT 12	Case, Gillum	SUF 105	Cash, Nathan	CAY 654	
Cary, Edward	MNT 99	Case, Horace	OND 181	Cash, Reuben	ORN 328	
Cary, Elihu	ORN 329	Case, Hosiah	STB 198	Cash, Rubin	SUF 104	
Cary, Francis	MNT 99	Case, Ido	OTS 41	Cash, Silvenas	GRN 326	
Cary, eorg	MNT 99	Case, Israel	SUF 75	Cash, William	DUT 126	
Cary, Jabez	OND 201	Case, James	OND 183	Cash, William Junr	DUT 126	
Cary, James	MNT 50	Case, James	ONT 414	Casharus, Valantine	MNT 35	
Cary, James	MNT 99	Case, James	SUF 75	Casheriee, John	ALB 24	
Cary, James	OND 201	Case, James	WSH 231	Cashman, Joshua	HRK 541	
Cary, James	WSH 291	Case, Jehab_d	DEL 280	Cashore, Andrew M.	COL 193	

Name	Code	No.	Name	Code	No.	Name	Code	No.
Chandler, Danl	ALB	12	Chapin, Thadeus	ONT	430	Chapman, Noah	SRA	45
Chandler, Enos	ORN	288	Chapin, Uriah	COL	184	Chapman, Olion	RNS	108
Chandler, Isaac	CAY	660	Chapin, Zadock	HRK	483	Chapman, Richd	COL	219
Chandler, Jacob	ONN	191	Chapins, David	OTS	37	Chapman, Richard	DUT	96
Chandler, John	ORN	350	Chapins, Gad Senr	OTS	37	Chapman, Robert	WSH	228
Chandler, John	ORN	397	Chapins, Gideon	OTS	47	Chapma_, Rockwell	SCH	169
Chandler, Jonah	CHN	982	Chapins, Israel	OTS	33	Chapman, Roswell	ALB	23
Chandler, Joseph	ORN	397	Chapins, Israel	OTS	37	Chapman, Roswell R.	HRK	466
Chandler, Joseph	WSH	270	Chapins, Jonathan	ONT	492	Chapman, Samuel	GRN	345
Chandler, Joseph Junr	ORN	398	Chapins, Saml	OTS	37	Chapman, Saml	OTS	58
Chandler, Joshua	ONN	158	Chapins, Uriah	OTS	37	Chapman, Samuel	RNS	110
Chandler, Josiah	TIO	230	Chaple, Amesias	MNT	65	Chapman, Samuel	SRA	41
Chandler, Mathew	CHN	982	Chap[le?], Noah	MNT	41	Chapman, Shubal	OND	186
Chandler, Moses	WSH	273	Chaple, Wm	MNT	65	Chapman, Silas	HRK	466
Chandler, Nathaniel	ORN	397	Chapler, Samuel	NYK	123	Chapm_, St__y	ONT	498
Chandler, Rebecca	ORN	331	Chapley, Mahitable	WSH	277	Chapman, Stephen	SRA	24
Chandler, Robert	DUT	49	Chapley, Otter	WSH	277	Chapman, Stephen	WSH	279
Chandler, Samuel	ORN	295	Chaplin, Benjamin	NYK	39	Chapman, Stephen Jur	WSH	279
Chandler, Solomon	GRN	330	Chaplin, Samuel	OND	200	Chapman, Sumner	OND	172
Chandler, Stephen	RNS	91	Chapman, _a h	CAY	544	Chapman, Thomas	ALB	25
Chandler, William	CAY	720	Chapman, Amasa	ONN	160	Chapman, Thomas	DUT	175
Chandler, William	WSH	273	Chapman, Amos	WSH	208	Chapman, Thomas	ONT	448
Chandler, William	WSH	272	Chapman, Asa	OND	172	Chapman, Thomas	ORN	335
Chandonet, Francis	CLN	169	Chapman, Asa	ONT	310	Chapman, Troup	WSH	289
Chaney, Wm	MNT	70	Chapman, Asa	RNS	111	Chapman, Uriah	ORN	317
Chaning, Nathaniel	ONN	192	Chapman, Benjamin	OND	163	Chapman, Washington	SRA	25
Chanpencus, Margaret	NYK	104	Chapman, Benjamin	ONT	408	Chapman, Wm	ALB	136
Chapel, Aaron	DUT	44	Chapman, Benjamin	ORN	325	Chapman, William	DUT	46
Chapel, Asel	ONN	161	Chapman, Benjamin	SRA	25	Chapman, William	ONT	430
Chapel, Daniel	ONN	131	Chapman, Benjamin T.	WSH	282	Chapman, William	WST	144
Chapel, James C.	OTS	22	Chapman, Benjamine	GRN	342	Chapman, Zachariah	RNS	101
Chapel, Jedediah	DUT	8	Chapman, Caleb	RNS	108	Chapman, Zepheniah	SCH	169
Chapel, Robert	DEL	282	Chapman, Charles	COL	210	Chapman, Zilpha	SRA	50
Chapel, William	ALB	31	Chapman, Comfort	HRK	505	Chappal, Wm	OTS	38
Chapel, Wm	OTS	7	Chapman, Dan	HRK	434	Chappel, James	NYK	54
Chapell, Curtiss	ONN	145	Chapman, Daniel	CHN	762	Chappel, Robart	GRN	344
Chapen, Artimus	CHN	916	Chapman, Daniel	CLN	158	Chappel, Russel	SRA	36
Chapen, Benjaman	CHN	746	Chapman, Daniel	TIO	229	Chappel, Silas	ALB	87
Chapen, Darius	WSH	305	Chapman, David	SRA	42	Chappell, Roswell	NYK	121
Chapen, David	CHN	904	Chapman, David	WST	161	Chappell, Samuel	RNS	26
Chapen, David	WSH	275	Chapman, De_nie	CAY	516	Chappin, Joseph	ALB	116
Chapen, Enoch	SRA	16	Chapman, Ebenezer	WSH	289	Chappin, Julius	ALB	30
Chapen, Enos	CHN	970	Chapman, Ebenezer	WSH	302	Chapple, Roger	WSH	187
Chapen, Gad	WSH	264	Chapman, Ebenezer	WSH	306	Charbonnie, John	NYK	31
Chapen, Joel	CHN	752	Chapman, Edward	SCH	169	Chard, Consider	SRA	13
Chapen, John	WSH	265	Chapman, Elisha	WSH	208	Chard, Elijah	SRA	13
Chapen, Prudence	WSH	268	Chapman, Eroch	MNT	125	Chard, Hugh	DUT	87
Chapen, Roderick	WSH	288	Chapman, Ezekel	OTS	40	Chard, Joseph	SRA	13
Chapen, Serenus	CHN	902	Chapman, Ezekiel	SRA	41	Chardavoyne, Isaac	NYK	40
Chapen, Uriah	STB	197	Chapman, George	ALB	135	Chardavoyne, William	NYK	94
Chapens, Seth	CHN	782	Chapman, Gurdon	DEL	275	Charet, Louis	CAY	530
Chapin, Aaron	DEL	272	Chapman, Haynes	OND	191	Charish, David	NYK	65
Chapin, Charles	ALB	133	Chapman, Himan	TIO	245	Charitan, John	CAY	676
Chapin, Charles	HRK	466	Chapman, Isaac	DUT	175	Charity a Negro Woman	ALB	142
Chapin, Dan	OTS	37	Chapman, Israel	DUT	46	Charl, Lydia	NYK	150
Chapin, Daniel	ONT	396	Chapman, Jehial	WSH	208	Charles a free Negro	ALB	141
Chapin, Elijah	CAY	666	Chapman, Jeremiah	CAY	626	Charles	QNS	60
Chapin, Ezekiel	OTS	31	Chapman, Jeremiah	DUT	79	Charles	QNS	78
Chapin, Gad Junr	OTS	37	Chapman, Joel	NYK	127	Charles	QNS	79
Chapin, Garner	WSH	265	Chapman, John	DEL	283	Charles	QNS	79
Chapin, Herman	ONT	398	Chapman, John	NYK	48	Charles	QNS	79
Chapin, Israel	ONT	430	Chapman, John	NYK	70	Charles	QNS	81
Chapin, Jeremiah	OND	193	Chapman, John	ONT	408	Charles	QNS	84
Chapin, Jona	OTS	22	Chapman, John	RNS	25	Charles (free Negro)	RNS	6
Chapin, Joseph	OTS	22	Chapman, John	RNS	43	Chas a Negro	SUF	67
Chapin, Joshua	ONT	410	Chapman, John	SRA	25	Chas a Negro	SUF	68
Chapin, Josiah	OND	177	Chapman, John C.	GRN	355	Charles	SUF	80
Chapin, Josiah	OND	180	Chapman, Johnson	CLN	174	Charles	SUF	90
Chapin, Jotham	OTS	46	Chapman, Jonathan	COL	219	Charles a Free Negro	WST	112
Chapin, Luke	CHN	986	Chapman, Joseph	COL	208	Charles, George	ALB	126
Chapin, Luke	OTS	22	Chapman, Joseph	ONN	160	Charles, George	ONT	502
Chapin, Oliver	ONT	398	Chapman, Joseph Jur	ONN	160	Charles, Henry	WSH	241
Chapin, Phineas	OND	182	Chapman, Josiah	RNS	92	Charles, John	NYK	71
Chapin, Rufus	HRK	483	Chapman, Mary	NYK	43	Charles, Mericha	ALB	128
Chapin, Samuel	CAY	714	Chapman, Mary	OND	186	Charlick, Henry	WST	134
Chapin, Samuel	RNS	94	Chapman, Nathan	ORN	335	Charlick, John	QNS	77
Chapin, Seth	ALB	121	Chapman, Nathaniel	RNS	90	Charlick, Thomas	WST	135

Charlock, Abraham	DUT 27	Chase, Stephen	ONN 169	Cheeseman, Ezekiel	CAY 590
Charlock, Henry	DUT 26	Chase, Susanna	DUT 90	Cheeseman, Isaac	CAY 592
Charlott, Aaron	COL 246	Chase, Thomas	GRN 325	Cheeseman, John	NYK 78
Charlott, William	COL 251	Chase, Thomas	MNT 104	Cheeseman, Joshua	DUT 126
Charlton, John	NYK 19	Chase, Thomas	ORN 285	Cheeseman, Nathaniel	DUT 124
Charnley, Robert	NYK 45	Chase, Walter	ONT 476	Cheeseman, Richard	QNS 69
Charter, Alexr	WSH 285	Chase, William	NYK 143	Cheesman, Abel	ALB 33
Charters, Alexander	WSH 306	Chase, William	OND 166	Cheesman, Eliza	NYK 66
Charters, George	NYK 56	Chase, William	WSH 238	Cheesman, Forman	WST 145
Charters, John	NYK 57	Chas[on?], Augustus	ONN 183	Cheesman, Samuel	NYK 75
Chase, Abner	DUT 52	Chatfield, Asa	SRA 22	Cheessbroock, James	CHN 830
Chase, Abner	OND 176	Chatfield, Henry	CLN 162	Cheessbroock, William	CHN 830
Chase, Abner	WSH 189	Chatfield, Henry	SUF 107	Cheetham, Benjamin	NYK 35
Chase, Abraham	SRA 52	Chatfield, Josiah	CAY 712	Cheetham, James	NYK 106
Chase, Abraham	WSH 202	Chatfield, Mary	SRA 40	Cheetham, Jane	NYK 91
Chase, Ama	NYK 128	Chatfield, Roswell	SRA 22	Cheetham, John C.	NYK 91
Chase, Asa	OTS 43	Chatfield, Samuel	GRN 337	Chee[v?]er, William M.	OND 157
Chase, Benjamin	ALB 23	Chatfield, Thomas	ORN 356	Cheild, Samuel	SRA 59
Chase, Benjamin	CAY 670	Chatfield, William	NYK 104	Chemerhorn, Cornelius	NYK 44
Chase, Benjamin	DUT 53	Chatham, John	WSH 197	Chena, Daniel	RNS 49
Chase, Benjn	OTS 43	Chatham, Robert	SUF 69	Chena, Jonathan	RNS 49
Chase, Benjamin	SRA 24	Chatkete, Lyrcontic		Chenett, Lewis	NYK 148
Chase, Benjamine	GRN 333	a Black	NYK 123	Cheney see Chainny &
Chase, Caleb	WSH 299	Chatman, Amos B.	WSH 207	Chaney
Chase, Charles	DUT 153	Chatman, Benjamin	NYK 56	Cheney, Amos	COL 252
Chase, Charles	SRA 51	Chatman, Doct	OTS 41	Cheney, Benjamin	ONN 169
Chase, Clark	OND 209	Chatman, Stephin	SCH 169	Cheney, Ebenr	OTS 12
Chase, David	DUT 45	Chatres, John	NYK 57	Cheney, Joseph	OTS 12
Chase, David	MNT 14	Chatsey, Benjamin	ESS 305	Cheney, Will[iam?]	OTS 13
Chase, David	RNS 17	ChatterDen, Jonathan	SCH 147	Cheney, Zack	OTS 52
Chase, Ebenezer	ORN 271	Chatterden, Lewis	SCH 147	Cheny, Enoch	OND 158
Chase, Ebenezer	RNS 21	Chatterden, Michl	ALB 106	Cheny, Reuben	WSH 222
Chase, Ebenezer	WSH 236	Chatterden, Michael	SCH 148	Cheny, Willerd	WSH 222
Chase, Eleazer	DUT 115	Chatterdon, Jonathan	SCH 135	Cherchell, James	WST 162
Chase, Elehu	WSH 185	Chatterton, Cornelias	WST 162	Cherchell, Jedidiah	ONN 186
Chase, Elijah	DUT 95	Chatterton, Jacob	DUT 6	Cherchell, John	WST 162
Chase, Elmer	DUT 90	Chatterton, James	WST 161	Cherchester, James	KNG 8
Chase, Enoch	CLN 162	Chatterton, Joshua	DUT 29	Cheriot, Henry	NYK 29
Chase, Enoch	CLN 163	Chatterton, Peter	DUT 121	Cherney, Isaac	CHN 886
Chase, Esther	OND 196	Chatterton, Peter	WST 146	Cherrard, Seamore	SUF 92
Chase, Hannah	NYK 145	Chatterton, Sarah	NYK 78	Cherry, Abm	SUF 66
Chase, Haviland	OTS 56	Chatterton, William	DUT 5	Cherry, Abraham	ULS 242
Chase, Henry	WSH 189	Chattin, Abraham	WSH 226	Cherry, Enus	SUF 66
Chase, Isaac	GRN 352	Chatwood, Charles	NYK 62	Cherry, James	WSH 251
Chase, Isaac	ONT 332	Chauncey, Isaac	ONN 178	Cherry, Joseph	WST 113
Chase, Isaih	OND 180	Chauncey, Josiah	ALB 30	Cherry, Reuben	CAY 598
Chase, James	OND 194	Chauncey, Moses	ALB 31	Cherry, Samuel	OND 190
Chase, Jeremeah	WSH 298	Chauncey, Rozel	TIO 260	Cherrytree, Briggs	DEL 281
Chase, Jeremiah	OND 196	Chaundler, Jonathan	CHN 984	Cherubub Shunmaker	SCH 172
Chase, Jeremiah	OTS 37	Chauviteau, Joseph	NYK 64	Chervill, S. N.	NYK 91
Chase, Job	ALB 65	Chavaro, William	NYK 80	Chesborough, Nehemiah	RNS 83
Chase, John	NYK 82	Cheavers, William	NYK 116	Chesebrock, Thomas	WSH 236
Chase, John	NYK 105	Cheedle, ...jamin	MNT 11	Chesebrook, Abel	WSH 190
Chase, John	ORN 371	Cheedle, . za	MNT 11	Cheshier, Jeremiah	QNS 81
Chase, John	SRA 33	Cheedle, Increase	SRA 35	Cheshier, Joseph	QNS 78
Chase, Jonathan	ORN 270	Cheedle, Samuel L.	SRA 35	Cheshier, Nehemiah	QNS 80
Chase, Joseph	DUT 113	Cheeny, Thomas	WSH 274	Cheshier, Samuel	QNS 80
Chase, Joseph	GRN 357	Cheesborough, Rebecca	ALB 135	Cheshier, Thomas	QNS 80
Chase, Joseph	MNT 91	Cheesbrough, Christr	ALB 68	Cheshire, Amos	QNS 79
Chase, Joseph	OND 201	Cheesbrough, Daniel	ALB 68	Cheshire, Benjamin	QNS 84
Chase, Joseph	SRA 14	Cheesbrough, Elijah	ALB 71	Cheshire, John	QNS 81
Chase, Joshua	ALB 66	Cheesbrough, Harris	RNS 67	Cheshire, William	QNS 73
Chase, Joshua	WSH 212	Cheesbrough, Isaac	RNS 67	Chesman, Anson	ALB 39
Chase, Josiah	OTS 43	Cheesbrough, Joseph	RNS 67	Chesman, Calvin	ALB 38
Chase, Lemuel	CAY 646	Cheesbrough, Robert	NYK 53	Chesney, James	ALB 136
Chase, Lemuel	WSH 189	Cheesbrough, Wm	ALB 77	Chaster, Elias	OTS 43
Chase, Levy	WSH 299	Cheeseborough, John	CHN 834	Chester, Hannah	WSH 285
Chase, Mark	CAY 670	Cheesebrook, James	CHN 834	Chestley, John	RNS 55
Chase, Nathan	DUT 45	Che_sebrook, Jesse	ONN 169	Chestny, John	SCH 158
Chase, Nathan	ONN 168	Cheesebrough, Christo-		Chevalier, Abner	DUT 134
Chase, Nechemiah	WSH 188	pher	RNS 67	Chevalier, Elias	DUT 134
Chase, Philander	DUT 65	Cheesebrough, Henry	OND 172	Chevalier, Richard	DUT 137
Chase, Richard	OND 196	Cheeseman, Anthony	QNS 71	Chevallie, John A.	NYK 37
Chase, Samuel	WSH 189	Cheeseman, Benjamin	CAY 592	Chevee, James B.	NYK 36
Chase, Seth	ONT 328	Cheeseman, Benjamin	QNS 71	Chevelier, John	NYK 152
Chase, Seth	OTS 43	Cheeseman, Benjamin		Chever, Ebenezer G.	HRK 429
Chase, Stephen	OND 169	Junr	QNS 71	Chever, Ezekiel	HRK 429

Name	Loc	No	Name	Loc	No	Name	Loc	No
Chever, Ezekiel	HRK	532	Chittenden, Moses	COL	187	Christopher, John	RCH	91
Chevers, William	NYK	147	Chittenden, Nathaniel	CLN	164	Christopher, Joseph	RCH	93
Chichester, Daniel	SUF	80	Chittendon, Benjamin	COL	187	Christopher, Peter	RCH	90
Chichester, Ebenezar	SUF	84	Chittendon, Dill	OTS	43	Christophers, John G.	TIO	212
Chichester, Elijah	SUF	80	Chittendon, Nathan	COL	187	Christram, Charles	NYK	25
Chichester, Hannah	SUF	86	Chittendon, Truman	TIO	216	Christy, Alexander	NYK	139
Chichester, Jeremiah	ALB	117	Chittendon, Wise	HRK	599	Christy, Nath..	MNT	55
Chichester, Mary	OTS	27	Chittenten, Lyman	ONT	402	Christy, Rachel	NYK	22
Chichester, Sivanus	SUF	87	Chittester, David	CHN	924	Chronk, James	HRK	421
Chichester, Sophia	ALB	117	Chittester, James	GRN	352	Chronk, Jasper	HRK	419
Chichester, Wm	OTS	27	Chiver, Ebenezer	SRA	38	Chruysler, Abraham	COL	233
Chichister, James	ALB	110	Choat, W___	SCH	140	Chruysler, John J.	COL	232
Chickens, Benjamin	DUT	44	Choate, Francis	RNS	80	Chrysler, Mary	ALB	101
Chidester, Daniel	SRA	18	Choate, Jonathan	RNS	80	Chrysler, Philip	ALB	101
Chidester, Eliphalet Junr	SUF	79	Choee, Isaac	SCH	137	Chubb, Gideon	COL	179
			Chogham, Benjamin	DUT	133	Church, Amasa	OTS	34
Chidester, Eliphalet Senr	SUF	79	Chogham, Samuel	DUT	133	Church, Amos	CHN	792
			Choten, Cornelius	ONN	156	Church, Benjamin	DUT	105
Chidsey, Augustus	CAY	650	Chowan, John	QNS	72	Church, Benjamin	NYK	119
Chidsey, Samuel	CAY	650	Chrenewolt, Mathias	STB	200	Church, Bethue	WSH	223
Chighzaler, Evangiles	NYK	138	Chreyste_, Adam	MNT	61	Church, Cade	CHN	842
Child, Abner	CHN	906	Chrislier, Jacob	OTS	40	Church, Caleb	ULS	241
Child, Abraham	NYK	28	Chrisman, Frederick	OND	198	Church, Chester	WSH	249
Child, Ephraim	SRA	46	Chrisman, Jacob	OND	185	Church, Daniel	SRA	56
Child, Francis	NYK	69	Chrisman, John	OND	185	Church, Daniel	WSH	278
Child, Increase	SRA	17	Christe, Peter	WSH	254	Church, David	OTS	50
Child, Thomas	CHN	972	Christean, Jonathan			Church, Deborah	NYK	45
Child, Timothy	DUT	142	a Black	NYK	70	Church, Ebenezer	COL	202
Child, Timothy	ULS	186	Christen, Zachariah	WST	148	Church, Eber	CHN	752
Child, William	SRA	12	Christian, Adam	MNT	43	Church, Eber	CHN	862
Childs, Daniel	CHN	882	Christian, Cornelius	DUT	6	Church, Eleazer	CHN	752
Childs, David	HRK	435	Christian, George	ULS	198	Church, Eli	OND	222
Childs, Evander	NYK	59	Christian, James	HRK	463	Church, Elijah	CAY	726
Childs, Francis	NYK	96	Christian, Jemima	HRK	463	Church, Ephraim	OND	216
Childs, Isaac	WSH	272	Christian, John	DEL	282	Church, George	NYK	114
Childs, Isaiah	RNS	69	Christian, John	HRK	460	Church, Grove	ONN	153
Childs, Jesse	OND	215	Christian, John	ONN	173	Church, Harison	WSH	187
Childs, John	OND	198	Christian, John	SRA	50	Church, Hubbard	OTS	32
Childs, John Junr	OND	198	Christian, Martin	DUT	6	Church, Ira C.	WSH	226
Childs, Jonathan	WSH	196	Christian, Rachel	DUT	79	Church, Isaac	CHN	752
Child, Noadiah	HRK	501	Christian, Richard	DUT	80	Church, Israiel	CHN	878
Childs, Silas	WSH	301	Christian, Richard Junr	DUT	80	Church, James	NYK	32
Childs, Theodore	RNS	69				Church, James	OTS	2
Childs, Thodore	RNS	14	Christian, William	DUT	80	Church, James	OTS	32
Childs, William	NYK	68	Christiance, Asuwurus	ALB	19	Church, James Junr	OTS	32
Chiles, John F.	WST	162	Christiance, Corns_	ALB	19	Church, Jesse	ONN	192
Chillet, Hanna	OTS	40	Christiance, Isaac	ALB	19	Church, Joel W.	DUT	175
Chilley, William	ALB	54	Christie, Andrew	ORN	323	Church, John	CHN	772
Chilliss, John	ESS	293	Christie, David	ORN	323	Church, John	NYK	40
Chilsen, Nathl	OTS	9	Christie, George	NYK	46	Church, John	OTS	42
Chilson, Alexr	OTS	10	Christie, James	DUT	36	Church, John	RNS	77
Chilson, David	GRN	340	Christie, John	DUT	9	Church, John	SRA	47
Chinele, Francis	MNT	35	Christie, John	ONT	316	Church, John Junr	CHN	772
Chiney, Abiel	COL	252	Christie, Mary	NYK	35	Church, John B.	NYK	19
Chinn, Edward	COL	195	Christie, Richard	DUT	9	Church, Jonathan	DEL	282
Chip, Joseph	ULS	228	Christie, Richard	NYK	23	Church, Josep.	MNT	103
Chipman, Cyrus	ONT	332	Christie, Thomas	WSH	287	Church, Josiah	CHN	772
Chipman, Lemuel	ONT	332	Christie, William	ALB	105	Church, Josiah	OND	209
Chipman, Moses	CHN	954	Christie, William	DUT	7	Church, Nathaniel	RNS	77
Chisam, George	COL	257	Christie, William	NYK	48	Church, Oliver	OTS	22
Chisholm, Andrew	ALB	27	Christie, William	NYK	84	Church, Primus a Black	NYK	140
Chisholm, Kenneth	DEL	286	Christion, Huffnaget	MNT	49	Church, Richard	CHN	754
Ch_holm, Robert	ONT	458	Christly, John	DEL	267	Church, Russell	OND	169
Chisholm, William	DEL	286	Christly, Peter	DEL	267	Church, Russle	WSH	223
Chissoha, John	NYK	16	Christly, Philip	DEL	267	Church, Samuel	CHN	754
Chitendon, Guidean	GRN	341	Christly, Wilhelmus	DEL	267	Church, Samuel	DUT	98
Chitendon, Jarius Jun	GRN	341	Christman, Frederick	HRK	495	Church, Samuel	SRA	33
Chitendon, Jerris Jun	GRN	341	Christman, .rederick	MNT	56	Church, Silus	CHN	820
Chitingdon, Leverrett	GRN	341	Christman, Jacob	MNT	53	Church, Simeon	ALB	83
Chitingdon, Jarias	GRN	341	Christman, John	MNT	52	Church, Thomas	DUT	132
Chitester, Samuel	GRN	326	Christman, John	MNT	54	Church, Timothy	CHN	750
Chittenden, Benjamin	CAY	606	Christmas, Jane	ORN	390	Church, Whitman	OTS	32
Chittenden, George	COL	246	Christmas, Thomas	NYK	104	Church, Willard	OTS	34
Chittenden, Jacob	ALB	52	Christmas, William	NYK	16	Church, Willard Junr	OTS	34
Chittenden, Jared	OND	168	Christopher, Edward	RCH	91	Church, William	CAY	608
Chittenden, Jesse	CAY	606	Christopher, George	OND	166	Church, William H.	WSH	187
Chittenden, Joseph	CAY	606	Christopher, Mrs HesterRCH		90	Church__, Elihu	ONT	482

69

Name	Code	No.	Name	Code	No.	Name	Code	No.
Churchel, Samuel	SRA	51	Clapp, Joseph	DUT	59	Clark, Caleb	OTS	29
Churchel, William	WSH	233	Clapp, Joseph	ULS	257	Clark, Caleb	OTS	49
Churchell, Asel	TIO	212	Clapp, Nathaniel	SRA	46	Clark, Cary	RNS	99
Churchell, Asel	TIO	213	Clapp, Paul	ONN	133	Clark, Cary	RNS	105
Churchell, Isaac	TIO	227	Clapp, Paul Junr	ONN	133	Clark, Charles	GRN	331
Churchell, Samuel	ONN	186	Clapp, Samuel	WST	130	Clark, Charles	GRN	335
Churchhill, Abner	NYK	120	Clapp, Thomas	NYK	61	Clark, Cornelius	HRK	455
Churchhill, James	MNT	55	Clapper, Catherine	ALB	119	Clark, Cornelius	WST	140
Churchill, Amos	MNT	120	Clapper, David	ALB	119	Clark, Cornelius D.	RCK	107
Churchill, Benjamin	MNT	12	Clapper, Elish.	MNT	87	Clark, Cornelus	SUF	67
Churchill, Benjamin	OND	169	Clapper, Frederick	COL	197	Clark, Cyrenus	OTS	9
Churchill, Danl	OTS	49	Clapper, John	COL	264	Clark, Cyrus	OTS	9
Churchill, Edward	DUT	162	Clapper, John P.	RNS	15	Clark, Cyrus	WSH	245
Churchill, Isaac	HRK	435	Clapper, Maria	COL	197	Clark, Dan	DEL	282
Churchill, Isaac Junr	HRK	466	Clapper, Peter	RNS	15	Clark, Daniel	DEL	268
Churchill, John	HRK	441	Clapper, Peter 3d	RNS	8	Clark, Daniel	DUT	46
Churchill, John	HRK	466	Clapsettle, Andrew	HRK	407	Clark, Daniel	DUT	135
Churchill, Jonas	HRK	449	Clapsettle, Andrew Junr	HRK	473	Clark, Daniel	ORN	359
Churchill, Lemuel	TIO	265	Clapsettle, Dennis	HRK	407	Clark, Daniel	OTS	5
Churchill, Nancy	NYK	18	Clapsettle, George	HRK	407	Clark, Daniel	SRA	16
Churchill, Robert	DUT	60	Clapsettle, William	HRK	407	Clark, Daniel	WST	113
Churchill, Sage	ESS	317	Clarck, Abraham	CHN	778	Clark, Danl D.	RCK	107
Churchill, Silas	COL	207	Clarck, Asa	CHN	840	Clark, Darcus	WSH	272
Churchill, Stephen	DEL	288	Clarck, Caleb	CHN	756	Clark, David	DEL	290
Churchill, William	CAY	666	Clarck, Cornelius	CHN	798	Clark, David	HRK	475
Churchill, Willm	COL	218	Clarck, Daniel	CHN	798	Clark, David	ORN	286
Churchward, James	RCH	88	Clarck, Ethan	CHN	822	Clark, David	ORN	311
Churchwell, Benjamin	ULS	212	Clarck, Henery	CHN	822	Clark, David	ORN	354
Churchwell, Henry	DUT	36	Clarck, Henery Junr	CHN	822	Clark, David	ORN	394
Churchwell, John	DUT	40	Clarck, Israel	CHN	774	Clark, David	RCK	97
Churchwell, John Junr	DUT	40	Clarck, John	CHN	798	Clark, David	TIO	209
Churchwell, Rachel	DUT	33	Clarck, Joseph	CHN	824	Clark, Deadama	WSH	294
Cills, Wessle	SUF	68	Clarck, Joshua	CHN	820	Clark, Deodatus	ONN	132
Cimmel, Samuel	ALB	44	Clarck, Nathan	CHN	818	Clark, Dirck D.	RCK	97
Cissel, George	WHS	198	Clarck, Stephen	CHN	822	Clark, Douglass	DUT	135
Cissen, John a Black	NYK	136	Clarck, Waters	OTS	22	Clark, Ebenezar	SUF	93
Cisson, Elisha	SUF	76	Clark, Aaron	OND	157	Clark, Ebenerzer	NYK	124
Cits, Henry	MNT	76	Clark, Aaron	ORN	329	Clark, Elam	ULS	268
Civel, Martinus	MNT	36	Clark, Aaron	SUF	107	Clark, Elias	ORN	322
Civils, John	MNT	30	Clark, Abel	OTS	16	Clark, Elihu	ORN	340
Cizner, Jacob	ALB	55	Clark, Abel	OTS	46	Clark, Elijah	DUT	134
Cl___, Caleb	ONT	380	Clark, Abel	WST	161	Clark, Elijah	OND	210
Clachner, Philip	ALB	82	Clark, Abijah Junr	SRA	18	Clark, Elijah	OND	215
Clack, William	NYK	65	Clark, Abner	SRA	29	Clark, Eliphalet	ONN	158
Cladus, Augustus	ALB	135	Clark, Adam	ALB	113	Clark, Eliphalet	OTS	16
Claflin, Amos	WSH	258	Clark, Alexander	MNT	114	Clark, Elisha	ONN	134
Claflin, Moses	OND	218	Clark, Alexander	NYK	106	Clark, Elisha	SRA	21
Claghorn, Wm	OTS	23	Clark, Ambrose	OTS	17	Clark, Elisha	WST	166
Claghorne, Joseph	NYK	112	Clark, Amos	NYK	127	Clark, Eliza	NYK	40
Clair, Lodwick	SRA	10	Clark, Amos	ONN	152	Clark, Elizabeth	ORN	317
Clakossey, Nancy	NYK	32	Clark, Amos	TIO	229	Clark, Ephraim	WST	126
Claksen, Levinus	NYK	100	Clark, Amos	WSH	226	Clark, Erastus	OND	160
Clamford, Susanah	ONT	460	Clark, Andrew	HRK	456	Clark, Ester	NYK	92
Clamon, John	GRN	327	Clark, Andrew	MNT	74	Clark, Ethan	OND	166
Clap, Benjamin	MNT	30	Clark, Andrew	MNT	114	Clark, Ezekiel	OND	159
Clap, Eddy	COL	260	Clark, Andrw	NYK	150	Clark, Ezekiel	OND	209
Clap, Gilbert	COL	260	Clark, Andrew	OND	209	Clark, Ezekiel	OTS	16
Clap, Isaac	WSH	222	Clark, Andrew F.	MNT	60	Clark, Ezra	DUT	135
Clap, Isreal	CAY	698	Clark, Ann	ALB	138	Clark, Ezra	WST	137
Clap, Lemuel	SRA	14	Clark, Ann	RCK	100	Clark, Flavel	HRK	478
Clap, Stephen	WSH	222	Clark, Anthony	ORN	330	Clark, Francis	DEL	286
Clapp, Allen	NYK	136	Clark, Arthur	SCH	159	Clark, Francis	SUF	77
Clapp, Allen	WST	145	Clark, Asa	MNT	88	Clark, Freeman	ONN	141
Clapp, Cornbury	DUT	142	Clark, Asher	RNS	87	Clark, Freeman	SRA	32
Clapp, David	SRA	42	Clark, Augustus	MNT	90	Clark, Gabriel	ALB	12
Clapp, Elias	DUT	59	Clark, Benjamin	NYK	69	Clark, Gardner	MNT	108
Clapp, Elias	WST	154	Clark, Benjn	OTS	46	Clark, George	HRK	447
Clapp, Ezra	OND	221	Clark, Benjamin	RNS	24	Clark, George	HRK	573
Clapp, Henry	DUT	120	Clark, Benjamin	SUF	90	Clark, George	NYK	24
Clapp, Henry	WST	140	Clark, Benjamin	TIO	212	Clark, George	ONN	130
Clapp, James	DUT	114	Clark, Benoni	ORN	286	Clark, George	ORN	306
Clapp, James	DUT	142	Clark, Benoni	ULS	233	Clark, George	SCH	123
Clapp, James	ULS	256	Clark, Birdsey	OND	162	Clark, George	WSH	300
Clapp, Jesse	DUT	14	Clark, Brewster	OTS	19	Clark, Gershom	ORN	382
Clapp, Jesse I.	DUT	18	Clark, Caleb	MNT	45	Clark, Gulielmus	ORN	282
Clapp, John	DUT	111	Clark, Caleb	OND	176	Clark, Henry	ALB	45
Clapp, John	ORN	397	Clark, Caleb	ORN	317	Clark, Henry	DEL	288

Name	Place	No.
Clark, Henry	ONN	132
Clark, Henry	RCK	101
Clark, Henry	WST	166
Clark, Hisekeah	MNT	76
Clark, Hugh	NYK	120
Clark, Icabod	NYK	132
Clark, Isaac	ESS	309
Clark, Isaac	OND	176
Clark, Isaac	ORN	377
Clark, Isaac	WST	141
Clark, Jabez	OND	175
Clark, Jabus	WST	161
Clark, Jacob	NYK	17
Clark, Jacob	ORN	313
Clark, Jacob	ORN	364
Clark, James	ALB	135
Clark, James	CHN	970
Clark, James	DEL	290
Clark, James	GRN	339
Clark, James	NYK	56
Clark, James	OND	176
Clar., James	ONN	183
Clark, James	ONN	183
Clark, James	ONT	324
Clark, James	ORN	322
Clark, James	ORN	340
Clark, James	ORN	379
Clark, James	ORN	383
Clark, James	ORN	393
Clark, James	OTS	57
Clark, James	ULS	187
Clark, James	WSH	292
Clark, James Junr	ORN	322
Clark, James Junr	ORN	341
Clark, James ye 3d	ORN	328
Clark, James B.	NYK	25
Clark, James D.	ORN	378
Clark, James D.	RCK	107
Clark, James D.	RCK	107
Clark, James D. Junr	RCK	107
Clark, Jared	OTS	9
Clark, Jemma	SRA	36
Clark, Jephther	SRA	56
Clark, Jeremiah	HRK	464
Clark, Jeremiah	ORN	394
Clark, Jerh	OTS	9
Clark, Jeremuah	RNS	6
Clark, Jeremiah	WST	146
Clark, Jerimiah	WSH	301
Clark, Jerremiah	CHN	932
Clark, Jesse	ORN	359
Clark, Jesse	SRA	30
Clark, Joel	MNT	119
Clark, John	CLN	165
Clark, John	DEL	288
Clark, John	MNT	90
Clark, John	NYK	74
Clark, John	NYK	97
Clark, John	OND	202
Clark, John	ONN	130
Clark, John	ONN	157
Clark, John	ORN	322
Clark, John	ORN	377
Clark, John	OTS	41
Clark, John	OTS	41
Clark, John	OTS	41
Clark, John	QNS	66
Clark, John	RNS	69
Clark, John	SRA	18
Clark, John	SRA	29
Clark, John	SUF	74
Clark, John	SUF	91
Clark, John	WSH	227
Clark, John	WSH	292
Clark, John	WSH	301
Clark, John	WST	154
Clark John Junr	MNT	90
Clark, John Junr	RNS	69
Clark, John Junr	RNS	82
Clark, John Junr	WST	160
Clark, John Senr	RNS	81
Clark, Jonathan	ALB	92
Clark, Jonathan	DUT	7
Clark, Jonathan	MNT	69
Clark, Jonathan	SUF	69
Clark, Jonathan	WSH	254
Clark, Jonathan	WST	161
Clark, Joseph	HRK	451
Clark, Joseph	ORN	292
Clark, Joseph	OTS	9
Clark, Joseph	RNS	73
Clark, Joseph	SRA	34
Clark, Joseph	WSH	269
Clark, Joseph	WST	137
Clark, Joseph Junr	OTS	9
Clark, Joseph Junr	RNS	66
Clark, Joshua	ALB	87
Clark, Joshua	ORN	395
Clark, Joshua	SUF	74
Clark, Josiah	DEL	285
Clark, Josias	SCH	119
Clark, Lucretia	ALB	94
Clark, Ludlow	SUF	69
Clark, Luke	RNS	66
Clark, Martha	ORN	331
Clark, Martin	CAY	520
Clark, Mary	NYK	151
Clark, Mary	WST	153
Clark, Matthew	OND	209
Clark, Matthew	ONT	342
Clark, Matthias	ALB	6
Clark, Moses	DEL	288
Clark, Moses	OND	176
Clark, Moses	ORN	377
Clark, Moses	ORN	391
Clark, Moses	ORN	394
Clark, Moses	SUF	104
Clark, Moses	WST	149
Clark, Moses	WST	149
Clark, Nathan	ALB	18
Clark, Nathan	WST	137
Clark, Nathan	WST	140
Clark, Nathan 3rd	WST	140
Clark, Nathaniel	DEL	268
Clark, Nathaniel	ORN	397
Clark, Nathaniel	WSH	220
Clark, Nehemiah	ORN	317
Clark, Nehemiah	ORN	348
Clark, Noah	OND	201
Clark, Oliver	CHN	978
Clark, Oliver	OND	164
Clark, Olivr	MNT	90
Clark, Paul	ALB	135
Clark, Pellatiah	DEL	273
Clark, Peter	NYK	27
Clark, Peter	OTS	13
Clark, Phillip	DUT	8
Clark, Phineas	DEL	288
Clark, Phinehas	ORN	377
Clark, Rachael	WST	139
Clark, Rachel	ALB	115
Clark, Ransom	NYK	81
Clark, Rebecca	NYK	131
Clark, Reuben	ORN	394
Clark, Reuben	ULS	185
Clark, Richard	ONN	167
Clark, Richard	ORN	325
Clark, Richard S.	NYK	48
Clark, Robert	SRA	24
Clark, Robert	STB	201
Clark, Robert	WSH	213
Clark, Russel	HRK	497
Clark, Salmon	WSH	280
Clark, Samuel	CHN	898
Clark, Samuel	DUT	22
Clark, Samuel	DUT	119
Clark, Samuel	NYK	21
Clark, Samuel a Black	NYK	22
Clark, Samuel	OND	159
Clark, Samuel	OND	182
Clark, Samuel	ONN	183
Clark, Samuel	ORN	380
Clark, Samuel	SRA	48
Clark, Samuel	SRA	48
Clark, Samuel	TIO	217
Clark, Samuel	ULS	188
Clark, Samuel	WSH	272
Clark, Sanford	HRK	434
Clark, Sarah	NYK	58
Clark, Silas	OND	162
Clark, Silas	ORN	313
Clark, Siles	WSH	249
Clark, Simon	ALB	20
Clark, Simon	GRN	335
Clark, Simon	HRK	480
Clark, Simon	HRK	483
Clark, Smith	ORN	396
Clark, Solomon	DUT	148
Clark, Solomon	ONN	151
Clark, Solomon	OTS	10
Clark, Stanton	MNT	90
Clark, Stephen	OND	216
Clark, Stephen	OTS	5
Clark, Stephen	OTS	41
Clark, Stephen B.	ALB	116
Clark, Stephen J.	ALB	116
Clark, Thomas	ALB	138
Clark, Thomas	CHN	902
Clark, Thomas	CHN	930
Clark, Thomas	CHN	936
Clark, Thomas	GRN	358
Clark, Thomas	ORN	352
Clark, Thomas	SRA	24
Clark, Thomas	SRA	41
Clark, Thoma_	SRA	57
Clark, Thomas	SRA	60
Clark, Thomas	SCH	160
Clark, Thomas	ULS	180
Clark, Thomas	WSH	208
Clark, Thomas	WSH	213
Clark, Thomas	WST	158
Clark, Thomas Junr	CHN	936
Clark, Thomas M.	ORN	346
Clark, Thomas N.	WSH	255
Clark, Thomas R.	OND	176
Clark, Timothy	ORN	361
Clark, Timothy	ORN	375
Clark, Uriah	DEL	281
Clark, Vincent	ORN	339
Clark, Walter	MNT	90
Clark, Waters	OTS	39
Clark, Wellett	MNT	90
Clark, Wells	OND	162
Clark, Wesson	CHN	776
Clark, Widow	SRA	25
Clark, William	ALB	53
Clark, William	DEL	290
Clark, Wm	MNT	37
Clark, Wm	MNT	110
Clark, William	NYK	56
Clark, William	NYK	74
Clark, William	NYK	94
Clark, William	NYK	143
Clark, William	OND	161
Clark, Willaim	OND	173
Clark, Wm	ONN	178
Clark, William	ORN	302
Clark William	ORN	377
Clark, William	ORN	383
Clark, William	ORN	394
Clark, Wm_	OTS	38

Name	Ref	Name	Ref	Name	Ref
Clark, William	RNS 6	Clarke, Phin..s	CAY 564	Clauson, Garret	CAY 562
Clark, William	SRA 34	Clarke, Richard	NYK 71	Clauson, John	CAY 524
Clark, William	SRA 35	Clarke, Richard H.	NYK 60	Claver, Nicholas	ALB 49
Clark, Wm	SUF 64	Clarke, Robert	CAY 584	Clavis, Benjamin	CAY 604
Clark, William	ULS 208	Clarke, Robert	NYK 104	Clavis, Daniel	CAY 602
Clark, William	WSH 192	Clarke, Robert	NYK 128	Claw, Andrew	COL 263
Clark, William 1st	CAY 610	Clarke, Roliff	COL 222	Claw, Gilbert	ALB 7
Clark, William B.	ULS 233	Clarke, Rowland	RNS 86	Claw, Hendrick	COL 190
Clarke, Abraham	CAY 708	Clarke, Rufus	COL 208	Claw, Henry H.	COL 258
Clarke, Andrew	COL 214	Clarke, Samuel	CAY 600	Claw, Henk P. & Mary	COL 263
Clarke, Asael	RNS 26	Clarke, Samuel	CAY 662	Claw, Jacob M.	COL 263
Clarke, Benjm	COL 206	Clarke, Samuel	NYK 125	Claw, John	SRA 51
Clarke, Benjamin	COL 221	Clarke, Samuel	ONT 348	Claw, Lambert	COL 263
Clarke, Benjamin	ONT 336	Clarke, Samuel	ONT 378	Claw, Mary & Henk P	COL 263
Clarke, Benjamin	ONT 346	Clarke, Samuel	ONT 458	Claw, Samuel	COL 261
Clarke, Benoni	CAY 698	Clarke, Sarah	ONT 458	Clawson, Enock	WST 142
Clarke, Caleb	COL 192	Clarke, Shubal	ONT 446	Clawson, Isaac	NYK 20
Clarke, Caleb	ONT 432	Clarke, Stephen	HRK 566	Clawson, Jacob	WST 129
Clarke, Caleb	ONT 454	Clarke, Thomas	NYK 63	Clawson, Jonathan	RCH 90
Clarke, Calvin	ONT 362	Clarke, Thomas	ONT 464	Clawson, Josiah	COL 261
Clarke, Catherine	NYK 26	Clarke, Thomas	ONT 484	Clawson, Nehemiah	COL 179
Clarke, Christopher	RNS 105	Clarke, Timothy	CAY 522	Clawson, Reuben	WST 142
Clarke, Cornelius	NYK 127	Clarke, Tristam	COL 249	Clay, Jack a Black	NYK 109
Clarke, Daniel	COL 250	Clarke, Walter	NYK 17	Clay, James	ALB 34
Clarke, David	COL 181	Clarke, William	COL 184	Clay, James	NYK 35
Clarke, Desire	RNS 20	Clarke, Willm	COL 203	Clay, Stephen S.	NYK 27
Clarke, Ebenezer	COL 252	Clarke, William	COL 216	Clayton, John	NYK 121
Clarke, Ebenezer	WSH 255	Clarke, William	COL 232	Clayton, Peter	ALB 30
Clarke, Edward	NYK 105	Clarke, William	NYK 94	Clear, Battus	OND 209
Clarke, El__	CAY 586	Clarke, William	ONT 336	Clear, Battus	OND 209
Clarke, Elijah	ONT 336	Clarke, William	ONT 440	Clear, John	OND 209
Clarke, Elijah Junr	ONT 336	Clarke, Wm	RNS 67	Clear, John	OND 209
Clarke, Elisha	CAY 518	Clarke, Wm	RNS 109	Clear, Joseph	RNS 68
Clarke, Eliza	NYK 80	Clarke, William Junr	CAY 612	Clear, Lewis	OND 209
Clarke, Ezekiel	COL 183	Clarke, William Junr	COL 216	Clear, Mary	DUT 46
Clarke, Gabrial	ONT 482	Clarke, William Junr	ONT 338	Clear, Peter	OND 211
Clarke, George	COL 250	Clarke, Wm Junr	RNS 67	Clearwater, Abraham	ULS 201
Clarke, George	RNS 104	Clarke, William 3d	COL 202	Clearwater, Benjamin	ORN 297
Clarke, Gideon	RNS 78	Clarke, Wm Jsh	COL 219	Clearwater, Benjamin Junr	ORN 297
Clarke, Henry	CAY 614	Clarke, William M.	CAY 612	Clearwater, Daniel	ULS 201
Clarke, Henry	COL 217	Clarke, Zepheniah	CAY 562	Clearwater, Evert	ULS 247
Clarke, Henry	COL 250	Clarksen, David M.	NYK 103	Clearwater, Jacob	ORN 342
Clarke, Henry 2d	COL 222	Clarkson, Fruman	NYK 51	Clearwater, Jacob	ULS 248
Clarke, Henry 3d	COL 222	Clarkson, Joshua	DUT 12	Clearwater, Jeremiah	ULS 205
Clarke, Henry W.	COL 223	Clarkson, Mathew	NYK 16	Clearwater, John	ULS 199
Clarke, Isaac	COL 219	Clarkson, Mathew	NYK 26	Clearwater, Joseph	ULS 201
Clarke, Isaac	ONT 382	Clarkson, Stratfield	NYK 20	Clearwater, Joseph	ULS 259
Clarke, Israel	COL 211	Clarey, Isaac	HRK 513	Clearwater, Martin	ULS 198
Clarke, James	CAY 692	Clarey, Samuel	HRK 411	Clearwater, Matthew	ORN 298
Clarke, James	NYK 23	Clarry, Danl	CHN 958	Clearwater, Phillip	DUT 152
Clarke, James W.	NYK 73	Clary, Abel	WSH 264	Clearwater, Thomas	ULS 201
Clarke, Jedediah	COL 251	Clary, Arad	DUT 141	Clearwater, Zachariah	NYK 135
Clarke, Jehiel	CAY 704	Clary, Samuel	DUT 141	Cleary, Adolphus	NYK 135
Clarke, Jesse	COL 182	Clary, Uriah	WSH 295	Cleary, William	NYK 78
Clarke, Job	RNS 20	Clashorn_, James	NYK 94	Cleaveland, Abel	ONT 326
Clarke, Joel	GRN 355	Clason, Aaron	ORN 318	Cleaveland, Abel	WSH 226
Clarke, Joel	ONT 422	Clason, George	ORN 381	Cleaveland, Anson	OND 178
Clarke, John	CAY 554	Clason, Isaac	WST 145	Cleaveland, Beaj_	CHN 984
Clarke, John	CAY 600	Clason, Nathaniel	NYK 140	Cleaveland, Benjamin	WSH 226
Clarke, John	CAY 664	Class a free Negro	ALB 131	Cleaveland, Clark	ONT 326
Clarke, John	COL 216	Classmann, George		Cleaveland, Curtis	DEL 284
Clarke, John	DUT 169	Augustus	KNG 8	Cleaveland, Daniel	DEL 285
Clarke, John	NYK 35	Classon, Robert	RNS 31	Cleaveland, Diar	WSH 251
Clarke, John	NYK 63	Claus a free Negro	ALB 18	Cleaveland, Ephm	CHN 924
Clarke, John	NYK 74	Claus	RCK 107	Cleaveland, Fredrick	WSH 231
Clarke, John	NYK 120	Claus, Christian	NYK 130	Cleaveland, Gardner	OND 198
Clarke, John	NYK 143	Claus, Garret	CAY 544	Cleaveland, James	ONT 326
Clarke, John	ONT 430	Claus, John	ALB 112	Cleaveland, Job	WSH 226
Clarke, Joseph	COL 251	Clausa, John B.	NYK 111	Cleaveland, John	CAY 684
Clarke, Joseph	ONT 422	Clause, Andrew	MNT 11	Cleaveland, John	WSH 214
Clarke, Lemuel	COL 209	Clause, John	MNT 4	Cleaveland, Jonas	WSH 278
Clarke, Luman	NYK 77	Clause, John	MNT 51	Cleaveland, Josiah	DEL 278
Clarke, Martin	NYK 54	Clause, Peter	MNT 2	Cleaveland, Palmer	WSH 226
Clarke, Mary	COL 249	Clause, Peter Junr	MNT 12	Cleavland, Bradford	COL 230
Clarke, Nathan	ONT 430	Clausen, Abraham	WSH 238	Cleavland, Ezekiel	OND 198
Clarke, Nathaniel	NYK 82	Clausen, John	WSH 231	Cleavland, James	SUF 76
Clarke, Oliver	ONT 346	Clausin, Stephen	WSH 196		

Name	Loc	Pg	Name	Loc	Pg	Name	Loc	Pg
Cleavland, Josiah	OND	209	Clemmons, Thomas	QNS	75	Clinton, James	ORN	292
Cleavland, Mary	SUF	76	Clemont, Samuel	ONN	133	Clinton, John	ALB	41
Cleavland, Moses	SUF	76	Clench, Thomas	ALB	9	Clinton, John	OTS	12
Cleavland, William	SRA	6	Clendennan, Alexander	NYK	22	Clinton, John junr	ALB	41
Cleavland, William	SRA	7	Clendennan, Alexander	NYK	78	Clinton, Joseph	DUT	57
Cleavs, Beriah	SUF	74	Clendenning, John	NYK	38	Clinton, Simeon	DUT	54
Cleavs, David	SUF	67	Cleom, Adam	RNS	86	Clinton, Simeon	OTS	27
Cleeveland, Isaac	OTS	40	Clerk, Conrod	MNT	100	Clinton, William	DUT	172
Cleeves, Danl	SUF	73	Clerk, Thomas	RNS	90	Clipp, Jacob	RNS	63
Clefford, Dennis	NYK	87	Clerk, Thomas	RNS	112	Clitz, John	NYK	21
Cleghorn, William	WSH	300	Cleuit, John	NYK	52	Clitzer, John	NYK	95
Cleland, Margaret	NYK	52	Cleveland, Asa	OTS	40	Clock, Crestion	MNT	20
Cleland, Norman	HRK	488	Cleveland, Benjamin	CHN	862	Clock, [F?]obe	MNT	62
Cleland, Salmon	HRK	488	Cleveland, Benj:	ONN	174	Clock, Gideon	NYK	73
Cleland, Samuel	HRK	488	Cleveland, Elijah	WSH	278	Clock, Jacob	WST	112
Cleland, Thomas	ONT	360	Cleveland, Ephraim	ONT	336	Clock, Jacob J.	MNT	3
Cleland, William	DUT	30	Cleveland, Ephraim	ONT	342	Clock, Jacob J.	MNT	3
Clem, John	ALB	146	Cleveland, Ephraim Junr	ONT	336	Clock, Jacob John Junr	MNT	19
Clem_, Jabes	CHN	884	Cleveland, Frederick	KNG	2	Clock, Johanis	MNT	1
Cleman, George	NYK	106	Cleveland, Gardner	ALB	34	Clock, John	MNT	2
Clemans, Aaron	WST	122	Cleveland, George	DUT	176	Clock, John Jb	MNT	19
Clemans, William	WST	126	Cleveland, Griffin	ONT	336	Clock, Joseph	MNT	19
Clemen, Frederick	SRA	12	Cleveland, Jacob	SRA	26	Clock, Joseph Junr	MNT	11
Clemence, Daniel	ORN	288	Cleveland, James	GRN	357	Clock, Joseph G.	MNT	20
Clemens, Jacob	HRK	455	Cleveland, John	GRN	342	Cloe, John	GRN	334
Clemens, Samuel P.	OND	195	Cleveland, Jonas	ONN	139	Clopman, Henry	NYK	95
Clement, Asa	OTS	53	Cleveland, Jonas	RNS	89	Clopper, Coonrod	RNS	10
Clement, Bartholemew	MNT	70	Cleveland, Joseah	WSH	274	Clopper, Henry	NYK	120
Clement, Bartlet	ORN	298	Cleveland, Joseph	GRN	331	Clopper, Henry	RNS	8
Clement, Daniel	ORN	298	Cleveland, Ralph	ONT	428	Clopper, Henry F.	COL	197
Clement, Darius	WSH	299	Cleveland, Robert	RNS	89	Clopper, Jacob	RNS	8
Clement, Henry	NYK	92	Cleveland, Samuel	ALB	87	Clopper, Peter	ALB	17
Clement, James	CAY	688	Cleveland, Waitstill	SCH	132	Clopper, Peter	NYK	26
Clement, Jarvis	QNS	71	Cleveland, William	RNS	89	Clopper, William	COL	195
Clement, Joel	ONN	143	Clever, Adam	MNT	31	Close, Abraham	SRA	18
Clement, John	MNT	117	Cleves, Joshua	ORN	286	Close, Benjamin	SRA	61
Clement, John	NYK	87	Cleves, Thomas	ORN	358	Close, Benjamin	WST	127
Clement, Lewis	MNT	30	Clevland, Asa	WSH	187	Close, David	NYK	57
Clement, Martha	NYK	44	Clew, Samuel	NYK	82	Close, Elnathan	CAY	614
Clement, Peter	SCH	168	Clibe, James	SRA	29	Close, Ezra	DUT	92
Clement, Stephen	DUT	175	Clice, Henry	ONT	462	Close, Henry	SRA	40
Clement, Stephen	QNS	69	Clickner, Philip	RNS	84	Close, Jabus	WST	157
Clements, Abraham	WSH	285	Clicner, George	RNS	84	Close, Jesse	WST	125
Clements, Charles	DUT	104	Clide, James	NYK	143	Close, John	SRA	3
Clements, Cornelius	DUT	12	Cliff, Joseph	CAY	686	Close, Jonathan	DUT	92
Clements, David	CHN	970	Clifford, James	NYK	127	Close, Jonathan	DUT	143
Clements, Henry	WSH	298	Clifford, James Junr	NYK	127	Close, Nathaniel	WST	126
Clements, Isaac	WSH	298	Clifford, Thomas	NYK	41	Close, Peter	SRA	61
Clements, James	OTS	54	Clift, Lemuel	DUT	177	Close, Stephen	CAY	688
Clements, James	WSH	298	Clightman, Lawrence	ALB	64	Close, Stephen	WST	151
Clements, Jonathan	WSH	285	Cliland, George	NYK	48	Closson, Ebenr	TIO	229
Clements, Joseph	WSH	285	Climons, Thomas	SRA	9	Closson, James	GRN	337
Clements, Samuel	CHN	970	Climson, William	NYK	143	Closson, Moses	TIO	229
Clements, Thomas	DUT	11	Clinch, John	NYK	113	Closson, Nathan	RNS	84
Clemins, Christopher	SRA	25	Clinchman, Christopher	OND	222	Clothier, Ambrose	SRA	53
Clemint, Josep	MNT	69	Cline, Elizabeth	COL	230	Clothier, Catharine	SRA	53
Clemman, Partrick	GRN	327	Cline, George	ALB	49	Clothier, John	SRA	53
Clemmans, Tobias	SRA	39	Cline, Henry	GRN	335	Clothier, Salmon	SRA	53
Clemmens, James	SRA	29	Cline, Henry	MNT	15	Clothur, Lyman	CLN	166
Clemment, Charles a Black	NYK	140	Cline, Jacob	COL	190	Clough, Abel	CHN	890
Clemmins, James	SRA	25	Cline, Jacob	COL	230	Clough, Benjamin	OTS	21
Clemmons, Benjn	SRA	39	Cline, Jacob	SCH	119	Clough, Ephriam	CHN	886
Clemmons, Colbun	ESS	307	Cline, Jacob C.	COL	230	Clough, Ithamer	WSH	264
Clemmons, Cornelius	SRA	40	Cline, Jacob V.	COL	240	Clough, John	CHN	888
Clemmons, David	ESS	321	Cline, John C.	COL	237	Clough, John	ONN	155
Clemmons, Francis	CHN	880	Cline, Martin Jun	MNT	114	Clough, John	WSH	290
Clemmons, ilbert	QNS	75	Cline, Nicholas	ALB	48	Clough, Jonathan	WSH	290
Clemmons, Hynd	ESS	308	Cline, Wido Sarah	COL	190	Clough, Rosena	CHN	886
Clemmons, James	SRA	43	Cling, Henry	NYK	123	Clound, Erastus	CHN	884
Clemmons, John	RNS	54	Clingan, Edward	NYK	129	Clover, John	GRN	345
Clemmons, John	RNS	109	Clink, John	ALB	113	Clow, Cosper	GRN	331
Clemmons, Jonothan	CHN	886	Clintick, Samuel	ORN	363	Clow, Cosper	GRN	358
Clemmons, Joseph	SRA	40	Clinton, Betsey	OTS	12	Clow, Evert	GRN	358
Clemmons, Peter	SRA	44	Clinton, Charles	ORN	282	Clow, Francis	GRN	348
Clemmons, Samuel	CHN	876	Clinton, DeWit	QNS	62	Clow, Francis	GRN	350
Clemmons, Stephen	CHN	822	Clinton, George	NYK	52	Clow, Francis	GRN	356
			Clinton, George Junr	NYK	27	Clow, Garret	GRN	348

Clow, Garret	GRN 350	Clute, John	ALB 15	Cobb, William	SUF 91
Clow, Henry	COL 190	Clute, John	ALB 17	Cobbe, Daniel	ONN 159
Clow, Henry G.	COL 262	Clute, John	ALB 57	Cobby, Joseph	DEL 286
Clow, Jamee	SRA 4	Clute, John	MNT 100	Cobby, Susannah	NYK 73
Clow, Jeremiah	GRN 358	Clute, John Junr	MNT 100	Cobern, Henery	CHN 762
Clow, Jeremiah	GRN 358	Clute, John B. T.	ALB 12	Cobern, Nathaniel	CHN 768
Clow, John	GRN 358	Clute, John F.	ALB 7	Cobet, Peter	TIO 236
Clow, John	QNS 73	Clute, John F.	ALB 54	Cobin, James	DEL 279
Clow, John C.	GRN 349	Clute, Nichs	ALB 9	Cobland, George	NYK 29
Clow, John G.	COL 262	Clute, Nicholas	ALB 42	Coble, William	WST 152
Clow, Laurance	ALB 10	Clute, Nicholas	ALB 56	Cobler, Enoch	DEL 287
Clow, Peter	GRN 356	Clute, Nicholas	MNT 97	Cobler, Ruben	WSH 187
Clow, Peter	RNS 35	Clute, Peter	ALB 54	Cobler, Samuel	WSH 187
Clowbridge, Chrit.	OND 221	Clute, Richard	ALB 8	Cobrn, Edward	CHN 762
Clower, Benjamin	KNG 8	Clyde, Caty	OTS 3	Coburn, Asher	ONT 414
Clowes, Grodus	QNS 73	Clyde, Matthew	OTS 3	Coburn, Benjn	TIO 222
Clowes, Samuel	QNS 73	Clyde, Samuel	HRK 558	Coburn, David	OTS 32
Clows, Gelbert a		Clyne, Peter	MNT 15	Coburn, Jonathan	CAY 590
mulatto	NYK 17	Co, Mary a Black	NYK 92	Coburn, William	OND 193
Clow, George	NYK 40	Co....an, _ a,	MNT 33	Coburn, Zedediah	OND 184
Clows, Isaac	QNS 74	Co..lman, John	MNT 72	Coch, David	QNS 69
Clows, Joseph	QNS 74	Co_, John	TIO 251	Cochone, Rebecca	NYK 95
Clows, Thomas	QNS 74	Coachman, Cornelius	NYK 81	Cochran, Andw	OTS 7
Cloyd, David	NYK 102	Coan, Elisa	ONT 402	Cochran, Betsey	NYK 91
Cloyes, Luther	HRK 422	Coals, Billings	OTS 15	Cochran, David	CAY 608
Cloys, Cage	CHN 870	Coan, Timothy	WSH 276	Cochran, David	CLN 154
Cloys, Daniel	OND 183	Coat, Aaron	CHN 984	Cochran, Francis	NYK 88
Cloys, Ezery	CHN 870	Coates, Benjn	ONN 143	Cochran, John	CLN 157
Cloyt, Josep	MNT 118	Coates, Benjn Junr	ONN 143	Cochran, John	MNT 1
Cluet, Peter P.	ALB 6	Coates, Christopher	RNS 78	Cochran, John	NYK 109
Clukton, David	SRA 57	Coates, Timothy	ONT 316	Cochran, John	OTS 5
Clum, Adam	COL 224	Coates, Zebulon	ONN 143	Cochran, John	WSH 197
Clum, George	COL 243	Coats see Coals		Cochran, John Junr	ESS 323
Clum, Henry	RNS 87	Coats, Alden	OTS 15	Cochran, Margaret	NYK 42
Clum, John P.	COL 225	Coats, Cary	OTS 49	Cochran, Patrick	NYK 15
Clum, Margaret	COL 224	Coats, John	CHN 776	Cochran, Peter	CAY 556
Clum, Peter	COL 240	Coats, John	OTS 56	Cochran, Philip	NYK 16
Clum, Phillip	COL 190	Coats, John H.	NYK 71	Cochran, Robert	CLN 157
Clum, Phillip	COL 191	Coats, Joseph	OTS 6	Cochran, Robert	ORN 299
Clum, Phillip	COL 243	Coats, Joseph	OTS 51	Cochran, Robert	ULS 182
Clum, Phillip A.	COL 190	Coats, Joseph	RNS 47	Cochran, Robert	WSH 219
Clum, Phillip H.	COL 225	Coats, Moses	OTS 5	Cochran, Silas	CLN 157
Clum, William	COL 199	Coats, Samuel	CHN 926	Cochrane, Widow	MNT 66
Clumeche, Darius	RNS 15	Coats, Samuel Junr	CHN 920	Cochron, Mary	GRN 325
Clumond, George	NYK 64	Coats, Saml R.	CHN 926	Cock, Andrew	NYK 80
Clump, Zachariah	DUT 39	Coats, [Semeon?]	ESS 292	Cock, Benjamin	QNS 63
Clung, Henery D.	CHN 964	Coats, Stephen	NYK 121	Cock, Betsey	NYK 83
Clute, Abraham F.	ALB 51	Coats, Thomas	NYK 33	Cock, Charles	QNS 82
Clute, Barthw	ALB 10	Coats, Uriah	COL 213	Cock, Clark	QNS 82
Clute, Catharine	ALB 8	Coats, Wm	OTS 38	Cock, Daniel	QNS 82
Clute, Cornelius	ALB 17	Coats, William Junr	OTS 39	Cock, Daniel	QNS 83
Clute, Daniel T.	ALB 21	Cob, Harmer	GRN 351	Cock, Dorothy	QNS 84
Clute, Dirck	ALB 50	Cob, Holden	NYK 87	Cock, Elijah	NYK 44
Clute, Douw	ALB 10	Cob, Justus	WSH 286	Cock, Garret	COL 189
Clute, Douw	ALB 18	Cob, Miner	GRN 345	Cock, George	NYK 83
Clute, Evert	SRA 40	Cob, William	NYK 84	Cock, George	QNS 72
Clute, Fredk	ALB 7	Coban, Jacob	CHN 754	Cock, George	WST 115
Clute, Frederick	ALB 8	Cobart, Jacob	NYK 134	Cock, Henry	ORN 284
Clute, Frederick	ALB 50	Cobb, Aaron	SCH 139	Cock, Isaac	NYK 80
Clute, Frederick	MNT 100	Cobb, Cyprian	ORN 334	Cock, Isaac	QNS 82
Clute, Frederick F.	ALB 67	Cobb, Daniel	ONN 163	Cock, Isaac	WST 115
Clute, Gererdus	ALB 50	Cobb, David	ONN 179	Cock, Israel	WST 115
Clute, Gererdus	ALB 53	Cobb, Ebenezer	SRA 26	Cock, Jacob	HRK 452
Clute, Gerret	SRA 40	Cobb, Elijah	ULS 252	Cock, James	NYK 139
Clute, Gerrit	ALB 45	Cobb, Henry	ORN 320	Cock, James	WSH 236
Clute, Gerrit	ALB 51	Cobb, Isaac	ONN 172	Cock, Job	WST 115
Clute, Gerrit F.	ALB 50	Cobb, Jacob	ONN 172	Cock, John	NYK 80
Clute, Grandus	SRA 11	Cobb, John	OND 209	Cock, John	QNS 82
Clute, Grandus	SRA 11	Cobb, John	ONT 380	Cock, John	WST 149
Clute, Henry	SRA 10	Cobb, John	OTS 55	Cock, Joshua	NYK 62
Clute, Henry	SRA 10	Cobb, Jonathan	ONN 180	Cock, Joshua	WST 114
Cl.te, Isaac	MNT 97	Cobb, Matthias	ESS 308	Cock, Levy	QNS 80
Clute, Jacob	ALB 5	Cobb, Nathaniel	RNS 60	Cock, Margaret	NYK 48
Clute, Jacob	ALB 55	Cobb, Noah	ORN 325	Cock, Noah	WST 115
Clute, Jacob	ALB 56	Cobb, Thomas	OND 172	Cock, Richard	QNS 82
Clute, Jacob	MNT 93	Cobb, Wm	OND 209	Cock, Samuel	QNS 82
Clute, Jellis	ALB 7	Cobb, William	ONN 159	Cock, Samuel	SRA 56

Cock, Samuel	WST 166	Coe, Daniel	ULS 235	Coffin, George G.	COL 246
Cock, Samuel Junr	QNS 82	Coe, David	OND 188	Coffin, Gideon	COL 255
Cock, Solomon	SRA 55	Coe, Edward	ULS 265	Coffin, Jared	COL 250
Cock, Thomas	QNS 82	Coe, Hannah	TIO 212	Coffin, Job	COL 250
Cock, Thomas Junr	QNS 82	Coe, Ichabud	COL 249	Coffin, John	ALB 98
Cock, Townsend	QNS 82	Coe, Isaac	ORN 375	Coffin, Judith	RNS 93
Cock, William	ORN 398	Coe, Ithamer	OND 202	Coffin, Latham	SRA 35
Cock, William	QNS 82	Coe, James	GRN 335	Coffin, Mark	NYK 44
Cock, Zoah	QNS 84	Coe, Joel	CAY 640	Coffin, Nathen	WSH 235
Cockburn, William	ULS 224	Coe, Joel	OND 219	Coffin, Noah	COL 222
Cocklan, Michael	ONN 190	Coe, Joel	OTS 39	Coffin, Paul	DUT 102
Cockle, Cornelius	ESS 298	Coe, John	DUT 139	Coffin, Salmon	DUT 104
Cockle, John	NYK 145	Coe, John	HRK 555	Coffin, Shubael	DUT 104
Cocknich, John E.	MNT 59	Coe, John	RCK 108	Coffin, Stephen	COL 247
Cockran, Michael	NYK 77	Coe, John D.	RCK 108	Coffin, Uriah	COL 248
Cockrin, John	COL 258	Coe, John S.	RCK 106	Coffin, Uriah	ULS 239
Cocks, Isaac	WST 124	Coe, Jonas	RNS 93	Coffin, Uriah Junr	COL 248
Cocks, Robert Senior	NYK 30	Coe, Jonas	TIO 265	Coffin, Uriel	COL 221
Cocks, Zachariah	CAY 590	Coe, Justice	GRN 333	Coffin, Aepheniah	COL 214
Cocksan, Nathaniel	ONN 151	Coe, Mathew	RCK 108	Cofford, John	SRA 26
Cocksdale, Silas	SRA 6	Coe, Nathan	OND 221	Cogden, John	ALB 3
Cocksure, Jonas	DUT 6	Coe, Nehemiah	QNS 65	Coggin, John	NYK 54
Codd, Matthew	WST 148	Coe, Rachel	RCK 108	Coggin, Timothy	DUT 108
Codding, Faunce	ONT 416	Coe, Reuben	WST 113	Cog_shall, Gideon	WST 148
Codding, George	ONT 416	Coe, Rial	OTS 18	Coggswell, Asahel	CAY 658
Codding, George Ju.	ONT 416	Coe, Robt	OTS 18	Coggswell, Elish	WSH 233
Codding, John	ONT 416	Coe, Samuel	CHN 876	Coggswell, John	RNS 31
Codding, Liscum	ONT 412	Coe, Saml	RCK 105	Coggswell, John	WSH 285
Coddington, Abraham	NYK 57	Coe, Samuel	TIO 215	Coggswell, Robert	WSH 233
Coddington, Benjamin	NYK 148	Coe, Samuel	ULS 236	Coggswell, Salmon	SRA 47
Coddington, Benjamin	ULS 217	Coe, Saml J.	RCK 108	Coggswell, Sarah	ONT 458
Coddington, Daniel	ULS 216	Coe, Saml W.	RCK 108	Coghill, Robert	NYK 79
Coddington, David	NYK 87	Coe, Seth	GRN 341	Coghlan, Michael	ORN 307
Coddington, David	RCH 88	Coe, Simeon	ALB 111	Cogner, John	SCH 121
Coddington, David	ULS 200	Coe, Simeon	HRK 555	Cogswell see Gogswell	
Coddington, Easias	NYK 58	Coe, Simeon	OND 183	Cogswell, Elisha	SRA 20
Coddington, Enoch	ORN 277	Coe, Thomas	KNG 9	Cogswell, Nathan	ALB 137
Coddington, Jacob	ULS 215	Coe, William	CLN 160	Cogswell, Reuben	SRA 30
Coddington, John	CAY 568	Coe, William	DUT 151	Cogswell, Robert	OND 167
Coddington, John	ULS 212	Coe, William	QNS 60	Cogswell, Smith	ALB 137
Coddington, Jonathan	ORN 338	Coe, Zachariah	OTS 39	Cogswell, Stephen	SRA 19
Coddington, Joseph	DEL 273	Coehutius	RCK 102	Cogswell, William	ONT 342
Coddington, Joseph	ORN 337	Coen, Beriah	COL 210	Cogswell, William Junr	ONT 342
Coddington, Joseph	ULS 234	Coen, Daniel	NYK 38	Cohenhaven, Peter	RNS 81
Coddington, Moses	NYK 96	Coen, Phillip	COL 232	Cohenhoven, Isaac	MNT 95
Coddington, Richard	ORN 339	Coen, Ray	COL 187	Cohernall, Adam	MNT 6
Coddington, Sarah	NYK 99	Coenradt, Johannis	ALB 90	Cohler, Charles	NYK 114
Coddington, William	ORN 276	Coesar	QNS 82	Cohoon, John	RNS 110
Coddon, Samuel	SCH 168	Coff, Jacob	CAY 520	Cohoon, Joseph	RCK 100
Codington, John	NYK 59	Coffee, Anthony	ESS 305	Cohoon, Joseph	WSH 186
Codman, William	NYK 28	Coffee, Barnabey	QNS 62	Cohound, Elexeander	GRN 340
Codner, Amos	CAY 702	Coffee, John	ORN 388	Coil, Barnabas	DUT 32
Codner, David	CAY 702	Coffee, John	WSH 288	Coil, Micajah	SRA 38
Codner, John	MNT 93	Coffee, Patrick	ALB 127	Coirrington, Isaac	NYK 96
Codner, Saml	RNS 111	Coffeen, Daniel	OND 222	Coit, David	NYK 133
Codner, Stephen	MNT 93	Coffeen, David	OND 220	Coit, Joseph	OTS 58
Codney, Samuel	WSH 214	Coffeen, Eleazer G.	WST 130	Coit, Levy	NYK 20
Codwice, George Junr	NYK 62	Coffeen, Goldsmith	OND 220	Coit, William	NYK 28
Codwise, Christopher	DUT 39	Coffeen, Henry(?)	OND 220	Coit, William	NYK 70
Codwise, Christopher	NYK 62	Coffeen, Moses	OND 222	Coker, Cornelius	SCH 135
Codwise, George	QNS 67	Coffen, Edward	HRK 440	Col see Coe	
Cody, Edward	ALB 43	Cofferty, Josiah	TIO 214	Col, Danel	NYK 110
Cody, Lydia	RCH 89	Coffey, William	NYK 29	Col, Moses	NYK 110
Cody, Samuel	OND 169	Coffin, Aaron	COL 201	Colbert, Hugh	NYK 144
Cody, William	ONT 354	Coffin, Abishai	DUT 98	Colbert, James	SRA 39
Coe see Col		Coffin, Albert	WSH 233	Colbert, Widow S.	DEL 275
Coe, Aaron	DUT 169	Coffin, Alexander	COL 247	Colboth, Susanna	WST 129
Coe, Amos	HRK 554	Coffin, Alesander Junr	COL 250	Colbourn, Pa_	MNT 41
Coe, Amos	OND 180	Coffin, Benjamin	NYK 132	Colbourn, Valentine	DUT 15
Coe, Andrew	HRK 554	Coffin, Edward	NYK 127	Colbourne, Ellis	OTS 48
Coe, Andrew Jun	HRK 555	Coffin, Eliab	COL 253	Colbourne, Jona	OTS 48
Coe, Benjamin	QNS 60	Coffin, Elihu	COL 248	Colbourne, Lewis	OTS 48
Coe, Benj. Esqr	RCK 104	Coffin, Eliphalet	ALB 35	Colbrath, Hester	OND 215
Coe, Branard	OND 220	Coffin, Elizabeth	COL 251	Colburn, Amos	OND 213
Coe, Canfield	OND 186	Coffin, Elizabeth	COL 253	Colburn, Joseph	HRK 420
Coe, Daniel	GRN 341	Coffin, Elizabeth	NYK 77	Colburn, Silas	OND 215
Coe, Danl	RCK 108	Coffin, Geer	COL 251	Colby, Henry	WSH 228

Name	Co	Pg
Colby, John	ALB	69
Colby, Thomas	ORN	337
Colchamer, Coonradt	RNS	83
Colchanmer, George	RNS	84
Colden, Alexander	ORN	305
Colden, Cadwallader	ORN	304
Colden, Cadwallader Junr	ORN	306
Colden, Cadwallader D.	NYK	28
Colden, James a Black	NYK	130
Colden, Thomas	ORN	305
Coldgrove	CHN	904
Cole, ...y	TIO	209
Cole, .arton	MNT	87
Cole, Aaron	CAY	686
Cole, Aaron	DUT	31
Cole, Aaron	OND	222
Cole, Aaron	RNS	56
Cole, Aaron Junr	DUT	28
Cole, Abigal	NYK	120
Cole, Abraham	ALB	21
Cole, Abraham	DUT	153
Cole, Abraham	HRK	483
Cole, Abraham	HRK	556
Cole, Abm	RNS	7
Cole, Abraham	RCH	90
Cole, Abraham	RCH	94
Cole, Abraham	RCH	95
Cole, Abrm	RCK	100
Cole, Abrm	RCK	103
Cole, Abrm	RCK	103
Cole, Abraham	SRA	8
Cole, Abraham	SRA	41
Cole, Abraham	ULS	255
Cole, Abraham Junr	ULS	255
Cole, Adam	COL	265
Cole, Adam	RNS	83
Cole, Adonijah	ONN	144
Cole, Albertus	SRA	14
Cole, Alida	COL	182
Cole, Amasiah	OTS	44
Cole, Ambrose	WSH	303
Cole, Amos	CHN	800
Cole, Amos	ESS	309
Cole, Amosa	WSH	217
Cole, Andrew	GRN	335
Cole, Andrew	MNT	89
Cole, Andrew	WSH	186
Cole, Andries	COL	199
Cole, Ansel	TIO	226
Cole, Archibald	ONT	498
Cole, Asa	COL	212
Cole, Asa	OTS	54
Cole, Azor	OTS	12
Cole, Barnebass	WSH	220
Cole, Bathuel	ONN	161
Cole, Bela	OND	196
Cole, Benjamin	CAY	632
Cole, Benjamin	HRK	569
Cole, ..njamin	MNT	87
Cole, Benjamin	OND	203
Cole, Benjamin	ONT	364
Cole, Benjamin	ORN	323
Cole, Benjamin	RNS	100
Cole, Benjamin	RCH	92
Cole, Benjamin	SRA	28
Cole, Benjamin	SRA	55
Cole, Benjamin	WSH	293
Cole, Benjamin Junr	MNT	87
Cole, Berry	DUT	86
Cole, Catharine	RCH	95
Cole, Charles	OTS	54
Cole, Cornelius	RCH	94
Cole, Cornelius	TIO	209
Cole, Curtis	WSH	193
Cole, Cyrus	DUT	141
Cole, Daniel	DUT	96
Cole, Daniel	DUT	108
Cole, Daniel	TIO	209
Cole, David	CAY	554
Cole, David	CHN	840
Cole, David	DUT	153
Cole, David	GRN	345
Cole, David a Black	NYK	92
Cole, David	OTS	33
Cole, David	SRA	35
Cole, David	SUF	69
Cole, David	ULS	191
Cole, Ebenezer	DUT	79
Cole, Ebenezer	HRK	540
Cole, Ebenezer	HRK	576
Cole, Edmund	CAY	670
Cole, Eddy	MNT	84
Cole, Edward	WSH	193
Cole, Eleazer	DUT	86
Cole, Elias	DUT	153
Cole, Eliazer	ONT	414
Cole, Elijah	TIO	236
Cole, Elisha	DUT	86
Cole, Elisha Junr	DUT	86
Cole, Esau	HRK	551½
Cole, Ez[ra?]	ONT	474
Cole, Francis	WSH	248
Cole, Freegift	WSH	219
Cole, Gerrit	ALB	122
Cole, Gilbert	TIO	225
Cole, Hendrick	SRA	51
Cole, Henery	SRA	18
Cole, Henry	COL	237
Cole, Henry J.	COL	235
Cole, Ira	ALB	86
Cole, Isaac	ALB	85
Cole, Isaac	CLN	156
Cole, Isaac	CLN	159
Cole, Isaac	COL	235
Cole, Isaac	GRN	324
Cole, Isaac	MNT	87
Cole, Isaac	RCH	94
Cole, Isaac	RCH	94
Cole, Isaac	SRA	45
Cole, Isaac	SCH	129
Cole, Isaac Junr	COL	238
Cole, Jabez	ONN	153
Cole, Jacob	ALB	121
Cole, Jacob	CAY	650
Cole, Jacob	CAY	710
Cole, Jacob	COL	211
Cole, Jacob	DUT	156
Cole, Jacob	HRK	411
Cole, Jacob	MNT	87
Cole, Jacob	ORN	323
Cole, Jacob Junr	COL	211
Cole, Jacob S.	COL	234
Cole, James	GRN	330
Cole, James	OND	165
Cole, James	OND	213
Cole, James	ONT	488
Cole, James	OTS	2
Cole, James	OTS	54
Cole, James	RNS	24
Cole, James	RNS	55
Cole, James	SRA	59
Cole, James	SRA	60
Cole, James	TIO	236
Cole, Jane	NYK	77
Cole, Jeremiah	MNT	83
Cole, Jeremiah	ULS	263
Cole, Jeremiah	WSH	240
Cole, John	CAY	660
Cole, John	COL	199
Cole, John	DEL	273
Cole, John	DEL	289
Cole, John	DUT	72
Cole, John	DUT	89
Cole, John	DUT	153
Cole, John	DUT	157
Cole, John	HRK	537
Cole, John	HRK	576
Cole, John	KNG	8
Cole, John	MNT	15
Cole, John	MNT	21
Cole, John	ONN	146
Cole, John	ONT	340
Cole, John	ONT	458
Cole, John	ORN	354
Cole, John	OTS	12
Cole, John	OTS	52
Cole, John	RNS	7
Cole, John	RNS	112
Cole, John	RCH	89
Cole, John	RCH	94
Cole, John	RCK	103
Cole, John	SRA	53
Cole, John	SRA	53
Cole, John	SRA	58
Cole, John Junr	DEL	273
Cole, John Junr	DUT	86
Cole, John J.	RCK	108
Cole, John S.	COL	235
Cole, Jonathan	HRK	534
Cole, Joseph	CAY	630
Cole, Joseph	DUT	86
Cole, Joseph	HRK	551½
Cole, Joseph	NYK	94
Cole, Joseph	SRA	15
Cole, Joseph	SRA	53
Cole, Joseph Junr	DUT	86
Cole, Joseph S.	ONN	138
Cole, Joshua	DUT	90
Cole, Josias	ORN	316
Cole, Lambert	ALB	44
Cole, Leonard	STB	200
Cole, Levi	ESS	296
Cole, Levi	HRK	576
Cole, Levi	WSH	193
Cole, Lewis	ESS	304
Cole, Luther	ONN	188
Cole, Luther	ONT	428
Cole, Mary	COL	227
Cole, athew	ONT	472
Cole, Matthew	ONN	188
Cole, Morgan	NYK	88
Cole, Moses	CAY	544
Cole, Moses	CAY	670
Cole, Moses	COL	208
Cole, Moses	HRK	413
Cole, Myndert	SRA	4
Cole, Nathan	DEL	273
Cole, Nathan	DUT	90
Cole, Nathan	GRN	339
Cole, Nathan	HRK	544
Cole, Nathan	RNS	21
Cole, Nathan	SRA	29
Cole, Nathl	TIO	232
Cole, Nehemiah	OTS	54
Cole, Newman	CAY	670
Cole, Noah	OTS	57
Cole, Obadiah	DUT	89
Cole, Oliver	OTS	32
Cole, Pardon	RNS	18
Cole, Patience	RCH	88
Cole, Peleg	OTS	33
Cole, Peter	CAY	620
Cole, Peter	CHN	780
Cole, Peter	COL	260
Cole, Peter	DEL	273
Cole, Peter	DUT	5
Cole, Peter	DUT	153
Cole, Peter	NYK	31
Cole, Peter	NYK	56
Cole, Peter	NYK	62

Cole, Peter	ULS 192	Coleman, Ben. Junr	SUF 104	Coles, James	NYK 80
Cole, Peter	ULS 255	Coleman, Caleb	ORN 353	Coles, James	WST 166
Cole, Peter P.	DUT 153	Coleman, Calvin	RNS 106	Coles, Jarvis	QNS 83
Cole, Phenias	OTS 53	Coleman, Charles	DUT 125	Coles, Jesse	NYK 84
Cole, Philip	HRK 544	Coleman, Charles	NYK 130	Coles, Jesse	OND 176
Cole, Reuben	DUT 89	Coleman, Daniel	DEL 280	Coles, Job	OTS 11
Cole, Reuben	WSH 267	Coleman, David	ORN 336	Coles, John	NYK 125
Cole, Richard	RCH 89	Coleman, Dennis	ULS 250	Coles, John	OND 194
Cole, Robert	WSH 219	Coleman, Eli	OND 215	Coles, John	WST 121
Cole, Royal	OTS 44	Coleman, Elihu	COL 250	Coles, John B.	NYK 16
Cole, Rufus	ESS 296	Coleman, Elijah	ORN 353	Coles, Jordon	KNG 8
Cole, Russel	WSH 219	Coleman, George	ORN 389	Coles, Joseph	WST 120
Cole, S___	TIO 232	Coleman, Gideon	ORN 355	Coles, Joseph	WST 148
Cole, Samuel	COL 224	Coleman, Isaac	ORN 319	Coles, Nathaniel	QNS 84
Cole, Samuel	DUT 86	Coleman, Israel	ORN 336	Coles, Nathaniel Junr	QNS 84
Cole, Samuel	ESS 296	Coleman, Jesse	COL 182	Coles, Robert	ALB 68
Cole, Samuel	OND 210	Coleman, Jethro	DUT 125	Coles, Robert	NYK 125
Cole, Saml	OTS 54	Coleman, Joab	ORN 396	Coles, Robert	WST 150
Cole, Samuel	RNS 29	Coleman, Joel	ORN 350	Coles, Salmon	GRN 345
Cole, Samuel	TIO 217	Coleman, John	CHN 742	Coles, Samuel	OND 176
Cole, Samuel	WSH 209	Coleman, John	NYK 53	Coles, Samuel	STB 201
Cole, Seth	OND 196	Coleman, John	NYK 60	Coles, Stephen	NYK 62
Cole, Silus	CHN 782	Coleman, John	ORN 289	Coles, Thomas	QNS 67
Cole, Simeon	OND 191	Coleman, John	ORN 336	Coles, Willet	NYK 62
Cole, Simon S.	DUT 160	Coleman, John	OTS 14	Coles, Wright	QNS 84
Cole, Sisson	OTS 54	Coleman, John	RNS 106	Colester, Charles	OND 179
Cole, Solomon	DEL 280	Coleman, John	RNS 106	Coley, Daniel	TIO 257
Cole, Southard	ONT 446	Coleman, John	ULS 211	Colgrove, Andw	OTS 41
Cole, Spencer	HRK 576	Coleman, Jonathan	ORN 336	Colgrove, Asaph	OTS 54
Cole, Spencer	RNS 42	Coleman, Joseph	STB 205	Colgrove, Christopher	RNS 72
Cole, Stephen	RCH 88	Coleman, Martha	ORN 356	Colgrove, Major	OTS 36
Cole, Stephen	RCH 91	Coleman, Michael	ORN 275	Colgrove, Stephen	OTS 35
Cole, Subel	ALB 112	Coleman, Noah	OTS 18	Colier, Benjamine	GRN 345
Cole, Sylvester Ju.	ONT 364	Coleman, Otis	RNS 106	Colier, Cosper	GRN 350
Cole, Teunis	ALB 73	Coleman, Ozias	WSH 303	Colier, Derrick	GRN 332
Cole, Teunis J.	COL 237	Coleman, Ozias Jur	WSH 303	Colier, Jacob	MNT 49
Cole, Thomas	HRK 576	Coleman, Paul	COL 250	Colier, Joel	GRN 350
Cole, Thomas	RNS 7	Coleman, Peter	QNS 79	Colier, John	MNT 49
Cole, Thomas	WSH 265	Coleman, Richard	ORN 351	Colier, Tunis	GRN 351
Cole, Thomas Senior	ONT 340	Coleman, Rowland	RNS 105	Colken, Samuel	SRA 8
Cole, Tilniss	WSH 193	Coleman, Ruth	ORN 289	Colkin, Abraham	SRA 3
Cole, Tobias	GRN 356	Coleman, Samuel	ONN 145	Colkins, Asa	COL 189
Cole, Tom.	WST 144	Coleman, Samuel	ORN 276	Colkins, Daniel	SRA 10
Cole, Tyler	CAY 664	Coleman, Samuel	ORN 339	Colkins, Elijah	COL 186
Cole, Wheter	OTS 41	Coleman, Saml	OTS 14	Colkins, Joseph	SRA 10
Cole, Wilhelmas	ORN 316	Coleman, Samuel	RNS 106	Colkins, Nathan	ALB 24
Cole, William	CHN 828	Coleman, Silas	NYK 147	Colkins, Nathan H.	ALB 23
Cole, William	HRK 413	Coleman, Silas	ORN 283	Colkins, Phebe	COL 187
Cole, William	ONT 364	Coleman, Thadeus	COL 249	Coll, Silas	ESS 297
Cole, Wm	OTS 54	Coleman, Thomas	ORN 394	Collall, Ventura	NYK 84
Cole, William	RCH 88	Coleman, Timothy	ONN 135	Collar, Abraham	WSH 284
Cole, William	SRA 28	Coleman, William	NYK 28	Collar, Abraham	WSH 305
Cole, William	SRA 45	Coleman, William	ORN 275	Collar, Elisha	WSH 284
Cole, William	WSH 193	Coleman, William	ORN 335	Collar, Isaac	OTS 51
Cole, Wilson	WSH 216	Coleman, William ye 2d	ORN 335	Collar, Jacob	ONT 326
Cole, Zepheniah	ALB 81	Colen, A___ m	MNT 44	Collar, Jesse	ONT 322
Coleback, John J.	COL 241	Colen, Abr...m	MNT 48	Collar, Joseph	ONT 322
Coleburn, David	OTS 46	Colepaugh, Adam	DUT 151	Collar, Thomas	ONT 322
Coleburn, Edward	OTS 46	Colepaugh, Christian	DUT 150	Collard, Abraham	NYK 88
Coleburn, George	NYK 113	Coles, Abraham	QNS 82	Collard, Anna	NYK 71
Coleby, Abner	ESS 318	Coles, Albert	QNS 83	Collard, Isaac	NYK 68
Coleby, William	ONN 137	Coles, Andrew	NYK 84	Collard, James	WST 132
Colegrove, Asa	WSH 197	Coles, Ann	QNS 83	Collard, Mary	NYK 92
Colegrove, Ely	CHN 924	Coles, Barrek	QNS 83	Collard, Thomas	ORN 338
Colegrove, James	DUT 47	Coles, Benjamin	QNS 83	Collegrove, Frances	NYK 147
Colegrove, John	DUT 74	Coles, Benjamin	QNS 83	Collemer, Thomas	SRA 16
Colegrove, John	WST 122	Coles, Benjamin	SUF 86	Collenbergh, George	ALB 106
Colegrove, Silas	SCH 158	Coles, Caleb	QNS 84	Collens, Hezekiah	CHN 832
Colegrove, William	DUT 80	Coles, Caleb	WST 84	Collens, Mikel	OND 222
Colegrove, William Junr	DUT 80	Coles, Christopher	WST 162	Coller, Isaac	DUT 45
Colehamer, Anthony	RNS 89	Coles, Daniel	QNS 84	Coller, Norris	DUT 45
Coleman, ...	QNS 84	Coles, Daniel	QNS 84	Colles, John	WSH 241
Coleman, Abner	ORN 353	Coles, David	SUF 69	Colles, John Jur	WSH 241
Coleman, Absalom	CAY 602	Coles, Gideon	OND 194	Colles, Richard	NYK 111
Coleman, Asahel	ORN 352	Coles, Hank	CHN 856	Collester, James	CHN 892
Coleman, Benjamin	ORN 348	Coles, Isaac	QNS 83	Collet, Charles	NYK 41
Coleman, Benjamin	SUF 104	Coles, Jacob	QNS 84	Collett, John	NYK 81

Colley, Alexander	NYK 74	Collins, Joshua	DUT 122	Colter, Jane	NYK 101
Colley, Elizabeth	CAY 558	Collins, Julias	ALB 23	Colter, John	NYK 100
Collier, Abraham	NYK 124	Collins, Keeder	OTS 25	Colter, Mark	NYK 16
Collier, Charles	SUF 79	Collins, Keziah	NYK 128	Colteral, Samuel	NYK 17
Collier, Frederick	NYK 119	Collins, Laurence	NYK 113	Coltes, James	NYK 102
Collier, George	ALB 44	Collins, Mark	NYK 27	Colton see Cotton	
Collier, George	ALB 46	Collins, Matthew	DUT 8	Colton, Aaron	WSH 302
Collier, Isaac	OTS 27	Collins, Nathan	COL 225	Colton, Eli	OTS 33
Collier, Jacob	QNS 60	Collins, Nathaniel	CHN 844	Colton, John	OTS 33
Collier, James	NYK 127	Collins, Nathaniel	ESS 305	Colton, John Junr	OTS 33
Collier, Jerh	OTS 27	Collins, Nathen	WSH 192	Colton, Jonathan	OTS 23
Collier, John	QNS 62	Collins, Normor	GRN 337	Colton, Joseph	ONN 148
Collier, Joseph	CHN 792	Collins, Oliver	OND 168	Colton, Joseph	WSH 266
Collier, Mathew	NYK 140	Collins, Oliver	OND 184	Colton, Nathan	WSH 304
Collier, Noah	DEL 282	Collins, Patrick B.	DUT 157	Colton, Quartus	OTS 33
Collier, Theodorus	QNS 60	Collins, Pitman	SRA 22	Colton, Reuben	WSH 276
Collier, William	OTS 27	Collins, Raney	WSH 271	Colton, Rowland	ONT 352
Collin, David	COL 178	Collins, Samuel	ALB 23	Colton, Walter	ONN 148
Collin, John	SRA 36	Collins, Samuel	NYK 114	Colver, Asa	ALB 82
Collin, Joseph	NYK 139	Collins, Samuel	NYK 153	Colvil, Wm	MNT 59
Collin, Thomas	SRA 29	Collins, Samuel	OND 173	Colvill, Anna	NYK 133
Collings, Gamaliel	OTS 55	Collins, Samuel	WSH 194	Colvill, James	ALB 116
Collins, Aaron	DEL 269	Collins, Stephen	CHN 784	Colvill, John	NYK 35
Collins, Abraham	CLN 164	Collins, Stephen	CHN 826	Colvin, Benjamin	WSH 190
Collins, Abraham	CLN 166	Collins, Thadeus	ONT 480	Colvin, Caleb	HRK 560
Collins, Abm	RNS 34	Collins, Thomas	CAY 724	Colvin, John	ALB 119
Collins, Abraham	RNS 88	Collins, Thomas	NYK 32	Colvin, Joseph	OTS 29
Collins, Amos	WSH 288	Collins, Thomas	WSH 222	Colvin, Joshua	OTS 30
Collins, Andrew	ESS 304	Collins, W. John	OND 202	Colvin, Josiah	SCH 158
Collins, Benjamin	CAY 584	Collins, Willeam	WSH 281	Colvin, Obadiah	WSH 191
Collins, Benjamin	CAY 696	Collins, William	ALB 92	Colvin, Obadiah	WSH 217
Collins, Benjamin	OTS 46	Collins, William	CHN 806	Colvin, Oliver	WSH 217
Collins, Benjamin	WSH 194	Collins, Wm	MNT 83	Colvin, Peleg	ESS 309
Collins, Benjamin	WSH 303	Collins, William	NYK 17	Colvin, William	WSH 217
Collins, Bersheba	SUF 102	Collins, William	NYK 25	Colwell, David	WST 136
Collins, Caleb	WSH 184	Collins, William	NYK 31	Colwell, Isaac	NYK 74
Collins, Catherin	NYK 78	Collins, William	NYK 102	Colwell, Jacob	NYK 122
Collins, Charles	CLN 163	Collins, Wm	OTS 46	Colwell, James	NYK 15
Collins, Charles	HRK 576	Collins, William	RNS 6	Colyer, Charles	KNG 11
Collins, Christopher	ESS 304	Collins, William	SRA 58	Colyer, Jacobus	KNG 11
Collins, Cornelius	SCH 162	Collis, Barry	NYK 72	Colyer, John	GRN 348
Collins, Cornelius	SCH 170	Collis, Benjn	OTS 32	Colyer, Peter	KNG 7
Collins, Cyprian	ONT 384	Collis, George	NYK 71	Colyer, Peter	KNG 11
Collins, Daniel	ESS 304	Collis, John	OTS 53	Coman, Isaac	WSH 228
Collins, Daniel a Black	NYK 146	Collis, Thustin	WSH 249	Coman, Nathen	WSH 228
Collins, David	DUT 136	Collison, Francis	RNS 86	Comar, Benjamin	DUT 127
Collins, David	OTS 46	Collister, Thomas	NYK 37	Comb, John	DEL 282
Collins, Edward Jun	GRN 351	Collock, William	NYK 137	Comb, Timothy	CAY 524
Collins, Elisabeth	CHN 762	Collogon, Patrick	SRA 25	Combs see Conbs	
Collins, Elizabeth	COL 251	Collord, Thomas	NYK 44	Combs, Alexander	NYK 107
Collins, Enos	STB 203	Collow, James	NYK 51	Combs, Cage	QNS 76
Collins, George	HRK 587	Collum, Jehoida	ULS 262	Combs, David	SUF 65
Collins, George	NYK 49	Colly, Sophia	ORN 295	Combs, Elexander	QNS 73
Collins, Giles	SRA 56	Colman, Elehu	MNT 81	Combs, George	WST 162
Collins, Harriot	NYK 134	Colman, John	MNT 124	Combs, Henry	QNS 76
Collins, Hezekiah	DUT 9	Colon, David	NYK 37	Combs, James	ALB 27
Collins, Hezekiah	ONT 334	Colon, John	NYK 108	Combs, James	NYK 127
Collins, Isaac	CLN 166	Colon, Margaret	NYK 67	Combs, John	ALB 21
Collins, Isaac	NYK 29	Colong, George	RCH 91	Combs, John	ALB 57
Collins, Jacob	NYK 153	Colong, James	RCH 92	Combs, John a Black	NYK 153
Collins, James a Black	NYK 146	Colony, Benjamin	MNT 34	Combs, John	OND 219
Collins, John	CAY 584	Colony, Henry	WSH 273	Combs, John	SCH 146
Collins, John	CHN 826	Colony, Isaaa	SRA 36	Combs, John	SUF 83
Collins, John	CHN 846	Colony, Jacob	MNT 88	Combs, Lawrence	QNS 74
Collins, John	COL 178	Colpays, Eliza	NYK 21	Combs, Nathaniel	QNS 76
Collins, hn	COL 178	Colsen, Abijah	CHN 916	Combs, Noah	CAY 518
Collins, John	NYK 135	Colson, Joseph	WSH 88	Combs, Noxh	QNS 76
Collins, John	NYK 136	Colson, Joseph Junr	GRN 332	Combs, Peter	OTS 58
Collins, John	SRA 59	Colson, Peter	ALB 41	Combs, Phebe	QNS 78
Collins, John	STB 203	Colsten, Abijah	CHN 912	Combs, Reuben	WSH 204
Collins, John	WSH 210	Colt, Jabez	OND 182	Combs, Samuel	ALB 91B
Collins, John	WSH 221	Colt, Joseph	ONT 508	Combs, Solomon	OND 219
Collins, John Junr	COL 177	Colt, Peter	OND 216	Combs, Solomon	WST 138
Collins, Jonathan	OND 221	Colt, Peter	QNS 78	Combs, Thomas	ALB 25
Collins, Joseph	CHN 806	Colt, Theod_rus	MNT 35	Combs, Thomas	CAY 528
Collins, Joseph	ONN 152	Colten, Edward B.	CHN 888	Combs, Thomas	QNS 76
Collins, Joseph	WSH 184	Colter, James	ORN 283	Combs, William	QNS 73
Collins, Joseph	WSH 199				

Comel, James	WSH 248	Comstock, H_man	OTS 12	Conckright, Mary	COL 255
Comel, Samuel	OTS 34	Comstock, Israel	OTS 57	Conclin, Isaac	ONN 140
Comer, Abraham	COL 244	Comstock, Jeremiah	RNS 82	Conda, Jesse	SRA 23
Comer, John	COL 242	Comstock, John	RNS 17	Conda, John	SRA 23
Comes, Ebenezer	HRK 528	Comstock, John	SRA 56	Condell, Benoni	HRK 476
Comestock, Ebenezer	COL 248	Comstock, Joshua	WSH 264	Condell, Biddy Lynch	NYK 72
Comestock, Thomas	COL 248	Comstock, Luther	OTS 10	Condey, Adam	ALB 22
Comfort, Benjamin	ORN 301	Comstock, Matthew	DUT 101	Condey, Albert	ALB 25
Comfort, Benjamin	ULS 188	Comstock, Nathan	SRA 28	Condey, Peter	ALB 22
Comfort, Daniel	ORN 301	Comstock, Phelix	CHN 790	Condfield, Caleb	MNT 116
Comfort, Edward	ORN 314	Comstock, Roswell	WSH 272	Condfield, Samuel	MNT 116
Comfort, Jacob	ORN 314	Comstock, Russel	DEL 273	Condict, Moses	ORN 356
Comfort, John	ORN 274	Comstock, Samuel	ONT 410	Condit, Samuel	COL 246
Comfort, John	ORN 301	Comstock, Samuel	WSH 300	Condit, Sophia	NYK 146
Comfort, John	ORN 314	Comstock, Solomon	OTS 10	Cone, Adam	ONN 193
Comfort, Joshua	ORN 298	Comstock, Solomon	OTS 39	Cone, Benjaman	CHN 824
Comfort, Richard	ORN 314	Comstock, Stephen	SRA 45	Cone, Calvin	ULS 207
Comfort, Samuel	ORN 387	Comstock, Stephen Junr	SRA 46	Cone, Eleazer	WSH 302
Comfort, Thomas	ULS 258	Comstock, Theophilus	RNS 17	Cone, Elihu	OTS 56
Comfort, William	ORN 298	Comstock, William	HRK 562	Cone, Elijah	OTS 30
Comin, Henry	CLN 168	Comstock, Wm	OTS 43	Cone, Elisher	OND 221
Comins, Abel	HRK 498	Comstock, William	SRA 11	Cone, Ephraim	OND 178
Comins, Benjamin	HRK 523	Comstock, William	SRA 60	Cone, George	CHN 924
Comins, Charles	HRK 521	Comstock, Zachariah	ESS 321	Cone, Gurdon	OND 175
Comins, James	HRK 521	Conant, Archibald	HRK 442	Cone, Hall	CHN 792
Comins, James Junr	HRK 521	Conant, Daniel	HRK 442	Cone, Hez.	CHN 924
Comins, Jennings	HRK 597	Conant, Ebenezer	HRK 540	Cone, Hosea	ONT 446
Comins, Jonathan	HRK 597	Conant, Gurdon	HRK 487	Cone, Ichabod	GRN 330
Comins, Jonathan Junr	HRK 597	Conant, John	CAY 606	Cone, Ira	OTS 30
Comins, John	HRK 520	Conant, Robert	HRK 522	Cone, Joseph	CAY 624
Comins, Thomas	HRK 446	Conant, Samuel	HRK 570	Cone, Joseph O.	OTS 31
Commandigne, Lodevick	NYK 134	Conant, Timothy	ALB 30	Cone, Oliver	OND 164
Commandinger, Lewis	NYK 125	Conant, Timothy	HRK 484	Cone, Ozias	OND 178
Commeran, Thomas a		Conbs, John	MNT 114	Cone, Samuel	OND 173
Black	NYK 141	Concklin, Abrm	RCK 105	Cone, Samuel C.	OND 174
Commings, Stephen	OND 209	Concklin, Amos	RCK 104	Cone, Stephen	DUT 51
Commins, Francis	RNS 18	Concklin, Cornelius	COL 233	Cone, Walter	OND 174
Commins, Wm	GRN 346	Concklin, Deliverance	COL 196	Coneey, Elijah	WSH 194
Commodore, John free		Concklin, Edward	RCK 99	Conel, Catherine	NYK 60
Negro	RNS 80	Concklin, Ezekiel	RCK 99	Conell, Mary	NYK 124
Compson, Edward	CAY 700	Concklin, Gabriel	RCK 104	Conent, Sylvanus	ONT 354
Compstock, Allen	CAY 722	Concklin, Gabriel	RCK 109	Conent, Timothy	ONT 352
Compstock, Darius	ONT 352	Concklin, Hannah	RCK 100	Conett, Josiah	COL 217
Compstock, Ebenezer	ALB 28	Concklin, Hannah	RCK 109	Coneway, Francis	TIO 257
Compstock, Hillius	ONT 456	Concklin, Isaac	NYK 60	Coney, Daniel	ONN 159
Compstock, Nathan	ONT 352	Concklin, Isaac	RCK 108	Coney, Elijah	ONN 159
Compstock, Nathan	ONT 438	Concklin, Jacob	COL 230	Coney, John	ULS 186
Compstock, Otis	ONT 438	Concklin, Jacob	RCK 110	Coney, Joseph	ONN 159
Compstock, Rufus	ALB 100	Concklin, James	COL 233	Coney, Wm	MNT 5
Compton, Andrew	TIO 240	Concklin, James	RCK 99	Congar, David	ORN 286
Compton, David	TIO 223	Concklin, James	RCK 101	Congdell, Robert	RNS 9
Compton, Ebenezer	NYK 117	Concklin, James	RCK 107	Congden, Charles	OND 198
Compton, Fran	ORN 384	Concklin, James	RCK 109	Congden, Ephraim	OND 197
Compton, Jacob	CHN 844	Concklin, John	COL 200	Congden, James	OND 203
Compton, Jacob	ORN 387	Concklin, John	COL 227	Congden, Jonathan	OND 202
Compton, James	DEL 278	Concklin, John	RCK 97	Congden, Joseph	OND 166
Compton, John	DEL 278	Concklin, John	RCK 99	Congden, Stephen	WSH 235
Compton, John	DUT 34	Concklin, John	RCK 106	Congden, Stuteley	OND 158
Compton, John Junr	DEL 278	Concklin, John Junr	RCK 106	Congdin, Gardner	CAY 664
Compton, Joseph	TIO 225	Concklin, Joseph	RCK 104	Congdon, Benjamin	DUT 148
Compton, Vincent	ORN 385	Concklin, Joseph	RCK 105	Congdon, Ephraim	DUT 107
Compton, William	ORN 349	Concklin, Joseph	RCK 106	Congdon, James	DUT 8
Compton, Wm	OTS 10	Concklin, Lewis	RCK 106	Congdon, John	DUT 136
Compton, William Junr	ORN 382	Concklin, Laverence	RCK 102	Congdon, John	WSH 266
Comstock, Aaron	SRA 11	Concklin, Mary	COL 234	Congdon, John	WSH 298
Comstock, Aaron	SRA 60	Concklin, Minardt	RCK 109	Congdon, Joseph	SUF 105
Comstock, Abner	COL 181	Concklin, Nicholas	RCK 105	Congdon, Joseph	WSH 265
Comstock, Adam	SRA 55	Concklin, Nicholas	RCK 109	Congdon, Nicholas	HRK 590
Comstock, Benajah	OTS 13	Concklin, Nic. Junr	RCK 105	Congdon, William	DUT 107
Comstock, Caleb	SRA 38	Concklin, Nicholas W.	RCK 109	Conger, Azeriah	WSH 192
Comstock, Daniel	MNT 32	Concklin, Silas	OTS 57	Conger, Elizabeth	NYK 20
Comstock, Daniel	RNS 24	Concklin, Thos	RCK 109	Conger, Hoziah	ALB 80
Comstock, Danl	SUF 68	Concklin, Wm	RCK 99	Conger, Jacob	CAY 594
Comstock, Daniel	WSH 264	Concklin, Wm	RCK 104	Conger, James	ALB 76
Comstock, David	CAY 720	Concklin, Wm	RCK 107	Conger, John	ORN 293
Comstock, David	RNS 71	Concklin, Wm N.	RCK 104	Conger, Joseph	COL 242
Comstock, Elisha	ORN 311	Conckln, Bridgett	COL 235	Conger, Mary	WSH 192

Name	Ref	Name	Ref	Name	Ref
Conger, Samuel	ONT 446	Conklin, Jeremiah Junr	DUT 140	Conkline, Burnett	SUF 108
Conger, Stephen	ALB 42	Conklin, John	ALB 29	Conkline, Carpenter	RNS 57
Conger, William	ALB 74	Conklin, John	ALB 72	Conkline, David	SUF 83
Congross, Jacob	MNT 40	Conklin, John	ALB 96	Conkline, David	SUF 108
C[ongross?], Jacob Junr	MNT 41	Conklin, John	CAY 592	Conkline, Davis	SUF 108
Congson, David	CLN 161	Conklin, John	CAY 678	Conkline, Edward	SUF 106
Congton, Henry	MNT 16	Conklin, John	DUT 116	Conkline, Elisha	SUF 107
Conick, Jonathan	RNS 64	Conklin, John	NYK 85	Conkline, Epinetus	SUF 85
Conies, James	ALB 91	Conklin, John	ORN 358	Conkline, Ezekiel	SUF 87
Conine, Casparus	COL 196	Conklin, John	ORN 364	Conkline, Ezra	SUF 86
Conine, Jane	COL 196	Conklin, John	ORN 387	Conkline, Gamaleel	SUF 92
Conine, Peter	MNT 65	Conklin, John	ULS 215	Conkline, Gilbert	RNS 57
Conine, Peter	RNS 64	Conklin, John	ULS 253	Conkline, Hall	SUF 81
Conker, Peter	RNS 11	Conklin, John	WST 166	Conkline, Henry	SUF 108
Conkey, John	WSH 222	Conklin, John I.	DUT 116	Conkline, Henry	SUF 108
Conkey, Joshua	WSH 227	Conklin, Josep	GRN 345	Conkline, Hubbard	SUF 86
Conkey, Richard	WSH 227	Conklin, Joseph	NYK 90	Conkline, Isaac	SUF 80
Conkey, Siles	WSH 249	Conklin, Joseph	ORN 295	Conkline, Isaac	SUF 108
Conkhite, James	WSH 249	Conklin, Joseph	ORN 355	Conkline, Israel	SUF 80
Conkins, Hezekiah	SCH 160	Conklin, Joseph Junr	ORN 360	Conkline, Israel	SUF 96
Conklin, Abijal	SRA 8	Conklin, Joseph L.	ORN 353	Conkline, Jacob	SUF 80
Conklin, Abraham	CAY 602	Conklin, Joshua	NYK 98	Conkline, Jacob Senr	SUF 80
Conklin, Abm	HRK 443	Conklin, Joshua	SRA 5	Conkline, Jedediah	SUF 108
Conklin, Abraham	ORN 348	Conklin, Josiah	ALB 82	Conkline, Jeremiah	SUF 106
Conklin, Abrm	RCK 99	Conklin, Lemuel & Benj	DUT 122	Conkline, Jeremiah	SUF 108
Conklin, Absolam	ULS 180	Conklin, Lewis	NYK 90	Conkline, Jessee	SUF 81
Conklin, Ananias	ORN 336	Conklin, Liwes	SRA 14	Conkline, Jessee	SUF 91
Conklin, Anthony	NYK 91	Conklin, Luther	OND 211	Conkline, John	RNS 37
Conklin, Bathuel	NYK 95	Conklin, Mary	DUT 37	Conkline, John	SUF 80
Conklin, Benjn & Lemuel	DUT 122	Conklin, Mary	DUT 82	Conkline, John	SUF 86
Conklin, Benjamin	ORN 361	Conklin, Mary	NYK 95	Conkline, John	SUF 104
Conklin, Benjamin Junr	ORN 361	Conklin, Mathias	NYK 53	Conkline, Jonathan	SUF 102
Conklin, Daniel	ALB 82	Conklin, Matthias	WST 162	Conkline, Jonathan S.	SUF 106
Conklin, Daniel	DUT 80	Conklin, Michael	CAY 544	Conkline, Lyneas	SUF 108
Conklin, Daniel	NYK 16	Conklin, Nathan	DUT 85	Conkline, Martha	SUF 87
Conklin, DAniel	ORN 362	Conklin, Nathan	DUT 140	Conkline, Nathan	SUF 86
Conklin, Daniel Junr	ALB 82	Conklin, Nathaniel	DUT 81	Conkline, Nathaniel	SUF 94
Conklin, David	DUT 141	Conklin, Nathaniel	ORN 361	Conkline, Philip	SUF 87
Conklin, David	NYK 15	Conklin, Nathaniel Junr	ORN 361	Conkline, Richard	SUF 87
Conklin, David	ORN 397	Conklin, Nicholas	NYK 134	Conkline, Richard	SUF 87
Conklin, David	WSH 217	Conklin, Nicholas	ULS 181	Conkline, Samuel	SUF 87
Conklin, David Junr	ORN 397	Conklin, Peter	ORN 384	Conkline, Saml	SUF 90
Conklin, Edmund	ORN 271	Conklin, Philip	NYK 91	Conkli_, Saml	SUF 108
Conklin, Egons	GRN 355	Conklin, Rebecca	SRA 9	Conkline, Shadrick	SUF 105
Conklin, Eleazer	DEL 276	Conklin, Richard	CAY 682	Conkline, Stephen	SUF 106
Conklin, Eleazer	DUT 142	Conklin, Samuel	DUT 87	Conkline, Strong	SUF 86
Conklin, Elias	MNT 30	Conklin, Samuel	NYK 141	Conkline, Timothy	SUF 87
Conklin, Elias	ORN 385	Conklin, Samuel	ORN 333	Conkline, Zebulon	SUF 108
Conklin, Elias	ULS 181	Conklin, Samuel	ORN 385	Conkling, Abigail	WST 152
Conklin, Elijah	WST 162	Conklin, Sarah	ALB 72	Conkling, Cornelus	SUF 66
Conklin, Elkanah	NYK 83	Conklin, Sarah	ORN 353	Conkling, David	SUF 73
Conklin, Ephraim	QNS 72	Conklin, Simon	MNT 29	Conkling, David	WST 155
Conklin, Ephraim	QNS 75	Conklin, Stephen	SCH 123	Conkling, Drake	WST 127
Conklin, Ezra	SRA 13	Conklin, Thomas	ALB 13	Conkling, Ebenezer	WST 134
Conklin, Georte	NYK 89	Conklin, Thomas	ALB 106	Conkling, Edmund	ALB 91B
Conklin, Henry	ALB 82	Conklin, Thomas	MNT 43	Conkling, Eleanor W.	WST 160
Conklin, Henry	GRN 356	Conklin, Thomas	ORN 389	Conkling, Francis	WST 160
Conklin, Isaac	CAY 678	Conklin, Thomas	SRA 9	Conkling, .saac	MNT 86
Conklin, Isaac	DEL 286	Conklin, Timothy	DUT 99	Conkling, Isaac	WST 153
Conklin, Isaac	DUT 110	Conklin, Timothy	DUT 118	Conkling, Jacob	WST 154
Conklin, Isaac	ORN 397	Conklin, Titus	NYK 74	Conkling, James	SUF 65
Conklin, Isaac	WST 166	Conklin, Toll	QNS 80	Conkling, James	WST 156
Conklin, Jacob	ALB 31	Conklin, William	ALB 28	Conkling, Joel	KNG 8
Conklin, Jacob	CAY 678	Conklin, William	ORN 270	Conkling, John	SUF 72
Conklin, Jacob	MNT 29	Conklin, William	ORN 389	Conkling, John	WST 123
Conklin, Jacob	NYK 34	Conklin, William	ULS 181	Conkling, John	WST 123
Conklin, Jacob	QNS 81	Conklin, William	ULS 193	Conkling, John	WST 127
Conklin, Jacob	WST 166	Conklin, Zedekiah	DUT 87	Conkling, John Nursery	
Conklin, Jafit	GRN 354	Conkline, Abel	SUF 86	Conkling, Jonathan	SUF 76
Conklin, Jame	NYK 68	Conkline, Abiel	SUF 87	Conkling, Jonathan	WST 126
Conklin, James	DUT 33	Conkline, Abm	RNS 57	Conkling, Joseph	KNG 8
Conklin, James	DUT 107	Conkline, Abm Junr	RNS 57	Conkling, Joseph	WST 122
Conklin, James	SRA 7	Conkline, Alexander	SUF 82	Conkling, Joseph	WST 152
Conklin, Jeremeah	WSH 300	Conkline, Annanias	SUF 86	Conkling, Judah	SUF 76
Conklin, Jeremiah	DUT 82	Conkline, Benjamin	SUF 108	Conkling, Lewis	SUF 74
Conklin, Jeremiah	DUT 140	Conkline, Ben_ Jun	SUF 105	Conkling, Nancey	WST 153
				Conkling, Samuel	ONN 157

Name	Co.	Pg.
Conkling, Stoddard	TIO	259
Conkling, Thos	SUF	76
Conkling, Thos	SUF	76
Conkling, Timothy	WST	155
Conkling, William	WST	153
Conkling, Zefeniah	SUF	65
Conkright, Casps	ALB	120
Conkright, Gilbert	ALB	120
Conkright, Simon	ALB	92
Conkright, Dan.	SRA	60
Conktright, Peter	ALB	131
Conley, Catharine	KNG	8
Conley, Fraderick	SRA	43
Conllins, Edward	GRN	351
Conllins, Enos	GRN	351
Conllins, Israel	GRN	351
Co[nn?], John	CHN	990
Connald, Peter	WST	116
Connallee, James	WSH	251
Connard, Nicholas	NYK	84
Connee, Martin	SRA	44
Connel, Alexander	WST	117
Connel, Isaac C.	SRA	7
Connel, John C.	SRA	7
Connell, Christopher	WSH	199
Connell, John	NYK	79
Connell, John	RNS	94
Connelly, James	NYK	49
Connelly, Partrick	NYK	110
Connely, Abraham	NYK	131
Connely, Jeremiah	NYK	75
Connely, John	NYK	74
Connely, William	NYK	74
Conner, Adriana	ALB	5
Conner, Cliff a Black	NYK	79
Conner, Daniel	ALB	44
Conner, Edward	ONN	193
Conner, Francis	DEL	286
Conner, Ira	ESS	323
Conner, James	COL	186
Conner, John	COL	186
Conner, John	GRN	325
Conner, John	SRA	3
Conner, John	WSH	228
Conner, Mary	NYK	67
Conner, Nicholas	NYK	41
Conner, Richard a mulatto	NYK	84
Conner, Richard	RCH	93
Conner, Richard	WST	111
Conner, Sarah	ALB	141
Conner, Sarah	COL	186
Conner, Timothy	WSH	290
Conner, Wm	ONN	151
Conner, Wm	ONN	152
Conner, William	WSH	228
Connerley, John	GRN	354
Connet, Anthony	WSH	249
Conney, William	MNT	16
Connike, John	OTS	18
Connike, Wm	OTS	18
Conning, William	ORN	346
Connolly, Martin	ORN	388
Connolly, Michael	DUT	148
Connolly, Richard	DUT	148
Connolly, Robert	NYK	139
Connolly, Tully	NYK	109
Connoly, Patrick	MNT	112
Connor, Aaron a mulatto	NYK	35
Connor, Charles	CAY	724
Connor, Charles	DUT	17
Connor, Dennis	NYK	104
Connor, Henry	ULS	200
Connor, Jacobus	ULS	200
Connor, James	DUT	17
Connor, Jane	NYK	120
Connor, Jeremiah	NYK	121
Connor, John	DUT	109
Connor, John	NYK	55
Connor, John	ORN	355
Connor, John	ULS	193
Connor, John	ULS	200
Connor, Joseph	ORN	340
Connor, Joseph ye 2d	ORN	343
Connor, Lawrence	DUT	13
Connor, Michael	ORN	331
Connor, Michael	ORN	383
Connor, Robert	ORN	344
Connor, Thomas	DUT	17
Connor, William	ORN	343
Connoss, Daniel	NYK	138
Connoyne, Derrick	GRN	357
Connoyne, Jeremiah	GRN	356
Connoyne, John	GRN	332
Connoyne, John C.	GRN	332
Connoyne, Peter	GRN	356
Connoyne, Peter G.	GRN	356
Connoyne, Phillip	GRN	350
Connoyne, Phillip	GRN	357
Connoyne, Phillip Jun	GRN	358
Conoley, Daniel	SRA	47
Conolly, John	HRK	408
Conover, James	NYK	16
Conover, Suzannah	NYK	44
Conoyne, Jesper	GRN	335
Conoyne, Leoynard Z.	GRN	358
Conrad, John	ONN	170
Conrad, John	SCH	168
Conrad, Nicholas	NYK	138
Con.adt, Henry	MNT	75
Conradt, Henry	OTS	15
Conradt, Nichs	OTS	15
Conradts, Azubah	OTS	3
Conradts, Joseph	OTS	3
Conraw, Peter	NYK	63
Conray, Jonathan	NYK	71
Conray, Thomas	NYK	88
Conray, William	NYK	15
Conrey, Thomas	NYK	91
Conrodt, Shalhanmer	MNT	115
Conroe, William	COL	236
Conroed, William	NYK	120
Conroy, John	NYK	54
Conruth, Peter	NYK	135
Consaul, John	DEL	280
Conselyee, Andrew	KNG	11
Conselyee, Ann	KNG	10
Conselyee, John	KNG	10
Conselyee, William	KNG	11
Conshaft, Michael	NYK	134
Consollus, John	ALB	54
Consolus, David	ALB	7
Consolus, Herms	ALB	13
Consolus, Peter	ALB	19
Constable, Elizabeth	ORN	307
Constable, Garret	ULS	209
Constable, James	NYK	32
Constable, Jane	NYK	27
Constable, John	ULS	198
Constable, John	ULS	254
Constable, Joseph	MNT	42
Constable, William	NYK	152
Constable, Wm	OTS	27
Constant, St. John	WST	153
Constant, Silas	WST	126
Constantine, Margaret	NYK	19
Constantinople, Michael	SRA	11
Constene, Daniel	CHN	934
Content, Henry	ULS	202
Content, Jacob	ULS	207
Content, Peter	ULS	259
Content, Samuel	ULS	207
Content, William	ULS	243
Content, Zachariah	ULS	257
Conterman, Abrahan	MNT	35
Conterman, Adam M.	MNT	27
Conterman, George	MNT	27
Conterman, George	MNT	28
Conterman, Jacob	MNT	27
Conterman, John A.	MNT	27
Conterman, John C.	MNT	35
Conterman, Joh M.(?)	MNT	33
Conterman, Nicholas	MNT	35
Contoct, John H.	NYK	20
Contreman, Conradt M.	MNT	24
Convass, Jesse	RNS	100
Converce, Isaac	WSH	286
Converse, David	OND	203
Converse, David Junr	OND	203
Converse, Joshua	DUT	52
Conver__, Mary	WSH	277
Converse, Samuel	CHN	806
Converse, Theron	OND	205
Converse, Thomas	OND	205
Converse, Willet	OND	203
Converse, William R.	CLN	170
Conway, Cornelius	ULS	209
Conway, Fraderic	OND	209
Conway, James	NYK	74
Conway, John	SCH	129
Conway, John	WSH	292
Conway, Michael	CLN	159
Conway, William	NYK	37
Conway, William	WSH	246
Conway, William	WSH	292
Conwey, William	WSH	225
Conyers, Frederick	ULS	224
Conyers, Jacob	ULS	220
Conyngham, Elisha	OTS	25
Conyngham, Grove	DUT	95
Conyngham, Thos	OTS	32
Conynham, Laten	OTS	26
Conynham, Wm	OTS	26
Coo, Elizabeth	NYK	41
Cooch, Abraham	KNG	10
Coock, Jacob	CHN	862
Coock, Stephen	SRA	53
Cook, Abiel	RNS	113
Cook, Abner	OTS	58
Cook, Abraham	DUT	54
Cook, Alexander	DUT	56
Cook, Amasa	WSH	275
Cook, Amos	GRN	339
Cook, Asher	SRA	26
Cook, Assaph	WSH	276
Cook, Assher	NYK	16
Cook, Beadus	MNT	10
Cook, Benjn	OTS	38
Cook, Benjamin	RNS	33
Cook, Benjamin	WSH	198
Cook, Bennit	ALB	71
Cook, Brasilla	RNS	33
Cook, Brian	SCH	150
Cook, Bryan	SCH	168
Cook, Caleb	GRN	346
Cook, Caleb	WSH	204
Cook, Calvin	SUF	71
Cook, Case	OND	190
Cook, Casper	MNT	7
Cook, Cester	WSH	218
Cook, Charles	OTS	6
Cook, Charles	WSH	272
Cook, Charles Junr	OTS	6
Cook, Comfort	OTS	12
Cook, Daniel	MNT	116
Cook, Daniel	OND	189
Cook, Daniel	SUF	95
Cook, Daniel	WSH	216
Cook, Daniel	WSH	218
Cook, Darius	DUT	57
Cook, David	CHN	950

Name		Name		Name		Name	
Cook, David	NYK 123	Cook, Joshua	ALB 107	Cook, Widow	OTS 36	Cook, Joseph R.	OTS 57
Cook, David	ONT 476	Cook, Joshua	SCH 168	Cook, Widow	SUF 107		
Cook, David	ORN 293	Cook, Leonard	WSH 237	Cook, William	DEL 275		
Cook, David	RNS 62	Cook, Levy	STB 200	Cook, William	ONN 144		
Cook, David	STB 200	Cook, Lewis	CHN 954	Cook, William	ONT 344		
Cook, David	SUF 101	Cook, Lyman	CHN 858	Cook, William	ORN 353		
Cook, David	WSH 204	Cook, Mary	DUT 54	Cook, Wm	OTS 19		
Cook, David	WSH 237	Cook, Mary	ONT 312	Cook, Wm	TIO 216		
Cook, David Junior	STB 200	Cook, Memnon	SRA 48	Cook, William D.	GRN 342		
Cook, Dick	RCK 107	Cook, Michael	ALB 33	Cook, Worthy	ONN 131		
Cook, Ebenezr	TIO 247	Cook, Miles	SCH 146	Cook, Zacheus	COL 263		
Cook, Edward	WSH 194	Cook, Mr	GRN 346	Cook, Zebula F.	OTS 10		
Cook, Elias	OTS 23	Cook, Moses	WSH 221	Cooke, Adam	COL 253		
Cook, Elihu	OND 189	Cook, Moses B.	TIO 225	Cooke, David	ONT 508		
Cook, Elijah	CHN 794	Cook, Nathan	DEL 278	Cooke, Edward	NYK 95		
Cook, Elijah	RNS 105	Cook, Nathan	DUT 133	Cooke, Elijah	HRK 555		
Cook, Elisha	CHN 938	Cook, Nathan	OND 209	Cooke, Francis	CAY 590		
Cook, Elisha	OND 201	Cook, Nathan	ULS 189	Cooke, George W.	HRK 554		
Cook, Elisha	SCH 146	Cook, Nathan T.	SUF 101	Cooke, James	DUT 67		
Cook, Enoch	QNS 68	Cook, Nathaniel	DEL 278	Cooke, John	DUT 64		
Cook, Ephrain	TIO 247	Cook, Nathaniel	SRA 25	Cooke, John	NYK 41		
Cook, Ephriam	WSH 218	Cook, Obediah	SUF 100	Cooke, John	QNS 66		
Cook, George	ALB 75	Cook, Paul	OTS 57	Cooke, John M.	DUT 62		
Cook, George	ESS 295	Cook, Peabody	OTS 57	Cooke, Joseph	DUT 140		
Cook, George	ORN 335	Cook, Peggy a Negro	NYK 41	Cooke, Joseph	NYK 68		
Cook, George	SUF 89	Cook, Peter	NYK 144	Cooke, Matthias	DUT 41		
Cook, Gideon	CHN 794	Cook, Peter	OND 221	Cooke, Michael	HRK 443		
Cook, Gideon	OND 187	Cook, Phenea	SRA 26	Cooke, Michael	NYK 93		
Cook, Hannah	OTS 21	Cook, Phinias	OTS 28	Cooke, Moses	DUT 140		
Cook, Henry	COL 249	Cook, Polly	NYK 106	Cooke, Philip	HRK 511		
Cook, Henry	SUF 99	Cook, Raphael	CAY 722	Cooke, Rachael	NYK 79		
Cook, Hons	GRN 348	Cook, Reubin	ESS 293	Cooke, Rebeca	ONT 500		
Cook, Isaac	CHN 982	Cook, Richard	ALB 5	Cooke, _muel(?)	ONT 310		
Cook, Isaac	OND 207	Cook, Richard	CHN 788	Cooke, Samuel	ORN 299		
Cook, Isaiah	SCH 168	Cook, Richard	DUT 94	Cooke, Thomas	CAY 594		
Cook, Jabis	GRN 345	Cook, Richard	GRN 343	Cooke, Thomas a Black	NYK 101		
Cook, Jair	OTS 28	Cook, Robert	DEL 274	Cooke, William	NYK 70		
Cook, James	CAY 626	Cook, Robert	OTS 29	Cooke, William H.			
Cook, James	ESS 320	Cook, Robert	OTS 29	Cookenham, Daniel	DUT 151		
Cook, James	GRN 341	Cook, Robert	SCH 147	Cookenham, Daniel	DUT 165		
Cook, James	GRN 356	Cook, Rudolp	MNT 53	Cookenham, David	DUT 112		
Cook, James	NYK 119	Cook, Rufus	OTS 29	Cookenham, Frederick	DUT 111		
Cook, James	OTS 28	Cook, Samuel	CHN 858	Cookenham, George	DUT 152		
Cook, James	WSH 234	Cook, Saml	CHN 886	Cookenham, Michael	DUT 111		
Cook, Joab	OND 215	Cook, Samuel	DUT 107	Cookenham, Peter	DUT 149		
Cook, Joab	WSH 301	Cook, Samuel	OND 164	Cookingham, John	RNS 35		
Cook, Job	NYK 144	Cook, Samuel	ONN 156	Cooky, Thomas	SCH 147		
Cook, Job	WSH 216	Cook, Samuel	OTS 29	Cool, Abraham	ULS 206		
Cook, John	DEL 274	Cook, Samuel	SRA 25	Cool, Benjamin	DUT 171		
Cook, John	GRN 327	Cook, Samuel	STB 200	Cool, Cornelius	ULS 206		
Cook, John	GRN 348	Cook, Samuel	SUF 101	Cool, Cornelius	ULS 250		
Cook, John	NYK 25	Cook, Samuel	WSH 207	Cool, Cornelius Junr	ULS 206		
Cook, John	NYK 39	Cook, Samuel	WSH 218	Cool, Cornelius C.	ULS 203		
Cook, John	ONT 442	Cook, Samuel	WSH 237	Cool, Daniel	SRA 44		
Cook, John	ORN 321	Cook, Samuel	WSH 264	Cool, Jacob	ULS 247		
Cook, John	OTS 29	Cook, Samuel	WSH 301	Cool, Jacob J.	COL 231		
Cook, John	RNS 109	Cook, Saverenus	SCH 169	Cool, Nicholas	SRA 44		
Cook, John	SRA 34	Cook, Selah	ONN 131	Cool, William	ULS 245		
Cook, John	SCH 131	Cook, Selah	OTS 18	Cooledge, Charles	OND 182		
Cook, John	SCH 151	Cook, Silus	CHN 950	Cooledge, Danl	CHN 926		
Cook, John	SUF 99	Cook, Simeon	DUT 137	Cooledge, Isaac	CHN 972		
Cook, John Jun	SRA 35	Cook, Simeon	MNT 12	Cooledge, Jonathan	WSH 234		
Cook, John B.	MNT 9	Cook, Simon	WST 134	Cooledge, Obediah	ESS 308		
Cook, John L.	OTS 6	Cook, Solomon	DUT 138	Cooley, Adanijah	DEL 278		
Cook, John R.	MNT 6	Cook, Solomon	GRN 327	Cooley, Ame	COL 252		
Cook, Jonathan	STB 199	Cook, Stephen	OTS 10	Cooley, Aruna	DEL 278		
Cook, Jonathan	SUF 95	Cook, Stephen	SUF 99	Cooley, Asahel	CAY 714		
Cook, Joseph	COL 185	Cook, Stephen	WSH 237	Cooley, Baruch	OND 197		
Cook, Joseph	COL 185	Cook, Theophilus	SUF 101	Cooley, Clarke	ONT 422		
Cook, Joseph	COL 205	Cook, Thomas	GRN 358	Cooley, Daniel	ORN 329		
Cook, Joseph	OND 220	Cook, Thomas a Black	NYK 64	Cooley, Daniel	ORN 354		
Cook, Joseph	RNS 54	Cook, Thomas	OND 163	Cooley, Darius	OND 222		
Cook, Joseph	RNS 109	Cook, Thomas	ORN 289	Cooley, David	ORN 330		
Cook, Joseph	SRA 26	Cook, Tryon	SCH 146	Cooley, David Junr	ORN 330		
Cook, Joseph	WSH 204	Cook, Uphemia	NYK 19	Cooley, Elijah	ONT 390		
Cook, Joseph	WSH 264	Cook, Warham	OND 201	Cooley, Freegift	ORN 325		
				Cooley, James	CAY 540		

Cooley, James	DEL 287	Coon, John	ULS 197	Coons, John	RNS 8
Coo_ey, James	ORN 363	Coon, John G.	COL 238	Coons, Jonathan	RNS 78
Cooley, James	WSH 221	Coon, John H.	COL 224	Coons, Mathias	RNS 87
Cooley, Jesse	ORN 378	Coon, John J.	COL 239	Coons, Nicholas	ALB 80
Cooley, John	OND 209	Coon, Jonathan	WSH 213	Coons, Peter	RNS 84
Cooley, John Ju.	ONT 420	Coon, Joseph	CAY 668	Coons, Philip	RNS 4
Cooley, Jonathan	ORN 394	Coon, Joseph	CLN 164	Coons, Phillip P.	COL 240
Cooley, Joseph	ALB 28	Coon, Joseph	OTS 47	Coons, William	RNS 84
Cooley, Joseph	CHN 988	Coon, Joseph	QNS 79	Coons, William Junr	RNS 84
Cooley, Justin	OND 190	Coon, Joseph	RNS 22	Coop, David	COL 246
Cooley, Justus	ULS 256	Coon, Joshua	OTS 46	Coop, Edward	KNG 9
Cooley, Levi	ESS 307	Coon, Jost	ULS 197	Coop, John	ALB 12
Cooley, Nathan	ORN 385	Coon, Luke	OTS 30	Coop, Thomas	SRA 7
Cooley, Nathaniel	ORN 329	Coon, Luke	RNS 69	Cooper, ...	CAY 576
Cooley, Nathen	WSH 205	Coon, Marks	COL 240	Cooper, _m_	MNT 100
Cooley, Peleg	WST 137	Coon, Matthew	DUT 10	Cooper, A- Allen	SUF 95
Cooley, Reuben	ONN 132	Coon, Michael	CAY 560	Cooper, Abigail	ORN 363
Cooley, Richard	MNT 112	Coon, Michael	ULS 197	Cooper, Abner	TIO 260
Cooley, Samuel	ALB 33	Coon, Nathan	RNS 112	Cooper, Abraham	RNS 7
Cooley, Samuel	RNS 60	Coon, Nathan	SRA 55	Cooper, Abrm	RCK 100
Cooley, Seth	OND 182	Coon, Nathaniel	WSH 255	Cooper, Abrm	RCK 100
Cooley, Seth	WSH 222	Coon, Nicholas	COL 241	Cooper, Albert	NYK 91
Cooley, Thomas	OND 215	Coon, Peter	COL 238	Cooper, Albert	NYK 96
Cooly, Jacob	COL 207	Coon, Peter	RNS 22	Cooper, Alexander	RNS 51
Cooly, Johial	GRN 341	Coon, Peter B.	DUT 43	Cooper, Andrew	ORN 385
Cooly, Moses	CHN 916	Coon, Philip	RNS 69	Cooper, Andrew	TIO 225
Cooly, Samuel	GRN 341	Coon, Phillip H.	COL 240	Cooper, Anna	OTS 29
Coombs, Andrew	DUT 151	Coon, Phillip J.	COL 240	Cooper, Annanias	SUF 99
Coomer, Windser	CHN 872	Coon, Samuel	DUT 45	Cooper, Apollus	OND 158
Coomer, Zebe	CHN 872	Coon, Saml	RNS 64	Cooper, Asa	CHN 804
Coon, Aaron	SRA 6	Coon, Sarah	RNS 78	Cooper, Benjamin	HRK 571
Coon, Abraham	DEL 268	Coon, Simon	COL 233	Cooper, Benjamin a	
Coon, Abrm	OTS 47	Coon, Simon Junr	COL 233	mulatto	NYK 68
Coon, Adam	ALB 86	Coon, Solomon	RNS 18	Cooper, Caleb	SUF 96
Coon, Adam	COL 236	Coon, Solomon	RNS 22	Cooper, Christopher	RNS 4
Coon, Alexander	HRK 424	Coon, Spencer	OTS 57	Cooper, Claus	RCK 99
Coon, Alexander	RNS 70	Coon, Sylvanus	DUT 99	Cooper, Closs	WST 166
Coon, Alexander	RNS 108	Coon, Thos	SUF 77	Cooper, Coonrad	RNS 4
Coon, Amos	OTS 30	Coon, Timothy	DEL 287	Cooper, Cornelius	NYK 86
Coon, Asa	ALB 34	Coon, Timothy	RNS 76	Cooper, Cornelius	RCK 108
Coon, Barnard	OND 159	Coon, timothy	SRA 32	Cooper, Cornelius	ULS 241
Coon, Benjamin	SCH 132	Coon, Timothy	SRA 33	Cooper, Daniel Young	RNS 94
Coon, Caleb	DUT 17	Coon, Wilhelmus	COL 225	Cooper, David	OND 207
Coon, Charles	OTS 18	Coon, William	COL 225	Cooper, David	ONT 380
Coon, Christian	ORN 301	Coon, Wm	RNS 70	Cooper, David	SUF 97
Coon, Coenrad	ALB 104	Coon, William	WSH 252	Cooper, Dowa	RCK 100
Coon, Daniel	HRK 593	Coon, William Junr	COL 225	Cooper, Elias	WST 147
Coon, Danl	OTS 48	Coone, Ruliff	GRN 331	Cooper, Elijah	ESS 292
Coon, Daniel	WSH 224	Coonhoven, Samuel	ALB 55	Cooper, Elizabeth	DUT 161
Coon, David	HRK 592	Cooning, Andrew	ALB 107	Cooper, Ephraim	DUT 47
Coon, David	RNS 22	Coonley, George	ALB 117	Cooper, Ezra	OND 222
Coon, Dennis	ORN 372	Coonley, Jeremiah	GRN 353	Cooper, Francis	NYK 24
Coon, Ebenezer	SRA 16	Coonley, John	GRN 353	Cooper, George	GRN 346
Coon, Elias	DUT 20	Coonley, Solomon	ALB 117	Cooper, George	TIO 254
Coon, Elijah	CAY 642	Coonly, Daniel	DUT 129	Cooper, George	WSH 230
Coon, Falter	ALB 122	Coonly, Jacob	DUT 130	Cooper, George	WSH 297
Coon, George	ALB 104	Coonly, John	DUT 104	Cooper, George D.	NYK 28
Coon, Godrey	NYK 48	Coonly, John	DUT 108	Cooper, Gilbert	NYK 94
Coon, Hans	ALB 86	Coonly, Samuel	DUT 104	Cooper, Gilbert T.	RCK 109
Coon, Hendrick	COL 237	Coonrad, Henry	CAY 580	Cooper, Hendrick	RCK 110
Coon, Henry S.	COL 233	Coonradt, Adam	RNS 84	Cooper, Henry	RNS 7
Coon, Hezekiah	RNS 73	Coonradt, Henry	RNS 84	Cooper, Henry	RNS 15
Coon, Jacob	ALB 86	Coonradt, Philip	RNS 84	Cooper, Hugh	NYK 134
Coon, Jacob	COL 232	Coonradt, Philip H.	RNS 86	Cooper, Jacob	DUT 35
Coon, Jacob	GEN 332	Coonradt, William	RNS 86	Cooper, Jacob	HRK 463
Coon, Jacob	ULS 197	Coonrod, Peter	CAY 580	Cooper, Jacob	NYK 125
Coon, Jacob J.	COL 237	Coonrod, Peter	CAY 696	Cooper, Jacob	NYK 125
Coon, Jacob S.	COL 233	Coonrodt, Philip Junr	RNS 87	Cooper, jacobus	RCK 99
Coon, Jeremiah	DUT 20	Coons, Abraham	RNS 8	Cooper, James	DUT 30
Coon, Jeremiah Junr	DUT 20	Coons, Andries	COL 239	Cooper, James	GRN 328
Coon, Jesse	ALB 34	Coons, Avery	RNS 78	Cooper, Ja_mes	GRN 347
Coon, Johanna a white		Coons, David	RNS 4	Cooper, James	NYK 38
woman and child	SRA 29	Coons, Harms	ALB 90	Cooper, James	OTS 10
Coon, Johannis	COL 225	Coons, Jacob	GRN 358	Cooper, James	RCK 100
Coon, John	COL 241	Coons, Jacob	RNS 8	Cooper, James	SRA 34
Coon, John	RNS 12	Coons, Jacob	RNS 84	Cooper, James	SRA 44
Coon, John	SRA 15	Coons, Jeremiah	SRA 7	Cooper, John	CAY 622

Cooper, John	COL 224	Cooper, Thomas	TIO 223	Corbin, Hannah	DUT 53
Cooper, John	DUT 35	Cooper, Tunis T.	RCK 100	Corbin, Jabez	DUT 52
Cooper, John	ESS 309	Cooper, William	ALB 106	Corbin, Job	DUT 144
Cooper, John	NYK 22	Cooper, William	COL 244	Corbin, John	CLN 172
Cooper, John	NYK 99	Cooper, William	DUT 38	Corbin, John	WSH 305
Cooper, John	OND 159	Cooper, William	DUT 47	Corbin, Joseph	CLN 173
Cooper, John	SUF 95	Cooper, William	NYK 55	Corbin, Micajah	DUT 53
Cooper, John	WSH 199	Cooper, William	NYK 114	Corbin, Moses	CLN 167
Cooper, John	WSH 230	Cooper, William	NYK 134	Corbin, Moses	RNS 90
Cooper, John	WSH 297	Cooper, William	OND 220	Corbin, Moses Junr	CLN 167
Cooper, John	WST 159	Cooper, Wm	OTS 19	Corbin, Peter	DUT 51
Cooper, John I.	DUT 153	Cooper, Wm	RNS 7	Corbin, Samuel	DUT 53
Cooper, John M.	NYK 55	Cooper, Wm	RNS 15	Corbin, Thomas	DUT 53
Cooper, Jonathan	OND 191	Cooper, William	SRA 44	Corbin, William	CLN 173
Cooper, Joseph	ALB 35	Cooper, William	WSH 197	Corbit, Daniel	COL 253
Cooper, Joseph	DUT 22	Cooper, William	WSH 225	Corbit, Thomas	STB 198
Cooper, Joseph	HRK 431	Cooper, William Junr	DUT 52	Cord, Elisha	SRA 56
Cooper, Joseph	HRK 474	Cooper, William Junr	WSH 197	Cordeir, Hubert	NYK 123
Cooper, Joseph	NYK 41	Cooper, William Senr	DUT 56	Cordner, Asmael	SCH 137
Cooper, Joseph	ORN 363	Cooper, Zebulon	ALB 86	Cordner, George	SCH 137
Cooper, Joseph	WSH 225	Cooper, Zopher	SUF 95	Cordner, Steward	SCH 137
Cooper, Josiah	ULS 260	Coopernail, William	DUT 151	Cordon, Benjamin	STB 203
Cooper, Junias A.	NYK 150	Coopman, Jacob	DUT 69	Cordon, James	CLN 160
Cooper, Letty	QNS 60	Coopman, John	DUT 61	Cordouse, Joseph a Black	NYK 122
Cooper, Levi	ALB 18	Coopman, John Junr	DUT 141	Corduvan, Lewis	NYK 119
Cooper, Luke	RCK 109	Coopper, Luther	SRA 52	Core, Isaac	SUF 64
Cooper, Margaret	RCK 100	Cooradt, John	RNS 83	Corey, Alexander	ORN 332
Cooper, Martin	COL 260	Cooshman, Wm	RNS 44	Corey, Anthoney	SRA 34
Cooper, Mathew	SUF 99	Coovert, Adolph	QNS 82	Corey, Benjamin	HRK 425
Cooper, Miles	GRN 341	Coovert, Isaac	QNS 75	Corey, Benjamin	HRK 550
Cooper, Myndert	ORN 352	Coovert, Luke	QNS 77	Corey, David	CAY 656
Cooper, Nathan	NYK 152	Coovert, Morris	NYK 80	Corey, David	SRA 22
Cooper, Nathan	SUF 97	Coovert, Tunic	QNS 75	Corey, Eliakim	SRA 21
Cooper, Nathaniel	NYK 86	Coovert, Tunis	QNS 68	Corey, Elisha	ORN 396
Cooper, Nathaniel	SRA 38	Coovert, Tunis	QNS 77	Corey, Elizabeth	NYK 107
Cooper, Obadiah	ALB 103	Coovert, Walter	QNS 75	Corey, Elizabeth	ORN 363
Cooper, Obadiah	ALB 133	Cop___, Joseph	OND 219	Corey, Elnathan	ORN 335
Cooper, Obediah	RNS 7	Cope, Samuel	DUT 35	Corey, Gabriel	ULS 180
Cooper, Obediah	SUF 95	Copeland, Benjamin	WSH 298	Corey, George	ONN 151
Cooper, Obediah I.	DUT 24	Copeland, Jacob	ALB 86	Corey, Gideon	ESS 302
Cooper, Obediah W.	DUT 34	Copeland, John	ALB 110	Corey, Gilbert	HRK 550
Cooper, Owen	WSH 280	Copeland, Luther	ESS 317	Corey, Isaac	ORN 327
Cooper, Paul	CAY 558	Copeland, William	SRA 50	Corey, Jacob	HRK 502
Cooper, Peter	COL 265	Copeley, Calvin	ALB 43	Corey, Jacob	WSH 211
Cooper, Peter	HRK 465	Copely, William	MNT 8	Corey, James	HRK 489
Cooper, Peter	ORN 387	Copeman, Abraham	MNT 33	Corey, James	NYK 109
Cooper, Peter	RNS 4	Copernall, Jn	OTS 58	Corey, John	SRA 34
Cooper, Peter	RCK 99	Copernall, Wm	OTS 58	Corey, John	WSH 211
Cooper, Pheebe	DUT 64	Copley, Wm	MNT 62	Corey, John Junr	WSH 211
Cooper, Phillip	DUT 14	Coply, Samuel	MNT 62	Corey, Joseph	ONT 470
Cooper, Phillip	ULS 237	Copp, Timothy	ONN 157	Corey, Lemuel	ORN 352
Cooper, Price	DUT 53	Coppen, John	NYK 121	Corey, Lucy	ORN 360
Cooper, Reuben	DEL 290	Copper, Jeremiah	WST 157	Corey, Nathan	ESS 308
Cooper, Richard	CAY 578	Coppernoll, John	HRK 577	Corey, Oliver	SRA 35
Cooper, Richard	WSH 301	Copsie, Catharine	ULS 201	Corey, Peleg	MNT 83
Cooper, Robert	DUT 162	Coquillet, Danl	RCK 105	Corey, Phillip	ESS 310
Cooper, Ruth	SUF 96	Coquillet, Peter	RCK 106	Corey, Phinehas	OND 209
Cooper, Samuel	COL 251	Cora, Silas	RNS 26	Corey, Rufus	HRK 424
Cooper, Samuel	DUT 40	Corben, Ebenezer	CHN 926	Corey, Thomas	ONN 192
Cooper, Samuel	DUT 47	Corben, Horace	WSH 282	Corey, Thomas	WSH 189
Cooper, Samuel	HRK 574	Corben, John	WSH 304	Corey, Timothy	NYK 134
Cooper, Samuel	SRA 45	Corben, Luther	CHN 920	Corey, William	HRK 593
Cooper, Saml	SUF 96	Corben, Samuel	CHN 756	Cork, Solomon	QNS 84
Cooper, Samuel	WSH 223	Corben, Samuel Junr	CHN 756	Corkhill, John	NYK 73
Cooper, Sarah	RCK 100	Corbert, James	SUF 65	Corkins, Ebenezer	COL 242
Cooper, Seth	CHN 794	Corbet, David	CLN 171	Corkins, Eli	WSH 209
Cooper, Shadrach	ORN 398	Corbet, Eldad	OND 203	Corkins, James	COL 241
Cooper, Silas	SUF 98	Corbet, Peter	TIO 239	Corkins, Richard	CLN 155
Cooper, Stephen	NYK 99	Corbet, Zachariah	NYK 81	Corkins, Semion	WSH 209
Cooper, Susan	NYK 148	Corbett, Joseah	WSH 264	Corkman, John	RNS 86
Cooper, Thomas	ALB 103	Corbett, Sarah	NYK 119	Corl, George	HRK 427
Cooper, Thomas	CLN 174	Corbey, John	WSH 299	Corl, Henry	ALB 7
Cooper, Thomas	NYK 67	Corbin, Ahijah	DUT 176	Corl, Henry Junr	SRA 23
Cooper, Thomas	NYK 125	Corbin, Asa	RNS 109	Corl, John	ALB 7
Cooper, Thomas	NYK 128	Corbin, Benjn	OTS 53	Corless, John Junr	WSH 234
Cooper, Thomas	ORN 352	Corbin, Edward E.	ESS 323	Corless, John Senr	WSH 242
Cooper, Thomas	SCH 123	Corbin, Ephraim	RNS 109	Corlis, George	HRK 510

Name	Loc	Name	Loc	Name	Loc
Corlus, George	NYK 63	Cornell, Seth	RNS 31	Cornwell, Edward	QNS 68
Corman, Wm	TIO 240	Cornell, Sylvanus	COL 178	Cornwell, Edward	WSH 236
Cormer, Joseph	COL 263	Cornell, Thomas	WST 119	Cornwell, Elish Jur	SRA 29
Cormick, John	ONT 326	Cornell, Whithed	QNS 73	Cornwell, Elisha	SRA 29
Corn, John	HRK 560	Cornell, William	DEL 291	Cornwell, Elizabeth	KNG 8
Cornal, Joab	SRA 31	Cornell, William	DUT 19	Cornwell, Elizabeth	KNG 9
Corne, Peter	NYK 48	Cornell, Willit	WST 115	Cornwell, Elizabeth	QNS 64
Cornel, erris	WST 119	Corney, Joshua	OND 171	Cornwell, George	QNS 65
Cornel, Aaron	WSH 234	Corning, Amos	NYK 102	Cornwell, Haviland	WST 128
Cornel, Benjamin	WSH 211	Cornington, Morton	SRA 47	Cornwell, Henry	QNS 64
Cornel, James	WSH 236	Cornish, Aaron	DUT 139	Cornwell, Hewlet	QNS 72
Cornel, John	WSH 214	Cornish, Benjamin	QNS 62	Cornwell, Holder	ALB 71
Cornel, Mathew	WSH 198	Cornish, Benjamin Junr	QNS 62	Cornwell, Isaac	CHN 764
Cornel, Stephen	WSH 235	Cornish, Daniel	GRN 347	Cornwell, Isaac	KNG 8
Cornel, Thomas	WSH 236	Cornish, Danil	GRN 339	Cornwell, Isaac	OND 202
Cornelise, Cland	NYK 56	Cornish, Eber	GRN 335	Cornwell, Isaac	WSH 305
Cornelison, Abrm	RCK 102	Cornish, Elkanor	SUF 85	Cornwell, James	WST 128
Cornelison, Michael	RCK 97	Cornish, Jabez	CHN 758	Cornwell, John	ALB 36
Cornelius	QNS 78	Cornish, Jabez Junr	CHN 758	Cornwell, John	KNG 8
Cornelius, Alias	WST 130	Cornish, John	KNG 10	Cornwell, John	NYK 146
Cornelius, David	ORN 388	Cornish, Joseph	DUT 66	Cornwell, John	NYK 146
Cornelius, John	COL 214	Cornish, Stephen	OND 213	Cornwell, John	QNS 64
Cornelius, John	ORN 387	Cornu, Da.iel	MNT 39	Cornwell, John	QNS 75
Cornelius, John	QNS 78	Cornu, Peter	MNT 39	Cornwell, John	QNS 75
Cornelius, John	SUF 79	Cornwall, Aspinwall	DUT 123	Cornwell, Joseph	ALB 70
Cornelius, Jonathan	QNS 73	Cornwall, Barack	QNS 71	Cornwell, Joseph	COL 208
Cornelius, Nancy	QNS 78	Cornwall, Benjamin	DUT 40	Cornwell, Joseph	SRA 29
Cornelius, Peter	ALB 75	Cornwall, Benjamin	DUT 99	Cornwell, Joseph	WST 131
Cornelius, Samuel	DUT 120	Cornwall, Catharine	DUT 16	Cornwell, Joshua	QNS 65
Cornelius, Tobias	ORN 387	Cornwall, Clements	DUT 40	Cornwell, Joshua	QNS 71
Corneliuson, John	KNG 9	Cornwall, Daniel	ULS 256	Cornwell, Joshua	WST 131
Cornell, Aspenwall	NYK 136	Cornwall, David	WSH 186	Cornwell, Lemuel	CHN 764
Cornell, Benjamin	MNT 91	Cornwall, Elijah	QNS 76	Cornwell, Lewis	QNS 63
Cornell, Benjamin	WST 119	Cornwall, Elisha	DUT 123	Cornwell, Lewis	QNS 65
Cornell, Ceaser a mulatto	NYK 39	Cornwall, Gabriel	ORN 369	Cornwell, Malson	QNS 75
Cornell, Charles	NYK 17	Cornwall, Gideon	DUT 129	Cornwell, Menson	QNS 72
Cornell, Charles	NYK 34	Cornwall, Gilbert W.	DUT 137	Cornwell, Moses	QNS 75
Cornell, Charles	QNS 69	Cornwall, Hait	SCH 143	Cornwell, Nathan	SRA 35
Cornell, Daniel	QNS 70	Cornwall, James	QNS 71	Cornwell, Nicholas	ALB 84
Cornell, David	CAY 664	Cornwall, Jesse	DUT 24	Cornwell, Obadiah	QNS 65
Cornell, Dowe	DUT 71	Cornwall, John	DUT 132	Cornwell, Oliver	QNS 64
Cornell, Elihu	SCH 117	Cornwall, John	ORN 367	Cornwell, Peleg	WSH 289
Cornell, Elijah	COL 251	Cornwall, John the 2d	DUT 130	Cornwell, Rebecca	COL 222
Cornell, Elizabeth	NYK 63	Cornwall, Joseph	WSH 185	Cornwell, Richard	QNS 73
Cornell, Ezra	WST 144	Cornwall, Josiah	ULS 257	Cornwell, Samuel	CHN 752
Cornell, George	QNS 69	Cornwall, Melancton	DUT 127	Cornwell, Saml	QNS 65
Cornell, Gilbert	QNS 70	Cornwall, Paul	WSH 185	Cornwell, Samuel	QNS 68
Cornell, Gilliam	NYK 34	Cornwall, Peleg	ALB 22	Cornwell, Silvester	QNS 77
Cornell, Henry	QNS 69	Cornwall, Peter	DUT 116	Cornwell, Smith	KNG 9
Cornell, Isaac	KNG 3	Cornwall, Samuel	DUT 166	Cornwell, Stephen	QNS 65
Cornell, Isaac	NYK 143	Cornwall, Samuel	ORN 390	Cornwell, Stephen	QNS 74
Cornell, Jacob	CAY 618	Cornwall, Stephen	NYK 130	Cornwell, Stephen	QNS 75
Cornell, Jacob	DUT 120	Cornwall, Thomas	DUT 76	Cornwell, Thomas	ONT 346
Cornell, James	DUT 12	Cornwall, Walter	DUT 105	Cornwell, Thomas	QNS 64
Cornell, John	DEL 291	Cornwall, William	DUT 137	Cornwell, Thomas	QNS 73
Cornell, John	DUT 14	Cornwall, William	ULS 256	Cornwell, Thomas	WST 166
Cornell, John	DUT 24	Cornwall, Zebulon	WSH 185	Cornwell, Timothy	QNS 75
Cornell, John	NYK 17	Cornway, John	GRN 355	Cornwell, Whitehead	QNS 73
Cornell, John	OTS 16	Cornwell, Abijah	CHN 766	Cornwell, William	COL 221
Cornell, John	SRA 6	Cornwell, Alexander	ALB 48	Cornwell, William	KNG 8
Cornell, John	WST 118	Cornwell, Amos	WSH 305	Cornwell, William	KNG 9
Cornell, Jupiter a Black	NYK 56	Cornwell, Asa	CHN 766	Cornwell, William	QNS 75
Cornell, Lavinia a mulatto	NYK 77	Cornwell, Barrak	QNS 65	Cornwell, Wm Junr	QNS 75
Cornell, Morris	QNS 69	Cornwell, Benjamin	CHN 766	Corol, John	
Cornell, Nathen	OTS 18	Cornwell, Benjamin	QNS 73	Corothers, Rober	WSH 187
Cornell, Patty	CLN 158	Cornwell, Benjamin	QNS 75	Corp, Benajah	HRK 591
Cornell, Peleg	CAY 664	Cornwell, Benjamin	WSH 303	Corp, John	HRK 562
Cornell, Peter	DUT 41	Cornwell, Caleb	QNS 72	Corp, Samuel	NYK 29
Cornell, Peter	NYK 69	Cornwell, Charles	QNS 63	Corps, David	OND 189
Cornell, Quinby	DUT 120	Cornwell, Charles	QNS 69	Corps, Joseph	CLN 169
Cornell, Reuben	SRA 28	Cornwell, Charles Junr	QNS 69	Correll, William	ALB 6
Cornell, Richard	DUT 12	Cornwell, Dan	GRN 346	Correy, Abijah	SUF 105
Cornell, Richard	WST 118	Cornwell, Daniel	GRN 346	Correy, Bradock	SUF 102
Cornell, Richardus	DUT 12	Cornwell, Daniel	MNT 119	Correy, John	SUF 104
		Cornwell, David	CAY 726	Correy, Phineas	SUF 102
		Cornwell, Ebenezer	CHN 766	Corry, Joseph	NYK 98
		Cornwell, Edward	ALB 113	Corsa, Andrew	WST 146

Name	Loc	Name	Loc	Name	Loc
Corsa, Benjamin	WST 145	Corwin, Thos	SUF 74	Coswell, Jonath_n	CAY 600
Corsa, Benjamin Senr	WST 145	Corwine, Gilbert	RCK 100	Cote, John	GRN 345
Corsa, Catherine	ORN 313	Corwithy, Bennett	SUF 99	Cotel, John	ALB 34
Corsa, Frederick	WST 145	Corwithy, Caleb	SUF 99	Cotes, Caleb	RNS 108
Corsa, Isaac	KNG 2	Corwithy, Caleb	SUF 100	Cotes, Daniel	OND 193
Corsakine, John	SRA 14	Corwithy, Henry	SUF 100	Cotes, Elephalet	OND 188
Corsate, John	SRA 24	Corwithy, John	SUF 100	Cotes, Eliphalet Junr	OND 188
Corsen, Cornelius	RCH 91	Cory	GRN 346	Cotes, Robert	RNS 51
Corsen, Daniel	RCH 91	Cory, Benjn	OTS 19	Cotes, Robert	RNS 88
Corsen, Daniel	RCH 93	Cory, Benjn	OTS 57	Cothone, Alexander	WST 166
Corsen, Daniel Junr	RCH 93	Cory, Casarus	MNT 82	Cothrell, Daniel	CAY 648
Corsen, Mrs	RCH 87	Cory, Clement	OND 167	Cothrell, Daniel	WSH 302
Corsen, Nelly	RCH 91	Cory, John	WSH 265	Coths, John	NYK 16
Corsen, Richard	RCH 91	Cory, Moses	GRN 337	Cotman, Abel	SCH 169
Corsey, Joseph	CLN 173	Cory, Oliver	OTS 19	Cotner, Fraderick	RNS 58
Cort, Elisha	NYK 36	Coryell, Abm	TIO 250	Cotong, Phoebe	NYK 122
Cortelyou, Isaac	KNG 5	Coryell, Danl	TIO 250	Cotrel, Nathaniel	WSH 251
Cortelyou, Jacob	RCH 92	Coryell, Joseph	NYK 137	Cotren, Nicholas	SRA 53
Cortelyou, Jaques	KNG 6	Coryell, Micheal	CAY 558	Cotrill, Saml	RNS 25
Cortelyou, John	KNG 2	Cosart, James	CAY 602	Cots, Rufus	GRN 340
Cortelyou, Peter	RCH 92	Cosbert, D..ick	QNS 67	Cott see Colt	
Cortelyou, Peter J.	KNG 7	Cosbin, Sylvester	CHN 754	Cott, Daniel	QNS 74
Cortelyou, Peter S.	KNG 6	Cosby, John	ALB 31	Cott, Garret	QNS 79
Cortelyou, Simon	KNG 6	Cose see Cox		Cott, Joseph	GRN 338
Cortin[eer?], John	MNT 96	Cose, Abraham	NYK 37	Cottell, James	NYK 138
Cortland, Elizabeth	NYK 19	Cose, Peter	NYK 81	Cotten, John	WSH 217
Cortney, John	ALB 127	Cosemore, William	NYK 90	Cotten, William	NYK 23
Cortright, Caleb	SRA 30	Cosey, Abraham	NYK 95	Cottendon, Joseph	GRN 332
Cortright, Jacob a Black	NYK 92	Cosey, Thomas	NYK 108	Cottephins, Benjamin	WST 170
Cortrite, Thomas	STB 200	Coshow, Andrius	QNS 80	Cotteral, George	NYK 16
Cortwright, Abraham	CAY 658	Coshow, Jacob	QNS 82	Cotterall, Richard	NYK 17
Cortwright, Daniel	CAY 686	Coshow, John	QNS 81	Cottin, John B.	DUT 60
Cortwright, James	CAY 658	Coshow, Ram	QNS 80	Cotting, Henry	DUT 159
Cortwright, Joel	CAY 686	Coshow, Robert W.	NYK 104	Cottle, Grant	NYK 106
Cortwright, Moses	CAY 684	Coshowe, Frederick	CHN 800	Cottle, Peter	COL 206
Cortwright, Moses Junr	CAY 686	Coshowe, John	CHN 800	Cotton see Colton	
Corvin, Mathias	SUF 71	Coshowe, John Jun	CHN 798	Cotton, Daniel	NYK 153
Corwan, Silas	SUF 95	Cosine, Cornelius	KNG 2	Cotton, David	MNT 96
Corwell, Henry	GRN 357	Cosine, Cornelius	QNS 67	Cotton, Ezra	CHN 756
Corwill, Leah	NYK 15	Cosine, Garret	KNG 3	Cotton, James	COL 258
Corwin, Abel	SUF 71	Cosine, Garret	RCK 98	Cotton, James	NYK 44
Corwin, Abner	ORN 335	Cosine, Jacob	KNG 8	Cotton, Michael	COL 189
Corwin, Abner	ORN 335	Cosine, John	KNG 3	Cotton, Nathaniel	MNT 96
Corwin, Ameca	SUF 74	Cosman, John	ORN 271	Cotton, Samuel	DUT 141
Corwin, Daniel	ORN 292	Cosman, Jonathan	ORN 271	Cotton, Silas	WSH 266
Corwin, Daniel	ORN 311	Cosman, Roeliff	ORN 271	Cotton, Thomas	DEL 282
Corwin, Daniel	ORN 332	Cosort, Anthony	OND 158	Cotton, Thomas	OTS 25
Corwin, Daniel Junr	ORN 334	Cosort, David	CAY 716	Cotton, William	CAY 596
Corwin, David	ORN 312	Cosort, John	OND 172	Cottrell, Garret	CAY 660
Corwin, David	SUF 74	Cosper, John	ALB 72	Cottrell, Samuel	DEL 288
Corwin, Eli	ORN 343	Cosper, John	QNS 62	Cottrell, Thomas	DUT 9
Corwin, Eli Junr	ORN 332	Cosper, Peter	KNG 7	Cottrell, Thomas	NYK 76
Corwin, Ezra	ORN 321	Coss, Azareah	WSH 297	Cou_ing, Daniel	OTS 21
Corwin, George	ORN 308	Coss, Coenradt	ALB 58	Couch, Daniel	SRA 18
Corwin, Gershom	ORN 336	Coss, Joseph	NYK 99	Couch, Ebenezer	SRA 18
Corwin, Heny	SUF 74	Coss, Mathias	SCH 168	Couch, Ebenezer	SRA 58
Corwin, James	ORN 277	Cossart, John Joseph	QNS 75	Couch, Ira H.	SRA 51
Corwin, James	ORN 333	Cossen, Cornelius	NYK 134	Couch, John G.	ALB 139
Corwin, James	SUF 74	Cosset, Timothy	ONN 147	Couch, Jonathan	CAY 720
Corwin, Jedediah	SUF 72	Cossett, Zadock	CAY 550	Couch, Joseph	OND 177
Corwin, Jemma	ORN 272	Cossey, Miles Z(?)	NYK 53	Couch, Solomon	SRA 17
Corwin, John	ORN 335	Cossit, Martin	ONN 159	Couch, Stephen	ONN 175
Corwin, John	SUF 71	Cossman, Valentine	ALB 82	Couch, Stephen Jur	ONN 178
Corwin, John	SUF 74	Coster, Flora D. a		Couchman, Henry	ALB 89
Corwin, John	ULS 249	Black	NYK 41	Couden, David	SCH 169
Corwin, John Jur	SUF 74	Coster, Henry A.	NYK 28	Coudred, Francis	ALB 142
Corwin, John Sen	SUF 71	Coster, John	CHN 754	Couenhoven, Benjamin	NYK 122
Corwin, Joseph	ORN 312	Coster, John	NYK 67	Coulter, Alexr	ALB 32
Corwin, Joseph	ORN 344	Coster, John G.	NYK 28	Coulter, Alexander	WSH 257
Corwin, Joshua	ORN 335	Costigan, Francis	ALB 47	Coulter, George	WSH 191
Corwin, Mary	SUF 74	Costigan, Michael	NYK 152	Coulter, James	WSH 191
Corwin, Nathan	SUF 73	Costillow, Thomas	WST 125	Coulthard, Isaac	NYK 111
Corwin, Peter	ORN 325	Costin, Bishop	HRK 541	Coulton, Elisha	CAY 604
Corwin, Prudence	SUF 75	Costin, Ebenezer	HRK 541	Coulton, John	CAY 604
Corwin, Saml	SUF 75	Costin, Ebenezer Jun	HRK 541	Coulton, John	CAY 604
Corwin, Samuel	ULS 188	Costin, Samuel	HRK 527	Coun, John	QNS 80
		Coswell, John	WSH 217	Counenhoven, Henry	NYK 52

Counsellman, John	TIO 218	Covenhoven, Catherine	NYK 55	Cowan, John	WSH 196
Counsellor, Jacob	DUT 39	Covenhoven, Danl	SCH 138	Cowan, John	WSH 302
Countlin, Laurence	GRN 358	Covenhoven, Francis	NYK 104	Cowan, Joseph	WSH 265
Countriman, Fredk	OTS 15	Covenhoven, George	NYK 57	Cowan, Moses	WSH 252
Countryman see Conterman		Covenhoven, James	NYK 109	Cowan, Peter	ALB 11
Countryman, Adam	OTS 15	Covenhoven, John	DUT 34	Cowan, Peter	WSH 280
Countryman, Elias	ULS 201	Covenhoven, John R.	QNS 61	Cowan, Robert	WSH 199
Countryman, Frederick	ULS 201	Covenhoven, Luke	QNS 61	Cowan, Stephen	WSH 280
Countryman, Hendrick	ULS 201	Covenhoven, Peter	DUT 33	Cowan, William	NYK 78
Countryman, Henry	OTS 15	Covenhoven, Peter	MNT 110	Cowan, William	NYK 148
Countryman, John	OTS 15	Covenhoven, Rachael	NYK 57	Cowan, William	WSH 258
Countryman, John	ULS 209	Coventry, Alexander	DUT 141	Cowbach, Christopher	DUT 161
Countryman, Levi	CAY 620	Coventry, Alexander	OND 199	Cowden, John	WSH 224
Countryman, Matthew	ULS 201	Coventry, Elizabeth	NYK 28	Cowden, Sarah	WSH 190
Countryman, Paul	ULS 201	Coventry, John H.	NYK 23	Cowden, Simpson	WSH 190
Couphman, John F.	WSH 244	Coventry, Robert	COL 255	Cowdry, Benjamin	NYK 119
Courbe, Cyprien	NYK 51	Coventry, William	COL 254	Cowdry, Jonathan	NYK 140
Courey, Michael	NYK 45	Coverly, William	NYK 137	Cowdry, Jonathan	TIO 216
Courey, Peter	NYK 72	Covert, Abraham	CAY 542	Cowdy, David	SCH 120
Coursa, William	NYK 66	Covert, Abraham Jun.	CAY 542	Cowel, Benjamine	GRN 355
Court, John	DUT 107	Covert, Bergen	CAY 556	Cowel, John	GRN 351
Court, John	HRK 419	Covert, David	WST 166	Cowel, Joshua	GRN 351
Courtious, Constant	GRN 340	Covert, Eder	CAY 542	Cowel, Samuel	GRN 355
Courtland, James	CHN 754	Covert, Elisha	COL 234	Cowel, Truman	GRN 351
Courtlin, Benjamin	GRN 346	Covert, Elisha	DUT 72	Cowell, Benjn	OTS 49
Courtlin, Benjamine	GRN 341	Covert, Gabriel	QNS 82	Cowell, John	ALB 94
Courtlin, Chales	GRN 346	Covert, Hause	CAY 542	Cowell, Joshua	DEL 288
Courtlin, Daniel	GRN 345	Covert, Isaac	DUT 82	Cowen, Charity	NYK 19
Courtlin, Daniel	GRN 346	Covert, Jacob	WST 122	Cowen, James	SRA 16
Courtlin, Ebenezar	GRN 340	Covert, James	ORN 311	Cowen, Margaret	DUT 176
Courtlin, Martin	GRN 346	Covert, Job	DUT 82	Cowen, Roger	DUT 176
Courtney, John	MNT 101	Covert, John	CAY 544	Cowen, Silus	SUF 73
Courtney, Laurence	NYK 114	Covert, John	CAY 546	Cowen, William	WSH 186
Courtney, William	ALB 28	Covert, John	COL 194	Cowenhoven, Garret	KNG 3
Courtney, William	CHN 762	Covert, John	DUT 62	Cowenhoven, George	KNG 5
Courtright, David	TIO 237	Covert, John	NYK 138	Cowenhoven, Jane	KNG 5
Courtright, Gideon	TIO 237	Covert, John	WST 122	Cowenhoven, Johannas	KNG 5
Cour_right, Tony	TIO 234	Covert, John B.	CAY 556	Cowenhoven, John	KNG 8
Courtrigt	GRN 338	Covert, John J.	CAY 544	Cowenhoven, Nelly	KNG 5
Cous, Andrew	DUT 147	Covert, Joshua	CAY 556	Cowenhoven, Nicholas R.	KNG 8
Cous, Han Tice	DUT 147	Covert, Luke	CAY 544	Cowenhoven, William	KNG 3
Cous, Jacob	DUT 147	Covert, Matthew	DUT 82	Cowin, Edward	DEL 274
Cous, Peter	DUT 147	Covert, Peter	CAY 544	Cowin, Jabez	SUF 73
Couse, Henry	DEL 283	Covert, Richard	ULS 207	Cowin, Jacob	SUF 71
Couse, John	ALB 84	Covert, Smith	CAY 602	Cowing, William	CHN 954
Cousin, George	NYK 131	Covert, Stephen	ALB 121	Cowise, Gilbert	GRN 353
Cousins, Ezekiel	NYK 21	Covert, Sylvanus	DUT 25	Cowland, Elizabeth	NYK 39
Cousins, Laban	ESS 320	Covert, Tunis	CAY 548	Cowles, Ebenezer	SRA 30
Cousins, Mathew	NYK 99	Covert, Walter	QNS 80	Cowley, Jonathan	DEL 291
Coutant, David	WST 149	Covey, Alpheus	RNS 32	Cowley, Widow	DEL 288
Coutant, Gilbert	NYK 149	Covey, Amos	SRA 5	Cowley, William	NYK 42
Coutant, Isaac	WST 149	Covey, Benjamin	COL 237	Cowly, William	SCH 141
Coutant, Isaac	WST 150	Covey, Hope	OTS 21	Cownover, Garrett	CAY 678
Coutant, Isaiah	WST 150	Covey, James	GRN 352	Cownover, Thomas	ONT 370
Coutman, Robert	NYK 137	Covey, John	CHN 794	Cox see Cose & Cocks	
Couts, Edward	CHN 824	Covey, John	RNS 18	Cox, Anne	WST 145
Couvert, Frederick	STB 207	Covey, Joseph	CHN 764	Cox, Charles	NYK 73
Couvert, Johannas	KNG 10	Covey, King	CHN 764	Cox, Charles	NYK 146
Co_vert, John	KNG 10	Covey, Walter	DUT 91	Cox, Ebenezer	MNT 25
Covel, Heman	SCH 161	Covey, William	OTS 22	Cox, Elizabeth	ULS 246
Covel, James	DEL 274	Covil, Henry	COL 205	Cox, Esas	WST 166
Covel, Joseph	SRA 33	Covil, Henry	DUT 171	Cox, Fanny a Black	NYK 133
Covel, Stephen	MNT 47	Covil, Warren	DUT 171	Cox, Gabriel	NYK 78
Covel, Zenus	DEL 276	Covill, Jacob	ESS 297	Cox, George	DUT 162
Covell, Benjamin	RNS 49	Covill, John	COL 201	Cox, George	MNT 25
Covell, Benjamin	RNS 92	Covill, Zacheus	COL 185	Cox, George	ULS 244
Covell, James	CHN 930	Coville, John	NYK 133	Cox, Isaac	NYK 54
Covell, James	WSH 265	Cowan, Alexander	WSH 257	Cox, Isabella	NYK 42
Covell, John	RNS 49	Cowan, Andrew	ALB 10	Cox, Jacob	DUT 113
Covell, Jonathan	WSH 265	Cowan, Barnet	NYK 148	Cox, James	DUT 111
Covell, Lemuel	RNS 41	Cowan, Ephraim	WSH 302	Cox, James	RNS 84
Covell, Richard	RNS 25	Cowan, George	NYK 137	Cox, James	WST 115
Covell, Seth	RNS 49	Cowan, Jacob	MNT 118	Cox, James	WST 130
Covell, Silas	RNS 92	Cowan, James	OND 192	Cox, Jemmison	NYK 67
Covenhaven, Jacob	WST 162	Cowan, James	WSH 190	Cox, Jesse	WST 132
Covenhoven, Abm	ALB 40	Cowan, James	WSH 196	Cox, John	DUT 162
Covenhoven, Adrian	DUT 69	Cowan, John	NYK 48	Cox, John	NYK 136

Name	Loc	Pg
Cox, John	ORN	276
Cox, John	ORN	344
Cox, John	RNS	23
Cox, John	RCX	108
Cox, John Junr	DUT	160
Cox, Joseph	HRK	440
Cox, Joseph	OTS	21
Co_, Jourden	WST	122
Cox, Lewis	NYK	143
Cox, Mary	NYK	55
Cox, Michael	ALB	136
Cox, Moses a Black	NYK	134
Cox, Moses	WSH	256
Cox, Nicholas	NYK	54
Cox, Nicholas	WST	166
Cox, Phinehas	ORN	316
Cox, Reeve	ORN	339
Cox, Robert	NYK	114
Cox, Robert	NYK	140
Cox, Robert	ULS	249
Cox, Saml	OTS	56
Cox, Samuel	SRA	43
Cox, Samuel C.	NYK	29
Cox, Silvenus	SRA	53
Co_, Tephen	DUT	108
Cox, Thomas	HRK	416
Cox, Thomas	NYK	98
Cox, Thomas	WSH	200
Cox, Thomas Junr	NYK	104
Cox, Wm	MNT	112
Cox, William	NYK	124
Cox, William	ORN	341
Cox, William	ORN	396
Cox, William	QNS	72
Cox, Wm	STB	205
Coxs, Stephen	NYK	66
Coy, David	OND	181
Coy, David Junr	OND	181
Coy, John	COL	215
Coy, John	GRN	337
Coy, John	SCH	142
Coy, John Jun	GRN	337
Coy, luke	ALB	78
Coy, Luke	SCH	145
Coy, Rufus	ALB	78
Coy, Shuble	CHN	768
Coye, Nathan	OTS	28
Coye, Nathl	OTS	21
Coye, Willard	OTS	21
Coyl, Jason	OTS	22
Coze, John	NYK	131
Cozine, Jacob	RCH	92
Cozine, John	NYK	152
Cozine, John R.	NYK	64
Cozine, Margaret	NYK	72
Cozine, Wilhelmus	RCH	92
Cozart, Benjamin	NYK	102
Crab, Henry	WSH	202
Crab, Jonathan	WST	120
Crabb, John	RNS	30
Crabb, Richard	WST	143
Crabb, Thomas	NYK	32
Crabb, Wm	RNS	29
Crabbtree, John	ORN	356
Crabtree, Benjm	COL	216
Crack, Joseph	NYK	149
Cracker, Samuel	GRN	344
Craeghton, Robert	WSH	292
Craford, John	WSH	257
Craft, Abraham	DUT	77
Craft, Benjamin	MNT	117
Craft, Benjamin	SRA	51
Craft, Caleb	DUT	86
Craft, Caleb	WST	124
Craft, Charles	WST	166
Craft, Daniel	QNS	73
Craft, Derrick	QNS	84
Craft, Edward	ONT	454
Craft, Fredereck	OTS	27
Craft, Henry	QNS	83
Craft, Jacob	DEL	267
Craft, James	QNS	72
Craft, James	QNS	84
Craft, John	ONT	454
Craft, John	RNS	15
Craft, Joseph	DUT	84
Craft, Joseph	NYK	130
Craft, Joseph	OTS	9
Craft, Jurden	QNS	83
Craft, Moses	RNS	95
Craft, Peter	QNS	84
Craft, Phebe	QNS	70
Craft, Richard	WST	117
Craft, Robert	QNS	71
Craft, Samuel	WST	111
Craft, Solomon	QNS	82
Craft, Stephen	NYK	130
Craft, Sutton	WST	128
Craft, Thomas	ALB	118
Craft, Thomas	DUT	76
Craft, Thomas	NYK	101
Craft, Thomas	QNS	84
Craft, William	CHN	788
Craft, William	WST	128
Craft, Wright	QNS	84
Crafts, Griffen	OTS	29
Crafts, James	DUT	174
Crafts, John	ULS	240
Crafts, Moses	ULS	240
Crafts, Samuel	OTS	55
Crafts, Walter	OTS	55
Crague	SRA	55
Crague, David	SRA	22
Crague, John	SRA	22
Craig, Alexander	NYK	90
Craig, Andrew	DEL	279
Craig, David	ORN	337
Craig, Elizabeth	NYK	129
Craig, Hector	ORN	350
Craig, James	NYK	42
Craig, James	ORN	348
Craig, John	CLN	158
Craig, John	NYK	90
Craig, John	NYK	150
Craig, John	NYK	152
Craig, John	RCH	92
Craig, Joseph	WSH	295
Craig, Mary	NYK	87
Craig, Moses	MNT	85
Craig, Thomas	ORN	310
Craig, Wm	GRN	331
Craig, William	NYK	20
Craig, William	NYK	76
Craige, Bristol	COL	219
Craige, Eli	ONT	448
Crain, Elijah	WSH	240
Crain, Samuel	WSH	201
Crall, Abraham	ALB	60
Cram, Francis	OND	191
Cramaty, James	COL	208
Cramer, Barent	COL	224
Cramer, Catharine	COL	226
Cramer, Conrad	HRK	457
Cramer, Conradt	MNT	33
Cramer, Frederick	RNS	14
Cramer, John	HRK	578
Cramer, John	MNT	35
Cramer, John	MNT	35
Cramer, John J.	COL	266
Cramer, Richard	ONT	386
Crammer, Jeremiah	ONT	492
Crammond, Abel	NYK	67
Crammond, James	NYK	105
Crampton, _eri	DEL	280
Crampton, Batson	SRA	42
Crampton, John	SRA	42
Crandal, Abner	SCH	170
Crandal, Archibald	OND	169
Crandal, Daniel	NYK	87
Crandal, Elur	SRA	22
Crandal, John	ONN	166
Crandal, John	ONT	350
Crandall, Abm	RNS	112A
C.andall, Daniel	ONN	181
Crandall, David	RNS	75
Crandall, Ebenezar	RNS	113
Crandall, Edward	DEL	280
Crandall, Edward	OND	192
Crandall, Gardner	RNS	98
Crandall, Gideon	RNS	73
Crandall, James	HRK	522
Crandall, Jeremiah	RNS	69
Crandall, Jesper	RNS	98
Crandall, Levi	OND	204
Crandall, Peleg	RNS	73
Crandall, Peter	OND	203
Crandall, Robert	RNS	33
Crandall, Roswell	RNS	73
Crandall, Samuel	RNS	75
Crandall, Stephen	ALB	85
Crandall, Thomas	RNS	98
Crandall, Wm	RNS	59
Crandall, William	RNS	112A
Crandel, Amos	DUT	127
Crandel, Azariah	DUT	54
Crandel, Eber	DUT	129
Crandel, Eber	WSH	255
Crandel, Elisha	OTS	46
Crandel, E[zra?]	DUT	146
Crandel, James	DUT	147
Crandel, Jeremiah Junr	DUT	59
Crandel, Jeremiah Senr	DUT	59
Crandel, John	DUT	148
Crandel, John Junr	DUT	148
Crandel, Joseph	DUT	56
Crandel, Joseph	WSH	255
Crandel, Laban	DUT	147
Crandel, Nathaniel	DUT	13
Crandel, Richard	DUT	146
Crandel, Samuel	DUT	146
Crandel, Samuel	WSH	255
Crandel, Simeon	DUT	148
Crandel, Thos	OTS	25
Crandell, William	WSH	250
Crandell, Benedict	RNS	104
Crandell, Caleb	WSH	298
Crandell, Clemon	RNS	72
Crandell, Eber	COL	184
Crandell, George	COL	222
Crandell, Gideon	COL	219
Crandell, Hannah	NYK	77
Crandell, Henry	RNS	70
Crandell, Isaiah	RNS	68
Crandell, James	COL	195
Crandell, James	RNS	71
Crandell, James	RNS	104
Crandell, Jarid	OTS	46
Crandell, John	RNS	74
Crandell, John	RNS	98
Crandell, John	ULS	234
Crandell, Joseph	RNS	59
Crandell, Michael	RNS	59
Crandell, Nathl	OTS	52
Crandell, Reuben	DUT	149
Crandell, Samuel	COL	179
Crandell, Samel	COL	212
Crandell, Samuel	COL	217
Crandell, Samuel	COL	258
Crandell, Simeon	ULS	238
Crandell, Stennet	RNS	70
Crandell, Timothy Junr	COL	221

Name	Loc		Name	Loc		Name	Loc
Crandell, Willm	COL 222		Crane, Josiah	HRK 491		Craver, David	RNS 13
Crandell, Wm	OTS 52		Crane, Josiah	MNT 102		Craver, Henry	RNS 11
Crandle, Able	WSH 186		Crane, Josiah	ORN 339		Craver, John	RNS 12
Crandle, Asa	WSH 207		Crane, Martha	NYK 25		Craver, Peter	RNS 84
Crandle, Asa	WSH 234		Crane, Michael	NYK 117		Craver, William	RNS 12
Crandle, Benjamin	RNS 66		Crane, NathanL	CHN 902		Cravin, John Junr	RNS 11
Crandle, Caleb	SRA 51		Crane, Noah	DUT 142		Craw, Ebenezar	CAY 642
Crandle, Daniel	WSH 231		Crane, Peter	RNS 61		Craw, Elias	WST 126
Crandle, Ezra	WSH 231		Crane, Roger	CAY 610		Craw, Israel	SRA 53
Crandle, Georg	GRN 339		Crane, Rufus	HRK 488		Craw, Joseph	SRA 53
Crandle, Henery	CHN 826		Crane, Sabine	CAY 618		Crawbarger, Daniel	RNS 37
Crandle, Henry	SRA 40		Crane, Samuel	MNT 105		Crawbeck, Elizabeth	NYK 94
Crandle, James	CHN 828		Crane, Samuel	WSH 293		Crawbeck, Godfrey	NYK 150
Crandle, John	CHN 810		Crane, Shederick	CAY 700		Crawbeck, Peter	NYK 148
Crandle, John	CHN 826		Crane, Simeon	DEL 289		Crawbeth, Elizabeth	NYK 145
Crandle, Jonathan	WSH 204		Crane, Solomon	DUT 172		Crawfoot, Archibald	SRA 42
Crandle, Jonathan	WSH 232		Crane, Stephen	ALB 132		Crawfoot, Archibald	SRA 42
Crandle, Joseph	CHN 850		Crane, [St?]ephen	CAY 516		Crawfoot, Daniel	SRA 42
Crandle, Joseph	WSH 258		Crane, Stephen	DUT 87		Crawfoot, David	SRA 42
Crandle, Joshua	SRA 51		Crane, Stephen	DUT 174		Crawfoot, Henderson	SRA 42
Crandle, Lewis	COL 218		Crane, Stephen	OND 163		Crawfoot, John	SRA 48
Crandle, Pardon	WSH 291		Crane, Stephen	ORN 359		Crawfoot, Robert	SRA 42
Crandle, Peter	WSH 209		Crane, Stephen	SRA 34		Crawfoot, Robert	SRA 42
Crandle, Reuben	WSH 193		Crane, Stephen Junr	ORN 359		Crawfoot, Samuel	SRA 14
Cr_ndle, Richard	SRA 5		Crane, Thaddeus	WST 123		Crawfoot, Stephen	SRA 42
Crandle, Robert	HRK 449		Crane, _mothy	MNT 105		Crawfoot, Wallace	SRA 41
Crandle, Samuel	OTS 22		Crane, Timothy	NYK 93		Crawford, Alexander	DEL 279
Crandol, Augustin	CHN 836		Crane, Timothy	SRA 23		Crawford, Alexander	NYK 38
Crandol, Ezekeil	CHN 836		Crane, William	DUT 176		Crawford, Andrew	ALB 28
Crandol, Ezekiel	CHN 836		Crane, William	ORN 358		Crawford, Caleb	WST 131
Crandol, Hoyea	CHN 948		Crane, Zebulon	DUT 178		Crawford, Charles	OND 207
Crandol, Mumford	CHN 836		Crane, Zeloc	ONT 432		Crawford, Charles	ULS 262
Crandol, Nathan	CHN 828		Cranedel, Joseph	CHN 746		Crawford, Daniel	ULS 186
Crandwall, Freeman	SCH 169		Cranell, Martin	RNS 41		Crawford, David	ORN 346
Crane, Aaron	CAY 700		Crank	SUF 105		Crawford, David	WST 131
Crane, Abraham	ORN 339		Crank, John	WST 124		Crawford, Donis a Black	NYK 90
Crane, Ambrose	ULS 249		Crankite, Jacob	MNT 92		Crawford, Elijah	WST 116
Crane, Asa	ULS 180		Crankshaw, Moses	ALB 53		Crawford, Francis	ORN 289
Crane, Belden	DUT 172		Cranmer, John	DUT 162		Crawford, Frederick	ONT 324
Crane, Benjamin	ORN 339		Cranmer, John	ONT 330		Crawford, George	COL 227
Crane, Benjamin	ORN 362		Crann, James	SRA 46		Crawford, George	WST 119
Crane, Caleb E(?)	MNT 105		Crannel, Nicholas	ALB 44		Crawford, George	WST 148
Crane, Caroline	MNT 10		Crannel, Peter	ALB 80		Crawford, Henry	ULS 262
Crane, Casper	SCH 158		Crannel, Robert	WSH 215		Crawford, Isaac	WSH 289
Crane, Charles	OND 174		Crannel, Wm, W.	ALB 148		Crawford, James	NYK 16
Crane, Daniel	ALB 138		Crannell, Henry	RNS 94		Crawford, James	NYK 52
Crane, David	MNT 105		Crannell, Isaac	RNS 15		Crawford, James	ORN 275
Crane, David	TIO 243		Crannell, Jacob	RNS 5		Crawford, James	ORN 303
Crane, Edmund	CAY 700		Crannell, Moses	RNS 92		Crawford, James	ORN 309
Crane, Elam	ONT 444		Cranson, Walter	RNS 78		Crawford, James	WSH 194
Crane, Elisha	ALB 127		Cranston, James	OTS 24		Crawford, James	WST 146
Crane, Ezekiel	CAY 516		Crants, Henry	HRK 431		Crawford, James	WST 158
Crane, Ezekiel	CAY 700		Crantz, Mark	HRK 499		Crawford, Jane	NYK 57
Crane, Francis	NYK 78		Crapo, Hezekiah	SRA 14		Crawford, Job	DUT 54
Crane, Frederick	OND 201		Crapo, Samuel	SRA 14		Crawford, Joel	CHN 890
Crane, George	CHN 852		Crapo, Seth	SRA 14		Crawford, John	ALB 40
Crane, Gilbert	COL 223		Crapser, Albertus	DUT 111		Crawford, John	CHN 752
Crane, Henry	OND 179		Crapser, Gertruyde	DUT 111		Crawford, John	NYK 136
Crane, Ira	DUT 176		Crapse_, James	SRA 57		Crawford, John	NYK 144
Crane, Isaac	HRK 491		Crapser, John Junr	DUT 111		Crawford, John	ORN 299
Crane, Isaac	HRK 526		Crapser, Sebastian	DUT 113		Crawford, John	SRA 42
Crane, Isaac Junr	HRK 492		Crarke, Thomas B.	NYK 141		Crawford, John	ULS 222
Crane, Isaac B.	NYK 97		Crary, Isaac	ALB 68		Crawford, John	WSH 291
Crane, James	CAY 724		Crary, Joseph	OND 221		Crawford, John	WST 146
Crane, James	DEL 275		Crary, Nathanl	COL 224		Crawford, Jonathan	ORN 300
Crane, John	DEL 267		Crary, Samuel	RNS 18		Crawford, Jonathan	WST 162
Crane, John	DUT 86		Crary, Thomas	ALB 68		Crawford, Joseph	ALB 41
Crane, John	HRK 456		Crary, Thomas	CHN 774		Crawford, Joseph	DEL 278
Crane, John	MNT 105		Crass, Bastian	ALB 63		Crawford, Joseph	ORN 303
Crane, John	NYK 58		Crass, Cronemus	ALB 63		Crawford, Joseph	OTS 44
Crane, John Junr	DUT 86		Crass, Elija	STB 204		Crawford, Joseph	ULS 189
Crane, Jonathan	DUT 173		Crass, George	ALB 63		Crawford, Margaret	NYK 56
Crane, Jonothan	CHN 796		Crat_inge_, Jacob	MNT 50		Crawford, Margaret	ORN 299
Crane, Joseph	DUT 86		Craumer, Christopher	SCH 136		Crawford, Moses	ORN 297
Crane, Joseph	DUT 172		Craumer, William	SCH 136		Crawford, Nathan	ORN 300
Crane, Joseph	NYK 15		Craumer, William	SCH 151		Crawford, Nehemiah	TIO 213
Crane, Josiah	DUT 173		Craven, Mercy	NYK 88		Crawford, Peter	NYK 128

Crawford, Robert	NYK 105	Crendall, Abraham	NYK 113	Crist, David	ORN 297
Crawford, Robert	ORN 338	Cresey, Hezekiah	CAY 662	Crist, Henry	ORN 296
Crawford, Robert	OTS 42	Cressy, Robert	NYK 134	Crist, John J.	ORN 300
Crawford, Robert	ULS 189	Crest, Philip	RNS 11	Crist, Jonathan	ORN 295
Crawford, Robert	WSH 246	Creth, Posper	ONN 174	Crist, Margaret	ORN 309
Crawford, Robert	WSH 291	Creveth, John	ONN 174	Crist, Martinus	ORN 310
Crawford, Robert	WST 126	Creveth, James	ONN 174	Crist, Matthew	ORN 297
Crawford, Samuel	ALB 83	Crevith, Robert	ONN 174	Crist, Philip	HRK 580
Crawford, Samuel	WST 118	Crevith, Samuel	ONN 174	Crist, Stephen	ORN 297
Crawford, Samuel J.	ORN 300	Crew, Ezra	NYK 16	Crist, William	ORN 310
Crawford, Samuel S.	ORN 303	Crewel, Balus	ALB 99	Cristeman, Frederick	MNT 32
Crawford, Silus	WST 163	Crewell, Henry	ALB 98	Cristman, Jacob F.	HRK 429
Crawford, Simeon	OTS 43	Cri , Adam	MNT 29	Cristman, John	HRK 445
Crawford, Solomon	ULS 189	Criddington, Noah	WSH 195	Critinton, Stog ste_	CHN 954
Crawford, Stephen	CAY 610	Criddington, Samuel	WSH 195	Crittenden, Inner	ONT 506
Crawford, Thomas	NYK 31	Criger, John	GRN 351	Crittendon, Ebenezr	ONN 189
Crawford, Thomas	ONT 496	Crigger, James	GRN 351	Crittendon, Hollibert	ONN 132
Crawford, Thomas	ORN 287	Crigier, Nicholas	NYK 25	Crittendon, Leverett	COL 249
Crawford, William	CHN 866	Crill, Thomas	MNT 33	Crittenton, Ebenr	TIO 215
Crawford, William	COL 204	Crimer, Francis	NYK 77	Crittenton, Jason	HRK 494
Crawford, William	DUT 174	Crimsher, Aletta	NYK 39	Crittington, Jerh	OTS 22
Crawford, William	ORN 300	Crine, Mark	RNS 64	Crittinten, Hosea	ONT 480
Crawford, William	ULS 190	Crinner, Cilleon	GRN 356	Croate, Cohan Dederick	COL 229
Crawford, William	WST 148	Crippen, Benjm	COL 204	Crocheron, Abraham	RCH 89
Crawford, William	WST 156	Crippen, Ezra	HRK 573	Crocheron, Abraham	RCH 93
Crawfort, Daniel	TIO 226	Crippen, Hosea	WSH 286	Crocheron, Daniel	RCH 90
Crawfort, Eliakim	TIO 226	Crippen, Ichabod	SCH 134	Crocheron, Daniel	RCH 90
Crawfort, John	ONN 183	Crippen, John	SCH 133	Crocheron, Henry	RCH 90
Crawle, Ebenezar	CAY 626	Crippen, Joseph	WSH 286	Crocheron, Jacob	NYK 15
Crawley, Dewsbury	NYK 35	Crippen, Nathan R.	COL 183	Crocheron, Jacob	RCH 90
Crawnag, Paulis	NYK 151	Crippen, Ransom	HRK 573	Crocheron, Capt John	RCH 91
Crawyer, Nanny Negro	QNS 71	Crippen, Samuel	SRA 51	Crocheron, John	RCH 92
Cray, James	DEL 277	Crippen, Silas	OTS 42	Crocheron, Nicholas	RCH 90
Crazvan, John	NYK 91	Crippen, Thaddeus	COL 181	Crocker, Benjamin	HRK 598
Creal, Anthony	SRA 59	Crippen, Thos	OTS 4	Crocker, David	ALB 86
Creamer, Catharine	SRA 10	Crippen, Thos	OTS 56	Crocker, Ebenezer	COL 257
Creamer, Christopher	SRA 8	Crippen, William	HRK551½	Crocker, Eliazer	WSH 184
Creamer, George	SRA 8	Crippin, Noah	CAY 670	Crocker, Enoch	ALB 86
Creamer, George	SRA 39	Crippin, Reuben	RNS 110	Crocker, Ephraim	ALB 83
Creamer, James	SRA 39	Crippin, Stephen	CAY 670	Crocker, Ephraim	WSH 243
Creamer, Jeremiah	SRA 8	Cripple, William	WSH 186	Crocker, Ezekiel	TIO 223
Creamer, John	SRA 8	Cripps, Peter	ORN 391	Crocker, Hazen	OND 163
Creamer, Peter	SRA 8	Crips, Elisha	RCH 90	Crocker, Jabez	CHN 932
Credit, Amos	DUT 165	Crips, Laurence	RCH 91	Crocker, Jesse	ORN 366
Credit, Benjamin	ORN 338	Crips, Thomas	RCH 93	Crocker, Job	ONN 131
Creed, Augustine	DUT 60	Crips, William	RCH 92	Crocker, John	COL 255
Creed, Benjamin	QNS 15	Crisler, John	ALB 28	Crocker, Jonathan	ALB 83
Creed, Cornelius	QNS 67	Crisley, Cranston	ALB 81	Crocker, Jonathn Junr	ALB 84
Creed, Gilbert	QNS 67	Crispel, Anthony	DEL 283	Crocker, Lemuel	HRK 547
Creed, Hewlet & Caleb		Crispell, Anthony	ULS 206	Crocker, Lemuel	WSH 300
Mills	QNS 66	Crispell, Anthony	ULS 249	Crocker, Lois	WSH 243
Creed, Richard	QNS 67	Crispell, Benjamine	GRN 334	Crocker, Nathaniel	WSH 186
Creed, William	QNS 67	Crispell, David	ULS 196	Crocker, Oliver	TIO 211
Creed, William Junr	QNS 67	Crispell, Eleazer	ULS 196	Crocker, Peter	RNS 101
Creel, James	SRA 56	Crispell, Henry	ULS 196	Crocker, Peter	WSH 294
Creell, John	ULS 203	Crispell, Jacob	ULS 242	Crocker, Russell	COL 219
Creesy, Josiah	OTS 2	Crispell, Jan	ULS 249	Crocker, Samuel	COL 219
Cregeier, Martin	MNY 37	Crispell, John	ULS 196	Crocker, Samuel	HRK 547
Cregier, John	NYK 56	Crispell, Peter	ULS 194	Crocker, Seth	WSH 188
Cregier, Peter	NYK 52	Crispell, Peter	ULS 206	Crocker, Stephen	SCH 120
Crigier, Augustus	NYK 57	Crispell, Solomon	ULS 196	Crocker, Walter	WSH 268
Crigier, Simon	NYK 57	Crispell, Thomas	ULS 196	Croel, Isaiah	SCH 161
Crego, Abraham	HRK 481	Crissell, Jacob	SCH 168	Croel, Seth	SCH 161
Crego, Chauncy	COL 213	Crissell, John	SCH 168	Croel, William	OND 221
Crego, David	COL 212	Crissell, Samuel	QNS 82	Croesby, John	WSH 193
Crego, George	COL 213	Crissey, Abijah	WST 132	Croft, James	DUT 73
Creg_, John	HRK 480	Crissey, Ebenezer	ORN 283	Croheron, Ann	RCH 89
Crego, Joseph	COL 213	Crissey, Elliot	NYK 103	Crokshanks, Hugh	WSH 258
Crego, Richard	COL 213	Crissey, John	ORN 395	Crolius, Clarkson	NYK 107
Crego, William	DUT 137	Crissey, Liberty	RNS 109	Crolius, John	NYK 105
Cregor, Richard	RNS 9	Crissey, Moses	WST 138	Crolius, John	NYK 110
Cregor, Stephen	RNS 9	Crissey, Moses Junr	WST 137	Crolius, William	NYK 105
Creidder, Catherine	NYK 121	Crissey, Stephen	ORN 395	Crom, Sarah	NYK 153
Creighton, James	NYK 31	Crissey, Sylvenus	SRA 55	Cromber, Stephen	RNS 37
Creighton, Peter	NYK 147	Crissey, William	WST 138	Cromeline, Joseph	QNS 65
Creiff, Charles	WSH 190	Crist, Adam	ORN 344	Cromiwell, John	NYK 94
Crelain, Wm	GRN 332	Crist, Christian	ORN 308	Crommelin, Charles	KNG 8

Crommeline, Charles	KNG 8	Crooke, John	DUT 106	Crosby, Richard	STB 206		
Crommeline, Elizabeth	NYK 18	Crooke, Mary	DUT 17	Crosby, Robert	MNT 110		
Crommeline, Robert	NYK 86	Crooker, Abraham	QNS 83	Crosby, Samuel	COL 203		
Cromner, John	NYK 56	Crooker, Jacob	QNS 82	Crosby, Samuel	HRK 537		
Cromp, Frances	NYK 130	Crooker, James	NYK 82	Crosby, Saml	OTS 46		
Cromp, Peter	ALB 134	Crooker, Jarvis	QNS 83	Crosby, Samuel	TIO 215		
Cromp, Peter	NYK 130	Crooker, Sarah	QNS 71	Crosby, Simon	CHN 900		
Cromp, William	NYK 125	Crooker, William	QNS 81	Crosby, Solomon	DUT 172		
Cromwell, Anna	NYK 120	Crookes, John	NYK 34	Crosby, Stephen	DUT 167		
Cromwell, Aron	MNT 61	Crooks, David	ONT 330	Crosby, Stephen	OND 166		
Cromwell, Benjamin	DUT 72	Crookshank, Alexander	WSH 283	Crosby, Sylvanus	HRK 556		
Cromwell, Caleb	DUT 69	Crookshank, Benjamin	NYK 36	Crosby, Tartelius	OTS 46		
Cromwell, Christopher	ORN 297	Crookshank, John	WSH 293	Crosby, Theodorus	DUT 175		
Cromwell, Daniel	NYK 44	Crookshanks, Peter	WSH 226	Crosby, Theodorus	WST 166		
Cromwell, Harmonus	MNT 71	Crookston, Eleanor	DUT 84	Crosby, Thomas	COL 209		
Cromwell, Isaac	KNG 10	Crooney, David	NYK 47	Crosby, Thomas	DEL 273		
Cromwell, Jacob a Black	NYK 81	Cropsey, Andrew	KNG 6	Crosby, Thomas	DUT 167		
Cromwell, James a Black	NYK 121	Cropsey, Andrew	ULS 266	Crosby, William	HRK 513		
Cromwell, James	ORN 382	Cropsey, Cosper	KNG 6	Crose, Hanmathy	SCH 168		
Cromwell, Jesse	HRK 459	Cropsey, Harmanous	RCH 94	Croshtwaite, Peter	NYK 88		
Cromwell, John	DUT 31	Cropsey, Jacob	CHN 958	Crosier, Cuff a Negro	ALB 132		
Cromwell, John	WST 111	Cropsey, James	KNG 6	Crosley see Crosby			
Cromwell, John	WST 145	Cropsey, Jasper	NYK 86	Crosley, Elisha	CHN 786		
Cromwell, Joseph	ULS 266	Cropsey, John	RNS 97	Crosley, Obediah	CHN 786		
Cromwell, Joseph	WST 111	Cropsey, Matthew	ULS 265	Cross, Abel	WSH 215		
Cromwell, Joseph	WST 145	Cropsey, Robert	ULS 257	Cross, Able	WSH 188		
Cromwell, Judith	DUT 72	Cropsey, Valentine	KNG 6	Cross, Alpheus	CHN 844		
Cromwell, Margaret	NYK 101	Cropsey, William	KNG 5	Cross, Arastes	WSH 214		
Cromwell, Oliver	WST 146	Cropsy, Adam	ULS 265	Cross, Benjamin	SRA 19		
Cromwell, William	DUT 145	Cropsy, Henry	ORN 291	Cross, Benjamin	SRA 55		
Cronck, James	WST 158	Cropsy, Henry	ULS 265	Cross, David	WSH 251		
Crone, David	NYK 18	Crosbey, Aaron	ESS 307	Cross, Ebenezar	RNS 25		
Crone, Thomas	NYK 67	Crosbey, Dyer	ONT 446	Cross, Ebenezer	OTS 4		
Cronin, William	COL 247	Crosbey, Isaac	SRA 5	Cross, Ebenr Junr	OTS 4		
Cronk, Abraham	WST 155	Crosbey, Winthrop	ESS 308	Cross, Edward	ONT 454		
Cronk, Abraham Junr	WST 155	Crosby see Crosley		Cross, Eleazer	OTS 27		
Cronk, Absalom	WST 152	Crosby, Abner	DUT 167	Cross, Eleazer Junr	OTS 26		
Cronk, Andrw	NYK 128	Crosby, Benjamin	STB 205	Cross, Ellih	CHN 844		
Cronk, Dennis	WST 162	Crosby, Cyrenius	DUT 136	Cross, Henry	SRA 61		
Cronk, Henry	WST 146	Crosby, Darius	DUT 89	Cross, Isaac	OTS 4		
Cronk, Hebry	WST 166	Crosby, David	DUT 176	Cross, Jacobus	MNT 3		
Cronk, Isaac	ORN 399	Crosby, Ebenezer	NYK 131	Cross, Jaduah	SCH 169		
Cronk, Isaac	WST 152	Crosby, Edward	DUT 167	Cross, James	MNT 20		
Cronk, James	ORN 391	Crosby, Eleazer	HRK 539	Cross, Jarus	SCH 169		
Cronk, John	ESS 307	Crosby, Eli	DUT 166	Cross, Jason	ONT 394		
Cronk, Mary	WST 166	Crosby, Elijah	HRK 583	Cross, Jeremiah	SCH 159		
Cronk, Robert	NYK 93	Crosby, Elisha	ONN 184	Cross, Joel	WSH 215		
Cronk, Simon	RNS112A	Crosby, Wido Elizth	COL 183	Cross, Joel Junr	WSH 215		
Cronk, Teunis	ORN 389	Crosby, Enoch	DUT 178	Cross, John	NYK 81		
Cronk, Thomas	WST 159	Crosby, Enoch Junr	DUT 175	Cross, John	ORN 291		
Cronk, Tunis	WST 122	Crosby, Enos	DUT 90	Cross, John	OTS 4		
Cronkhite, Andrew	ORN 393	Crosby, Increase	ORN 299	Cross, John	WST 161		
Cronkhite, Henry	MNT 24	Crosby, Isaac	DUT 167	Cross, John Junr	WST 151		
Cronkhite, John ye 1st	ORN 396	Crosby, Isaac	DUT 175	Cross, Josep	MNT 91		
Cronkhite, John ye 2d	ORN 393	Crosby, Israel	MNT 60	Cross, Joseph	CHN 812		
Cronkhite, William	ORN 393	Crosby, James	DUT 167	Cross, Joseph	OND 211		
Cronkright, Annee	RNS 22	Crosby, James	HRK 537	Cross, Joshua	GRN 335		
Cronkright, Aury	RNS 22	Crosby, James	OTS 12	Cross, Lemuel	ALB 94		
Cronkright, Ezekiel	RNS 22	Crosby, Joel	WSH 297	Cross, Levi	OTS 27		
Cronkright, John	ALB 83	Crosby, John	ALB 71	Cross, Lockwood	WST 161		
Cronkright, John	RNS 22	Crosby, John	ONN 152	Cross, Michael	ALB 76		
Cronkright, John	RNS 34	Crosby, John	WSH 303	Cross, Natha_il	CAY 630		
Cronkrite, Gilbert	DUT 44	Crosby, Joseph	HRK 537	Cross, Nathel	COL 217		
Cronkrite, John	SCH 123	Crosby, Joseph a Black	NYK 131	Cross, Noah	ULS 201		
Croocker, Sampson	GRN 333	Crosby, Joshua	DUT 175	Cross, Noah	WSH 214		
Croocker, William	GRN 346	Crosby, Josiah	HRK 556	Cross, Penn	QNS 84		
Croofoot, Malcam	SRA 53	Crosby, Lot	OTS 12	Cross, Peter	NYK 90		
Crook, Henry	ULS 230	Crosby, Morton	HRK 540	Cross, Reuben	OND 209		
Crook, Jacob	ULS 230	Crosby, Moses	DUT 167	Cross, Robert	ONT 474		
Crook, John	ULS 247	Crosby, Nathan	DUT 91	Cross, Robert	ORN 292		
Crook, Joseph	OND 195	Crosby, Nathan Junr	DUT 93	Cross, Salem	OTS 4		
Crook, Margaret	NYK 53	Crosby, Nathaniel	ALB 71	Cross, Samuel	WSH 248		
Crook, Martin	ULS 228	Crosby, Patrick	OND 194	Cross, Sarah	OTS 4		
Crook, Nathaniel	OND 181	Crosby, Peter	DUT 176	Cross, Silbester	NYK 132		
Crook, Robert	NYK 132	Crosby, Reuben	DUT 167	Cross, Solomon	WSH 214		
Crook, Samuel	SUF 105	Crosby, Reuben	STB 205	Cross, Thophilus	SRA 10		
Crook, Thomas	OND 195	Crosby, Rial	OTS 20	Cross, Timothy	WSH 252		

Name	Ref	Name	Ref	Name	Ref
Culver, David	CLN 173	Cummings, Stephen	OTS 32	Cunningham, William	NYK 32
Culver, David	DEL 273	Cummings, Stephen Junr	OTS 32	Cunningham, William	ORN 291
Culver, David	WSH 296	Cummings, Thomas	ONT 338	Cunninghams, Shubael	DUT 16
Culver, Deborah	TIO 260	Cummings, Thos	OTS 32	Cuppen, Mark	WSH 186
Culver, Ebenezar	SUF 96	Cummings, William	ALB 45	Cupper, John	WST 137
Culver, Edward	SUF 96	Cummings, William	DUT 43	Cupples, William	ORN 350
Culver, Elias	SUF 96	Cummings, William	NYK 150	Curan, Debrah	ALB 119
Culver, Ephraim	NYK 116	Cummings, Wm	OTS 10	Curan, John	NYK 104
Culver, Francis	CLN 161	Cummins, Aaron	COL 203	Curands, James	ALB 104
Culver, George	ONT 346	Cummins, Abel	RNS 112	Curbey, Seth	SRA 26
Culver, Gideon	OTS 23	Cummins, Abraham	OND 219	Curby, Caleb	WST 131
Culver, Hosias	CAY 658	Cummins, Chapman	RNS 109	Curby, Elihu	WSH 195
Culver, Jacob	SRA 43	Cummins, Clark	WSH 230	Curby, John	GRN 329
Culver, James	CAY 588	Cummins, Cornelius	RNS 109	Curby, Ruth	SRA 12
Culver, James	DUT 115	Cummins, Cornelius	SRA 25	Curby, Thomas	WST 131
Culver, Jeremiah	SUF 95	Cummins, Daniel	RNS 5	Curd, William	CAY 672
Culver, Jeremiah	SUF 96	Cummins, Daniel	ULS 180	Cure, Elias	DEL 286
Culver, John	CLN 164	Cummins, Ephraim	RNS 60	Cure, John	GRN 353
Culver, John	DUT 114	Cumming, Gaylord	DEL 286	Cureden, John	SRA 10
Culver, John	DUT 143	Cummins, James	OND 157	Curler, Aaron	WSH 184
Culver, Joseph	OTS 4	Cummins, James	WSH 195	Curley, Agnetias	NYK 110
Culver, Joseph	OTS 27	Cummins, John	QNS 74	Curlice, Comfort	OTS 57
Culver, Joshua	DUT 146	Cummins, John	TIO 259	Curlis, James	HRK 509
Culver, Joshua	SCH 152	Cummins, Nathan	COL 210	Curlis, Uriah	HRK 509
Culver, Koraham	QNS 62	Cummins, Peter	RNS 55	Curney, Barney	SCH 158
Culver, Lewis	RNS 106	Cummins, Robert	WSH 195	Curney, William	TIO 246
Culver, Moses	ONT 346	Cummins, Samuel	COL 202	Currain, Asa	SUF 73
Culver, Moses	SUF 97	Cummins, Sarah	RNS 43	Currain, Selah	SUF 73
Culver, Nathaniel	CLN 171	Cumper, Frances a		Curran, Vincent	OND 186
Culver, Nathen	WSH 195	Black	NYK 119	Curran, William	CAY 590
Culver, Peter	COL 233	Cumpston, Edward	ALB 32	Currant, Nicholas	NYK 138
Culver, Pheneas	CLN 172	Cumstock, Anson	WSH 209	Curren, Heny	SUF 72
Culver, Phinehas	CAY 564	Cumstock, David	OND 202	Curren, Heny	SUF 72
Culver, Richard	NYK 32	Cumstock, Ichobud	OND 209	Curren, Jeremiah	SUF 72
Culver, Robert S.	ONN 146	Cumstock, Jeremiah	WSH 218	Curren, Joseph	SUF 72
Culver, Samuel	CAY 674	Cune, Joseph	ULS 187	Curren, Nathan	SUF 66
Culver, Samuel	CAY 714	Cuney, Thomas	NYK 135	Curren, Richd	SUF 69
Culver, Silas	OND 220	Cuningham, Aaron	ORN 388	Curren, Saml	ALB 69
Culver, Truman	OND 189	Cuningham, Abner	ORN 386	Currey, Joshua	WSH 250
Culver, William	CAY 658	Cuningham, Andrew	ORN 386	Currey, Mary	WSH 258
Culver, William	NYK 49	Cuningham, Charles	ORN 386	Currey, Robert	CAY 564
Culver, Wm	ONN 168	Cuningham, Mary	SRA 18	Currey, Thomas	WST 128
Culver, William	SUF 96	Cuningham, Moses	ORN 385	Currie, Archibald	NYK 35
Culverhouse, William	NYK 111	Cuningham, Obadiah	ORN 386	Currie, Archibald	NYK 75
Culyer, Richard	NYK 67	Cuningham, Thos	RNS 25	Currie, Charles	DUT 79
Cumber, Tennant D. a		Cunnagum, Joseph	KNG 4	Currie, Frances	NYK 81
Black	NYK 78	Cunneham, Andrew	MNT 34	Currie, James	COL 195
Cumberson, Cornelius	QNS 62	Cunnel, Danl	OTS 32	Currie, James	DUT 73
Cumberson, Thomas	QNS 62	Cunning, Alexr	ALB 40	Currie, Jane	NYK 51
Cumbole, Labus	MNT 45	Cunning, William	NYK 39	Currie, John	NYK 20
Cumbstock, Thomas	OND 207	Cunningham, Alexander	STB 197	Currie, John	ULS 183
Cumming, Jedediah	ONT 364	Cunningham, Archibald	ORN 385	Currie, Lewis	DUT 84
Cummings, Abner	OTS 57	Cunningham, Benjamin	ORN 349	Currie, Nathaniel	SUF 95
Cummings, Abraham	DUT 47	Cunningham, David	CHN 868	Currie, Stephen	ULS 184
Cummings, Anson	OTS 34	Cunningham, David	NYK 118	Currien	NYK 78
Cummings, Caleb	OTS 21	Cunningham, David	OTS 54	Curring, Henry	NYK 151
Cummings, David	OTS 32	Cunningham, Fredk	OTS 10	Currington, Benjamin	SUF 86
Cummings, David	OTS 37	Cunningh.m, George	ONN 154	Curry, Archibald	RNS 23
Cummings, Edward	OTS 46	Cunningham, James	NYK 46	Curry, Benjamin	ORN 379
Cummings, Elijah	OTS 32	Cunningham, James	SRA 25	Curry, George	COL 193
Cummings, Ethiel	WSH 267	Cunningham, Jane	ORN 393	Curry, John	ALB 121
Cummings, George	NYK 138	Cunningham, John	ALB 6	Curry, John	SCH 121
Cummings, Isaac	OTS 8	Cunningham, John	HRK 430	Curry, Joseph	ORN 378
Cummings, Jacob	OTS 8	Cunningham, John	NYK 121	Curry, Richard	WST 158
Cummings, James	DUT 44	Cunningham, John	NYK 137	Curry, Richard Junr	WST 158
Cummings, Jedediah	ONT 374	Cunningham, John	ONN 166	Curry, Robert	ESS 295
Cummings, John	ALB 52	Cunningham, John	ORN 285	Curry, Samuel	DUT 63
Cummings, John	ALB 99	Cunningham, John D.	NYK 50	Curry, Stephen	WST 152
Cummings, John	DUT 44	Cunningham, Mathew	NYK 122	Cursio, Jacob Junr	NYK 97
Cummings, John	DUT 80	Cunningham, Nathaniel	NYK 62	Curswell, Samuel	CAY 542
Cummings, John	OTS 10	Cunningham, Ralph	ALB 128	Curt, John	RCK 110
Cummi[ngs?], John	OTS 21	Cunningham, Richard	NYK 62	Curter, Henry	WSH 186
Cummings, John	OTS 46	Cunningham, Samuel	NYK 121	Curtes, Joseph	WSH 188
Cummings, Joseph	ONT 316	Cunningham, Samuel	ORN 385	Curtice, Ager	OTS 49
Cummings, Nathan	CLN 172	Cunningham, Sarah	CAY 670	Curtice, Asa	OTS 41
Cummings, Samuel	MNT 55	Cunningham, Thomas	OND 209	Curtice, Ebenr	OTS 52
Cummings, Simeon	DUT 44	Cunningham, Walter	NYK 139	Curtice, Ebenr B.	OTS 49

Curtice, Edmund	OTS 4	Curtis, Orsis	ONN 156	Cushing, Benjamin	NYK 75
Curtice, Nathl	OTS 52	Curtis, Pardon	RNS 104	Cushing, Matthew	OND 195
Curtinnus, Peter	NYK 96	Curtis, Philo	WSH 212	Cushing, Stephen	DUT 53
Curtis, __eb	RNS 90	Curtis, Phineas	MNT 114	Cushing, Thomas	CHN 956
Curtis, Abner	HRK 585	Curtis, Richard	NYK 81	Cushing, William	DUT 53
Curtis, Ambrose	OND 190	Curtis, Robert	CHN 882	Cushion, John	MNT 120
Curtis, Andrew	SRA 25	Curtis, Robert	NYK 35	Cushman, Benjn	OTS 37
Curtis, Assahel	WSH 277	Curtis, Samuel	CHN 772	Cushman, Charles	WSH 267
Curtis, Benjamin	WST 147	Curtis, Samuel	CHN 894	Cushman, Consider	DUT 95
Curtis, Caleb	WSH 273	Curtis, Samuel	OND 193	Cushman, Ebenezer	WSH 198
Curtis, Charles	NYK 142	Curtis, Samuel J.	OND 192	Cushman, Joseph	OTS 13
Curtis, Comfort	WSH 185	Curtis, Sarah	NYK 58	Cushman, Leveret	OTS 41
Curtis, Daniel	ONT 312	Curtis, Solomon	CHN 768	Cushman, Minerva	OTS 48
Curtis, Daniel	ONT 388	Curtis, Stephen	ALB 110	Cushman, Seth	CAY 672
Curtis, Daniel	WSH 212	Curtis, Stephen	WSH 186	Cushnahan, Charles	ULS 199
Curtis, Daniel	WSH 272	Curtis, Stephen	WSH 303	Cushnahan, John	ULS 199
Curtis, Daniel	WSH 276	Curtis, Thaddeus	SRA 57	Cussaboom, David	SUF 79
Curtis, David	CHN 808	Curtis, Thaddeus	SRA 57	Custer, Paul	HRK 428
Curtis, David	OND 168	Curtis, Thomson	CHN 882	Cutchalk, Sebastian	NYK 147
Curtis, Eanaes	WSH 208	Curtis, Thomas	HRK 449	Cutendon, Benjamin	OND 209
Curtis, Ebenezar	ONT 388	Curtis, Thomas	SUF 89	Cutendon, Benj. Junr	OND 209
Curtis, Ebenezer	HRK 592	Curtis, Thomas	WSH 208	Cutendon, James	OND 209
Curtis, Ebenezer	MNT 122	Curtis, Thos Junr	RNS 104	Cutgrave, Wm	GRN 346
Curtis, Edward	CHN 920	Curtis, William	NYK 146	Cuthbert, Benjm	ALB 107
Curtis, Edward	SRA 15	Curtis, Wm	QNS 73	Cuthbert, Benjamin	DUT 126
Curtis, Elihu	OND 207	Curtis, Wm B.	OND 215	Cuthill, Alexander	NYK 44
Curtis, Elijah	SRA 29	Curtis, William P.	OND 199	Cutland see Culland	
Curtis, Eliphalet	OND 207	Curtis, Zachariah	SRA 41	Cutland, William G.	GRN 342
Curtis, Elisha	OND 207	Curtis, Zachaus H.	WSH 213	Cutlar, Abraham	NYK 128
Curtis, Elisha	WSH 277	Curtiss, Agustus	ONT 314	Cutlar, Ebenezer	NYK 141
Curtis, Ezra St. John	WSH 269	Curtis, Amasa	ORN 353	Cutlar, Peter	NYK 145
Curtis, Felex	WSH 276	Curtis, Amaziah	COL 216	Cutler see Cutter	
Curtis, Harry	CHN 822	Curtiss, Amos	ORN 280	Cutler, Abigail	DUT 101
Curtis, Henry	SRA 41	Curtiss, Ashbel	CAY 720	Cutler, Abner	OND 181
Curtis, Hiram	TIO 213	Curtiss, Benjamin	ORN 348	Cutler, Benjamin	WSH 302
Curtis, Horace	OND 182	Curtiss, Caleb	ORN 293	Cutler, Bradley	OTS 52
Curtis, Hosea	ONN 136	Curtiss, Daniel	CAY 690	Cutler, David	CHN 856
Curtis, Isaac	OND 191	Curtiss, Daniel	COL 218	Cutler, David	OTS 47
Curtis, Israel	SRA 26	Curtiss, Daniel	DUT 130	Cutler, Henry	ULS 257
Curtis, James	MNT 114	Curtiss, David	CAY 594	Cutler, Joel	CHN 838
Curtis, James	OND 192	Curtiss, Eden	DUT 93	Cutler, John	WSH 294
Curtis, Jarus	OND 186	Curtiss, Elijah	CAY 670	Cutler, John Jur	WSH 294
Curtis, Jesse	OND 200	Curtiss, Ethan	ORN 290	Cutler, Jonas	ONT 338
Curtis, Jesse	OND 207	Curtiss, Israel	DUT 145	Cutler, Jonas	WSH 302
Curtis, Joel	RNS 93	Curtiss, Isreal	CAY 720	Cutler, Jonathan	ALB 120
Curtis, Joel	RNS 102	Curtiss, James	COL 193	Cutler, Jonathan	CHN 856
Curtis, Joel	SRA 51	Curtiss, John	DUT 132	Cutler, Jonathan	GRN 325
Curtis, Joel Junr	RNS 101	Curtiss, Joshua	ORN 353	Cutler, Joseph	DUT 47
Curtis, John	NYK 65	Curtiss, Josiah	HRK 554	Cutler, Joseph	OND 193
Curtis, John	NYK 94	Curtiss, Josiah	ULS 211	Cutler, Joseph	WST 165
Curtis, John	OND 161	Curtiss, Lewis	DUT 131	Cutler, Nathan	CHN 862
Curtis, John	OND 209	Curtiss, Lydia	DUT 129	Cutler, Peter	NYK 125
Curtis, John	ONN 155	Curtiss, Martin	CAY 548	Cutler, Samuel	DUT 48
Curtis, John	RNS 104	Curtiss, Mary	CAY 590	Cutler, Seth L.	OND 181
Curtis, John	SRA 15	Curtiss, Moses	DUT 58	Cutler, Stephen	DUT 101
Curtis, John	SUF 91	Curtiss, Robert	TIO 248	Cutler, William	DUT 47
Curtis, Jonah	CHN 780	Curtiss, Rosanna	COL 217	Cutter see Cutler	
Curtis, Jonathan	OND 167	Curtiss, Samuel	COL 184	Cutter, Ellen	CAY 612
Curtis, Jonathan	SRA 12	Curtiss, Samuel	DUT 8	Cutter, John	ALB 20
Curtis, Jonathan	TIO 228	Curtiss, Samuel	DUT 132	Cutter, Saml	RNS 23
Curtis, Joseph	ALB 32	Curtiss, Samuel Junr	COL 187	Cutter, Simeon	RNS 23
Curtis, Joseph	CHN 878	Curtiss, Samuel A.	COL 205	Cutterback, Pet_r G.	CAY 596
Curtis, Joseph	RNS 104	Curtiss, Samuel Dean	CAY 670	Cutting, Alpheus	OTS 41
Curtis, Joshua	OND 168	Curtiss, Selden	COL 217	Cutting, William	NYK 51
Curtis, Jotham	ONT 312	Curtiss, Seth	CAY 622	Cutting, Zackariah	CHN 972
Curtis, Jotham W.	TIO 229	Curtiss, Sylvester	ONT 330	Cuvvey, Elish	WSH 211
Curtis, Judson	OND 201	Curtter, Forde	NYK 19	Cuyes, Henry	ONT 408
Curtis, Lawrin	CHN 800	Curver, John	MNT 122	Cuyle, Ephm	OTS 18
Curtis, Ledeas	WSH 277	Curwan, Barnabas	CAY 594	Cuyler, Abraham N.	ALB 43
Curtis, Levi	ONN 150	Curwin, George	ULS 195	Cuyler, Glenn	CAY 628
Curtis, Levy	WSH 294	Curwin, Joseph	SUF 71	Cuyler, Henry	DUT 80
Curtis, Luther	ONT 374	Curwin, Phinehas	ORN 276	Cuyler, Henry	MNT 110
Curtis, Margaret	NYK 52	Curwood, John	NYK 104	Cuyler, Henry	RNS 5
Curtis, Mark	RNS 33	Cury, Jeremiah	WST 132	Cuyler, Jacob	ALB 46
Curtis, Nathaniel	MNT 123	Curzon, Jonathan	DUT 45	Cuyler, Jacob	ALB 147
Curtis, Nathaniel	WSH 212	Cusack, George	ULS 193	Cuyler, Jacob J.	OTS 41
Curtis, Newman	HRK 415	Cuse, Henry	WST 166	Cuyler, John J.	ALB 135

Name	Loc	Name	Loc	Name	Loc
Cuyler, Joseph	MNT 71	Dakin, Benjamin	DUT 93	Damoth, Richard	ONN 166
Cuyler, Philip	ALB 140	Dakin, Caleb	DUT 135	Damouth, George	HRK 465
Cuyler, Stephen	ESS 304	Dakin, Ebenezer K.	DUT 142	Damouth, John	HRK 437
Cuyler, Tobias	SCH 118	Dakin, Elisha	DUT 93	Damund, George	RNS 81
Cuyler, Wm	STB 199	Dakin, Jacob	DUT 143	Dan, Abijah	GRN 355
Cuyper, Gilbert	RCK 110	Dakin, Johnson	DUT 40	Dan, Selleck	DUT 174
Cuyper, Gilbert	RCK 110	Dakin, Joshua	DUT 143	Dan, Thaddeus	DUT 89
Cuyper, Jacob	RCK 109	Dakin, Paul	COL 249	Dan, William	DUT 89
Cuyper, Theunis	RCK 110	Dakin, Preserved	DUT 166	Dana, Edmund	NYK 69
Cyler, John	GRN 356	Dakin, Simon Senr &		Dana, Francis	ONT 508
Cypher, Jacob	WST 162	Junr	DUT 142	Dana, Joseph	OND 172
Cypher, Manassa a		Dakin, Timothy	DUT 55	Dana, Samuel	ONT 488
mulatto	NYK 41	Dakin, William	DUT 166	Danalds, John	WST 141
Cypher, William	WST 166	Dakin, Zebulon	COL 238	Dance, John	ALB 51
Cyphers, John	WST 146	Dakins, Ebenezer	SRA 50	Dance, Joseph	ALB 7
		Dakins, Joshua	COL 182	Dance, Walter	ALB 8
D		Dakins, Woster	CHN 798	Dandee, Timothy	NYK 69
		Dalabee, George	OND 170	Dandford, Ephraem	MNT 64
D___, Joseph	CAY 554	Dalack, Partrick	GRN 357	Dandley, James	WSH 213
D...., Joseph	MNT 100	Dalaney, Peter	HRK 487	Dandling, Henry	MNT 107
D...., Wenstone	ONN 164	Dale, Lydia a mulatto	NYK 39	Dando, Stephen	NYK 48
D_g_n, Samuel	ONT 428	Dale, Robert	NYK 59	Dane, Daniel	ORN 356
D...., J_n	ONT 474	Dale, William	ALB 140	Danels, John	CHN 956
D_smore, Thomas	ONT 482	Dale, William	DEL 284	Danes, Henry	ORN 349
D_ean, Richard	ORN 384	Dales, Alexander	DEL 285	Danes, Saml	SUF 71
D_ane, Elnathan	OTS 48	Daley, Abraham	HRK 541	Danford, Samuel	SRA 41
D...ea, Jacob	QNS 64	Daley, Abraham Jun	HRK 541	Danforth, Abijah	ALB 12
D___, Joseph	RNS 92	Daley, Absalom	WSH 281	Danforth, Asa	ONN 150
D_ke, Benjamin	WST 148	Daley, David	WSH 298	Danforth, Cyrus	ONN 138
Da_ah, Rossel	CHN 812	Daley, Ethiel	WSH 305	Danforth, Daniel	ONN 138
Dacker, Cornelius	GRN 333	Daley, Jacob	OTS 37	Danforth, Elisha	WSH 210
Daddey, William	WSH 199	Daley, Nathaniel	ALB 24	Danforth, Francis	ALB 49
Dady, Nathaniel	ONN 181	Daley, Samuel	CHN 746	Danforth, Isaac	RNS 21
Daget, Elisha	OND 216	Daley, Samuel	WSH 305	Danforth, John	ONN 154
Dagget, Levi	WSH 248	Daley, William	ONT 380	Danforth, Jonathan	SCH 127
Daggett, Harman	SUF 95	Dalie, Waterman	RNS 17	Danforth, Prince	ORN 289
Daggett, Job	RNS 51	Dall, Nathaniel	NYK 142	Dangordus free Black	
Daggett, Mahue	RNS 41	Dallaby, William	NYK 33	Man	SRA 15
Daggett, Thomas	RNS 41	Dallas, Chas	SUF 67	Daniel	QNS 62
Dailands, John	WSH 214	Dallass, John	WST 129	Daniel	QNS 80
Dailey, David	CAY 562	Dallemot, Jacob	ALB 16	Daniel	SUF 89
Dailey, Edward	GRN 345	Dallemot, John	ALB 16	Daniel, James	ALB 134
Dailey, James	CAY 560	Dal[lis?], Jacob	GRN 346	Daniel, Mathew	NYK 25
Dailey, Jeremiah	WSH 211	Dally, Abraham	NYK 136	Daniel, Sands	NYK 124
Dailey, John	OTS 13	Dally, Charles	NYK 16	Daniels, Abraham	OND 209
Dailey, John	OTS 22	Dally, George	NYK 116	Daniels, Amos	OTS 14
Dailey, John	TIO 253	Dally, Joseph	NYK 129	Daniels, Andrew	OND 201
Dailey, Robert	CAY 560	Dally, Mary	NYK 113	Daniels, Benjamin	ESS 298
Dailey, Samuel	ULS 180	Dally, Phillip	NYK 69	Daniels, Bennajah	ESS 302
Dailey, Samuel	WSH 211	Dally, Phillip	NYK 132	Daniels, Charles	DEL 267
Dailey, Sarah	OTS 36	Dally, William	NYK 124	Daniels, Daniel	ONT 390
Dailey, Thadeus	OTS 49	Dalrimple, Paul	NYK 39	Daniels, David J.	NYK 31
Dailey, William	CAY 560	Dalrymple, Ebenezer	WSH 266	Daniels, Ephraim	NYK 65
Dailey, William	CAY 580	Dalsby, Thomas	ORN 297	Daniels, Frederick	HRK 509
Dailey, William	ONT 434	Dalsen Abraham	ORN 373	Daniels, George	HRK 474
Dailey, William	WSH 213	Dalsen, Asa	ORN 330	Daniels, George	OTS 15
Daily, Archibald	ORN 304	Dalsen, Isaac	ORN 373	Daniels, James	DUT 76
Daily, Benjamin	ORN 330	Dalsen, James	ORN 330	Daniels, James	ESS 307
Daily, Benjamin	ULS 239	Dalsen, Samuel	ORN 330	Daniels, James	NYK 64
Daily, Dennis	ORN 292	Dalson, Edward	ORN 378	Daniels, Jasper	COL 250
Daily, Henry	ULS 245	Dalson, Jacob	ORN 282	Daniels, Jeremiah	ESS 304
Daily, James	DEL 272	Dalson, Peter	ULS 265	Daniels, Joel	DUT 139
Daily, John	ULS 211	Dalson, Samuel	ORN 273	Daniels, John	ESS 304
Daily, Nathan	SCH 170	Dalton, John	DUT 73	Daniels, John	NYK 32
Daily, Peter	ULS 255	Dalton, William	ALB 120	Daniels, John	ONN 176
Daily, Silas	ORN 335	Dalway, Andrew	DUT 39	Daniels, John	ULS 180
Dains, John	ONT 430	Daly, Daniel	NYK 123	Daniels, Joseph	ONN 154
Dains, David	ONT 432	Daly, Martin	NYK 145	Daniels, Lemuel	COL 180
Dairagh, James	CAY 614	Daly, William	WSH 246	Daniels, Nahum	HRK 565
Dairah, Alexander	CAY 614	Damarest, Albert	CAY 680	Daniels, Nathan	OND 186
Dake, Augustus	SRA 58	Damarist, David	NYK 58	Daniels, Nathl	OTS 32
Dake, Bartlet	SRA 58	Dames, Caty	NYK 19	Daniels, Reuben	OND 166
Dake, Charles	SRA 58	Damewood, Hannah	OND 198	Daniels, Richard	STB 197
Dake, Charles	SRA 58	Damewood, John	OND 198	Daniels, Samuel	ESS 304
Dake, John	SRA 58	Damewood, Richard	OND 198	Daniels, Samuel	NYK 20
Dake, William	SRA 58	Damon, David	CHN 938	Daniels, Samuel	WSH 218
Dakes, Oliver	CAY 676	Damoth, Marks	ONN 166	Daniels, Starling	DEL 268

Name	Loc	Name	Loc	Name	Loc
Daniels, Starling	ESS 298	Darling, Garret	SUF 89	Dates, Henry	DUT 122
Daniels, Thomas	CHN 842	Darling, Gershem	WSH 214	Dates, Henry	RNS 88
Daniels, William	CAY 640	Darling, Hamilton	SUF 89	Dates, John	DUT 5
Daniels, Wm	MNT 94	Darling, Hamilton	SUF 89	Dates, Mary	DUT 69
Daniels, William	OND 221	Darling, Hannah	ALB 107	Dates, William	CAY 710
Daniels B, John	ESS 304	Darling, Ichabod	ONT 410	Daton, David	SRA 55
Danielson, Altimont	OTS 22	Darling, Jacob	ESS 323	Daton, David	WST 112
Danielson, Calvin	OTS 23	Darling, Jedediah	OND 168	Daton, Fraderick	RNS 47
Danielson, Ebenezer	WST 124	Darling, Jeremiah	WSH 214	Daton, Gilbert	WST 124
Danielson, Fredk	OTS 22	Darling, John	COL 208	Daton, Heny	SUF 69
Danielson, John	OTS 22	Darling, John	SUF 84	Daton, Heny	SUF 69
Danielson, Nathl	OTS 22	Darling, John	SUF 89	Daton, James	SUF 69
Danielson, Timo	OTS 22	Darling, John	SUF 89	Daton, James	SUF 69
Danilds, Samuel	RNS 85	Darling, Jonathan	DUT 137	Daton, John	SUF 66
Danker, Jacob	RNS 92	Darling, Joseph	SCH 146	Daton, Nathl	SUF 70
Danks, Isaac	ONN 150	Darling, Joseph	SCH 148	Daton, Nathl	SUF 70
Danks, Shaverick	CLN 165	Darling, Levi	RNS 101	Dauney, John	CHN 944
Danley, John	WSH 264	Darling, Michl	OTS 36	Daunton, Elijah	ESS 317
Danley, Merril	WSH 264	Darling, Naham	ESS 319	Daunton, Thomas	ESS 317
Dann, Abraham	WST 152	Darling, Nathaniel	GRN 335	Dauph, Edward	SRA 16
Dann, Abram Junr	WST 153	Darling, Nathaniel	OND 184	Davall, Phineas	SUF 104
Dann, Ebenezer	WST 139	Darling, Nicholas	DUT 148	Davan, John	NYK 53
Dann, Ebenezer	WST 152	Darling, Peter	DUT 153	Davenport, Anne	ULS 227
Dann, Enoch	WST 152	Darling, Roswell	COL 208	Davenport, Cornelius	ULS 201
Dann, James	WST 152	Darling, Samuel	OND 166	Davenport, David	ALB 89
Dann, James	WST 160	Darling, Solomon	DUT 152	Davenport, Gabriel	ORN 381
Dann, James Junr	WST 160	Darling, William	ULS 184	Davenport, Garret	ORN 318
Dann, Richard	MNT 77	Darling, Zepheniah	ULS 187	Davenport, Henry	ORN 385
Dann, Squire	WST 160	Darner, Russel	OTS 4	Davenport, Isaac	DUT 72
Dann, Thaddeus	WST 153	Darnley, Charles	NYK 100	Davenport, Isaac	NYK 134
Danniels, James	RCH 93	Darnold, Nathaniel	SRA 61	Davenport, Jesse	ORN 390
Danniels, John	NYK 112	Darra, John	NYK 131	Davenport, Jesse	TIO 228
Danniels, John	RCH 92	Darren, Josiah	COL 201	Davenport, John	CAY 518
Danninger, George	COL 225	Darren, Seba	COL 200	Davenport, John	NYK 148
Danniston, John	DEL 285	Darrough, Joseph	CAY 628	Davenport, John	NYK 148
Dannon, Partrick	NYK 136	Darrow, Abel	WSH 238	Davenport, John	ULS 250
Danse, John	ESS 296	Darrow, Amrons	OND 219	Davenport, John F.	QNS 79
Dansmore, John	SCH 170	Darrow, Azariah	DUT 133	Davenport, Jonathan	COL 187
Danton, Amasa	WSH 187	Darrow, Christopher	ULS 184	Davenport, Joseph	CAY 596
Danton, Ebenezer	WSH 192	Darrow, Christopher	WSH 238	Davenport, Lewis	DUT 54
Danton, Thomas	ALB 85	Darrow, Daniel	ALB 41	Davenport, Mary	DUT 72
Darbey, Dudley	OND 216	Darrow, Daniel	RNS 32	Davenport, Nathaniel	CAY 572
Darbey, George	WSH 272	Darrow, George	COL 205	Davenport, Newberry	WST 149
Darbey, James	WSH 271	Darrow, George	DEL 279	Davenport, Robert	ORN 390
Darbey, Jason	WSH 295	Darrow, Guy	MNT 48	Davenport, Samuel	DUT 63
Darbey, Lemuel	OND 216	Darrow, Guy Junr	MNT 48	Davenport, Samuel	QNS 69
Darbey, Peter	WSH 271	Darrow, Isaac	DEL 276	Davenport, Samuel	ULS 210
Darby, Daniel	COL 248	Darrow, Isaac	WSH 203	Davenport, Stephen	ORN 390
Darby, Elizabeth	NYK 97	Darrow, Jeddedeah	WSH 296	Davenport, Thomas	NYK 94
Darby, George	NYK 110	Darrow, Jeremiah	WSH 296	Davenport, William	DUT 72
Darby, George	WSH 224	Darrow, John	COL 215	Davenport, William Junr	DUT 72
Darby, James	TIO 218	Darrow, Jonathan	CLN 172	Davey, Adam	OTS 15
Darby, John	NYK 70	Darrow, Nathaniel	RNS 31	Dav[ice?], Thomas J.	OND 224
Darby, John	ORN 285	Darrow, Paul	DUT 67	David Negro	QNS 73
Darby, John	SRA 7	Darrow, Paul	NYK 136	David a Negro	SUF 68
Darby, John	SRA 9	Darrow, Saml	OTS 48	David, Daniel	RNS 56
Darby, John	SUF 79	Darrow, Thomas	SRA 18	David, Elizabeth	NYK 37
Darby, Ruth	NYK 135	Darrow, Walter	CLN 170	David, Henry	ORN 335
Darby, Saml	OTS 28	Darrow, Widow	SRA 30	David, Henry	ULS 253
Darby, Samuel	ULS 182	Darrow, William	OND 222	David, Isaac	COL 259
Darby, Willet	QNS 78	Dart, Jeremiah	DEL 268	David, Isaac	MNT 85
Darby, William	ONN 132	Dart, Nathan	OTS 33	David, Jesse	OTS 57
Darby, Wm	ONN 168	Dart, Nathan Junr	OTS 33	David, John	NYK 103
Darby, William	SUF 79	Dart, Nathun	WSH 266	David, Jonathan	COL 258
Darbyshare, David	WST 130	Dart, Roswell	WSH 266	David, Peter	ALB 132
Darbyshire, Matthw	OTS 10	Dart, William	DEL 287	David, Samuel	SCH 147
Darbyshire, William	DUT 88	Darwin, Daniel	COL 178	David, Wm	RNS 10
Darcey, James	NYK 79	Daryee, Abraham	DUT 32	David, Wm	RNS 55
Darg, John	NYK 147	Dash, John B.	NYK 47	Davids, Benjamin	ULS 226
Darley, James	MNT 68	Dash, John B. Junr	NYK 50	Davids, Isaac	WST 156
Darling, Abner	OND 170	Da Sylva, John	ULS 265	Davids, Joseph	ULS 226
Darling, Adam	SUF 89	Datche, Jeremiah	RNS 23	Davids, Richard	MNT 95
Darling, Benjamin	SRA 41	Date, Christopher	GRN 336	Davids, Thadeus	MNT 95
Darling, Davi	WSH 214	Dater, Adam	RCK 106	Davids, Wm	MNT 93
Darling, David	CHN 796	Dater, John	RCK 100	Davids, William	ULS 233
Darling, Ebenezer	RNS 47	Dater, Philip	RNS 87	Davidson, Amy	NYK 93
Darling, Ebenezer	COL 208	Dates, Abraham L.	DUT 40	Davidson, Andrew	HRK 531

Davidson, Charles	NYK 28	Davis, Daniel	RNS 42	Davis, Gershom	DEL 288		
Davidson, Charles	ONT 368	Davis, Danl	SUF 68	Davis, Gilbert	ORN 367		
Davidson, Daniel	DUT 7	Davis, Daniel Jun	ONT 314	Davis, Gilbert	SUF 71		
Davidson, Daniel	RNS 94	Davis, David	CAY 620	Davis, Gilbert	SUF 75		
Davidson, David	NYK 105	Davis, David	CAY 672	Davis, Goldsmith	SUF 69		
Davidson, George	NYK 57	Davis, David	CHN 776	Davis, Henry	DUT 81		
Davidson, James	ALB 27	Davis, David	DUT 104	Davis, Henry	DUT 157		
Davidson, James	NYK 93	Davis, David	NYK 76	Davis, Henry	HRK 577		
Davidson, James	NYK 102	Davis, David	NYK 90	Davis, Henry	RNS 77		
Davidson, James	NYK 102	Davis, David	ONT 366	Davis, henry	SRA 45		
Davidson, James	NYK 102	Davis, David	OTS 49	Davis, Heny	SUF 68		
Davidson, John	NYK 103	Davis, David	RNS 33	Davis, Henry	ULS 191		
Davidson, John	NYK 104	Davis, David	RNS 71	Davis, henry	ULS 199		
Davidson, John	WSH 219	Davis, David	SUF 69	Davis, Hezekiah	RNS 32		
Davidson, Robert	ORN 324	Davis, David	SUF 74	Davis, Hiel	SRA 22		
Davidson, Robert Junr	ORN 323	Davis, David	SUF 81	Davis, Horace	ONT 368		
Davidson, William	NYK 104	Davis, David	WST 166	Davis, Ichabod	GRN 358		
Davie, Archibald	NYK 27	Davis, David Junr	RNS 71	Davis, Ichabod	WSH 264		
Davie, John	ORN 383	Davis, David Jr	SUF 69	Davis, Isaac	ALB 80		
Davies, William	DUT 68	Davis, David Sr	SUF 69	Davis, Isaac	CHN 956		
Davinish, John a		Davis, David A.	NYK 147	Davis, Isaac	DUT 162		
mulatto	NYK 98	Davis, Davis	MNT 70	Davis, Isaac	GRN 335		
Davinson, Thomas	SRA 24	Davis, Dennis	COL 261	Davis, Isaac	ONT 368		
Davis	GRN 343	Davis, Ebenesar	GRN 345	Davis, Isaac	SUF 66		
Davis	RNS 22	Davis, Ebenezar	GRN 357	Davis, Isaac	SUF 69		
Davis, ___	GRN 359	Davis, Ebenezar	RNS 76	Davis, Isaac	SUF 74		
Davis, Aaron	HRK 414	Davis, Ebenezer	ALB 92	Davis, Isaac	ULS 199		
Davis, Aaron	OND 178	Davis, Ebenezer	OND 219	Davis, Isaac	WST 166		
Davis, Aaron	OND 181	Davis, Edmond	SRA 12	Davis, Isaac C.	ULS 203		
Davis, Abijah	OND 182	Davis, Edward	ALB 46	Davis, Isaiah	CAY 722		
Davis, Abner	DEL 287	Davis, Edward	CHN 792	Davis, Isaiah	ULS 194		
Davis, Abraham	NYK 147	Davis, Edward	NYK 120	Davis, Ishmael	DUT 62		
Davis, Abraham	ONT 494	Davis, Edward	SRA 10	Davis, Ishmal	OTS 35		
Davis, Abraham	QNS 78	Davis, Eleazer	COL 217	Davis, Israel	HRK 423		
Davis, Abraham	WST 162	Davis, Eliakim	SRA 18	Davis, Israel	SUF 71		
Davis, Abraham	WST 162	Davis, Elias	GRN 345	Davis, Jabez	OTS 21		
Davis, Abraham	WST 167	Davis, Elias	ULS 181	Davis, Jabez	OTS 43		
Davis, Abraham Junr	WST 167	Davis, Elias	ULS 207	Davis, Jacob	COL 246		
Davis, Alben	DEL 288	Davis, Elicom	SUF 68	Davis, Jacob a Black	NYK 42		
Davis, Alpheus	SRA 39	Davis, Elijah	SUF 68	Davis, Jacob	SRA 22		
Davis, Amos	GRN 350	Davis, Elisha	SRA 45	Davis, Jacobus	ORN 315		
Davis, Amos	MNT 112	Davis, Elisha	SUF 68	Davis, Jacobus	ULS 198		
Davis, Andrew	ORN 312	Davis, Eliud	SRA 23	Davis, Jacobus	ULS 209		
Davis, Andrew	SRA 18	Davis, Elizabeth	ALB 138	Davis, James	ALB 134		
Davis, Andrew Junr	ULS 196	Davis, Elizabeth	KNG 9	Davis, James	ESS 307		
Davis, Andries	ULS 199	Davis, Elizabeth	NYK 40	Davis, James	ESS 310		
Davis, Annenias	SUF 66	Davis, Elizabeth	NYK 42	Davis, James	MNT 73		
Davis, Archibald	COL 241	Davis, Elizabeth	NYK 92	Davis, James	NYK 22		
Davis, Asa	OND 181	Davis, Elizabeth	ULS 207	Davis, James	NYK 78		
Davis, Asa	OTS 10	Davis, Ellis	ORN 398	Davis, James	NYK 149		
Davis, Benajh	OTS 32	Davis, Elnathan	SUF 68	Davis, James	ORN 292		
Davis, Benjaman	CHN 824	Davis, Ephraim	COL 265	Davis, James	RNS 36		
Davis, Benjamin	DUT 17	Davis, Ephraim	DEL 272	Davis, James	RNS 41		
Davis, Benjamin	DUT 117	Davis, Ephraim	OND 182	Davis, James	SRA 10		
Davis, Benjamin	ORN 370	Davis, Ephraim	TIO 213	Davis, James	SUF 67		
Davis, Benjn	SUF 75	Davis, Even	SRA 12	Davis, James	SUF 68		
Davis, Benjamin	SUF 108	Davis, Even	WSH 215	Davis, James	ULS 205		
Davis, Benjamin	ULS 204	Davis, Ezekiel	ALB 110	Davis, James	WSH 195		
Davis, Benjamin Junr	ORN 370	Davis, Ezekiel	ORN 277	Davis, James Jur	SUF 68		
Davis, Benjamin J.	ULS 196	Davis, Ezra	CAY 650	Davis, James Ser	SUF 68		
Davis, Billa	ONT 318	Davis, Ezra	SRA 15	Davis, Jane	NYK 91		
Davis, Briant	SUF 69	Davis, Ezra	SUF 64	Davis, Jane	NYK 126		
Davis, Caleb	SUF 91	Davis, Ferrend	WSH 185	Davis, Jane	WST 167		
Davis, Charles	NYK 96	Davis, Frames	NYK 30	Davis, Japhet	DUT 17		
Davis, Charles	OND 203	Davis, Frederick	ULS 196	Davis, Japhet Junr	DUT 17		
Davis, Charles	SRA 12	Davis, Frederick	ULS 208	Davis, Jared	ONN 180		
Davis, Charles F.	GRN 332	Davis, Gardner	OTS 35	Davis, Jeddediah	SUF 91		
Davis, Chasman	SUF 71	Davis(?), Garrit	ONT 312	Davis, Jeremiah	ALB 118		
Davis, Clement	OTS 40	Davis, George	CLN 158	Davis, Jeremiah Jn	ALB 118		
Davis, Cornelius	NYK 34	Davis, George a Black	NYK 21	Davis, Jesee	SUF 68		
Davis, Danl	CHN 840	Davis, George	NYK 22	Davis, Jesse	CHN 792		
Davis, Daniel	CLN 157	Davis, George	RNS 64	Davis, jesse	OTS 42		
Davis, Daniel	COL 217	Davis, George	SRA 39	Davis, Job	CHN 798		
Davis, Daniel	DUT 9	Davis, George	SUF 67	Davis, Joel	NYK 78		
Davis, Daniel	DUT 51	Davis, George	ULS 204	Davis, Joel	OND 172		
Davis, Daniel	NYK 133	Davis, George	WSH 236	Davis, Joel	SUF 81		
Davis, Daniel	ONT 314	Davis, George	WSH 267	Davis, John	ALB 30		

97

Name	Loc	Pg	Name	Loc	Pg	Name	Loc	Pg
Davis, John	ALB	92	Davis, Margaret	NYK	49	Davis, Samuel	RNS	106
Davis, John	CAY	588	Davis, Martha	SUF	91	Davis, Samuel	SRA	12
Davis, John	CAY	636	Davis, Mary	ORN	370	Davis, Samuel	SUF	68
Davis, John	CAY	704	Davis, Mason	OTS	35	Davis, Saml	SUF	69
Davis, John	COL	204	Davis, Mathew	SUF	109	Davis, Saml	SUF	75
Davis, John	DUT	17	Davis, Mathew L.	NYK	62	Davis, Sarah	SUF	75
Davis, John	DUT	64	Davis, Mathias	SUF	75	Davis, Solomon	ORN	315
Davis, John	GRN	344	Davis, Matthew	CHN	798	Davis, Solomon	OTS	32
Davis, John	HRK	588	Davis, Matthew	ORN	345	Davis, Spicer	SUF	68
Davis, John	MNT	25	Davis, Matthias	SUF	69	Davis, Squire	CAY	704
Davis, John	NYK	59	Davis, Merritt	SUF	92	Davis, Stephen	ALB	37
Davis, John	NYK	76	Davis, Moses	CHN	956	Davis, Stephen	DUT	17
Davis, John	NYK	78	Davis, Nancy	NYK	112	Davis, Stephen	DUT	58
Davis, John	NYK	94	Davis, Nathan	CAY	608	Davis, Stephen	DUT	114
Davis, John	NYK	143	Davis, Nathan	DUT	17	Davis, Susannah	SRA	38
Davis, John	OND	175	Davis, Nathan	OND	178	Davis, Sylvanus	HRK	422
Davis, John	OND	192	Davis, Nathan	ONN	148	Davis, Sylvester	ONT	440
Davis, John	OND	205	Davis, Nathan	SRA	30	Davis, Thadeus	ALB	61
Davis, John	OND	213	Davis, Nathan	SRA	31	Davis, Thomas	HRK	421
Davis, John	ORN	307	Davis, Nathan	SUF	68	Davis, Thomas	HRK	430
Davis, John	ORN	344	Davis, Nl a free			Davis, Thomas	OND	177
Davis, John	ORN	382	Negro	ALB	131	Davis, Thomas	ONT	368
Davis, John	OTS	7	Davis, Nathaniel	CHN	792	Davis, Thomas	ORN	344
Davis, John	OTS	40	Davis, Nathaniel	DEL	284	Davis, Thomas	QNS	84
Davis, John	OTS	46	Davis, Nathaniel	ORN	370	Davis, Thomas	RNS	95
Davis, John	OTS	53	Davis, Nathl	SUF	67	Davis, Thomas	ULS	204
Davis, John	QNS	70	Davis, Nathl	SUF	68	Davis, Thomas B.	DUT	67
Davis, John	QNS	81	Davis, Nathl	SUF	68	Davis, Timothy	DEL	271
Davis, John	RNS	92	Davis, Nehemiah	DEL	288	Davis, Timy	SUF	68
Davis, John	SRA	33	Davis, Nehemiah	HRK	594	Davis, Uriah	GRN	348
Davis, John	SRA	39	Davis, Nelly	DUT	37	Davis, Uriah	GRN	348
Davis, John	SUF	93	Davis, Nelly	ORN	327	Davis, Uriah	HRK	414
Davis, John	TIO	225	Davis, Nemiah	HRK	414	Davis, Valentine	ULS	203
Davis, John	ULS	267	Davis, Nicholas	ORN	344	Davis, Widow	DEL	290
Davis, John	WSH	202	Davis, Noah	ESS	319	Davis, Willeam	WSH	286
Davis, John	WSH	253	Davis, Oliverson	DUT	51	Davis, William	ALB	37
Davis, John	WSH	275	Davis, Orimell	OTS	42	Davis, William	ALB	61
Davis, John	WST	166	Davis, Pardon	SRA	33	Davis, William	ALB	118
Davis, John	WST	166	Davis, Parker	WSH	267	Davis, William	CHN	824
Davis, John Junr	COL	204	Davis, Parris	SRA	33	Davis, William	GRN	334
Davis, John Junr	SRA	38	Davis, Patrick	ORN	344	Davis, William	GRN	343
Davis, John Junr	WST	166	Davis, Paul	DUT	49	Davis, Wm	GRN	348
Davis, John B.	ULS	199	Davis, Peggy a mulatto	NYK	22	Davis, William	HRK	461
Davis, John D.	MNT	103	Davis, Peleg	OTS	35	Davis, Wm	MNT	108
Davis, John R.	ULS	215	Davis, Peter	ORN	359	Davis, William	NYK	24
Davis, Johnathan	GRN	350	Davis, Peter	SRA	7	Davis, William	NYK	79
Davis, Jonathan	OND	181	Davis, Peter	ULS	195	Davis, William	NYK	146
Davis, Jonathan	ONT	466	Davis, Peter	WSH	233	Davis, William	ONT	462
Davis, Jonathan	RNS	93	Davis, Philander	ONT	368	Davis, William	ONT	488
Davis, Jonathan	SUF	71	Davis, Phineas	SUF	66	Davis, William	ORN	298
Davis, Jonathan Junr	OND	181	Davis, Phinehas	HRK	509	Davis, William	ORN	312
Davis, Jonas	ONT	370	Davis, Phinehas	OND	210	Davis, William	ORN	397
Davis, Jonas	SUF	66	Davis, Reuben	CHN	798	Davis, William	OTS	51
Davis, Joseph	CAY	720	Davis, Richard	DUT	67	Davis, William	QNS	79
Davis, Joseph	CHN	792	Davis, Richard	NYK	92	Davis, William	QNS	81
Davis, Joseph	CLN	172	Davis, Richard	ORN	345	Davis, Wm	QNS	81
Davis, Joseph	COL	206	Davis, Richard	SRA	40	Davis, Wm	RNS	71
Davis, Joseph	DEL	287	Davis, Richd	SUF	68	Davis, Wm	SUF	66
Davis, Joseph	DUT	99	Davis, Richard	ULS	215	Davis, Wm	SUF	68
Davis, Joseph	SRA	18	Davis, Robert	NYK	37	Davis, Wm	SUF	71
Davis, Joseph	SUF	66	Davis, Robert	NYK	118	Davis, Wm	SUF	71
Davis, Joseph	SUF	67	Davis, Robert	QNS	77	Davis, William	ULS	197
Davis, Joseph	SUF	68	Davis, Robert	RNS	72	Davis, William	ULS	209
Davis, Joseph	WSH	249	Davis, Roger	SRA	30	Davis, William	WST	115
Davis, Joshua	CAY	726	Davis, Roland	TIO	213	Davis, William	WST	120
Davis, Joshua	OND	185	Davis, Rosanna a			Davis, William	WSH	284
Davis, Joshua	ORN	326	mulatto	NYK	35	Davis, William A.	NYK	102
Davis, Joshua	RNS	71	Davis, Roswell	COL	204	Davison	GRN	338
Davis, Joshua	WSH	202	Davis, Samuel	ALB	45	Davison, Alexander	SRA	14
Davis, Joshua Junr	ORN	326	Davis, Samuel	CAY	618	Davison, Asa	RNS	76
Davis, Lemuel	COL	210	Davis, Samuel	DEL	270	Davison, Ezra	RNS	76
Davis, Lemuel	SRA	38	Davis, Samuel	ONN	186	Davison, Isaac	GRN	340
Davis, Levi	DEL	283	Davis, Samuel	ONT	314	Davison, John	DEL	272
Davis, Live	RNS	32	Davis, Samuel	ONT	498	Davison, John	MNT	36
Davis, Luke	ORN	274	Davis, Samuel	ORN	349	Davison, John	OTS	9
Davis, Luther	HRK	512	Davis, Saml	OTS	51	Davison, Jn Junr	OTS	9
Davis, Malchia	ONT	466	Davis, Samuel	RNS	19	Davison, Joseph	WSH	285

Name	Loc	Pg	Name	Loc	Pg	Name	Loc	Pg
Dean, Peter	QNS	84	Dearing, John	DUT	69	Decker, Andries G.	COL	237
Dean, Richard	NYK	16	Dearley, Arthur	NYK	25	Dacker, Andries G.	COL	244
Dean, Samuel	ALB	3	Dearman, George	ORN	379	Decker, Barnt	RCH	91
Dean, Samuel	DUT	149	Dearman, Justis	NYK	87	Decker, Benjamin	ALB	91B
Dean, Samuel	QNS	82	Dearmot, James	ALB	143	Decker, Benjamin	ORN	317
Dean, Samuel	WST	111	Deas, David	NYK	149	Decker, Benjamin	RCH	89
Dean, Samuel	WST	159	Deas, Euphemia	NYK	113	Decker, Benjamin	ULS	245
Dean, Saun a mulatto	NYK	41	Deas, John	NYK	73	Decker, Bornt	RCH	90
Dean, Seth	ONT	478	De Barras, Claude	NYK	91	Decker, Brewer	TIO	243
Dean, Seth	ONT	484	Debaugh, Mr	OND	223	Decker, Catharine	RCH	88
Dean, Seth	SCH	144	Debaun, Abrm	RCK	107	Decker, Charles	RCH	91
Dean, Seth Junr	SCH	144	Debaun, Abrm	RCK	107	Decker, Christopher	ORN	379
Dean, Silas	DEL	283	De Baun, Abrm	RCK	107	Decker, Christopher	RNS	44
Dean, Solomon	WSH	191	Debaun, Abrm Junr	RCK	107	Decker, Coenradt	COL	200
Dean, Solomon	NYK	127	Debaun, Andrew	RCK	107	Decker, Coenradt G.	COL	235
Dean, Thomas	QNS	78	Debaun, Christian	RCK	107	Decker, Coenradt J.	COL	228
Dean, Thomas	WST	115	Debaun, David	RCK	107	Decker, Cornelius	COL	190
Dean, Willets	WSH	215	Debaun, Jacob	RCK	107	Decker, Cornelius	COL	226
Dean, William	COL	211	Debaun, Jacob	RCK	109	Decker, Cornelius	COL	238
Dean, William	OND	178	Debaun, John	RCK	107	Decker, Cornelius	DEL	278
Dean, William	OND	186	Debaun, Saml	RCK	103	Decker, Cornelius	ORN	294
Dean, William	QNS	61	Debay, John	WST	162	Decker, Cornelius	ORN	374
Dean, William	SRA	28	Debbin, John	NYK	85	Decker, Cornelius	ULS	246
Dean, William	TIO	264	Debell, Nathaniel	MNT	125	Decker, Cornelius L.	COL	230
Dean, Zepheniah	DUT	149	Deberard, Charles J.	OND	176	Decker, Daniel	ORN	319
Deane, Abigail	DUT	55	Debeshiere, Daniel	SRA	9	Decker, Daniel	ORN	369
Deane, Anna	COL	217	De Bevoe, Frederick	KNG	11	Decker, David	ORN	308
Deane, Benjamin	ONT	464	DeBevoice, George	QNS	63	Decker, David	ORN	340
Deane, Caleb	DUT	90	DeBevoice, John	QNS	60	Decker, Derrick	GRN	333
Deane, Cato	ORN	394	De Bevoice, John	QNS	61	Decker, Dorothy	COL	232
Deane, Daniel S.	DUT	6	De Bevoice, John	QNS	63	Decker, Elias	ULS	246
Deane, David	DUT	92	De Bevoice, John	QNS	63	Decker, Ephraim	ULS	232
Deane, Dennis	ONT	456	De Bevois, Abraham	KNG	7	Decker, Evert	ULS	249
Deane, Elijah	DUT	169	De Bevois, Robert	KNG	8	Decker, Frederick	ONT	442
Deane, Elizabeth	DUT	73	De Bevoise, Charles	KNG	11	Decker, Frederick	ORN	309
Deane, Elizabeth	DUT	169	De Bevoise, Coert	KNG	10	Decker, Gabriel	ORN	366
Deane, Ezekiel	DUT	90	De Bevoise, Isaac	KNG	10	Decker, Garret	COL	244
Deane, Ezra	COL	182	De Bevoise, Jac___	KNG	10	Decker, Carret	ORN	367
Deane, Ezra	ORN	272	Deboe, John	NYK	138	Decker, Garret Ye 2d	ORN	367
Deane, Gideon	ULS	238	De Boies, Laurence	ALB	87	Decker, Garrett	GRN	347
Deane, James	DUT	90	De Bois, Abrahan	ALB	91B	Decker, George	COL	256
Deane, Jeremiah	COL	255	Debois, Gideon	SRA	9	Decker, George A.	COL	245
Deane, John	CAY	680	Debois, James	ALB	10	Decker, Gerard	COL	241
Deane, John	DUT	90	De Bois, James	ALB	113	Decker, Gibert	GRN	335
Deane, Jonathan	DUT	117	Debois, John	ALB	91	Decker, Hannah	CHN	770
Deane, Jonathan R.	DUT	6	Debon, Peter	NYK	149	Decker, Hannah	ORN	310
Deane, Joseph	DUT	89	Deboue, Jacob	SCH	159	Decker, Hendrick	COL	198
Deane, Joseph S.	DUT	109	De Bow, Gerret	NYK	59	Decker, Hendrick	COL	239
Deane, Josiah	COL	205	De Boyce, Peter	WST	162	Decker, Henry	COL	248
Deane, Margaret	DUT	49	Debu, Andrus	CLN	154	Decker, Henry	RNS	57
Deane, Mary L.	DUT	6	De Camp, David	NYK	76	Decker, Ida	ORN	308
Deane, Moses	DUT	118	De Camp, Henry	RNS	90	Decker, Isaac	COL	229
Deane, Moses	ORN	272	De Camp, Job	NYK	84	Decker, Isaac	GRN	332
Deane, Nathanl	ONN	139	DeCamp, John	RNS	93	Decker, Isaac	RNS	57
Deane, Nicholas	ULS	259	De Camp, Matthias	ALB	54	Decker, Isaac	RCH	90
Deane, Paley	ONT	472	De Cantillon, Richard	DUT	114	Decker, Isaac	ULS	224
Deane, Peter	ORN	382	De Cay, George	WST	118	Decker, Isaac Junr	ORN	315
Deane, Richard	DUT	83	Dechay, David	NYK	120	Decker, Isaac ye 3d	ORN	328
Deane, Richard	DUT	90	Decker see Deeker			Decker, Isaac A.	COL	228
Deane, Robert	COL	255	Decker	GRN	335	Decker, Isaac L.	COL	245
Deane, Thomas	DUT	70	Decker, Aaron	ORN	369	Decker, Isaac M.	ORN	315
Deane, William	COL	182	Decker, Abner	RCH	88	Decker, Israel	RCH	88
Deane, William	DUT	88	Decker, Abraham	COL	228	Decker, Jacob	COL	234
Deane, William	DUT	151	Decker, Abraham	ORN	374	Decker, Jacob	COL	256
Deane, Zebulon	ONT	468	Decker, Abraham	RCH	90	Decker, Jacob	ORN	351
De Angelis, Pascal C.	T.OND	187	Decker, Abraham	RCH	91	Decker, Jacob	ORN	368
Deans, Castle	ONT	466	Decker, Abraham	TIO	233	Decker, Jacob	RCH	88
Deans, Ephraim	ONT	466	Decker, Abraham	ULS	246	Decker, Jacob	RCH	90
Deans, Jesse	ONT	466	Decker, Abraham	ULS	255	Decker, Jacob	SCH	159
Deans, Jonathan	ONT	468	Decker, Abraham	ULS	264	Decker, Jacob	TIO	255
Deany, James	SCH	151	Decker, Abraham	COL	232	Decker, Jacob A.	COL	228
Deany, Joseph	SCH	151	Decker, Abram J.	COL	233	Decker, Jacob C.	COL	235
Deany, Thomas	SCH	151	Decker, Abraham V.	COL	238	Decker, Jacob E.	ULS	245
Deany, William	SCH	151	Decker, Adam	ORN	375	Decker, Jacob F.	COL	228
Dearbourne	CAY	656	Decker, Andrew	ORN	366	Decker, Jacob J.	ULS	246
Dearing, James	DUT	69	Decker, Andrew J.	COL	231	Decker, Jacob J.	ULS	250
Dearing, James	NYK	104	Decker, Andries A.	COL	234	Decker, Jacob L.	COL	233

Name	Ref
Decker, Jacobus	COL 231
Decker, Jacobus Junr	COL 237
Decker, Jacobus	COL 234
Decker, Jacobus A.	COL 239
Decker, Jacobus B.	COL 226
Decker, Jacobus J.	COL 227
Decker, James	ORN 367
Decker, Jemima	RCH 91
Decker, Johannis	ORN 351
Decker, John	COL 239
Decker, John	ONT 326
Decker, John	ORN 317
Decker, John	ORN 375
Decker, John	RCH 91
Decker, John	SCH 159
Decker, John	ULS 240
Decker, John	WSH 199
Decker, John Junr	ORN 316
Decker, John C.	COL 235
Decker, John G.	ALB 69
Decker, John G.	COL 237
Decker, John J.	COL 231
Decker, Jonathan	ULS 248
Decker, Joseph	ORN 297
Decker, Joseph	RCH 88
Decker, Joseph	ULS 246
Decker, Lawrence	COL 229
Decker, Lawrence	GRN 333
Decker, Lawrence Isaac	COL 230
Decker, Lawrence J.	COL 233
Decker, Levi	ORN 324
Decker, Margaret	COL 238
Decker, Margaret	RCH 91
Decker, Martin	ORN 377
Decker, Martinus	ORN 316
Decker, Mary	COL 239
Decker, Mary	ORN 323
Decker, Matthew	RCH 89
Decker, Matthew	RCH 92
Decker, Matthew	ULS 248
Decker, Matthias	RCH 90
Decker, Matthias	RCH 91
Decker, Matthias	RCH 92
Decker, Minor	ALB 80
Decker, Moses	ORN 374
Decker, Moses	RCH 91
Decker, Myndert	COL 239
Decker, Nicholas	COL 235
Decker, Oliver	ONT 326
Decker, Peter	COL 228
Decker, Peter	ORN 315
Decker, Peter	RCH 90
Decker, Peter	SCH 137
Decker, Peter	ULS 224
Decker, Peter	ULS 250
Decker, Peter A.	COL 229
Decker, Peter G. Junr	ULS 246
Decker, Peter M.	ULS 245
Decker, Phillip	COL 225
Decker, Phillip	ORN 309
Decker, Phillip W.	COL 245
Decker, Phillup	CHN 770
Decker, Rewben	KNG 2
Decker, Richard	ORN 316
Decker, Richard	RCH 90
Decker, Richard	RCH 91
Decker, Richard son of C. Decker	RCH 91
Decker, Samuel	ORN 369
Decker, Samuel	RCH 92
Decker, Simon	TIO 243
Decker, Thomas	RCH 91
Decker, Tunis	SCH 145
Decker, Uriah	ORN 308
Decker, William	CAY 622
Decker, William	ULS 248
Decker, William	ULS 256
Decker, Zachariah	ULS 249
Deckline, Francis	NYK 95
De Clark, Jacob	RCK 106
Declen, Margret	NYK 109
Declene, Philip	MNT 65
Decline, Barnet	NYK 150
Decline, Leonard	NYK 150
De Coster, Joseph J.	NYK 60
Decous, Adam	NYK 98
Dederee, Christian	NYK 60
Dederick, Christian	COL 196
Dederick, Christian	COL 224
Dederick, David	HRK 419
Dederick, John	ALB 111
Dederick, John	COL 201
Dederick, Philip	COL 265
Dederick, Willm	COL 201
Dederrick, John	NYK 134
Dedrick, Andrew	DUT 165
Dedrick, Christian	ULS 221
Dedrick, Frederick	GRN 343
Dedrick, Garret	DUT 113
Dedrick, George	DUT 111
Dedrick, Gilbert	ULS 221
Dedrick, Jacobus	ULS 222
Dedrick, Matthias	ULS 222
Dedrick, Peter	DUT 111
Dedrick, Peter	GRN 327
Dedrick, Sachariah	GRN 326
Dedrick, William	DUT 165
Dedrick, William	GRN 326
Dedrick, Wm	GRN 355
Dedrick, William	ULS 225
Deeker see Decker	
Deeker, Isaac	COL 199
Deeland, Job	WSH 290
Deeland, Joseph	WSH 269
Deelew, Joseph	NYK 144
Deer, David	ONN 151
Deer, Jonathan	ALB 89
Dee Reen see Val Dee Reen	
Deering, Henry	SUF 104
Deering, Silvester	SUF 105
Deerstine, Abraham	RNS 5
Deerstine, Henry	RNS 6
Deerstine, John	RNS 5
D. Farest, Peter	CHN 812
Defendorf, George	MNT 24
Defendorf, George	NYK 105
Defore, Henry	NYK 40
de Forest, Abel	OTS 24
de Forest, Abel	OTS 36
Deforest, Abraham	NYK 145
De Forest, Curtis	ALB 116
Deforest, David	RNS 11
Deforest, David	RNS 84
De Forest, David L.	DUT 172
Deforest, David M.	RNS 5
Deforest, Derick	RNS 11
Deforest, Ebenezer	NYK 141
De Forest, Gerradus	NYK 100
de Forest, Gideon	OTS 36
De Forest, Hezekiah	ORN 386
Deforest, Jacob	RNS 5
Deforest, Jacob	RNS 6
Deforest, Jesse	RNS 11
Deforest, John	NYK 113
Deforest, John	NYK 145
De Forest, John	RNS 5
De Forest, Joseph	DUT 43
Deforest, Martin	RNS 5
De Forest, Peter	RNS 5
De Forest, Philip	ALB 104
Deforest, Samuel	SRA 15
De Forest, Stephen	ULS 192
Deforest, Theodorus	KNG 8
de Forest, Thos	OTS 24
De Forest, William	ALB 104
De Forest, William	NYK 38
de Forest, Wm	OTS 24
Deforett, Benjamin	MNT 112
Deforett, Isaa	MNT 112
Deforrist, Benjamin	WST 166
De Forrist, Ebenezer	WST 160
DeForrist, Hezekiah	WST 155
Defreeze, Anthony	RNS 53
Defres, Catherine	RCK 102
DeFres, John	RCK 102
Defreze, Stephen	RNS 57
Defries, Jacob	WSH 305
De Garmeau, Peter	DUT 114
De Garmo	ALB 137
De Garno	COL 201
Degauldier, James	SRA 28
D. Goulder, John	WSH 300
De Graaff, Abraham	DUT 66
De Graaff, Barent	DUT 41
De Graaff, Cornelius	ULS 241
De Graaff, Evert	DUT 117
De Graaff, Hannah	DUT 66
De Graaff, Jacobus	DUT 32
De Graaff, John	ULS 232
De Graaff, Michael	DUT 31
De Graaff, Moses	DUT 41
De Graaff, Moses	DUT 116
De Graaff, Simon	DUT 41
De Graaff, Solomon	ULS 210
De Graaff, Ursula	ULS 233
De Graaffstein, John	DUT 105
Degrafdt, John	NYK 122
De Graff, Abraham	ALB 25
De Graff, Abm	SCH 170
De Graff, Andrew	ALB 41
De Graff, Catlinta	ALB 12
Degraff, David	MNT 110
Degraff, Emanuel	MNT 108
Degraff, Fredereck	MNT 108
Degraff, Garrett	MNT 108
De Graff, Hers	ALB 13
De Graff, Isaac	ALB 3
De Graff, Isaac	ALB 18
Degraff, Jeremiah	MNT 107
De Graff, Jesse	ALB 22
De Graff, Jesse D.	ALB 11
De Graff, John	ALB 25
Degraff, John	MNT 107
De Graff, William	ALB 25
De Graff, William	CAY 684
Degrau, Garret	SRA 35
Degrauw, Abraham	NYK 36
Degrave, Aaron	KNG 5
Degrave, Abraham	SRA 9
Degrave, Gedion	SRA 7
Degrave, Isaac	KNG 9
Degrave, James a Black	NYK 116
Degrave, Moses A.	SRA 7
Degrave, Moses G.	SRA 7
Degrave, Nancy	NYK 128
De Graw, Aaron	ORN 352
Degraw, Abraham	SRA 7
Degraw, Abraham	SRA 7
De Graw, Benjamin	ONT 396
De Graw, Cornelius	ONT 396
Degraw, Garret	RCK 106
Degraw, Michael	NYK 78
Degraw, Thomas	NYK 138
Degraw, Walter	NYK 58
Degraw, Walter	RCK 106
De Graze, John	ORN 381
De Groat, Corns	ALB 35
Degroat, Cornelius	GRN 332
Degroat, John	NYK 116
Degroat, John	RCH 93
De Groat, John	RCK 104

Degroat, Peter	RCH 92	De La Clere, John	NYK 69	Delany, Micheal	CAY 518
Degroat, Peter Junr	RCH 93	De La Croix, Joseph	NYK 21	Delany, Peter	CAY 700
Degroat, Robert	RCH 93	De La Ferriere	NYK 107	Delany, Wm	MNT 48
De Groat, Samuel	OND 180	Delafield, John	NYK 56	Delap, Robert	OND 216
Degroat, William	RCH 93	Delafield, John	QNS 63	Delap, William	OND 216
Degroff, Abram	COL 218	Delamanta, Manderville	NYK 120	D. La Pierre, David	NYK 37
De Groff, Corns	ALB 11	Delamare, Louis A.	NYK 101	Delaplain, Samuel	NYK 146
Degroff, John	COL 218	de la Massne, Joseph	NYK 91	Delaplane, James R.	NYK 45
Degroff, John	MNT 98	De La Mater, Abraham	DUT 162	Delaplyne, Uphima	NYK 44
De Groff, Simon	ALB 3	Delamater, Abraham	NYK 91	Delareaue, Louisa	NYK 87
De Groit, Daniel	TIO 238	De La Mater, Abraham	ULS 207	De La Rue, Francis	ORN 302
Degroodt, John	NYK 128	De La Mater, Abraham	ULS 232	Delavan, Daniel	WST 166
Degroodt, Peter	NYK 124	De La Mater, Abraham D.		De La Van, David	DUT 43
Degrooe, Adolph	NYK 72	Junr	ULS 207	Delavan, James	WST 166
De Groot, Jacob	ULS 265	De La Mater, Anthony	DUT 163	De La Van, Jesse	DUT 173
De Groot, Jacob Junr	ULS 265	Delamater, Barnet	WST 167	Delavan, Jonathan D.	WST 166
De Groot, Joseph	ULS 263	De La Mater, Benjamin	DUT 109	Delavan, Lewis	WST 166
Degroot, Richard	NYK 117	Delamater, Benjamin	WSH 281	De La Van, Mary	DUT 169
Degroot, Samuel	NYK 40	De La Mater, Benjamin		De La Van, Nathaniel	DUT 169
Degrote, Wm	RCK 102	Junr	ULS 219	De La Van, Stephen	DUT 43
De Grou, Daniel	ORN 368	De Lamater, Cornelius	DEL 271	De La Van, Timothy	DUT 173
De Grou, John	ORN 368	De La Mater, Cornelius	DUT 155	Delavere, Avraham	NYK 147
De Grou, Lucas	ORN 376	De La Mater, Cornelius		De La Vergne, Benjamin	DUT 106
De Grout, William	ORN 270	Junr	ULS 219	De La Vergne, Ebenezer	DUT 105
Degrove, Elizabeth	NYK 83	De La Mater, Cornelius		De La Vergne, Giles	DUT 137
Degrove, Jane	NYK 94	J.	ULS 233	De La Vergne, Henry	DUT 137
Degrove, John	NYK 104	De La Mater, David	ULS 228	De La Vergne, Isaac	DUT 106
Degrove, Joseph	NYK 137	Delamater, Evert	WST 166	De La Vergne, John	DUT 41
Degrove, Robert C.	NYK 80	Delamater, Isaac	NYK 50	De La Vergne, Lewis	DUT 137
Degrow, Peter	GRN 354	Delamater, Isaac	NYK 64	De Lavigne, Cassimere	NYK 86
De Grushe, Aaron	NYK 44	Delamater, Isaac	NYK 104	De La Zan, Joseph	DUT 79
De Grushe, John	NYK 38	De La Mater, Jacob J.	ULS 199	Delemater, Abraham	COL 189
De Grushe, Robert	NYK 101	De Lamater, John	DEL 272	Delemater, Claudius	COL 254
De Grushe, Thomas	WST 115	Delamater, John	NYK 69	Delemater, Claudius D.	COL 256
Degulleir, Joseph	MNT 89	De La Mater, John	ULS 233	Delemater, Claudius J.	COL 254
Deha.., James	TIO 223	Delamater, John S.	NYK 26	Delemater, Derick	COL 256
Deharsh, Abraham	MNT 14	De La Mater, Martin	DUT 134	Delemater, George	MNT 51
Deharsh, Isaaeh	MNT 14	De Lamater, Moses	DEL 271	Delemater, Isaac	COL 237
D..arsh, Marten	MNT 14	De La Mater, Nicholas	DUT 137	Delemater, Isaac	WST 167
Deharsh, Philip	MNT 14	Delamater, Samuel	NYK 53	Delemater, James J.	COL 192
De Hart, Abigail	RCH 88	Delamater, Sarah	NYK 59	Delemater, Jerreh	COL 191
De Hart, Andries	ORN 296	De La Mater, William B.	ULS 207	Delemater, Jerreh J.	COL 193
De Hart, Balthazer	TIO 223	De La Matter, Abm	ALB 29	Delematter, John	RNS 59
De Hart, Catharine	RCH 88	De La Matter, Abraham	ALB 97	Delevarge, James	WSH 232
De Hart, Cyrus	DUT 162	De La Matter, Benjm	ALB 27	Delew, John	NYK 27
De Hart, Jacob	ORN 296	De La Matter, Isaac	ALB 30	Deligne, Dominick	NYK 107
De Hart, John	NYK 133	De La Matter, Jacob	ALB 31	Delin, William	OND 170
De Hart, Matthias	RCH 88	Delamatter, Samuel	RNS 4	Deline, Benjamin	MNT 76
De Hart, Samuel	RCH 88	Delamontayne, Jacob	NYK 98	Deline, Isaac	MNT 97
Deheland & Bordon	QNS 66	Delamontayne, John	NYK 57	Deline, Lewis	MNT 71
Dehuse, John	NYK 128	Delanaux, Dolly	NYK 67	Deline, Wm	MNT 114
Deil, John	OTS 2	Delance, Delavan	ESS 298	Deling, Maria	NYK 38
Deitz, Adam	ALB 72	Delance, Delavan Jr	ESS 298	Delingham, Joshua	WSH 237
Deitz, Adam A.	ALB 72	Delance, John	OND 223	Delino, Nathan	SCH 139
Deitz, Henry	ALB 72	De Lancey, Abraham	ORN 286	Delino, Nathaniel	WSH 240
Deitz, John	ALB 72	De Lancey, Oliver	WST 144	Delivan, Abraham	WST 153
Deitz, John	NYK 118	Delancey, Susanna	WST 123	Delivan, Agnes	WST 126
Deitz, Maria	SCH 119	Delancy see Delaney		Delivan, John	WST 125
Deitz, Philip	SCH 119	Delancy, John	NYK 82	Delivan, John Junr	WST 124
Deitz, Willm	SCH 119	Delancy, Moses F.	SCH 155	Delivan, Matthew	WST 124
Deitzell, Johannis	ULS 221	Deland, Philip	OND 180	Delivan, Matthew Junr	WST 124
De Joy, Josephus	ALB 139	Delaney see Delancy		Delivan, Timothy	WST 124
Dekato, Francis	NYK 72	De. Laney, John	ONN 166	Dilivern, Nichs	SCH 119
De Kay, George	CAY 538	Delaney, John Peter	WST 121	Dellaffre, Anna	NYK 30
De Kay, Jacobus	ORN 347	Delang, James	SRA 53	Dellebach, David	MNT 35
De Kay, Michael	ORN 359	Delano, Calvin	COL 243	Dellebach, John M.	MNT 35
De Kay, Thomas	ORN 372	Delano, Izrael	ONT 354	Dellebach, Jonas	MNT 27
De Kay, William	CAY 540	De La No, Jethro	DUT 133	Dellebach, Nicholas	MNT 27
Dekker, Daniel	SCH 132	Delano, Nathaniel	TIO 225	Delleback, Baltus	MNT 35
Dekker, Michael	SCH 131	Delance, Abraham	WST 166	Delleback, Henry	MNT 34
Dekker, Peter	SCH 142	Delance, Benjn	OTS 12	Dellenback, Andrew J.	MNT 7
Dekker, Thomas	SCH 136	Delance, Daniel	WST 166	Delleverge, Josep	MNT 28
Dekkers, Nichs	SCH 136	Delance, Frederick	CAY 628	Dellihu, John	NYK 34
Deklyn, Leonard	NYK 53	Delance, James	WST 166	Dellinbach, John	MNT 7
De La Bigarre, Pierre	DUT 63	Delance, John	WST 166	Dellinbach, John B.	MNT 23
Delacharine, Gabriel	NYK 96	Delance, Roger	CAY 630	Dellinbach, Richard	MNT 7
Delachiere, Mary	NYK 96	Delance, William	WST 166	Dellingham, Joseph	WSH 236

Dellingham, Stephen	WSH 237	Demarest, Philip	RCK 106
Dellon, John	NYK 138	Demarest, Richard	RCK 105
Delmas, Anthony	NYK 56	Demarest, Ruelf	NYK 97
Delong, Abraham	SRA 5	Demarest, Samuel	ORN 365
De Long, Arie	DUT 14	Demarest, Simon	NYK 144
De Long, Benjamin	DUT 123	Demarest, Simon	RCK 107
Delong, Benjamin	SRA 10	Demarest, Smith	ULS 263
De Long, Charles	DUT 19	Demarest, Thomas	NYK 93
Delong, Corneleus	MNT 36	Demarets, Samuel	NYK 99
Delong, Danl	OTS 57	Demask, Ebenezer	WSH 209
Delong, David	ALB 100	De: Merry, Newcomb	ONN 164
Delong, Elias	ALB 37	Demby, John a Black	NYK 73
De Long, Elias	DUT 60	Deme, Charles	OTS 31
Delong, Ezekiel	CLN 171	Demear, John	GRN 328
Delong, Henry	ALB 100	Demell, Benjamin	NYK 130
Delong, Isaac	CLN 161	Demelt(?), John	ALB 77
Delong, Isaac	HRK 507	Demerass, David	GRN 336
Delong, Jacob	RNS 39	Demeress, John	ALB 50
De Long, James	DUT 14	Demerist, Henry	GRN 328
Delong, James	HRK 508	Demest(?), Barentt	SRA 8
Delong, James	MNT 36	Demick, Elijah	WSH 283
De Long, John	DEL 268	Demick, John	SRA 53
De Long, John	DUT 14	De Mill, Garret	ULS 193
De Long, John	DUT 24	De Mill, Lawrence	ULS 192
De Long, John	ONT 338	demill, Peter	NYK 63
Delong, John	RNS 48	Demlt, Isaac	NYK 42
De Long, John E.	DUT 60	Demlt, Isaac	NYK 46
De Long, Jonas	DEL 268	Demlt, Isaac	NYK 84
De Long, Laurance	ALB 60	De Milt, Obadiah	QNS 71
De Long, Michael	DUT 112	Demilt, Peter	NYK 38
De Long, Peter	CLN 162	Deming, Asa	COL 260
Delong, Reuben	HRK 508	Deming, Daniel	SRA 35
De Long, Richard	DUT 15	Deming, David	OND 173
De Long, Thomas	DEL 268	Deming, Elias	COL 180
Delonguermar, Nicholas	NYK 26	Deming, Elisha	COL 180
Deloo, John T.	COL 199	Deming, John	SRA 61
De Loran, Reymond	ALB 120	Deming, Joseph	OND 166
De Lord, Henry	CLN 156	Deming, Simeon	NYK 43
Deloy, James	MNT 119	Deming, Solomon	OND 177
Delphie, Polly	NYK 138	Deming, Solomon	SRA 61
Delpuech, Henry P.	NYK 64	Demirest, Jacob	NYK 58
Delsin, Michael M.	OND 196	Demman, Abraham	SUF 107
Delson, Tunis	NYK 144	Demman, David	SUF 106
Delves, Thomas	NYK 28	Demman, Isaac	SUF 107
Demamara, David Jun	NYK 99	Demman, John	SUF 107
Deman, Joseph	OND 222	Demman, Joseph	SUF 107
Demarce, Daniel	NYK 90	Demmara, David	NYK 99
Demarest, Albert	RCK 109	Demming, Abel	OTS 31
Demarest, Cornelius	NYK 93	Demming, Annans	OTS 37
Demarest, Cornelius	ORN 373	Demming, Charles	SRA 46
Demarest, Cornelius	RCK 108	Demming, Davis	ONN 158
Demarest, Danl	RCK 109	Demming, Edmond	OND 177
Demarest, David	ORN 372	Demming, Isaac	SRA 34
Demarest, David	ORN 378	Demming, Jason	OND 200
Demarest, David	RCK 100	Demming, Roger	OTS 31
Demarest, David	ULS 204	Demming, Zebulan	OTS 8
Demarest, David C.	NYK 98	Demmon, Da__	ONT 414
Demarest, David J.	NYK 59	Demmon, Jonathan	SUF 73
Demarest, David J.	NYK 144	Demmon, Joseph	RNS 110
Demarest, Jacob	RCK 108	Demmon, Simeon	ALB 24
Demarest, Jacobus	ULS 235	Demmon, William	ALB 98
Demarest, James	RCK 101	Demmons, Samuel	WSH 199
Demarest, John	NYK 91	Demon, Joseph	TIO 240
Demarest, John	ORN 377	Demond, Anthony	GRN 329
Demarest, John	RCK 97	Demont, Abigail	CAY 702
Demarest, John	RCK 103	Demont, Joseph	CAY 702
Demarest, John J.	NYK 91	Demont, Joseph	CAY 726
Demarest, Joseph	NYK 93	Demont, Margaret	CAY 726
Demarest, Mathew	RCK 108	deMont, Peter	OTS 44
Demarest, Nicholas	ORN 377	Demont, Richard	CAY 518
Demarest, Oliver	NYK 93	Demont, Samuel	SRA 3
Demarest, Peter	ORN 317	Demora, Nicholas	RNS 40
Demarest, Peter	RCK 101	Demore.t, Gidion	MNT 88
Demarest, Peter	RCK 103	Demorest, Peter D.	MNT 88
Demarest, Peter	RCK 107	Demorest, Samuel	MNT 90
Demarest, Peter	RCK 108	Demorist, David	MNT 87
Demarest, Peter	RCK 108	Demot, Daniel	NYK 142

Demot, Willm	COL 189	Denham, David	OND 174
De Mott, Abraham	CAY 560	Denice, Denice	KNG 5
De Mott, Antoney	QNS 75	Denice, Denice	KNG 6
De Mott, Benjamin	ORN 273	Denice, Denice	KNG 6
Demott, David	QNS 78	Denice, Jaques	KNG 6
De Mott, Isaac	ORN 271	Denice, John	KNG 4
Demott, Jacob	QNS 75	Denike, Isaac	WST 156
De Mott, James	ORN 272	Denike, Jacob	WST 158
Demott, James	QNS 75	Denike, Robert	WST 152
Demott, John	CHN 806	Denio, Israel	OND 216
Demott, John	NYK 128	Denio, Joseph	DEL 290
Demott, John	NYK 132	Denio, William	DEL 289
Demott, John	QNS 75	Denish, Easter	CHN 872
Demott, John	QNS 75	Denison, Andrew	ONN 178
Demott, John	QNS 75	Denison, Daniel	ALB 76
Demott, John	QNS 77	Denison, David	ONN 178
Demott, John	QNS 77	Denison, George	ONN 173
De Mott, Michael	ORN 272	Denison, Griswell	RNS 99
Demott, Michael	QNS 76	Denison, James	ORN 389
Demott, Samuel	QNS 77	Denison, James P.	OTS 39
De Mott, Thomas	QNS 77	Denison, Joseph	SRA 58
De Mott, William	ORN 278	Denison, Liverick	GRN 342
Dempsey, Elizabeth	NYK 56	Denison, Thomas	TIO 212
Dempster, James	NYK 85	Denison, William	CHN 776
Demsey, Mark	ALB 83	Deniston, Abraham	ORN 290
Demun, Isaac	TIO 240	Deniston, Alexander	ORN 289
Demund, Walter	RNS 64	Deniston, Charles	RNS 99
De Myer, Benjamin	ULS 219	Deniston, David	ALB 76
De Myer, Nicholas	ULS 224	Deniston, Eleazer	WSH 264
Dence, Dominy	ORN 379	Deniston, George	ORN 290
Denfield, Catherine	NYK 50	Deniston, George	ORN 337
		Deniston, George A.	ORN 289
		Deniston, Isaac	ORN 288
		Deniston, James	ORN 290
		Deniston, John	ORN 288
		Deniston, Jonathan	RNS 99
		Deniston, Joseph	ALB 104
		Deniston, Mathew	ONT 476
		Deniston, Robert	ALB 68
		Deniston, Samuel	ONT 478
		Deniston Samuel M.	ORN 288
		Deniston, William	ORN 397
		Denjman, Jacob	TIO 254
		Denman, Isaac	ORN 341
		Denman, William	ULS 184
		Denmark, Barnabas	CAY 620
		Denmark, Christian	SCH 159

Denmark, George	MNT 66	Dennison, Joseph	CHN 776	Denton, Daniel	KNG 10
Denmark, Suffel	SCH 150	Dennison, Joseph	CHN 830	Denton, Daniel	ORN 339
Denmon, Daniel	QNS 62	Dennison, Nathanl	CHN 830	Denton, Daniel	ORN 362
Denmon, Samuel	QNS 61	Dennison, Palmer	CHN 826	Denton, David	DUT 55
Denn, Christopher	ORN 340	Dennison, Samuel	GRN 342	Denton, David	DUT 140
Denn, Lucy	ORN 320	Dennison, Samuel	SUF 102	Denton, George	NYK 128
Denn, Samuel	ORN 311	Dennison, Stanton	HRK 478	Denton, Henry	ORN 357
Denn, Samuel	WST 159	Dennison, Stephen	GRN 344	Denton, Isaac	DUT 7
Denn, Solomon	CAY 644	Dennison, William	COL 219	Denton, Isaac	QNS 73
Denn, Thomas	ULS 186	Denniston, Alexander	ORN 282	Denton, Isaac	QNS 76
Dennend, Ezra	DEL 283	Denniston, Asa	ONT 330	Denton, Isaac	SRA 47
Dennend, John	DEL 290	Denniston, Charles	ALB 26	Denton, Israel	SRA 45
Dennett, Andrew	CAY 538	Denniston, Charles	ORN 277	Denton, Jacob	ORN 332
Dennet, George	NYK 104	Denniston, Ezekiel	ALB 26	Denton, James	ORN 356
Denney, Jacob	MNT 69	Denniston, Henry	ALB 68	Denton, James	QNS 67
Denney, William	NYK 95	Denniston, Isaac	ALB 135	Denton, Jeremiah	KNG 7
Dennice, Jaques	KNG 6	Denniston, James	ALB 135	Denton, Jo_	DEL 267
Denning, Frederick	NYK 60	Denniston, James Junr	ORN 352	Denton, Joel	DUT 140
Denning, Humphrey	ONT 356	Denniston, John	ALB 127	Denton, John	DUT 140
Denning, Isaac	CHN 960	Denniston, Rosannah	NYK 97	Denton, John	ORN 283
Denning, William	NYK 56	Denny, Abraham	DUT 58	Denton, John	ORN 360
Denning, William a		Denny, Absalom	DUT 140	Denton, John	ORN 362
mulatto	NYK 108	Denny, Andrew	DUT 77	Denton, John	SUF 66
Denning, William	RCK 103	Denny, Asahel	OND 178	Denton, Jonas	QNS 69
Dennis, Benjamin	SUF 85	Denny, Bargo	DUT 10	Denton, Joseph	KNG 3
Dennis, Britton	WSH 211	Denny, Charles	GRN 340	Denton, Joseph	ORN 360
Dennis, Charles	COL 236	Denny, Clark	DUT 140	Denton, Joseph	QNS 69
Dennis, Charles	WSH 239	Denny, Edward	DUT 58	Denton, Joshua	QNS 61
Dennis, Daniel	QNS 84	Denny, Elisha	DUT 77	Denton, Josiah	WSH 237
Dennis, David	NYK 122	Denny, Isaac	DUT 10	Denton, Levina	ORN 271
Dennis, Elihu	RNS 31	Denny, Isaac	MNT 83	Denton, Mary	ORN 359
Dennis, Frederick	ALB 29	Denny, Jacob	DUT 77	Denton, Nathl	HRK 447
Dennis, Frederick Junr	ALB 27	Denny, John	ALB 134	Denton, Nathaniel	QNS 69
Dennis, George	WSH 256	Denny, John	DUT 140	Denton, Nehemiah	ORN 358
Dennis, Howard	DUT 10	Denny, John	RNS 95	Denton, Nehemiah	RNS 44
Dennis, Humphrey	WSH 235	Denny, John Junr	DUT 77	Denton, Oliver	QNS 73
Dennis, Humphry	OTS 51	Denny, John Senr	DUT 79	Denton, Peter	NYK 37
Denn[is?], Is_c	CAY 554	Denny, Joseph	DUT 10	Denton, Preston	SRA 60
Dennis, Isaac	SUF 85	Denny, Peter	DUT 124	Denton, Reuben	CAY 536
Dennis, Jacob	SRA 40	Denny, Richard	ALB 119	Denton, Richard	SRA 44
Dennis, Joacim C.	NYK 24	Denny, Richard	DUT 10	Denton, Robert	KNG 5
Dennis, John	COL 241	Denny, Richard	DUT 77	Denton, Robert	ORN 272
Dennis, John	DUT 11	Denny, Roger	DUT 77	Denton, Samuel	ORN 372
Dennis, John	KNG 5	Denny, Samuel	DUT 77	Denton, Samuel	QNS 66
Dennis, John	NYK 58	Denny, Samuel	NYK 24	Denton, Samuel	QNS 69
Dennis, John	QNS 78	Denny, Solomon Junr	DUT 10	Denton, Samuel	SRA 44
Dennis, John	WSH 239	Denny, Solomon Senr	DUT 58	Denton, Simeon	QNS 62
Dennis, Jonathan	DUT 11	Denny, Thomas	DUT 77	Denton, Solomon Junr	DUT 17
Dennis, Jonathan	HRK 502	De Noyelles, John	RCK 103	Denton, Solomon Senr	DUT 55
Dennis, Jonathan	NYK 79	De Noyells, Peter	RCK 103	Denton, Stephen	SRA 58
Dennis, Jos:	SCH 124	Denslow, Benjn	HRK 527	Denton, Thomas	ORN 273
Dennis, Joseph	DUT 47	Denslow, Chapman	COL 192	Denton, Thomas	WSH 192
Dennis, Joseph Junr	DUT 43	Denslow, James	OND 211	Denton, Timothy	QNS 66
Dennis, Miner	DUT 80	Denslow, William	OND 198	Denton, William	QNS 74
Dennis, Nicholas	COL 241	Densmore, Dyre	WSH 284	Denton, Wm	RNS 33
Dennis, Peter	ALB 50	Densmore, Elipht	OTS 52	Denyck, John	QNS 64
Dennis, Petrus	COL 242	Densmore, John	OTS 53	Denys, William	KNG 5
Dennis, Phillip	COL 241	Densmore, John Junr	OTS 53	Deo, Christopher	CHN 740
Dennis, Reuben	DUT 10	Densmore, Leonard	ESS 292	Deo, Daniel	RNS 54
Dennis, Robert	OTS 51	Densmore, Obed	WSH 284	Deo, David	GRN 357
Dennis, Shedrick	WSH 198	Densmore, Thomas	NYK 114	Deo, James	COL 182
Dennis, Simeon	RNS 34	Densmore, Uri	OTS 37	Deo, James	RNS 46
Dennis, Stephen a Black	NYK 76	Densmore, Willeam	WSH 285	Deo, John	RNS 47
Dennis, Thomas	DEL 278	Densmore, William	OND 170	Deo, Levi	GRN 351
Dennis, Thomas	WSH 239	Denten, Jesse	SRA 43	Deo, Peter	COL 182
Dennis, Wilbert	CAY 652	Denton, Abel & Jonathan		Deo, Peter	COL 201
Dennis, William	COL 241	Morrell	QNS 60	Deo, Peter	RNS 48
Dennis, William	NYK 130	Denton, Alexander	SUF 87	Deo, Richard	COL 199
Dennis, William	WSH 239	Denton, Alexander	WST 137	Deo, Simeon	RNS 59
Dennisen, William	NYK 150	Denton, Amos	QNS 67	Deo, William	CHN 182
Dennison, Daniel	CHN 776	Denton, Anthony	DUT 17	Deo, William	COL 182
Dennison, Daniel	HRK 476	Denton, Anthony	ULS 258	De One, Silas	TIO 240
Dennison, David	NYK 28	Denton, Asa	CHN 974	Depeesswell, Melanie	NYK 123
Dennison, Ebenezer	ALB 76	Denton, Benjamin	DUT 103	Depeest, Benjamin	RNS 53
Dennison, Elihu	ALB 75	Denton, Benjamin	DUT 140	De Pew, Abrm	RCK 100
Dennison, George	CHN 830	Denton, Benjamin	QNS 75	De Pew, Abrm	RCK 105
Dennison, John	NYK 79	Denton, Caleb	DUT 173	Depew, Abraham	WST 155

Name	Loc	Name	Loc	Name	Loc
Devoo, Henry	ALB 76	Dewey, Loan	ALB 9	De Witt, Thomas	ULS 228
Devoo, James	SRA 10	Dewey, Martin	ALB 3	De Witt, Tjierck C.	ULS 218
Devoo, John	ALB 59	Dewey, Nathaniel	CHN 880	De Witt, William	ULS 210
Devoo, John	ALB 77	Dewey, Peleg	WSH 281	De Witt, William	ULS 246
Devoo, John	SRA 11	Dewey, Ralph	WSH 244	De Witt, William Junr	ULS 210
Devoo, John	SRA 12	Dewey, Robert	OTS 12	De Witt, William A.	ULS 204
Devoo, John J.	SRA 8	Dewey, Samuel R.	WSH 297	Dewolf, Daniel	SRA 30
Devoo, Martinus	SRA 10	Dewey, Solomon	OND 165	Dewolf, E	ONT 392
Devoo, Samuel	SRA 11	Dewey, Solomon	WSH 303	De Wolf, Russel	CHN 928
Devoo, William	RNS 36	Dewey, Stephen	DEL 280	Dewolf, Willm W.	HRK 481
Devoo, William	SRA 11	Dewey, Thaddeus	WSH 303	Dewsnbury, Charles	WST 152
Devorsney, John	KNG 7	Dewey, Thomas	WSH 306	Dewyre, Jeremy	OTS 36
Devos, Wynant	NYK 135	Dewey, Trueman	OTS 10	Dewzenbury, Charles	WST 162
Devou, Anthony	HRK 490	Dewey, William	MNT 17	Dexcow, Daniel	WST 127
Devou, David	KNG 10	Dewfreiy, James	NYK 52	Dexemer, John	NYK 113
Devoue, Abraham	CAY 640	Dewick, John	SUF 67	Dexen	NYK 49
De Voue, Elisha	CAY 684	Dewick, Richd	SUF 67	Dexter, Daniel	NYK 58
Devow, Charles	NYK 136	De Wint, John	DUT 37	Dexter, Daniel	OND 195
Devzenbury, Henry	WST 162	Dewit, Hester	NYK 149	Dexter, Elijah	WSH 185
De Waal, William	ULS 227	De Wit, John	NYK 71	Dexte., Jabez B.	ONT 508
Dewals, Peter	OTS 57	Dewit, Peter	NYK 153	Dexter, John	SCH 167
Dewalt, Oswald	ULS 205	Dewitt	GRN 340	Dexter, Jonathan	ONN 154
Dewandeller, John	MNT 6	De Witt, Aaron	ULS 183	Dexter, Jonathan	ULS 181
Dewas, Francis	OND 220	De Witt, Abraham	DUT 22	Dexter, Joseph	ESS 320
De Weaver, Abm	ALB 44	De Witt, Abraham	ULS 221	Dexter, Joseph	WST 133
Dewel, Abraham	SRA 38	De Witt, Abraham T. E.	ULS 214	Dexter, Levi	HRK 423
Dewel, Edmond	SRA 56	Dewitt, Abram	TIO 223	Dexter, Philip	WST 130
Dewel, Jonathan	SRA 56	De [Wi?]tt, Andrew	ONT 490	De_ter, Philo	MNT 65
Dewel, Joseph	ALB 65	De Witt, Andrew	ULS 209	Dexter, Samuel	ALB 136
Dewel, Joseph	SRA 40	De Witt, Andrew Junr	ULS 242	Dexter, Samuel	HRK 438
Dewel, Silas	SRA 42	De Witt, Andries	ULS 218	Dexter, Thomas	OTS 21
Dewell, Abner	ALB 34	De Witt, Andries A.	ULS 213	Dexter, Wm	OTS 51
Dewell, Benjamin	ALB 65	De Witt, Andries J.	ULS 205	Dey, Anthony	NYK 27
Dewell, Benjamin	DUT 50	De Witt, Andrus A.	ULS 211	Dey, David	RCH 92
Dewell, Daniel	DUT 132	De Witt, Anthony	ULS 212	Dey, John	RCH 93
Dewell, Ezra	WSH 291	De Witt, Benjamin	HRK 520	Dey, Richard	CHN 814
Dewell, Isaac	DUT 129	De Witt, Catharine	DUT 22	Dey, Samson a Black	NYK 79
Dewell, Israel	DUT 128	Dewitt, Cornelius	MNT 118	Dey, Samuel	CHN 814
Dewell, Jacob	OTS 53	De Witt, Cornelius D.	CAY 678	Dey, Samuel	NYK 76
Dewell, John	DUT 50	De Witt, Daniel	TIO 260	Dey, Thomas	CHN 826
Dewell, Jonathan	DUT 104	De Witt, Egbert	ULS 210	Dey, Vincent	NYK 140
Dewell, Jonathan	DUT 131	De Witt, Elizabeth	ULS 211	Dey, William	CHN 778
Dewell, Jonathan	DUT 144	De Witt, Ezekiel	DUT 129	Dey, William	CHN 826
Dewell, Jonathan	WSH 293	De Witt, Garret	ULS 209	Dey, William	NYK 149
Dewell, Joseph	COL 265	Dewitt, Hendrick	GRN 327	Deyarment, Michael	NYK 108
Dewell, Joseph	DUT 128	De Witt, Henry	DUT 157	Deyg_ot, Peter	MNT 14
Dewell, Joshua	DUT 50	De Witt, Henry	ULS 206	Deygert, Peter S. Junr	MNT 9
Dewell, Mary	ALB 65	De Witt, Henry Junr	ULS 214	Deygert, Severinus	MNT 9
Dewell, Reuben	DUT 50	Dewitt, Ichabud	CHN 948	Deyo, Jonas	DEL 272
Dewell, Silas T.	DUT 101	De Witt, Jacob	CAY 678	De Yoe, Abraham	ULS 237
Dewell, Silas W.	DUT 102	De Witt, Jacob	QNS 60	De Yoe, Abraham B.	ULS 236
Dewell, Wilbour	DUT 102	Dewitt, James	GRN 342	De Yoe, Abraham D.	ULS 242
Dewer, Edward	MNT 9	De Witt, James	NYK 57	De Yoe, Benjamin	ULS 236
Dewer, Lewis	SRA 29	Dewitt, James	ULS 210	De Yoe, Benjamin H.	ULS 238
Dewey, Aaron	CLN 165	De Witt, Jan L.	ULS 224	De Yoe, Bridget	ULS 240
Dewey, Andrew	COL 203	De Witt, Johannis	QNS 63	De Yoe, Christian	ULS 243
Dewey, Benjamin	COL 220	De Witt, Johannis	ULS 224	De Yoe, Christopher	ULS 258
Dewey, Benjamin Junr	COL 222	De Witt, John	DUT 108	De Yoe, Daniel	ULS 242
Dewey, David	HRK 442	Dewitt, John	GRN 328	De Yoe, David	ULS 243
Dewey, E.	OND 220	Dewitt, John	SRA 16	De Yoe, Elizabeth	DUT 62
Dewey, Eleazer	WSH 264	De Witt, John	ULS 185	De Yoe, Henrick	ULS 239
Dewey, Eli	OTS 9	De Witt, John	ULS 210	De Yoe, Henry Junr	ULS 239
Dewey, Elias	CLN 170	De Witt, John A.	ULS 205	De Yoe, Jacob	ULS 244
Dewey, Elias	OND 202	De Witt, John C.	ULS 209	Deyoe, James	COL 192
Dewey, Elijah	TIO 215	De Witt, John Van Leuven	ULS 201	De Yoe, Jane	ULS 240
Dewey, Emannuel	ONN 161	De Witt, Joseph	CAY 548	De Yoe, Johannis	ULS 242
Dewey, Ezekiel	ESS 305	De Witt, Levi	ULS 201	De Yoe, John B.	ULS 236
Dewey, Ezra	OND 202	Dewitt, Luke	GRN 339	De Yoe, Jonathan	ULS 235
Dewey, Heman	DEL 267	Dewitt, Lu e	GRN 343	De Yoe, Joseph	ULS 235
Dewey, James	ALB 127	De Witt, Moses	ULS 254	De Yoe, Josiah	ULS 243
Dewey, Jedediah	ONT 442	De Witt, Peter	DUT 42	De Yoe, Levi	ULS 233
Dewey, John	COL 182	De Witt, Peter	DUT 117	De Yoe, Levi	ULS 244
Dewey, John	DEL 281	De Witt, Petrus	ULS 201	De Yoe, Lucas	ULS 250
Dewey, John	ESS 311	De Witt, Samuel	ULS 201	De Yoe, Matthew	ULS 243
Dewey, John Junr	DEL 281	De Witt, Simeon	ALB 134	De Yoe, Nathaniel	ULS 242
Dewey, Joseph	COL 187	De Witt, Stephen	ULS 210	De Yoe, Peter	DUT 9
Dewey, Joshua	OTS 17			De Yoe, Phillip	ULS 242

Name	Code	Name	Code	Name	Code
De Yoe, Simon	ULS 239	Dick, Phillip	COL 194	Dickey, David	OTS 36
De Yoe, William	ULS 236	Dick, Thomas	NYK 40	Dickey, Elizabeth	NYK 118
De Yoe, William	ULS 242	Dick, Thomas	NYK 147	Dickey, Mathew	WSH 200
Deyoo, Nathan	COL 261	Dick_, Thomas	CHN 890	Dickey, William	COL 258
Deyoung, John Jacob	NYK 143	Dickason, Elisha	GRN 340	Dickey, William	OND 165
Deys, Moses	TIO 225	Dickens, Arnold	DUT 177	Dickins, Arnol	WST 134
Dezell, John	ALB 133	Dickens, Edward	WST 134	Dickins, John	CHN 778
De Zeng, Frederick A.	ULS 230	Dickens, James	DUT 21	Dickins, John	HRK 560
Di__, Christiani	NYK 87	Dickens, John	CHN 780	Dickinson, Abraham	ORN 309
Diah, David	SUF 96	Dickens, Joseph	DUT 35	Dickinson, Amos	ONN 142
Diamond see Dymond		Dickens, Joseph Junr	DUT 35	Dickinson, Benjamin	ORN 299
Diamond, Henry	SRA 10	Dickens, Michael	WST 131	Dickinson, Braddock	HRK 519
Diamond, John	ONT 390	Dickens, Nathaniel	DUT 89	Dickinson, Charles	NYK 79
Diamond, Matthew	SRA 10	Dickens, Roger	DUT 49	Dickinson, David	ONT 322
Diamond, William	ALB 126	Dickens, Samuel	WST 131	Dickinson, David	ORN 298
Dian a free wench	ALB 48	Dickens, Thomas	WST 123	Dickinson, David	WST 167
Dibart, Urbain	NYK 106	Dickens, Thomas	WST 152	Dickinson, Ebenezer	SRA 48
Dibbin, Alexander	NYK 88	Dickens, William	WST 152	Dickinson, Eleanor	DUT 72
Dibble, Aaron	RNS 111	Dickensan, Daniel	SRA 47	Dickinson, Elisha	ORN 299
Dibble, Andrew	DEL 289	Dickensen, Benjamin	NYK 67	Dickinson, Gabrial	WSH 212
Dibble, Asa	OTS 12	Dickerson see Dickerson		Dickinson, Giddeon	RNS 25
Dibble, Asa	WSH 214	Dickenson, Amos	QNS 80	Dickinson, Jacob	NYK 131
Dibble, Carmi	SRA 30	Dickenson, Augustus	ONT 476	Dickinson, James	DUT 89
Dibble, Charles	ONN 188	Dickenson, Benjamin	WSH 248	Dickinson, James	ORN 270
Dibble, Christopher	DUT 131	Dickenson, Charles	NYK 47	Dickinson, James	SRA 44
Dibble, Cornish	WSH 279	Dickenson, Christopher	ULS 183	Dickinson, Jeremiah	OND 216
Dibble, Daniel	DEL 289	Dickenson, Cott	ONT 476	Dickinson, John	ALB 22
Dibble, Danl	SCH 136	Dickenson, Elias	ONT 476	Dickinson, John	DEL 278
Dibble, Daniel	WST 132	Dickenson, Elijah	SRA 47	Dickinson, John	SRA 44
Dibble, Ebenezer	SRA 48	Dickenson, Elisha	CAY 704	Dickinson, John	WSH 207
Dibble, Elijah	DEL 285	Dickenson, Henry	WST 139	Dickinson, John D.	RNS 83
Dibble, Elisha	SCH 136	Dickenson, Isaac	SRA 46	Dickinson, Jonatham B.	RNS 17
Dibble, Henry	DEL 275	Dickenson, James	WST 132	Dickinson, Joseph	HRK 485
Dibble, Henry	DEL 285	Dickenson, John	ALB 3	Dickinson, Joseph	ORN 308
Dibble, Henry Junr	DEL 285	Dickenson, John	ORN 278	Dickinson, Joseph	SRA 44
Dibble, Hutton	WSH 216	Dickenson, John	QNS 82	Dickinson, Joseph	ULS 234
Dibble, Isaac	SCH 136	Dickenson, Jonathan	SUF 67	Dickinson, Joseph	WSH 239
Dibble, Isaiah	DUT 145	Dickenson, Jonathan	SUF 67	Dickinson, Joseph	WSH 287
Dibble, Jethro	SCH 136	Di.kenson, Lewis	CAY 594	Dickinson, May	NYK 98
Dibble, Joel	DUT 55	Dickenson, Mordekey	MNT 125	Dickinson, Nathan	ULS 234
Dibble, John	ALB 78	Dickenson, Robert	ULS 235	Dickinson, Nathaniel	ESS 308
Dibble, John	CHN 766	Dickenson, Samuel	NYK 72	Dickinson, Nathaniel	ORN 270
Dibble, John	DEL 289	Dickenson, Samuel	OTS 22	Dickinson, Philemon	WSH 207
Dibble, John	SCH 136	Dickenson, Saml	SUF 75	Dickinson, Samuel	WSH 207
Dibble, Jonathan	WST 157	Dicke_son, Selah	SUF 75	Dickinson, Thomas	WSH 211
Dibble, Joseph	COL 187	Dickenson, Tartulous	WST 127	Dickinson, Thomas	WSH 242
Dibble, Joseph	SCH 131	Dickenson, Thomas	WSH 248	Dickinson, Vasales	WSH 211
Dibble, Joseph	SCH 132	Dickenson, Wm	SUF 67	Dickinson, William	CAY 640
Dibble, Joseph P.	COL 187	Dicker, Alexander	TIO 237	Dickinson, William	ORN 306
Dibble, Levi	ESS 320	Dicker, John	TIO 237	Dickman, Charles	RNS112A
Dibble, Patrick	SCH 131	Dickerson see Dickenson		Dickman, Cornelius	NYK 146
Dibble, Patrick Jr	SCH 132	Dickerson, Abraham	NYK 132	Dickman, Frederick	NYK 147
Dibble, Patrick Senr	SCH 132	Dickerson, Asahel	OND 174	Dickman, Jonathan	SRA 59
Dibble, Samuel	HRK 434	Dick___n, Charles	CAY 538	Dicksinson, Isaac	NYK 82
Dibble, Silas	SCH 136	Dickerson, Charles Ju	CAY 538	Dicksnson, Robert	WSH 244
Dibble, Silas	WSH 245	Dickerson, Christopher	COL 213	Dicksom, John	MNT 117
Dibble, Thomas	CHN 856	Dickerson, Ebenezer	OND 176	Dickson see Dixon	
Dibble, Thomas	DUT 130	Dickerson, Ebenezer		Dickson, Amos	WST 160
Dibble, Thomas	OND 203	Junr	OND 176	Dickson, Benard	WSH 269
Dibble, Tompkins	WSH 282	Dickerson, Elihu	OND 186	Dickson, Berry a Black	NYK 119
Dibblee, Ebenezer	DUT 146	Dickerson, Elijah	OND 186	Dickson, Curt	WSH 269
Dibbs, John	NYK 77	Dickerson, George	COL 213	Dickson, Daniel	NYK 140
Dible, John	GRN 338	Dickerson, Henry	GRN 352	Dickson, Daniel	WST 161
Dick a Negro man	ALB 81	Dickerson, James	COL 213	Dickson, David	NYK 30
Dick Free Black	COL 240	Dickerson, Jesse	WST 139	Dickson, Francis	OTS 41
Dick a Black	NYK 152	Dickerson John	CAY 538	Dickson, James	WSH 226
Dick Negro	QNS 60	Dickerson, Jonathan	SUF 68	Dickson, James	WSH 257
Dick Negro	QNS 74	Dickerson, Nathan	SUF 71	Dickson, James	WSH 280
Dick	QNS 84	Dickerson, Obediah	GRN 352	Dickson, James	WSH 295
Dick a free Negro	RNS 53	Dickerson, Sarah	NYK 144	Dickson, Jedothan	WSH 294
Dick, David	WST 117	Dickerson, Seth	TIO 216	Dickson, John	NYK 103
Dick, Henry	COL 189	Dickerson, Sherman B.	TIO 232	Dickson, John	NYK 115
Dick, Henry	MNT 27	Dickerson, Waitstill	OND 183	Dickson, John	NYK 138
Dick, John	MNT 33	Dickerson, Waitstill	OND 186	Dickson, John	OTS 2
Dick, John	RNS 88	Dickerson, William	DEL 273	Dickson, Joseph	CHN 798
Dick, John	WSH 290	Dickeson, Daniel	CHN 766	Dickson, Lewis	NYK 145
Dick, Perry	RNS 70	Dickeson, Josiah	CHN 782	Dickson, Nathl	SCH 136

Dolph, Amos	COL 211	Donnar, John	ALB 132	Dorland, Joseph	ORN 364
Dolph, John	COL 211	Donnaven, William	NYK 46	Dorland, Samuel	DUT 18
Dolph, Joseph	WSH 303	Donnelly, Partrick	NYK 68	Dorland, Samuel	ORN 363
Dolph, Robert R.	ORN 279	Donnelly, Thomas	ALB 43	Dorland, William	DUT 120
Dolph, Solomon	STB 200	Donnerly, Charles	COL 225	Dorman, Ambrose	ALB 109
Dolphin, Eli a free		Donneshe, John	SRA 14	Dorman, Ezra	HRK 560
Negro	ALB 88	Donnile, Nicholas	MNT 120	Dorman, Jacob	ALB 109
Dolphin, Rebecca	NYK 56	Donnoldson, John	NYK 128	Dorman, Jacob	RNS 56
Dolten, William	KNG 4	Donnougher, Henry	NYK 147	Dorman, Jared	HRK 560
Domine, Jane	SUF 109	Donnoughky, John	NYK 128	Dorman, Jeremiah	ALB 109
Domine, John	CLN 161	Donolly, Henry	OND 209	Dorman, Jesse	OND 202
Dominic, Francis	NYK 70	Donolly, James	ORN 279	Dorman, John	ONT 460
Dominick, Francis J.	NYK 123	Donom, Samuel	GRN 329	Dorman, Robert	ALB 109
Dominick, George	NYK 78	Donovan, George	WST 118	Dorman, Thomas	ALB 109
Dominick, George	SCH 124	Donovan, Richard	NYK 32	Dornbergh, Philip	SCH 128
Dominick, John	SCH 124	Dony, John	SCH 135	Dornbergh, Simon	SCH 128
Dominick, John Jr	SCH 124	Dony, Samuel	SCH 135	Dorph, Earl (Rupt)	SCH 172
Dominick, Partrick	NYK 140	Dony, William	SCH 135	Dorr, Edward	COL 220
Dominick, Peter	SCH 124	Dooley, Mathus	NYK 30	Dorr, Elisha	ALB 140
Dominick, William	NYK 124	Doolin, Moses	ORN 370	Dorr, Joseph	RNS 17
Dommine, Nathaniel	SUF 106	Doolittle, Abel	TIO 228	Dorr, Mathew	COL 220
Dommine, Nathl Junr	SUF 106	Doolittle, Asa	ONT 420	Dorrance, Daniel	CAY 522
Domnick, Francis	SCH 124	Doolittle, Charles	OND 175	Dorrance, David	ULS 187
Domp, Frederick	ALB 54	Doolittle, Ebenezer	HRK 532	Dorrance, James	OND 172
Domp, Philip	ALB 54	Doolittle, George	ALB 55	Dorrell, Daniel	HRK 427
Donaghe, Henry	OTS 39	Doolittle, George	OND 157	Dorrington, Thomas	NYK 79
Donaghy, William	ESS 306	Doolittle, Harvey	ONT 396	Dorris, William	NYK 147
Donalds	ALB 48	Doolittle, Hopkins	ULS 255	Dorrow, Samuel	WSH 227
Donalds, Asa	SRA 61	Doolittle, Ichabod	DUT 172	Dorset, John	RCH 92
Donalds, Isaac	WST 115	Doolittle, Jared	OND 190	Dorset, Lawrence	RNS 96
Donalds, James	MNT 12	Doolittle, Jesse	HRK 532	Dorsey see Darcey &	
Donalds, Peter	CHN 956	Doolittle, Jesse	OND 189	Dorcy	
Donalds, Philip	WST 116	Doolittle, Joel	HRK 408	Dorsey, Partrick	NYK 131
Donaldson, Abraham	ULS 234	Doolittle, John	OND 190	Dorton, John	NYK 67
Donaldson, Abraham Junr	ULS 234	Do.little, John	TIO 232	Dorus, Sarah	ALB 132
Donaldson, Boyd	WSH 289	Doolittle, Jonathan	ORN 347	Dorwell, Daniel	HRK 476
Donaldson, Daniel	WSH 268	Doolittle, Joseph	ORN 346	Dosen, Thomas	MNT 114
Donaldson, James	NYK 101	Doolittle, Luther	CHN 970	Dossayres, Mary	NYK 69
Donaldson, James	ULS 234	Doolittle, Philemon	OND 190	Dossen, Joel	RNS 64
Donaldson, James	WSH 289	Doolittle, Reuben	SRA 47	Dotty, Alphaus	WSH 216
Donaldson, James	WST 166	Doolittle, Ruben	WSH 288	Dotty, Benjamine Junr	GRN 345
Donaldson, Jesse	WST 149	Doolittle, Stephen	NYK 101	Dotty, Chilius	WSH 222
Donaldson, John	DUT 120	Doolittle, Thompson	HRK 536	Dotty, Thadius	WSH 215
Donaldson, John	WSH 246	Doolittle, Timothy	ULS 188	Dotty, Timothy	SRA 10
Donaldson, Peter	ULS 184	Doolittle, Uri	OND 184	Doty, Benjamin	COL 183
Donaldson, Peter	WST 121	Doolittle, Wait	WSH 265	Doty, Benjamin Junr	ORN 327
Donaldson, Robert	DUT 125	Doop, John	ULS 235	Doty, Benjamine	GRN 345
Donaldson, Robert	NYK 94	Doop, Zachariah	DUT 116	Doty, Charles	DUT 110
Donaldson, Robert	WSH 206	Door, Benjamin	QNS 82	Doty, Charles	WST 145
Donaldson, William	NYK 48	Dooreman, George G.	NYK 97	Doty, Danforth	HRK 591
Donaldson, William	ULS 240	Doorman, Christopher	RNS 19	Doty, David	ALB 73
Donaway, James	ALB 126	Dop, David	CLN 160	Doty, David	WST 115
Done, James	GRN 357	Dop, Peter	CLN 163	Doty, Dorus	HRK 521
Done, John	GRN 330	Dophinee, John B. a		Doty, Edward	GRN 342
Done, John	HRK 525	Black	NYK 104	Doty, Elias	WST 144
Done, John	WSH 184	Dopp, Henry	OND 209	Doty, Elijah	ALB 91
Done, Joseph	GRN 346	Dor, Jonathin	WSH 190	Doty, Elijah	GRN 330
Done, Josiah	GRN 345	Doran, Abraham	ALB 40	Doty, Elisha	CAY 636
Done, Mary	WSH 192	Doran, John	ALB 40	Doty, Isaac	CAY 636
Done, Wm	GRN 346	Doran, John Junr	ALB 40	Doty, Isaac	DUT 119
Donegan, William	ULS 215	Dorand, William	NYK 102	Doty, Isaac	NYK 45
Donelly, _____	GRN 330	Dorcas, Alexander	ORN 303	Doty, Isaac	ORN 327
Donelson, Alexander	RNS 41	Dorchester, Alexander	OND 179	Doty, Isaac	WSH 286
Doney, James	SRA 13	Dorchester, James	OND 160	Doty, Isaac	WST 167
Doney, John	SRA 13	Dorcy, Margaret	NYK 92	Doty, Jacob	DUT 119
Doney, Pamela	ONT 392	Doresley, Solomon	RNS 46	Doty, Jacob	RNS 30
Dongan, Walter	RCH 93	Dorgan, Andrw	NYK 74	Doty, Jesse	ALB 30
Doniver, Daniel	GRN 330	Dorgan, Timothy	NYK 28	Doty, John	ALB 125
Donley, Partrick	NYK 132	Doring, James	NYK 122	Doty, John	OND 209
Donley, Stephen	KNG 5	Dorland, Benjamin	DUT 120	Doty, John	RNS 105
Donnald, Anna M.	NYK 118	Dorland, Charles	ORN 328	Doty, John	WST 144
Donnald, Jane	NYK 85	Dorland, Enoch	DUT 18	Doty, Joseph	COL 204
Donnaldson, James	NYK 73	Dorland, Garret	ORN 319	Doty, Joseph	DUT 7
Donnally, Joseph	ALB 103	Dorland, Gilbert	DUT 18	Doty, Joseph	DUT 126
Donnally, Peter	ALB 129	Dorland, Jacobus	DUT 25	Doty, Joseph	NYK 89
Donnally, Robert	RCH 94	Dorland, Jane	ORN 363	Doty, Joseph	RNS 29
Donnally, William	ALB 145	Dorland, John	ORN 317	Doty, Joseph	RNS 44

Name	Loc	Name	Loc	Name	Loc
Downing, John	RNS 87	Drake, Aaron	SUF 102	Drake, Perez	OTS 43
Downing, John	SRA 58	Drake, Aaron	ULS 186	Drake, Peter	DUT 6
Downing, Levi	WSH 195	Drake, Abiel	COL 206	Drake, Peter	ESS 294
Downing, Moses	DUT 60	Drake, Abraham	NYK 135	Drake, Reuben	ULS 255
Downing, Moses Junr	DUT 74	Drake, Alpheus	ONN 139	Drake, Richard	ORN 352
Downing, Mumford	OTS 30	Drake, Andrew	RCH 92	Drake, Richd	SUF 75
Downing, Peter	COL 186	Drake, Apollus	CHN 846	Drake, Roger	HRK 564
Downing, Samuel	NYK 60	Drake, Asa	ONN 139	Drake, Samuel	COL 222
Downing, Samuel	ORN 279	Drake, Augustus	WST 144	Drake, Samuel	TIO 259
Downing, Silas	QNS 83	Drake, Benjamin	ORN 317	Drake, Samuel	ULS 265
Downing, Stephen	CAY 704	Drake, Benjamin	ORN 360	Drake, Susannah	NYK 116
Downing, William	CAY 700	Drake, Benjn	TIO 233	Drake, Theoas	RNS112B
Downniger, Jacob	QNS 81	Drake, Benjamin	WSH 265	Drake, Tho as	CAY 556
Downs, Abel	DEL 275	Drake, Burgess	ORN 364	Drake, Uriah	ULS 256
Downs, Benjn	SUF 64	Drake, Caleb	DUT 90	Drake, Warner	OND 197
Downs, Danl	SUF 74	Drake, Chrles	CHN 888	Drake, Wm	GRN 355
Downs, Danl	SUF 74	Drake, Charles	MNT 120	Drake, William	NYK 142
Downs, David	SUF 73	Drake, Charles	RCH 94	Drake, Wm	OTS 43
Downs, Edward	ORN 281	Drake, Chauncey	OND 197	Drake, Wm	RNS 46
Downs, James	ESS 321	Drake, Cornelius Junr	MNT 125	Drake, William	RCH 95
Downs, James	SUF 76	Drake, Curtiss	ORN 379	Drake, William	ULS 235
Downs, John	ORN 281	Drake, Daniel	ORN 360	Drake, William	ULS 256
Downs, John	SUF 72	Drake, Daniel	TIO 239	Drake, William	WST 156
Downs, Mary	DUT 65	Drake, David G.	ORN 364	Drake, William Junr	ORN 365
Downs, Nathl	SUF 72	Drake, Ebenezer	SUF 89	Drake, William S.	ULS 264
Downs, Nicols	SUF 65	Drake, Elijah	CAY 602	Drake, Zepheniah	ULS 180
Downs, Peter	SUF 72	Drake, Elijah	CAY 602	Drake, Zepheniah Junr	ULS 186
Downs, Reuben	CAY 634	Drake, Elijah	CAY 650	Draper, Ebenezer	OTS 21
Downs, Samuel	WSH 222	Drake, Francis	CAY 556	Draper, Friend	ALB 110
Downs, Samuel	WSH 266	Drake, Francis	CAY 594	Draper, Gideon	SRA 30
Downs, Samuel	WST 156	Drake, Francis	ORN 347	Draper, James	NYK 126
Downs, Seth	WST 112	Drake, Francis	SRA 13	Draper, James	WSH 277
Downs, Truman	CAY 634	Drake, George	RCH 95	Draper, Joel	OTS 29
Downs, Wm	SUF 72	Drake, Gilbert	GRN 330	Draper, John	DUT 50
Downse, William	WST 144	Drake, Gilbert	WST 127	Draper, John	OND 209
Downy, Thomas	NYK 63	Drake, Girardus	DUT 114	Draper, John	OTS 21
Dows, Eleazer	SRA 25	Drake, Hannah	NYK 30	Draper, John	RNS 74
Dows, Thomas whiteman	SRA 25	Drake, Henry	DUT 141	Draper, John	WSH 251
Dowse, John	OTS 15	Drake, Jacob	NYK 116	Draper, Jonathan	WSH 302
Dowse, William	OTS 2	Drake, James	NYK 78	Draper, Joseph	DUT 46
Dowse, Wm	OTS 15	Drake, James	OND 209	Draper, Joseph	TIO 248
Dox, Isaac	SRA 11	Drake, James	TIO 250	Draper, Joshua	OTS 43
Dox, John	SRA 11	Drake, Jasper	CAY 602	Draper, Nathan	WSH 277
Dox, Mary	MNT 69	Drake, Jasper	NYK 123	Draper, Nathaniel	WSH 278
Dox, Peter	ALB 48	Drake, Jasper	NYK 148	Draper, Reuben	DUT 46
Dox, Peter	ALB 146	Drake, Jeremiah	ORN 346	Draper, Richard	DUT 53
Doxey, Amos	SUF 93	Drake, Jeremiah	RCH 88	Draper, Samuel	ONN 143
Doxey, Benjamin	QNS 76	Drake, Jeremiah	ULS 183	Draper, Samuel	WSH 238
Doxey, Isaiah	QNS 73	Drake, John	DUT 32	Draper, Solomon	WSH 253
Doxey, Jacob	QNS 77	Drake, John	DUT 79	Draper, William	OND 216
Doxey, Obadiah	QNS 77	Drake, John	DUT 115	Draper, Wm	OTS 49
Doxey, Philip	QNS 76	Drake, John	DUT 141	Dratt, John	SRA 12
Doxey, Samuel	COL 249	Drake, John	NYK 61	Drawer, Aaron	QNS 75
Doxey, Samuel	QNS 76	Drake, John	NYK 81	Drawer, Anthony	QNS 81
Doxsie, James	ORN 285	Drake, John	ORN 396	Drawer, John	QNS 75
Doxsie, John	DUT 24	Drake, John	SUF 75	Drawer, Martin	QNS 76
Doxsie, John	ORN 287	Drake, John	WST 162	Drawyer, Abraham	QNS 75
Doxtrader, Jacob	ALB 138	Drake, John the 2d	DUT 38	Drawyer, Allin	CHN 964
Doxtrader, John F.	MNT 7	Drake, Jonathan	RCH 91	Drawyer, John	KNG 9
Doxy, Gabriel	OTS 47	Drake, Jonathan	TIO 253	Drawyer, William Negro	QNS 70
Doxy, Thomas	ESS 298	Drake, Joseph	ORN 363	Dreamer, Jacob	SRA 25
Doxy, Thomas	QNS 81	Drake, Joseph	TIO 242	Dreamer, Peter	SRA 25
Doy, Jacob	NYK 85	Drake, Joseph	TIO 253	Drean, James	RCK 105
Doyer, William	NYK 123	Drake, Joseph	ULS 180	Dreher, Adam	COL 251
Doyl, Samuel	STB 198	Drake, Joseph	ULS 256	Dresser, Elijah	OND 194
Doyle, Abraham	ULS 230	Drake, Joseph	WST 148	Drew, Ephriam	SCH 170
Doyle, Charles	DUT 162	Drake, Joshua	ORN 363	Drew, Gilbert	DUT 93
Doyle, Elizabeth	DUT 78	Drake, Joshua	WST 156	Drew, Isaac	DUT 96
Doyle, Elizabeth	NYK 132	Drake, Josiah	ULS 235	Drew, John	RNS 22
Doyle, James	NYK 27	Drake, Josias	DUT 118	Drew, John	RNS 56
Doyle, Moses	DUT 162	Drake, Lyman	OTS 41	Drew, Oliver	DUT 65
Doyle, Thomas	NYK 27	Drake, Moses	GRN 330	Drew, Partrick	NYK 150
Doyle, Thomas	NYK 145	Drake, Moses	NYK 116	Drew, Samuel	ORN 375
Doyson, John	MNT 74	Drake, Nathan	ORN 314	Drew, William	DUT 89
Dr___, .saac	ONT 510	Drake, Nathaniel	WST 158	D Ridder, Waller	WSH 241
Drader, Nichs	SCH 162	Drake, Oliver	NYK 24	Driesback, Jost	MNT 26
Drake, Aaron	COL 184	Drake, Ovid	COL 204	Driesback, Philip	SCH 122

Name	Ref	Name	Ref	Name	Ref
Drigg, Barthalemew	GRN 332	Du Bois, Coonradt	ULS 197	Du Bois, Tobias	ULS 204
Driggs, Daniel	ONN 163	Dubois, Cornelius	RNS 55	Du Bois, Tobias Junr	ULS 196
Driggs, David	SUF 84	Dubois, Cornelius	RNS 57	Du Bois, Walter	ULS 253
Driggs, Elisha	DUT 143	Du Bois, Cornelius	ULS 206	Du Bois, Wessels	ULS 253
Driggs, Elliot	GRN 332	Du Bois, Cornelius	ULS 244	Du Bois, Wilhelmus	ULS 266
Driggs Geore	GRN 358	Dubois, Cort	NYK 88	Du Bois, William	ULS 219
Driggs, Grissel	GRN 332	Du Bois, Daniel	ULS 237	Du Boyes, Daniel	TIO 212
Driggs, Rozel	ONN 192	Du Bois, David	ULS 223	DuBoyes, Mattheus	TIO 212
Drinkwater, Amos	RNS 17	Du Bois, David Junr	ULS 224	Dubuar, Mary	NYK 48
Drinnan, John	NYK 107	Du Bois, Elias	ULS 259	Ducet, John	ALB 34
Drisback, Jost	ALB 45	Dubois, Elisha	NYK 128	Duche, Rene Rock	NYK 37
Drisburg(?), James	NYK 140	Du Bois, Ephraim	DUT 71	Ducher, Abraham	DUT 32
Driscol, David	NYK 25	Du Bois, Ephraim	ULS 239	Ducher, Barent	DUT 41
Driskel, Jacob	NYK 71	Dubois, Francis	CLN 160	Ducher, Benjamin	WSH 185
Driskill, William	CHN 740	Du Bois, Garret	DUT 31	Ducher, Christopher	DUT 43
Driver, Richard	NYK 143	Du Bois, Garret	HRK 555	Ducher, Cornelius Junr	DUT 45
Drown, Levi	GRN 356	Du Bois, Garret	ULS 205	Ducher, Cornelius Senr	DUT 44
Drown, Samuel	ONT 402	Du Bois, Garret	ULS 242	Ducher, David	DUT 32
Dru_e, Samuel	ONT 510	Dubois, Henry	RNS 55	Ducher, David	DUT 41
Druce, Andrew	OTS 51	Du Bois, Hezekiah	ULS 223	Ducher, David	DUT 61
Druce, James	OTS 57	Du Bois, Isaac	ORN 394	Ducher, David	ORN 380
Druce, Stephen	OTS 54	Du Bois, Isaac	ULS 204	Ducher, Gideon Junr	DUT 43
Druce, Stephen	OTS 57	Du Bois, Isaac	ULS 237	Ducher, Gideon Senr	DUT 43
Drue, William	ALB 120	Du Bois, Isaac	ULS 249	Ducher, Isaac M.	DUT 41
Druley, Nichs	ALB 141	Du Bois, Jacob	DUT 40	Ducher, Jacob	DUT 78
Drum, Andrew	DUT 158	Du Bois, Jacob	HRK 555	Ducher, John	DUT 44
Drum, Andries	DUT 151	Du Bois, Jacob	ULS 196	Ducher, John	MNT 11
Drum, Anthony	COL 235	Du Bois, Jacob	ULS 242	Ducher, Matthew	DUT 48
Drum, Frederick	COL 197	Du Bois, Jacobus	ULS 219	Ducher, Moses	DUT 48
Drum, George & John	DUT 150	Du Bois, Jacobus	ULS 232	Ducher, Silas	DUT 43
Drum, Jacob	COL 225	Du Bois, Jacobus Junr	ULS 224	Duchesne, Arnauld	NYK 126
Drum, Jacob	DUT 153	Dubois, James	ORN 290	Duck, Daniel	NYK 94
Drum, Jacob Junr	COL 228	Dubois, James	WST 145	Duclos, Baptist	NYK 73
Drum, Johannis	COL 232	Du Bois, Jeremiah	DUT 6	Ducsten, Parley	MNT 51
Drum, John George	DUT 150	Du Bois, Jeremiah	ULS 228	Dudley, Abraham	GRN 338
Drum, John Junr	COL 227	Du Bois, Joel	DUT 67	Dudley, Belia	WSH 196
Drum, Marcus	COL 227	Du Bois, Joel	ORN 310	Dudley, George	DUT 172
Drum, Mathias	COL 237	Du Bois, Joel Junr	DUT 68	Dudley, George	GRN 354
Drum, Nicholas	DUT 150	Du Bois, Johannis	DUT 31	Dudley, George	HRK 541
Drum, Peter	DUT 76	Du Bois, Johannis	ULS 206	Dudley, Isaac	OND 177
Drum, Peter	DUT 156	Du Bois, Johannis J.	ULS 219	Dudley, John	SUF 97
Drum, Wm	OTS 27	Du Bois, John	DUT 121	Dudley, Martin	ONT 430
Drum, Zachariah	DUT 150	Dubois, John	GRN 327	Dudley, Miles	ONT 410
Drum, Zacheriah	COL 245	Dubois, John	GRN 358	Dudley, Miss	GRN 355
Drumer, John	SRA 4	Dubois, John	RCH 89	Dudley, Nathan	GRN 338
Drumman, James	RCK 104	Dubois, John	RCH 94	Dudley, Nathan	GRN 338
Drummond, George	NYK 150	Du Bois, John	ULS 254	Dudley, Peter	GRN 338
Drummond, James	NYK 35	Dubois, John Junr	GRN 327	Dudley, Subbell	TIO 217
Drummond, John	WSH 199	Du Bois, John H.	DUT 69	Dudley, William	NYK 34
Drummond, Robert	NYK 141	Du Bois, John N.	ULS 219	Dudrey, Abraham	ULS 196
Drummond, Robert	ULS 221	Du Bois, Jonathan	ULS 242	Due, Jeremiah	MNT 24
Drummond, William	NYK 45	Du Bois, Joshua	ULS 228	Due, Mary	WSH 196
Druyare, Lurentia	NYK 135	Du Bois, Koert	DUT 29	Duel see Deuel, Dewel	
Drurey, Martha	CHN 912	Du Bois, Koert	DUT 116	& Duwl	
Drury, Ebenezer	HRK 532	Du Bois, Lewis	ULS 268	Duel, Abraham	SRA 9
Drury, Ebenezer	HRK 533	Du Bois, Louis J.	ULS 242	Duel, Benjamin	OND 194
Drury, Lewis	HRK 532	Dubois, Lucy	RCH 91	Duel, Benjamin	SRA 56
Dryin, Michael	NYK 76	Du Bois, Martin	ULS 196	Duel, Cornelius	WSH 196
Duane, James C.	ALB 29	Du Bois, Matthew	ULS 225	Duel, Ebenezer	WSH 238
Duane, Mary	ALB 12	Du Bois, Matthew M.	ORN 289	Duel, James	SRA 56
Dubey, Philip	RCK 89	Du Bois, Methusaleh	ULS 244	Duel, Jasper	WSH 201
Dublin, Andrew	NYK 55	Du Bois, Nathaniel	DUT 41	Duel, Joseph	SRA 56
Dublin, Flora a Black	NYK 26	Du Bois, Nathaniel	ORN 279	Duel, Joseph	WSH 213
Dublin, Jacob	NYK 107	Dubois, Nathaniel	RCK 99	Duel, Joseph Junr	SRA 56
Du Bois, Abraham	DUT 36	Du Bois, Peter	DUT 5	Duel, Levi	WSH 201
Du Bois, Abraham	ULS 243	Du Bois, Peter	DUT 36	Duel, Richard	WSH 213
Dubois, Allias	GRN 358	Du Bois, Peter	NYK 84	Duel, Seth	WSH 213
Du Bois, Andries	ULS 252	Dubois, Peter	NYK 147	Duel, Trustam	SRA 45
Du Bois, Anne	ORN 352	Dubois, Peter	SRA 11	Duel, William	WSH 237
Dubois, Augustus	RCH 89	Du Bois, Peter	ULS 206	Duell, Robert	SCH 123
Du Bois, Benjamin	DUT 5	Du Bois, Peter	ULS 225	Duer, Caesar a Black	NYK 64
Dubois, Benjamine	GRN 327	Du Bois, Peter P.	DUT 71	Duer, Catherine	NYK 87
Dubois, Bornet	GRN 330	Dubois, Richard	RCH 94	Duers, David	WSH 216
Dubois, Charles	NYK 93	Du Bois, Samuel	ULS 192	Duesenberry, Anaziah	NYK 84
Du Bois, Charles	ULS 244	Du Bois, Samuel	ULS 243	Duesenburry, Richard	NYK 84
Du Bois, Christian	DUT 31	Du Bois, Simon	ULS 251	Dueslar, Elisabeth	MNT 19
Dubois, Col_	GRN 358	Du Bois, Teunis	DUT 36	Dueslar, Jacob Junr	MNT 18

Name	Loc	Pg	Name	Loc	Pg	Name	Loc	Pg
Dueslar, John Jacob	MNT	18	Dumerest, Abraham	ALB	22	Duncan, Samuel	COL	182
Dueslar, Marcus	MNT	18	Dummond, John	NYK	66	Duncan, Sarah	NYK	135
Duester, Martinus	MNT	34	Dumom, Jonathan	MNT	13	Duncan, Solomon	DUT	127
Duewey, Isaah	MNT	89	Dumond, David	DEL	272	Duncan, Stephen	NYK	99
Duey, Benjamin	WSH	196	Dumond, Egnus	DEL	272	Duncan, Thomas	DUT	127
Duey, David	GRN	341	Dumond, Harmanus	DEL	272	Duncan, Thomas Junr	DUT	125
Duey, Elijah	GRN	341	Dumond, John	DEL	272	Duncan, William	DUT	8
Duey, Russle	WSH	219	Dumond, John B.	GRN	327	Duncebox, Henry	RNS	10
Dufendorf, Abraham D.	MNT	26	Du Mond, John P.	ULS	218	Duncombe, Charles H.	DUT	68
Dufendorf, Henry	MNT	24	Dumond, Joseph	ALB	71	Dundfee, Cornelius	WSH	230
Dufendorf, Jacob	MNT	28	Du Mond, Joshua	ULS	214	Dunfie, Laurence	NYK	22
Dufendorf, Jacob H.	MNT	26	Dumond, Waldring	GRN	327	Dunham, Abner	OTS	8
Dufendorf, Solomon	MNT	28	Dumond, William V.	ALB	138	Dunham, Benjamin	NYK	122
Dufer, David	OND	165	Du Mont, Coonradt	ULS	192	Dunham, Charles	CLN	164
Duff, Alexander	SRA	43	Du Mont, Cornelius	ULS	192	Dunham, Corne_ius	SRA	6
Duff, Deborah	NYK	111	Du Mont, James	ULS	254	Dunham, Daniel	ONN	129
Duff, Edward	WST	146	Du Mont, John	CAY	702	Dunham, Daniel	SRA	52
Duff, James	NYK	133	Du Mont, John	DUT	111	Dunham, Daniel	WSH	286
Duff, Nicholas	NYK	53	Du Mont, John	ULS	234	Dunham, Danil	WSH	246
Duff, Richard	NYK	25	Du Mont, Margaret	ULS	230	Dunham, David	ONN	177
Duffee, Mary	NYK	73	Dumont, Peter(?)	CAY	576	Dunham, David	RNS	42
Duffee, William	ALB	135	Dumont, Peter	NYK	29	Dunham, David	SRA	52
Duffel, Edward	NYK	46	Dumont, Peter	SRA	48	Dunham, Edward	SRA	52
Duffel, Edward	NYK	112	Du Mont, Peter	ULS	230	Dunham, Elias	CHN	862
Duffie, Arthur	WSH	306	Du Mont, Peter	ULS	232	Dunham, Elias Junr	CHN	862
Duffie, Barbary	NYK	47	Du Mont, Phillip	ULS	230	Dunham, Elijah	SRA	52
Duffie, Edward	QNS	67	Dumont, William	CAY	520	Dunham, Epharim	SRA	3
Duffie, Frances	NYK	120	Dun, George	WSH	254	Dunham, Ephraim	DEL	274
Duffie, Henry	NYK	108	Dun, Jane	OND	184	Dunham, Ephraim	SRA	9
Duffie, James	NYK	15	Duna__, Jonat...	MNT	81	Dunham, Ezekiel	ONN	180
Duffie, James	NYK	92	Dunbar, Amos	CAY	578	Dunham, Ezra	CAY	674
Duffie, James	QNS	67	Dunbar, Asa	ONT	362	Dunham, Gideon	ONT	378
Duffie, John	NYK	24	Dunbar, David	CHN	858	Dunham, Hazel	CHN	866
Duffie, Ross	NYK	118	Dunbar, Calup	CHN	872	Dunham, Hezikeah	SRA	40
Duffield, John	ULS	262	Dunbar, George	QNS	75	Dunham, Isaac	RNS	106
Duffill, Margaret	KNG	10	Dunbar, Jesse	OTS	29	Dunham, Jermi	ONN	178
Dugal, William	NYK	145	Dunbar, Joel	OND	207	Dunham, John	ALB	80
Dugan see Augan			Dunbar, John	CAY	618	Dunham, John	ALB	93
Dugan, Alexander	NYK	99	Dunbar, John	DUT	48	Dunham, John	DUT	120
Dugan, Alexander	NYK	143	Dunbar, John	OTS	18	Dunham, John	DUT	134
Dugarhy, John	RNS	82	Dunbar, Joshua	ONT	498	Dunham, John	NYK	49
Dugat, George	ALB	28	Dunbar, Laurence	ONT	358	Dunham, John	NYK	94
Duggan, James	SRA	11	Dunbar, Levinus	ALB	146	Dunham, John	NYK	129
Duglas, Benjamin	SRA	53	Dunbar, Lucy a mulatto	NYK	20	Dunham, John	ORN	383
Duglas, Isaac	CHN	864	Dunbar, Nathaniel	GRN	331	Dunham, Jonathan	COL	217
Duglas, John	CHN	864	Dunbar, Noomie	NYK	34	Dunham, Jonathan	OND	189
Duglas, Zebulon	CHN	946	Dunbar, Philip	ALB	50	Dunham, Jonathan	TIO	222
Duglass, George	RNS	46	Dunbar, Prince	DUT	44	Dunham, Jonathan	WSH	191
Duglass, John	SRA	40	Dunbar, Richd	RNS	34	Dunham, Jonathan	WSH	239
Duglass, Joseph	GRN	329	Dunbar, Robert	ALB	102	Dunham, Joseph	CAY	674
Duglass, Wm Junr	RNS	100	Dunbar, Robert	ALB	146	Dunham, Josiah	ALB	142
Dugless, Samuel	RNS	43	Dunbar, Robert Junr	ALB	45	Dunham, Mary	WSH	245
Duher, Stephen	NYK	88	Dunbar, Samuel	COL	212	Dunham, Morgan	SRA	8
Duhurst, John	NYK	101	Dunbar, Seth	CHN	938	Dunham, Naham	WSH	191
Duke, John	ORN	306	Dunbar, Seth	OND	208	Dunham, Nathl	ONN	180
DuKee(?), Cornelius	TIO	214	Dunbar, William	ALB	145	Dunham, Nathaniel	RNS	42
Dukelin, Claudius	HRK	409	Dunbar, Nehemiah	SRA	60	Dunham, Richardson	WSH	223
Dukelin, Stephen	HRK	428	Dunber, Tine	SRA	3	Dunham, Robert	WSH	223
Dukson, Patrick	NYK	17	Duncan, Abigail	ORN	328	Dunham, Samuel	ORN	368
Dul, Henry	MNT	47	Duncan, Benjamin	DUT	8	Dunham, Samuel	SRA	46
Dulittle, Joell	CHN	954	Duncan, Charles E.	WST	121	Dunham, Samuel	WSH	239
Dulittle, Patridge	SRA	16	Duncan, Daniel	COL	182	Dunham, Silas	COL	191
Dulittle, Samuel	CHN	954	Duncan, Daniel Junr	COL	182	Dunham, Silvenus	CHN	878
Dull, Elizabeth	ALB	148	Duncan, Elizabeth	NYK	34	Dunham, Simeon	SRA	52
Dull, Wm	TIO	213	Duncan, Freeborn	DUT	5	Dunham, Smith	SRA	52
Dulston, Widow Mary	TIO	258	Duncan, George	DUT	59	Dunham, Solomon	SRA	40
Duly, Philip	ALB	32	Duncan, John	ORN	319	Dunham, Thomas	ORN	370
Duma, George	SRA	48	Duncan, John	WSH	228	Dunham, William	CLN	163
Du Mais, Enos	CLN	173	Duncan, John	WSH	293	Dunham, William	DEL	276
Dumas, Peter	CAY	518	Duncan, Joseph	COL	192	Dunham, Youngholt	WSH	240
Dumb, Adam	MNT	1	Duncan, Mc Vain	MNT	76	Dunhill, Thomas	NYK	133
Dumb, Conrod	MNT	2	Duncan, Mary	DUT	47	Dunihu, James	WSH	196
Dumb, David	MNT	2	Duncan, Nancy	ONT	326	Dunihu, John	WSH	191
Dumb, Nicholas	MNT	4	Duncan, Nicholas	MNT	51	Dunihu, John	WSH	196
Dumbleton, Nathl	OTS	44	Duncan, Peter	COL	249	Dunin, Noah	OND	222
Dumbleton, Saml	OTS	2	Duncan, Richd	ALB	11	Duning, Alexander	SRA	29
Dumbolton, Gad	NYK	102				Duning, Philo	SRA	23

114

Name			Name			Name		
Dunkhile, Nicholas	MNT	46	Dunn, Reuben	ORN	377	Dupuy, Mary	RCH	92
Dunkhill, Francis	MNT	43	Dunn, Richard	ALB	134	Dupuy, Nicholas	RCH	91
Dunkin, John	RNS	17	Dunn, richard	NYK	50	Dupuy, Nicholas	RCH	92
Dunkley, Cec_l ia	NYK	78	Dunn, Robert	NYK	26	Dupy, Nicholas	NYK	103
Dunkley, Joseph	NYK	81	Dunn, Samuel	NYK	105	Dura, Joseph	NYK	85
Dunkley, William	NYK	130	Dunn, Stephen	CAY	662	Duran, Marinus Fs	CLN	160
Dunks, Joel	ONT	434	Dunn, Susan	NYK	43	Duran, Semeon	ESS	318
Dunlap, Andrew	CAY	542	Dunn, Thomas	NYK	43	Durand, Bryan	DUT	94
Dunlap, Eliza	NYK	68	Dunn, Thomas	NYK	74	Durand, Frances	NYK	127
Dunlap, Ellenor	NYK	38	Dunn, Thomas a Black	NYK	118	Durand, George	NYK	95
Dunlap, James	ALB	141	Dunn, Thomas	ULS	181	Durand, John	WSH	220
Dunlap, James	DEL	273	Dunn, thomas	ULS	204	Durand, John P.	NYK	141
Dunlap, James	NYK	52	Dunn, Wm	STB	199	Durand, Joseph	ESS	318
Dunlap, James	ORN	289	Dunn, William	ULS	181	Durand, Mirari	ULS	212
Dunlap, John	MNT	47	Dunnam, Nathaniel	OND	222	Durands, Stephen	DUT	63
Dunlap, John	NYK	75	Dunnavan, Thomas	NYK	44	Durant, Allen	ALB	92
Dunlap, John	NYK	80	Dunnegan, Hugh	NYK	132	Durant, Eleazer	OTS	31
Dunlap, John	OTS	2	Dunnim___, Jonathan D.	MNT	4	Durborow, Joseph	NYK	123
Dunlap, John	STB	197	Dunning, Able	MNT	81	Durell, Jonathan	NYK	73
Dunlap, John	WSH	190	Dunning, Abraham	CAY	644	Durell, Stephen	CAY	604
Dunlap, John H.	OTS	4	Dunning, Abraham	ORN	331	Durell, Stephen	CAY	626
Dunlap, Margaret	NYK	129	Dunning, Allen	ESS	295	Durell, William	NYK	29
Dunlap, Peter	ORN	338	Dunning, Benjamin	ORN	358	Durfee, Mrs	DEL	278
Dunlap, Robert	CAY	630	Dunning, Calvin	SRA	44	Durfee, William	OND	186
Dunlap, Robert	NYK	92	Dunning, Charles	ORN	321	Durfee, William	SRA	33
Dunlap, Thomas	MNT	52	Dunning, Daniel	ORN	331	Durfey, Edward	ONT	348
Dunlap, Thomas	NYK	105	Dunning, David	ONN	191	Durfey, Gideon	ONT	348
Dunlap, William	ALB	10	Dunning, Ebenezer	CLN	171	Durfey, Gideon Jun	ONT	346
Dunlap, Wm	MNT	97	Dunning, Ebenezer	ORN	357	Durfey, Job	ONT	348
Dunlap, William	NYK	100	Dunning, Ely	CLN	171	Durfey, Lemuel	ONT	348
Dunlap, William	ULS	199	Dunning, Ephraim	ULS	189	Durfey, Lemuel	WSH	198
Dunlap, William	WSH	234	Dunning, Isaac	ORN	357	Durfey, Stephen	ONT	348
Dunlap, William	WST	162	Dunning, Jacob	ORN	340	Durgie, Andrew	CAY	632
Dunlavey, James	SUF	66	Dunning, James	ORN	360	Durgie, Ebenezar	CAY	640
Dunleavey, James	ALB	142	Dunning, James	SRA	61	Durgie, Elisha	CAY	644
Dunlive, George	NYK	108	Dunning, Jesse	ULS	184	Durgie, Wilks	CAY	632
Dunmore, Cirus a Black	NYK	140	Dunning, John	ORN	343	Durham, Andrw	NYK	67
Dunmore, Larrey	ONN	145	Dunning, John	SRA	44	Durham, Asa	WSH	214
Dunn, Alexander	NYK	70	Dunning, Jonathan	ORN	343	Durham, Benjamin	ONT	466
Dunn, Alexander	ONT	360	Dunn[ing?], Joseph	NYK	117	Durham, David	NYK	15
Dunn, Andrew	ONT	466	Dunning, Lewis	SRA	44	Durham, Ezra	WSH	198
Dunn, Cary	QNS	66	Dunning, Luther	COL	254	Durham, John	TIO	264
Dunn, Cary Junr	NYK	27	Dunning, Michael	ORN	331	Durham, Joseph	WSH	198
Dunn, Christopher	ALB	108	Dunning, Michael	SRA	34	Durham, Josiah	COL	220
Dunn, David	OND	174	Dunning, Michael	SRA	48	Durham, Michael	COL	220
Dunn, David	ORN	291	Dunning, Michael	SRA	48	Durham, Simeon	COL	246
Dunn, Dennis	RNS	27	Dunning, Moses	SRA	48	Durham, Stephen	ALB	102
Dunn, Duncan	ESS	306	Dunning, Rhoda	DUT	65	Durham, Stephen	WSH	232
Dunn, Elizabeth	NYK	42	Dunning, Samuel	ORN	343	Durham, Trey	WSH	198
Dunn, Enoch	NYK	15	Dunning, Silas	CAY	704	Durham, Unis	CHN	766
Dunn, George	CAY	560	Dunning, Timothy	ONT	448	Durkee, Andrew W.	SRA	30
Dunn, George	ONT	360	Dunning, Timothy	ORN	356	Durkee, Benjamin	OND	168
Dunn, Gersham	NYK	97	Dunning, William	SRA	48	Durkee, Daniel	HRK	551
Dunn, Henry	ORN	292	Dunning, Wolcot	OTS	32	Durkee, Harvey	OND	164
Dunn, Henry	SRA	43	Dunphy, Thomas	NYK	153	Durkee, James	WSH	245
Dunn, Jacob	SCH	132	Dunsbaugh, Phillip	COL	198	Durkee, John	WSH	242
Dunn, James	COL	249	Dunscomb, Charles	DEL	269	Durkee, Joseph	OND	168
Dunn, James	MNT	116	Dunscomb, Daniel	NYK	39	Durkee, Lydeas	WSH	244
Dunn, James	ULS	241	Dunscomb, Edward	NYK	52	Durkee, Moses	WSH	185
Dunn, James	WST	120	Dunscomb, Ezra	NYK	17	Durkee, Nathan	WSH	244
Dunn, Jane	NYK	71	Dunscomb, Mathia	NYK	15	Durkee, Pineas	NYK	117
Dunn, John	ALB	99	Dunscomb, Thomas	DEL	269	Durkee, Pilgrim	SRA	30
Dunn, John	NYK	76	Dunspagh, John	COL	225	Durkee, Robert	OND	168
Dunn, John	QNS	67	Dunston, Robert	WSH	186	Durkee, Silas	OND	168
Dunn, John	RNS	111	Dunton, William	ONT	338	Durkee, Solomon	WSH	244
Dunn, John	RCH	92	Duntz, George P.	COL	232	Durkin, Sarah	NYK	95
Dunn, John	ULS	236	Dupan, John	NYK	106	Durlam, John O.	WSH	278
Dunn, Jonathan D.	NYK	65	Dupee, Charles	COL	204	Durland, George	ONT	340
Dunn, Joseph	CAY	568	Dupee, James	COL	207	Durland, James	NYK	88
Dunn, Joseph	HRK	465	Dupin, Joseph	CLN	169	Durland, Peter	NYK	88
Dunn, Joseph	NYK	105	Duplex, George	NYK	50	Durlen, Elizabeth	SUF	81
Dunn, Joseph	TIO	266	Du Pont, Victor	NYK	51	Durling, Benjamin	QNS	76
Dunn, Joseph	ULS	254	Dupoy	NYK	67	Durling, Charles	QNS	76
Dunn, Levi	ONT	324	Duppe, Charles	SRA	19	Durling, Charles	QNS	78
Dunn, Michael	WST	145	Dupper, Samuel	SRA	19	Durling, David	QNS	76
Dunn, Mitchell	NYK	107	Dupuy, Elizabeth	RCH	94	Durling, Elias	QNS	74
Dunn, Peter	SRA	43	Dupuy, John	RCH	90	Durling, Garret	QNS	67

Name	Loc	Pg	Name	Loc	Pg	Name	Loc	Pg
Durling, Henry	QNS	82	Dusenbery, Moses	RNS	84	Duvine, Wm	GRN	352
Durling, James	RCH	89	Dusenburry, Berzilla	NYK	109	Duwl, Abel	SRA	56
Durling, John	QNS	76	Dusenburry, Henry	NYK	147	Duy, Ira	GRN	331
Durling, Joseph	QNS	76	Dusenbury, Benjamin	ONT	370	Duy, Josiah	MNT	84
Durling, Joseph	QNS	78	Dusenbury, Daniel	ORN	371	Duy, Stephen	GRN	331
Durling, Lennington	QNS	76	Dusenbury, Denton	WST	153	Duyck, Jacob	COL	244
Durling, Lennington	QNS	78	Dusenbury, Gabriel	DUT	149	Duyck, Nicholas	COL	244
Durling, Morris	QNS	75	Dusenbury, Gilbert	QNS	72	Duyck, Nicholas Junr	COL	244
Durling, Samuel	QNS	76	Dusenbury, Henry	DUT	123	Duycker, Henry	COL	258
Durling, Thomas	QNS	60	Dusenbury, Henry	DUT	149	Duyckin, Daniel	NYK	35
Durling, Thomas	QNS	78	Dusenbury, Israel	DUT	61	Duyckinack, Christopher	NYK	36
Durning, Daniel R.	NYK	38	Dusenbury, Jarvis	ORN	278	Duyckinck, Anna	NYK	27
Durphe, Elisha	SRA	50	Dusenbury, John	NYK	117	Duyckinck, Catherine	NYK	39
Durphie, Putnam	NYK	43	Dusenbury, John	ULS	182	Duyckinck, Evert	NYK	30
Durrah, John	NYK	44	Dusenbury, Peter	DUT	110	Duyckink, Gerardus	DUT	63
Durry, Thomas	NYK	80	Dusenbury, Peter Junr	DUT	8	Duyken, Betsey	NYK	17
Durston, Parley	WSH	291	Dusenbury, Samuel	ORN	285	Duzenburry, William	NYK	146
Durtignare, John Babtis	NYK	80	Dusenbury, Stephen	DUT	7	Dwelley, Abner	RNS	29
Dury, Thomas	WST	132	Dusenbury, Totten	DUT	123	Dwell_y, Lemmon	WSH	251
Duryea, Aaron	QNS	65	Dusenbury, William	DUT	79	Dwellry, Abner	WSH	251
Duryea, Abraham	QNS	60	Dusinborough, Henry	WST	111	Dwenel, Ebenezer	WSH	185
Duryea, Abraham	QNS	62	D.sinborough, Henry Junr	WST	121	Dwight, Cornelius	MNT	43
Duryea, Abm	SUF	70				Dwight, Elihue	SRA	47
Duryea, Charles	SUF	79	Dusinborough, Nehemiah	WST	111	Dwight, Israel	OTS	11
Duryea, Cornelius	QNS	79	Dusinbrow, Gilbert	WST	111	Dwight, Israel	SUF	79
Duryea, Daniel	QNS	79	Dussenburry, Hannah	NYK	147	Dwight, Jonathan	MNT	40
Duryea, Daniel Junr	QNS	79	Dussenburry, John	NYK	109	Dwight, Joseph	OTS	18
Duryea, Dow	QNS	67	Dust, John	HRK	455	Dwight, Margaret	NYK	140
Duryea, Francis	QNS	63	Dust, Martinus	HRK	455	Dwight, Mary	NYK	64
Duryea, Gabriel	QNS	79	Dustan, James	NYK	31	Dwight, Solomon	OTS	18
Duryea, Garret	ORN	348	Dustan, Peter	NYK	31	Dwinnell, William	ONT	374
Duryea, George	ORN	299	Dustan, William	NYK	89	Dyar, Boardwin	ALB	114
Duryea, George	ORN	350	Dustin, Nathaniel	OND	219	Dyar, Charles	ALB	114
Duryea, George	QNS	67	Duston, Preston	SCH	135	Dyars, Robert	ALB	132
Duryea, George	QNS	81	Dutch, Thomas	WST	156	Dyching, Jedediah	CAY	654
Duryea, George	QNS	82	Dutcher see Ducher			Dyckman, Abraham	WST	157
Duryea, John	QNS	67	Dutcher, Abraham	COL	240	Dyckman, Benjamin	DUT	178
Duryea, John	QNS	67	Dutcher, Abraham	WST	166	Dyckman, Benjamin	WST	157
Duryea, John	QNS	75	Dutcher, Abraham	WST	167	Dyckman, Daniel	DUT	17
Duryea, Joshua	SUF	83	Dutcher, Catherine	WST	162	Dyckman, Jacobus	NYK	153
Duryea, Paul	QNS	67	Dutcher, Charles	ONT	490	Dyckman, Joseph	DUT	91
Duryea, Rulaf	QNS	67	Dutcher, Corneleus	WSH	272	Dyckman, Joseph	DUT	178
Duryea, Rulef Junr	QNS	67	Dutcher, David	GRN	326	Dyckman, Josiah	QNS	74
Duryea, Rulif	QNS	73	Dutcher, David	RCK	97	Dyckman, Peter	DUT	168
Duryea, William	QNS	69	Dutcher, David	WST	167	Dyckman, States	WST	157
Duryea, William	QNS	81	Dutcher, Dirck D.	RNS	92	Dyckman, Tunis	QNS	78
Duryee, Abraham	KNG	6	Dutcher, Henry	ONN	172	Dyckman, William	WST	162
Duryee, Abraham	NYK	33	Dutcher, Isaac	RCK	97	Dye, Abel	SRA	29
Duryee, Charles	NYK	24	Dutcher, Isaac Junr	RCK	97	Dye, Amos	MNT	117
Duryee, Christian	KNG	3	Dutcher, Jacob	ALB	37	Dye, Asa	ALB	95
Duryee, Elizabeth	NYK	28	Dutcher, Jacob	RCK	97	Dye, Danl	CHN	960
Duryee, Fulkert	KNG	10	Dutcher, John	OTS	3	Dye, James	MNT	65
Duryee, Gabriel	KNG	10	Dutcher, John	RNS	21	Dye, James	ORN	321
Duryee, George	KNG	7	Dutcher, John	RCK	97	Dye, John	MNT	120
Duryee, George	NYK	141	Dutcher, John	WST	162	Dye, Nathan	HRK	537
Duryee, Jacob	KNG	10	Dutcher, Lawrance	OTS	3	Dye, Peter	OND	195
Duryee, Jacob	NYK	98	Dutcher, Lawrence	DUT	99	Dyer see Dier		
Duryee, Jacob	NYK	145	Dutcher, Peter	NYK	105	Dyer, Benj:	ONN	152
Duryee, Johannas	KNG	10	Dutcher, Philip	RNS	13	Dyer, Benjn N.	RNS	97
Duryee, John	KNG	7	Dutcher, Revaland	WSH	271	Dyer, Elizabeth	NYK	79
Duryee, John T.	NYK	30	Dutcher, Simeon	RNS	8	Dyer, Robert	DUT	109
Duryee, Peter	KNG	11	Dutcher, Solomon	WSH	254	Dyer, Robert	WSH	186
Duryee, Richard	NYK	29	Duterick, George	NYK	62	Dyer, Samuel	COL	236
Duryee, Samuel	NYK	149	Dutervay, Louis	NYK	145	Dyer, Samuel	OND	191
Duryer, Abraham	NYK	81	Dutman, Jacob	MNT	105	Dyer, Silvenus	CHN	898
Dusanyar, George	WSH	205	Dutimore, Alexander	CHN	740	Dyer, Thomas	ALB	81
Dusenberry, Ann	NYK	131	Dutten, Samuel	CHN	932	Dyer, William	ALB	41
Dusenberry, Gabriel	SRA	41	Dutton, Jesse	OND	209	Dyer, William Junr	ALB	42
Dusenberry, John	RCK	110	Dutton, Sarah	CHN	750	Dyess, Bogert a Black	NYK	58
Dusenberry, Margaret	RCK	108	Dutton, Titus	DUT	107	Dygart, George	HRK	418
Dusenberry, Stephen	RCK	109	Duval, Aron	NYK	152	Dygart, Jost	HRK	411
Dusenberry, Wm	RCK	108	Du Val, George	ORN	278	Dygart, Peter	HRK	418
Dusenbery, Daniel	RNS	57	Duval, James	MNT	99	Dygart, William	HRK	417
Dusenbery, Enock	RNS112A		Du Val, Stephen	ORN	380	Dygart, William Junr	HRK	417
Dusenbery, Gabriel	RNS112A		Duvall, Thomas	NYK	97	Dygert, David	HRK	426
Dusenbery, Henry	RNS112A		Duvall, William	CAY	700	Dygert, Peter	OND	198
Dusenbery, Jacob	RNS	15	Duvall, William	NYK	48	Dygert, Samuel	ALB	55

Dygert, Severinus	MNT 22	Eagleston, Samuel	WSH 248	Earle, Jacob	OND 209

Name	Loc	Name	Loc	Name	Loc
Easton, Isaac	CAY 688	Eaton, Wyman	HRK 572	Eckly, Ezra Junr	SCH 157
Easton, Isaac	HRK 552	Eaustice, Sarah	NYK 133	Eday, Benjamin	SRA 38
Easton, Isaac	MNT 77	Eavory, Daniel	WST 134	Eddenton, Philip	CAY 522
Easton, Job	WSH 240	Eavory, Ebenezer	WST 153	Eddington, James	NYK 42
Easton, Joseph	OND 215	Eavory, Elisha	WST 153	Eddy, Abel	WSH 278
Easton, Joshua	WSH 186	Eavory, Elisha	WST 161	Eddy, Abiel	OND 192
Easton, Josiah	CAY 528	Eavory, Enoch	WST 161	Eddy, Amos	COL 206
Easton, Obed	CHN 876	Eavory, Enos	WST 161	Eddy, Andrew	NYK 144
Easton, Rufus	OND 215	Eavory, Henry	WST 151	Eddy, Asa	RNS112A
Easton, Samuel	CAY 528	Eavory, John	WST 161	Eddy, Barns	OTS 31
Easton, William	ALB 124	Eavory, Stephen	WST 151	Eddy, Barns Junr	OTS 31
Eastter, Valantine	CAY 648	Eavory, William	WST 151	Eddy, Calvin	OTS 10
Eastwood, Daniel	OTS 21	Eb....h, Christion	MNT 44	Eddy, Charles	SRA 35
Eastwood, David	CHN 778	Ebbets, Daniel S.	NYK 24	Eddy, Eaden	WSH 277
Eastwood, David	CHN 780	Ebbetts, Daniel	NYK 18	Eddy, Edward	OTS 10
Eastwood, George	DUT 86	Ebbetts, Jenny	NYK 202	Eddy, Ellice	OTS 10
Eastwood, John	OTS 21	Ebbins, Samuel	WSH 302	Eddy, Enos	OTS 53
Eastwood, Martin	RNS 44	Ebert, John	ALB 68	Eddy, Eseck	SRA 56
Eastwood, Nathaniel	RNS 82	Ebo	QNS 80	Eddy, George	ULS 219
Easty, Elijah	OND 173	Eccles, William	CAY 624	Eddy, Hannah	OTS 35
Easty, Siles	WSH 223	Ecfort, Henry	KNG 10	Eddy, Henry	WSH 236
Eatin, Aaron	ONN 168	Eckar, David	COL 201	Eddy, Jacob	OND 200
Eaton, Abel	COL 219	Ecker see Coker		Eddy, Jeremiah	SRA 55
Eaton, Abner	CHN 898	Ecker, Cornelius	SCH 127	Eddy, Jeremiah	SRA 60
Eaton, Alexander	ORN 320	Ecker, Daniel	MNT 69	Eddy, Jesse	OTS 54
Eaton, Alpheus	SRA 47	Ecker, George J.	NYK 27	Eddy, John	OND 158
Eaton, Amos	CHN 944	Ecker, Jacob	MNT 39	Eddy, John	OND 192
Eaton, Amos	COL 214	Ecker, John	SCH 127	Eddy, John	OTS 21
Eaton, Asa	RNS 18	Ecker, Thomas	SCH 127	Eddy, Levi	OTS 35
Eaton, Asel	ONN 168	Ecker, Thomas Junr	SCH 127	Eddy, Mark	OND 196
Eaton, Benjamin	OND 196	Ecker, Tunis	SCH 127	Eddy, Naboth	OTS 31
Eaton, Benjamin	ORN 288	Ecker, William	ORN 270	Eddy, Nathen	WSH 236
Eaton, Calvin	COL 216	Eckerson, Thomas	SCH 154	Eddy, Noah	OTS 10
Eaton, Calvin	OTS 28	Eckerson, Thomas	SCH 157	Eddy, Ode	OND 196
Eaton, Cyrell	ALB 69	Eckert, Frederick	NYK 89	Eddy, Samuel	WSH 266
Eaton, Ebenezer	ONT 508	Eckert, Philip	NYK 64	Eddy, Seth	WSH 278
Eaton, Ebenr	OTS 53	Eckhart, Abraham	DUT 112	Eddy, Solomon	RNS 95
Eaton, Eleazer	ONN 168	Eckhart, Adam	DUT 17	Eddy, Tabitha	OND 201
Eaton, Elijah	OTS 4	Eckhart, Adam	ULS 195	Eddy, Thomas	NYK 150
Eaton, Elisha	HRK 572	Eckhart, Albertus	COL 195	Eddy, Thomas	OND 202
Eaton, Ephraim	OTS 50	Eckhart, Andrew	DUT 162	Eddy, Welcome	HRK 414
Eaton, Ezra	OTS 8	Eckhart, Coonrat	DUT 166	Eddy, William	OTS 10
Eaton, James	OTS 33	Eckhart, Cornelius	ULS 232	Eddy, Wm	OTS 52
Eaton, Jane	NYK 81	Eckhart, Daniel	DUT 110	Eddy, William	RCH 94
Eaton, John	ALB 30	Eckhart, Daniel	DUT 112	Eddy, Zachariah	OTS 38
Eaton, John	HRK 572	Eckhart, David	DUT 163	Eddy, Zephaniah	OTS 8
Eaton, John	OND 210	Eckhart, George	DUT 156	Edenborough	QNS 62
Eaton, John	RNS 59	Eckhart, George	DUT 162	Ediener, George	ORN 286
Eaton, Jonathan	ONT 334	Eckhart, George	DUT 165	Edes, Samuel	OND 215
Eaton, Joseph	OND 196	Eckhart, George A.	DUT 160	Edes, Samuel	ONT 438
Eaton, Joseph	ONN 165	Eckhart, George Adam	ULS 195	Edesel, Thomas	QNS 62
Eaton, Joseph	OTS 44	Eckhart, Jacob	ULS 195	Edey, Levi	HRK 520
Eaton, Joshua	ONT 422	Eckhart, Jacob	ULS 232	Edgar, James	NYK 132
Eaton, Joshua	OTS 53	Eckhart, Jacob W.	DUT 156	Edgar, Samuel	NYK 101
Eaton, Joshua 1t	WSH 277	Eckhart, James	DUT 124	Edgar, William	NYK 20
Eaton, Joshua 2d	WSH 277	Eckhart, Jeremiah	ULS 233	Edge__b, Roger	WSH 206
Eaton, Joshua 3	WSH 277	Eckhart, Jeremiah Junr	ULS 232	Edgecomb, Thomas	ALB 63
Eaton, Lemuel	ALB 30	Eckhart, Johannis	ULS 233	Edger, Joseph	WSH 221
Eaton, Lot	RNS 106	Eckhart, John	DUT 19	Edger(?), Wm	GRN 331
Eaton, Nathaniel	OND 186	Eckhart, John	DUT 119	Edger, William	WSH 194
Eaton, Nathl	OTS 4	Eckhart, John	DUT 164	Edger, William	WST 102
Eaton, Noah	CLN 173	Eckhart, Joshua	ULS 205	Edgerton, Jedediah	ALB 75
Eaton, Origin	ALB 65	Eckhart, Martin	DUT 166	Edgerton, Nathan	DEL 281
Eaton, Peter	OTS 2	Eckhart, Martinus	ULS 232	Edgerton, Nathan Junr	DEL 281
Eaton, Rice	WSH 277	Eckhart, Martinus Junr	ULS 231	Edgerton, Nathel	COL 208
Eaton, Robert	ORN 320	Eckhart, Peter	DUT 163	Edgerton, Richard	ORN 287
Eaton, Rufus	HRK 551	Eckhart, Peter	DUT 164	Edgerton, Rozel	OND 215
Eaton, Samuel	ALB 65	Eckhart, Peter	ULS 245	Edget, Abel	HRK 461
Eaton, Samuel	OND 195	Eckhart, Peter J.	DUT 159	Edget, Edward	ALB 86
Eaton, Saml	OTS 52	Eckhart, Peter M.	DUT 165	Edget, William	DUT 129
Eaton, Simeon	SCH 170	Eckhart, Samuel	ULS 247	Edick, Christopher	DEL 279
Eaton, Squire	OND 196	Eckhart, Solomon	DUT 162	Edie, David	CAY 648
Eaton, Stephen	ALB 65	Eckhart, Solomon	ULS 231	Edie, Joseph	CAY 638
Eaton, Thomas	ALB 30	Eckhart, Stephen	ULS 232	Edin, Joseph	NYK 152
Eaton, Titus	GRN 335	Eckhart, Stephen	ULS 245	Edington, James	QNS 60
Eaton, Willard	OTS 53	Eckhart, Zachariah	DUT 111	Edir, James	GRN 341
Eaton, Wm	OTS 53	Eckly, Ezra	SCH 157	Edjet, Stephen	HRK 461

Name	Loc.
Edkin, George	NYK 143
Edkins, Thomas	SRA 8
Edmans, Aandrew	WSH 205
Edmans, Jeremiah	WSH 237
Edmendson, Christopher	
a Black	NYK 107
Edmerston, Robert	WSH 244
Edminston, Joseph	TIO 217
Edmond	QNS 81
Edmond, George	SRA 35
Edmond, John	SCH 129
Edmond, Reuben	SCH 170
Edmond, Robert	CHN 868
Edmonds, Andrew	DEL 273
Edmonds, Andrew	OND 219
Edmonds, Canada	DUT 43
Edmonds, Eliphelet	OND 220
Edmonds, Isaac	SRA 56
Edmonds, Jasper	TIO 221
Edmonds, John	COL 179
Edmonds, Mat..w	MNT 82
Edmonds, Nathaniel	SRA 56
Edmonds, Richards	MNT 82
Edmonds, Samuel	COL 250
Edmonds, Samuel	DUT 43
Edmonds, William	DUT 43
Edmonds, William	OND 188
Edmondson, Benjamin	ORN 371
Edmondson, David	ORN 288
Edmondson, James	ORN 398
Edmondson, William	ORN 287
Edmunds, Benjamin	CHN 782
Edmunds, John	ALB 93
Edmunds, Joseph	ALB 11
Edmunds, Joseph	ALB 37
Edmunds, Robert	SRA 44
Edmunds, Rufus	ALB 71
Edmunds, William	SRA 44
Edmuston, Thomas	WSH 291
Edsall, Barton	ORN 369
Edsall, James	ORN 343
Edsall, Peter	ORN 371
Edsall, Richard	ORN 326
Edsall, William	ORN 358
Edsill, Samuel	TIO 263
Edson, Adam	SRA 4
Edson, Barnabas	OND 164
Edson, Isaac	OTS 26
Edson, John	OND 165
Edson, Nathan	OND 165
Edson, Obid	OTS 51
Edson, Thos	OTS 17
Educt, Conrad	TIO 222
Educt, Jared	TIO 222
Edward	QNS 80
Edward a Negro	SUF 70
Edward	SUF 93
Edward	SUF 108
Edward, Abraham	SUF 106
Edward, Thomas	ORN 384
Edwards, Alanson	ONN 164
Edwards, Benajah	ULS 186
Edwards, Benjn	SUF 69
Edwards, Bethuel	SUF 107
Edwards, Charles	ALB 91
Edwards, Charles	SCH 145
Edwards, Christian	NYK 48
Edwards, Christopher	CHN 776
Edwards, Daniel	OTS 7
Edwards, Danl	SUF 71
Edwards, Danl	SUF 71
Edwards, Daniel	SUF 101
Edwards, Daniel	WST 145
Edwards, Danl Junr	OTS 8
Edwards, David	RCK 97
Edwards, Ebenezer	COL 184
Edwards, Edward	NYK 123
Edwards, Edward	TIO 220
Edwards, Eldridge	OND 199
Edwards, Elihue	SUF 107
Edwards, Elijah	OTS 55
Edwards, Ephriam	SUF 109
Edwards, Esten	SUF 101
Edwards, Garret	RCK 97
Edwards, George	NYK 127
Edwards, Gilbert	ORN 276
Edwards, Henery	SRA 12
Edwards, Henry	DEL 290
Edwards, Henry	SUF 101
Edwards, Isaac	NYK 141
Edwards, isaac	SUF 108
Edwards, Jacob	MNT 50
Edwards, James	DEL 290
Edwards, James	RCK 97
Edwards, Jeremiah	SUF 108
Edwards, Jestus	OTS 36
Edwards, John	NYK 66
Edwards, John	OND 209
Edwards, John	SRA 47
Edwards, John	SUF 64
Edwards, John	SUF 92
Edwards, John	SUF 99
Edwards, John	SUF 109
Edwards, John	WSH 250
Edwards, Jonathan	ALB 4
Edwards, Jonathan	ONT 460
Edwards, Jonathan	SUF 108
Edwards, Jonathan	TIO 218
Edwards, Jonathan Junr	SUF 108
Edwards, Joseph	DEL 290
Edwards, Joseph	SUF 101
Edwards, Lemuel	ORN 273
Edwards, Ludovic	HRK 546
Edwards, Luther	CLN 157
Edwards, Mary	ORN 328
Edwards, Mary	ULS 207
Edwards, Mathew	SUF 92
Edwards, Mehitable	SUF 101
Edwards, Nathaniel	SRA 29
Edwards, Pheneas	OTS 8
Edwards, Phillip	COL 262
Edwards, Ralph	OND 181
Edwards, Rice	WSH 299
Edwards, Richd	OTS 19
Edwards, Ruth	NYK 40
Edwards, Samuel	MNT 12
Edwards, Samuel	ONN 170
Edwards, Saml	OTS 7
Edwards, Samuel Junr	MNT 10
Edwards, So...on	ONN 164
Edwards, Sten	SUF 67
Edwards, Stephen	OTS 31
Edwards, Stephen	SUF 92
Edwards, Stephen	SUF 100
Edwards, Stephen	TIO 217
Edwards, Tamage	MNT 58
Edwards, Thaddeus	ONN 164
Edwards, Thomas	ORN 276
Edwards, Thomas	SCH 149
Edwards, Thomas	SUF 108
Edwards, Thos	RCK 105
Edwards, Thomas	WST 145
Edwards, Thomas Jr	SCH 153
Edwards, William	ALB 91
Edwards, Wm	GRN 349
.dwards, Wm	MNT 92
Edwards, William	SUF 95
Edwards, William	SUF 106
Edwards, William F.	SRA 36
Edwords, Gersham	SUF 71
Edy, Amos	HRK 423
Edy, Asaph	RNS 102
Edy, Gilbert	CHN 760
Edy, Gilbert	RNS 40
Edy, James	WSH 190
Edy, James	WSH 196
Edy, John	RNS 87
Edy, John	RNS 93
Edy, Jonathan	RNS 41
Edy, Jonathan	RNS 43
Edy, Obadiah	RNS 43
Edy, Robert	RNS 88
Edy, Shermon	RNS 88
Edy, Tisdil	RNS 39
Edy, Willard	CHN 810
Edy, William	WSH 196
Edy, Zacheus	CHN 810
Edy, Zephaniah	SRA 46
Eegle, Michael	MNT 61
Eellis, Jeremiah	SRA 42
Eels, Daniel	OND 178
Eels, John	CLN 156
Eels, John	DEL 277
Eels, Nathaniel	HRK 420
Eels, Semeon	CLN 156
Eels, Waterman	CLN 156
Effer, Valentine	SCH 138
Effnor, Henry	SRA 3
Effnor, Phillip	SRA 4
Egalston, Alexr	ALB 40
Egalston, Amos	ALB 31
Egalston, Asa	ALB 31
Egalston, Benjamin	ALB 31
Egalston, John	ALB 23
Egalston, John	ALB 40
Egan, Ebenezer	ALB 17
Egan, John	ALB 46
Eganor, Jacobus	ALB 90
Egberson, Bonard	GRN 332
Egbert, Abraham	NYK 22
Egbert, Anna	NYK 144
Egbert, Benjamin	NYK 62
Egbert, Henry	NYK 102
Egbert, James	ORN 283
Egbert, John	NYK 135
Egbert, Moses	NYK 150
Egbert, Peter	NYK 137
Egbert, Tunis	NYK 101
Egberts, Abraham	RCH 90
Egberts, Abraham	RCH 90
Egberts, Abraham	RCH 92
Egberts, Anthony	ALB 121
Egberts, Edward	RCH 92
Egberts, Elizabeth	RCH 90
Egberts, James	RCH 92
Egberts, James	RCH 92
Egberts, John	RCH 92
Egberts, Richard	RCH 90
Egberts, Samuel	RCH 90
Egberts, Tunis	RCH 92
Egelston, Samuel	STB 197
Eget, Annanias	HRK 461
Eggar, Eghart	ONN 172
Eggelston, Abraham	ESS 304
Eggelston, Ebenezer	ESS 302
Eggelston, Elisha	ESS 304
Eggelston, Judah	ESS 304
Eggelston, Moses	CLN 166
Eggelston, Richard	ESS 304
Egget, Henry	GRN 354
Eggiton, Samuel	OND 178
Eggleston, Aaron	OND 200
Eggleston, David & Samuel	DUT 143
Eggleston, Elisha Junr	RNS 107
Eggleston, Ezekiel	OND 163
Eggleston, James	DUT 144
Eggleston, James	DUT 176
Eggleston, Jeremiah	SRA 44
Eggleston, John	HRK 569
Eggleston, John	SRA 55

Name	Ref	Name	Ref	Name	Ref
Eggleston, Josiah	ONT 404	Elderd, Cornelia	KNG 3	Alexander, Rufus	GRN 335
Eggleston, Nathaniel	ONT 392	Elderd, Maria	KNG 3	Eley, Richard	CAY 564
Eggleston, Nicholas	DUT 143	Elderidge, Jesper	WST 155	Eley, Wells	SUF 74
Eggleston, Samuel & David	DUT 143	Eld_ridge, John	RNS 20	Eley, Zeloph	ONT 388
Eggleston, Samuel	SRA 55	Elderkin, Rudols	OTS 16	Elgar, Gideon	OND 186
Egglestone, Elisha	RNS 102	Eldred, Elisha	ORN 331	Eli, William	SRA 23
Egglestone, Daml	HRK 491	Eldred, Everitt	ORN 332	Eli__, John	MNT 97
Eggliste, Moses	ONT 378	Eldred, Israel	QNS 74	Eligh, Andries	ULS 222
Egglston, Mary	SRA 55	Eldred, James	SRA 6	Eligh, Jeremiah	ULS 222
Eglestan, Edward	GRN 336	Eldred, Job	OTS 33	Eligh, Johannis	ULS 221
Egleston, Amos	STB 198	Eldred, Robert	SRA 6	Elihu, Horton	ORN 364
Egleston, David	CHN 774	Eldred, Zebulan	OTS 33	Elijah	QNS 74
Egleston, Erd	GRN 336	Eldredge, Joseph	NYK 90	Elijah, Lewis	DUT 50
Egleston, James	OTS 6	Eldredge, Samuel	WSH 268	Eliot, Daniel	WSH 219
Egleston, Jesse	MNT 115	Eldredge, William	WSH 291	Eliot, Joseph	SRA 17
Egleston, John	ALB 23	Eldredge, William	WSH 184	Eliot, Laban	ONN 161
Egleston, Squire	CHN 776	Eldredge, William C.	WSH 230	Eliot, Macajah	WSH 219
Egleston, William	GRN 342	Eldrick, Ann	DUT 154	Eliot, Walter	RNS 12
Egleston, Winlock	CHN 776	Eldrick, John	KNG 4	Eliott, Benjn	ONN 161
Egner, Peter	GRN 325	Eldridge, Barney	SCH 159	Eliott, John	ONN 161
Egnew, George	STB 205	Eldridge, Benedict	DUT 134	Elis, John	SRA 52
Egnew, Samuel	STB 205	Eldridge, Benjn	OTS 30	Elisha	SUF 92
Ehle, ____	MNT 5	Eldridge, Caleb	RNS 74	Elison, Peter	WST 113
Ehle, ...us	MNT 5	Eldridge, Charles	OTS 30	Elison, Richard	OTS 41
Ehle, Anthony	MNT 48	Eldridge, Christopher	WSH 185	Eliston, Wm	MNT 117
Ehle, Harmanus	MNT 40	Eldridge, Daniel	CAY 706	Elkenbragh, Peter	COL 264
Ehle, John E.	MNT 24	Eldrid_, Danl	OTS 33	Elkins, Robert	NYK 31
Ehreitz, John	DUT 87	Eldridge, Ebenezer	WSH 230	Ellar, John	ULS 216
Eigabrout, Peter	MNT 1	Eldridge, Edward	DUT 74	Ellathorp, Henry	ONN 158
Eigenbrot, Lewis	QNS 66	Eldridge, Elisha	CAY 706	Ellbert, Ellinor	NYK 108
Eigerbroat, Christion	MNT 1	Eldridge, Elisha	OTS 9	Elle_, Gideon Junr	MNT 77
Eigerbroa_t, George	MNT 1	Eldridge, Ezra	SUF 104	Ellenezer	NYK 48
Eigerbrout, Frederick	MNT 25	Eldridge, Francis	WSH 185	Ellenwood, Hananiah	OND 188
Eig.brout, Hon	MNT 25	Eldridge, Henry 1st	OTS 30	Ellenwood, Samuel	OND 197
Eighener, Abraham	ULS 221	Eldridge, Henry 2d	OTS 30	Ellerton, Lucretia	DUT 53
Eighener, Peter	ULS 221	Eldridge, James	ESS 302	Ellet, William	NYK 98
Eighener, Zachariah	ULS 222	Eldridge, James	RNS 74	Elletson, Samuel	DUT 80
Eights, Abraham	ALB 149	Eldridge, James	RNS 77	Ellett, Daniel	SUF 104
Eights, Jonathan	ALB 121	Eldridge, James	WSH 186	Ellice, David	SCH 145
Eilderman, Henry	NYK 88	Eldridge, James	WSH 256	El[lice?], Gedeon	MNT 71
Eimigh, George	DUT 11	Eldridge, Jerome	WSH 185	Ellice, James	SCH 142
Eimigh, George L. Junr	DUT 10	Eldridge, John	OTS 30	Ellice, Jared	SCH 143
Eimigh, Henry	DUT 11	Eldridge, John	RNS 27	Ellice, Mary	MNT 66
Eimigh, Jeremiah	DUT 12	Eldridge, John	RNS 74	Ellice, Samuel	SCH 142
Eimigh, John G.	DUT 11	Eldridge, Joseph	RNS 103	Ellick, Frederik	SRA 30
Eimigh, Lawrence	DUT 11	Eldridge, Joseph	WSH 265	Ellinwood, Jacob	HRK 540
Eimigh, Nicholas	DUT 11	Eldridge, Joseph	WST 167	Elliot, Augustine	NYK 40
Eimigh, Nicholas H.	DUT 11	Eldridge, Joshua	SUF 104	Elliot, Benjamin	RNS 90
Eimigh, Nicholas N.	DUT 12	Eldridge, Lemuel	CAY 704	Elliot, Catharine	DUT 48
Eimigh, Phillip	ULS 194	Eldr.dge, Michael	WST 161	Elliot, Christopher Junr	DUT 43
Ein, Abraham	ULS 237	Eldridge, Nathan	OTS 30	Elliot, Christopher Senr	
Ein, Elias	ULS 237	Eldridge, Pelick	GRN 353	Elliot, Dan...	RNS 39
Eisenburgh, Peter	NYK 69	Eldridge, Seth	SCH 170	Elliot, David	DEL 281
Eisenhart, Christopher	WST 114	Eldridge, Seth	SUF 99	Elliot, David	ORN 309
Eisenl_d, John	MNT 17	Eldridge, Siles	WSH 229	Elliot, Francis	DUT 113
Eisman, Robert	NYK 72	Eldridge, Stephen	ESS 302	Elliot, Gidion	OTS 4
Eker, John	RNS 32	Eldridge, Stephen	OND 192	Elliot, Jacob	ULS 265
Eker, Peter	MNT 124	Eldridge, Sylvanus	OTS 55	Elliot, James	NYK 152
Elbesty, Barnard	GRN 341	Eldridge, Thankfull	RNS 82	Elliot, James	OND 178
Elconar, Ebeneser	MNT 99	Eldridge, Thomas	OTS 30	Elliot, James	ULS 188
Elcot, Isaac	SCH 170	Eldridge, Thomas	RNS 18	Elliot, Jane	ULS 265
Elcot, Johntn	SCH 170	Eldridge, Thomas	RNS 56	Elliot, John	ALB 105
Eldard, Abraham	QNS 77	Eldridge, Thomas	WSH 217	Elliot, John	DUT 45
Eldard, Elnathan	QNS 75	Eldridge, William	ESS 302	Elliot, John	NYK 101
Eldard, James	QNS 77	Eldridge, Wm	OTS 30	Elliot, Lewis	WST 140
Eldard, John	QNS 74	Eldridge, William	WSH 271	Elliot, Robert	NYK 67
Eldard, John	QNS 75	Eldridge, Wm Secd	OTS 30	Elliot, Romer	NYK 102
Eldard, Lucas	QNS 75	Eldrige, Abner	SUF 104	Elliot, Samuel	DUT 45
Eldard, Samuel	QNS 67	Eldrige, Thomas	TIO 212	Elliot, Thomas	CHN 748
Eldard, Samuel	QNS 78	Eldrige, Thomas Jur	TIO 212	Elliot, Thomas	NYK 73
Eldard, Smith	QNS 77	Ele, Israel	WSH 291	Elliot, William	ORN 291
Eldard, William	QNS 77	Ele_, Richard	ONT 340	Elliott, Aden	CHN 742
Eldard, William	QNS 78	Elensworth	OND 220	Elliott, Andrew	MNT 114
Elder, John	ALB 39	Eles, William	WST 131	Elliott, Archibald	ORN 278
Elder, Joseph	ORN 298	Elesworth, Philip	OND 208	Elliott, De[sire?]	CHN 748
Elder, William	KNG 9	Elevell, Samuel	TIO 228		
		Elevin, George	ALB 9		

Name			Name			Name		
Elliott, Gideon	CAY	686	Ellis, Jonathan	DUT	105	Elmendorph, Catharine	ALB	3
Elliott, Henry	ORN	365	Ellis, Jonathan	ONN	154	Elmendorph, Coonradt C.	ULS	209
Elliott, Itt	CHN	742	Ellis, Joseph	DUT	46	Elmendorph, Coonradt C.	ULS	230
Elliott, Jacob	MNT	114	Ellis, Joseph	ORN	334	Elmendorph, Coonradt E.	ULS	228
Elliott, James	ALB	134	Ellis, Joseph	WST	155	Elmendorph, Coonradt G.	ULS	218
Elliott, James	ALB	148	Ellis, Josiah Foster	DUT	178	Elmendorph, Coonradt J.	ULS	228
Elliott, Jane	ALB	143	Ellis, Lazarus	CAY	560	Elmendorph, Coonradt W.	ULS	206
Elliott, Joab	CHN	748	Ellis, Lemuel	ESS	323	Elmendorph, Cornelius C.	DUT	159
Elliott, John	NYK	25	Ellis, Levi	CAY	560	Elmendorph, Cornelius I.	DUT	155
Elliott, John	ONN	151	Ellis, Lovey	COL	252	Elmendorph, Frederick S.	ULS	202
Elliott, John	ULS	242	Ellis, Margaret	NYK	75	Elmendorph, Henrica	ULS	206
Elliott, John	WST	138	Ellis, Marvel	RNS	94	Elmendorph, Hubert	ULS	202
Elliott, Lewis	WST	135	Ellis, Mary	NYK	63	Elmendorph, Jacob	ULS	208
Elliott, Nathan	ALB	93	Ellis, Mary	NYK	109	Elmendorph, James	ULS	222
Elliott, Nathan	ALB	93	Ellis, Mordecai	HRK	489	Elmendorph, Johannis	ULS	218
Elliott, Robert	ONN	152	Ellis, Moses	OND	197	Elmendorph, John	COL	214
Elliott, William	COL	236	Ellis, Nathan	OTS	30	Elmendorph, John A.	ULS	226
Elliott, William	ORN	356	Ellis, Nathan	RNS	78	Elmendorph, Jonathan	ULS	208
Elliott, William	WST	138	Ellis, Nicholas	RNS	113	Elmendorph, Joseph	COL	200
Ellis, Aaron	RNS	60	Ellis, Nicolls	RNS	77	Elmendorph, Lucas	ULS	229
Ellis, Abner	HRK	469	Ellis, Noah	DEL	273	Elmendorph, Martin	ULS	229
Ellis, Abraham	WSH	189	Ellis, Oliver	HRK	583	Elmendorph, Peter	ULS	206
Ellis, Amasa	RNS	106	Ellis, Oliver	OND	221	Elmendorph, Peter	ULS	224
Ellis, Archibald	CAY	560	Ellis, Peleg	HRK	583	Elmendorph, Peter Junr	ULS	218
Ellis, Asa	OND	185	Ellis, Philip	QNS	79	Elmendorph, Peter Edmd	ALB	144
Ellis, Bastian	RCH	87	Ellis, Pineas	ONT	378	Elmendorph, Roman	ORN	316
Ellis, Benjamin a			Ellis, Reuben	OTS	32	Elmendorph, Samuel	DUT	155
mulatto	NYK	135	Ellis, Richard	NYK	33	Elmendorph, Tobias Junr	SCH	151
Ellis, Benjn	OTS	41	Ellis, Richmond	TIO	239	Elmendorph, Willm	SCH	159
Ellis, Benjamine	GRN	336	Ellis, Robert	MNT	110	Elmer, Anna	ORN	366
Ellis, Caleb	OND	210	Ellis, Robert	SRA	42	Elmer, Caleb	GRN	334
Ellis, Caleb	SRA	42	Ellis, Samuel	MNT	110	Elmer, Ephriam	SCH	170
Ellis, Calvin	OTS	30	Ellis, Samuel	RNS	71	Elmer, Jesse	ORN	375
Ellis, Catherene	NYK	114	Ellis, Samll	TIO	241	Elmer, Jonathan	COL	213
Ellis, Charles	ORN	357	Ellis, Simeon	DUT	178	Elmer, Nathaniel	ORN	332
Ellis, Daniel	DUT	166	Ellis, Squire	DUT	178	Elmer, Thadeus	COL	212
Ellis, Daniel	ESS	317	Ellis, Turner	OND	191	Elmer, William	ORN	359
Ellis, Daniel J.	ESS	311	Ellis, Warren	ONN	154	Elmore, Ambrose	ULS	242
Ellis, Ebenezar	TIO	241	Ellis, William	DEL	283	Elmore, Asa	CLN	158
Ellis, Ebenezar Jur	TIO	242	Ellis, William	HRK	455	Elmore, Daniel	ULS	184
Ellis, Ebenezer	DUT	178	Ellis, William	ULS	190	Elmore, Darius	SCH	170
Ellis, Edward	CAY	674	Ellis, William	WSH	188	Elmore, David	SCH	170
Ellis, Effy a mulatto	NYK	97	Ellise, Edward	GRN	328	Elmore, Elijah	DEL	288
Ellis, Eleasar	MNT	110	Ellise, John	GRN	328	Elmore, Hezekiah	OND	208
Ellis, Eleazer	OND	177	Ellison, Abraham	ALB	136	Elmore, Isaac	SCH	170
Ellis, Elijah	ONT	446	Ellison, Benjamin	ORN	271	Elmore, James	CHN	806
Ellis, Elijah	ONT	448	Ellison, Benjamin	QNS	81	Elmore, Joel	OTS	18
Ellis, Elijah	SRA	55	Ellison, Crandel	DUT	127	Elmore, John	CLN	158
Ellis, Elisha	WST	154	Ellison, David	QNS	76	Elmore, Joseph B.	ALB	146
Ellis, Ezekel	WSH	213	Ellison, Elizabeth	NYK	47	Elmore, Levi	OND	168
Ellis, Freeman	CHN	804	Ellison, Gabriel	DUT	63	Elmore, Lot	CLN	158
Ellis, Garret	RCH	94	Ellison, George	NYK	89	Elmore, Simon	ULS	209
Ellis, George	RNS	71	Ellison, James	QNS	71	Elms, Leweretee	SRA	46
Ellis, Giddeon	RNS	20	Ellison, John	CHN	756	Elns, Rodolphus	SRA	16
Ellis, Henry	DUT	65	Ellison, John	ORN	287	Elsbre, Jonathon	DUT	102
Ellis, Henry	NYK	34	Ellison, Joseph	NYK	87	Elsbre, William	DUT	103
Ellis, Humphry	DUT	46	Ellison, Michael	NYK	55	Elsbre, William Junr	DUT	103
Ellis, Jacob	DUT	178	Ellison, Owen	ORN	290	Elsiver, David	DUT	160
Ellis, Jacob	OND	175	Ellison, Peter	NYK	47	Elsiver, Lodowick	DUT	160
Ellis, James	ORN	362	Ellison, Peter	NYK	60	Elston, Abraham	ORN	322
Ellis, Jeremiah	ULS	260	Ellison, Samuel	QNS	75	Elston, Jacob	SRA	25
Ellis, Joel	CHN	804	Ellison, Thomas	ALB	140	Elston, Jeremiah	ORN	322
Ellis, John	CAY	672	Ellison, Thomas	NYK	19	Elston, Joseph	ORN	319
Ellis, John	DUT	178	Ellison, Thos	SUF	65	Elston, Lewis	ORN	322
Ellis, John	NYK	22	Ellison, Thomas	WST	115	Elston, Warren	RCK	91
Ellis, John	NYK	143	Ellison, Timothy	WST	113	Elstone, Benjamin	OND	161
Ellis, John	ONN	154	Ellison, Wm	ORN	286	Elsworth, Abraham	SRA	4
Ellis, John	ONN	183	Ellison, Wm	OTS	19	Elsworth, Ahasuerus	DUT	100
Ellis, John	ORN	330	Ellison, William	QNS	71	Elsworth, Anthony	DUT	48
Ellis, John	RNS	71	Elliston, John F.	DUT	161	Elsworth, Anthony	ULS	194
Ellis, John	RNS	104	Ellot, Nathan	GRN	325	Elsworth, Benjn	OTS	27
Ellis, John	SRA	43	Ellsworth, Henry	OND	168	Elsworth, Benjamin	ULS	240
Ellis, John	WSH	225	Ellsworth, William	OND	168	Elsworth, Catherine	NYK	42
Ellis, John	WST	145	Ellsworth, Wm	RCK	98	Elsworth, Charles	SRA	7
Ellis, John Junr	SRA	43	Ellwood, P ter	MNT	34	Elsworth, Elijah	MNT	35
Ellis, John F.	NYK	54	Elmendorph, Abraham	ULS	230	Elsworth, Elkanah	OTS	34
Ellis, Jonathan	DUT	44	Elmendorph, Benjamin	ULS	229			

Name	Loc	Pg
Elsworth, Frances	NYK	136
Elsworth, Geoge	SRA	7
Elsworth, Henry	ONN	150
Elsworth, James	SRA	7
Elsworth, Jeremiah	KNG	3
Elsworth, Jesper	CHN	958
Elsworth, John	DUT	79
Elsworth, John	NYK	19
Elsworth, John	NYK	38
Elsworth, John	OTS	26
Elsworth, John	ULS	235
Elsworth, John	WSH	184
Elsworth, John W.	NYK	30
Elsworth, Joseph	DEL	288
Elsworth, Joseph	ULS	238
Elsworth, Perry G.	OTS	30
Elsworth, Philip	OTS	27
Elsworth, Samuel	NYK	93
Elsworth, Silas	DUT	16
Elsworth, Theophilus	ULS	227
Elsworth, Theopholus	NYK	42
Elsworth, Thomas	KNG	3
Elsworth, Verdine	NYK	55
Elsworth, William	ALB	142
Elsworth, William	KNG	8
Elsworth, William	NYK	99
Elsworth, Wm	OTS	27
Elsworth, William	SRA	10
Elsworth, William	ULS	232
Elsworth, William	ULS	233
Elting, Edward	NYK	46
Elting, James	COL	255
Elting, James	GRN	339
Elting, John	COL	255
Elting, John	ULS	218
Elting, Peter	NYK	24
Elting, Peter Senior	NYK	29
Elting, Rhesa	COL	192
Elting, Wm	GRN	328
Eltinge, Cornelius	ULS	206
Eltinge, Ezekiel	ULS	237
Eltinge, Henry	ULS	229
Eltinge, Henry Junr	ULS	229
Eltinge, Henry A.	ULS	238
Eltinge, Isaac	ULS	192
Eltinge, Jacobus	ULS	192
Eltinge, James	ULS	227
Eltinge, John	ULS	237
Eltinge, Josiah	ULS	237
Eltinge, Josiah R.	ULS	236
Eltinge, Noah	ULS	238
Eltinge, Phillip	ULS	237
Eltinge, Solomon	ULS	206
Eltinge, Solomon	ULS	240
Eltinge, Thomas	ULS	218
Eltinge, William	ULS	192
Elton, Anthony	NYK	123
Elversdorf, Abrahan	GRN	328
Elvington, Andrew	NYK	117
Elwell, Abner	DUT	171
Elwell, Ebenezer	DUT	172
Elwell, Elizabeth	DUT	171
Elwell, Ezra	DUT	175
Elwell, Jabez	DUT	171
Elwell, Jabez Junr	DUT	171
Elwell, .oses	MNT	82
Elwell, Samuel	DEL	281
Elwell, Thomas	WSH	186
Elwood, Benjamin	MNT	25
Elwood, Benjamin	MNT	52
Elwood, Ebraham	WSH	222
Elwood, Isaac	MNT	25
Elwood, Isaac	OND	205
Elwood, John	MNT	25
Elwood, Nathan	DEL	288
Elwood, Richard	MNT	28
Elwood, Samuel	RNS	80

Name	Loc	Pg
Ely, Andrew	ULS	266
Ely, Benjamin	ULS	263
Ely, Catherine	NYK	50
Ely, Elisha	TIO	244
Ely, Enoch	NYK	86
Ely, Gad	NYK	37
Ely, John	GRN	355
Ely, John	NYK	89
Ely, John	TIO	244
Ely, Oliver	HRK	510
Ely, Samuel	HRK	510
Ely, Simeon	HRK	510
Ely, Simeon Jun	HRK	510
Ely, William	DUT	121
Ely, Worthington	ALB	120
Emanuel, Solomon	NYK	91
Embler, Andrew	ORN	344
Embler, George	ULS	241
Embler, John	ULS	251
Embler, Silas	NYK	126
Embree, Abigail	QNS	66
Embree, Effingham	QNS	65
Embree, John	NYK	124
Embree, John	RCK	103
Embree, Thomas	WSH	278
Emburry, Peter	NYK	49
Emerick, Francis	COL	197
Emerick, George	ALB	146
Emerick, Mathew T.	COL	258
Emerick, Mathias	COL	197
Emerick, Peter	ALB	90
Emerson, Benjamen	WSH	299
Emerson, Ephraim	RNS	78
Emerson, Jonathan	OND	175
Emerson, Nathaniel	DEL	277
Emerson, Richd	OTS	32
Emerson, Robert	ULS	182
Emery, Isaac	OTS	53
Emery, Robert	SRA	8
Emery, Rowland	SRA	47
Emey, Elias	SRA	9
Emey, John	SRA	9
Emey, Nicholas	SRA	9
Emey, Nicholas	SRA	12
Emigh, John	SRA	58
Emiup, John	STB	204
Emmans, Abraham	NYK	135
Emmans, Isaac	NYK	144
Emmans, William	NYK	54
Emmens, James	NYK	97
Emmens, John	CAY	554
Emmerick, Adam	COL	193
Emmerick, Adam G.	COL	193
Emmerson, Broadstreet	SRA	53
Emmerson, Broadstreet Senr	SRA	53
Emmerson, Joseph	WSH	275
Emmerson, William	NYK	46
Emmet, Abraham	NYK	106
Emmet, Tunis	RCK	104
Emmet, Wm	RCK	105
Emmins, Unis	SUF	71
Emmonds, Elisha	OTS	34
Emmons, Abraham	KNG	4
Emmons, Abraham S.	KNG	4
Emmons, Andrew	KNG	6
Emmons, Asa	DEL	288
Emmons, Danl	SUF	71
Emmons, Hannah	COL	207
Emmons, Hendrick	DUT	24
Emmons, Hendrick	QNS	67
Emmons, Jacobus	KNG	5
Emmons, James	DUT	24
Emmons, John	KNG	4
Emmons, Jonathan	RNS	109
Emmons, Jonathan Jur	RNS	109
Emmons, Nicholas	ONT	394

Name	Loc	Pg
Emmons, Oliver	RNS	109
Emmons, Russel	GRN	325
Emmons, Samuel	ONN	147
Emmet, James	NYK	106
Emoch, John	DUT	68
Emory, Mathias Junr	COL	257
Emott, William	DUT	63
Empie, Fredereck	MNT	9
Empie, Jacob	MNT	8
Empie, John	ALB	6
Empie, John F.	MNT	8
Empie, Philip	MNT	14
Empsom, John	ULS	247
Empy, Anthony	WSH	188
Empy, George	MNT	123
Empy, John	SCH	162
Empy, John Junior	SCH	163
Emrigh, William	ULS	222
Enderley, Anne	ULS	215
Enderley, Michael	ULS	216
Enders, Jacob	SCH	124
Enders, Johannes	SCH	120
Enders, John	SCH	122
Enders, Peter	SCH	119
Enders, William	SCH	122
Enderson, Henry J.	COL	201
Endevour, John	MNT	78
Enerton, Anna	NYK	69
Enfield, Sebastian	SCH	171
Eng___, Jo..	MNT	43
Engan, Benjamin	SRA	59
Engersol, Nathaniel	SRA	59
England, Benjamin	MNT	7
England, James	NYK	22
England, William	RCH	87
Engle, John	SCH	151
Engles, George	SCH	160
Engles, Joseph	ONT	384
English, James	NYK	111
English, John	TIO	234
English, Mary	NYK	19
English, Robert	DEL	288
English, Robert	HRK	562
English, William	GRN	336
English, Wm	TIO	253
Enman, Arnold	DEL	267
Enman, Belabra	SRA	41
Enman, Caleb	SRA	41
Enman, Moses	SRA	41
Enman(?), Nathan	GRN	336
Ennis, Amelia	NYK	18
Ennis, George	NYK	85
Ennis, James	ONN	165
Ennis, Phebe	WST	112
Ennis, Sarah	NYK	123
Ennis, William	NYK	98
Ennist, Cornelius	ULS	198
Ennist, George	ULS	198
Ennist, William	ULS	198
Eno, John	OND	165
Eno, Orange	OND	201
Eno, Skinner	OND	178
Eno, Stephen	DUT	126
Enos, Abejah	MNT	70
Enos, Alexander	OND	164
Enos, Alexander Junr	OND	176
Enos, Amanah	RNS	75
Enos, Elisha	HRK	598
Enos, Erasmus	ONT	392
Enos, John	NYK	134
Enos, Joseph	COL	207
Enos, Park	HRK	523
Enos, Samuel	DUT	135
Enoss, Benjamin	CHN	796
Enoss, Ebenezer	CHN	768
Enoss, Henry	CHN	794
Enoss, Joab	CHN	794

Name	Ref		Name	Ref		Name	Ref		Name	Ref
Enseen, Henry	COL 251		Etchard, Samuel	QNS 60		Everdall, James	NYK 84
Ensell, Edward	NYK 127		Etheridge, Nathl	HRK 453		Everest, Noah	ALB 43
Ensell, Peter	COL 240		Etick, Frederick	RNS 4		Everet, Hovencamp	RCK 103
Ensigh, Chancy	GRN 357		Eton, Benjamin	STB 202		Everet, John	SRA 34
Ensign, Amos	WSH 279		Etsell, Henry	ORN 326		Everet, Thomas	QNS 71
Ensign, Asa	DUT 45		Ett, Jacob	DUT 58		Everett, Abigal	SRA 15
Ensign, Bela	OND 165		Etz, Willm	SCH 170		Everett, Jeremiah	COL 233
Ensign, Daniel	ONT 426		Euman, Gecorg(?)	MNT 71		Everett, Jesse	COL 249
Ensign, Elijah	DUT 126		Euphemia	NYK 109		Everett, John	NYK 22
Ensign, Ely	COL 221		Eus[tace?], Margaret	ORN 347		Everett, Nehemiah	QNS 75
Ensign, Ezekiel	SRA 47		Evans, Abel	DUT 55		Everidge, Evan	NYK 138
Ensign, Martin	WSH 276		Evans, Asa	COL 213		Everill, Isaac	DUT 41
Ensign, Ormond	ORN 319		Evans, Benjamin	OND 162		Evering, Martin	NYK 121
Ensign, Samuel	OND 171		Evans, Charles	NYK 52		Everist, Samuel	COL 179
Ensign, Samuel Junr	OND 167		Evans, Daniel	ORN 276		Everit, Jeremiah	CHN 768
Ensley, Daniel	NYK 95		Evans, Elzy	CLN 154		Everit, John	ONT 368
Ensley, John	NYK 92		Evans, Errad	OND 193		Everit, Oliver	CHN 768
Ensley, Joseph	STB 199		Evans, Henry	ORN 274		Everitt see Averitt	
Ensley, William	NYK 76		Evans, Henry	ULS 245		Everitt, Abraham	DUT 89
Enslow, John	COL 181		Evans, Hugh	OND 182		Everitt, Benjamin	DUT 40
Ensworth, Asael	ONT 348		Evans, Jacob	NYK 108		Everitt, Benjamin	QNS 68
Entrekin, James	ONT 442		Evans, James	ULS 257		Everitt, Benjamin	QNS 68
Ephrim a Negro	SUF 69		Evans, Jesse	NYK 97		Everitt, Clear	DUT 11
Epim, Joh	MNT 108		Evans, John	DUT 49		Everitt, Daniel	ORN 360
Ephnnger, John			Evans, John	NYK 96		Everitt, Daniel	QNS 68
Christopher	NYK 111		Evans, John a mulatto	NYK 107		Everitt, Daniel	ULS 259
Eppland, John	NYK 111		Evans, John	NYK 140		Everitt, Edward	CLN 158
Erasmus, John	NYK 129		Evans, John	OND 189		Everitt, Elias	CHN 764
Erbun, Peter	NYK 64		Evans, John	ULS 211		Everitt, Ephraim	ORN 338
Erills, Enoch	SCH 133		Evans, John	ULS 250		Everitt, Ephraim	ORN 341
Erkenbreck, Willm	COL 239		Evans, Jonathan	DUT 48		Everitt, George	SUF 79
Erkenbush, Phillip	SRA 8		Evans, Jonathan	OND 177		Everitt, Isaac	DUT 177
Erkson, John	ALB 23		Evans, Joseph	OND 166		Everitt, Isaac	ORN 323
Errickson, Peter	NYK 101		Evans, Lewis	DUT 87		Everitt, Israel	OTS 24
Errill, Nathan	SCH 159		Evans, Lewis	NYK 133		Everitt, James	ORN 383
Ersenburgh, John	NYK 57		Evans, Lewis	ORN 383		Everitt, John	HRK 533
Ervine, Henry	COL 240		Evans, Luther	NYK 15		Everitt, John	ORN 341
Ervine, Henry Junr	COL 240		Evans, Michael	DUT 93		Everitt, John	ORN 360
Ervine, John	COL 239		Evans, New Year a			Everitt, John	QNS 68
Erving, ...as	MNT 78		Black	NYK 65		Everitt, John	SUF 79
Erving, Andrew	WST 167		Evans, Oliver	COL 222		Everitt, John	SUF 82
Erwin, George	QNS 79		Evans, Oliver	DUT 127		Everitt, John Jun	HRK 533
Erwin, Henry	OND 223		Evans, Owen	NYK 85		Everitt, John Junr	ORN 341
Erwin, James	ALB 60		Evans, Randal	OND 193		Everitt, Jonas	HRK 533
Erwin, James	TIO 264		Evans, Samuel	DUT 56		Everitt, Meliscent	ORN 376
Erwin, John	ALB 101		Evans, Samuel	HRK 585		Everitt, Nehemiah	DUT 119
Erwin, William	ORN 306		Evans, Septi...	ONT 510		Everitt, Nicholas	QNS 67
Esdale, Walter	NYK 72		Evans, Shadrach	DUT 11		Everitt, Nicholas	QNS 68
Eslick, Isaac	RNS 60		Evans, Silas	COL 186		Everitt, Richard	DUT 61
Esmond, Isaiah	DUT 99		Evans, Simon	OND 164		Everitt, Samuel	ORN 322
Esmond, Thomas	DUT 12		Evans, Stephen	DUT 86		Everitt, Susannah	NYK 85
Esmund, Cornelius	SRA 40		Evans, Thomas	DUT 58		Everitt, Walter	ORN 341
Esmund, Jacob	SRA 40		Evans, Titus	NYK 101		Evermgham, Gelbert	NYK 34
Esmund, Jacob	SRA 40		Evans, Titus	NYK 112		Evermore, ...	MNT 78
Esmunds, Samuel	SRA 40		Evans, William	ALB 61		Everrit, Daniel	GRN 343
Escmes, Nathel	ONN 177		Evans, William	DEL 280		Everritt, William	NYK 146
Esqire, Clark	GRN 354		Evans, William	DUT 93		Everson, Barnabas	DUT 95
Esquerol, John	NYK 68		Evans, William	NYK 60		Everson, George	NYK 59
Esquire, Samuel	GRN 354		Evans, William	NYK 126		Everson, George B.	DUT 67
Essex, Benjamin	ALB 103		Evans, Ziva(?)	TIO 237		Everson, George R.	ORN 296
Este, William	ONT 504		Evarts, Linus	HRK 575		Everson, Henry	GRN 358
Estelstyne, Cornelius	COL 191		Eveleth, Amariah	OTS 22		Everson, Jacob	DUT 117
Estelstyne, Gabriel	COL 197		Evelin, W[illiam?]	CAY 584		Everson, John	CAY 674
Estelsyne, Jacob	COL 193		Evener, Michael	NYK 151		Everson, Nicholas	DEL 267
Esterwood, Lewis	NYK 149		Evenham, John	CHN 922		Everson, Thomas	ORN 334
Estes, James	ALB 29		Evens, Amos	RNS 60		Evert, Asariah	MNT 71
Estes, Joseph	ALB 33		Evens, Andrew	SRA 9		Evert, John	ONT 386
Estes, Philip	ALB 37		Evens, Benjamin	SRA 13		Evert, Phillip	NYK 123
Estes, Robert	ALB 37		Evens, Doney	ONT 420		Evert, Sally	KNG 9
Estes, Thomas	ALB 29		Evens, Henery	CHN 758		Everton, Esraiel	CHN 926
Estherbrook, Rial	SRA 57		Evens, Nathan	SRA 6		Everton, John	CHN 926
Estis, Benjamin	RNS 60		Evens, Oliver	GRN 349		Everts, Charles	COL 256
Estrastrenger, Peter	MNT 65		Evens, Trey	WSH 215		Everts, Edmund	COL 207
Estrestrenger, John	MNT 65		Evens, William	WSH 238		Everts, Henry	OND 210
Estus, Stephen	ESS 319		Eventon, Caleb	WST 158		Everts, Jacob	COL 256
Eta, Jacob Negro	QNS 71		Eveors, Mrs Susan	QNS 60		Everts, Jedediah	DUT 135
Etchard, Philip	QNS 60		Everan, Adam	MNT 62		Everts, Jeremiah	COL 227

123

Name	Ref	Name	Ref	Name	Ref
Everts, John	COL 254	Failing, Henry J.	MNT 45	Faivill, Jacob	MNT 52
Everts, John	ULS 184	Failing, John Jur	MNT 40	Fake, George	RNS 45
Everts, John Junr	COL 185	Failing, John H.	MNT 43	Fake, George Junr	RNS 44
Everts, Martin	DUT 133	Failing, John J.	MNT 20	Fake, John	MNT 57
Everts, Mathias	COL 177	Failing, John R.	MNT 2	Fake, John	RNS 45
Evertson, Anthony	MNT 44	Failix, Geo.	SCH 121	Fakes, George	MNT 63
Evertson, Benjamin	NYK 149	Failix, John	SCH 121	Falconer, John	WST 118
Evertson, Bernerdus	ALB 144	Failix, Peter	SCH 121	Falconer, Jonathan	WST 117
Evertson, Evert	ALB 45	Fairbank, Silas	HRK 533	Falconer, William	NYK 30
Evertson, Henry	ALB 129	Fairbank, Thos	HRK 423	Faling, Philip	MNT 32
Evertson, Jacob	ALB 146	Fairbanks, Abel	MNT 103	Faling, Richard	MNT 32
Evertson, Lewis	RCH 88	Fairbanks, Eleazar	ONT 356	Falkaneer, John	QNS 67
Evertson, Nicholas	NYK 18	Fairbanks, Ephraim	OND 200	Falkaneer, Roger	WST 167
Every, Benjamin	ALB 94	Fairbanks, Gamaliel	WST 167	Falkburg, Lisher	SCH 132
Every, Isaac	DEL 272	Fairbanks, Jeremeah	MNT 104	Falkenbury, Levy	WSH 280
E ery, James	GRN 344	Fairbanks, Joseph	CHN 862	Falkener, Agnes	ORN 337
Every, John	DEL 272	Fairbanks, Nahum	OND 167	Falkener, James	ORN 293
Every, John	ULS 198	Fairbanks, Samuel F.	DUT 176	Falkener, John	ORN 345
Every, Joseph	DEL 272	Fairbern, Francis	NYK 39	Falkener, Joseph	DUT 135
Every, Richard	ULS 198	Fairchild, Aaron	ESS 305	Falkener, Josiah	DUT 85
Every, Uriah	DEL 272	Fairchild, Abijah	OTS 13	Falkener, Samuel	DUT 138
Everyman, John	ORN 380	Fairchild, Able	CHN 984	Falkener, Samuel	ORN 337
Eves, Thomas	NYK 149	Fairchild, Alpheus	ULS 210	Falkener, William	CHN 808
Evills, Charles	WSH 271	Fairchild, Amos	CHN 776	Falkener, William	DUT 85
Evins	RNS 36	Fairchild, Benjaman	CHN 984	Falkener, William	ORN 347
Evins, Barna	RNS 77	Fairchild, Benjamin	COL 250	Falkerson, Philip	NYK 20
Evins, Isaac	RNS 102	Fairchild, Benjamine	GRN 336	Falkiner, Joseph	CHN 746
Evins, John	RNS 110	Fairchild, Danl	CHN 984	Falkiner, Nicholus	CHN 746
Evins, Thomas	WSH 222	Fairchild, Daniel	ULS 212	Falkner, John	WSH 286
Evitts, Amaziah	WSH 306	Fairchild, David	CHN 776	Falkner, John Junr	WSH 221
Evitts, Daniel	CAY 564	Fairchild, David	ONT 388	Falkner, Saml	RNS 44
Evitts, Elihu	WSH 271	Fairchild, Ebin	ONT 396	Fall, Benjamin	ONT 498
Evitts, Hervy	ONT 408	Fairchild, Elijah	DUT 170	Fall, Henry	HRK 421
Evitts, Jerad	ONT 390	Fairchild, Freeman	CHN 984	Fall, Israel	ORN 349
Evitts, Jesse	WSH 271	Fairchild, Hamlet	NYK 86	Fallet, Levy	CHN 850
Evitts, John	WSH 272	Fairchild, Isaac	ULS 210	Falls, Alexander	ORN 282
Evitts, Judah	WSH 272	Fairchild, James	DUT 52	Falls, James	DUT 164
Evitts, Stephen	WSH 271	Fairchild, James	DUT 170	Falls, Mary	ORN 291
Ewen, Catherine	NYK 67	Fairchild, John	CHN 796	Falls, William	ORN 351
Ewer, James	OND 163	Fairchild, John	COL 212	Falshaw, John	WSH 277
Ewer, Thomas	ONN 154	Fairchild, John	ONT 396	Falshaw, Lemuel	WSH 277
Ewer, Thomas Jun	ONN 155	Fairchild, John	OTS 26	Fan, James	RNS 96
Ewing, Alexander	NYK 20	Fairchild, John Junr	OTS 26	Fancher, Abm	RNS 57
Ewing, Gazalene	NYK 121	Fairchild, Jonathan	ONT 486	Fancher, Andrew	WST 160
Ewing, Jane	NYK 54	Fairchild, Jonathan	ULS 212	Fancher, Benjamin	MNT 16
Ewing, John	CAY 654	Fairchild, Levi	ULS 210	Fancher, David	RNS 109
Ewing, John	NYK 132	Fairchild, Oliver	ULS 210	Fancher, Jerred	WST 158
Ewing, Samuel	ONT 386	Fairchild, Ransford	OTS 23	Fancher, John	RNS 57
Ewings, Joshua	DUT 71	Fairchild, Robert	NYK 52	Fancher, John	WST 160
Ewles, William	DEL 290	Fairchild, Rubin	CLN 171	Fancher, Joseph	WST 159
Exceen, Jeremiah	SUF 87	Fairchild, Seth	ULS 212	Fancher, Nehemiah	WST 158
Eyesblister, John	ULS 250	Fairchild, Stephen	ULS 210	Fancher, Peter	RNS 57
Eyet, John	DUT 11	Fairchild, Thomas	NYK 48	Fancher, Rufus	DUT 169
Eyres, Simon	SUF 108	Fairchild, Thomas Jun	NYK 15	Fancher, Samuel	TIO 228
		Fairchild, Widow	STB 202	Fancher, Samuel	WST 159
F		Fairchild, Zalmon	OTS 31	Fancher, Seth	RNS 60
		Fairchildes, Daniel	WSH 215	Fancher, Silvanus Junr	WST 157
F____,	DEL 267	Fairchilds, Jesse	WSH 190	Fancher, Squire	WST 160
F....ng, John	MNT 4	Fairchilds, Peter	WSH 282	Fancher, Thaddeus	DUT 20
F____, John	MNT 5	Fairchilds, Samuel	OND 224	Fancher, Wm	TIO 227
F ller, Godfrey	MNT 31	Fairchilds, Sweeting	WSH 275	Fancher, William	WST 159
F....., Arent	MNT 43	Fairclo, George	NYK 78	Fancher, Wm Junr	WST 159
F....., Daniel	MNT 83	Fairfield, Archabald	ONN 193	Fanchier, Joseph	CAY 714
F.....son, Jeremiah	MNT 87	Fairle, Alexander	NYK 100	Fane, Thomas	RNS 109
Faber, George	NYK 50	Fairle, Hugh	NYK 100	Fanham, Jonah	CHN 972
Fabrick, Lewis	HRK 478	Fairlee, Jonathan	DUT 143	Fanichur, Richard	MNT 114
Face, Andrew	RNS 8	Fairley, Hugh	WSH 227	Fank, Conrad	MNT 30
Face, Coonrod	RNS 57	Fairley, James	QNS 84	Fanning, David	SUF 76
Face, Frederick	COL 225	Fairley, Joseph	NYK 60	Fanning, Edmond	OND 189
Fach, Elizabeth	NYK 68	Fairlie, James	NYK 51	Fanning, Edward	NYK 62
Fader, Henry	OND 222	Fairman, Amasa	CLN 166	Fanning, Elizabeth	NYK 62
Fady, Thomas	SRA 34	Fairman, Frederick	CLN 166	Fanning, Hannah	WST 113
Faft, James	WSH 267	Fairman, Gideon	ALB 149	Fanning, James	SUF 96
Fagal, William	NYK 89	Fairman, James	CLN 160	Fanning, James Junr	SUF 96
Fagen, Daniel	QNS 60	Fairman, Richard	COL 252	Fanning, John	ONT 428
Failing, Elisabeth	MNT 39	Fairnham, Benjamin	ONT 328	Fanning, John	SUF 96
Failing, Henry J.	MNT 40	Fairwell, Isaac M.	OND 183	Fanning, Jonathan	ALB 74

Fanning, Joshua	CHN	776	Farquahar, James	NYK	30	Fassett, John	OND	179
Fanning, Mary	SUF	74	Farr, A_	OTS	42	Fassy, Andrew	NYK	56
Fanning, Nathl	SUF	73	Farr, Archibald	ULS	186	Fastemire, John	COL	261
Fanning, Patrick	DUT	77	Farr, Eli	OND	185	Faster, Alujah	TIO	243
Fanning, Phinehas	CHN	774	Farr, Eli Junior	OND	185	Faster, Edward	SCH	146
Fanning, Walter	SCH	138	Farr, James	OTS	52	Faster, Jacob	SCH	163
Fanning, William	HRK	588	Farr, John	NYK	40	Faster, Jacob	SCH	168
Fanning, William	OND	202	Farr, John	ULS	209	Faster, Luther	TIO	238
Fanshaw, Henry	NYK	55	Farr, Jonah	SRA	53	Faste_, Robert	TIO	223
Fansworth, Aron	ALB	3	Farr, Jonas	MNT	33	Faster, Seth	SCH	147
Fansworth, Ebenezer	WSH	304	Farr, Lent	WSH	299	Fatin, Thomas	NYK	37
Fansworth, John	WSH	304	Farr, Levi	ESS	320	Fatoute, George	QNS	66
Fansworth, Josiah	WSH	304	Farr, Phebe	DUT	137	Fatz, Samuel	NYK	64
Fansworth, Nicholas	ONT	396	Farr, Reuben	WSH	299	Faucet, Cox	MNT	95
Fansworth, Solomon	WSH	304	Farr, Richard	CAY	566	Faukiner, Anthony	OND	193
Fant, Uriah	DEL	281	Farr, Stephen	WSH	299	Faulconbergh, Samuel	CAY	630
Fanton, James	NYK	62	Farrchilds, Samuel	GRN	333	Faulk, Corns_	ALB	61
Faquin, Joseph	NYK	72	Farre_, Anthony	MNT	54	Faulk, Daniel	ALB	61
Farble, __y	QNS	60	Farrell, Elihu	OTS	47	Faulk, James	ALB	107
Fardon, Abraham	NYK	34	Farrell, James	NYK	45	Faulk, Jehoicham	ALB	111
Fardon, Caleb	NYK	129	Farrell, Jane	NYK	150	Faulk, Jeronomus	ALB	111
Fardon, John	NYK	98	Farren, Hugh	NYK	79	Faulk, Laurance	ALB	87
Fardon, Thomas	KNG	7	Farren, John	NYK	120	Faulk, Matthias	ALB	74
Fardon, Thomas	NYK	82	Farren, John	NYK	123	Faulk, Peter	ALB	111
Farest see D. Farest			Farren, Joseph	CAY	700	Faulkner, Caleb	MNT	1
Fareweell, John	OND	223	Farren, Stephen	NYK	111	Faulkner, George	NYK	74
Farewell, Elisha	ONT	316	Farren, William	NYK	41	Faulkner, Joseph	NYK	65
Farewell, Joseph	OND	205	Farrend, Moses	CAY	702	Faulkner, Patrick	ALB	77
Farewell, Nathan	ONT	328	Farrend, Samuel	CAY	702	Faulkner, Samuel	STB	207
Fargay, James	NYK	57	Farriar, John	NYK	103	Faulkner, Thomas	DEL	279
Fargay, John	NYK	57	Farrier, Robert	ORN	369	Faulkner, Wm	OTS	6
Fargeson, David	NYK	82	Farrin, John	NYK	15	Fauman, Hannah	NYK	117
Fargo, Aaron	OND	208	Farrington, Abner	RNS	49	Faunk, Christian	SCH	168
Fargo, Calvin	ONT	460	Farrington, Charles	QNS	66	Faunk, David	SCH	168
Fargo, Daniel	HRK	431	Farrington, Daniel	QNS	62	Fauqeres, Louis	NYK	42
Fargo, Daniel	NYK	139	Farrington, Ebenezer M.	COL	207	Faurgason, John	MNT	89
Fargo, Flavel	CHN	856	Farrington, Edward	WST	127	Fausborough, Abraham	GRN	344
Fargo, Jason	CHN	798	Farrington, Elijah	QNS	64	Fausbury, Phillip	GRN	356
Fargo, Zebediah	HRK	431	Farrington, Elizabeth	QNS	66	Fauset, Lansing	WSH	227
Farguarson, Joshua	MNT	89	Farrington, Ezery	QNS	83	Fawcitt, Lyman	RNS	90
Faringdon, Palatine	GRN	333	Farrington, Frederick	ONN	137	Fawler, Samuel	COL	265
Farington, Ephraim	RNS	58	Farrington, George	QNS	66	Fawpell, John	NYK	86
Farington, Mathew	QNS	63	Farrington, George	WST	148	Faxen, Allen	RNS	102
Farington, Robert	MNT	46	Farrington, Jacob	WST	114	Faxen, Reuben	RNS	17
Farley, John	ALB	5	Farrington, James	NYK	123	Faxen, Samuel	RNS	17
Farley, John	HRK	501	Farrington, James	NYK	154	Fay, Asa	CHN	936
Farling, Andrew	DUT	142	Farrington, John	NYK	86	Fay, Asa	SRA	31
Farman, Joab	OND	202	Farrington, John	QNS	64	Fay, Charles	DEL	272
Farman, Moody	OND	163	Farrington, Joseph	DUT	94	Fay, David	CHN	928
Farmer, Anna	NYK	37	Farrington, Joseph	WST	147	Fay, Elisha	ONT	418
Farmer, Henry	HRK	438	Farrington, Joshua	NYK	146	Fay, Isaac	SRA	29
Farmer, Jacob	MNT	61	Farrington, Lawrence	QNS	61	Fay, Jacob	NYK	113
Farmer, James	HRK	438	Farrington, March	DEL	289	Fay, John	SRA	29
Farmer, John	DUT	5	Farrington, Margaret	WST	148	Fay, Jonathan	ONN	155
Farmer, John	HRK	448	Farrington, Mathew	QNS	66	Fay, Joseph	NYK	24
Farmer, John	SRA	17	Farrington, Matthew	DUT	22	Fay, Joseph	ONN	155
Farmer, Simon	HRK	438	Farrington, Matthew	WST	127	Fay, Moses	WSH	184
Farmer, Thomas	NYK	19	Farrington, Matthew	WST	152	Fay, Nicholas a mulatto	NYK	98
Farmer, Thomas a Black	NYK	150	Farrington, Putman	DEL	289	Fay, Pall	WSH	217
Farmer, Thomas	SRA	35	Farrington, Robert	WST	146	Fay, Sherebiah	OND	165
Farmer, Uriah	OTS	34	Farrington, Solomon	DUT	96	Fay, Wm	ONN	154
Farmer, William	OTS	34	Farrington, Thomas	ALB	88	Fayard, Frances	NYK	131
Farmer, Wm	OTS	56	Farrington, Thomas	DEL	289	Fazer, Moses	NYK	133
Farmington, Pelletire	GRN	336	Farrington, Thomas	NYK	131	Feader, Phillip	OND	223
Farnet, Barnet	SRA	10	Farrington, Thomas	WST	146	Feagles, Jacob	ORN	378
Farnham, Calvin	CHN	968	Farrington, Timothy	QNS	83	Feagles, Jacob Junr	ORN	364
Farnham, Elisha	CHN	966	Farrington, Walter	QNS	65	Feagles, John	ORN	378
Farnham, Joel	TIO	236	Farrington, William	DUT	95	Feather see Fether &		
Farnham, Joel	TIO	239	Farrow, John	CAY	716	Teather		
Farnham, Jonathan	ONN	143	Farrow, Nathan	OTS	46	Feather, Jacob	RNS	107
Farnham, Jonathan Jr	ONN	144	Farthe, Nicholas	CHN	978	Featherly, Christopher	DUT	112
Farnham, Levi	ONN	132	Farthings, Abraham	NYK	34	Featherly, John	ONT	488
Farnham, Philo	ONN	145	Farver, John	GRN	325	Featherly, John	QNS	74
Farnsworth, Nathaniel	OND	174	Fash, John	CHN	958	Featherly, John	RNS	64
Farnsworth, William	DUT	64	Fash, John	QNS	60	Featherly, Thomas	QNS	74
Farnum, Samuel	ESS	307	Fassair, Elizabeth	NYK	98	Featte, Benajah	ONN	172
Farnum, Zebediah	ESS	304	Fasset, Shubel	WSH	221	Fecks, Robert	QNS	80

Name	Loc	Name	Loc	Name	Loc
Fecter, William	HRK 459	Felter, Abrm	RCK 110	Ferguson, Abraham	DUT 9
Fectes, Wm	MNT 52	Felter, Benjamin	ULS 227	Ferguson, Abraham	DUT 73
Federly, Philip	ALB 65	Felter, David	ORN 296	Ferguson, Alexr	ALB 9
Feek, Cornelius	SCH 131	Felter, David	RCK 102	Ferguson, Alexander	ORN 299
Feek, Jacob	SCH 131	Felter, Eliza	RCK 102	Ferguson, Allen	SRA 47
Feek, Nicholas	SCH 131	Felter, Jacob	ALB 93	Ferguson, Barbara	ALB 73
Feek, Peter	SCH 131	Felter, Johanis	RCK 102	Ferguson, Benjamin	DUT 12
Feeks, Daniel	QNS 83	Felter, Johannis	ULS 219	Ferguson, Bezaleel	ULS 235
Feeks, Daniel Junr	QNS 83	Felter, Johannis P.	ULS 219	Ferguson, Daniel	DEL 284
Feeks, Henry	ORN 369	Felter, John	NYK 57	Ferguson, David	ALB 54
Feeks, Joseph	WST 113	Felter, John	ORN 296	Ferguson, Gabriel	ULS 257
Feeks, Joseph Junr	WST 114	Felter, John	RCK 102	Ferguson, Henry	ALB 31
Feeks, Lockwood	WST 113	Felter, John	ULS 245	Ferguson, Isaac	DUT 88
Feeks, Prior	WST 114	Felter, Matthew	ULS 190	Ferguson, James	DEL 271
Feeld, Josiah L.	NYK 30	Felter, Peter	RCK 102	Ferguson, James	DEL 285
Feeling, Cornelius	SRA 5	Felter, Peter	RCK 103	Ferguson, James	ORN 324
Feely, Aaron	COL 242	Felter, Phillip	ULS 224	FerguSon, James	OTS 3
Feetsout, Isaac	GRN 326	Felter, William	NYK 100	Ferguson, James	OTS 4
Fegan, Alexander	DUT 32	Felter, William	ORN 271	Ferguson, James	OTS 30
Fegoler, John	ALB 107	Felter, Wm	RCK 102	Ferguson, James	SCH 154
Feild, David	COL 206	Felter, Wm Junr	RCK 101	Ferguson, Jeams	OND 223
Feis, John William	NYK 73	Felthousen, Henry	NYK 125	Ferguson, John	ALB 37
Feitner, Frances	NYK 152	Felton, Daniel	OND 208	Ferguson, John	ALB 39
Fel_, Nath.n	MNT 12	Felton, James	RNS 51	Ferguson, John	DEL 275
Felch, John	WSH 272	Felton, John	OTS 27	Ferguson, John	DUT 88
Felcher, John	WSH 274	Felton, Jonathan	OND 177	Ferguson, John	DUT 146
Felix, Augustus	NYK 86	Felton, Moses	ONN 190	Ferguson, John	NYK 114
Felker, John	COL 242	Felton, Robert	OND 208	Ferguson, John	ORN 292
Fell, James	RNS 21	Felton, Robert	ONN 189	Ferguson, John	ORN 318
Fellars, David	WSH 188	Felts, Albert	COL 236	Ferguson, John	ORN 327
Feller, David	DUT 150	Felts, Coonrad	WST 158	Ferguson, John	OTS 56
Feller, George	DUT 161	Felts, John	COL 241	Ferguson, John	WSH 242
Feller, Henry	DUT 156	Felts, Phillip	COL 241	Ferguson, John	WST 145
Feller, Jacob	COL 232	Fene, Jenny a Black	NYK 26	Ferguson, Lewis	DEL 275
Feller, Jacob	RNS 11	Fenis, Jonothan	CHN 780	Ferguson, Lot	ALB 104
Feller, James	NYK 70	Fenn, Amos	DUT 132	Ferguson, Mary	DUT 19
Feller, John	DUT 150	Fenn, James	DUT 73	Ferguson, Michael	DUT 91
Feller, John I.	DUT 160	Fenn, Stephen	DEL 287	Ferguson, Peter	ULS 248
Feller, Nicholas	COL 244	Fenn, Theophilus	DEL 290	Ferguson, Richard	ORN 326
Feller, Nicholas	RNS 11	Fennell, John	NYK 118	Ferguson, Robert	OTS 56
Feller, Peter	COL 225	Fennell, Thomas	NYK 113	Ferguson, Samuel	DUT 14
Feller, Peter	DUT 160	Fenner, Daniel	HRK 551	Ferguson, Samuel	MNT 60
Feller, Philip	RNS 11	Fenner, George	HRK 566	Ferguson, Samuel	OND 157
Feller, Philip J.	RNS 90	Fenner, Nicholas	ORN 381	Ferguson, Samuel	ORN 322
Feller, Phillip P.	DUT 154	Fen.er, Reuben	CAY 596	Ferguson, Samuel	WSH 192
Feller, Wilhelmus	DUT 161	Fenner, Thomas	HRK 519	Ferguson, Samuel	WSH 296
Feller, Zachariah	DUT 156	Fenner, William	HRK 518	Ferguson, Thomas	DUT 86
Feller, Zachariah	RNS 11	Fenney, Jesse	RNS 45	Ferguson, Thos	OTS 29
Fellers, John	RNS 11	Fenny, Partrick	NYK 94	Ferguson, Uriah	DUT 14
Felley, Jonathan	ALB 25	Fenton, Asa	OND 223	Ferguson, Uriah	ORN 323
Fellger, Phillip W.	COL 238	Fenton, Berry	SRA 53	Ferguson, William	DUT 73
Fellhousen, Jacob	ALB 13	Fenton, Daniel	COL 184	Ferguson, William	NYK 101
Fellhousen, Sarah	ALB 13	Fenton, Elijah	OND 208	Ferguson, William	ORN 368
Fellors, William	RNS 110	Fenton, Jacob	OTS 34	Ferguson, Wm	OTS 29
Fellows, Cyrus	OND 215	Fenton, Joseph	CAY 532	Ferguson, Wm	OTS 56
Fellows, David	NYK 86	Fenton, Joshua	SRA 53	Fermon, Robert	QNS 60
Fellows, Henry	SCH 140	Fenton, Malichi	OTS 32	Fernam, _m berst	CAY 634
Fellows, Hiram	OND 215	Fenton, Nathl	OTS 34	Fero, Abraham	RNS 94
Fellows, James	ONN 157	Fenton, Peter	NYK 103	Fero, Henry	RNS 94
Fellows, John	SRA 43	Fenton, Peter	NYK 106	Fero, John	GRN 327
Fellows, John G.	SRA 31	Fenton, Robert	OTS 34	Fero, John	GRN 328
Fellows, Joseph	TIO 260	Fenton, Wm	MNT 110	Fero, Paul	GRN 327
Fellows, Joshua	COL 252	Fenwich, Joseph	NYK 74	Ferran, Barnabas	HRK 539
Fellows, Josiah	SRA 54	Fenwick, Joseph	NYK 149	Ferran, Jarerd	WSH 249
Fellows, Lewis	SCH 140	Fenwick, Thomas	NYK 99	Ferred, Sherman	TIO 247
Fellows, Reuben	OTS 44	Fera[ts?], John	MNT 72	Ferrel, Andrew	NYK 19
Fellows, Rozel	OND 215	Ferbeck, John	ALB 105	Ferrell, Anna	NYK 142
Fellows, Warner	OTS 44	Ferdig, George	CAY 518	Ferrell, Peter	NYK 75
Fellows, William	SRA 34	Ferdon, Abraham A.	DUT 71	Ferrell, Richard	NYK 21
Fellows, William	SRA 43	Ferdon, John I.	DUT 71	Ferrell, Robert	OTS 46
Felshow, Christopher	NYK 147	Ferdon, Peter	ULS 185	Ferrell, Simeon	OTS 46
Felt, David	CHN 848	Ferdon, Thomas	NYK 75	Ferrell, Wm	STB 197
Felt, Elum	CHN 848	Ferend, Elisha	TIO 238	Ferren, Abraham	ESS 317
Felt, Ichial	CHN 848	Fergason, Andrew	WSH 233	Ferrer, John	ONN 170
Felt, Jacob	WSH 277	Fergasson, Thomas	ONT 502	Ferrers, John	NYK 17
Felt, Samuel	CHN 848	Fergerson, Stephen	COL 261	Ferres, Ahasuerus	CAY 604
Felt, Samuel Jur	CHN 848	Ferguson, Aaron	ORN 323	Ferres, James	CAY 604

INDEX TO THE 1800 CENSUS OF NEW YORK

Ferres, Jonah	CAY 604	Ferris, Seillick	WST 153	Field, John	WST 122
Ferres, Josiah	NYK 125	Ferris, Seth	SRA 36	Field, Jonathan	DUT 25
Ferrier, John	NYK 137	Ferris, Silvanus	WST 151	Field, Jonathan	RNS 94
Ferrier, John F.	NYK 114	Ferris, Simeon	GRN 344	Field, Joseph	KNG 9
Ferril, Hannah	ALB 3	Ferris, Solomon	COL 239	Field, Joseph C.	DUT 173
Ferrill, John	ALB 106	Ferris, Solomon	ULS 238	Field, Letty	QNS 63
Ferrill, Philip	ALB 135	Ferris, Solomon	WSH 213	Field, Martin	RNS 111
Ferrill, Thoms	ONN 190	Ferris, Stephen	WST 162	Field, Nathan	OTS 12
Ferrill, William	ALB 36	Ferris, Stephen	WST 167	Field, Nathan	OTS 20
Ferrin, Benoni	ESS 317	Ferris, Sylvanus	HRK 559	Field, Oliver	NYK 122
Ferrin, Bernard	WSH 249	Ferris, Sylvenus	ALB 115	Field, Oliver	ONT 478
Ferrin, Justice	WSH 248	Ferris, Thomas	SRA 57	Field, Oliver	QNS 63
Ferriole, John A.	CLN 169	Ferris, Thomas	WST 114	Field, Perservid	SUF 75
Ferris, Aaron	ESS 319	Ferris, Timothy	CHN 802	Field, Peter	NYK 43
Ferris, Alpherd	WSH 208	Ferris, Warren	WSH 208	Field, Peter a Black	NYK 133
Ferris, Andrew	DUT 168	Ferris, William	SCH 152	Field, Reuben	WSH 230
Ferris, Benjamin	CAY 548	Ferrisle, Joseph	ESS 310	Field, Robart	GRN 343
Ferris, Benjamin	CHN 800	Ferriss, Alexander	ESS 317	Field, Robeart	GRN 342
Ferris, Benjamin	DUT 51	Ferriss, Gilbert	OTS 22	Field, Robert	ONT 476
Ferris, Benjamin	NYK 53	Ferriss, Jedediah	ESS 295	Field, Samuel	ULS 266
Ferris, Benjamin	WST 144	Ferriss, Pitt	DUT 53	Field, Solomon	DUT 174
Ferris, Caleb	WST 149	Ferriss, Seneca	DUT 53	Field, Stephen ye 1st	DUT 173
Ferris, Charity	WST 149	Ferriss, Wayman	DUT 56	Field, Stephen ye 2d	DUT 174
Ferris, Cornul	NYK 74	Ferrote, Benjamin	ORN 393	Field, Stephen ye 3d	DUT 173
Ferris, Daniel	DUT 74	Ferrote, Henry	ORN 393	Field, Waterman	CHN 790
Ferris, Daniel	DUT 129	Ferrote, Henry Junr	ORN 393	Field, Whitehead	QNS 63
Ferris, Daniel	WST 137	Ferrote, Mary	ORN 392	Field, William	DEL 287
Ferris, David	WST 156	Ferry see Terry		Field, William	DUT 173
Ferris, Ebenezar	WST 113	Ferry, Asa	DEL 279	Field, William	NYK 148
Ferris, Edmund	DUT 54	Ferry, Elijah	OTS 28	Field, Wm	OTS 12
Ferris, Edward	NYK 75	Ferry, Henry	OND 215	Field, Wm	OTS 20
Ferris, Elijah	ULS 185	Ferry, John	ONN 143	Field, William	WST 111
Ferris, Elisabeth	WST 156	Ferry, Lewis	RNS 75	Fields, Benjamin	WST 111
Ferris, Elisabeth	WST 159	Ferry, Pyre	NYK 148	Fields, Charles	ORN 395
Ferris, Elisha	NYK 43	Fersol, Robert	RNS 96	Fields, Daniel	WST 126
Ferris, Eliza	NYK 58	Fescout, Margaret	NYK 104	Fields, David	WST 111
Ferris, Enoch	RNS112A	Fether, Catrean	GRN 328	Fields, Elijah	SRA 53
Ferris, George	WST 122	Fether, John	GRN 328	Fields, Ilisha	OTS 11
Ferris, Gould	WST 160	Fetterlee, Daniel	HRK 471	Fields, Hazard	WST 122
Ferris, Henry	DUT 129	Fetterlee, Eve	HRK 471	Fields, Israel	CHN 752
Ferris, Isaac	CLN 154	Fetterlee, Henry	HRK 471	Fields, Jesse	WST 159
Ferris, Isaac	NYK 140	Fetterlee, Peter	HRK 471	Fields, John	NYK 60
Ferris, Israel	CHN 788	Fetterlee, Thomas	HRK 471	Fields, Josiah	CHN 752
Ferris, Israel Jun	CHN 800	Fetterley, Philip	ALB 58	Fields, Mary	WST 111
Ferris, Jacob	WST 144	Fetterly, George	MNT 29	Fields, Moses	CHN 790
Ferris, James	DUT 83	Few, David	MNT 122	Fields, Oliver	WST 167
Ferris, James	NYK 71	Few, John	ORN 347	Fields, Peluck	CHN 784
Ferris, James	WSH 208	Few, William	COL 254	Fields, Phillip	NYK 143
Ferris, John	NYK 58	Few, William	NYK 150	Fields, Reubin	OND 223
Ferris, John	ULS 184	Fi_t, Caleb	MNT 87	Fields, Robert a Black	NYK 39
Ferris, John	WST 149	Fice, Jacob	MNT 51	Fields, Samuel	NYK 20
Ferris, John	WST 159	Fichard, Isaac	GRN 356	Fields, Samuel	WST 154
Ferr[is?], John	WST 167	Fick, Peter	GRN 326	Fields, William Junr	WST 112
Ferris, John Junr	WST 115	Fidler, John	DUT 162	Fiero, Abraham	ULS 221
Ferris, John A.	WSH 208	Fidler, Robert	COL 246	Fiero, Christian	DUT 158
Ferris, Jonathan	SRA 32	Field, Abijah	DUT 78	Fiero, Christian	ULS 222
Ferris, Jonathan	WST 156	Field, Abraham	NYK 54	Fiero, Coonradt	ULS 220
Ferris, Jonathan D.	NYK 52	Field, Amelia	SUF 108	Fiero, Peter &	
Ferris, Joseph	DUT 74	Field, Austin	QNS 63	H. Almendorp	DUT 157
Ferris, Joseph	WSH 213	Field, Cesar	KNG 9	Fiero, Peter	ULS 222
Ferris, Joseph	WST 132	Field, Charles J.	NYK 107	Fiero, Stephen	ULS 221
Ferris, Josiah	NYK 82	Field, Daniel	QNS 66	Fiero, William	ULS 221
Ferris, Lewis	CLN 154	Field, Daniel	ULS 182	Fierson, John Lewis	NYK 41
Ferris, Matthew	DUT 13	Field, Edward	NYK 123	Fifer, Andrew	SCH 170
Ferris, Morris	WSH 209	Field, Elnathan	DUT 172	Fifer, Jacob	CAY 678
Ferris, Nathan	CLN 156	Field, Frances	WST 153	Figler, Peter	ALB 113
Ferris, Nathan	DUT 149	Field, Frederick	QNS 65	Fik_es, Peter	MNT 29
Ferris, Noah	ESS 311	Field, George	QNS 65	Fikener, Peter	NYK 86
Ferris, Orange	WSH 300	Field, Gilbert	WST 125	Fikes, Adam	MNT 77
Ferris, Peter	CLN 161	Field, Hezi	QNS 60	Fikes, Henry	MNT 76
Ferris, Reed	DUT 51	Field, Isaac	DUT 174	Fikes, Nicholas	MNT 28
Ferris, Richard	WST 156	Field, Jacob	KNG 9	Fikes, Peter	MNT 77
Ferris, Richard	WST 162	Field, Jacob	QNS 62	File, Christopher	RNS 85
Ferris, Samuel	DEL 288	Field, James	SUF 108	File, Christopher	RNS 89
Ferris, Samuel	NYK 143	Field, Jesse	DUT 176	File, Malkert	RNS 89
Ferris, Samuel	WST 112	Field, John	DUT 64	Filer, Alenson	HKR 478
Ferris, Samuel	WST 115	Field, John	ULS 182	Filer, Jonathan	HRK 474

127

Name	Loc	No.	Name	Loc	No.	Name	Loc	No.
Filer, Jonathan Jun	HRK	474	Finch, John	CHN	790	Finger, Jeremiah	COL	238
Filer, Thomas	SUF	106	Finch, John	DUT	50	Finger, John	COL	236
Filer, Zephaniah	RNS	95	Finch, John	MNT	60	Finigan, Charles	NYK	24
Files, Peter	ORN	391	Finch, John	ONT	492	Fink, Adam	NYK	147
Filkin, Abraham	DUT	67	Finch, John	ORN	371	Fink, Alexander	NYK	69
Filkin, Abraham	RNS	39	Finch, John	SRA	55	Fink, Alexander Jun	NYK	150
Filkin, Bernard	DUT	106	Finch, John	STB	203	Fink, Andrew	MNT	17
Filkin, Francis	DEL	277	Finch, John	WST	124	Fink, Ezra	ALB	83
Filkin, Germond	RNS	56	Finch, Jonathan	SRA	32	Fink, Henry	NYK	148
Filkin, Isaac	DUT	121	Finch, Jonnathan	GRN	357	Fink, John	NYK	41
Filkin, John	RNS	87	Finch, Joseph	NYK	55	Fink, John	NYK	145
Filkin, Jonathan	RNS112B		Finch, Joseph	RNS	55	Fink, John	RNS	88
Filkin, Lewis	DUT	115	Finch, Joseph	SRA	40	Fink, John	SCH	137
Filkin, Peter	DUT	121	Finch, Joseph	WST	113	Fink, Peter	SCH	142
Filkins, ...	RNS112A		Finch, Joshua	ESS	323	Fink, Phillip	NYK	134
Filkins, Abraham	CAY	636	Finch, Justus	DUT	100	Fink, Wm	MNT	13
Filkins, Cornelius	RNS	39	Finch, Lewis	RNS	48	Fink, William	SCH	137
Filkins, Henry	OND	208	Finch, Libius	DEL	287	Fink, William Jr	MNT	28
Filkins, Henry B.	RNS	39	Finch, Margaret	ORN	339	Finkle, John	COL	238
Filkins, Isaac	RNS	88	Finch, Mary	NYK	121	Finkle, John	RNS	87
Filkins, Jacob	RNS	45	Finch, Micheal	CAY	718	Finkle, William	COL	245
Filkins, James	DUT	124	Finch, Moses	ONT	492	Finkly, John	SCH	154
Filkins, John	CAY	636	Finch, Nathaniel	OND	178	Finks, William	CHN	810
Filkins, John J.	RNS	45	Finch, Nehemiah	COL	221	Finlap, Susannah	NYK	43
Filkins, Langdon	RNS112A		Finch, Pastor	SCH	117	Finlay, Charles	ORN	312
Filkins, Nathaniel	SRA	34	Finch, Peleg	DEL	287	Finlay, Elizabeth	ORN	292
Filkins, Peter	RNS112A		Finch, Peter	CHN	806	Finlay, James	ORN	287
Filkins, Timothy	RNS	39	Finch, Peter	RNS	55	Finley, Samuel	NYK	30
Fill, Isaac	RNS	88	Finch, Phillip	DUT	177	Finley, Stephen	NYK	42
Fillbout, John	SCH	168	Finch, Reuben	COL	221	Finley, Thomas	ORN	396
Fillen, Mitchell	NYK	117	Finch, Reuben	SCH	123	Finlinson, Mathew	RNS	80
Filley, Arune	CAY	722	Finch, Richd	OTS	36	Finn, Catharine	ORN	371
Filley, Jesse	CAY	704	Finch, Samuel	CAY	598	Finn, Elizabeth	NYK	93
Filley, Remembrance	ALB	89	Finch, Samuel	SRA	48	Finn, Henery	CHN	808
Fillmore, Henery	SRA	58	Finch, Selah	OND	179	Finn, John	DUT	68
Filmore, Calvin	CAY	624	Finch, Selvenus	SCH	123	Finn, William	ORN	371
Filmore, Nathaniel	CAY	624	Finch, Seth	WST	152	Finneer, John	SUF	96
Fin_, Francis	MNT	98	Finch, Shubil	RNS	112	Finney, Elizabeth a		
Finagan, Anna	NYK	38	Finch, Silvinus	SCH	117	mulatto	NYK	30
Finch, Abigal	SRA	40	Finch, Simeon	ALB	32	Finney, Jabez	COL	253
Finch, Abraham	DUT	139	Finch, Simeon	RNS	112	Finney, James	ONT	346
Finch, Abraham	SRA	46	Finch, Smith	COL	221	Finney, Jonathan	DEL	289
Finch, Adam Junr	NYK	60	Finch, Solomon	HRK	461	Finney, Uriah	CHN	876
Finch, Albert	SCH	159	Finch, Solomon	ORN	384	Finney, Ire	CHN	858
Finch, Albert Junr	SCH	159	Finch, Stephen	COL	221	Finns, John W.	NYK	28
Finch, Allum	GRN	341	Finch, Stephen	SCH	168	Finster, John	HRK	455
Finch, Alpheas	ALB	36	Finch, Stephen	WSH	288	Fint, James	COL	181
Finch, Amos	DUT	138	Finch, Thaddeus	ORN	368	Finton, Benjamin	WSH	194
Finch, Amos	GRN	349	Finch, Timothy	CAY	600	Finton, John	DUT	85
Finch, Andrew	RNS	4	Finch, William	CLN	158	Finton, John	ORN	326
Finch, Asahel	ORN	333	Finch, William	DEL	267	Finton, Oliver	WSH	193
Finch, Benjamin	RNS	112	Finch, William	OTS	31	Finton, Orange	WSH	193
Finch, Caleb	COL	242	Finch, William	WST	113	Finton, Samuel	WSH	193
Finch, Daniel	ORN	329	Finch, Zela	GRN	325	Finton, Thomas	WSH	200
Finch, David	CHN	788	Finch, Zuriah	SUF	85	Finton, William	CAY	562
Finch, David	ORN	287	Fincher, Abraham	NYK	152	Finton, William	ORN	383
Finch, David	SRA	28	Fincher, Isaac	WSH	209	Finster, Catherine	NYK	65
Finch, Ebenezer	COL	242	Fincher, Jesse	ONT	500	Finucane, John B.	ALB	149
Finch, Elnathan	ONT	444	Fincher, Joseph	NYK	151	Fiprite, Jacob	SRA	40
Finch, Esrar	GRN	355	Finchut, Hellen	NYK	32	Firm, Molly	NYK	32
Finch, Ezekiel	CHN	788	Finck, Elizabeth	COL	254	Firman, Jacob	OND	213
Finch, Foster	SCH	123	Finckel, Nicholas	COL	223	Firman, John	OND	213
Finch, Henery	CHN	782	Findly, Amos	MNT	108	Firnhower, Catherine	NYK	43
Finch, Ira	ESS	323	Findly, Deacon	MNT	107	Firth, Eliza	NYK	40
Finch, Isaac	CLN	158	Fine, Jacobus	NYK	34	Fise, Philip	ONT	490
Finch, Isaac Junr	CLN	158	Fineer, Francis	SUF	96	Fish, Abner	ESS	317
Finch, Jabez	COL	221	Fineer, Peter	SUF	96	Fish, Alexander	DUT	159
Finch, Jacob	DEL	287	Finehout, Arndt	DUT	160	Fish, Allen	WSH	188
Finch, James	CLN	157	Finehout, Cornelius	DUT	154	Fish, Benjamin	QNS	76
Finch, James	DEL	275	Finehout, Cornelius	DUT	160	Fish, Benjamin	WSH	213
Finch, James	ORN	313	Finehout, John	ALB	102	Fish, Benjamin	WSH	239
Finch, James	ORN	356	Finehout, Peter	ALB	17	Fish, Caleb	SRA	42
Finch, James Junr	ORN	313	Finehout, Peter	ALB	110	Fish, Cyrus	OTS	46
Finch, Jeremiah	GRN	345	Finger, Catharine	COL	232	Fish, Daniel	QNS	65
Finch, Jeremiah	NYK	57	Finger, Coeradt	COL	189	Fish, Daniel	WSH	229
Finch, Jeremiah	WSH	218	Finger, Jacob	COL	230			
Finch, Jesse	ONT	386	Finger, Jacob	DUT	149			

Fish, David	ALB	63	Fisher, Elijah	WST	167	Fisk, Jonathan	OND	208
Fish, David	CLN	155	Fisher, Elijah Junr	WST	167	Fisk, Jona	OTS	12
Fish, David	DUT	126	Fisher, Elizabeth	ORN	367	Fisk, Jona	OTS	15
Fish, David	MNT	117	Fisher, Fredrick	WST	167	Fisk, Jonathan	SRA	40
Fish, David	ONT	464	Fisher, George	DEL	290	Fisk, Joseph	DEL	291
Fish, Ebenezer	SRA	41	Fisher, George	WSH	183	Fisk, Mrs	HRK	450
Fish, Edmund	ALB	68	Fisher, George L.(?)	NYK	121	Fisk, Nathan	ONT	358
Fish, Elias	OTS	46	Fisher, Gilbert	WST	167	Fisk, Nathan	OTS	12
Fish, Eliphalet Junr	SRA	45	Fisher, Henry	NYK	122	Fisk, Rufus	OTS	26
Fish, Eliphalet Senr	SRA	45	Fisher, Henry a Black	NYK	123	Fisk, Saml	OTS	28
Fish, Elisha	ALB	82	Fisher, Henry	WSH	232	Fisk, Silvanus	CAY	588
Fish, Elisha	SCH	124	Fisher, Ichabod	OND	196	Fisk, Solomon	OTS	13
Fish, Ephraim	CHN	774	Fisher, Isaac	COL	259	Fisk, Thomas	RNS	111
Fish, Isaac	COL	208	Fisher, James	NYK	107	Fisk, William	CAY	588
Fish, Isaac	WSH	200	Fisher, James	WST	163	Fisk, Wm	RNS	105
Fish, Jared	COL	254	Fisher, Jane	DUT	169	Fisk, William	WSH	302
Fish, Jason	ULS	182	Fisher, Jerry	WST	167	Fisk, Wm Junr	RNS	105
Fish, Jerathmael	OND	185	Fisher, John	ALB	65	Fister, Henry	SCH	159
Fish, Jesse	QNS	65	Fisher, John	ALB	140	Fitch, Abel	COL	257
Fish, Jesse	WST	146	Fisher, John	CHN	920	Fitch, Abel Junr	COL	257
Fish, Job	RNS	31	Fisher, John	CHN	950	Fitch, Asa	WSH	222
Fish, John	COL	241	Fisher, John	KNG	8	Fitch, Asel	CHN	844
Fish, John	DUT	147	Fisher, John	MNT	51	Fitch, Ashel	SRA	58
Fish, John	KNG	2	Fisher, John	NYK	35	Fitch, Benjamin	WSH	224
Fish, John	RNS	17	Fisher, John	NYK	94	Fitch, Chauncey	CLN	165
Fish, John	WSH	238	Fisher, John	NYK	142	Fitch, Christopher	NYK	79
Fish, John	WST	163	Fisher, John	OTS	37	Fitch, Cyprean	COL	221
Fish, John Junr	WSH	238	Fisher, John	RCK	105	Fitch, David	CHN	772
Fish, Jonathan	ALB	81	Fisher, John	WSH	183	Fitch, David H.	CHN	844
Fish, Jonathan	QNS	65	Fisher, John	WST	163	Fitch, David Y.	OND	167
Fish, Joseph	DEL	284	Fisher, John Junr	WST	167	Fitch, Ebenezer	SRA	41
Fish, Joseph	GRN	350	Fisher, Joseph	DUT	84	Fitch, Edward	NYK	45
Fish, Joseph	RNS	39	Fish[er?], Joshua	WSH	238	Fitch, Elijah	CHN	746
Fish, Joshua	SRA	45	Fisher, Joshua	WSH	254	Fitch, Elijah	OTS	38
Fish(?), Joshua	WSH	238	Fisher, Josiah	ONT	316	Fitch, Eliphalet	NYK	17
Fish, Levi	SRA	45	Fisher, Leonard	NYK	68	Fitch, Elisha	CAY	648
Fish, Mary	DUT	165	Fisher, Lille	OND	219	Fitch, Elisha	WSH	224
Fish, Mercy	ALB	84	Fisher, Luke	OND	219	Fitch, Elisha Junr	CAY	646
Fish, Moses	GRN	350	Fisher, Luther	OND	215	Fitch, Erastus	OTS	38
Fish, Moses	OND	215	Fisher, Margaret	NYK	24	Fitch, Ezekiel	GRN	351
Fish, Nathan	CAY	702	Fisher, Margaret	NYK	98	Fitch, Ezra	SUF	90
Fish, Nathan	WST	163	Fisher, Margaret	ORN	398	Fitch, Haines	ORN	376
Fish, Pardon	SRA	41	Fisher, Moses	CHN	954	Fitch, Henly	SCH	143
Fish, Perry	OND	185	Fisher, Moses a Black	NYK	134	Fitch, Henry	OTS	38
Fish, Peter	DUT	141	Fisher, Nathl	HRK	521	Fitch, Jabez	CLN	170
Fish, Peter	OND	185	Fisher, Nathaniel	ONT	410	Fitch, James	ESS	308
Fish, Peter N.	ESS	318	Fisher, Nicholas	NYK	151	Fitch, James	OTS	10
Fish, Phebe	OND	185	Fisher, Nicholas	WST	117	Fitch, John	CHN	772
Fish, Preservad	NYK	82	Fisher, Nicholas	WST	163	Fitch, John	DUT	101
Fish, Preserved	DUT	9	Fisher, Peter	NYK	125	Fitch, John M.	NYK	93
Fish, Samuel	DEL	284	Fisher, Richard	WST	114	Fitch, Jona	OTS	25
Fish, Samuel	QNS	61	Fisher, Robert	CHN	922	Fitch, Lemuel	OTS	51
Fish, Sebree	GRN	356	Fisher, Ryneer	WSH	267	Fitch, Lindel	DEL	277
Fish, Silas	ALB	81	Fisher, Samuel	WST	118	Fitch, Luke	RNS	40
Fish, Thomas	OTS	46	Fisher, Samuel	WST	167	Fitch, Margaret	NYK	113
Fish, Thomas	WSH	238	Fisher, Stephen	SRA	10	Fitch, Mathew	COL	183
Fish, Thustin	OND	208	Fisher, Stophel	ONT	504	Fitch, Mathew Junr	COL	183
Fish, Titus	ALB	81	Fisher, William	NYK	138	Fitch, Nathan	HRK	506
Fish, Walter	HRK	434	Fisher, William	OTS	44	Fitch, Nathaniel	ESS	308
Fish, Whitehead	NYK	35	Fisher, William	WSH	183	Fitch, Nathaniel	OND	208
Fish, Wm M.	OTS	37	Fisher, William	WST	148	Fitch, Nehemiah	OTS	15
Fisher	NYK	111	Fisher, William	WST	163	Fitch, Nehemiah	OTS	46
Fisher, Abel S.	NYK	143	Fisher, William	WST	167	Fitch, Peabody	OND	204
Fisher, Abijah	CLN	162	Fisher, Zachariah	WSH	183	Fitch, Peletiah Junr	WSH	221
Fisher, Adam	ONT	504	Fisk, Abraham	OND	171	Fitch, Roger	GRN	338
Fisher, Albert	NYK	145	Fisk, Abrm	OTS	12	Fitch, Roswell	OND	170
Fisher, Alexander	NYK	32	Fisk, Asa	DEL	273	Fitch, Seth	OTS	38
Fisher, Amos	KNG	9	Fisk, Bezaleel	OND	187	Fitch, Seymour	DEL	277
Fisher, Amos	OTS	57	Fisk, Danl	OTS	56	Fitch, Silas	DEL	282
Fisher, Bartholmew	NYK	48	Fisk, David	OTS	10	Fitch, Silas	SRA	61
Fisher, Benjamin	WST	152	Fisk, Ezra	SRA	40	Fitch, Simeon	ALB	121
Fisher, Charles	NYK	141	Fisk, Isaac	OND	208	Fitch, Stephen	NYK	42
Fisher, Christian	ONT	504	Fisk, Job	OND	219	Fitch, Stephen	OTS	16
Fisher, Daniel	CHN	780	Fisk, John	OTS	13	Fitch, Thomas	DEL	289
Fisher, Daniel	WST	114	Fisk, John	WSH	274	Fitch, Thomas a Black	NYK	78
Fisher, Elijah	WST	117	Fisk, Jonathan	OND	172	Fitch, Thomas	SCH	143
Fisher, Elijah	WST	167				Fitch, William	NYK	80

Fitch, William	OTS 25	Flander, Philip	MNT 10	Fletcher, James	CAY 672
Fitch, William	SRA 20	Flander, Thomas	NYK 104	Fletcher, James	COL 241
Fitcher, Minor	COL 190	Flandereau, Benjamin	WST 150	Fletcher, John	CHN 838
Fitchet, Isaac	DUT 61	Flandereau, Daniel	WST 150	Fletcher, John	COL 241
Fitch patrick, John	WST 160	Flandereau, Elias	WST 150	Fletcher, John	NYK 63
Fithean, David	SUF 106	Flandereau, Peter	WST 150	Fletcher, Lemuel	OTS 42
Fithean, Elisha	SUF 106	Flanders, Augustinus	MNT 17	Fletcher, Nicholas	NYK 70
Fithean, Jonathan	SUF 106	Flanders, George	MNT 3	Fletcher, Oliver	ONT 478
Fitsgerald, John	ALB 17	Flanders, George	MNT 17	Fletcher, Robert	NYK 118
Fitsgerald, Patten	HRK 417	Flanders, Henry	MNT 3	Fletcher, Solomon	WSH 253
Fits Givens	WST 155	Flanders, Henry	MNT 17	Fletcher, Thomas	CLN 167
Fitsimmons, Felix	SRA 39	Flanders, Jacob	MNT 11	Fletcher, Thomas	CLN 168
Fitsjerels, Wm	WST 132	Flanders, Jacob	ONT 332	Fletcher, Wm	ALB 89
Fitszsimmons, John	TIO 263	Flanders, Thomas	WSH 229	Fleuri, Peter	NYK 65
Fitz, Lucy	ALB 61	Flanigem, Edward	WSH 208	Flewman, Jacob	MNT 28
Fitz, Nathan	ALB 58	Flann, James	NYK 151	Flewwellin, Francis	DUT 23
Fitz, Nathaniel	NYK 60	Flannagan, Dennis	NYK 91	Flewwellin, John	DUT 27
Fitzburn, Anna	NYK 21	Flannagan, Owen	NYK 55	Flewwellin, Ogden	ULS 187
Fitzerald, Ebenezer	NYK 18	Flansborough, Andw	ALB 98	Flewwelling, Robert	WST 124
Fitzgerald, Edmund	NYK 80	Flansborough, Daniel	ALB 98	Flewwelling, Robert	WST 130
Fitzgerald, Edward	ORN 310	Flansborough, David	ALB 98	Flewwelling, Robert Junr	WST 124
Fitz Gerald, Elizabeth	ORN 395	Flansborough, John	ALB 98	Fliechman, Abraham	NYK 51
Fitz Gerald, Jacob	DUT 128	Flansborough, Mary	ALB 98	Flin, James	NYK 151
Fitz Gerald, Jeremiah	ORN 337	Flansborough, Matthias	ALB 56	Flin, William	CHN 922
Fitzgerald, John	NYK 112	Flansborough, Peter	ALB 97	Fling, Abrm	OTS 7
Fitz Gerald, John	ORN 381	Flansborough, Richd	ALB 41	Flinn, Elizabeth	NYK 16
Fitzgerald, Robert	ORN 297	Flansborough, Wm	ALB 76	Flinn, James	NYK 64
Fitz Gerald, William	ORN 381	Flansburgh, Anthony	MNT 11	Flinn, James	NYK 130
Fitz Gerald, William	ORN 384	Flansburgh, Mathew	MNT 69	Flinn, John	CAY 636
Fitzgereld, Edmond	SRA 8	Flansburgh, William	WSH 238	Flinn, John	NYK 62
Fitzpartrick, Edward	NYK 100	Flashner, John F.	OND 215	Flinn, John	NYK 118
Fitz Partrick, James	NYK 89	Flatt, James	NYK 137	Flinn, Lewis D.	NYK 32
Fitz Partrick, James	NYK 128	Flatt, John	NYK 131	Flinn, Michael	NYK 130
Fitzpartrick, John	NYK 110	Flatt, Phenes	ALB 13	Flinn, Patrick	CHN 836
Fitz Partrick, Thomas	NYK 139	Flavill, Bartle	MNT 119	Flinn, Thomas	NYK 74
Fitz Randolph, David	NYK 121	Fleet, Alexander	SUF 84	Flint, Adam H.	MNT 40
Fitz Randolph, Martha	NYK 118	Fleet, Arnold	QNS 80	Flint, Alexander	MNT 49
Fitz Simmons, David	DUT 44	Fleet, Arnold	SUF 81	Flint, Asa	MNT 96
Fitzwater, George	ONT 462	Fleet, David	SUF 88	Flint, Asher	OND 202
Fix, John	WST 145	Fleet, Deborah	SUF 84	Flint, Charles	NYK 82
Fl___, Nicholas Junr	MNT 18	Fleet, Gilbert	SUF 84	Flint, David	COL 211
Flack, James	WSH 289	Fleet, Jeremiah	SUF 94	Flint, Edward	DEL 290
Flack, James 2d	WSH 289	Fleet, Jessee	QNS 79	Flint, Elisha	ALB 114
Flack, John	WSH 289	Fleet, John	QNS 80	Flint, Elisha	OTS 5
Flack, Richard	WSH 289	Fleet, Melancton	SUF 88	Flint, Frederick	COL 238
Flag, John C.	NYK 108	Fleet, Ranselear	SUF 84	Flint, How	OTS 7
Flagan, Charles	NYK 27	Fleet, Samuel	SUF 85	Flint, Jabez	DUT 139
Flageler, Abraham	DUT 121	Fleet, imon	NYK 98	Flint, Jacob	NYK 141
Flageler, John	DUT 6	Fleet, Stephen	SUF 85	Flint, Jacob	OTS 42
Flageler, John	ULS 211	Fleet, Thomas	SUF 80	Flint, James	COL 180
Flageler, Paul	DUT 42	Fleet, Thomas	SUF 85	Flint, John M.	COL 205
Flageler, Peter	DUT 117	Fleet, Thomas	SUF 88	Flint, John O.	MNT 40
Flageler, Phillip Junr	DUT 16	Fleet, Thomas Junr	SUF 88	Flint, Joseph	OTS 42
Flageler, Phillip Senr	DUT 16	Fleming, Andries	ALB 117	Flint, Joseph Junr	OTS 42
Flageler, Richard	DUT 16	Fleming, Benoni	ESS 293	Flint, Luther	OTS 42
Flageler, Simon	DUT 117	Fleming, George	ORN 392	Flint, Richard	COL 205
Flageler, Solomon	DUT 121	Fleming, James	KNG 10	Flint, R ber	MNT 41
Flageler, Thomas	DUT 14	Fleming, James	ONT 382	Flint, Robert A.	OTS 4
Flageler, Zachariah	DUT 16	Fleming, Ma y	CAY 532	Flint, Thos	OTS 42
Flageler, Zachariah	DUT 24	Fleming, Nelly	DUT 52	Flint, Thos	OTS 42
Flageler, Zachariah	DUT 121	Fleming, Peter	WST 141	Flint, William	COL 205
Flagg, Bazaleel	ESS 317	Fle[ming?], Thomas W.	ONT 420	Flint, Zacheus	OTS 39
Flagg, Elijah	OND 223	Flemming, Blair	NYK 69	Flirt, ..ber	MNT 50
Flagg, Isaac	ESS 292	Flemming, George	ALB 137	Flitcher, Conrad	SCH 163
Flagg, John	ALB 56	Flemming, James	NYK 22	Flitcher, Conrad	SCH 168
Flagg, John H.	ALB 59	Flemming, James	NYK 97	Flocher, John	NYK 141
Flagg, Joseph	ALB 57	Flemming, James	WSH 191	Flock, Henry	NYK 146
Flagg, Peter	HRK 469	Flemming, Joseph	CAY 698	Flock, John	NYK 146
Flagler, Barton	COL 262	Flemming, Malcom	CAY 574	Flood, Alexander	ORN 391
Flagler, John	WSH 255	Flemming, Margaret	NYK 66	Flood, John	NYK 116
Flagler, Philip	RNS 85	Flemming, Pierre	NYK 56	Floot, David	SRA 50
Flamburgh, John	SRA 35	Flemming, Thomas	WSH 217	Florence, Abraham	ORN 393
Flamburgh, Nicholas	SRA 35	Flesh, John George	ORN 388	Florence, Abraham	WST 119
Flanagan, Dorcus	NYK 20	Fletcher, Benjn	CHN 936	Florence, Gideon	ORN 390
Flanagan, Christopher	NYK 36	Fletcher, Benjamin	SRA 4	Florence, John	ORN 388
Flanagen, Charles	NYK 153	Fletcher, Cotton	CAY 522	Florence, Peter	WST 121
Flander, John	MNT 20	Fletcher, George	NYK 56	Florentine, Thomas	NYK 111

Flory, Benjamin	MNT 56	Follet, Robert	DEL 267	Foot, Aron	MNT 82
Flotter, Samuel	CLN 167	Follet, Thaddeus	WST 126	Foot, Asa	ALB 134
Flower, Harmon	QNS 75	Follett, Francis	NYK 51	Foot, Bernice	OTS 34
Flower, John	QNS 75	Follett, John	RNS 50	Foot, Brunson	OND 202
Flower, Therral	CHN 926	Follett, William	RNS 50	Foot, Daniel	CAY 628
Flower, Timothy	QNS 75	Follett, Wm Junr	RNS 50	Foot, Danl	CHN 792
Flower, Uthrel(?)	CHN 960	Follier, John	ALB 121	Foot, Daniel	DEL 269
Flower, Warren	HRK 525	Follin, Augustus	NYK 117	Foot, Ebenezer R.	OND 204
Flower, William	QNS 75	Follock, Isaac	GRN 348	Foot, Elsha	MNT 82
Flowers, Aboill	CLN 159	Follot, Ezeke_	OTS 26	Foot, Epapheodilus	CHN 864
Flowers, Benjamin	DUT 128	Follott, Frederick	ONT 448	Foot, Hazard a Black	NYK 113
Flowers, Elijah	ONT 432	Folsom, Araspes	WSH 249	Foot, Heli	OND 197
Flowers, Gabriel	OND 168	Folsom, John	WSH 249	Foot, Hyol	SRA 6
Flowers, Thomas	QNS 76	Folter, Allen	WSH 253	Foot, Ira	OND 201
Flowrs, John	NYK 96	Folton, Samuel	GRN 357	Foot, Isaac	CHN 768
Floyd, David R.	QNS 78	Folts, Conrad	HRK 418	Foot, Isaac	CHN 802
Floyd, John	SUF 91	Folts, Conrad	HRK 445	Foot, Isaac	GRN 351
Floyd, Nicolls	SUF 65	Folts, George	HRK 436	Foot, Jacob	NYK 123
Floyd, Richd	SUF 67	Folts, Jacob	HRK 417	Foot, James	ALB 40
Floyd, Thomas	SUF 91	Folts, Jacob	HRK 436	Foot, Jarus	OND 202
Floyd, William	ESS 311	Folts, Jost	HRK 445	Foot, John	CHN 794
Floyd, Wm	SUF 65	Folts, Melcher	HRK 435	Foot, John	COL 219
Fluellan, Jesse	ONT 442	Folts, Melcher	HRK 445	Foot, John	NYK 15
Flunno, John	RNS 69	Folts, Peter	HRK 459	Foot, Joseph	COL 189
Fluskey, John	HRK 434	Folts, Warner	HRK 417	Foot, Joseph	NYK 20
Flusky, James	OND 196	Fonda, Abraham	NYK 150	Foot, Joseph	SRA 39
Flurrence, Abraham	WST 148	Fonda, Abraham J.	COL 229	Foot, Josiah W.	CHN 984
Flyn, Charles	DEL 268	Fonda, Abraham L.	COL 193	Foot, Lewis	SRA 20
Flynn, ...n	SRA 8	Fonda, Adam	MNT 68	Foot, Luther	OND 202
Flynn, Daniel	DUT 168	Fonda, Cornelius	COL 197	Foot, Mallica	WST 162
Flynn, Mary	DUT 145	Fonda, Cornelius	MNT 117	Foot, Miles	SCH 141
Foa, Partrick,	NYK 102	Fonda, Cornelus	SRA 12	Foot, Moses	OND 202
Foalks, John	COL 255	Fonda, Daniel	RNS 84	Foot, Oleton C.	OTS 5
Foard, Barthosomew	GRN 348	Fonda, David	ALB 149	Foot, Peter	RCK 105
Fobes, Christian	ULS 183	Fonda, David	MNT 72	Foot, Peter	SRA 13
Fod, Samuel a Black	NYK 143	Fonda, David	MNT 74	Foot, Reuben	SCH 141
Fodner, Prague	MNT 97	Fonda, Douw	ALB 49	Foot, Ruben	CHN 864
Foe, Phillip	NYK 106	Fonda, Dow	NYK 59	Foot, Samuel	CHN 804
Fogerly, Barthw	ALB 104	Fonda, Dowe	COL 253	Foot, Samuel	COL 217
Foght, John M.	ORN 373	Fonda, Dowed	SRA 13	Foot, Stephen	OND 224
Fogison, Francis	GRN 330	Fonda, Edward	RNS 21	Foot, Stilman	OND 224
Foiullalle, Louis	NYK 72	Fonda, Elsia	MNT 50	Foot, Timothy	MNT 117
Foland, Henry	RNS 63	Fonda, Henderick H.	ALB 50	Foot, Zeruiah	COL 185
Folandt, George	COL 261	Fonda, Hendrica	ALB 49	Foote, Allen	TIO 229
Folandt, Henry	COL 265	Fonda, Henry	MNT 68	Foote, Ba_ley	DEL 288
Folandt, Phillip	COL 264	Fonda, Herman	ALB 49	Foote, David	TIO 221
Folant, Zachariah	COL 230	Fonda, Isaac D. B.	COL 229	Foote, Ebenezer	DEL 290
Folconer, Archibald	NYK 55	Fonda, Isaac J.	ALB 50	Foote, George	DEL 288
Foler, Cosper	MNT 57	Fonda, Jacob	ALB 2A	Foote, Isaac	TIO 232
Foley, Mary Ann	NYK 74	Fonda, James	ALB 148	Foote, John	CAY 612
Folger, Aaron	WSH 210	Fonda, Jane	MNT 68	Foote, Justin	ORN 279
Folger, Abisha	COL 250	Fonda, Jeremiah	COL 194	Foote, Simon	TIO 229
Folger, Benjamin	COL 247	Fonda, John	ALB 50	Foote, William	WSH 285
Folger, Benjamin S.	RNS 91	Fonda, John Junr	ALB 145	Foott, Thomas	NYK 71
Folger, Daniel	WSH 235	Fonda, John Junr	RNS 11	Foqurt, John L.	CLN 164
Folger, Deborah	COL 248	Fonda, John A.	COL 229	Forbe., Peter	MNT 72
Folger, Elisha	WSH 210	Fonda, John J.	RNS 11	Forbe, John C.	ALB 70
Folger, Mathew	COL 251	Fonda, Lawrence	COL 193	Forbes, Abraham	OND 166
Folger, Nathan	COL 251	Fonda, Peter	RNS 84	Forbes, Abraham G.	NYK 66
Folger, Reuben	COL 247	Fonda, Sarah	ALB 147	Forbes, Alexander	NYK 110
Folger, Robert	COL 247	Fonda, Walter	RNS 11	Forbes, Alexander	SRA 41
Folger, Thomas	WSH 234	Fonda, Widow	MNT 74	Forbes, Asa	ESS 298
Folinsbe, George	RNS 58	Fonda, William	ALB 130	Forbes, Christopher	NYK 144
Foliott, Elisha	OND 218	Fonday, Dow	SRA 48	Forbes, Colin Van	
Folk, John	ORN 383	Fonday, Elsie	ALB 145	Gelder	NYK 21
Folk, John	QNS 62	Fonday, Isaac D.	SRA 48	Forbes, Daniel	NYK 92
Folkinson, Caleb	TIO 258	Fondebergh, Cornels	HRK 492	Forbes, Elisha	TIO 210
Folkner, John	WSH 192	Fondey, Jacob G.	ALB 5	Forbes, Flora	NYK 43
Follensbee, James	RNS 64	Fondey, Jellis A.	ALB 5	Forbes, Gitty	NYK 40
Follensbee, Jer[ome?]	RNS 64	Fondey, Jellis J.	ALB 5	Forbes, Jacob	MNT 16
Foller, Henry	MNT 34	Fones, John	NYK 98	Forbes, James	NYK 101
Follerton, James	NYK 73	Fontain, Benjn	RNS 48	Forbes, John	NYK 19
Follet, Francis	ALB 129	Fontaine, Roche	ORN 281	Forbes, John G.	ONN 170
Follet, James	DEL 280	Fontbonne, Mary Vin-		Forbes, Joseph	OND 166
Follet, John	RNS 29	cent Frances	NYK 141	Forbes, Joseph Junr	OND 166
Follet, John	SRA 26	Fooley see Tooley		Forbes, Luke	CAY 672
Follet, Joseph	RNS 29	Foot, Adonijah	WSH 278	Forbes, Nathaniel	ALB 127

Name	Loc	No.
Forbes, Ralph B.	NYK	20
Forbes, Thomas	NYK	146
Forbes, Verner	MNT	52
Forbes, William	NYK	92
Forbes, William A.	NYK	64
Forbes, William G.	NYK	21
Forbish, Peter	MNT	59
Forbos, Isaac	NYK	51
Forbs, Elijah	WSH	216
Forbs, John	ONT	418
Forbus, John	DUT	68
Forbus, Martha	NYK	37
Forbus, Peter	NYK	112
Forbus, Sarah a Black	NYK	75
Forbus, Winslow	DUT	106
Forbush, Jacob P.	MNT	22
Forbush, John	QNS	66
Forbush, John	WSH	301
Forbush, Nicholas	MNT	21
Force, Baldin	NYK	103
Force, Daniel	DUT	58
Force, Joseph	WSH	211
Force, Munson	NYK	102
Force, Sylvester	DUT	58
Force, William	NYK	102
Ford, Abel	ALB	86
Ford, Abel	RNS	75
Ford, Abijah	HRK	590
Ford, Abijah	MNT	125
Ford, Adden Iger	GRN	333
Ford, Amasa	RNS	91
Ford, Ansyl	DEL	282
Ford, Bela	ALB	37
Ford, Benjamin	HRK	521
Ford, Benjamin	NYK	128
Ford, Benjamin	RNS	9
Ford, Benoni	HRK	520
Ford, Charles	WSH	192
Ford, David	WST	154
Ford, David	WST	161
Ford, Eliakem	NYK	80
Ford, Elijah	GRN	335
Ford, Elijah	MNT	125
Ford, Elisha	ALB	94
Ford, Ephraim	DUT	140
Ford, Esther	SRA	46
Ford, George	ONT	372
Ford, Hezekiah	OND	183
Ford, Hubbard	OND	159
Ford, Jacob	COL	183
Ford, Jacob	MNT	30
Ford, Jacob	OTS	26
Ford, James	MNT	91
Ford, James	TIO	222
Ford, Jesse	COL	202
Ford, Joel	GRN	335
Ford, John	DUT	79
Ford, John	MNT	28
Ford, John	NYK	62
Ford, John	NYK	120
Ford, John	OTS	44
Ford, John	RNS	102
Ford, John	SRA	46
Ford, John	SCH	117
Ford, John	STB	202
Ford, John G.	OTS	6
Ford, Johnathan	GRN	335
Ford, Jonathan	COL	202
Ford, Jonathan	RNS	9
Ford, Joseph	QNS	64
Ford, Lewis	NYK	99
Ford, Lewis	NYK	126
Ford, Lifelet	GRN	336
Ford, Mathew	NYK	57
Ford, Moses	OTS	26
Ford, Nathan	OND	224
Ford, Nathanl	CHN	896
Ford, Nathaniel	MNT	28
Ford, Nathaniel	SRA	6
Ford, Nathaniel Junr	MNT	28
Ford, Nehemh	OTS	26
Ford, Noah	OTS	26
Ford, Patrick	ORN	389
Ford, Patty	NYK	49
Ford, Peter	MNT	30
Ford, Phillis	WST	148
Ford, Reuben	ALB	89
Ford, Richard	ALB	30
Ford, Sambil	SRA	19
Ford, Stephen	MNT	122
Ford, Stephen	OND	158
Ford, Sylvester	ALB	80
Ford, Timothy	SRA	44
Ford, William	ALB	37
Ford, William	OND	222
Ford, William E.	SRA	44
Ford, Zebulon	SRA	39
Forde, Gitty	NYK	79
Fordham, Abraham	SUF	96
Fordham, Daniel	SUF	104
Fordham, Ephraim	SUF	104
Fordham, George	ULS	254
Fordham, James	SUF	97
Fordham, James	SUF	102
Fordham, Jerrus	SUF	102
Fordham, John	SUF	104
Fordham, John N.	SUF	102
Fordham, Nathan	SUF	102
Fordham, Nathaniel	SUF	102
Fordham, Phineas	SUF	69
Fordham, Saml	SUF	104
Fordham, Steohen	SUF	95
Fordham, Thadeus	SUF	107
Fordman, Silas	GRN	343
Fordyce, Benjamin	CAY	642
Foredom, Taylor	RNS	81
Foreman, Miles	TIO	234
Forest, Abijah	WSH	283
Forest, Betsey a Black	NYK	67
Forest, Charles	NYK	53
Forest, David	NYK	101
Forest, James	NYK	53
Foresyth, Oliver	OTS	39
Forfener, William	GRN	336
Forgarthy, Betty	NYK	53
Forgason, Dunscum	SRA	29
Forgason, Elijah	RNS	10
Forgason, Israel	RNS	58
Forgason, Jeremiah	RNS	58
Forgason, Jeremiah Junr	RNS	58
Forgason, Leonard	RNS	12
Forgus, James a mulatto	NYK	27
Forguson, Enos	MNT	99
Forguson, James	WST	155
Forguson, Joel	WST	156
Forguson, John	WSH	192
Forguson, John	WST	132
Forguson, Millison	WST	142
Forguson, Reuben	WST	135
Forguson, Reuben	WST	140
Forguson, Thomas	WST	133
Forham, George	NYK	136
Forington, Benjamin	NYK	103
Forks, Bartholemew	MNT	52
Forman, Aaron	DUT	59
Forman, Abraham	DUT	24
Forman, Enoch	WSH	269
Forman, George	NYK	29
Forman, George	NYK	132
Forman, Henry	NYK	86
Forman, Isaac	DUT	60
Forman, Isaac	ULS	184
Forman, John	ULS	233
Forman, John	WSH	243
Forman, Jonathan	CHN	966
Forman, Joseph	DUT	21
Forman, Josiah	ULS	238
Forman, Lydia	DUT	60
Forman, Nathan	ORN	370
Forman, Nouell	ULS	244
Forman, Paul	DUT	109
Forman, Samuel	CHN	772
Forman, Samuel	DUT	111
Forman, Samuel S.	CHN	966
Forman, Stephen	WST	156
Forman, Thomas Junr	WST	140
Forman, William	ALB	130
Formon, Chaveneau	NYK	142
Formon, Lewis	NYK	122
Forniquet, Louis	NYK	39
Forrest, James	NYK	125
Forrest, John	ALB	124
Forrest, Loes	WSH	226
Forrest, Robert	NYK	81
Forrester, Widow	SCH	121
Forris, Ezra	SRA	12
Forry, Abner	RNS	26
Forsha, James	NYK	128
Forshell, John	NYK	144
Forshure, John	RCK	109
Forshure, John Junr	RCK	110
Forshure, Peter	RCK	110
Forsith, James	WST	156
Forsithe, Alexander	ALB	140
Forster, Sheffield	ULS	218
Forsyth, Jacob	NYK	16
Forsyth, John	NYK	30
Forsythe, Alexander	ONT	378
Forsythe, John	ONT	312
Forsythe, William	HRK	564
Forsythe, William	ULS	253
Fort, Abraham	DUT	70
Fort, Abraham J.	WSH	198
Fort, Charles	HRK	567
Fort, Costleman	MNT	73
Fort, Hannah	RNS	95
Fort, Isaac	RNS	90
Fort, Jacob	WSH	198
Fort, John	ALB	6
Fort, John	ALB	51
Fort, John	RNS	82
Fort, John	WSH	198
Fort, John J.	RNS	34
Fort, Lewis	WSH	198
Fort, Nicholas	ALB	51
Fort, Peter	RNS	34
Fort, Peter	SRA	41
Fort, Rhody	WSH	198
Fort, Richard	ALB	53
Fort, Sibrian	SRA	41
Fort, Thomas W.	ALB	146
Fortt, Daniel	SRA	3
Fortt, Nicholas	SRA	3
Fortune, Enoch	OND	201
Fortune, Glode	NYK	45
Fortune, John a Black	NYK	80
Fortune, Peter	RCK	99
Fortune, Samuel	HRK	451
Fortune, William	NYK	94
Forward, Jesse	RNS	106
Forwett, Mathew	NYK	121
Fosbrook, William	NYK	141
Fosburgh, Abraham	MNT	78
Fosburgh, John	WSH	213
Fosbury, Richard	TIO	230
Fosbury, Thomas	SCH	142
Fosdick, Edward	CHN	982
Fosdick, John	CHN	982
Fosdick, Lawrence	WSH	279

Fosdick, Morris	QNS 73	Foster, Israel	OTS 11
Fosdick, Nathaniel	ORN 278	Foster, Jabez	OND 174
Fosdick, Nathen	WSH 265	Foster, Jacob	ALB 42
Fosdick, Samuel	GRN 352	Foster, Jacob	QNS 69
Fosdick, Silas	DUT 113	Foster, James	ALB 42
Fosdick, Solomon	ORN 279	Foster, James	ALB 113
Fosdick, Willeam	WSH 267	Foster, James	DUT 175
Fosdick, William	WSH 290	Foster, James	ONN 171
Fosgate, Ezekiel	DUT 24	Foster, James	ORN 361
Fosget, Belia	WSH 229	Foster, James	QNS 66
Fosh, Christian	MNT 30	Foster, James	RNS 21
Foshay, David	WST 167	Foster, James	WSH 292
Foshay, James	WST 167	Foster, James	WST 117
Foshay, John	WST 162	Foster, James	WST 128
Foshay, John	WST 163	Foster, James Junr	DUT 175
Foshay, John Hatter	WST 167	Foster, Jared	OTS 11
Foshay, John	WST 167	Foster, Jedediah	ONT 344
Foshay, John Junr	WST 167	Foster, Jesse	ONN 134
Foshay, Mathew	WST 167	Foster, Joel	ONT 348
Foshay, William	WST 167	Foster, John	CHN 944
Foshe, Amiable	OND 223	Foster, John	DUT 134
Foshee, James	NYK 145	Foster, John	GRN 357
Fosket, James	OND 168	Foster, John	HRK 521
Foskett, William	NYK 131	Foster, John	NYK 136
Fosmire, John Junr	COL 262	Foster, John	NYK 147
Foss, Catherine	NYK 53	Foster, John	OTS 2
Foss, George	NYK 104	Foster, John	QNS 69
Fossett, George	CAY 562	Foster, John	QNS 73
Fost, Francis	SCH 163	Foster, John	QNS 75
Fost, John	GRN 350	Foster, John	SUF 81
Foster, ___rus	GRN 328	Foster, John	SUF 102
Foster, Aaron	CHN 942	Foster, John	SUF 107
Foster, Abel	WSH 285	Foster, John	ULS 265
Foster, Abner	RNS 90	Foster, John	WSH 292
Foster, Abraham	CAY 718	Foster, John	WST 117
Foster, Abraham	CAY 718	Foster, John Junr	WST 117
Foster, Abraham	HRK 521	Foster, Jonah	SRA 22
Foster, Abraham	ONT 482	Foster, Jonathan	ONN 169
Foster, Abraham	SUF 102	Foster, Jonathan	ONT 332
Foster, Abraham	WSH 202	Foster, Joseph	CHN 858
Foster, Abraham	WSH 202	Foster, Joseph	DUT 89
Foster, Absalom	CAY 568	Foster, Joseph	NYK 59
Foster, Agnes	DUT 151	Foster, Joseph	OND 196
Foster, Albert	ORN 358	Foster, Joseph	WSH 268
Foster, Ambrose	OTS 11	Foster, Josiah	SUF 95
Foster, Andrew	NYK 40	Foster, Josiah Junr	SUF 97
Foster, Asa	ALB 110	Foster, Justus	SUF 96
Foster, Benjm	ALB 115	Foster, Lebbeus	ONN 171
Foster, Benjamin	GRN 325	Foster, Lenard	CHN 952
Foster, Benjamin	SUF 102	Foster, Lydia	DUT 167
Foster, Caleb	ALB 113	Foster, Mary	NYK 126
Foster, Charity	DUT 167	Foster, Mary	NYK 145
Foster, Charles	NYK 127	Foster, Mathew	SUF 98
Foster, Chillingworth	DUT 45	Foster, Mermaduke	WST 167
Foster, Christopher	SUF 97	Foster, Michael	WST 117
Foster, Coonrod	CAY 724	Foster, Nathan	CHN 856
Foster, Cyrus	ONT 350	Foster, Nathan	OTS 2
Foster, Daniel	ONT 446	Foster, Nathaniel	KNG 9
Foster, David	CAY 624	Foster, Nathaniel	MNT 123
Foster, David	DEL 267	Foster, Nathaniel	ONN 133
Foster, David	HRK 521	Foster, Nathaniel	QNS 64
Foster, David	SRA 31	Foster, Oliver	ALB 15
Foster, David	SUF 98	Foster, Parlee	COL 185
Foster, David H.	ONT 348	Foster, Peter	SCH 143
Foster, Denniston	ONT 386	Foster, Peter	SCH 149
Foster, Edmund	DUT 167	Foster, Peter	SUF 102
Foster, Edward	ALB 92	Foster, Prudence	OND 193
Foster, Elijah	CHN 800	Foster, Raymond R.	HRK 442
Foster, Elisha	HRK 552	Foster, Richard	SUF 96
Foster, Elizabeth	NYK 147	Foster, Richard	WSH 294
Foster, Elnathan	ORN 280	Foster, Robert	DUT 72
Foster, Emerson	SUF 77	Foster, Robert	WST 153
Foster, Erastus	SRA 32	Foster, Rufus	SUF 95
Foster, Erastus	SRA 33	Foster, Samuel	CAY 718
Foster, Gilbert	DUT 178	Foster, Samuel	CAY 718
Foster, Hackeliah	SRA 31	Foster, Samuel	DUT 12
Foster, Henry	NYK 78	Foster, Samuel	DUT 122

Foster, Samuel	DUT 136
Foster, Samuel	GRN 325
Foster, Samuel	OND 220
Foster, Saml	OTS 46
Foster, Samuel	WSH 294
Foster, Sarah	DUT 122
Foster, Sarah	WSH 249
Foster, Seth	DUT 90
Foster, Silas	SRA 31
Foster, Simeon	RNS 100
Foster, Stephen	CHN 740
Foster, Stephen	SUF 98
Foster, Thomas	CHN 830
Foster, .homas	MNT 84
Foster, Thomas	ONN 132
Foster, Thos	OTS 33
Foster, Thomas	RNS 93
Foster, Timothy	HRK 537
Foster, Vincent	SRA 41
Foster, Whitehead	SUF 102
Foster, Whitman	SUF 96
Foster, William	ESS 297
Foster, William	ONT 332
Foster, William	ORN 316
Foster, William	QNS 68
Foster, William	SUF 98
Foster, William	WSH 285
Fothard, Isaac	ALB 5
Fotheringham, Thomas	NYK 54
Fott, James	ALB 139
Fought, Jacob	NYK 69
Fougier, Emenuel	NYK 110
Fouhr, John	COL 190
Fouler, William	SCH 148
Foulk, Abraham	NYK 88
Foulk, Arnout	ULS 223
Foulk, Jacob	ULS 223
Foulk, Johannis	ULS 223
Foulk, Jonas	ULS 221
Foulk, Wilhelmus	ULS 222
Foulkner, James	STB 202
Foulton, John	ONT 506
Fountain, Anthony	RCH 90
Fountain, Anthony	RCH 91
Fountain, Anthony	RCH 92
Fountain, Cornelius	RCH 90
Fountain, Elijah	NYK 55
Fountain, Ezra	WST 137
Fountain, Garret	NYK 15
Fountain, James	WST 137
Fountain, Margaret	NYK 55
Fountain, Moses	CAY 608
Fountain, Peter	RCH 92
Fountain, Vincent	RCH 91
Fourcroy, Charles	NYK 115
Fourgason, Farrington	SRA 6
Fournier, Stephen	NYK 87
Fousha, Reuben	ALB 119
Fow, John	GRN 333
Fo[wellellet?], Dupont	NYK 79
Fowle, Isaac	WSH 190
Fowler, Abel	DUT 146
Fowler, Abel	WSH 190
Fowler, Abel Junr	WSH 190
Fowler, Abijah	NYK 123
Fowler, Abijah	WST 158
Fowler, Abner	ESS 303
Fowler, Abraham	WST 147
Fowler, Abraham	WST 150
Fowler, Alexander	WST 149
Fowler, Alexander Junr	WST 148
Fowler, Amon	WSH 199
Fowler, Amon	WST 141
Fowler, Amos	SRA 35
Fowler, Andrew	ULS 259
Fowler, Ann	DUT 22
Fowler, Anna	NYK 73

Fowler, Anson S.	OND	198	Fowler, Joseph	SRA	9	Fox, Anthony	DUT	60
Fowler, Anthoney	WST	163	Fowler, Joshua	ULS	267	Fox, Asa	SRA	13
Fowler, Augustus	ALB	5	Fowler, Joshua	WST	121	Fox, Caty	RCK	106
Fowler, Benjamin	ALB	63	Fowler, Joshua	WST	167	Fox, Christopher	HRK	469
Fowler, Benjamin	QNS	65	Fowler, Josiah	WST	147	Fox, Christopher	MNT	3
Fowler, Benjamin	WST	147	Fowler, Justus	ONN	136	Fox, Christopher C.	MNT	17
Fowler, Benjamine	GRN	334	Fowler, Levi	OND	213	Fox, Christopher W.	MNT	1
Fowler, Caleb	DUT	177	Fowler, Levi	ONN	136	Fox, Christopher W.	MNT	2
Fowler, Caleb	SRA	9	Fowler, Lewis	ALB	77	Fox, Consider	MNT	90
Fowler, Caleb Junr	DUT	179	Fowler, Lott	CAY	632	Fox, Daniel	MNT	2
Fowler, Daniel	NYK	87	Fowler, Major	DUT	178	Fox, Daniel	OND	215
Fowler, David	DUT	67	Fowler, Mark	OTS	46	Fox, Daniel	SCH	150
Fowler, David	NYK	105	Fowler, Mary	WST	149	Fox, Daniel C.	MNT	17
Fowler, David	NYK	112	Fowler, Moses	DUT	91	Fox, David	ALB	91
Fowler, David	ORN	270	Fowler, Moses	DUT	178	Fox, David	MNT	20
Fowler, Deleware	COL	258	Fowler, Moses	WST	149	Fox, David	ONN	175
Fowler, Drake	NYK	142	Fowler, Moses	WST	167	Fox, Eli	WSH	212
Fowler, Duncan	QNS	71	Fowler, Newberry	WST	132	Fox, Elisha	COL	243
Fowler, Edmund	DUT	19	Fowler, Oliver	DUT	130	Fox, Elizabeth	HRK	409
Fowler, Elijah	ULS	267	Fowler, Oliver	KNG	7	Fox, Ephraim	OTS	14
Fowler, Eliphalet	ONN	136	Fowler, Pexill	NYK	92	Fox, Gelbert	NYK	88
Fowler, Elizabeth	NYK	132	Fowler, Pexsel	NYK	58	Fox, George	NYK	34
Fowler, Elizabeth	ORN	277	Fowler, Phalix	QNS	73	Fox, Hari[ot?]	NYK	58
Fowler, Felix	QNS	75	Fowler, Phe_	CHN	960	Fox, Hedman	WST	115
Fowler, Frederick	NYK	95	Fowler, Philemon	WST	148	Fox, Hendrick	RNS	59
Fowler, Gabriel	ULS	259	Fowler, Philo	OND	186	Fox, Heziah	ONT	364
Fowler, George	NYK	71	Fowler, Reuben	DUT	25	Fox, Jabez	ONT	314
Fowler, George	ORN	386	Fowler, Richard	DUT	19	Fox, Jacob	MNT	2
Fowler, George	OTS	5	Fowler, Richard	QNS	74	Fox, Jacob	MNT	21
Fowler, George	QNS	73	Fowler, Richard	SUF	98	Fox, Jacob M.	COL	212
Fowler, George	WSH	190	Fowler, Richard	WST	149	Fox, James	NYK	95
Fowler, Gilbert	DUT	111	Fowler, Richardson	NYK	121	Fox, Jedediah	HRK	477
Fowler, Gilbert	NYK	147	Fowler, Samuel	ORN	272	Fox, Jeheal	WSH	212
Fowler, Gilbert	QNS	73	Fowler, Samuel	WSH	189	Fox, Jeremiah	RNS	54
Fowler, Gilbert	RCK	98	Fowler, Sarah	NYK	70	Fox, Jeremiah	WST	127
Fowler, Gilbert	ULS	217	Fowler, Silas	GRN	333	Fox, Jeremiah	WST	155
Fowler, Hannah	WST	122	Fowler, Silas	OND	213	Fox, John	HRK	409
Fowler, Henry	DUT	97	Fowler, Simon	WSH	190	Fox, John	MNT	2
Fowler, Henry	DUT	117	Fowler, Solomon	DUT	91	Fox, John	NYK	148
Fowler, Henry	WST	147	Fowler, Solomon	ULS	267	Fox, John	ORN	301
Fowler, Isaac	NYK	58	Fowler, Solomon	WST	126	Fox, John	OTS	15
Fowler, Isaac	ORN	271	Fowler, Stephen	DUT	178	Fox, John	RNS	74
Fowler, Isaac	WST	122	Fowler, Stephen	ULS	255	Fox, John	WSH	191
Fowler, Isaac Junr	WSH	190	Fowler, Theodosius	WST	149	Fox, John C.	HRK	429
Fowler, Israel	DUT	8	Fowler, Thomas	CHN	820	Fox, Joseph	CAY	674
Fowler, Jabez	WST	146	Fowler, Thomas	OND	199	Fox, Joseph	KNG	9
Fowler, Jacob	DUT	8	Fowler, Thomas	QNS	65	Fox, Joseph	NYK	133
Fowler, James	ULS	267	Fowler, Thomas	QNS	74	Fox, Joseph	ONT	390
Fowler, James	WST	125	Fowler, Thomas	SRA	24	Fox, Joseph	ONT	484
Fowler, James	WST	130	Fowler, Victory L.	CAY	632	Fos, Lemuel	ONN	191
Fowler, James	WST	163	Fowler, Vincent	WST	147	Fox, Levet	WSH	212
Fowler, James Junr	WST	125	Fowler, Walter	WST	159	Fox, Levi	ONN	171
Fowler, James Jr	WST	163	Fowler, William	ALB	149	Fox, Mathew	NYK	143
Fowler, Jedediah	HRK	443	Fowler, William	DUT	8	Fox, Nathan	CHN	928
Fowler, Jeremiah	QNS	75	Fowler, William	DUT	89	Fox, Nathan	SCH	154
Fowler, Jeremiah	SRA	31	Fowler, William	DUT	97	Fox, Nathaniel	RNS	32
Fowler, Jeremiah	WST	111	Fowler, William	DUT	135	Fox, Oliver	COL	218
Fowler, Jesse	WST	122	Fowler, Wm	ONN	163	Fox, Oliver	SRA	59
Fowler, John	COL	258	Fowler, William	QNS	66	Fox, Peter	CAY	674
Fowler, John	DUT	168	Fowler, William	SRA	12	Fox, Peter	HRK	460
Fowler, John	NYK	72	Fowler, William	SUF	96	Fox, Peter	MNT	2
Fowler, John	ONN	136	Fowler, William	ULS	256	Fox, Peter	MNT	32
Fowler, John	ORN	270	Fowler, William	WST	145	Fox, Peter	MNT	38
Fowler, John	ORN	342	Fowler, William Junr	ULS	254	Fox, Peter C.	MNT	20
Fowler, John	ORN	387	Fowler, Woodard	WSH	194	Fox, Peter F.	HRK	409
Fowler, John	QNS	64	Fowler, Woolsey	NYK	71	Fox, Peter G.	MNT	17
Fowler, John	ULS	267	Fowler, Zebulon	SUF	97	Fox, Peter P.	HRK	481
Fowler, John	WST	131	Fowler, Zepheniah	DUT	127	Fox, Pe_er R.	MNT	48
Fowler, John Junr	QNS	64	Fowles, John	NYK	38	Fox, Peter W.	MNT	17
Fowler, Jonathan	ALB	64	Fowlks, John	DUT	161	Fox, Pheneas	CLN	173
Fowler, Jonathan	DUT	168	Fox, Aaron	MNT	44	Fox, Philip	CAY	674
Fowler, Jonathan	SCH	124	Fox, Aaron	WSH	209	Fox, Robert	NYK	30
Fowler, Jonathan	WST	144	Fox, Abraham	CHN	978	Fox, Russel	CHN	904
Fowler, Joseph	ALB	120	Fox, Allen	DEL	284	Fox, Samuel	ONN	175
Fowler, Joseph	COL	258	Fox, Amasa	OTS	54	Fox, Silas	RNS	74
Fowler, Joseph	ESS	323	Fox, Amos	SRA	20	Fox, Thomas	CLN	170
Fowler, Joseph	NYK	123	Fox, Amosa	WSH	212	Fox, Thomas	NYK	82

Name	Loc	Pg	Name	Loc	Pg	Name	Loc	Pg
Fox, Thomas	OTS	46	Francis, Ephraim	ONT	412	Franklin, Walter	QNS	80
Fox, William	HRK	441	Francis, Jobe	GRN	340	Franklin, William	CHN	814
Fox, William	HRK	477	Francis, John	HRK	438	Frankline, Abel	SUF	104
Fox, William	MNT	20	Francis, Lemuel	MNT	97	Frankline, Frederick	SUF	104
Fox, William	OTS	40	Francis, Reubin	ONT	416	Frankline, John	SUF	104
Fox, William	SRA	28	Francis, Richard	CAY	590	Frankline, Walter	SUF	104
Fox, Wm P.	MNT	35	Francis, Richard	HRK	422	Franks, John	ALB	44
Fox, Zebediah	ONT	398	Francis, Roswell	CAY	590	Franks, John	SUF	76
Foxe, William	OND	171	Francis, Samuel	CLN	155	Franks, Nicholas	ALB	140
Foxhole, William a			Francis, Sarah	NYK	51	Franneser, John	MNT	85
mulatto	NYK	42	Francis, Selah	DEL	283	Franscisco, Levi	RNS	48
Foy, John	NYK	108	Francis, Simeon	OND	219	Fransickle, Philip	ALB	22
Fozer, John	NYK	93	Francis, Thomas	DUT	121	Fransickle, Philip	ALB	22
Fra_k, Francis	MNT	25	Francis, Thomas	QNS	70	Fransisco, Abm	RNS	39
Fraanes, Peggy a Black	NYK	71	Francis, Thomas	SRA	35	Fransisco, Cornelius	RNS	45
Fradenburgh, Isaac	SCH	159	Francis, William	ONT	412	Fransisco, George	RNS	37
Fraderick, Abrm	RCK	106	Francisco, ...	MNT	86	Fransisco, Henry	RNS	45
Fraderick, Henry	RCK	109	Francisco, Cornelius	MNT	89	Fransisco, Jeremiah	RNS	37
Fraderick, Isaac	RCK	106	Franciscko, John R.	DEL	276	Fransisco, John	RNS	45
Fraderkirk	RNS	24	Frandenburgh, John	ALB	5	Fransisco, John T.	RNS	88
Fradgley, Thomas	NYK	36	Franicko, Franiss	SRA	11	Frante, Christian	SCH	170
Fraghtenburgh Peter	RNS	19	Fran[ics?], Jacob	SRA	53	Frarry, Justice	SCH	168
Frail, Towl	NYK	118	Frank a free Negro	ALB	140	Frary, Asa	COL	248
Fraileigh, Clement	MNT	40	Frank free Black	COL	234	Frary, Giles	COL	248
Frair, John	RNS	95	Frank, Albert	MNT	110	Frary, John S.	CHN	960
Fraisure, Andrew	SRA	11	Frank, Andrew	MNT	113	Fraser, Adam	DUT	145
Fraitenburg, Peter	SUF	65	Frank, David	WSH	280	Fraser, Andrew	DUT	169
Fralick, John	GRN	326	Frank, Frederick	HRK	428	Fraser, Archd	ALB	137
Fralig, Lewis	DUT	164	Frank, Henry	HRK	429	Fraser, Daniel	NYK	40
Frallrik, Benjamin	CHN	762	Frank, Henry	MNT	105	Fraser, Donald	NYK	41
Frame, Hugh	ULS	255	Frank, Jacob	SCH	123	Fraser, Fernando	DUT	146
Frame, Samuel	ULS	202	Frank, John	HRK	429	Fraser, James	ALB	32
France, Adam	ULS	226	Frank, John H.	HRK	421	Fraser, James	MNT	74
France, Bastian	SCH	161	Frank, John M.	ONN	183	Fraser, John	ALB	137
France, Catharine	ULS	220	Frank, John S.	HRK	428	Fraser, John	SCH	159
France, Christian	ULS	190	Frank, Laerence	HRK	424	Fraser, Simon	NYK	119
France, Cornelius	ULS	223	Frank, Martin	ALB	9	Fraser, Simon	NYK	129
France, Henry	SCH	168	Frank, Nicholas	HRK	428	Fraser, Stephen	SCH	159
France, Jacob	SCH	153	Frank, Peter	ALB	107	Fraser, Stuart	CLN	163
France, Jacob	ULS	228	Frank, Stephen	HRK	429	Fraser, William	ALB	96
France, John	ULS	250	Frank, Timothy	HRK	496	Fraser, William	ALB	135
France, Joseph	ULS	190	Frank, Tothy	SCH	154	Fraser, William	NYK	77
France, Jost	ORN	302	Frankinson, Sylvia	DUT	138	Fraseur, Wm	GRN	332
France, Lawrence	SCH	161	Franklen, David	WSH	305	Fraseure, Robart	GRN	347
France, Philip	ALB	87	Franklin, Abel	CHN	750	Frasier, Agnes	NYK	97
France, Stuffle	SCH	161	Franklin, Abraham	QNS	65	Frasier, Hetty	NYK	88
France, Wilhelmus	ULS	219	Franklin, Amos	DUT	51	Frasier, Nancy	SRA	13
Frances	NYK	152	Franklin, Anthony	QNS	64	Frasier, Robert a		
Frances, Adam a Black	NYK	42	Franklin, Ashel	CHN	758	mulatto	NYK	18
Frances, Cuffy a Black	NYK	152	Franklin, Benjamin	DUT	57	Frasier, Robert	NYK	112
Frances, Dinah	NYK	104	Franklin, Caleb	OTS	34	Frasure, John	WSH	193
Frances, Euphemia	NYK	142	Franklin, Daniel	ORN	323	Frasy, Aaron	SCH	138
Frances, Jacob a Black	NYK	87	Franklin, Ebenezer	RNS	26	Frasy, Ann	SCH	138
Frances, John a Black	NYK	83	Franklin, George	COL	213	Frasy, Benjamin	SCH	138
Frances, John a			Franklin, Geo.	OTS	31	Frate, James	ONN	153
mulatto	NYK	104	Franklin, Gideon	NYK	82	Fratenbery, Robert	RNS	29
Frances, John	NYK	153	Franklin, Gloriana	WST	149	Fratenbery, Wm	RNS	29
Frances, Joseph	NYK	119	Franklin, Henry	NYK	71	Fratenburgh, James	RNS	26
Frances, Joseph	NYK	120	Franklin, James	OTS	45	Fratt, Casper	RNS	90
Frances, Lewis a			Franklin, Jane	RNS	19	Fratts, Willm	SCH	169
mulatto	NYK	110	Franklin, Jehiel	ONT	344	Frautz, John	SCH	169
Frances, Martha	WSH	256	Franklin, John	COL	213	Fraver, Frances	OTS	13
Frances, Pero	NYK	130	Franklin, John	ESS	293	Fraver, Wm	OTS	13
Frances, Thomas	NYK	112	Franklin, John	HRK	574	Fraw, Corbon	MNT	97
Francher, Abm	ALB	84	Franklin, John	NYK	62	Frayer, Abraham	RNS	90
Francher, Elijah	GRN	355	Franklin, John	NYK	77	Frayer, Alexander	COL	210
Francher, Nathaniel	GRN	355	Franklin, John	RNS	30	Frayer, David	COL	242
Francher, Rufus	TIO	228	Franklin, Joshua	SUF	107	Frazee, Isaac	NYK	86
Franchot, Paschal	OTS	22	Franklin, Mary	NYK	70	Frazer, John	ULS	223
Francis	GRN	330	Franklin, Moses	OTS	56	Frazer, Roderick C.	HRK	541
Francis a free Negro	RNS	95	Franklin, Nathaniel	NYK	79	Frazer, Simon	CAY	516
Francis, Aaron	OND	213	Franklin, Noah	CHN	752	Frazer, Thomas	CLN	167
Francis, Cipio a Black	NYK	76	Franklin, Reuben	OND	183	Frazer, Widow	DEL	268
Francis, Daniel	ONT	428	Franklin, Roswell	CAY	650	Frazer, William	ONT	372
Francis, Daniel	QNS	83	Franklin, Samuel	NYK	43	Frazer, William	RNS	94
Francis, David	GRN	342	Franklin, Simeon	GRN	332	Frazier, Daniel	OND	189
Francis, David	OTS	25	Franklin, Thomas ..	NYK	45	Frazier, Duncan	NYK	75

Name	Code	No.	Name	Code	No.	Name	Code	No.
Frazier, George	OND	188	Freeland, Michael	CAY	728	Freeman, Silas	MNT	21
Frazier, Grace	NYK	56	Freeland, Phineas	COL	194	Freeman, Smieth	HRK	501
Frazier, James	CHN	750	Freeland, Simon	CAY	658	Freeman, Solomon	DUT	134
Frazier, James	COL	251	Freelon, Abraham	NYK	30	Freeman, Stephen	WSH	233
Frazier, James	OTS	44	Freelove, Gedeon	MNT	91	Freeman, Vincent	SCH	159
Frazier, John	CHN	936	Freeman see Treeman			Freeman, Wm	OTS	36
Frazier, John	NYK	63	& Trueman			Freer, Daniel Junr	COL	265
Frazier, Josiah	NYK	75	Freeman, Adam	HRK	528	Freer, Jacob	CHN	920
Frazier, Michael	NYK	67	Freeman, Amos	OND	166	Freer, Michael	DEL	275
Frazier, Orris	COL	189	Freeman, Ananeas	WSH	187	Freer, Nathaniel	SRA	57
Frazier, William	NYK	22	Freeman, Andrew	WSH	221	Frehout, Joseph	RNS	88
Frazier, William	OND	189	Freeman, Artello a			Freightenburgh, Abraham	NYK	142
Frazine, Peter	ULS	254	Black	NYK	102	Freigliegt, Jacob	MNT	43
Frazure, James	OTS	6	Freeman, Asa	OND	223	Freindt, Ingle	NYK	124
Fream, John	NYK	86	Freeman, Asa	MNT	112	Freith, Margaret	NYK	90
Frear, Peter	ONN	144	Freeman, Ashbell	COL	263	Freitz, Nicholas	ALB	53
Freary, Festus	OTS	33	Freeman, Asher	CAY	660	Freleigh, John	ALB	143
Freary, Jesse	OTS	33	Freeman, Assa	WSH	275	Freleigh, Wilhelmus	ALB	100
Freborn, David	CHN	934	Freeman, Bradley	OND	208	Freligh, Abraham	DUT	113
Freborn, Gideon	CHN	934	Freeman, Cesar Free			Freligh, Elizabeth	DUT	157
Frecker, John	MNT	19	Black	COL	244	Freligh, Hendrick	ULS	221
Frecketon, Evans	NYK	112	Freeman, Charles	DUT	16	Freligh, Isaac	DUT	113
Fredenburgh, David	WSH	187	Freeman, Cuffey a			Freligh, Michael	ALB	50
Fredereck, Peter	MNT	112	Black	NYK	41	Freligh, Moses	ULS	249
Frederick, Charles	COL	177	Freeman, Cyrenus	RNS	44	Freligh, Peter	DUT	163
Frederick, Charles	NYK	76	Freeman, Daniel	HRK	434	Freligh, Peter B.	DUT	157
Frederick, Christian	ALB	35	Freeman, Daniel	OND	163	Freligh, Phillip	DUT	109
Frederick, Francis	MNT	29	Freeman, Dick	WST	158	Freligh, Samuel	ULS	221
Frederick, Geo:	SCH	168	Freeman, Eli	WSH	268	Freligh, Stephen	DUT	163
Frederick, Henery	NYK	103	Freeman, Elisha	CHN	960	Freman, Joseph	WSH	227
Frederick, Henry	NYK	47	Freeman, Elisha	OTS	41	Freman, Saml	RCK	97
Frederick, Henry	NYK	85	Freeman, Elisha	SCH	159	Freman, Timothy	CHN	942
Frederick, Henry	QNS	68	Freeman, Frederick	CAY	688	French, Abner	CAY	642
Frederick, Henry	RCK	105	Freeman, Gaius	COL	181	French, Asa	MNT	41
Frederick, Henry	RCK	106	Freeman, Gideon	CAY	650	French, Asa L.	NYK	82
Frederick, Jacob	ORN	385	Freeman, Henry a			French, Asher	CHN	782
Frederick, James	NYK	129	mulatto	NYK	22	French, Benjamin	NYK	125
Frederick, John	DUT	109	Freeman, Henry	NYK	67	French, Benjamin	SRA	41
Frederick, John	NYK	114	Freeman, Hezekiah	CAY	696	French, Benjamin	WSH	187
Frederick, John	ULS	236	Freeman, Hezekiah	NYK	127	French, Benjamin	WSH	222
Frederick, John C.	MNT	13	Freeman, Isaac	CAY	696	French, Daniel	OTS	27
Frederick, Martin	ALB	60	Freeman, Isaac	HRK	437	French, David	OTS	26
Frederick, Michael	ALB	60	Freeman, Isaac	MNT	35	French, David	WSH	196
Frederick, Michael	SCH	168	Freeman, James	SRA	4	French, David	WSH	287
Frederick, Michael Jr	ALB	60	Freeman, James	SRA	28	French, David Junr	OTS	26
Frederick, Peter	MNT	61	Freeman, James	SRA	28	French, Ebeneser	MNT	115
Frederick, Peter	QNS	68	Freeman, Jedediah	OND	214	French, Ebenezer	ONT	394
Frederick, Peter	ULS	234	Freeman, John	ALB	15	French, Ebenezer	SRA	21
Frederick, Philip	MNT	112	Freeman, John	CAY	520	French, Effee	NYK	31
Frederick, Prince	ORN	321	Freeman, John	DUT	134	French, Elijah J.	SRA	26
Frederick, Tebalt	ALB	61	Freeman, John	OTS	43	French, Enos	ONT	394
Frederick, William	QNS	68	Freeman, John	SRA	40	French, Ezara	WSH	187
Fredericus, Adam	NYK	50	Freeman, Jonathan	DEL	276	French, Henry	ESS	306
Free, Deen	ULS	250	Freeman, Jonathan	HRK	550	French, Henry	MNT	102
Free, Ezekiel	DUT	61	Freeman, Jonathan	ORN	397	French, Ja[bez?]	ONT	452
Free, Ezekiel	ULS	243	Freeman, Joseph	MNT	12	French, James	ONN	133
Free, Hannah	DUT	152	Freeman, Joseph	OND	223	French, James	OTS	28
Free, Isaac	WST	149	Freeman, Judith a			French, Jasper	CHN	808
Free, Jacob	ORN	313	mulatto	NYK	17	French, Jeremiah	DEL	282
Free, John	DUT	116	Freeman, Junich	CHN	864	French, Jeremiah	RNS	83
Free, Rhoda	ORN	359	Freeman, Moses	HRK	507	French, Jeremi.h	TIO	236
Freeborn, Robert	CHN	932	Freeman, Nathan	SRA	20	French, John	NYK	125
Freeborn, Robert	NYK	133	Freeman, Nathan	WSH	273	French, John	OND	175
Freeborn, Stephen	CHN	936	Freeman, Natl	OTS	36	French, John	OTS	26
Freeborn, Thomas	NYK	63	Freeman, Peleg	HRK	431	French, John	OTS	35
Freeborn, Thomas	NYK	104	Freeman, Peter	OTS	18	French, John	RNS	6
Freebush, Jean	NYK	24	Freeman, Primus	DUT	24	French, John	WSH	188
Freedom, Richard	DUT	71	Freeman, Prince	CHN	796	French, Jonathan	WSH	188
Fr[eeer?], Solomon	CHN	962	Freeman, Prince	WSH	210	French, Joseph	CHN	872
Fr[eeier?], Richard	CHN	962	Freeman, Rebecca	NYK	137	French, Joseph	HRK	436
Freeke, John C.	KNG	7	Freeman, Richard	ALB	21	French, Joseph	HRK	456
Freelan, Peter	RCK	106	Freeman, Richard a			French, Joseph	ULS	184
Freeland, Andrw	NYK	116	Black	NYK	77	French, Manassa	CAY	694
Freeland, John	NYK	106	Freeman, Richard	OND	208	French, Nathan	OTS	35
Freeland, John	NYK	148	Freeman, Robin	ULS	203	French, Peter P.	WSH	287
Freeland, Maria	NYK	83	Freeman, Samuel	COL	243	French, Reuben	ESS	306
Freeland, Michael	CAY	520	Freeman, Silas	CAY	696	French, Sally	OND	175

Name	Loc		Name	Loc		Name	Loc	
French, Samuel	MNT	108	Frey, Philup J.	MNT	45	Frist see Trist		
French, Stephen	OTS	5	Frey, Rhodes	OTS	20	Fritat, Charles	NYK	45
French, Thomas	NYK	95	Freydendall, Frederick	ALB	59	Frith, Henry	NYK	98
French, Wheeler	OTS	28	Freydenryck, John C.	ALB	136	Fritts, Adam	COL	240
French, William	DEL	282	Freyer, Isaac	ALB	61	Fritts, Francis	RNS	53
French, William	NYK	126	Freyer, John	ALB	61	Fritts, Herman	COL	240
French, Wm	OTS	19	Freyer, Mathew	RNS	6	Fritts, John	COL	195
French, Zepheniah	OTS	35	Freyland, John	ALB	144	Fritts, John	COL	232
Frencherd, John	ALB	78	Frezel, James	CHN	920	Fritts, John	COL	242
Frend, John	NYK	135	Frezel, Saml	CHN	920	Fritts, William	COL	190
Frendenbergh, Isaac	ALB	81	Frezon, John	RNS	62	Fritts, William	COL	238
Frenk, Margaret	ALB	9	Frickelton, James	NYK	108	Fritz, Christian	ORN	389
Frere, Abraham Junr	DUT	62	Friday, Abraham	ALB	137	Fritz, Conrod A.	NYK	145
Frere, Abraham Senr	DUT	61	Friday, Coenrad	ALB	109	Fritz, Eliza	NYK	144
Frere, Anthony	ULS	216	Friday, Jacob	NYK	80	Fritz, John	NYK	95
Frere, Benjamin	ULS	236	Friday, Paul	NYK	118	Frizle, Saml	OTS	54
Frere, Benjamin B.	ULS	241	Frieday, Christian	NYK	69	Frolick, Jacob	MNT	31
Frere, Benjamin H.	ULS	207	Frier, John	RNS	8	Froman, Alexander	WSH	242
Frere, Cornelius	ULS	200	Frier, Saml	RNS	8	Fromant, Peter	NYK	36
Frere, Daniel	ULS	243	Frier, Simeon	ONN	146	Frome, John	RCH	89
Frere, Daniel D.	ULS	207	Fries, Adam	CAY	708	Froome, Christian	RCH	89
Frere, David	ULS	241	Friesnos, John E.	MNT	13	Froome, Christian	RCH	92
Frere, Elias	DUT	70	Frigleth, Edward	NYK	105	Froome, Matthias	RCH	91
Frere, Elias Junr	DUT	68	Frim, Benjamin	ONN	150	Froot, William	NYK	80
Frere, Elisha	ULS	259	Frinehager, Elizabeth	QNS	69	Frosk, John	TIO	217
Frere, Garret	ULS	243	Frink see French			Frost, Aaron	WSH	249
Frere, Garret Junr	ULS	218	Frink, Arthur	TIO	234	Frost, Abner	CHN	746
Frere, Garret I.	ULS	219	Frink, Asa	CHN	816	Frost, Allen	ALB	133
Frere, Hugo	ULS	210	Frink, Asa Junr	CHN	816	Frost, Allen	ALB	142
Frere, Isaac	ULS	241	Frink, Charles	ALB	69	Frost, Benjamin	ALB	36
Frere, Isaac Junr	ULS	241	Frink, Charles	CHN	776	Frost, Benjamin	DUT	114
Frere, Jacob	ULS	200	Frink, Elias	ALB	43	Frost, Bial	WSH	204
Frere, Jacob	ULS	207	Frink, Fraderic	OND	215	Frost, Caleb	QNS	83
Frere, Jacob & Peter	ULS	219	Frink, Gorge	CHN	816	Frost, Charles	QNS	81
Frere, Jacob I.	ULS	243	Frink, Henry	SRA	22	Frost, Charles	WST	115
Frere, Jacoba	DUT	69	Frink, Jabez	ALB	69	Frost, Daniel	DUT	87
Frere, Jacobus	DUT	69	Frink, Jabez Junr	ALB	69	Frost, Daniel	QNS	84
Frere, Jacobus	ULS	199	Frink, James	RNS	18	Frost, David	CLN	172
Frere, Jan	ULS	219	Frink, John	MNT	41	Frost, David	DUT	56
Frere, Jeremiah	ULS	243	Frink, Jones	RNS	19	Frost, David	DUT	87
Frere, John	DUT	62	Frink, Luke	RNS	21	Frost, David Junr	DUT	93
Frere, John Junr	DUT	68	Frink, Nathan	RNS	18	Frost, Edward	NYK	36
Frere, John E.	ULS	259	Frink, Nathan	SRA	20	Frost, Elijah	SRA	53
Frere, John I.	ULS	237	Frink, Pe_is	ALB	88	Frost, Enos	ONT	370
Frere, Jonas	ULS	237	Frink, Samuel	ALB	83	Frost, Ephram	CHN	864
Frere, Jonathan	ULS	236	Frink, Samuel	SRA	20	Frost, Ezra	NYK	140
Frere, Joseph	ULS	241	Frink, Stephen	CHN	784	Frost, Ezra	RNS	55
Frere, Maria	ULS	230	Frink, Theophilus	RNS	18	Frost, George	DUT	112
Frere, Martinus	ULS	243	Frink, Thomas	CHN	784	Frost, George	QNS	84
Frere, Martinus	ULS	254	Frink, William	COL	259	Frost, George P.	ULS	217
Frere, Martinus E.	ULS	260	Frisbe, Janus	COL	184	Frost, Isaac	WST	153
Frere, Nathan	DUT	69	Frisbe, Phillip	COL	203	Frost, Jacob	NYK	45
Frere, Paulus	ULS	243	Frisbee, Benjamin	ALB	84	Frost, Jacob	QNS	76
Frere, Peter	DUT	68	Frisbee, Ebenezer	ALB	31	Frost, Jacob	QNS	84
Frere, Peter	ULS	185	Frisbee, Ezra	ALB	94	Frost, James	NYK	60
Frere, Peter & Jacob	ULS	219	Frisbee, Hezekiah	ALB	31	Frost, James	NYK	113
Frere, Petrus	ULS	243	Frisbee, John	ALB	84	Frost, James	NYK	147
Frere, Samuel	ULS	228	Frisbee, Reuben	ALB	84	Frost, James	WST	156
Frere, Samuel Junr	ULS	226	Frisbee, Samuel	ALB	29	Frost, Jedidiah	WST	144
Frere, Simeon Junr	DUT	68	Frisbee, Semeon	ESS	323	Frost, Joel	WST	153
Frere, Simeon Senr	DUT	68	Frisbee, Susannah	COL	203	Frost, John	CAY	586
Frere, Simeon I.	DUT	69	Frisbee, Thomas	ALB	70	Frost, John	COL	214
Frere, Simon	ULS	208	Frisbey, Samuel	OND	173	Frost, John	COL	227
Frere, Simon	ULS	260	Frisbie, Abel	CAY	530	Frost, John	DUT	88
Fresghdenberg, Margerit	NYK	42	Frisbie, Benjamin	DEL	267	Frost, John	QNS	69
Fretcher, Henry	MNT	96	Frisbie, Gideon	DEL	289	Frost, John	QNS	82
Frets, John	MNT	77	Frisbie, Lawman	DEL	287	Frost, Jonathan B.	ALB	88
Fretz, Ernest	SCH	161	Frisbie, Samuel	DEL	290	Frost, Jordon	DUT	111
Fretz, Henry	NYK	111	Frisbie, Widow	DEL	289	Frost, Joseph	NYK	133
Fretz, John	SCH	161	Frisby, Augustus	MNT	125	Frost, Lot	ALB	36
Frevaw, George	OTS	14	Frisby, Eli	OND	169	Frost, Michael	OND	215
Frevaw, Peter	OTS	14	Frisby, John H.	ONN	189	Frost, Mordecai	DUT	111
Frey, Abraham	MNT	18	Frisby, Joseph	OND	168	Frost, Obadiah	WST	135
Frey, Henry Junr	MNT	48	Frisby, Pardy	OND	169	Frost, Peter	RNS	83
Frey, James	MNT	18	Friskney, Sarah	NYK	18	Frost, Prior	WST	125
Frey, John	MNT	8	Friss, Peter	COL	235	Frost, Robert	ULS	243
Frey, Philip	ALB	89	Frissle, Elisha	WSH	226	Frost, Samuel	ALB	54

Name	Code	Name	Code	Name	Code
Frost, Samuel	COL 179	Fuller, Abner	WSH 238	Fuller, John	DEL 268
Frost, Samuel	RNS 81	Fuller, Abner	WSH 273	Fuller, John	DUT 142
Frost, Samuel	WST 125	Fuller, Abner Junr	WSH 238	Fuller, John	NYK 98
Frost, Sarah	WST 122	Fuller, Abrm	OTS 25	Fuller, John	OND 215
Frost, Solomon	DUT 112	Fuller, Adna	WSH 245	Fuller, John	ONN 142
Frost, Stephen	QNS 69	Fuller, Amos	ALB 103	Fuller, John	ONT 356
Frost, Stephen	QNS 84	Fuller, Amos	COL 179	Fuller, John	WSH 217
Frost, Stephen	WST 153	Fuller, Amos	ONN 192	Fuller, Joseph	CHN 866
Frost, Tartelus	RNS 55	Fuller, Amos	RNS 73	Fuller, Joseph	DEL 275
Frost, Thomas	DUT 19	Fuller, Arnon	ESS 296	Fuller, Joseph	NYK 56
Frost, Thomas	RNS 55	Fuller, Asa	OND 215	Fuller, Joseph	WSH 272
Frost, Underhill	DUT 26	Fuller, Beckman	COL 209	Fuller, Joseph	WSH 281
Frost, William	DUT 87	Fuller, Benjamin	DEL 283	Fuller, Joshua	WSH 295
Frost, William	DUT 89	Fuller, Benjamin	DUT 61	Fuller, Josiah	SRA 39
Frost, Wright	QNS 83	Fuller, Benjamin	DUT 82	Fuller, Josiah	WSH 191
Frost, Wright	WST 122	Fuller, Benjn	OTS 11	Fuller, Josiah	WSH 219
Frost, Wright	WST 153	Fuller, Benjn	TIO 218	Fuller, Josiah	WST 152
Frost, Zebulon	QNS 83	Fuller, Benjamin	WSH 211	Fuller, Judah	WSH 281
Frost, Zophar	DUT 124	Fuller, Benjamin	WSH 291	Fuller, Judah Jur	WSH 281
Frotenham, David	SUF 102	Fuller, Benjamine	GRN 347	Fuller, Lemuel	COL 178
Frothingham, Thomas	COL 248	Fuller, Boyls	DUT 35	Fuller, Levi	COL 243
Frott, John	NYK 81	Fuller, Calvin	SRA 30	Fuller, Levi	ONN 156
Fruger, Jacob	MNT 117	Fuller, Calvin	TIO 215	Fuller, Lot	OND 192
Fruger, John	MNT 117	Fuller, Comfort	ORN 304	Fuller, Mathew	WSH 211
Fruger, Peter	MNT 117	Fuller, Comfort	SCH 159	Fuller, Mathew	WSH 283
Fry, Abiel	TIO 256	Fuller, Cornelius	DUT 82	Fuller, Matthew	CHN 764
Fry, Derik	SRA 11	Fuller, Daniel	ESS 298	Fuller, Micajah	WST 127
Fry, Francis	MNT 105	Fuller, Daniel	OND 199	Fuller, Michael	CHN 762
Fry, Henry Cox	MNT 51	Fuller, Danl	OTS 40	Fuller, Nathan	DEL 275
Fry, Jacob	MNT 4	Fuller, Daniel	RNS 70	Fuller, Nathan	DUT 90
Fry, Jacob Senior	MNT 4	Fuller, Darius	WSH 187	Fuller, Nathan Jun	DEL 275
Fry, James	QNS 82	Fuller, Daton	COL 214	Fuller, Nathaniel	COL 243
Fry, John	MNT 118	Fuller, David	CHN 980	Fuller, Noah	DEL 275
Fry, Martin	MNT 105	Fuller, David	COL 185	Fuller, Oliver	OND 169
Fry, Michael	SRA 11	Fuller, David	DUT 27	Fuller, Oliver	RNS 14
Fry, Philip	MNT 4	Fuller, David	ONT 314	Fuller, Rebecca	WSH 274
Fryar, Barant	ALB 80	Fuller, David	WSH 284	Fuller, Reuben	ALB 142
Fryar, David	ALB 90	Fuller, Dayton	WSH 283	Fuller, Reynhart	ALB 102
Fryar, Isaac	ALB 126	Fuller, Derius	WSH 213	Fuller, Rial	CHN 850
Fryar, Jacob	ALB 90	Fuller, Eben	OTS 27	Fuller, Richard	WSH 281
Fryar, John	ALB 90	Fuller, Ebenezer	COL 182	Fuller, Richard	WSH 283
Fryar, John	ALB 126	Fuller, Ebenezer	WSH 268	Fuller, Rufus	SRA 39
Fryar, John	ALB 129	Fuller, Edmund	OND 213	Fuller, Samuel	ALB 85
Fryer, Casparus	OTS 25	Fuller, Edward	WSH 216	Fuller, Samuel	CHN 862
Fryer, Eli	ALB 46	Fuller, Edward	WST 127	Fuller, Samuel	DEL 268
Fryer, Isaac	ALB 44	Fuller, Elezar	ALB 61	Fuller, Saml	OTS 42
Fryer, Jacob	ALB 48	Fuller, Elihu	DUT 35	Fuller, Saml	OTS 48
Fryer, Peter	SCH 124	Fuller, Elijah	DUT 90	Fuller, Samuel	SCH 159
Fryer, Thomas	SCH 128	Fuller, Elijah	OTS 24	Fuller, Samuel	WSH 238
Frymyer, John Jr	SCH 131	Fuller, Eliphalet	HRK 535	Fuller, Samuel	WSH 284
Frymyer, Michael	SCH 170	Fuller, Elisha	CHN 866	Fuller, Silvester	CHN 862
Frymyers, John	SCH 128	Fuller, Elisha	WST 124	Fuller, Simeon	OND 213
Frynt, Hendrick	ORN 307	Fuller, Elisha Junr	WST 125	Fuller, Simon	WSH 207
Frynt, Henry	ULS 242	Fuller, Ephraim	WSH 284	Fuller, Solomon	COL 231
Fryon, John	CLN 173	Fuller, Esery	CHN 864	Fuller, Solomon	WSH 213
Fryover, Jacob	DUT 165	Fuller, Eszery N.	CHN 866	Fuller, Subel	WSH 206
Fu_erson, Josiah	CAY 594	Fuller, Farley	HRK 592	Fuller, Thomas	ONT 350
Fuale, Patrick	KNG 8	Fuller, George	SCH 159	Fuller, Thos	OTS 19
Fueter, Daniel	NYK 73	Fuller, Gersham	ALB 101	Fuller, Thomas	WSH 190
Fule[npon?], Henry	CAY 552	Fuller, Henry	WSH 281	Fuller, Thomas W.	NYK 57
Fulford, David	OND 184	Fuller, Hubbard	OTS 18	Fuller, Versal	WSH 243
Fulkinson, Cornelius	OND 175	Fuller, Isaac	CHN 762	Fuller, William	OTS 17
Fulkinson, Cornelius Jr	OND 175	Fuller, Isaac	CHN 764	Fuller, William	WSH 223
Full, Simon	COL 248	Fuller, Isaac	ULS 186	Fuller, William Junr	OTS 16
Fullam, Elisha	OTS 29	Fuller, Isaiah	SRA 33	Fullerton, Alexander	STB 207
Fullam, Mary	NYK 45	Fuller, Jabez	ONT 442	Fullerton, Alexander	WSH 289
Fullarton, Samuel	ORN 314	Fuller, Jabus	WST 156	Fullerton, Daniel	ORN 329
Fuller	RNS 9	Fuller, Jacob	WSH 293	Fullerton, Henry	WSH 257
Fuller, _____	CHN 832	Fuller, James	COL 189	Fullerton, Henry	WSH 289
Fuller, Aaron	OTS 34	Fuller, Jedidiah	OTS 38	Fullerton, Phinehas	ORN 325
Fuller, Aaron	WSH 284	Fuller, Jeduthan	OTS 47	Fullerton, Samuel	COL 191
Fuller, Aaron	WSH 284	Fuller, Jehebal	MNT 112	Fullerton, William	ORN 325
Fuller, Abel	GRN 351	Fuller, Jeptha	ORN 311	Fullerton, William	WSH 289
Fuller, Abel	GRN 354	Fuller, Jeremiah	ALB 5	Fullington, Grace	SRA 43
Fuller, Abel	SCH 159	Fuller, Jesse	OTS 11	Fulmer, George	HRK 432
Fuller, Abial	OND 213	Fuller, John	CAY 644	Fulmer, Jacob	HRK 432
Fuller, Abijah	OTS 21	Fuller, John	COL 243	Fulmer, John	SRA 6

Name	Loc	Name	Loc	Name	Loc
Gale, Jacob	ORN 349	Gallup, Joshua	ALB 76	Gansy, Nathaniel	SCH 129
Gale, Jessee	QNS 73	Gallup, Nathaniel	ALB 75	Gantley, Sarah	NYK 140
Gale, John	ORN 360	Gallup, Nathaniel	OND 204	Gants, Paul	GRN 330
Gale, John	RNS 47	Gallup, Samuel	ALB 76	Ganty, Frances	NYK 124
Gale, John	WST 163	Gallup, Samuel Jur	ALB 75	Ganty, Francis	NYK 117
Gale, John the 2d	ORN 360	Gally, Hugh	DUT 153	Gantz, Gabriel	NYK 135
Gale, John Ye 3d	ORN 356	Gally, James	WSH 258	Ganung, Edward	WST 127
Gale, Joseph	DUT 78	Galor, Zachariah	DUT 156	Ganung, Peter	WST 127
Gale, Joseph	RNS112A	Galowwey, John	WSH 197	Ganyard, James	ONT 420
Gale, Marinus	NYK 44	Galpin, David	SRA 4	Ganyard, Peter	ONT 418
Gale, Nehemiah	COL 213	Galpin, Joseph	ESS 296	Garbet, William	ONT 494
Gale, Nicholas	TIO 264	Galpin, Lucy	RNS 81	Garbrance, Peter	NYK 36
Gale, Noah	DUT 132	Galusha, Jacob	ALB 71	Garbutt, John	NYK 142
Gale, Peter	ORN 357	Galusha, Thomas	WSH 243	Gard, Andrew	NYK 83
Gale, Phebe	ORN 346	Galutiah, Biram	WSH 254	Garden, Thomas	NYK 67
Gale, Reuben	DUT 79	Galutia, William	WSH 183	Gardeneer, Jacob	MNT 98
Gale, Richard	ORN 342	Galway, James	ORN 382	Gardeneer, John Junr	MNT 98
Gale, Roger	ALB 66	Galway, James Junr	ORN 386	Gardener, John	NYK 59
Gale, Samuel	ALB 28	Galway, John	ORN 291	Gardener, Levy	CHN 778
Gale, Samuel	NYK 15	Galway, Thomas	DUT 72	Gardener, Peter a mulatto	NYK 130
Gale, Samuel	RNS 112	Galway, Thomas	ORN 390	Gardener, Stephen	OTS 13
Gale, Samul	NYK 24	Gamage, John	NYK 48	Gardenier, William	NYK 134
Gale, Silvanus	WST 114	Gamage, Samuel	COL 248	Gardenner, Cosper	GRN 348
Gale, Stephen	WST 163	Gambey, Joseph	WSH 204	Gardinear, Henry	RNS 62
Gale, Thaddes	WSH 278	Gambey, William	WSH 254	Gardinear, Henry H.	RNS 85
Gale, Thomas	ORN 332	Gamble, Benjamin	NYK 66	Gardineer, Aaron	COL 259
Gale, Thomas	WST 163	Gamble, Hugh	DUT 146	Gardineer, Andrew	ALB 46
Galer, Mathias	RNS 35	Gamble, James	SRA 48	Gardineer, Andrew	COL 261
Gales, Samuel	WST 127	Gamble, James	WSH 289	Gardineer, Cornelius	RNS 62
Gales, William	ALB 15	Gamble, Samuel	WSH 227	Gardineer, David	COL 259
Galey, Andrew	ORN 300	Gamble, William	COL 180	Gardineer, Derick	COL 262
Galey, Josiah	ORN 304	Gamboll, Andew	NYK 125	Gardineer, Henry A.	ALB 46
Galey, William	ORN 304	Gamel, George	NYK 102	Gardineer, Jacob Junr	MNT 98
Galiway, John	WST 160	Gammell, John	NYK 120	Gardineer, John	COL 257
Gall, Jacob	ORN 379	Gammott, Thomas	WST 156	Gardineer, John S.	MNT 98
Gall, Townsend a Black	NYK 127	Gammut, Paul	OTS 29	Gardineer, Nicholas	MNT 74
Gallagher, Partrick	NYK 132	Gamuel	QNS 67	Gardineer, Nicholas	MNT 98
Gallagher, Partrick	NYK 132	Gan, John	SUF 106	Gardineer, Peter J.	COL 261
Gallahan, George	NYK 32	Gance, Caspar	DUT 39	Gardineer, Philip	ALB 47
Gallahar, Benjamin	NYK 68	Gannet, Jacob	ONT 354	Gardineer, Samuel	MNT 60
Gallalee, Mathew	NYK 42	Gannet, Joseph	ONT 354	Gardineer, Samuel	MNT 98
Gallandt, Elisha	NYK 134	Gannon, Benjamin	ORN 374	Gardineir, Barent	ULS 228
Gallant, James	NYK 118	Gannon, William	ORN 374	Gardineir, Bilbert	COL 265
Gallard, Josiah	SCH 154	Ganoe, James	OTS 48	Gardiner, Abel a Black	NYK 76
Gallaspie, John	WST 144	Ganoe, John	OTS 51	Gardiner, Alexes	NYK 147
Gallaudet, Joseph	WST 149	Ganong, Daniel	DUT 178	Gardiner, Andrew	NYK 81
Gallaway, Jacob	CHN 868	Ganong, Ebenezer	DUT 89	Gardiner, Benjamin	NYK 42
Gallaway, James	ONT 346	Ganong, Gilbert	DUT 94	Gardiner, Benjamin	ORN 273
Galley, James	OND 204	Ganong, Isaac	DUT 88	Gardiner, Calvin	ORN 356
Galley, William	OND 204	Ganong, Isaac	DUT 89	Gardiner, Charles	NYK 42
Gallipee, George	SRA 25	Ganong, Isaac Junr	DUT 88	Gardiner, Charles	NYK 77
Gallon, Christopher	NYK 72	Ganong, Jacob	DUT 88	Gardiner, Daniel D.	CHN 798
Gallop, Benjamin	NYK 25	Ganong, Jeremiah	DUT 88	Gardiner, David	ORN 277
Gallop, Ebe	OTS 37	Ganong, Jesse	DUT 88	Gardiner, David	ORN 336
Gallop, Fear	WSH 294	Ganong, John	CLN 156	Gardiner, David	ORN 354
Gallop, Job	OTS 8	Ganong, John	DUT 74	Gardiner, Edward	NYK 101
Gallop, John	ALB 67	Ganong, John	DUT 86	Gardiner, Elijah	MNT 108
Gallop, Joshua	ALB 68	Ganong, John	DUT 177	Gardiner, Elijah	ULS 266
Gallop, Levi	ALB 68	Ganong, Jonathan	DUT 178	Gardiner, Gaius	DUT 145
Gallop, Lucias	RNS 74	Ganong, Rachel	DUT 89	Gardiner, George	ORN 284
Gallop, Nathl	OTS 8	Ganong, Reuben	DUT 88	Gardiner, Isaac	DUT 98
Gallop, Sarah	NYK 52	Gansen, James	ONT 312	Gardiner, James	DUT 11
Galoop, Thomas	TIO 209	Gansen, John	ONT 312	Gardiner, James	NYK 28
Gallop, Wm	OTS 8	Gansevert, Leonard Junr	RNS 7	Gardiner, James	NYK 44
Gallop, Wm	RNS 27	Gansevoort, Conrod	MNT 46	Gardiner, James	NYK 120
Gallop, William	RNS 73	Gansevoort, Hugh	MNT 69	Gardiner, Jeptha	ORN 358
Gallow, John	ORN 285	Gansevoort, Leonard	ALB 108	Gardiner, Jetur	DEL 277
Gallow, Joseph	DUT 133	Gansevoort, Peter	ALB 147	Gardiner, John a Black	NYK 56
Galloway, Elizabeth	NYK 144	Gansevoort, Peter Jr	ALB 148	Gardiner, John	NYK 111
Galloway, Francis	NYK 126	Gansevourt, Conradt	MNT 26	Gardiner, Joseph	NYK 99
Galloway, James	NYK 127	Gansey, Hester	ALB 97	Gardiner, Joseph	ULS 257
Galloway, John	NYK 126	Gansey, Isaac	WST 154	Gardiner, Joshua	WSH 186
Gallowwey, William	WSH 197	Gansey, Jaunsey	ALB 10	Gardiner, Luke	DUT 125
Gallup, Ezra	ALB 75	Gansey, John	WSH 194	Gardiner, Margaret	NYK 74
Gallup, Gideon	ALB 64	Gansey, Silas	NYK 95	Gardiner, Mary	DUT 129
Gallup, John P.	ALB 92	Gansy, James	SCH 117	Gardiner, Michael	NYK 103

Name	Loc	Name	Loc	Name	Loc
Gardiner, Nathaniel	DUT 98	Gardner, Ira	ALB 79	Gardner, William	ALB 81
Gardiner, Nathaniel	NYK 133	Gardner, Jacob	COL 255	Gardner, William	ALB 92
Gardiner, Resolved	DUT 12	Gardner, James	COL 200	Gardner, William	ALB 93
Gardiner, Rhodes	CAY 572	Gardner, James	OTS 19	Gardner, William	NYK 68
Gardiner, Richd	HRK 512	Gardner, James	SUF 72	Gardner, Wm	RNS 72
Gardiner, Robert	ORN 282	Gardner, James	WSH 216	Gardner, William	RNS 110
Gardiner, Samuel	ORN 273	Gardner, James D.	COL 231	Gardner, Willm	SCH 161
Gardiner, Samuel	ORN 277	Gardner, Jeremiah	COL 183	Gardner, William	TIO 262
Gardiner, Samuel	ORN 277	Gardner, Jeremiah	SUF 106	Gardner, Zepheniah	ALB 81
Gardiner, Samuel	ORN 366	Gardner, Jerone	COL 249	Gardnor, Lion	SUF 70
Gardiner, Sears	ULS 180	Gardner, Jesse	RNS 73	Garfield, Jesse	HRK 581
Gardiner, Silas	ORN 275	Gardner, Job	RNS 108	Garison, David	GRN 326
Gardiner, Solomon	ORN 283	Gardner, Job B.	ALB 81	Garison, Hellmus	NYK 93
Gardiner, Stephen	DUT 98	Gardner, John	ALB 93	Garison, Martin	NYK 82
Gardiner, Stephen	ULS 219	Gardner, John	COL 200	Garl(?), Harmonus	GRN 334
Gardiner, Thomas	NYK 143	Gardner, John	HRK 553	Garl(?), Nicholas	GRN 334
Gardiner, Thomas	NYK 143	Gardner, John	HRK 561	Garland, Abigal	NYK 111
Gardiner, Thomas	ORN 280	Gardner, John	NYK 24	Garland, Alexander	NYK 125
Gardiner, Timothy	NYK 129	Gardner, John	ONT 360	Garland, John	NYK 75
Gardiner, William	DUT 120	Gardner, John	OTS 25	Garlick, Phineas	RNS 34
Gardiner, William	OND 163	Gardner, John	OTS 37	Garlinghouse, Benjamin	ONT 334
Gardiner, William	SUF 104	Gardner, John	RNS 74	Garlinghouse, J___	ONT 332
Gardinier, Adam	HRK 552	Gardner, John	RCK 106	Garlinghouse, James	ONT 332
Gardinier, Cornelia	COL 264	Gardner, John	SUF 84	Garloch, Jacob	OTS 4
Gardinier, Henry	ALB 83	Gardner, John	SUF 106	Garlock see Carlock	
Gardner, Abail	ALB 93	Gardner, John	TIO 231	Garlock, Charles	MNT 34
Gardner, Abial	ONT 360	Gardner, John Junr	ALB 93	Garlock, Christian	MNT 21
Gardner, Abraham	COL 255	Gardner, John L.	ALB 86	Garlock, Elias	MNT 33
Gardner, Abm	SUF 69	Gardner, John Lyon	SUF 108	Garlock, George	SCH 139
Gardner, Adam	OTS 22	Gardner, Jonathan	SCH 137	Garmen, Obediah	CHN 780
Gardner, Andrw	SCH 119	Gardner, Jonathan	SCH 144	Garmo, Bastian	ALB 140
Gardner, Andw	SCH 126	Gardner, Jones	WSH 237	Garmo, William D.	NYK 60
Gardner, Asahel	RNS 29	Gardner, Joseph	OND 205	Garner, Andrew	SRA 29
Gardner, Barbary	COL 223	Gardner, Joseph	OTS 29	Garner, Christopher	ALB 108
Gardner, Benjamin	COL 253	Gardner, Joshua	RNS 102	Garner, Daniel	ULS 202
Gardner, Benjamin	ONT 384	Gardner, Lyon	COL 183	Garner, Frederick	NYK 45
Gardner, Benjn	OTS 33	Gardner, Mary	ONT 466	Garner, James	ALB 40
Gardner, Benjamin	RNS 103	Gardner, Mary	OTS 32	Garner, John	SUF 76
Gardner, Benjn 2d	RNS 110	Gardner, Mary	SUF 106	Garner, John	ULS 202
Gardner, Caleb	ONT 502	Gardner, Michael	COL 195	Garner, John Junr	ULS 202
Gardner, Caleb	OTS 15	GArdner, Mills	RCK 105	Garner, Josep	SUF 74
Gardner, Caleb	RNS 42	Gardner, Nathan	OTS 25	Garner, Samuel	GRN 353
Gardner, Caleb	RNS 103	Gardner, Nathan	RNS 100	Garnet, John	ORN 362
Gardner, Caleb Ju.	ONT 502	Gardner, Nathan	TIO 227	Garnett, Wm	SUF 94
Gardner, Caleb Junr	RNS 77	Gardner, Nathaniel	RNS 110	Garnice, Thomas	WST 167
Gardner, Champlin	ALB 93	Gardner, Nathaniel	SUF 106	Garnrite, Zachariah	RNS 85
Gardner, Daniel	ALB 81	Gardner, Nicholas	OND 191	Garnrite, Zachariah	RNS 85
Gardner, Daniel	RNS 74	Gardner, Oldin	RNS 103	Garnrycke, Godlope	ULS 221
Gardner, Daniel	RNS 74	Gardner, Mrs Olive	STB 198	Garnrycke, Hieronimus	ULS 221
Gardner, David	CHN 964	Gardner, Oliver	OTS 12	Garnrycke, John	ULS 221
Gardner, David	COL 209	Gardner, Oliver	OTS 37	Garnrycke, Peter	ULS 218
Gardner, David	MNT 103	Gardner, Paul Junr	OTS 37	Garnryke, David	ULS 197
Gardner, David	OND 197	GArdner, Paul Senr	OTS 37	Garnsey, Daniel	SRA 28
Gardner, David	QNS 63	Gardner, Peregrine	ONT 388	Garnsey, David	DEL 287
Gardner, Derick	COL 200	Gardner, Phoebe	SUF 106	Garnsey, David	TIO 228
Gardner, Derick	COL 226	Gardner, Powel	RNS 102	Garnsey, Ebenezer	TIO 227
Gardner, Elisha	COL 252	Gardner, Robert	COL 217	Garnsey, Enoch	NYK 43
Gardner, Ezekiel	WSH 300	Gardner, Robert	SCH 162	Garnsey, Isaac	DEL 287
Gardner, Ezra	COL 221	Gardner, Sallivan	OTS 35	Garnsey, Isaac	TIO 227
Gardner, Gayer	COL 247	Gardner, Saml	OTS 29	Garnsey, Joel	TIO 226
Gardner, George	COL 209	Gardner, Saml	OTS 37	Garnsey, John	DUT 136
Gardner, George	OND 162	Gardner, Samuel	QNS 73	Garnsey, Nathan	SRA 5
Gardner, George	ONT 312	Gardner, Samuel	WSH 295	Garnsey, Peter	DUT 131
Gardner, Geo.	OTS 30	Gardner, Samuel H.	COL 262	Garnung, Jason	CHN 840
Gardner, George	RNS 67	Gardner, Seth	OTS 22	Garow, Daniel	NYK 59
Gardner, George	TIO 265	Gardner, Simeon	HRK 484	Garrabrant, Lucenda	NYK 149
Gardner, Gilbert	COL 214	Gardner, Simeon	RNS 103	Garrabrants, Jacob	NYK 149
Gardner, Godfrey	COL 260	Gardner, Solomon	ONT 492	Garrat, Robert	OTS 38
Gardner, Godfrey	COL 265	Gardner, Stephen	ALB 91B	Garratt, John	OTS 32
Gardner, Henry	COL 183	Gardner, Stephen	ONN 165	Garratt, William	OTS 32
Gardner, Henry	OTS 47	Gardner, Stephen	OTS 15	Garremoe, Matthew	SRA 50
Gardner, Henry	RNS 108	Gardner, Sylvanus	COL 221	Garrems, Jacob	RNS 45
Gardner, Henry G.	HRK 553	Gardner, Sylvanus Junr	COL 209	Garrenow, Lewis	WST 147
Gardner, Hiram	NYK 21	Gardner, Thos	OTS 35	Garreson, Dennis	WST 145
Gardner, Howland	RNS 105	Gardner, Thomas	RNS 108	Garreson, Garret	WST 146
Gardner, Hugh	SRA 58	Gardner, Wilkinson	ALB 93	Garreson, Isaac	WST 145
Gardner, Hutchings	RCK 102	Gardner, Wm	ALB 12	Garreson, John	WST 145

Garreson, Nicholas	WST 144	Garrison, Thomas	ORN 392	Gates, Joseph	OND 175
Garret, Ephraim	GRN 353	Garrison, Thomas	ULS 195	Gates, Joseph	SRA 13
Garret, George	WST 111	Garrison, William	ALB 64	Gates, Joshua	ONN 169
Garret, John	DUT 114	Garrison, William	COL 238	Gates, Joshua	OTS 36
Garret, John	ORN 271	Garrit, John	NYK 149	Gates, Lemuel	MNT 45
Garret, Magnus	NYK 113	Garritson, Elsa	KNG 2	Gates, Lemuel	MNT 93
Garret, Mary	NYK 148	Garritson, John	CAY 588	Gates, Levy	WSH 266
Garret, Peter	SRA 43	Garritson, Mary	CAY 552	Gates, Malachi	DUT 140
Garret, Robert	DUT 113	Garrow, Frances	NYK 119	Gates, Marvin	ONT 390
Garret, Samuel	OND 159	Garrow, John	CAY 704	Gates, Michael	NYK 91
Garret, Simeon	GRN 353	Garson, Sarah	NYK 52	Gates, Moses	SRA 48
Garret, Wait	SRA 40	Garston, Henry	NYK 64	Gates, Nathaniel	WSH 207
Garrets, John	GRN 353	Garter, Leonard	MNT 15	Gates, Noadiah	RNS 108
Garretson, Abraham	RCH 90	Garter, Robert	CHN 942	Gates, Noah	SRA 48
Garretson, Contentment	RCH 93	Gartley, Andrw	NYK 104	Gates, Oldham	ALB 90
Garretson, Harmanous	RCH 89	Garve, Noah	TIO 228	Gates, Oliver	COL 208
Garretson, Hartshorn	ONN 172	Garvey, Francis	ALB 71	Gates, Parly	ONT 450
Garretson, Hendrick	RCH 92	Garvey, William	COL 261	Gates, Phinehas	HRK 430
Garretson, Jacob	RCH 90	Garvin, William	WST 149	Gates, Rufus	TIO 218
Garretson, John	KNG 9	Garvy, Cornelius	COL 215	Gates, Saml	OTS 28
Garretson, John	RCH 91	Garvy, Thomas	COL 220	Gates, Samuel	SRA 48
Garretson, John	RCH 92	Gary, Saml	OTS 7	Gates, Seth	HRK 535
Garretson, Jonathan	WST 163	Gary, Saml	OTS 18	Gates, Simon	WSH 207
Garretson, Marvel	WST 167	Gasharie, Joseph	ULS 227	Gates, Stephen	ALB 52
Garretson, Mary	RCH 89	Gasharie, Joseph	ULS 246	Gates, Stephen	WSH 207
Garretson, Nathanel		Gashin, William	NYK 94	Gates, William	ALB 13
Junr	WST 167	Gaskil, Silas	TIO 246	Gates, William	SRA 47
Garretson, Peter	OTS 56	Gaskil, Uriah	TIO 246	Gates, Willm	SCH 169
Garretson, Samuel	KNG 4	Gaskil, Wilder	TIO 246	Gates, Zebulon	WSH 207
Garrett, Cheney	OND 187	Gaskill, Jonathan	TIO 243	Gates, Zephaniah	ONN 171
Garrett, Daniel	CHN 750	Gaslor, Adam	MNT 46	Gates, Zephoniah	CHN 978
Garrett, James	SRA 17	Gasner, Henry	NYK 125	Gatfield, Benjamin	NYK 38
Garrett, John	OND 187	Gaspier, Peter	SCH 161	Gathan, Thomas	NYK 64
Garrett, Joseph	SRA 15	Gassar, William	ALB 138	Gatier, Louis A.	NYK 108
Garrett, Peter	OND 187	Gassner, John	NYK 53	Gatter, Samuel	NYK 24
Garrick, Mary	NYK 143	Gassner, Peter	NYK 55	Gatty, Henry	NYK 46
Garrigeus, Thomas	NYK 129	Gaster, Henry	HRK 578	Gaudessard, Lawrence	NYK 107
Garrison, Abraham	DUT 74	Gastin, John	RNS 81	Gauf, James	NYK 34
Garrison, Abraham	MNT 85	Gastin, Stephen	RNS 29	Gauff, Sam l	NYK 103
Garrison, Abrm	RCK 105	Gaston, Thomas G.	NYK 16	Gaul, Jacob	COL 195
Garrison, Abraham J.	NYK 97	Gates see Yates		Gaul, Jacob Junr	COL 195
Garrison, Andrew	ULS 257	Gates, Aaron	COL 208	Gauledet, Paul	NYK 76
Garrison, Benjamin	ORN 271	Gates, Abraham	ALB 137	Gault, James	OTS 2
Garrison, Beverley	ORN 392	Gates, Alfred	TIO 218	Gault, James	OTS 52
Garrison, David	GRN 336	Gates, Ambrose	OTS 49	Gault, John	OTS 2
Garrison, David	ORN 385	Gates, Azel	OTS 55	Gault, Luther	WSH 292
Garrison, Elizabeth	ALB 54	Gates, Caleb	ALB 22	Gault, Thomas	WSH 292
Garrison, Elizabeth	ORN 392	Gates, Caleb	ALB 146	Gault, Wm	OTS 2
Garrison, Fredk	ALB 135	Gates, Colman	SRA 48	Gault, William	WSH 297
Garrison, Freeborn	DUT 163	Gates, Daniel	ONT 446	Gause, John	GRN 333
Garrison, Harry Free		Gates, Daniel	RNS 96	Gause, John	SCH 132
Negro	COL 184	Gates, Daniel Ju	ONT 446	Gause, Nicholas	GRN 336
Garrison, Harry	DUT 73	Gates, David	CHN 830	Gauthiek Paul	CAY 558
Garrison, Henry	COL 245	Gates, David	WSH 266	Gautier, Samuel	NYK 95
Garrison, Ira	RNS 64	Gates, Elijah	ONT 480	Gavet, Samuel	SCH 145
Garrison, Isaac	ORN 398	Gates, Elijah	OTS 46	Gaviston, John	NYK 111
Garrison, Isaac	ULS 257	Gates, Elisha	HRK 535	Gavitt, Isaiah	RNS 72
Garrison, Jacob	DUT 150	Gates, Elisha	SCH 169	Gavoit, John	ALB 80
Garrison, Jacob	RCK 99	Gates, Elizur	SCH 160	Gawley, Hugh	RNS 35
Garrison, James	NYK 111	Gates, Ephraim	WSH 266	Gay, Abigal	NYK 105
Garrison, James	ORN 388	Gates, Ezra	COL 208	Gay, Abner,	DUT 178
Garrison, James	ULS 195	Gates, Ezra	HRK 535	Gay, Barnet	DUT 106
Garrison, John	ALB 91B	Gates, Fredom	MNT 122	Gay, Daniel	DUT 178
Garrison, John	NYK 106	Gates, Freeman	MNT 11	Gay, Elisha	HRK 495
Garrison, John	NYK 108	Gates, George D.	OND 174	Gay, Elizabeth	NYK 17
Garrison, John	ORN 329	Gates, Hannah	ONN 176	Gay, Fisher	DUT 134
Garrison, John	RCK 101	Gates, Hart	OND 172	Gay, Jane	NYK 76
Garrison, Joseph	DUT 72	Gates, Hortatio	NYK 143	Gay, Jason	ORN 325
Garrison, Joseph	RNS 57	Gates, Jacob	OTS 26	Gay, John	ALB 28
Garrison, Joseph	RCK 104	Gates, Jacob	RNS 67	Gay, John	GRN 357
Garrison, Joseph	SRA 26	Gates, James	RNS 32	Gay, John	HRK 477
Garrison, Peter	NYK 131	Gates, Jerremiah	CHN 976	Gay, John	HRK 582
Garrison, Reuben	WST 122	Gates, Jirah	WSH 266	Gay, John B.	DUT 59
Garrison, Reuben	WST 125	Gates, John	ALB 146	Gay, Joseph	HRK 415
Garrison, Richard	ALB 41	Gates, John	OTS 37	Gay, Nathaniell	GRN 351
Garrison, Samuel	WST 124	Gates, John	WSH 207	Gay, Oliver	SRA 60
Garrison, Samuel	WST 125	Gates, Jonathan	MNT 122	Gay, Robard	GRN 350

Gay, Rosewell	HRK 443	Geer, Lydia	OND 208	George, Semion	WSH 229

Name	Ref	Name	Ref	Name	Ref
Gewey, John	ALB 46	Gibson, Robert	WSH 226	Gifford, Ebunez..	MNT 84
Ghoram, Jonathan	NYK 100	Gibson, Thomas	NYK 26	Gifford, Elihu	ALB 91B
Gi___, Elihu	ONT 478	Gibson, Thomas a Black	NYK 112	Gifford, Elijah	ONT 370
Gibb, Oliver	SCH 142	Gibson, Thomas	NYK 145	Gifford, Elisha	DUT 168
Gibbon, James	NYK 89	Gibson, Thomas	QNS 64	Gifford, Elizabeth	ORN 392
Gibbons, James	ALB 133	Gibson, Thomas	WSH 247	Gifford, Enos	CHN 876
Gibbons, John	ALB 112	Gibson, William	CHN 796	Gifford, Giddeon	RNS 51
Gibbons, John Senr	ALB 112	Gibson, William	NYK 38	Gifford, Gideon	OND 208
Gibbons, Robert	ALB 130	Gibson, William	ONT 392	Gifford, Henry	ALB 91
Gibbons, Thomas	ULS 253	Gibson, William	ONT 394	Gifford, Herculus	WSH 197
Gibbony, John	WSH 292	Gibson, William	WSH 246	Gifford, Humphrey	COL 250
Gibbrey, William	ALB 146	Gichrist, Robert	WST 145	Gifford, Jabaze	RNS 51
Gibbs, Caleb	DEL 287	Gidby, William	SRA 39	Gifford, James	HRK 515
Gibbs, Charles	WSH 277	Gidding, James	HRK 534	Gifford, Jeremiah	ALB 91
Gibbs, Cyrenus	DEL 287	Giddings, Joshua	ONT 432	Gifford, Jeremiah	HRK 477
Gibbs, Daniel	CAY 620	Giddions, Harris	GRN 343	Gifford, Jesse	GRN 333
Gibbs, Danl	OTS 54	Giddions, Miss	GRN 343	Gifford, John	DUT 130
Gibbs, David	SUF 102	Gideon	SUF 93	Gifford, John	MNT 84
Gibbs, Elijah	SRA 32	Gideon, Crowfoot	MNT 109	Gifford, John	RNS 49
Gibbs, Israel	GRN 356	Gideon, Niles	WSH 274	Gifford, John	WSH 185
Gibbs, Jabez	SRA 31	Gideon, Sarles	WSH 288	Gifford, Joseph	RNS 50
Gibbs, James	CAY 582	Gidersleve, David	QNS 75	Gifford, Joseph	SRA 15
Gibbs, James E.	TIO 213	Gidley, Daniel	DUT 7	Gifford, Joshua	COL 214
Gibbs, Job	RNS 43	Gidley, Jasper	ALB 104	Gifford, Lewis	HRK 515
Gibbs, John	CAY 640	Gidley, Jonathan	DUT 6	Gifford, Mary	COL 249
Gibbs, John	ESS 309	Gidley, Timothy	DUT 6	Gifford, Obadiah	ALB 71
Gibbs, John	OTS 36	Gidney, Absalom	WST 117	Gifford, Perry	SRA 46
Gibbs, Jonas	ESS 319	Gidney, Absolum	WST 167	Gifford, Peter	ONT 468
Gibbs, Jonas	SCH 140	Gidney, Benjamin	WST 115	Gifford, Roger	WST 161
Gibbs, Joseph	OTS 52	Gidney, Caleb	WST 111	Gifford, Rowland	COL 219
Gibbs, Joseph	RNS 43	Gidney, Daniel	ORN 284	Gifford, Silas	SRA 57
Gibbs, Justus	OTS 56	Gidney, Daniel	WST 115	Gifford, Thomas	ALB 39
Gibbs, Leonard	WSH 300	Gidney, Eleazer	ORN 278	Gifford, Thomas	SRA 50
Gibbs, Ozias	HRK 588	Gidney, Elezar	WST 111	Gifford, Timothy	MNT 84
Gibbs, Preserve	OTS 56	Gidney, Elizabeth	NYK 68	Gifford, Wilkinson	DUT 8
Gibbs, Richard	CAY 620	Gidney, Elizabeth	WST 115	Gifford, William	DUT 51
Gibbs, Samuel	CAY 580	Gidney, Elizabeth	WST 120	Gifford, Wm	MNT 84
Gibbs, Samuel Junr	CAY 584	Gidney, .ilbert	WST 111	Gifford, William B.	KNG 2
Gibbs, Sheldon	WSH 306	Gidney, Jacob	ORN 277	Giggie, William	ORN 315
Gibbs, Simeon	OTS 56	Gidney, James	NYK 138	Gil_, Benjamin	CAY 564
Gibbs, Sovell	ONN 164	Gidney, James	WST 115	Gil_on, Jacob	TIO 233
Gibbs, Uriah	DUT 109	Gidney, John	ORN 279	Gilbert & Nathan Negroes	CHN 932
Gibbs, W___	CAY 580	Gidney, John	WST 116	Gilbert	SUF 72
Gibbs, Warren	WSH 281	Gidney, Joseph	ULS 234	Gilbert, Abijah	ALB 9
Gibbs, Weram	WSH 294	Gidney, Joseph	WST 147	Gilbert, Abijah	WST 155
Gibbs, William	ALB 141	Gidney, Robert	WST 149	Gilbert, Allen	SCH 169
Gibbs, Willm	SCH 142	Gidney, Samuel	ORN 284	Gilbert, Amos	CAY 600
Gibbs, Woodruff	WSH 296	Gidney, Solomon	WST 115	Gilbert, Amos	OND 166
Gibbs, Zenas	OND 183	Gidney, Thomas	WST 115	Gilbert, Ashley	GRN 330
Gibes, Isaac	NYK 73	Gidney, William	ORN 272	Gilbert, A ger	CHN 882
Gibs, Oliver	GRN 340	Gidney, William	WST 115	Gil[bert?], Augustus	ONN 177
Gibson, Abel	CHN 762	Gifferd, Benjamin	WSH 210	Gilbert, Benjn	OTS 6
Gibson, Abel [Junr?]	CHN 762	Gifferd, Charles	WSH 238	Gilbert, Benjamin	RNS 35
Gibson, Alexander	NYK 75	Gifferd, Eli	WSH 233	Gilbert, Benjamin	RNS 90
Gibson, Alexander	WSH 258	Gifferd, Elihu	WSH 198	Gilbert, Butler	OTS 30
Gibson, Archd	ALB 139	Gifferd, Gedion	WSH 196	Gilbert, Daniel	ORN 366
Gibson, Collin	WSH 191	Gifferd, Justice	WSH 198	Gilbert, Darius	SRA 58
Gibson, ..niel	SRA 3	Gifferd, Phileps	WSH 196	Gilbert, David	CHN 740
Gibson, David	ALB 127	Giffin, Jonathan	WSH 209	Gilbert, David	ONT 418
Gibson, David	KNG 10	Giffin, William	NYK 86	Gilbert, David	WSH 288
Gibson, Henry	ORN 388	Gifford, Aaron	COL 250	Gilbert, Dinah a Black	NYK 41
Gibson, Hughe	RCH 92	Gifford, Abel	WSH 198	Gilbert, Ebenezar	KNG 10
Gibson, James	ALB 33	Gifford, Abner	DUT 49	Gilbert, Egbert	NYK 139
Gibson, James	NYK 44	Gifford, Abraham	DUT 103	Gilbert, Eleazer	SRA 46
Gibson, James	NYK 76	Gifford, Absalom	HRK 494	Gilbert, Eli	WSH 251
Gibson, James	NYK 115	Gifford, Alexander	NYK 90	Gilbert, Elias	ONT 450
Gibson, James	WSH 225	Gifford, Amaziah	COL 202	Gilbert, Elias	SRA 59
Gibson, Janes	NYK 47	Gifford, Andrw	NYK 101	Gilbert, Elijah	COL 208
Gibson, John	CHN 796	Gifford, Andrew	SRA 30	Gilbert, Elisha	CHN 740
Gibson, John	MNT 1	Gifford, Asa	HRK 434	Gilbert, Elisha	COL 207
Gibson, John	NYK 135	Gifford, Benjamin	DUT 130	Gilbert, Elisha	STB 200
Gibson, John	SRA 13	Gifford, Benjamin	NYK 33	Gilbert, Elisha Junr	CHN 740
Gibson, John	WSH 305	Gifford, Benjamin	RNS 50	Gilbert, Elisha Junr	COL 202
Gibson, Jones	WSH 203	Gifford, Caleb	WSH 189	Gilbert, Elmore	SRA 19
Gibson, Lewes	NYK 109	Gifford, Caleb	WSH 198	Gilbert, Ephraim	WST 155
Gibson, Mathew	WSH 190	Gifford, Daniel	DUT 148	Gilbert, Ezekiel	COL 246
Gibson, Richard	DUT 48				

144

Name	Loc	Name	Loc	Name	Loc
Gilbert, Frederick	CHN 944	Gilchrist, John W.	SRA 24	Gill, Napthali	RNS 80
Gilbert, Garrit	NYK 52	Gilchrist, Robert	NYK 16	Gill, Robert	DUT 70
Gilbert, Gershum	SRA 48	Gilchrist, Thomas	WSH 289	Gill, Samuel	CHN 952
Gilbert, Hezekiah	SRA 59	Gilchrist, Wm	ALB 34	Gill, Stephen	SCH 169
Gilbert, Hezekiah Jr	SRA 53	Gilchrist, William	SRA 25	Gill, Thomas	NYK 49
Gilbert, Jacob	WST 155	Gilchrist, William	ONN 154	Gillam, Ezekiel	ULS 247
Gilbert, James	NYK 96	Gilchrust, John Junr	WSH 258	Gillam, Henry	WSH 292
Gilbert, Jeduthen	WSH 252	Gilcrest, Alexander	WSH 246	Gillan, Peter	ORN 392
Gilbert, Jesse	DEL 288	Gilcriest, James	WSH 247	Gillan, Suzannah	NYK 58
Gilbert, Joel	OND 210	Gilcrust, Archibald	WSH 246	Gillan, Thomas	ULS 190
Gilbert, John	CAY 522	Gild, John	TIO 244	Gillard, Robert	CAY 522
Gilbert, John	DUT 90	Gildersleaves, Joseph	RNS 91	Gillaspey, Robert	WSH 292
Gilbert, John	NYK 91	Gildersleeve see Geld-		Gillaspie, Andrew	RNS 82
Gilbert, John	ONT 488	erslieve, Gidersleve		Gillaspie, Andrew	WST 144
Gilbert, John	OTS 21	& Gindersleaf		Gillaspie, Benjamin	RNS 29
Gilbert, John	SRA 29	Gildersleeve, Asa	TIO 259	Gillaspie, James	RNS 82
Gilbert, John	WSH 255	Gildersleeve, Benjamin	DUT 22	Gillaspie, James	RNS 82
Gilbert, John	WSH 258	Gildersleeve, Finch	DUT 174	Gillaspie, Joseph	RNS 80
Gilbert, John W.	NYK 48	Gildersleeve, Henry	DUT 123	Gillaspie, Matthew	RNS 82
Gilbert, Jonathan	COL 200	Gildersleeve, James	DUT 23	Gillcot, Theodore	CHN 934
Gilbert, Jonathan	HRK 464	Gildersleeve, John	QNS 77	Gillend, Bryan	NYK 121
Gilbert, Jonathan	OTS 22	Gildersleeve, Nathan-		Gillender, James	NYK 39
Gilbert, Joseph	GRN 328	iel	DUT 24	Gilles, Alexander	WSH 258
Gilbert, Joseph	ONN 132	Gildersleeve, Phillip	DUT 103	Gilles, Archibald	WSH 247
Gilbert, Joseph	ONT 390	Gildersleeve, Silas	ORN 311	Gilles, Huton	WSH 259
Gilbert, Joseph	SRA 6	Gildersleeve, Stephen	SUF 83	Gilles, James	WSH 258
Gilbert, Joseph	SRA 55	Gildersleeve, Thomas	DUT 34	Gilles, John	WSH 258
Gilbert, Joseph	WSH 190	Gildersleeve, Wight-		Gilles, Robert	WSH 297
Gilbert, Joseph	WSH 200	head	SUF 83	Gilles, Samuel	WSH 225
Gilbert, Josiah	GRN 341	Gildersleeve, William	DUT 125	Gillespey, James	ALB 24
Gilbert, Josiah	WSH 200	Gildersleeves, Joseph	WST 149	Gillespie, Charles	NYK 104
Gilbert, Justus	ULS 193	...dersleve, ...	QNS 78	Gillespie, Francis	NYK 69
Gilbert, Lazarus	COL 252	Gildersleve, George	QNS 78	Gillespie, Joseph	CAY 566
Gilbert, Mary	COL 243	Gildersleve, James	QNS 74	Gillespie, Kitty	NYK 105
Gilbert, Medad	DUT 135	Gildersleve, Jonathan	QNS 74	Gillespie, Thomas	HRK 407
Gilb_t, Moses	CAY 698	Gildersleve, Richard	QNS 74	Gillespie, William	KNG 7
Gilbert, Nancy	NYK 93	Gildersleve, Richard		Gillespy, Neil	WSH 250
Gilbert, Nathan	OTS 24	Junr	QNS 74	Gillet, Aaron	COL 178
Gilbert, Nathaniel	CAY 612	Gildersleve, Richard		Gillet, Abijah	HRK 527
Gilbert, Othniel	ONT 418	Senr	QNS 74	Gillet, Abraham	CHN 942
Gilbert, Phoebe	SUF 101	Gildersleve, Simeon	QNS 74	Gillet, Abraham	HRK 421
Gilbert, Reuben	ONT 418	Gildersleve, Wright	QNS 76	Gillet, Asa	DEL 279
Gilbert, Rufus	ONT 454	Gildersleves, John	SRA 10	Gillet, Asa	ULS 234
Gilbert, Samuel	CAY 684	Gile, Benjamin	SRA 56	Gillet, Asahel	ULS 184
Gilbert, Samuel	COL 213	Gile, Ray	SCH 169	Gillet, Austin	ULS 184
Gilbert, Samuel	HRK 464	Gilead, Jabesh	DUT 101	Gillet, Barnibas	WSH 192
Gilbert, Samuel	ONN 180	Gilees, Thomas	CHN 834	Gillet, Benjamin	DUT 43
Gilbert, Saml	OTS 53	Giles, Aquila	KNG 2	Gillet, Benjamin	ULS 184
Gilbert, Seth	CHN 944	Giles, Hamlin	MNT 46	Gillet, Benajmin Junr	ULS 184
Gilbert, Sewell	ONT 420	Giles, Isaac	COL 240	Gillet, Calvin	COL 210
Gilbert, Silas	OTS 30	Giles, Isaiah	ORN 316	Gillet, Charles	COL 215
Gilbert, Thaddeus	DUT 140	Giles, James	HRK 563	Gillet, Charles	OND 208
Gilbert, Thaddeus Junr	DUT 136	Giles, Janet	ORN 356	Gillet, Charles	ORN 313
Gilbert, Theodore	OND 195	Giles, Joab	RNS 22	Gillet, Charles Junr	ORN 313
Gilbert, Theodore Junr	OND 195	Giles, Joel	OND 183	Gillet, Daniel	CAY 592
Gilbert, Thomas	CAY 522	Giles, John	NYK 143	Gillet, Daniel	COL 264
Gilbert, Thomas	NYK 102	Giles, John	OTS 34	Gillet, David	DUT 44
Gilbert, Thomas	OND 215	Giles, Joseph	WSH 275	Gillet, Eli	HRK 527
Gilbert, Thomas	WSH 249	Giles, Phillip a		Gillet, Elijah	COL 221
Gilbert, Thomas	WST 151	mulatto	NYK 66	Gillet, Elisha	SUF 66
Gilbert, Thomas	WST 155	Giles, Robert	NYK 67	Gillet, Ezekiel	ULS 184
Gilbert, Timothy	DUT 139	Giles, Robert	NYK 150	Gillet, Gershom	ONT 380
Gilbert, Titus	OND 195	Giles, Samuel	HRK 585	Gillet, Horace	ULS 184
Gilbert, Truman	TIO 215	Giles, William	ALB 141	Gillet, Isaac	DEL 279
Gilbert, William	ONT 472	Giles, William	DUT 28	Gillet, Israel	ULS 265
Gilbert, William W.	NYK 150	Gilespie, Collin	NYK 28	Gillet, Jabez	ONT 426
Gilbert W., Eunice	WST 155	Gilespy, Jacob	WSH 247	Gillet, Jacob	HRK 599
Gilbet, John	SRA 55	Gilfert, George	NYK 52	Gillet, Job	ONT 442
Gilbons, Margaret	NYK 34	Gilford, Henry	NYK 119	Gillet, Joel	DUT 137
Gilbs, Itheman	OND 213	Gilford, John	WSH 198	Gillet, John	ORN 311
Gilchrest, Saml	RCK 102	Gilford, Samuel	NYK 40	Gillet, Jonth	COL 211
Gilchriest, John	WSH 257	Gilford, Samuel Junior	NYK 40	Gillet, Joseph	OND 164
Gilchrist see Gichrist		Gill, George	RNS 82	Gillet, Moses	COL 264
Gilchrist, Alexander	SRA 25	Gill, James	NYK 90	Gillet, Moses	ULS 184
Gilchrist, Andrus	NYK 57	Gill, Johh	ALB 45	Gillet, Moses Junr	COL 266
Gilchrist, John	SRA 24	Gill, John	ONN 174	Gillet, Nathan	COL 221
Gilchrist, John	SRA 24	Gill, Matthew	ALB 128	Gillet, Nathel	COL 211

Name	Loc		Name	Loc		Name	Loc	
Gillet, Noadiah	RNS	54	Gilmore, James	NYK	111	Glass, Sarah	NYK	113
Gillet, Oliver	HRK	531	Gilmore, James	WSH	194	Glass, Thomas	OND	205
Gillet, Olliver	CHN	862	Gilmore, John	CHN	810	Glass, Widow	MNT	108
Gillet, Richard	DUT	44	Gilmore, John	KNG	9	Glasure, William	WSH	203
Gillet, Ruben	CHN	976	Gilmore, John	NYK	65	Glatier, Jacob	WSH	221
Gillet, Rufus	DUT	77	Gilmore, John	NYK	145	Glazier, Jacob	OTS	42
Gillet, Samuel	DUT	44	Gilmore, John	OND	224	Gle__, John S.	MNT	14
Gillet, Samuel	WSH	190	Gilmore, John	WSH	191	Gleason, Bazaleel	OND	186
Gillet, Seth	CAY	550	Gilmore, Joseph	NYK	26	Gleason, Daniel	OND	186
Gillet, Seth	ULS	185	Gilmore, Mary	NYK	66	Gleason, David	COL	187
Gillet, Solomon	OND	189	Gilmore, Mathew	NYK	131	Gleason, Ephraim	COL	184
Gillet, Thomas	DEL	289	Gilmore, Richard	CAY	562	Gleason, John	SRA	53
Gillet, Timothy	CHN	932	Gilmore, Robert	ULS	254	Gleason, Solomon	OND	200
Gillet, Timothy	OND	173	Gilmore, Robert	WST	146	Gleason, Thomas	COL	194
Gillet, William	COL	206	Gilmore, Thomas	DEL	274	Gleason, William	SRA	43
Gillet, William	ORN	313	Gilmore, William	WSH	189	Gleason, William T.	SRA	47
Gilletond, Catherine	NYK	120	Gilson, Giles	WSH	265	Gleaston, David	WSH	214
Gillett, Abraham	ULS	210	Gilson, Jacob	ALB	77	Gleaston, Henry	WSH	214
Gillett, Adonijah	WSH	272	Gilson, Joseph	ORN	334	Gleeson, John	CLN	159
Gillett, Assahel	WSH	302	Gilson, Samuel	ORN	344	Gleeson, Assa	WSH	264
Gillett, Daniel	ONN	136	Gilson, Sarah	ORN	344	Gleeson, James	ALB	87
Gillett, Elihu	MNT	53	Gilson, Susannah	WSH	189	Gleeson, Joel	WSH	243
Gillett, Jeremiah	ONT	472	Gilston, Joel	ONN	136	Gleeson, Luther	SUF	90
Gillett, Joel	CHN	828	Gilston, John	DEL	284	Gleeston, Whilltesey	TIO	218
Gillett, Rhoda	WSH	301	Gilston, John	ONT	354	Glen, Alexander	SRA	22
Gillett, Samuel	CHN	976	Giltren, Francis	TIO	214	Glen, Allen	SRA	22
Gillett, Samuel	RNS	95	Giltson, Jonathan	ALB	112	Glen, Cornelius	ALB	43
Gillett, Samuel	WSH	274	Gilyoe, Jasper	WST	158	Glen, Henry	ALB	12
Gillett, Simmeon	CHN	874	Gin a Black Woman and			Glen, Jacob	ALB	6
Gillett, William	CHN	962	Child	SRA	29	Glen, Jacob S.	SCH	137
Gilliam, Thomas	SCH	148	Ginaway, Joseph M.	NYK	83	Glen, John	ALB	12
Gillias, Alexander	NYK	114	Ginay, Lewis	ALB	46	Glen, John S.	ALB	4
Gillidet, Thomas	HRK	599	Gindar, Thomas	NYK	104	Glenn, Charles	CAY	606
Gilligan, Peggy	NYK	22	Ginder, Molly	NYK	104	Glenn, William	WST	145
Gillin, Hugh	RCK	109	Gindersleaf, Elkanah	ALB	21	Glenny, James	ONN	183
Gillis, Jonathan	ORN	323	Gingly, Saml	SCH	117	Glenny, John	ONN	183
Gillis, Joseph	CHN	816	Gingon, Ishreet	NYK	124	Gleson, Eleazer	OTS	51
Gillis, Joseph	SRA	60	Ginks, Thomas	CHN	804	Gleves, Mathew	KNG	10
Gillis, Matchiah	ULS	263	Gipson, Michael	HRK	516	Gliechman, Frederick	ALB	76
Gillis, Sarah	ORN	273	Girand, Joseph	NYK	23	Glin, James	WST	152
Gillisbie, Daniel	SUF	82	Giraud, Anna	NYK	42	Glines, Abner	WSH	222
Gillislie, Jonas	SUF	83	Gird, Henry	NYK	42	Gliston, Amose	WSH	214
Gillislie, Thos	SUF	81	Gireau, Benjamin	DUT	39	Glochlin, Daniel	MNT	72
Gillispie, David	ULS	181	Gireau, Daniel	DUT	30	Glorianna	SUF	84
Gillispie, James	ULS	206	Gireau, Elias	ULS	257	Glover, Andrew	DUT	84
Gillispie, John	ORN	284	Gireau, James	DUT	39	Glover, Benjn	OTS	23
Gillispie, John	ORN	298	Gireau, John	ULS	258	Glover, Chas	SUF	75
Gillispie, John	ULS	223	Gireau, Oliver	ULS	258	Glover, Christopher	RNS	59
Gillispie, John Junr	ULS	224	Gireau, William	ULS	258	Glover, Davis	SUF	65
Gillispie, Matthew	ORN	296	Girsel, Levi	GRN	341	Glover, Elizabeth	NYK	48
Gillispie, Robert	ORN	302	Gisbrowe, Henry D.	NYK	122	Glover, Ezekiel	SUF	77
Gillispie, Samuel	ORN	307	Gisner, John	RCK	97	Glover, Ezra	WSH	237
Gillispie, William	ORN	294	Gisner, Nicholas	RCK	99	Glover, Grover	SUF	77
Gillispie, William Junr	ORN	309	Gisselbergh, Henry	COL	194	Glover, Isaac B.	RNS	60
Gillitt, Daniel	RNS	40	Gitchel, Eaton	SRA	35	Glover, Jacob	MNT	107
Gillman, Charles	NYK	122	Gitman, James	NYK	148	Glover, James	CHN	774
Gillman, Daniel	ALB	135	Given, John	ALB	138	Glover, Jeremeah	WSH	247
Gillman, Daniel	SRA	17	Given, Joseph	SRA	34	Glover, John J.	NYK	38
Gillman, Joseph	RNS	90	Given, Margaret	ORN	293	Glover, Joseph	SUF	75
Gillmore, Bathsheba	RNS	82	Given, Resolved	SRA	13	Glover, Thomas	SCH	169
Gillmore, John	NYK	112	Given, Robert	WST	144	Glover, Zadock	CAY	710
Gillmore, John	SRA	55	Givens, Fits	WST	155	Goave, Robt	OTS	7
Gillmore, Perez	CHN	750	Givens, _muel	CAY	608	Gobair, Isaac	NYK	25
Gills, Felix	SCH	169	Givet, John	WSH	247	Gobble, Hugh	NYK	96
Gillson, Amariah	RNS	92	Gla..an, Robert	MNT	91	Gobble, Usial	OTS	50
Gillson, Asa	ORN	366	Gladwin, William	HRK	419	Gobert, Charles	NYK	29
Gillson, Asaph	ORN	367	Glann, James	ORN	322	Goble, Abner	DEL	278
Gillson, Isaac	ORN	287	Glann, John	ULS	240	Goble, George	ORN	360
Gillson, James	RNS	92	Glann, William	ULS	240	Goble, Jacob	OTS	49
Gillson, John	ORN	367	Glasgow, Hugh	OND	199	Goble, James	CAY	530
Gilky, Samuel	ONT	344	Glasher, Eleakim	WSH	269	Goble, Jona	OTS	49
Gilman(?), Eli___	ONT	390	Glasier, Abel	WSH	270	Godard, Edward	OTS	43
Gilman, Phillip	STB	199	Glass, Boswell	MNT	106	Godard, Lewis	OND	222
Gilman, Samuel	SRA	46	Glass, James	MNT	106	Godby, William	NYK	112
Gilmer, John	HRK	502	Glass, James	NYK	29	Goddard, Ebel	OTS	43
Gilmore, Benjamine	NYK	133	Glass, John	OTS	52	Goddard, Mary	NYK	73
Gilmore, James	CHN	784	Glass, Philetes	OND	199	Godden, John	ALB	16

Name	Loc		Name	Loc		Name	Loc
Godfree, John free Negro	RNS 110		Goff, Potter	OTS 35		Golden, Hugh	NYK 22
Godfree, Jonathan	RNS 27		Goff, Richard	CHN 766		Golden, Jacob	QNS 61
Godfree, Josiah	RNS 70		Goff, Robert	ALB 88		Golden, James	NYK 114
Godfree, Molburn	RNS 70		Goff, Roswell	TIO 256		Golden, James	WST 113
Godfree, Robert	RNS 71		Goff, Solomon	ONN 176		Golden, Jesse	HRK 449
Godfree, Robert Junr	RNS 71		Goff, Tertullus	CAY 560		Golden, John	ALB 112
Godfrey, Daniel	ULS 188		Goff, Timothy	ULS 188		Golden, John	DUT 91
Godfrey, David	CAY 548		Goff, Wm	OTS 38		Golden, John	QNS 74
Godfrey, David	ORN 313		Goffe, David	ULS 234		Golden, John	ULS 182
Godfrey, George	OND 195		Gogelett, Henry	QNS 62		Golden, Joseph	DUT 79
Godfrey, Isaac	ALB 24		Goggan, Thomas	NYK 146		Golden, Justus	HRK 447
Godfrey, James	SRA 9		Gogswell see Cogswell			Golden, Margaret	NYK 128
Godfrey, John	ALB 128		Gogswell, Samuel	SRA 53		Golden, Nathl	ALB 70
Godfrey, Jonathan	DUT 172		Gohuties, Danl	RCK 100		Golden, Nathaniel	RNS 36
Godfrey, Jonathan	ULS 188		Gohutius, Abrm	RCK 109		Golden, Reuben	WST 113
Godfrey, Josiah	OND 172		Goin, Thomas	NYK 106		Golden, Robert	ORN 280
Godfrey, Richard	ALB 83		Goit, Samuel	ONT 410		Golden, Samuel	DUT 9
Godfrey, Seth	MNT 117		Gold, Abraham	DEL 268		Golden, Susanna	ALB 70
Godfrey, Spencer a Black	NYK 127		Gold, Benjn	SUF 70		Golden, Thomas	DUT 79
Godfrey, Thomas	SCH 136		Gold, Daniel	ONT 364		Golder, Abraham	QNS 75
Godfrey, Wm	OND 208		Gold, Daniel	ONT 374		Golder, Andrew	QNS 75
Godfrey, John	MNT 88		Gold, Daniel Ju.	ONT 364		Golder, Benjamin	QNS 68
Godgrove, Ury	CHN 980		Gold, Daniel Ju.	ONT 374		Golder, Isaac	QNS 68
Godley see Godby			Gold, David	HRK 525		Golder, John	DUT 115
Godwin, Job	ONT 412		Gold, David	ONT 438		Golder, Joseph	QNS 74
Godwin, William	ONT 410		Gold, David	RNS 108		Golder, Morris	QNS 77
Goehutias, Joseph	RCK 107		Gold, Ebenezer	WSH 229		Golder, William	QNS 68
Goelet, Peter Senior	NYK 27		Gold, Edward	ESS 308		Golder, William	QNS 68
Goelet, Peter P.	NYK 31		Gold, Eli	DEL 277		Golding, Abraham	WST 161
Goelet, Robert R tsey	NYK 29		Gold, Eli	WSH 206		Golding, Amos	WST 138
Goes, Barent A.	COL 266		Gold, Elijah	ALB 68		Golding, Bernerd	ALB 148
Goes, Barent J. Junr	COL 264		Gold, Geor..	CAY 696		Golding, Elias	COL 213
Goes, Bernard	ORN 297		Gold, Hannah	ONN 162		Golding, George	WST 150
Goes, Christopher	RNS 58		Gold, Isaac	DEL 269		Golding, Isaiah	CAY 706
Goes, Derick	COL 187		Gold, Jabez	CAY 718		Golding, James	WST 150
Goes, Derick, J.	RNS 48		Gold, James	ALB 92		Golding, John	WST 150
Goes, Dirck D.	COL 266		Gold, James	CAY 556		Golding, Phebee	WST 133
Goes, Ephraim	COL 262		Gold, James	MNT 31		Golding, Robert	ALB 117
Goes, George	RNS 60		Gold, James	MNT 36		Golding, Simeon	SUF 93
Goes, Hendrick	ESS 311		Gold, Jeremiah	ONN 137		Golding, Simeon	WST 150
Goes, Henry	RNS 58		Gold, Job	ALB 134		Golding, William	WST 150
Goes, Isaac	COL 257		Gold, Joel	CHN 900		Goldsmith, Abigal	SUF 75
Goes, John Junr	COL 263		Gold, John	MNT 28		Goldsmith, Benjamin	ORN 325
Goes, John B.	COL 266		Gold, John	ONN 152		Goldsmith, Benjn	SUF 73
Goes, John J.	RNS 59		Gold, John	ONT 370		Goldsmith, Benjn	SUF 74
Goes, John L.	COL 257		Gold, John	ONT 382		Goldsmith, Benjn	SUF 75
Goes, Laurane D.	RNS 92		Gold, Jonathan	ONT 370		Goldsmith, Caleb	ORN 344
Goes, Lawrence	COL 264		Gold, Levi	DEL 277		Goldsmith, Daniel	ORN 351
Goes, Lucas	COL 259		Gold, Levi	RNS 86		Goldsmith, Danl	OTS 29
Goes, Lucas J.	COL 266		Gold, Lewis	RNS 33		Goldsmith, Danl	SUF 75
Goes, Lucas J.	COL 266		Gold, Luther	DEL 278		Goldsmith, David	ULS 211
Goes, Mary	COL 258		Gold, Nathan	DEL 269		Goldsmith, Elisha Junr	ORN 351
Goes, Mathew	RNS 49		Gold, Noah	RNS 49		Goldsmith, Elizabeth	SUF 74
Goes, Nancy	RNS 62		Gold, Samuel	ALB 113		Goldsmith, Elizabeth	SUF 75
Goes, Ope free Black	COL 263		Gold, Samuel	CAY 718		Goldsmith, Hellen	NYK 67
Goes, Peter D.	RNS 48		Gold, Shem	DUT 29		Goldsmith, James	ORN 276
Goes, Richard	COL 258		Gold, Solomon	HRK 454		Goldsmith, Jemima	ORN 296
Goes, Richard J.	COL 261		Gold, Solomon	ONT 426		Goldsmith, Jeremiah	ULS 183
Goes, William	COL 263		Gold, Talcott	DEL 269		Goldsmith, John	ORN 353
Goetchius, Henry	ULS 242		Gold, Thomas	CAY 714		Goldsmith, John	SUF 75
Goetchius, Henry Junr	ULS 250		Gold, Thomas Junr	CAY 714		Goldsmith, Jonathan	SUF 74
Goetchius, John	ULS 251		Gold, Thomas R.	OND 157		Goldsmith, Joseph	SUF 75
Goetschius, Stephen	ULS 204		Gold, William	ONT 364		Goldsmith, Joshua	ORN 357
Goeway, John	ALB 42		Gold, William	ONT 374		Goldsmith, Joshua	SUF 75
Goeway, Solomon	ALB 41		Gold, Wm	RNS 102		Goldsmith, Luther	SUF 75
Goff, Anthy	OTS 38		Gold, Wm	SUF 66		Goldsmith, Martin	SUF 75
Goff, Benjamin	OND 167		Golden a Negro	QNS 66		Goldsmith, Nathl	SUF 75
Goff, Caleb	ALB 100		Golden, Amos	HRK 448		Goldsmith, Paul	ONT 348
Goff, David	OTS 38		Golden, Anna	RNS 48		Goldsmith, Richard	ORN 351
Goff, Job	OTS 38		Golden, Charles	NYK 146		Goldsmith, Richard Junr	ORN 353
Goff, John	HRK 544		Golden, Charles	RNS 83		Goldsmith, Thomas	ONT 350
Goff, John	ONT 470		Golden, Daniel	DUT 9		Goldsmith, Thomas Jun	ONT 346
Goff, Nathan	CHN 842		Golden, Daniel	OTS 13		Goldsmith, Timothy	SRA 47
Goff, Nathan	OTS 38		Golden, David V.W.	HRK 487		Goldsmith, Wilmot	ORN 305
Goff, Oliver	HRK 588		Golden, Ephraim	QNS 83		Goldsmith, Zacheas	SUF 75
			Golden, Garrett	SUF 86		Goldthrite, Thomas	OND 183
			Golden, Harman	RNS 48		Goldtrap, Thos	RCK 110

Name	Ref
Goliway, _____	OND 224
Golloway, George	NYK 152
Golpin, Abel	TIO 238
Gomar, Saul	DUT 40
Gomez, Abraham Jun	NYK 24
Gomez, Benjamin	NYK 38
Gomez, Isaac	NYK 31
Gomez, Moses	NYK 37
Gomier, Nicholas	DUT 78
Gondron, Francis	CLN 168
Gonell, Daniel	COL 181
Gones, Augustus W.	NYK 81
Goney, John	MNT 98
Gonong, Marquis	NYK 105
Gonsalus, Benjamin	ULS 187
Gonsalus, Daniel	ULS 186
Gonsalus, Manuel	ULS 187
Gooches, Jacob	GRN 329
Goo[ches?], Silvenus	GRN 330
Good, George	DUT 83
Good, John	NYK 69
Good, William	NYK 146
Goodal, Stephen	MNT 16
Goodale, David	COL 221
Goodale, Ebenezer	HRK 528
Goodale, Ezekiel	HRK 528
Goodale, Fredrick	TIO 226
Goodale, John	CHN 768
Goodale, Joseph	SUF 96
Goodale, Joseph	SUF 98
Goodale, Josiah	SUF 96
Goodale, Jude	CHN 794
Goodale, Moses	OND 208
Goodale, Sarah	SUF 96
Goodale, Silas	SUF 105
Goodale, Simeon	OTS 2
Goodale, Solomon	ONT 482
Goodale, Thomas	CHN 924
Goodale, Warner	CHN 924
Goodale, William	ONT 434
Goodall, George	CHN 802
Goodanough, Jones	WSH 196
Goodbartlat, John	NYK 65
Goodby, John	SUF 104
Goodday, Lewis	NYK 132
Goodel, Josiah	WSH 223
Goodell, Abijah	HRK 577
Goodell, Ezekiel	WSH 268
Goodemont, Jacob	COL 265
Goodemont, John J.	COL 265
Goodenot, Nichola.	MNT 73
Goodenough, David	CHN 746
Goodenough, Isaiah	OND 184
Goodenough, John	SCH 141
Goodenow, Assahel	WSH 275
Goodens, Jothum	CHN 876
Goodeve, John	NYK 17
Goodfellow, Amos	ALB 61
Goodfellow, Corns	ALB 61
Goodfellow, Ichabod	ONN 166
Goodfellow, James	GRN 340
Goodfellow, John	GRN 340
Goodfellow, Moses	GRN 340
Goodfellow, Samuel	COL 209
Goodfellow, Samuel Junr	COL 209
Goodfellow, Timothy	ONN 166
Goodfellow, William	DEL 272
Goodger, Asa(?)	GRN 339
Goodgion, William	ULS 247
Good Hal_, Robert	MNT 116
Goodhart, George	NYK 145
Goodhue, George	ONT 318
Goodhue, John	OND 164
Goodill, Assahel	WSH 299
Goodin, Asa	CLN 154
Goodin, John	CAY 548
Goodin, Richard	CAY 576
Goodin, Simon	RNS 96
Gooding, James	ONT 416
Goodland, Jeremiah	NYK 22
Goodman, Eliazer	WSH 206
Goodman, Enos	DEL 279
Goodman, Frederick	MNT 120
Goodman, Henry	MNT 118
Goodman, John	ULS 255
Goodman, John	WST 167
Goodman, Mathew	NYK 148
Goodman, Peter	NYK 146
Goodman, Simeon	ALB 12
Goodman, William	NYK 83
Goodnow, Jonathan	MNT 31
Goodnuff, James	MNT 70
Goodrich, Allen	SRA 26
Goodrich, Amos	COL 209
Goodrich, Ashley	CAY 692
Goodrich, Benjamin	ALB 15
Goodrich, Widow C.	DEL 282
Goodrich, Charles	ESS 317
Goodrich, Daniel	GRN 346
Goodrich, David	CHN 792
Goodrich, Elihew Chancy	GRN 331
Goodrich, Elezur	CAY 728
Goodrich, Elnathan	DEL 277
Goodrich, Enock	RNS 83
Goodrich, Ethan	DUT 136
Goodrich, Ezekiel	CAY 692
Goodrich, Ezekiel	WSH 272
Goodrich, Gideon	SRA 19
Goodrich, Hubbard	OTS 31
Goodrich, Isaac	CAY 692
Goodrich, Isaac	DEL 277
Goodrich, Isaac	ONT 396
Goodrich, James	DEL 284
Goodrich, James	ESS 312
Goodrich, Jared	DEL 284
Goodrich, Jesse	COL 204
Goodrich, Jesse	RNS 101
Goodrich, John	ESS 293
Goodrich, Josiah	OND 218
Goodrich, Justus	DEL 282
Goodrich, Levi	HRK 441
Goodrich, Marvin	OND 215
Goodrich, Menus	DEL 282
Goodrich, Michael	DEL 277
Goodrich, Michael Jun	DEL 277
Goodrich, Mrss(?)	GRN 325
Goodrich, Peter	ESS 293
Goodrich, Philander	ALB 84
Goodrich, Roswell	ALB 51
Goodrich, Roswell	OND 170
Goodrich, Samuel	CAY 692
Goodrich, Samuel	DUT 140
Goodrich, Samuel	HRK 418
Goodrich, Samuel	RNS 112
Goodrich, Samul	RNS 94
Goodrich, Shelden	CAY 692
Goodrich, Silas	DEL 285
Goodrich, Timothy	RNS 34
Goodrich, William	COL 202
Goodrich, William	DUT 59
Goodrich, Zenus	DEL 282
Goodrich, Zenus	GRN 339
Goodridge, Ebenezer	SRA 21
Goodridge, Jacob	SRA 21
Good Ridge, Jonah	MNT 91
Goodridge, Levy	SUF 93
Goodridge, Samuel	ONT 372
Goodsal, Joseph	COL 186
Goodsal, Samuel	GRN 339
Goodsbey, Richard	ALB 99
Goodsel, Jacob	WSH 183
Goodsel, Jesse	GRN 336
Goodsell, Isaac	DUT 48
Goodsell, Sexto	WSH 302
Goodsill, Peter	OTS 9
Goodspead, John	SRA 58
Goodspeed, Abner	ALB 31
Goodspeed, Anthony	CHN 754
Goodspeed, Anthony	RNS 92
Goodspeed, Daniel	SRA 48
Goodspeed, DAvid	CHN 754
Goodspeed, Isaac	OTS 51
Goodspeed, Isaac	OTS 54
Goodspeed, Joseph	WSH 201
Goodspeed, Shubal	WSH 277
Goodspeed, Wenslow	WSH 277
Goodwen, Phinehas	GRN 337
Goodwin, Charles	CHN 906
Goodwin, Daniel	ONT 508
Goodwin, David	WSH 185
Goodwin, Eleazer	OND 205
Goodwin, Elizabeth	NYK 90
Goodwin, Francis	NYK 81
Goodwin, George	RNS 82
Goodwin, Hezekiah	CAY 720
Goodwin, Ira	RNS 97
Goodwin, James	CHN 904
Goodwin, James	ONT 424
Goodwin, James	SRA 34
Goodwin, John	MNT 89
Goodwin, John	NYK 152
Goodwin, Mathew	WSH 269
Goodwin, Nathaniel	WSH 243
Goodwin, Norman	CHN 908
Goodwin, O.	CHN 960
Goodwin, Oliver	NYK 28
Goodwin, Samuel	DUT 115
Goodwin, Seth	HRK 533
Goodwin, Solomon	ALB 64
Goodwin, Willeam C.	WSH 269
Goodwin, William	CAY 582
Goodwin, Wm	ONN 173
Goodwin, Zaphania W.	ONT 412
Goodyard, Church	SCH 154
Goodyear, Aaron	HRK 537
Goodyear, Henry	HRK 537
Goodyear, Jared	SCH 152
Goodyear, William	CAY 602
Gool, Henry	COL 197
Gold, Daniel	ULS 180
Gold, Edward	NYK 28
Gold, Elihue	SRA 52
Gold, Elijah	GRN 354
Gold, Frances a Black	NYK 39
Gold, Hannah	NYK 49
Gold, Jesse	SRA 45
Gold, John	NYK 89
Gold, John	NYK 136
Gold, Robert	NYK 124
Gold, Stephen	NYK 126
Gold, William	ULS 180
Goolden, Barney	NYK 69
Goolden, Charles	NYK 105
Gooldsmith, Thomas	NYK 130
Goonch, Jeremiah	CHN 786
Goord, John	NYK 80
Goorich, Calvin	OTS 11
Goorlack, Edward a mulatto	NYK 73
Goos, William	DUT 65
Goose, Benjamin	ONT 410
Goram, Jacob	WST 126
Goram, Joel	SRA 6
Gordanier, Nicholas	SRA 47
Gorden, Henery	CHN 770
Gorden, James	SRA 15
Gorden, James	SRA 16
Gorden, John	CHN 814
Gorden, John	NYK 95
Gorden, John	TIO 216

Graham, Felix	ORN 350	Grainger, Joseph	GRN 332	Grant, John	NYK 121
Graham, Frances	NYK 131	Grammund, Micheal	CAY 624	Grant, John	ONN 174
Graham, Francis	ULS 213	Gran see Green		Grant, John	STB 199
Graham, Frederick	ULS 195	Granadier, John	SCH 169	Grant, John Junr	DEL 268
Graham, George	COL 185	Granby, Mark	ONT 384	Grant, Joseph	STB 202
Graham, George	DUT 140	Grandby, Richard	SCH 137	Grant, Joshua Junr	ULS 183
Graham, George	HRK 479	Grandene, Elizabeth	NYK 39	Grant, Joshua Senr	ULS 185
Graham, George	NYK 88	Grandine, Jacob	RCH 88	Grant, Lewis	DEL 286
Graham, George	WSH 223	Grandon, Samuel	NYK 49	Grant, Melzer	OND 162
Graham, George	WST 145	Grandy, Alpheus	WSH 242	Grant, Michael	NYK 32
Graham, George Junr	WSH 223	Grandy, Bezelius	WSH 252	Grant, Peter	CAY 598
Graham, Hannah	NYK 105	Grandy, Henry	NYK 73	Grant, Peter	DEL 269
Graham, Hector a Negro	ALB 132	Grandy, John	OND 189	Grant, Peter	DEL 269
Graham, Hugh	NYK 140	Grandy, Parker	WSH 205	Grant, Peter	NYK 76
Graham, Isaac	ULS 195	Granfield, Thomas	NYK 75	Grant, Peter	RNS 46
Graham, Isaac G.	WST 167	Granger, Charles	SRA 52	Grant, Richard	NYK 44
Graham, Jacob	NYK 132	Granger, Daniel	COL 204	Grant, Robert	DEL 269
Graham, James	ALB 77	Granger, Daniel	DEL 286	Grant, Samuel	CAY 652
Graham, James	CHN 752	Granger, Ebenr	OTS 7	Grant, Sophia	NYK 130
Graham, James	NYK 42	Granger, Eldad	OTS 2	Grant, Thomas	ONT 328
Graham, James	NYK 105	Granger, Eli	ONT 318	Grant, William	DUT 99
Graham, James	ULS 189	Granger, Elias	ONT 486	Grant, Wm	MNT 60
Graham, James	ULS 249	Granger, Elisha	ONN 164	Grant, Wm	MNT 64
Graham, James G.	ULS 251	Granger, John	ALB 5	Grant, William	NYK 64
Graham, James W.	ORN 303	Granger, John	NYK 85	Grant, William	ULS 185
Graham, John	ALB 143	Granger, John	ONN 163	Grant, Wilson	ONT 444
Graham, John	CHN 866	Granger, Levi	OTS 2	Grarnwright, John	RNS 14
Graham, John	NYK 121	Granger, Moses	CAY 654	Grass see Crass	
Graham, John	NYK 151	Granger, Moses	RNS 110	Grassfield, Henry	ALB 71
Graham, John	ORN 300	Granger, Moses	WSH 224	Grast, John	WSH 283
Graham, John	ORN 337	Granger, Nathon	SRA 52	Grataeah, Peter	NYK 98
Graham, John	WSH 223	Granger, Oliver	OND 174	Graton, James	WSH 268
Graham, John	WST 145	Granger, Peter	WSH 285	Gratsinger, Christian	ULS 233
Graham, John Junr	CHN 866	Granger, Robert	ONN 161	Gratsinger, John	ULS 233
Graham, John Junr	WSH 223	Granger, Samuel	ONN 174	Gratt, Jacob	COL 198
Graham, John C.	NYK 60	Granger, Silas	ONN 164	Gratt, Peter	COL 192
Graham, Jonathan	ALB 129	Granger, Zacharias	ONN 160	Gratt, Wilhelmus	COL 192
Graham, Joseph	GRN 330	Granger, Zeba	OTS 2	Graub, George	NYK 26
Graham, Joseph	NYK 148	Grangy, Mathew	NYK 126	Graughton, James	NYK 133
Graham, Joseph	WSH 267	Grannis, Edward	OND 192	G[rause?], Wm	GRN 333
Graham, Levi P.	NYK 71	Grannis, Robert	GRN 342	Gravalt, Charles	SCH 154
Graham, Malcom	NYK 89	Grant, Abraham	CAY 558	Graver, William	ULS 194
Graham, Margaret	RCK 97	Grant, Alexander	DEL 268	Graves, Abner	DEL 283
Graham, Morris	WST 145	Grant, Alexander 2d	DEL 269	Graves, Abner	OTS 8
Graham, Moses	OND 198	Grant, Allen	DEL 268	Graves, Abrm	SRA 22
Graham, Pale	NYK 31	Grant, Anna	NYK 18	Graves, Adam a Black	NYK 144
Graham, Peter	DUT 34	Grant, Anna	NYK 27	Graves, Ambrose	DUT 132
Graham, Richard	ORN 309	Grant, Widow B.	DEL 269	Graves, Amos	CHN 844
Graham, Richard	RNS 82	Grant, Christie Ann	DUT 53	Graves, Ansel	RNS 18
Graham, Robert	NYK 70	Grant, Daniel	NYK 56	Graves, Ariel	OTS 53
Graham, Robert	WSH 270	Grant, Donald	DEL 268	Graves, Bela	DEL 288
Graham, Robert	WST 122	Grant, Ebenezer	OND 172	Graves, Benjamin	CLN 165
Graham, Roswell	WSH 280	Grant, Eleazer	COL 206	Graves, Benjamin	HRK551½
Graham, Samuel	CAY 596	Grant, Eleazer Junr	COL 206	Graves, Benjamin	OND 194
Graham, Samuel	CAY 604	Grant, Elisher	OND 219	Graves, Chandler	CLN 172
Graham, Samuel	WSH 228	Grant, Elizabeth	ULS 247	Graves, Charles	CHN 782
Graham, Sarah	RCK 97	Grant, George	ALB 39	Graves, Chauncey	OND 194
Graham, Silus	CHN 866	Grant, Gregor	ALB 124	Graves, Cornelius	OND 179
Graham, Simeon	COL 177	Grant, Hugh	ALB 128	Graves, Daniel	TIO 228
Graham, Theods V. W.	ALB 146	Grant, Isaac	ORN 371	Graves, David	SRA 59
Graham, Thomas	ORN 307	Grant, James	DEL 268	Graves, David	WSH 270
Graham, William	ORN 306	Grant, James	DUT 54	Graves, Eldad	COL 204
Graham, William	ORN 321	Grant, James	DUT 76	Graves, Eleazer	CLN 172
Graham, William	ORN 349	Grant, James	NYK 73	Graves, Elihu	SCH 140
Graham, William	ULS 244	Grant, James	RNS 32	Graves, Eliphalet	SCH 140
Graham, William	WST 163	Grant, James	SCH 134	Graves, Ezra	CLN 174
Graham, William Junr	WSH 223	Grant, James Jun	DEL 269	Graves, Ezra	HRK 589
Graham, Winthrop	CAY 690	Grant, Jesse	GRN 329	Graves, Hubbard	ULS 198
Graham, Zachariah	ULS 213	Grant, Jesse	GRN 329	Graves, Israel	CHN 782
Grahams, Daniel	WSH 255	Grant, John	ALB 91B	Graves, Jacob	OND 179
Grahams, John	WSH 195	Grant, John	ALB 124	Graves, Jahue	NYK 135
Grahams, Joseph	WSH 184	Grant, John	COL 254	Graves, James	CAY 582
Grahams, Robert	WSH 267	Grant, John	DEL 268	G.aves, James	SCH 140
Grahams, Samuel	WSH 193	Grant, John	DEL 272	Graves, Jedediah	HRK 573
Grahan, William	WSH 223	Grant, John	NYK 34	Graves, John	HRK 589
Graig, Laurence	CLN 166	Grant, John	NYK 39	Graves, John	MNT 36
Grai_er, John	ONT 486	Grant, John	NYK 78	Graves, John B.	NYK 31

Graves, Jonah	COL 183	Gray, James	OTS 11	Greatrase, Sylvanus	ALB 94
Graves, Jonathan	ESS 319	Gray, James	RNS 45	Greek, James	DUT 81
Graves, Jonathan	OND 208	Gray, James	WSH 297	Green, ...	SCH 133
Graves, Josiah	HRK 420	Gray, Jeduthen	CHN 742	Green, ...othy	SCH 133
Graves, Josiah	RNS 4	Gray, Joe a mulatto	NYK 20	Green, Abraham	NYK 90
Graves, Lebbeus	ONN 162	Gray, Joel	CHN 880	Green, Abraham	ULS 213
Graves, Lewis	SRA 59	Gray, John	ALB 134	Green, Allen	OTS 16
Graves, Martin	OND 215	Gray, John	CAY 542	Green, Ambrose	MNT 38
Graves, Mattheus	ONN 163	Gray, John	CHN 808	Green, Amos	WSH 251
Graves, Matthew	CHN 782	Gray, John	COL 234	Green, Andrew	WST 151
Graves, Moses	CHN 752	Gray, John & Richard	DUT 142	Green, Anna	TIO 245
Graves, Moses	OTS 13	Gray, John	NYK 42	Green, Anson	OTS 55
Graves, Nathaniel	OND 198	Gray, John	NYK 70	Green, Anthony	SRA 40
Graves, Noah	WSH 212	Gray, John	NYK 111	Green, Archelaus	OTS 32
Graves, Phineas	COL 202	Gray, John	OND 176	Green, Archibald	CAY 690
Graves, Recompence	OTS 19	Gray, John	ONT 500	Green, Arthur M.	QNS 69
Graves, Richard	HRK 420	Gray, John	ORN 313	Green, Asa	RNS 76
Graves, Roswell	NYK 33	Gray, John	ORN 382	Green, Asher	ULS 183
Graves, Rufus	CLN 172	Gray, John	OTS 4	Green, Assa	WSH 244
Graves, Russel	SCH 140	Gray, John	RNS 74	Green, Augustus	SRA 41
Graves, Seth	CLN 172	Gray, John	WSH 183	Green, Benjamin	ALB 78
Graves, Stephen	CAY 574	Gray, John Junr	CHN 800	Green, Benjamin	CLN 155
Graves, Stephen	COL 184	Gray, John Junr	WSH 222	Green, Benjamin	DUT 97
Graves, Sterling	OND 175	Gray, John Senr	WSH 226	Green, Benjamin	ONT 486
Graves, Sylvanus	DEL 288	Gray, John D.	NYK 15	Green, Benjn	OTS 11
Graves, Thomas	NYK 130	Gray, Jonathan	ULS 209	Green, Benjn	OTS 39
Graves, Timothy	RNS 24	Gray, Jordan	HRK 423	Green, Benjamin	WSH 271
Graves, Waters	OND 164	Gray, Joseph	CHN 742	Green, Benjamin	WST 130
Graves, William	COL 250	Gray, Joseph a mulatto	NYK 86	Green, Benjamin	WST 161
Graves, William	HRK 589	Gray, Joseph	WSH 293	Green, Bowen	ALB 111
Graves, Wm	ONN 162	Gray, Joseph	WSH 294	Green, Branerd	OTS 49
Graves, Zenos	ESS 322	Gray, Matthew	CAY 544	Green, Brinton	OTS 48
Gravestein, Herman	DUT 127	Gray, Moses	OND 181	Green, Caleb	OND 204
Gravett, Robert	CAY 682	Gray, Nathaniel	CHN 798	Green, Caleb	WSH 236
Gravey, Daniel	QNS 68	Gray, Nathaniel	WSH 227	Green, Caleb	WSH 291
Gray, Aaron	RNS 22	Gray, Nathaniel Jun	CHN 808	Green, Calvin	CHN 912
Gray, Abraham	ORN 312	Gray, Peter a Black	NYK 50	Green, Chaffe	OTS 53
Gray, Abraham Junr	ORN 336	Gray, Peter	ULS 180	Green, Charles	CHN 788
Gray, Adam	HRK 411	Gray, Richard & John	DUT 142	Green, Charles	CHN 818
Gray, Amos	CHN 742	Gray, Robert	MNT 3	Green, Charles	OND 169
Gray, Andrew	MNT 10	Gray, Robert	MNT 19	Green, Charles	OND 205
Gray, Andrew	STB 205	Gray, Samuel	SRA 19	Green, Charles	RNS 71
Gray, Asahel	OND 195	Gray, Samuel Junr	MNT 7	Green, Charles	WST 113
Gray, Benjamin	ONT 370	Gray, Sarsfield	COL 210	Green, Charles Junr	WST 113
Gray, Benoney	WST 167	Gray, Silas	ALB 116	Green, Chris	OTS 26
Gray, Cooly	COL 208	Gray, Simeon	ONT 370	Green, Christopher	RNS 106
Gray, Daniel	COL 243	Gray, Thaddeus	ULS 209	Green, Christopher	ULS 244
Gray, Daniel	NYK 70	Gray, Thadeus	COL 208	Green, Coggwell	RNS 23
Gray, Daniel	RNS 70	Gray, Thomas	ALB 83	Green, Daniel	COL 211
Gray, Dan...	RNS 92	Gray, Thomas	TIO 229	Green, Daniel	ORN 335
Gray, Daniel	SRA 30	Gray, Thomas	ULS 212	Green, Danl	OTS 35
Gray, Daniel	WSH 289	Gray, Titus	MNT 1	Green, Daniel	SRA 18
Gray, David	CAY 542	Gray, Widow	MNT 8	Green, Daniel	SCH 151
Gray, David	DUT 20	Gray, William	DUT 159	Green, Daniel	SCH 154
Gray, David	SRA 22	Gray, William	DUT 170	Green, Daniel	WST 167
Gray, David	WSH 230	Gray, Wm	GRN 348	Green, David a Black	NYK 153
Gray, Dugal	NYK 124	Gray, Wm	GRN 348	Green, David	ONN 130
Gray, Edward	WSH 296	Gray, Wm	GRN 350	Green, David	ULS 235
Gray, Eleazer	ORN 391	Gray, William	NYK 129	Green, David	WSH 236
Gray, Elihu	WSH 292	Gray, William	ORN 349	Green, David Junr	ULS 235
Gray, Elijah	CHN 798	Gray, William	SRA 30	Green, Deidamia	DUT 14
Gray, Elijah	OTS 48	Gray, Wm	STB 206	Green, Dexter	RNS 84
Gray, Elisha	CHN 808	Gray, William	WST 123	Green, Duty	DUT 104
Gray, Elkana	SRA 55	Gray, William D.	HRK 575	Green, Duty	TIO 245
Gray, Ephraim	COL 208	Graydes, Gasper	NYK 90	Green, Dyer	OTS 53
Gray, Godfrey	DUT 150	Grayer, George	SUF 107	Green, Ebenezar	CAY 656
Gray, Henry	CAY 526	Grayham, Austin	SRA 42	Green, Ebenezer	CHN 890
Gray, Henry	WSH 230	Grayham, Filander	RNS 13	Green, Ebenezer	ORN 340
Gray, Isaac	CHN 936	Grayham, Henry	RNS 13	Green, Ebenezer	SRA 32
Gray, Isaac	WSH 292	Grayham, Isaac	RNS 13	Green, Ebenezer	TIO 210
Gray, Jabez	SRA 55	Grayson, Anthony	NYK 113	Green, Ebenr	TIO 255
Gray, Jacob	ONN 186	Grayson, John	NYK 28	Green, Ebenezer	ULS 187
Gray, Jacob	TIO 266	Grayson, John	ULS 255	Green, Edward	CHN 794
Gray, James	ALB 96	Grayson, William	NYK 82	Green, Edward	CHN 814
Gray, James	CAY 584	Grayton, Crary	OND 170	Green, Edward	CHN 816
Gray, James	NYK 18	Grd..y, Eli,.	ONN 151	Green, Edward	HRK 453
Gray, James	NYK 55	Greatman, Uriah	SUF 81	Green, Eliot	SRA 41

Name	Code	Name	Code	Name	Code
Green, Elisha	CLN 155	Green, John	DUT 121	Green, Northroup	ULS 235
Green, Elisha	WSH 184	Green, John	MNT 23	Green, Obadiah	RNS 60
Green, Elizabeth	ORN 328	Green, John	MNT 110	Green, Obediah	HRK 550
Green, Ephra_m	MNT 54	Green, John	NYK 28	Green, Oliver	RNS 98
Green, Enoch	DUT 87	Green, John	NYK 37	Green, Oliver	WST 131
Green, Es1c	OTS 54	Green, John	NYK 42	Green, Ocniel(?)	RNS 23
Green, Ethan	CHN 820	Green, John	ONT 332	Green, Othniel	WSH 288
Green, Ezekiel	DUT 35	Green, John	ORN 325	Green, Partrick	NYK 132
Green, Ezra	OND 213	Green, John	OTS 54	Green, Patty	NYK 96
Green, Felix	MNT 22	Green, John	RNS 50	Green, Paul	NYK 63
Green, Gardner	RNS 108	Green, John	RNS 70	Green, Perry	CHN 816
Green, George	DUT 14	Green, John	RNS 72	Green, Peter	ALB 16
Green, George	SRA 4	Green, John	RCK 97	Green, Peter	ORN 382
Green, Hannah	CAY 574	Green, John	RCK 108	Green, Peter	RNS 30
Green, Henry	CLN 158	Green, John	SRA 18	Green, Peter Junr	ORN 382
Green, Henry	DUT 148	Green, John	SUF 92	Green, Philander	RNS 71
Green, Henry	NYK 72	Green, John	SUF 97	Green, Philip	SRA 28
Green, Henry	ONT 450	Green, John	TIO 245	Green, Plinna	RNS 77
Green, Henry	WSH 299	Green, John	ULS 210	Green, Randall	RNS 20
Green, Increase	NYK 98	Green, John	WSH 197	Green, Reuben	WST 128
Green, Isaac	CHN 786	Green, John	WSH 302	Green, Richard	ALB 36
Green, Isaac	DUT 35	Green, John 2d	RNS 76	Green, Richard	ORN 364
Green, Isaac	GRN 354	Green, John J.	RNS 98	Green, Richd	OTS 54
Green, Isaac	OTS 7	Green, John R.	ALB 51	Green, Richard	QNS 76
Green, Isaiah	SRA 48	Green, John R.	DUT 128	Green, Richard	RNS 30
Green, Isaiah	WST 131	Green, John R.	ONT 508	Green, Richard	RNS 76
Green, Israel	CLN 163	Green, Jonas	RCK 106	Green, Robert	ALB 29
Green, Israel	OND 173	Green, _onas	STB 205	Green, Robert	ALB 145
Green, Israel	WST 130	Green, Jonathan	RNS 71	Green, Robert	NYK 131
Green, Jabes	WSH 217	Green, Jonathan	RNS 98	Green, Robert	OTS 28
Green, Jabez	CAY 632	Green, Jonathan	SRA 48	Green, Robert	WSH 211
Green, Jack	WST 144	Green, Jones	WSH 209	Green, Rowland	SRA 28
Green, Jacob	HRK 491	Green, Joseph	CHN 814	Green, Rowland	SCH 133
Green, Jacob	ORN 381	Green, Joseph	DUT 35	Green, Rufus	CLN 156
Green, Jacob	RNS 105	Green, Joseph	DUT 115	Green, Samuel	NYK 77
Green, Jacob	SUF 91	Green, Joseph	GRN 352	Green, Saml	OTS 28
Green, Jacob	TIO 240	Green, Joseph	OTS 48	Green, SamI	RNS 26
Green, James	CHN 930	Green, Joseph	RNS 98	Green, Samuel	RNS 69
Green, James	DEL 279	Green, Joseph	TIO 256	Green, Samuel	RNS 71
Green, James	DUT 34	Green, Joseph	ULS 192	Green, Samuel	WSH 196
Green, James	DUT 172	Green, Joseph	WSH 209	Green, Samuel	WST 130
Green, James	MNT 68	Green, Jospeh	WST 131	Green, Samuel Junr	WSH 195
Green, James	MNT 117	Green, Joseph Junr	RNS 98	Green, Samuel P.	DEL 274
Green, James	NYK 26	Green, Joseph Junr	WST 131	Green, Sarah	NYK 49
Green, James	NYK 63	Green, Joseph 2d	RNS 102	Green, Seth	GRN 336
Green, James	ORN 288	Green, Joseph J.	CLN 164	Green, Seth L.	GRN 336
Green, James	ORN 318	Green, Joshua	CLN 155	Green, Silas	DEL 289
Green, James	RNS 45	Green, Joshua	OND 173	Green, Simeon	OND 203
Green, James	RNS 98	Green, Joshua	ORN 290	Green, Simon	ORN 288
Green, James	SRA 41	Green, Joshua	QNS 84	Green, Solomon	DEL 281
Green, James	SRA 60	Green, Josiah	CAY 584	Green, Stephen	OTS 4
Green, James(?)	SCH 133	Green, Josiah	CHN 820	Green, Stephen	RNS 30
Green, James	WSH 193	Green, Lankford	RNS 99	Green, Stephen	WST 161
Green, James	WSH 250	Green, Leucretia	NYK 87	Green, Susanna	DUT 39
Green, James	WSH 289	Green, Levi	SCH 133	Green, Tempe	QNS 64
Green, Jamew	WSH 295	Green, Luke	RNS 72	Green, Thomas	NYK 90
Green, James	WST 155	Green, Manzer	RNS 69	Green, Thomas	OND 204
Green, Jedediah	CHN 958	Green, Mary	NYK 126	Green, Thomas	OTS 11
Green, Jehiel	ORN 319	Green, Nad	MNT 26	Green, Thomas	OTS 48
Green, Jered	WST 134	Green, Nancey	WST 129	Green, Thomas	RNS 82
Green, Jeremiah	DUT 38	Green, Nancy	RNS 91	Green, Thomas	TIO 216
Green, Jeremiah	RNS 108	Green, Nathan	DUT 174	Green, Thomas	WSH 193
Green, Jeremiah	WSH 217	Green, Nathan	OND 178	Green, Thomas	WST 131
Green, Jeremiah	WST 113	Green, Nathan	OND 219	Green, Timothy	DEL 281
Green, Jerry	RNS 19	Green, Nathan	ONN 166	Green, Timothy	GRN 353
Green, Jesse	OTS 57	Green, Nathan	OTS 35	Green, Timothy	MNT 120
Green, Job	OND 204	Green, Nathan	OTS 35	Green, Timothy	MNT 120
Green, Job	RNS 42	Green, Nathan	RNS 21	Green, Timothy	NYK 48
Green, Job	RNS 69	Green, Nathan	RNS 74	Green, Timothy	SCH 169
Green, Joel	OND 192	Green, Nathan	SRA 9	Green, Tobias	DUT 104
Green, John	ALB 115	Green, Nathan	SRA 45	Green, Turpen	SRA 29
Green, John	CAY 526	Green, Nathan Junr	OTS 35	Green, Wardwell	SCH 133
Green, John	CAY 552	Green, Nathaniel	CHN 788	Green, Warren	OTS 14
Green, John	CAY 590	Green, Nathaniel	SRA 51	Green, Weaver	SRA 29
Green, John	CLN 155	Green, Nathaniel	SRA 52	Green, Williett	SUF 92
Green, John	DUT 13	Green, Nicholas	GRN 353	Green, William	ALB 117
Green, John	DUT 32	Green, Nicholas	RCK 97	Green, William	CHN 776

Griffen, Bartholemew	WST	116	Griffin, Heth	DEL	269	Griffin, Thomas	WSH	284
Griffen, Benjn	OTS	20	Griffin, Isaac	CLN	166	Griffin, Thomas	WST	129
Griffen, David	OTS	48	Griffin, Isaac	DUT	37	Griffin, William	DEL	272
Griffen, Ebenezer	HRK	421	Griffin, Isaac	DUT	104	Griffin, William	DEL	289
Griffen, Esther	WST	121	Griffin, Isaiah	DUT	128	Griffin, William	DUT	153
Griffen, Isaac	OTS	30	Griffin, Jabez	COL	207	Griffin, William	NYK	86
Griffen, Isaiah	COL	251	Griffin, Jacob	ALB	113	Griffin, William	ONT	358
Griffen, Jacob	WSH	200	Griffin, Jacob	NYK	150	Griffin, William	ONT	504
Griffen, James	OTS	38	Griffin, James	COL	211	Griffin, Wm	SUF	72
Griffen, James	WST	112	Griffin, James	DUT	118	Griffin, Zopher	WST	124
Griffen, Jesse	COL	212	Griffin, James	OND	169	Griffing, Augustin	SUF	77
Griffen, John	HRK	565	Griffin, James	WST	132	Griffing, James	SUF	77
Griffen, John a mulatto	NYK	97	Griffin, Jesper	RNS	97	Griffing, Jared	HRK	576
			Griffin, Jesse	WST	122	Griffis, Daniel	HRK	573
Griffen, John	NYK	137	Griffin, John	DEL	284	Griffis, Jerremeah	CHN	958
Griffen, John	QNS	66	Griffin, John	DUT	16	Griffith, Anna	NYK	36
Griffen, John	SRA	61	Griffin, John	DUT	87	Griffith, Barnabas	HRK	488
Griffen, John	WST	112	Griffin, John	OND	201	Griffith, Daniel	CAY	722
Griffen, John	WST	114	Griffin, John	ONT	462	Griffith, David	ALB	36
Griffen, John	WST	118	Griffin, John	RNS	61	Griffith, Eli	ONT	318
Griffen, Jonathan	SRA	38	Griffin, John	SUF	72	Griffith, Hugh	OND	213
Griffen, Joseph	OTS	19	Griffin, John	WSH	211	Griffith, Hugh M.	NYK	70
Griffen, Joseph	WST	121	Griffin, John	WSH	283	Griffith, Jabez	SRA	40
Griffen, Joseph Junr	WST	121	Griffin, John	WST	127	Griffith, James	ONN	136
Griffen, Joshua	OTS	3	Griffin, John	WST	130	Griffith, James	ONN	136
Griffen, Mary	QNS	64	Griffin, John	WST	137	Griffith, Jeremiah	DUT	177
Griffen, Oliver	WST	116	Griffin, John Junr	WST	122	Griffith, [Ow?]en	OND	213
Griffen, Saml	OTS	6	Griffin, John Hunr	WST	124	Griffith, Robert	OND	213
Griffen, Uriah	WSH	220	Griffin, John Senr	WST	124	Griffith, Robert	ORN	307
Griffen, Willm	COL	205	Griffin, Johnathan	GRN	352	Griffith, Saml J.	COL	212
Griffen, William	WST	111	Griffin, Jonathan	WST	124	Griffith, Se hen	ALB	36
Griffen, Zachareah	OTS	5	Griffin, Jonathon	CLN	156	Griffith, Thomas	NYK	100
Griffeth, Evan	OND	213	Griffin, Joseph	ALB	78	Griffith, William	OND	213
Griffeth, John	OND	213	Griffin, Joseph	DUT	42	Griffith, Wm	OTS	42
Griffeth, Moses	OND	208	Griffin, Joseph	DUT	103	Griffiths, Daniel	OTS	29
Griffeths, Clement	OTS	42	Griffin, Joseph	WST	129	Griffiths, Eli	WSH	285
Griffeths, N ah	OTS	29	Griffin, Joseph	WST	142	Griffiths, James	NYK	27
Griffets, Stephen	MNT	111	Griffin, Joshua	DEL	289	Griffiths, James	SUF	84
Griffets, Wm	MNT	111	Griffin, Joshua	DUT	30	Griffiths, John	NYK	35
Griffin, Abijah	GRN	336	Griffin, Joshua	DUT	55	Griffiths, Jona	OTS	29
Griffin, Adam	DUT	124	Griffin, Joshua	RNS	59	Griffiths, Nathaniel C.	NYK	27
Griffin, Adam	ULS	258	Griffin, Josiah	DUT	51	Griffiths, Richard	NYK	139
Griffin, Adam	WST	140	Griffin, Justus	HRK	476	Griffiths, Stephen	SUF	84
Griffin, Amos	DUT	58	Griffin, Kirkland	OND	183	Griffiths, Thomas	NYK	138
Griffin, Andrew	ONT	324	Griffin, Lad	CHN	824	Griffiths, Thomas	ORN	391
Griffin, Ann	SUF	76	Griffin, Lawrence	ULS	216	Griffiths, William	NYK	25
Griffin, Aron	MNT	21	Griffin, Mary	DUT	101	Grigery, Jonathan	WSH	206
Griffin, Austin	ALB	78	Griffin, Michael	WSH	283	Grigery, Thomas	WSH	201
Griffin, Bartlett	SUF	72	Griffin, Michael	WSH	284	Grigg, Asa	OTS	53
Griffin, Benjamin	ALB	115	Griffin, Moses	DUT	118	Grigg, John	ONT	414
Griffin, Benjamin	DUT	89	Griffin, Moses	SUF	105	Grigg, John	TIO	265
Griffin, Benjn	SUF	72	Griffin, Nathan	RNS	97	Grigg, Samuel	COL	211
Griffin, Catherine	NYK	72	Griffin, Nathaniel	OND	200	Grigg, William	KNG	9
Griffin, Clande	NYK	16	Griffin, Nathl	SUF	72	Griggs, Alexander	SRA	8
Griffin, Cornelius	DEL	284	Griffin, Obadiah	DUT	121	Griggs, Amos	TIO	227
Griffin, Cornelius	DUT	28	Griffin, Palmer	ULS	236	Griggs, Betsey	NYK	38
Griffin, Daniel	ULS	184	Griffin, Peter	DEL	274	Griggs, Charles	ALB	92
Griffin, David	CAY	656	Griffin, Phebe	QNS	66	Griggs, Daniel	ALB	110
Griffin, David	WSH	284	Griffin, Rebecca	DUT	42	Griggs, Ichabod	OTS	56
Griffin, David	WST	130	Griffin, Richard	DUT	37	Griggs, John	GRN	352
Griffin, Ebenezer	WSH	284	Griffin, Ruth	DUT	29	Griggs, John	ORN	273
Griffin, Edward	DUT	37	Griffin, Samuel	CHN	952	Griggs, Joshua	RNS	108
Griffin, Edward	DUT	121	Griffin, Samuel	COL	211	Griggs, Nathl	OTS	44
Griffin, Elihue	WST	128	Griffin, Samuel	DUT	103	Griggs, Noah	TIO	227
Griffin, Elizabeth	ULS	257	Griffin, Samuel a mulatto	NYK	133	Griggs, Parker	SCH	169
Griffin, Ezekiel	DUT	20	Griffin, Saml	RNS	59	Griggs, Samuel	ORN	273
Griffin, Ezekiel	WST	125	Griffin, Saml	SUF	72	Griggs, Solomon	OND	208
Griffin, Ezra	ALB	95	Griffin, Smith	ALB	94	Griggs, Thomas	NYK	48
Griffin, Gashum	GRN	336	Griffin, Solomon	DUT	17	Griggs, William	CAY	708
Griffin, Gashum	GRN	353	Griffin, Stephen	ALB	114	Grigory, Hezekiah	OTS	32
Griffin, Gilbert	DUT	128	Griffin, Stephen	DUT	11	Grigory, Silas	OTS	22
Griffin, Gilbert	SRA	57	Griffin, Stephen	RNS	68	Grim, Adam	HRK	492
Griffin, Gilbert	WST	142	Griffin, Stephen	SUF	72	Grim, Charles	NYK	113
Griffin, Gilbert S.	DUT	127	Griffin, Sten	WSH	201	Grim, David	NYK	47
Griffin, Henry	ALB	112	Griffin, Stephen	CHN	818	Grim, Hector a mulatto	NYK	92
Griffin, Henry	DUT	52	Griffin, Thomas			Grim, Henry	HRK	491
Griffin, Henry	NYK	81	Griffin, Thomas	NYK	94	Grim, Henry	NYK	146

Grim, Jacob	NYK 148	Griswold, Miles	OTS 21
Grim, Peter	NYK 56	Griswold, Moses	HRK 454
Grim, Peter	NYK 129	Griswold, Oliver	ONT 468
Grim, Philip	NYK 50	Griswold, Samuel	WSH 213
Grimes, Elizabeth	NYK 24	Griswold, Seth	CHN 914
Grimes, James	ONT 424	Griswold, Simeon	HRK 581
Grimes, Patrick	NYK 65	Griswold, Thomas	NYK 79
Grimes, Richard	GRN 325	Griswold, Walter	DUT 118
Grimes, Richard	GRN 332	Griswold, William	HRK 581
Grimes, Thomas	WSH 295	Griswold, Zed	CAY 656
Grimes, William	HRK 439	Griswould, Amaziah	COL 206
Grimes, William	OND 177	Griswould, David	WSH 298
Grimes, Wm	TIO 263	Griswould, Elias	DEL 290
Grimes, William Junr	HRK 439	Griswould, Elisha	WSH 295
Grimzebeach, John	NYK 69	Griswould, Ephraim	WSH 299
Grindall, John	ORN 326	Griswould, Frances	OTS 17
Grindle, Caleb	MNT 60	Griswould, Jabez	COL 186
Grindman, Adley	MNT 113	Griswould, Jarid	OTS 25
Grindman, F--	MNT 104	Griswould, John	COL 186
Grindman, Halut	MNT 113	Griswould, John	WSH 303
Grinell, Daniel	COL 204	Griswould, Jonah	COL 240
Grineway, James E.	WSH 240	Griswould, Noah	WSH 276
Grinmon, Nathan	CHN 816	Griswould, Oliver	COL 233
Grinmon, Nathan Junr	CHN 816	Griswould, Samuel	CHN 746
Grinmon, William G.	CHN 826	Griswould, Thomas W.	DEL 276
Grinnel, Asa	SRA 35	Griswould, Timo	OTS 9
Grinnel, John	SRA 35	Griswould, Wm	OTS 9
Grinnell, Benjamin	SRA 58	Gritchman	NYK 113
Grinnell, Daniel	SRA 58	Gritman, John Junr	DUT 62
Grinnell, Gideon	ONT 436	Gritman, John Senr	DUT 67
Grinnell, John	ONT 436	Gritmon, Richard	QNS 77
Grinnell, Nathaniel	ONT 436	Gritmon, William	QNS 77
Grinnels, Aaron	SRA 31	Gritton, Wm	GRN 349
Grinnolds, Isaiah	OND 163	Groat, Abraham	ALB 10
Grinold, Mathew	HRK 524	Groat, Abraham	ALB 51
Grinold, Samuel	HRK 524	Groat, Abraham	COL 230
Grippen, Elijah	COL 263	Groat, Abm A.	ALB 12
Grippen, Ichabod	ALB 35	Groat, Andrew	ALB 6
Grippen, Jabez	COL 211	Groat, Catharine	ALB 111
Grippen, Jeffrey	COL 208	Groat, Cornelius	ALB 38
Grippen, Roswell	DEL 275	Groat, Cornelius	ALB 51
Grippen, William	SRA 48	Groat, Corns A.	ALB 51
Grippin, Jabaza	RNS 9	Groat, Dirck	ALB 54
Grippin, Robert	SRA 25	Groat, Dirck A.	ALB 51
Grisol, Abraham	GRN 346	Groat, Dirck S.	ALB 51
Grissel, Elijah	ALB 64	Groat, Eldrad	ALB 54
Grissel, Jeremiah	GRN 346	Groat, Elias	SRA 4
Grist, John	NYK 23	Groat, Gerolemus	OTS 5
Griswald, Asel	ESS 294	Groat, Henry	COL 261
Griswelld, John	SRA 14	Groat, Henry	MNT 23
Griswold, Aaron	ONT 464	Groat, Henry	SRA 4
Griswold, Anson	HRK 437	Groat, Jacob	SRA 35
Griswold, Benajah	CHN 916	Groat, John	ALB 59
Griswold, Benjamin	OND 165	Groat, John	OND 208
Griswold, Chauncy	ORN 281	Groat, Nicholas	OND 208
Griswold, Daniel	HRK 582	Groat, Nichs	SCH 161
Griswold, Daniel 2d	HRK 549	Groat, Philip	OND 208
Griswold, David	TIO 262	Groat, Simon	ALB 23
Griswold, Edmund	ORN 282	Groat, Simon A.	ALB 12
Griswold, Edward	HRK 581	Groat, Stephen	COL 234
Griswold, Elihu	HRK 434	Groate, John	GRN 339
Griswold, Elijah	TIO 255	Groatvalt, Hendrick	RCK 104
Griswold, Elijah	TIO 262	Groatvalt, Henry	RCK 108
Griswold, Elisha	TIO 255	Groatvalt, Joseph	RCK 105
Griswold, Ezekiel	ONN 160	Grodus	QNS 84
Griswold, Francis	HRK 582	Grodvant, George	ALB 83
Griswold, Francis	ONT 472	Grodvant, Peter	ALB 83
Griswold, Gaylord	HRK 434	Groen, Jacob Marius	ULS 229
Griswold, Gideon	TIO 255	Groen, Peter Marius	ULS 228
Griswold, Ira	DUT 153	Groen, William Marius	ULS 229
Griswold, Jacob	DUT 136	Groenhof, Eliza	NYK 138
Griswold, J nna	MNT 60	Groesbeck, Harman	RNS 34
Griswold, Jedediah	NYK 132	Groesbeck, Harman J.	RNS 35
Griswold, Jedediah	ORN 282	Groesbeck, Jacob J.	RNS 36
Griswold, Joab	HRK 434	Groesbeck, John Junr	RNS 35
Griswold, John	HRK 426	Groesbeck, John W.	RNS 36
Griswold, John	OND 208	Groesbeck, Lewis	RNS 35

Groesbeck, Minard	RNS 35	Groom, John	SRA 12
Groesbeck, Nicholas	RNS 32	Groom, Joseph	GRN 332
Groesbeck, Nicholas	RNS 33	Groom, Peter	GRN 331
Groesbeck, Nicholas	RNS 49	Groom, William	SRA 5
Groesbeck, Peter	RNS 36	Groom, William	SCH 144
Groesbeck, Peter W.	RNS 35	Groomes, David	ONN 162
Groesbeck, Walter V.	RNS 35	Groonendyck, Peter	ONT 374
Groesbeck, Walter W.	RNS 35	Groosbeck, Hugh	SRA 6
Groesbeck, Wm	RNS 36	Groot, John D.	CHN 952
Groesbeck, Wm N.	RNS 32	Groover, Edward	SCH 144
Groff, Mathew	RNS 44	Groshoney, John	NYK 95
Grohins, Thomas	GRN 343	Groshong, William	NYK 124
Grom, Wm	GRN 332	Gross, Danie	MNT 49
Gromes, William	SRA 3	Gross, Dederick	NYK 144
Gronindike, John	CAY 550	Gross, George	CLN 160
Gront, Rohan D.	COL 238	Gross, Jabez	OTS 36
Groo, Samuel	ULS 184	Gross, Jabez Junr	OTS 36
Grooesbeck, Anthy	ALB 46	Gross, James	MNT 47
Grooesbeck, Corns	ALB 140	Gross, James	MNT 64
Grooesbeck, David J.	ALB 142	Gross, John	NYK 126
Grooesbeck, David W.	ALB 141	Gross, Johan Daniel	MNT 46
Grooesbeck, Gerrit	ALB 43	Gross, John	OTS 17
Grooesbeck, Gerrit	ALB 109	Gross, Joshua	NYK 117
Grooesbeck, Gisbert	ALB 109	Gross, [N?]owell	OTS 31
Grooesbeck, John	ALB 109	Gross, Thomas	NYK 122
Grooesbeck, John	ALB 141	Grosse, John	ALB 108
Grooesbeck, Peter W.	ALB 45	Grosvant, Andrew	SCH 154
Grooesbeck, Walter	ALB 147	Grotchlass, Gilbert	NYK 57
Grooesbeck, Wm W.	ALB 142	Groundson, Comfort	ESS 306
		Grovener, John	HRK 437
		Grover, Aaron	WSH 191
		Grover, Amasa	OTS 29
		Grover, Benjamin	CAY 686
		Grover, Benjn	OTS 30
		Grover, Eanes	WSH 203
		Grover, Eanes Junr	WSH 203
		Grover, Hesediah	CAY 686
		Grover, John	CAY 712
		Grover, John Senr	CAY 712
		Grover, Josep	MNT 103
		Grover, Joseph	CAY 714
		Grover, Joseph	ONT 416
		Grover, Mabel	OTS 30
		Grover, Manassa	CAY 686
		Grover, Mary	NYK 99
		Grover, Mathew	OTS 54
		Grover, Nehamiah	WSH 203
		Grover, Panuel	CAY 712

Name	Ref	Name	Ref	Name	Ref
H..kins, Asa	CNN 184	Hadley, Smith	ESS 305	Hagerman, Dennis	WSH 189
H...man, John	QNS 73	Hadley, William	NYK 91	Hagerman, Elbert	QNS 70
H.bbs, James	QNS 81	Hadley, William	WST 146	Hagerman, Jack	WST 148
H_ing, Robert	SCH 170	Hadlock, James	TIO 209	Hagerman, James	WSH 189
H_mond, States	WST 167	Hadlock, James	WSH 298	Hagerty, William	ALB 136
Ha_ser, James	MNT 54	Hadlock, Jonathan	CHN 756	Hagete, Thomas	SRA 57
Ha_sett, Barret	MNT 54	Hadlock, Samuel	WSH 298	Hagete, William	SRA 57
Ha..als, ...	MNT 84	Hadly, John	ONT 494	Haggard, Daniel	MNT 73
Ha___, Moses	ORN 384	Hadstele, Joseph	STB 205	Haggarthy, Wm	MNT 63
Ha__, Ele_	OTS 28	Hadway, Frederick K.	WSH 274	Hagger, Stephen	CHN 878
Haag, William	RNS 46	Haesar, Jacob	NYK 71	Haggerman, John	NYK 124
Haan, Andries	ORN 302	Haff, David	SUF 82	Haggerman, Peter	NYK 125
Haarz, Samuel	HRK 548	Haff, Isaac	SUF 83	Haggerman, Peter	NYK 143
Haase, Elizabeth	DUT 162	Haff, James	SUF 82	Haggert, Andrew	WSH 247
Hack, Benjamin	MNT 75	Haff, John	NYK 24	Hagget, Isaac	CNN 158
Hack, Eleazer	NYK 95	Haff, Joseph E.	DUT 103	Haggo, James	NYK 72
Hack, Walter	MNT 89	Haff, Lamen	MNT 120	Hagins, Jerh	COL 218
Hacker, Hogsteed	NYK 77	Haff, Lawrence	QNS 79	Hagle, Peter	OND 214
Hacker, John	NYK 76	Haff, Louy	SUF 89	Hagman, John	COL 177
Hackerly, Richard S.	NYK 51	Haffry, Cornelius	NYK 86	Hagne, John	NYK 129
Hacketoff, Lodovich	NYK 96	Haford, Saml1	TIO 246	Hagner, Hendrick	QNS 69
Hackett, Abil	CHN 772	Hag, Margaret	ALB 124	Hagner, Henry Junr	QNS 69
Hackett, Henery	CHN 770	Hagadorn, Adam	SCH 170	Hagonnene, St Catherine	NYK 49
Hackett, John	NYK 95	Hagadorn, Bartho	SCH 128	Hague, Stephen	OTS 28
Hackett, Joseph	CHN 770	Hagadorn, Jacob	SCH 146	Haight, Aaron	DUT 97
Hackett, Joseph	COL 184	Hagadorn, Samuel	SRA 4	Haight, Aaron	WSH 205
Hackett, Joseph	COL 186	Hagadorn, Samuel	SCH 131	Haight, Aaron, Junr	WSH 206
Hackett, Josiah	CHN 770	Hagadorn, Silas	SRA 36	Haight, Abijah	WST 167
Hackett, Lucy	COL 186	Hagadorn, Robert	SRA 36	Haight, Abraham	COL 221
Hackett, Thomas G.	NYK 26	Hagaman, Benjaman	QNS 76	Haight, Abraham	DUT 106
Hackitt, George	ONT 350	Hagaman, Isaac	COL 177	Haight, Amos	COL 209
Hackley, Andrew	COL 207	Hagaman, James	QNS 83	Haight, Benjm	ALB 10
Hackley, Levi	HRK 569	Hagaman, Joseph	QNS 83	Haight, Benjamin	DUT 101
Hackley, Simeon	COL 207	Hagaman, Peter	QNS 82	Haight, Benjamin	NYK 47
Hackley, Thos_	OTS 47	Hagaman, Peter	QNS 83	Haight, Benjn	OTS 15
Hackney, George	ALB 13	Hagaman, Ram	QNS 83	Haight, Beverly	DUT 31
Hackstone, Wm	OTS 57	Hagaman, Wm	RNS 10	Haight, Caleb	NYK 153
Had, Henry	OTS 10	Hagamine, David	COL 260	Haight, Caleb	WST 133
Hadcock, John	HRK 551	Hagar, Henry	DUT 95	Haight, Charles	WST 168
Hadcock, John	MNT 106	Hagarman, Elbert	QNS 83	Haight, Cornelius	DUT 22
Haddeman, Joseph	DUT 31	Hagarty, James	RNS 81	Haight, Cornelius	DUT 98
Hadden, Bartholemew	WST 115	Hararty, John	RNS 82	Haight, Cornelius	WSH 205
Hadden, Benjamin	WST 121	Hagatee, James	SRA 60	Haight, Cornelius I.	DUT 28
Hadden, Cezer	WST 137	Hagden, Henry	SRA 26	Haight, Daniel	DUT 74
Hadden, Elijah	WST 111	Hagedorn, Christopher	COL 195	Haight, Daniel	WST 111
Hadden, Frank	WST 132	Hagedorn, Jacob	COL 190	Haight, Daniel	WST 155
Hadden, .ilbert	WST 111	Hagedorn, Jonathan	SRA 30	Haight, David	WST 124
Hadden, Gilbert	WST 122	Hagedorn, Joseph	COL 238	Haight, David L.	NYK 52
Hadden, John Junr	WST 122	Hagedorn, Peter Junr	COL 235	Haight, Dorcas	ALB 85
Hadden, Lazarus	WST 129	Hagedorn, Samuel	SRA 32	Haight, Eben	ULS 257
Hadden, Moses	WST 130	Hageman, Benjamin	QNS 65	Haight, Ebenezer	DUT 100
Hadden, Thomas	NYK 141	Hageman, Cornelius	DUT 15	Haight, Elithan	WST 129
Haddock, George	WSH 193	Hageman, Dennee	DUT 116	Haight, Elnathan	WST 122
Haddock, Mary	NYK 64	Hageman, Hendrick	DUT 25	Haight, Ezekiel	CHN 760
Haddock, Samuel	HRK 411	Hageman, Isaac	DUT 127	Haight, George	OND 213
Haddock, William	NYK 23	Hageman, Jacob	DUT 166	Haight, Gilbert	DUT 100
Haddock, Zachariah	MNT 103	Hageman, John	DUT 116	Haight, Grove	NYK 151
Haddy, Charles	NYK 97	Hageman, John	QNS 65	Haight, Henry	ESS 307
Haden, Calup	CHN 888	Hageman, John A.	DUT 24	Haight, Isaac	GRN 345
Haden, Jonathan	ONT 350	Hageman, Samuel	DUT 33	Haight, Israel	DUT 130
Haden, Joseah	CHN 892	Hageman, Thomas	CAY 710	Haight, Jacob	DUT 100
Hadington, Henery	SRA 53	Hagen, Samuel	NYK 101	Haight, Jacob	GRN 330
Hadley	GRN 343	Hagencamp, John	ORN 383	Haight, Jacob	ORN 352
Hadley, Abraham	NYK 93	Hager, Adam	SCH 137	Haight, James	DUT 31
Hadley, Benjamine	GRN 338	Hager, Daniel	SCH 128	Haight, James	DUT 75
Hadley, Ebenezer	OTS 42	Hager, Henry	SCH 137	Haight, James	ORN 302
Hadley, Frederick	ORN 271	Hager, Jacob	SCH 137	Haight, James	WST 122
Hadley, George	NYK 93	Hager, John	SCH 128	Haight, James	WST 131
Hadley, Isaac	NYK 58	Hager, John Junr	SCH 128	Haight, James	WST 132
Hadley, James	NYK 134	Hager, Josias	SCH 128	Haight, James	WST 135
Hadley, James	STB 206	Hager, Peter	DEL 276	Haight, James	WST 159
Hadley, John	NYK 117	Hager, Tunis	SCH 130	Haight, Jesse	DUT 127
Hadley, John	WST 142	Hagerman, Adrean	SRA 4	Haight, Jesse	DUT 128
Hadley, Joseph	CAY 598	Hagerman, Andries	QNS 71	Haight, Jesse	GRN 345
Hadley, Lydia	NYK 132	Hagerman, Andries J.	QNS 71	Haight, Jesse	ULS 258
Hadley, Samuel	ESS 298	Hagerman, Benjamin	COL 232	Haight, John	ALB 139
Hadley, Samuel Jr	ESS 305	Hagerman, Cornelius	QNS 72	Haight, John	DUT 76

Name	Ref
Haight, John	DUT 98
Haight, John	DUT 107
Haight, John	WST 111
Haight, John Junr	WST 155
Haight, Jonathan	COL 212
Haight, Jonathan	DUT 97
Haight, Joseph	DUT 129
Haight, Joseph	NYK 132
Haight, Joseph	WST 168
Haight, Joseph Junr	DUT 127
Haight, Joshua	DUT 105
Haight, Joshua	WSH 300
Haight, Josiah	DUT 106
Haight, Lewis	DEL 275
Haight, Lidia	NYK 93
Haight, Ludlow	WST 133
Haight, Margaret	NYK 137
Haight, Moses J.	DUT 98
Haight, Nicholas	DUT 98
Haight, Nicholas	WST 111
Haight, Nicholas	WST 135
Haight, Obadiah	DUT 130
Haight, Oliver	WSH 228
Haight, Reuben	DUT 100
Haight, Reuben	WST 130
Haight, Reuben	WST 132
Haight, Richard	NYK 134
Haight, Robert	DUT 97
Haight, Robert	DUT 106
Haight, Samuel	CHN 808
Haight, Samuel	CLN 166
Haight, Samuel	DUT 94
Haight, Samuel	DUT 118
Haight, Samuel	GRN 329
Haight, Samuel	GRN 346
Haight, Samuel	TIO 263
Haight, Samuel	ULS 190
Haight, Samuel	WST 133
Haight, Samuel	WST 156
Haight, Samuel	WST 167
Haight, Silas	DUT 97
Haight, Solomon	DUT 100
Haight, Solomon	RNS 53
Haight, Solomon	WST 155
Haight, Stephen	DUT 31
Haight, Sylvanus	DUT 30
Haight, Sylvanus	DUT 73
Haight, Thomas	NYK 128
Haight, Thos	OTS 30
Haight, Thomas J.	GRN 352
Haight, William	CHN 808
Haight, William	DUT 74
Haight, William	NYK 111
Haight, William	WST 167
Haight, William	WST 168
Haight, William Junr	WST 168
Hail, Joel	WSH 237
Haile, Amos Jun	HRK 573
Haile, James	HRK 573
Haile, Nathan	HRK 572
Haile, Peleg	OND 200
Haile, Richard	HRK 573
Haile, Widow	HRK 571
Hain, John	SCH 154
Hainer, Samuel	SCH 160
Haines, Aaron	DUT 178
Haines, Asa	DUT 170
Haines, Caleb	DUT 54
Haines, Charles	ORN 305
Haines, Daniel	DUT 170
Haines, Daniel	ORN 374
Haines, David	ONT 384
Haines, David	ORN 304
Haines, David	ORN 305
Haines, David	SCH 161
Haines, Edward	ORN 279
Haines, Elihu	DUT 178
Haines, Elizabeth	ORN 282
Haines, Elizabeth	ORN 305
Haines, Enoch	DUT 170
Haines, George	OTS 22
Haines, Godfrey	DUT 29
Haines, Godfrey	WST 135
Haines, Godfrey Junr	WST 135
Haines, Henry	SCH 161
Haines, Henry	SUF 105
Haines, Job	SUF 100
Haines, John	DUT 35
Haines, John	DUT 178
Haines, John	ORN 303
Haines, John B.	ALB 76
Haines, Joseph	CAY 530
Haines, Lockwood	ALB 78
Haines, Mary	SUF 98
Haines, Nathan	ONT 498
Haines, Samuel	ORN 303
Haines, Sanford	DUT 54
Haines, Stephen	ALB 116
Haines, William	DUT 170
Hainey, Barnabas	ULS 210
Hainey, Charles	ALB 59
Hainis, Whitney P.	MNT 40
Hains, Benjamin	SUF 98
Hains, Benjamin	WSH 283
Hains, Benjamin	WST 163
Hains, Caleb	NYK 136
Hains, Cornelius	WSH 232
Hains, Daniel	WST 155
Hains, David	NYK 125
Hains, David	SUF 101
Hains, David	WST 111
Hains, Elijah	SCH 146
Hains, Gidney	WST 111
Hains, Jacob	SCH 131
Hains, James	ONT 382
Hains, James	WST 161
Hains, Jeremiah	NYK 137
Hains, Job	SUF 98
Hains, John	SUF 98
Hains, Joshua	WST 160
Hains, Lemuel	SUF 101
Hains, Mathew	WST 115
Hains, Mehitabel	SUF 101
Hains, Peter	WST 113
Hains, Samuel	WST 111
Hains, Sanders	ALB 88
Hains, William	WSH 239
Hainy, John	ONT 400
Hair, Daniel	ALB 110
Hair, Henry	ALB 110
Hair, Jacob	ALB 111
Hair, Nicholas	ALB 36
Hair, William	ALB 34
Hairn, James	WSH 283
Haise, William	WST 154
Hait, Abijah	ULS 259
Hait, Abijah	WST 158
Hait, Amos	ULS 259
Hait, Benjamin	WST 152
Hait, David	SRA 59
Hait, David	WST 141
Hait, Elnathan Junr	WST 125
Hait, Enoch	WST 161
Hait, Hannah	WST 159
Hait, Henry	WST 151
Hait, Israel	ULS 259
Hait, Israel Junr	ULS 259
Hait, Jacob	WST 140
Hait, Jesse	WST 158
Hait, Jesse	WST 159
Hait, Job	WST 158
Hait, John	ULS 259
Hait, John	WST 142
Hait, John	WST 158
Hait, Jonas	WST 158
Hait, Jonathan	WST 132
Hait, Joseph	WST 160
Hait, Nathaniel	WST 158
Hait, Nathaniel Junr	WST 132
Hait, Parson	WST 159
Hait, Samuel	WST 158
Hait, Samuel	WST 160
Hait, Silvanus	WST 161
Hait, Stephen	WST 158
Hait, Thaddeus	ULS 259
Hait, Thaddeus	WST 158
Hait, Walter	WST 132
Hait, William	GRN 343
Haitt, Abraham	WST 138
Haitt, John	NYK 114
Hakatt, Charles	NYK 123
Hake, Samuel	DUT 158
Hakes, Caleb	RNS 78
Hakes, Doneston	RNS 78
Hakes, George	CAY 698
Hakes, George	RNS 73
Hakes, George	RNS 97
Hakes, James	RNS 105
Hakes, Jesse	RNS 84
Hakes, Nathan	RNS 67
Hakes, Stephen	HRK 413
Hakes, Warden	RNS 67
Hakly, Philo	MNT 123
Halbert, Nathan	OND 214
Halbrook, Danl	CHN 882
Halburt, Levi	OTS 21
Halbur , Thomas	OTS 21
Hale, Aaron	CAY 718
Hale, Aaron	SRA 61
Hale, Abner	OND 189
Hale, Asal	MNT 122
Hale, Asal	MNT 124
Hale, Barnet	RNS 29
Hal , Benjamin	MNT 70
Hale, Catherine	NYK 153
Hal , Chrispner	MNT 118
Hale, Daniel	ALB 144
Hale, Daniel	SRA 47
Hale, Ebenezer	CHN 906
Hale, George	GRN 329
Hale, Israel	ONT 410
Hale, Jacob	CAY 718
Hale, James	OTS 32
Hale, Jesse	OND 205
Hale, John	CHN 814
Hale, John	OTS 5
Hale, John	WSH 279
Hale, John	WSH 306
Hale, Justus	CHN 902
Hale, Levi	OND 189
Hale, Levy	CHN 936
Hale, Luther	RNS 24
Hale, Manerva	CHN 902
Hale, Oliver	OTS 26
Hale, Reuben	OND 178
Hale, Reuben	WSH 274
Hale, Samuel	OND 189
Hale, Samuel	WSH 274
Hale, Simeon	SCH 121
Hale, Solomon	ALB 121
Hale, Theadore	MNT 110
Hale, Thomas	CHN 914
Hale, Thomas	GRN 329
Hale, William	CHN 936
Hale, m	MNT 94
Hale, Wm	MNT 95
Halenbake, Michael	RNS 30
Halenbrack, Wm	ALB 104
Haley, Ebenezar	CAY 694
Haley, Edward	NYK 82
Haley, Peter a Black	NYK 79

Name	Ref	Name	Ref	Name	Ref
Haley, Samuel	SRA 6	Hall, Elisha	DUT 177	Hall, Luther	OND 201
Haliday, Alexander	ORN 297	Hall, Elisha	WSH 264	Hall, Mary	NYK 93
Haliday, James	ULS 247	Hall, Elizabeth	NYK 49	Hall, Mary	OTS 16
Haliday, Samuel	ORN 375	Hall, Enoch	OND 211	Hall, Mathew	KNG 10
Haliday, William	ORN 388	Hall, Ephraim	WST 137	Hall, Michael	WSH 290
Hall see Hale		Hall, Ezriel	SCH 170	Hall, Morton	DUT 172
Hall, ...	MNT 84	Hall, Francis	SCH 139	Hall, Moses	CHN 806
Hall, Aaron	COL 230	Hall, Friend	ONT 312	Hall, Moses	HRK 572
Hall, Aaron	RNS 51	Hall, Gad	ALB 88	Hall, Moses	SRA 33
Hall, Abel	DUT 31	Hall, Garner	OTS 31	Hall, Nathan	DUT 174
Hall, Abigail	ORN 286	Hall, George	NYK 103	Hall, Nathan	GRN 340
Hall, A..er	ONT 456	Hall, George	WSH 257	Hall, Nathl	SCH 144
Hall, Abijah	OND 208	Hall, Gideon	DUT 12	Hall, Nathaniel	WSH 274
Hall, Abraham	CAY 554	Hall, Gilbert	ONT 314	Hall, Nathl Junr	SCH 144
Hall, Adam	DEL 289	Hall, Green	CHN 764	Hall, Nicholas	ALB 5
Hall, Alpheus	CHN 806	Hall, Henry	ORN 386	Hall, Noah	QNS 83
Hall, Ambrose	DUT 166	Hall, Henry	QNS 84	Hall, Noah Jur	OND 212
Hall, Amos	ONT 388	Hall, Henry	SRA 28	Hall, Oliver	RNS 71
Hall, Anan	OTS 14	Hall, Henry	SCH 154	Hall, Oliver	ULS 267
Hall, Andrew	QNS 80	Hall, Hezekiah	ALB 90	Hall, Orin Day H.(?)	GRN 330
Hall, Andrew	WSH 214	Hall, Ira	WSH 276	Hall, Pathiah	QNS 74
Hall, Aner	RNS 50	Hall, Isaac	DUT 16	Hall, Peter	COL 251
Hall, Archibald	NYK 138	Hall, Isaac	NYK 93	Hall, Peter	NYK 41
Hall, Aron	GRN 354	Hall, Isaac	OND 204	Hall, Peter	QNS 70
Hall, Asa	RNS 103	Hall, Isaac	ONN 138	Hall, Philemon	ONT 388
Hall, Augustus	RNS 101	Hall, Isaac	RNS 51	Hall, Powell	CHN 822
Hall, Azariah	ONN 156	Hall, Jacob	DEL 272	Hall, Reuben	ORN 319
Hall, Benajah	DUT 58	Hall, Jacob	DUT 15	Hall, Reuben	ORN 376
Hall, Benjamin	COL 210	Hall, Jaduthan	RNS 51	Hall, Reuben	QNS 80
Hall, Benjamin	DEL 269	Hall, James	CLN 154	Hall, Richd	OTS 7
Hall, Benjamin	DUT 11	Hall, James	DUT 80	Hall, Rivers	QNS 80
Hall, Benjamin	DUT 119	Hall, James	DUT 122	Hall, Robard	GRN 354
Hall, Benjamin	DUT 139	Hall, James	ESS 303	Hall, Robert	DEL 268
Hall, Benjamin	HRK 559	Hall, James	ORN 367	Hall, Robert	ORN 345
Hall, Benjamin	OND 200	Hall, James	ORN 382	Hall, Robert	QNS 80
Hall, Benjn	OTS 31	Hall, James	WST 131	Hall, Rowland	OTS 19
Hall, Benjn	OTS 38	Hall, Jeremiah	RNS 66	Hall, Rowland	RNS 99
Hall, Bennajah	MNT 120	Hall, Jesse	ONT 454	Hall, Rufus	OND 174
Hall, Bonajah	MNT 120	Hall, John	DEL 269	Hall, Ruphes	WSH 237
Hall, Bristol	ALB 88	Hall, John	DUT 126	Hall, Salman	OND 221
Hall, Burges	WSH 189	Hall, John	HRK 559	Hall, Samuel	CHN 766
Hall, Caleb	COL 206	Hall, John a Black	NYK 118	Hall, Samuel	CHN 806
Hall, Caleb	DUT 96	Hall, John	NYK 123	Hall, Samuel	CHN 822
Hall, Calup	CHN 876	Hall, John	OND 208	Hall, Samuel	DUT 5
Hall, Catharine	WST 143	Hall, John	ONN 140	Hall, Samuel	DUT 72
Hall, Charles	RNS 66	Hall, John	ONT 486	Hall, Samuel	DUT 174
Hall, Charles	RNS 74	Hall, John	ORN 345	Hall, Samuel	NYK 146
Hall, Chrisr	OTS 11	Hall, John	ORN 375	Hall, Samuel	OND 220
Hall, Dan	WST 155	Hall, John	RNS 99	Hall, Samuel	ONN 129
Hall, Daniel	DUT 52	Hall, John	ULS 199	Hall, Samuel	ONN 180
Hall, Daniel	HRK 559	Hall, John	WSH 205	Hall, Samuel	ORN 386
Hall, Daniel	MNT 47	Hall, John	WSH 258	Hall, Samuel	WSH 286
Hall, Daniel	NYK 71	Hall, John	WST 168	Hall, Sarah	NYK 62
Hall, Daniel	OND 177	Hall, John Jun	HRK 559	Hall, Shuball	ONN 155
Hall, Daniel	ORN 362	Hall, John Senr	ULS 184	Hall, Sillaman	WST 137
Hall, Daniel	QNS 80	Hall, John ye 2d	ULS 184	Hall, Silo	TIO 222
Hall, Daniel	QNS 84	Hall, John B.	ULS 240	Hall, Silvanus	OTS 9
Hall, Daniel	RNS 71	Hall, Jonathan	CAY 524	Hall, Solomon	QNS 82
Hall, Daniel	SUF 104	Hall, Jonathan	DUT 147	Hall, Stephen	COL 206
Hall, Daniel J.	HRK 549	Hall, Jonathan	ONN 164	Hall, Stephen	ONN 129
Hall, Darius	QNS 80	Hall, Jona	OTS 14	Hall, Stephen	ONN 180
Hall, David	DUT 172	Hall, Jonathan	WSH 266	Hall, Stephen	ORN 379
Hall, David	HRK 559	Hall, Josep	MNT 65	Hall, Stephen	SRA 33
Hall, David	OND 221	Hall, Joseph	ESS 320	Hall, Stephen	WST 121
Hall, David	QNS 84	Hall, Joseph	QNS 73	Hall, Sylvester	OND 213
Hall, David	RNS 43	Hall, Joseph	QNS 76	Hall, Sylvester Jur	OND 213
Hall, Dennis	CHN 828	Hall, Joseph	WSH 190	Hall, Thomas	ALB 133
Hall, Drew	NYK 30	Hall, Joseph	WSH 256	Hall, Thomas	CLN 163
Hall, Ephraim	ALB 28	Hall, Joshua	COL 210	Hall, Thomas	DUT 126
Hall, Easy	NYK 20	Hall, Joshua A.	DUT 125	Hall, Thomas	HRK 484
Hall, Ebenezer	NYK 103	Hall, Josiah	CHN 822	Hall, Thomas	NYK 136
Hall, Ebenezer	RNS 51	Hall, Jothum	CHN 824	Hall, Thomas	RNS 43
Hall, Edward	RCH 91	Hall, Justus	COL 207	Hall, Thomas	RNS 72
Hall, Elias	WSH 215	Hall, Lemuel	ONN 169	Hall, Thomas	WSH 289
Hall, Eliezer	SCH 139	Hall, Levi	ULS 256	Hall, Timothy	DUT 46
Hall, Elijah	ONN 141	Hall, Limon	WSH 254	Hall, Timothy	SRA 34
Hall, Elijah	WSH 254	Hall, Luke	CHN 806	Hall, Uriah	DUT 125

Name	Loc	Name	Loc	Name	Loc
Hall, William	CAY 600	Hallenbeck, Michl M.	COL 228	Hallock, Foster	ULS 267
Hall, William	DUT 8	Hallenbeck, Michael R.	COL 254	Hallock, George	SUF 67
Hall, William	DUT 138	Hallenbeck, Michael W.	COL 256	Hallock, Hendrick	SUF 68
Hall, William	GRN 335	Hallenbeck, Nichs	SCH 133	Hallock, Henry	OND 176
Hall, William	HRK 454	Hallenbeck, Nichs	SCH 146	Hallock, Heny	SUF 67
Hall, William	HRK 572	Hallenbeck, Richard	ALB 90	Hallock, Isaac	DUT 119
Hall, William	NYK 73	Hallenbeck, Robert	COL 254	Hallock, Isaac	DUT 125
Hall, William	NYK 121	Hallenbeck, Samel	COL 182	Hallock, Isaac	WSH 239
Hall, William	TIO 209	Hallenbeck, Samuel	COL 198	Hallock, Israel	ORN 328
Hall, William	ULS 189	Hallenbeck, Samel W.	COL 178	Hallock, Israel Junr	ORN 328
Hall, William	WSH 200	Hallenbeck, Willm	COL 182	Hallock, James	SUF 74
Hall, William	WST 121	Hallenbeck, William	COL 254	Hallock, James	ULS 239
Hall, Zebulon	WSH 242	Hallenbeck, William	GRN 340	Hallock, James	ULS 266
Hallace, Thomas	NYK 75	Hallenbeck, Wm	GRN 348	Hallock, James	WST 125
Hallam, Jonas	COL 265	Hallenbeck, William J.	COL 254	Hallock, Jesse	WST 122
Hallam. Lewis	NYK 48	Hallenbeck, Willm J.	COL 254	Hallock, John	ALB 115
Hallam, Mervin	NYK 68	Hallenbeck, Yocham	GRN 348	Hallock, John	ESS 306
Hallaway, Benjamin	DUT 48	Hallenbee, Andrus	COL 194	Hallock, John	ORN 328
Hallaway, John	DUT 53	Hallery, David	MNT 113	Hallock, John	SUF 66
Hallaway, Joseph	DUT 12	Hallet, Geo	OTS 45	Hallock, John	SUF 75
Hallaway, Joseph	DUT 53	Hallet, Jacob	SCH 155	Hallock, John	ULS 252
Hallaway, Niles	DUT 11	Hallet, Joseph	DEL 288	Hallock, John	WSH 298
Hallaway, William	DUT 53	Hallet, Moses	ORN 270	Hallock, John Jr	WST 145
Hallawick, John	ULS 250	Hallet, Nathan	STB 206	Hallock, Jonathan	ORN 382
Hallebert, John	SUF 102	Hallet, Samuel	DUT 32	Hallock, Jonathan	SUF 67
Hallebert, Joseph	SCH 149	Hallet, Samuel	STB 206	Hallock, Jonathan	SUF 68
Hallebrant, John	SCH 169	Hallet, Solomon	ALB 33	Hallock, Jonathan	SUF 69
Halleck, [F?]rederick	SUF 96	Hallet, William	NYK 81	Hallock, Joseph	ORN 276
Halleck, Thomas	SUF 91	Hallet, William	ORN 343	Hallock, Joseph	SUF 75
Halleck, Samuel	SUF 89	Hallet, Ednor	NYK 64	Hallock, Joshua	CAY 538
Halleck, William	SUF 95	Hallett, Elizabeth	NYK 50	Hallock, Joshua	DUT 9
Hallembeck, Abraham	CHN 740	Hallett, Elizabeth	NYK 139	Hallock, Joshua	DUT 105
Hallembeck, Ephram	CHN 746	Hallett, Gideon	QNS 62	Hallock, Josiah	SUF 68
Hallembeck, John	CHN 742	Hallett, Isaac	ORN 389	Hallock, Josiah Jr	SUF 68
Hallembeck, Michal	CHN 742	Hallett, Jacob W.	ONT 508	Hallock, Luther	SUF 74
Hallenbak_, Abraham C.	ESS 294	Hallett, James	NYK 44	Hallock, Moses	DUT 105
Hallenbake, Mary	RNS 91	Hallett, James	NYK 48	Hallock, Nathan	GRN 338
Hallenbeck, Aaron	ALB 76	Hallett, John	NYK 123	Hallock, Noah	SUF 68
Hallenbeck, Abraham	ALB 100	Hallett, Jonah	QNS 64	Hallock, Noah	SUF 68
Hallenbeck, Andrew	COL 254	Hallett, Joseph	ORN 279	Hallock, Peter	ALB 115
Hallenbeck, Anthony	ALB 125	Hallett, Nathaniel	QNS 63	Hallock, Peter	CLN 155
Hallenbeck, Billa	COL 254	Hallett, Richard S.	NYK 35	Hallock, Philip	SUF 68
Hallenbeck, Caspar	COL 266	Hallett, Samuel	NYK 142	Hallock, Reeve	SUF 69
Hallenbeck, Casoer	ALB 108	Hallett, Samuel	ORN 279	Hallock, Richard	ORN 320
Hallenbeck, Casper	GRN 348	Hallett, Samuel	QNS 63	Hallock, Richd	SUF 74
Hallenbeck, Corns	ALB 23	Hallett, Samuel Jun	NYK 142	Hallock, Richard	WST 126
Hallenbeck, Corns	ALB 103	Hallett, Stephen	QNS 61	Hallock, Richard Junr	WST 126
Hallenbeck, Derick	COL 256	Hallett, William	NYK 116	Hallock, Robert	WST 132
Hallenbeck, Elizth	ALB 90	Hallett, William	ORN 278	Hallock, Ruble	SUF 74
Hallenbeck, Ephriam	SCH 144	Halley, Abraham	ALB 115	Hallock, Ruport	SUF 74
Hallenbeck, Henry	ALB 125	Halley, Jesse	WST 140	Hallock, Samuel	OND 175
Hallenbeck, Henry	COL 254	Halley, John	ALB 35	Hallock, Samuel	ORN 276
Hallenbeck, Isaac	ALB 58	Hallibard, John	CNN 157	Hallock, Samuel	WST 151
Hallenbeck, Isaac	SRA 34	Hallibert, John	CAY 608	Hallock, Thomas	GRN 352
Hallenbeck, Jacob	ALB 101	Hallick, Cato a		Hallock, Thomas	ULS 196
Hallenbeck, Jacob	COL 254	mulatto	NYK 73	Hallock, Uriah	SUF 72
Hallenbeck, Jacob	GRN 328	Halliday, Gideon	ALB 33	Hallock, Uriah Ju	SUF 72
Hallenbeck, Jacob J.	ALB 101	Hall[in?], Adam	MNT 32	Hallock, William	ALB 120
Hallenbeck, Jacob J.	COL 254	Hallinbeck, Eleanor	ALB 125	Hallock, William	HRK 572
Hallenbeck, James	SCH 128	Hallinbeck, Isaac	ALB 125	Hallock, William	OND 201
Hallenbeck, Jeremiah	COL 255	Hallinbeck, Jacob Jn	ALB 122	Hallock, Wm	SUF 72
Hallenbeck, John	ALB 90	Hallker, Stephen	MNT 67	Hallock, Wm	SUF 72
Hallenbeck, John	ALB 102	Hallock, Amos	DUT 106	Hallock, Wm Jr	SUF 72
Hallenbeck, John	COL 261	Hallock, Azah	ALB 115	Hallock, Zebulon	ORN 320
Hallenbeck, John	GRN 329	Hallock, Benjn	SUF 75	Hallock, Zebulon Junr	ORN 320
Hallenbeck, John J.	COL 254	Hallock, Caleb	RNS 95	Hallock, Zepheniah	NYK 130
Hallenbeck, John R.	COL 254	Hallock, Daniel	ORN 389	Hallock, Zopher	SUF 66
Hallenbeck, Killian	COL 228	Hallock, Danl	SUF 74	Hallow, Jeremiah	GRN 339
Hallenbeck, Mathew	COL 256	Hallock, David	SUF 67	Hallowell, Samuel	NYK 20
Hallenbeck, Mathew R.	COL 256	Hallock, David	SUF 69	Hallsey, Luther	ALB 5
Hallenbeck, Mathias	COL 255	Hallock, Edward	CLN 154	Hallshaver, Lawrence	ALB 57
Hallenbeck, Mathias Junr	COL 255	Hallock, Deward	DUT 105	Hallstead, James	CAY 636
Hallenbeck, Matthias	ALB 58	Hallock, Edward	GRN 357	Hallstead, Timothy	CAY 648
Hallenbeck, Michl	ALB 90	Hallock, Edward	ULS 267	Hallsted, Phillip	NYK 125
Hallenbeck, Michael	COL 191	Hallock, Elisha	ORN 328	Halluway, Richard	NYK 98
Hallenbeck, Michael	COL 254	Hallock, Elizabeth	SUF 74	Hallworth, R..ert	MNT 66
Hallenbeck, Michael	GRN 349	Hallock, Ezra	SUF 73	Hally, James	GRN 354

Handtrot, Henry	DUT 80	Hanmore, Francis	ORN 276	Harden, Francis	WST 112
Handy, Brazilla	ESS 307	Hanmore, Moses	ULS 257	Harden, Isaac	ONT 482
Handy, George	SCH 169	Hanna, James	NYK 97	Harden, Moses	SRA 55
Handy, Jabez	WSH 236	Hanna, James	ORN 378	Harden, Rachael	NYK 85
Handy, James	CHN 814	Hanna, John	DUT 154	Harden, Silus	CHN 872
Handy, James	TIO 217	Hanna, John	NYK 102	Harden, Steven	MNT 100
Handy, John	SRA 7	Hanna, William	ORN 274	Harden, Theodore	CHN 872
Handy, John	WSH 235	Hanna, William	OTS 25	Harden, Thomas	DUT 104
Handy, Joseph	TIO 209	Hannah	SUF 93	Hardencergh, Abraham J.	ULS 244
Handy, Joy	CHN 814	Hannah	SUF 98	Hardenbergh, Benjamin	ULS 182
Handy, Martin	SCH 150	Hannah, David	WSH 225	Hardenbergh, Catharine	ULS 206
Handy, Monassah	SRA 42	Hannah, Hugh	ALB 9	Hardenbergh, Charles	ULS 208
Handy, Richard	SCH 150	Hannah, John	SRA 29	Hardenbergh, Elias	ULS 231
Handy, Robert	ULS 185	Hannah, John	WSH 183	Hardenbergh, Garret	ORN 275
Handy, Samuel	ONT 388	Hannah, John	WSH 225	Hardenbergh, Girardus	ULS 204
Handy, Thomas	TIO 257	Hannah, Robert	ALB 53	Hardenbergh, Isaac	DEL 267
Handy, William	OND 194	Hannah, Robert	WSH 225	Hardenbergh, Jacob	MNT 24
Handy, Wm	ONN 160	Hannah, Samuel	ALB 138	Hardenbergh, Johannis G.	ULS 213
Handy, Zebulon	SRA 35	Hannan, Andrew	NYK 69	Hardenbergh, John C.	ULS 206
Hanebal, Stephen a		Hannan, Henry	NYK 29	Hardenbergh, John E.	ULS 208
Black	NYK 139	Hannans, James	ALB 78	Hardenbergh, John J.	ULS 214
Hanecy, Medad	ONN 150	Hannas, John	TIO 241	Hardenbergh, Jonathan	ULS 208
Hanegar, Nancy	NYK 111	Hannas, Thomas	NYK 63	Hardenbergh, Leonard	ULS 204
Haneman, Andrew	RNS 89	Hanness, William	QNS 66	Hardenbergh, Lewis	ULS 208
Han more, John	MNT 73	Hannevert, Anne	ULS 201	Hardenbergh, Nicholas	ULS 248
Han_on, Benjamin	ORN 384	Hannien, David	NYK 151	Hardenbergh, Phillip	ULS 203
Haneon, Peter	ORN 380	Hanning, John Chris-		Hardenbrook, Abel	NYK 43
Haner, Coonrod	RNS 89	tian	NYK 56	Hardenbrook, Abel	NYK 151
Haner, Helma _	RNS 89	Hanning, Joseph	NYK 56	Hardenbrook, Gradus	NYK 111
Haner, Jacob	HRK 498	Hannum, John	DEL 280	Hardenbrook, John A.	NYK 48
Haner, Jeremiah	HRK 498	Hanny, Robert	OND 174	Hardenbrook, Phillip	NYK 135
Haner, John	RNS 89	Hanon, Daniel	WST 156	Hardenbrook, William	NYK 44
Haner, John	WST 123	Hanor, Peter	COL 201	Hardenbrook, William	
Haner, Philip	RNS 96	Hanor, Phillip	COL 194	Junr	NYK 40
Haner, Waples	TIO 229	Hans_, Ephram	CHN 838	Hardenbrook, William A.	NYK 114
Haner, William	HRK 498	Hanse, Thomas	CAY 652	Hardenburgh, Charity	QNS 61
Hanes, Daniel	COL 246	Hanseker, Henry	ORN 304	Hardenburgh, John L.	CAY 694
Hanes, Elias	NYK 15	Hansell, George	ORN 285	Harder, John	GRN 333
Hanes, John	GRN 336	Hansen, Aart	DUT 22	Harder, Martin	SCH 147
Hanes, Michael	ALB 47	Hansen, Albert	ALB 144	Harder, Martin Jr	SCH 148
Hanes, Samuel	QNS 63	Hansen, Benjm	ALB 144	Harder, William Junr	COL 266
Hanever, Flora	ALB 126	Hansen, Isaac	ALB 149	Hardick, Daniel J.	COL 254
Haney, Charles	MNT 81	Hansen, James	ALB 15	Hardick, Francis	GRN 358
Haney, Hugh	RNS 69	Hansen, John	ALB 139	Hardick, Garett	SRA 12
Haney, Peter A.	WSH 288	Hansen, John	ALB 144	Hardick, Jacob	GRN 358
Hanford, Abraham	OND 214	Hansen, Letty	NYK 153	Hardick, John	COL 255
Hanford, Alexr	OND 214	Hansen, Peter	MNT 72	Hardick, Jonathan	COL 252
Hanford, George	DUT 64	Hansen, William	ALB 16	Hardick, Joseph	COL 249
Hanford, Gershom	DEL 285	Hansen, William	NYK 132	Hardick, Leonard	COL 249
Hanford, Joseph	WST 125	Hanshe, Henry	NYK 151	Hardick, Leonard Junr	COL 252
Hanford, Lewis	WST 126	Hanshett, Isaac	CAY 674	Hardick, Leonard J.	COL 253
Hanford, Moses	DEL 278	Hanson, John	RNS 111	Hardick, Peter	COL 254
Hanford, Theophilus	ULS 265	Hanton, Jeremiah	NYK 140	Hardick, William F.	COL 249
Hankerson, James	SRA 25	Hanton, William	WSH 210	Hardie, Andrew	ESS 294
Hankin, John	NYK 82	Hantz, Andrew	ORN 390	Hardie, Thomas	NYK 39
Hankins, Ralph	ULS 181	Hantz, John	ORN 390	Hardin, Archibald	CAY 626
Hanks, Azariah	HRK 439	Hantz, Joseph	ORN 393	Hardin, _ary	CAY 626
Hanks, David	RNS 74	Hanyan, David	DUT 75	Harding, Abraham	ORN 313
Hanks, Hannah	RNS 77	Hanyan, Isaac	ORN 304	Harding, Abraham	ORN 321
Hanks, Isaac	WSH 253	Hanyan, Peter	DUT 160	Harding, Amos	ULS 188
Hanks, Isaac	WSH 253	Hanyan, Thomas	DUT 73	Harding, Benj Negro	QNS 70
Hanks, Joseph	OTS 33	Hanyay, Joseph	NYK 93	Harding, Charles	ULS 188
Hanks, Luthar	RNS 77	Hapeman, Frederick	COL 235	Harding, Daniel	TIO 237
Hanks, William	WSH 193	Hapeman, John	DUT 150	Harding, Ezekiel	WSH 264
Hanlenbeek, Isaac P	NYK 55	Hapeman, Peter	COL 235	Harding, George	OND 187
Hanley, Benjamin	WST 157	Hapgood, Jonathan	CLN 166	Harding, Isaac	TIO 221
Hanley, Joel	WST 123	Hapman, Frederick	COL 236	Harding, Jacob	MNT 18
Hanley, Matthew	CAY 576	Happy, George	ULS 193	Harding, James	ULS 252
Hanley, Patrick	ALB 15	Harbach, Henry	HRK 515	Harding, John	NYK 81
Hanley, William	KNG 11	Harbeck, John	ALB 43	Harding, John	ORN 314
Hanlon, John	HRK 451	Harbert, Henry	NYK 127	Harding, John	WSH 264
Hanmer, Andrew	ORN 290	Harcourt, Nathaniel	ULS 268	Harding, John Junr	ORN 313
Hanmer, David	MNT 30	Hard, Ezra	WSH 282	Harding, Maggey	NYK 39
Hanmer, John	ALB 138	Hard, James	WSH 282	Harding, Seth	NYK 32
Hanmore, Benjamin	ULS 198	Harda, Wm	RNS 104	Harding, Stephen	NYK 43
Hanmore, Cadwallader	ORN 273	Hardcastle, William	SUF 81	Harding, William	ULS 188
Hanmore, Edward	ORN 355	Harden, Elias milatto	NYK 128	Hardman, John	NYK 76

Harris, Ezekiel	SRA	57
Harris, Ezekiel	WST	141
Harris, Francis	DUT	61
Harris, Garret	CAY	544
Harris, Gilbert	SRA	10
Harris, Henry	ALB	29
Harris, Henry a Black	NYK	70
Harris, Henry	ONT	448
Harris, Henry	SUF	98
Harris, Isaac	ULS	237
Harris, Isaac	WST	163
Harris, Jacob	ALB	29
Harris, James	CAY	536
Harris, James	CAY	642
Harris, James	DEL	285
Harris, James	NYK	111
Harris, James	ONN	175
Harris, James	QNS	70
Harris, James	RNS	111
Harris, Jasper	NYK	136
Harris, Job	WSH	299
Harris, John	CAY	668
Harris, John	CAY	726
Harris, John	HRK	522
Harris, John	KNG	10
Harris, John	MNT	115
Harris, John a Black	NYK	90
Harris, John	OND	186
Harris, John	SRA	57
Harris, John C.	DEL	284
Harris, John W.	SRA	57
Harris, Joicy	KNG	7
Harris, Jonathan	ONN	130
Harris, Joseph	CHN	944
Harris, Joseph	CLN	163
Harris, Joseph	DEL	285
Harris, Joseph	HRK	421
Harris, Joseph	OND	191
Harris, Joseph	SRA	10
Harris, Joseph R.	DUT	7
Harris, Justus	SRA	4
Harris, Leuther	WSH	270
Harris, Mary a mulatto	NYK	108
Harris, Mary a Black	NYK	110
Harris, Moses	NYK	58
Harris, Moses	WST	163
Harris, Nathan	ONT	350
Harris, Nicholas	RNS	99
Harris, Olney	HRK	518
Harris, Paul	ONT	438
Harris, Peter	DUT	153
Harris, Peter	OND	213
Harris, Peter	ONT	348
Harris, Peter	ONT	356
Harris, Philip	OTS	15
Harris, Plyris	MNT	96
Harris, Richard	RCH	87
Harris, Robert	DEL	285
Harris, Robert	QNS	70
Harris, Robert	RNS112A	
Harris, Robert Junr	RNS112A	
Harris, Samuel	CAY	726
Harris, Samuel	KNG	7
Harris, Stephen	DUT	62
Harris, Stephen	SRA	57
Harris, Stephen	SUF	98
Harris, Thaddeus	OND	203
Harris, Thomas	ALB	35
Harris, Thomas	ALB	131
Harris, Thomas	CAY	644
Harris, Thomas	NYK	99
Harris, Thomas	OND	186
Harris, Thomas	ONT	348
Harris, Thomas	ONT	356
Harris, Thomas L.	SUF	102
Harris, William	ALB	64
Harris, William	GRN	325
Harris, Wm	MNT	54
Harris, William	ONT	320
Harris, William	OTS	54
Harris, Wm	RNS112B	
Harris, William	SRA	50
Harris, William	SRA	50
Harris, Zadock	WSH	269
Harrison, Adonijah	NYK	84
Harrison, Daniel	OND	183
Harrison, Danl	SUF	76
Harrison, David	SUF	88
Harrison, Denise Mary	NYK	107
Harrison, Edward	NYK	131
Harrison, Elias	ONT	324
Harrison, Ellenor	NYK	52
Harrison, Harmonus	MNT	103
Harrison, Hugh	ONT	326
Harrison, Hugh	ORN	279
Harrison, Isaac	ORN	319
Harrison, Jacob	OTS	30
Harrison, Jesse	ORN	398
Harrison, John	NYK	30
Harrison, John	NYK	38
Harrison, John	NYK	80
Harrison, Jonas	NYK	84
Harrison, Joseph	WSH	186
Harrison, Mathew	RNS	82
Harrison, Mary	NYK	40
Harrison, Nathaniel	SUF	85
Harrison, Richard	NYK	56
Harrison, Roswell	DEL	287
Harrison, Salmon	OTS	29
Harrison, Saml	OTS	30
Harrison, Sarah	ORN	397
Harrison, Silas	HRK	500
.arrison, Thomas	MNT	103
Harrison, William	ESS	321
Harrison, William	NYK	54
Harrison, William	NYK	105
Harriss, Benjamin	DUT	72
Harriss, David	COL	206
Harriss, David	ORN	303
Harriss, Evan	COL	210
Harriss, George	DUT	126
Harriss, James	ULS	258
Harriss, John	COL	181
Harriss, John	DUT	144
Harriss, John	ORN	280
Harriss, John	ORN	303
Harriss, John	ULS	193
Harriss, John	ULS	257
Harriss, John Junr	COL	181
Harriss, Joseph	COL	242
Harriss, Joseph	DUT	42
Harriss, Richard	DUT	64
Harriss, Robert	ORN	277
Harriss, Thomas	COL	186
Harriss, Thomas	DUT	155
Harriss, Thomas	ULS	245
Harriss, William	DUT	121
Harriss, William	ORN	272
Harrisson, Thomas	CHN	808
Harrity, Dennis	NYK	114
Harrou, Rufus	CHN	946
Harrower, David	DEL	277
Harrower, David	DEL	291
Harry a free Negro	ALB	140
Harse, David	ALB	86
Harse, Peter	SRA	21
Harsen, Cornelius	NYK	153
Harsen, Francis	ALB	73
Harsen, Jacob	NYK	152
Harsen, John	NYK	62
Harsha, John	WSH	244
Harsin, George	NYK	32
Harsons, Eli	MNT	75
Hart see Heart		
Hart, Aaron	SRA	31
Hart, Abel	TIO	234
Hart, Abel Jur	TIO	234
Hart, Abijah	NYK	28
Hart, Adam	TIO	253
Hart, Amasa	OND	197
Hart, Amos	OND	192
Hart, Bennett	CHN	778
Hart, Bennett	CHN	780
Hart, Bernard	NYK	18
Hart, Catharine	NYK	142
Hart, Christian	TIO	239
Hart, Daniel	MNT	53
Hart, Daniel	OND	162
Hart, Daniel	SRA	29
Hart, David	ALB	59
Hart, David	SRA	28
Hart, Deborah	WST	112
Hart, Ebenezr	SUF	69
Hart, Edward	RNS	34
Hart, Elemuel	SUF	91
Hart, Elihu	GRN	343
Hart, Elisha	OND	194
Hart, Elisha	WST	168
Hart, Elisabeth	WST	127
Hart, Enos	DUT	160
Hart, Ephraim	NYK	24
Hart, Ephraim	OND	202
Hart, Ezra	ONN	140
Hart, Ezra	ONN	147
Hart, George	NYK	43
Hart, George	SRA	36
Hart, Gilbert	DUT	83
Hart, Gilbert	SRA	32
Hart, Gilbert	SUF	93
Hart, Henry	MNT	10
Hart, Isaac	RNS	84
Hart, Isaac	WST	116
Hart, Jabez	ONT	404
Hart, Jacob	NYK	71
Hart, Jacob	OND	178
Hart, Jacob Senior	NYK	71
Hart, James	ALB	129
Hart, James	OND	208
Hart, James	WST	115
Hart, Jeoffery	SUF	82
Hart, Jeremiah	ONT	440
Hart, Jeremiah	SRA	45
Hart, Jessee	SUF	82
Hart, Jidediah	SUF	67
Hart, John	MNT	55
Hart, John	NYK	56
Hart, John	OND	190
Hart, John	SRA	45
Hart, John	SUF	75
Hart, John	WST	163
Hart, Jonathan	OND	198
Hart, Jonathan	WSH	185
Hart, Joseph	ONN	133
Hart, Joseph Junr	WST	116
Hart, Joshua	SUF	84
Hart, Josiah	SUF	80
Hart, Lemuel	OND	166
Hart, Levi	OND	221
Hart, Lewis a Black	NYK	46
Hart, Luke	WSH	186
Hart, Margret	SRA	4
Hart, Michael	SUF	82
Hart, Monmoth	WST	163
Hart, Morris	SUF	93
Hart, Munmouth	WST	126
Hart, Nehemiah	RNS	91
Hart, Ozias	OND	165
Hart, Peleg	ALB	30
Hart, Philetus	SUF	89
Hart, Philip	RNS	91
Hart, Phillip	DUT	104

Hart, Reuben	OND 181	Harvey, Asa	COL 187	Hasbrouck, Joseph B.	ULS 251
Hart, Reuben	SRA 44	Harvey, Benjamin	WSH 297	Hasbrouck, Joseph J.	ULS 250
Hart, Richard	DUT 158	Harvey, Bethuel	OTS 47	Hasbrouck, Josephat	ULS 241
Hart, Richard	RNS 29	Harvey, Charles	ALB 40	Hasbrouck, Josiah	ULS 237
Hart, Robert	RCK 97	Harvey, Charles	HRK 423	Hasbrouck, Lewis	ULS 203
Hart, ..muel	COL 178	Harvey, Charles	OND 174	Hasbrouck, Mary	ULS 203
Hart, Samuel	WSH 200	Harvey, David	WSH 300	Hasbrouck, Peter	ULS 225
Hart, Seth	WSH 189	Harvey, Ebenezer	WSH 273	Hasbrouck, Rodolphus	DUT 30
Hart, Stephen	OND 221	Harvey, Elijah	HRK 458	Hasbrouck, Roeliff	ULS 242
Hart, Stephen	SRA 45	Harvey, Ezra	CHN 776	Hasbrouck, Sally	DUT 23
Hart, Stephen	SUF 82	Harvey, George	NYK 125	Hasbrouck, Samuel	ULS 237
Hart, Terrence	NYK 117	Harvey, James	TIO 214	Hasbrouck, Solomon	ULS 230
Hart, Thomas	CHN 846	Harvey, James	WSH 221	Hasbrouck, Suffrein	ULS 203
Hart, Thomas	OND 202	Harvey, Joel	HRK 458	Hasbrouck, Tobias	ULS 229
Hart, Timothy	OND 181	Harvey, Joel	ONT 384	Hasbrouck, Wilhelmus	ULS 236
Hart, William	ALB 78	Harvey, John	TIO 240	Hasbrouck, Zachariah	ULS 240
Hart, William	COL 190	Harvey, Jonathan	WSH 296	Hascal, Simeon	CHN 968
Hart, William	SRA 12	Harvey, Joseph	OND 171	Hascall, John	HRK 459
Hart, Zadock	SUF 89	Harvey, Luther	WSH 295	Hascall, Zachariah	HRK 450
Harte, Silas	ONT 350	Harvey, Medad	WSH 216	Hascel, Jonathan	OTS 22
Hartell, Adam	NYK 142	Harvey, Moses	WSH 284	Haskill, Thos	OTS 53
Hartell, Solomon	OTS 41	Harvey, Ora	HRK 576	Hase, Amons	SRA 6
Harter, Lawrence	HRK 431	Harvey, Pall	WSH 209	Hase, Amos	GRN 344
Harter, Nicholas	OND 197	Harvey, Paul	CHN 826	Hase, Henry	SRA 28
Harter, Peter	MNT 27	Harvey, Pe[ter?]	CAY 602	Haselton, John	NYK 78
Harter, Philip	OND 197	Harvey, Phineas	WSH 284	Hasen, Mathew	NYK 17
Harterly, John	MNT 61	Harvey, Samuel	NYK 132	Hasford, Joseph	TIO 246
Hartgrowe, James	WSH 239	Harvey, Thomas	OND 192	Haskell, Moses	WSH 293
Harthen, William	WSH 192	Harvey, Thomas	RNS 67	Haskell, Nathanl	CHN 812
Harthorne, Jacob	MNT 74	Harvey, Uzziel	COL 228	Hasken, Heman	WSH 303
Harthorne, John	NYK 38	Harvey, William Junr	NYK 52	Haskens, Lemuel	CHN 756
Harthoway, Elisha	WSH 270	Harvy, Daniel	GRN 344	Haskill, Samuel	ONT 384
Hartin, Joseph	RNS 17	Harway, Lewis	NYK 107	Haskill, Samuel	WST 114
Hartin, Roger	RNS 17	Harway, Peter	ALB 76	Haskin, Benjamin F.	NYK 150
Harting, Jacob	MNT 3	Harwick, Conr.dt	MNT 29	Haskins, Abraham	WSH 296
Harting, John D.	NYK 38	Harwick, John	NYK 20	Haskins, Anthony	WSH 299
Hartley, Isaac	SRA 23	Harwick, Josep	MNT 29	Haskins, Asahel	DUT 146
Hartman, Adam	HRK 454	Harwood, Ambrose	HRK 543	Haskins, Asal	ESS 297
Hartman, Christian	NYK 134	Harwood, Ebenezer	HRK 569	Haskins, Daniel	ONN 167
Hartman, George	HRK 439	Harwood, Edward	NYK 65	Haskins, Eber	WSH 296
Hartman, John	NYK 97	Harwood, James	RCK 105	Haskins, Eliphalet	CLN 166
Hartman, Lewis	NYK 67	Harwood, Nathan	HRK 568	Haskins, Enoch	RNS 41
Hartman, Nicholas	WSH 215	Harwood, Oliver	HRK 568	Haskins, Franklen	WSH 299
Hartness, James	NYK 101	Harwood, Samuel	RNS 66	Haskins, Joel	DUT 131
Hartness, John	DEL 284	Harwood, Samuel	RNS 75	Haskins, John	WSH 306
Hartness, Thomas	DEL 284	Hasbrook, Clarissa	NYK 69	Haskins, Joseph	DUT 130
Harton, Benjamin	MNT 112	Hasbrouck, Abraham J.	ULS 227	Haskins, Lemuel	CLN 166
Hartsh___, David	CHN 846	Hasbrouck, Benjamin	DUT 23	Haskins, Lemuel	ONN 167
Hartshorn, Elijah	CHN 760	Hasbrouck, Benjamin	DUT 106	Haskins, Lott	ONN 176
Hartshorn, William	RNS 67	Hasbrouck, Benjamin	ULS 241	Haskins, Michael	OTS 27
Hartshorne, Beriah	ULS 258	Hasbrouck, Benjamin B.	ULS 251	Haskins, Paulo	ONN 176
Hartshorne, John	OTS 13	Hasbrouck, Benjamin J.	ULS 202	Haskins, Rossel	CHN 816
Hartshorne, Joseph	OTS 13	Hasbrouck, Cornelius	ULS 251	Haskins, Ryer	RNS 41
Hartshorne, Richard	NYK 67	Hasbrouck, Daniel	ORN 345	Haskins, William	ONN 137
Hartshorne, Saml	OTS 18	Hasbrouck, Daniel	ULS 193	Hasleton, Nathan	OND 223
Hartshorne, Saml	OTS 49	Hasbrouck, Daniel	ULS 244	Hasner, Jacob	DUT 22
Hartshorne, William	NYK 37	Hasbrouck, Daniel Junr	ULS 241	Hassam, Thomas	NYK 82
Hartwell, Abijah	OTS 42	Hasbrouck, David	ULS 243	Hassay, Henry J.	NYK 32
Hartwell, Abraham	DUT 142	Hasbrouck, David A.	ULS 202	Hassock, William	ULS 209
Hartwell, Daniel	SRA 50	Hasbrouck, Dinah	DUT 25	Hasson, Michael	MNT 58
Hartwell, Ebenezer	CHN 780	Hasbrouck, Elias	ULS 193	Hasswell, Anna	NYK 81
Hartwell, Ephm	ONN 171	Hasbrouck, Elizabeth	ULS 193	Haste, Reuben	ONT 402
Hartwell, James	DUT 52	Hasbrouck, Esaias	ULS 237	Hasteer, John	NYK 30
Hartwell, James	ORN 312	Hasbrouck, Henry	ULS 230	Hasteings, Nicholas	COL 221
Hartwell, James Junr	DUT 170	Hasbrouck, Isaac	ORN 284	Hasting, Jeheada	WSH 188
Hartwell, John	DEL 283	Hasbrouck, Jacob	ULS 237	Hasting, Warren	WSH 188
Hartwell, Lawrence	DUT 142	Hasbrouck, Jacob J.	ULS 204	Hastings, Daniel	COL 204
Hartwell, Peter	DUT 52	Hasbrouck, Jacobus	ULS 243	Hastings, Diah	CHN 844
Hartwell, Peter	WSH 277	Hasbrouck, Jacobus B.	ULS 202	Hastings, James	DEL 270
Hartwell, Phipps	WSH 277	Hasbrouck, James	ULS 230	Hastings, Jonas	ONT 432
Hartwell, Samuel	ONT 474	Hasbrouck, Johannis	ULS 237	Hastings, Jonathan	CAY 632
Hartwell, Thomas	OND 214	Hasbrouck, John	ULS 193	Hastings, Lemuel	WSH 300
Hartwell, William	DUT 53	Hasbrouck, John	ULS 229	Hastings, Seth	OND 191
Hartwell, Wm	ONN 171	Hasbrouck, Jonas	ULS 216	Hastings, Stephen	COL 207
Hartwick, Fraderick	RCK 106	Hasbrouck, Jonathan	ULS 229	Hastings, Stephen J.	COL 211
Hartwick, Margaret	ALB 69	Hasbrouck, Joseph	ULS 244	Hastings, Stepn S.	COL 207
Hartwick, Sarah	NYK 129	Hasbrouck, Joseph Junr	ULS 201	Hastings, Sylvanus	ONT 338

Hastings, Zaccheus ALB 133	Hatfield, Edmund ALB 134	Hatter, Mary WST 140
Haswell, Arthur ALB 62	Hatfield, Elias NYK 56	Hauahurst, Nathaniel NYK 34
Haswell, Edward ALB 97	Hatfield, Elizabeth NYK 75	Hauck, Peter COL 223
Haswell, Elizabeth NYK 107	Hatfield, Ephraim NYK 18	Hauck, Peter COL 235
Haswell, John ALB 106	Hatfield, Ephraim NYK 59	Hauck, Peter Junr COL 235
Haswell, Joseph ALB 62	Hatfield, Gilbert WST 118	Haugadorn, George DUT 162
Haswell, Robert ALB 97	Hatfield, Isaac NYK 89	Haugh, Amos OND 213
Haswell, Thomas ALB 42	Hatfield, Isaac WST 155	Haugh, Joel OND 193
Haswell, Thomas NYK 67	Hatfield, James RCH 89	Haughwout, Frans RCH 91
Hatch, Able CHN 886	Hatfield, Jemima NYK 44	Haughwout, Peter RCH 93
Hatch, Asa CAY 686	Hatfield, John NYK 121	Hauk, John RNS 48
Hatch, Asa CAY 688	Hatfield, John WST 168	Haukins, Peter RNS 107
Hatch, Asahel HRK 501	Hatfield, Joseph WST 117	Hauley, David ONT 420
Hatch, Bogardus COL 211	Hatfield, Joseph WST 163	Haulk, Arther ALB 111
Hatch, Charles ESS 304	Hatfield, Joseph WST 163	Haum, Adol[ph?] MNT 44
Hatch, Daniel CHN 874	Hatfield, Joshua QNS 80	Haum, Conrad Jur MNT 47
Hatch, Daniel COL 204	HAtfield, Joshua WST 168	Hauman, John D. NYK 108
Hatch, Daniel SRA 61	Hatfield, Mason HRK 548	Haun, Christian COL 199
Hatch, David HRK 501	Hatfield, Peter DUT 118	Haune, Henry OND 316
Hatch, Dorastus OTS 51	Hatfield, Peter HRK 567	Haunsekle, Jacob CAY 684
Hatch, Ebenezer ALB 30	Hatfield, Peter WST 118	Hause, Henry SCH 131
Hatch, Elephalet SRA 61	Hatfield, Richard WST 118	Hause, John MNT 54
Hatch, Elijah COL 181	Hatfield, Robert DUT 119	Hause, Peter COL 266
Hatch, Eliphalet SRA 42	Hatfield, Robert a	Hause, Samuel CAY 524
Hatch, Elisha WSH 280	Black NYK 88	Hausey, John KNG 10
Hatch, Esther ORN 279	Hatfield, Suzannah NYK 59	Hausinfrats, Peter NYK 124
Hatch, George WSH 186	Hatfield, William OND 203	Hauss, John H. QNS 77
Hatch, George W. MNT 59	Hatham, Oney SRA 56	Hautman, Jacob NYK 73
Hatch, Guy OND 186	Hathaway, Bailey COL 247	Hauver, Christian RNS 25
Hatch, Heman ULS 249	Hathaway, Benjamin CAY 530	Hauver, Jacob RNS 59
Hatch, Henry WSH 280	Hathaway, Benjamin SCH 118	Hauver, Peter COL 245
Hatch, Joel CHN 806	Hathaway, Ebenezar CAY 618	Hauxey, Joseph SRA 28
Hatch, John CHN 858	Hathaway, Henry HRK 597	Hauxley, James NYK 95
Hatch, John COL 181	Hathaway, Henry MNT 101	Hauze, George ALB 138
Hatch, John OTS 37	Hathaway, Isaac CAY 526	Hauze, Matthias ALB 45
Hatch, John RNS 90	Hathaway, Isaac COL 247	Haveland, James RNS 43
Hatch, John WSH 187	Hathaway, Isaac ONT 436	Haveland, John RNS 24
Hatch, John WSH 270	Hathaway, Isaac ONT 486	Havens, Abigail A. ORN 286
Hatch, John WSH 293	Hathaway, Israel OND 162	Havens, Abiram SUF 101
Hatch, Jonathan MNT 112	Hathaway, Israel OND 167	Havens, Abner HRK 598
Hatch, Jonathan SRA 20	Hathaway, Jacob CAY 528	Havens, Abra.am SRA 42
Hatch, Joseph CAY 666	Hathaway, James MNT 62	Havens, Asa OTS 21
Hatch, Joshua WSH 286	Hathaway, John CAY 526	Havens, Augustus SUF 105
Hatch, Levi COL 183	Hathaway, John COL 246	Havens, Benn OTS 7
Hatch, Lewis WSH 279	Hathaway, John SRA 30	Havens, Benjamin WSH 254
Hatch, Mathew WSH 280	Hathaway, Jno R. OTS 28	Havens, Constant OTS 7
Hatch, Meletiah CHN 844	Hathaway, Joseph CAY 526	Havens, Cornelius ESS 302
Hatch, Nathan ONT 418	Hathaway, Joshua OND 214	Havens, Daniel ALB 74
Hatch, Nathan Ju. ONT 418	Hathaway, Nathaniel NYK 130	Havens, Danl CHN 828
Hatch, Nathaniel ALB 30	Hathaway, Nicholas COL 247	Havens, Daniel SUF 91
Hatch, Nathaniel CHN 792	Hathaway, Phineas OND 162	Havens, Darling ONT 322
Hatch, Nathaniel HRK 487	Hathaway, Robert HRK 588	Havens, Desire SUF 105
Hatch, Oliver CAY 600	Hathaway, Seth ONT 412	Havens, Elizabeth ORN 304
Hatch, Peter HRK 469	Hathaway, Thomas ONT 466	Havens, Ezekiel SUF 105
Hatch, Reuben ALB 84	Hatherway, Jathro NYK 106	Havens, Francis SUF 104
Hatch, Samuel ULS 249	Hatheway, Eleazer DUT 113	Havens, Gerushe SUF 107
Hatch, Samuel WSH 280	Hatheway, Michael WSH 237	Havens, Gurdin SUF 105
Hatch, Seth ONT 382	Hatheway, Nathen WSH 199	Havens, Henry KNG 8
Hatch, Simeon OND 176	Hatheway, Stephen ORN 339	Havens, Jabez CAY 558
Hatch, Solomon CHN 976	Hatheway, Wilber WSH 222	Havens, James SUF 105
Hatch, Stephen COL 207	Hatheway, Eliazer WSH 238	Havens, Jeremiah SUF 69
Hatch, Timothy CHN 800	Hathins, Collins SRA 58	Havens, Jeremiah SUF 69
Hatch, Timothy OND 192	Hathorn, Andrew ORN 301	Havens, Jeriah ESS 304
Hatch, Timothy SRA 15	Hathorn, John ORN 374	Havens, Jessee SUF 102
Hatch, Timothy Junr SRA 15	Hathorn, Thomas ORN 372	Havens, John SUF 69
Hatch, William CHN 844	Hathorn, William ORN 287	Havens, John B. ORN 286
Hatch, Willm COL 204	Hathoway, Abia WSH 303	Havens, Jonathan SUF 104
Hatche, Alden NYK 123	Hathoway, Abner WSH 299	Havens, Joseph ESS 298
Hatchell, Michael SCH 170	Hathway, Benjn TIO 209	Havens, Joseph SRA 17
Hatchett, Elisha COL 179	Hathway, Benjn TIO 225	Havens, Joseph SRA 31
Hatchett, Nathan MNT 112	Hathway, Jacob DEL 279	Havens, Joseph SUF 105
Hatfield, Abner TIO 263	Hathway, Joanna NYK 73	Havens, Joseph WSH 244
Hatfield, Abraham WST 116	Hathway, John NYK 72	Havens, Lodowick SUF 105
Hatfield, Abraham WST 145	Hathway, Paul NYK 73	Havens, Nathan HRK 422
Hatfield, Absalum ALB 116	Hatmaker, Henry HRK 412	Havens, Nathaniel CHN 760
Hatfield, Daniel WST 117	Haton, Charles OND 213	Havens, Nathaniel SUF 85
Hatfield, David SCH 146	Hatt, William ORN 375	Havens, Nathaniel Junr CHN 770

Havens, Obediah	SUF 105	Haviland, Gilbert	WST 122	Hawkins, David	ORN 347
Havens, Paul	OTS 56	Haviland, Henry	DUT 171	Hawkins, David	ORN 375
Havens, Paul	OTS 58	Haviland, Isaac	DUT 52	Hawkins, Edward	ESS 306
Havens, Peleg	OND 172	Haviland, Isarel	NYK 44	Hawkins, Edward	WST 159
Havens, Peter	HRK 598	Haviland, Jacob	DUT 52	Hawkins, Elijah	CHN 748
Havens, Peter	SUF 65	Haviland, Jacob	DUT 171	Hawkins, Elijah	OTS 36
Havens, Peter	SUF 105	Haviland, Jacob	WST 111	Hawkins, Enoch	TIO 231
Havens, Ranseller	NYK 37	Haviland, Jerusha	NYK 42	Hawkins, Eseck	RNS 82
Havens, Samuel	ESS 302	Haviland, John	NYK 32	Hawkins, Ezra	SUF 66
Havens, Samuel	HRK 418	Haviland, John	WST 111	Hawkins, Gaylord	COL 215
Havens, Samuel	OND 179	Haviland, John	WST 112	Hawkins, George	NYK 125
Havens, Samuel	SUF 105	Haviland, John	WST 154	Hawkins, George	OND 201
Havens, Samuel	WSH 267	Haviland, Joseph	QNS 60	Hawkins, Gersham	SUF 93
Havens, Silas	SUF 104	Haviland, Joseph	QNS 78	Hawkins, Gilbert	ORN 289
Havens, Smith	ORN 280	Haviland, ..seph	WST 111	Hawkins, Hezebiah	HRK 566
Havens, Stephen	SRA 45	Haviland, Nathaniel	DUT 50	Hawkins, Isa	SUF 70
Havens, Thomas	CHN 760	Haviland, Partrick	NYK 110	Hawkins, Isaac	WST 157
Havens, Thomas	ONT 322	Haviland, Peter	DUT 171	Hawkins, Isabella	DUT 95
Havens, Thomas	ONT 324	Haviland, Roe	QNS 66	Hawkins, Israel	SUF 67
Havens, Thomas	ULS 265	Haviland, Samuel	DUT 171	Hawkins, Jacob	SUF 67
Havens, Walter	SUF 96	Haviland, Samuel	QNS 84	Hawkins, James	DUT 95
Havens, Walter	SUF 105	Haviland, Samuel	WST 153	Hawkins, James	SRA 18
Havens, William	COL 182	Haviland, Solomon	WST 111	Hawkins, James	SUF 66
Havens, William	WSH 266	Haviland, Stephen	WST 111	Hawkins, James	SUF 67
Havens, William B.	SUF 104	Haviland, Thomas	DUT 171	Hawkins, Jesse	OND 194
Havens, Zedekiah	OND 183	Haviland, Thomas Junr	DUT 171	Hawkins, John	NYK 136
Haver, Abraham	ALB 16	Haviland, Timothy	DUT 171	Hawkins, John	OND 208
Haver, Andrew	COL 189	Haviland, .imothy	WST 111	Hawkins, John	ORN 375
Haver, Benjamin	COL 190	Haviland, William	WST 117	Hawkins, John	SRA 45
Haver, Christian	COL 266	Havillen, Dennis	NYK 110	Hawkins, John	SUF 91
Haver, Christian	DUT 113	Havins, Nathl	SUF 69	Hawkins, John	WST 115
Haver, Frederick	COL 232	Havoy, James	MNT 58	Hawkins, John Jur	OND 208
Haver, Frederick	DUT 119	Havsworth, Abraham	SRA 48	Hawkins, Jonas	SUF 66
Haver, Frederick	ULS 195	Haward, Josiah L.	COL 265	Hawkins, Joseph	NYK 99
Haver, Harman	COL 233	Haward, Thomas	SCH 155	Hawkins, Joseph	OTS 46
Haver, Herman	DUT 151	Hawber, Adam	OTS 57	Hawkins, Joseph	SRA 40
Haver, Isaac	DUT 128	Hawe, Samuel	OND 211	Hawkins, Joseph	SUF 66
Haver, Jacob	COL 227	Hawe, Samuel Jnr	OND 211	Hawkins, Joseph	SUF 69
Haver, Jacob	COL 243	Hawes, George	NYK 143	Hawkins, Luther	HRK 519
Haver, Jacob	DUT 150	Hawes, John	ORN 374	Hawkins, Mathew	NYK 119
Haver, Jacob G.	COL 235	Hawes, Lyman	COL 181	Hawkins, Mermaduke	SRA 44
Haver, Jacob H.	COL 230	Hawes, Simon	ORN 376	Hawkins, Mitchel	NYK 64
Haver, Jacob H. Junr	COL 231	Hawes, Stephen	COL 189	Hawkins, Moses	ORN 355
Haver, John	COL 189	Hawes, William	ORN 375	Hawkins, Olive	SUF 67
Haver, John	DUT 150	Hawk, George	OND 214	Hawkins, Oliver	ORN 342
Haver, John	DUT 150	Hawk, Jacob	SRA 18	Hawkins, Orpheus	SUF 67
Haver, John	SCH 143	Hawk, Nicholas	OND 214	Hawkins, Rhodolphus	OND 169
Haver, John	SCH 161	Hawk, Peter	NYK 20	Hawkins, Samuel	DUT 67
Haver, John Junr	COL 266	Hawk, Peter	NYK 79	Hawkins, Samuel	DUT 93
Haver, Peter	COL 265	Hawke, George	DEL 274	Hawkins, Samuel	ORN 283
Haver, Rachel	COL 238	Hawke, John	DEL 274	Hawkins, Samuel	ORN 312
Haverland, Joseph	ALB 78	Hawke, Mathew	OND 208	Hawkins, Saml	SUF 67
Haverland, Roger	WSH 209	Hawkenback, Peter	OTS 4	Hawkins, Semion	SUF 67
Haverland, William	DEL 273	Hawkens, Isaac	SUF 67	Hawkins, Solomon	OND 201
Haverland, William	QNS 69	Hawkens, Joseph	SUF 65	Hawkins, Stephen	HRK 566
Haverley, John	ALB 24	Hawkens, Mary	SUF 66	Hawkins, Stephen	WSH 201
Haverly, Jacob	ALB 70	Hawkens, Nathl Jr	SUF 70	Hawkins, Susannah	HRK 473
Haverly, Philip	SCH 154	Hawkens, Nathl Sr	SUF 70	Hawkins, Thomas	ESS 305
Havey, George	NYK 123	Hawkens, Robert	SUF 64	Hawkins, Timothy	OND 172
Havey, John	NYK 148	Hawkens, Zacariah	SUF 67	Hawkins, Toby L.	COL 218
Havey, John	WST 144	Hawkes, Aphas	ONT 484	Hawkins, William	OTS 31
Haviland, Abraham	WSH 299	Hawkes, Asa	CLN 167	Hawkins, William	SRA 16
Haviland, Benjamin	DUT 171	Hawkes, Eleazer	ONT 478	Hawkins, Wm	SUF 65
Haviland, Benjamin	WST 112	Hawkes, James	SUF 82	Hawkins, Wm	SUF 66
Haviland, Benjamin	WST 145	Hawkes, Joseph	ONT 480	Hawkins, William	WSH 204
Haviland, Birdsall	DUT 167	Hawkhurst, Hannah	NYK 70	Hawkins, William	WST 115
Haviland, Charles	RNS 22	Hawkhurst, Thomas	NYK 41	Hawkins, Zachariah	NYK 83
Haviland, Daniel	DUT 171	Hawkins, Abel D.	ALB 140	Hawkins, Zopher	SUF 65
Haviland, Daniel Junr	DUT 171	Hawkins, Alaxr	SUF 67	Hawks, Abijah	OTS 54
Haviland, David	DUT 171	Hawkins, Andrew	COL 149	Hawks, Caleb	NYK 138
Haviland, Deborah	SUF 87	Hawkins, Benjn	SUF 67	Hawks, Daniel	OTS 51
Haviland, Ebenezer	WST 145	Hawkins, Benjamin	WST 115	Hawks, Daniel	WST 114
Haviland, Edward	DUT 50	Hawkins, Christopher	DUT 14	Hawks, Eleazer	ONT 488
Haviland, Eleazer	DUT 171	Hawkins, Christopher	HRK 566	Hawks, Israel	NYK 138
Haviland, Elias	NYK 107	Hawkins, Daniel	SRA 14	Hawks, Jacob	QNS 74
Haviland, Elijah	DUT 167	Hawkins, Danl	SUF 68	Hawks, James	QNS 63
Haviland, Garrison	RNS 25	Hawkins, David	OND 172	Hawks, John	QNS 63

Name	Loc	Name	Loc	Name	Loc
Hawks, Josham	WST 151	Haxton, John	COL 217	Haynes, Edward	GRN 336
Hawks, Nathan	OTS 54	Haxton, Timothy	COL 233	Haynes, Elisha	GRN 336
Hawks, Olive	OTS 51	Hay, [Al?]ary	ESS 295	Haynes, Joseph	SRA 46
Hawks, Phillip	ULS 259	Hay, Daniel	SCH 143	Haynes, Joseph	SRA 47
Hawks, Richard	NYK 138	Hay, James	NYK 32	Haynes, Nicholas	CLN 172
Hawks, Richard	QNS 78	Hay, James	WSH 199	Haynes, Samuel Jun	GRN 336
Hawkshurst, Henry	QNS 70	Hay, John	WSH 253	Haynes, Samull	GRN 344
Hawkshurst, Joseph	QNS 82	Hay, Martha	RCK 103	Haynes, Silas	CAY 702
Hawkshurst, Sarah	QNS 82	Hay, Mary	DUT 68	Haynes, Thomas	NYK 54
Hawkshursts, William	QNS 82	Hay, Michael	RCK 103	Hayness, Samuel	GRN 336
Hawksley, Solomon	CHN 824	Hay, Samuel	ORN 278	Hayness, William	GRN 336
Hawksley, Stephen	CHN 824	Hay, Sarah	NYK 90	Hayney, Coonrod	WSH 215
Hawl, Thomas	CHN 884	Hay, Thos	RCK 103	Hayns, John	RNS 24
Hawl, William	WST 158	Hay, William	ORN 278	Hays, Abraham	WST 153
Hawlan, Silas	SRA 38	Hay, William	WSH 191	Hays, Ahaz	RNS 111
Hawley, Abel	OND 196	Haya_, Wm	MNT 92	Hays, Asa	CLN 161
Hawley, Abraham	DEL 267	Hayard, Morris	GRN 347	Hays, Asahel	OTS 32
Hawley, Amos	SRA 50	Hayden, Alpheus	DUT 89	Hays, Benjamin	WSH 207
Hawley, Andrew	ALB 70	Hayden, Edmund	RNS 40	Hays, Benjamin	WSH 272
Hawley, Assa	WSH 284	Hayden, Elijah	DUT 101	Hays, Benjamin	WST 143
Hawley, Benjamin	DEL 276	Hayden, Elijah	ONN 184	Hays, Caleb	OTS 32
Hawley, Benjamin	DEL 279	Hayden, Saml	OTS 56	Hays, Caziah	WST 134
Hawley, Chapman	ONT 314	Haydock, Henry	NYK 43	Hays, Coenradt, Jur	WSH 242
Hawley, Clawson	QNS 80	Haydock, William	NYK 39	Hays, Coonrod	WSH 232
Hawley, Daniel	COL 209	Haydon, Abijah	HRK 567	Hays, David	WST 167
Hawley, Daniel	OTS 51	Hayer, Peter	NYK 59	Hays, Edward	CHN 764
Hawley, David	OND 170	Hayes, Aaron	ESS 321	Hays, Eli	RNS 111
Hawley, David	ONT 434	Hayes, Abraham	DUT 113	Hays, Freegift	WST 153
Hawley, Ebe.... R.	ONN 164	Hayes, Caleb	GRN 343	Hays, Henry	NYK 21
Hawley, Enos	ONT 434	Hayes, Denniston	ONT 384	Hays, Hezikiah	COL 241
Hawley, Ezra	DUT 17	Hayes, Eli	ONN 159	Hays, Ire	CHN 764
Hawley, Francis	HRK 504	Hayes, Enark	GRN 343	Hays, Isaac	CAY 690
Hawley, Gideon	SRA 23	Hayes, John	DEL 269	Hays, Isaac	WST 152
Hawley, Henry	OND 197	Hayes, Levi	OTS 13	Hays, Israel	SUF 87
Hawley, Henry	ONT 436	Hayes, Martin	ONN 159	Hays, Jacob	NYK 91
Hawley, Ichabud	SRA 51	Hayes, Moses	DEL 290	Hays, James	CHN 764
Hawley, Isaac	DEL 284	Hayes, Nathaniel	GRN 343	Hays, James	DUT 169
Hawley, James	WSH 222	Hayes, Nehemiah	DEL 268	Hays, James	NYK 95
Hawley, James	WSH 274	Hayes, Phinny	ONN 159	Hays, James	NYK 125
Hawley, John	ESS 306	Hayes, Rufus	OND 187	Hays, Jeremeah	WSH 287
Hawley, John	MNT 91	Hayes, Stephen	OND 214	Hays, John	ALB 69
Hawley, Jonathan	OND 165	Hayes, Tilus	ONT 422	Hays, John	GRN 343
Hawley, _nathan	ONT 434	Hayes, William	CAY 550	Hays, John	NYK 80
Hawley, Joseph	DEL 275	Hayes, William	DEL 290	Hays, John	NYK 113
Hawley, Levi	OTS 51	Hayford, Jonathan	WSH 223	Hays, John	SRA 25
Hawley, Moses	ONT 434	Hayford, Webster	WSH 223	Hays, John Junr	RNS 111
Hawley, Nathan	ALB 84	Hayght, Cornelius	QNS 62	Hays, Jonathan	WSH 271
Hawley, Nathan	OND 168	Hayght, Elkan	QNS 62	Hays, Jonathan Jur	WSH 271
Hawley, Nicholas	ESS 302	Hayght, Jesse	NYK 140	Hays, Joseph	NYK 127
Hawley, Riggs	SRA 26	Hayght, Thomas	QNS 62	Hays, Josephus	HRK 516
Hawley, Salmon	ULS 184	Hayley, Elizabeth	COL 247	Hays, Philip	OTS 28
Hawley, Samuel	ESS 306	Hayman, William	NYK 74	Hays, Phillip	RNS 18
Hawley, Samuel S.	CHN 786	Hayne_, Aaron	RNS 24	Hays, Rachel	NYK 16
Hawley, Thomas	ONT 402	Hayner, Abraham	COL 180	Hays, Richard	OND 197
Hawley, Zadock	DEL 276	Hayner, Christopher	COL 196	Hays, Richard	RNS 24
Hawn, George	MNT 24	Hayner, Coonradt	RNS 86	Hays, Samuel	WST 153
Haws, Jason	OTS 29	Hayner, David	RNS 87	Hays, Thatcher	WST 152
Haws, John	COL 246	Hayner, George	COL 185	Hays, Thomas	ALB 73
Haws, Lois	OND 214	Hayner, George Junr	COL 179	Hays, Thomas	NYK 62
Haws, Palatiah	WST 153	Hayner, George B.	RNS 7	Hays, Thomas	RNS 49
Haws, Pelletia	NYK 131	Hayner, Henry P.	RNS 7	Hays, William	RNS 111
Haws, Peter	NYK 34	Hayner, Jacob	COL 197	Hayse, Nathen	WSH 210
Haws, Seth	WST 159	Hayner, Jacob	WSH 232	Hayse, Thomas	WSH 210
Haws, Solomon	WST 156	Hayner, John	RNS 75	Hayt, Abel	DUT 56
Hawse, George	ORN 301	Hayner, John	RNS 86	Hayt, Benjaman	CHN 846
Hawsen, Hunnaval	NYK 124	Hayner, John Junr	RNS 86	Hayt, Benjamin	DUT 56
Hawsler, Sampson	SRA 34	Hayner, John P.	RNS 7	Hayt, Catherine	NYK 127
Hawver, Frederick	WST 157	Hayner, Martinus	RNS 86	Hayt, Charles	ULS 257
Hawxhurst, James	WST 144	Hayner, Peter	RNS 86	Hayt, Daniel	ULS 213
Hawxhurst, Jessee	QNS 83	Hayner, Peter	RNS 88	Hayt, Dorothy	DUT 56
Hawxhurst, Jotham	QNS 83	Hayner, Peter P.	RNS 7	Hayt, Isaac	WST 134
Hawxhurst, Simeon	QNS 82	Hayner, Philip P.	RNS 36	Hayt(?), Jacob	WST 124
Hawyer, Wm	OTS 58	Hayner, Phillip Junr	COL 196	Hayt, James	NYK 31
Haxteen, Jeremiah	COL 257	Haynes, Caty	OTS 4	Hayt, John	DUT 170
Haxton, Benjm	COL 217	Haynes, David	ONN 177	Hayt, Jonas	WST 134
Haxton, Benjamin	COL 246	Haynes, David	ONN 191	Hayt, Joseph	DUT 56
Haxton, Ely	COL 217	Haynes, Edmund	RNS 22	Hayt, Major	WST 139

Hayt, Martha	DUT 84	Head, John
Hayt, Monson	NYK 31	Head, John
Hayt, Rachael	NYK 144	Head, Jonathan
Hayt, Samuel	DUT 166	Head, Jonathan
Hayt, Stephen	DUT 169	Head, Jonathan Junr
Hayt, Zepheniah	DUT 166	Head, Loring
Haytt, Thomas	QNS 61	Head, Lovett
Hayward, Reuben	COL 255	Head, Michael
Hayward, William	DUT 119	Head, Reuben
Haywood, John	COL 241	Head, Smith
Haywood, Thomas	COL 242	Head, William
Haywood, Thomas	DUT 116	Headen, Elijah
Haywood, Thomas	WSH 225	Headen, Joab
Hazard, Edward	OTS 41	Headen, John
Hazard, Evens	CHN 764	Headen, Peter
Hazard, Green	WSH 200	Head lock, Davd
Hazard, Griffin B.	ONT 468	Headsteel, Elisha
Hazard, James	KNG 11	Heady, Amos
Hazard, James	ORN 390	Heal, Elisha
Hazard, John	COL 231	Healy, Dennis
Hazard, John	COL 263	Healy, Eleazar
Hazard, John	NYK 136	Healy, Elizabeth
Hazard, Joseph	SUF 76	Heard, Abraham
Hazard, Joshua	COL 249	Heard, James
Hazard, Morris	NYK 136	Heard, Jennet
Hazard, Robert	OND 214	Heard, Philo
Hazard, Sarah a mulatto	NYK 69	Heard, Phinehas
Hazard, Stephen a Black	NYK 29	Hearl, Catharine
		Hearlin, David
Hazard, Steward	CHN 764	Hearon, James
Hazard, Steward Junr	CHN 164	Heart see Hart
Hazard, Thomas	NYK 108	Heart, Humphry
Haze, James	SRA 30	Heart, Joseph
Hazel, Phillup	CHN 948	Heart, Joseph Jun
Hazelton, Alpheus	CHN 972	Heartshorn, Widdow
Hazelton, Royal	CHN 972	Heartt, Benjamin
Hazen, Anne	ORN 321	Heath, Arden
Hazen, Benjamin	HRK 457	Heath, Azariah
Hazen, Caleb	DUT 87	Heath, Daniel
Hazen, Edward	ONT 332	Heath, David
Hazen, Isaiah	ORN 321	Heath, Ebenezer
Hazen, Jeremiah	ORN 319	Heath, Hezekiah
Hazen, Jesse	HRK 450	Heath, Hezekiah
Hazen, John	ORN 327	Heath, Horace
Hazen, Joseph	NYK 69	Heath, Hosea
Hazen, Joshua	DUT 95	Heath, Jesse
Hazen, Levi	CLN 173	Heath, John
Hazen, Moses	RNS 93	Heath, Joseph
Hazen, Moses	ULS 189	Heath, Joseph
Hazen, Nathl	OTS 43	Heath, Joseph
Hazen, Samuel	ORN 323	Heath, Joseph
Hazen, Silas	HRK 457	Heath, Josiah
Hazen, William	HRK 450	Heath, Josiah
Hazlet, James	NYK 43	Heath, Levi
Hazleton, Hannah	DUT 91	Heath, Richard
Hazzard, Clarke	RNS 100	Heath, Samuel
Hazzard, Robert	RNS 99	Heath, Samuel
Hdden, Thomas	WST 111	Heath, Samuel Junr
Hdgiss, Stephen	ONN 141	Heath, Seth
He son, Martin	ALB 129	Heath, Simeon
He t, Phillep	MNT 65	Heath, Thomas
He cks, Asa	ONT 400	Heath, Thomas
Hea ck, Daniel	CAY 534	Heath, Timothy
Heaccock, Benjn	CHN 906	Heath, Winslow
Heacock, David	GRN 342	Heather, John
Heacock, George	ONT 424	Heather, Jona
Heacock, John	ONT 408	Heaton, Aaron
Heacock, Levi	ONT 422	Heaton, Adna
Heacock, Levi	ONT 430	Heaton, Benjn
Heacock, Noah	ONT 434	Heaton, Isaac
Heacock, Rufus	ONT 422	Heaton, Jacob
Heacock, Wm	GRN 354	Heaton, James(?)
Heacock, Warren	ONN 165	Heaton, Robert
Head, Fobes	OND 197	Heaveland, Benjamine
Head, Henry	COL 229	Hebart, Ebenezard
Head, Henry	COL 265	Hebbats, Debborah
Head, John	ALB 33	Hebberd, Abigail

COL 265	Hebron, John
WST 129	Hebuton, John
COL 259	Heccle, Robert
OND 183	Heckle, David
COL 265	Heckle, William
NYK 78	Hecock, Chauncey
RNS 44	Hecock, Elisha
COL 260	Hecock, Francis
DUT 128	Hecock, Guidean
CAY 582	Hecock, Guidean Jun
ALB 91B	Hecock, Isaac
ALB 22	Hecock, Johnston
SRA 30	Hecock, Richard
WST 163	Hecock, Thomas
NYK 116	Hecock, Thomas
TIO 250	Hecocks, Asahel
SCH 155	Hecocks, James
WSH 270	Hecocks, James
NYK 111	Hecocks, Salmon
NYK 32	Hecocks, Simon
DUT 76	Hecox, Samuel
DUT 76	Hecter see Herter
NYK 90	Hector, William
NYK 35	Hedden, Daniel
NYK 81	Hedden, Elijah
HRK 522	Hedden, Isarel
ORN 350	Hedden, Jacob
ORN 301	Hedden, Josias
STB 202	Hedden, Moses
NYK 92	Hedden, Polly
	Hedden, Reuben
SRA 32	Hedden, Samuel
GRN 344	Hedden, William
GRN 344	Hedden, William
GRN 340	Hedden, Wm
RNS 18	Hedden, Zadock
WSH 191	Heddin, Samuel
TIO 221	Heddy, Dennis
WSH 191	Heddy, Henry a mulatto
DEL 286	Heddy, Hiseph
WSH 223	Hede, Joseph
HRK 439	Hedgeley, John
NYK 29	Hedgen, Thomas
WSH 248	Hedger, Evert
WSH 270	Hedger, Joseph
ESS 303	Hedger, Rachael
SRA 19	Hedger, Robert
ALB 109	Hedger, Thomas
WSH 247	Hedger, William
WSH 268	Hedges, Abraham
WSH 269	Hedges, Anthony &
OTS 57	Davis
OTS 58	Hedges, Benjamin
HRK 459	Hedges, Caleb
ONT 392	Hedges, Christopher
COL 251	Hedges, Daniel
WSH 222	Hedges, David
WSH 249	Hedges, David
OND 198	Hedges, David
WSH 290	Hedges, David Junr
NYK 62	Hedges, Davis &
NYK 87	Anthony
WSH 270	Hedges, Ebenezar
WSH 248	Hedges, Edward
COL 250	Hedges, Elezar
OTS 2	Hedges, Elias
CAY 694	Hedges, Elias
ULS 256	Hedges, Elihue
SUF 68	Hedges, Elizabeth
ONT 482	Hedges, Isaac
SUF 68	Hedges, Jacob
CAY 666	Hedges, Jeremiah
WST 149	Hedges, Jessee
GRN 331	Hedges, Job
MNT 50	Hedges, John
NYK 39	Hedges, John
NYK 135	

COL 198	
NYK 118	
NYK 105	
NYK 106	
NYK 105	
TIO 226	
TIO 231	
GRN 340	
GRN 340	
GRN 340	
SCH 141	
OTS 8	
ORN 384	
TIO 227	
TIO 232	
OND 194	
OND 180	
OND 186	
OND 180	
OND 194	
OND 173	
DUT 54	
DUT 83	
DUT 78	
NYK 86	
DUT 81	
RCK 107	
DUT 87	
NYK 40	
DUT 77	
DUT 109	
DUT 82	
NYK 87	
RCK 107	
NYK 95	
ONT 486	
WST 144	
NYK 38	
GRN 336	
CHN 892	
ORN 280	
NYK 74	
ULS 251	
DUT 143	
NYK 121	
DUT 83	
WST 145	
ULS 252	
SUF 106	
OTS 49	
ORN 280	
SUF 108	
SUF 101	
SUF 108	
SUF 107	
SUF 75	
SUF 101	
SUF 106	
SUF 101	
ORN 280	
SUF 109	
ONT 486	
GRN 342	
SRA 17	
SUF 64	
SUF 106	
NYK 106	
OTS 11	
SUF 106	
SUF 102	
SUF 104	
SRA 30	
SUF 75	

Name	Loc		Name	Loc		Name	Loc
Hedges, Jonathan	SRA 48		Heith, Ira	SRA 56		Hely, Arthermar	NYK 91
Hedges, Jonathan	SUF 101		Heith, Salmon	SRA 56		Hely, David	MNT 94
Hedges, Joseph	SUF 64		Heldaw, Mathew	MNT 71		Hemba, Enos	GRN 349
Hedges, Mathew	SUF 107		Heldman, John	NYK 112		Hemenway, Jason	HRK 533
Hedges, Nathan	SUF 107		Helebrant, Jacob	MNT 60		Hemenway, Moses	HRK 536
Hedges, Paul	SUF 76		Heley, Bennona	RNS 25		Hemenway, Rufus	HRK 515
Hedges, Philip	SUF 108		Heliker, David	WST 160		Hemestrat, Chas	ALB 49
Hedges, Reuben	SUF 107		Helister, Thoms	TIO 234		Heminway, William	ORN 324
Hedges, Silvenus	OTS 49		Helldrithe, Joseph	MNT 100		Hemminway, Isaac	OND 178
Hedges, Stephen	ONN 176		Hellebolt, Adolph	MNT 12		Hemmingway, Nathan	OND 168
Hedges, Stephen	RNS 51		Hellegars, Frederick	ALB 69		Hemmion, Jacob	RCK 106
Hedges, Stephen	SUF 101		Hellegars, John	ALB 69		Hemp, Jacob	MNT 84
Hedges, Stephen Junr	SUF 101		Helleger, David	NYK 114		Hempstead, James	RNS 107
Hedges, Susannah	SUF 101		Heller, Abraham	NYK 109		Hempstead, Nathaniel	KNG 8
Hedges, Thos	OTS 49		Hellibrant, John	WSH 301		Hempstead, Thos	SUF 76
Hedges, Wilkes	SUF 101		Helli..s, Conrod	MNT 5		Hempsted, Isaac	RNS 5
Hedges, William	COL 245		Hellicos, Peter	MNT 5		Hempsted, John	COL 219
Hedges, William	SUF 106		Hellicot, Esekiel	MNT 73		Hempsted, Nathaniel	RNS112A
Hedges, Zephiniah	SUF 107		Helligas, Christian	ALB 69		Hempstradt, Philip	ALB 16
Hedgeum, William	COL 230		Helligass, Frederick	COL 200		Hempstraw, David	TIO 245
Hedley, Henry	NYK 87		Helliger, Samuel	SRA 43		Hemrod, William	CAY 558
Heeler, Beltus	ALB 99		Hellman, Benjamin	OND 222		Hemshott, Jacob	SRA 55
Heeler, Jacob	ALB 99		Hellsinger, Abm	SCH 170		Hemson, William	WST 147
Heely, John	ONN 189		Hellsinger, Barent	SCH 155		Hemstradt, Dicarus	ALB 23
Heeny, Coarnelius	NYK 30		Hellsinger, Elisha	SCH 155		Hemstradt, Richd	ALB 23
Heermance, Henry	RNS 6		Hellsinger, John	SCH 122		Hemstradt, Wm	ALB 23
Heermance, Israel	RNS 6		Hellyer, William	NYK 15		Hemstrat, Francis	ALB 50
Heermance, John W.	RNS 95		Helm, Abraham	ULS 206		Hemstrat, John	ALB 50
Heermanse, Abraham	ULS 212		Helm, Anselm	ORN 352		Hamstrock, Derrick	MNT 95
Heermanse, Abraham	ULS 228		Helm, Christina	COL 197		Hemstroot, Dirck	SRA 3
Heermanse, Andreus H.	DUT 156		Helm, Daniel	ULS 187		Henchman, Benjamin	KNG 7
Heermanse, Andrew	DUT 155		Helm, Levi	ULS 209		Henchman, Thomas	KNG 6
Heermanse, Andrew G.	DUT 155		Helm, Peter	ULS 208		Henderer, Herms	ALB 141
Heermanse, Henry	DUT 163		Helm, Simon	ULS 245		Henderick, Peter	SRA 61
Heermanse, Jacob	ULS 206		Helm, Thomas	ORN 335		Hendershot, Michael	ORN 321
Heermanse, Jacob	ULS 211		Helm, Vincent	ORN 394		Hendershult, Michael	DEL 267
Heermanse, John	DUT 156		Helm, Woodhull	ORN 348		Henderson, Alexander	CAY 614
Heermanse, John	ULS 230		Helman, Marlin	MNT 73		Henderson, Alexander	NYK 128
Heermanse, Martin	DUT 162		Helme, Pompey	SUF 105		Henderson, Alexander	WST 120
Heermanse, Phillip	DUT 33		Helmer, Adam	HRK 495		Henderson, Alexander	WST 148
Heermanse, Phillip	DUT 40		Helmer, Adam	HRK 496		Henderson, Andrew	WSH 227
Heermanse, Phillip	DUT 156		Helmer, Adam	MNT 104		Henderson, Aron	GRN 346
Heermanse, Ryer	DUT 150		Helmer, Adam Junr	HRK 495		Henderson, Benjamin	QNS 75
Heermanse, Simon	DUT 155		Helmer, Conrad	HRK 435		Henderson, Charles	NYK 30
Heermanse, William	ULS 225		Helmer, Daniel	HRK 446		Henderson, Daniel	ONT 358
Hees, Abraham	HRK 579		Helmer, George	HRK 445		Henderson, David	DUT 159
Hees, Isaac	HRK 579		Helmer, George	HRK 482		Henderson, David	WSH 268
Heesck, Silas	HRK 549		Helmer, George	OTS 28		Henderson, Ebenezer	HRK 463
Hegerman, Adrian	KNG 3		Helmer, George Junr	HRK 482		Henderson, Edward	HRK 558
Hegerman, Adrian	KNG 6		Helmer, Henry	HRK 445		Henderson, Hendrick	RCK 97
Hegerman, Cornelius	NYK 31		Helmer, Henry	HRK 495		Henderson, Henry	WSH 218
Hegerman, Jacobus	KNG 2		Helmer, Jacob	NYK 52		Henderson, Jacob	NYK 62
Hegerman, John	KNG 2		Helmer, Jacob	OTS 28		Henderson, James	ONT 322
Hegerman, Johnson	KNG 6		Helmer, James	MNT 104		Henderson, James	SRA 18
Hegerman, Joseph	KNG 2		Helmer, John	HRK 437		Henderson, James	WSH 227
Hegerman, Peterus	KNG 2		Helmer, John	HRK 446		Henderson, James	WSH 228
Hegerman, Rem	KNG 3		Helmer, John	OTS 28		Henderson, James	WSH 268
Hegerman, Vansansus	KNG 3		Helmer, Peter	HRK 410		Henderson, Jane	NYK 51
Heggerman, Andrew	NYK 53		Helmer, Peter	HRK 445		Henderson, John	DUT 22
Heggerman, Elbert	NYK 135		Helmer, Philip	HRK 445		Henderson, John	SRA 26
Heggerman, Jacob	NYK 40		Helmer, Philip	OTS 28		Henderson, John	WSH 266
Heggerman, Peter	NYK 152		Helmer, William	HRK 437		Henderson, John T.	NYK 25
Heggins, Sally	NYK 20		Helmes see Helmer			Henderson, Joseph	OND 174
Heibner, Daniel	COL 193		Helmes, Adam	NYK 70		Henderson, Josiah	WST 136
Heibner, John	COL 193		Helmes, Charles	NYK 57		Henderson, Lemull	OND 214
Heibner, John Junr	COL 193		Helmes, John	NYK 32		Henderson, Phinehas	ONN 173
Heicox, William	ONT 398		Helmes, John	NYK 40		Henderson, Rachel	NYK 107
Height, Isaih	WSH 210		Helmes, Robe	OTS 53		Henderson, Reuben	WSH 227
Hein, John	SCH 118		Helmes, Samuel	CAY 596		Henderson, Richard	ONT 466
Heir, Daniel	SCH 121		Helmis, Benjamin	MNT 104		Henderson, Richard	RCH 92
Heir, Silas	SCH 117		Helms, Thos	SUF 68		Henderson, Robert	NYK 124
Heir, Willm Junr	SCH 117		Helms, William	ORN 382		Henderson, Samuel	DUT 22
Heir, Willm N.	SCH 117		Helms, Wm	SUF 77		Henderson, Samuel	NYK 22
Heirds, Arm	NYK 120		Helmus, John a free			Henderson, Sarah	NYK 101
Heiser, Henry	NYK 59		Negro	ALB 8		Henderson, Thomas	CAY 614
Heisler, Frederick	CAY 526		Helmus, John	ALB 47		Henderson, Willeam	WSH 267
Heister, Daniel	NYK 148		Helton, Benjamin	MNT 74		Henderson, William	CHN 822

Name	Loc	Pg	Name	Loc	Pg	Name	Loc	Pg
Henderson, William	NYK	27	Hendrickson, John	QNS	79	Henry, James	MNT	103
Henderson, William	NYK	89	Hendrickson, John	SUF	89	Henry, James	ONT	370
Henderson, William	NYK	120	Hendrickson, Joseph	RNS	83	Henry, James	RNS	42
Henderson, William	WSH	228	Hendrickson, Joseph	ULS	214	Henry, James	ULS	265
Henderson, William Junr	WSH	228	Hendrickson, Matthew	ALB	101	Henry, James	WSH	221
Hendickson, Carman	SUF	87	Hendrickson, Nicholas	QNS	75	Henry, James M.	SCH	141
Hendreke, Johnson	MNT	95	Hendrickson, Oliver	QNS	68	Henry, John	ALB	22
Hendrekson, Barnardus	SUF	79	Hendrickson, Peter	NYK	94	Henry, John	ALB	76
Hendrekson, Peter	ONN	178	Hendrickson, Peter	QNS	75	Henry, John	ALB	97
Hendrick, Aaron	WSH	206	Hendrickson, Peter	TIO	230	Henry, John	DEL	285
Hendrick, _artle	COL	178	Hendrickson, Philip	MNT	61	Henry, John	MNT	86
Hendrick, Cornelius	CHN	988	Hendrickson, Simon	SUF	81	Henry, John	MNT	109
Hendrick, Francis	DUT	164	Hendrickson, Stephen	DUT	64	Henry, John	ONT	508
Hendrick, Heny	SUF	73	Hendrickson, Stephen	KNG	10	Henry, John	ORN	291
Hendrick, Heth	CHN	750	Hendrickson, Stephen	QNS	79	Henry, John	OTS	8
Hendrick, Jacob	CAY	574	Hendrickson, Thomas	QNS	79	Henry, John	OTS	14
Hendrick, Jacob	DUT	164	Hendrickson, Thomas	QNS	79	Henry, John	ULS	187
Hendrick, Joel	CHN	766	Hendrickson, Thomas	QNS	79	Henry, John S.	NYK	31
Hendrick, John	ALB	73	Hendrickson, Thomas	SUF	87	Henry, John V.	ALB	133
Hendrick, John	CHN	988	Hendrickson, Uriah	QNS	68	Henry, Jonathan	CAY	638
Hendrick, John	MNT	103	Hendrickson, Uriah	QNS	79	Henry, Jonathan	DEL	285
Hendrick, John	SRA	28	Hendrickson, Will	WSH	252	Henry, Joseph	RNS	83
Hendrick, Joseph	SRA	60	Hendrickson, William	QNS	68	Henry, Joseph	WSH	189
Hendrick, Lawrence	DUT	156	Hendrison	GRN	345	Henry, Michael	RNS	81
Hendrick, Walter	NYK	48	Hendry, David	DEL	287	Henry, Robert	ALB	121
Hendrick, William	CHN	988	Hendry, Thomas	DEL	287	Henry, Robert	NYK	96
Hendricks, Abraham	STB	203	Hendry, William	DEL	287	Henry, Robert	ONT	446
Hendricks, Abraham	WSH	210	Hen.y, John B.	ONN	189	Henry, Robert	RCK	103
Hendricks, Benjamin	STB	203	Hendy, Obed	ONN	147	Henry, Robert R.	ALB	147
Hendricks, Benjamin	WSH	211	Hendy, Samuel	TIO	257	Henry, Sarah	NYK	150
Hendricks, Cornelius	NYK	30	Heneman, Elizabeth	QNS	66	Henry, Shelena	NYK	129
Hendricks, Dayton	ONT	482	Henen, Catherine	NYK	121	Henry, Sylvester	WSH	278
Hendricks, Harmer	NYK	30	Henery, James	SRA	13	Henry, Thomas	MNT	106
Hendricks, Hendrick	COL	257	Henigan, Adam	NYK	134	Henry, Wells	SCH	169
Hendricks, Hugh	RCK	103	Henkley, Reuben	DEL	272	Henry, William	ALB	125
Hendricks, Jacob	CAY	524	Henly, Thomas	ORN	391	Henry, William	HRK	529
Hendricks, Jacob	ULS	227	Henman, Elijah	TIO	252	Henry, William	NYK	41
Hendricks, John	DUT	108	Henman, Lewis	WSH	281	Henry, William a Black	NYK	47
Hendricks, John	RCK	99	Henman, Mary	OTS	55	Henry, William	NYK	76
Hendricks, John	ULS	187	Henman, Nathan	SRA	23	Henry, William	NYK	83
Hendricks, John	ULS	192	Henman, Reuben	OTS	55	Henry, William a Black	NYK	85
Hendricks, Lawrence	ULS	245	Henmon, James	CHN	936	Henry, William mulatto	NYK	88
Hendricks, Nathaniel	STB	203	Hennebergher, Christ-			Henry, William	WSH	251
Hendricks, Peter	ULS	226	ian	ULS	194	Hensdale, David	ONN	134
Hendricks, Phillip	ULS	227	Hennegan, David	WSH	303	Henshaw, ...	MNT	78
Hendricks, Simon	ULS	245	Hennegan, John	WSH	303	Henshaw, Daniel	ALB	144
Hendricks, Wonzer	WSH	205	Hennegan, Joseph	ONN	150	Henshaw, James	CAY	624
Hendrickson, ...	QNS	77	Hennegar, George	NYK	118	Henshaw, Mary	ALB	129
Hendrickson, Aaron	QNS	69	Hennery, Abraham	CHN	888	Henshaw, Nathaniel	CAY	592
Hendrickson, Abigail	QNS	75	Hennery, Francis	CHN	852	Henshaw, Samuel	NYK	64
Hendrickson, Abraham	QNS	66	Hennery, Robert	CHN	782	Henshaw, William	CAY	592
Hendrickson, Abraham	QNS	68	Hennery, William	CHN	856	Henshaw, William	ONT	318
Hendrickson, Bernardus	QNS	68	Hennica, Emeniel	ALB	27	Henshaw, Zacchius	NYK	88
Hendrickson, Bernardus	QNS	79	Henniger, Christopher	NYK	142	Hensler, Phillip	ORN	342
Hendrickson, Daniel	QNS	79	Henniger, John	NYK	123	Henson, Levi	GRN	336
Hendrickson, Elias Junr	ULS	215	Hennybolt, James	MNT	56	Henson, Samuel	GRN	335
Hendrickson, Garret	NYK	131	Henrey see Hervey			Henson, William	GRN	335
Hendrickson, Hendrick	QNS	68	Henrigius, Philip	NYK	135	Henyon, Cornelius	RCH	91
Hendrickson, Hendrick	QNS	70	Henry	SUF	82	Henyon, Peter	OND	223
Hendrickson, Hendrick	QNS	75	Henry, Aaron	NYK	81	Hepburn, Peter	DUT	171
Hendrickson, Hendrick	QNS	76	Henry, Aaron	ULS	187	Hepman, Michael	SCH	170
Hendrickson, Hendrick	ULS	213	Henry, Andrew	NYK	148	Herbert, Edward	NYK	97
Hendrickson, Henry a			Henry, Babary	NYK	82	Herbert, Felin	NYK	35
Black	NYK	140	Henry, Catherine	NYK	75	Herb_t, Samuel	NYK	65
Hendrickson, Isaac	QNS	65	Henry, Charles	NYK	39	Herbert, William	NYK	146
Hendrickson, Isaac	QNS	68	Henry, Daniel	MNT	123	Hercles, Thomas	TIO	261
Hendrickson, Isaac	QNS	69	Henry, David	RNS	83	Herd, Daniel	WSH	273
Hendrickson, Jacob	NYK	58	Henry, Edward	NYK	110	Herd, David	WSH	200
Hendrickson, Jacobus	ULS	213	Henry, Enoch T.	ESS	303	Herd, Jedediah	ONT	446
Hendrickson, Jacobus			Henry, Francis	OTS	14	Herd, Johnathan	GRN	339
Junr	ULS	213	Henry, George	MNT	55	Herd, Jotham	WSH	287
Hendrickson, Jacobus J.	ULS	213	Henry, George a Black	NYK	36	Herd, Samuel	RNS	33
Hendrickson, James	QNS	75	Henry, Gerard	MNT	52	Herd, Samuel	WSH	198
Hendrickson, John	ALB	129	Henry, Gosbert J.	MNT	55	Herd, Truman	COL	263
Hendrickson, John	COL	252	Henry, Hugh	NYK	40	Herder, Adam Junr	COL	192
Hendrickson, John	QNS	75	Henry, Hugh	OTS	48	Herder, Benjamin	COL	194
Hendrickson, John	QNS	75	Henry, James	ALB	97	Herder, George	COL	198

Name	Ref	Name	Ref	Name	Ref
Herder, George M.	COL 191	Hermon, John	WSH 305	Herring, Daniel	CAY 718
Herder, Jacob J.	COL 193	Hern, Wm	RNS 73	Herring, Isaac	RCK 101
Herder, Jacob P.	COL 195	Herne, Thomas	NYK 121	Herring, John	ALB 67
Herder, Jacob W.	COL 227	Heron, Elizabeth	ORN 300	Herring, John	MNT 15
Herder, John	COL 190	Heron, Herculas	WST 116	Herring, John	NYK 91
Herder, John	COL 254	Heron, Michal	CHN 978	Herring, John	RCK 97
Herder, John Junr	COL 190	Heroy, Charles	DUT 84	Herring, John	RCK 98
Herder, John J.	COL 255	Heroy, Clarkson	DUT 85	Herring, John	WSH 199
Herder, Margaret	COL 191	Heroy, James	ALB 122	Herring, John James	MNT 67
Herder, Margaret P.	COL 195	Herreck, Rebecca	MNT 60	Herring, Leonard	MNT 10
Herder, Michael	COL 190	Herren, James	WSH 293	Herring, Lodiwick	MNT 10
Herder, Michael	COL 196	Herrick, Amasa	OND 204	Herring, Oliver	WSH 199
Herder, Michael J.	COL 198	Herrick, Amaziah	RNS 46	Herring, Philip	MNT 15
Herder, Michael Jno	COL 195	Herrick, Amos	CAY 588	Herring, Thomas	NYK 49
Herder, Michael M.	COL 200	Herrick, Artimus	CHN 786	Herrington, Aaron	OTS 30
Herder, Nicholas	COL 222	Herrick, Benjamin	DUT 141	Herrington, Abel	SRA 5
Herder, Nicholas	COL 259	Herrick, Cyprean	OTS 55	Herrington, Abraham	ONT 440
Herder, Nicholas P.	COL 260	Herrick, Daniel	DEL 286	Herrington, Ahab	OND 223
Herder, Peter Junr	COL 226	Herrick, Daniel	GRN 352	Herrington, Allen	OTS 29
Herder, Peter M.	COL 200	Herrick, Daniel	MNT 114	Herrinton, Amosa	WSH 233
Herder, Peter P.	COL 224	Herrick, David	OTS 47	Herrington, Archibald	DEL 279
Herder, Peter W.	COL 231	Herrick, Denniston	ALB 29	Herrington, Asel	ALB 112
Herder, Phillip	COL 199	Herrick, Ebenezer	DEL 268	Herrington, Basseli	WSH 210
Herder, Phillip	COL 261	Herrick, Ebenezer	OND 175	Herrington, Benjn	OTS 37
Herder, Teunis	COL 218	Herrick, Eliazer	WSH 201	Herrington, Chad	WSH 233
Herder, William	COL 259	Herrick, Elijah	ALB 27	Herrington, Charles	OTS 33
Herder, Willm P.	COL 218	Herrick, Elisha	COL 209	Herrington, Charles	WSH 233
Herder, Willm R.	COL 223	Herrick, Ephraim	DUT 152	Herrington, David	WSH 278
Herdick, John	COL 197	Herrick, Francis	OTS 55	Herrington, Eber	OTS 37
Herdick, William J.	COL 254	Herrick, Hannah	SUF 96	Herrington, Edmund	OTS 38
Herendeen, Eleazer	CHN 794	Herrick, Henery	CHN 798	Herrington, Elias	ONT 440
Hereson, Abel	SRA 34	Herrick, Hugh	CHN 798	Herrington, Elijah	OTS 37
Herichman, Joseph	TIO 265	Herrick, Israel	DUT 121	Herrington, Elisha	WSH 201
Herington, ...	RNS 113	Herrick, John	ALB 27	Herrington, Ephraim	OTS 29
Herington, Atm	RNS 12	Herrick, John	DUT 139	Herrington, Ezekiel	ONT 436
Herington, Benjn	RNS 12	Herrick, John	SCH 121	Herrington, Francis	OTS 31
Herington, Benjn	RNS 22	Herrick, Jonathan	ALB 27	Herrington, Francis	OTS 37
Herington, Benjn	RNS 104	Herrick, Joseph	CHN 810	Herrington, Henry	WSH 185
Herington, Crandall	RNS 98	Herrick, Josiah	DUT 125	Herrington, Isaac	GRN 351
Herington, James	RNS 12	Herrick, Lemuel	CAY 668	Herrington, Isaac	OTS 33
Herington, James	RNS 59	Herrick, Leonard	DUT 101	Herrington, Jacob	TIO 248
Herington, John	RNS 6	Herrick, Leonard	OND 223	Herrington, James	CAY 716
Herington, John	RNS 58	Herrick, Lewis	DUT 100	Herrington, James	GRN 332
Herington, Nicholas	RNS 98	Herrick, Mary	DUT 131	Herrington, James	HRK 443
Herinton, Isaac	RNS 102	Herrick, Micah	SUF 97	Herrington, James	OTS 33
Herinton, James	RNS 102	Herrick, Nathan	ALB 29	Herrington, Jeams	OND 223
Herinton, Jes..	RNS 100	Herrick, Nathan	COL 209	Herrington, Jeremiah	WSH 252
Herinton, Samuel	RNS 100	Herrick, Reuben	ONN 172	Herrington, Job	OTS 29
Herinton, Samuel Junr	RNS 100	Herrick, Rufus	CHN 784	Herrington, Job	OTS 37
Herinton, Theophilus	RNS 102	Herrick, Rufus	DUT 101	Herrington, Job	SRA 51
Heriot, Israel	WST 116	Herrick, Rufus Junr	DUT 132	Herrington, John	ALB 104
Herkemer, George	OTS 13	Herrick, Samuel	DUT 132	Herrington, John	WSH 258
Herkemer, Jost	HRK 409	Herrick, Saml	OTS 55	Herrington, Jonathan	WSH 201
Herkermer, Henry	OTS 13	Herrick, Simeon	CAY 668	Herrington, Jos:	SCH 121
Herkimer, Abraham	MNT 22	Herrick, Smith	DUT 100	Herrington, Joseph	SRA 51
Herkimer, Aledaw	MNT 22	Herrick, Stephen	ALB 27	Herrington, Joseph	WSH 274
Herkimer, John	MNT 22	Herrick, Stephen	DUT 99	Herrington, Joshua	ONT 440
Herkimer, John Jost	MNT 22	Herrick, Stephen	OTS 13	Herrington, Levi	ALB 112
Herkimer, Nicholas	MNT 22	Herrick, Stephen	WSH 201	Herrington, Lot	OTS 21
Jerman, Daniel	OND 178	Herrick, Willeam	WSH 264	Herrington, Nathan	ONT 440
Herman, Gares	SRA 24	Herrick, William	ALB 27	Herrington, Nathaniel	ONT 444
Herman, Geers	SRA 24	Herrick, William	SUF 97	Herrington, Nathl	OTS 30
Herman, Jacob	ALB 83	Herrien, John	CAY 714	Herrington, Noah	WSH 258
Herman, John	HRK 451	Herril, William	SRA 12	Herrington, Obadh	OTS 38
Herman, John	ONT 318	Herriman, James	QNS 66	Herrington, Pearly	OTS 5
Herman, Jonathan	WSH 287	Herriman, Jesse	CAY 568	Herrington, Peter	WSH 274
Herman, Joshua	SRA 33	Herriman, Thomas	ONT 386	Herrington, Philip	ALB 17
Herman, William	ALB 132	Herrin, David	ONN 156	Herrington, Presarved	WSH 233
Herman, William	WSH 305	Herring, Abraham	NYK 30	Herrington, Reserved	
Hermance, Andrew W.	COL 199	Herring, Abrm	RCK 109	Junr	WSH 233
Hermance, Henry	COL 191	Herring, Abrm	RCK 109	Herrington, Richard	WSH 233
Hermance, James free		Herring, Adam	MNT 63	Herrington, Rufus	OTS 33
Black	COL 249	Herring, Albert	CAY 710	Herrington, Samuel	ESS 293
Hermance, Jane	COL 255	Herring, Albert	MNT 120	Herrington, Shiffield	OTS 33
Hermance, Nicholas	COL 231	Herring, Benjamin	NYK 95	Herrington, Simeon	CAY 728
Hermance, Phillip H.	COL 196	Herring, Cornelius	MNT 59	Herrington, Solomon	OTS 18
Hermance, Wilhelmus	COL 197	Herring, Cornelius D.	NYK 55	Herrington, Stephen	OTS 33

Name	Co.	Pg.	Name	Co.	Pg.	Name	Co.	Pg.
Hickcox, Jonas	DUT	84	Hicks, Perus	CHN	840	Hifield, John	NYK	105
Hickey, George	MNT	43	Hicks, Rodman	QNS	69	Higbee, Edward	KNG	9
Hickey, John	QNS	76	Hicks, Rufus	OND	177	Higbee, Levi	RNS	40
Hickman, Michael	WST	157	Hicks, Rufus	OTS	2	Higbey, Daniel	QNS	67
Hickock, Theodore	RNS	82	Hicks, Samuel	CAY	614	Higbey, John	SRA	15
Hickocks, Preserved	OND	159	Hicks, Samuel	CLN	173	Higbey, John	SRA	15
Hickocks, Reuben	OND	201	Hicks, Samuel	DUT	122	Higbey, John Junr	QNS	68
Hickok, Ezra	RNS	80	Hicks, Samuel	ONT	318	Higbey, Lewis	SRA	31
Hickox, Jabez	OND	196	Hicks, Samuel	QNS	65	Higbey, Nathaniel	QNS	69
Hicks, Aaron	ONT	412	Hicks, Samuel	QNS	75	Higbey, Nehimiah	SUF	93
Hicks, Abraham	DUT	147	Hicks, Samuel	QNS	75	Higbey, Orrey	QNS	68
Hicks, Adrian B.	NYK	32	Hicks, Samuel	SRA	7	Higbey, Stephen	QNS	68
Hicks, Anna a mulatto	NYK	92	Hicks, Samuel Junr	QNS	75	Higby see Higley		
Hicks, Asa	SRA	46	Hicks, Sarah	QNS	69	Higby, Abigail	DEL	269
Hicks, Asa	WSH	213	Hicks, Semion	SRA	10	Higby, Amby	WSH	265
Hicks, Assa	WSH	272	Hicks, Silas	QNS	73	Higby, Amos	OND	221
Hicks, Benjamin	DUT	147	Hicks, Smith	NYK	123	Higby, Asahel	OND	175
Hicks, Benjamin	HRK	489	Hicks, Solomon	WSH	296	Higby, Benjam	MNT	94
Hicks, Benjamin	NYK	86	Hicks, Solomon S.	WSH	296	Higby, Benjamin	OND	220
Hicks, Benjamin	ONT	318	Hicks, Stephen	OND	208	Higby, Cheney	NYK	137
Hicks, Benjn	OTS	57	Hicks, Stephen	QNS	66	Higby, Daniel	OND	220
Hicks, Benjamin	QNS	70	Hicks, Stepehn	QNS	73	Higby, Daniel	SUF	85
Hicks, Bernard	ALB	117	Hicks, Stephen	SRA	39	Higby, Dudly	WSH	279
Hicks, Caleb	ALB	116	Hicks, Thomas	COL	247	Higby, Edward	OND	175
Hicks, Charles	QNS	64	Hicks, Thomas	KNG	8	Higby, Elijah	TIO	213
Hicks, Daniel	RNS	49	Hicks, Thomas	OND	189	Higby, Enoch	OND	176
Hicks, Daniel	WSH	272	Hicks, Thos	OTS	57	Higby, George	MNT	112
Hicks, David	OND	208	Hicks, Thomas	QNS	60	Higby, Heming	SRA	4
Hicks, Deborah	WST	119	Hicks, Thomas	QNS	65	Higby, Henry	NYK	75
Hicks, Dinah a Black	NYK	104	Hicks, Thomas	RNS112B		Higby, Henry	QNS	72
Hicks, Durphe	SRA	35	Hicks, Valentine	QNS	80	Higby, Isaac	ONT	388
Hicks, Eben & Mary Boss	QNS	60	Hicks, Wheaton	ALB	16	Higby, Jacob	GRN	336
Hicks, Edward	QNS	65	Hicks, Whitehead	NYK	140	Higby, James	OND	169
Hicks, Elias	DUT	124	Hicks, Willet	NYK	45	Higby, James	ORN	359
Hicks, Elias	QNS	80	Hicks, William	ALB	15	Higby, John	QNS	67
Hicks, Elizabeth	QNS	66	Hicks, William	ALB	29	Higby, Johon	OND	221
Hicks, George	ALB	37	Hicks, William	ALB	32	Higby, Joseph	OND	175
Hicks, George	DUT	34	Hicks, William/Lieut.	QNS	69	Higby, Joseph	SUF	85
Hicks, George	KNG	8	Hicks, William 2	QNS	69	Higby, Joseph Junr	OND	183
Hicks, George	MNT	19	Hicks, Zachariah	SUF	108	Higby, Levy	WSH	300
Hicks, Gideon	ONT	412	Hickson, Amos	ORN	372	Higby, Luther	CAY	690
Hicks, Isaac	NYK	62	Hickson, James	ALB	147	Higby, Moses	ORN	279
Hicks, Isaac	QNS	69	Hickson, James	WSH	210	Higby, Nicholas	NYK	68
Hicks, Israel a mulatto	NYK	105	Hiclin, John	SRA	48	Higby, Noah	OND	221
Hicks, Jabez	ONT	412	Hicock, David	DUT	168	Higby, Peter	DEL	281
Hicks, Jack a Black	NYK	145	Hicock, David Junr	DUT	169	Higby, Seth	DUT	99
Hicks, Jacob	CAY	696	Hicock, Gamaliel	DUT	168	Higby, Stephen	OND	175
Hicks, Jacob	QNS	73	Hicock, Gideon	RNS	26	Higby, Stephen	SUF	85
Hicks, Jacob	SRA	41	Hicock, Heman	SCH	141	Higby, Thomas	QNS	68
Hicks, Jacob	KNG	8	Hicock, Lemuel	DUT	168	Higby, Thomas	SUF	85
Hicks, James	DUT	40	Hicock, Nathan	SRA	59	Higby, Zekeus	OND	221
Hicks, James	SRA	39	Hicocks, James	OND	177	Higens, Timothy	WSH	229
Hicks, John	DUT	148	Hide see Hyde			Higens, William	WSH	183
Hicks, John	KNG	9	Hide, Ambrus	CHN	786	Higgenbotom, Niles	OTS	42
Hicks, John	NYK	111	H[ide?], Benjamine	GRN	330	Higgens, Elijah	WST	130
Hicks, John	NYK	143	Hide, Clerk	RNS	34	Higgenson, Saml	RCK	107
Hicks, John	OND	187	Hide, Eber	HRK	488	Higgins, Abner	NYK	122
Hicks, John	OND	197	Hide, Eliphalet	RNS	50	Higgins, Amy	NYK	88
Hicks, John	QNS	65	Hide, Erastus	WSH	270	Higgins, Benjamin	DUT	81
Hicks, John	RNS112B		Hide, Gesham	CHN	752	Higgins, Benjamin	NYK	53
Hicks, John	SCH	145	Hide, Gideon	GRN	340	Higgins, Charles	NYK	74
Hicks, John	WSH	218	Hide, Henry	NYK	78	Higgins, Cormbeus	ONN	145
Hicks, John	WST	119	Hide, Jonathan	WSH	216	Higgins, Daniel	RNS	40
Hicks, John B.	QNS	64	Hide, Joseph Jur	WSH	288	Higgins, David	WST	138
Hicks, Joseph	DUT	146	Hide, Nathaniel	WSH	280	Higgins, Diah	OND	186
Hicks, Joseph	QNS	80	Hide, Noah	CHN	756	Higgins, Edward	NYK	45
Hicks, Latham	SRA	33	Hide, Theophilus	WSH	270	Higgins, Edward	NYK	82
Hicks, Latham	SRA	35	Hide, [Thomus?]	RNS	20	Higgins, Elias	OTS	48
Hicks, Levi	WSH	218	Hide, William	WSH	215	Higgins, Elijah	WST	167
Hicks, Lewis	QNS	76	Hidecker, John	ALB	112	Higgins, Elisha Junr	ESS	307
Hicks, Marten	WSH	265	Hidla, John	RNS	11	Higgins, Elizabeth	NYK	81
Hicks, Moses	WSH	293	Hidla, John Junr	RNS	11	Higgins, Elkanan	OTS	48
Hicks, Mott	NYK	66	Hidla, Michael	RNS	11	Higgins, Gabriel	WST	134
Hicks, Oliver	QNS	69	Hiell, William	HRK	513	Higgins, Gabriel	WST	138
Hicks, Otis	ONT	412	Hiferd, Joseph	SRA	51	Higgins, Isaac	ALB	33
Hicks, Paedon	OND	186	Hiferds, Ira	SRA	51	Higgins, Isaac	ESS	305
			Hiffer, Abial	MNT	106	Higgins, Isaac	ESS	307

175

Name	Code	Name	Code	Name	Code
Higgins, John	COL 179	Hill, Africa	DUT 145	Hill, John	NYK 117
Higgins, John	ORN 275	Hill, Agusts	CHN 944	Hill, John	ONN 136
Higgins, John	ULS 260	Hill, Alexander	WSH 195	Hill, John	ONT 499
Higgins, John Junr	ORN 281	Hill, Allice	NYK 78	Hill, John	ORN 341
Higgins, Joseph	WST 168	Hill, Amasa	OTS 41	Hill, John	OTS 14
Higgins, Josiah	ESS 303	Hill, Amos	OTS 14	Hill, John	SRA 50
Higgins, Laurence	NYK 62	Hill, Andrew	ULS 196	Hill, John	SCH 143
Higgins, Live	OTS 51	Hill, Asa	OND 195	Hill, John	SUF 68
Higgins, Margaret	NYK 89	Hill, Asa	RNS 29	Hill, John	TIO 233
Higgins, Moses	OTS 48	Hill, Augustus	ULS 246	Hill, John	TIO 236
Higgins, Moses	WST 138	Hill, Barnett	CHN 786	Hill, John	ULS 201
Higgins, Nathaniel	SRA 33	Hill, Barthalomew	ALB 103	Hill, John	ULS 267
Higgins, Nehemiah	DUT 131	Hill, Benajah	WSH 275	Hill, John	WSH 193
Higgins, Richard	OTS 48	Hill, Benjamin	DUT 77	Hill, John	WSH 199
Higgins, Samuel	WST 126	Hill, Bethuel	SUF 102	Hill, John	WST 141
Higgins, Seth	DUT 172	Hill, Caleb	ORN 339	Hill, John Junr	ORN 339
Higgins, Simeon	OTS 43	Hill, Caleb	WSH 275	Hill, John ye 3d	ORN 342
Higgins, Thomas	CLN 164	Hill, Calup	CHN 786	Hill, John B.	SRA 45
Higgins, Thomas	DUT 172	Hill, Charles	CHN 956	Hill, Johnathan	GRN 330
Higgins, Waters	NYK 138	Hill, Charles	DUT 77	Hill, Johnathan	GRN 348
Higgins, William	CHN 758	Hill, Charles	QNS 82	Hill, Jonathan	COL 252
Higgins, Wm	RNS 66	Hill, Cornelius	CHN 740	Hill, Jonathan	DUT 77
Higgins, Wm	RNS 75	Hill, Cornelius	DUT 84	Hill, Joseph	DEL 269
Higgs, Samuel	DUT 21	Hill, Daniel	HRK 421	Hill, Joseph	DUT 150
High, Charles	WSH 215	Hill, Danl	OTS 53	Hill, Joseph	HRK 413
High, Danl	WSH 217	Hill, Daniel	RNS 98	Hill, Joseph	MNT 55
High, Hebron	WSH 217	Hill, Daniel	SRA 25	Hill, Joseph	NYK 38
High, Hoperven	WSH 215	Hill, David	ALB 77	Hill, Joseph	OND 203
High, John	WSH 215	Hill, David	DUT 77	Hill, Joseph	ONT 428
High, Nathen	WSH 220	Hill, David	DUT 108	Hill, Joshua	RNS 23
High, William	WSH 220	Hill, David	ONN 190	Hill, Joshua	WSH 291
Higham, Abm	ALB 12	Hill, David	WSH 287	Hill, Josiah L.	ESS 305
Highstead, Thadeus	SRA 43	Hill, David Junr	ALB 78	Hill, Leah	NYK 92
Hight, Elias	STB 204	Hill, Ebenezar	ONN 140	Hill, Levi	CAY 644
Hight, John	STB 204	Hill, Ebenezar	RNS 102	Hill, London Jun	DUT 44
Highton, Josiah	WSH 299	Hill, Ebenezar	RNS 110	Hill, London Sen	DUT 44
Higins, Edward	SCH 137	Hill, Ebenezer	WSH 238	Hill, Michael	NYK 81
Higler, John	SRA 53	Hill, Ebenezer	WSH 239	Hill, Nancy	TIO 221
Higley see Higby		Hill, Eleazer	CAY 642	Hill, Nathan	COL 178
Higley, David	CAY 566	Hill, Elezer	RNS 75	Hill, Nathan	DEL 282
Higley, David	HRK 505	Hill, Elezur	ONT 414	Hill, Nathaniel	WST 157
Higley, Nathaniel	COL 211	Hill, Elijah	DEL 282	Hill, Noah	DUT 84
Higley, Nathaniel	RNS 12	Hill, Ensign	ONN 144	Hill, Norman	ONT 414
Higley, Rozel	TIO 227	Hill, Ephraim	DUT 111	Hill, Oliver	SCH 121
Higley, Samuel	CAY 640	Hill, Ferris	DUT 167	Hill, Orin	SCH 148
Higley, Seba	WSH 293	Hill, Francis	NYK 82	Hill, Parly	ONT 356
Higley, Seth	CAY 700	Hill, George	COL 197	Hill, Paul	OTS 55
Higleys, Rozel	TIO 228	Hill, George	ONT 424	Hill, Rachael a mulatto	NYK 118
Higman, Abraham	ALB 115	Hill, George Junr	COL 197	Hill, Rachel	WST 141
Hikock, James	RNS 81	Hill, George Junr	COL 227	Hill, Reuben	ALB 90
Hikok, Samuel	RNS 80	Hill, Guy	RNS 40	Hill, Reuben	ONT 404
Hilard, Joseph	SRA 53	Hill, Hegason	WSH 258	Hill, Reubin	WSH 196
Hildreath, Daniel	SUF 98	Hill, Henry	ONN 174	Hill, Richard	DUT 150
Hildreath, David	SUF 100	Hill, Henry	RNS 66	Hill, Richard	GRN 329
Hildreath, John	SUF 100	Hill, Henry	WSH 265	Hill, Robert	WSH 206
Hildreath, Levy	SUF 100	Hill, Hezekiah	OTS 41	Hill, Robert	WSH 304
Hildreath, Jonathan	SUF 101	Hill, Hezekiah	OTS 42	Hill, Roby	NYK 38
Hildreath, Luther	SUF 102	Hill, Hilliand	GRN 329	Hill, Rufus	SUF 102
Hildreath, Peter	SUF 102	Hill, Ichobod	OND 208	Hill, Samuel	ALB 53
Hildreth, Benjamin	COL 252	Hill, Ira	ALB 54	Hill, Samuel	ALB 136
Hildreth, Esekiah	MNT 124	Hill, Isaac	DUT 144	Hill, Samuel	GRN 346
Hi reth, James	MNT 58	Hill, Isaac	SCH 154	Hill, Saml	OTS 57
Hildreth, John	ORN 281	Hill, Isaac	ULS 267	Hill, Saml Junr	OTS 57
Hildreth, Reuben	HRK 439	Hill, Isabella	ORN 303	Hill, Selah	CHN 946
Hildrick, Isaac	SUF 99	Hill, Jacob	TIO 218	Hill, Seth	COL 206
Hildridge, Samuel	SUF 96	Hill, James	NYK 22	Hill, Silas	ONT 370
Hileman, Michael	NYK 143	Hill, James	OND 214	Hill, Solomon	ESS 302
Hiley, Catharine	NYK 145	Hill, James	ONT 506	Hill, Solomon	OTS 41
Hilf, Loron	CHN 948	Hill, James	ORN 309	Hill, Stephen	TIO 221
Hill	GRN 344	Hill, James	SUF 89	Hill, Thomas	ALB 82
Hill, Aaron	CHN 946	Hill, James	ULS 185	Hill, Thomas	OND 221
Hill, Aaron	RNS 75	Hill, James	WSH 195	Hill, Thomas	RNS 22
Hill, Aaron	SRA 40	Hill, Jeremiah	NYK 37	Hill, Thomas	TIO 233
Hill, Aaron	WSH 291	Hill, Jesse	GRN 336	Hill, Thomas H.	NYK 48
Hill, Abiel J.	ORN 311	Hill, John	CHN 944	Hill, Tilton	ORN 341
Hill, Abner	ONT 356	Hill, John	CLN 172	Hill, Timothy	WSH 201
Hill, Abraham	DUT 84	Hill, John	COL 215	Hill, Uriah	NYK 95
Hill, Abraham	DUT 167				

Hill, Uriah	ULS 196	Hillson, John	MNT 66	Hinderer, Samuel	ALB 47
Hill, Wiat	OND 168	Hillyard, Benjamin	NYK 137	Hindman, John	ONT 380
Hill, Willeam	WSH 278	Hillyard, Daniel	CLN 159	Hinds, Henry	SCH 171
Hill, William	DEL 271	Hillyard, Joshua	CLN 162	Hinds, John	ONN 140
Hill, William	DUT 84	Hillyer, Jacob	NYK 15	Hinds, Joseph	RNS 51
Hill, William	NYK 17	Hillyer, John	RCH 89	Hinds, Reuben	WSH 277
Hill, William	NYK 70	Hillyer, Lawrence	RCH 95	Hinds, Richard	NYK 38
Hill, William	NYK 145	Hillyer, William	RCH 89	Hinds, Robert	ONT 348
Hill, William	ORN 302	Hilman, Henry	NYK 59	Hinds, Seth	WSH 242
Hill, William	OTS 14	Hilman, Sampson	WSH 197	Hinds, Willn	SCH 171
Hill, Wm	RNS 23	Hilmon, George	OND 224	Hine, Charles	DUT 177
Hill, Wm	RNS 103	Hilsimer, Charles	MNT 62	Hine, James	DUT 177
Hill, William	ULS 249	Hilt, Frederick	HRK 473	Hine, Lewis	ULS 234
Hill, William	WSH 195	Hilton, Amos	MNT 113	Hine, Walter	GRN 344
Hill, Zachariah	DUT 62	Hilton, Benjamin	ALB 129	Hineman, James	NYK 41
Hill, Zacheus	OND 208	Hilton, Benjamin	QNS 69	Hines, Edward	NYK 104
Hillager, Elizabeth	NYK 114	Hilton, Catharine	ALB 46	Hines, George	ALB 45
Hillard, Ezra	SRA 28	Hilton, David	ONT 372	Hines, Isaac	GRN 343
Hillard, Thurston	DUT 173	Hilton, Jacob	ALB 129	Hines, Isaac Junr	GRN 346
Hillart, Mary	NYK 134	Hilton, James	ALB 130	Hines, James	OTS 54
Hilldreth, Joshua	MNT 58	Hilton, John	ALB 61	Hines, Paul	RNS 97
Hillebrandt, Hendrick	COL 224	Hilton, John	ALB 129	Hines, Reuben	OTS 15
Hillebratt, John	ALB 106	Hilton, John	COL 264	Hines, Stephen	SRA 56
Hillebratt, Wendell	ALB 106	Hilton, John	MNT 119	Hines, Stephen	SRA 60
Hillegar, John	NYK 148	Hilton, Jonathan	WSH 248	Hinkley, Abel	ALB 75
Hillegar, Stephen	NYK 148	Hilton, Nathan	DUT 53	Hinkley, Elijah	WSH 188
Hillegas, Peter	COL 183	Hilton, Nicholas	ALB 59	Hinkley, Gershom	OND 214
Hilleker, Henry	DUT 18	Hilton, Nicholas	ALB 126	Hinkley, Gershom Jnr(?)	OND 211
Hilleker, Henry	DUT 104	Hilton, Peter	ALB 61	Hinkley, Isaac Junr	DUT 17
Hilleker, Herman	DUT 23	Hilton, Peter	ALB 125	Hinkley, Isaac Senr	DUT 17
Hilleker, John	DUT 117	Hilton, Peter	ALB 127	Hinkley, John	DEL 273
Hilleker, Soliss	DUT 23	Hilton, Peter	WSH 246	Hinkley, Jonah (poss-	
Hilleker, William	DUT 18	Hilton, Richard	ALB 41	ibly Josiah)	DEL 272
Hillequist, Caspar	DUT 63	Hilton(?), Richard	ALB 106	Hinkley, Joshua	ALB 114
Hiller, David	DUT 53	Hilton, Richard	ALB 131	Hinkley, Josiah	ALB 114
Hiller, Frederick	SCH 169	Hilton, Richard	SRA 55	Hinkley, Nathan	DEL 272
Hiller, John	HRK 418	Hilton, Robert	ALB 105	Hinkley, Nathaniel	ESS 311
Hiller, John	SRA 58	Hilton, Samuel	MNT 102	Hinkley, Reuben Junr	DEL 272
Hiller, John	SCH 169	Hilton, Thomas	ALB 130	Hinkley, Samuel	RNS 106
Hiller, Jonathan	DUT 48	Hilton, William	ALB 58	Hinkley, Seth	DUT 103
Hiller, Nathan	DUT 58	Hilton, William	ALB 129	Hinkley, Thomas	CHN 750
Hiller, Nathaniel	ONN 159	Hilton, William	ONT 472	Hinkley, Thomas	ESS 320
Hiller, Prince	DUT 103	Hilton, William Ju.	ONT 472	Hinkly, George	SCH 136
Hillhouse, Thomas	RNS 91	Hilton, William P.	SCH 141	Hinkly, Walter	SCH 152
Hilliard, David	ALB 37	Hilton, Willm W.	SCH 137	Hinkly, Walter	SCH 154
Hilliard, David	RNS 53	Hilts, Frederick	HRK 577	Hinks, James	OND 180
Hillibrant, Jacob	ALB 97	Hilts, George	HRK 445	Hinman, Aaron	OND 200
Hillibrant, Wedell	ALB 97	Hilts, Godfrit	HRK 446	Hinman, Aaron B.	RNS 82
Hillier, Richard	WST 167	Hilts, John	HRK 436	Hinman, Benjamin	OND 160
Hilliker, Elzabethe	WST 163	Hilts, John	HRK 446	Hinman, Besteel	GRN 340
Hilliker, John	RCH 92	Hilts, Loring	ONN 165	Hinman, Clarles	GRN 325
Hilliker, John	WST 163	Hilts, Philip	HRK 445	Hinman, Curtis	OND 185
Hilliker, John	WST 167	Hilts, Phillip	MNT 6	Hinman, Ebenezer	COL 242
Hilliker, Nicholas	WST 167	Hiltz, John E.	NYK 132	Hinman, Edward	GRN 332
Hillin, Garret	RNS 19	Hilyman, Jacob	NYK 143	Hinman, Eleazer	HRK 517
Hillman, John	TIO 256	Himes, Benjamin	ONT 324	Hinman, Elihu	HRK 558
Hillman, Levi	OND 219	Himes, Frederick	CAY 726	Hinman, Elijah	GRN 355
Hillon, Richard	ALB 106	Hi melman, George	NYK 56	Hinman, Husted	DUT 53
Hillop, Thomas	NYK 17	Hinard, Michall	WST 133	Hinman, James	OND 168
Hills, Asahel	OND 182	Hinchbald, Wm	MNT 77	Hinman, James	ONN 132
Hills, Ebenezer Junr	ALB 53	Hinchman, Joanna	QNS 66	Hinman, Jonas	CHN 984
Hills, Elisha	OND 199	Hinchman, John	QNS 67	Hinman, Lewis	HRK 557
Hills, George	SCH 118	Hinchman, John Junr	QNS 67	Hinman, Michael	OND 168
Hills, George Junr	SCH 123	Hinchman, Nehemiah	NYK 117	Hinman, Nathaniel	GRN 331
Hills, Isaac	SRA 52	Hinchman, Obadiah	KNG 2	Hinman, Reuben	OND 180
Hills, Jabald	SCH 123	Hinchman, Sarah	QNS 66	Hinman, Samuel	CHN 752
Hills, Jesse	WSH 265	Hinckley, Elijah	HRK 592	Hinman, Samuel	CHN 754
Hills, John	SCH 143	Hinckley, Gardner	HRK 590	Hinman, Truman	GRN 340
Hills, Joseph	OTS 54	Hinckley, Joshua	DUT 173	Hinman, William	GRN 341
Hills, Nathan	WSH 269	Hinckley, Nathan	SRA 53	Hinman, Zachariah	DUT 170
Hills, Nathan	WSH 288	Hinckley, Paul	RNS 103	Hinmon, Justus	COL 205
Hills, Nicholas	HRK 435	Hinckley, Thomas	DUT 167	Hinney, Jacob	ALB 48
Hills, Peter	SCH 152	Hinckley, Voice	DUT 64	Hinton, David	QNS 75
Hills, Reuben	WSH 269	Hincksman, Robert	HRK 452	Hinton, John	NYK 45
Hills, Seth	OND 169	Hinckston, Joseph Junr	OND 167	Hinton, John	NYK 66
Hills, Seth Junior	OND 169	Hincman, Cornelius	NYK 47	Hipp, Isaac	KNG 9
Hills, Squire	MNT 50	Hinderer, Jacob	ALB 139	Hippolite, Vincent	DUT 80

Hird, Johiel	ALB 60	Hitchcock, William	WSH 275	Hoag, Wenchester	MNT 93
Hiscock, Gardner	RNS 73	Hitchcock, Zeni	WSH 216	Hoag, William	DUT 49
Hiscock, Isaac	DUT 148	Hitchcok, Noah	ONN 182	Hoag, William	DUT 149
Hiscock, Wm	RNS 73	Hitchell, George	ALB 38	Hoagg, Aaron	CAY 678
Hiscox, Simeon W.	WSH 246	Hitchings, Martha	NYK 41	Hoagg, Levi	GRN 353
Hiser, John	GRN 326	Hitchock, Solomon	OTS 16	Hoar, Daniel	ONN 185
Hislop, John	ONT 508	Hitherington, Joseph	ALB 31	Hoar, Dix	ONN 146
Hismon, James	MNT 77	Hitsman, Henry	SCH 122	Hoar, Edward	ONN 147
Hisscock, James	ALB 31	Hitsman, John	SCH 150	Hoar, Jacob	ONN 147
Hisscock, Levi	ONN 155	Hitsman, John	SCH 155	Hoar, Jacob	ONN 182
Hisscock, Richard	ONN 135	Hitt, Dennis	DEL 276	Hoar, Jonathan	ONN 180
Hisscock, Thankfull	WSH 239	Hitt, Henry	DEL 276	Hoar, Leonard	CAY 602
Hisscock, William	ALB 31	Hitt, Henry	WST 130	Hoar, Samuel	HRK 444
Hist, George	WSH 251	Hitt, James	DEL 276	Hoard, David	RNS 104
Hitchcock, Alpheus	OND 175	Hitt, Jared	DEL 276	Hoard, George	RNS 105
Hitchcock, Amariah	DUT 133	Hitt, Jerid	WST 132	Hoard, Isaac	OTS 5
Hitchcock, Amos	OND 167	Hitt, John	DEL 276	Hoard, Jonathan	RNS 30
Hitchcock, Amos	WSH 306	Hitt, John	ULS 235	Hoard, Samuel	RNS 98
Hitchcock, Asahel	WSH 219	Hitt, John	WST 131	Hoard, Simeon	RNS 104
Hitchcock, Barnum	WSH 219	Hitt, Samuel	DUT 106	Hoatt, Barent	COL 245
Hitchcock, Benjamen	WSH 274	Hitt, Samuel	WST 133	Hoatt, Joseph	COL 245
Hitchcock, Bethuel	ONT 416	Hix, Ambrose	DEL 268	Hobart, Jesse	MNT 106
Hitchcock, Brshabel	WSH 219	Hix, John	RNS 13	Hobart, Dolly	ONT 454
Hitchcock, Caleb	GRN 349	Hix, Levi	DEL 268	Hobart, John H.	QNS 78
Hitchcock, Collins	WSH 219	Hix, Thomas	DEL 271	Hobart, John S.	WST 150
Hitchcock, Daniel	ALB 78	Hizer, Jacob	OND 161	Hobart, Samuel	ORN 305
Hitchcock, Daniel	NYK 64	Hizer, Jacob	OND 196	Hobart, Saml	SUF 77
Hitchcock, Daniel M.	NYK 62	Hizer, Michael Thomas	DUT 110	Hobbard, John	WSH 188
Hitchcock, David	CHN 752	Hoack, George	ALB 99	Hobble, Abijah	MNT 63
Hitchcock, David	DUT 84	Hoadley, Daniel	TIO 229	Hobby, Abraham	DUT 147
Hitchcock, David	OTS 22	Hoadley, Ira	TIO 229	Hobby, Caleb	WST 138
Hitchcock, David Jnr	OTS 22	Hoadley, Nathaniel	OND 175	Hobby, David	WST 113
Hitchcock, Ebenezer	HRK 533	Hoag, Abel	DUT 49	Hobby, David	WST 136
Hitchcock, Ebenezer	OTS 22	Hoag, Abner	DUT 50	Hobby, David Junr	WST 113
Hitchcock, Ebenezer	WSH 274	Hoag, Abner	RNS 49	Hobby, Drake	ORN 282
Hitchcock, Elizth	COL 207	Hoag, Abraham	DUT 42	Hobby, Enos	WST 113
Hitchcock, Enoch	OND 172	Hoag, Abraham	DUT 128	Hobby, Epinetus	OND 161
Hitchcock, Ezra	OTS 22	Hoag, Abraham	ULS 264	Hobby, Henry	WST 112
Hitchcock, George	HRK 414	Hoag, Andw	OTS 29	Hobby, John	OND 161
Hitchcock, Gideon	WSH 273	Hoag, Asa	DUT 55	Hobby, Jonathan	ORN 282
Hitchcock, Isaac	WSH 218	Hoag, Benjamin	ALB 115	Hobby, Lott	WST 112
Hitchcock, Jacob	GRN 337	Hoag, Benjamin	DUT 48	Hobby, Peter a Black	NYK 118
Hitchcock, James	COL 206	Hoag, Benjamin	OTS 36	Hobby, Vashti	WST 113
Hitchcock, James	DUT 22	Hoag, Charles	DUT 144	Hoben, John	NYK 141
Hitchcock, Jarid	OTS 43	Hoag, David	DUT 125	Hoben, Nicholas	DUT 147
Hitchcock, Jarvis	CHN 890	Hoag, Ebenezar	RNS 25	Hobs, Mary	NYK 145
Hitchcock, Jedediah	GRN 334	Hoag, Elisha	RNS 44	Hobs, Robert	NYK 71
Hitchcock, Jeremiah	ONN 185	Hoag, Ellit	RNS 22	Hobsen, George	NYK 63
Hitchcock, Jeremiah	WST 144	Hoag, Enoch	DUT 50	Hobsen, James	NYK 63
Hitchcock, John	WSH 218	Hoag, Ezeil	RNS 44	Hobson, Simon	RNS 26
Hitchcock, John	WST 147	Hoag, Henry	DUT 125	Hochkins, Brier	GRN 340
Hitchcock, Joseph	CHN 890	Hoag, Hiram	ALB 113	Hochland, Chris	SCH 138
Hitchcock, Joseph	DUT 21	Hoag, Ichabod	RNS 25	Hochland, Jacob	SCH 138
Hitchcock, Levi	ALB 78	Hoag, Isaac	DUT 50	Hochland, John	SCH 138
Hitchcock, Levi	GRN 344	Hoag, Isaac	OTS 29	Hochom, Enos	ONT 390
Hitchcock, Levi	WSH 203	Hoag, Isaiah	DUT 50	Hochstrasser, Jacob	OND 189
Hitchcock, Lewis	WST 154	Hoag, Jacob	OTS 29	Hochstrasser, Paul J.	ALB 69
Hitchcock, Marten	WSH 300	Hoag, Jedediah	SRA 45	Hochtaling, Jacob	SCH 132
Hitchcock, Martin	MNT 114	Hoag, Jeremiah	DUT 50	Hochtaling, Tunis	SCH 131
Hitchcock, Miles	NYK 40	Hoag, John	DUT 54	Hocknell, Richar	ALB 52
Hitchcock, Nathaniel	NYK 88	Hoag, John	DUT 97	Hockten, John	SUF 95
Hitchcock, Oliver	COL 207	Hoag, Jonathan	RNS 53	Hocome, Anthony	NYK 120
Hitchcock, Pheneas	WSH 291	Hoag, Levi	DUT 50	Hocum, Catharine	COL 198
Hitchcock, Poundwell	RNS 8	Hoag, Michael	DUT 50	Hocum, Dane	ONT 420
Hitchcock, Rueby	NYK 77	Hoag, Moses	OTS 29	Hocum, John	CHN 794
Hitchcock, Saml	ALB 42	Hoag, Nathaniel	DUT 50	Hocum, Levy	CHN 792
Hitchcock, Samuel	GRN 349	Hoag, Nehemiah	ULS 264	Hocum, Oriter	CHN 906
Hitchcock, Samuel	RNS 63	Hoag, Obadiah	RNS 45	Hocum, Seth	ONT 420
Hitchcock, Solomon	DUT 133	Hoag, Patience	DUT 50	Hocum, Zeturn	CHN 792
Hitchcock, Stephen	NYK 66	Hoag, Paul	DUT 125	Hodeley, Daniel	TIO 226
Hitchcock, Thomas	OND 184	Hoag, Peter	RNS 43	Hodeley, Noah	TIO 226
Hitchcock, Thos	RNS 64	Hoag, Phillip	DUT 7	Hodge, ame	SCH 170
Hitchcock, Timothy	CAY 638	Hoag, Samuel	COL 241	Hodge, Abel	RNS 57
Hitchcock, Volentine	GRN 334	Hoag, Solomon	DUT 103	Hodge, Abel	ULS 182
Hitchcock, William	DUT 21	Hoag, Thomas	COL 216	Hodge, Abraham	CHN 832
Hitchcock, William	GRN 337	Hoag, Thomas	WSH 282	Hodge, Andrew	SCH 170
Hitchcock, William	OTS 22	Hoag, Timothy	DUT 51	Hodge, Assahel	WSH 264

Hodge, Assahel	WSH 268	Hoff, Adam	RNS 57	Hoffnagel, John Junr	ESS 304		
Hodge, Benjn	OTS 49	Hoff, John	CLN 156	Hoffnagel, Michael	ESS 298		
Hodge, Curtis	CHN 768	Hoff, Laurence	RNS 33	Hofftail, Albert	COL 247		
Hodge, Daniel	SCH 170	Hoff, Levi	OND 220	Hofftail, Henry	COL 235		
Hodge, Elijah	COL 202	Hoff, Rich..d	MNT 94	Hofftail, Rachel	COL 229		
Hodge, Israel	WSH 223	Hoff, Stephen	QNS 78	Hofman, Frederick	ONT 376		
Hodge, Jacob	ONN 146	Hoff, William	COL 225	Hofstodom, Christion	MNT 31		
Hodge, James	ALB 133	Hoff, William	COL 240	Hofstodom, Jacob	MNT 31		
Hodge, John	MNT 43	Hoff, William	NYK 147	Hog, John George	MNT 63		
Hodge, John	MNT 49	Hofferlick, Chas	ALB 69	Hogabomb, Jacob	MNT 92		
Hodge, John	SCH 170	Hofferlick, Chrs	ALB 69	Hogaboom, Barthw	ALB 96		
Hodge, John Junr	MNT 49	Hoffman, Abraham	DUT 64	Hogaboom, Christion	MNT 92		
Hodge, Joshua	WSH 290	Hoffman, Abraham	ULS 227	Hogoboom, Jacob	SCH 134		
Hodge, Nahum	OND 208	Hoffman, Adam	RNS 29	Hogaboom, John L.	ALB 101		
Hodge, Noah	DUT 167	Hoffman, Adam	ULS 203	Hogadon, Dirck H.	ALB 20		
Hodge, Ralph	NYK 45	Hoffman, Andrew	ALB 134	Hogadon, Dirick D.	ALB 19		
Hodge, Reuben	MNT 49	Hoffman, Anthony	DUT 64	Hogadon, Henry D.	ALB 19		
Hodge, Robert	KNG 9	Hoffman, Anthony	MNT 54	Hogadoon, Hannah	ALB 91B		
Hodge, Sally	NYK 36	Hoffman, Anthony M.	DUT 147	Hogadoon, Henry	ALB 20		
Hodge, Samuel	WSH 290	Hoffman, Archibald	MNT 45	Hogadoon, Herms	ALB 20		
Hodge, Samuel Jur	MNT 43	Hoffman, Bastian	COL 244	Hogadorn, Elizabeth	NYK 124		
Hodge, Timothy	ULS 180	Hoffman, Betsey	NYK 134	Hogaford, Charles	MNT 111		
Hodgekinson, John	NYK 49	Hoffman, Cha	MNT 37	Hogan, Daniel	COL 215		
Hodgekiss, Jeremiah	WSH 213	Hoffman, Charles	DUT 70	Hogan, Dennis	NYK 113		
Hodges, Amos	WSH 207	Hoffman, Charles A.	NYK 34	Hogan, Edward	ALB 111		
Hodges, Benjamin	DEL 280	Hoffman, Coonradt	DUT 156	Hogan, James	ORN 280		
Hodges, Cornelius	CLN 167	Hoffman, Cornelius	NYK 44	Hogan, John	NYK 79		
Hodges, David	ONN 161	Hoffman, Daniel	COL 200	Hogan, John	ULS 208		
Hodges, Druces	WSH 256	Hoffman, Daniel	COL 238	Hogan, Jurian	ALB 98		
Hodges, Ezekiel	CLN 167	Hoffman, Daniel	DUT 24	Hogan, Patrick	ORN 335		
Hodges, Ezekiel	RNS 22	Hoffman, David	RCK 106	Hogan, Peter	ALB 120		
Hodges, Hezekiah	DEL 280	Hoffman, Evert	ULS 245	Hogan, Pett	ULS 208		
Hodges, Isaac	DEL 280	Hoffman, Frederick	COL 193	Hogan, Philip	ALB 55		
Hodges, Isaac	MNT 113	Hoffman, Frederick	COL 244	Hogan, William	COL 218		
Hodges, James	ONN 161	Hoffman, Frederick	NYK 121	Hogan, Zachariah	ULS 191		
Hodges, James	RNS 83	Hoffman, George	DUT 156	Hogben, Charles	NYK 81		
Hodges, Joseph	ONT 310	Hoffman, Heman	COL 244	Hogden, Samuel	SRA 19		
Hodges, Josiah	ONN 161	Hoffman, Henry	COL 235	Hogebome, Peter	SRA 48		
Hodges, Mathew	RNS 20	Hoffman, Herman	COL 225	Hogeboom, Abraham	COL 215		
Hodges, Philip	DEL 282	Hoffman, Isaac	DUT 66	Hogeboom, Barthow	COL 192		
Hodges, Sam	RNS 20	Hoffman, Jacob	NYK 153	Hogeboom, Daniel	COL 180		
Hodges, Samuel	HRK 515	Hoffman, Jacobus	ULS 249	Hogeboom, David	COL 180		
Hodges, Samuel	RNS 82	Hoffman, John	HRK 443	Hogeboom, Henry	DEL 275		
Hodges, Wm	RNS 21	Hoffman, John	MNT 53	Hogeboom, Jacob	COL 180		
Hodgkin, George	DUT 132	.offman, John	ONT 490	Hogeboom, James	COL 181		
Hodgkin, Noah	DUT 136	Hoffman, John	ORN 335	Hogeboom, John	COL 194		
Hodgkins, Thomas	WSH 302	Hoffman, John	ULS 249	Hogeboom, John White-			
Hodgkiss, Michael	NYK 51	Hoffman, John C.	NYK 139	man	SRA 26		
Hodgman, Amos	SRA 46	Hoffman, Joseph	ORN 283	Hogeboom, John C.	COL 193		
Hodgman, Daniel	ONN 193	Hoffman, Josiah O.	ALB 147	Hogeboom, John J.	COL 180		
Hodgson, George	WSH 203	Hoffman, Laurence	NYK 151	Hogeboom, Lawrence	COL 196		
Hodgson, Ralph	ORN 396	Hoffman, Martin	ALB 22	Hogeboom, Peter	COL 254		
Hodgson, Stephen	RNS 37	Hoffman, Martin	DUT 66	Hogeboom, Peter C.	COL 262		
Hodkins, Aaron	OND 196	Hoffman, Martin	NYK 31	Hogeboom, Stephen	COL 193		
Hodler, Solomon	ULS 232	Hoffman, Martin H.	COL 192	Hogeboom, Stephen J.	COL 194		
Hodskess, Christopher	WSH 245	Hoffman, Mathew	COL 241	Hogedone, Jacob	HRK 493		
Hodskin, Samuel	OTS 26	Hoffman, Matthias	CAY 708	Hogedone, William	HRK 493		
Hodskiss, Isaac	WST 156	Hoffman, Nicholas	COL 201	Hogedorn, Henry	SRA 28		
Hodswell, Joseph	DEL 286	Hoffman, Nicholas	DUT 156	Hogedorn, Jacob	COL 195		
Hoeagg, John	GRN 353	Hoffman, Nicholas	ULS 249	Hogevout, Egbert	RCH 89		
Hoeg, Amaziah	COL 193	Hoffman, Peter	HRK 450	Hogevout, Elenor	RCH 89		
Hoeg, Amos	WSH 188	Hoffman, Peter	RCK 104	Hogevout, Peter	RCH 89		
Hoeg, Amos	WSH 189	Hoffman, Philip	ALB 142	Hogg, James	NYK 80		
Hoeg, Andrew	WSH 208	Hoffman, Phillip L.	COL 237	Hogg, John	NYK 58		
Hoeg, Beman	WSH 189	Hoffman, ..chard	MNT 93	Hogg, John	NYK 80		
Hoeg, Elijah	WSH 189	Hoffman, Robert	DUT 62	Hogg, Samuel	CAY 622		
Hoeg, Elisha	WSH 236	Hoffman, Simon	DUT 156	Hogg, Wintrup	WST 128		
Hoeg, Friend	WSH 207	Hoffman, Uriah	RCK 102	Hoggs, Moses	SRA 56		
Hoeg, Jonathen	WSH 237	Hoffman, William	COL 200	Hoghland, Benjamin	NYK 106		
Hoeg, Moses	COL 219	Hoffman, William	DUT 70	Hoghstawlings, Wm	MNT 72		
Hoeg, Salvenus	WSH 236	Hoffman, Wm	RCK 102	Hoghtalin, Phillip	COL 235		
Hoeg, Stephen	WSH 237	Hoffman, Wm	RCK 102	Hogins, Amos	RNS 97		
Hoegg, Abner	GRN 353	Hoffman, Wynsell	ALB 55	Hogins, Jesse	RNS 113		
Hoel, John	ORN 310	Hoffman, Zacharias	DUT 153	Hogland, Albert	QNS 65		
Hoet, Thos	RCK 164	Hoffman, William	NYK 37	Hogland, Cornelius	QNS 78		
Hofbusy, Thomas	MNT 93	Hoffmire, Isaac	RCK 100	Hogland, Cornelius	QNS 82		
Hoff, Adam	COL 201	Hoffnagel, John	ESS 304	Hogland, Elizabeth	NYK 94		

Hogland, Tunis	QNS	82	Holcomb, Levy	WSH	298	Holket, John	DUT	87
Hogland, William	NYK	52	Holcomb, Michael	HRK	427	Holladay, Catherine	NYK	54
Hogle, Abraham	WSH	246	Holcomb, Michael	RNS	110	Holland, Elihu	OTS	18
Hogle, Benoni	WSH	191	Holcomb, Oliver	ESS	318	Holland, Ivary	OTS	51
Hogle, Cathrine	WSH	185	Holcomb, Phinehas	HRK	511	Holland, James	RNS	59
Hogle, Cornelius	WSH	215	Holcomb, Reuben	ULS	188	Holland, Jane	COL	260
Hogle, Elisha	SCH	170	Holcomb, Saml	RNS	106	Holland, John	MNT	58
Hogle, Francis	RNS	12	Holcomb, Selah	HRK	535	Holland, John W.	OTS	51
Hogel, Francis	RNS	27	Holcomb, Timothy	DEL	287	Holland, Joseph	DUT	100
Hogle, Isaac	WSH	214	Holcomb, Zephiniah	OTS	21	Holland, Richard	QNS	75
Hogle, Isaac	WSH	246	Holden, Abel	NYK	103	Holland, Robert	ONT	360
Hogle, Jeremiah	WSH	185	Holden, Anthony	SCH	128	Holland, William	NYK	132
Hogle, Nicholas	RNS	12	Holden, Asa	NYK	149	Holland, William	ORN	372
Hogner, Isaac	QNS	69	Holden, Caleb	WSH	215	Hollander, Jeremiah	NYK	23
Hogoboom, Derick	RNS	64	Holden, David	NYK	117	Hollarday, Robard	GRN	354
Hogoboom, Jacob	RNS	110	Holden, David	WSH	215	Hollay, David	NYK	130
Hogoboom, James L.	RNS	41	Holden, Ebenezar	RNS	10	Hollay, Rachael	NYK	119
Hogoboom, John	RNS	112	Holden, Jacob Ju.	ONT	418	Holldridge, Roswell	RNS	4
Hogovout, Nicholas	RCH	93	Holden, Jeduthan	OTS	31	Hollebut, Eleazer	CLN	157
Hogovout, Winant	RCH	93	Holden, John	CAY	608	Holleck, Benjamin	QNS	78
Hogskins, Jonas	OTS	29	Holden, John	RNS	26	Holleck, Jabez	OND	208
Hogston, Amos	MNT	95	Holden, Josiah	HRK	486	Holleck, Parker	OND	214
Hohnes, Nathaniel	WST	168	Holden, Oliver	DUT	59	Holleck, Thomas	SUF	89
Hoick, Levi	ALB	92	Holden, Robert	NYK	117	Holleday, Rogers	WSH	265
Hoig, Eliab	WST	131	Holden, Thomas	NYK	70	Hollenbake, _ niel	RNS	12
Hoig, Reuben	COL	209	Holden, William	DUT	59	Hollenbake, John	CLN	171
Hoigg, Ezra	CHN	794	Holden, William	NYK	73	Hollenbake, William	CLN	171
Hoit, Charles	SRA	58	Holderidge, Isaac	ALB	82	Hollenbeck, Abraham	GRN	357
Hoit, Eliphalet	CAY	686	Holderidge, Lucretia	ALB	82	Hollenbeck, Abraham	GRN	358
Hoit, Enos	ONT	378	Holderidge, Joseph	ALB	82	Hollenbeck, Cornelius	GRN	340
Hoit, Ephraim	OND	211	Holdman, David	HRK	440	Hollenbeck, Cornelius	GRN	359
Hoit, Gideon	SRA	59	Holdon, James	OTS	57	Hollenbeck, Cosper	GRN	357
Hoit, Levi	ONT	382	Holdredge, John	STB	203	Hollenbeck, Jacob N.	GRN	350
Hoit, Silas	SRA	59	Holdridge, Abraham	COL	177	Hollenbeck, Jacob N.	GRN	357
Hoit, Silas	SRA	59	Holdridge, Arnold	COL	189	Hollenbeck, Johaicam	GRN	350
Hoit, Solomon	SRA	59	Holdridge, Artems	OTS	31	Hollenbeck, John	GRN	348
Hoitt, Hezekiah	SRA	15	Holdridge, Asa	COL	203	Hollenbeck, John	GRN	357
Hoitt, John	SRA	13	Holdridge, Augustus	DUT	13	Hollenbeck, John	MNT	30
Hoitt, Phebe	SRA	16	Holdridge, Danl	OTS	48	Hollenbeck, John	RNS	12
Hokam, Elishama	WSH	283	Holdridge, David	HRK	415	Hollenbeck, John C.	GRN	348
Hoke, John	MNT	35	Holdridge, Epaphroditas	WSH	282	Hollenbeck, John C.	GRN	358
Holbert, Abijah	SCH	146	Holdridge, Felix	MNT	83	Hollenbeck, John W.	GRN	358
Holbert, Azariah	OTS	4	Holdridge, Felix	OTS	31	Hollenbeck, Martain A.	GRN	357
Holbert, Ebenezer	ORN	361	Holdridge, Gersham	COL	203	Hollenbeck, Martin	GRN	350
Holbert, John	ORN	361	Holdridge, Hezkiah	ALB	92	Hollenbeck, Martin A.	GRN	350
Holbert, John Junr	ORN	361	Holdridge, Isaac	COL	203	Hollenbeck, Peter	GRN	348
Holbert, Reuben	SCH	146	Holdridge, Israel	COL	182	Hollenbeck, Peter	GRN	348
Holbert, Timothy	SCH	146	Holdridge, Nathl	OTS	4	Hollenbeck, Robart	GRN	349
Holbert, Joel	OTS	10	Holdridge, Rebecca	COL	189	Hollenbeck, Robbard	GRN	339
Holbrook, Barick	ONN	141	Holdridge, Richard	COL	203	Hollenbeck, Samuel	GRN	332
Holbrook, Josiah	ONN	141	Holdridge, Richd	HRK	415	Hollenbeck, William	GRN	345
Holbrook, Luke	ONN	141	Holdridge, Thos	OTS	31	Hollenbeck, Wm	RNS	46
Holbrook, Reuben	TIO	243	Holdridge, Thomas	OTS	38	Hollenbeck, Yockam	GRN	348
Holbrook, Silas	CAY	672	Holdridge, Willm	COL	214	Hollenburgh, Isaac	GRN	348
Holburt, Caleb	OTS	26	Holdridge, William	QNS	78	Hollester, Smith	OTS	47
Holburt, John	OTS	22	Holdron, John	NYK	50	Hollester, William	WSH	276
Holbut, David	OTS	32	Holdup, Thomas	NYK	83	Hollet, Cristion	MNT	107
Holby, Elisha	COL	237	Hole, Jonathan	MNT	124	Hollet, Joseph	MNT	64
Holchkess, Harres	WSH	244	Holebrock, Daniel	WSH	195	Holley, Daniel	WST	153
Holchkess, Rufus	WSH	280	Holeday, Adam	TIO	228	Holley, George	COL	178
Holchkiss, Simon	WSH	284	Holeday, Amariah	ESS	320	Holley, Henry	WST	153
Holcom, Peggy	NYK	20	Holenbeck, Daniel	RNS	19	Holley, Jonah	WST	140
Holcomb, Abel	ONN	158	Holenbeck, Ephraim	RNS	46	Holley, Joseph	ONN	186
Holcomb, Abram	COL	202	Holenbeck, Hons	GRN	348	Holley, Josiah	COL	236
Holcomb, Almon	ESS	311	Holenbergh, Peter	MNT	117	Holley, Lemuel	RNS	84
Holcomb, Azariah	RNS	9	Holester, Solomon	SRA	13	Holley, Myron	OTS	19
Holcomb, Bariah	RNS	101	Holford, Edward	TIO	216	Hollibart, June	GRN	332
Holcomb, Benjamin	ESS	311	Holister, Abner	OND	200	Hollibert, Arrenus	SRA	4
Holcomb, Bethuel	RNS	9	Holister, David	OTS	49	Hollibert, Moses	WSH	304
Holcomb, Butler	HRK	525	Holister, Derastus	SRA	14	Holliburt, Lewis	ALB	88
Holcomb, Cyrus	ONN	158	Holister, Francis	OND	183	Holliburt, Zachariah	CLN	162
Holcomb, Ebenzer	ULS	188	Holister, Hiel	OND	159	Hollice, Daniel	OTS	34
Holcomb, Ebenezer Junr	ULS	188	Holister, Nathan	GRN	325	Holliday, Elihu	CAY	614
Holcomb, Edad	RNS	9	Holister, Reuben	SRA	14	Holliday, James	ALB	75
Holcomb, Jedediah	ESS	318	Holister, Robert	OND	170	Hollida_, James	MNT	115
Holcomb, Josiah	RNS	101	Holister, Samuel	SRA	12	Holliday, John	CHN	810
Holcomb, Josiah	RNS	106	Holister, Silas	SRA	14	Holliday, John	NYK	57

Holliday, Mathew	ONT 442	Holmes, Ebenezar	RNS 65	Holmes, Roswell	SRA 39
Holliday, Richard	NYK 68	Holmes, Ebenezer	SRA 18	Holmes, Ruben	CHN 974
Holliday, William	DEL 275	Holmes, Edward	CHN 926	Holmes, Rufus	COL 242
Holliday, William	SCH 135	Holmes, Eldad	NYK 80	Holmes, Rufus Junr	COL 243
Holliday, William	SCH 148	Holmes, Eleazor	NYK 140	Holmes, Samuel	ALB 93
Hollinbeck, Isaac	ONT 460	Holmes, Elijah	CHN 866	Holmes, Samuel	COL 187
Hollinbergh, Isaac	MNT 31	Holmes, Elijah	HRK 523	Holmes, Samuel	DUT 100
Hollister, ...thy	GRN 359	Holmes, Elijah	HRK 570	Holmes, Samuel	OTS 22
Hollister, Amos	OTS 34	Holmes, Elizabeth	RCH 95	Holmes, Samuel	RCH 91
Hollister, Asa	DUT 139	Holmes, Ethan	HRK 511	Holmes, Seth	OND 169
Hollister, Benjamin	DUT 134	Holmes, Ezra	WSH 229	Holmes, Seth	OTS 56
Hollister, Elisha	COL 216	Holmes, Gilbert	WST 136	Holmes, Shubel	ALB 60
Hollister, Ephraim	OND 211	Holmes, Henry	DUT 141	Holmes, Silas	SRA 61
Hollister, Ezra	CAY 542	Holmes, Henry	QNS 65	Holmes, Simeon	ALB 71
Hollister, Ezra	CAY 542	Holmes, Hester	NYK 112	Holmes, Simeon	ALB 104
Hollister, Francis	CAY 604	Holmes, Ichabod	DUT 141	Holmes, Stephen	COL 247
Hollister, Francis	CAY 612	Holmes, Isaac	COL 179	Holmes, Stephen	DUT 106
Hollister, Isaac	ULS 197	Holmes, Isaac	SRA 24	Holmes, Stephen	NYK 80
Hollister, John	HRK 417	Holmes, Isaac Junr	COL 187	Holmes, Stephen	ULS 207
Hollister, Josiah	ULS 197	Holmes, Israel	DUT 141	Holmes, Stephen	WST 140
Hollister, William	ORN 348	Holmes, Jabez	ALB 79	Holmes, Thomas	ALB 77
Hollister, William	SRA 59	Holmes, Jacob	DUT 100	Holmes, Thomas	NYK 67
Hollister, William	ULS 239	Holmes, Jacob a Black	NYK 81	Holmes, Widow	SRA 42
Hollman, Eliphalet	ALB 27	Holmes, Jacob	WSH 275	Holmes, William	COL 185
Hollock, Jeremiah	CAY 722	Holmes, James	ALB 77	Holmes, William	DUT 122
Hollock, John	WST 132	Holmes, James	ALB 81	Holmes, William	NYK 59
Hollock, Nathan	GRN 338	Holmes, James	ALB 128	Holmes, William	NYK 89
Hollock, Thomas	GRN 352	Holmes, James	DUT 126	Holmes, William	NYK 118
Hollock, William	GRN 338	Holmes, James	ORN 370	Holmes, William	ORN 283
Hollock, William	GRN 343	Holmes, James	SRA 23	Holms, Absalom	WST 152
Holloday, Jonah	OND 193	Holmes, James	SRA 25	Holms, James	MNT 98
Holloway, Daniel	ONT 426	Holmes, James	WST 136	Holms, James	SUF 64
Holloway, John	NYK 98	Holmes, Jeremiah	WST 136	Holms, Jedediah	ONT 466
Holloway, Thos	RCK 102	Holmes, Jessemiah	HRK 570	Holms, John	CAY 584
Holly, Abraham	NYK 153	Holmes, Joel	NYK 116	Holms, Nathaniel	SRA 4
Holly, Benjamin	ORN 320	Holmes, Joel	WSH 219	Holms, Samuel	WST 134
Holly, Benjamin	WSH 265	Holmes, John	ALB 94	Holnby, John	TIO 257
Holly, Daniel	COL 177	Holmes, John	CHN 770	Holsbrook, David	ONN 170
Holly, Daniel	ORN 396	Holmes, John	COL 204	Holsey, Abraham	SUF 99
Holly, Ebenezer	ORN 317	Holmes, John	DEL 276	Holsey, Annanias	SUF 97
Holly, Increase	ORN 368	Holmes, John	DUT 89	Holsey, Elias	SUF 99
Holly, Ira	RNS 32	Holmes, John	DUT 120	Holsey, Epinitus	CLN 163
Holly, John	CLN 167	Holmes, John	DUT 131	Holsey, Frederick	CLN 164
Holly, John	DUT 143	Holmes, John	HRK 415	Holsey, Hezekiah	SUF 99
Holly, John	ORN 364	Holmes, John	NYK 91	Holsey, Isaac	SUF 97
Holly, Joseph	ORN 368	Holmes, John	NYK 127	Holsey, Jane	SUF 99
Holly, Josiah	ORN 359	Holmes, John	ORN 274	Holsey, Paul	SUF 99
Holly, Noah	ORN 367	Holmes, John	QNS 72	Holsey, Paul Junr	SUF 99
Holly, Sally	DEL 276	Holmes, John	QNS 76	Holsey, Silvenus	SUF 99
Holly, Samuel	ORN 367	Holmes, John	SRA 23	Holsey, Stephen	SUF 99
Holly, Silas	ORN 368	Holmes, John	SRA 24	Holsey, Stephen	SUF 99
Holly, Sillick	WSH 276	Holmes, John	SRA 24	Holsey, William	SUF 99
Holly, Squires	WSH 267	Holmes, John	WSH 298	Holsey, William	SUF 99
Holly, Sylvenus	WSH 276	Holmes, John	WST 161	Holsey, Zebulon	SUF 98
Holly, Timothy	ORN 367	Holmes, John Junr	CHN 770	Holsinger, Charles	SCH 169
Holman, David	OND 181	Holmes, John M.	SRA 42	Holsinger, Jacob	SCH 169
Holman, Samuel	HRK 489	Holmes, Jonathan	KNG 3	Holsinger, Peter	SCH 169
Holmes	RNS 24	Holmes, Jonathan	WSH 275	Holson, Isaac	GRN 336
Holmes, Aaron	COL 187	Holmes, Jonathan	WST 136	Holstead, Isaac	QNS 81
Holmes, Abijah	WST 142	Holmes, Joseph	COL 183	Holstead, Joseph	OND 188
Holmes, Abner	RNS 40	Holmes, Joseph	WSH 275	Holstead, Phebe	RCK 108
Holmes, Abraham	OND 162	Holmes, Joseph	WST 136	Holsted, David	GRN 352
Holmes, Alexander	OND 167	Holmes, Jotham	SRA 42	Holsted, James	GRN 352
Holmes, Amey	WST 136	Holmes, Lester	CHN 768	Holsted, Joshua	SRA 6
Holmes, Asa	CAY 554	Holmes, Lewis	WST 142	Holsted, Samuel	SRA 28
Holmes, Asa	COL 231	Holmes, Margaret	RCH 90	Holsted, Samuel	SRA 33
Holmes, Assahel	WSH 299	Holmes, Moses	DUT 91	Holsted, Samuel	WST 131
Hoomes, Azel	HRK 511	Holmes, Nathl	OTS 52	Holt, Amos	OND 158
Holmes, Belcher	ALB 94	Holmes, Obadiah	SRA 23	Holt, Benjamin	RNS 85
Holmes, Burroughs	ORN 272	Holmes, Orsamus	CHN 810	Holt, Elijah	CHN 838
Holmes, Caleb	SRA 23	Holmes, Palmer	COL 200	Holt, Elijah	OTS 2
Holmes, Charles	NYK 29	Holmes, Palmer	COL 259	Holt, Elisha	WSH 212
Holmes, Cornelius	WSH 227	Holmes, Peter	DEL 275	Holt, George	OTS 14
Holmes, Daniel	WST 138	Holmes, Peter	QNS 75	Holt, Isaac	OND 175
Holmes, David	ORN 273	Holmes, Phebe	NYK 23	Holt, James	NYK 74
Holmes, David	WST 136	Holmes, Reuben	ORN 272	Holt, James	WSH 199
Homes, Debroah	WST 137	Holmes, Roswell	CHN 962	Holt, Joseph	OTS 19

Name	Loc	Pg
Holt, Jotham	OTS	41
Holt, Lester	OTS	2
Holt, Peter	NYK	70
Holt, Widow	OTS	2
Holton, Elijah	OTS	41
Holton, Rufus	OND	187
Holton, William	ONT	454
Holtsapple, Henry	COL	192
Holtsapple, John	COL	196
Holtsapple, John	COL	240
Holtsapple, Martin	COL	179
Holtsapple, Nichs	COL	225
Holtsapple, Phillip H.	COL	192
Holtsapple, Wm Z.	COL	196
Holtsapple, Zacheriah	COL	190
Holumb, John	RNS	94
Holyday, Amos	ONN	147
Holyday, Jonathan	ONN	147
Homan, Benjamin	ORN	289
Homan, Benjn	SUF	72
Homan, Danl	SUF	64
Homan, Danl	SUF	69
Homan, David	SUF	65
Homan, Ebenezer S.	ULS	268
Homan, Gilbert	SUF	90
Homan, Isaac	SUF	64
Homan, Isaac	SUF	66
Homan, James	SUF	65
Homan, Joel	DUT	167
Homan, John	ORN	279
Homan, John	SRA	35
Homan, John	SUF	64
Homan, John	SUF	65
Homan, John	SUF	66
Homan, Joseph	SUF	64
Homan, Joseph	SUF	76
Homan, Joshua	ORN	352
Homan, Mordeca	SUF	65
Homan, Mordian Jr	SUF	64
Homan, Mordian Ser	SUF	64
Homan, Morris	OND	208
Homan, Nathl	SUF	69
Homan, Paul	SUF	65
Homan, Robert	SUF	64
Homan, Robert	SUF	69
Homan, Samuel	SUF	94
Homan, Theophilus	OND	181
Homan, Willet	DEL	282
Homan, Zebulon	DUT	167
Homer, John	OND	157
Homes, John	STB	197
Homes, Nathan	TIO	212
Homes, Nathaniel	OND	195
Homfedt, Henry	NYK	80
Homing, George	SCH	169
Homing, William	SCH	169
Homston, Titus	TIO	226
Hommedin, Benjn	SUF	72
Hommister, Abraham	GRN	338
Hone, Christian	SCH	169
Hone, Jacob	OTS	4
Hone, John	NYK	51
Hone, John a mulatto	NYK	75
Hone, Samuel	NYK	23
Honewill, Jane	WST	163
Honewill, Phillip	WST	163
Honeywell, Enoch	WST	137
Honeywell, Gilbert	NYK	134
Honeywell, Israel	WST	144
Honeywell, James	NYK	71
Honeywell, John	OND	214
Honeywell, Matthew	DUT	172
Honeywell, Stephen	WST	137
Honeywell, William	DEL	289
Honiwell, Enoch	WST	168
Honnes, Elisha	TIO	248
Honnicunt, Jonathan	MNT	119
Honson, John	KNG	6
Honson, Stephen	RNS	13
Honson, Tunis	RNS	13
Honywell, James	SRA	53
Hoo_e, Israel	DEL	271
Hood, Andrew	CAY	530
Hood, George	CAY	530
Hood, George	RNS	108
Hood, J ne	CAY	530
Hood, John	CAY	530
Hood, John	OTS	55
Hood, Timothy Junr	MNT	76
Hood, William	CAY	530
Hood, William	COL	253
Hood, William	ULS	238
Hoodges, Abraham	SRA	43
Hoof, Adam	RNS	53
Hoof, Ellis	RNS	56
Hoof, Joshua	RNS	56
Hoofcoot, George	DUT	44
Hoofcoot, John	DUT	44
Hooff, Mary	ULS	223
oofman, ...	RNS	37
Hoofman, Andrew	HRK	443
Hoofman, George	SRA	23
Hoofman, Mary	NYK	65
Hoofman, Nicholas	RNS	39
Hoofman, Peter	RNS	59
Hoofman, Rinhart	NYK	86
Hoofman, Tobias	NYK	111
Hoofmire, Peter	NYK	99
Hoofurth, Nicholas	RNS	10
Hoogeboom, Anthony	ULS	227
Hoogeboom, Dirck	ULS	183
Hooghteling, Abraham	ULS	219
Hooghteling, Anna M.	ULS	230
Hooghteling, Cornelius	ULS	231
Hooghteling, Isaac	DUT	147
Hooghteling, Jeremiah	ULS	231
Hooghteling, Jeremiah Junr	ULS	206
Hooghteling, John	DUT	145
Hooghteling, John Junr	DUT	5
Hooghteling, John Senr	DUT	5
Hooghteling, Peter	DUT	147
Hooghteling, Phillip	ULS	218
Hooghteling, Teunis	ULS	231
Hooghteling, Thomas	ULS	230
Hooghteling, William	DUT	162
Hooghteling, William	ULS	231
Hoogland, Abraham	DUT	40
Hoogland, Abraham	NYK	76
Hoogland, Albert	QNS	79
Hoogland, Dirck	DUT	40
Hoogland, Ellenor	NYK	123
Hoogland, Jemima	DUT	37
Hoogland, John	NYK	70
Hoogland, Margaret	NYK	86
Hoogland, Peter	DUT	26
Hoogland, William	DUT	34
Hook, Thomas	NYK	50
Hook_, Increase	ONN	176
Hooker, Charles	ONT	428
Hooker, Gilbert	SRA	47
Hooker, Jared J.	HRK	528
Hooker, Jonathan	HRK	539
Hooker, Levi	WSH	218
Hooker, Philip	ALB	143
Hooker, Samuel	OND	160
Hooker, Samuel	WSH	288
Hooks, John	MNT	114
Hoolbrook, Griffin	GRN	355
Hoolbrooks, Ephraim	ALB	120
Hooly, John	NYK	132
Hoony, Mercy	DUT	87
Hooper, Abraham	RCH	89
Hooper, Calvin	COL	184
Hooper, Daniel	RCH	88
Hooper, Isaac	WSH	241
Hooper, John	ONN	156
Hooper, Judith	ULS	230
Hooper, Lawrance	SRA	48
Hooper, Stephen	CAY	516
Hoopper, Pontus	SRA	48
Hoops, Jacob	QNS	79
Hoornbeck, Benjamin	ULS	213
Hoornbeck, Benjamin I.	ULS	211
Hoornbeck, Cornelius	ULS	245
Hoornbeck, Cornelius Junr	ULS	215
Hoornbeck, Cornelius P.	ULS	214
Hoornbeck, Evert	ORN	315
Hoornbeck, Garret S.W.	ULS	244
Hoornbeck, Henry	ULS	212
Hoornbeck, Isaac	ULS	213
Hoornbeck, Jacob	ULS	213
Hoornbeck, James	ULS	212
Hoornbeck, Joel	ULS	245
Hoornbeck, Johannis	ULS	211
Hoornbeck, Lawrence	ULS	213
Hoornbeck, Lodowick	ULS	215
Hoornbeck, Phillip	ULS	214
Hoornbeck, Tobias	ULS	220
Hoory, Robert	NYK	127
Hoory, John	NYK	127
Hoos, Mathias	GRN	356
Hoos, Mathias Jun	GRN	356
Hoose	GRN	350
Hoose, Jacob	ALB	77
Hoose, Lowrance	SRA	6
Hoose, Matthew	ONN	144
Hoot, John	ALB	126
Hootches, Doctor	WST	157
Hooten, William	NYK	128
Hoover, Henry	HRK	450
Hoover, Henry Junr	HRK	450
Hoover, Jacob	HRK	450
Hoover, John	HRK	450
Hopeleus, Christian	OND	208
Hopeleus, John	OND	208
Hopewell, William	NYK	76
Hopkins, Abner	OTS	38
Hopkins, Anthony a Black	NYK	124
Hopkins, Benjamin	DUT	20
Hopkins, Benjamin	NYK	120
Hopkins, Benj:	ONN	153
Hopkins, Benjamin	ONT	346
Hopkins, Benjn	OTS	38
Hopkins, Berry	DUT	172
Hopkins, Caleb	ALB	135
Hopkins, Caleb	ONT	358
Hopkins, Chancery	OTS	35
Hopkins, Charles	CHN	874
Hopkins, Danl	OTS	9
Hopkins, Daniel	QNS	83
Hopkins, Daniel	WSH	294
Hopkins, Daniel	WST	116
Hopkins, David	DUT	93
Hopkins, David	WSH	295
Hopkins, David Esqr	WSH	295
Hopkins, Duty	OTS	30
Hopkins, Edmund	DUT	94
Hopkins, Ehud	ONT	396
Hopkins, Eli	WSH	211
Hopkins, Elias	OND	189
Hopkins, Elisha	WSH	228
Hopkins, Elizabeth	DUT	67
Hopkins, Freeman	DUT	143
Hopkins, George	WSH	226
Hopkins, George F.	NYK	30
Hopkins, Gideon	OTS	31

Hopkins, Isaiah	DUT 93	Hopper, Cornelius	TIO 260	Horseford, John	GRN 346
Hopkins, James	DUT 36	Hopper, Daniel	SUF 107	Horsfield, Israel	NYK 33
Hopkins, James	NYK 76	Hopper, Edward	ALB 113	Horsford, Ashbil	SRA 39
Hopkins, James	WSH 242	Hopper, Edward	DUT 74	Horsford, David	GRN 332
Hopkins, James	WSH 277	Hopper, Elizabeth	KNG 8	Horsford, Joseph	ALB 132
Hopkins, James	WSH 294	Hopper, Elizabeth	WST 148	Horsted, Edward	WSH 298
Hopkins, Jeremiah	DUT 96	Hopper, Garret	RCK 107	Horstford, Gideon	GRN 334
Hopkins, Jeremiah	OTS 9	Hopper, George	CAY 522	Horten, Nancy	NYK 128
Hopkins, Jerh Junr	OTS 9	Hopper, Gerret	NYK 60	Hortenborough, Ram	QNS 81
Hopkins, Joel	WSH 295	Hopper, Henry	COL 185	Horth, Frances	WSH 269
Hopkins, John	HRK 408	Hopper, Jacob	NYK 144	Horth, James	MNT 8
Hopkins, John	NYK 148	Hopper, James	SCH 162	Horton, Abraham	DUT 25
Hopkins, John	ONT 344	Hopper, Jasper	ALB 135	Horton, Abraham	WST 116
Hopkins, John	ONT 486	Hopper, John	DUT 73	Horton, Alithea	DUT 7
Hopkins, Jonah	OTS 36	Hopper, John	NYK 69	Horton, Ambrose	WST 113
Hopkins, Jonathan	DUT 188	Hopper, John	NYK 104	Horton, Amos	DUT 137
Hopkins, Joseph	ALB 74	Hopper, John	SRA 48	Horton, Asa	OTS 43
Hopkins, Joseph	ALB 85	Hopper, Joseph	DUT 74	Horton, Azariah	WST 116
Hopkins, Joseph	DUT 87	Hopper, Joseph	WSH 203	Horton, Barnabas	ONT 346
Hopkins, Joseph	NYK 43	Hopper, Lambert	CLN 162	Horton, Barnabas	ORN 325
Hopkins, Judah	ONN 158	Hopper, Mary	NYK 48	Horton, Benjamin	CAY 694
Hopkins, Lemwell	GRN 339	Hopper, Nathaniel	CLN 166	Horton, Benjamin	ORN 379
Hopkins, Lybius	DEL 279	Hopper, Neathur	NYK 103	Horton, Benjn	SUF 72
Hopkins, Margaret	NYK 137	Hopper, Peter	RCK 105	Horton, Benjn	SUF 74
Hopkins, Mark	OND 188	Hopper, Richard	DUT 74	Horton, Benjn	SUF 75
Hopkins, Martin	OTS 37	Hopper, Rinard	RCK 110	Horton, Benjn	SUF 76
Hopkins, Martin	WSH 242	Hopper, Samuel	QNS 60	Horton, Benjn	TIO 238
Hopkins, Mary	NYK 117	Hopper, Yellis	NYK 152	Horton, Caleb	DUT 9
Hopkins, Moses	CHN 798	Hoppin, Aaron	CAY 720	Horton, Caleb	DUT 86
Hopkins, Moses	ONN 184	Hoppin, Jehiel	ONN 191	Horton, Caleb	WST 111
Hopkins, Nathaniel	WSH 228	Hopping, Ephraim	NYK 116	Horton, Caleb	WST 128
Hopkins, Nathen	WSH 227	Hopping, Samuel	NYK 112	Horton, Casiah	SUF 105
Hopkins, Noris	WSH 203	Hopple, George	NYK 108	Horton, Daniel	WST 118
Hopkins, Oliver	OTS 36	Hopple, John	NYK 137	Horton, Daniel	WST 122
Hopkins, Pitts	ONT 408	Hoppole, Francis	ALB 57	Horton, Daniel	WST 154
Hopkins, Reuben	ORN 359	Hops, Franciss	SRA 58	Horton, Daniel	WST 159
Hopkins, Richard	WSH 209	Hops, James	WST 114	Horton, Daniel Junr	WST 122
Hopkins, Robert	RNS 20	Hops, Joseph	WST 114	Horton, Daniel Junr	WST 122
Hopkins, Robert	WSH 306	Hopson, Lyman	GRN 346	Horton, David	COL 205
Hopkins, Roderick	OND 176	Hopson, Clement	HRK 575	Horton, David	DUT 137
Hopkins, Saml	SUF 68	Hopson, Philo	HRK 574	Horton, David	RNS 43
Hopkins, Samuel	WSH 227	Hopson, William	WST 116	Horton, David	RNS 69
Hopkins, Samuel	WST 130	Hopwood, Rachael	NYK 145	Horton, David	SUF 72
Hopkins, Sewal	OND 199	Horace, James	MNT 63	Horton, David	SUF 76
Hopkins, Stephen	ONT 390	Hording, Benajah	ONT 336	Horton, David	ULS 190
Hopkins, Stephen	ONT 406	Hore, Mathew	NYK 74	Horton, Deborah	WST 120
Hopkins, Stephen	OTS 35	Horgan, Patrick	RCK 101	Horton, Ebenezer	GRN 358
Hopkins, Stephen	OTS 37	Horgerman, Peter	NYK 136	Horton, Elihu	SRA 60
Hopkins, Stephen	QNS 83	Horman, Pad	MNT 120	Horton, Elijah	DUT 81
Hopkins, Sylvanus	WSH 229	Horn, Jacob	GRN 344	Horton, Elijah	ORN 394
Hopkins, Telly	CHN 858	Horn, John	ALB 47	Horton, Elijah	WSH 183
Hopkins, Thatcher	DUT 89	Horn, Joseph G.	COL 250	Horton, Elijah	WST 119
Hopkins, Thomas	CHN 858	Hornakey, Charles	NYK 96	Horton, Elijah	WST 148
Hopkins, Thomas	DUT 177	Hornbeck, Abraham	ULS 210	Horton, Elijah Junr	WSH 183
Hopkins, Thomas	NYK 136	Hornbeck, Elisha	ULS 210	Horton, Eliphalet	OND 214
Hopkins, Thos	OTS 54	Hornbeck, Garret	NYK 105	Horton, Elisha	CAY 642
Hopkins, Thomas	QNS 83	Hornbeck, Gideon	COL 191	Horton, Elisha	SUF 64
Hopkins, Thomas	WSH 244	Hornbeck, Peter	ULS 210	Horton, Esquier	SUF 64
Hopkins, Thomas	WST 113	Hornbeck, Samuel	CAY 682	Horton, Ezra	ORN 358
Hopkins, Thomas Jur	WSH 242	Hornbeck, Timothy	NYK 105	Horton, Frederick	ORN 357
Hopkins, Thomas Junr	WST 116	Hornbeck, Warner	ULS 200	Horton, Galreel	MNT 96
Hopkins, William	CHN 874	Hornbek, John	ONN 161	Horton, George	TIO 237
Hopkins, William	DEL 274	Hornbook, Christopher	MNT 99	Horton, Gilbert	DUT 23
Hopkins, William	HRK 473	Horne, Fanton	ORN 378	Horton, Gilbert	NYK 33
Hopkins, William	NYK 76	Horne, Jacob	NYK 151	Horton, Gilbert	SUF 75
Hopkins, Wm	OTS 29	Horne, John	NYK 151	Horton, Gilbert	WST 131
Hopkins, William	QNS 83	Horne, Martha	NYK 129	Horton, Hannah	SUF 75
Hopkins, Zadock	OND 185	Horne, Peter	ALB 43	Horton, Henry	DEL 275
Hopkinson, Caleb	ONN 172	Horneker, Andrew	RNS 8	Horton, Henry	ONN 165
Hopole, George	ALB 4	Horner, David	ALB 138	Horton, Henry	ORN 327
Hopp, Thomas	COL 193	Horner, George	STB 207	Horton, Henry	SCH 169
Hoppen, John	NYK 152	Horner, Jacob	MNT 31	Horton, Hicks	TIO 245
Hoppensteed, Frederick	ULS 244	Horner, James	NYK 102	Horton, Isaac	ORN 354
Hopper, Albert	NYK 99	Hornes, Daniel	QNS 69	Horton, Isaac	ORN 393
Hopper, Andrew	NYK 49	Hornfager, Christopher	COL 194	Horton, Israel	TIO 239
Hopper, Benjamin	SUF 107	Horning, Leonard	MNT 33	Horton, Jacob	COL 195
Hopper, Christian	NYK 107	Horry, John	ULS 253	Horton, Jacob	COL 211

Howard, John	OND 210	Howe, Joseph	ONN 138	Howell, Jabes	CHN 790
Howard, John	ONN 173	Howe, Joseph	ONN 156	Howell, James	NYK 99
Howard, John	RNS 34	Howe, Josiah	ESS 306	Howell, James	NYK 113
Howard, John	RNS 95	Howe, Lebbeus	DUT 21	Howell, James	NYK 124
Howard, John	SRA 19	Howe, Lot	NYK 77	Howell, James	ORN 341
Howard, John	SUF 91	Howe, Moses	HRK 548	Howell, James	SUF 104
Howard, John E.	OND 191	Howe, Obid	ESS 322	Howell, Jeremiah	SUF 99
Howard, Jonathan	RNS 102	Howe, Oliver	ORN 285	Howell, Jeremiah	ULS 258
Howard, Joseph	COL 258	Howe, Pearley	ONN 158	Howell, Jeremiah Junr	ULS 258
Howard, Joseph	HRK 459	Howe, Richard	ALB 26	Howell, John	ONT 376
Howard, Joseph	KNG 3	Howe, Sarah	NYK 80	Howell, John	SUF 74
Howard, Joseph	OND 166	Howe, Searls	ONN 157	Howell, John	SUF 95
Howard, Joseph	OND 181	Howe, Solomon	HRK 553	Howell, John M.	SUF 95
Howard, Joseph	ULS 184	Howe, Thomas	ORN 272	Howell, Jonah	ONT 350
Howard, Josiah	RNS 102	Howe, Timothy	CAY 658	Howell, Jonah Junior	ONT 350
Howard, Leavet	DUT 102	Howe, Timothy Junr	CAY 654	Howell, Jonathan	SUF 74
Howard, Mary	QNS 61	Howe, Titus	CAY 654	Howell, Joseph	ONT 310
Howard, Mathew	SRA 31	Howe, William	CAY 676	Howell, Joshua	ALB 41
Howard, Moses	CHN 788	Howe, Zarah D.	ONN 138	Howell, Joshua	HRK 563
Howard, Nathan	TIO 211	Howeg, Enos	TIO 227	Howell, Joshua	SUF 102
Howard, Nathaniel	OND 187	Howeg, John	TIO 227	Howell, Joshua Jun	HRK 563
Howard, Nathaniel	WSH 271	Howel, Abraham	DEL 281	Howell, Josiah	SUF 95
Howard, Noah	WSH 303	Howel, David	SUF 69	Howell, Lewis	ORN 361
Howard, Oliver	WSH 223	Howel, Gilbert	SUF 71	Howell, Lidia	SUF 75
Howard, Peter	CAY 686	Howel, Isaac	DEL 281	Howell, Mathew	NYK 45
Howard, Philip	CAY 602	Howel, Isaac	SUF 65	Howell, Mathew	SUF 72
Howard, Phinehas	ONT 328	Howel, Isaac Junr	DEL 282	Howell, Mathew	SUF 97
Howard, Pontus	DUT 58	Howel, Israel	SUF 71	Howell, Merrit	SUF 72
Howard, Richard	DUT 37	Howel, James	SUF 66	Howell, Mitchel	SUF 74
Howard, Richard	DUT 53	Howel, Jessee	SUF 64	Howell, Moses	ORN 319
Howard, Richard	RCK 99	Howel, John	SUF 65	Howell, Moses	SUF 100
H.ward, Robert	MNT 74	Howel, Jonathan	SUF 65	Howell, Nathaniel	ORN 348
Howard, Robert a Black	NYK 88	Howel, Joseph	SUF 71	Howell, Nathaniel W.	ONT 428
Howard, Samuel	ALB 132	Howel, Michael	SUF 71	Howell, Noble	ORN 378
Howard, Samuel	CHN 858	Howel, Reeve	SUF 69	Howell, Obediah	ORN 341
Howard, Samuel	HRK 548	Howel, Richd Jur	SUF 71	Howell, Oliver	SUF 97
Howard, Samuel	WSH 190	Howel, Richd Ser	SUF 71	Howell, Paul	ORN 348
Howard, Silas	TIO 220	Howel, Silas	SUF 67	Howell, Phebe	SUF 73
Howard, Silas Jur	TIO 220	Howell, ...	CAY 544	Howell, Philetus	ORN 359
Howard, Silus	CHN 926	Howell, Aaron	NYK 109	Howell, Philip	SUF 99
Howard, Smith	OND 182	Howell, Aaron	ORN 319	Howell, Phinehas	ONN 173
Howard, Stephen	DUT 51	Howell, Abraham	SUF 101	Howell, Phinehas	ORN 328
Howard, Stephen	NYK 139	Howell, Ann	SUF 73	Howell, Price	SUF 100
Howard, Sylvester	DUT 58	Howell, Anthony	CHN 964	Howell, Recompence	SUF 76
Howard, Thomas	CHN 840	Howell, Benjamin	ORN 331	Howell, Richd	SUF 74
Howard, Thomas	CHN 842	Howell, Caleb	SUF 100	Howell, Roger	ORN 369
Howard, Thomas	DUT 54	Howell, Cathrine	SUF 76	Howell, Saml	SUF 74
Howard, Thomas	DUT 130	Howell, Charles	ORN 353	Howell, Samuel	SUF 99
Howard, Thomas	ONT 512	Howell, Charles	SUF 98	Howell, Sarah	ORN 328
Howard, Thos	RCK 105	Howell, Daniel	SUF 79	Howell, Selah	SUF 94
Howard, Timothy	HRK 458	Howell, Daniel	SUF 100	Howell, Seth	ONT 346
Howard, Uriah	HRK 457	Howell, David	ORN 378	Howell, Silas	ORN 277
Howard, Vine	OTS 5	Howell, David	SUF 99	Howell, Silas	SUF 102
Howard, Widow	RNS 6	Howell, Ebenezar	SUF 96	Howell, Silas W.	ALB 129
Howard, William	DUT 58	Howell, Edward	ORN 282	Howell, Silus	SUF 72
Howard, William	KNG 3	Howell, Edward	ORN 337	Howell, Silvenus	SUF 97
Howard, Wm	MNT 74	Howell, Eli	ORN 296	Howell, Silvenus	SUF 102
Howard, William	NYK 107	Howell, Elias	ORN 351	Howell, Stephen	SUF 97
Howard, William	ONN 131	Howell, Elihue	SUF 101	Howell, Stephen	SUF 100
Howard, William	WSH 217	Howell, Elizabeth	ORN 348	Howell, Stephen	SUF 102
Howard, Zepheniah	DUT 59	Howell, Esther	ORN 282	Howell, Theophilus	ORN 359
Howd, Josiah	COL 251	Howell, Ezekiel	SUF 97	Howell, Theophilus	SUF 100
Howe, Benjamin	ALB 56	Howell, Ezekiel	SUF 100	Howell, Thomas	DUT 123
Howe, Bezabeel	NYK 67	Howell, Ezra	ORN 362	Howell, Urias	SUF 94
Howe, Brigham	NYK 39	Howell, Florah	OND 174	Howell, Walter	SUF 100
Howe, Daniel	CAY 668	Howell, Floyd	ONN 173	Howell, Widow	SUF 98
Howe, Darius	CAY 654	Howell, Garius	ONT 486	Howell, Wm	MNT 24
Howe, Darius	CAY 658	Howell, George	SUF 95	Howell, William	NYK 27
Howe, Ebenezar	CAY 612	Howell, Gilbert	ORN 377	Howell, William	ONT 310
Howe, Ebenezer	ORN 299	Howell, Hampton	SUF 95	Howell, William	ORN 358
Howe, Eleazar	CAY 614	Howell, Hezekiah	ORN 352	Howell, Zebulon	SUF 97
Howe, Ira	CLN 162	Howell, Isaac	CAY 702	Howell, Zopher	SUF 96
Howe, James A.	ONN 159	Howell, Isaac	ORN 396	Howen, John	MNT 69
Howe, Jeriah	TIO 247	Howell, Isaac	SUF 94	Howen, Wm	MNT 64
Howe, John	CLN 155	Howell, Isaac	ULS 207	Howes, Alvis	OTS 52
Howe, John	CLN 162	Howell, Isaiah	ORN 322	Howes, Daniel	DUT 176
Howe, John S.	CLN 164	Howell, Israel	SUF 94	Howes, Haman	WSH 187

Name	Loc/Pg	Name	Loc/Pg	Name	Loc/Pg
Howes, Job	DUT 174	Hoxey, Zebulon	WSH 236	Hubbard,	DEL 282
Howes, John	DUT 175	Hoxie, Christopher	COL 246	Hubbard, Abner	WSH 281
Howes, John	OTS 52	Hoxsie, Joshua Bill	DUT 127	Hubbard, Abraham	CHN 858
Howes, Moody	DUT 174	Hoxsie, Lodowick	DUT 8	Hubbard, Amas	GRN 334
Howes, Moody Junr	DUT 174	Hoxsie, Peleg	DUT 8	Hubbard, Amos	OND 203
Howes, Noah	DUT 171	Hoxsie, Thomas	DUT 100	Hubbard, Amos Jun	GRN 334
Howes, Philip	OND 199	Hoxley, Jacob	ALB 100	Hubbard, Asa	COL 210
Howes, Prince	DUT 171	Hoxy, John	RNS 106	Hubbard, Asa	GRN 339
Howes, Reuben	DUT 98	Hoxy, William	RNS 106	Hubbard, Ashebil	OND 220
Howes, Samuel	DUT 174	Hoy, Agness	WSH 224	Hubbard, Bela	OND 158
Howey, Daniel	ORN 316	Hoy, Bartholomew	ORN 384	Hubbard, Benjamine	GRN 344
Howey, Thomas	ONT 320	Hoy, James	WSH 194	Hubbard, Butler	QNS 84
Howil, John	GRN 339	Hoy, Richard	WSH 224	Hubbard, Caleb	GRN 333
Howke, Andrew	OND 220	Hoy, William	WSH 224	Hubbard, Chancey	OTS 53
Howke, Garret	OND 163	Hoy, William Junr	WSH 224	Hubbard, Clark	GRN 345
Howke, Johnson	OND 220	Hoy., ...fer	SCH 132	Hubbard, David	OTS 44
Howl , Stephen	GRN 352	Hoyer, George	HRK 492	Hubbard, David G.	NYK 18
Howlagan, James	NYK 44	Hoyer, Peter	HRK 492	Hubbard, Ebenr	OTS 11
Howland, Allen	NYK 80	Hoyl, Christian	NYK 86	Hubbard, Edward	TIO 233
Howland, Azariah	DUT 50	Hoyle, George	DEL 267	Hubbard, Eli	OND 191
Howland, Benjamin	CAY 652	Hoyt, Abijah	WST 134	Hubbard, Eli Junior	OND 192
Howland, Benjamin	CAY 664	Hoyt, Andrew	WST 153	Hubbard, Elias	KNG 4
Howland, Benjamin	SRA 40	Hoyt, Asa	DUT 172	Hubbard, Elijah	COL 258
Howland, Benjamin	WSH 197	Hoyt, Benjamin S.	ORN 376	Hubbard, Elijah	GRN 345
Howland, Benjamine	GRN 331	Hoyt, Caleb	WST 153	Hubbard, Elijah	OTS 34
Howland, Cathrine	WSH 200	Hoyt, Daniel	COL 249	Hubbard, Elijah	WSH 278
Howland, Charles	DUT 25	Hoyt, Daniel	HRK 491	Hubbard, Elisa	GRN 352
Howland, Charles Junr	DUT 50	Hoyt, David	WST 155	Hubbard, Elisha	ALB 76
Howland, David	MNT 82	Hoyt, Ebenezer	OND 174	Hubbard, Ephraim	OND 204
Howland, Edward	SRA 40	Hoyt, Elnathan	MNT 110	Hubbard, Ephraim B.	GRN 336
Howland, Elisha	SRA 40	Hoyt, Ezekiel	SRA 24	Hubbard, Ezekiel	CLN 163
Howland, Elisheb	WSH 200	Hoyt, Ezra	DEL 270	Hubbard, Fairchild	OND 221
Howland, Elizabeth	RNS 10	Hoyt, Ezra	DEL 281	Hubbard, Frederick	NYK 111
Howland, Gershom	DEL 276	Hoyt, Gates	CLN 167	Hubbard, Griffen	OTS 49
Howland, Gershom Junr	DEL 291	Hoyt, Henry	DUT 175	Hubbard, Isaac	GRN 341
Howland, Gilbert	ONT 440	Hoyt, Hezekiah	WST 153	Hubbard, Isaac	GRN 341
Howland, Isaac	OTS 44	Hoyt, Isaac	ORN 374	Hubbard, Isaac	OND 188
Howland, Isaac	RNS 46	Hoyt, Isaac	WST 152	Hubbard, Isaac	ONN 141
Howland, Jeremiah	DUT 101	Hoyt, Isaac	WST 153	Hubbard, Isreal	GRN 345
Howland, Job	DEL 276	Hoyt, Jackin	RNS112B	Hubbard, Ithuel	OND 191
Howland, Job	ONT 438	Hoyt, Jacob	WST 155	Hubbard, Jacob	OND 185
Howland, John	DUT 51	Hoyt, Jacob Junr	WST 155	Hubbard, James	KNG 5
Howland, Jonath.	SRA 38	Hoyt, James	WST 155	Hubbard, Jedediah	GRN 334
Howland, Joseph	DEL 291	Hoyt, Jared	DEL 276	Hubbard, Jedediah Junr	GRN 334
Howland, Nathaniel	DUT 53	Hoyt, Jeremiah	WST 155	Hubbard, Joel	DEL 287
Howland, Notton	SRA 44	Hoyt, Jesse	WST 152	Hubbard, John	ALB 81
Howland, Obediah	DUT 171	Hoyt, Joel	ORN 325	Hubbard, John	COL 208
Howland, Peleg	DUT 54	Hoyt, John	DEL 281	Hubbard, John	DUT 169
Howland, Phineas	DEL 276	Hoyt, John	RNS 54	Hubbard, John	OND 204
Howland, Reuben	NYK 119	Hoyt, John C.	OND 159	Hubbard, John	ONN 184
Howland, Samuel	DEL 276	Hoyt, Jonathan	ONN 137	Hubbard, John	ONT 330
Howland, Samuel	DUT 100	Hoyt, Lewis	ONN 139	Hubbard, John	OTS 10
Howland, Seth	DEL 291	Hoyt, Moses	DUT 78	Hubbard, John	OTS 34
Howland, Solomon	DUT 111	Hoyt, Moses	NYK 82	Hubbard, John	WST 128
Howland, Timothy	DUT 100	Hoyt, Nathan	MNT 110	Hubbard, John Junr	COL 206
Howland, Wesson	DUT 105	Hoyt, Noah	OND 168	Hubbard, Jonas	OND 193
Howland, William	CAY 660	Hoyt, Peter	ORN 336	Hubbard, Jonathan	DEL 288
Howland, William	DUT 171	Hoyt, Peter	WST 152	Hubbard, Jonathan	HRK 516
Howland, Wm	RNS 9	Hoyt, Phineas	RNS 93	Hubbard, Joseph	OND 220
Howland, William	WSH 185	Hoyt, Rice	WST 152	Hubbard, Joseph	OTS 16
Howland, Zimri	OND 204	Hoyt, Samuel	ALB 20	Hubbard, Joseph	OTS 16
Howlet, Parley	ONN 155	Hoyt, Samuel	NYK 23	Hubbard, Michael	DEL 287
Howlett, Samuel	NYK 45	Hoyt, Sarah	NYK 17	Hubbard, Nathan	ONN 168
Howlett, Thomas	NYK 99	Hoyt, Silas	ORN 340	Hubbard, Nathaniel	DUT 85
Howley, Abner	ONT 402	Hoyt, Simeon	DEL 277	Hubbard, Nathaniel	ONT 432
Howley, James	ONT 402	Hoyt, Stephen	DEL 281	Hubbard, Nathl	OTS 44
Howlin, John	SRA 28	Hoyt, Stephen	DUT 64	Hubbard, Noediah	OND 222
Howlin, William	SRA 36	Hoyt, Sylvanus	MNT 104	Hubbard, Obediah	WSH 287
Howlks, Aron	MNT 123	Hoyt, Thaddeus	DEL 277	Hubbard, Peter	ORN 303
Howord, Daniel	ONN 179	Hoyt, Uriah	WST 152	Hubbard, Richard S.	ORN 350
Hows, Ebenezer	WST 135	Hoyt, William	ALB 117	Hubbard, Robert	RNS 9
Hows, John	WSH 187	Hualey, Sylvunus	SRA 55	Hubbard, Roswell	RNS 108
Hows, Seth	NYK 102	Hub., Job	QNS 81	Hubbard, Samuel	KNG 5
Hows, Samuel	SCH 137	Hubart, Mary	NYK 33	Hubbard, Samuel	OND 192
Howser, Frederick	COL 194	Hubb, Amos	GRN 332	Hubbard, Samuel	OND 198
Howser, George	ORN 350	Hubband, James	SCH 140	Hubbard, Saml	OTS 34
Hoxey, Abraham	WSH 236	Hubbard	GRN 341	Hubbard, Samuel	WSH 302

Hubbard, Shadrach	ULS 192	
Hubbard, Simon	OND 185	
Hubbard, Solomon	GRN 345	
Hubbard, Stephen	KNG 5	
Hubbard, Timothy	GRN 334	
Hubbard, William	OND 220	
Hubbard, Wm	RNS 10	
Hubbart, Aaron	SCH 143	
Hubbart, Aurvin	SCH 144	
Hubbart, Daniel	NYK 131	
Hubbart, Daniel Senr	SCH 143	
Hubbart, Heny	SUF 70	
Hubbart, Jeremiah	SUF 70	
Hubbart, Joel	OND 213	
Hubbart(?), Mary	SUF 74	
Hubbart, Moses	SCH 143	
Hubbart, Noah	CLN 155	
Hubbart, Oliver	WST 145	
Hubbart, Samuel	OND 213	
Hubbart, Saml Jur	SUF 77	
Hubbart, Selah	ESS 310	
Hubbart, Thos	SUF 74	
Hubbel, Abel	DEL 269	
Hubbel, Abijah	OTS 13	
Hubbel, Almerin	ALB 69	
Hubbel, Enoch	DEL 273	
Hubbel, Ezra	DUT 77	
Hubbel, Gershom	OND 178	
Hubbel, Isaac	DEL 269	
Hubbel, John	DEL 269	
Hubbel, Mathew	OND 162	
Hubbel, Matthew	DEL 273	
Hubbel, Peter	ALB 88	
Hubbel, Peter	WST 153	
Hubbel, Richard	OND 163	
Hubbel, Samuel	DEL 269	
Hubbel, Syllivant	HRK 497	
Hubbell, Andrew	DUT 174	
Hubbell, Elijah	COL 259	
Hubbell, Elijah	OTS 6	
Hubbell, Ichabod	HRK 484	
Hubbell, Jabez	OTS 17	
Hubbell, John	CAY 634	
Hubbell, John	DUT 175	
Hubbell, Lemuel	OTS 38	
Hubbell, Levi	COL 249	
Hubbell, Noah	OTS 6	
Hubbell, Shederick	CAY 648	
Hubbell, Shedrick	CAY 634	
Hubbell, Silas	OTS 26	
Hubbell, Silas Jnr	OTS 25	
Hubbell, Thomas	COL 248	
Hubbell, Walter	NYK 73	
Hubbell, William G.	COL 250	
Hubbert, Benj.	SUF 77	
Hubbert, Bershaba	SUF 65	
Hubbert, Nathan	WSH 246	
Hubbert, Nathl	SUF 74	
Hubbert, Thomas	HRK 565	
Hubbil, Shederick	GRN 351	
Hubble, Abijah	SRA 13	
Hubble, Abijah	WSH 230	
Hubble, David	SRA 23	
Hubble, Ebenezer	WSH 230	
Hubble, Ephraim	WSH 297	
Hubble, Hannah	WSH 211	
Hubble, Icabode	WSH 210	
Hubble, Iseble	SRA 15	
Hubble, James	SCH 134	
Hubble, Nehemiah	STB 202	
Hubble, Onisimus	SRA 15	
Hubble, Peter	MNT 58	
Hubble, Prudence	SRA 23	
Hubble, Sullivan D.	SRA 32	
Hubbs, Alexander	WST 114	
Hubbs, Charles	SRA 7	
Hubbs, Charles	SUF 83	
Hubbs, Daniel	WST 112	
Hubbs, Ira	SUF 83	
Hubbs, James C.	SUF 83	
Hubbs, Jonathan	WSH 241	
Hubbs, Nathaniel	WST 113	
Hubbs, Selah	QNS 78	
Hubbs, Tabitha	SUF 92	
Hubbs, Uriah	SUF 83	
Hubburt, John	SUF 74	
Hubby, Ebenezer	DEL 270	
Hubby, Jonathan	CHN 842	
Hubby, Joshua	DEL 270	
Hubert, Daniel	CHN 886	
Hubert, James	KNG 9	
Hubert, Phillip	MNT 91	
Hubkinson, Alexander	SRA 4	
Hubles, Amos	NYK 133	
Hubren, James	NYK 99	
Hubs, Alexander	MNT 48	
Hubs, Joseph	SRA 6	
Huchens, Jacob	OND 223	
Huck, Michael	NYK 34	
Hucker, Richard	STB 207	
Hucksmo., Nathaniel	CAY 536	
Huddleston, George	COL 230	
Huddleston, John	SCH 160	
Huddleston, Richard	HRK 582	
Huddleston, Sarah	DUT 149	
Huddleton, William	COL 229	
Huddy, Thomas	SUF 102	
Hudson see Hutson		
Hudson, Abraham	ONT 510	
Hudson, Agelo	COL 218	
Hudson, Amos	ONN 136	
Hudson, Asa	ALB 86	
Hudson, Benoni	CLN 170	
Hudson, Bernard	MNT 24	
Hudson, Daniel	RNS 92	
Hudson, Daniel	TIO 210	
Hudson, David	CAY 704	
Hudson, Ebenezer	ALB 133	
Hudson, Eleazer	ORN 353	
Hudson, Ephraim	OTS 2	
Hudson, Ester	ALB 7	
Hudson, George	ORN 395	
Hudson, Giles	QNS 66	
Hudson, Heny	SUF 73	
Hudson, Henry	SUF 98	
Hudson, Isaac	NYK 116	
Hudson, Jane	KNG 9	
Hudson, John	ORN 354	
Hudson, John	QNS 64	
Hudson, John	SUF 69	
Hudson, John B.	OTS 25	
Hudson, Jonathan	ALB 33	
Hudson, Joseph	SUF 84	
Hudson, Lydia	COL 222	
Hudson, Lyndes	COL 221	
Hudson, Moses	ALB 105	
Hudson, Nathaniel	COL 218	
Hudson, Nathaniel	RNS 89	
Hudson, Nathl	SUF 69	
Hudson, Obadiah	SUF 74	
Hudson, Oliver	SUF 71	
Hudson, Richard	CAY 640	
Hudson, Richard	ORN 279	
Hudson, Samuel	COL 216	
Hudson, Samuel	QNS 77	
Hudson, Saml	SUF 74	
Hudson, Thomas	OTS 2	
Hudson, Wealthy	SRA 41	
Hudson, William a mulatto	NYK 19	
Hudson, William	ORN 353	
Hudson, William	SUF 89	
Huel, John	CHN 760	
Hues, George	ONN 153	
Hues, Samuel	ONN 152	
Huested, Benjamine	GRN 349	
Huested, John	GRN 349	
Huesten, Patallas	SRA 4	
Huestis, Benjamin	WST 131	
Huestis, Thaddeus	WST 125	
Hueston, Thomas	CHN 868	
Hueston, William	CHN 868	
Huestus, David	HRK 505	
Huestus, Edward	HRK 506	
Huestus, Michael	HRK 506	
Huet, Palmer	OND 203	
Huff, Abra	CAY 544	
Huff, Asael	GRN 336	
Huff, Gamaliel	WST 154	
Huff, Gershom	RCK 108	
Huff, Jacob	ALB 27	
Huff, Jacob	QNS 78	
Huff, James	CAY 558	
Huff, John	ORN 317	
Huff, John	ORN 367	
Huff, John	SUF 93	
Huff, Lawrence	COL 220	
Huff, Neal	COL 215	
Huff, Nicholas	CAY 544	
Huff, Peter	CAY 532	
Huff, Peter	RNS 21	
Huff, Richard	CAY 544	
Huff, Theson	GRN 336	
Huff, William	CAY 546	
Huff, William	DUT 97	
Huff, William	ULS 189	
Huff, Zephineah	STB 204	
Huffman, Hamand	WSH 208	
Huffman, Jacob	CHN 780	
Huffman, James	NYK 98	
Huffman, Peter	GRN 325	
Huffnagle, Christion	MNT 49	
Huftaling, Coonrodd	GRN 357	
Huftaling, Garret	GRN 357	
Huftaling, Hendrick	GRN 356	
Huftaling, Hendrick	GRN 357	
Huftaling, John	HRK 408	
Huftaling, Jonathan	GRN 354	
Huftaling, Miss	GRN 357	
Hug_, Joseph	CAY 566	
Hugan, John J.	ALB 57	
Hugg, Abraham	ULS 243	
Hugg, Isaac	TIO 233	
Hugg, Wm	TIO 233	
Huggeboom, Peter	GRN 334	
Huggenott, Christian	MNT 46	
Huggens, Willeam	WSH 271	
Hugget, Edward a Black	NYK 70	
Hugget, Segesmind	NYK 147	
Huggingg t_, Rockbe	CHN 954	
Huggins, Elizabeth	CAY 628	
Huggins, James	ULS 230	
Huggins, John	CAY 706	
Huggins, John	NYK 20	
Huggins, Levi	CAY 674	
Huggins, Zenas	CAY 706	
Huggoboom, Leo_nard	GRN 334	
Huggobo_m, Tobias	GRN 334	
Huggons, Samuel	GRN 328	
Hughes see Hues		
Hughes, Anthony	NYK 109	
Hughes, Arthur	NYK 118	
Hughes, Christopher	DUT 108	
Hughes, Christopher	NYK 67	
Hughes, Christopher Junr	DUT 109	
Hughes, Daniel	OTS 55	
Hughes, David	NYK 137	
Hughes, David	RNS 40	
Hughes, Henry	NYK 100	
Hughes, Hugh	RCK 99	

Name	Ref	Name	Ref	Name	Ref
Hunter, Elijah	WST 167	Huntington, Joseph	RNS 9	Hurlburt, Peter	ORN 320
Hunter, Elisha	CAY 632	Huntington, Joseph	RNS 9	Hurlburt, Thomas	COL 216
Hunter, Elisha	OTS 52	Huntington, Reuben	ALB 97	Hurlburt, Thomas	OND 171
Hunter, Euphemia	NYK 67	Huntington, Samuel	GRN 355	Hurlburt, Thomas	OND 179
Hunter, Ezra	WST 167	Huntington, Saml	OTS 19	Hurlburt, Truman	OND 194
Hunter, Francis	CAY 690	Huntington, Susannah	WST 150	Hurlbut, Daniel	ESS 293
Hunter, George	NYK 28	Huntington, Thomas	WSH 256	Hurlbutt, Daniel	HRK 562
Hunter, George	NYK 33	Huntington, Wm	OTS 35	Hurlbutt, Uriah	HRK 583
Hunter, George	ORN 386	Huntinton, Reubin	GRN 348	Hurley, Bartholomew	RNS 27
Hunter, George	SRA 43	Huntler, Johia	GRN 351	Hurley, John	CAY 540
Hunter, Gilbert	WST 126	Huntley, Abner	HRK 483	Hurley, John	NYK 133
Hunter, Gilbert	WST 167	Huntley, Abraham	DEL 276	Hurley, William	ORN 397
Hunter, Henry	WST 131	Huntley, Andrew	CLN 172	Hurly, Thomas	ORN 387
Hunter, James	ALB 142	Huntley, Ashur	ONT 420	Hurman, John	MNT 116
Hunter, James	CAY 572	Huntley, Bethuel	CLN 167	Hurn, Roger A.	ESS 298
Hunter, James	NYK 17	Huntley, Calvin	OTS 35	Hurne, Peter	MNT 67
Hunter, James	RNS 95	Huntley, Ebenesar	GRN 351	Hurse, Christian	ONT 358
Hunter, James	ULS 251	Huntley, Elisha	OTS 55	Hurst, Margaret	NYK 43
Hunter, James	WST 122	Huntley, Ezekiel	WSH 303	Hurst, Robert	ALB 135
Hunter, Jeremiah	RNS 47	Huntley, Ezra	ONN 166	Hurst, Robert Junr	ALB 67
Hunter, John	CAY 574	Huntley, Jabez	COL 216	Hurst, Timothy	NYK 148
Hunter, John	NYK 51	Huntley, James	OTS 48	Hurt, William	NYK 119
Hunter, John	SRA 46	Huntley, Jasper	ONN 166	Hurtin, Christian	ORN 356
Hunter, John	STB 204	Huntley, Jehial	GRN 351	Hurtin, John H.	NYK 25
Hunter, John	WST 128	Huntley, John	CAY 566	Hurtin, William	ORN 342
Hunter, John	WST 167	Huntley, Ranar	SRA 57	Hurvy, Obid	GRN 338
Hunter, John Junr	CAY 574	Huntley, Richard	COL 187	Husbands, William a mulatto	NYK 40
Hunter, Jonathan	CAY 566	Huntley, Timothy	ONN 166		
Hu.ter, Joseph	CAY 566	Huntley, William	COL 178	Huse, David	GRN 332
Hunter, Joseph	ULS 249	Huntly, Andrew	WSH 268	Huse, James	WSH 193
Hunter, Matthew	ORN 300	Huntly, Eleanor	DUT 26	Husen, James	GRN 338
Hunter, Moses	SRA 46	Huntly, Elijah	RNS 107	Huskins, Shedrack	SRA 32
Hunter, Robert	NYK 114	Huntly, Eliphalet	RNS 107	Huskwell, ...is	MNT 78
Hunter, Robert	ORN 307	Huntly, Ira	ONN 165	Huson, Cittura	SUF 74
Hunter, Robert	ORN 328	Huntly, Mathew	RNS 107	Huson, Eliakim	COL 243
Hunter, Robert	RNS 47	Huntly, Wm	ONN 165	Huson, James	CHN 780
Hunter, Robert	SRA 48	Huntly, Zadock	MNT 11	Huson, John	OND 214
Hunter, Ruth	NYK 51	Huntly, Zenas	SCH 170	Huson, William	WST 126
Hunter, Samuel	ORN 305	Huntlys, Stephen	SCH 169	Huss, Casparus	COL 235
Hunter, Samuel	ORN 309	Hunts, Joseph	GRN 349	Hussen, George	QNS 63
Hunter, Samuel	SRA 21	Huntswarght, William	NYK 41	Hussey, Jonathan	CAY 652
Hunter, Samuel	SRA 46	Hupp(?), Abraham	ORN 386	Hussey, Patrick	RCH 94
Hunter, Thomas	ESS 296	Hupson, Edward	MNT 96	Hussey, Sylvanus	CAY 650
Hunter, Timothy	ESS 294	Hurbut, William	ESS 293	Hustace, Stephen	NYK 31
Hunter, William	NYK 140	Hurd, Allen	DUT 47	Hustas, Benjamin	NYK 59
Hunter, William	OND 185	Hurd, Asa	ALB 33	Hustead, Jesse	NYK 141
Hunter, William	ORN 398	Hurd, Asa	HRK 597	Hustead, Solomon	SRA 39
Hunter, William	SRA 21	Hurd, Asahel A.	OND 162	Husted, Abm	RNS 54
Hunter, William	SRA 59	Hurd, Calvin	OND 214	Husted, Ananias	DUT 127
Hunter, William	ULS 190	Hurd, Cooley	WSH 207	Husted, Caleb	DUT 129
Hunter, William	WST 122	Hurd, Daniel	ALB 31	Husted, Charity	DUT 75
Hunter, William	WST 167	Hurd, David	DUT 54	Husted, David	SRA 6
Hunter, William Junr	ULS 189	Hurd, Ebenezer	DUT 133	Husted, Ebenezer	DUT 100
Hunting, Abraham	SUF 106	Hurd, Ebenezer Senr	DUT 47	Husted, Ebenezer	DUT 129
Hunting, Benjamin	SUF 97	Hurd, Elijah	ONT 450	Husted, Ingelhart	QNS 84
Hunting, Edward	DUT 35	Hurd, George A. H.	OND 163	Husted, Jethro	DUT 124
Hunting, Isaac	DUT 129	Hurd, Joseph	DEL 268	Husted, Jonathan	DUT 59
Hunting, Isaac M.	DUT 129	Hurd, Joseph	OND 168	Husted, Joseph	DUT 75
Hunting, John	SUF 106	Hurd, Joseph	ONN 153	Husted, Joseph	DUT 121
Hunting, Joseph	RNS 107	Hurd, Medad	SRA 15	Husted, Joseph	DUT 129
Hunting, Jos:	SCH 124	Hurd, Nathan	CAY 668	Husted, Joseph	RNS 58
Hunting, Nathaniel	SUF 106	Hurd, Wallis	COL 205	Husted, Joseph	RNS 58
Hunting, William	SUF 106	Hurd, Walliston	DUT 137	Husted, Lewis	RNS 58
Huntingdon, Ezekiel	RNS 111	Hurder, George	COL 199	Husted, Lott	WST 145
Huntington, Aaron	SRA 55	Hurding, John	MNT 8	Husted, Moses	DUT 98
Huntington, Abel	SUF 107	Hurdman, John	ORN 282	Husted, Nicholas	COL 222
Huntington, Caleb	SCH 133	Hurlbert, Gidean	GRN 341	Husted, Noah	WST 167
Huntington, Daniel	SCH 133	Hurlbert, Joshua	OND 222	Husted, Peter	DUT 146
Huntington, Eliphlet	GRN 355	Hurlbert, Noediah	OND 222	Husted, Peter	SRA 6
Huntington, Ezekiel	SCH 133	Hurlburt, Benjm	COL 216	Husted, Reuben	DUT 59
Huntington, Frederick	GRN 331	Hurlburt, Ebenezer	COL 222	Husted, Reuben	DUT 127
Huntington, George	OND 214	Hurlburt, Grove	OND 172	Husted, Robert	DUT 75
Huntington, Gurdon	OTS 25	Hurlburt, Hezh	COL 216	Husted, Silas	DUT 145
Huntington, Henry	OND 214	Hurlburt, Jonathan	OND 174	Husted, Solomon	DUT 59
Huntington, John	GRN 354	Hurlburt, Joseph	OND 188	Husted, Solomon	WST 145
Huntington, John	SCH 133	Hurlburt, Josiah Junr	COL 263	Husted, Stephen	WST 144
Huntington, Jonathan	ALB 133	Hurlburt, Matthias	OND 182	Husted, Titus	RNS 58
				Husted, William	DUT 75

Husten, Ephraim	GRN 339	Hutchinson, Asa	ALB 59
Husten, James	SRA 13	Hutchinson, Benjm	COL 219
Hustes, Jacob	WSH 251	Hutchinson, Elisha	HRK 503
Hustfield, Charles	RNS 50	Hutchinson, Heny	SUF 71
Hustice, Joshua	WST 119	Hutchinson, Isaac	RCH 93
Hustis, David	WST 144	Hutchinson, James	NYK 77
Hustis, Joseph	DUT 110	Hutchinson. James	NYK 106
Hustis, Joseph Junr	DUT 110	Hutchinson. James	QNS 70
Hustis, Joshua	WST 148	Hutchinson, John	CAY 664
Hustis, Samuel	WST 146	Hutchinson, John	HRK 442
Hustis, William	DUT 109	Hutchinson, John	NYK 18
Huston, Alexr	TIO 251	Hutchinson, John	NYK 23
Huston, Cornelus	SRA 4	Hutchinson, John	NYK 54
Huston, David	CAY 662	Hutchinson, Lemuel	CAY 660
Huston, Elizabeth	WSH 188	Hutchinson, Robert	WST 149
Huston, J...	TIO 251	Hutchinson, Samel	COL 204
Huston, James	DEL 280	Hutchinson, Samuel	NYK 113
Huston, Joseph	WSH 251	Hutchinson, Silas	CAY 596
Hutch, George W.	MNT 68	Hutchinson, Solomon	COL 181
Hutchan, Charles	WSH 289	Hutchinson, Stephen	OND 173
Hutchan, William	WSH 290	Hutchinson, Thomas	NYK 32
Hutchens, Isaac	WST 126	Hutchinson, Wheeler	COL 214
Hutchens, Saml	OTS 14	Hutchinson, Zenas	OND 208
Hutchens, Stephen	OTS 33	Hutchinsons, Esias	NYK 57
Hutchenson, Benjn	SUF 71	Hutchkins, Asahel	ORN 323
Hutchenson, Benjn Jr	SUF 71	Huthwaite, Ellinor	NYK 68
Hutchenson, Stephen	OND 211	Hutson, Andrew	NYK 148
Hutchenson, Thos	SUF 75	Hutson, John	NYK 55
Hutcherson, Daniel	KNG 4	Hutt, John	SCH 169
Hutcheson, Aaron	CHN 802	Hutt__, Wm M.	MNT 56
Hutcheson, Daniel	SRA 48	Hutton, Christopher	RNS 90
Hutcheson, David	CHN 956	Hutton, George	ALB 149
Hutcheson, Ephraim	CHN 780	Hutton, George	NYK 57
Hutcheson, George	WSH 301	Hutton, John	ALB 39
Hutcheson, Jesse	CHN 804	Hutton, John	OND 208
Hutcheson, John	OTS 6	Hutton, John	RCK 107
Hutcheson, Joss	CHN 944	Hutton, Richard	DUT 75
Hutcheson, Noah	CHN 804	Hutton, Thomas	NYK 97
Hutcheson, Stephen	CHN 742	Hutton, William	NYK 94
Hutchesons, Able	CHN 802	Hutton, William	WSH 306
Hutchin, John	ONT 386	Huver, Henry	MNT 56
Hutching, Samuel	NYK 91	Huxford, William	SRA 53
Hutchings, Calvin	OTS 52	Huxley, John	CAY 522
Hutchings, John	OTS 2	Huxren, Peter M.	MNT 58
Hutchings, John	OTS 52	Huyck, Abm	RNS 61
Hutchings, John	RCK 101	Huyck, Berger	COL 257
Hutchingson, Alexander	NYK 125	Huyck, Burger J.	COL 260
Hutchins, Amos	ALB 120	Huyck, Christina	COL 260
Hutchins, Benjamin	CAY 720	Huyck, Cornelius	COL 264
Hutchins, Benjamin	DUT 26	Huyck, Cornelius	DEL 282
Hutchins, Charles	HRK 444	Huyck, Henry	DEL 272
Hutchins, David	NYK 111	Huyck, Isaac	DEL 278
Hutchins, Edward	WSH 201	Huyck, Jacob	RNS 61
Hutchins, Isaac	DEL 276	Huyck, John	COL 239
Hutchins, Isaac	DUT 128	Huyck, John	DUT 155
Hutchins, Jacamiah	DUT 15	Huyck, Nicholas	RNS 63
Hutchins, Jacob	DUT 17	Huyck, Peter	COL 236
Hutchins, James	QNS 72	Huyck, Peter	DEL 278
Hutchins, John	QNS 71	Huysdrot, Henry	COL 241
Hutchins, John	ULS 191	Huyser, Jacob	COL 234
Hutchins, Jonathan	NYK 72	Huyser, John	COL 190
Hutchins, Joshua	ULS 264	Huyser, Peter	COL 189
Hutchins, Leavens	HRK 414	Huystradt, Hendrick A.	COL 240
Hutchins, Mary	NYK 39	Huystradt, John A.	COL 242
Hutchins, Nathan	RCK 107	Huystrant, James	COL 200
Hutchins, Noah	HRK 414	Huzza, Margaret	COL 250
Hutchins, Reuben	QNS 72	Hyack, ...d	MNT 86
Hutchins, Richard	DEL 288	Hyans, Elizabeth	NYK 109
Hutchins, Richard	NYK 74	Hyat, Mynah	OND 182
Hutchins, Samuel	ULS 208	Hyat, Roger	RNS 25
Hutchins, Thomas	DUT 106	Hyatt, Aboyle	WST 123
Hutchins, William	OTS 55	Hyatt, Abraham	DUT 28
H.tchinson, ...	MNT 78	Hyatt, Abraham	NYK 135
Hutchinson, Alexander	NYK 61	Hyatt, Abraham	SRA 47
Hutchinson, A asa	CAY 594	Hyatt, Caleb	ORN 374
Hutchinson, Amasa	HRK 551	Hyatt, David M.	WST 122
Hutchinson, Amos	COL 181	Hyatt, Elijah	WST 128

Hyatt, Elisha	WST 111
Hyatt, Ezekiel	WST 123
Hyatt, Hezekiah	WST 125
Hyatt, Jacob	WST 147
Hyatt, James	COL 249
Hyatt, James	WST 145
Hyatt, James	WST 156
Hyatt, John	DUT 82
Hyatt, John	WST 123
Hyatt, John Junr	WST 123
Hyatt, Joseph	DUT 96
Hyatt, Joseph	WST 130
Hyatt, Mary	WST 123
Hyatt, Nathaniel	WST 123
Hyatt, Samuel	DUT 129
Hyatt, William	WST 146
Hyatt, William	WST 151
Hyatte, Samuel	ONN 137
Hycks, Adam	MNT 72
Hyde see Hide	
Hyde, Anne	WST 144
Hyde, Azel	DEL 277
Hyde, Benjamin	NYK 36
Hyde, Benjamin	SCH 133
Hyde, Caleb	DUT 156
Hyde, Caleb	TIO 217
Hyde, Calvin	TIO 217
Hyde, Chauncey	TIO 216
Hyde, Christopher	DUT 108
Hyde, Dan	CAY 692
Hyde, Daniel	COL 194
Hyde, David	OND 200
Hyde, Elli	MNT 12
Hyde, Enock	GRN 325
Hyde, Henry	KNG 7
Hyde, Isaac	ALB 84
Hyde, J__	MNT 16
Hyde, James	OTS 51
Hyde, Jesse	HRK 545
H.de, Joel	MNT 16
Hyde, John	ALB 139
Hyde, John	COL 178
Hyde, John	NYK 29
Hyde, John	QNS 83
Hyde, John	QNS 83
Hyde, John	WST 150
Hyde, Moses	SCH 133
Hyde, Oliver	NYK 142
Hyde, Simon	OND 172
Hyde, William	QNS 83
Hyderick, John	QNS 82
Hydla, George	RNS 11
Hydorn, Adam	COL 256
Hydorn, Coonrodt	RNS 86
Hydorn, Henry	RNS 86
Hydorn, Peter	RNS 86
Hyer, Andrew	NYK 108
Hyer, Cornelius	NYK 18
Hyer, Mary C.	NYK 123
Hyer, William	CAY 668
Hyer, William	NYK 51
Hyer, William	NYK 106
Hyleman, Peggy	NYK 112
Hyler, Abraham	NYK 55
Hyler, Adam	NYK 135
Hyler, George	NYK 135
Hyller, Isaac	SCH 162
Hymer, George	NYK 141
Hymes, Anstye	NYK 49
Hymes, George	DEL 275
Hymes, Nathan	COL 218
Hymes, William	CAY 702
Hymrought, Coonradt	ULS 213
Hynckley, Wyott	CHN 828
Hyne, Ambrose	TIO 229
Hyne, Bildad	GRN 344

Name	Loc	Pg
Irish, Samuel	SRA	4
Irish, Smith	CAY	720
Irish, Smith	ONN	189
Irons, Asa	OTS	20
Irons, Edi	OTS	54
Irons, Jeremiah	OTS	51
Irons, John	OTS	12
Irons, Saml	OTS	52
Irons, Wm	OTS	52
Irvin	NYK	107
Irvin, Edward	NYK	40
Irvin, Isaac	WSH	258
Irvin, James	WSH	193
Irvin, Samuel	ULS	260
Irvin, William	NYK	136
Irvin, William	NYK	144
Irvin, William	WSH	258
Irvin, William Junr	NYK	45
Irvine, Allen	ULS	243
Irvine, Francis	NYK	101
Irvine, James	ULS	209
Irvine, Richard	ULS	199
Irvine, William	ULS	237
Irving see Erving		
Irving, William	NYK	40
Irwan, James	NYK	68
Irwan, Robert	NYK	118
Irwin see Erwin		
Irwin, Anna	NYK	121
Irwin, James	ONT	502
Irwin, James	ULS	254
Irwin, John	ORN	306
Irwin, Peter	CAY	680
Irwin, Robert	ULS	255
Isaac	QNS	80
Isaac	QNS	80
Isaac	QNS	82
Isaac	QNS	84
Isaac	QNS	84
Isaac Free Negro Family	SRA	35
Isaacs, Aaron	SUF	107
Isaacs, Benjamin	WST	139
Isaacs, Isaac	SUF	106
Isaacs, Joshua	NYK	96
Isaacs, Mary	SUF	106
Isaacs, Rachel	NYK	25
Isaacs, Samuel	SUF	106
Isaac's, Samuel	WST	156
Isaacs, William	WST	138
Isaman, Jacob	HRK	499
Isaman, John	HRK	452
Isaman, Peter	HRK	452
Isaman, Stephen	HRK	470
Isan a Negro	SUF	67
Isarel, Sarah	NYK	47
Isbel, Ebenezer	SRA	26
Isbel, Joel	OND	201
Isbel, Oliver	SRA	26
Isbell, Bishop	NYK	83
Isbell, Israel	OND	170
Isbill, Lyman	ONT	408
Isdell, John	DUT	23
Isenbergh, Charity	ORN	295
Isenbergh, Christian	ORN	309
Isenlord, Peter	MNT	44
Isenlord, Peter	MNT	44
Isget, Francis	DEL	286
Isham, Zebulon	HRK	491
Ishaw, Abel	NYK	123
Ishbald, Eleaz	CHN	868
Ishbald, Stephen	CHN	868
Isherwood, Benjamin	NYK	40
Isleton, Patty	NYK	129
Isman, Elias	COL	214
Isman, Elias	COL	221
Isman, Joseph	RNS	46

Name	Loc	Pg
Isman, Thomas	RNS	30
Isme, Thomas	ALB	60
Ismon, James	ESS	303
Isong, John	MNT	120
Israel	QNS	64
Israel, Moses	MNT	113
Israel, Richard	ONT	476
Israels, John	WST	129
Isum, Chauncey	CHN	864
Isum, Isaac	CHN	864
Italy, Tobias	MNT	66
Ittig, Conrad	HRK	419
Ittig, Frederick	HRK	501
Ittig, George	HRK	484
Ittig, George	HRK	502
Ittig, George J.	HRK	495
Ittig, Henry	HRK	431
Ittig, Jacob	HRK	495
Ittig, John	HRK	499
Ittig, Michael	HRK	409
Ittig, Michael Junr	HRK	409
Ivers, Gregory	NYK	143
Ivers, Mary	NYK	23
Ivers, Thomas	NYK	140
Ivers, William	NYK	140
Ivery, John	WSH	220
Ives, Abner	OND	205
Ives, Abraham	CHN	766
Ives, Amon	OND	201
Ives, Amos	HRK	423
Ives, Amos	OND	173
Ives, Benjamin	OTS	43
Ives, Christopher	RNS	87
Ives, Elias	CHN	766
Ives, Ephraim	ORN	314
Ives, Isaac	NYK	62
Ives, Isaac	OND	202
Ives, Jesse	OND	163
Ives, Joel	CHN	820
Ives, John	OND	220
Ives, John	SRA	46
Ives, Joseph	DUT	36
Ives, Lazarus	RNS	4
Ives, Lazarus Junr	RNS	4
Ives, Lent	OND	213
Ives, Levi	OND	220
Ives, Lymon	CHN	766
Ives, Samuel	CHN	766
Ives, Samuel	GRN	334
Ives, Saml	GRN	333
Ives, Seth	OTS	58
Ives, Titus	MNT	43
Izarman, John	RCK	99
Izarman, Joseph	RCK	110
Izenhart, Nathan	NYK	

J

Name	Loc	Pg
Jabez	SUF	84
Jac...n, Jane	ONT	510
Jack a free Negro	ALB	97
Jack Negro	QNS	70
Jack Negro	QNS	74
Jack	QNS	74
Jack	QNS	81
Jack	QNS	83
Jack (a free Negro)	RNS	64
Jack a free Negro	RNS	95
Jack a Negro	SUF	67
Jack a Negro	SUF	76
Jack	SUF	93
Jack: Ben	SUF	108
Jack, Edward	NYK	24
Jack, Louis	ORN	270
Jack, Negro	QNS	82
Jack, Robert	NYK	94
Jack, William	DUT	178

Name	Loc	Pg
Jacket, John	WSH	287
Jackett, Michael	WSH	285
Jacklin, Joseph	DEL	286
Jackson	GRN	349
Jackson, Aaron	RNS	97
Jackson, Aaron	SRA	12
Jackson, Abm a free Negro	ONN	139
Jackson, Abm a free Negro	ALB	131
Jackson, Alexander	ORN	328
Jackson, Amasa	NYK	17
Jackson, Amos	ULS	197
Jackson, Andrew	SRA	19
Jackson, Archibald	COL	204
Jackson, Asa	CAY	710
Jackson, Asahel	OND	177
Jackson, Asel	CHN	928
Jackson, Benjamin	ORN	354
Jackson, Benjn	OTS	49
Jackson, Benjamin	ULS	190
Jackson, Benjamine	GRN	325
Jackson, Benoni	NYK	54
Jackson, Caesar a Black	NYK	39
Jackson, Ceaser a Black	NYK	118
Jackson, Calvin	ONN	156
Jackson, Charity	COL	185
Jackson, Charles	QNS	81
Jackson, Comfort	GRN	325
Jackson, Cyrus	OTS	24
Jackson, Daniel	CLN	155
Jackson, Daniel	GRN	325
Jackson, Daniel	ORN	354
Jackson, David	DUT	174
Jackson, David	ONN	139
Jackson, David	ONN	189
Jackson, David	QNS	74
Jackson, David	QNS	78
Jackson, David	SUF	80
Jackson, David	WST	149
Jackson, Ebenr	ALB	82
Jackson, Edward a Black	NYK	59
Jackson, Eliphalet	CHN	928
Jackson, Elizabeth	DUT	126
Jackson, Elizabeth	NYK	112
Jackson, Elizabeth	NYK	119
Jackson, Elizabeth	ORN	279
Jackson, Enoch	ORN	373
Jackson, Ephiam	CHN	922
Jackson, Ephraim	DUT	108
Jackson, George	ALB	140
Jackson, George Kinelvell	NYK	31
Jackson, Gershom	DEL	271
Jackson, Gertrude	COL	180
Jackson, Gilbert	NYK	70
Jackson, Hamilton	ORN	331
Jackson, Hannibal	ULS	192
Jackson, Hy a free Negro	ALB	9
Jackson, Henry	NYK	114
Jackson, Henry	ORN	360
Jackson, Increase	DUT	126
Jackson, Isaac	HRK	481
Jackson, Isaeah	DEL	289
Jackson, Jabus	WST	156
Jackson, Jack a free Negro	ALB	131
Jackson, Jack	COL	208
Jackson, Jacob	HRK	580
Jackson, Jacob	QNS	73
Jackson, Jacob	QNS	74
Jackson, James	CAY	544
Jackson, James	CAY	560
Jackson, James	COL	259

Name	Ref.
Jackson, James	DUT 113
Jackson, James	HRK 519
Jackson, James	HRK 522
Jackson, James	HRK 551½
Jackson, James	NYK 90
Jackson, James	ORN 293
Jackson, James	ORN 373
Jackson, James	QNS 74
Jackson, James A.	CAY 558
Jackson, Jede	CHN 928
Jackson, Jehial	WSH 208
Jackson, Jehiel	OTS 32
Jackson, Jeremiah	ALB 82
Jackson, Jeremiah	ONN 168
Jackson, Joel	COL 213
Jackson, John	ALB 26
Jackson, John	ALB 105
Jackson, John a free man	ALB 143
Jackson, John	GRN 356
Jackson, John	KNG 8
Jackson, John a Black	NYK 22
Jackson, John a Black	NYK 22
Jackson, John Black	NYK 118
Jackson, John	ORN 294
Jackson, John	ORN 325
Jackson, John	ORN 363
Jackson, John	OTS 18
Jackson, John	OTS 38
Jackson, John	QNS 74
Jackson, John	QNS 76
Jackson, John	QNS 80
Jackson, John	SUF 82
Jackson, John Junr	ALB 26
Jackson, Joseph	DUT 40
Jackson, Joseph	ONN 145
Jackson, Joseph	QNS 77
Jackson, Joseph	WSH 285
Jackson, Joshua	TIO 215
Jackson, Louis	ULS 233
Jackson, Lyman	OTS 48
Jackson, Mary	ORN 357
Jackson, Mary	QNS 72
Jackson, Mecher	DEL 273
Jackson, Michael	COL 185
Jackson, Michael	ORN 331
Jackson, Michael	ORN 372
Jackson, Michael	OTS 48
Jackson, Michael	QNS 74
Jackson, Nancy a mulatto	NYK 20
Jackson, Naomi	ORN 356
Jackson, Nathan	SUF 81
Jackson, Nathan	WSH 293
Jackson, Nathan	WST 142
Jackson, Obadiah	QNS 73
Jackson, Obadiah	QNS 80
Jackson, Patten	RCK 108
Jackson, Patton	ORN 361
Jackson, Peter	NYK 93
Jackson, Peter	RNS 43
Jackson, Richard	DUT 28
Jackson, Richard	ORN 354
Jackson, Richard	QNS 72
Jackson, Richard	ULS 204
Jackson, Robert	DUT 72
Jackson, Robert	DUT 126
Jackson, Robert	HRK 455
Jackson, Robert	MNT 116
Jackson, Robert	NYK 50
Jackson, Robert	QNS 75
Jackson, Robert	WSH 292
Jackson, Ruthey	QNS 76
Jackson, Samuel	DUT 29
Jackson, Samuel	DUT 107
Jackson, Samuel	ESS 310
Jackson, Samuel	HRK 551½
Jackson, Samuel	MNT 113
Jackson, Samuel	QNS 72
Jackson, Samuel	QNS 74
Jackson, Samuel	QNS 74
Jackson, Saml	SUF 90
Jackson, Selah	SCH 151
Jackson, Selah Jr	SCH 151
Jackson, Selia	SCH 155
Jackson, Silas	SRA 23
Jackson, Stephen	HRK 551½
Jackson, Stephen	ORN 356
Jackson, Stephen	RNS 43
Jackson, Stephen	SRA 19
Jackson, Theophilus	HRK 485
Jackson, Thomas	QNS 74
Jackson, Thomas	QNS 80
Jackson, Thomas	QNS 81
Jackson, Townsend	QNS 79
Jackson, Uri	ONT 414
Jackson, Uri	OTS 22
Jackson, William	COL 264
Jackson, Wm	MNT 116
Jackson, William	ONT 498
Jackson, William	ORN 294
Jackson, William	ORN 361
Jackson, William	ORN 362
Jackson, Wm	RNS 39
Jackson, William J.	ONT 492
Jackway, Gamaliel	COL 259
Jackway, Seth	COL 259
Jackways, Frederick	WSH 281
Jackways, Hosea	WSH 281
Jackways, Jesse	WSH 301
Jackways, John	NYK 124
Jackways, Jonathan	WSH 267
Jackways, Samuel	WSH 281
Jacob Negro	QNS 65
Jacob	QNS 80
Jacob	QNS 82
Jacob	SUF 89
Jacob	SUF 93
Jacob, Ezekil	OTS 10
Jaco, Frances	NYK 139
Jacob, Francis mulatto	NYK 26
Jacob, Joseph	SUF 100
Jacobea, Wm	RNS 53
Jacobee, Henry	COL 234
Jacobie, Bastian	COL 231
Jacobie, Francis	RNS 85
Jacobie, Henry	COL 191
Jacobie, John	COL 197
Jacobie, John	COL 235
Jacobie, Michael	COL 239
Jacobie, Nicholas	COL 231
Jacobie, Peter	COL 231
Jacobie, William	COL 244
Jacobs, Aaron a Black	NYK 48
Jacobs, Abraham	NYK 127
Jacobs, Anthony	SRA 50
Jacobs, Cornelius	DUT 164
Jacobs, David	NYK 107
Jacobs, Henry	DUT 40
Jacobs, Jacob	ALB 105
Jacobs, Jacob	QNS 70
Jacobs, Joel	SUF 97
Jacobs, John	CHN 792
Jacobs, John	MNT 88
Jacobs, John	RNS 89
Jacobs, John	RNS 111
Jacobs, Joseph	NYK 16
Jacobs, Joseph	SRA 43
Jacobs, Moses	NYK 114
Jacobs, Nathaniel	RNS 81
Jacobs, Nicholas	ALB 70
Jacobs, Nicholas	NYK 91
Jacobs, Oliver	SUF 84
Jacobs, Phillip	NYK 92
Jacobs, Phillip	ULS 193
Jacobs, Samuel	KNG 10
Jacobs, Samuel	WST 158
Jacobs, Sarah	NYK 48
Jacobs, Thomas	NYK 67
Jacobs, Uriah	DEL 273
Jacobs, William	DUT 46
Jacobs, William	NYK 49
Jacobs, William	NYK 144
Jacobson, Jacob	HRK 492
Jacobson, John	RCH 90
Jacobus, Abraham	ORN 379
Jacobus, James	CAY 536
Jacobus, Peter	NYK 87
Jacobus, Roelof	NYK 89
Jacorhes, Thomas	NYK 93
Jacovy, Tobias	DUT 150
Jacques, Asa	OTS 35
Jacques, James	OTS 35
Jacques, Oliver	NYK 88
Jacquish, John	DEL 284
Jacson, Jonathan	ONN 139
Jacson, Matthew	ONN 139
Jadwin, Jesse	RNS 34
Jafferies, Thomas	NYK 90
Jafferies, William	NYK 87
Jagger, David & Stephen	ORN 303
Jagger, David	SUF 72
Jagger, Ebenezar	SUF 97
Jagger, Enock	SUF 95
Jagger, James	SUF 97
Jagger, Jeremiah	SUF 95
Jagger, Jeremiah	SUF 97
Jagger, John	ORN 276
Jagger, Jonathan	SUF 95
Jagger, Matthew	CAY 558
Jagger, Nathan	SUF 97
Jagger, Nathaniel	SUF 97
Jagger, Pheneas	ESS 310
Jagger, Phoebe	SUF 97
Jagger, Rufus	NYK 116
Jagger, Stephen & David	ORN 303
Jagger, Stephen	SUF 97
Jaggir, Daniel	ONT 346
Jakeways, Samuel	WSH 184
Jakeways, William C.	OND 187
Jakins, George	COL 204
Jakways, George A.	WSH 256
James] Peters] Negroes	CHN 932
James Negro	QNS 65
James	QNS 78
James	QNS 79
James	QNS 80
James	QNS 80
James	QNS 81
James	QNS 82
James	QNS 82
James	QNS 82
James	QNS 83
James	QNS 84
James	SUF 69
James	SUF 89
James	SUF 90
James	SUF 91
James	SUF 93
James	SUF 94
James, Abel	OND 199
James, Abraham a Black	NYK 111
James, Amos	SRN 111
James, Chalkley	NYK 86
James, Cyrus	NYK 41
James, Daniel	ESS 296
James, Daniel	ONT 368
James, David	WSH 196
James, Ebenezer	SUF 87

INDEX TO THE 1800 CENSUS OF NEW YORK

Name	Code	Name	Code	Name	Code
James, George	NYK 116	Jaquelin, Titus	DUT 32	Jauncey, John	ALB 145
James, Henry	RNS 33	Jaques, Asahel	OND 208	Jauncey, William	NYK 26
James, Howard	OND 199	Jaques, Daniel	ONN 173	Jauncy, Sarah	NYK 41
James, Jacob	ULS 184	Jaques, Moses	HRK 503	Javery, Didea	CHN 778
James, James	WSH 231	Jaques, Richard	NYK 126	Javis, Elizabeth	NYK 92
James, Jesse	SRA 53	Jaques, Samuel	OND 208	Javis, George	NYK 108
James, Jesse	SRA 58	Jaques, William	ONT 350	Javis, Jemima	NYK 108
James, John	ALB 47	Jaques, Wm C.	OTS 36	Javis, Jesse	WST 156
James, John	ORN 391	Jaquess, David	RCH 93	Jay, David	TIO 237
James, John	WSH 231	Jaquez, Wait	DUT 163	Jay, John	ALB 136
James, John L.	CHN 780	Jaquish, Henry	ORN 354	Jay, John	NYK 29
James, Jonathan	SRA 58	Jaret, William	ALB 129	Jay, John	ORN 354
James, Joseph	WSH 253	Jaringer see Taringer		Jay, Peter	NYK 19
James, Joseps	NYK 86	Jarman, Charles	QNS 84	Jay, Peter	WST 115
James, Martin	OND 199	Jarman, John	WST 133	Jay, Sarah	TIO 247
James, Paul	RCK 101	Jarmon, Peter	CHN 840	Jay, Upheam	NYK 26
James, Randall	RNS 23	Jarmon, Simmons	QNS 64	Jaycocks see Jeacocks	
James, Rebecca	NYK 42	Jarnum, Jesee	SUF 76	Jaycocks, David	ALB 79
James, Rebecca	NYK 81	Jarrard, Mat.	SUF 76	Jaycocks, Elias	RCK 99
James, Robert	CHN 814	Jarred a Negro	SUF 71	Jaycocks, Ezekiel	ALB 79
James, Robert	SRA 7	Jarrington, Gelbert	TIO 238	Jaycocks, Francis	ALB 79
James, Thomas	NYK 86	Jarves, James a Black	NYK 21	Jaycox, Bowers	RCK 97
James, Thomas	SRA 30	Jarving, Peter	NYK 48	Jayne, James	SUF 70
James, Townsed	QNS 63	Jarvis Negro	QNS 64	Jayne, James	SUF 90
James, William	ALB 7	Jarvis, Abraham	SUF 85	Jayne, James Junr	SUF 90
James, William	ALB 133	Jarvis, Abraham	SUF 88	Jayne, John	SUF 67
James, William	NYK 110	Jarvis, Andrw	NYK 75	Jayne, Joseph	SUF 67
James, Wm	RCK 102	Jarvis, Augustine	SUF 88	Jayne, Joseph	SUF 90
Jameson, Alexander	ULS 244	Jarvis, Austin	SUF 83	Jayne, Jotham	ORN 290
Jamison, Hugh	ONT 432	Jarvis, Bennijah	SUF 94	Jayne, Samuel	KNG 8
Jamison, Wm	MNT 95	Jarvis, Catharine	WST 159	Jayne, Samuel	ORN 366
Jane a free wench	ALB 137	Jarvis, Danl	SUF 83	Jayne, Moses	SUF 67
Jane a Black	NYK 92	Jarvis, Daniel	SUF 94	Jayne, Robert	SUF 67
Jane (free Black)	RNS 36	Jarvis, David	QNS 72	Jayne, Robert	SUF 67
Jane	SUF 108	Jarvis, Elijah	NYK 31	Jayne, Stephen	SUF 90
Jane, Thomas	CAY 578	Jarvis, Eliphalet	SUF 85	Jayne, Timothy	CAY 536
Janeaay, George	NYK 109	Jarvis, Ellenor	NYK 134	Jayne, Wm	SUF 67
Janeaay, William	NYK 111	Jarvis, Frederick	TIO 257	Jeacocks see Jaycocks	
Janes, Benjamine	GRN 336	Jarvis, Henry	SUF 85	Jeacocks, Abijah	DUT 77
Janes, David	WSH 257	Jarvis, Icabod	SUF 85	Jeacocks, Benjamin F.	DUT 71
Janes, Elijah	RNS 80	Jarvis, Ickabod	NYK 60	Jeacocks, David	DUT 77
Janes, Elisha	COL 212	Jarvis, Isaac	SUF 82	Jeacocks, David	DUT 100
Janes, Elishama	COL 209	Jarvis, Isaiah	SUF 81	Jeacocks, Gershom	DUT 169
Janes, James	CHN 782	Jarvis, Isaiah	SUF 86	Jeacocks, Guy	ORN 392
Janes, James	CHN 784	Jarvis, James	NYK 122	Jeacocks, Isaiah	DUT 77
Janes, James	COL 208	Jarvis, John	ORN 319	Jeacocks, Jonathan	DUT 32
Janes, John	DUT 177	Jarvis, John	SUF 85	Jeacocks, Joshua	DUT 169
Janes, Mary	ONT 312	Jarvis, John	SUF 89	Jeacocks, Reuben	DUT 98
Janes, Nathel	COL 210	Jarvis, John F.	NYK 64	Jeacocks, Solomon	ORN 392
Janes, Roger	COL 209	Jarvis, Jonathan	SUF 79	Jeacocks, Thomas Ye 1st	DUT 71
Jansen, Abraham	ULS 199	Jarvis, Joseph	SUF 85	Jeacocks, Thomas T.	DUT 70
Jansen, Benjamin	ULS 217	Jarvis, Kezia	NYK 80	Jeacocks, Thomas W.	DUT 70
Jansen, Daniel	ULS 241	Jarvis, Lemuel	NYK 150	Jearomes, John	DEL 289
Jansen, Egbert & John	ULS 218	Jarvis, Locey	SUF 85	Jearomes, Timothy	DEL 289
Jansen, Isaac	ULS 240	Jarvis, Mathew	NYK 148	Jearst, John a Black	NYK 92
Jansen, Jacobus	ORN 306	Jarvis, Moses	NYK 78	Jed a Negro	SUF 75
Jansen, Jermiah	DUT 19	Jarvis, Nathaniel	DUT 166	Jeff	QNS 83
Jansen, Johannis	ULS 246	Jarvis, Nicholas	NYK 135	Jeffards, Nathan	OTS 54
Jansen Johannis I.	ULS 229	Jarvis, Nicholas	SUF 89	Jefferds, Benjamin	OTS 51
Jansen John & Egbert	ULS 218	Jarvis, Noah	NYK 33	Jefferds, Dodat	WSH 215
Jansen, John	ULS 258	Jarvis, Peter	NYK 82	Jefferds, Joseph	OTS 51
Jansen, Levi	ORN 301	Jarvis, Philip	SUF 82	Jefferery, John	ONN 187
Jansen, Matthew	ULS 213	Jarvis, Robt	SUF 79	Jefferies, William	NYK 58
Jansen, Nicholas	ULS 248	Jarvis, Samuel	OND 208	Jeffers, George	ALB 87
Jansen, Peter	ULS 205	Jarvis, Sands	WST 159	Jeffers, Gilbert	CAY 696
Jansen, Peter	ULS 241	Jarvis, Seth	SUF 89	Jeffers, Isa_c	CHN 864
Jansen, Rachel	ULS 248	Jarvis, Silvenus	GRN 326	Jeffers, John	RNS 107
Jansen, Richard	ULS 259	Jarvis, Stephen	NYK 150	Jeffers, John	WST 148
Jansen, Teunis	ULS 217	Jarvis, Stephen	SUF 82	Jeffers, Rachel M.	ALB 135
Jansen, Thomas	ULS 205	Jarvis, Stephen	SUF 85	Jeffers, Samuel	DUT 73
Jansen, Thomas1	ULS 247	Jarvis, Thomas	ALB 97	Jeffers, Thomas	CHN 912
Jansen, Thomas B.	NYK 45	Jarvis, Thomas	SUF 86	Jefferson, Joseph	NYK 86
Jansen, William	ULS 246	Jarvis, Timothy	NYK 114	Jefferson, Partrick	NYK 108
Jansen, Zachariah	ULS 248	Jarvis, Timothy	OND 214	Jefferst, Wm	MNT 19
January, John	SUF 94	Jarvis, William	NYK 99	Jeffery, Mary	NYK 27
Janus, Thomas	NYK 137	Jarvis, Wm	OTS 17	Jeffords, Alpheus	OTS 14
Jaquelin, George a Black	NYK 110	Jarvis, William	SUF 86	Jeffords, Asa	OTS 54

196

Name	Loc	Pg	Name	Loc	Pg	Name	Loc	Pg
Jeffords, Joseph	SRA	45	Jenkins, William	NYK	110	Jeoffery	SUF	94
Jeffords, Thomas	SRA	42	Jenkins, William	ORN	382	Jephson, William	OND	176
Jefforey, Umphry	CHN	790	Jenkins, Wm	TIO	262	Jepperson, Amos	OND	214
Jeffries see Jaffries			Jenkins, William	WSH	299	Jepperson, Solomon	OND	214
Jeffries, Christopher	CAY	698	Jenkinson, Francis	NYK	128	Jerams, Moses	GRN	358
Jeffries, John	NYK	147	Jenks, Elisha	TIO	239	Jerard, Joseph	NYK	135
Jeffries, Partrick	NYK	79	Jenks, Joel	OND	219	Jeraw, Andrew	WST	124
Jefries, Jeremiah	CAY	568	Jenks, Joseph	COL	205	Jeraw, Reubin	WST	124
Jeiris, Wm	MNT	107	Jenks, Laban	TIO	239	Jeraw, Solomon	WST	124
Jeleton, Jonathan	NYK	124	Jenks, Michael	TIO	239	Jeremiah, John	NYK	16
Jelson, Ananias	OTS	24	Jenks, Otis	ONN	131	Jeremiah, Augustus	SRA	10
Jemison, Elizabeth	NYK	35	Jenks, Stephen	WSH	243	Jerman, Andrew	SRA	10
Jemison, Henry a Black	NYK	49	Jenks, Willeam	WSH	264	Jerman, Henery	SRA	9
Jamison, John	STB	206	Jenne, Cornelius	OTS	24	Jerman, Isaac	SRA	24
Jemmerman see Temmerman			Jenney, Elisha	SRA	24	Jermins, Silas	GRN	349
Jemmison, Margaret	NYK	105	Jenning, Hezekiah	SRA	24	Jernett, Jonas	SUF	93
Jemmison, Robert	NYK	84	Jennings see Gennings			Jernon, Caesar a Black	NYK	43
Jenar, Thomas	NYK	31	& Jinnings			Jeroloman, Jacob	NYK	47
Jencks, Dickinson	OTS	29	Jennings, Andrw	NYK	84	Jeroloman, Nicholas	ALB	98
Jencks, Gideon	HRK	518	Jennings, Asa	ORN	370	Jerolomon, Ns Junr	ALB	98
Jencks, Jerh	OTS	29	Jennings, Benjamin	ORN	361	Jerolsman, John	CAY	682
Jencks, John S.	ORN	340	Jennings, David	ORN	287	Jerom, Augustus	RNS	98
Jencks, Joseph	OND	193	Jennings, Doras a			Jerom, Timothy	ONN	178
Jencks, Levi	OTS	29	mulatto	NYK	47	Jerome, Chancy	ONN	148
Jencks, Lory	OTS	29	Jennings, Ebenezer	ALB	91	Jerome, John	ONN	145
Jenings, Joseph	OND	171	Jennings, Edmond	SRA	17	Jerome, John	ONN	148
Jenington, Daniel	MNT	102	Jennings, Elias	SUF	98	Jerome, Levi	ONN	145
Jenkens, John	RCK	105	Jennings, Elnathan	OTS	2	Jeroms, Robert	OND	201
Jenkenson, Philep	MNT	43	Jennings, Ezra	DUT	170	Jeroms, Samuel	ONT	396
Jenkine, George	NYK	86	Jennings, G. H.	SUF	98	Jeroms, Zerubibel	OND	201
Jenkings, James	NYK	84	Jennings, Gideon	ORN	365	Jerons, John	KNG	8
Jenkins, _____ netus	GRN	353	Jennings, Henry	SRA	20	Jerow, John J.	NYK	59
Jenkins, Abia	WSH	305	Jennings, Henry	SUF	95	Jerrard, Joseph	SUF	64
Jenkins, Charles	COL	254	Jennings, Hezekiah	SUF	76	Jerret, Benjn	SUF	66
Jenkins, Christopher	ALB	37	Jennings, Isaac	OTS	41	Jerret, Chas	SUF	65
Jenkins, Deborah	COL	247	Jennings, Isaac	QNS	82	Jerret, Gilbert	SUF	66
Jenkins, Dinah	COL	247	Jennings, Isbon	SRA	26	Jerret, Isaac	SUF	66
Jenkins, Ebenezer	COL	251	Jennings, James	ORN	287	Jerret, Joseph	SUF	68
Jenkins, Elisha	COL	246	Jennings, James	SUF	72	Jerret, Nathl	SUF	66
Jenkins, Elizabeth	COL	248	Jennings, James	SUF	98	Jerret, Wm	SUF	66
Jenkins, Ezra	DUT	157	Jennings, Jesse	ORN	370	Jerret, Wm	SUF	68
Jenkins, Francis	COL	250	Jennings, John	RCH	90	Jerrume, Aaron	ONN	146
Jenkins, Frederick	COL	246	Jennings, John	TIO	263	Jerry	QNS	78
Jenkins, Garret	ORN	385	Jennings, John R.	SUF	72	Jersey, Abrm	RCK	108
Jenkins, George	WSH	293	Jennings, Jonathan	NYK	117	Jersey, Elizabeth	DUT	124
Jenkins, George	WSH	295	Jennings, Joseph	NYK	71	Jersey, Hannah	RCK	109
Jenkins, Gideon	DUT	10	Jennings, Joseph	SUF	72	Jersey, Henry	CLN	163
Jenkins, Gilbert	COL	246	Jennings, Justice	SRA	22	Jersey, Henry	DUT	123
Jenkins, Hannah	NYK	58	Jennings, [Le?]muel	ONT	386	Jersey, John	CLN	162
Jenkins, Jabez	SRA	40	Jennings, Lemuel	OTS	38	Jersey, John	RCK	108
Jenkins, James	ULS	257	Jennings, Lemuel	SUF	101	Jersey, John	RCK	109
Jenkins, Jededeah Junr	WSH	210	Jennings, Lidia	SUF	75	Jersey, Richard	GRN	336
Jenkins, Joel	DUT	74	Jennings, Luke	ORN	305	Jersey, William a Black	NYK	119
Jenkins, John	ORN	382	Jennings, Nathan	NYK	49	Jervaige, Frances G.	NYK	91
Jenkins, John	ULS	241	Jennings, Nicholas	SUF	98	Jervers, James	NYK	139
Jenkins, Joseph	COL	202	Jennings, Peter	DEL	269	Jessee	QNS	81
Jenkins, Joseph	WSH	305	Jennings, Peter Junr	DEL	269	Jessee	SUF	97
Jenkins, Lemuel W.	COL	253	Jennings, Redman	ORN	380	Jessop, Caleb	COL	205
Jenkins, Margaret	MNT	36	Jennings, Reuben	OTS	38	Jessop, William	COL	252
Jenkins, Marshall	COL	250	Jennings, Reuben	SRA	22	Jessup, Abraham	DEL	275
Jenkins, Mary	COL	247	Jennings, Richard	NYK	82	Jessup, Benjamin	NYK	117
Jenkins, Nathan	DEL	267	Jennings, Richard	ORN	361	Jessup, Benjamin	WST	128
Jenkins, Nathaniel	DEL	267	Jennings, Richd	SUF	72	Jessup, Blackleach	DUT	168
Jenkins, Phillip	GRN	350	Jennings, Samuel	MNT	16	Jessup, Daniel	ORN	360
Jenkins, Robert	COL	247	Jennings, Saml	SUF	98	Jessup, Edward	NYK	69
Jenkins, Samuel	ALB	84	Jennings, Seth	SRA	21	Jessup, Henry	SUF	95
Jenkins, Samuel	COL	250	Jennings, Silvenus	SUF	98	Jessup, Isaac	ORN	362
Jenkins, Samuel	DEL	267	Jennings, Silvenus Junr	SUF	98	Jessup, Isaac	SUF	100
Jenkins, Samuel	TIO	262	Jennings, Stephen	DEL	274	Jessup, Jared	ORN	305
Jenkins, Seth	COL	247	Jennings, Thomas	NYK	130	Jessup, Jeremiah	ORN	359
Jenkins, Simeon	WSH	293	Jennings, William	NYK	15	Jessup, John	SUF	95
Jenkins, Solomon	ALB	65	Jennings, William	SUF	98	Jessup, Joseph	HRK	484
Jenkins, Thomas	COL	246	Jennison, Joseph	ONT	394	Jessup, Mathew	SUF	95
Jenkins, Thomas	NYK	138	Jenny, Seth	COL	223	Jessup, Samuel	ORN	361
Jenkins, Thomas Junr	COL	246	Jenson, Richard	OTS	21	Jessup, Stephen	SUF	95
Jenkins, Valentine	DUT	48	Jentle, Robert	NYK	109	Jessup, Stephen	SUF	105
Jenkins, Wilks	TIO	261	Jen[unge?], Cors	OTS	49	Jessup, Thomas	SUF	97

Jessup, Thomas Jun<u>r</u>	SUF 97	
Jessup, William	CAY 592	
Jessup, Zebulon	SUF 97	
Jesup, Silv..us	WST 131	
Jewel, George	SRA 31	
Jewel, Herman	SRA 50	
Jewel, John	SRA 42	
Jewel, John	WST 163	
Jewel, Jonathan	WST 119	
Jewel, Stephen	SRA 42	
Jewell, Aaron	OTS 9	
Jewell, Abraham	WST 124	
Jewell, Adin<u>h</u>	OTS 27	
Jewell, Asen<u>as</u>	OTS 9	
Jewell, Daniel	DUT 27	
Jewell, Ellice	OTS 52	
Jewell, George	DUT 28	
Jewell, George	WST 122	
Jewell, George H.	DUT 32	
Jewell, Henry	DUT 32	
Jewell, Herman	DUT 32	
Jewell, Isaac	ORN 393	
Jewell, Isaac	OTS 27	
Jewell, John	OTS 45	
Jewell, John	WST 122	
Jewell, John H.	DUT 18	
Jewell, John I.	DUT 28	
Jewell, John Morris	OTS 45	
Jewell, Joseph	MNT 9	
Jewell, Nath<u>l</u>	HRK 456	
Jewell, Penu<u>el</u>	OTS 26	
Jewell, Richard	DUT 28	
Jewell, William	DUT 32	
Jewell, W<u>m</u>	OTS 9	
Jewell, W<u>m</u>	OTS 45	
Jewell, Whitney	OTS 45	
Jewesson, George	NYK 109	
Jewet, Arron	DUT 46	
Jewet, Briggs	DEL 288	
Jewet, David	OND 198	
Jewet, Eleazer	ULS 205	
Jewet, Isaac	DUT 56	
Jewet, John	DUT 91	
Jewett, Amos	MNT 124	
Jewett, Caleb	COL 208	
Jewett, Ezekiel	TIO 220	
Jewett, Jacob	OTS 56	
Jewett, Nathan	SRA 29	
Jewett, Solomon	COL 183	
Jewit, Samuel	OND 175	
Jewitt, Nathaniel	ESS 310	
Jiffinna, W<u>m</u>	GRN 349	
Jillet, Eliphalet	ALB 135	
Jillet, Job	ONT 426	
Jillet, Noah	ALB 50	
Jime, Jacob	NYK 15	
Jincks, Nicholas	CHN 940	
Jingly, Daniel	SCH 128	
Jinings, Nathaniel	SRA 15	
Jinkens, Jededeah	WSH 210	
Jinkins, John	WSH 217	
Jinkins, Joshua	WSH 185	
Jinkins, Palmer	WSH 211	
Jinkins, Semion	WSH 212	
Jinkins, Stephen	WSH 217	
Jinkins, Thomas	WSH 212	
Jinkins, W<u>m</u>	MNT 71	
Jinks, Amos	ONT 500	
Jinks, Benjamin	WSH 202	
Jinks, Oliver	CHN 752	
Jinks, Thomas	ONT 352	
Jinks, William	DUT 134	
Jinney, John	CAY 658	
Jinnings, Enoch	CHN 870	
Jinnings, Israel	SRA 15	
Jinnins, Robert	GRN 349	
Joakim, Gulick	MNT 98	

Joanson, Christophel	CAY 606	
Job, Euphemia	NYK 63	
Job, James	SRA 28	
Job, James Jur	SRA 28	
Jobs, John	NYK 95	
Jobs, Joseph	ULS 235	
Jocelin, John	DUT 105	
Jocelin, Joseph	ONT 480	
Joceylin, Rufus	HRK 425	
Jock, Thomas	SUF 96	
Jodal, ...	MNT 86	
Johmson, David	MNT 124	
John a free Negro	ALB 132	
John a Black	NYK 106	
John a free Negro	RNS 96	
John a Negro	SUF 76	
John a free Negro	WST 121	
John, Jacob	RNS 63	
John Joseph	DUT 128	
John, Thomas	HRK 421	
John, Thomas	MNT 110	
Johnes, John a Black	NYK 99	
Johnno Black		
Johns, Abraham a Black	NYK 19	
Johnson see Johmson, Johnston & Jonson		
Johnson	GRN 338	
Johnson	HRK 502	
Johnson a Black	NYK 21	
Johnson, Aaron	OTS 33	
Johnson, Abigail	SUF 88	
Johnson, Abigal	CHN 782	
Johnson, Abraham	CAY 574	
Johnson, Abraham	CAY 682	
Johnson, Abraham	RCH 94	
Johnson, Abraham	RCH 94	
Johnson, Abr<u>m</u>	RCK 110	
Johnson, Abraham	SRA 26	
Johnson, Abraham	SRA 43	
Johnson, Abraham	ULS 210	
Johnson, Abrm J.	RCK 110	
Johnson, Ab<u>m</u> P.	COL 215	
Johnson, Adams	OND 167	
Johnson, Alderman	ONT 450	
Johnson, Amasa	OND 164	
Johnson, Amos	COL 181	
Johnson, Andrew	CAY 674	
Johnson, Andrew	ORN 393	
Johnson, Anna	NYK 35	
Johnson, Anthony	OND 197	
Johnson, Asa	OND 171	
Johnson, Asa	ONT 380	
Johnson, Barrend	KNG 4	
Johnson, Barrend	KNG 5	
Johnson, Benjamin	COL 242	
Johnson, Benjamin	HRK 578	
Johnson, Benjamin	OND 171	
Johnson, Betsey a Black	NYK 22	
Johnson, Betsey	NYK 87	
Johnson, Betty a Black	NYK 98	
Johnson, Brister a Black	NYK 85	
Johnson, Bryan	OND 160	
Johnson, Bryant	HRK 553	
Johnson, Cale.	MNT 63	
Johnson, Caleb	OTS 34	
Johnson, Calep	MNT 58	
Johnson, Calvin	HRK 497	
Johnson, Catherine	NYK 58	
Johnson, Cather<u>m</u>	NYK 34	
Johnson, Charles	GRN 346	
Johnson, Charles	NYK 39	
Johnson, Charles	OND 214	
Johnson, Charles	ONT 436	
Johnson, Charles	QNS 62	

Johnson, Charles	RNS 63	
Johnson, Charles R.	RCK 103	
Johnson, Chloe	HRK 497	
Johnson, Christiana	NYK 105	
Johnson, Christopher	HRK 418	
Johnson, Christopher	NYK 21	
Johnson, Coert	KNG 5	
Johnson, Cornelius	CAY 720	
Johnson, Cornelius	ONT 334	
Johnson, Cuff	KNG 9	
Johnson, Cyrus M.	HRK 579	
Johnson, Daniel	CHN 766	
Johnson, Daniel	ESS 294	
Johnson, Daniel	MNT 96	
Johnson, Daniel	ONT 402	
Johnson, Dan<u>l</u>	OTS 33	
Johnson, Daniel	SRA 56	
Johnson, David	ALB 9	
Johnson, David	CHN 848	
Johnson, David	CHN 904	
Johnson, David	GRN 333	
Johnson, David	HRK 579	
Johnson, David	OTS 30	
Johnson, David	RNS 63	
Johnson, David	ULS 180	
Johnson, Derick	MNT 23	
Johnson, Dirck	COL 266	
Johnson, Duke	ULS 190	
Johnson, Dyer	OND 167	
Johnson, Ebenezar	GRN 333	
Johnson, Ebenezar	ONT 430	
Johnson, Ebner	SCH 160	
Johnson, Edmund	SRA 46	
Johnson, Edmund S.	NYK 15	
Johnson, Edward a Black	NYK 64	
Johnson, Edward	NYK 107	
Johnson, Edward	OND 221	
Johnson, Edward	RCH 93	
Johnson, Edward	SUF 81	
Johnson, Edward	TIO 220	
Johnson, Edward Jur	TIO 220	
Johnson, Eleazer	CHN 966	
Johnson, Elenor	RCH 92	
Johnson, Elhana	NYK 63	
Johnson, Elijah	CHN 916	
Johnson, Elijah	ESS 297	
Johnson, Elijah	GRN 334	
Johnson, Eliphalet	RNS 71	
Johnson, Elisha	CHN 812	
Johnson, Elisha	DUT 140	
Johnson, Elisha	ONN 182	
Johnson, Elisha	OTS 34	
Johnson, Elisha	OTS 36	
Johnson, Elisher	OND 220	
Johnson, Elizabeth	NYK 41	
Johnson, Elizabeth	NYK 57	
Johnson, Elizabeth	NYK 63	
Johnson, Elizabeth	NYK 92	
Johnson, Elizabeth	ONT 312	
Johnson, Elkanah	OND 200	
Johnson, Ephraim	RCH 94	
Johnson, Esa	ALB 75	
Johnson, Ester	NYK 105	
Johnson, Ezekiel	DEL 284	
Johnson, Francis	NYK 36	
Johnson, George	NYK 92	
Johnson, George	ONT 450	
Johnson, George	ONT 994	
Johnson, George	ONT 498	
Johnson, George	ULS 251	
Johnson, George W.	SRA 23	
Johnson, Gideon	HRK 461	
Johnson, Gilbert	QNS 77	
Johnson, Gilbert	RCK 109	
Johnson, Gilbert	RCK 109	
Johnson, Harman Jun<u>r</u>	NYK 27	
Johnson, Harmen	NYK 72	

Name	Loc	Name	Loc	Name	Loc
Johnson, Harris	OTS 34	Johnson, John	OND 204	Johnson, Peter	CAY 548
Johnson, Hendrick	KNG 5	Johnson, John	ONN 169	Johnson, Peter	COL 215
Johnson, Henry	GRN 338	Johnson, John	ONT 336	Johnson, Peter	GRN 329
Johnson, Henry	RNS 23	Johnson, John	ONT 376	Johnson, Peter	GRN 348
Johnson, Henry	SCH 127	Johnson, John	ORN 356	Johnson, Peter	MNT 31
Johnson, Horace	NYK 86	Johnson, John	OTS 32	Johnson, Peter	ONN 154
Johnson, Hugh	RCK 109	Johnson, John Negro	QNS 71	Johnson, Peter	ORN 335
Johnson, Ira	OTS 35	Johnson, John	QNS 76	Johnson, Peter	ORN 384
Johnson, Ira	SRA 48	Johnson, John	QNS 77	Johnson, Peter	QNS 67
Johnson, Isaac	ALB 75	Johnson, John	RNS 8	Johnson, Peter	QNS 67
Johnson, Isaac	CAY 534	Johnson, John	RNS 46	Johnson, Peter	SRA 6
Johnson, Isaac	COL 215	Johnson, John	RNS 89	Johnson, Peter Jun	ONN 156
Johnson, Isaac	NYK 54	Johnson, John	RNS 96	Johnson, Philup a mulatto	NYK 62
Johnson, Isaac	NYK 93	Johnson, John	RCH 87	Johnson, Potter	SRA 57
Johnson, Isaac	ONT 330	Johnson, John	RCK 99	Johnson, Reuben	SUF 86
Johnson, Isaac	RNS 81	Johnson, John	RCK 109	Johnson, Richard	COL 213
Johnson, Isaac	SRA 16	Johnson, John	SRA 11	Johnson, Richard	ORN 360
Johnson, Isaiah	HRK 590	Johnson, John	SRA 26	Johnson, Richard	ORN 373
Johnson, Isaiah	OND 184	Johnson, John	SCH 127	Johnson, Richard	QNS 77
Johnson, Jacob	ESS 304	Johnson, John	SCH 160	Johnson, Robbard	GRN 334
Johnson, Jacob	GRN 350	Johnson, John	ULS 190	Johnson, Robert	DUT 85
Johnson, Jacob	ONN 141	Johnson, John Junr	COL 215	Johnson, Robert a Black	NYK 35
Johnson, Jacob	ORN 280	Johnson, John Junr	RCK 99	Johnson, Robert a Black	NYK 39
Johnson, Jacob	RCH 93	Johnson, John Jun	SCH 160	Johnson, Robert	NYK 42
Johnson, Jacob	RCH 93	Johnson, John Junr	SUF 88	Johnson, Robert	NYK 63
Johnson, Jacob Jur	ONN 141	Johnson, John P.	COL 215	Johnson, Robert a Black	NYK 64
Johnson, James	CAY 542	Johnson, John R.	NYK 60	Johnson, Robert	RCK 110
Johnson, James	CAY 574	Johnson, Jonathan	ESS 312	Johnson, Rufus	RNS 23
Johnson, James	CHN 906	Johnson, Jonathan	HRK 517	Johnson, Ruliph	RNS 61
Johnson, James	COL 183	Johnson, Jonathan	OND 199	Johnson, Russel	OTS 30
Johnson, James	COL 258	Johnson, Jonathan	OTS 30	Johnson, Rutluff	MNT 96
Johnson, James	MNT 15	Johnson, Jonathan	ULS 247	Johnson, Samuel	CHN 764
Johnson, James	NYK 52	Johnson, Joseph	ALB 74	Johnson, Samuel	DEL 277
Johnson, James	NYK 84	Johnson, Joseph	CHN 770	Johnson, Samuel	DUT 41
Johnson, James	ORN 334	Johnson, Joseph	COL 215	Johnson, Samuel	DUT 66
Johnson, James	ORN 351	Johnson, Joseph	GRN 345	Johnson, Samuel	GRN 345
Johnson, James	ORN 390	Johnson, Joseph	MNT 118	Johnson, Samuel	ONT 460
Johnson, James	RCH 93	Johnson, Joseph	RNS 47	Johnson, Samuel	ORN 272
Johnson, James	RCH 93	Johnson, Joseph	SRA 25	Johnson, Samuel	ORN 373
Johnson, James	RCH 94	Johnson, Joseph	ULS 243	Johnson, Samuel	QNS 77
Johnson, James	RCH 94	Johnson, Joshua	OND 181	Johnson, Samuel Junr	QNS 77
Johnson, James	RCH 94	Johnson, Josiah	OND 190	Johnson, Sarah	NYK 63
Johnson, James	RCK 104	Johnson, Lemuel	COL 180	Johnson, Sarah	RCK 109
Johnson, James	SRA 26	Johnson, Lemuel	OND 169	Johnson, Sebin	ALB 74
Johnson, Jani_a	NYK 105	Johnson, Letty a Black	NYK 114	Johnson, Seth	CHN 856
Johnson, Jeremiah	CHN 786	Johnson, Levi	TIO 221	Johnson, Seth	HRK 424
Johnson, Jeremiah	KNG 7	Johnson, Lewis	RCH 89	Johnson, Seth	NYK 98
Johnson, Jeremiah	ONN 191	Johnson, Luther	HRK 497	Johnson, Shelden	OND 220
Johnson, Job	GRN 330	Johnson, Margaret	NYK 72	Johnson, Shubael	DEL 277
Johnson, Joel	CHN 766	Johnson, Marrit	SCH 155	Johnson, Shubal	RNS 10
Johnson, John	ALB 13	Johnson, Mary	NYK 88	Johnson, Shubill	RNS 107
Johnson, John	ALB 72	Johnson, Mary a Black	NYK 98	Johnson, Silas	COL 238
Johnson, John	CHN 906	Johnson, Mary	NYK 104	Johnson, Silas	DEL 277
Johnson, John	COL 190	Johnson, Mechael	MNT 62	Johnson, Silas	HRK 447
Johnson, John	COL 207	Johnson, Moses	CAY 596	Johnson, Simeon	RNS 81
Johnson, John	COL 217	Johnson, Moses	ESS 294	Johnson, Simon	QNS 78
Johnson, John	COL 228	Johnson, Moses	MNT 16	Johnson, Solomon	DEL 277
John[son?], John	DEL 285	Johnson, Naham	OND 214	Johnson, Solomon	HRK 423
Johnson, John	DUT 27	Johnson, Nathan	HRK 551	Johnson, Solomon	NYK 72
Johnson, John	DUT 73	Johnson, Nathan	OTS 30	Johnson, Stephen	GRN 333
Johnson, John	DUT 131	Johnson, Nathanl	CHN 884	Johnson, Stephen	ONN 159
Johnson, John	GRN 329	Johnson, Nathaniel	CLN 172	Johnson, Stephen H.	HRK 565
Johnson, John	HRK 413	Johnson, Nathaniel	RCH 93	Johnson, Stewart	OND 181
Johnson, John	KNG 4	Johnson, Nathaniel B.	OND 214	Johnson, Sylvester	ONT 330
Johnson, John	KNG 6	Johnson, Nehemiah	DUT 57	Johnson, There	RNS 104
Jo[hn?[son, John	MNT 67	Johnson, Nehemiah	RCK 104	Johnson, Thomas	DEL 274
Johnson, John	MNT 103	Johnson, Nelly	RCK 108	Johnson, Thomas	GRN 345
Johnson, John	NYK 16	Johnson, Nicholas	RNS 63	Johnson, Thomas a Black	NYK 36
Johnson, John a Black	NYK 41	Johnson, Nicholas	SRA 5	Johnson, Thomas a Black	NYK 50
Johnson, John a mulatto	NYK 41	Johnson, Noble	RNS 89	Johnson, Thomas	NYK 83
Johnson, John	NYK 62	Johnson, Noell	CHN 968	Johnson, Thomas	ONN 156
Johnson, John	NYK 83	Johnson, Nouh	MNT 42	Johnson, Thomas	ONT 394
Johnson, John	NYK 93	Johnson, Obadiah	COL 204	Johnson, Thomas	RNS 12
Johnson, John	NYK 103	Johnson, Ot...(?)	ONT 422	Johnson, Thomas	RNS 89
Johnson, John	NYK 118	Johnson, Otis	ONT 330	Johnson, Thos	RCK 106
Johnson, John	OND 164	Johnson, Paul	NYK 42	Johnson, Thos	TIO 255

Name	Loc	Pg	Name	Loc	Pg	Name	Loc	Pg
Johnson, Thomas Senr	CAY	682	Johnston, George	OTS	44	Johnston, William	NYK	70
Johnson, Timothy	HRK	558	Johnston, Henry	NYK	120	Johnston, William	NYK	136
Johnson, ..mothy	MNT	103	Johnston, Henry	OTS	2	Johnston, William	NYK	147
Johnson, Timothy	ONN	161	Johnston, Horatio	OTS	13	Johnston, William	ORN	284
Johnson, Titus	ORN	380	Johnston, Hugh	DEL	279	Johnston, Wm	OTS	6
Johnson, Tovile(?)	MNT	65	Johnston, Hugh	WSH	290	Johnston, Wm	OTS	10
Johnson, Tunis	KNG	10	Johnston, Isaac	ALB	12	Johnston, William	WSH	204
Johnson, Walter	COL	249	Johnston, Isaac	ALB	102	Johnston, William	WSH	231
Johnson, William	CHN	972	Johnston, Isaac	NYK	119	Johnston, William	WSH	268
Johnson, William	CHN	974	Johnston, Jabez	OTS	7	Johnston, Witter	DEL	279
Johnson, William	COL	180	Johnston, Jacob	NYK	63	Johson, Johnothan	CHN	782
Johnson, Willm	COL	212	Johnston, Jacob a Black	NYK	119	Johson, Marvirck	SCH	151
Johnson, William	COL	223	Johnston, Jakeways	WSH	185	Joice see Joyce		
Johnson, William	DUT	13	Johnston, James	ALB	6	Joice, Benjamin	NYK	52
Johnson, William	DUT	33	Johnston, James	ALB	71	Joice, George	ALB	141
Johnson, William	DUT	84	Johnston, James	ALB	103	Joice, John	ALB	5
Johnson, William	DUT	107	Johnston, James	NYK	125	Joice, Mary	NYK	63
Johnson, William	DUT	120	Johnston, James	NYK	146	Joice, William	NYK	59
Johnson, William	ESS	298	Johnston, James	OTS	2	Joine, John	NYK	128
Johnson, William	HRK	490	Johnston, Jane	NYK	132	Joiner, Asahel	OND	157
Johnson, William	NYK	16	Johnston, Jane	ORN	299	Joiner, Robert	OND	200
Johnson, William	NYK	28	Johnston, Jeremiah	ALB	126	Joiner, William	OND	187
Johnson, William	NYK	37	Johnston, Jesse	NYK	125	Joiner, William	OND	210
Johnson, William a Black	NYK	75	Johnston, John	ALB	25	Joline, John	ORN	366
Johnson, William a mulatto	NYK	76	Johnston, John	ALB	133	Jolley, Edward	WST	168
Johnson, William	OND	214	Johnston, John	DUT	106	Jolly, Hugh	ALB	97
Johnson, William	OND	219	Johnston, John	NYK	119	Jolly, James	ALB	136
Johnson, Wm	ONN	186	Johnston, John	NYK	129	Jolly, John	CAY	524
Johnson, William	ONT	310	Johnston, John	NYK	146	Jolly, William	NYK	122
Johnson, William	ONT	364	Johnston, John	ORN	284	Jonah a Negro	SUF	68
Johnson, William	ORN	273	Johnston, John	TIO	221	Jonathan, Benjamin	MNT	114
Johnson, William	ORN	310	Johnston, John	WSH	257	Jonathan, Ox	MNT	88
Johnson, William	ORN	373	Johnston, John	WSH	304	Jone, David	TIO	241
Johnson, Wm	OTS	33	Johnston, John B.	ALB	147	Jones, ..a....s	RNS	80
Johnson, William	QNS	75	Johnston, Jona	OTS	4	Jones, Abel	RNS	69
Johnson, William	QNS	76	Johnston, Joseph	ALB	19	Jones, Abijah	ALB	33
Johnson, William	RNS	7	Johnston, Joseph	ALB	50	Jones, Abraham	MNT	41
Johnson, Wm	RNS	71	Johnston, Kindle	WSH	187	Jones, Abraham	RCH	90
Johnson, William	SRA	21	Johnston, Levy	NYK	135	Jones, Abraham	SCH	142
Johnson, William	SRA	57	Johnston, Luis	WSH	215	Jones, Alexander	QNS	75
Johnson, William	SUF	88	Johnston, Luther	WSH	216	Jones, Amasa	ALB	102
Johnson, Wm	TIO	225	Johnston, Masten	WST	160	Jones, Amasa Junr	ALB	102
Johnson, William ye 2d	ORN	372	Johnston, Michael	ULS	250	Jones, Ambrose	OTS	58
Johnson, Winant	RCH	94	Johnston, Nathaniel a Black	NYK	141	Jones, Ambrose	RNS	57
Johnson, Winant Junr	RCH	94	Johnston, Ns	ALB	8	Jones, Amos	ALB	75
Johnson, Zephaniah	TIO	260	Johnston, Peter	NYK	120	Jones, Amos	DEL	282
Johnsten, Jane	NYK	70	Johnston, Rachael	NYK	109	Jones, Amos	ESS	310
Johnston, Abel	WSH	212	Johnston, Richard	ORN	338	Jones, Amos	GRN	341
Johnston, Abigal	NYK	70	Johnston, Robert	DUT	64	Jones, Amos	HRK	508
Johnston, Abm	ALB	107	Johnston, Robert	NYK	79	Jones, Amos	OTS	32
Johnston, Agnis	ORN	295	Johnston, Robert	ORN	276	Jones, Amos	SCH	171
Johnston, Amond	NYK	133	Johnston, Roswell	ALB	43	Jones, Ananias	DUT	96
Johnston, Andrew	SRA	53	Johnston, Sarah	NYK	107	Jones, Andrew	ORN	358
Johnston, Archellus	WSH	273	Johnston, Seth	ALB	10	Jones, Anna	NYK	56
Johnston, Barakh	OTS	13	Johnston, Stepehn	ALB	78	Jones, Anthony	NYK	147
Johnston, Benjamin	NYK	129	Johnston, Stephen	ALB	127	Jones, Arthur	NYK	99
Johnston, Benjn	OTS	2	Johnston, Stephen	NYK	126	Jones, Asa	MNT	60
Johnston, Daniel a Black	NYK	116	Johnston, Stephen	WSH	268	Jones, Asael	GRN	342
Johnston, Danl	OTS	13	Johnston, Thias	WSH	188	Jones, Asael	GRN	343
Johnston, David	DUT	102	Johnston, Thomas	ALB	126	Jones, Ashur	WST	120
Johnston, David	NYK	111	Johnston, Thomas	NYK	77	Jones, Ben	RCK	99
Johnston, David	NYK	111	Johnston, Thomas a Black	NYK	122	Jones, Benijah	ALB	3A
Johnston, David	NYK	112	Johnston, Thomas	NYK	138	Jones, Benjamin	ALB	62
Johnston, David a Black	NYK	149	Johnston, Thomas	OTS	9	Jones, Benjamin	CAY	566
Johnston, David	OTS	58	Johnston, Thos	OTS	14	Jones, Benjamin	CHN	746
Johnston, Edward	ALB	13	Johnston, Thomas	SRA	53	Jones, Benjamin	DUT	170
Johnston, Edward	NYK	111	Johnston, Thomas Junr	WSH	268	Jones, Benjamin	NYK	57
Johnston, Elijah	NYK	126	Johnston, Timothy	OTS	17	Jones, Benjamin	OND	218
Johnston, Elijah	WSH	243	Johnston, Timothy	WSH	203	Jones, Benjamin	ONN	135
Johnston, Elijah	WSH	302	Johnston, Timothy	WSH	271	Jones, Benjamin	RNS	69
Johnston, Elizth	ALB	122	Johnston, Willeam	WSH	281	Jones, Benj.	RCK	108
Johnston, Evert	ALB	105	Johnston, Wm	ALB	105	Jones, Benjn	SUF	67
Johnston, George	ALB	133	Johnston, Wm	ALB	137	Jones, Benj:	TIO	221
Johnston, George	NYK	128	Johnston, William	NYK	32	Jones, Benjamin	WSH	285
Johnston, George	OTS	13				Jones, Bornt	RCH	89
						Jones, Briggs	CAY	628
						Jones, Burgoen	SRA	5

Jones, Caleb	ORN 339	Jones, Henry	WSH 296	Jones, John	SUF 70
Jones, Caleb	SCH 139	Jones, Herman	HRK 455	Jones, John	TIO 241
Jones, Caty	RCH 92	Jones, Hewlit	NYK 116	Jones, John	WSH 203
Jones, Charles	GRN 326	Jones, Hezekiah	OND 219	Jones, John	WST 158
Jones, Christopher	HRK 581	Jones, Hollett	SUF 87	Jones, John	WST 160
Jones, Christopher P.	WSH 277	Jones, Horatio	ONT 386	Jones, John Junr	MNT 113
Jones, Comfort	WSH 278	Jones, Hosea	SUF 91	Jones, John Junr	RCK 102
Jones, Cornelius	WST 168	Jones, Hugh	NYK 137	Jones, John Junr	WST 156
Jones, Cornelius	ORN 371	Jones, Hugh	NYK 139	Jones, John P.	WSH 258
Jones, Cornelius	WSH 283	Jones, Hulet	QNS 80	Jones, John S.	NYK 34
Jones, Cornelius Junr	ORN 371	Jones, Increase	WSH 277	Jones, Jonas	RCK 105
Jones, Cyrus	DUT 133	Jones, Isaac	CAY 650	Jones, Jonathn	CHN 924
Jones, Daniel	CLN 159	Jones, Isaac	DUT 25	Jones, Jona	OTS 52
Jones, Daniel	COL 257	Jones, Isaac	DUT 46	Jones, Jonathan	QNS 67
Jones, Daniel	KNG 4	Jones, Isaac	DUT 67	Jones, Jonathan	SUF 71
Jones, Daniel	ONN 152	Jones, Isaac	ESS 307	Jones, Joseph	COL 195
Jones, Danl	RCK 102	Jones, Isaac	MNT 107	Jones, Joseph	DUT 170
Jones, Daniel	SRA 28	Jones, Isaac	MNT 107	Jones, Joseph	MNT 107
Jones, Danl	SUF 67	Jones, Isaac	NYK 25	Jones, Joseph	OND 173
Jones, Daniel	WST 155	Jones, Isaac	NYK 52	Jones, Joseph	ONN 135
Jones, David	CAY 646	Jones, Isaac	NYK 126	Jones, Joseph	ONN 150
Jones, David	OND 213	Jones, Isaac	OND 172	Jones, Joseph	ONT 460
Jones, David	ORN 377	Jones, Isaac	RCK 109	Jones, Joseph	ORN 398
Jones, David	OTS 55	Jones, Isaac	SUF 70	Jones, Joseph	RCK 109
Jones, David Esqr	QNS 79	Jones, Isaac	WST 120	Jones, Joseph	WST 168
Jones, David	SRA 51	Jones, Isaiah	TIO 241	Jones, Joseph Junr	RCK 108
Jones, David	SCH 139	Jones, Israel	HRK 535	Jones, Joshua	NYK 19
Jones, David	TIO 244	Jones, Jacob	ORN 387	Jones, Joshua	OND 184
Jones, Dyer	COL 212	Jones, James	NYK 139	Jones, Joshua	SRA 18
Jones, , Ebenr	ONN 188	Jones, James	ONN 188	Jones, Joshua	SCH 140
Jones, Ebenezar	ONT 334	Jones, James	OTS 10	Jones, Josiah	OTS 10
Jones, Ebenezer	WST 158	Jones, James	RNS 99	Jones, Josiah	WST 151
Jones, Ebeser	GRN 325	Jones, James	SRA 6	Jones, Laban	RNS 69
Jones, Ebunezar	RNS 90	Jones, James	TIO 220	Jones, Levi	DUT 158
Jones, Edward	ALB 88	Jones, James	WST 158	Jones, Levi	SRA 32
Jones, Edward	ONN 131	Jones, James Senr	RNS 108	Jones, Levy	CHN 964
Jones, Edward	RCH 89	Jones, Jared	COL 207	Jones, Lewis	ALB 37
Jones, Edward	RCK 108	Jones, Jemina	NYK 38	Jones, Lewis	ULS 195
Jones, Edward	SUF 107	Jones, Jeremiah	DUT 29	Jones, Lewis	WST 158
Jones, Eleakim	STB 202	Jones, Jeremiah	OTS 21	Jones, Louis	NYK 28
Jones, Eleanor	ALB 8	Jones, Jeremiah	SUF 107	Jones, Luis	WSH 192
Jones, Elias	HRK 537	Jones, Jesse	ESS 310	Jones, Major	STB 205
Jones, Elias	OND 204	Jones, Jesse	SCH 171	Jones, Marcus	ONT 392
Jones, Elias	OTS 48	Jones, Jichard Jr	MNT 36	Jones, Margaret	NYK 19
Jones, Elias C.	COL 249	Jones, Jillet	ALB 73	Jones, Mary	NYK 72
Jones, Elihu	OND 222	Jones, Job	ULS 181	Jones, Mary	SRA 5
Jones, Elijah	NYK 110	Jones, Joel	WSH 281	Jones, Mary	WSH 200
Jones, Elijah	RNS 99	Jones, John	ALB 132	Jones, Mary	OND 184
Jones, Elijah	WSH 216	Jones, John	CAY 574	Jones, Matthew	CAY 574
Jones, Elisabeth	GRN 355	Jones, John	CHN 762	Jones, Moses	COL 207
Jones, Elisha	DUT 54	Jones, John	CHN 782	Jones, Nathan	HRK 509
Jones, Eliza	SUF 107	Jones, John	CHN 934	Jones, Nathan	SRA 57
Jones, Elizabeth	DUT 168	Jones, John	CLN 174	Jones, Nathaniel	ALB 28
Jones, Elnathan	ONT 418	Jones, John	COL 187	Jones, Nathaniel	DUT 166
Jones, Enias	SRA 5	Jones, John	DEL 271	Jones, Nehemiah	DUT 167
Jones, Enoch	TIO 231	Jones, John	DEL 277	Jones, Nehemiah	OND 178
Jones, Ephraim	RNS 54	Jones, John	DUT 33	Jones, Nicholas	ORN 271
Jones, Esra	GRN 344	Jones, John	ESS 296	Jones, Nicholas	QNS 67
Jones, Evan	NYK 141	Jones, John	MNT 112	Jones, Noel	RNS 69
Jones, Ezekiel	ONT 450	Jones, John	MNT 117	Jones, Obadiah	RCH 88
Jones, Ezekiel	SUF 107	Jones, John	NYK 28	Jones, Oliver	WSH 285
Jones, Ezekiel	WSH 282	Jones, John	NYK 39	Jones, Peter	DEL 277
Jones, Ezra	HRK 458	Jones, John	NYK 101	Jones, Peter Junr	MNT 120
Jones, Flint	MNT 119	Jones, John	NYK 125	Jones, Phillip	NYK 116
Jones, Francis	CAY 720	Jones, John	OND 222	Jones, Phillip	WST 168
Jones, Francis	HRK 530	Jones, John	ONN 167	Jones, Platt	WST 120
Jones, Francis	NYK 67	Jones, John	ONT 320	Jones, Rescom	RNS 69
Jones, Garderner	NYK 53	Jones, John	ONT 324	Jones, Reuben	WSH 280
Jones, Garner	ALB 112	Jones, John	ONT 426	Jones, Reuben	WSH 283
Jones, George	WST 152	Jones, John	ONT 476	Jones, Richard	DEL 274
Jones, Gersham	ALB 93	Jones, John	ORN 318	Jones, Richard	HRK 455
Jones, Gilbert	ORN 272	Jones, John	QNS 79	Jones, Richard	MNT 36
Jones, Gilbert	WST 146	Jones, John	QNS 80	Jones, Richard	OND 186
Jones, Griffin	SRA 7	Jones, John	RNS 29	Jones, Richard	ONT 340
Jones, Henry a Black	NYK 96	Jones, John	RCK 101	Jones, Richard	QNS 79
Jones, Henry	ORN 274	Jones, John	RCK 109	Jones, Robert	ALB 94
Jones, Henry	SCH 171	Jones, John	SRA 12	Jones, Robert	OND 213

Name	Loc	No.
Jones, Roger	ALB	75
Jones, Roger	ORN	278
Jones, Roswell	CLN	159
Jones, Rufus	OTS	25
Jones, Russell	CLN	160
Jones, Russell	SCH	140
Jones, Samuel	ALB	11
Jones, Samuel	ALB	84
Jones, Saml	CHN	892
Jones, Samuel	COL	206
Jones, Samuel	DUT	96
Jones, Samuel	ESS	321
Jones, Samuel	MNT	36
Jones, Samuel	MNT	103
Jones, amuel	MNT	107
Jones, Samuel	NYK	67
Jones, Samuel	NYK	139
Jones, Samuel	OND	203
Jones, Samuel	ONN	129
Jones, Samuel	ORN	352
Jones, Saml	OTS	7
Jones, Saml	OTS	48
Jones, Samuel	QNS	78
Jones, Samuel	QNS	79
Jones, Saml	RNS	33
Jones, Samuel	RNS	69
Jones, Samuel	RNS	78
Jones, Samuel	SRA	5
Jones, Samuel	SRA	14
Jones, Samuel	SCH	134
Jones, Samuel	WST	168
Jones, Samuel Junr	NYK	26
Jones, Samuel Junr	ONN	131
Jones, Samel F.	COL	206
Jones, Sarah	DUT	166
Jones, Seth	COL	252
Jones, Seth	DUT	38
Jones, Seth	ONT	412
Jones, Silas	RNS	69
Jones, Silvanus	WST	158
Jones, Simeon	OND	159
Jones, Simeon	ORN	363
Jones, Simon	CHN	746
Jones, Smith	ALB	36
Jones, Smith W.	DUT	25
Jones, Solomon	CHN	804
Jones, Solomon	CHN	868
Jones, Squire	SRA	42
Jones, Stephen	ALB	93
Jones, Stephen	DUT	38
Jones, Stephen	HRK	537
Jones, Stephen	WST	146
Jones, Stephenson	GRN	343
Jones, Sylvanus	ONT	414
Jones, Sylvester	ALB	112
Jones, Talmage	SUF	107
Jones, Thomas	HRK	535
Jones, Thomas	HRK	583
Jones, Thomas a Black	NYK	66
Jones, Thomas	NYK	117
Jones, Thomas	NYK	147
Jones, Thomas	OND	161
Jones, Thomas	RNS	69
Jones, Thomas	RNS	94
Jones, Thomas	SUF	97
Jones, Thomas	ULS	236
Jones, Thomas	ULS	251
Jones, Thomas	WSH	276
Jones, Victor	MNT	76
Jones, Vincent	SUF	67
Jones, Walter	QNS	78
Jones, Willeam	WSH	264
Jones, William	CHN	786
Jones, William	CHN	978
Jones, William	DEL	270
Jones, William	DUT	93
Jones, William	GRN	338
Jones, Wm	MNT	77
Jones, Wm	MNT	87
Jones, William	NYK	58
Jones, William	NYK	77
Jones, William	NYK	89
Jones, William	NYK	130
Jones, William	NYK	149
Jones, William	OND	195
Jones, Wm	OND	213
Jones, William	ONT	340
Jones, William	ONT	356
Jones, William	ORN	395
Jones, William	QNS	79
Jones, William	QNS	79
Jones, Wm	RCK	102
Jones, William	SRA	53
Jones, Wm 2nd	OND	213
Jones, William C.	HRK	527
Jones, William H.	QNS	79
Jones, Zophar	DUT	33
Jones, Zopher	WST	158
Joney see Toney		
Jonson, John	SUF	68
Jonson, Stephen	CLN	166
Jonston, Stephen	NYK	145
Joraleman, Tunis	KNG	8
Jordan, Edward	ULS	246
Jordan, Gilbert	MNT	118
Jordan, James	ONT	352
Jordan, John	ORN	333
Jordan, John	ORN	338
Jordan, John	ORN	393
Jordan, Jonathan	ULS	248
Jordan, Phillip	NYK	126
Jordan, Robert	ORN	298
Jordan, Robert	ULS	247
Jordan, Rufus	ESS	322
Jordan, Stephen	DUT	56
Jordan, William	ORN	379
Jorden, James	WST	161
Jordon, Conrod	NYK	88
Jordon, Conrod	NYK	124
Jordon, Mathew	NYK	142
Jordon, Willm	COL	185
Joseph a Black	NYK	110
Joseph a Black	NYK	121
Joseph	QNS	78
Joseph	QNS	80
Joseph, Abraham	NYK	133
Joseph, John	NYK	87
Joseph, John	NYK	119
Joslin, Abel	OND	172
Joslin, Abijah	OND	176
Joslin, Anna	RNS	50
Joslin, Benjamin	WSH	186
Joslin, Clark	OTS	29
Joslin, Daniel	ALB	73
Joslin, Daniel	OTS	29
Joslin, Eleanor	OTS	29
Joslin, Eleazer	OTS	5
Joslin, Freeborn	OTS	29
Joslin, Hannah	ALB	110
Joslin, Henry	OTS	29
Joslin, Hezekiah	OND	172
Joslin, John	OND	172
Joslin, John	OND	178
Joslin, Potter	WSH	186
Joslin, Reuben	OND	180
Josling, Thomas Senr	OTS	21
Joslyn, Darius	OTS	36
Joslyn, Joshua	OTS	40
Jott, Pierce	CLN	168
Jouneay, Richard	NYK	55
Jourdan, Stephen	OTS	27
Jourdon, John	OTS	4
Journeay, Albert	RCH	95
Journeay, John	RCH	95
Journeay, Nicholas	RCH	95
Journeay, William	RCH	88
Jowls, Jeremiah	RNS	101
Jowls, Thomas	RNS	101
Joy, Albertus	ULS	225
Joy, Charles	RNS	34
Joy, David	ONN	180
Joy, Ebenezer	OND	193
Joy, Gershom	DEL	276
Joy, John	HRK	592
Joy, John	NYK	98
Joy, Levy	COL	248
Joyce see Joice		
Joyce, Charles	DUT	175
Joyce, Charles	ONN	182
Joyce, Jonathan	SCH	133
Ju.ing, Joseph	MNT	87
Judah, Benjamin J.	NYK	25
Judd, Abner	GRN	344
Judd, Alexander	CLN	158
Judd, Alveny	ONN	177
Judd, Daniel	ONN	132
Judd, Daniel C.	ONN	132
Judd, Ebenezer	HRK	538
Judd, Elkanah	TIO	230
Judd, Ethel	HRK	538
Judd, Freeman	SCH	141
Judd, Giles	ONN	177
Judd, Gridley	RNS	111
Judd, Harmon	CHN	858
Judd, Ithea	CHN	900
Judd, Job	TIO	239
Judd, John	TIO	221
Judd, Marvin	SCH	142
Judd, Nathanl	CHN	858
Judd, Ozias	ONN	152
Judd, Randall	DUT	129
Judd, Richard S.	COL	194
Judd, Shelden	CAY	630
Judd, Silas	OND	184
Judd, Stephen	SCH	141
Judd, Supplina	DEL	279
Judd, Thomas	ONT	464
Judd, William	DEL	287
Jude a free wench	ALB	8
Jude a free wench	ALB	48
Judey	QNS	61
Judey Negro	QNS	75
Judey	QNS	76
Judge, Hugh	NYK	63
Judge, Johial	GRN	346
Judgson, Noah	SCH	141
Judgson, Samuel	SCH	141
Judson, Andrew	SRA	20
Judson, Darius F.	MNT	67
Judson, David	SRA	21
Judson, Eben	OND	205
Judson, Eli	RNS	80
Judson, Elihu	MNT	64
Judson, Ephraim	OND	201
Judson, Ephm.	ONN	179
Judson, Ephraim	SRA	20
Judson, Herman	SRA	38
Judson, James	NYK	131
Judson, John B.	DEL	269
Judson, Nathaniel	ALB	137
Judson, Noadiah	OND	174
Judson, Timothy	ALB	115
Judson, William	ALB	115
Judas		
Juel, Chole	MNT	107
Juel, Sely	CHN	902
Juel, William	NYK	93
Juell, Moses	CHN	806
Juell, Ruben	CHN	812
Juett, Banjaman	CHN	916
Juglar, John	NYK	149

Jugle, Jonathan	ONT 448	Kane, Martin	ORN 381	Keech, David	NYK 132
Jugle, Thomas	ONT 448	Kane, Patrick	SRA 35	Keech, David	ULS 238
Jugle, William	ONT 448	Kane, Phillip	DUT 115	Keech, George	NYK 133
Juhel, John	NYK 22	Kane, Powelis	COL 262	Keech, George	OTS 24
Juitt, David	GRN 339	Kane, Priscilla	ORN 367	Keech, Isaac	RNS 95
Julian, Daniel	TIO 257	Kane, Robert S.	ULS 249	Keech, Israel	OTS 25
Juliard, Joseph	CHN 742]	Kane, Thomas	HRK 462	Keech, Job	DUT 38
Jump, Amos	WST 158	Kane, Thomas	RNS 80	Keech, Reuben	RNS 100
Jump, Amos	WST 160	Kane, Warren	ALB 25	Keech, Robert	ULS 238
Jump, James	WST 159	Kane, William	ALB 43	Keech, William	RNS 95
Jump, James	WST 160	Kane, William	HRK 462	Keeck, Thomas	NYK 83
Jump, Reubin	GRN 355	Kane, Wm	OTS 16	Keefer, Baltus	ULS 226
June see Tune		Kane, William A.	ALB 43	Keefer, Beltus	ALB 110
June, Abner	DUT 16	Kane, Wm A.	ALB 148	Keefer, Lawrence	ULS 229
June, Abner	WST 158	Kanuff, John	ALB 124	Keelar, Daniel	GRN 336
June, Abraham	DUT 127	Kap, John C.	NYK 87	Keelar, Helmus	GRN 325
June, Abraham	ORN 390	Kaple, Leanard	MNT 51	Keelar, Hezekiah	GRN 332
June, Abrm	RCK 101	Kard, Elisha	MNT 112	Keelar, James	GRN 356
June, Baxter	RCK 101	Karhoon see Harhoon		Keelar, Thomas	GRN 358
June, Benjamin	COL 180	Karker, Solomon	SCH 152	Keeler see Kuler	
June, Isaac	ALB 60	Karner, Silas	ESS 318	Keeler, Aaron	WST 155
June, Israel	WST 158	Karns, John	NYK 42	Keeler, Aaron Junr	WST 156
June, Joel	ORN 369	Karr, Jacob	WST 168	Keeler, Abner	SRA 50
June, John	DUT 138	Karrie, John	NYK 100	Keeler, Catherine	NYK 109
June, Joshua	GRN 344	Karson, Robert	MNT 89	Keeler, Christopher	COL 228
June, Pathiel	RCK 101	Karus, Roeliff	ORN 379	Keeler, Coleman T.(?)	ONN 170
June, Phebe a mulatto	NYK 41	Kasback, John	MNT 53	Keeler, Daniel	ONN 170
June, Phinehas	ORN 282	Kaslor, Peter	RCK 102	Keeler, David	DUT 55
June, Stephen	NYK 109	Kass, Henry	ALB 69	Keeler, David	SRA 48
June, Zabid	WST 125	Kast, George	HRK 445	Keeler, Ebenezer	DEL 278
June, Zebulon	RCK 101	Kast, Peter	HRK 551	Keeler, Ebenezer	QNS 70
Junk, Wm	GRN 354	Kast, Severinus	HRK 461	Keeler, Elijah	ONN 150
Jupane, Peter a Black	NYK 152	Kator, Gideon	NYK 146	Keeler, Elijah	ONN 170
Jupiter a Black	NYK 112	Kave, Francis	NYK 65	Keeler, Ezra	CAY 566
Jupiter	SUF 86	Kay, William	WSH 250	Keeler, Ezra	OTS 35
Jurden	QNS 83	Kaynes see Haynes		Keeler, Fenias	WST 123
Jurden, James	CHN 914	Kayns, Solomon	MNT 113	Keeler, Gutridge	SRA 44
Jurden, John	SRA 50	Ke_s, John Gen	MNT 48	Keeler, Isaac	SRA 20
Jurdon, John	COL 183	Ke_p, Caleb	ONN 182	Keeler, Jeremiah	ONN 150
Jury, John	ULS 192	Keaga Blackman and		Keeler, Jeremiah	WST 126
Justus, Charles	DUT 60	wife	SRA 14	Keeler, Jeremiah	WST 151
		Kearce, Lazarus	SRA 19	Keeler, Jeremiah	WST 153
K		Kearce, William	SRA 4	Keeler, Jeremiah Junr	WST 153
		Kearnes, Elizabeth	CAY 520	Keeler, Jesse	WST 126
K...ood, John	CAY 546	Kearney, John	NYK 90	Keeler, John P. Junr	COL 240
K_ter, Daniel	MNT 61	Kearney, Margaret	NYK 68	Keeler, Jonas	SRA 30
K_, Jacob	MNT 62	Kearney, Partrick	NYK 69	Keeler, Jonas	WST 126
K_y, Theodore	MNT 84	Kearse, Jacobus	DUT 14	Keeler, Josiah	SRA 28
K_se, John	ONT 442	Kearser, John	DUT 77	Keeler, Lewis	RNS 29
Kaho, John	NYK 152	Keasley, William	SRA 30	Keeler, Lewis	TIO 210
Kaho, Thomas	NYK 152	Keater, Abraham	ULS 196	Keeler, Martin	ONN 177
Kahow, Mary	NYK 39	Keater, Benjamin	ULS 199	Keeler, Nathan	NYK 142
Kaine, James	NYK 31	Keater, Cornelius	ULS 204	Keeler, Nathan	OTS 23
Kaitland, Roswell	ALB 74	Keater, Gideon	DUT 156	Keeler, Nathaniel	SRA 5
Kanada, Henry	MNT 106	Keater, Henry	ULS 198	Keeler, Obadiah	WST 153
Kane, Anna	NYK 82	Keater, Jacob N.	ULS 204	Keeler, Thomas	ULS 189
Kane, Barnabus	HRK 462	Keater, Jacob T.	ULS 207	Keeler, Ureah	WSH 274
Kane, Charles	WSH 301	Keater, James	ULS 199	Keeler, Zachariah	COL 239
Kane, Cornelius	DUT 160	Keater, Johannis Junr	ULS 200	Keeley, Christian	ALB 58
Kane, Daniel	CAY 592	Keater, Johannis F.	ULS 199	Keeley, William	NYK 139
Kane, Dennis	NYK 103	Keater, John	ULS 204	Keeling, Adam	RNS 92
Kane, Elias	NYK 86	Keater, Matthew	ULS 198	Keeling, Catherine	NYK 32
Kane, George	ALB 35	Keater, Peter	ULS 199	Keen, Jacob	ORN 341
Kane, Henry	COL 237	Keater, Peter	ULS 202	Keen, Joseph	ORN 340
Kane, Isaac	DUT 145	Keater, William	ULS 230	Keen, Matthias	ORN 329
Kane, James	NYK 59	Keath, Henry	RNS 42	Keenbergh, David	ORN 295
Kane, James	SCH 155	Keating, John	ORN 317	Keenbergh, George	ULS 253
Kane, James	ULS 250	Keating, Robert	ORN 386	Keenbergh, George	ULS 254
Kane, John	ALB 4	Keator, John	DEL 267	Keenbergh, Matthew	ORN 309
Kane, John	HRK 461	Keator, Joseph	DEL 267	Keenbergh, Matthew	ULS 254
Kane, John	NYK 43	Keator, William	DEL 267	Keener, John	CAY 572
Kane, John	ORN 367	Kebbe, Edward	ONT 336	Keeney, John	COL 246
Kane, John	ULS 204	Kebbe, Joseph	ONT 336	Keeny, George	COL 187
Kane, John O.	COL 228	Kecthum, Jonathan	SRA 52	Keep, Isaac	GRN 325
Kane, John R.	ULS 250	Kedar, David	DUT 50	Keep, Jacob	GRN 325
Kane, Jost	HRK 561	Kedney, Henry	NYK 54	Keep, John	ONN 181
Kane, Matthias	ORN 329	Keech, Abm	RNS 22	Keep, Mathew	SRA 35

Keeper, William	ULS 219	Kelley, John	ALB 94
Keers, Peter	WST 125	Kelley, Jon	OND 213
Kees, Henry	MNT 11	Kelley, Joshua	ALB 113
Kees, Simson	MNT 103	Kelley, Nathan	ALB 114
Keese, John	ALB 28	Kelley, Reuben	WSH 251
Keese, John	CLN 155	Kelley, Richard	WSH 281
Keese, John	NYK 26	Kelley, Robert	NYK 15
Keese, Oliver	CLN 156	Kelley, Samuel	OND 222
Keese, Richard	CLN 155	Kelley, Stephen	ALB 87
Keese, Stephen	CLN 156	Kelley, Sylvenus	ALB 115
Keese, William	CLN 156	Kelley, Tente	OTS 25
Kegwin, Elias	OND 176	Kelley, William	SRA 29
Kegwin, Thomas	OND 177	Kellis, Stephen	QNS 76
Keif, Arthur	NYK 16	Kelloc, Thomas	RCH 92
Keip, Martin	ONN 185	Kellock, Elisha	CHN 866
Keir, Ceasar (Black)	NYK 16	Kellock, Martin	CHN 762
Keir, Henry	WST 168	Kellock, Wm	MNT 103
Keirsted, William	ULS 206	Kellog, ...	MNT 86
Keisler, Frederick	CAY 528	Kellog, ...	MNT 86
Keith, James	HRK 441	Kellog, Aaron	COL 205
Keith, Oliver	OND 188	Kellog, Aaron Junr	COL 209
Keith, Phinehas	OND 208	Kellog, Amasa	COL 184
Keith, William	OND 197	Kellog, Azuba	COL 250
Kelburn, Thomas	MNT 39	Kellog, Benjamin	COL 182
Kelcey see Kelsee, Kill-		Kellog, Benjamin	COL 264
sey & Kilsay		Kellog, Charles	WSH 275
Kelcey, Ebenezer	DUT 11	Kellog, Israel	COL 205
Kelcey, Jonas	ALB 87	Kellog, Jason	WSH 288
Kelcey, Jonas	DUT 60	Kellog, Lovell	OND 193
Kelcey, Peter	HRK 552	Kellog, Pliney	COL 183
Kelcey, Richard	DUT 60	Kellog, Stephen	ONT 426
Kelcey, Simeon	DUT 143	Kellog, Truman	RNS 39
Kelch, Philip	HRK 420	Kellogg, Aaron	CAY 666
Kelcy, Abraham	ORN 383	Kellogg, Aaron	OND 197
Kelcy, Daniel	ULS 262	Kellogg, Amos	OND 202
Kelcy, Eber	OND 219	Kellogg, Asa	SRA 31
Kelcy, John	HRK 569	Kellogg, Belden	CAY 590
Kelcy, Nathaniel	ULS 262	Kellogg, Charles	CAY 676
Kelcy, Resolved	CHN 812	Kellogg, Daniel	CLN 171
Kelcy, William	ORN 355	Kellogg, Daniel	OND 189
Keley see Kelcy		Kellogg, Daniel	SRA 59
Kelder, Coon	RNS 74	Kellogg, Ebenezer	HRK 442
Kelder, Felter Junr	ULS 215	Kellogg, Eleazer	OND 188
Kelder, Godfrey	DEL 282	Kellogg, Elijah	ESS 318
Kelder, Henry J.	COL 265	Kellogg, Elijah	OND 189
Kelder, Joseph	ULS 215	Kellogg, Eliphlet	SRA 13
Kelder, William	ULS 215	Kellogg, Enoch	SRA 42
Kelderhouse, William	COL 245	Kellogg, Ezekiel	OTS 17
Kele, Robert	ESS 309	Kellogg, Ezra	COL 252
Kellak, Soloman	CHN 770	Kellogg, Ezra	SRA 30
Kellam, Ephraim	OND 174	Kellogg, Horace	OND 159
Keller, Andrew	CAY 618	Kellogg, Ichabod	HRK 429
Keller, Andrew	MNT 25	Kellogg, Isaac	ESS 295
Keller, Henry	HRK 450	Kellogg, Isaac	OND 189
Keller, Henry	MNT 26	Kellogg, Isaac	SRA 48
Keller, Henry	MNT 48	Kellogg, Jacob	OND 194
Keller, Henry	MNT 54	Kellogg, Jason	DEL 269
Keller, Jacob	HRK 449	Kellogg, Jesse	ONN 163
Keller, Jacob	MNT 48	Kellogg, Joel	SRA 16
Keller, Jacob	SCH 171	Kellogg, Jonathan	OND 213
Keller, Jacob A.	MNT 25	Kellogg, Joseph	OND 168
Keller, John	DUT 157	Kellogg, Joseph	OND 188
Keller, John	MNT 52	Kellogg, Joseph	OND 213
Keller, John	MNT 92	Kellogg, Joseph	SRA 55
Keller, John Junr	HRK 578	Kellogg, Josiah	ULS 244
Keller, John Junr	MNT 52	Kellogg, Keziah	ESS 319
Keller, John P.	COL 234	Kellogg, Levi	OTS 52
Keller, Michael	MNT 11	Kellogg, Loomis	OND 177
Keller, Robert	MNT 52	Kellogg, Martin	HRK 569
Kellett, Stephen	MNT 68	Kellogg, Martin	SRA 29
Kelley, Adam	ALB 38	Kellogg, Nathan	COL 180
Kelley, Charles	ONN 150	Kellogg, Nathan	DEL 277
Kelley, David	SUF 85	Kellogg, Noah	OND 188
Kelley, Ebenezer	ALB 114	Kellogg, Philip	SRA 26
Kelley, Edmund	ALB 94	Kellogg, Phineas	OND 176
Kelley, Edy	ALB 91B	Kellogg, Ruth	OND 202
Kelley, Freeman	ALB 70	Kellogg, Samuel	DUT 157

Kellogg, Seth	OND 168		
Kellogg, Soloman	CAY 592		
Kellogg, Solomon	OND 177		
Kellogg, Stephen	SRA 59		
Kellogg, Thos	HRK 441		
Kellogg, Timothy	OND 181		
Kellogg, Truman	OND 181		
Kellogg, Webster	OND 181		
Kellogg, Wells	OND 209		
Kellogg, Whiting	OND 188		
Kellogg, William	ESS 318		
Kelloth, Daniel	WSH 231		
Kells, Conradt	MNT 23		
Kells, Elizabeth	COL 197		
Kells, Hendrick	COL 197		
Kells, John	COL 197		
Kells, Peter	COL 197		
Kellum, Ebenezar	SUF 88		
Kellum, Jessee	SUF 88		
Kellum, Jonas	SUF 81		
Kellum, Obediah	SUF 80		
Kellux, John	RNS 53		
Kelly, Abraham	DUT 43		
Kelly, Alexander	ALB 11		
Kelly, Alexander	ORN 335		
Kelly, Amaziah	RNS 113		
Kelly, Ann	OTS 19		
Kelly, Anna	NYK 72		
Kelly, Benjamin	CAY 622		
Kelly, Bryan	NYK 48		
Kelly, Charles	CAY 554		
Kelly, Charles E.	NYK 107		
Kelly, Craig	WST 145		
Kelly, Daniel	CAY 724		
Kelly, Daniel	COL 180		
Kelly, Daniel	ONT 384		
Kelly, David	DUT 178		
Kelly, Dennis	SRA 12		
Kelly, Esic	OTS 42		
Kelly, Francis	NYK 109		
Kelly, George	MNT 6		
Kelly, Jacob	NYK 67		
Kelly, James	CHN 750		
Kelly, James	DEL 279		
Kelly, James	NYK 127		
Kelly, James	NYK 141		
Kelly, James	OTS 56		
Kelly, Jeremiah	DUT 89		
Kelly, John	DUT 90		
Kelly, John	NYK 109		
Kelly, John	NYK 112		
Kelly, John	ORN 382		
Kelly, John	ORN 389		
Kelly, John	RNS 77		
Kelly, John	STB 204		
Kelly, John	TIO 243		
Kelly, John	WSH 293		
Kelly, John Junr	DUT 90		
Kelly, Jonathan	DUT 178		
Kelly, Joseph	ULS 257		
Kelly, Josiah	DUT 90		
Kelly, Judah	DUT 90		
Kelly, Mary	NYK 38		
Kelly, Mary	NYK 118		
Kelly, Merchant	DUT 90		
Kelly, Michail	ESS 295		
Kelly, Neomy	SUF 67		
Kelly, Oliver	ORN 386		
Kelly, Partrick	NYK 19		
Kelly, Partrick	NYK 108		
Kelly, Patrick	ONT 326		
Kelly, Reuben	DUT 178		
Kelly, Richard	WST 120		
Kelly, Robbins	GRN 352		
Kelly, Robert	DEL 284		
Kelly, Robert	DUT 98		
Kelly, Robert	NYK 37		

Kelly, Roger	OTS 43	Kemble, David	MNT 96	Kennedy, Robert	SRA 6
Kelly, Samuel	GRN 352	Kemble, Henry	NYK 69	Ken..dy, Samuel	MNT 87
Kelly, Samuel	WST 145	Kemble, Isaac	SCH 171	Kennedy, Thomas	DUT 161
Kelly, Samuel W.	DUT 54	Kemble, John	NYK 114	Kennedy, Thomas	MNT 88
Kelly, Seth	DUT 92	Kemble, Levi	DEL 274	Kennedy, Thomas H.	NYK 86
Kelly, Shubil	RNS 64	Kemble, Nathan	MNT 96	Kennedy, Wm	OTS 36
Kelly, Thomas	DEL 272	Kemble, Robert T.	NYK 152	Kennedy, William	SCH 133
Kelly, Thomas	HRK 480	Kemmens, Isabella	NYK 129	Kenney, Asa	OTS 18
Kelly, Thomas	NYK 98	Kemmins, Richard	NYK 79	Kenney, Benjamin	CHN 790
Kelly, Thomas	NYK 100	Kemp, Asa	RNS 24	Kenney, Danl	OTS 10
Kelly, Thomas	OND 163	Kemp, John	NYK 57	Kenney, Ethel	ONN 173
Kelly, Timothy	SCH 171	Kemp, John	STB 197	Kenney, Heny	CHN 988
Kelly, William	ALB 17	Kempe, Edward	RCK 102	Kenney, Jacob	OTS 42
Kelly, William	CAY 684	Kempe, Thos	RCK 101	Kenney, Jeremi	SUF 68
Kelly, William	NYK 101	Kempe, Wm	RCK 102	Kenney, Levy	STB 200
Kelly, William	ONT 324	Kemper, Daniel	NYK 25	Kenney, Patrick	RCK 103
Kelly, William	ORN 274	Kemper, John	COL 251	Kennicitt, John	SRA 34
Kelly, William	ORN 382	Kemple, John	COL 190	Kennicut see Kinnicut &
Kelly, Wing	DUT 53	Kempton, Martha	NYK 63	Kinnikut
Kelly, Zebudee	DEL 273	Kenada, Samuel	MNT 76	Kennicut, Elijah	DUT 86
Kelly, Zepheniah	ORN 382	Kenault, Nicholas	NYK 48	Kennicut, Luther	DUT 87
Kelmaster, Nathaniel	NYK 91	Kinby, Jacob	QNS 80	Kennion, Benjamin	CHN 774
Kelog, Seth	RNS 27	Kendall, Asa	ONN 129	Ke[nnion?], Thomas	CHN 832
Kelogg, Josiah	ONT 408	Kendall, Charles	CAY 658	Kenny, Amos	ONN 176
Kelsay, Benedick	WSH 237	Kendall, John	HRK 529	Kenny, Barnabas	CHN 792
Kelsay, Daniel	WSH 237	Kendig, Martin	ONT 510	Kenny, Cyrus	ONN 166
Kelsee, Samuel	GRN 335	Kendig, Martin Jun	CAY 518	Kenny, Denneson	WSH 303
Kelsey, Abner	TIO 261	Kendleman, David	MNT 68	Kenny, Didimus	CHN 784
Kelsey, Charles	OND 220	Kendrick, John	DUT 110	Kenny, Elias	CHN 790
Kelsey, Daniel	SUF 83	Kendrick, John	SRA 40	Kenny, Elijah	ONN 175
Kelsey, David	CAY 616	Kendrick, Zibeth	ORN 391	Kenny, Elisha	COL 204
Kelsey, Ebenezer	OND 191	Kendrick, John	MNT 93	Kenny, Ezra	ONN 173
Kelsey, Eben	SUF 82	Kene, Joseph	CLN 154	Kenny, James	NYK 103
Kelsey, Elijah	OND 170	Keneda, Robert	CHN 830	Kenny, Jesse	ONN 178
Kelsey, Elijah	ONT 470	Kenedy, Alexander	WSH 246	Kenny, John	NYK 78
Kelsey, Enoch	SCH 155	Kener, Joseph	ALB 107	Kenny, John	WSH 198
Kelsey, Gideon	OND 186	Kennada, Morris	QNS 63	Kenny, Prentice	ONN 173
Kelsey, James	OTS 31	Kennady, Josiah	OTS 36	Kenny, Rufus	COL 204
Kelsey, John	SUF 81	Kennals, Jonas	NYK 123	Kenny, Russell	ONN 176
Kelsey, Jonathan	TIO 220	Kennan, Peter	NYK 34	Kenny, Selah	SUF 67
Kelsey, Nathan	OND 173	Kennard, Albert	NYK 113	Kenny, Silas	ONN 137
Kelsey, Nathan	ONN 162	Kennard, Jane a		Kenny, Simon	ONN 176
Kelsey, Nathaniel Junr	SUF 85	Black	NYK 105	Kenny, Simon Jur	ONN 176
Kelsey, Nathaniel Senr	SUF 85	Kenne, Daniel	OTS 22	Kenny, Stephen	CHN 790
Kelsey, Pardon	OND 186	Kenne, Jona	OTS 55	Kenny, Thomas	ONN 178
Kelsey, Platt	SUF 88	Kenne, Roger	OTS 22	Kenny, Zacharias	ONN 166
Kelsey, Roswell	OND 189	Kenne, Roger Junr	OTS 22	Kennyon, Job	MNT 90
Kelsey, Samuel	CAY 612	Kenne, Rosel	OTS 25	Kenshamer, Peter	DUT 29
Kelsey, Samuel	CHN 802	Kennecutt, Levi	SRA 17	Kent, Abner	OND 195
Kelsey, Samuel	WSH 224	Kenneday, Peter Jay	NYK 72	Kent, Amos	OND 209
Kelsey, Sary	NYK 65	Kennedy, Ama	NYK 93	Kent, Asa	OND 195
Kelsey, Solomon	OTS 38	Kennedy, Bartholemew	NYK 88	Kent, Bartholemew	MNT 114
Kelsey, Stephen	CHN 802	Kennedy, Charles	NYK 75	Kent, Bella	ALB 20
Kelsey, Stephen	SUF 87	Kennedy, George	SRA 19	Kent, Carol	OND 163
Kelsey, Stephen	SUF 88	Kennedy, Gideon	DUT 44	Kent, Eli	OND 213
Kelsey, Thomas	RNS 10	Kennedy, Hugh	RNS 95	Kent, Elijah	ONT 318
Kelsey, Timothy	WSH 196	Kennedy, Hugh	SRA 5	Kent, Honor	NYK 74
Kelsey, Zina	HRK 583	Kennedy, Jacob	CHN 846	Kent, I...c	MNT 50
Kelso, David	NYK 119	Kennedy, James	COL 253	Kent, Jacob	CLN 161
Kelso, Henry	NYK 41	Kennedy, Ja.es	MNT 88	Kent, Jacob	ULS 189
Kelso, John	ORN 291	Kennedy, James	OTS 36	Kent, James	ALB 147
Kelso, John	OTS 44	Kennedy, James	SCH 155	Kent, James	NYK 89
Kelso, Robert	NYK 75	Kennedy, James Junr	MNT 88	Kent, Jeremiah	NYK 106
Kelso, Samuel	NYK 99	Kennedy, James Junr	OTS 36	Kent, John	ALB 31
Kelso, Thomas	NYK 42	Kennedy, John	CAY 524	Kent, John	CLN 165
Kelso, Thomas	ORN 278	Kennedy, John	CAY 552	Kent, John a mulatto	NYK 49
Keltch, John	CHN 948	Kennedy, John	CHN 862	Kent, John	OND 213
Keltch, Nichs(?)	OTS 27	Kennedy, John	HRK 486	Kent, John	ONT 414
Kelter, Felter Senr	ULS 215	Kennedy, John	HRK 552	Kent, John	OTS 52
Kelton, John	OTS 11	Kennedy, John	NYK 33	Kent, Joseph	ORN 303
Kelton, Robert	ONT 358	Kennedy, John	ORN 365	Kent, Joseph M.	HRK 567
Kelts, Conrod	MNT 17	Kennedy, Neil	WSH 247	Kent, Moss	OTS 19
Kelts, Nicholas	HRK 459	Kennedy, Pat	MNT 56	Kent, Noah	OND 213
Kemball, Asa	CHN 788	Kennedy, Patrick	MNT 13	Kent, Oliver	ALB 31
Kemberly, Gedeon	NYK 78	Kennedy, Robert	NYK 34	Kent, Samuel	CHN 766
Kemble see Remble		Kennedy, Robert	NYK 81	Kent, Samuel	HRK 567
Kemble, Daniel	MNT 96	Kennedy, Robert	OTS 56	Kent, Simeon	CAY 586

Kent, Simeon	TIO 261	Ketcham, Edward	ORN 370	Ketchum, Joel	SRA	5
Kent, Thomas	ORN 275	Ketcham, Elijah	DUT 90	Ketchum, Joel	SRA	45
Kent, Warren	OND 195	Ketcham, Elisabeth	WST 156	Ketchum, Joseph	DEL	272
Kent, Warren	OND 213	Ketcham, Elizabeth	ORN 397	Ketchum, Joseph	SUF	93
Kenter, Anna	ALB 13	Ketcham, Epenetus	ONT 344	Ketchum, Joshua	ONT	358
Kenter, John	ALB 5	Ketcham, Ezekiel	WST 142	Ketchum, Mary	QNS	74
Kentner, John	CLN 166	Ketcham, Ezra	CHN 982	Ketchum, Matthew	OND	186
Kenyan, Enoch	TIO 262	Ketcham, Horace	ORN 349	Ketchum, Matthew	SRA	53
Kenyon see Henyon		Ketcham, Isaac	DUT 14	Ketchum, Nathan	SRA	58
Kenyon, Amasa	RNS 19	Ketcham, Isaac	DUT 56	Ketchum, Nathaniel	ESS	320
Kenyon, Arnold	COL 225	Ketcham, Isaac	DUT 129	Ketchum, Nathaniel	SUF	84
Kenyon, Benjamin	RNS 31	Ketcham, Jacob	SUF 84	Ketchum, Nehemeah	SUF	84
Kenyon, Benjamin	STB 205	Ketcham, James	DUT 43	Ketchum, Oliver	SUF	66
Kenyon, Benjamin Junr	RNS 31	Ketcham, James	ORN 312	Ketchum, Parah	NYK	136
Kenyon, Comford	STB 206	Ketcham, Jedediah	ORN 286	Ketchum, Richd	SUF	65
Kenyon, Gardner	OND 213	Ketcham, Jessee	SUF 80	Ketchum, Samuel	SRA	61
Kenyon, Ira	OTS 33	Ketcham, John	DUT 26	Ketchum, Selah	SUF	84
Kenyon, Job	RNS 31	Ketcham, John	ORN 331	Ketchum, Seth	WSH	243
Kenyon, Lord	SCH 155	Ketcham, John	ORN 335	Ketchum, Stephen	CLN	156
Kenyon, Remington	OTS 33	Ketcham, John	ORN 395	Ketchum, Stephen	SRA	11
Kenyon, Remington	WSH 270	Ketcham, John	SUF 87	Ketchum, Thaddeus	HRK	457
Kenyon, Richd	COL 186	Ketcham, John S.	ORN 328	Ketchum, Thomas	SUF	80
Kenyon, Robert	MNT 118	Ketcham, Jonas	CHN 976	Ketchum, Widow	SRA	41
Kenyon, Thos	RNS 101	Ketcham, Joseph	DUT 81	Ketchum, Youngs	HRK	569
Kenyon, Thomas	SCH 155	Ketcham, Joseph	ORN 312	Ketchum, Zebulon	SUF	80
Kenyon, William	NYK 44	Ketcham, Joseph	ORN 397	Ketchum, Zopher	SUF	79
Ker, George	ONT 340	Ketcham, Joseph	TIO 213	Keteras, John	MNT	98
Ker, John	OTS 33	Ketcham, Joshua	DUT 8	Keth, Ebenezer	CHN	910
Ker, Joseph	NYK 151	Ketcham, Joshua	DUT 26	Keth, James	OTS	35
Ker, Nathan	ORN 360	Ketcham, Joshua	ONT 402	Keth, Lewis	CHN	910
Ker, Samuel	ONT 366	Ketcham, Losee	DUT 170	Keth, Luther	OTS	35
Kerker, John	SCH 150	Ketcham, Mary	DUT 59	Ketham, Nathaniel	CHN	750
Kerley, William A.	QNS 72	Ketcham, Nathaniel	ORN 376	Ketteltas, Gerrit	NYK	17
Kermit, Henry	NYK 26	Ketcham, Peleg	KNG 8	Ketteltas, Phillip	DUT	174
Kern, John	MNT 15	Ketcham, Philip	SUF 80	Ketter, Jacob	CHN	940
Kernaghan, Alexander	ORN 281	Ketcham, Reuben	DUT 7	Ketter, John	CHN	940
Kernaghan, Charles	ORN 289	Ketcham, Ruben	SUF 80	Ketter, Nicholas	CHN	940
Kernaghan, James	ORN 289	Ketcham, Saml	CHN 930	Ketterer, Jacob	NYK	121
Kernaghan, William	ORN 305	Ketcham, Samuel	ORN 377	Ketterley, John	MNT	74
Kerner, Barbara	NYK 110	Ketcham, Samuel	ORN 397	Kettle, Edward	OTS	48
Kerney, Samuel	CAY 550	Ketcham, Solomon	NYK 46	Kettle, Frederick	DEL	273
Kerr, Alexander	ORN 311	Ketcham, Stephen	CHN 740	Kettle, John	COL	260
Kerr, Elijah	ONT 470	Ketcham, Stephen	RNS 45	Kettle, [L?]imon	WSH	243
Kerr, Henry	CAY 630	Ketcham, Thomas	SUF 80	Kettle, Nicholas	COL	262
Kerr, James	CAY 648	Ketcham, Timothy	DUT 37	Kettles, David	OTS	44
Kerr, Job	CAY 568	Ketcham, Timothy	WST 140	Kettletas, Sarah	QNS	67
Kerr, John	ORN 292	Ketcham, Titus	ULS 240	Kettletas, Stephen	RCH	90
Kerr, John	ORN 345	Ketcham, William	NYK 97	Kettletas, William	NYK	85
Kerr, Joseph	CAY 532	Ketcham, Zephiniah	SUF 84	Kettletas, William N.	NYK	34
Kerr, Robert	ORN 367	Ketcham, Zopher	ORN 349	Keuen, Robert	NYK	72
Kerr, William	OND 214	Ketchum, Abiel N.	CLN 158	Keune, Roger	MNT	111
Kerr, William	ORN 326	Ketchum, Abijah	SUF 93	Kevan, Andrew	NYK	45
Kersey, James	RNS 58	Ketchum, Amos	SRA 48	Kever, Hendrick	COL	238
Kersey, Margaret	NYK 16	Ketchum, Beather	WSH 243	Kewan, Moses	NYK	139
Kersey, Wm	STB 199	Ketchum, Benjamin	SUF 84	Key, Thomas a Black	NYK	49
Kershow, Jacob	KNG 7	Ketchum, Caleb	SUF 83	Keyes see Kyes		
Keslor, Paul	RCK 102	Ketchum, Daniel	SRA 5	Keyes, David	OTS	45
Keslor, Peter	RCK 99	Ketchum, Danl	SUF 83	Keyes, Francis	ONT	480
Keslor, Rachel	RCK 110	Ketchum, David	SUF 79	Keyes, Samuel	OTS	24
Kessler, Adam	MNT 33	Ketchum, David	SUF 84	Keyes, Sarah	DUT	128
Kessler, Joseph	MNT 19	Ketchum, David	SUF 93	Keyes, Seplin	OTS	45
Kessler, Thomas	MNT 50	Ketchum, Elizabeth	SUF 65	Keyes, Stephen	OND	165
Kesslman, W	MNT 64	Ketchum, Elizabeth	SUF 65	Keyes, Thadeus	ONT	478
Kestand, Henry	MNT 107	Ketchum, Ephraim	OTS 45	Keyhoon, Reynolds	MNT	122
Ketcham see Khetcham		Ketchum, Ezekiel	SUF 83	Keyler, Frederic	NYK	98
Ketcham, A. Hawkins	ORN 325	Ketchum, Ezra	KNG 8	Keylor, Joseph	ONN	177
Ketcham, Abijah	RNS 45	Ketchum, George	CLN 167	Keyne, Samuel	ONN	182
Ketcham, Azariah	ORN 376	Ketchum, Hezekiah	SRA 5	Keyne, Zebulon	ONN	182
Ketcham, Benjamin	ORN 396	Ketchum, Hoel	TIO 239	Keys, David	CHN	760
Ketcham, Carll	SUF 82	Ketchum, Hubbard	SUF 84	Keys, Faderick	SRA	50
Ketcham, Charity	DUT 17	Ketchum, Isaac	SRA 58	Keys, Johnathan	GRN	328
Ketcham, Conkline	SUF 87	Ketchum, Isaac	SUF 66	Keys, Moses	CHN	760
Ketcham, Daniel	DUT 176	Ketchum, Israel	SUF 80	Keyse, Elihu	OTS	48
Ketcham, Daniel	SUF 80	Ketchum, Israel	SUF 87	Keyse, Paul	OTS	58
Ketcham, Daniel	WSH 278	Ketchum, James	TIO 202	Keyse, Saml	OTS	47
Ketcham, Daniel Junr	DUT 176	Ketchum, Jeremiah	HRK 457	Keysen, Jacob	NYK	108
Ketcham, David	QNS 80	Ketchum, Jesse	CLN 167	Keyser	NYK	96

Name	Code	No.
King, Earl	RNS	106
King, Ebenezer	WSH	268
King, Elias	NYK	150
King, Elisha	ORN	275
King, Elisha W.	NYK	76
King, Ephriam	SUF	105
King, Esaw	WST	163
King, Francis	CAY	574
King, Frederick	SUF	77
King, George	CHN	790
King, George	CHN	794
King, George	NYK	95
King, George	SUF	66
King, Gideon	ONT	410
King, Gilbert	ORN	388
King, Hannah	NYK	67
King, Hannah	SUF	77
King, Hawkins	ORN	274
King, Heman	DUT	177
King, Henry	DUT	154
King, Henry	MNT	83
King, Henry	NYK	59
King, Henry	WST	163
King, Hezekiah	WSH	200
King, Isaac	CHN	908
King, Israel	SRA	52
King, Jacob	NYK	58
King, Jacob	NYK	71
King, James	HRK	552
King, James	NYK	60
King, James	RNS	69
King, James	WST	168
King, Jason	SUF	77
King, Jehiel	COL	209
King, Jehiel	COL	215
King, Jepther	OND	219
King, Jeremeah	WSH	274
King, Jeremiah	SUF	77
King, Jeremiah	SUF	105
King, Jeremiah	SUF	109
King, Joab	SRA	35
King, Joel	SUF	77
King, John	CAY	598
King, John	CAY	726
King, John	CHN	790
King, John	COL	206
King, John	COL	251
King, John	HRK	553
King, John a Black	NYK	29
King, John	NYK	34
King, John	NYK	69
King, John	NYK	85
King, John	NYK	87
King, John	ONN	160
King, John	ONT	398
King, John	ORN	299
King, John	ORN	314
King, John	ORN	378
King, John	ORN	389
King, John	RCK	101
King, John	SRA	26
King, John	SRA	46
King, John	SRA	53
King, John	SUF	77
King, John	SUF	105
King, John	SUF	109
King, John	WSH	274
King, John Junr	CAY	598
King, Jonah	COL	215
King, Jonathan	HRK	526
King, Jonathan	OND	188
King, Jonathan	OND	192
King, Jonathan	SRA	46
King, Jonathan	SUF	70
King, Joseph	CLN	169
King, Joseph	NYK	62
King, Joseph	NYK	65
King, Joseph	ONT	398
King, Joseph	ORN	350
King, Joseph	ORN	378
King, Joseph	SRA	35
King, Joshua	WSH	268
King, Josiah	RNS	47
King, Jotham	OND	183
King, Keneth	NYK	67
King, Lemuel	TIO	210
King, Ludwick	SCH	171
King, Luther	SUF	72
King, Lydia	NYK	75
King, Martha	NYK	29
King, Martin	ORN	318
King, Martin	ULS	186
King, Mary	NYK	104
King, Mary	NYK	110
King, Mathew	NYK	67
King, Mehitable	SUF	72
King, Merrick	CAY	568
King, Moses	COL	206
King, Nancy	NYK	72
King, Nancy	NYK	103
King, Nathan	NYK	87
King, Nathan	SCH	155
King, Nathaniel	CAY	552
King, Nathl Jun	SUF	77
King, Nathl Sen	SUF	77
King, Nathl D.	ALB	25
King, Nehemiah	RNS	44
King, Newton a Black	NYK	54
King, Obadiah	ORN	283
King, Obediah	CHN	902
King, Obediah	GRN	352
King, Orange	ONN	138
King, Paul	ONN	138
King, Peter	NYK	67
King, Peter	NYK	88
King, Peter	ORN	378
King, Pheneas	SUF	105
King, Philip	CAY	700
King, Philip	OND	213
King, Rachel	SUF	109
King, Reuben	ALB	84
King, Reuben	CAY	552
King, Reuben	COL	206
King, Reuben	OND	218
King, Reuben	RNS	81
King, Richard	NYK	109
King, Robert	SRA	9
King, Robert	SRA	55
King, Roger	ALB	42
King, Rufus	SUF	77
King, Samuel	CAY	544
King, Saml	RNS	23
King, Samuel	ULS	189
King, Samuel Junr	ULS	189
King, Sarah	NYK	82
King, Seth	RNS	108
King, Seth	WSH	267
King, Seymore	WSH	192
King, Simeon	OND	210
King, Simon	ONT	318
King, Solomon	WSH	187
King, Solomon	WSH	217
King, Stephen	CAY	642
King, Stephen	ORN	274
King, Stephen	ORN	292
King, Stephen	RNS	66
King, Stephen	SRA	53
King, Sybele	SUF	99
King, Sylvanus	HRK	541
King, Tertullus	CAY	552
King, Thomas	CHN	910
King, Thomas	COL	196
King, Thomas	ONT	318
King, Thos	RCK	99
King, Thomas	ULS	189
King, Thurstin	CHN	852
King, Titus	OND	179
King, William	ALB	84
King, William	HRK	425
King, William	NYK	16
King, William	NYK	64
King, William	NYK	79
King, William	OND	218
King, William	ONT	398
King, William	OTS	26
King, William	SRA	5
King, William	SRA	52
King, Wm	SUF	74
King, William	SUF	106
King, William	WSH	187
King, William the 3d	SRA	52
King, Zebulin	SUF	76
Kingly, Thomas	SCH	148
Kingman, John	ONN	188
Kingman, John	ONT	354
Kingsbearry, Joseah	CHN	908
Kingsbeaury, Jonathan	CHN	812
Kingsbeaury, Lemuel	CHN	934
Kingsbry, Elijah	OND	219
Kingsbury, Ar[euls?]	OND	219
Kingsbury, Daniel	OND	166
Kingsbury, Elias	OND	219
Kingsbury, Elijah	OND	188
Kingsbury, Thomas	OND	224
Kingsland, Aaron	NYK	116
Kingsland, Anna	NYK	55
Kingsland, Cornelius	NYK	65
Kingsland, Cornelius	ORN	392
Kingsland, Daniel	NYK	116
Kingsland, John	NYK	60
Kingsland, Josiah	NYK	129
Kingsland, Phillip	NYK	149
Kingsland, Richard	NYK	31
Kingsley, Bela	ONN	158
Kingsley, Daniel	WSH	276
Kingsley, Isaiah	COL	205
Kingsley, James	WSH	304
Kingsley, Jeremiah	WSH	305
Kingsley, John	WSH	283
Kingsley, John	WSH	304
Kingsley, Jonathan	WSH	276
Kingsley, Nathan	WSH	283
Kingsley, Nathan	WSH	304
Kingsley, Peleg	WSH	286
Kingsley, Philip	SCH	149
Kingsley, Simion	ONN	176
Kingsley, Sylvanus	WSH	221
Kingsley, Thaddeus	WSH	266
Kingsley, Thomas	WSH	304
Kingsley, Vine	TIO	244
Kingsley, Zephaniah	WSH	305
Kingsly, Nathon	SRA	52
Kingston, James	SUF	71
Kingston, John	NYK	47
Kingston, John	NYK	142
Kingston, Thomas	RCH	88
Kingston, William	RCH	87
Kingwood, Thomas	NYK	39
Kinholt, Charles	ALB	68
Kin on, Benjamin	WSH	252
Kinkim, Thomas	RNS	43
Kinne, Amos	HRK	523
Kinne, Coggeswell	ULS	187
Kinne, Ebenezer	DUT	140
Kinne, Ebenezer Junr	DUT	141
Kinne, Nathan	ULS	186
Kinne, Roswell	DUT	132
Kinne, Theodore	ONN	143
Kinne, Thomas	DUT	137
Kinnear, Anthony	WSH	281
Kinnear, Susannah	ALB	141

Kinnecut, Edwd	ALB 33	Kip, Thomas (F.?)	NYK 72	Kircum, Thomas	DUT 83
Kinner, Ann	ORN 363	Kipp, Aaron	DUT 166	Kirk, George	NYK 37
Kinner, Asa	ORN 381	Kipp, Abraham	DUT 35	Kirk, George	WSH 289
Kinner, John	CAY 572	Kipp, Abraham	DUT 114	Kirk, Gerrit	ALB 126
Kinner, John	ORN 363	Kipp, Abraham	DUT 122	Kirk, Jesse	DUT 36
Kinner, John Junr	ORN 363	Kipp, Abm	RNS 13	Kirk, John	ALB 149
Kinner, Nathaniel	ORN 361	Kipp, Abraham A.	DUT 161	Kirk, John	NYK 121
Kinner, William	ORN 364	Kipp, Abraham I.	DUT 160	Kirk, John	NYK 148
Kinney, Anson	OTS 42	Kipp, Abraham R.	DUT 161	Kirk, John	QNS 81
Kinney, Bernard	ALB 31	Kipp, Andrew	DUT 163	Kirk, Nancy	NYK 19
Kinney, Charles	ORN 370	Kipp, Barney	CAY 682	Kirk, Richard	QNS 70
Kinney, David	OTS 18	Kipp, Benjamin	DUT 155	Kirk, Thomas	KNG 8
Kinney, Elijah	CAY 542	Kipp, Benjamin	DUT 161	Kirk, Thomas	NYK 108
Kinney, Elijah Jun.	CAY 536	Kipp, Benjamin	WST 131	Kirk, William	ORN 331
Kinney, Ephraim	CAY 538	Kipp, Benoni	DUT 115	Kirkaldie, David	NYK 50
Kinney, Henry	RNS 4	Kipp, Caleb	WST 168	Kirkam, John	WSH 241
Kinney, James	OND 202	Kipp, Catharine	DUT 161	Kirkby, Miles	NYK 30
Kinney, Joel	ONT 330	Kipp, Catharine	ULS 227	Kirkcum, Seth	DUT 81
Kinney, John	CAY 638	Kipp, Francis	DUT 61	Kirker, David	ALB 54
Kinney, John	CAY 666	Kipp, Garret	DUT 161	Kirker, Henderick	ALB 53
Kinney, Joseph	ONT 368	Kipp, Gilbert	WST 131	Kirker, Henry	ALB 54
Kinney, Miss(?)	GRN 334	Kipp, Hannah	DUT 68	Kirker, Jacob	ALB 53
Kinney, Peabody	ONT 330	Kipp, Isaac	ALB 88	Kirker, John	ALB 53
Kinney, Pearly	CAY 646	Kipp, Isaac & John	DUT 155	Kirkim, Adonijah	WSH 259
Kinney, Peter	ULS 235	Kipp, Isaac	DUT 162	Kirkland, Henry	OND 208
Kinney, William	OND 165	Kipp, Isaac	WST 168	Kirkland, Joseph	OND 176
Kinney, William	ORN 324	Kipp, Isaac A.	NYK 18	Kirkland, Samuel	OND 202
Kinney, Wm	OTS 18	Kipp, Isaac L.	NYK 21	Kirkland, William	ALB 124
Kinnikut, Edward	RNS 40	Kipp, Jacob	WSH 213	Kirkner, George	ALB 99
Kinny, Dedymus	CHN 774	Kipp, Jacob A.	DUT 65	Kirkner, Nicholas	ALB 99
Kinny, Joseph	NYK 25	Kipp, Jacob J.	DUT 155	Kirkpatrick, James	NYK 119
Kinny, Solomon	CHN 760	Kipp, Jacob J.	DUT 162	Kirkpatrick, John	ORN 274
Kinsberry, Thomas	NYK 89	Kipp, Jacobus	DUT 160	Kirkpatrick, Samuel	ULS 190
Kinsey, Jean	NYK 19	Kipp, James	WST 132	Kirkum, James	ONN 157
Kinsey, John	NYK 86	Kipp, Jeremiah	DUT 160	Kirkum, Sameel	CHN 902
Kinsey, Zebina	ORN 393	Kipp, John	CAY 518	Kirns, Thomas	NYK 109
Kinsharm, Willm	SCH 171	Kipp, John	CAY 524	Kirpatrick, Alexander	NYK 31
Kinshart, Jost	SCH 171	Kipp, John	COL 224	Kirpatrick, Jane	NYK 34
Kinslea, Thomas	SCH 146	Kipp, John & Isaac	DUT 155	Kirsmire, George	NYK 111
Kinsley, Apollos	NYK 140	Kipp, John	RNS 44	Kirtland, Alexr	ALB 104
Kinsley, Jedediah	HRK 420	Kipp, John	ULS 192	Kirtland, Roger	HRK 548
Kinsley, Joseph	ALB 4	Kipp, John	WST 128	Kirtland, William	ALB 62
Kinsley, Nathan	WSH 235	Kipp, John	WST 132	Kirtland, William	ALB 104
Kinsley, William	SRA 12	Kipp, John Junr	COL 225	Kise, Purley	OND 220
Kintch, David	WSH 186	Kipp, John A.	DUT 162	Kisler, George	ULS 182
Kintch, David	WSH 189	Kipp, John I.	DUT 153	Kisler, Teunis	ULS 256
Kintch, John	WSH 186	Kipp, John I.	DUT 161	Kissam, Benjamin	QNS 72
Kintchen, William	NYK 18	Kipp, Martin	DUT 160	Kissam, Charles	QNS 70
Kinvill, Joseph	NYK 123	Kipp, Mary	WST 132	Kissam, Daniel	NYK 122
Kinyan, Mumferd	GRN 349	Kipp, Peter	DUT 61	Kissam, Daniel	QNS 65
Kinyon, Abial	OND 208	Kipp, Peter	DUT 100	Kissam, Daniel	QNS 69
Kinyon, David	TIO 243	Kipp, Peter	DUT 156	Kissam, Daniel W.	QNS 72
Kinyon, Peleg	HRK 522	Kipp, Peter	NYK 127	Kissam, Daniel W.	SUF 85
Kinyon, Peter	DUT 68	Kipp, Peter	RNS 12	Kissam, Hewlet	QNS 64
Kinyon, Peter	DUT 91	Kipp, Peter I.	DUT 164	Kissam, John	QNS 71
Kinyon, Samuel	ULS 183	Kipp, Teunis	RNS 35	Kissam, Joseph	QNS 72
Kinyon, Sheffield	HRK 523	Kipp, Thomas	DUT 162	Kissam, Tredwell	QNS 65
Kinyon, Robert	WSH 248	Kippard, Wm	GRN 347	Kissam, Wm Negro	QNS 71
Kip, Abraham	NYK 24	Kippen, Mary	NYK 53	Kissan, Gill Negro	QNS 63
Kip, Anna	NYK 47	Kipple see Ripple		Kissane, John	NYK 122
Kip, Francis	OND 164	Kirby see Curbey		Kisselbrack, Abm	COL 224
Kip, Garret	NYK 85	Kirby, Daniel	QNS 83	Kisslebrack, Gerret	COL 224
Kip, Isaac	NYK 91	Kirby, George	DUT 51	Kissom, Benjamin	NYK 51
Kip, Isaac Junior	NYK 89	Kirby, John	ESS 295	Kisterd, Mrss	GRN 329
Kip, James	NYK 71	Kirby, Joseph	QNS 83	Kitcham, John & Wm
Kip, James	OND 213	Kirby, Reuben	CHN 756	Leverage	QNS 61
Kip, James H.	NYK 51	Kirby, Rosanna	QNS 83	Kitchell, Demas	CAY 700
Kip, James S.	OND 161	Kirby, Stephen	WST 116	Kitchell, Isaac	NYK 89
Kip, Jane	NYK 64	Kirby, Thomas	COL 194	Kitchell, James L.	ORN 388
Kip, Jedith	NYK 44	Kirby, Thomas	RCH 89	Kitchell, Josiah	ORN 356
Kip, John	NYK 39	Kirby, Willets	QNS 80	Kitchell, Lewis	CAY 700
Kip, Leonard	NYK 60	Kirby, William	NYK 25	Kitchem, Benjamin	WSH 239
Kip, Luke	NYK 82	Kirby, William	ORN 334	Kitchum, Hannah	NYK 25
Kip, Samuel	NYK 89	Kircum, Ezekiel	COL 196	Kitchum, Joshua	WSH 291
Kip, Samuel	NYK 151	Kircum, Joseph	DUT 96	Kitchum, Phoebe	NYK 43
Kip, Samuel Junr	NYK 151	Kircum, Peter	DUT 83	Kithcart, Siles	WSH 232
Kip, Thomas	NYK 78	Kircum, Solomon	DUT 85	Kitler, John	NYK 131

Kitridge, George	WSH 234	
Kitter, John	ALB 51	
Kittle, Abraham	ULS 213	
Kittle, Benjamin	ALB 30	
Kittle, Daniel	ALB 20	
Kittle, Douw	ALB 38	
Kittle, Dow	WSH 256	
Kittle, Ephraim	RNS 105	
Kittle, Ephraim	RNS 105	
Kittle, Hendrick	ULS 212	
Kittle, Henry	RNS 59	
Kittle, John	RNS 61	
Kittle, Jonathan	GRN 328	
Kittle, Maglin	RNS 105	
Kittle, Nichs D.	ALB 103	
Kittle, Nicholas J.	RNS 61	
Kittle, Samuel	RNS 105	
Kittle, Sybrant	ALB 142	
Kittle, Wm	RNS 37	
Kittle, William	RNS 103	
Kittle, Wm Junr	RNS 103	
Kitton, Daniel	NYK 95	
Kitts, Abraham	MNT 53	
Kitts, John	OND 222	
Kitts, John	OND 222	
Kitts, _than	MNT 53	
Kitts, Peter	MNT 52	
Kitz, George	NYK 151	
Kizer, John	RNS 35	
Klack, Adam	MNT 57	
Klapp, Rebecca	RCH 90	
Klause, Jacob	MNT 20	
Klause, John	MNT 20	
Klause, Peter	MNT 20	
Klause, Samuel	MNT 43	
Kledey, Isaac	CAY 702	
Klein, Frederick	DUT 162	
Klesimer, John	RNS 50	
Kliff, Joseph	ONN 152	
Klim, Leonard	NYK 123	
Klimp, John	DUT 160	
Klinck, George	ALB 145	
Kline see Klyne		
Kline, Anthony	NYK 134	
Kline, Betsey a		
mulatto	NYK 124	
Kline, Frederick	NYK 131	
Kline, John	ALB 37	
Kline, John	NYK 142	
Kline, John	RNS 46	
Kline, Joseph	RNS 34	
Kline, Joseph Junr	RNS 31	
Kline, Margaret	NYK 124	
Kline, Nicholas	COL 236	
Kline, Wm	MNT 104	
Kline, Wm	MNT 109	
Kline, William	NYK 142	
Klinebergh, Frederick	NYK 145	
Kling, Nichs	SCH 163	
Kling, Nichs Junr	SCH 163	
Klisimer, Peter J.	RNS 44	
Klock see Clock		
Klock, Adam	MNT 25	
Klock, Charles	HRK 456	
Klock, George G.	MNT 16	
Klock, George J.	MNT 17	
Klock, George Jb	MNT 20	
Klock, Henry	HRK 454	
Klock, Henry	MNT 42	
Klock, Jacob	HRK 495	
Klock, John J. Junr	MNT 16	
Klock, Peter	HRK 454	
Klock, William	ULS 194	
Kluber, Henry	MNT 65	
Klum, Henry	DUT 154	
Klum, John	DUT 154	
Klum, John P.	DUT 154	

Klum, Peter	DUT 151	
Klump, Thos	OTS 14	
Klunish, John	MNT 96	
Klynchrout, George	DUT 154	
Klyne see Kline		
Klyne, Abraham	DUT 11	
Klyne, Ad.m	DUT 146	
Klyne, Coonradt	ULS 185	
Klyne, Coonradt	ULS 246	
Klyne, Fronache	DUT 133	
Klyne, Henry	DUT 10	
Klyne, Jacob	DUT 146	
Klyne, James	COL 191	
Klyne, Johannis	ULS 248	
Klyne, John	DUT 133	
Klyne, Jonas	ULS 185	
Klyneman, Thomas	ORN 306	
Knap, Abel	RCK 109	
Knap, Abial	RNS 54	
Knap, Asa	OND 213	
Knap, Benjamin	NYK 149	
Knap, Benjamin	OND 185	
Knap, Benj.	RCK 104	
Knap, Benjamin	WST 113	
Knap, Caty	RCK 99	
Knap, Charles	OTS 19	
Knap, David	RNS 93	
Knap, David	WSH 291	
Knap, Ebenezer	GRN 338	
Knap, Ebenezer	RNS112B	
Knap, Esther	RNS 94	
Knap, Ezrael	SCH 150	
Knap, Henry	RCK 99	
Knap, Isaac	RCK 104	
Knap, James	MNT 6	
Knap, Jared	RCK 100	
Knap, John	NYK 141	
Knap, Joseph	RCK 104	
Knap, Joseph Junr	RCK 109	
Knap, Joshua	NYK 139	
Knap, Joshua	RNS112B	
Knap, Joshua	WST 112	
Knap, Josiah	ALB 114	
Knap, Josiah	SCH 155	
Knap, Lemuel	WSH 278	
Knap, Libeus	RCK 100	
Knap, Lucias	RNS 54	
Knap, Moses	ALB 85	
Knap, Olivel	RNS 109	
Knap, Reuben	RNS112B	
Knap, Reuben	RCK 108	
Knap, Reuben Junr	RNS 112	
Knap, Samuel	RNS 112	
Knap, Simeon	WST 112	
Knap, Wheeler	SRA 34	
Knap, Wm	RNS112B	
Knap, Zadock	GRN 326	
Knapp, Aaron	ONN 184	
Knapp, Abigail	NYK 128	
Knapp, Abraham	NYK 128	
Knapp, Amos	ALB 116	
Knapp, Amos	COL 196	
Knapp, Amos	DUT 128	
Knapp, Amos	HRK 461	
Knapp, Asa	DUT 143	
Knapp, Benjamin	DUT 83	
Knapp, Benjamin	NYK 111	
Knapp, Benjamin	WSH 213	
Knapp, Benjamin K.	NYK 90	
Knapp, Brundage	WST 154	
Knapp, Charles	ORN 368	
Knapp, Comfort	COL 211	
Knapp, Daniel	NYK 139	
Knapp, Daniel	ONN 185	
Knapp, Danl	OTS 26	
Knapp, Daniel	WST 122	
Knapp, Daniel	WST 127	

Knapp, David	COL 196	
Knapp, David	COL 222	
Knapp, David	DUT 76	
Knapp, David	DUT 82	
Knapp, David	MNT 116	
Knapp, David	WST 126	
Knapp, Eben	NYK 128	
Knapp, Ebenezer	OTS 22	
Knapp, Eli	NYK 56	
Knapp, Elijah	ALB 23	
Knapp, Elijah	DUT 75	
Knapp, Elijah	HRK 575	
Knapp, Elijah	NYK 141	
Knapp, Elijah	NYK 149	
Knapp, Ellen	NYK 128	
Knapp, Enoch	DEL 275	
Knapp, Ezekiel	COL 221	
Knapp, Gabriel	WST 123	
Knapp, Hannah	WST 123	
Knapp, Henry	HRK 461	
Knapp, Henry	WSH 213	
Knapp, Isaac	DUT 24	
Knapp, Isaac	DUT 65	
Knapp, Isaac	DUT 99	
Knapp, Isaac	ESS 318	
Knapp, Isaac	ORN 347	
Knapp, Israel	DUT 94	
Knapp, Israel	NYK 141	
Knapp, Israel	WSH 213	
Knapp, Israel Junr	DUT 94	
Knapp, Jacob	OTS 30	
Knapp, Jacob	WST 151	
Knapp, James	CAY 600	
Knapp, James	DUT 22	
Knapp, James	HRK 483	
Kna.., James	ONN 183	
Knapp, Jehu	DEL 287	
Knapp, Jeremiah	ORN 368	
Knapp, Jeremiah	WST 168	
Knapp, Jesse	ONN 137	
Knapp, Joel	WST 168	
Knapp, John	DEL 287	
Knapp, John	DUT 76	
Knapp, John	DUT 94	
Knapp, John	DUT 138	
Knapp, John	ONT 458	
Knapp, John	ORN 326	
Knapp, John	ORN 347	
Knapp, John	ORN 358	
Knapp, John	ORN 377	
Knapp, John	ULS 186	
Knapp, John B.	OTS 32	
Knapp, Jonas	HRK 461	
Knapp, Jonathan	DUT 21	
Knapp, Jonathan	ORN 320	
Knapp, Jona	OTS 5	
Knapp, Jonathan	WST 157	
Knapp, Joseph	ALB 116	
Knapp, Joseph	COL 210	
Knapp, Joseph	DUT 92	
Knapp, Joseph	MNT 111	
Knapp, Joseph	ORN 333	
Knapp, Joseph	ULS 183	
Knapp, Joseph	WST 122	
Knapp, Joseph	WST 161	
Knapp, Joseph 2d	COL 211	
Knapp, Joshua	NYK 139	
Knapp, Joshua	OTS 43	
Knapp, Josiah	DUT 142	
Knapp, Lockwood	NYK 129	
Knapp, Lucius	ESS 318	
Knapp, Luke	COL 185	
Knapp, Martha	ORN 365	
Knapp, Mary	NYK 128	
Knapp, Matthew	ORN 363	
Knapp, Moses	DUT 94	
Knapp, Moses	ONN 135	

Name	Code	Pg
Knapp, Moses	WST	153
Knapp, Nathaniel	CAY	614
Knapp, Nathaniel	DUT	132
Knapp, Nathl	ONN	184
Knapp, Nathaniel	ORN	364
Knapp, Nathaniel	ORN	377
Knapp, Nehemiah	DUT	24
Knapp, Obadiah	WSH	213
Knapp, Oliver	NYK	105
Knapp, Peter	DEL	270
Knapp, Peter	ULS	221
Knapp, Phineas	COL	223
Knapp, Phinehas	DUT	126
Knapp, Right	TIO	229
Knapp, Roger	DUT	123
Knapp, Saml	ALB	76
Knapp, Samuel	DEL	287
Knapp, Samuel	ONT	432
Knapp, Samuel	ORN	368
Knapp, Samuel	WST	138
Knapp, Seth	OTS	7
Knapp, Shadrach	ORN	376
Knapp, Silas	DEL	270
Knapp, Solomon	CAY	604
Knapp, Solomon	MNT	118
Knapp, Stephen	DUT	88
Knapp, Stephen	DUT	100
Knapp, Susannah	COL	209
Knapp, Thomas	OTS	32
Knapp, Timothy	WST	126
Knapp, Uriah	CAY	600
Knapp, Walter	ORN	287
Knapp, William	DUT	94
Knapp, William	DUT	138
Knapp, William	ORN	364
Knapp, William	ORN	365
Knapp, William	ORN	371
Knapp, Wm	RNS	42
Knapp, Wright	HRK	516
Knapp, Zadock	COL	185
Knaringar, John	NYK	62
Kneeland, Asa	HRK	436
Kneeland, Ichabod	WSH	276
Kneeland, Saml	ALB	128
Kneeland, Seth R.	NYK	70
Kneffen, Peter	WSH	241
Kneffen, Roger	NYK	151
Knesher, Peter	MNT	25
Kneshern, John	MNT	28
Knettles, John	CAY	618
Knickabacker, Jacob	MNT	99
Knickabacker, Solomon	GRN	342
Knickebacher, Samuel	SRA	48
Knickebacker, Benjm	COL	239
Knickebacker, Theos	COL	237
Knickerbacher, Solomon	DEL	275
Knickerbacker, Abraham	CAY	672
Knickerbacker, Benjamin	DUT	144
Knickerbacker, Benjamin Junr	DUT	144
Knickerbacker, Darius	CAY	672
Knickerbacker, Herman	OTS	4
Knickerbacker, Herman J.	DUT	163
Knickerbacker, Hermanus	DUT	138
Knickerbacker, Hermanus ye 2d	DUT	139
Knickerbacker, Hugh	DUT	149
Knickerbacker, John	RNS	36
Knickerbacker, John Junr	RNS	36
Knickerbacker, John C.	DUT	144
Knickerbacker, John H.	DUT	10
Knickerbacker, John P.	DUT	149
Knickerbacker, Laurence	DUT	149
Knickerbacker, Peter	DUT	149
Knickerbacker, Phillip	DUT	147
Kickerbacker, Roeliff	DUT	138
Knickerbacker, Wm	RNS	36
Knies, Thomas Y.	DUT	134
Knifer, Michael	GRN	356
Kniff, Isaac	SRA	10
Kniffen, Amos	NYK	100
Kniffen, Benjamin	WST	154
Kniffen, Charles	NYK	143
Kniffen, Daniel	CAY	516
Kniffen, John	NYK	143
Kniffen, John the 2d	ORN	271
Kniffen, Lewis	NYK	130
Kniffen, Obediah	HRK	523
Kniffin, Amos	DUT	178
Kniffin, Daniel	DUT	168
Kniffin, Daniel	ORN	271
Kniffin, Daniel Junr	ORN	271
Kniffin, David	ULS	191
Kniffin, Gilbert	ORN	271
Kniffin, Israel	ULS	207
Kniffin, Jacob Junr	DUT	87
Kniffin, James	WST	154
Kniffin, Jeremiah	ORN	275
Kniffin, John	ORN	270
Kniffin, Jonathan	DUT	87
Kniffin, Jonothan	WST	129
Kniffin, Mary	DUT	21
Kniffin, Roger	DUT	18
Kniffin, Samuel	DUT	89
Knifier, David	ALB	119
Knight, Andrew	CHN	786
Knight, Caleb	COL	215
Knight, Charles	CHN	876
Knight, Daniel W.	OND	213
Knight, David	ONN	179
Knight, Edward	HRK	413
Knight, George	HRK	457
Knight, Isreal	CAY	556
Knight, James	DUT	59
Knight, James	SRA	3
Knight, Job	OND	201
Knight, John	CAY	556
Knight, John	COL	263
Knight, John	HRK	413
Knight, Joseph	HRK	541
Knight, Joseph	HRK	564
Knight, Joseph	OND	199
Knight, Michael	ALB	24
Knight, Nicholas	ORN	362
Knight, Noel	CHN	934
Knight, Peter	NYK	130
Knight, Philip	ALB	33
Knig__, Richard	ONT	484
Knight, Samuel	ORN	298
Knight, Thomas	ORN	299
Knight, Thomas	ORN	315
Knight, William	HRK	498
Knights, Catharine	SRA	10
Knights, Moses	WSH	269
Kniskern, Abraham	SCH	149
Kniskern, Jacob	SCH	120
Kniskern, John	SCH	119
Kniskern, John	SCH	137
Kniskern, John Jost	SCH	137
Kniskern, Jost	SCH	119
Kniskern, Peter	SCH	137
Kniskern, Peter	SCH	142
Kniskern, Tunis	SCH	120
Knittle, John	ALB	55
Kniver, George	COL	232
Kniver, Henry	COL	232
Kniver, Henry	DEL	279
Kniver, John	COL	241
Kniver, Marks J.	COL	245
Knochett, James	NYK	102
Knock, Abner	SCH	156
Knoles, Joseph	ALB	92
Knoll, Andrew	ALB	120
Knoll, Coenradt	ALB	117
Knoll, Henry Junr	ALB	121
Knoll, John	ALB	120
Knoll, Samuel	COL	252
Knolton, Joshua	ONN	167
Knott, James	MNT	68
Knott, Thomas	NYK	42
Knouls, Jo__	MNT	33
Knouts, Georg	MNT	29
Knower, Benjamin	DUT	63
Knowlan, John	DUT	91
Knowlan, Michael	DUT	91
Knowlan, William	DUT	91
Knowland, John	ESS	305
Knowlen, Manasseh	RNS	7
Knowlen, Nathaniel	RNS	7
Knowles, Arthur	CLN	156
Knowles, Haden	OTS	9
Knowles, Isaac	RNS	90
Knowles, Jacob	OTS	26
Knowles, Jesse	CLN	155
Knowles, John	RNS	90
Knowles, Reynold	ALB	92
Knowlin, John	WST	120
Knowls, Ebenezar	GRN	340
Knowls, L.	GRN	340
Knowls, Thomas	GRN	340
Knowls, Thomas	GRN	343
Knowls, William	WST	157
Knowlton, Benjamin	ESS	321
Knowlton, Daniel	ORN	387
Knowlton, Ephraim	HRK	582
Knowlton, Henry	ESS	310
Knowlton, Jerad	RNS	8
Knowlton, John	NYK	36
Knowlton, John	SRA	12
Knowlton, Robert	HRK	582
Knowlton, Stephen	ALB	75
Knowlton, Thomas	ORN	388
Knox, Abraham	WST	126
Knox, Alexander	WST	155
Knox, Andrew	DUT	89
Knox, Archibald	DUT	50
Knox, Frederick	DUT	173
Knox, George	NYK	19
Knox, George	NYK	50
Knox, James	COL	189
Knox, James	MNT	51
Knox, James	NYK	83
Knox, James	TIO	229
Knox, James	ULS	186
Knox, Janus	NYK	126
Knox, John	ESS	292
Knox, John	ORN	307
Knox, John	SCH	120
Knox, John	STB	202
Knox, John	WST	124
Knox, Joseph	WST	124
Knox, Margaret	NYK	63
Knox, Robert	WST	124
Knox, Thomas	NYK	28
Koergan, Nichs	SCH	171
Koergar, Philip	SCH	171
Koespot, Christian	SCH	171
Koespot, Gotless	SCH	171
Koespot, John	SCH	171
Kohenhoven, Canine	MNT	99
Kolb, John	DUT	57
Kolman, Christian	NYK	68
Konckite, James	ONN	170
Koncle, Daniel	CAY	582
Kopelman, Johanis	MNT	62
Koons, Jacob	STB	204
Korckright, Henry	HRK	498
Korey, Thankfull	WSH	255
Korning, Joh.nderick K.	MNT	49
Korton, Joseph	MNT	116

Kortright, Aaron	ONT 510	Kronkhite, John	DUT 125	Kurves, James	NYK 100
Kortright, Edward	WST 146	Kronkite, Elijah	OTS 18	Kuse, John	NYK 21
Kortright, James	NYK 57	Kronkite, Henry	OTS 18	Kuslyn, John	NYK 127
Kortright, Jane	TIO 253	Kronkite, Saml	OTS 18	Kutz, Henry	NYK 142
Kortright, John	NYK 153	Kronkite, Stephen	OTS 18	Kuykendal, Wilhelmus	ULS 187
Kortright, Joseph	NYK 146	Kronkrite, Abraham	DUT 74	Kuykendall, Elias	ORN 316
Kortrite, Benjamin	ULS 213	Kronkrite, Cornelius	DUT 79	Kuykendall, Henry	ORN 316
Kortrite, Bowdoine	ORN 319	Kronkrite, Giradus	DUT 82	Kuykendall, Jacob	ONT 488
Kortrite, Daniel	ORN 318	Kronkrite, Jacob	DUT 92	Kuykendall, Martinus	ORN 316
Kortrite, Harry	ULS 203	Kronkrite, Nathaniel	DUT 58	Kuykindall, Benjamin	CAY 572
Kortrite, Henry	ULS 213	Kronkrite, Samuel	DUT 58	Kuykindall, Henry	CAY 678
Kortrite, John	ORN 357	Kronkrite, Solomon	DUT 11	Kuykindall, James	CAY 572
Kortrite, Lawrence	ORN 358	Kronkrite, Teunis	DUT 73	Ku kindall, Joel	CAY 546
Kortrite, Lawrence	ULS 213	Kronkrite, William	DUT 69	Kuyse, Charles	NYK 135
Kortrite, Ryer	DUT 72	Krouse, Gertrude	MNT 50	Kyes, Charles	OTS 37
Kortrite, Sylvester	ORN 317	Krouse, John	MNT 3	Kyes, Chester	HRK 508
Kortz, James	ULS 222	Krouse, Widow	MNT 2	Kyes, Marshal	SCH 151
Kortz, John	COL 189	Krouskoup, George	DEL 273	Kyes, Marshal	SCH 155
Kough, Andries	ALB 67	Krouskoup, John	DEL 273	Kyle, John	OTS 29
Kovan, Laurence	NYK 62	Krows, Johannis	ULS 233	Kynion, David	WSH 204
Kram, John	MNT 20	Krows, Leonard	ULS 231	Kynion, David	WSH 252
Kramer, Frederick	DUT 157	Kruislar, Maths Junr	COL 224	Kynion, David Junr	WSH 204
Kramer, Frederick Junr	DUT 157	Krum, Abrahan	ULS 201	Kynion, Freeman	WSH 258
Kramer, George	DUT 157	Krum, Alex.	RCK 103	Kynion, Gardner	WSH 258
Kramer, Hendrick	DUT 28	Krum, Benjamin A.	ULS 205	Kynion, Holden	WSH 204
Kramer, Joham Jesse	MNT 51	Krum, Cornelius	ULS 198	Kynion, James	WSH 238
Kramer, John N.	DUT 163	Krum, Cornelius	ULS 209	Kynion, James	WSH 250
Kramer, Phillip	DUT 17	Krum, Dirck	ULS 219	Kynion, John	WSH 204
Kramer, William	DUT 130	Krum, Elizabeth	ULS 205	Kynion, John	WSH 211
Krandall, Christopher	ONN 177	Krum, Henry	COL 179	Kynion, John	WSH 252
Krankins, Henry	MNT 24	Krum, Henry	ULS 198	Kynion, John	WSH 258
Krans, Adam	ULS 250	Krum, Henry	ULS 205	Kynion, Joseph	WSH 252
Krans, Ezekiel	ORN 299	Krum, Jacob	COL 179	Kynion, Mumford	WSH 197
Krans, Henry	ORN 297	Krum, Jacob	ULS 197	Kynion, Nathaniel	WSH 234
Krans, John	ORN 298	Krum, Jacob De Witt	ULS 214	Kynion, Nathaniel Junr	WSH 234
Krans, John	ULS 188	Krum, Jacobus	ULS 205	Kynion, Phenius	WSH 234
Krans, John Junr	ORN 297	Krum, Jacobus	ULS 214	Kynion, Phenius	WSH 256
Krans, John G.	ORN 301	Krum, Johannis	ULS 200	Kynion, Robert	WSH 252
Krans, Michael	ORN 302	Krum, John	RCK 103	Kynion, Ronalds	WSH 234
Krans, Peter	ULS 189	Krum, John	ULS 244	Kynion, Samuel	WSH 249
Krans, Samuel	ORN 368	Krum, John G.	ULS 206	Kynion, Samuel	WSH 252
Krans, William	ORN 286	Krum, John H.	ULS 215	Kynion, Serrel	WSH 231
Kransoen, Samuel	DEL 268	Krum, John I.	ULS 205	Kynion, Thuston	WSH 204
Krapp, Us	SRA 52	Krum, Jonathan	ULS 209	Kynion, William	WSH 204
Krassenbarough, Conrod	MNT 74	Krum, Martin	COL 218	Kynion, William	WSH 232
Kraw, Asa	DUT 142	Krum, Martin Junr	COL 218	Kynion, William	WSH 254
Kraw, Ebenezer	DUT 140	Krum, Matthew	ULS 197	Kynion, Zebulon	WSH 258
Kraw, Geoffry	DUT 106	Krum, Matthew	ULS 201	Kypers, Gerardus	
Kraw, Jacob	DUT 142	Krum, Peter	ULS 203	Arence	NYK 36
Kraw, Jacob	DUT 177	Krum, Peter	ULS 214	Kyser, Abraham	SCH 128
Kress, George	TIO 255	Krum, Reuben	ULS 215	Kyte, John	OND 177
Kr.ss, John	TIO 254	Krum, Simon	ULS 202	Kyte, William	CHN 966
Kress, Mary	TIO 255	Krum, Simon	ULS 216		
Kress, Saml	TIO 254	Krum, Solomon	ULS 216		
Kri.., Jacob	MNT 4	Krum, Solomon Junr	ULS 215	L	
Krin., John	MNT 4	Krum, William	ULS 199	L s , James	MNT 43
Krine, George	COL 240	Krum, William	ULS 205	L...., Christoher	MNT 44
Krine, Peter	COL 240	Kruysler, Johannis	COL 199	La ..., James	MNT 70
Kring, Catharine	MNT 18	Kruysler, Nicholas	COL 199	L cy, Gershom	MNT 85
Kring, Jacob	MNT 18	Kuby, Archibald	NYK 70	L om s, Nathan	ONT 452
Kring, John	MNT 18	Kuck, Stephen	NYK 124	La , John	CHN 934
Kring, John Junr	MNT 18	Kuck, William	NYK 55	La ghin, James	DEL 286
Kring, John Ludwig	MNT 19	Kugin, Laurence	NYK 114	La daw, Joseph	MNT 76
Kritler, Leonard	MNT 19	Kuhn, Marcus	OTS 27	La daw, J..es	MNT 76
Kroat, Ephraem	MNT 108	Kuler, Isaac	NYK 138	La...., Wm	MNT 81
Kroat, Sem	MNT 106	Kuline, Daniel	NYK 62	La oway, Martin	NYK 56
Kroft, George	OTS 40	Kumble, William	NYK 45	La den, Zebulon	ONT 484
Kroft, Fredk	OTS 40	Kump, John	NYK 91	Labagh, Abraham	NYK 50
Kroft, John	OTS 40	Kunan, Barnet	NYK 66	Laban, Christopher	ONT 318
Krom, Peter	COL 259	Kuney, Robert	NYK 90	Labartow, Peggy	NYK 39
Kroneholm, Christian	NYK 144	Kuntz, George	DUT 9	Labateaux, Jacob	CAY 708
Kronk, Abraham	DUT 96	Kuntz, John	DUT 153	Labateaux, William	CAY 708
Kronk, Abraham	MNT 109	Kunze, John C.	NYK 111	Laben, Allen	MNT 92
Kronk, Frederick	ULS 259	Kunzel, Simon	NYK 46	Laberton, Letiteia	NYK 113
Kronk, Garret	ULS 248	Kurry, John	MNT 104	La Bonta, John Br	CLN 170
Kronk, Teunis	DUT 96	Kursted, James	NYK 97	Labouesse, John	NYK 107
Kronk, Timothy	DUT 93	Kursted, John	NYK 51	Labre, Joseph	NYK 98

Labuzan, Bartholemew	NYK 126	
Laby, John	MNT 55	
Lacey, Isaac	WSH 185	
Lacey, James	SRA 15	
Lacey, Samuel	SRA 14	
Lacey, William	ONT 492	
Lacock, John	NYK 66	
La count, Josiah	WST 149	
Lacour, Peter	NYK 150	
Lacutteau, Lewis	ALB 48	
Lacy, Abraham	CAY 522	
Lacy, Edmond	SRA 15	
Lacy, Edward	SRA 26	
Lacy, Enoch	DUT 150	
Lacy, Frederick	MNT 99	
Lacy, Gilbert A.	RNS 81	
Lacy, John	CAY 528	
Lacy, John	MNT 85	
Lacy, John	NYK 116	
Lacy, John Jun.	CAY 528	
Lacy, Nathan	MNT 85	
Lacy, Sanford	OTS 36	
Lad, John	ALB 31	
Lad, Thomas	ALB 31	
Lad, William Junr	ALB 31	
Lad, William Senr	ALB 31	
Ladaw, Jacob	MNT 15	
Ladaw, John	MNT 15	
Ladd, Amasa	CLN 169	
Ladd, Bodwell	HRK 476	
Ladd, Cyrus	OTS 34	
Ladd, Elisha	OND 204	
Ladd, Henry	CLN 173	
Ladd, Jesse	ESS 312	
Ladd, John	HRK 415	
Ladd, Phineas	OND 204	
Ladd, Samuel	OND 171	
Ladd, Whiting	HRK 488	
Lader, Pettit	WST 155	
Ladley, Thomas	NYK 103	
Ladowan, Abraham	MNT 93	
Ladu, Peter	RNS 83	
Ladue, Abraham	SRA 48	
Ladue, Stephen	SRA 18	
La[er?], Jos:	SCH 120	
Laeraway, Jonas	DEL 267	
Laers, Joshua	CAY 662	
Lafergey, Peter	WST 163	
Lafergy, Martin	WST 163	
La Fevre, Louis	CAY 538	
Laff, John S.	SCH 152	
Lafferts, P a free		
Negro	ALB 48	
Lafferty, John	OTS 2	
Lafflin, Sp_dy	ESS 302	
Lafforge, Charles	RCH 88	
Lafforge, Peter	RCH 93	
Lafler, Coenrad	ONT 504	
Lafler, Lenah	ONT 504	
Lafler, Peter	ONT 510	
La Foe see Ta Foe		
Laforge, James	RCH 89	
Laforge, Philip	RCH 88	
La Forgee, Benjamin	ORN 374	
Laforque, Gloriana	NYK 58	
Laforque, John	NYK 37	
Lafort, John	WST 168	
Lafortune, Benjamin	CLN 169	
Lafromboise, Jacque	CLN 168	
Lafromboise, John Br	CLN 168	
Lafuge, Lamick	NYK 93	
Lagar, John	NYK 49	
Lagendorph, Hermanus J.	COL 191	
Lager, Thomas	ONN 173	
Laglere, Joshua	WSH 206	
Lagow, Francis	NYK 107	
Lagrange, Christian	ALB 108	

Lagrange, Coenrad	ALB 105	
Lagrange, Henry	ALB 104	
La Grange, Jacob	ALB 56	
Lagrange, Jacob O.	ALB 104	
La Grange, James	ALB 55	
La Grange, James	ALB 130	
La Grange, Johannis	ALB 61	
La Grange, John	ALB 105	
La grange, John	TIO 212	
La Grange, Omy	SCH 171	
La Grange, Peter	ALB 59	
Lags, John	TIO 251	
Laight, Elisha	DUT 92	
Laight, Elizabeth	NYK 70	
Laight, Henry	DUT 95	
Laight, Henry Junr	DUT 92	
Laight, John	DUT 95	
Laight, John	DUT 110	
Laight, William	DUT 34	
Laight, William	NYK 50	
Laight, Woolsey	DUT 81	
Laine see Lane		
Laine, Elisha	WST 123	
Laine, Henry	WST 168	
Laine, Notheniel	WST 123	
Laine, Peter	WST 123	
Laing see Lang		
Laing, John	NYK 104	
Laing, Peter	NYK 70	
Laing, William	SRA 24	
Laird, Samuel	OND 172	
Laird, Wm	ONN 154	
Laird, Wm Jun	ONN 152	
Lake, Abraham	DEL 272	
Lake, Abm	RNS 21	
Lake, Brownell	ALB 36	
Lake, Casparus	WSH 298	
Lake, Catharine	CAY 639	
Lake, Cornelius	CHN 798	
Lake, Cornelius	RCH 91	
Lake, Court	RCK 109	
Lake, Curtiss	COL 212	
Lake, Daniel	ALB 113	
Lake, Daniel	COL 212	
Lake, Daniel	KNG 5	
Lake, Daniel	QNS 69	
Lake, Daniel	RCH 90	
Lake, David	ALB 88	
Lake, David	ALB 114	
Lake, David Junr	ALB 77	
Lake, Ebenezar H.	GRN 333	
Lake, Edward	GRN 340	
Lake, Edward Junr	ALB 114	
Lake, Garret	OTS 48	
Lake, Garret	WSH 189	
Lake, Gersham	ALB 94	
Lake, Hannah	GRN 354	
Lake, Henry	ALB 50	
Lake, Henry	ONT 406	
Lake, Henry	OTS 48	
Lake, Henry	RNS 23	
Lake, Isaac	DEL 271	
Lake, Jacob	OND 190	
Lake, James	OND 190	
Lake, James	OTS 48	
Lake, Jeremeah	WSH 243	
Lake, Joel	CAY 704	
Lake, John	KNG 4	
Lake, John	OTS 48	
Lake, Joseph a Black	NYK 148	
Lake, Joseph	RCH 87	
Lake, Joseph	RCH 90	
Lake, Joseph	RCH 91	
Lake, Joseph	RCH 91	
Lake, Matthew	ALB 77	
Lake, Matthew	ALB 113	
Lake, Nicholas	OND 190	

Lake, Peleg	ULS 212	
Lake, Peter	KNG 3	
Lake, Reuben	ULS 234	
Lake, Richard	RCH 91	
Lake, Roger	OTS 45	
Lake, Seth	GRN 352	
Lake, Thomas	ALB 33	
Lake, Timothy	ALB 77	
Lake, Warner	DEL 285	
Lake, William	MNT 50	
Lake, Wm	MNT 96	
Lake, William	NYK 25	
Lake, William	RCH 91	
Lakeman, John	NYK 126	
Lakerman, Richard	ORN 287	
Lakin, Joel	DEL 274	
Lakin, Jonas	DEL 274	
Lakin, Wm	ONN 190	
Lallor, Margaret	NYK 147	
Lallor, William	NYK 111	
Lam, Asa	CHN 768	
Lam, Elvin	CHN 840	
Lam, James	CHN 784	
Lam, Michal	CHN 780	
Lam, Solomon	ONN 179	
Lam_ary, Joshua	GRN 354	
Lamaire, John	NYK 54	
Lamata, Joseph	NYK 122	
Lamatty, Lewis	NYK 137	
Lamb, Abigil	RNS 43	
Lamb, Abraham	NYK 102	
Lamb, Alexander	NYK 74	
Lamb, Alexander	NYK 108	
Lamb, Amos	CAY 722	
Lamb(?), Asa	CHN 832	
Lamb, Benjamin	OND 179	
Lamb, Caleb	SCH 160	
Lamb, Caleb	WSH 207	
Lamb, Charles	WSH 225	
Lamb, Christian	SCH 162	
Lamb, Christian Junr	SCH 162	
Lamb, Daniel	WSH 280	
Lamb, David	CAY 526	
Lamb, David	NYK 104	
Lamb, David	WSH 207	
Lamb, Eleanor	WST 160	
Lamb, George	CAY 526	
Lamb, Isaac	OTS 34	
Lamb, Isaac	TIO 213	
Lamb, Isaac	WSH 284	
Lamb, Isrel	WSH 273	
Lamb, James	CAY 526	
Lamb, Jeduthen	WSH 231	
Lamb, Jehial	ALB 94	
Lamb, John	DEL 282	
Lamb, John	NYK 96	
Lamb, John	ONN 143	
Lamb, John	ORN 333	
Lamb, John	WSH 273	
Lamb, Joseph	CAY 656	
Lamb, Joseph	SRA 9	
Lamb, Joshua	RNS 78	
Lamb, Lemuel	DEL 268	
Lamb, Martin	WSH 269	
Lamb, Nathaniel	WSH 207	
Lamb, Nehemiah	HRK 494	
Lamb, Patrick	DEL 270	
Lamb, Pricella	NYK 75	
Lamb, Reuben	OTS 27	
Lamb, Samuel	RNS 78	
Lamb, Thomas	WSH 269	
Lamb, Thomas	DEL 268	
Lamb, William	DEL 287	
Lamb, William Junr	DEL 287	
Lambe, Thomas	NYK 54	
Lambert, David	MNT 99	
Lambert, David	ORN 316	

Name	Loc	Pg	Name	Loc	Pg	Name	Loc	Pg
Lane, Nathan	DUT	82	Langdon, Willeam	WSH	298	Lansing, Obadiah	RNS	62
Lane, Nathan	TIO	221	Langerthy, Oliver	OND	202	Lansing, Peter	ALB	143
Lane, Nathaniel	SRA	36	Langerthy, Sanford	OND	185	Lansing, Peter	DUT	65
Lane, Peter	QNS	60	Langley, Susan	NYK	84	Lansing, Philip	MNT	105
Lane, Peter Jun	QNS	60	Langlow, Vincent	NYK	146	Lansing, Richard	SRA	11
Lane, Primus	ORN	395	Langrall, Margaret	NYK	71	Lansing, Sander	MNT	14
Lane, Rachel	DUT	76	Languithe, Amon	WSH	254	Lansing, Sanders	ALB	147
Lane, Robert	WST	123	Languithe, Phnius	WSH	254	Lansing, Sanders Senr	ALB	147
Lane, Samuel	ONT	394	Languthey, Sanford	WSH	188	Lansing, Thomas	ALB	137
Lane, Samuel	STB	203	Languthy, Robert	WSH	188	Lansing, William	ALB	49
Lane, Samuel	WST	112	Langworth, Benjamin	WSH	201	Lansmu__, Duty	CHN	928
Lane, Smith	WST	123	Langworth, Robert	WSH	201	Lanson, Goncott	MNT	92
Lane, Thomas	NYK	108	Laning, Judah	SCH	149	Lant, Casparus	WSH	247
Lane, Thomas	QNS	60	Lank, William	COL	201	Lant, Christina	COL	196
Lane, Thomas	SCH	171	Lankano, Richard	NYK	19	Lant, Henry	COL	201
Lane, Timothy	MNT	92	Lankman, Jacob	RNS	19	Lant, Jeremiah	MNT	36
Lane, Timothy	NYK	22	Lankman, John	RNS	19	Lant, Lawrence	COL	196
Lane, Timy	SUF	64	Lankton, Benjamin	KNG	7	Lant, William	WSH	247
Lane, Timy	SUF	71	Lankton, John	ULS	250	Lantaliere, Louisa	NYK	114
Lane, William	COL	220	Lanman, Peter Junr	NYK	25	Lanterman, Isaac	DUT	168
Lane, William	DUT	119	Lanniere, Joseph	NYK	138	Lantman, Casparus	COL	231
Lane, William	NYK	123	Lannieur, Augustus	NYK	21	Lantman, Casparus Junr	COL	231
Lane, William	ORN	327	Lanning, Conradt	ALB	26	Lantman, Hendrick	COL	228
Lane, William	ULS	194	Lanning, Edward	ALB	26	Lantman, Nicholas	COL	200
Lane, William	ULS	235	Lanpher, Rowland	RNS	70	Lanton, Lewis	SCH	155
Lane, William	WSH	211	Lanqier, Nicholas B.	NYK	39	Lanz, John	CHN	942
Lane, William	WST	113	Lansdone, Edward	NYK	121	Lape, Jacob	COL	194
Lane, William Junr	ULS	196	Lanseer, Georg	MNT	46	Lape, Thomas	COL	195
Lanegar, Frederick	RNS	88	Lansey, Archabald	WSH	214	Lapeire, James	NYK	21
Laneman, Jacob	NYK	151	Lansier, Stepher	MNT	50	Laper, David	MNT	47
Lanemore, James	KNG	11	Lansing, Abraham	RNS	5	Lapham, Abraham	ONT	354
Lanen, George a Black	NYK	104	Lansing, Abraham	RNS	18	Lapham, Benjamin	DUT	131
Laney, John	NYK	135	Lansing, Abraham	RNS	80	Lapham, David	DUT	125
Lanfair, David	SRA	26	Lansing, Abraham	RNS	83	Lapham, Isaac	ONT	440
Lang see Laing			Lansing, Abm A.	ALB	133	Lapham, Noah	CAY	658
Lang, George	NYK	50	Lansing, Abm D.	ALB	133	Lapham, Reuben	DUT	124
Lang, John	NYK	30	Lansing, Abraham G.	ALB	145	Lapham, Solon	DUT	130
Lang, John	SRA	53	Lansing, Abm H.	ALB	49	Lapham, Stephen	WSH	210
Lang, John M.	SUF	105	Lansing, Alexander	ALB	21	Lapham, Thomas	CAY	650
Lang, Joseph	NYK	100	Lansing, Christopher	ALB	46	Laping, Jonathan	SRA	6
Lang, Robert	WST	123	Lansing, Cornelius	RNS	80	Laplace, John	NYK	133
Lang, Thomas	SRA	53	Lansing, David	ALB	133	Lappon, William	HRK	434
Lang, Thomas	WSH	193	Lansing, Garret	DUT	65	Laquay, Peter	NYK	69
Lang, Walter	SRA	53	Lansing, Garret	RNS	6	Laques, Jonathen	NYK	102
Lang, William	SRA	53	Lansing, Garret Junr	HRK	473	Larabee, Artimes	RNS	104
Langatha, Andrew B.	COL	248	Lansing, Garret G.	WSH	250	Larabee, Ezra	RNS	67
Langathe, Elisha	SRA	16	Lansing, Gerrett(?)	WSH	241	Larabee, Nathan	RNS	27
Langden, Benjamin	CAY	652	Lansing, Gerrit A.	ALB	133	Larabee, Paul	RNS	83
Langden, Benjamin	WSH	216	Lansing, Gerrit R.	ALB	50	Larabee, Paul	RNS	93
Langden, Samuel	WSH	216	Lansing, Gerudus	ALB	143	Larabee, Richard	RNS	109
Langden, Timothy	WST	144	Lansing, Harpert	RNS	86	Larabee, Samuel	HRK	575
Langden, William	WSH	216	Lansing, Henry R.	ALB	134	Larabee, Seth	ONN	183
Langdon, Annanias	QNS	76	Lansing, Isaac	ALB	54	Larabee, Theophilus	RNS	66
Langdon, Archelus	QNS	73	Lansing, Isaac Junr	ALB	54	Larabee, Tyler	RNS	23
Langdon, Edward	WSH	267	Lansing, Jacob	ALB	50	Laraby, James	COL	249
Langdon, Ezekiel	QNS	76	Lansing, Jacob	RNS	21	La ramma, Antoine	CLN	169
Langdon, Jared	SUF	74	Lansing, Jacob	RNS	37	Laraway, John	GRN	334
Langdon, John	DUT	88	Lansing, Jacob Junr	ALB	49	Laraway, Martinas	GRN	334
Langdon, John	SUF	65	Lansing, Jacob H.	ALB	49	Laraway, Peter	GRN	334
Langdon, John	WSH	282	Lansing, Jacob John	NYK	18	Lare, Mary	ORN	301
Langdon, John	WSH	298	Lansing, Jacob Js	ALB	44	Laremore, Ralph	NYK	79
Langdon, Jonathan	SUF	76	Lansing, James	MNT	66	Laren, William	WST	130
Langdon, Joseph	DEL	276	Lansing, Jane	ALB	49	Largin see Cargin		
Langdon, Joseph	OND	177	Lansing, Jeremiah	ALB	144	Lark, Andrew	MNT	72
Langdon, Joseph	QNS	76	Lansing, Johannis	ALB	50	Larken, Laurence	NYK	80
Langdon, Lewis	OTS	41	Lansing, John	ALB	125	Larkens, Edward	CHN	832
Langdon, Martin	OND	177	Lansing, John	ONN	179	Larkin, Gideon	SCH	120
Langdon, Mary	SUF	76	Lansing, John	SRA	5	Larkin, James	ONN	152
Langdon, Noah	OND	177	Lansing, John Junr	ALB	147	Larkin, John	SCH	121
Langdon, Patty	NYK	17	Lansing, John E.	RNS	63	Larkin, John	SCH	155
Langdon, Philip	DEL	281	Lansing, John Jacob	ALB	147	Larkin, Joseph	RNS	106
Langdon, Rueben	OND	177	Lansing, John V. A.	ALB	52	Larkin, Nathan	RNS	39
Langdon, Richard	QNS	76	Lansing, Lena	ALB	52	Larkin, Thomas W.	DEL	279
Langdon, Rufus	OND	196	Lansing, Levinus	RNS	80	Larkin, Timothy	RNS	106
Langdon, Samuel	DEL	276	Lansing, Levinus F.	ALB	52	Larkin, Timothy Junr	RNS	107
Langdon, Samuel	QNS	73	Lansing, Myndert	ALB	134	Larkin, Wm	RNS	112
Langdon, Thomas	NYK	66	Lansing, Revd Nicholas	RCK	98	Larkins, Adam	WSH	208

Name	Code		Name	Code		Name	Code	
Larkins, Amos	SRA	14	Lasher, Marcus Jr	ALB	106	Latourrette, David	RCH	89
Larkins, John	COL	251	Lasher, Marcus Junr	ALB	106	Latourrette, John	RCH	88
Larkins, Nicholas	CHN	832	Lasher, Margaret	NYK	125	Latourrette, John	RCH	90
Larkins, Scovel	CHN	896	Lasher, Marks	COL	190	Latourrette, Mary	RCH	88
Larmouth, Hugh	WSH	197	Lasher, Mary	COL	225	Latourrette, Paul	RCH	88
Larnard, Daniel	CHN	960	Lasher, Peter	COL	234	Latourrette, Sarah	RCH	95
Larned, Benjn	HRK	415	Lasher, Peter B.	COL	190	Latsurrett, Peter	NYK	130
Larns, John	SRA	8	Lasher, Phillip C.	COL	189	Latta, Elizabeth	ORN	296
Laroche, Francis	CLN	165	Lasher, Samuel B.	COL	242	Latta, James	ONT	494
Laroche, John	NYK	68	Lasher, Samuel L.	COL	231	Latta, James	ONT	496
Laroque, Joseph	NYK	91	Lasher, William	COL	192	Latta, Samuel	ONT	496
La Roy see Le Roy			Lasher, William	COL	233	Latten, Daniel	QNS	81
La Roy, Daniel	TIO	210	Lashere, Abraham	WSH	292	Latten, Isaac	QNS	81
Laroza, John	NYK	123	Lashier, John S.	COL	231	Latten, Joseph	QNS	79
Larrabee, Joseph	DEL	273	Lashley	GRN	340	Latten, William	QNS	84
Larraby, Thomas	ULS	197	Lashley, James	GRN	346	Latter, John	ONT	360
Larraway, Abraham	SCH	139	Lashley, James Junr	GRN	346	Lattimore, Robert N.	ONT	468
Larraway, David	DEL	267	Lashley, Margaret	NYK	58	Lattimore, Thomas	ALB	124
Larraway, John B.	DEL	267	Lashorne, Garret	NYK	139	Lattin, Adolph	DUT	116
Larriby, Thomas	QNS	79	Lasley, Thomas	OND	207	Lattin, Benjamin	DUT	116
Larrow, Simeon	MNT	42	Lason, Micah	DUT	152	Lattin, Jabe	COL	212
Larrow, Simon	MNT	47	Lason, Micajah	DUT	120	Lattin, Jacob	ULS	208
Larrow, William	ALB	27	Lassel, Joshua	ALB	79	Lattin, Josiah	ALB	114
Larrowbey, John	WSH	233	Lassley, John	GRN	343	Lattin, Pharoah	ULS	264
Larroway, Isaac	ALB	71	Laster, Enock	SCH	136	Lattin, Richard	QNS	80
Larroway, Isaac	ALB	139	Laster, James	SCH	136	Lattin, William	DUT	117
Larroway, Jacob	ALB	55	Lasure, Amasa	WSH	186	Latting, Jacob	NYK	32
Larroway, Wm	ALB	98	Lasure, Paul	WSH	186	Latting, Lydia a		
Larue, Joseph	SRA	23	Lasure, Siles	WSH	199	Black	NYK	138
Larue, Lewis	NYK	88	Latemore, Alexander	WSH	300	Lauback, Isaac	COL	257
Larway, Phillip	SRA	56	Laten, Isaac	WSH	197	Laudie, Joseph	CAY	630
Larwood, Thomas	DUT	164	Latham, Daniel	SUF	102	Laudin, Ezekiel	CAY	660
Lary, Nancy	NYK	41	Latham, David	NYK	136	Laughton, James	NYK	91
Larzelaer, Benjamin	RCH	94	Latham, Hubbard	SUF	102	Lauks, Peter Junr	MNT	76
Larzel er, Richard	ONT	508	Latham, John L.	COL	244	Laumer, Lem el	KNG	10
Las, Jacob Brawalibiga	ORN	391	Latham, Jonathan	ONT	456	Laune, Stephen P.	NYK	89
Lascelles, Edward	ORN	391	Latham, Jonathan	SUF	77	Launsbury, James	WST	125
Lascels, Edward	RCK	102	Latham, Joseph	QNS	84	Laurance see Lawrence &		
Lasee, Israel	ORN	299	Latham, Lewis	QNS	61	Lourence		
Lash, George	COL	259	Latham, Peleg	SUF	104	Laurance, Clark	DEL	289
Lasher, Adam	GRN	327	Latham, Saml	OTS	48	Laurance, James	WSH	239
Lasher, Bastian	COL	225	Latham, Saml Junr	OTS	48	Laurance, Oliver	ALB	80
Lasher, Bastian	DUT	154	Latham, Stanton	NYK	26	Laurance, Salas	OND	224
Lasher, Bastian J.	COL	224	Latham, Stephen	NYK	70	Laurance, Thomas	WSH	239
Lasher, Bastian M.	COL	228	Latham, Thomas	DUT	31	Laure, James	ONT	378
Lasher, Coenradt B.	COL	191	Latham, Wilhelmus	COL	244	Laurence see Laurenel		
Lasher, Coenradt J.	COL	190	Lathan, Hulbard	SUF	102	Laurence, Ariel	ONN	155
Lasher, Coenradt P.	COL	189	Lathen, Joseph	WSH	250	Laurence, Augustus	NYK	100
Lasher, Conradt	MNT	22	Lather, Henry	NYK	147	Laurence, Benjamin	NYK	91
Lasher, Conrod J.	MNT	6	Lathon, Peleg	WSH	197	Laurence, Benjamin	NYK	134
Lasher, Elizabeth	ULS	221	Lathon, Peleg Junr	WSH	197	Laurence, Daniel	NYK	42
Lasher, Garret	COL	226	Lathrop, Gurdon	HRK	523	Laurence, Daniel	NYK	117
Lasher, Garrit	MNT	7	Lathrop, Hezekiah	ONN	140	Laurence, Daniel	ULS	255
Lasher, George	ALB	28	Lathrop, Isaac	OND	213	Laurence, David	ONN	152
Lasher, George	COL	190	Lathrop, Joseph	NYK	43	Laurence, David	ORN	365
Lasher, George	COL	223	Lathrop, Melatiah	SRA	48	Laurence, David	SRA	46
Lasher, George	MNT	7	Lathrop, Roswell	HRK	495	Laurence, Domonic	NYK	66
Lasher, George	COL	223	Lathrop, Uriah	OND	178	Laurence, Elezar	RNS	21
Lasher, George C.	COL	189	Lathrop, Wm	MNT	29	Laurence, Elijah	ONN	155
Lasher, George P.	COL	190	Latimer, Ebenezer	ULS	215	Laurence, Ezekiel &		
Lasher, Gerret B.	COL	225	Latimer, James	COL	250	Joseph	DUT	118
Lasher, Gerrit	MNT	22	Latimer, John	DUT	120	Laurence, Isaac	NYK	38
Lasher, Henry	MNT	7	Latimer, Thomas	DUT	36	Laurence, Isaiah	RNS	112
Lasher, Herman	SRA	41	Latimore, Elisha	GRN	336	Laurence, Israel	ORN	293
Lasher, Jacob	COL	190	Latimore, Elisha Junr	GRN	336	Laurence, Jacob	NYK	134
Lasher, Jacob P.	COL	223	Latimore, Frederick	MNT	42	Laurence, James	RNS	104
Lasher, John	COL	190	Latimore, Mathew	NYK	90	Laurence, Jesse	DUT	75
Lasher, John	COL	223	Latimore, Rainbow	MNT	50	Laurence, Job	ONN	159
Lasher, John	MNT	7	Latine, John	STB	200	Laurence, Johanna	KNG	8
Lasher, John	NYK	96	Lating, Joanna	COL	177	Laurence, John	MNT	101
Lasher, John a Black	NYK	101	Laton, David	QNS	81	Laurence, John	NYK	61
Lasher, John	SRA	11	Laton, David Junr	QNS	82	Laurence, John	ONT	460
Lasher, John Junr	MNT	7	Laton, Garret	QNS	82	L..rence, Jonathan	CAY	616
Lasher, John B.	COL	225	Laton, Jacob	QNS	82	Laurence, Jonathan	NYK	25
Lasher, John P.	ALB	18	Laton, William	COL	246	Laurence, Jonathan H.	NYK	21
Lasher, Joseph	ALB	11	Latour, Anthony	NYK	26	Laurence, Joseph &		
Lasher, Joseph	ALB	98	Latourrette, David	RCH	88	Ezekiel	DUT	118

216

Name	Loc	No
Laurence, Joseph W.	ONT	384
Laurence, Lebeus	RNS	75
Laurence, Levi	ONN	159
Laurence, Marchant	GRN	326
Laurence, Mary	NYK	38
Laurence, Nancy	NYK	99
Laurence, Obediah	DUT	118
Laurence, Peter	MNT	104
Laurence, Peter	ONN	159
Laurence, Polly	NYK	37
Laurence, Richard	DUT	118
Laurence, Richard	NYK	38
Laurence, Richard T.	NYK	38
Laurence, Robert	NYK	96
Laurence, Rufus	ONN	159
Laurence, Samuel	DUT	114
Laurence, Samuel	DUT	176
Laurence, Sarah	NYK	43
Laurence, Sarah	NYK	43
Laurence, Silas	NYK	45
Laurence, Stephen	DUT	118
Laurence, Thomas	DUT	37
Laurence, Thomas	NYK	74
Laurence, Thomas E.	DUT	109
Laurence, William	CLN	169
Laurence, Wm	MNT	44
Laurence, William	NYK	70
Laurence, William	NYK	124
Laurence, William	NYK	134
Laurenel, Nicholas	NYK	88
Laurenel, William	NYK	88
Lauron, Saml	RNS	37
Lauton, Edward	RNS	106
Lauton, Josiah	RNS	66
Lauton, William	RNS	42
Lauvelt, Harman	NYK	93
Lavarnois, Toussaint	CLN	170
Laver, Adam	ALB	19
Laver, Phillip	NYK	119
Laveretts, Richard	QNS	60
Laverty, Alexr	OTS	34
Laverty, Henry	NYK	72
Lavillay, Peter a Black	NYK	134
Lavinus, Joseph	WST	163
Lavinus, Thomas	WST	163
Lavor, Augustus	NYK	132
Lavy, Jacob	MNT	46
Law see Low		
Law, Consider	OND	187
Law, David	NYK	49
Law, Elizabeth	RNS	83
Law, George	ONT	400
Law, Jacob	CHN	980
Law, John	WSH	187
Law, John	WSH	228
Law, John Junr	WSH	229
Law, Joseph	COL	207
Law, Nathan	WSH	277
Law, Robert	WSH	188
Law, Samuel	RNS	43
Law, Samuel	WSH	249
Law, Saml And:	DEL	288
Law, Thomas	COL	207
Law, Thomas	WSH	224
Law, William	COL	252
Lawk, Michael	DUT	159
Lawless, ...an	MNT	78
Lawless, John	DUT	110
Lawless, Joseph	DUT	114
Lawlow, Ellen	NYK	118
Lawnsberry, Daniel	CAY	706
Lawnsbury, John	WST	171
Lawny, David T.	NYK	86
Lawpaw, Peter	GRN	328
Lawrance see Laurance		
Lawrance, Abel	OND	190
Lawrance, Amos	DEL	288
Lawrance, Ariel	OND	173
Lawrance, Chauncey	DEL	284
Lawrance, David	DEL	268
Lawrance, Edward	OND	223
Lawrance, Filander	WST	156
Lawrance, Grove	OND	103
Lawrance, John	WSH	245
Lawrance, Minor	WST	154
Lawrance, Richard	WST	154
Lawrance, Roger	OND	204
Lawrance, Samuel	WST	154
Lawrance, Semion	SRA	59
Lawrance, Thomas	QNS	61
Lawrance, Abel	TIO	246
Lawrance, Abraham	MNT	46
Lawrance, Andrew	ULS	216
Lawrance, Augustus H.	NYK	28
Lawrance, Benjamin	CAY	518
Lawrance, Benjamin	QNS	65
Lawrance, Calvin	COL	240
Lawrance, Calvin	ONN	159
Lawrance, Catherine	NYK	24
Lawrance, Charles	QNS	70
Lawrance, Charles	WST	118
Lawrance, Christian	COL	220
Lawrance, Consider	TIO	246
Lawrance, Daniel	DUT	128
Lawrance, Daniel	QNS	61
Lawrance, Daniel	QNS	65
Lawrance, Daniel	WST	163
Lawrance, David	COL	247
Lawrance, Edward & Richd	QNS	61
Lawrance, Edward	QNS	63
Lawrance, Effingham	QNS	66
Lawrance, Eliza	KNG	11
Lawrance, Elizabeth	WST	145
Lawrance, Ellenor	NYK	63
Lawrance, Elvin	WST	163
Lawrance, Elwin	WST	148
Lawrance, Frank Jun.	HRK	424
Lawrance, Gedeon	MNT	63
Lawrance, George	WST	163
Lawrance, Gilbert	WST	120
Lawrance, Gilbert	WST	148
Lawrance, Henry	QNS	64
Lawrance, Ira	COL	181
Lawrance, Isaac	COL	201
Lawrance, Isaac	ORN	394
Lawrance, Isaac	WST	146
Lawrance, Isaac	WST	147
Lawrance, Jacob & William	DUT	118
Lawrance, Jacob	QNS	73
Lawrance, James	NYK	143
Lawrance, James	QNS	65
Lawrance, James	WSH	288
Lawrance, James	WST	116
Lawrance, John	COL	202
Lawrance, John	DUT	167
Lawrance, John	MNT	8
Lawrance, John	NYK	18
Lawrance, John	ORN	382
Lawrance, John	QNS	61
Lawrance, John	QNS	75
Lawrance, John	RCK	99
Lawrance, John	RCK	108
Lawrance, John	ULS	216
Lawrance, John	WSH	288
Lawrance, John	WST	111
Lawrance, John	WST	148
Lawrance, John	WST	163
Lawrance, John Junr	ULS	217
Lawrance, John B.	NYK	45
Lawrance, Jno Free Black	COL	244
Lawrence, Jonathan	NYK	87
Lawrence, Jonathan	RCK	99
Lawrence, Jonathan Junr	RCK	99
Lawrence, Joseph	QNS	64
Lawrence, Joseph	RCK	108
Lawrence, Joseph	WST	148
Lawrence, Joseph	WST	163
Lawrence, Joshua	WST	168
Lawrence, Judah	COL	189
Lawrence, Judah M.	COL	189
Lawrence, Michael	WST	119
Lawrence, Monis	COL	194
Lawrence, Nathaniel	NYK	70
Lawrence, Noah	WST	149
Lawrence, Olliver	GRN	354
Lawrence, Peter	COL	225
Lawrence, Peter	NYK	90
Lawrence, Peter Junr	COL	226
Lawrence, Philip	QNS	69
Lawrence, Phillip	NYK	125
Lawrence, Pompey Black	QNS	69
Lawrence, Richard	QNS	61
Lawrence, Richd & Edward Lawrence	QNS	61
Lawrence, Richard R.	NYK	45
Lawrence, Robert	ULS	217
Lawrence, Sampson	CAY	696
Lawrence, Samuel	QNS	61
Lawrence, Samuel	WSH	282
Lawrence, Samuel	WST	117
Lawrence, Samuel	WST	146
Lawrence, Stephen	DUT	167
Lawrence, Stephen	NYK	83
Lawrence, Stephen	QNS	65
Lawrence, Stephen	SCH	118
Lawrence, Stephen	WST	146
Lawrence, Thaddeus	DUT	107
Lawrence, Thankfull	WSH	305
Lawrence, Thomas	COL	248
Lawrence, Thomas	DUT	156
Lawrence, Thomas	QNS	65
Lawrence, Thos	RCK	99
Lawrence, Thos	RCK	108
Lawrence, Thomas	WST	163
Lawrence, Thomas P.	WST	148
Lawrence, Uriah M.	DUT	142
Lawrence, Whitehead	QNS	70
Lawrence, William & Jacob	DUT	118
Lawrence, William	NYK	53
Lawrence, William	QNS	65
Lawrence, William	QNS	71
La[ws?], Benjn	SUF	68
Lawson, Abraham	DUT	71
Lawson, Abraham	ULS	263
Lawson, Andrew	ALB	73
Lawson, Andrew	DUT	71
Lawson, Andrew P.	ALB	80
Lawson, Benjamin	ULS	185
Lawson, Daniel	DUT	17
Lawson, George	DUT	18
Lawson, George	ULS	219
Lawson, Henry	ALB	79
Lawson, Isaac	ALB	62
Lawson, Isaac	DUT	34
Lawson, Jacob	ULS	258
Lawson, James	ALB	32
Lawson, James	OND	204
Lawson, John	ALB	23
Lawson, John	NYK	121
Lawson, John	NYK	136
Lawson, John D.	ORN	282
Lawson, John P.	DUT	71
Lawson, John W.	ULS	182
Lawson, Joseph	RNS	42
Lawson, Lawrence	ALB	110
Lawson, Mathew	WSH	228

Lawson, Matthew	DUT	70	Layton, Daniel	CAY	600	Leake, Thomas	DUT	117
Lawson, Matthew Ye 2d	DUT	71	Layton, Daniel	ORN	369	Leake, William	CAY	522
Lawson, Peter	ALB	96	Layton, John	OTS	57	Leake, William	DUT	120
Lawson, Peter	NYK	58	Layton, John	QNS	81	Leal, Alexander	DEL	290
Lawson, Peter	NYK	84	Layton, Richard	NYK	59	Leal, Henry	DEL	290
Lawson, Peter	NYK	143	Layton, Samuel	ORN	369	Leancourt, Stephen	NYK	36
Lawson, Peter A.	DUT	69	Layton, Thomas	OTS	54	Learner, Adam	ONT	490
Lawson, Richard	OND	173	Layton, Thomas	TIO	257	Leary, Daniel	NYK	33
Lawson, Samuel	DUT	21	Layton, William	OND	166	Leary, John	OTS	22
Lawson, Samuel	WSH	188	Layton, Wm	TIO	263	Leaseman, John	NYK	72
Lawson, Simon	DUT	71	Laytor, William	ONT	366	Leasenby, Thomas	NYK	80
Lawson, Simon	NYK	104	Lazellier, Daniel	ONT	464	Lea[sh?], Levi	WST	129
Lawson, Simon	ULS	186	Lazen, Fredrick	TIO	211	Leason, Caleb	TIO	247
Lawson, William	DUT	41	Lazerbeer, Abraham	NYK	89	Leason, Daniel	TIO	247
Lawson, William	DUT	70	Lazerbeer, Abraham	NYK	89	Leason, Jesse	TIO	247
Lawson, William	NYK	61	Lazere, Jacob	RCH	92	Leason, Joseph	TIO	249
Lawton, Abigail	QNS	66	Lazier, Cornelius	ORN	372	Leason, Noah	ALB	87
Lawton, Benjamin	HRK	586	Lazier, Henry	ORN	304	Leason, Peter	SRA	60
Lawton, Clark	WSH	190	Lazurus, Fanny	NYK	26	Leath, Luther	SRA	16
Lawton, David	DUT	106	Lazy, Richard	NYK	65	Leath_y, James	NYK	74
Lawton, David	HRK	586	Le___, James	DEL	285	Leavens, Benjamin	DUT	102
Lawton, George	HRK	586	Le..., Sarah	TIO	209	Leavenworth see Leven-		
Lawton, James	OTS	23	Leab, George	ALB	67	worth		
Lawton, Joseph	HRK	517	Leab, Johannis	ALB	67	Leavenworth, Amos	OND	200
Lawton, Oliver	HRK	517	Leach, Alexander	COL	181	Leavenworth, Ebeneser	MNT	66
Lawton, Robert	COL	252	Leach, Alexander	ONN	189	Leavenworth, Elisha	NYK	78
Lawton, Stephen	HRK	524	Leach, Archibald	NYK	117	Leavenworth, Lemuel	OND	157
Lawton, Thomas	HRK	524	Leach, Caleb	NYK	100	Leavenworth, Lemuel Junr	OND	157
Lawton, Wm	OTS	52	Leach, Ebenezer	OND	163	Leavett, Asaph	ESS	309
Lawyer, Abraham	SCH	118	Leach, Ephraim	DUT	46	Leavey, Michael	ALB	31
Lawyer, Abraham	SCH	128	Leach, Jacob	SRA	4	Leavings, Calvin	OTS	16
Lawyer, Caleb	CAY	662	Leach, James	CHN	814	Leavinworth, James	MNT	77
Lawyer, Christian	SCH	118	Leach, Jane	NYK	104	Leavitt, David	ORN	389
Lawyer, Christopher	COL	190	Leach, John D.	WSH	293	Leaycraft, John R.	NYK	109
Lawyer, David	SCH	152	Leach, Jonathan	CHN	896	Leaycraft, Richard	NYK	27
Lawyer, David Ju	SCH	118	Leach, Jonathan	ONN	189	Leayercraft, William	NYK	69
Lawyer, Eber	SCH	124	Leach, Obediah	CHN	902	Le Bar, Charles	CAY	580
Lawyer, Henry	SCH	118	Leach, Oby	QNS	69	Le Bar, Philip	CAY	580
Lawyer, Jacob	ALB	24	Leach, Oliver	WSH	268	Le Bar, William	CAY	580
Lawyer, Jacob	SCH	125	Leach, Pheneas	MNT	59	Lebarn, Alden	RNS	24
Lawyer, Jacob F.	SCH	118	Leach, Thomas	CHN	814	Lebarn, John	RNS	24
Lawyer, Jacob Fred_	SCH	125	Leach, Thomas	CHN	882	Lebastone, William	SCH	154
Lawyer, Jacob J.	SCH	118	Leache, George	NYK	113	Lebert, Abraham	CHN	966
Lawyer, John	SCH	125	Leache, William	NYK	72	Lebrun, Marin	NYK	33
Lawyer, John J.	SCH	118	Lea.ock, David	CAY	544	Le Conte, John	NYK	52
Lawyer, John L.	SCH	128	Leacraft, James	NYK	106	Le Cost, Francis	ORN	377
Lawyer, Lambert	SCH	150	Leacraft, Willett	QNS	64	Le Count, John	DUT	74
Lawyer, Laurence	SCH	150	Leacraft, William	NYK	51	Le Count, John	WST	149
Lawyer, Lawrence	SCH	127	Leader, Henry	NYK	75	Le Count, Joseph	ORN	273
Lawyer, Lawrence L.	SCH	128	Leader, John	ORN	348	Le Count, Josiah	WST	149
Lawyer, Peter	SCH	122	Leak, Clark	SCH	146	Lecoy, David	NYK	102
Lay, Edward	COL	222	Leak, David	SUF	64	Lecquah, Elijah	NYK	105
Lay, John	OND	202	Leak, Philip	SUF	64	Le Cunte, Charles	NYK	75
Lay, Joseph	OND	213	Leake, Abraham	SUF	109	Leddie, John	NYK	97
Lay, Reuben	COL	219	Leake, Benjamin	DUT	6	Ledell, George	CAY	582
Lay, Reuben	OND	213	Leake, Coonrod	CAY	522	Ledens, John	ALB	98
Lay, Samuel	CAY	518	Leake, Crapo	DUT	6	Lederman, George	ALB	46
Laybolt, Adam	ULS	188	Leake, Daniel	DUT	46	Ledgard, George	SUF	76
Laybolt, John	ULS	188	Leake, David	SUF	106	Ledgard, Thos	SUF	76
Laybolt, Nicholas	ORN	297	Leake, Elias	SUF	93	Ledger, John	MNT	95
Layer, Jacob	TIO	258	Leake, Elijah	DUT	130	Le Dieu, Abraham	CAY	724
Laylor, Annestatia	NYK	71	Leake, Henry	CAY	522	Le Dieu, Ambrose	DUT	36
Layman, ...ah	SCH	145	Leake, Henry	DUT	7	Le Dieu, Daniel	ULS	195
Layman, Andrew	SCH	145	Leake, Henry	DUT	122	Le Dieu, John	DUT	97
Layman, Clament	GRN	327	Leake, Henry	DUT	129	Le Dieu, Nathaniel	DUT	27
Layman, Ephraim	GRN	326	Leake, James	DUT	7	Le Dieu, Oliver	DUT	27
Layman, Jacob	GRN	327	Leake, James	DUT	114	Le Dieu, Peter	DUT	27
Layman, Jeremiah	GRN	326	Leake, James	DUT	120	Le Dieu, Roger	DUT	44
Layman, John	GRN	325	Leake, James Junr	DUT	122	Le Dieu, William	DUT	26
Layman, John	MNT	3	Leake, John	DUT	6	Le Dieu, William Junr	DUT	27
Layman, Mathias	GRN	327	Leake, John	DUT	103	Ledius, Beltishazer	ALB	136
Laymant, George	COL	236	Leake, John	DUT	114	Ledson, Daniel	WSH	254
Laymant, William	ONT	394	Leake, John G.	NYK	21	Ledson, William	WSH	254
Layn, Josiah	NYK	48	Leake, Orange	DUT	135	Le Due, Joseph	CLN	168
Layne see Lane & Laine			Leake, Peter	DUT	114	Ledyard, Benjamin	CAY	628
Layne, Eliza	NYK	55	Leake, Stephen	DUT	48	Ledyard, Isaac	QNS	60
Layton, Andrw	NYK	71	Leake, Ruth	ORN	375	Ledyard, Peter V.	NYK	29

Name	Co	Pg
Leir, ..phus	MNT	11
Leister see Liester, Luster & Luyster		
Leister, Benjamin	NYK	114
Leister, Charles	CAY	666
Leister, Daniel	CAY	668
Leister, Derrick	NYK	128
Leister, Ichabod	COL	216
Leister, Isaac	CAY	710
Leister, James	COL	238
Leister, James Junr	COL	178
Leister, Jason	COL	219
Leister, Jehoikim	CAY	708
Leister, John	COL	177
Leister, Nathaniel	SUF	109
Leister, Richard	NYK	79
Leister, Samuel	COL	241
Leister, Thomas	COL	185
Leland, Isaac	ONT	444
Leland, James	ONT	444
Leland, Joshua	CHN	812
Leller, Martin	MNT	66
Lellobridge, Edward	WSH	251
Lemains, John	NYK	128
Le Masteney, Edmund	ORN	301
Leming, Aaron	COL	257
Lemmon, Isaac	CAY	722
Lemmon, John	KNG	8
Lemmon, John	ONT	328
Lemmon, John	ORN	327
Lemmon, Mathias	ONT	384
Lemon a Negro	SUF	73
Lemon, John	SCH	131
Lemon, Thomas	ONT	324
Lemon, William	ONT	324
Lemons, Archibald	SCH	131
Lemons, John	SCH	132
Lempson, Humphrey	OTS	47
Le Munyon, James	ULS	242
Le Munyon, John	ULS	240
Le Munyon, Phillip	ULS	240
Lender, Christion	MNT	63
Lenhart, John	ALB	66
Lenhart, Simon	ALB	57
Lenicre, James	ALB	139
Lening, Richard	OND	213
Lenk, Jacob	NYK	95
Lennington, Thomas	ALB	130
Lennington, Thomas	ALB	143
Lennon, John ye 1st	DUT	148
Lennon, John ye 2d	DUT	124
Lenon, Peter	DUT	118
Lenos, Hathaway	MNT	89
Lenox, David	NYK	146
Lenox, James	ALB	104
Lenox, James	NYK	18
Lenox, Robert	NYK	28
Lenox, Robert	ONT	474
Lensey, James Jur	MNT	47
Lenssy, Samuel	SRA	56
Lent, Abraham	ALB	62
Lent, Abraham	DUT	33
Lent, Abraham	ORN	390
Lent, Abrm	RCK	98
Lent, Abraham	WSH	239
Lent, Abraham	WST	147
Lent, Abraham	WST	155
Lent, Abraham	WST	160
Lent, Abraham	WST	160
Lent, Abraham D.	NYK	149
Lent, Albert	WST	160
Lent, Benjamin	WST	168
Lent, Charles	DUT	177
Lent, David	RNS	6
Lent, David	WST	154
Lent, David	WST	157
Lent, Dennis	WST	146
Lent, Garret	WST	163
Lent, George	ORN	394
Lent, Harculaus	WST	158
Lent, Harculous Junr	WST	155
Lent, Henderick	WST	157
Lent, Hendrick	WST	160
Lent, Henry	NYK	81
Lent, Henry	WSH	238
Lent, Henry	WSH	240
Lent, Henry Capt.(?)	WST	158
Lent, Henry	WST	159
Lent, Henry Bus.	WST	159
Lent, Henry Crum.	WST	159
Lent, Herman	WST	160
Lent, Isaac	DUT	78
Lent, Isaac	WST	152
Lent, Isaac	WST	159
Lent, Isaac Junr	WST	163
Lent, Jacob	OND	195
Lent, Jacob	ORN	389
Lent, Jacob	RCK	102
Lent, Jacob	RCK	102
Lent, Jacob	WST	124
Lent, Jacob	WST	130
Lent, Jacob	WST	147
Lent, Jacob Botman	WST	156
Lent, Jacob Clip.	WST	157
Lent, Jacob	WST	160
Lent, Jacob Junior	WST	160
Lent, Jacob 3rd	WST	154
Lent, James	RCK	98
Lent, James	WST	156
Lent, James	WST	157
Lent, James W.	NYK	24
Lent, Jocob	WSH	239
Lent, John	DUT	25
Lent, John	NYK	45
Lent, John	WSH	239
Lent, John	WST	155
Lent, John longfly	WST	157
Lent, John Clip.	WST	157
Lent, John	WST	158
Lent, John Clip.	WST	160
Lent, John	WST	161
Lent, John 3rd	WST	160
Lent, Margaret	WST	157
Lent, Matthew	WST	155
Lent, Moses	CAY	700
Lent, Peter	WST	147
Lent, Peter	WST	168
Lent, Phillip	SRA	55
Lent, Tobias	WST	159
Lent, Tobias Senr	WST	155
Lent, William	WST	157
Lent, William	WST	159
Lent, William	WST	160
Lentner, John	NYK	31
Lentz, Frederick	NYK	37
Lentz, Lewis	NYK	48
Lentz, Paul	NYK	58
Leon, Louis	NYK	69
Leon, Moses	NYK	71
Leonard, Abm	SCH	161
Leonard, Abraham	WSH	286
Leonard, Amos	OND	199
Leonard, Asa	TIO	247
Leonard, Benjn	OTS	40
Leonard, Chauncy	ORN	272
Leonard, Daniel	ALB	108
Leonard, Danl	OTS	52
Leonard, Daniel A.	NYK	116
Leonard, David	COL	189
Leonard, David	DEL	274
Leonard, Ebenr	OTS	34
Leonard, Enoch	ALB	146
Leonard, Ephraim	OND	207
Leonard, Francis	NYK	73
Leonard, Henry	SRA	19
Leonard, Isaac	RNS	23
Leonard, Jacob	NYK	74
Leonard, Jacob	NYK	105
Leonard, Jacob	SRA	19
Leonard, James	DEL	178
Leonard, James	NYK	84
Leonard, Jeffry	NYK	109
Leonard, Job	WSH	275
Leonard, John	ALB	108
Leonard, John	CAY	542
Leonard, John	NYK	24
Leonard, John	NYK	98
Leonard, John	NYK	101
Leonard, John	RNS	96
Leonard, John	WSH	268
Leonard, John	WSH	286
Leonard, Jonathan	ONT	318
Leonard, Joseph	CAY	686
Leonard, Joseph	TIO	210
Leonard, Joshua	CHN	966
Leonard, Levi	OTS	37
Leonard, Livingston	NYK	77
Leonard, Manassa	CAY	700
Leonard, Moses	SRA	19
Leonard, Nathan	CAY	688
Leonard, Nathan Junr	CAY	688
Leonard, Nathaniel	SRA	22
Leonard, Nathaniel	WSH	256
Leonard, Noah	OND	163
Leonard, Reuben	DUT	17
Leonard, Rhuben	CHN	824
Leonard, Robert	NYK	59
Leonard, Robert	RNS	83
Leonard, Robert	SRA	12
Leonard, Rufus	HRK	516
Leonard, Sarah	NYK	86
Leonard, Solomon	HRK	515
Leonard, Solomon	ONN	143
Leonard, Stephen	HRK	442
Leonard, Thomas	DUT	17
Leonard, Thomas	NYK	25
Leonard, Thomas	NYK	108
Leonard, Thomas	RNS	23
Leonard, Timothy	WSH	276
Leonard, Walter	TIO	253
Leonard, William	DUT	123
Lepper, Conradt	MNT	19
Lepper, Fredirick	MNT	105
Lepper, Jacob	MNT	23
Lepper, Joh.	MNT	30
epper, John	MNT	62
Lepper, John Junr	MNT	62
Lepwing, John	MNT	100
Lequer, Abraham	KNG	8
Lequere, Abraham	ORN	310
Lerghthizen, Henry	NYK	67
Le Roy see La Roy		
Le Roy, Crynus	ORN	378
Le Roy, David	NYK	125
Le Roy, Elizabeth	DUT	32
Le Roy, Francis	DUT	63
Leroy, Francis	NYK	80
Le Roy, Francis	ULS	239
Le Roy, Henry	DUT	61
Le Roy, Herman	NYK	19
Leroy, Jacob	NYK	50
Le Roy, John	DUT	64
Le Roy, John F.	DUT	32
Le Roy, John I.	DUT	41
Le Roy, Michael	ULS	239
Le Roy, Middaugh	ULS	262
Le Roy, Peter	DUT	71
Leroy, Peter	MNT	71
Le Roy, Peter	ULS	216
Le Roy, Robert	NYK	19
Le Roy, Robert	ULS	234

Le Roy, Simeon	ALB 106	Leverse, Anthony	SRA 11	Lewis, Benjn Jur	ONN 143
Le Roy, Simon	ULS 235	Leversee, Lavinus	RNS 85	Lewis, Charles	ONT 334
Lesco, Wm	TIO 253	Levi, Solomon	WST 158	Lewis, Charles	OTS 49
Leseure, Hyacinth	COL 247	Leving, James	NYK 62	Lewis, Clark	RNS 76
Leshey, John	NYK 98	Levingo, Joseph	ALB 129	Lewis, Clark	RNS 76
Leshmell, Robert	COL 253	Levingstone, Saml	RNS 33	Lewis, Comfort	OTS 21
Leslie, George	ALB 9	Levins, Isaac	RNS 30	Lewis, Cornelius	DUT 160
Leslie, John	COL 193	Levintts, ...riel	QNS 60	Lewis, Cyrus	OTS 38
Leslie, Thomas	NYK 77	Levinus, James	WST 119	Lewis, Daniel	CHN 764
Lesnia, Daniel	MNT 52	Levinus, John	NYK 60	Lewis, Daniel	DEL 290
Lespanard, Anthony	NYK 102	Levinus, Joseph	NYK 149	Lewis, Daniel	DUT 129
Lessanna, John	NYK 77	Levirsee, Douw	ALB 49	Lewis, Daniel	OND 198
Lessly, George	WSH 249	Levirsee, Maria	ALB 49	Lewis, Danl	OTS 2
Lester, Allen	ULS 265	Levisee, Isaac	WSH 241	Lewis, Danl	OTS 38
Lester, Andw	NYK 90	Levisee, Isaac	WSH 251	Lewis, Daniel	WST 114
Lester, Catharine	DUT 65	Levisier, Belthazer	NYK 87	Lewis, David	NYK 79
Lester, David	ALB 113	Leviss, Richard	OND 197	Lewis, David	RNS 67
Lester, Elisha	ULS 239	Levisson, Daniel	NYK 105	Lewis, David	ULS 209
Lester, Henry	MNT 77	Levit, Josiah Gold	SRA 25	Lewis, Dennis	WST 115
Lester, John	ULS 240	Levit, Sherwood	SRA 25	Lewis, Dunning	ORN 344
Lester, Mordecai	DUT 67	Levorce, Levinus	SRA 6	Lewis, Ebenezer	COL 180
Lester, Mordica	ALB 36	Levvins, Thurlow	WSH 214	Lewis, Eber	ONT 364
Lester, Thomas	DUT 6	Levvins, William	WSH 214	Lewis, Edward	OND 162
Lester, Timothy	DUT 6	Levy	QNS 82	Lewis, Edward	OTS 30
Lesuer, Samuel	HRK 437	Levy	SUF 96	Lewis, Edward Junr	OND 162
Lesure, David	CAY 642	Levy, Ahas	NYK 52	Lewis, Eli	TIO 233
Le Sure, John	CAY 678	Levy, David a Black	NYK 44	Lewis, Elijah	CAY 690
Le Sure, John Junr	CAY 678	Levy, Eleazer	NYK 16	Lewis, Elijah	ULS 268
Le Sure, Nathan	CAY 678	Levy, Elizabeth	DUT 155	Lewis, Elisha	DUT 168
Letcher, Cornelius	RNS 77	Levy, Frances a		Lewis, Elisha	ONN 151
Lete, Allen	SCH 134	Black	NYK 148	Lewis, Elisha	ONN 153
Leth, Phebe	NYK 33	Levy, Henry	COL 224	Lewis, Elisha 2d	ONN 153
Letson, George	RNS 73	Levy, Isaac H.	NYK 29	Lewis, Elizabeth	NYK 138
Letson, Isaiah	OND 164	Levy, Jacob	DUT 156	Lewis, Elizabeth	ULS 268
Letson, James	DUT 60	Levy, Joshua	NYK 16	Lewis, Elkanan	SUF 88
Letson, John	OND 164	Levy, William	WSH 280	Lewis, Ellen	NYK 123
Letson, Jonathan	RNS 73	Lew Negro	QNS 73	Lewis, Elnathan	CHN 776
Letson, Michael	OND 164	Lew	QNS 78	Lewis, Enoch	DUT 117
Letson, Robert	RNS 73	Lew	SUF 93	Lewis, Enoch	DUT 170
Letson, William	DUT 32	Lewellan, Lewis	CAY 636	Lewis, Erasmus	NYK 97
Letson, William	OND 164	Lewer, Michael	WSH 220	Lewis, Esekiel	MNT 82
Letsow, John	NYK 66	Lewillen, Richard	NYK 138	Lewis, Evan	NYK 121
Letterett, Mary	NYK 75	Lewis Negro	QNS 71	Lewis, Eve	ALB 130
Lettle, Eleazer	NYK 109	Lewis	SUF 81	Lewis, Ezekiel	OND 169
Letts, John	WSH 187	Lewis a Free Negro	WST 112	Lewis, Ezekiel	OND 203
Letz, Abraham	ORN 390	Lewis see Louis & Luis		Lewis, Ezra	ALB 72
Leuer, Joshua	ONN 190	Lewis, ...	MNT 84	Lewis, Felix	DUT 65
Levalle, Benjn	HRK 417	Lewis, as	QNS 71	Lewis, Frances	NYK 122
Levally, Christopher	OND 193	Lewis, Abel	ONN 143	Lewis, Francis	NYK 102
Levally, Cookley	ALB 98	Lewis, Abel	RNS 68	Lewis, Francis Junr	NYK 52
Levally, George	OND 213	Lewis, Abner	RNS 29	Lewis, Frederick	CHN 958
Levally, James	OND 193	Lewis, Abner	ULS 238	Lewis, Frederick	MNT 44
Levally, John	QNS 79	Lewis, Abraham	MNT 82	Lewis, Fredk	OTS 28
Levans, Hezekeah	WSH 274	Lewis, Abraham	MNT 116	Lewis, George	ALB 145
Levany, Joseph	CLN 158	Lewis, Abrm	OTS 55	Lewis, George	NYK 52
Levelly, Peleg	ALB 74	Lewis, Abraham	RNS 68	Lewis, George	NYK 99
Levengslone, Richard	OND 222	Lewis, Adres	GRN 345	Lewis, George	SUF 84
Levens, Noah	RNS 30	Lewis, Alexander	SUF 89	Lewis, George K.	SRA 52
Levens, Samuel	SRA 47	Lewis, Alexander	ULS 243	Lewis, Gilbert	WST 150
Levenworth, David	COL 209	Lewis, Amos	HRK 560	Lewis, Grace	WSH 186
Levenworth, John	COL 209	Lewis, Andrew	NYK 112	Lewis, Hannah a Black	NYK 41
Levenworth, Truman	COL 209	Lewis, Anthony	DUT 155	Lewis, Hannah	NYK 62
Leverage, Caleb	ONN 151	Lewis, Arnold	SRA 26	Lewis, Henry	ALB 73
Leverage, Jessee	QNS 62	Lewis, Asa	RNS 70	Lewis, Henry	ALB 87
Leverage, Richard	QNS 62	Lewis, Augustus	RNS 68	Lewis, Henry	DEL 275
Leverage, Sackett	QNS 62	Lewis, Avery	QNS 84	Lewis, Henry	MNT 100
Leverage, Sarah & Elias		Lewis, Barent	ULS 191	Lewis, Henry	NYK 66
Bailey	QNS 61	Lewis, Barent Junr	ULS 191	Lewis, Henry	WSH 298
Leverage, Wm & John		Lewis, Beal A.	NYK 116	Lewis, Henry Junr	MNT 100
Kitcham	QNS 61	Lewis, Benedict	ALB 125	Lewis, Howell	ORN 398
Leverage, William	QNS 62	Lewis, Benjamin	HRK 512	Lewis, Ichabod	ORN 347
Leverett, Michael	NYK 145	Lewis, Benjamin	ONT 370	Lewis, Ichabud	WST 121
Leveretts, Samuel	QNS 60	Lewis, Benjn	RNS 24	Lewis, Isaac	ALB 20
Leverich, James	KNG 9	Lewis, Benjamin	SRA 53	Lewis, Isaac	COL 219
Levericks, John	SUF 66	Lewis, Benjamin	SRA 60	Lewis, Isaac	DEL 275
Leveridge, John	WST 112	Lewis, Benj	TIO 211	Lewis, Isaac	NYK 141
Levering, Samuel	NYK 82	Lewis, Benjn Jur	ONN 142	Lewis, Isaac	ORN 387

Name	Ref	Name	Ref	Name	Ref
Lewis, Isaac	OTS 19	Lewis, Leonard B.	DUT 61	Lewis, Thos	OTS 18
Lewis, Isaac	OTS 35	Lewis, Levy	NYK 60	Lewis, Thomas	QNS 71
Lewis, Isaac	WST 136	Lewis, Lodowick	OTS 49	Lewis, Thomas W.	OND 183
Lewis, Isarel	NYK 96	Lewis, Margaret	SRA 26	Lewis, Timothy	TIO 243
Lewis, Israel	DUT 129	Lewis, Margaret	WST 151	Lewis, Truman	ONN 147
Lewis, Jacob	DUT 163	Lewis, Martial	GRN 337	Lewis, Uriah	RNS 68
Lewis, Jacob	ORN 387	Lewis, Mary	SUF 86	Lewis, Valentine	ULS 268
Lewis, Jacob	QNS 81	Lewis, Mathew	HRK 491	Lewis, Vintor	OTS 11
Lewis, James	ALB 53	Lewis, Mathew	RNS 14	Lewis, Wait	OTS 57
Lewis, James	CHN 790	Lewis, Matthew	HRK 476	Lewis, William	CHN 906
Lewis, James	OND 158	Lewis, Matthew	ULS 191	Lewis, William	CLN 155
Lewis, James	ONT 450	Lewis, Morgan	DUT 108	Lewis, William	CLN 172
Lewis, James	OTS 7	Lewis, Moses	SRA 28	Lewis, William	DUT 73
Lewis, James	QNS 73	Lewis, Moses	SRA 51	Lewis, Wm	MNT 43
Lewis, James	QNS 77	Lewis, Nathan	ALB 81	Lewis, Wm	MNT 88
Lewis, James	RNS 8	Lewis, Nathan	ESS 311	Lewis, William	NYK 32
Lewis, James	RNS 77	Lewis, Nathan	HRK 567	Lewis, William	NYK 149
Lewis, James	RCH 91	Lewis, Nathan	MNT 22	Lewis, William	ONT 450
Lewis, James	WSH 273	Lewis, Nathan	ONN 171	Lewis, William	ORN 386
Lewis, James	WST 115	Lewis, Nathan	RNS 76	Lewis, William	OTS 33
Lewis, James	WST 144	Lewis, Nathan	RNS 76	Lewis, William	QNS 66
Lewis, James Junr	RNS 88	Lewis, Nathan Junr	ESS 318	Lewis, William	QNS 69
Lewis, Jedson	CHN 882	Lewis, Nathaniel	ORN 334	Lewis, William	RNS 55
Lewis, Jeptha	WSH 270	Lewis, Nathl	OTS 49	Lewis, William	ULS 211
Lewis, Jesse	WST 121	Lewis, Nehemiah	CHN 778	Lewis, Zadoc	ULS 266
Lewis, Job	ALB 84	Lewis, Nehemiah	OTS 35	Lewis, Zebulon	RNS 67
Lewis, Joel	MNT 68	Lewis, Nicholas	ONN 174	Leydenburgh, Joseph	ULS 201
Lewis, John	ALB 111	Lewis, Nicholas	SRA 26	Leyster, Gerrit	ALB 45
Lewis, John	CAY 524	Lewis, Oliver	ORN 318	Leyster, Jacob	QNS 80
Lewis, John	CHN 946	Lewis, Peter	GRN 333	Leyster, Jeromus	QNS 80
Lewis, John	DUT 154	Lewis, Peter	KNG 10	Leyster, Peter	QNS 80
Lewis, John	HRK 408	Lewis, Peter	ONT 376	Lezar, Laurence	NYK 100
Lewis, John a Black	NYK 91	Lewis, Philo	DUT 19	Lezen, Aza Junr	ULS 188
Lewis, John	NYK 92	Lewis, Prince a mulatto	NYK 35	Lezen, Aza Senr	ULS 188
Lewis, John	NYK 127			Lezotte, Luis	CLN 168
Lewis, John	OND 162	Lewis, Randall	DEL 289	Lezure, Bethuel	OTS 24
Lewis, John	OND 170	Lewis, Reuben	CAY 660	Lhomedue see Lomedu,	
Lewis, John	ONT 498	Lewis, Reuben	OTS 34	Lommidieu & Lonmediew	
Lewis, John	ORN 309	Lewis, Reuben	SRA 34	Lhomedue, Joseph	SUF 90
Lewis, John	ORN 333	Lewis, Richard	DUT 107	Lhomidue, Constant	SUF 76
Lewis, John	ORN 389	Lewis, Richard	NYK 54	L. Homme' Dieu, Ezra	ORN 351
Lewis, John	RNS 55	Lewis, Richard	NYK 87	Lhommedieu, Saml	SUF 73
Lewis, John	RNS 76	Lewis, Richard	ORN 398	Lhommedue, Charles	SUF 102
Lewis, John	RNS 78	Lewis, Richard	SUF 87	Lhommedue, Danl	SUF 72
Lewis, John	RNS 99	Lewis, Robert	ESS 296	Lhommedue, David	SUF 90
Lewis, John	RCH 88	Lewis, Roswell	COL 210	Lhommedue, Gehiel	SUF 92
Lewis, John	ULS 190	Lewis, Samuel	ALB 111	Lhommedue, James	SUF 90
Lewis, John	ULS 192	Lewis, Samuel	CHN 894	Lhommedue, Mehitable	SUF 102
Lewis, John	WSH 267	Lewis, Samuel	DEL 274	Lhommedue, Saml	SUF 102
Lewis, John Junr	ULS 211	Lewis, Samuel	DUT 57	L Hommidue, Ezra	SUF 76
Lewis, Jonathan	ALB 71	Lewis, Samuel	MNT 22	Lhomnidue, Mary	SUF 72
Lewis, Jonathan	CAY 532	Lewis, Samuel	ORN 387	Lhonmedieu, Benjn	SUF 73
Lewis, Jonathan	DUT 65	Lewis, Saml	OTS 18	Liberty, John	HRK 482
Lewis, Jonathan	ORN 390	Lewis, Samuel	SRA 34	Liberty, Thomas	DUT 58
Lewis, Jonathan	RCH 95	Lewis, Samuel	SRA 50	Licett, William	SUF 85
Lewis, Jonathan	SRA 58	Lewis, Samuel	WSH 282	Lick, David	MNT 11
Lewis, Joseph	CAY 534	Lewis, Samuel H.	CLN 170	Lickly, James	DUT 80
Lewis, Joseph	CLN 165	Lewis, Sarah	ALB 138	Lickly, John	DUT 78
Lewis, Joseph	COL 211	Lewis, Sarah	CAY 520	Liddell, James	NYK 69
Lewis, Joseph	DUT 95	Lewis, Scudder	SUF 85	Liddle, James	ESS 304
Lewis, Joseph	NYK 31	Lewis, Seth	ONT 318	Liddle, John	WSH 257
Lewis, Joseph	NYK 71	Lewis, Seth	OTS 49	Liddle, Mark	WSH 257
Lewis, Joseph	ORN 387	Lewis, Shubill	RNS 29	Lidle, Wm	OTS 13
Lewis, Joseph	OTS 26	Lewis, Silus	CHN 882	Liebeneau, Frederic	NYK 55
Lewis, Joseph	OTS 51	Lewis, Solomon	ONT 450	Liens, Henry	NYK 58
Lewis, Joseph	RNS 103	Lewis, Sophia	WST 116	Liester see Leister	
Lewis, Joseph Junr	MNT 84	Lewis, Spencer	HRK 408	Liester, Ebenezar	CAY 668
Lewis, Joseph G.	HRK 567	Lewis, Spencer	OTS 2	Lift, Royal	CHN 930
Lewis, Joshua	CAY 698	Lewis, Stephen J.	NYK 34	Light see Laight & Liht	
Lewis, Joshua	OTS 57	Lewis, Stewart	ALB 132	Light, John	WST 142
Lewis, Joshua	RNS 35	Lewis, Tamer	ULS 193	Light, Lemuel	WST 139
Lewis, Joshua	RNS 95	Lewis, Thomas	CHN 750	Light, Roderick	TIO 235
Lewis, Joshua	WSH 186	Lewis, Thomas	COL 181	Lightbody, Gabriel	ORN 397
Lewis, Justice	OTS 42	Lewis, Thomas	COL 210	Lightbody, James as	
Lewis, Lendert	ULS 238	Lewis, Thomas	DUT 155	the gaoler of the	
Lewis, Leonard	ALB 131	Lewis, Thomas a Black	NYK 73	city & county	ALB 145
Lewis, Leonard Junr	DUT 60	Lewis, Thomas	NYK 109		

Name	Loc	Name	Loc	Name	Loc
Lightbody, James	ALB 145	Linds, John	HRK 540	Linsley, Solomon	OND 223
Lightfhart, Barnabes	SRA 42	Lindsay, Gedion	WSH 214	Linsley, William	CHN 892
Lighthall, Abraham	ALB 21	Lindsey, Aaron Jur	CHN 972	Linsow, Gilbert	NYK 112
Lighthall, Abrm	OTS 54	Lindsey, Alexander	RCK 101	Lintler, Albert	MNT 37
Lighthall, Abm J.	ALB 20	Lindsey, Daniel	OND 185	Lintler, George	MNT 37
Lighthall, Francis	MNT 2	Lindsey, David	NYK 169	Lintler, George Jr	MNT 37
Lighthall, George	OTS 54	Lindsey, George	NYK 150	.intler, John	MNT 37
Lighthall, James	ALB 13	Lindsey, Hugh	ORN 296	Lints, Philip	HRK 418
Lighthall, Jellis	ALB 20	Lindsey, James	NYK 129	Lintz, Peter	HRK 577
Lighthall, John	ALB 20	Lindsey, John	NYK 84	Linvell, James	NYK 64
Lighthall, Nicholas	ALB 26	Lindsey, Peter	DUT 72	Linzey, Robert	COL 210
Lighthall, Wm	ALB 20	Lindsley, Abiel	OND 167	Lion see Lyon	
Lighthall, Wm N.	ALB 3	Lindsley, Daniel	ONT 328	Lion, Aaron	ONT 392
Ligir, Gattien	NYK 123	Lindsley, Eleasor	STB 200	Lion, David	SRA 48
Lihte, John	MNT 59	Lindsley, James	OND 180	Lion, Eli	ONT 398
Lilienthal, Hankie	NYK 81	Lindsley, John	CAY 556	Lion, Horace	ONT 398
Lille, Samuel	CHN 894	Lindsley, John	ONT 328	Lion, Zebulon	RNS 9
Lilley, Eleanor W.	WST 160	Lindsley, Jonathan	OND 190	Lipe, Abraham	MNT 34
Lilley, John	NYK 126	Lindsley, Judah	CHN 972	Lipe, Adam	MNT 26
Lilley, Lemuel	OTS 26	Lindsley, Ozias	OND 185	Lipe, Cashe	MNT 26
Lilley, Reuben	WSH 256	Lindsley, Samuel	STB 200	Lipe, David	MNT 26
Lilley, Samuel	ALB 47	Line, James	WST 168	Lip_, Johanes	MNT 26
Lillia, William	WST 168	Lineback, Henry	HRK 447	Lipe, John	MNT 26
Lillie, John	ORN 392	Lines, Hosea	OTS 4	Lippencut, Hannah	NYK 42
Lilly, Aaron	WSH 241	Lines, Thomas	ORN 288	Lippencut, John	NYK 68
Lilly, Abiather	CHN 746	Lingo, Cornelius	NYK 129	Lippet, Loudon	OTS 12
Lilly, Daniel	ULS 211	Linham, George	NYK 47	Lippett, Joseph	OTS 10
Lilly, Jeremiah	ULS 181	Lininson, William	ULS 263	Lippett, Waterman	RNS 58
Lilly, Moses	ONN 148	Linis, Oliver W.	OTS 46	Lisbeacepin, Renne	NYK 87
Lilly, Silas	ONN 130	Link, David	ALB 35	Liscomb, Pelateah	WSH 299
Lilly, William	ALB 146	Link, Henry	COL 199	Liscomb, Robert	ALB 32
Limbert, George	NYK 145	Link, Jacob	HRK 472	Liscomb, Samuel	SRA 36
Limmerman, Hannah	DUT 161	Link, John	COL 224	Liscum, Elias	SUF 66
Limon, Aratus	RNS 84	Link, John	COL 230	Liscum, Isaac	SUF 95
Limon, Siles	WSH 206	Link, Lewis	NYK 134	Liscum, Isaac	SUF 96
Limons, Aaron	COL 261	Link, Nicholas	COL 199	Liscum, John	ORN 287
Limpkins, Ephraim	CAY 616	Link, Peter	RNS 7	Liscum, John	SUF 95
Linbacker, John	ORN 353	Link, Peter	RNS 15	Liscum, Samuel	ORN 287
Linch, Jacob	MNT 31	Link, Phillip	COL 199	Lisk, Benjamine	GRN 353
Linch, John	ALB 144	Link, Phillip	COL 225	Lisk, Catharine	RCH 90
Linch, Joshua	OND 210	Link, Wilhelmus	COL 199	Lisk, Charles	GRN 353
Linchela n, John	CHN 966	Link, Wilhelmus Junr	COL 199	Lisk, Daniel	RCH 90
Linckletter see Lynck-letter		Link, Willm	COL 232	Lisk, Ebenr	OTS 15
Linckletter, John	RCK 103	Link, William P.	COL 197	Lisk, James	ALB 117
Lincolin, Benjamin	NYK 117	Link, Zachariah	COL 224	Lisk, John	RCH 88
Lincoln, Appoles	RNS 24	Linkfuller, ..a..	MNT 78	Lisk, Thomas	RCH 88
Lincoln, Elizabeth	NYK 42	Linley, Nehemiah	DEL 275	Lismond, Edmond	MNT 66
Lincoln, Gideon	ORN 381	Linley, Samuel	ALB 83	Lispenard, John	WST 149
Lincoln, James	WSH 303	Linly, Abraham	GRN 339	Lisswell, John	ALB 45
Lincoln, Joseph	OTS 40	Linly, Abraham Jun	GRN 345	Listen, Tho.as	MNT 83
Lincoln, Levi	OTS 40	Linly, Mrs	GRN 341	Lister, Ephraem	WSH 271
Lincoln, Nathaniel	SUF 102	Linly, Philleman	GRN 345	Lister, George	WSH 257
Lincoln, Ormel	OTS 31	Linn, Daniel	SCH 117	Lister, Jacob	WSH 271
Lincoln, Otis	OTS 46	Linn, Mary	NYK 76	Lister, Silvester	SUF 76
Lincoln, Samuel	CAY 672	Linnen, George	NYK 104	Listlet, Charles	ONN 171
Lincoln, Silas	COL 208	Linnen, John	ALB 87	Liswell, Thomas	ALB 127
Lincoln, Thoms	TIO 248	Linnen, John	NYK 109	Lit_, William	ULS 233
Lincon, Anna	NYK 59	Linsey, Allen	SRA 48	Litchfield, James	ALB 113
Linda, George	WSH 303	Linsey, Daniel	SRA 48	Litchfield, Leonard	ALB 78
Lindaman, Catharine	NYK 134	Linsey, James	MNT 42	Litchfield, Mark	ALB 78
Lindbergh see Lyndbergh		Linsey, Jonah	WST 130	Litterman, Joseph	NYK 61
L d man, Cornelius	CAY 578	Linsey, Liub	SRA 48	Little see Lettle & Lytle	
Linden, Henry	NYK 72	Linsey, Wm	MNT 44		
Linderbach, John	DUT 31	Linsley see Lynsley		Little, Andw	SCH 163
Linderman, David	CAY 608	Linsley, A aron	CHN 970	Little, Andrew	WSH 221
Linderman, Ezekiel	ORN 298	Linsley, Archabald	CHN 764	Little, Benjamin	WSH 286
Linderman, Henry	ORN 339	Linsley, David	ALB 32	Little, David	OTS 56
Linderman, Jacob	ORN 298	Linsley, David	ONN 181	Little, David	SRA 59
Linderman, John	ORN 338	Linsley, Eliada	DEL 287	Little, David	WSH 225
Linderman, Justus	CAY 608	Linsley, Elijah	ONN 192	Little, Eleanor	WSH 221
Lindes, Clarissa	HRK 543	Linsley, Eliphalet	CHN 764	Little, Ephraim	DEL 280
Lindley, Eliada	ONT 398	Linsley, Isaac	ONN 192	Little, Francis	ULS 250
Lindley, Moses	CAY 618	Linsley, Matthew	DEL 287	Little, George	ORN 332
Lindley, Samuel	HRK 465	Linsley, Obed	CHN 764	Little, George	OTS 28
Lindly, Aron	MNT 106	Linsley, Oliver	OND 223	Little, Henry	ORN 283
Lindoll, John	SRA 51	Linsley, Oliver	OND 223	Little, Henry	SCH 137
				Little, Henry	WSH 228

Little, Hypsthabee	SRA 21	Livingston, Gilbert R.	ALB 6	Lobdel, Jacob	WST 126
Little, Isaac	NYK 87	Livingston, Henry	COL 227	Lobdell, Caleb Junr	MNT 85
Little, Isaac	ORN 332	Livingston, Henry	DUT 69	Lobdell, Daniel	MNT 85
Little, Jacob	ALB 68	Livingston, Henry	SCH 171	Lobdell, Isaac	ALB 78
Little, James	WST 143	Livingston, Henry A.	DUT 67	Lobdell, Jacob	ONT 400
Little, James Junr	WST 143	Livingston, Henry B.	DUT 162	Lobdell, James	HRK 452
Little, Jane	WSH 225	Livingston, Henry G.	NYK 16	Lobdell, John	ESS 317
Little, John	ESS 305	Livingston, Jacob	SCH 126	Lobdell, Joseph	HRK 436
Little, John	MNT 73	Livingston, James	CHN 952	Lobdell, Joshua	ALB 93
Little, John	MNT 92	Livingston, James	MNT 58	Lobdell, Levi	RNS 54
Little, John	NYK 141	Livingston, James	RNS 14	Lobdell, Simon	ALB 93
Little, John	NYK 146	Livingston, Johannis	ALB 61	Lobdell, William	ORN 376
Little, John	NYK 153	Livingston, John	CAY 564	Lobden, John	GRN 354
Little, John	OND 223	Livingston, John	HRK 411	Lobd-n, Stephen	GRN 348
Little, John	TIO 230	Livingston, John	MNT 59	Lobden, Stephen	GRN 355
Little, John	WSH 183	Livingston, John	OND 193	Lobdile, Daniel	MNT 124
Little, John P.	OND 188	Livingston, John	SCH 126	Lobdill, Abijah	MNT 59
Little, Jonathan	NYK 48	Livingston, John	WSH 292	Lobdill, Sylvanus	ESS 317
Little, Joseph	NYK 75	Livingston, John A.	COL 237	Lobdle, John	WST 126
Little, Joseph	ONN 140	Livingston, John H.	NYK 149	Lobrman, _odoch	MNT 125
Little, Joseph	ORN 386	Livingston, John O.	DUT 63	Loce, Silas	ONT 362
Little, Justin	OND 200	Livingston, John R.	NYK 20	Locee, Abraham	WST 163
Little, Michael	NYK 18	Livingston, John W.	WST 144	Locee, Cornelias	WST 163
Little, Moses	CAY 670	Livingston, Joseph	WSH 292	Locee, Joseph	WST 163
Little, Peter	NYK 140	Livingston, Margaret	ALB 140	Locey see Lorey	
Little, Robert	ORN 379	Livingston, Margaret	NYK 57	Locey, James	QNS 76
Little, Robert	WSH 225	Livingston, Molborne	ONN 172	Locey, Peter	SUF 81
Little, Samuel	WSH 225	Livingston, Peter	ALB 61	Loch, Nathaniel	CHN 774
Little, Smith	CAY 696	Livingston, Peter J.	ALB 61	Lochiere, Peter	NYK 88
Little, Stephen	OND 213	Livingston, Peter R.	NYK 19	Lochlan, John	OTS 2
Little, Thomas	ALB 27	Livingston, Peter W.	NYK 86	Lock, Amius	CHN 766
Little, William	ORN 330	Livingston, Philip J.	WST 145	Lock, Collins	HRK 462
Little, William	WSH 221	Livingston, Phillip	NYK 19	Lock, Henry	NYK 35
Littlebrandt, Hartman	COL 225	Livingston, Phillip	WST 163	Lock, Henry	SRA 61
Littlefield, Benjamin	WSH 282	Livingston, Phillip H.	DUT 153	Lock, John	HRK 535
Littlefield, Limon	WSH 219	Livingston, Richard	MNT 74	Lock, Josiah	CHN 828
Littlefield, Samuel	HRK 536	Livingston, Robert	WSH 201	Lo.k, Rufus	CHN 910
Littlefield, Samuel	WSH 283	Livingston, Robert	WSH 291	Locker, John	ALB 42
Littlefield, Sanders	WSH 218	Livingston, Robert H.	DUT 64	Locker, Samuel	RCH 89
Littlefield, Thomas	SRA 50	Livingston, Robert L.	COL 223	Lockerman, Isaac	RCH 93
Littlefield, Walden	RNS 75	Livingston, Robert R.	COL 223	Lockerman, John	RCH 88
Little John, John	HRK 529	Livingston, Samuel	WSH 293	Lockerman, Nathaniel	RCH 90
Littleton, Benjamin	TIO 261	Livingston, Sarah	NYK 51	Lockerman, Rebecca	RCH 90
Littlewood, William	NYK 45	Livingston, Sears free		Lockerman, Richard	RCH 91
Litts, Daniel	RNS 58	Black	COL 255	Lockerman, William	RCH 94
Litz, Daniel	ULS 186	Livingston, Suzan	NYK 60	Lockero, Anthony	RNS 89
Litz, Hendrick	ULS 233	Livingston, Thomas	WSH 194	Lockero, Charles	RNS 89
Lively, Simon	RNS 83	Livingston, Willeam	WSH 291	Lockerson, John a	
Livemore, Josiah	WSH 256	Livingston, William	KNG 3	mulatto	NYK 71
Liver, Catherine	NYK 43	Livingston, William	NYK 86	Lockery, William	NYK 108
Liveridge, John	NYK 77	Livingston, Willm	SCH 171	Lockman, Abraham	NYK 75
Livermoor, Danl	CHN 984	Livingstone see Leveng-		Lockman, Jacob	NYK 50
Livermore, Abner	CHN 910	slone		Lockman, James	NYK 91
Livermore, Daniel	CHN 910	Livingstone, __bert T.	COL 227	Lockman, Samuel	NYK 15
Livermore, Enos	TIO 216	Livingstone, __nes S.	COL 227	Lockward, James	NYK 69
Livermore, Solomon	HRK 546	Livingstone, Walter T.	COL 227	Lockward, Nathan	GRN 347
Livimore, Daniel	WSH 203	Livingsworth, Whitman	RNS 111	Lockwood, Aaron	ULS 186
Livingston, __nerief	COL 227	Livinsworth, David	RNS 111	Lockwood, Abraham	DUT 27
Livingston, __nelia	COL 227	Livinus, Nathaniel	NYK 88	Lockwood, Abraham	DUT 89
Livingston, __n	COL 227	Livire, Jasper	WST 145	Lockwood, Abraham	OND 173
Livingston, __ery W.	COL 227	Lizell, William D.	NYK 129	Lockwood, Abraham	WST 125
Livingston, Abraham	SRA 47	Lloyd see Loyd		Lockwood, Abraham	WST 159
Livingston, Alexander	WSH 195	Lloyd, Aaron	ALB 33	Lockwood, Amos	DUT 83
Livingston, Alexander	WSH 250	Lloyd, Amelia	SUF 86	Lockwood, Anna	NYK 70
Livingston, Alfred	WST 145	Lloyd, Anthony	DEL 276	Lockwood, Carey	NYK 85
Livingston, Beekman	DUT 5	Lloyd, James	ALB 137	Lockwood, Charles	KNG 2
Livingston, Benjamin	WSH 257	Lloyd, Joseph	ALB 33	Lockwood, Daniel	ALB 78
Livingston, Brockholst	NYK 20	Lloyd, Samuel	DEL 286	Lockwood, Daniel	ULS 268
Livingston, Cirus a		Llyd, Paul B.	NYK 31	Lockwood, Daniel	WST 160
Black	NYK 49	Loadman, Mary	ALB 120	Lockwood, Daniel	WST 161
Livingston, Eaward	NYK 51	Loag, Robert	ALB 7	Lockwood, David	ALB 93
Livingston, Edward P.	COL 223	Loatwall, David	ALB 110	Lockwood, David	ULS 241
Livingston, Eleanor	WSH 249	Loatwall, Jacob	ALB 110	Lockwood, Ebenezer	DUT 177
Livingston, Frances	WSH 292	Lobb, Jacob	WST 149	Lockwood, Ebenezer	WST 160
Livingston, Gilbert	DUT 163	Lobdal_, Da	MNT 84	Lockwood, Ebenezer Junr	WST 159
Livingston, Gilbert	SRA 6	Lobdel, Daniel	WST 125	Lockwood, Enoch	NYK 75
Livingston, Gilbert H.	DUT 153	Lobdel, Ebenezer	WST 126	Lockwood, Ezekiel	ESS 323

Lockwood, Ezra	WST 159	Lockwood, Zephaniah	SRA 53	Longbottom, Nathl	SUF 66
Lockwood, Gilbert	QNS 82	Lockyear, Benjamin	DUT 169	Longbottom, Saml	SUF 66
Lockwood, Gilbert	ULS 197	Locnard, Simmeon	CHN 912	Longbottom, Wm	SUF 66
Lockwood, Henery	SRA 10	Lodadwick, Cosper	MNT 1	Longendyke, Cornelius	ULS 224
Lockwood, Henry	ALB 28	Lodamer, Christopher	ORN 302	Longendyke, Cornelius	
Lockwood, Henry	DUT 90	Loder, Abijah	ULS 187	Junr	ULS 220
Lockwood, Henry	ULS 256	Loder, John	WST 112	Longendyke, John	ULS 196
Lockwood, Henry	ULS 260	Loder, John Junr	WST 112	Longendyke, Lucas	ULS 224
Lockwood, Hezekiah	QNS 84	Loder, Jonathan	WST 125	Longenhawh, Geo:	SCH 171
Lockwood, Ichabod	ORN 286	Loder, Jonathan	WST 160	Longhead, Joseph	ONT 470
Lockwood, Ira	ALB 78	Loder, Samuel	WST 113	Longman, Peter	MNT 2
Lockwood, Isaac	ORN 275	Lodewick, John	RNS 63	Longo, Lana	HRK 471
Lockwood, Isaac	WST 116	Lodges, John	MNT 93	Longshore, Richard	SRA 50
Lockwood, Israel	NYK 118	Lodine, Andrew	NYK 153	Longstaff, Charles	ALB 55
Lockwood, Israel	WST 156	Lodiwick, Abraham	MNT 3	Longville, Thomas	CLN 164
Lockwood, Jacob	WST 160	Lod....k, Bardolph	MNT 100	Longwall, David	DUT 84
Lockwood, James	COL 209	Lodiwick, Peter	MNT 3	Longwall, John	DUT 96
Lockwood, James	COL 214	Lodi[wick?], Peter	MNT 100	Longwood, Christopher	COL 230
Lockwood, James	MNT 12	Loff, Philip Laurence	NYK 56	Longworth, David	NYK 49
Lockwood, James	NYK 38	Logan, Aaron	NYK 101	Longyear, Christopher	ULS 194
Lockwood, James	ONN 177	Logan, Alexander	ONT 502	Longyear, John	ULS 194
Lockwood, Jane	ULS 262	Logan, Catherine	NYK 75	Longyear, John	ULS 232
Lockwood, Jared	ALB 135	Logan, George	NYK 46	Longyear, Solomon	ALB 6
Lockwood, Jemima	ULS 262	Logan, John	DUT 164	Longyear, William	ULS 194
Lockwood, Jeremiah	CAY 604	Logan, Samuel	ORN 286	Lonis, Henry	ALB 82
Lockwood, Jeremiah	ULS 256	Logan, Sheldon	ONN 192	Lonmediew, Nathaniel	NYK 64
Lockwood, Jersham	WST 153	Loggan, Daniel	HRK 591	Lonos, George M.	MNT 30
Lockwood, Jesse	WST 152	Loggin, Joseph	DUT 137	Loo, John	ULS 255
Lockwood, Job	CHN 948	Loines, James	NYK 62	Loocker, Othniel	SRA 30
Lockwood, John	COL 180	Loines, John	QNS 72	Loofborraw, Isaac	NYK 139
Lockwood, John	NYK 97	Lolridge, John	CHN 838	Look, Martha	CHN 908
Lockwood, John	ONN 161	Lomarex, James	TIO 223	Look, Thomas	COL 215
Lockwood, John	RNS 29	Lomax, Charles	ULS 245	Look, William	CHN 908
Lockwood, Jonathan	ONN 177	Lombaire, Edward	NYK 80	Looker, John	HRK 593
Lockwood, Josenaway	RNS 56	Lombart, John B.	NYK 122	Looker, Lynus	NYK 89
Lockwood, Joseph	ALB 138	Lomedu see Lhomedue		Lookey, Richard	NYK 77
Lockwood, Joseph	DUT 9	Lomedu, Henry	GRN 358	Loomas see Lomis, Lomm-	
Lockwood, Joseph	OND 159	Lomerce, Peter	COL 240	is & Lummis	
Lockwood, Joseph Junr	OND 161	Lomes see Loomis		Lommas, Asa	OTS 17
Lockwood, Mary	DUT 86	Lomes, Enos	WSH 273	Loomas, Charles	OTS 17
Lockwood, Mazor	RNS 69	Lomis, Ezekiel	WSH 296	Loomas, Eleaszer	OTS 12
Lockwood, Michael	WST 153	Loms, Zachareah	WSH 274	Loomas, Ezekiel	OTS 17
Lockwood, Michael Junr	WST 153	Lommdieu, William	NYK 55	Loomas, Israel	OTS 13
Lockwood, Morey	WST 158	Lommis, Benjamin	OND 214	Loomas, Silas	OTS 12
Lockwood, Moses	WST 157	Lommis, Martin	OND 214	Loomas, Thomas	OTS 10
Lockwood, Nathan	GRN 340	Lommis, Moses	OND 211	Loomis, Aaron	OND 197
Lockwood, Nathan	WST 160	Londegreen, Charles	NYK 73	Loomis, Abijah	TIO 213
Lockwood, Nathanel	WST 163	London, Charles	OND 174	Loomis, Abner	OND 162
Lockwood, Nathaniel	WST 113	London, Elijah	SUF 75	Loomis, Benjamin	ONT 452
Lockwood, Nathaniel	WST 116	London, Zachariah	NYK 127	Loomis, Calvin	ONT 452
Lockwood, Peter	COL 187	Lone, Dauphine a		Loomis, Daniel	CAY 648
Lockwood, Peter	DUT 82	Black	NYK 88	Loomis, Daniel	DEL 278
Lockwood, Peter	MNT 110	Loness, Adam	RNS 86	Loomis, Danl	OTS 47
Lockwood, Peter	SRA 25	Loness, Andrew	RNS 86	Loomis, David	CAY 712
Lockwood, Phillup	NYK 77	Loness, Bastian	RNS 86	Loomis, Dudley	HRK 509
Lockwood, Philo	RNS 92	Long, Abner	WSH 293	Loomis, Ebenezer	OND 176
Lockwood, Phineas	NYK 77	Long, Adam	ALB 101	Loomis, Ebenezer	OTS 24
Lockwood, Robert	ORN 277	Long, Benjamin	ALB 8	Loomis, Ezra	OTS 9
Lockwood, Samuel	ORN 286	Long, Betsey	NYK 31	Loomis, Gamaliel	OND 189
Lockwood, Samuel	ULS 197	Long, Christian	SCH 138	Loomis, Grove	OND 173
Lockwood, Samuel	WSH 282	Long, Coenrad	ALB 101	Loomis, Israel	HRK 507
Lockwood, Samuel	WST 113	Long, David	WSH 295	Loomis, Israel	OND 162
Lockwood, Samuel	WST 151	Long, Frederick	NYK 115	Loomis, Israel Jun	HRK 507
Lockwood, Seth	GRN 333	Long, Gerrit	ALB 59	Loomis, Jabez	OND 176
Lockwood, Solomon	ALB 71	Long, Hannah	SUF 86	Loomis, Jerome	ONT 504
Lockwood, Solomon	ALB 125	Long, Henry	CAY 630	Loomis, Job	CAY 648
Lockwood, Stephen	DUT 5	Long, Job	RCK 97	Loomis, John	ALB 67
Lockwood, Sylvanus	DUT 78	Long, John	ESS 295	Loomis, John	COL 232
Lockwood, Theophilas	COL 214	Long, Peter	ALB 101	Loomis, John	DEL 281
Lockwood, Thomas	DUT 173	Long, Reuben	OND 157	Loomis, Jonathan	COL 205
Lockwood, Timothy	GRN 336	Long, Richard	ONT 366	Loomis, Joseph	OND 203
Lockwood, Timothy	ULS 258	Long, Richard	ONT 374	Loomis, Micheal	CAY 610
Lockwood, Timothy	WST 159	Long, Robert	WSH 295	Loomis, Nathaniel	OND 174
Lockwood, Titus	DUT 177	Long, Thomas C.	DUT 19	Loomis, Nathaniel Junr	OND 176
Lockwood, Walter	DUT 15	Long, William	NYK 111	Loomis, Reuben	COL 240
Lockwood, William	QNS 82	Longbothom, Jacob	SUF 90	Loomis, Samuel	CAY 710
Lockwood, William	ULS 189	Longbothom, Saml	SUF 90	Loomis, Samuel	OND 197

Loomis, Seth	COL 205	Lord, Hezekiah	NYK 63	Losey, William	QNS 76
Loomis, Silas	ORN 311	Lord, Hezekiah	SRA 41	Loss, Charles	NYK 149
Loomis, Simon	CHN 766	Lord, John	ALB 70	Loss, John	OND 172
Loomis, Stephen	ONT 510	Lord, John	DUT 174	Loss, Samuel	OND 167
Loomis, Thadeus	OTS 52	Lord, John	GRN 330	Lossing, Henry	DUT 11
Loomis, Thomas	COL 180	Lord, John	SRA 23	Lossing, John	DUT 8
Loomis, Thomas	COL 230	Lord, John	ULS 182	Lossing, Nicholas	DUT 14
Loomis, Thomas Junr	COL 240	Lord, Jonath	SRA 51	Lossing, Peter	DUT 14
Loomis, William	ESS 295	Lord, Joseph	CAY 634	Losson, James	GRN 352
Loomis, Zadoch	OND 197	Lord, Joseph	COL 209	Losson, Peter J.	DEL 286
Loomson, Nichs	ONN 192	Lord, Russel	RNS 92	Loswells, ...	MNT 78
Loomiss, Timothy	DUT 164	Lord, Samuel	HRK 484	Lot, Abraham	QNS 67
Loop, Andrew	WSH 214	Lord, Samuel	WST 168	Lot, Dennis	QNS 60
Loop, David	GRN 338	Lord, Sebens	OND 218	Lot, Johannis	QNS 67
Loop, Henry	WSH 214	Lord, Silas	NYK 55	Lot, Johannis	QNS 67
Loop, Jacob	COL 196	Lord, Silvanus	OTS 16	Lot, Nathan	WSH 185
Loop, John	COL 227	Lord(?), Solomon	OND 213	Lothop, Ebenezer	SRA 14
Loop, John	WSH 210	Lord, Solomon	ULS 190	Lothrip, Samuel	WSH 190
Loop, Josiah	DUT 155	Lord, Timothy	ALB 83	Lothrop, Aruna	DEL 280
Loop, Lucy	TIO 265	Lord, William	NYK 122	Lothrop, Azariah	ONN 168
Loop, Marton	WSH 214	Lord, William	SRA 22	Lothrop, Ebenezer	MNT 51
Loop, Peter	COL 178	Lord, Zelotis	OND 213	Lothrop, Elisha	OTS 26
Loop, Peter	WSH 214	Loree, Hezekiah	ORN 326	Lothrop, Hezekiah	COL 192
Loop, Peter Jur	TIO 265	Loree, Samuel	ORN 331	Lothrop, Isaac	DEL 282
Loose, Henry	ALB 126	Loree, Sylvanus	ORN 323	Lothrop, Israel	OTS 56
Loosely, Titus Free		Loree, Tounsend	RNS 111	Lothrop, John H.	OND 202
Black	COL 252	Loreman, Henry	RNS 94	Lothrop, Nathel	COL 209
Lootz, Godfrey	ORN 319	Lorensus, Simon	OND 189	Lothrop, Rufus	DUT 135
Lootz, Peter	ORN 321	Lorey see Locey		Lothrop, Simon	COL 213
Lope, John	RNS 12	Lorey, Isaac	SUF 86	Lothrop, Solomon	COL 213
Lope, Samuel	RNS 12	Lorillard, Bla[ce?]	NYK 111	Lothrop, Wm	OTS 16
Lopee, Abraham	RNS 7	Loring, Inocent	NYK 138	Lothrop, Wyllys	CAY 692
Loper see Soper		Loring, James	NYK 27	Lothrop, Zephaniah	DEL 282
Loper, Amos	SUF 99	Loring, John	MNT 99	Lothroup, Nathaniel	DUT 153
Loper, Caleb	SUF 99	Loring, Mary	NYK 19	Lothroup, Walter	DUT 138
Loper, David	DUT 131	Loring, William	ALB 17	Lothroup, William	DUT 104
Loper, David	WSH 301	Lorrillard, Peter	NYK 109	Lothroup, William	DUT 138
Loper, Eliza	SUF 109	Lorton, Lewis	NYK 57	Lothrup, Eleazar	CHN 808
Loper, Henry	SUF 108	Lorton, Paul	NYK 135	Lothrup, Ezera	CHN 810
Loper, Isaac	SUF 101	Lory, John	MNT 87	Lothrup, Isaiah	CHN 800
Loper, Jacob	DUT 131	Lo_ybee, John	NYK 130	Lothrup, John	CHN 808
Loper, James	SUF 98	Loryd, Demons	NYK 103	Lothrup, Ransom	RNS 49
Loper, Jason	SUF 104	Lo[se?], Nathan	STB 197	Loton, Clark	WSH 199
Loper, Job	DUT 141	Losee, Abraham	DUT 99	Lotrage, Robert	RNS 18
Loper, Labeus	SUF 104	Losee, Abraham A.	DUT 14	Lotrip, Philander	WSH 265
Loper, Levi	SCH 156	Losee, Abraham L.	DUT 28	Lott, Abraham	ALB 113
Loper, Live	SCH 145	Losee, Chauncy	DUT 18	Lott, Abraham	MNT 92
Loper, Lyon	SUF 109	Losee, Cornelius	DUT 23	Lott, Abraham	QNS 75
Loper, Roger	SCH 145	Losee, Daniel	WST 125	Lott, Abraham	WSH 207
Loper, Sarah	SUF 99	Losee, David	QNS 71	Lott, Andrw	NYK 84
Loper, William	SUF 106	Losee, Dorland	DUT 65	Lott, Bartholomew	ORN 372
Lopes, Joseph	NYK 65	Losee, Elizabeth	DUT 18	Lott, Charles	KNG 6
Lopez, Isaac	NYK 142	Losee, George	DUT 18	Lott, Christopher	KNG 2
Lopez, Lewis a mulatto	NYK 64	Losee, James	DUT 14	Lott, Engelbert	KNG 5
Lopez, Moses	NYK 86	Losee, James	DUT 97	Lott, George	KNG 6
Lopie, John	RNS 10	Losee, James	ORN 372	Lott, Gertrude	NYK 50
Lopier, William	RNS 10	Losee, John	DUT 117	Lott, Harmanus	QNS 76
Lepough, Charles	ALB 95	Losee, John	RNS 47	Lott, Hendrick	KNG 2
Lopough, Philip	ALB 92	Losee, John F.	DUT 18	Lott, Hendrick	QNS 67
Loraner, Alexander	OND 206	Losee, John I.	DUT 59	Lott, Hendrick J.	KNG 4
Lord see Ford		Losee, Joseph	DUT 68	Lott, Henry	WSH 207
Lord, Amos	OTS 29	Losee, Joseph	DUT 124	Lott, Ichabod	ORN 384
Lord, Andrew	OND 207	Losee, Langdon	DUT 121	Lott, Isaac	SCH 138
Lord, Asa	HRK 555	Losee, Martin	SRA 24	Lott, Jacob	ONN 133
Lord, Asa	OND 219	Losee, Primus	DUT 18	Lott, James	NYK 131
Lord, Daniel	NYK 31	Losee, Richard	QNS 71	Lott, Johannas	KNG 3
Lord, David	COL 202	Losee, Richard	SRA 24	Lott, Johannas J.	KNG 2
Lord, David	SRA 53	Losee, Simon	DUT 103	Lott, Johannes E.	KNG 2
Lord, Deborah	ALB 84	Losey, Cornelius	NYK 60	Lott, John	KNG 2
Lord, Ebenezer	SRA 15	Losey, David	QNS 69	Lott, John H.	KNG 3
Lord, Ebenezer Junr	SRA 15	Losey, [H?]iram	GRN 351	Lott, John J.	KNG 4
Lord, Ephraim	ONN 144	Losey, Isaac	QNS 69	Lott, Margaret	NYK 131
Lord, Freedom	SRA 40	Losey, John	QNS 68	Lott, Peter	NYK 118
Lord, George	NYK 124	Losey, Martha	QNS 76	Lott, Peter	SCH 142
Lord, George H.	OND 187	Losey, Simeon	GRN 351	Lott, Simon	KNG 5
Lord, Widow H.	DEL 273	Losey, Stephen	GRN 351	Lott, Simon P.	KNG 3
Lord, Henry	RNS 112A	Losey, William	NYK 147		

Lott, Stephen	KNG 3	Lounsbury, Wyntie	ULS 203	Lovendal, John a		
Lott, Stephen	QNS 67	Loure, John Jur	CHN 910	mulatto	NYK	46
Lotterage, Hannah	ALB 48	Louree, John	CHN 908	Loveridge, Abner	DUT	135
Lotteridge, George	HRK 472	Louree, Jones	RNS 40	Loveridge, David	OTS	16
Lottice, James	MNT 101	Lourence, Nathaniel	NYK 137	Lovet, John	SUF	64
Louck Jeremiah	SCH 130	Lourey, William	NYK 35	Lovett, Benjm	COL	208
Loucks see Lucks		Loury, Valentine	NYK 113	Lovett, Daniel	NYK	67
Loucks, Andrew	SCH 130	Loux, Frederick	MNT 16	Lovett, Henry	NYK	76
Loucks, Andw Jr	SCH 172	Loux, George	MNT 10	Lovett, John	COL	263
Loucks, Catharine	SCH 163	Loux, Jacob	MNT 17	Lovett, John	NYK	20
Loucks, Cornelius	SCH 171	Love, Arthur	OTS 31	Lovett, Peter	ULS	238
Loucks, Geo. John	SCH 172	Love, David	DUT 146	Lovett, William	NYK	63
Loucks, Hendrick	COL 243	Love, David	NYK 77	Lovitt, John	RNS	80
Loucks, Jacob	SCH 171	Love, George	WSH 267	Lovlat, Abraham	WST	116
Loucks, Jeremiah Jr	SCH 130	Love, James	ONT 404	Low, Aaron	DUT	59
Loucks, John	SCH 169	Love, John	GRN 343	Low, Abraham	ULS	229
Loucks, John	SCH 171	Love, John	NYK 119	Low, Abraham	ULS	246
Loucks, John Jr	SCH 171	Love, John	OND 204	Low, Abraham Junr	ULS	220
Loucks, Peter	SCH 172	Love, John	ONN 193	Low, Abraham D.	ULS	220
Loucks, Willm	SCH 130	Love, Johne	WSH 220	Low, Andrew	ULS	241
Loucks, Willm	SCH 171	Love, Joseph	DEL 267	Low, Anthoney	ONT	416
Louder, Catherine	NYK 22	Love, Richard	OND 204	Low, Benjamin	ULS	217
Loudin, David	SCH 155	Love, Robert	OND 204	Low, Charles	NYK	27
Loudin, Silvenius	SCH 155	Love, Robert	ULS 235	Low, Cornelius	ULS	210
Loudon, John	RNS 94	Love, Samuel	WSH 268	Low, Cornelius	ULS	246
Loudon, Robert	WSH 297	Love, Thomas	CAY 524	Low, Cornelus	TIO	250
Loughhen, Michael	NYK 18	Love, William	CHN 956	Low, Daniel	ALB	35
Loughneet, Hous	MNT 62	Lovecock, Charles	ALB 80	Low, Daniel	ORN	301
Louick, Abraham	SRA 10	Lovecock, Nichs	ALB 80	Low, David	ULS	244
Louis see Lewis & Luis		Lovee, Ephraim	MNT 51	Low, Edward	ONT	338
Louis, Aaron a Black	NYK 51	Loveell, Gideon	CHN 884	Low, Elizabeth	ULS	230
Louis, Thomas	GRN 339	Lovegrove, Herman	ALB 52	Low, Ephraim	ULS	232
Louis, Toby a Black	NYK 111	Lov_it, Roger	CHN 834	Low, Ezekiel	ULS	242
Louks, Gerard	MNT 53	Lovejoy, Andrew	COL 216	Low, Henry	NYK	152
Louks, Henry G.	MNT 53	Lovejoy, Andrew	COL 262	Low, Hooker	ONT	420
Louks, Peter	MNT 53	Lovejoy, Asa	OTS 46	Low, Isaac	ULS	238
Louks, Peter P.	MNT 52	Lovejoy, Benjamin	COL 216	Low, Jacob	ALB	114
Loummerux see L'Amoreux		Lovejoy, Ebenezer	COL 216	Low, Jacob	ALB	145
Loummerux, Andrew	WST 126	Lovejoy, Ezra	CHN 968	Low, Jacob	ORN	300
Lound, Bastian	COL 232	Lovejoy, Jonas	CHN 964	Low, Jacob	ULS	244
Lound, David	COL 232	Lovejoy, Justus	COL 216	Low, Jacob G.	ULS	244
Louning, John	NYK 63	Lovejoy, Nathan	ALB 30	Low, Jacobus	ULS	232
Lounsberry, Benjn	TIO 234	Lovejoy, Preston	OTS 2	Low, Jocobus	WSH	201
Lounsbery, Phineus	RNS 93	Lovejoy, Theodore	ONN 170	Low, James	CAY	622
Lounsbery, Thos	RNS 31	Lovel, Heaman	SRA 33	Low, James	ORN	303
Lounsbery, Thos Junr	RNS 31	Lovel, James	TIO 222	Low, James	SRA	25
Lounsborough, Michael	TIO 222	Lovel, Reuben	WST 120	Low, Jeremiah	ULS	237
Lounsborough, Peter	NYK 139	Lovel, Simeon	TIO 252	Low, John	NYK	39
Lounsburry, Gideon	WST 140	Lovelace, Crandel	RNS 48	Low, John	NYK	81
Lounsbury, Edward	ULS 203	Lovelace, Jeremiah	DUT 75	Low, John	OTS	45
Lounsbury, Epinetus	ORN 276	Lovelace, John	MNT 15	Low, John	ULS	208
Lounsbury, Henry	DUT 86	Lovelace, Joseph	DEL 274	Low, John	ULS	217
Lounsbury, Henry	ORN 389	Lovelace, Thomas	DEL 274	Low, John	ULS	244
Lounsbury, Henry	WST 125	Lovelace, William	DUT 75	Low, John Junr	OTS	45
Lounsbury, Henry	WST 127	Loveland	GRN 342	Low, John J.	ULS	230
Lounsbury, Isaac	DUT 23	Loveland, Amos	RNS 10	Low, John M.	DUT	108
Lounsbury, Isaac	DUT 85	Loveland, David	CAY 706	Low, Laurence	NYK	119
Lounsbury, Isaac	SCH 124	Loveland, David	DEL 280	Low, Lawrence	DUT	62
Lounsbury, John	ORN 391	Loveland, Elephaz Jun	DEL 281	Low, Narinus	WST	169
Lounsbury, John	SCH 117	Loveland, Eliphas	DEL 281	Low, Nicholas	NYK	19
Lounsbury, John	SCH 123	Loveland, Enos	ESS 317	Low, Peter	DUT	59
Lounsbury, John	ULS 203	Loveland, Gad	ONN 145	Low, Peter	KNG	2
Lounsbury, Joshua	ULS 264	Loveland, Gad	ONN 148	Low, Peter	ORN	303
Lounsbury, Michael	DUT 141	Loveland, Nathan	OTS 54	Low, Peter	OTS	5
Lounsbury, Nathan	ALB 91B	Loveland, William	DEL 280	Low, Peter	SCH	161
Lounsbury, Nehemiah	WST 160	Loveless, David	WSH 214	Low, Peter	ULS	223
Lounsbury, Phinehas	DUT 103	Loveless, Ezrom	MNT 15	Low, Peter Junr	DUT	67
Lounsbury, Reuben	SCH 117	Loveless, George	ONN 160	Low, Peter W.	DUT	40
Lounsbury, Reuben	SCH 123	Loveless, George	ONN 166	Low, Samuel	NYK	35
Lounsbury, Richard	ULS 204	Loveless, James	SRA 18	Low, Samuel	STB	198
Lounsbury, Richard	WST 154	Loveless, John	SRA 56	Low, Samuel	ULS	213
Lounsbury, Robert	WST 128	Loveless, Joseph	MNT 19	Low, Sarah	DUT	60
Lounsbury, Robert Junr	WST 128	Loveless, Joseph	RNS 47	Low, Simeon	ULS	237
Lounsbury, Samuel	DUT 88	Lovell, Henry	ONT 342	Low, Thomas	CHN	838
Lounsbury, Stephen	WST 139	Lovell, John	NYK 145	Low, Tjierk	ULS	224
Lounsbury, Sylvenus	ALB 91B	Lovell, Nathan	WSH 270	Low, William	NYK	136
Lounsbury, Thomas	DUT 85	Loveman, John	COL 230	Low, Wilson	ESS	303

Name	Loc	Name	Loc	Name	Loc
Lowberch, John	ALB 39	Loyd, Robert	OTS 48	Ludentun, Elisha	DUT 20
Lowd, John	NYK 128	Loyd, Samuel L.(?)	QNS 61	Ludentun, Henry	DUT 92
L[owden?], Jacob	CAY 528	Loyd, Thomas	DUT 59	Ludentun, Samuel	DUT 5
Lowden, James	NYK 22	Loyd, Thomas	NYK 63	Ludentun, Thomas	DUT 20
Lowden, John	DEL 284	Loyd, William	OND 202	Ludentun, Zalmon	ORN 321
Lowden, Robert	DEL 284	Loyde, Charles	WSH 234	Ludington, Collins	TIO 239
Lowden, Thomas	CAY 526	Lozier, Elelrant	NYK 122	Ludkins, Emanuel	TIO 266
Lowdon, Guyld	COL 202	Lozier, Jacob	NYK 108	Ludley, Daniel	QNS 69
Lowdon, John	COL 202	Lozier, Nicholas	NYK 52	Ludley, James	NYK 113
Lowdon, John Junr	COL 208	Lozier, Nicholas	NYK 59	Ludlo, Samuel	GRN 356
Lowdry, John H.	NYK 120	Lozier, Oliver	ORN 343	Ludlow, Abraham	SRA 52
Lowell, Willoughby	OND 178	Lubheart, John	ONT 336	Ludlow, Anna	NYK 17
Lower, Conrad	ONN 166	Lucas, Andrew	CHN 952	Ludlow, Carey	NYK 16
Lower, Conrad Jun	ONN 166	Lucas, Daniel	OND 164	Ludlow, Christopher B.	NYK 55
Lower, John	ONN 166	Lucas, David	WSH 187	Ludlow, Daniel	COL 262
Lower, Peter	TIO 230	Lucas, Elnathan	DUT 142	Ludlow, Daniel	NYK 19
Lowers, Robert	ORN 291	Lucas, Icabod	SUF 100	Ludlow, Daniel	WST 145
Lowery, Peter	ALB 27	Lucas, Isaiah	CAY 526	Ludlow, Elizabeth	ORN 282
Lowes, George	NYK 62	Lucas, James	WSH 201	Ludlow, Francis	CAY 552
Lowger, Nicholas	RNS 51	Lucas, Oliver	OND 201	Ludlow, Francis	NYK 29
Lowk, Adam	DUT 144	Lucas, Wm	ONN 182	Ludlow, Gabraiel V.	NYK 17
Lowk, Adam	DUT 154	Luce see Luse		Ludlow, Gabriel W.	NYK 26
Lowk, Jacob	DUT 154	Luce, Abraham	OND 214	Ludlow, Guhan	NYK 17
Lowk, Peter	DUT 143	Luce, Daniel	WSH 193	Ludlow, Henry	CAY 586
Lowk, Wendell	DUT 144	Luce, Edy	WSH 250	Ludlow, Peter R.	ORN 332
Lowke, Jacob	OND 165	Luce, Ephraim	OND 179	Ludlow, Silas	CAY 552
Lowman, Jacob	TIO 255	Luce, Ezra	WSH 195	Ludlow, Silas	CAY 586
Lowman, Peter	COL 261	Luce, Harvey	ONN 148	Ludlow, Thomas	CAY 586
Lown, David	COL 195	Luce, Icabode	WSH 195	Ludlow, Thomas	NYK 19
Lown, David & John	DUT 157	Luce, Ivery	CHN 908	Ludlow, Thomas	OND 164
Lown, David	DUT 159	Luce, John	OTS 17	Ludlow, William	NYK 29
Lown, George	COL 195	Luce, John	WSH 233	Ludlow, William	NYK 150
Lown, Jacob	ALB 65	Luce, Jonathan	HRK 597	Ludlow, Wm H.	COL 191
Lown, Jacob	DUT 159	Luce, Joseph	OND 194	Ludlum, Anthony	SUF 99
Lown, Jacob	DUT 164	Luce, Moses	WSH 233	Ludlum, Charles	QNS 80
Lown, John & David	DUT 157	Luce, Nathan	OTS 17	Ludlum, Christian	ORN 360
Lown, John	DUT 160	Luce, Othaniel	OTS 7	Ludlum, Daniel	QNS 80
Lown, John B.	DUT 157	Luce, Rufus	OND 182	Ludlum, Ebenezer	NYK 92
Lownds, Thomas	NYK 51	Luce, Seth	OTS 52	Ludlum, Ephraim	NYK 33
Lownes, William	NYK 67	Luce, Shubal	HRK 596	Ludlum, Gershom	QNS 65
Lownsborough, Joshua	WST 112	Luce, Uriah	OTS 17	Ludlum, Henry	QNS 80
Lownsborough, Silus	WST 112	Luce, William	OND 192	Ludlum, Isaac	ORN 360
Lownsbury, James	TIO 258	Luce, William	OND 194	Ludlum, Jacob	NYK 15
Lownsbury, John	WST 145	Lucee, John	CLN 168	Ludlum, Jacob	ORN 354
Lownsbury, Stephen	WST 168	Lucet, Eugene	NYK 96	Ludlum, Jeremiah	SUF 98
Lowree, Abm	SUF 65	Lucette, Eugene	ORN 391	Ludlum, John	ORN 361
Lowree, Coorod	CHN 944	Lucey, Abm	SUF 73	Ludlum, John	QNS 62
Lowree, Wm	RNS 65	Lucey, Benjn	SUF 73	Ludlum, John	QNS 75
Lowrey, Francis	NYK 47	Lucey, Mehetable	SUF 72	Ludlum, John	TIO 259
Lowrey, John	NYK 87	Lucie, John Br(?)	CLN 168	Ludlum, Joseph	NYK 95
Lowrie, Abraham	QNS 64	Luck, William	ALB 44	Ludlum, Phoebe	SUF 100
Lowrie, Charles	QNS 66	Lucker, Major	SRA 25	Ludlum, Samuel	TIO 259
Lowrie, Henrie	QNS 64	Luckey, John	ORN 378	Ludlum, Stephen	NYK 66
Lowrie, John	QNS 66	Luckey, Mary	DUT 70	Ludlum, Thomas	QNS 82
Lowrie, John	QNS 66	Luckey, Samuel	DUT 69	Ludlum, William	NYK 58
Lowrie, Martha	QNS 64	Luckly, James	SCH 125	Ludlum, William	ORN 361
Lowrie, Thomas	QNS 64	Lucks, Stephen	MNT 118	Ludlum, William	QNS 68
Lowry, Edward	NYK 36	Lucky, George	ORN 365	Ludlum, William	QNS 80
Lowry, James	CAY 726	Lucky, Henry	ORN 366	Ludlum, William Junr	QNS 68
Lowry, James	NYK 98	Lucky, James	ALB 83	Ludlun, Nathaniel	QNS 67
Lowry, Jane	NYK 57	Lucky, John	ORN 370	Ludum, Nehemiah	QNS 68
Lowry, John	DUT 5	Lucky, Joseph	ALB 83	Ludum, Nicholas	QNS 66
Lowry, Memucan	DEL 278	Lucky, Joseph	ORN 369	Ludwic, Giffers	MNT 52
Lowry, Thomas	DUT 5	Lucky, Samuel	ORN 370	Lue	SUF 82
Lowry, William	NYK 123	Lucky, Thomas	CAY 630	Lufborrow, Thomas	NYK 68
Lowther, Henry	NYK 149	Lucky, William	GRN 325	Luff, Catherine	NYK 123
Lowther, Robert	NYK 123	Lucour, John	ONT 452	Luff, Mathias	NYK 123
Lowthrop, Frederick	MNT 29	Lucus	CHN 982	Luff, Nicholas	NYK 18
Lowttit, Thomas	NYK 136	Lucus, Aaron	WSH 185	Luff, Valentine	NYK 139
Loyd see Lloyd		Lucus, Benoni	WSH 207	Luger, Christopher	SUF 102
Loyd, Edward	NYK 26	Lucus, Ire	CHN 930	Luh_, Frederic	NYK 143
Loyd, Henry	QNS 80	Luddington, Archd	COL 227	Luis see Louis & Lewis	
Loyd, James	DUT 135	Luddington, Jerh	ONN 171	Luis, Amos	WSH 219
Loyd, James	ORN 349	Luddington, Nathl	HRK 509	Luis, Amos	WSH 258
Loyd, John	RNS 67	Luddington, Stephen	HRK 508	Luis, Andrew	WSH 208
Loyd, Joseph	NYK 15	Luddington, William	ESS 296	Luis, Silus	GRN 337
Loyd, Richard	NYK 55	Ludentun, Comfort	DUT 20	Luke, Coenrad Junr	ALB 106

Luke, John	HRK 474	Lute, Lambert	ONT 394	Lynch, Henry B.	OTS 25
Luke, Mark	CHN 762	Luthe, Amos	WSH 219	Lynch, James	NYK 15
Luke, Nathen	WSH 197	L_ther, Abia	OTS 10	Lynch, James	NYK 114
Luke, Peter	NYK 128	Luther, Abner	WSH 249	Lynch, James	ORN 397
Luke, Sarah	NYK 41	Luther, Edward	ORN 280	Lynch, Jane	NYK 27
Luke, Solomon	ALB 97	Luther, Elisha	ONT 466	Lynch, John	NYK 118
Lukentary, George	COL 241	Luther, Esick	HRK 561	Lynch, John	ORN 397
Luker, Elesar	GRN 338	Luther, Ezra	DUT 127	Lynch, John	WST 163
Luker, William	SRA 24	Luther, Gideon	SRA 14	Lynch, Mark	NYK 54
Lukes, Daniel	MNT 117	Luther, Gilbert	HRK 447	Lynch, Matthew	ALB 131
Lull, Abner	OTS 33	Luther, James	DUT 125	Lynch, Partrick	NYK 74
Lull, Benjamine	GRN 344	Luther, John	ALB 48	Lynch, Samuel	ORN 349
Lull, Caleb	OTS 33	Luther, Joshua	OTS 11	Lynch, Sarah	NYK 48
Lull, James	OTS 33	Luthe_, [Loved?]	ONT 458	Lynch, Stephen	ORN 357
Lull, Joseph	OTS 24	Luther, Martin	OTS 36	Lynch, Thomas	ORN 398
Lull, Joseph	OTS 25	Luther, Martin	WSH 248	Lynck, Phillip	DUT 151
Lull, Nathan	OTS 24	Luther, Nathen	WSH 285	Lynd, Jonathan	OND 213
Lull, Timo W.	OTS 23	Luther, Reuben	ONT 466	Lyndbergh, John	ORN 305
Lull, Wm_	OTS 33	Luther, Robert	ALB 128	Lyndbergh, John	ULS 245
Lum, Jehial	ALB 28	Luther, Sheffield	ONT 466	Lynde, Jonathon	ESS 305
Lum, Jonathan	MNT 112	Luther, Squire	OTS 9	Lyndes, Egnacius	ALB 79
Lum, Reuben	MNT 112	Luther, Theophilus	HRK 596	Lynes, David	COL 235
Lumb, George	MNT 42	Lutis, John	MNT 115	Lyngester, William	NYK 74
Lumbard, Philip	ONN 143	Lutterage, Robert	ALB 49	Lynk, Johannis	DUT 151
Lumbard, Roswell	COL 182	Lutterman, Martha	WST 149	Lynklater, John	ORN 374
Lumbers, Daniel	SRA 7	Lutton, Benjamin	HRK 486	Lynn, John	ONN 166
Lumbly, George	WST 168	Lutton, Seth	HRK 486	Lynn, William	NYK 36
Lumley, Elizabeth	NYK 121	Luts, John	NYK 146	Lynsen, Abraham	NYK 97
Lummis see Loomas		Luw	QNS 78	Lynsen, David B.	RNS 92
Lummis, Benajah	CHN 742	Luyck, David	COL 242	Lynsley, Wm	ONN 191
Lummis, Daniel	RNS 9	Luyck, John	COL 241	Lyon see Lion	
Lummis, Ebenezer	WSH 256	Luyster see Liester		Lyon, Aaron	ALB 73
Lummis, Edward	CHN 746	Luyster, Cornelius	DUT 23	Lyon, Aaron	CHN 756
Lummis, Edward	CHN 772	Luyster, James	DUT 25	Lyon, Aaron	HRK 484
Lummis, Zacheriah	CHN 782	Luyster, Matthias	DUT 40	Lyon, Aaron	ORN 280
Lumsey, Mary	SUF 64	Luyster, Peter	DUT 40	Lyon, Aaron Junr	HRK 484
Lumsey, Samuel	SUF 64	Luyster, Peter J.	DUT 25	Lyon, Abel	MNT 50
Lundy, John	NYK 137	Luzer, Gershom	TIO 266	Lyon, Abel	SRA 22
Lunmore, Andrew	WST 147	Lyatt, Abraham	WST 131	Lyon, Abel	SRA 51
Lunn, John	NYK 72	Lyck, Andries	DUT 159	Lyon, Abiel	OTS 30
Lunn, Peter	NYK 136	Lydacker, Abrm	RCK 97	Lyon, Abiel	OTS 53
Lupton, Augustine	ORN 295	Lydacker, John	RCK 107	Lyon, Abraham	WST 134
Lupton, David	SUF 99	Lyde, Edward	NYK 28	Lyon, Alanson	HRK 563
Lupton, James	SUF 71	Lyde, Edward	NYK 53	Lyon, Alexander	CHN 784
Lupton, John	NYK 77	Lydig, David	NYK 41	Lyon, Amos	CAY 606
Lupton, Josiah	SUF 71	Lydig, Margaret	NYK 44	Lyon, Andrew	WST 113
Lupton, Mary	SUF 96	Lyell, Fenwick	NYK 25	Lyon, Asa	SRA 51
Lupton, William	NYK 35	Lyell, Peter	NYK 57	Lyon, Augustus	DUT 171
Lurey, Alexander	WSH 194	Lyell, Sarah	NYK 99	Lyon, Benjamen	MNT 1
Lurrine, John	NYK 134	Lyke, David	COL 232	Lyon, Benjamin	CHN 798
Lusdrof, John H.	NYK 140	Lyke, Jerone	COL 254	Lyon, Benjamin	ORN 278
Luse see Luce		Lyke, John	COL 232	Lyon, Benjamin	WST 117
Luse, Benjamin	ONT 346	Lyke, Peter	COL 264	Lyon, Caleb	CAY 606
Luse, Isreal	CAY 580	Lyker, Henry	MNT 45	Lyon, Caleb Junr	CAY 606
Lush, Richard	ALB 147	Lyle, Henry	DUT 157	Lyon, Charles	CAY 602
Lush, Stephen	ALB 147	Lyle, Margaret	ALB 34	Lyon, Charles	CAY 606
Lush, Stephen	ONT 362	Lyllie, Zenas	ONN 185	Lyon, Daniel	CHN 768
Lusk, Amos	ONT 400	Lyman, Edmund	WSH 282	Lyon, Daniel	WSH 190
Lusk, Asel	ONT 404	Lyman, Eleazer	WSH 269	Lyon, Daniel	WST 116
Lusk, E_ur	ONT 404	Lyman, Frederick	WSH 294	Lyon, David	DUT 24
Lusk, George	COL 259	Lyman, William	COL 181	Lyon, David	NYK 133
Lusk, Jacob	COL 194	Lymon, Isaac	CHN 934	Lyon, David	OTS 26
Lusk, James	ORN 354	Lymons, David	WSH 271	Lyon, David	WST 113
Lusk, James	TIO 214	Lyn, Archibald	RNS 4	Lyon, David	WST 131
Lusk, Wido Jane	COL 204	Lyn, Francis	NYK 23	Lyon, Denny	CHN 926
Lusk, John	COL 205	Lyn, Hillena	RNS 5	Lyon, Ebnr	CHN 930
Lusk, John	DEL 282	Lyn, John	RNS 4	Lyon, Elisha	OTS 26
Lusk, John	OND 170	Lyn, Leonard	RNS 4	Lyon, Elnathan	DUT 119
Lusk, Joseph	WSH 212	Lynch, Cornelius	KNG 10	Lyon, Elvan	WST 124
Lusk, Michael	COL 195	Lynch, Daniel	DEL 267	Lyon, Enon	CAY 606
Lusk, Nathan	COL 262	Lynch, David	ORN 354	Lyon, Esehiah	STB 202
Lusk, Salmon	OND 169	Lynch, Dominick	NYK 20	Lyon, Ezekiel	SRA 22
Lusk, Thomas Ju.	ONT 404	Lynch, Domonick	WST 144	Lyon, Ezra	SRA 22
Lusk, Willm	COL 205	Lynch, Francis	NYK 45	Lyon, George	ULS 195
Luster, David Junr	SUF 109	Lynch, Francis	NYK 79	Lyon, Gilbert	WST 116
Luster, David Senr	SUF 109	Lynch, Gabriel	WST 116	Lyon, Henry	HRK 481
Lut, Solomon	GRN 343	Lynch, Henry	ORN 398	Lyon, Henry	NYK 47

Name	Ref
Lyon, Isaac	ORN 306
Lyon, Isaac	SRA 9
Lyon, Israel	WST 137
Lyon, Israel Junr	WST 136
Lyon, Jabez	HRK 548
Lyon, Jabez	HRK 562
Lyon, Jacob	RCK 110
Lyon, James	NYK 116
Lyon, James	NYK 127
Lyon, James	NYK 128
Lyon, James	RNS 34
Lyon, James	SRA 7
Lyon, James	TIO 211
Lyon, James	WST 114
Lyon, James	WST 139
Lyon, James	WST 143
Lyon, Jeremy	HRK 481
Lyon, Jesse	COL 181
Lyon, Jesse	WST 140
Lyon, John	CHN 936
Lyon, John	NYK 143
Lyon, John	OND 224
Lyon, John	ONT 310
Lyon, John	SRA 28
Lyon, John	ULS 246
Lyon, John	WST 116
Lyon, John	WST 134
Lyon, Jonathan	DUT 119
Lyon, Jonathan	NYK 125
Lyon, Jonathan	WSH 192
Lyon, Jonathan	WST 142
Lyon, Joseph	CAY 606
Lyon, Joseph	NYK 38
Lyon, Joseph	NYK 76
Lyon, Joseph a Black	NYK 152
Lyon, Joseph	RCK 106
Lyon, Joseph	WST 116
Lyon, Joseph C.	OTS 32
Lyon, Lewis	NYK 124
Lyon, March	WST 113
Lyon, Mary	WST 113
Lyon, Mathew	NYK 119
Lyon, Matthias C.	NYK 59
Lyon, Michael	COL 181
Lyon, Michal	COL 252
Lyon, Michael	ULS 200
Lyon, Moses	CAY 706
Lyon, Moses	MNT 45
Lyon, Moses	OND 182
Lyon, Moses	WST 137
Lyon, Nemiah	WST 113
Lyon, Nicholas	NYK 114
Lyon, Noah	CAY 606
Lyon, Oliver	ONT 330
Lyon, Peter	WST 116
Lyon, Roger	WST 142
Lyon, Rufus	ONN 144
Lyon, Russekey	CAY 632
Lyon, Samuel	CHN 768
Lyon, Samue.	MNT 83
Lyon, Samuel	NYK 59
Lyon, Saml	RNS 34
Lyon, Samuel	SRA 5
Lyon, Samuel	SRA 35
Lyon, Samuel	WST 113
Lyon, Samuel	WST 113
Lyon, Samuel	WST 134
Lyon, Samuel	WST 147
Lyon, Samuel Junr	WST 141
Lyon, Sarah	WST 114
Lyon, Seth	DEL 269
Lyon, Seth Junr	DEL 269
Lyon, Silvanus	WST 114
Lyon, Simeon	ONT 336
Lyon, Sirus	CHN 798
Lyon, Sparden	WST 137
Lyon, Stephen	DUT 171
Lyon, Stephen	NYK 80
Lyon, Thomas	CHN 768
Lyon, Thomas	COL 210
Lyon, Thomas	NYK 107
Lyon, Thomas	WST 113
Lyon, Thomas Junr	CHN 768
Lyon, Thomas Junr	WST 113
Lyon, Timothy	MNT 82
Lyon, Walter	DEL 269
Lyon, Walter	QNS 65
Lyon, William	DUT 108
Lyon, William	WST 112
Lyon, William	WST 139
Lyons, David	ALB 6
Lyons, David	NYK 105
Lyons, Elbert a mulatto	NYK 27
Lyons, Francis	ULS 252
Lyons, Hannah	NYK 113
Lyons, Henry	OTS 58
Lyons, Jacob	ALB 8
Lyons, James	WST 148
Lyons, Jesse	TIO 242
Lyons, Joseph	NYK 90
Lyons, Nelly	NYK 91
Lyons, Samuel	ULS 266
Lyons, Sarah	NYK 37
Lyons, Thomas	WSH 284
Lyons, William	WST 168
Lypert, David	ALB 20
Lypert, Jacob	ALB 20
Lyster see Liester	
Lyster, Cornelius	QNS 61
Lyster, Elbert	QNS 61
Lyster, John	QNS 83
Lyster, John Junr	QNS 83
Lyster, Peter	QNS 83
Lytle see Little	
Lytle, Andrew	WSH 293
Lytle, Isaac	WSH 290
Lytle, James	WSH 245
Lytle, William	WSH 292
Lyttle, Alexr	ONN 175
Lyver, Gersham	NYK 61

M

Name	Ref
M_ maker, C____	CAY 574
M_d_, Johsua	CAY 664
M_en, Widow	CHN 842
M_t_, Abraham	CHN 928
M_nn, Whit[ing?]	DEL 288
M..., Oliver	MNT 50
M..ah, Isaac	ONT 490
M.ttack, Joseph Negro	QNS 72
M_lear, Peter	TIO 251
M_son, John	WST 163
Ma_in, Nathin	ONT 392
Maaimore, _eter a mulatto	NYK 47
Maarts, Philip P.	HRK 473
Maatten, James	SRA 41
Mabb, John	RNS 36
Mabb, John	SCH 161
Mabbet, Israel	WSH 185
Mabbett, Jonathan	SRA 20
Mabbett, Richard	DUT 100
Mabbett, Ruth	DUT 101
Mabbitt, Joseph S.	RNS 81
Mabbitt, Titus	DUT 8
Mabe, Isaac	WST 117
Mabee, Abraham	DEL 290
Mabee, Abraham	MNT 24
Mabee, Daniel	DEL 289
Mabee, Debroah	WST 130
Mabee, John	DEL 290
M[abee?], John	WST 122
Mabee, Silas	WST 130
Mabee, Sylvanus	ONT 310
Mabee, William	WST 154
Maben, George	WSH 250
Maben, John	GRN 335
Mabie, Abrm	RCK 98
Mabie, Abrm	RCK 105
Mabie, Casporus	RCK 108
Mabie, Cornelius	RCK 101
Mabie, Joost	RCK 98
Mabie, Peter	NYK 34
Mabie, Peter	RCK 101
Maby, Abrm	OTS 14
Maby, Abrm	RCK 97
Maby, Abrm Junr	RCK 97
Maby, Adam	NYK 99
Maby, Cornelius	NYK 101
Maby, David	OTS 13
Maby, Jasper	RCK 97
Maby, John	NYK 60
Maby, John	RCK 99
Maby, Peter	NYK 101
Maby, Peter	RCK 98
Maby, Peter	RCK 99
Maby, Stephen	SCH 141
Mabye, Frederic	NYK 109
Mac see Mack	
Mac, John	WSH 226
McAdam, Anna	NYK 20
McAdam, John	NYK 124
McAdams, Andrew	ALB 23
McAdams, James	ALB 23
McAlister, Daniel	WSH 224
McAlister, Ebenezer	WSH 224
McAlister, John	COL 263
McAlister, John	WSH 224
McAlister, William	COL 263
McAlley see McCalley	
McAlley, Angus	MNT 63
McAllister, James	HRK 570
McAlpin, Daniel	DUT 142
McAlpin, Eliza	NYK 102
McAlpin, John	DUT 142
McAlpin, John	OND 177
McAlpin, John William	NYK 70
McAlpin, Walter	DUT 142
McAmburgh, Joseph	CHN 908
McAmly, David	ORN 371
McAmly, Samuel	ORN 371
McAnerly, Martin	NYK 136
McArdle, Philip	NYK 145
McArther see McCarther	
McArther, Archibald	MNT 88
McArther, Arther	COL 249
McArther, .aniel	MNT 61
McArther, Duncan	WSH 250
McArther, John	COL 239
McArther, Duncan	WSH 287
McArthur, Elizabeth	NYK 30
McArthur, John	MNT 13
McArthur, John Mc	MNT 58
McArthur, Neil	ORN 290
McArthur, William	CLN 160
McAulay see McCalley	
McAulay, William	ESS 295
McAyley, John	ORN 283
McAuley, Margaret	ORN 383
McAuley, Peter	WSH 258
McAuley, William	WSH 193
McAuther, Alexr	COL 180
McAwen, Duncan	WSH 204
McAwley, Hugh	WSH 205
McBaine, John	NYK 117
McBaine, John Junr	NYK 117
McBarnse, John	GRN 357
McBean, James	ALB 32
McBeath, Alexander	NYK 127

Name	Ref
McBeth, James	NYK 127
McBride, Alexander	MNT 106
McBride, Andrew	NYK 77
McBride, Archibald	ORN 345
McBride, Daniel	WSH 212
McBride, George	ONT 310
McBride, Irvin	NYK 89
McBride, James	NYK 132
McBride, James	ORN 302
McBride, James	SRA 46
McBride, John	NYK 123
McBride, John	OND 216
McBride, John	SRA 44
McBride, Levi	OTS 48
McBride, Robert	CAY 664
McBride, Robert	OND 198
McBride, Sarah	ORN 294
McBride, Thomas	SCH 156
McBride, Walter	NYK 111
McBride, William	ALB 138
McBride, William	NYK 102
McBurney, William	NYK 101
McBurney, William	ORN 307
McCabe, Benjamin	DUT 80
McCabe, Catharine	ULS 207
McCabe, Edward	DUT 38
McCabe, Henry	NYK 120
McCabe, Israel	DUT 33
McCabe, James	NYK 133
McCabe, Matthew	DUT 79
M'Cabe, Owen	HRK 465
McCabe, William	DUT 34
McCabe, William	NYK 106
McCade, Stephen	GRN 353
McCag, Hannah	RNS112A
McCagg, James	DEL 269
McCahan, Peter	NYK 62
McCale, Barnet	NYK 110
McCall, Agness	WST 152
McCall, Ansell	CAY 720
McCall, Benajah	DEL 276
McCall, Daniel	DEL 281
McCall, Daniel	NYK 23
McCall, Dougal	WSH 294
McCall, Dugal	MNT 65
McCall, Duncan	WSH 293
McCall, Ephraim	DEL 281
McCall, Hugh	MNT 73
McCall, Ira	DEL 281
McCall, James	CAY 720
McCall, James	OND 182
McCall, Jona	MNT 65
McCalley see McAlley, McAwley & McAuley	
McCalley, James	WSH 203
McCalley, William	WSH 203
McCally, William	DEL 285
McCalp, Salla	SRA 10
McCalpin, James	OTS 25
McCalpin, Thos	OTS 25
McCalpin, William	CHN 774
McCalvry, William	ORN 354
McCalvy, John	ORN 388
McCammon, John	NYK 147
McCan, Samuel	RNS 85
McCann, George	ORN 285
McCann, James	ALB 41
McCann, John	ULS 191
McCannegan, Patrick	SCH 154
McCannon, Patrick	SRA 30
McCarger, Joseph	WSH 271
McCarger, Rebecca	DUT 91
McCargill, James	CLN 157
McCarl, Partrick	NYK 118
McCarld, Philip	NYK 95
McCarn, John	NYK 151
McCarne, John	MNT 48
McCarrel, John	SRA 34
McCarrick, Francis	DUT 33
McCarteney, Daniel	DUT 163
McCarter, Duncan	COL 208
McCarter, John	DEL 280
McCarter, John	NYK 30
McCarter, John	ORN 341
McCarter, John	WSH 194
McCarter, John	WSH 226
McCarter, John Junr	ORN 342
McCarter, Joseph	WSH 257
McCarter, Patrick	WSH 229
McCarter, Robert	WSH 247
McCarter, Robert	WSH 291
McCarter, Samuel	WSH 226
McCarter, Wm	CHN 942
McCarter, William	WSH 247
McCartey, William	ALB 34
McCarther see McArther	
McCarther, William	GRN 329
McCarthey, William	ONT 324
McCarthy, Daniel	DUT 162
McCarthy, John	MNT 58
McCarthy, Walter	DUT 60
McCartney see McCarthy	
McCartney, Dennis	RNS 27
McCartney, James	ONT 486
McCartney, John	ONT 488
McCarty, Andrew	ALB 121
McCarty, Auther	COL 238
McCarty, Charles	NYK 70
McCarty, Clerk	OND 219
McCarty, David	ALB 121
McCarty, Duncan	COL 243
McCarty, George	RNS 46
McCarty, James	NYK 106
McCarty, James	NYK 139
McCarty, James	SRA 41
McCarty, Jeremiah	NYK 39
McCarty, Jeremiah	NYK 147
McCarty, John	COL 238
McCarty, John D.	COL 244
McCarty, Michael	HRK 416
McCarty, Peter	ALB 121
McCarty, Polly	ONN 177
McCarty, Rebecca	RNS 46
McCarty, Reuben	COL 241
McCarty, Richard	GRN 354
McCarty, Ruliff	COL 218
McCarty, Samuel	COL 238
McCarty, Thomas	RNS 100
McCarty, William	SRA 29
McCarty, William	SRA 41
McCashlin, John	WSH 258
McCauley, Anthony	ONT 504
McCauley, William	NYK 132
McCausey, James	WSH 237
McCave, Jacob	NYK 77
McCave, Mary	NYK 131
McCay see McKay & Makay	
McCay, Alexander	SRA 58
McCay, William	RNS 26
McChain, James	WST 164
McChain, James Junr	WST 165
McChain, John	WST 123
McChelchran, Geo	ALB 140
McChesney, John H.	ALB 128
McChesney, Hugh	RNS 86
McChesney, John	RNS 86
McChesney, John Junr	RNS 86
McChesney, Joseph	RNS 85
McChesney, Robert	RNS 86
McChesney, Samuel	RNS 86
McChesney, Stephen	RNS 86
McChestney, Walter M.	RNS 87
McCl___, John	ONT 462
McClain, Peter	RNS 48
McClain, William	WST 166
McClair, Cuffey a Black	NYK 55
McClallen, Archd	ALB 9
McClallen, John	SRA 29
McClallen, Robert	ALB 124
McClallen, Wm	ALB 12
McClallen, William	ALB 124
McClanagan, Elizabeth	NYK 26
McClanathen, James	CHN 894
McClanathen, William	CHN 894
McClanehan, William	RNS 81
McClann, James	ESS 297
McClannen, Hugh	ORN 393
McClarren, John	WSH 202
McClarry, Luke	GRN 344
McClary, Isaac	WSH 264
McClary, James	RCK 102
McClaskey, William	NYK 121
McClasky, John	NYK 35
McClaughrey, Richard	WSH 224
McClaughry, Andrew	DEL 284
McClaughry, James	DEL 285
McClaughry, Joseph	DEL 285
McClaughry, Richard	DEL 284
McClaughry, Thomas	DEL 285
McClaurin, John	ONT 314
McClean see McLean	
McClean, Catherine	NYK 54
McClean, Charles	COL 234
McClean, Daniel	WSH 247
McClean, Henry	DUT 116
McClean, Hugh	NYK 37
McCleary, Elizabeth	WSH 226
McCleary, John	WSH 194
McCleary, John	WSH 227
McCleary, Thomas	WSH 226
McCleen, David	SRA 48
McCleland, James	RNS 37
McCleland, Joseph	NYK 118
McClelen, Daniel	SRA 5
McClellan, Alexander	WSH 291
McClellan, James	WSH 293
McClellan, John	COL 237
McClellan, John	WSH 193
McClellan, Robert	WSH 292
McClellan, Thomas	ORN 280
McClellan, William	WSH 291
McClellan, William	WSH 292
McClelland, Henry	CAY 568
McClelland, James	ONT 394
McClelland, John	CAY 524
McClelland, John	CAY 568
McClelland, John	DEL 289
McClelland, Samuel	ONT 368
McClemon, Andrew	ALB 40
McClemon, Andrew Jr	ALB 40
McClenithen, Thomas	WSH 222
McClennan, Barney	NYK 107
McClennan, Robert	COL 251
McClentick, Samuel	ONT 446
McClentoch, John	WSH 272
McClerren, John	WSH 202
McClery, Alexander	CAY 576
McCleun, John	TIO 233
McCleur, Wm	TIO 222
McCleve, John	ALB 32
McCleve, William	ALB 33
McClevren, Agness	WSH 190
McClintick, George	ORN 302
McClouchn, Joseph	ORN 293
McClouchn, Robert	ORN 298
McCloud see McLeod	
McCloud, Angus	ONT 326

McCloud, John	NYK 37	McConnel, Joseph	TIO 259	McCoy, Alexr	OND 215
McCloud, John	NYK 129	McConnel, Matthew	TIO 259	McCoy, Alexander	SRA 26
McCloud, Lewis	SCH 137	McConnel, Samuel	TIO 260	McCoy, Catharine	WST 153
McCloud, Norman	COL 194	McConnell, Charles	ORN 367	McCoy, Eneas	NYK 124
McCloud, Robert	CHN 762	McConnell, Eli	OND 194	McCoy, Flora a Black	NYK 79
McCloud, Robert	ONT 408	McConnell, Hugh	ORN 319	McCoy, Henry	COL 198
M Cloud, Wm	MNT 91	McConnell, John	ORN 288	McCoy, John	ALB 27
McCloughen, William	NYK 74	McConnell, Peter	ORN 367	McCoy, John	ALB 105
McCloughken, Samuel	NYK 87	McConnell, Phillip	ORN 369	McCoy, John	COL 263
McClue, William	NYK 54	McConnell, Robert	ALB 124	McCoy, John	NYK 89
McCluer, James	NYK 89	McConnell, Robert	NYK 148	McCoy, John	OND 161
McCluer, William	NYK 145	McConnell, Thaddeus S.	OND 197	McCoy, John	RCK 99
McClum, Thomas	STB 207	McConnely, David	SRA 18	McCoy, John	WSH 245
McClumfry, John	ALB 32	McConnll, Guian	CAY 524	McCoy, John	WST 153
McClung, James	CAY 524	McConnoghkey, Peter	NYK 120	McCoy, Neil	STB 207
McClung, James	CAY 612	McConny, Jacob	NYK 63	McCoy, Patrick	ALB 128
McClure, Daniel	ORN 345	McConoghy, Danl	RCK 105	McCoy, Robert	NYK 101
McClure, George	STB 198	McCool, Elizabeth	WSH 290	McCoy, Rosanna	COL 264
McClure, James	ONN 143	McCoon, Richard	SUF 92	McCoy, Willeam Junr	WSH 245
McClure, John	OTS 27	McCoon, Samuel	SUF 82	McCoy, William	NYK 97
McClure, John	TIO 250	McCord, Andrew	DUT 6	McCoy, William	WSH 245
McClure, Joseph	NYK 101	McCord, Andre_	ORN 347	McCrackan, David	CAY 666
McClure, Thos	TIO 250	McCord, Benjamin	DUT 117	McCracken, Andrew	SRA 48
McClure, William	DEL 284	McCord, Benjamin	WST 154	McCracken, George W.	WSH 226
McClure, William	ORN 369	McCord, Benjamin Junr	WST 154	McCracken, Hannah	DUT 116
McCluskey, John	ALB 107	McCord, Benjamin Junr	WST 156	McCracken, John	NYK 69
McColister, Archibald	COL 243	McCord, James	WST 163	McCracken, John	WSH 227
McColister, Hamleton	WSH 222	M'Cord, James	WST 166	McCracken, Joseph	WSH 225
McColl, John	ALB 40	McCord, John	DUT 7	McCracken, Joseph	WSH 226
McColl, John	WSH 294	McCord, John	ULS 250	McCracken, Joseph	WSH 255
McColle, Robert	NYK 89	M'Cord, John	WST 166	McCracken, Joseph Junr	WSH 227
McCollick, John	ALB 70	McCord, Jurden	WST 154	McCracken, Mary	WSH 226
McCollick, William	NYK 88	McCord, Robert	WST 160	McCrada, George	SRA 40
McCollop, John	NYK 58	McCord, Robt	WST 166	McCrada, James	SRA 50
McCollum, Alexr	OTS 7	McCord, Samuel	ORN 344	McCradey, William	SRA 39
McCollum, Benjn	OTS 7	McCord, William	DUT 5	McCraken, Samuel	WSH 305
McCollum, Danl	OTS 7	McCord, William	WST 151	McCraken, Samuel Jur	WSH 306
McCollum, Danl	OTS 54	McCormick see McComick		McCraken, William	WSH 290
McCollum, Daniel	WSH 257	& McOrmick		McCrany, William	DEL 284
McCollum, Elizabeth	ORN 295	McCormick, Abigal	NYK 78	McCrarry, Widow	DEL 288
McCollum, Isaac	ORN 275	McCormick, Archd	ALB 107	McCray see McGrea,	
McCollum, James	ULS 258	McCormick, David	CAY 540	McRay & McCrey	
McCollum, John	ALB 32	McCormick, David	NYK 28	McCray, James	DEL 268
McCollum, John	WSH 257	McCormick, Elizabeth	NYK 131	McCray, Samuel	SRA 16
McCollum, John Junr	WSH 257	McCormick, Henry	STB 203	McCray, Thomas	DEL 285
McCollum, Matthew	ORN 275	McCormick, Hugh	NYK 106	McCrea, Alexander	WSH 239
McCollum, Reuben	OTS 7	McCormick, James	NYK 67	McCrea, James	ESS 307
McCollum, Reuben	OTS 7	McCormick, James	NYK 106	McCrea, James	SRA 17
McCollum, Robert	CAY 642	McCormick, James	ORN 382	McCrea, John	WSH 227
McCollum, Robert	ULS 250	McCormick, Robert	NYK 59	McCrea, Martha	WSH 228
McCollum, Thomas	ORN 274	McCormick, Susannah	NYK 119	McCready see McReady	
McColom, Thomas	WST 115	McCorte, Moses	SRA 45	McCready, Andrw	NYK 82
McComb, Alexander	NYK 20	McCorty, William	CAY 628	McCready, Charles	CLN 159
McComb, Ashbell	MNT 45	McCotter, James	COL 248	McCready, James	NYK 119
McComb, John	NYK 92	McCoughtry, Jas	ALB 132	McCready, John	HRK 493
McComb, John	NYK 96	McCough_y, John	ALB 105	McCready, John	NYK 132
McComb, William	NYK 116	McCoun see McKoon		McCready, Robert	HRK 493
McComber, Archibald	DUT 105	McCoun, Austin	QNS 80	McCready, Thomas	CLN 159
McComber, John	DUT 105	McCoun, Gilbert	QNS 80	McCready, Thomas	NYK 18
McComber, Roscom	DUT 106	McCoun, Henry	ORN 380	McCready, Thomas	NYK 28
McCombs, Alexr	ALB 39	McCoun, Isaac	QNS 79	McCready, Volkey	ALB 146
McCombs, Archd	ALB 39	McCoun, Jacob	QNS 79	McCready, William	ALB 121
McCombs, George	HRK 571	McCoun, James	ORN 342	McCready, William	NYK 50
McCombs, James	ALB 39	McCoun, James	QNS 79	McCready, William	NYK 104
McCombs, John	HRK 429	McCoun, Jerusha	QNS 79	McCready, William	NYK 134
McCombs, John	HRK 453	McCoun, John	RNS 90	McCreary, John	ORN 299
McComick, Willm	TIO 250	McCoun, Justus	QNS 80	McCreary, Joseph	ORN 337
McComson, Gaune	ORN 345	McCoun, Peter	ULS 267	McCreary, Robert	ORN 299
McConchay, Robert	NYK 71	McCoun, Pomp free		McCreddy, William	ALB 148
Mc[Conn?], John	ALB 51	Negro	RNS 95	McCrellis, William	CHN 872
McConnallee, Daniel	WSH 256	McCoun, Samuel	ORN 283	McCrery, John	ALB 92
McConnallee, Neil	WSH 256	McCoun, Tounsend	RNS 90	McCrey see McCray	
McConnel, Charles	ONT 482	McCoun, William	QNS 80	McCrey, Mary	NYK 140
McConnel, Daniel	TIO 260	McCowan, Mary	NYK 65	McCrille, William Junr	CHN 872
McConnel, Hugh	DUT 30	McCowen, Henry	ONN 136	McCrillis, James	ONN 189
McConnel, James	NYK 74	McCown, Joseph	COL 179	McCrum, George	ONT 414
McConnel, James	OTS 27	McCoy see McKoy		McCrumber, Moses	RNS 66

Name	Loc	No	Name	Loc	No	Name	Loc	No
McCuchen, George	SRA	40	McDonald, Alexander	NYK	51	McDougal, Ann	WSH	257
McCullam, Randall	ALB	47	McDonald, Alexander	NYK	73	McDougal, Archibald	NYK	31
McCullen, Andrew	NYK	54	McDonald, Alexander	ONT	322	McDougal, Daniel	WSH	246
McCullen, Mary	NYK	39	McDonald, Alexander	WSH	225	McDougal, Duncan	NYK	58
McCullen, Robert	NYK	15	McDonald, Alexander L.	NYK	28	McDougal, Duncan	WSH	247
McCuller, James	CHN	776	McDonald, Andries	ALB	68	McDougal, Elizabeth	NYK	87
McCuller, James	CHN	784	McDonald, Anges	WSH	250	McDougal, James	WSH	250
McCullich, George	STB	202	McDonald, Annanias	COL	228	McDougal, Margaret	NYK	126
McCulloch, Alexr	OTS	17	McDonald, Archibald	WST	117	McDougal, Mary	ALB	32
McCulloch, Alexander	WSH	217	McDonald, Augustus	DUT	12	McDougal, William	WSH	247
McCulloch, Isa...	ONT	496	McDonald, Charles	WST	135	McDougal, William Junr	WSH	247
McCulloch, John	OTS	17	McDonald, Christopher	NYK	51	McDougald, Alexander	WSH	257
McCulloch, William	WSH	217	McDonald, Cornelius	COL	197	McDougald, Dougald	WSH	257
McCullock, John	ONT	494	McDonald, Cornelius	STB	201	McDougald, Duncan	WSH	257
McCullock, William	ALB	64	McDonald, Dan	MNT	45	McDougald, John	WSH	255
McCullough, William	NYK	145	McDonald, Daniel	MNT	106	McDougald, Ronald	WSH	257
McCullugh, Alexr	OTS	22	McDonald, Daniel	WSH	293	McDougall, Ann	ALB	6
McCullum, Fenally	MNT	89	McDonald, David	HRK	472	McDougall, Duncan R.	WSH	290
McCullum, Finly	MNT	108	McDonald, Donald	ALB	127	McDougall, Hugh	NYK	21
McCully, Frances	NYK	106	McDonald, Donald	DUT	13	McDougall, Hugh	NYK	43
McCulm, Archibald	NYK	92	McDonald, Duncan	NYK	46	McDougall, John	ALB	6
McCumber, Dier	OND	210	McDonald, Enos	ORN	376	McDougall, John	NYK	36
McCumber, Elijah	HRK	595	McDonald, Hugh	ORN	389	McDougall, Peter	ALB	62
McCumber, George	OND	175	McDonald, Jacob	MNT	106	McDouguld, Archibald	WSH	257
McCumber, James	ONT	342	McDonald, James	COL	223	McDowal see McDauel		
McCune see McKeun			McDonald, James	OTS	28	McDowal, John	STB	203
McCune, Clark	OND	169	McDonald, James	STB	199	McDowel, Andrew	TIO	257
McCune, David	NYK	135	McDonald, James	WSH	202	McDowel, James	ORN	288
McCune, Samuel	OND	169	McDonald, James	WSH	204	McDowel, William	DUT	104
McCurdy, Archibald	ORN	301	McDonald, James	WST	143	McDowell, Alexander	ORN	312
McCurdy, Jacob	ORN	328	McDonald, James D.	WSH	204	McDowell, Daniel	ORN	303
McCurdy, John	ORN	297	McDonald, John	CLN	166	McDowell, Henry	ORN	291
McCurdy, Robert	ORN	300	McDonald, John	DUT	81	McDowell, John	ORN	350
McCutchen, David	ORN	289	McDonald, John	DUT	124	McDowell, Jonathan	ORN	304
McCutchen, Robert	ORN	278	McDonald, John	NYK	56	McDowell, Mathew	NYK	89
McCutchen, Robert	ORN	293	McDonald, John	NYK	81	McDowell, Obadiah	ORN	321
McDaniel, Duncan	SCH	121	McDonald, John	NYK	101	McDowell, Robert	CAY	576
McDaniel, James	OND	201	McDonald, John	NYK	140	McDowell, Robert	NYK	77
McDaniel, John	COL	266	McDonald, John	OND	190	McDowell, Thomas	ORN	289
McDaniel, John	DEL	286	McDonald, John	SCH	155	McDowell, William	ORN	312
McDaniel, John	WSH	272	McDonald, John	SCH	162	McDowl, Hugh	NYK	77
McDaniel, Michael	WSH	272	McDonald, John	SCH	164	McDuff, Michael	OTS	19
McDaniel, Michal	CHN	800	McDonald, John	ULS	197	McDuffy, Daniel	DUT	103
McDaniel, Peter	COL	243	McDonald, John	WSH	191	McDugal, John	ONN	187
McDaniel, Reuben	WSH	271	McDonald, John	WSH	202	McDugle, James	SRA	52
McDaniel, Thomas	NYK	62	McDonald, John	WSH	293	McDunnock, Jeremiah	NYK	94
McDaniel, William	WSH	271	McDonald, Joseph	NYK	89	Mace, Abraham	COL	239
McDannell, Elias	COL	235	McDonald, Joseph	OTS	27	Mace, John	ESS	321
McDanniel, Jane	NYK	80	McDonald, Levi P.	ULS	237	Mace, Lydia	RNS	22
McDanold, James	SRA	48	McDonald, Michael	SRA	14	Mace, Simeon	DEL	286
McDanold, John	NYK	136	McDonald, Michael Junr	SRA	17	Mace, Thomas	NYK	36
McDauel see McDowal			McDonald, Moses	DUT	81	Mace, Vendal	NYK	97
McDauel, James	MNT	59	McDonald, Moses	TIO	259	McEacharn, John	COL	182
McDavid, Dennis	NYK	128	McDonald, Patrick	ULS	230	McEachron, Corneleus	WSH	247
McDavid, Mary	KNG	8	McDonald, Richard	RNS	82	McEachron, Jacob	WSH	247
McDavit, Charles	ORN	276	McDonald, Robert	SRA	29	McEachron, Neil	WSH	247
McDermet, Angus	SRA	21	McDonald, Roger	ORN	341	McEachron, Peter	WSH	247
McDermot, Daniel	NYK	119	McDonald, Sarah	ORN	398	McEachron, Peter Junr	WSH	246
McDermot, Gabriel	NYK	118	McDonald, Walter	NYK	121	McElevain, Thomas	NYK	120
McDermot, Hugh	NYK	125	McDonald, William	NYK	79	McElroy, James	ALB	125
McDermot, John	COL	237	McDonald, William	NYK	95	McElroy, James	ALB	138
McDermot, John	NYK	120	McDonald, William	ORN	397	McElroy, John	ALB	138
McDermot, Lawrence	COL	229	McDonald, William	ULS	237	McElroy, Samuel	ALB	148
McDole, Alexander	SCH	155	McDonald, William	WSH	246	McElwaine see McIllwain		
McDole, George	ALB	108	McDonalds, Marten	WST	151	McElwaine, David	DEL	283
McDole, James	WSH	193	McDonnald, Catherine	NYK	52	McElwaye, Guyne	DEL	286
McDole, John	ALB	129	McDonnel, Angus	ALB	40	McEntee, Bernard	HRK	515
McDole, John	SRA	48	McDonnel, James	ALB	38	McEntee, Charles	OND	207
McDole, John	WSH	195	McDonnel, Jas Junr	ALB	38	McEntire see McIntire		
McDole, Robert	SCH	162	McDonnell, Angus	ALB	130	McEntire, Abraham	ESS	298
McDole, Robert	WSH	192	McDonnell, Donald	ALB	124	McEntire, Ebenezer	CLN	165
McDoll, Danl	TIO	253	McDonogh, James	QNS	63	McEntire, James	OND	179
McDonagh, Hugh	ALB	129	McDonold, John	NYK	144	McEntire, John	CHN	886
McDonal, Randall	NYK	84	McDormont, Robert	NYK	119	McEntire, John	OND	180
McDonald, Aaron	DUT	80	McDossell, Alexander	MNT	116	McEntire, Joseph	ESS	298
McDonald, Alexander	DEL	268	McDougal, Alexander	NYK	59	McEntire, Levi	OND	180
McDonald, Alexander	DEL	270	McDougal, Alexander	RCH	93	McEntire, Peter	CHN	824

McEntire, Price	CHN 824	McFarlane, William	NYK 94	McGilvray, William	DUT 170
McEntire, Richard	CLN 161	McFarlane, Isabella	NYK 81	McGinnely, John	NYK 114
McEntire, Stephen	CLN 161	McFarlen, Robert	MNT 26	McGinnes, Catherine	NYK 94
McEntire, William	OND 179	McFarlin, Alexander	MNT 105	McGinnis, Alexander	ULS 203
McEntosh see McIntosh		McFarlin, Andrw	ALB 11	McGinnis, Bryan	ORN 380
McEntosh, John	CHN 788	McFarlin, Andrw Junr	ALB 11	McGinnis, Hester	NYK 96
McEuen see McCune &		McFarlin, Daniel	WSH 226	McGinnis, Peter	ORN 343
McKeun		McFarlin, Daniel	WSH 228	McGinnis, William	ULS 203
McEuen, Duncan	ORN 338	McFarlin, Daniel Junr	WSH 228	McGlarhan, Peter	MNT 88
McEuen, Hugh	MNT 64	McFarlin, Duncan	MNT 87	McGlarhan, Robert	MNT 88
McEuen, James	NYK 91	McFarlin, James	WSH 228	McGlasky, James	RNS 48
McEuen, John	ORN 303	McFarlin, Jane	ALB 13	McGlasshen, Alexr	ALB 124
McEuen, Malcom	NYK 45	McFarlin, Jane	ALB 52	McGlaughlan, Charles	ORN 335
McEuen, Robert	ORN 280	McFarlin, John	WSH 193	McGlaughlan, John	ORN 301
McEvers, Charles	NYK 28	McFarlin, Malcomb	ALB 32	McGlaughlin, Archibald	ORN 343
McEvers, Guhan	NYK 50	McFarlin, Norman	ALB 40	McGlaughlin, Joseph	ORN 350
McEvers, James	CLN 155	McFarlin, Robert	WSH 225	McGlaughlin, Patrick	ORN 350
McEvers, James	NYK 17	McFarlin, William	WSH 222	McGlaughlin, Peter	ORN 343
McEvers, James	NYK 142	McFarlin, William	WSH 225	McGlaughry, Agnis	ORN 290
McEvers, James	ONN 146	McFarlin, William Junr	WSH 222	McGlaughry, John	ORN 290
McEvers, J.hn	NYK 43	McFarling, Andrew	GRN 328	McGlaughry, John	ORN 341
McEvoy, Malcom	WST 145	M.Far_ing, James	WST 163	McGlaughry, Robert	ORN 341
McEwen, Mary	NYK 32	McFarren, John	WSH 283	McGlaughry, Thomas	ORN 341
McEwen, Mary	NYK 120	McFarren, Robert	ALB 82	McGlaughry, William	ORN 341
McEy, Robert	NYK 143	McFees, Alex	OTS 4	McGlave, James	NYK 84
Macey see Macy		McFerrin, William	WSH 195	McGlowen, Partrick	NYK 66
Macey, Abraham	COL 219	McGahagan, Dennis	NYK 81	McGlue, Theopholus	NYK 81
Macey, George	COL 211	McGalpin, James	SRA 10	McGonigal, John	COL 181
Macey, Nathel	COL 214	McGarey, Christian	NYK 139	McGonigall, Thomas	COL 181
Macey, Reuben	COL 255	McGarey, Richard	NYK 139	McGoon, Alexander	WSH 222
Macey, Reuben 2d	COL 252	McGarrah, John	ORN 388	McGorgy, Anne	ORN 369
Macey, Richard	COL 252	McGarron, James	NYK 73	McGouch, John	ALB 40
Macey, Robert	COL 214	McGarty, Thomas	ORN 365	McGougen, Stephen	NYK 120
Macey, Seth G.	COL 248	McGarvee, Anthony	NYK 108	McGoun, John	MNT 72
Macey, Simeon	COL 217	McGathlin, Wm	OTS 52	McGoun, John	ORN 346
Macey, Willm	COL 214	McGauger, Michael	RNS 48	McGourachy, Robert	ALB 139
McFadden, Alexander	WSH 244	McGaw, William	RNS 7	McGourchy, James	ALB 141
McFadden, Hugh	WSH 244	McGee see McKee		McGourchy, John	ALB 141
McFadden, John	WSH 244	McGee, Abraham	ALB 59	McGourk, James	ALB 128
McFaddon, George	WSH 246	McGee, David	WSH 217	McGorvern, John	NYK 62
McFaddon, Samuel	WSH 246	McGee, Ephraim	GRN 328	McGowan, Andrw	NYK 152
McFail, John	WSH 244	McGee, Hannah	ALB 141	McGowan, James	NYK 120
McFall see McPhall		McGee, Henry	ONT 322	McGowan, John	NYK 119
McFall, Daniel	NYK 42	McGee, Henry	STB 205	McGowan, John	NYK 125
McFall, Hendrick	COL 238	McGee, James	ORN 291	McGowan, Mary	NYK 32
McFall, Henry	COL 229	McGee, James	WSH 256	McGowan, Robert	NYK 137
Mcfall, John	GRN 332	McGee, James Junr	ALB 105	McGowen, Hugh	MNT 59
McFall, John	SCH 155	McGee, John	ALB 56	McGown, Cutter	SRA 50
McFall, Patrick	COL 192	McGee, John	ORN 376	McGown, Stephen	OTS 42
McFall, Patrick	COL 229	McGee, Joseph	OTS 57	McGrager, Jame	GRN 354
McFall, Robert	NYK 113	McGee, Samuel	ORN 274	McGrath, John	NYK 22
McFall, Thomas	DEL 270	McGee, Samuel	ULS 228	McGrath, John	NYK 54
McFall, Thomas	OTS 37	McGee, Thomas	WSH 217	Ma_grath, Mary	NYK 101
McFall, Wm	OTS 34	McGee, Wm	CHN 940	McGratick, John	NYK 31
McFarlain, Andrew	WSH 287	McGee, Wm	MNT 111	McGraw, Christopher	HRK 416
McFarlain, John	WSH 287	McGee, William	ONT 322	McGraw, Dennis	ALB 65
McFarlain, John	WSH 297	McGellevra, Duncan	WSH 242	McGraw, Duncan	NYK 41
McFarlain, Thomas	WSH 283	McGellevra, John	WSH 242	McGraw, Edward	ALB 34
McFarlain, William	WSH 282	McGellevrey, Archabald	WSH 255	McGraw, Geo.	OTS 41
McFarlaine, William	ESS 294	McGenghgin, John	NYK 22	McGraw, John	SRA 7
McFarlan, James	HRK 548	McGeoach, John	NYK 89	McGraw, Marica	ALB 139
McFarlance, Dugal	NYK 47	McGerrahan, Hugh	NYK 18	McGraw, Samuel	HRK 563
McFarlance, John	NYK 134	McGibbons, Peter	ALB 48	McGraw, Thomas	GRN 352
McFarland, David	DEL 285	McGilfry, Alexander	DEL 270	McGrea see McCray	
McFarland, James	DEL 285	McGilfrey, Daniel	DEL 270	McGrea, Jeremiah	SCH 117
McFarland, John	DEL 284	McGill, Arthur	ULS 233	McGregor, Alexander	NYK 30
McFarland, Josep	ONT 366	McGill, Hugh	ORN 288	McGregor, Alexander	NYK 33
McFarland, Joseph	WSH 248	McGill, Hugh	WSH 306	McGregor, Alexander	ORN 297
McFarland, Samuel	WSH 249	McGill, John	COL 224	McGregor, Alexander	QNS 79
McFarland, W.	TIO 251	McGill, John	HRK 451	McGregor, Alexander	WSH 246
McFarlane, Daniel	DUT 121	McGill, John	WSH 231	McGregor, Ann	ALB 137
McFarlane, Eleazer	NYK 88	McGill, Joseph	TIO 250	McGregor, Duncan	MNT 63
McFarlane, James	DUT 91	McGill, Peter	WSH 194	McGregor, John	NYK 19
McFarlane, Jane	NYK 140	McGill, Robert	NYK 47	McGregor, John	NYK 21
McFarlane, John	NYK 100	McGill, William	ALB 46	McGregor, Jonas	MNT 118
McFarlane, John	ORN 372	McGillevrey, Daniel	WSH 255	McGregor, Malcomb	ALB 54
McFarlane, Peter	NYK 148	McGillvrey, Archabald	WSH 256	McGregor, Peter	ALB 40

D.

McGregor, William	SRA	53	McIntire, Murphey	COL	239	McKay, Paul	DUT 167
McGreg_y, Duncan	GRN	336	McIntire, Murphy	WSH	246	Mackdormet, William	GRN 327
McGregory, Samuel	SRA	13	McIntire, Nathan	WSH	294	Macke, Jerremiah	CHN 884
McGriner, John	ALB	149	McIntire, Nicholas	COL	241	McKean, Elizabeth	NYK 35
McGuffen, John	ALB	136	McIntire, Oliver	OTS	44	McKean, William	ORN 369
McGuigan, Frs	ALB	7	McIntire, Peter	DUT	57	McKean, William Junr	ORN 369
McGuines, Jacob	GRN	334	McInti[re?], Peter	MNT	73	McKe_y, James	NYK 82
McGuire see McQuire			McIntire, Peter	WSH	246	McKeblun, Joseph	NYK 127
McGuire, Andrew	RNS	77	McIntire, Samuel	ONT	500	McKee see McGee &
McGuire, Betsey	NYK	91	McIntire, Thomas	OTS	42	McKey
McGuire, Christian	NYK	64	McIntire, Wm	MNT	70	McKee, Eleazer	HRK 418
McGuire, Edward	NYK	70	McIntire, Wm	MNT	89	McKee, Francis	OND 187
McGuire, Hugh	DUT	151	McIntire, William	NYK	105	McKee, James	ALB 105
McGuire, John	ORN	281	McIntire, William	ONT	500	McKee, James	DEL 286
McGuire, Partrick	NYK	29	McIntosh see McEntosh			McKee, James	WSH 184
McGuire, Sarah	NYK	100	McIntosh, Alexr	COL	236	McKee, John	ALB 40
McGuire, Thomas	NYK	103	McIntosh, Alexander	NYK	131	McKee, John	OND 175
McGuire, Thomas	ONT	474	McIntosh, Andrew	ALB	131	McKee, Joseah	WSH 297
McGunnagal, Felix	NYK	113	McIntosh, Angus	ALB	39	McKee, Joseph	HRK 417
McGunty, Barney	NYK	152	McIntosh, Angus Junr	ALB	39	McKee, Robert	NYK 105
McGuyre, John	CHN	966	McIntosh, Daniel	CAY	728	McKee, Samuel	ALB 39
Machan, Jachamiah	OTS	34	McIntosh, Daniel	SCH	164	McKee, Thomas	NYK 105
McHarg, John	ALB	137	McIntosh, Geo.	SCH	123	McKee, William	DEL 286
McHarg, John Junr	ALB	148	McIntosh, Gilbert	ALB	148	McKee, William	OND 187
McHarry, John	ONN	191	McIntosh, James	NYK	148	McKee, Wm	ONN 168
Machary, Richard	ALB	47	McIntosh, John	ALB	51	McKee, William	WSH 257
McHarz, Peter	ALB	106	McIntosh, John	ALB	107	McKee, William	WSH 257
McHenny, John	KNG	8	McIntosh, John	ALB	132	McKeel, Isaac	WST 123
McHenry, Henry	STB	206	McIntosh, Margaret	NYK	48	McKeel, John	ORN 390
McHenry, John	TIO	263	McIntosh, Matthias	ALB	72	McKeel, Josiah	DUT 74
McHenry, Mathew	STB	205	McIntosh, Timothy	DUT	76	McKeel, Michael	ORN 390
Machet, John	NYK	149	McIntosh, William	ALB	26	McKeel, Michael	WST 163
McHinch, James	ALB	100	McIntosh, William	ALB	52	McKeel, Thomas	DUT 72
McHinch, Robert	NYK	35	McIntosh, William	ALB	139	McKeel, Tunis	DEL 273
Machon, Patrick	ALB	48	McIntosh, William	NYK	40	McKeel, Uriah	DUT 72
McHony, James	ULS	249	McIntyre, John	GRN	353	McKeen, James	ONT 420
McHue, Justus	TIO	227	McIver, John	DEL	286	McKeen, Laughton B.	ONT 424
McHugh, James	ALB	18	McJimpsey, John	ORN	309	McKeen, Levi	DUT 66
McHugh, John	ORN	299	Mack see Mac & Mark			McKeen, Saml	OTS 3
McIlheny, William	ONT	382	Mack, Abijah	OND	189	McKelerick, Wm	ALB 35
McIllwain see McElwaine			Mack, Anna	OTS	32	McKell, Patrick	STB 199
McIllwain, Moses	OTS	53	Mack, Benjamin	ONT	420	McKeller, Archibald	WSH 254
McIllwane, Saml	OTS	46	Mack, Daniel	NYK	65	McKellip, John	OTS 56
McIlwaine, David Junr	DEL	283	Mack, Edward	NYK	20	Macken, Nicholas	NYK 120
McIlwaine, John	ONT	482	Mack, Gad	DEL	281	Mackenburgh, Abner	SRA 31
Macin, Dezire	NYK	93	Mack, Jesse	ULS	245	Mackenburgh, Gour	SRA 31
McInburgh, Elihu	ONN	169	Mack, Joel	DEL	286	Mackenburgh, John	SRA 31
McInroy, John	WSH	247	Mack, John	ONT	378	Mackenburgh, John	SRA 31
McIntier, William	ULS	264	Mack, John	ONT	388	Mackenburgh, Parden	SRA 31
McIntire see McEntire			Mack, John	ULS	211	Mackenburgh, Peter	SRA 31
McIntire, Alexander	ONT	352	Mack, John	WSH	187	McKenna, Andrew	ALB 141
McIntire, Archibald	MNT	70	Mack, Josiah	OTS	38	McKennan, Peter	NYK 64
McIntire, Archibald	MNT	87	Mack, Orlando	DEL	286	McKenncy see McKenney
McIntire, Benjamin	WSH	287	Mack, Orlando	TIO	245	McKenney, Andrew	ALB 17
McIntire, Daniel	COL	241	Mack, O[rlando?] Junr	DEL	283	McKenney, Daniel	MNT 112
McIntire, Daniel	MNT	70	Mack, Stephen	TIO	245	McKenney, John	ALB 55
McIntire, Daniel	MNT	87	Mack, Warren	HRK	514	McKenney, John	WSH 241
McIntire, Daniel	NYK	127	Mack, Zebulon	ONT	424	McKenney, Robert	SRA 24
McIntire, Daniel	SRA	13	McKabie, Patrick	ONN	157	McKenney, William	SUF 83
McIntire, Daniel Junr	MNT	88	Mackable, Catherine	NYK	68	McKenny, Danl	ALB 10
McIntire, Dougal	DEL	288	McKain, Daniel	MNT	68	McKenny, John	NYK 51
McIntire, Duncan	MNT	87	McKallor, Dougald	WSH	255	McKenny, Mathew	SRA 23
McIntire, Duncan	WSH	246	Mackaness, Thomas	NYK	53	McKenny, William	NYK 21
McIntire, Dutey	WSH	236	Mackarel, James	QNS	67	McKensey, Daniel	STB 199
McIntire, Eli	DEL	291	Mackarel, James Junr	QNS	67	McKensey, Geo.	OTS 16
McIntire, Elizabeth	NYK	79	McKay see McCay			McKenster, John	SRA 40
McIntire, Experce	OTS	31	McKay, Angus	ORN	288	McKenzie, John	OND 183
McIntire, Hugh	NYK	90	McKay, David	NYK	124	Mackenzie, Kenneth	NYK 79
McIntire, Jacob	COL	243	McKay, Hector	ONT	322	Mackercey, George	NYK 70
McIntire, James	MNT	92	Mackay, James	ALB	124	McKerley, Alexr	ALB 23
McIntire, John	ALB	5	McKay, James	NYK	31	McKerley, John	ALB 40
McIntire, John	COL	239	McKay, John	NYK	21	McKerley, Michael	ALB 134
McIntire, John	NYK	43	McKay, John	RCH	36	McK[eu?]en, James	NYK 130
McIntire, John	NYK	74	McKay, Miranda	ORN	279	McKeun see McCune, Mc-
McIntire, John	WSH	225	McKay, Montgomery	ALB	90	Euen, McEwen, & McKuen
McIntire, Marey	WSH	190	McKay, Murdoch	DUT	133	McKeun, James	RNS 26
McIntire, Moses	NYK	105	McKay, Partrick	NYK	108	McKever, William	NYK 73

Name	Ref	Name	Ref	Name	Ref
McKew, John	NYK 120	McKinstry, Stephen	ORN 296	McLaughlin, Dennis	TIO 264
Mackey see McKee		McKin[zey?], John	ONT 510	McLaughlin, James	CAY 664
Mackey, Alexander	ALB 87	McKinzie, Alexander	NYK 82	McLaughlin, Lean	HRK 469
McKey, Alexander	NYK 130	McKinzie, Alexander	ULS 225	McLawren, Duncan	NYK 102
McKey, George	NYK 65	McKinzie, Collier	NYK 147	McLean see McClean	
Mackey, Jacob Ogden	NYK 16	McKinzie, John	NYK 145	McLean, Anna	NYK 90
Mackey, James	ALB 91B	McKinzie, John	ULS 222	McLean, Charles	NYK 101
McKey, John	MNT 27	McKinzie, Mary	NYK 21	McLean, Charles	OND 212
McKey, John	NYK 15	McKinzie, Mary	NYK 26	McLean, Cornelius	NYK 88
McKey, John	NYK 76	McKinzie, Mary	NYK 27	McLean, Cornelius	RCH 90
Mackey, Peter	NYK 140	McKinzie, Murdock	NYK 22	McLean, Daniel	CLN 168
McKey, Reuben	MNT 123	McKinzy, William	DEL 270	McLean, Donnold	NYK 137
McKey, Samuel	NYK 130	McKissac, James	NYK 29	McLean, Hector	ALB 26
Mackey, Solomon	ALB 87	McKissick, Thomas	ORN 306	McLean, James	NYK 26
Mackey, William	ALB 87	McKisson, John	NYK 37	McLean, John	ALB 29
McKicker, Daniel	MNT 90	McKissuk, James	NYK 108	McLean, John	DEL 270
McKie, Alexander	NYK 57	Mackling, William	NYK 132	McLean, John	DUT 166
Mackie, Alexander	ULS 262	McKneeley see McNeeley		McLean, John	NYK 79
Mackie, Alexander	ULS 266	McKneeley, Peter	ALB 28	McLean, John	NYK 110
Mackie, Charles	ULS 260	McKnight see McNight		McLean, John	ORN 295
Mackie, David	ORN 288	McKnight, Andrew	CAY 532	McLean, John	ORN 360
McKie, David	SUF 97	McKnight, Barnabas	OND 167	McLean, John	ULS 228
Mackie, Elias	ULS 262	McKnight, David	OND 167	McLean, John Junr	ALB 29
McKie, George	SUF 97	McKnight, George	WSH 292	McLean, Jonas	ORN 298
McKie, James	RCK 108	McKnight, James	CAY 528	McLean, Joseph	DUT 74
Mackie, John	ORN 295	McKnight, James	NYK 36	McLean, La[ncklan?]	OND 212
Mackie, John	ULS 262	McKnight, James	WSH 292	McLean, Neil	NYK 38
Mackie, John	ULS 262	McKnight, John	NYK 109	McLean, Neil	ULS 247
Mackie, John Ye 2d	ULS 263	McKnight, Samuel	OND 162	McLean, Obadiah	ONN 161
Mackie, Jurion	ULS 262	McKnight, Willm	COL 212	McLean, Obid	ESS 309
Mackie, Jurion Ye 2d	ULS 266	McKollough, John	DEL 287	McLean, William	NYK 55
Mackie, Jurion the 3d	ULS 263	McKollough, Samuel	DEL 287	McLean, William	OND 160
Mackie, Levi	ULS 262	McKonnegal, Patrick	RCH 91	McLee, Benjn M.	OTS 16
Mackie, Matthew	ULS 267	Mackoon see McCoun		McLees, James	DUT 12
McKie, Peter	NYK 31	Mackoon, Gesham	CHN 904	McLees, James Junr	DUT 14
Mackie, Samuel	ULS 264	McKoon, James	HRK 498	McLees, Peter	DUT 12
Mackie, Thomas	NYK 56	McKoon, James Jun	HRK 498	McLeod see McCloud	
Mackie, Thomas	ULS 262	McKoon, Martin	HRK 498	McLeod, Alexander	ORN 283
McKilip, John	WSH 192	McKoun, James	RNS 63	McLeod, Daniel	NYK 35
McKill, Jane	NYK 52	McKoun, Wm	RNS 27	McLeod, Daniel	ORN 277
McKillip, Archd	OTS 3	McKown, Joseph	COL 185	McLeod, Donald	ALB 145
McKillip, Archd Junr	OTS 3	McKown, William	ALB 137	McLeod, Henry	ORN 394
McKillip, Thomas	WSH 187	McKoy see McCoy		McLeod, John	ORN 289
McKinley, Duncan	ALB 71	McKoy, Getray	SRA 11	McLeod, John	WSH 291
McKinley, Hugh	ORN 283	McKoy, Joel	SRA 5	McLeod, Norman	WSH 291
McKinley, John	MNT 70	McKoy, John	NYK 18	McLeod, Roderic	NYK 29
McKinley, John	NYK 105	McKoy, Thomas	NYK 29	McLeughlin, Patrick	NYK 133
McKinley, John	SRA 29	Mackraell, William	NYK 130	McLocklan, John	NYK 120
McKinley, Neal	NYK 106	McKrell, Partrick	NYK 116	McLoghlan, Daniel	NYK 58
McKinley, Peter	NYK 34	Macksfield, John	SRA 25	Mclough, Jeremiah	NYK 64
McKinley, Richard	ULS 238	Mackuen see McKeun		McLough, John	ONT 440
McKinley, William	ORN 279	Mackuen, Charles	SRA 26	McLough, Peter	ONT 440
McKinney, Anna	NYK 86	McKutchen, Hugh	NYK 78	McLoughlane, George	NYK 76
McKinney, Charles	ORN 332	Macky, Elexander	GRN 335	McLoughlin, Susannah	NYK 123
McKinney, Cornelius	MNT 25	McLaben, Mary	NYK 124	McLouth, Laurence	ONT 440
McKinney, Daniel	ONT 448	McLachlan, Archibald	NYK 77	McMacken, Terrence	NYK 62
McKinney, George	SCH 139	McLachlan, Benjamin	NYK 79	McMaclean, Murdock	NYK 83
McKinney, Jacob a		McLachlan, James	NYK 79	McMahan, Jane	ORN 294
Black	NYK 119	McLachlan, Michale	NYK 76	McMahon, Michel	NYK 80
McKinney, James	ORN 308	McLallin, Archibald	MNT 68	McMahon, Patrick	NYK 17
McKinney, James	SRA 26	McLane, Allen	WSH 255	McMallom, James	NYK 71
McKinney, Mathew	SRA 24	McLane, Frances	WSH 196	McMamara, Peter	NYK 122
McKinney, Matthew	ORN 308	McLane, James	WSH 192	McManners, Hugh	RNS 84
McKinney, Samuel	ALB 52	McLane, John	WSH 192	McManners, Kinney	ORN 385
McKinney, Seth	CAY 648	McLane, Laughlan	WSH 183	McMannon, Christopher	TIO 209
McKinney, Thomas	CAY 648	McLane, Murdick	WSH 202	McManus, John	NYK 145
McKinnon, Neal	NYK 80	McLane, Peter	MNT 91	McManus, William	ALB 139
McKinnon, Neil	NYK 42	McLane, Thomas	WSH 252	McMarten, Peter	MNT 60
McKinny, Arthur	ORN 304	McLane, William	WSH 192	McMartin, Duncan	MNT 58
McKinny, Robert	NYK 25	McLaren, Daniel	NYK 51	McMartin, Peter	MNT 58
McKinsey, Hector	STB 199	McLaren, Margaret	NYK 38	McMartin, Peter	SRA 30
McKinsey, James	ALB 22	McLaren, Neal	NYK 82	McMaster, Dann	CHN 806
McKinsey, James	SCH 137	McLarey, John	NYK 65	McMaster, David	CHN 756
McKinstry, Charles	COL 177	McLanghlin, Garret	NYK 73	McMaster, James	MNT 103
McKinstry, Charles Junr	COL 180	McLaughlen, Daniel	NYK 108	McMaster, James	NYK 139
McKinstry, Daniel	COL 177	McLaughlen, James	NYK 108	McMaster, James	TIO 244
McKinstry, George	COL 214	McLaughlen, John	NYK 102	McMaster, James W.	SRA 17

Name	Loc	Pg	Name	Loc	Pg	Name	Loc	Pg
McMaster, John	ALB	40	McMurray, James	NYK	101	McNight, John	SRA	23
McMaster, John	ALB	130	McMurray, James	RNS	81	McNight, Robert	ONN	187
McMaster, John	CHN	806	McMurray, John	DUT	164	McNish, Andrew Clark	ORN	341
McMaster, John	ONT	498	McMurray, John	NYK	108	McNish, George	ORN	332
McMaster, John	SRA	16	McMurray, Robert	ALB	132	McNitt, Andw	OTS	47
McMaster, Partrick	NYK	52	McMurray, Robert	WSH	228	McNitt, Saml	OTS	47
McMaster, Thomas	TIO	236	McMurray, Thomas	ALB	140	McNulty, Daniel	DUT	167
McMaster, Thoms	TIO	239	McMurray, James	ALB	47	McNulty, Daniel	WST	121
McMaster, William	SRA	15	McMirry, Andrew	ALB	125	McNut, Alexander	WSH	224
McMasters, David	SRA	17	McMurtry, Alexander	ORN	380	McNut, Alexander Junr	WSH	224
McMasters, James	NYK	39	McMurtry, Henry	ORN	380	McNut, Daniel	WSH	224
McMasters, James	ULS	200	McMurtry, John	ALB	71	McNut, John	WSH	186
McMasters, Jeremiah	TIO	244	McNab, Hugh	ALB	103	McNutley, John	CAY	578
McMath, Alla	CAY	528	McNab, John	NYK	112	McNutt, Alexander	CAY	522
McMath, John	CAY	542	McNable, Widow	MNT	65	McNutt, Andrew	OTS	21
McMechan, Alexander	COL	263	McNair, Hugh	ONT	320	McNutt, Barnard	ONT	342
McMenomy, Robert	NYK	35	McNair, John	ONT	320	McNutt, David	STB	202
McMichael, Alexr	ALB	16	McNair, John	ONT	452	McNutt, Eleanor	ALB	9
McMichael, Charles	ONT	450	McNair, John Ju.	ONT	452	McNutt, James	HRK	420
McMichael, John	ALB	62	McNair, Robert	ONT	452	McNutt, John	CHN	796
McMichael, Mary	ALB	4	McNair, William	ONT	320	McNutt, John	ONT	316
McMichael, Jane	NYK	78	McNair, William	ONT	326	McNutt, Samuel	HRK	567
McMichael, John	HRK	585	McNall, Samuel	CLN	165	McNutt, William	SRA	59
McMichel, John	WSH	230	McNamee, William	DUT	110	Macomb, John N.	NYK	86
McMicken, James	DEL	283	McNames, Abram	ONN	180	Mcormick, Alaxr	SUF	64
McMickle, John	ORN	384	McNara, John	OND	183	McPhall see McFall		
McMillan, John	ALB	136	McNaughon, John	MNT	70	McPhall, John	NYK	89
McMillen, Alexander	NYK	85	McNaughten, Alexander	WSH	227	McPhall, John	NYK	121
McMillen, Andrew	WSH	228	McNaughten, Alexander	WSH	254	McPhall, William	NYK	92
McMillen, Arther	WSH	224	McNaughten, David	WSH	254	McPhearson, Molly	NYK	75
McMillen, Hugh	WSH	204	McNaughten, Duncan	WSH	250	McPhearson, Thomas	NYK	78
McMillen, James	NYK	116	McNaughten, John	ONT	316	McPherson, Alexander	DEL	270
McMillen, John	ALB	105	McNaughten, Peter	MNT	105	McPherson, Charles	ALB	62
McMillen, John	NYK	127	McNaughten, Robert	WSH	229	McPherson, Daniel	DEL	285
McMillen, John	WSH	191	McNaughten, Robert	WSH	250	McPherson, Daniel	ONT	316
McMillen, John	WSH	201	Mc aughton, Malcom	WSH	244	McPherson, Even	ALB	143
McMillen, John	WSH	228	McNeal, Archibald	SRA	48	McPherson, John	ALB	137
McMillen, Thomas	CHN	890	McNeal, Charles	QNS	66	McPherson, John	CLN	169
McMillian, Andrew	WSH	289	McNeal, James	COL	258	McPherson, John	DEL	268
McMinderse, Wm	ALB	21	McNeal, James	NYK	80	McPherson, John	MNT	66
McMinn, David	DEL	284	McNeal, John	CHN	770	McPherson, John	NYK	81
McMinn, John	ORN	271	McNeal, John	NYK	22			
McMitchell, Assa	WSH	301	McNeal, John	SRA	47	McPherson, John a mulatto	NYK	85
McMoran, Thomas	NYK	105	McNeal, Willm	COL	186	McPherson, John	ONT	448
McMorris, Armstrong	DEL	286	McNear, John	NYK	71	McPh.rson, William	ONT	494
McMullan, Charles	NYK	51	McNear, Mary	NYK	109	McPhie, John	NYK	59
McMullen, Adam	DEL	279	McNeary, Martin	DUT	31	McPuny, Thomas	TIO	264
McMullen, Andrew	OND	167	McNeash, Alexander	WSH	224	McQoid, John ye 1st	ORN	334
McMullen, Archibald	DEL	279	McNeash, Andrew	WSH	229	McQoid, John the 2d	ORN	340
McMullen, Charles	QNS	60	McNeash, John	WSH	227	McQuade, James	RNS	55
McMullen, Daniel	ALB	39	McNechar, John	NYK	56	McQueen, Cathrine	WSH	225
McMullen, Danl	OTS	42	McNeeley see McKneeley			McQueen, John	MNT	120
McMullen, George	MNT	38	McNeeley, Andrew	ALB	42	McQueen, John	NYK	44
McMullen, James	ALB	32	McNeely, Sarah	ORN	291	McQueen, John	QNS	81
McMullen, James	SRA	29	McNeil, Aaron	WSH	221	McQueen, John	WSH	224
McMullen, John	ALB	101	McNeil, Alexande	WSH	257	McQueen, Robert	NYK	107
McMullen, John	DEL	279	McNeil, Archibald	WSH	250	McQueen, Robert	SRA	35
McMullen, John	ORN	337	McNeil, Daniel	ULS	257	McQueen, William	DEL	270
McMullen, John	WSH	188	McNeil, Elizabeth	DUT	19	McQuerg, Daniel	WSH	246
McMullen, Mary	ORN	337	McNeil, Hannah	ORN	345	McQuig, Patrick	ORN	381
McMullen, Nancy	ULS	250	McNeil, Henry	DUT	19	McQuigg, John	TIO	248
McMullen, William	ORN	326	McNeil, Isaac	ORN	345	McQuilhin, John	NYK	133
McMullin, Alexander	CLN	168	McNeil, John	ORN	345	McQuire see McGuire		
McMullin, David	CLN	167	McNeil, John	ULS	227	McQuire, Isaac	WSH	274
McMullin, Dennis	ALB	138	McNeil, John	WSH	250	McQuire, Isaac Jur	WSH	274
McMullin, John	MNT	105	McNeil, Neil	WSH	257	McQuire, Silas	WSH	275
McMunn, Elijah	ORN	296	McNeil, Theodore	MNT	20	McQuithy, Abraham	CAY	690
McMunn, James	ORN	294	McNeil, William	DUT	30	McQuithy, James	CAY	694
McMurday, Anthony	ALB	133	McNeil, William E.	ORN	339	McQuithy, Reuben	CAY	690
McMurdy, Benjamin	DEL	285	McNichel, Arthur	NYK	132	McQuort, Robert	NYK	105
McMurdy, Jonathan	DEL	285	McNichols, Neil	NYK	71	McRay see McCray		
McMurdy, Sarah	ORN	288	McNiel, Charles	OND	200	McRay, Sylvester	TIO	210
McMurphey, James	WSH	293	McNiel, Cornelias	MNT	25	McReady see McCready		
McMurray, Alexander	NYK	106	McNiel, Henry	OND	193	McReady, James	NYK	46
McMurray, Francis	WSH	242	McNiel, John	SCH	132	McReady, James	WST	116
McMurray, James	ALB	126	McNiel, John C.	SCH	156	McRinley see McKinley		
McMurray, James	NYK	79	McNight see McKnight	SRA	23	McShunkin, Augustus	NYK	65

McSparon, William	NYK 137	Maguire, John	ONT 378	Mallaby, Francis	NYK 26	
McSwain, John	RCH 92	Mahallen, Daniel	STB 206	Mallary, James	NYK 81	
McTuckin, Hugh Boyd	NYK 44	Mahan, James	ORN 310	Mallary, James	RNS 33	
Macumber, Benjamin	ESS 307	Mahan, Samuel	OND 169	Mallary, John	CHN 936	
Macumber, Daniel	ONT 444	Mahan, Thomas	NYK 47	Mallenbury, Christian	NYK 81	
Macumber, Elizabeth	RNS 72	Mahan, William	OND 169	Mallery, Ashbell	OND 180	
Macumber, Hugh	COL 246	Mahar, William	ALB 130	Mallery, Azariah	DUT 135	
Macumber, John	ESS 307	Maharey, Mary	NYK 54	Mallery, Burr	ONN 168	
Macumber, John	ONT 444	Maharr, William	WST 147	Mallery, David	COL 189	
Macumber, Richard	ONT 444	Mahew, Abijah W.	COL 183	Mallery, David	DUT 136	
Macumber, Roger	COL 263	Mahew, Zepheniah	COL 182	Mallery, .iah	COL 178	
Macumber, Samuel	ONT 444	Mahom, Sarah	NYK 17	Mallery, Ebenezer	COL 183	
Macumbur, Philip	SRA 28	Mahon, John	HRK 428	Mallery, Edmund	DUT 135	
McVain, Duncan	MNT 64	Mahony, Timothy	NYK 138	Mallery, Eli	HRK 594	
McVain, James	MNT 71	Mahue, Lemuel	ONN 168	Mallery, Elijah	ALB 74	
McVain, John	MNT 68	Maigley, Christian	COL 245	Mallery, Elijah Junr	ALB 74	
McVain, Peter	MNT 64	Maigley, Frederick	COL 237	Mallery, Isaac	COL 179	
McVeagh, Alexander	ORN 347	Maigley, John	COL 236	Mallery, Jiles	WST 156	
McVeagh, Benjamin	ORN 289	Maigley, Willm	COL 236	Mallery, Luther	ESS 308	
McVeagh, Daniel	ORN 343	Main see Mane & Mayne		Mallery, Nathaniel	ESS 323	
McVeagh, James	ORN 344	Main, Andrew	NYK 85	Mallery, Oliver	COL 179	
McVeagh, John	ORN 311	Main, David	WSH 303	Mallery, Oliver Junr	COL 179	
McVean, John	ONT 314	Main, Henry	HRK 539	Mallery, Samuel	COL 183	
McVickar, John	RCH 92	Main, James	CLN 163	Mallery, Sheldon	HRK 554	
McVicker, Archabald	WSH 190	Main, James	NYK 38	Mallery, Willm	COL 177	
McVicker, John	STB 205	Main, James	NYK 91	Mallett, Samuel	DUT 129	
McWay, Patrick	DUT 166	Main, James	RNS 72	Mallison, Joseph	COL 204	
McWay, William	NYK 131	Main, Jeremiah	OND 203	Mallock, James	ULS 235	
McWhorter, Gilbert	ORN 378	Main, Jeremiah Jun	HRK 539	Mallory, Lemuel	DEL 274	
McWhorter, John	ONN 188	Main, Jeremy	HRK 539	Mallson, John	ONN 151	
McWhorter, John	ORN 369	Main, John	NYK 39	Malony, Bartholomew	DUT 9	
McWhorter, John Junr	ORN 369	Main, John	WSH 305	Malony, Bryant	DUT 120	
McWhorter, Thomas	ORN 371	Main, Joseph	WSH 248	Malony, John	ORN 277	
McWhorter, Thomas	STB 199	Main, Lathrop	HRK 539	Maloy, Thomas	NYK 81	
McWhorther, Mathew Jur	WSH 227	Main, Peter	WSH 248	Malrey, Peter	WSH 215	
McWilliams, Andrew	ALB 133	Main, Rachel	NYK 20	Malrey, William	WSH 215	
McWilliams, George	SRA 25	Main, Stephen Junr	RNS 104	Maltby, Joseph	OND 192	
McWilliams, James	ALB 12	Maine, George	NYK 70	Maltby, Morris	OND 183	
McWilliams, James	ALB 75	Maine, Gilbert	RNS 78	Maltby, Timothy	OND 182	
McWilliams, John	DEL 285	Maine, Joshua	DUT 169	Maltison, Abraham	SRA 57	
McWilliams, John	ORN 343	Maine, Sibbeus	DUT 91	Mammerman, Derick	KNG 8	
Macy see Macey		Mains, Diademi	NYK 64	Man, Abrm	OTS 48	
Macy, John	COL 198	Mains, Francis	ORN 289	Man, Amos	SRA 58	
Maddison, Noah	CHN 786	Mains, James	ONT 496	Man, Andrew	WSH 234	
Maddison, Robert M.	NYK 74	Mains, James	WSH 254	Man, Anne	ORN 331	
Maddock, James	NYK 127	Mains, John	WSH 256	Man, Archabald	NYK 72	
Maddock, Roger W.	KNG 7	Mairs, George	WSH 255	Man, David	NYK 150	
Maddon, Anna	NYK 118	Mairs, Thomas	WSH 255	Man, Gideon	SRA 56	
Maddon, John	NYK 120	Maitland, Benjamin	NYK 53	Man, Hezekeah	WSH 269	
Maddon, Samuel	NYK 110	Maitland, James	NYK 147	Man, Israel	CHN 794	
Mader, Thomas	WST 168	Maitles, Sarah	NYK 87	Man, James	SRA 16	
Madin, Timothy	ONT 318	Maitling, Daniel	CAY 652	Man, Jesse	ORN 331	
Madin, Timothy Jun.	ONT 318	Major, John	SRA 29	Man, Jesse	SRA 58	
Madley, Joseph	CAY 594	Major, Samuel	NYK 74	Man, John	NYK 71	
Maes see Mays		Major, William	NYK 152	Man, Peter a mulatto	NYK 72	
Maes, John	SRA 9	Makay see McKay		Man, Rodolphus	SRA 14	
Maffitt, Samuel	DUT 60	Makay, William	NYK 19	Man, Samuel	SRA 19	
Ma Fo___, James	ORN 378	Makeham, Hamilton	ULS 190	Man, Solomon	WSH 199	
Mafre, Mary	NYK 91	Maker, Artemas	ONN 131	Man___, Harmanus	ONT 442	
Magee see McGee		Malberry, Joseph	HRK 504	Manar, Edward	NYK 43	
Magee, James	NYK 95	Malby, Jonathan	WSH 292	Manard, Joseph	CLN 160	
Magee, James	SRA 4	Malcom, Charles	SRA 47	Manchester, Archibald	RNS 67	
Magee, Patrick	ONN 193	Malcom, Henry	COL 248	Manchester, David	RNS 51	
Magee, Philup	CHN 948	Malcomb, Richard	KNG 9	Manchester, Elias	WSH 183	
Magee, Robert	ALB 130	Maldrum, Alexander	SRA 14	Manchester, Elizabeth	WSH 206	
Magee, Robert	ALB 133	Malery, Ebeneser	GRN 326	Manchester, Ephraim	NYK 110	
Mager, Peter	OTS 2	Malery, Gashum	GRN 326	Manchester, George	RNS 33	
Maggee, John	NYK 107	Malery, Samuel	ONT 414	Manchester, Jabez	SRA 32	
Maggee, Thomas	NYK 109	Maley, John	ALB 147	Manchester, James	MNT 87	
Maggeson, Peter	ULS 192	Maley, Margaret	NYK 68	Manchester, Job	CHN 878	
Maggie, Safety	NYK 63	Maley, Richard	MNT 106	Manchester, John	DUT 138	
Maggot, Isaac	ALB 80	Malick, John	SCH 164	Manchester, John	OND 166	
Maghie, Sarah	NYK 113	Malin, Achison	CAY 520	Manchester, John	RNS 18	
Magnac, John	NYK 107	Malin, Enoch	ONT 466	Manchester, John	WSH 216	
Mag_en, John	WSH 187	Maliss, Quaco Free Black	COL 250	Manchester, Joseph	CHN 892	
Magsen, Robert	NYK 15	Mallabae, Maria	NYK 38	Manchester, Jos_	OTS 31	
Maguire see McQuire						

Name	Loc	Pg
Manchester, Peleg	RNS	33
Manchester, Samuel	CLN	169
Manchester, Stephen	ALB	85
Manchester, Stephen	DUT	99
Manchester, Stephen	DUT	137
Manchester, Thomas	CAY	600
Manchester, Thomas	COL	251
Manchester, Wm	RNS	51
Manchester, Wm	RNS	77
Mancias, Wilhelmus	ALB	148
Mancius, George W.	ALB	134
Mancleif, Benjamin	NYK	129
Mancrief, James	NYK	54
Mandebu, John	NYK	54
Mandego, Rumbocet	SCH	147
Ma[nde?]gor, Peter	MNT	36
Mandell, Ephraim	COL	260
Mander, Catharine	ALB	80
Mandervell, Elizabeth	NYK	21
Mandervell, James	NYK	100
Mandervell, John	NYK	100
Manderville, Garret	ULS	214
Manderville, George Francis Gabriel	NYK	84
Mandevill, John	RNS	45
Mandevill, Rebec_a	NYK	141
Mandeville, Benoni	DEL	279
Mandeville, Daniel	WSH	282
Mandeville, Elead	WSH	283
Mandeville, Francis	ORN	344
Mandeville, Henry	ORN	292
Mandeville, Jacob	ORN	344
Mandeville, James	WSH	283
Mandeville, Jeremiah	COL	263
Mandeville, Juliana	ORN	292
Mandeville, Shearman	WSH	283
Mandewill, James	WST	153
Mandigoe, John	ORN	392
Mandigoe, Luke	ORN	392
Mandigoe, Sarah	ORN	392
Mandivell, Charles	NYK	99
Mandiville, John	ORN	279
Mandley, David	WST	158
Mandlyne, Mary a Black	NYK	89
Mane see Main		
Mane, David	CHN	990
Manee, Abraham	RCH	94
Manee, Peter	RCH	88
Manen, Elias	SRA	20
Maner, Daniel	WST	168
Manerwell, Mary a Black	NYK	39
Manes, Nathaniel	CHN	812
Manett, Abigail	NYK	125
Maney, Francis	NYK	69
Maney, Louy	SUF	85
Manfort, Isaac	SCH	140
Mangham, Betsey	WST	171
Mangin, Joseph T.	NYK	96
Mangle, Hannah	DUT	78
Manier, Abraham	CAY	584
Manihull, Thomas	CAY	658
Manley, George	OTS	18
Manley, John	NYK	29
Manley, Luther	OND	169
Manley, Robert	NYK	35
Manley, Robert	NYK	41
Manley, Thomas	HRK	553
Manly, Ceasar a Black	NYK	49
Manly, Samuel	RNS	75
Ma_n,	RNS	6
Mann, Abijah	HRK	582
Mann, Benjamin	RNS	96
Mann, Curtis	SRA	21
Mann, Daniel	DEL	282
Mann, Daniel	NYK	79
Mann, David	ALB	60
Mann, David	NYK	113
Mann, David	RCK	99
Mann, Elizabeth	NYK	53
Mann, George	RCK	99
Mann, George	SCH	152
Mann, Hugh	OTS	18
Mann, Isnall	SCH	136
Mann, Jacob	ALB	60
Mann, Jacob	SCH	117
Mann, James	OTS	18
Mann, Joel	SRA	19
Mann, John	ESS	306
Mann, John M.	COL	246
Mann, Mathias	NYK	113
Mann, Oliver	DEL	282
Mann, Peter	SCH	152
Mann, Reuben	OTS	18
Mann, William	SCH	118
Mannee, John	NYK	140
Mannel, Charity	RCK	103
Mannell, John	NYK	97
Manney, Benjamin	ORN	274
Manney, Catherine	NYK	35
Manney, John	DUT	63
Manney, Winants	DUT	62
Manney, Winants Junr	DUT	62
Mannifold, Peter	QNS	62
Mannin, Barnabas	OTS	6
Mannin, Stephen	RNS	105
Manning, Abraham	NYK	97
Manning, Amos	CAY	578
Manning, Caleb	DUT	115
Manning, Charles	DUT	115
Manning, Charles Junr	DUT	115
Manning, Daniel	NYK	65
Manning, David	TIO	218
Manning, Enoch	CAY	558
Manning, Isaac	ORN	317
Manning, Jacob	DUT	115
Manning, James	NYK	16
Manning, John	ALB	15
Manning, John	ALB	29
Manning, John	COL	206
Manning, John	DUT	115
Manning, John	ORN	317
Manning, John	ORN	317
Manning, Joseph	ORN	317
Manning, Joshua	NYK	148
Manning, Margaret	ORN	317
Manning, Nathl	ALB	79
Manning, Peter	SRA	61
Manning, Richard	CAY	576
Manning, Ripley	TIO	246
Manning, William	DUT	77
Manning, William	ESS	307
Manor see Mann		
M[anor?], Jacob	MNT	39
Manroe, Nathan	GRN	341
Manross, Theodore	OND	190
Mansell, Elizabeth	NYK	153
Mansell, Godfrey	NYK	151
Mansey, William	ONT	464
Mansfield, Charles	ULS	213
Mansfield, Daniel	NYK	72
Mansfield, Edward a mulatto	NYK	84
Mansfield, John	NYK	128
Mansfield, John	NYK	137
Mansfield, Jonathan	WSH	266
Mansfield, Josiah	OND	170
Mansfield, Samuel	NYK	47
Mansfield, Thomas	CAY	582
Mansfield, Thomas	WSH	290
Mansfield, Wm	GRN	357
Manson, Alexander	NYK	146
Manson, James	OTS	15
Manson, Nathan	OND	181
Mantange, Peter	SRA	30
Mantaye, John	RCK	101
Manter, Mathew	OTS	28
Mantin, James	NYK	29
Manury, Ezekiel	SUF	77
Manvill, David	OND	183
Manwaren, Wm	RNS	107
Manwaring, Gurdon	NYK	34
Manwaring, Jabez	OTS	22
Manwaring, Samuel	OND	167
Many, Augustus	MNT	125
Many, Barnabus	ORN	348
Many, Barnabus, Junr	ORN	348
Many, James	ORN	350
Manzer, John	RNS	57
Manzer, Laurence	RNS	13
Manzer, Laurence Junr	RNS	50
Mapes, Benjamin	ORN	349
Mapes, Benjn	SUF	71
Mapes, Benjn	TIO	222
Mapes, Bennona	RNS	86
Mapes, Daniel	ORN	351
Mapes, David	ORN	378
Mapes, David	ORN	386
Mapes, Enos	ORN	340
Mapes, Erastus	ORN	340
Mapes, George	ORN	340
Mapes, Henry	ONT	462
Mapes, Henry	ORN	340
Mapes, Isaac	ORN	388
Mapes, Israel	GRN	352
Mapes, James	ORN	349
Mapes, James	ORN	364
Mapes, James	SUF	90
Mapes, James	TIO	236
Mapes, Jemima	ORN	343
Mapes, John	ORN	363
Mapes, John	ORN	386
Mapes, John	SUF	71
Mapes, Jonas	NYK	46
Mapes, Jonathan	SUF	71
Mapes, Joseph	ORN	363
Mapes, Joseph	TIO	236
Mapes, Mary	ORN	364
Mapes, Nathan	ORN	386
Mapes, Pheneas	OTS	30
Mapes, Samuel	ORN	340
Mapes, Samuel Junr	ORN	340
Mapes, Seth	ONT	498
Mapes, Silas H.	ONT	470
Mapes(?), Smith	STB	204
Mapes, Thos	SUF	75
Mapes, Timothy	GRN	358
Mapes, William	ORN	335
Maples, Josiah	OTS	10
Maples, Stephen	OTS	9
Mappa, Adam G.	OND	189
Mar__, Joseph	GRN	328
Marander, Anthony a Black	NYK	35
Maranus, Chrisn	OTS	27
Maranus, Wm	OTS	27
Marble, Aaron	OTS	27
Marble, Ephraem	WSH	277
Marble, Ephraim	ONT	482
Marble, John	CHN	884
Marcade, Roso a Black	NYK	98
Marcealus, Peter	NYK	93
Marcellin, Anthony	NYK	47
Marcelno, Deborah	NYK	25
Marcenis, John	ALB	108
March, Benajah	CHN	986
March, Benjamin	MNT	53
March, Charles L.	GRN	325
March, David	MNT	119
March, Frs a free Negro	ALB	47
March, Stephen	MNT	2
March, Stephen	RCK	103

March, Thomas	MNT	31	Marks, Joseph	RNS112B	Marsh, Elnathan	ONN	135
Marchant, Peter	CLN	171	Marks, Martin	NYK	142	Marsh, Ely	CHN	808
Marchant, True.an	MNT	86	Marks, Nathan	MNT	92	Marsh, Ephraim	OTS	24
Marcum, Brazilla	ESS	323	Marks, Peter	COL	237	Marsh, Ephraim	WSH	281
Marcum, Israel	ESS	319	Marks, Richard	DUT	45	Marsh, George(?)	CLN	164
Marcus, George	NYK	146	Marks, Robert	COL	211	Marsh, George	KNG	8
Marcy, Ebenezer	DUT	48	Marks, Samuel	COL	211	Marsh, Isaac	ONT	404
Marcy, Griffin	DUT	47	Marks, Timothy	MNT	98	Marsh, Isaac	ONT	432
Marcy, Moses	DUT	48	Marks, Willm	COL	211	Marsh, Isaiah	DEL	277
Mare, John	SCH	120	Markum, Abijah Jr	CHN	894	Marsh, James	NYK	86
Marenous, Abraham	SCH	162	Markum, Erastus	ONN	140	Marsh, James	NYK	141
Marenous, David	SCH	163	Marlet, Elizabeth	NYK	53	Marsh, James	OND	189
Marenous, John	SCH	162	Marlet, James	ALB	21	Marsh, Jasper	OTS	37
Marenus, George	DEL	283	Marlett, John	MNT	100	Marsh, Jeremiah	DUT	157
Marenus, Jeremiah	DEL	283	Marlin, Christopher	CAY	702	Marsh, John	CAY	582
Marenus, Thomas	DEL	282	Marlin, Ebenezer Ju	OND	207	Marsh, John	DUT	51
Margaret a Black	NYK	97	Marlin, Henry	NYK	126	Marsh, John	MNT	119
Margetson, Frederick	DUT	96	Marlin, Jacob	MNT	56	Marsh, John	ONT	404
Margler, Christopher	DUT	65	Marlin, Thomas	MNT	111	Marsh, John	OTS	21
Margurd, Frederick	NYK	79	Marlin, William	ONT	326	Marsh, John	RCH	90
Marhes, Michael	WST	168	Marling, Benjamin	RCH	93	Marsh, Jonas	CHN	774
Maria, John	NYK	32	Marling, Benjamin Junr	RCH	93	Marsh, Joseph	MNT	124
Marien, Jacob	QNS	69	Marling, John	RCH	93	Marsh, Joseph	NYK	96
Marigold, Lawrence	ORN	380	Marling, John	RCH	93	Marsh, Joseph	NYK	118
Marihue, Abner	DUT	148	Marlow, John	MNT	101	Marsh, Joseph	OTS	38
Marihue, David	ULS	197	Marmer, Edward	NYK	21	Marsh, Joshua	ORN	283
Marihue, John	DUT	129	Marner, Richard	KNG	8	Marsh, Lewis	NYK	97
Marihue, John	ULS	197	Marney, Lewis	CLN	169	Marsh, Marshes	ONT	420
Marihue, Samuel	ULS	197	Marney, Luis	CLN	160	Marsh, Mary	RNS	48
Mariman, Caleb	CAY	576	Marot, Louisa	NYK	37	Marsh, Moses	COL	209
Marina, James	MNT	96	Marquart, George	DUT	165	Marsh, Nathan	OND	188
Mariner, Elizabeth	NYK	97	Marquart, Jacob	ULS	183	Marsh, Nathaniel	ULS	230
Mariner, Hercules	RNS	91	Marquart, Jeremiah	COL	261	Marsh, Obed	OND	188
Mariner, John	NYK	50	Marquart, Johannis	DUT	165	Marsh, Peter	CHN	940
Mariner, William	NYK	62	Marquart, John George	DUT	112	Marsh, Ralph	WST	150
Maring, John Frederic	RCH	92	Marqrum, James	NYK	57	Marsh, Richard	RCH	88
Mark a Black	NYK	131	Marrell, Levi	TIO	231	Marsh, Roswell	COL	247
Mark see Mack			Marrener, William	NYK	153	Marsh, Samuel	OND	185
Mark, Amos	RNS	22	Marrick, James	MNT	95	Marsh, Samuel	OND	214
Mark, Bridget	NYK	113	Marriot, Jonathan R.	DUT	125	Marsh, Silas	ALB	36
Mark, Isaac	ALB	62	Marriot, Phelix	SCH	120	Marsh, Silas	CAY	698
Mark, Jacob	NYK	20	Marriott, Henry	COL	248	Marsh, Si_es	CAY	628
Mark, John	DEL	267	Mars a Black	NYK	153	Marsh, Solomon	CLN	171
Mark, Miles	WSH	218	Mars, Cornelius	ONT	498	Marsh, William	ONN	130
Mark, Nancy	CAY	594	Mars, James	SRA	31	Marsh, William	ULS	238
Mark, Oliver	CAY	612	Marschalk, Francis	NYK	44	Marshal see Martial		
Mark, Samuel	CAY	586	Marschalk, Francis	NYK	132	Marshal, Alexander	NYK	65
Markell, James	MNT	53	Marschalk, Gamaliel	SUF	97	Marshal, Daniel	OND	207
Markell, Peter	MNT	41	Marschalk, Hester	NYK	32	Marshal, David	SRA	51
Markenber, Joshua	SRA	38	Marschalk, John	NYK	19	Marshal, Elihu	NYK	58
Markens, John	NYK	117	Marschalk, John	NYK	113	Marshal, James	NYK	22
Markham, Abiah	OTS	46	Marschalk, Joseph	NYK	77	Marshal, John	DUT	43
Markham, Asher	OND	198	Marschalk, Nelly	NYK	47	Marshal, John	OND	213
Markham, David	ONT	376	Marschalk, Philip	SUF	95	Marshal, Rebecca	NYK	74
Markham, Derias	OND	201	Marschalk, William	NYK	63	Marshal, William	DUT	43
Markham, Ebenezer Jr	OND	157	Marsden, John	RCH	92	Marshal, William	SRA	15
Markham, Ebenezer Senr	OND	157	Marsdien, George	OND	210	Marshall, Aaron	DUT	115
Markham, James	OND	177	Marselis, John	RNS	5	Marshall, Abraham	SRA	39
Markham, James	OTS	46	Marsellis, Asher	ALB	33	Marshall, Charles	DUT	118
Markham, John	OND	168	Marsellis, Aurant	ALB	21	Marshall, Corns	ALB	4
Markham, John	ONT	376	Marsellis, Hy	ALB	3	Marshall, Corns	ALB	145
Markham, Justus	OND	163	Marsellis, John	ALB	20	Marshall, Daniel	ALB	132
Markham, Samuel	OND	163	Marsellis, John J.	ALB	20	Marshall, Daniel	ORN	347
Markham, William	ONT	376	Marsellis, John N.	ALB	4	Marshall, Daniel	RNS	56
Markie, Anthony	NYK	117	Marsellis, Ns H.	ALB	2A	Marshall, Daniel	WST	129
Markle, Jacob	OTS	58	Marsellis, Ns N.	ALB	2A	Marshall, David	DUT	116
Markle, John	DEL	271	Marselus, Evert	RNS	34	Marshall, David	NYK	149
Markle, Michael	SCH	164	Marselus, Theophilus	WST	115	Marshall, Elihu	HRK	585
Marks, Comfort	OTS	2	Marsh	QNS	74	Marshall, Elihu	NYK	66
Marks, Corns	OTS	2	Marsh, Allen	ONN	167	Marshall, Elisha	HRK	483
Marks, Ebenezer	OTS	6	Marsh, Benjamen	WSH	279	Marshall, Elizabeth	DUT	166
Marks, George	RCK	103	Marsh, Benjamin	CAY	572	Marshall, Elnathan	DUT	121
Marks, Henry	NYK	141	Marsh, Charles	CLN	164	Marshall, Enos	DUT	167
Marks, Henry	ORN	323	Marsh, Charles	DEL	277	Marshall, Gertrude	ALB	42
Marks, Hezh	OTS	2	Marsh, Charles	NYK	42	Marshall, Harvey	OND	173
Marks, Isaac	DUT	140	Marsh, Daniel	SRA	47	Marshall, Henry	CAY	606
Marks, John	OTS	5	Marsh, David	NYK	148	Marshall, Henry	DEL	285

Marshall, Henry	DUT 110	Marten, Henry	DUT 157	Martin, Gold	DEL 282
Marshall, James	CAY 614	Marten, Jeremeah	WSH 266	Martin, Henry	DUT 155
Marshall, James & John	DUT 121	Marten, John	DUT 159	Martin, Henry	WSH 214
Marshall, James	ONT 344	Marten, John	ULS 195	Martin, Hugh	WSH 224
Marshall, James	SRA 39	Marten, Joseph	ULS 222	Martin, Ichabod	CHN 754
Marshall, James Junr	DUT 120	Marten, Joseph	WSH 264	Martin, Isaac	OTS 49
Marshall, James Junr	ONT 344	Marten, Reuben	RNS 10	Martin, Isaac	STB 201
Marshall, Jeremiah	HRK 489	Martendill, S__	WSH 252	Martin, Isaac N.	CAY 612
Marshall, Jeremiah	NYK 43	Martene, James	WST 163	Martin, Jacob	DUT 12
Marshall, John	DUT 109	Martene, Samuel	WST 163	Martin, Jacob	GRN 333
Marshall, John & James	DUT 121	Martense, Garret	KNG 2	Martin, ..cob	MNT 103
Marshall, John	RCH 94	Martense, Jane	KNG 2	Martin, Jacob	RNS 17
Marshall, John	SRA 38	Martensie, Adrian	KNG 2	Martin, James	DUT 47
Marshall, John	WST 121	Martensie, Adrian	KNG 3	Martin, James	DUT 50
Marshall, Joseah	WSH 268	Martensie, Garret	KNG 2	Martin, James	NYK 145
Marshall, Joseph	NYK 45	Marthers, John	ALB 15	Martin, James	QNS 67
Marshall, Joseph	NYK 137	Marthings, Abraham	NYK 17	Martin, James	RNS 54
Marshall, Josiah	ALB 89	Martial see Marshal		Martin, James	WSH 247
Marshall, Justus	DUT 118	Martial, Elisabeth	GRN 326	Martin, Jeremiah	DUT 69
Marshall, Levi	OND 173	Martial, Jeremiah	MNT 92	Martin, John	ALB 74
Marshall, Major	DUT 115	Martin see Marlin &		Martin, John	CAY 718
Marshall, Moses	WST 129	Martain		Martin, John	COL 192
Marshall, Nathaniel	RNS 58	Martin, ...	MNT 78	Martin, John	COL 241
Marshall, Nathaniel		Martin, Aaron	ALB 24	Martin, John	KNG 9
Junr	RNS112B	Martin, Aaron	ALB 39	Martin, John	MNT 51
Marshall, Nehemiah	DUT 118	Martin, Abijah	CHN 894	Martin, John	MNT 67
Marshall, Nehemiah	NYK 123	Martin, Abner	CHN 884	Martin, John a Black	NYK 17
Marshall, Peter	ALB 42	Martin, Abraham	DUT 66	Martin, John	NYK 56
Marshall, Peter	RNS 5	Martin, Adam	WSH 222	Martin, John	NYK 66
Marshall, Peter	WST 122	Martin, Agrippa	DUT 143	Martin, John	NYK 88
Marshall, Rachel	RCH 94	Martin, Alexander	ORN 355	Martin, John a Black	NYK 132
Marshall, Rebecah	WST 129	Martin, Allice	QNS 66	Martin, John	OND 210
Marshall, Reuben	DUT 111	Martin, Amaziah	ONN 152	Martin, John	ORN 300
Marshall, Samuel	SRA 39	Martin, Ammasa	RNS 42	Martin, John	OTS 49
Marshall, Simeon	CHN 930	Martin, Anderson	ONT 342	Martin, John	STB 201
Marshall, Stephen	DUT 121	Martin, Andrew	COL 254	Martin, John	WSH 256
Marshall, Thomas	ORN 325	Martin, Andrew a		Martin, John	WSH 288
Marshall, Totten	DUT 109	mulatto	NYK 99	Martin, John	WSH 292
Marshall, Widow	HRK 534	Martin, Artimus	WSH 192	Martin, John	WST 135
Marshall, William	ALB 97	Martin, Asa	ULS 267	Martin, Joseph	GRN 340
Marshall, William	CAY 562	Martin, Asel	RNS 60	Martin, Joseph	NYK 107
Marshall, William	NYK 121	Martin, Barbara	NYK 26	Martin, Joseph	OND 222
Marshall, Zaccheus	DUT 57	Martin, Benjamin	ALB 81	Martin, Joseph	SRA 14
Marshall, Zaccheus	DUT 114	Martin, Bethuel	OTS 48	Martin, Joshua	CAY 576
Marshall, Zaccheus I.	DUT 120	Martin, Burwick a		Martin, Josiah	NYK 146
Marshel, Alexander	WSH 196	Black	NYK 152	Martin, Jurden	SRA 59
Marshel, Anthoney	WST 161	Martin, Casper	SCH 138	Martin, Killeon	RNS 56
Marshel, Charles	WSH 235	Martin, Charles	ALB 11	Martin, Kingsley	WSH 303
Marshel, Daniel	WST 128	Martin, Charles	ORN 291	Martin, Ledia	WSH 222
Marshel, David	WSH 234	Martin, Christ	CAY 726	Martin, Levi	RNS 9
Marshel, Elias	NYK 110	Martin, Clement	NYK 56	Martin, Levi	RNS 105
Marshel, Frances	WSH 234	Martin, Cunrod	STB 207	Martin, Lucy	NYK 130
Marshel, John	WSH 258	Martin, Dan	STB 201	Martin, Manasseh	DUT 44
Marshel, Lebbeus	NYK 69	Martin, Daniel	DUT 53	Martin, Margaret	NYK 125
Marshel, Rebeca	WST 128	Martin, Danl	RCK 97	Martin, Martin	MNT 82
Marshel, Thomas	WSH 220	Martin, David	ALB 104	Martin, Mary	ALB 96
Marshell, Amon	WST 158	Martin, David	NYK 147	Martin, Mary	ORN 367
Marshell, Daniel	WST 131	Martin, David	WSH 272	Martin, Moses	NYK 150
Marshell, James	WST 129	Martin, Deliverance	RNS 69	Martin, Moses	WSH 222
Marshell, John	RCH 88	Martin, Dirck	ALB 74	Martin, Natha	OTS 49
Marshell, John	RCH 95	Martin, Ebenezar	RNS 112	Martin, Nicholas	GRN 334
Marsiells, Gerrit	MNT 18	Martin, Ebenezer	WSH 303	Martin, Nicholas	GRN 334
Marston, __on	QNS 67	Martin, Eli	RNS 49	Martin, Peter	NYK 122
Marston, Corns	ALB 24	Martin, Elijah	OTS 53	Martin, Peter	OND 169
Marston, John	QNS 68	Martin, Enoch	QNS 64	Martin, Primus	DUT 107
Marston, Thomas	NYK 152	Martin, Ephraim	RNS 49	Martin, Robert	ALB 120
Marston, William	QNS 66	Martin, Ezekiel	DUT 146	Martin, Robert	DUT 149
Martain, Charles	MNT 73	Martin, Francis	NYK 86	Martin, Robert	NYK 139
Martain, Isaac	WST 115	Martin, Gedeon	NYK 94	Martin, Robert	ONT 342
Martain, William	GRN 327	Martin, George	DUT 148	Martin, Robert	ORN 274
Marteline, William	ALB 47	Martin, George	NYK 150	Martin, Robert	OTS 49
Marten, Alexande	MNT 9	Martin, George	STB 201	Martin, Robert	RNS 54
Marten, Daniel	WSH 266	Martin, George	WSH 217	Martin, Robert	STB 201
Marten, David	DUT 158	Martin, Gershom	DUT 22	Martin, Robert	WSH 297
Marten, David M.	WSH 283	Martin, Gideon Jur	GRN 325	Martin, Saml	CHN 926
Marten, Elisha	WSH 283	Martin, Gideon	SRA 55	Martin, Samuel	NYK 25
Marten, Gilbert	WST 127	Martin, Godlope	DUT 157	Martin, Samuel a Black	NYK 56

Name	Loc	No.
Martin, Samuel	OTS	49
Martin, Samuel	QNS	73
Martin, Samuel	RNS	93
Martin, Samuel	WSH	288
Martin, Solomon	OTS	25
Martin, Stephen	DUT	22
Martin, Stephen	OTS	49
Martin, Tartulus	WST	135
Martin, Thomas	ALB	81
Martin, Thomas	CAY	572
Martin, Thomas	COL	266
Martin, Thomas	DUT	18
Martin, Thomas	DUT	22
Martin, Thomas	RNS	59
Martin, Timo	OTS	48
Martin, Ury	STB	201
Martin, Walter	WSH	221
Martin, William	ALB	94
Martin, William	NYK	77
Martin, William	NYK	116
Martin, William	OND	166
Martin, William	QNS	68
Martin, William	RNS	82
Martin, William	ULS	262
Martin, William	ULS	267
Martin, William	WSH	246
Martin, Zabathy	OND	207
Martindale, John	ALB	23
Martindale, Thomas	ESS	295
Martine, Abrm	RCK	104
Martine, Danl	RCK	103
Martine, Daniel	ULS	189
Martine, Daniel	ULS	256
Martine, Isaac	RCK	104
Martine, John	NYK	78
Martine, John	NYK	101
Martine, Peter	NYK	133
Martine, Thomas	ORN	337
Martinoe, Benjamin	RCH	90
Martinoe, Stephen	RCH	90
Martlett, Gedeon	MNT	93
Martlett, Mark	MNT	112
Martling, Abraham	NYK	37
Marton, Aaron	WSH	221
Martondale, Gray	WSH	242
Marts, Jacob	ONT	324
Martting, Abraham	WST	163
Martting, Abraham Jr	WST	163
Martting, Daniel	WST	163
Martting, David	WST	163
Martting, Deliverance	WST	163
Marven, Hannah	SUF	64
Marvill, Francis	DUT	56
Marvin, Aaron	OTS	12
Marvin, Abigail	DUT	172
Marvin, Abrm	OTS	12
Marvin, Adonijah	HRK	489
Marvin, Archibald	ORN	374
Marvin, Asa	OND	202
Marvin, Asa	RNS	41
Marvin, Asel	OTS	28
Marvin, Benjn	OTS	24
Marvin, Daniel	RNS	82
Marvin, David	GRN	346
Marvin, David	SRA	13
Marvin, Elihu	ORN	348
Marvin, Enoch	CHN	792
Marvin, Enock	OTS	28
Marvin, Ephraim	DUT	176
Marvin, Isaac	WST	156
Marvin, Isaiah	RNS	59
Marvin, Jacob	ALB	63
Marvin, James	ORN	349
Marvin, James	WST	156
Marvin, James Junr	MNT	49
Marvin, Jared	CLN	173
Marvin, Jedediah	SRA	39

Name	Loc	No.
Marvin, Jesse	ORN	387
Marvin, John	NYK	32
Marvin, John	OTS	17
Marvin, John C.	CLN	158
Marvin, John C.	WSH	273
Marvin, Martha	DUT	176
Marvin, Martin	HRK	487
Marvin, Mathew	HRK	551½
Marvin, Matthew	ONT	388
Marvin, Michael	CLN	173
Marvin, Nathan	GRN	339
Marvin, Nathan	ORN	349
Marvin, Nathan	ORN	364
Marvin, Nathan	OTS	28
Marvin, Nathaniel	RNS	112
Marvin, Ozias	OND	202
Marvin, Reynold	HRK	580
Marvin, Samuel	ALB	97
Marvin, Samuel	GRN	340
Marvin, Samuel	ONN	152
Marvin, Samuel	WST	115
Marvin, Selden	HRK	583
Marvin, Seth	ORN	348
Marvin, Seth Junr	ORN	387
Marvin, Timothy	ULS	266
Marvin, Uriah	RNS	6
Marvin, Widow	SRA	52
Marvin, William	SRA	48
Marvin, William	SRA	48
Marvine, Anthony	DEL	286
Marvine, Matthew	DEL	277
Marwin, Heman	OND	220
Mary a free wench	ALB	140
Masan, Daniel	WSH	265
Mase, Benjamin	SRA	5
Mase, John	SRA	7
Mase, Joseph	SCH	146
Mash see Nash		
Mash	HRK	509
Mash, Corolinah	WSH	189
Mash, Hensdale	HRK	514
Mash, Isaac	CHN	958
Mash, John	MNT	124
Mash, John	HRK	461
Mash, Joseph	ONT	454
Masher, Zebdiah	SRA	56
Masier, Christopher	GRN	328
Masmore, Jacob	NYK	69
Mason, Aaron	OND	220
Mason, Abner	CHN	932
Mason, Alexander	WSH	273
Mason, Andrew	WSH	218
Mason, Arnold	OND	183
Mason, Benjamin	RNS	54
Mason, Charles	OTS	43
Mason, Charles	RNS	54
Mason, Comer	WSH	304
Mason, Daniel	DUT	136
Mason, Daniel	NYK	75
Mason, Daniel	WSH	304
Mason, David	OTS	19
Mason, David	WSH	268
Mason, Edward	RNS	80
Mason, Elijah	OTS	9
Mason, Hale	WSH	304
Mason, Harman	GRN	336
Mason, Isaac	WSH	305
Mason, James	ALB	132
Mason, James	DEL	290
Mason, James	MNT	64
Mason, James	RNS	7
Mason, James	RNS	15
Mason, John	CAY	724
Mason, John	COL	248
Mason, John	NYK	35
Mason, John	NYK	75
Mason, John	NYK	125

Name	Loc	No.
Mason, John	ONT	396
Mason, John M.	NYK	21
Mason, Joseph	DUT	68
Mason, Joseph	DUT	137
Mason, Joseph	HRK	463
Mason, Joseph	HRK	518
Mason, Joseph Junr	DUT	134
Mason, Josiah	OTS	9
Mason, Levy	WSH	304
Mason, Luke	CAY	728
Mason, Malachi	HRK	466
Mason, Mary	RNS	91
Mason, Matthew	ESS	310
Mason, Nathan	WSH	304
Mason, Nathan Jur	WSH	304
Mason, Olney	CLN	156
Mason, Peleg	DUT	134
Mason, Robert	DEL	290
Mason, Royal	CAY	688
Mason, Russel	HRK	519
Mason, Samon 2d	WSH	305
Mason, Samson Jur	WSH	304
Mason, Samuel	DUT	122
Mason, Shubal	WSH	305
Mason, Simon	NYK	38
Mason, Stephen	CAY	668
Mason, Thaddeus	ESS	306
Mason, Thomas	DUT	100
Mason, William	DEL	290
Mason, Zephaniah	WSH	304
Masoner, John	MNT	113
Mass, Joseph	QNS	81
Massaboux, Peter	NYK	77
Masse, Jacques	NYK	87
Massen, John	QNS	63
Massingberg, Humphry	NYK	65
Masson, Benjamin	NYK	35
Massun, Thomas	QNS	62
Masten, Aart	ULS	252
Masten, Abraham	ULS	204
Masten, Abraham	ULS	228
Masten, Abraham P.	ULS	228
Masten, Barent	DUT	6
Masten, Caleb	DUT	122
Masten, Charles	DUT	141
Masten, Cornelius	ULS	252
Masten, Cornelius B.	ULS	229
Masten, Cornelius C.	ULS	230
Masten, Elkanen	RNS	90
Masten, Ezekiel	ULS	187
Masten, Ezekiel	ULS	253
Masten, George	DUT	97
Masten, Hazael	ULS	186
Masten, Henry	DUT	41
Masten, Jacob	ULS	187
Masten, Jacobus	ULS	228
Masten, Johannis	ULS	186
Masten, Johannis B.	ULS	229
Masten, Johannis C.	ULS	229
Masten, Johannis E.	ULS	229
Masten, John	DUT	111
Masten, John	DUT	122
Masten, John Junr	ULS	253
Masten, Joseph	ULS	242
Masten, Matthew	ULS	252
Masten, Samuel	DUT	113
Masten, Samuel	ULS	230
Masten, William	ULS	252
Masters, Daniel	OND	210
Masters, David	NYK	112
Masters, James	RNS	32
Masters, James S.	RNS	32
Masters, Josiah	RNS	32
Masters, Mary	RNS	50
Masters, Nicholas	RNS	32
Masters, Richard	WSH	299
Masters, Saml	OTS	3

Name	County	Page
Masters, Stephen	GRN	325
Masters, William	ONT	382
Masters, William	ONT	474
Masters, William	ORN	295
Masters, William	ORN	327
Masterton, David	NYK	34
Masterton, Peter	TIO	264
Mastin, Lawrence	QNS	72
Mastin, Thomas	QNS	75
Mat..., Thomas	MNT	76
Matcham, James	ALB	138
Matchcraft, John	ALB	44
Matchem, Jehoicham	ALB	82
Matchem, Simeon	ALB	82
Matchet, William	WSH	230
Materson, Solomon	CHN	982
Mates, Jonathan	COL	242
Mateson, Allen	RNS	98
Mateson, Caleb	RNS	20
Mateson, John	RNS	21
Mateson, Peleg	RNS	20
Mather, Andrew	NYK	22
Mather, Aseph	HRK	462
Mather, Cotton	ORN	326
Mather, Daniel	NYK	151
Mather, Daniel	ONT	432
Mather, Ebenezer	ORN	332
Mather, Fredk	OTS	34
Mather, Hezh	COL	214
Mather, Increase	ORN	327
Mather, John	ORN	327
Mather, John Junr	ORN	328
Mather, Joseph	ORN	327
Mather, Joseph	SRA	30
Mather, Joshua	HRK	463
Mather, Moses	HRK	560
Mather, Nathaniel	ORN	324
Mather, Reuben	HRK	463
Mather, Reuben nr	HRK	464
Mather, Richard	NYK	56
Mather, Samuel	ORN	327
Mather, Sarah	ORN	319
Mather, Silvenus	OTS	35
Mather, Thomas	OTS	34
Mather, Zacheriah	COL	204
Mathers, Eusebeus	SRA	41
Mathers, Josiah	ONT	368
Mathers, Obadiah	SRA	45
Mathers, Timothy	ONT	368
Matherson, Duncan	NYK	20
Mathes, Bethel	RNS	31
Mathes, David	WSH	228
Mathes, Isaih	WSH	238
Mathes, John	WST	169
Mathes, Joseph	WST	168
Mathes, Samuel	WSH	255
Mathew, Alaxr	SUF	68
Mathewes, Benajah	OND	213
Mathews see Matthews		
Mathews, Abigal	NYK	68
Mathews, Abraham a mulatto	NYK	50
Mathews, Abraham	NYK	145
Mathews, Andrew	NYK	35
Mathews, Barnabas	WSH	284
Mathews, Barnett	MNT	76
Mathews, Benjamin	WSH	275
Mathews, Daniel	WSH	254
Mathews, David	NYK	119
Mathews, Edwen	NYK	74
Mathews, James	WSH	191
Mathews, John	NYK	118
Mathews, John	NYK	120
Mathews, John	WSH	235
Mathews, Jonathn	CHN	884
Mathews, Joseph C.	OTS	26
Mathews, Mary	NYK	120
Mathews, Mathias	COL	200
Mathews, Robert	NYK	25
Mathews, Robert	NYK	102
Mathews, Samuel	HRK	535
Mathews, Thomas Junr	CHN	880
Mathews, William	NYK	31
Mathews, William	NYK	120
Mathews, William	WSH	226
Mathewson, John	NYK	108
Mathewson, Robert	NYK	80
Mathiew, Victoriene	NYK	27
Matison, Atwood	WSH	217
Matison, Charles	WSH	217
Matison, Jacob	WSH	217
Matison, William	WSH	217
Matistock, Adam	ULS	222
Matistock, Jacob	ULS	222
Matistock, Johannis	ULS	222
Matoon, Abel	WSH	206
Matoon, Christopher	SRA	18
Matoon, Eli	SRA	18
Matoon, Garshom	SRA	18
Matoon, John	CHN	934
Matrat, Peter	COL	264
Matross, Abraham	DUT	41
Matross, John	DUT	42
Matross, Samuel	DUT	119
Matshing, Thomas	SCH	164
Matson, Eber	OTS	33
Matson, Eber Junr	OTS	33
Mattauny, Abm	SCH	120
Matterson, Abel	OTS	36
Matterson, Asahel	OND	207
Matterson, Daniel	CHN	968
Matterson, David	OTS	12
Matterson, Eseck	SRA	51
Matterson, Henry	OTS	35
Matterson, James	OTS	35
Matterson, John	OTS	13
Matterson, Jona	OTS	38
Matterson, Reuben	OTS	35
Matterson, Silvenus	SRA	51
Matterson, Thos	OTS	38
Matterson, Wm	OTS	38
Matteson, Calvin	OND	194
Matteson, Henry	SRA	56
Matteson, Henry	WSH	289
Matteson, Jacob	SRA	57
Matteson, James	SRA	45
Matteson, Joab	WSH	296
Matteson, Joseph	WSH	289
Matthaner, Oliver	HRK	584
Matthews, Aaron	OND	208
Matthews, Abel	CAY	616
Matthews, Abner	OND	193
Matthews, Abner	OND	208
Matthews, Amasa	CAY	566
Matthews, Amos	CAY	516
Matthews, Daniel	DEL	272
Matthews, Elias	QNS	78
Matthews, Gilbert	DEL	272
Matthews, Gilbert	WST	128
Matthews, Henry	ULS	234
Matthews, Henry	WST	157
Matthews, Isaac	DUT	12
Matthews, James & Selah	TIO	258
Matthews, James	ULS	256
Matthews, Jeremiah	ULS	195
Matthews, John	CAY	538
Matthews, John	CLN	172
Matthews, John	WST	132
Matthews, Levi	OND	208
Matthews, Ozias	WST	132
Matthews, Peter	TIO	258
Matthews, Richard	QNS	78
Matthews, Richard	QNS	78
Matthews, Salmon	OND	199
Matthews, Samuel	DUT	71
Matthews, Selah & James	TIO	258
Matthews, Stephen	DEL	272
Matthews, Vincent	TIO	264
Matthews, William	WST	129
Matthews, William	WST	157
Matthewson, Abm	OTS	30
Matthewson, Amos	OTS	30
Matthewson, Asa	ORN	288
Matthewson, Bernard	DUT	131
Matthewson, Chs	OTS	30
Matthewson, John	OTS	29
Matthewson, Thos	OTS	30
Matthias, Barnet	WST	163
Matthis, Daniel	WST	168
Matthis, John	WST	168
Mattice, Adam	SCH	127
Mattice, Conradt	MNT	33
Mattice, Conrod	SCH	128
Mattice, David	SCH	128
Mattice, Frederick	SCH	128
Mattice, George	SCH	128
Mattice, Henry	SCH	127
Mattice, John	MNT	33
Mattice, Joh.	MNT	34
Mattice, John	SCH	128
Mattice, John	SCH	142
Mattice, John C.	SCH	129
Mattice, Jost	SCH	125
Mattice, Nichs	SCH	128
Mattice, Willm	SCH	125
Matticks, James	WSH	209
Matticks, John	WSH	209
Mattison, Alexander	HRK	549
Mattison, Asa	HRK	521
Mattison, David	HRK	550
Mattison, David	RNS	78
Mattison, Duty	HRK	425
Mattison, Francis	ORN	398
Mattison, Freeborn	COL	211
Mattison, James	HRK	420
Mattison, Jesse	HRK	425
Mattison, John	HRK	408
Mattison, John	HRK	524
Mattison, John Junr	HRK	408
Mattison, Joseph	HRK	521
Mattison, Ludwick	HRK	561
Mattison, Thomas	HRK	560
Mattocks, Robert	WST	168
Mattox, John	WSH	210
Maubray, Anning	SUF	94
Mauford, William	SRA	26
Maul, Thomas	NYK	28
Mauley, Ezekiel	WSH	285
Maurice, Isaac	DUT	164
Maurice, Thomas	ALB	135
Mauring, Peter	NYK	49
Mauy(?), Godfrey	MNT	61
Maverack, Peter R.	NYK	47
Mawling, William	RNS	80
Max, Elijah	WSH	227
Maxfield, Caleb	COL	199
Maxfield, Elias	OTS	7
Maxfield, James	MNT	30
Maxfield, John	COL	178
Maxfield, John	HRK	457
Maxfield, John	MNT	30
Maxfield, Partrick	NYK	137
Maxfield, Peggy	NYK	15
Maxfield, William	COL	199
Maxfield, William	COL	238
Maxfield, William	DEL	278
Ma_ham, Ellice	OND	223
Maxin, Asa	RNS	67

Name	Ref	Name	Ref	Name	Ref
Mead, John	DUT 174	Meads, Levi	SRA 56	Meeker, Silas	MNT 68
Mead, John	DUT 177	Meaker, Joshua	COL 177	Meeker, Solomon	DUT 174
Mead, John	NYK 83	Mears, James	ONN 180	Meeks, Amos	CAY 626
Mead, John	OTS 43	Mease, Francis	NYK 40	Meeks, Charles	NYK 53
Mead, John	SRA 25	Mease, John	ALB 107	Meeks, Edward	DUT 74
Mead, Jonathan	CAY 604	Measereau, Daniel	NYK 21	Meeks, Edward	NYK 57
Mead, Jonathan	DUT 151	Meastride, John	NYK 144	Meeks, Edward C.	NYK 65
Mead, Jonathan Junr	DUT 149	Measwrall, Charles	CAY 558	Meeks, John	DUT 78
Mead, Joseph	ALB 22	Meater, Caleb	SRA 14	Meeks, John	NYK 48
Mead, Joseph	DUT 79	Mecham, Titus	OND 209	Meeks, Joseph	NYK 25
Mead, Joseph	DUT 116	Mechum, Saml	OTS 29	Meeks, Josiah	CAY 716
Mead, Joseph	ORN 395	Mecklewee, William	RNS 83	Meeks, Michael	DUT 73
Mead, Joseph	SRA 60	Meckum, Ashbil	SRA 47	Meeks, Moses	DUT 73
Mead, Joseph	WST 152	Medah, Benjamin	ONT 488	Meeks, Richard	DUT 74
Mead, Joseph	WST 156	Medah, Dick	CAY 560	Meeks, Thomas	NYK 51
Mead, Joshua	DUT 75	Medah, Gasper	ONT 408	Meers, John	OND 179
Mead, Joshua	SRA 33	Medan, Jacob	TIO 237	Meesick, Derick H.	COL 192
Mead, Joshua	WST 151	Medaws, Abner	TIO 261	Meesick, Fite	COL 193
Mead, Josiah	SRA 60	Medaws, Samuel	TIO 261	Meesick, Hendrick T.	COL 199
Mead, Judah	ORN 375	Medbeaury, Benjamin. d.	CHN 790	Meesick, Henry J.	COL 195
Mead, King	DEL 277	Medbeaury, Hezekiah	CHN 790	Meesick, John	COL 199
Mead, Levi	DUT 30	Medbeaury, Nathaniel	CHN 790	Meesick, John	COL 200
Mead, Levi	SRA 55	Medbury, Abner	SRA 57	Meesick, John H.	COL 192
Mead, Levi	WST 113	Medbury, Darling	SRA 57	Meesick, John J.	COL 199
Mead, Lewis	DUT 92	Medbury, Joseph	OTS 32	Meesick, Peter	COL 196
Mead, Lewis	TIO 238	Medbury, Nathan	SRA 57	Meesick, Peter Junr	COL 257
Mead, Mary	WST 131	Medcalf see Metcalf		Meesick, Solomon	COL 199
Mead, Matthias	CAY 614	Medcalf, Jabez	ONT 336	Meesick, Richard	COL 199
Mead, Michael	CAY 536	Medcalf, Widow	STB 199	Meesick, Thomas	COL 200
Mead, Michael	ONN 177	Medcaugh, Elias	TIO 254	Meesick, Thomas	RNS 12
Mead, Moses	DUT 94	Medceff, William	QNS 62	Meesick, Thomas H.	COL 197
Mead, Moses Junr	DUT 94	Meddaght, John	KNG 9	Megaw, John	RNS 100
Mead, Nathan	DUT 137	Meddah, Benjamin	ONT 480	Mege, John	OND 213
Mead, Nathan	DUT 177	Meddlemast, Joseph	NYK 150	Meggs, Samuel	OND 202
Mead, Nathaniel	DUT 56	Mede, Amos	TIO 243	Megien, Daniel	NYK 96
Mead, Nathaniel	DUT 177	Medlar, Aaron	DUT 71	Meglone, Hugh	NYK 105
Mead, Nathl	ONN 152	Medlar, Abraham	DUT 71	Megomery, James	SRA 29
Mead, Nathaniel	ORN 395	Medlar, John	DUT 71	Megrath, Thomas	NYK 74
Mead, Nathaniel	RNS 55	Medlar, John A.	DUT 71	Megue, Samuel	NYK 75
Mead, Nehemiah	COL 223	Medles, Daniel	NYK 60	Mehary, William	NYK 125
Mead, Nehemiah	WST 153	Medon, John	ALB 44	Mehon, William	WST 163
Mead, Nicholas	NYK 49	Medor, Robert	WSH 234	Meiggs, Phineas	COL 227
Mead, Peter	GRN 335	Medre, John	NYK 36	Meigs, Phinehas	DUT 132
Mead, Peter	NYK 126	Meech, Aaron	ULS 210	Meit, Jotham	WSH 213
Mead, Peter	TIO 265	Meech, Lydia	COL 184	Melass, Jacob	ONN 191
Mead, Peter	TIO 266	Meed see Mead		Melat, John	NYK 142
Mead, Phillip	GRN 336	Meed, Caleb	WSH 213	Melatte, Peter	CAY 658
Mead, Samuel	CHN 788	Meed, Eli	WSH 212	Melcher, John	COL 254
Mead, Samuel	NYK 144	Meed, Gedion Senr	WSH 212	Meldrum, Jenet	NYK 23
Mead, Sarah	CHN 788	Meed, Isaac	WSH 213	Meldrum, John	NYK 101
Mead, Selah	WST 132	Meed, Isaih	WSH 217	Meleck, Cutlep	NYK 113
Mead, Sibbeus	WST 151	Meed, Israel Junr	WSH 217	Melick, John	RNS 82
Mead, Smith	NYK 125	Meed, Jabes	WSH 213	Melious, Anthony	COL 200
Mead, Solomon	WST 155	Meed, Jacob	GRN 351	Melious, Coenradt J.	COL 233
Mead, Solomon Junr	WST 154	Meed, Jacob	GRN 353	Melious, Coenradt W.	COL 231
Mead, Stephen	CAY 606	Meed, John	KNG 10	Melious, Jacob	COL 233
Mead, Stephen	OTS 25	Meed, Joseph	WSH 213	Melious, Jacob J.	COL 233
Mead, Susanna	WST 161	Meed, Levi	WSH 212	Melious, Jacob R.	COL 243
Mead, Thaddeus	WST 153	Meed, Nehemiah	GRN 353	Melious, Jacobus	COL 256
Mead, Thomas	NYK 135	Meed, Nehemiah	WSH 213	Melious, John J.	COL 233
Mead, Thompson	CHN 788	Meed, Nehemiah Junr	WSH 212	Melious, John W.	COL 231
Mead, Uriah	ALB 41	Meed, Noah	WSH 213	Melious, Peter W.	COL 236
Mead, Uriah	RNS 60	Meed, Nucum	WSH 212	Melious, Simon	COL 239
M[ead?], William	CAY 568	Meed, Stephen	WSH 219	Melious, William	COL 231
Mead, William	DUT 94	Meede, Daniel	WSH 213	Melious. William	COL 258
Mead, William	NYK 78	Meede, Eanes Junr	WSH 213	Melious, William W.	COL 231
Mead, William	OTS 17	Meede, James	WSH 213	Melious, William W.	COL 238
Mead, William	SRA 23	Meede, Justice	WSH 213	Melis, Jacob	MNT 48
Mead, William	SRA 43	Meeker, Abner	HRK 422	Melius, Benjamin	DUT 144
Mead, William	SRA 47	Meeker, Benjamin	KNG 9	Melius, Jacob	DUT 144
Mead, William Junr	DUT 95	Meeker, Ephm	OTS 31	Meller see Miller	
Mead, Wright	HRK 516	Meeker, Henry	ORN 323	Meller, John	MNT 68
Mead, Zachariah	ORN 359	Meeker, Jonothan	SCH 135	Mellington, John	NYK 112
Mead, Zadoc	ORN 318	Meeker, Peleg	ORN 324	Mellis, Catherine	NYK 63
Mead, Zecheriah	ALB 41	Meeker, Robert	SCH 135	Mellivan, Eliot	TIO 229
Mead, Zelek	HRK 516	Meeker, Robert	SCH 141	Mellman, Christopher	ULS 192
Meadder, John	ESS 296	Meeker, Samuel	ORN 392	Mellon, Henry	SCH 129

Mellus, Adam	OND 224	Merihu, John	WSH 250	Merrian, Thomas	CHN 964
Melmoth	NYK 65	Meril, Reuben	OND 213	Merrick, Abel	OTS 46
Meloy, Susanna	DUT 42	Meriman, Earl	WSH 227	Merrick, Charles	CHN 924
Melvin, Jabez	OTS 42	Meriman, Ichabod	GRN 344	Merrick, Constant	CHN 848
Melvin, Jonathan	ONT 480	Meritheu, Jeremiah	CAY 638	Merrick, David	CHN 922
Melvin, Jonathan Ju.	ONT 480	Merithew, Jeremeah	WSH 269	Merrick, David	ONN 184
Membrit, John	COL 237	Merithew, Saml	OTS 5	Merrick, Joseph	DEL 280
Memia, Henry	ALB 66	Meritt, Justin	COL 255	Merrick, Moses	DEL 274
Mengo, Peter a Black	NYK 73	Merkeil, Lawrence	GRN 329	Merrick, Robert	WSH 264
Menick, Jane	NYK 38	Merkel, Abraham	ULS 214	Merrick, Seth	OTS 47
Menick, Peter	RNS 15	Merkel, Barent, Junr	ULS 214	Merrick, Solomon	CHN 924
Menise, Mary	NYK 69	Merkel, Benjamin	ULS 194	Merrick, Thomas	CHN 922
Menler, Reuben	WSH 254	Merkel, Benjamin	ULS 214	Merrick, William	CHN 922
Menneck, Barnard	OND 221	Merkel, Christian	DUT 165	Merricle see Mirkle	
Mensing, Charles	NYK 123	Merkel, Cornelius	ULS 199	Merricle, John	ALB 101
Menter, Elijah	WSH 254	Merkel, Elias Senr	ULS 215	Merrifield, Abraham	SUF 102
Menter, Reuben	WSH 255	Merkel, Frederick	ULS 197	Merrifield, William	ALB 126
		Merkel, Jacob	ULS 194	Merrigo, Jeremiah	GRN 347
Mentfield, Rachael a		Merkel, Jacob	ULS 198	Merril, Brazela	RNS 107
Black	NYK 131	Merkel, Jane	ULS 203	Merril, Jesse	SRA 33
Menthorn see Minthorn		Merkel, William	ULS 199	Merrill, Frederick	NYK 55
Menthorn, Samll H.	TIO 239	Merkell, Henry	MNT 7	Merrill, Jesse	HRK 432
Menthorne, Philip	NYK 97	Merkell, John	MNT 7	Merrill, Joseph	OTS 35
Mentor, Felix	ESS 302	Merkels, Henry	NYK 134	Merrill, Mead	RNS 107
Mentor, Reuben	WSH 296	Merkill, Henry	SCH 126	Merrill, Oliver	WSH 295
Mentor, Richard	WSH 290	Merkle, Dewalt	MNT 7	Merrill, Philip	SCH 164
Menturn, Benjamin G.	NYK 38	Merkle, Frederick	SCH 161	Merrill, Samuel	DEL 272
Mentz, John	ULS 245	Merkle, Henry	RNS 27	Merrill, Truman	RNS 40
Meraman, Bennona	CHN 976	Merkle, Jacob	SCH 163	Merrill, William	NYK 70
Mercer, John	NYK 31	Merkle, Nichs	SCH 163	Merrills, Abraham	OND 201
Mercer, John	SRA 7	Merkle, Peter	MNT 7	Merrills, Anson	TIO 209
Mercer, Linor	ALB 4	Merkle, Peter	SCH 163	Merrills, Asher	COL 184
Mercer, Willm	COL 203	Merkle, Philip	RNS 37	Merrills, Benajah	OND 182
Mercereau, Elizabeth	RCH 88	Merl, Timy	SUF 76	Merrills, Bildad	OND 176
Mer.hant, __ did	TIO 232	Merlin, George	ONT 372	Merrills, Caleb B.	OND 173
Merchant, Abel	RNS 65	Merlin, John	ONT 372	Merrills, Elias Sen.	ONN 165
Merchant, Bernard	CAY 566	Merlin, Thomas	ONT 372	Merrills, Jacob	OND 169
Merchant, Charles	NYK 124	Merlin, William	ONT 372	Merrills, Jared	OND 185
Merchant, Ezra	TIO 229	Mermet, Aemac	NYK 66	Merrills, Jonathan	OND 182
Merchant, Frederick	NYK 107	Mernard, John	NYK 89	Merrills, Moses	ORN 362
Merchant, George	ALB 136	Mernek, Bullis	GRN 331	Merrills, Reuben	COL 204
Merchant, Heman	ALB 71	Mernene, Margaret	NYK 18	Merrils, Elijah	SCH 131
Merchant, Hezekeah	WSH 278	Merrell, Abraham	RCH 89	Merrils, James	SRA 17
Merchant, John	DUT 47	Merrell, Abraham	RCH 90	Merrils, Joseph	OTS 35
Merchant, John	DUT 133	Merrell, Andrew	NYK 69	Merriman see Meriman,	
Merchant, John	WSH 248	Merrell, Benjamin	SRA 51	Mariman & Merryman	
Merchant, Joseah	WSH 277	Merrell, Iyon	RCH 89	Merriman, Amasa	HRK 520
Merchant, Joseph	OND 198	Merrell, John	NYK 70	Merriman, Benjn	HRK 590
Merchant, Jurden	SRA 59	Merrell, John	RCH 89	Merriman, Benoni	ONN 169
Merchant, Peter	RNS 113	Merrell, John	RCH 89	Merriman, Charles	ONN 169
Merchant, Robin	WSH 304	Merrell, John	RCH 89	Merriman, Christopher	OND 171
Merchel, Robert	ALB 134	Merrell, John	RCH 89	Merriman, Enoch	CAY 610
Merchue, Preserved	ALB 71	Merrell, John	WSH 296	Merrit, Abraham	DUT 7
Mercien, Andreo	NYK 64	Merrell, Lambert	RCH 89	Merrit, Abraham	WST 116
Mercy, Andrew	WST 155	Merrell, Morris	RNS 45	Merrit, Caleb	WST 112
Meream, Samuel	WSH 284	Merrell, Nancy	RCH 89	Merrit, Charles	ALB 90
Meredith, John	KNG 8	Merrell, Richard	RCH 89	Merrit, Daniel	WST 113
Merenous see Marenous		Merrell, Richard	RCH 89	Merrit, Daniel	WST 113
Merenous, Abraham Jr	SCH 164	Merrell, Richard	RCH 89	Merrit, Daniel	WST 116
Merenous, David Junr	SCH 164	Merrell, Thomas	RCH 89	Merrit, Ebenezer	ALB 86
Merenous, Frederick	SCH 164	Merrell, Thomas	RCH 89	Merrit, Edward	WST 120
Merenous, John	SCH 164	Merrell, William	NYK 34	Merrit, Elijah	WST 111
Merenous, John Junr	SCH 164	Merrell, William	RCH 88	Merrit, Gilbert	WST 116
Merenous, Martinus	SCH 164	Merrells, Shubel	ESS 297	Merrit, Henry	WST 113
Merenous, Michael	SCH 164	Merrels, George	NYK 40	Merrit, Isaac	WSH 237
Merenous, Willm	SCH 164	Merret, Ebenezer	NYK 68	Merrit, Israel	WST 114
Merett, Anna	NYK 58	Merret, Isaac	OND 202	Merrit, James	SCH 121
Meriam, John	WSH 284	Merret, Jacob	WSH 185	Merrit, James	WST 117
Meriam, Marshal	OND 208	Merrett, Charaty	NYK 131	Merrit, Jessee	QNS 78
Meriam, William	WSH 284	Merrett, James	NYK 95	Merrit, Job	QNS 84
Merical see Mirakle		Merrett, James	WSH 273	Merrit, John	QNS 79
Merical, Anthony	SRA 11	Merrett, John	NYK 81	Merrit, John	SRA 26
Merick, James	OTS 22	Merrew, Andrew	MNT 41	Merrit, John	WST 114
Merick, Perus	DEL 280	Merrew, John	MNT 41	Merrit, Jonathan	WST 116
Merickle, Jacob	ALB 34	Merriam, Reuben	RNS 34	Merrit, Joseph	WST 111
Merickle, Matthew	ALB 57	Merriam, Samuel	CHN 904	Merrit, Jotham	WST 113
Merickle, Matthias	ALB 53	Merriam, William	HRK 543	Merrit, Nathan	CHN 834
Merihu see Marihue					

Name	Loc	No	Name	Loc	No	Name	Loc	No
Miller, Charles	ALB	12	Miller, Enoch Junr	DEL	291	Miller, Jacob	ALB	93
Miller, Charles	ESS	319	Miller, Enos	WST	136	Miller, Jacob	COL	229
Miller, Charles	NYK	30	Miller, Epenetus	WST	136	Miller, Jacob	DEL	290
Miller, Charles	RNS	84	Miller, Epenetus	WST	141	Miller, Jacob	DUT	158
Miller, Christian	ALB	149	Miller, Euphemia	NYK	83	Miller, Jacob	GRN	334
Miller, Christian	NYK	148	Miller, Eve	OTS	44	Miller, Jacob	HRK	497
Miller, Christoper	COL	197	Miller, Eve	SRA	60	Miller, Jacob	HRK	511
Miller, Christopher	SRA	4	Miller, Ezekel	CHN	954	Miller, Jacob	HRK	542
Miller, Christopher A.	COL	193	Miller, Ezra	DUT	137	Miller, Jacob	ONT	484
Miller, Coenradt	ALB	75	Miller, Ezra	TIO	235	Miller, Jacob	RNS	4
Miller, Coenradt	COL	200	Miller, Fite	COL	235	Miller, Jacob	RNS	59
Miller, Coenradt W.	COL	193	Miller, Francis	DUT	21	Miller, Jacob	RNS	59
Miller, Conradt	MNT	34	Miller, Frederick	DEL	276	Miller, Jacob	RNS	89
Miller, Constant	OND	222	Miller, Frederick	ONT	446	Miller, Jacob	SRA	9
Miller, Coonrod	WST	154	Miller, Frederick G.	DEL	276	Miller, Jacob	SRA	53
Miller, Cornelius	MNT	39	Miller, Frelove	WST	161	Miller, Jacob	SRA	60
Miller, Cornelius	QNS	77	Miller, Full	RNS	14	Miller, Jacob	TIO	263
Miller, Cornelius	RNS	4	Miller, Gad	ONN	171	Miller, Jacob	WSH	241
Miller, Cornelius	WST	139	Miller, Gardner	SUF	108	Miller, Jacob ye 2d	DUT	159
Miller, Cornelius C.	COL	199	Miller, Garret	RNS	89	Miller, Jacob C.	COL	180
Miller, Corns C. S.	COL	192	Miller, George	HRK	456	Miller, Jacob F.	COL	193
Miller, Cornelius J.	COL	104	Miller, George	NYK	29	Miller, Jacob F.	MNT	69
Miller, Cornelius S.	COL	191	Miller, George	NYK	74	Miller, Jacob H.	COL	190
Miller, Cornelius Z.	COL	194	Miller, George	NYK	119	Miller, Jacob H.	HRK	494
Miller, Dan	OND	207	Miller, George	ORN	338	Miller, Jacob J.	COL	193
Miller, Daniel	CAY	688	Miller, George	RNS	35	Miller, Jacob J.	COL	237
Miller, Daniel	GRN	354	Miller, George	SUF	108	Miller, Jacob P.	ALB	44
Miller, Daniel	NYK	87	Miller, George	WSH	193	Miller, Jacob S.	COL	198
Miller, Daniel	ORN	312	Miller, Gertrude	COL	193	Miller, Jacobus	ORN	300
Miller, Daniel	ORN	387	Miller, Gideon	WST	136	Miller, James	DEL	274
Miller, Danl	OTS	37	Miller, Gilbert	DUT	100	Miller, James	DUT	33
Miller, Daniel	SRA	58	Miller, Gilbert	WST	113	Miller, James	GRN	335
Miller, Danl	SCH	160	Miller, Gilbert	WST	114	Miller, James	NYK	73
Miller, Daniel	SCH	164	Miller, Godfrey	DUT	116	Miller, James	NYK	135
Miller, Daniel	WSH	218	Miller, Grant	OTS	14	Miller, James	OND	221
Miller, Daniel	WST	114	Miller, Gurdon	DUT	126	Miller, James	ORN	297
Miller, Daniel	WST	157	Miller, H__y	MNT	9	Miller, James	ORN	345
Miller, Daniel	WST	163	Miller, Hachaliah	WST	142	Miller, James	ORN	378
Miller, Daniel	WST	168	Miller, Harvey	ESS	297	Miller, James	ORN	386
Miller, Daniel Jr	SCH	155	Miller, Hendrick	ULS	216	Miller, James	ORN	396
Miller, David	CAY	714	Miller, Henry	ALB	103	Miller, James	OTS	50
Miller, David	CHN	808	Miller, Henry	COL	197	Miller, James	RNS	47
Miller, David	KNG	11	Miller, Henry	DUT	79	Miller, James	SRA	29
Miller, David	NYK	153	Miller, Henry	GRN	334	Miller, James	WSH	193
Miller, David	OND	204	Miller, Henry	GRN	334	Miller, James	WST	114
Miller, David	OND	205	Miller, Henry	HRK	494	Miller, James	WST	132
Miller, David	ONT	468	Miller, Henry	HRK	497	Miller, James	WST	159
Miller, David	ORN	345	Miller, Henry	NYK	26	Miller, James	WST	168
Miller, David	ORN	365	Miller, Henry	NYK	60	Miller, James S.	SUF	91
Miller, David	QNS	77	Miller, Henry	NYK	80	Miller, Jason	CHN	814
Miller, David	RNS	53	Miller, Henry	ONN	150	Miller, Jason	DUT	126
Miller, David	SUF	108	Miller, Henry	ORN	276	Miller, Jellis	MNT	9
Miller, David	SUF	109	Miller, Henry	QNS	77	Miller, Jeremiah	SUF	106
Miller, David	WST	137	Miller, Henry	RNS	12	Miller, Jeremiah	WST	136
Miller, David	WST	168	Miller, Henry	RCH	91	Miller, Jeremiah	WST	140
Miller, David Junr	SUF	108	Miller, Henry	RCH	92	Miller, Jeremiah Junr	SUF	106
Miller, David B.	OND	219	Miller, Henry	WSH	268	Miller, Jeremiah C.	COL	196
Miller, David Owen	ORN	388	Miller, Henry	WST	161	Miller, Jeremiah J.	COL	193
Miller, Derick	COL	179	Miller, Henry H.	COL	230	Miller, Jerre: C. S.	COL	196
Miller, Drake	SCH	164	Miller, Henry H.	COL	234	Miller, Jerre: Corns	COL	192
Miller, Ebenezer	SRA	13	Miller, Herman	ALB	146	Miller, Jerre: Jacob	COL	197
Miller, Ebenezer	WST	140	Miller, Herman	WST	119	Miller, Jerre: Johans	COL	194
Miller, Edward	NYK	50	Miller, Hezekiah	RNS	43	Miller, Jespar	WST	140
Miller, Edward	ORN	291	Miller, Hezikiah	WST	139	Miller, Jesse	OND	221
Miller, Elea.	MNT	83	Miller, Hugh	TIO	258	Miller, Jesse	ONT	434
Miller, Eleazar	SUF	108	Miller, Hugh	TIO	260	Miller, Jesse	ORN	391
Miller, Eleazer	CLN	165	Miller, Hunting	SUF	106	Miller, Jesse	OTS	27
Miller, Eliakim	OND	207	Miller, Ibrook	CLN	164	Miller, Jesse	TIO	235
Miller, Elias	ULS	164	Miller, Ichabod	ONT	364	Miller, Jesse Junr	ORN	386
Miller, Elihu	WSH	286	Miller, Increase	WST	136	Miller, Joachim	COL	193
Miller, Elisha	GRN	356	Miller, Increase	WST	141	Miller, Joel	OND	220
Miller, Elisha	SRA	13	Miller, Increase	WST	154	Miller, Joel	SUF	106
Miller, Elisha	SUF	109	Miller, Isaac	ALB	20	Miller, Johannes	CHN	778
Miller, Elisha Junr	SRA	16	Miller, Isaac	OND	192	Miller, Johannis	ORN	294
Miller, Eliza	NYK	144	Miller, Isaac	SUF	68	Miller, John	ALB	37
Miller, Elizabeth	NYK	122	Miller, Isaac	WST	139	Miller, John	ALB	56
Miller, Enoch	DEL	291	Miller, Israel	ALB	21	Miller, John	ALB	111

Name	Loc	No.	Name	Loc	No.	Name	Loc	No.
Miller, John	CHN	780	Miller, Jonathan	SUF	108	Miller, Peter	COL	197
Miller, John	CLN	162	Miller, Jonathan	WST	130	Miller, Peter	COL	224
Miller, John	COL	190	Miller, Jonathan Junr	WST	130	Miller, Peter	COL	240
Miller, John	COL	191	Miller, Jones	RNS	59	Miller, Peter	DUT	70
Miller, John	COL	192	Miller, Joseah	CHN	912	Miller, Peter	KNG	11
Miller, John	COL	241	Miller, Joseph	GRN	348	Miller, Peter	ONT	484
Miller, John	COL	254	Miller, Joseph	ORN	388	Miller, Peter	RNS	12
Miller, John	DEL	278	Miller, Joseph	OTS	52	Miller, Peter	SRA	5
Miller, John	DUT	53	Miller, Joseph	STB	200	Miller, Peter	ULS	192
Miller, John	DUT	171	Miller, Joseph	SUF	68	Miller, Peter	ULS	259
Miller, John	HRK	450	Miller, Joseph	SUF	108	Miller, Peter	WST	140
Miller, John	HRK	497	Miller, Joseph	TIO	263	Miller, Peter C S	COL	191
Miller, John	HRK	557	Miller, Joseph	ULS	184	Miller, Peter C S	COL	197
Miller, John	NYK	25	Miller, Joseph	ULS	219	Miller, Peter G.	MNT	32
Miller, John a mulatto	NYK	40	Miller, Joseph	WSH	258	Miller, Phebe	WST	114
Miller, John	NYK	53	Miller, Joseph	WST	111	Miller, Phelix	RNS	70
Miller, John	NYK	109	Miller, Joseph	WST	136	Miller, Philip	ALB	146
Miller, John	NYK	124	Miller, Joseph Junior	SUF	108	Miller, Phillip	COL	240
Miller, John	NYK	128	Miller, Joseph Junr	WST	136	Miller, Phillip	DUT	16
Miller, John	NYK	137	Miller, Joshua	OTS	57	Miller, Phillip	DUT	37
Miller, John	NYK	153	Miller, Joshua	SRA	6	Miller, Phillip	DUT	158
Miller, John	ONN	151	Miller, Josiah	RNS	46	Miller, Phillip	MNT	9
Miller, John	ONT	358	Miller, Josiah	SRA	6	Miller, Phillip	ULS	192
Miller, John	ORN	351	Miller, Jotham	OTS	31	Miller, Philo	WSH	283
Miller, John	ORN	373	Miller, Laurence	NYK	116	Miller, Pliny Junr	RNS	111
Miller, John	OTS	10	Miller, Lena	ALB	58	Miller, Pliny Senr	RNS	112A
Miller, John	OTS	19	Miller, Leonard	SCH	164	Miller, Polly	NYK	62
Miller, John	OTS	39	Miller, Levi	ORN	339	Miller, Polly	SCH	151
Miller, John	QNS	63	Miller, Levi	RNS	20	Miller, Polly	WSH	241
Miller, John	QNS	82	Miller, Levy	WSH	288	Miller, Powell	MNT	63
Miller, John	QNS	83	Miller, Lewis	WST	129	Miller, Reuben	ULS	207
Miller, John	QNS	84	Miller, Lucius	CHN	990	Miller, Rhebecca	SUF	107
Miller, John	RNS	14	Miller, Lyon	WST	111	Miller, Richard	WST	160
Miller, John	RNS	35	Miller, Margaret	NYK	80	Miller, Robert	RNS	46
Miller, John	RNS	89	Miller, Martha	CAY	690	Miller, Robert	RNS	58
Miller, John	SRA	3	Miller, Martin	COL	184	Miller, Robert	WSH	197
Miller, John	SRA	7	Miller, Martin	OND	207	Miller, Robert	WST	114
Miller, John	SRA	13	Miller, Martinus	COL	236	Miller, Roger	WST	115
Miller, John	SRA	45	Miller, Mary	NYK	32	Miller, Sally	HRK	444
Miller, John	SCH	134	Miller, Mary	NYK	126	Miller, Samuel	ALB	96
Miller, John	SCH	141	Miller, Mary	NYK	131	Miller, Samuel	CHN	914
Miller, John	STB	197	Miller, Mathias	COL	236	Miller, Samuel	DEL	272
Miller, John	SUF	107	Miller, Menoah	ESS	293	Miller, Samuel	DEL	283
Miller, John	TIO	262	Miller, Michael	ONT	486	Miller, Samuel	HRK	527
Miller, John	ULS	189	Miller, Moses	OND	222	Miller, Samuel	ONT	390
Miller, John	ULS	258	Miller, Moses	ORN	388	Miller, Samuel	ONT	486
Miller, John	WSH	195	Miller, Moses	RNS	47	Miller, Samuel	ORN	293
Miller, John	WSH	218	Miller, Moulton	OND	187	Miller, Samuel	ORN	309
Miller, John	WSH	241	Miller, Munmoth	WST	124	Miller, Samuel	QNS	77
Miller, John	WST	124	Miller, Nathan	ALB	109	Miller, Saml	RNS	39
Miller, John	WST	142	Miller, Nathan	ALB	121	Miller, Saml	RCK	105
Miller, John	WST	168	Miller, Nathan	CAY	698	Miller, Samuel	SCH	164
Miller, John Junr	DUT	21	Miller, Nathan	CHN	828	Miller, Samuel	SCH	164
Miller, John Junr	MNT	69	Miller, Nathan	DUT	16	Miller, Samuel	STB	198
Miller, John Junr	ORN	387	Miller, Nathan	SUF	108	Miller, Samuel	STB	199
Miller, John Junior	SUF	107	Miller, Nathan	SUF	108	Miller, Samuel	WST	129
Miller, John Jur	TIO	264	Miller, Nathan Junr	CHN	828	Miller, Samuel	WST	136
Miller, John Senr	DUT	21	Miller, Nathaniel	ALB	21	Miller, Samuel	WST	141
Miller, John Senr	ORN	388	Miller, Nathaniel	ESS	293	Miller, Samuel	WST	168
Miller, John	MNT	26	Miller, Nathaniel	GRN	349	Miller, Samuel A.	COL	191
Miller, John A.	COL	241	Miller, Nathl	OTS	2	Miller, Sarah	NYK	38
Miller, John B.	ORN	309	Miller, Nathaniel	WST	136	Miller, Sarah	ULS	205
Miller, John C.	COL	197	Miller, Nathaniel	WST	141	Miller, Sarah	WSH	241
Miller, John C.	WST	154	Miller, Nicholas	ALV	54	Miller, Sarah	WST	141
Miller, John Frederick	NYK	37	Miller, Nicholas	COL	242	Miller, Savia	ORN	385
Miller, John H.	COL	223	Miller, Nicholas	HRK	470	Miller, Seth	OND	220
Miller, John H.	COL	234	Miller, Nicholas	NYK	55	Miller, Seth	OTS	19
Miller, John J.	RNS	55	Miller, Nicholas	RNS	59	Miller, Seth	WST	168
Miller, John J.	RNS	63	Miller, Nicholas	ULS	188	Miller, Silas	COL	241
Miller, John J. Junr	RNS	63	Miller, Noah	WSH	270	Miller, Simeon	CAY	688
Miller, Johnson	TIO	253	Miller, Noath	NYK	100	Miller, Smith	OND	207
Miller, Jonas	HRK	497	Miller, Obadiah	SRA	41	Miller, Solomon	SRA	46
Miller, Jonas G.	COL	237	Miller, Ogden	SRA	24	Miller, Solomon	WST	141
Miller, Jonathan	GRN	353	Miller, Oliver	RNS	9	Miller, Stephen	COL	191
Miller, Jonathan	HRK	573	Miller, Peggy	TIO	254	Miller, Stephen	DUT	13
Miller, Jonathan	ORN	278	Miller, Peleg	COL	187	Miller, Stephen	HRK	486
Miller, Jonathan	ORN	296	Miller, Perry	WSH	231	Miller, Stephen	RNS	12

Name	Co.	Pg.
Miller, Stephen Junr	RNS	12
Miller, Stephen H.	COL	197
Miller, Susanna	DUT	161
Miller, Susanna	ORN	276
Miller, Thaddeus	WST	139
Miller, Thomas	CLN	164
Miller, Thomas	CLN	169
Miller, Thomas	NYK	23
Miller, Thomas a mulatto	NYK	38
Miller, Thomas	NYK	76
Miller, Thomas	NYK	78
Miller, Thomas	NYK	111
Miller, Thomas	RNS	89
Miller, Thomas	SRA	48
Miller, Thomas A.	ONN	162
Miller, Tillotson	TIO	245
Miller, Timothy	SRA	22
Miller, Timy	SUF	68
Miller, Timothy	SUF	109
Miller, Timothy Junr	SUF	109
Miller, Tobias	COL	241
Miller, Uriah	RNS	90
Miller, Uriah	SUF	99
Miller, Valentine	HRK	440
Miller, Valentine R.	NYK	150
Miller, Walter	NYK	108
Miller, Widdow	SRA	15
Miller, [Widow?]	QNS	83
Miller, William	ALB	36
Miller, William	ALB	73
Miller, William	CAY	688
Miller, William	CHN	814
Miller, William	COL	185
Miller, William	DUT	16
Miller, William	GRN	336
Miller, William	HRK	497
Miller, William	NYK	32
Miller, William	NYK	78
Miller, William	NYK	94
Miller, William	NYK	101
Miller, William a Black	NYK	111
Miller, William	OND	187
Miller, William	ONN	145
Miller, William	ORN	309
Miller, William	ORN	340
Miller, William	ORN	374
Miller, William	ORN	396
Miller, William	OTS	35
Miller, William	RNS	25
Miller, Wm	RNS	47
Miller, William	SUF	107
Miller, William	WSH	194
Miller, William	WSH	225
Miller, William	WSH	287
Miller, William	WST	134
Miller, William	WST	136
Miller, William	WST	168
Miller, William Junr	WST	143
Miller, William A.	COL	193
Miller, Willm C.	COL	195
Miller, William G.	NYK	48
Miller, William J.	COL	223
Miller, William J.	ORN	295
Miller, William S.	ORN	294
Miller, Zachariah	ORN	387
Miller, Zadock	RNS	25
Miller, Zeba	TIO	235
Miller, Zepheniah	ALB	37
Miller, Zepheniah	NYK	137
Miller, Zopher	SUF	71
Millet, Abraham	COL	225
Millet, Andrew	ONT	344
Millet, Frances	NYK	110
Millet, Samuel	ONT	352
Millett, Daniel	ONT	352
Millham, Abraham	DUT	158
Millham, Coonradt	DUT	157
Millham, Jacob	RNS	53
Millham, Martin	DUT	157
Millham, Simon	RNS	58
Milli_, Thomas	NYK	42
Millican, James	CAY	600
Millice, George	SCH	135
Millice, John C.	SCH	135
Millice, Willm	SCH	135
Milligan, Alexander	ORN	303
Milligan, David	ULS	190
Milligan, Hugh	ORN	302
Milligan, Hugh Junr	ORN	304
Milligan, Robert a mulatto	NYK	49
Milligan, Samuel	NYK	150
Milligan, Thomas	ALB	42
Milligan, Thomas	ONN	151
Milligan, William	NYK	90
Milligan, William	QNS	62
Milligon, Nathaniel	ORN	276
Milliman, Bryant	ONT	380
Milliman, Isaac	RNS	20
Milliman, John	RNS	20
Milliman, John Junr	RNS	20
Milliman, Rowland	WSH	289
Milliman, Samuel	RNS	21
Milliman, Thos	RNS	20
Millington, Jacob	HRK	509
Millington, John	HRK	589
Millington, Jonathan	HRK	595
Millington, Nathan	HRK	595
Millington, Peter	OTS	26
Millington, Peter	OTS	55
Millington, Samuel	WSH	203
Million, Daniel	NYK	76
Million, John	WSH	220
Millis, James	NYK	122
Millner, Ursulk	NYK	87
Millroy, Anthony	ALB	39
Millroy, John	ALB	27
Mills see Miles		
Mills, ...	MNT	78
Mills, Abijah	COL	177
Mills, Alexander	ONT	320
Mills, Amos	QNS	73
Mills, Amos	QNS	73
Mills, Amos	ULS	189
Mills, Andrew	OND	162
Mills, Andrew	SUF	91
Mills, Benjamin	DUT	145
Mills, Benjamin	SRA	57
Mills, Caleb & Hewlet Creed	QNS	66
Mills, Christopher	COL	197
Mills, Daniel	HRK	485
Mills, Danl	OTS	30
Mills, Daniel	WSH	214
Mills, Daniel Junr	WSH	214
Mills, David	CHN	766
Mills, David	OND	190
Mills, David	ORN	330
Mills, David	SCH	134
Mills, David	WSH	214
Mills, Ebenezer	ORN	339
Mills, Edward	OTS	43
Mills, Elkanah	OND	169
Mills, Ephraim	DUT	29
Mills, Frederick	MNT	38
Mills, George	CAY	666
Mills, George	NYK	80
Mills, George	SRA	35
Mills, George	SUF	67
Mills, Gilbert	SUF	65
Mills, Hannah	NYK	28
Mills, Henry	QNS	68
Mills, Henry	WSH	210
Mills, Hezekiah	COL	220
Mills, Hezekiah	DUT	176
Mills, Hugh	DEL	269
Mills, Increase	DUT	35
Mills, Isaac	CAY	548
Mills, Isaac	CHN	766
Mills, Isaac	COL	219
Mills, Isaac	SUF	90
Mills, Israel	SUF	91
Mills, Jacob	MNT	38
Mills, Jacob	ORN	342
Mills, Jacob	QNS	68
Mills, Jacob	SRA	55
Mills, Jacob Junr	ORN	337
Mills, James	DEL	284
Mills, James	DUT	105
Mills, James a Black	NYK	39
Mills, James	NYK	64
Mills, James	ORN	329
Mills, James	ULS	215
Mills, James	WSH	258
Mills, Jane	ORN	395
Mills, Jededeah	SUF	91
Mills, John	CAY	568
Mills, John	CAY	664
Mills, John	COL	255
Mills, John	HRK	483
Mills, John	NYK	48
Mills, John	NYK	131
Mills, John	ONT	310
Mills, John	QNS	67
Mills, John	QNS	75
Mills, John	QNS	78
Mills, John	RNS	55
Mills, John	RNS	76
Mills, John	TIO	241
Mills, John	ULS	233
Mills, John	WSH	243
Mills, John	WST	136
Mills, Jonas	SUF	91
Mills, Jonathan	ALB	88
Mills, Jonathan	ORN	337
Mills, Jonathan	SUF	67
Mills, Jonathan	WST	136
Mills, Joshua	NYK	77
Mills, Joshua	QNS	69
Mills, Josiah	WST	143
Mills, Louis	ONT	316
Mills, Louis	ONT	322
Mills, Micah	ORN	373
Mills, Moses	SUF	90
Mills, Nathaniel	QNS	68
Mills, Nathl	SUF	68
Mills, Nicholas	WSH	257
Mills, Pelatiah	OND	170
Mills, Peter	ORN	329
Mills, Peter Junr	ORN	329
Mills, Philip	SCH	148
Mills, Robert	DUT	34
Mills, Roger	MNT	44
Mills, Roger	OND	204
Mills, Rosel	OND	211
Mills, Samuel	NYK	41
Mills, Samuel	NYK	63
Mills, Samuel	ONT	320
Mills, Samuel	QNS	68
Mills, Samuel	QNS	68
Mills, Samuel	RNS	89
Mills, Samuel	SRA	20
Mills, Samuel	SUF	91
Mills, Samuel Junr	ALB	72
Mills, Samuel Sr	ALB	72
Mills, Sarah	DEL	284
Mills, Sarah	QNS	66
Mills, Stephen	SRA	57
Mills, Stephen	TIO	241

Mitchell, Allen	QNS 70	Mitter, James	GRN 334	Moll_y, Ebenezer	ONN 129
Mitchell, Amasa	ULS 241	Mix, Abel	GRN 336	Mollay, Henry	NYK 105
Mitchell, Anan	DEL 286	Mix, Amos	GRN 331	Molleaor, William	NYK 153
Mitchell, Andrew	NYK 28	Mix, Amos	GRN 340	Molleneaux, Jessee	QNS 66
Mitchell, Andrew	SCH 155	Mix, Benjamin	SRA 3	Mollery, John	CHN 968
Mitchell, Ann	ALB 126	Mix, Elihue	ALB 22	Mollery, John	SRA 46
Mitchell, Archibald	DEL 286	Mix, Elisha	SRA 34	Mollet, Philo	COL 262
Mitchell, Asa	HRK 598	Mix, Ephraim	COL 249	Molt, Jacob	CHN 740
Mitchell, Azariah	ONT 422	Mix, Giles	CHN 904	Molvey, John	NYK 128
Mitchell, Beriah	ESS 307	Mix, Joel	OND 222	Mon, Melachi	RCH 94
Mitchell, Charles	QNS 69	Mix, Josiah	DEL 281	Monache, Julut	NYK 104
Mitchell, Christopher	RNS 74	Mix, Levi	GRN 332	Monaughan, Patrick	OTS 3
Mitchell, Consider	OND 187	Mix, Reuben	HRK 451	Moncrief, Hugh	WSH 225
Mitchell, Daniel	ONN 137	Mix, Thomas	WSH 205	Moncrief, Thomas B.	NYK 29
Mitchell, David	NYK 43	Mix, William P.	NYK 34	Moncrief, William	WSH 225
Mitchell, Edward	NYK 106	Mo_e, David	CAY 590	Monday, Ezra	NYK 15
Mitchell, Elijah	RNS 91	Moake, Francis	ALB 99	Monde, Henry	NYK 40
Mitchell, Elizabeth	NYK 121	Moake, Henry	ALB 99	Monden, Stephen	ULS 260
Mitchell, Henry	NYK 43	Moake, Jacob	ALB 101	Mondy, Nathaniel	RCH 92
Mitchell, Henry	NYK 136	Moake, Johannis	ALB 99	Mondy, Nicholas	RCH 90
Mitchell, Hugh	OTS 2	Moake, John	ALB 105	Moneer, John	COL 234
Mitchell, Hugh Junr	OTS 2	Mode, John	NYK 102	Monell, David	ULS 208
Mitchell, Isaac	DUT 64	Moe, Abraham	SRA 8	Monell, George	COL 194
Mitchell, James	DUT 130	Moe, Ezra	ULS 208	Monell, George	ORN 282
Mitchell, James	ESS 322	Moe, Isaac	SRA 10	Monell, James	ORN 294
Mitchell, James	NYK 92	Moe, Joseph	ULS 207	Monell, John	ORN 346
Mitchell, James	QNS 64	Moe, Nun	CLN 173	Monell, Samuel	ORN 346
Mitchell, James	SUF 101	Moe, Peter	SRA 8	Monell, Thomas	ORN 337
Mitchell, James	ULS 251	Moffat, Alexander	ORN 298	Monell, William	ORN 279
Mitchell, John	ALB 132	Moffat, Bezelial	OTS 28	Monford, Hannah	QNS 65
Mitchell, John	NYK 18	Moffat, James	NYK 50	Monford, Peter	QNS 83
Mitchell, John	NYK 25	Moffat, John	ORN 358	Mongar, Timothy	GRN 346
Mitchell, John	NYK 72	Moffatt, Henry	DUT 155	Monger, Benja_n	CAY 546
Mitchell, John	NYK 75	Moffatt, John	ORN 352	Monger, Ichabod	ONT 328
Mitchell, John	NYK 92	Moffatt, Nathaniel	ORN 351	Monger, James	CHN 958
Mitchell, John	OND 203	Moffatt, Samuel	ORN 289	Mongomry, David	WSH 246
Mitchell, John	SCH 156	Moffatt, Samuel	ORN 351	Monigan, Hugh	NYK 112
Mitchell, Joseph	COL 210	Moffatt, Samuel	ORN 357	Monk, Christopher	MNT 35
Mitchell, Joseph	DEL 286	Moffatt, Samuel Junr	ORN 351	Monk, John	MNT 34
Mitchell, Joseph	DUT 138	Moffatt, Thomas	ORN 348	Monk, John Junr	MNT 24
Mitchell, Joseph	NYK 40	Moffatt, William	ORN 289	Monk, John W.	MNT 31
Mitchell, Joseph	ONT 420	Moffatt, William	ORN 352	Monk, William	SCH 156
Mitchell, Joseph	WSH 306	Moffet, Enoch	SRA 60	Monkhouse, Anna	NYK 41
Mitchell, Manuel	SCH 119	Moffet, Joel	HRK 511	Monnell, Charles	NYK 120
Mitchell, Nancy	NYK 57	Moffett, Isaac	DEL 287	Monro see Munroe
Mitchell, Nash	RNS 91	Moffit, Conkey	OTS 47	Monro, John	ULS 217
Mitchell, Nathan	ULS 181	Moffit, John	NYK 17	Monroe, Abel	RNS 108
Mitchell, Nathaniel	DEL 289	Moffitt, Alanson	OTS 47	Monroe, Archebald	RNS 20
Mitchell, Patrick	ALB 106	Moffitt, Aquilla	OTS 47	Monroe, Joel	OTS 6
Mitchell, Peter a		Moffitt, Harman	RNS 96	Monroe, John	OTS 28
Black	NYK 19	Moffitt, Hosea	RNS 101	Monroe, Phebe	RNS 74
Mitchell, Peter	RCH 90	Moffitt, Isaac	OTS 47	Monroe, Samuel	RNS 20
Mitchell, Richard	ALB 132	Moffitt, John	CAY 728	Monrow, Elijah	CHN 796
Mitchell, Robert	NYK 41	Moffitt, Jona	OTS 47	Monrow, Joseph	CHN 782
Mitchell, Samuel	NYK 122	Moffitt, Melvin	OTS 47	Monrow, Josiah	ORN 298
Mitchell, Samuel	WSH 305	Moger, Arthur	SUF 64	Monrow, William	CHN 782
Mitchell, Samuel _	NYK 136	Moger, Cristifer	SUF 64	Monsesinger, Conrod	RCK 106
Mitchell, Stephen	DUT 170	Moger, Henery	CHN 942	Monsey, Henry	RNS 74
Mitchell, Stephen	OTS 44	Moger, John Junr	CHN 942	Monson(?), Abel	GRN 339
Mitchell, Stephen	SUF 100	Moher, Jacob	MNT 10	Monson, Caleb	CHN 754
Mitchell, Thomas	DUT 67	Moke, Daniel	SCH 164	Monson, Mosses	CHN 754
Mitchell, Thomas	DUT 120	Moke, Jacob J.	ALB 99	Monson, Reuben	NYK 137
Mitchell, Thomas	NYK 25	Molbone, Charles	ESS 322	Montagnie, Benjamin	ULS 189
Mitchell, Thos D.	OTS 49	Molder, David	CHN 950	Montagnie, Coonradt	ORN 384
Mitchell, Uriah	DUT 52	Molhench, Thomas	WSH 291	Montagnie, Thomas	ORN 376
Mitchell, Uriah	DUT 121	Molineaux see Mulinox		Montague see Mortigue
Mitchell, Walter	NYK 28	& Mullineaux		Montague, Edward	MNT 98
Mitchell, Walter	NYK 75	Molineaux, Gideon	ULS 243	Montague, George a
Mitchell, William	COL 205	Molineaux, James	ORN 274	Black	NYK 50
Mitchell, William	DUT 103	Molineaux, John	DUT 168	Montague, Nathaniel	OND 178
Mitchell, William	ONT 440	Molineaux, Lawrence	ORN 274	Montague, Uriel	OND 182
Mitchell, William	ORN 271	Molineaux, Levi	DUT 178	Montaigne, Peter	ULS 199
Mitchell, William	QNS 50	Molineaux, Moses	DUT 100	Montandevert, Sarah	NYK 31
Mitchell, William	RNS 33	Molineaux, Thomas	ORN 274	Montayne, Isaac	NYK 22
Mitchell, Zeruel	WSH 280	Molineaux, William	ORN 290	Montayne, Isaac	NYK 55
Mith, Thomas	NYK 87	Molineux, John	NYK 77	Montayne, Isaac	NYK 90
Mitre, Thomas	RNS 80	Moll see Mott		Montayne, John	NYK 72

Montayne, John	NYK	99	Montross, Abraham	WST	156	Moon, Thomas	SRA	31
Montayne, Mary	NYK	71	Montross, Abram	WST	154	Moon, William	ONT	362
Montcath, Wm	MNT	91	Montross, Adam	DUT	25	Moone, Elizabeth	NYK	18
Montee, John	CLN	173	Montross, Cornelius	DUT	76	Mooney, David	DUT	169
Montey, Amable	CLN	168	Montross, Daniel	WST	124	Mooney, Edward	DUT	169
Montey, Glode Junr	CLN	173	Montross, David	WST	133	Mooney, Hannah	NYK	43
Montey, Francis	CLN	168	Montross, Gilbert	WST	124	Mooney, James	WSH	189
Montey, Francis Junr	CLN	168	Montross, Isaac	WST	158	Mooney, Magdalen	NYK	52
Montford, Abraham	QNS	82	Montross, Jacob	ULS	192	Mooney, Partrick	NYK	73
Montford, Jacobus	QNS	83	Montross, John	WST	156	Mooney, Robert	CAY	698
Montford, Sarah	QNS	81	Montross, Joseph	QNS	75	Mooney, William	DUT	21
Montfort, Adrian	DUT	26	Montross, Joseph	WST	132	Mooney, William	NYK	48
Montfort, Albert H.	DUT	34	Montross, Matthias	ULS	195	Mooney, William	NYK	73
Montfort, Albert J.	DUT	24	Montross, Nathaniel	WST	130	Mooney, William	WST	142
Montfort, Dominicus	DUT	40	Montross, Peter	DUT	73	Moony, Absalom	WST	124
Montfort, Elizabeth	ORN	304	Montross, Phebee	WST	124	Moony, John	ONN	146
Montfort, Garrett	SUF	93	Montross, Reuben	ULS	192	Moor, Alansen	OTS	22
Montfort, Henry	DUT	33	Mony, Barnet	ONN	167	Moor, Amos	CHN	742
Montfort, James	DUT	33	Mood, Able	MNT	116	Moor, Elijah	CHN	812
Montfort, John	DUT	163	Moodee, John	WSH	194	Moor, Francis	RNS	77
Montfort, John P.	DUT	22	Moody, Benjamin	WST	168	Moor, Henry	TIO	247
Montfort, Widow Kitty	QNS	65	Moody, Catherine a			Moor, Husted	WSH	299
Montfort, Martin	DUT	32	Black	NYK	78	Moor, Jacob	CHN	812
Montfort, Mary	DUT	31	Moody, David	CHN	906	Moor, Jacob	RNS	8
Montfort, Peter	DEL	288	Moody, Ellen	NYK	26	Moor, James	QNS	81
Montfort, Peter P.	DUT	33	Moody, Epiphras	OND	205	Moor, Job	RNS	106
Montfort, Stephen	DUT	32	Moody, Freiman	MNT	87	Moor, Joel F.	WSH	288
Montfort, Stephen P.	DUT	33	Moody, Harman	SRA	47	Moor, John	QNS	62
Montgomery see Mongom-			Moody, Hezekiah	WSH	206	Moor, John	RNS	10
ery			Moody, James	TIO	259	Moor, John	RNS	13
Montgomery, Arch	OND	223	Moody, John J. A.	TIO	261	Moor, John	TIO	248
Montgomery, Daniel	SRA	46	Moody, Nodiah	SRA	47	Moor, Jonah	CHN	774
Montgomery, Ebenezer	WSH	226	Moody, Perus	DEL	279	Moor, Jona	OTS	22
Montgomery, Elias	CHN	916	Moody, Wm	MNT	41	Moor, Joseph	OND	205
Montgomery, Elijah	SRA	46	Moody, William	NYK	25	Moor, Orson	OTS	22
Montgomery, Elisha	SRA	46	Mooers, Benjamin	CLN	160	Moor, Phinehas	SRA	50
Montgomery, Ezekiel	ESS	306	Mooers, John	CLN	160	Moor, Roderick	OTS	22
Montgomery, Henry	CAY	586	Mook, William	NYK	148	Moor, Roger Junr	OTS	33
Montgomery, Henry	WSH	230	Mooklar, James	COL	248	Moor, Solomon	CHN	790
Montgomery, Henry Junr	WSH	230	Mookler, John	COL	247	Moor, Stephen	CHN	958
Montgomery, Hugh	NYK	43	Moon see Moore			Moor, Sylvenus	CHN	774
Montgomery, Hugh	RNS	95	Moon, Andrew	ORN	386	Moor, Thaddeus	CHN	822
Montgomery, James	ALB	53	Moon, Benajah	SRA	31	Moor, William	RNS	25
Montgomery, James	MNT	111	Moon, Benoni	ONT	454	Moor, William A.	WSH	300
Montgomery, James	WSH	290	Moon, Benoni Jur	ONT	454	Moor, Zopha	CHN	852
Montgomery, Janet	DUT	163	Moon, Dake	RNS	68	Moore see Moher, Moone,
Montgomery, John	DEL	288	Moon, Daniel	RNS	77	More & Mower
Montgomery, John	NYK	25	Moon, Darius	OTS	8	Moore, iel	CAY	610
Montgomery, John	NYK	62	Moon, David	SCH	140	Moore, Abner	ESS	295
Montgomery, John	SRA	46	Moon, David	SCH	156	Moore, Abraham	CAY	548
Montgomery, John	WSH	226	Moon, Ebenezer	SRA	39	Moore, Abraham	COL	234
Montgomery, Peter	HRK	548	Moon, Hazard	RNS	77	Moore, Abraham	NYK	54
Montgomery, Robert	RNS	81	Moon, Herman	SCH	139	Moore, Abraham	NYK	102
Montgomery, Robert	SRA	46	Moon, Jacob	MNT	4	Moore, Abraham	NYK	135
Montgomery, Robert	WSH	226	Moon, Job	HRK	589	Moore, Abraham Jun	NYK	135
Montgomery, Robert Junr	WSH	227	Moon, Job	RNS	98	Moore, Alexander	DEL	267
Montgomery, Rosanna a			Moon, John	COL	179	Moore, Alexander	ORN	343
Black	NYK	116	Moon, John	COL	228	Moore, Alexander	ORN	395
Montgomery, Samuel	NYK	67	Moon, John	OTS	48	Moore, Alexander T.	DEL	267
Montgomery, Sandy	NYK	58	Moon, John	RNS	99	Moore, Almeron	OND	180
Montgomery, Wm	ALB	108	Moon, John	SRA	58	Moore, Alpheus	SRA	20
Montgomery, William	CAY	704	Moon, John	WSH	213	Moore, Andrew	DUT	149
Montgomery, William	ORN	291	Moon, John B.	COL	198	Moore, Andw	OTS	58
Montgomery, William	SRA	46	Moon, John R.	RNS	70	Moore, Anna	NYK	54
Montgomry, Reuben	SRA	46	Moon, Jonathan	ONT	454	Moore, Anna	NYK	127
Montius, Jaocum	NYK	19	Moon, Jonathan	WSH	268	Moore, Appollus	ALB	82
Montonia, Elijah	TIO	214	Moon, Mecaja	MNT	89	Moore, Arnold	COL	206
Montonia, Joseph	TIO	214	Moon, Paul	COL	198	Moore, Asa	CLN	171
Montonia, Joseph Junr	TIO	214	Moon, Richard	ONT	430	Moore, Benjamin	CLN	173
Montonye, John	KNG	9	Moon, Richard	WSH	203	Moore, Benjamin	DUT	120
Montonyey, Aurt	RCK	105	Moon, Robert	ONT	454	Moore, Benjamin	ESS	295
Montonyey, Conrod	RCK	105	Moon, Robert	OTS	38	Moore, Benjamin	NYK	48
Montonyey, Isaac	RCK	105	Moon, Robert	WSH	211	Moore, Benjamin	QNS	61
Montonyey, Isaac Junr	RCK	105	Moon, Robert Junr	WSH	211	Moore, Benjn	SUF	74
Montros, James	NYK	139	Moon, Silus	RNS	27	Moore, Benjn	SUF	76
Montrose, Isaac	ONT	468	Moon, Stephen	ONT	394	Moore, Bird	SRA	45
Montrose, James	NYK	92	Moon, Thomas	RNS	98	Moore, Blase	NYK	48

Name	Ref	Name	Ref	Name	Ref
Moory, Asel	CHN 958	Morehouse, Samuel	WSH 203	Morgan, David	NYK 140
Moose, Hendrick	ULS 222	Morehouse, Silas	DEL 279	Morgan, David	ONT 366
Moradoff, Geo.	OTS 44	Morehouse, Stephen	WSH 201	Morgan, David	ONT 366
Moran, Edward	NYK 81	Morehouse, Thomas	WSH 297	Morgan, David	WSH 288
Moran, John	NYK 133	Morehouse, William	WSH 291	Morgan, Desire	NYK 139
Morch, Casper	NYK 114	Morehouse, Zar D.	HRK 496	Morgan, Elijah	DUT 33
Morchead, Thomas	NYK 80	Moreland, James	ORN 334	Morgan, Elijah	ONT 366
Mordock, Andrew	NYK 142	Moreland, Stephen	SRA 21	Morgan, Elijah	WST 153
Mordock, John	CHN 944	Morell, William	WSH 273	Morgan, Elisha	RNS 18
More, Andrew	TIO 231	Mores, Robert	COL 251	Morgan, Ephraim	CAY 666
More, Benjamine	GRN 356	Morewise, John	NYK 134	Morgan, Ephraim	RNS 93
More, Cade	SUF 105	Morey, Adam	ALB 34	Morgan, Evans	CAY 582
More, Charles	WSH 199	Morey, Amos	ALB 34	Morgan, Gaius	OND 214
More, Coonradt	ORN 309	Morey, Augustus	COL 181	Morgan, Hezekeah	CHN 910
More, Daniel	TIO 211	Morey, Benjamin	ALB 32	Morgan, Horace	CLN 170
More, David	GRN 338	Morey, Benjamin	DUT 15	Morgan, Isaac	ALB 40
More, Ebenezer	WSH 223	Morey, David	HRK 581	Morgan, Isaac	OND 198
More, Elijah	GRN 335	Morey, David	RNS 45	Morgan, Isaac	ORN 393
More, Ellehu	GRN 341	Morey, David	ULS 188	Morgan, Isarel	NYK 100
More, Francis	RNS 18	Morey, David D.	RNS 46	Morgan, Israel	DUT 126
More, Frederick	MNT 72	Morey, Ephraim	CHN 810	Morgan, Jacob	ALB 68
More, Henry	SCH 144	Morey, Friend	DUT 45	Morgan, James	CHN 762
More, Hugh	WSH 188	Morey, Hazard	ALB 34	Morgan, James	CHN 900
More, Hugh	WSH 223	Morey, Hazard	COL 182	Morgan, James	COL 252
More, Jacob	SUF 86	Morey, Hazerd	WSH 201	Morgan, James	HRK 480
More, James	ONN 182	Morey, Isaac	WSH 236	Morgan, James	MNT 93
More, James	STB 204	Morey, James	CLN 164	Morgan, James	NYK 56
More, Jerutia	WSH 186	Morey, James	RNS 110	Morgan, James	RCH 94
More, Jiles	SRA 53	Morey, John	DUT 32	Morgan, James	SCH 145
More, John	GRN 326	Morey, John	WSH 224	Morgan, James Junr	WST 148
More, John	MNT 60	Morey, Jonah	WSH 233	Morgan, James Senr	WST 148
More, John	STB 206	Morey, Joseph	COL 182	Morgan, Jedediah	CAY 652
More, Michael	MNT 60	Morey, Joseph	ULS 263	Morgan, Jedediah	OND 203
More, Peter	SRA 16	Morey, Joshua	COL 182	Morgan, Jeseph	ONT 316
More, Peter	SRA 56	Morey, Latin	DUT 15	Morgan, Jesse	RCH 95
More, Samuel	SRA 59	Morey, Lattin	RNS112A	Morgan, Joel	SCH 161
More, Silas	TIO 228	Mo_ey, Leonard	OTS 26	Morgan, John	CAY 584
More, Solomon	TIO 212	Morey, Martha	ULS 263	Morgan, John	CLN 168
More, Stephen	MNT 121	Morey, Moses	RNS 14	Morgan, John	DUT 96
More, Wm	ONN 161	Morey, Nathan	OTS 26	Morgan, John	DUT 137
More, Wm	TIO 231	Morey, Nicholas D.	RNS 46	Morgan, John	HRK 569
More, William	WSH 220	Morey, Roger	DUT 15	Morgan, John	MNT 58
More, Zebulon	TIO 211	Morey, Roger	RNS112A	Morgan, John	ONN 135
More_, Josiah	ONN 178	Morey, Samuel	DUT 118	Morgan, John	ONT 366
Moreau, James	ESS 296	Morey, Semeon	CLN 154	Morgan, John	ORN 383
Morecraft, John	DEL 274	Morey, Silas	ONT 330	Morgan, John	RCH 92
Moredock, Eli	WSH 274	Morey, Silas	OTS 26	Morgan, John	ULS 262
Moredock, Samuel	WSH 274	Morey, Solomon	OND 175	Morgan, Jonas	RNS 81
Morehead, Isaac	NYK 122	Morey, Stephen	COL 179	Morgan, Jonathan	CHN 830
Morehouse see Moorehouse		Morey, Stephen	DUT 15	Morgan, Jonathan	SRA 34
& Morhous		Morey, Stephen	DUT 102	Morgan, Joseph	NYK 84
Morehouse, Aaron	SRA 13	Morey, Still	DUT 140	Morgan, Joseph	ORN 274
Morehouse, Abillebe	SRA 24	Morey, Sylvanus	OND 177	Morgan, Joseph	WSH 288
Morehouse, Andrew	COL 219	Morey, William	DUT 8	Morgan, Joseph	WST 155
Morehouse, Andrew	MNT 59	Morey, William	ONT 330	Morgan, Joshua	CHN 830
Morehouse, Andrew	NYK 63	Morfet(?), John	MNT 12	Morgan, Joshua Jur	CHN 830
Morehouse, Banks	COL 178	Morford, Elizth Free		Morgan, Lewis	CAY 584
Morehouse, Benj:	ONN 168	Black	COL 252	Morgan, Lucius	ONT 360
Morehouse, Daniel	OND 168	Morgan see Horgan		Morgan, Margaret	ONT 368
Morehouse, Daniel	ORN 350	Morgan, Abijah	CHN 864	Morgan, Nathan	HRK 569
Morehouse, Daniel	ORN 375	Morgan, Abraham	CAY 702	Morgan, Nathan	OTS 22
Morehouse, Elijah	DEL 278	Morgan, Abraham	WSH 288	Morgan, Nathaniel	ONT 372
Morehouse, Eneas	SRA 19	Morgan, Amos	HRK 432	Morgan, Peleteah	WSH 245
Morehouse, Gershom	SRA 58	Morgan, Augustus	DUT 40	Morgan, Peletiah	OTS 25
Morehouse, Hezekiah	ULS 187	Morgan, Benjamin	HRK 488	Morgan, Peter B.	DUT 63
Morehouse, Isaac	WSH 291	Morgan, Benjamin	WST 148	Morgan, Reuben	WSH 208
Morehouse, Jared	DUT 176	Morgan, Caleb	WST 122	Morgan, Sampford	CHN 776
Morehouse, Jeremiah	ORN 374	Morgan, Caleb	WST 148	Morgan, Samuel	RNS 75
Morehouse, Joel	SRA 28	Morgan, Charles	ONN 154	Morgan, Thadeus	CHN 856
Morehouse, John	HRK 437	Morgan, Charles	OTS 9	Morgan, Thadeus	CHN 866
Morehouse, John	ORN 362	Morgan, Charles	RCH 94	Morgan, Theodore	GRN 341
Morehouse, John	SRA 13	Morgan, Charles	WST 148	Morgan, Thomas	CAY 652
Morehouse, John L.	SRA 23	Morgan, Consider	DUT 51	Morgan, Thomas	NYK 52
Morehouse, Joseph	SRA 13	Morgan, Daniel	SRA 40	Morgan, Thomas	ONT 462
Morehouse, Joseph	SRA 58	Morgan, David	GRN 331	Morgan, Thomas	QNS 84
Morehouse, Mathias	NYK 70	Morgan, David	NYK 80	Morgan, Thomas	QNS 84
Morehouse, Reuben	MNT 59	Morgan, David	NYK 99	Morgan, Thos_	RNS 9

Name	Loc	Pg	Name	Loc	Pg	Name	Loc	Pg
Morgan, Walter	OTS	7	Morrell, John Junr	QNS	70	Morris, Levy	COL	216
Morgan, William	CAY	656	Morrell, Jona	OTS	27	Morris, Lewis	NYK	109
Morgan, William	HRK	432	Morrell, Joseph	QNS	76	Morris, Lewis	ONT	472
Morgan, William	HRK	489	Morrell, Robert	OTS	53	Morris, Lewis	WST	145
Morgan, William	NYK	95	Morrell, Robert	WST	148	Morris, Lyman	WSH	284
Morgan, William	NYK	95	Morrell, Thomas	ALB	9	Morris, Mary	NYK	18
Morgan, William	NYK	114	Morrell, Thomas	MNT	100	Morris, Moses	COL	212
Morgan, William	NYK	128	Morrell, Thomas	QNS	63	Morris, Moss	DEL	283
Morgan, William	OND	205	Morrell, William	NYK	138	Morris, Nathan	OTS	15
Morgan, William	ORN	324	Morres, Asahel	WSH	198	Morris, Nicholas	NYK	73
Morgan, William	ORN	383	Morrey, George	COL	207	Morris, Nicholas	NYK	74
Morgan, William	RCH	90	Morrihue, Desire	SRA	32	Morris, Nero	DUT	68
Morgin, Ephriam	WSH	225	Morril, James	QNS	67	Morris, Peter a Black	NYK	91
Morgin, John	WSH	207	Morrill, John	SCH	150	Morris, Richard	NYK	15
Morgin, Plena	OND	219	Morrill, John Jr	SCH	155	Morris, Richard	WST	119
Morgin, William	WSH	216	Morrill, Philip	QNS	78	Morris, Richard H.	NYK	29
Morgis, Charles	SCH	138	Morrill, Richard	NYK	140	Morris, Richard V.	NYK	19
Morhous see Moorehouse			Morrill, Salyer	NYK	137	Morris, Robert	COL	183
Morhous, John Junr	ESS	304	Morrill, William	NYK	53	Morris, Robert	DUT	164
Morhouse, John	CLN	158	Morrills, Benjamin	OND	182	Morris, Robert	NYK	89
Morhouse, William	CLN	158	Morriman, Ichabod	GRN	342	Morris, Robert	ONN	187
Moriatty, Peter	DUT	132	Morrin, John	NYK	131	Morris, Robt	WST	163
Morice, Bildad	SRA	3	Morris	QNS	64	Morris, Rufus	MNT	48
Morice, Jonathan	SRA	18	Morris Black	QNS	69	Morris, Samuel a Black	NYK	153
Morice, Thomas	SRA	18	Morris Negro	QNS	73	Morris, Samuel	OND	219
Moris, David	SRA	44	Morris	QNS	79	Morris, Saml	OTS	12
Moriser, Nathaniel	NYK	102	Morris	QNS	81	Morris, Solomon	WSH	288
Morison, Consider H.	SRA	52	Morris	QNS	83	Morris, Sshester	NYK	21
Morison, Edward	GRN	333	Morris, Aaron a Black	NYK	108	Morris, Sylvanus	OND	198
Morison, Hugh	SRA	17	Morris, Abraham	DUT	152	Morris, Thomas	CHN	870
Morison, Hugh	WSH	218	Morris, Abraham	NYK	105	Morris, Thomas	NYK	118
Morison, John	GRN	325	Morris, Abraham	ULS	206	Morris, Thomas	ONT	338
Morison, John	GRN	329	Morris, Abraham A.	NYK	103	Morris, Thomas	ONT	428
Morison, John	GRN	338	Morris, Andrew	NYK	16	Mo[rris?], Thomas	ORN	385
Morison, John	WSH	218	Morris, Anna	NYK	64	Morris, Thomas	WSH	288
Morison, John Junr	WSH	218	Morris, Artemus	ALB	70	Morris, Timothy	CAY	528
Morison, Nicholas	GRN	325	Morris, Arthur	ULS	213	Morris, Valentine	WST	145
Morison, Orange	GRN	339	Morris, Benjamin	NYK	58	Morris, Willeam	WSH	288
Morison, Samuel	WSH	218	Morris, Benjamin	OND	173	Morris, William	NYK	78
Morison, Walter	GRN	335	Morris, Bennet	ULS	220	Morris, Wm	OTS	15
Morisson, John A.	COL	239	Morris, Charles	ALB	9	Morris, Wm	RCK	105
Morisson, Henry	COL	238	Morris, Christian	GRN	336	Morris, Wm	SUF	64
Morley, John	CAY	694	Morris, Daniel	COL	217	Morris, Willm	WST	145
Morley, Obadiah	CAY	694	Morris, David	NYK	38	Morris, William H.	NYK	27
Morley, Thomas	CAY	694	Morris, David	OND	161	Morris, William W.	NYK	16
Morony, Thomas	NYK	30	Morris, David	OTS	8	Morrisan, James	SRA	45
Moross, Lewis	ESS	295	Morris, David	RNS	44	Morrison, Clarke	WST	159
Morrace, Andrew	GRN	326	Morris, Debborah	NYK	70	Morrison, Cornelius	DEL	278
Morre, Moses a Black	NYK	132	Morris, Eaton	NYK	128	Morrison, Daniel	ALB	26
Morrel, Abraham	QNS	61	Morris, Edward	OTS	18	Morrison, David	NYK	62
Morrel, Andrew	ALB	149	Morris, Elizabeth a			Morrison, Hamilton	ORN	294
Morrel, Jane	QNS	61	mulatto	NYK	132	Morrison, Henry	RNS	87
Morrel, Jessee	QNS	62	Morris, Gouverne_r	WST	145	Morrison, Henry	WSH	268
Morrel, John	QNS	64	Morris, Hyel	SRA	9	Morrison, James	DEL	287
Morrel, John	QNS	66	Morris, Isaac	RCK	99	Morrison, James	NYK	65
Morrel, John	WSH	218	Morris, Jacob	NYK	138	Morrison, James	NYK	95
Morrel, John	WST	118	Morris, Jacob	OTS	21	Morrison, James	NYK	130
Morrel, Jonathan &			Morris, Jacobus	ULS	205	Morrison, James	ORN	341
Abel Denton	QNS	60	Morris, James	NYK	19	Morrison, James	WSH	216
Morrel, Rachel	ALB	149	Morris, James	ULS	208	Morrison, John	ALB	32
Morrel, Richard	QNS	65	Morris, James	WST	145	Morrison, John	NYK	18
Morrel, Rivers	WST	116	Morris, Jesse	RNS	45	Morrison, John	NYK	32
Morrell, Abraham	QNS	60	Morris, John	COL	251	Morrison, John	NYK	47
Morrell, Andrw	NYK	66	Morris, John	COL	255	Morrison, John	NYK	139
Morrell, Daniel	ALB	142	Morris, John	NYK	40	Morrison, John	ORN	292
Morrell, Danl	OTS	27	Morris, John	NYK	83	Morrison, John	WST	169
Morrell, Gilbert	QNS	64	Morris, John	NYK	107	Morrison, John E.	ORN	393
Morrell, Heartman	CAY	636	Morris, John	NYK	116	Morrison, Joseph	NYK	22
Morrell, Isaac	QNS	60	Morris, John	NYK	137	Morrison, Martin	NYK	121
Morrell, Jacob	NYK	141	Morris, John	SRA	14	Morrison, Nathaniel	NYK	99
Morrell, Jacob	OTS	27	Morris, Joseph	NYK	25	Morrison, Richard a		
Morrell, John	ALB	141	Morris, Joseph	QNS	66	Black	NYK	40
Morrell, John	DUT	32	Morris, Joseph	SRA	23	Morrison, Richard	ORN	345
Morrell, John	KNG	11	Morris, Joseph	RNS	53	Morrison, Robert	NYK	40
Morrell, John	QNS	60	Morris, Josiah	ALB	91	Morrison, Roderick	OND	172
Morrell, John	QNS	62	Morris, Josiah	HRK	421	Morrison, Samuel	CAY	600
Morrell, John	QNS	70	Morris, Josiah	OND	161	Morrison, Simeon	DUT	91

Name	Loc		Name	Loc		Name	Loc
Morrison, Solomon	WSH 268		Morsell, Peter	DUT 151		Mosher, Willcox	RNS 20
Morrison, Thomas	RNS 88		Morsman, William	HRK 459		Mosher, William	WST 133
Morrison, Thomas	SRA 45		Morte, Coonradt	COL 266		Moshier, Cornelius	ALB 118
Morrison, Violet	DUT 166		Morte, Johannis	COL 266		Moshier, David	ALB 118
Morrison, William	GRN 345		Morte, Johannis Junr	COL 266		Moshier, Eliakim	COL 221
Morrison, William	NYK 54		Morten, Joel	CHN 784		Moshier, Gideon	ALB 111
Morrison, William	NYK 65		Mortigue, Orib	CHN 980		Moshier, John	ALB 111
Morrison, William	NYK 67		Mortimer, Wm	OTS 24		Moshier, Jonathan	ALB 110
Morrison, William	ORN 291		Mortinot, Genist	NYK 64		Moshier, Nathaniel	COL 221
Morrison, William	ORN 342		Morton, Abner	CHN 884		Moshier, Stephen	ALB 110
Morrison, William P.	RNS 7		Morton, Alexander	NYK 18		Mosh[ore?], Jonathan	SRA 38
Morrisson, Coenradt	COL 256		Morton, Alexander	ULS 183		Moshur, Solomon	MNT 11
Morrisson, Ephraim	ONT 358		Morton, Andrew	NYK 65		Moshure, Daniel	SRA 41
Morrisson, Jacob J.	COL 230		Morton, Jacob	NYK 149		Moshure, Elisha	WSH 189
Morrisson, James	COL 255		Morton, Joseah	WSH 275		Moshure, Henry	MNT 11
Morrisson, John	CAY 596		Morton, Levy	CHN 884		Moshure, Israel	MNT 12
Morrisson, John	COL 223		Morton, Matthias a			Moshure, Peter	MNT 1
Morrisson, Willm	COL 186		Mulatto	NYK 77		Mosier, Abner	ORN 380
Morrow see Muro & Murrow			Morton, Reuben	COL 248		Mosier, Abraham	MNT 41
Morrow, George	ORN 372		Morton, Reuben Junr	COL 249		Mosier, Absalom	DUT 117
Morrow, James	ALB 40		Morton, Simeon	ONT 320		Mosier, After	DUT 76
Morrow, John	NYK 142		Morton, Thomas	CHN 884		Mosier, Bardine	DUT 105
Morrow, Thomas	ORN 384		Morton, Thomas	NYK 30		Mosier, Benjamin	DUT 101
Morse, Aaron	OND 204		Morton, Washington	NYK 19		Mosier, Benjamin	DUT 110
Morse, Alpheus	OND 190		Morton, William	NYK 106		Mosier, Benjamin	SRA 36
Morse, Amos	COL 179		Morton, William	ORN 327		Mosier, Caleb	DUT 103
Morse, Asahel	OND 167		Morunn, Thomas	TIO 211		Mosier, Christopher	DUT 140
Morse, Asaph	ULS 251		Mory, George	CHN 760		Mosier, David	DUT 145
Morse, Benjn	CHN 876		Mory, Gideon	RNS 100		Mosier, Elijah	DUT 76
Morse, Daniel	HRK 569		Moscrip, Robert	DEL 270		Mosier, Ephraim	DUT 105
Morse, Daniel	NYK 130		Moscrip, William	DEL 270		Mosier, Ephraim	DUT 126
Morse, Daniel	OTS 14		Mose, John	NYK 120		Mosier, Eseck	DUT 106
Morse, Danl	OTS 39		Moseir see Mosher,			Mosier, .enry	MNT 56
Morse, Danl Junr	OTS 14		Mosur & Mozier			Mosier, Hiram	SRA 48
Morse, David	MNT 89		Moseir, John	CAY 668		Mosier, Ichabod	DUT 98
Morse, David	ONN 177		Moseir, Joseph	CAY 638		Mosier, Isaac	KNG 9
Morse, Elisha	DUT 118		Moseir, William	CAY 668		Mosier, Isaac	ULS 193
Morse, Gershom	CAY 670		Moseler, Joseph	COL 222		Mosier, Isreal	SRA 17
Morse, Ira	COL 181		Moseley, Elizur	OND 157		Mosier, James	DUT 103
Morse, Isaac	ESS 292		Moseley, John	CLN 157		Mosier, James	SRA 36
Morse, Jeduthan	OND 188		Moseley, Jonathan	RNS 17		Mosier, James	WST 113
M[orse?], John	ALB 132		Mosells, Alexander	MNT 26		Mosier, Jared	ORN 359
Morse, John	COL 177		Mosely, Ebenezer	WSH 212		Mosier, Joab	SRA 33
Morse, John	NYK 51		Mosely, Elisha	COL 218		Mosier, John	DUT 11
Morse, John	ONN 155		Mosely, Elisha	COL 222		Mosier, John	DUT 76
Morse, John	ONN 184		Moseman, Ebenezer	WST 135		Mosier, John	KNG 9
Morse, John	TIO 231		Moseman, Elisha	WST 142		Mosier, John	OND 180
Morse, John H.	NYK 135		Moseman, John	WST 142		Mosier, Jonathan	ALB 100
Morse, John T.	HRK 557		Moseman, Peter	WST 142		Mosier, Jonathan	DUT 10
Morse, Joseph	CHN 874		Moses Negro	QNS 73		Mosier, Jonathan	DUT 98
Morse, Joseph	COL 211		Moses	QNS 82		Mosier, Jonathan	SRA 36
Morse, J...ph	MNT 71		Moses, Enom	WSH 245		Mosier, Joseph	DUT 70
Morse, Joseph	OND 167		Moses, Isaac	NYK 20		Mosier, Joseph	DUT 98
Morse, Joshua	DUT 111		Moses, Isaac	NYK 30		Mosier, Joseph	DUT 124
Morse, Joshua	ESS 293		Moses, Jona	ONT 366		Mosier, Joseph	KNG 9
Morse, Joshua	ONN 178		Moses, Little	MNT 115		Mosier, Joseph	SRA 4
Morse, Josiah	COL 177		Moses, Parson	MNT 95		Mosier, Joseph	SRA 9
Morse, Lemuel	HRK 414		Moses, Peter	MNT 116		Mosier, Joseph	SRA 31
Morse, Peter	COL 181		Moses, Reuben	SRA 5		Mosier, Josiah	OND 180
Morse, Peter	COL 201		Moses, Shubel	ESS 292		Mosier, Lemuel	CHN 768
Morse, Philip	HRK 552		Moses, Zebulon	ONT 368		Mosier, Martha	DUT 136
Morse, Reuben	DUT 118		Moseur, John	WST 169		Mosier, Maxom	DUT 103
Morse, Robert	WST 116		Mosher, Abm	ALB 34		Mosier, Nathan	SRA 31
Morse, Rufus	MNT 53		Mosher, Abm	RNS 50		Mosier, Peter	DUT 99
Morse, Samuel	OND 207		Mosher, Adda	RNS 22		Mosier, Philip	SRA 31
Morse, Sephen	OTS 6		Mosher, Benjm	ALB 35		Mosier, Richard	DUT 128
Morse, Silas	OND 207		Mosher, Caleb	NYK 95		Mosier, Samuel	DUT 20
Morse, Staughton	ONN 139		Mosher, Daniel	RNS 40		Mosier, Samuel	DUT 105
Morse, Stephen	COL 246		Mosher, Franck Bl.	WST 153		Mosier, Samuel Junr	SRA 33
Morse, Stephen	OTS 39		Mosher, Gabriel	WSH 243		Mosier, Selah	WST 113
Morse, Theopholus	ESS 293		Mosher, Isaac	RNS 20		Mosier, Seth	ULS 227
Morse, Thomas	CLN 157		Mosher, James	WST 144		Mosier, Stephen	DUT 129
Morse, Thomas	ESS 297		Mosher, John	RNS 21		Mosier, Stephen Junr	ALB 99
Morse, Timo	OTS 39		Mosher, John	WST 130		Mosier, Thomas	DUT 128
Morse, Wait	OTS 30		Mosher, Jonathan	WST 138		Mosier, Thomas	WST 114
Morse, William	NYK 145		Mosher, Martha W.	WST 160		Mosier, Tripp	DUT 105
Morse, Zebediah	HRK 414		Mosher, Semans	WST 130			

Mower, Jacob	DUT 155	Mulford, Abm	SUF 76	Mumpford, Ezekiel	SUF 108
Mower, Jacob	ULS 221	Mulford, David	ULS 253	Mumpford, Jonathan	SUF 106
Mower, Jacob	ULS 222	Mulford, Ezekiel	ALB 53	Mumpford, Josiah	SUF 106
Mower, John	COL 259	Mulford, Ezekiel	STB 200	Mumpford, Marcey	SUF 106
Mower, John	HRK 479	Mulford, Hannah	DUT 108	Mumpford, William	SUF 106
Mower, John	ULS 222	Mulford, Jeremiah	DUT 108	Mun, Prudence	SRA 16
Mower, Lendert	ULS 223	Mulford, Jonathan	SUF 109	Muncey, Jamima	SUF 81
Mower, Nicholas	ULS 223	Mulford, Lemuel	RNS 44	Muncy, Benjamin	OND 213
Mower, Peter	ULS 220	Mulford, Matthew	ALB 84	Munday, Elijah	ULS 238
Mower, Peter Junr	ULS 223	Mulford, Nathan	SUF 70	Mundoor, Jeduthan	DUT 138
Mowers, Henry	ULS 198	Mulford, Rachel	SUF 107	Mundy, Benjn	TIO 241
Mowers, Peter	ULS 198	Mulford, Samuel	DUT 147	Mungar, Benjamin	DUT 386
Mowers, Samuel	ULS 198	Mulford, Saml	SUF 108	Mungar, David	DUT 136
Mowrey, Richard	CHN 968	Mulford, Stephen	CAY 588	Mungar, James	DUT 40
Mowrey, Silvenus	CHN 968	Mulgrove, John	CAY 722	Mungar, John	DUT 40
Moxam, Elizabeth	WSH 203	Mulhallen, Wm	STB 203	Mungar, Lemuel	DUT 96
Moyer, Anthony	COL 244	Mulheran, John	NYK 106	Mungar, Samuel	DUT 96
Moyer, Catharine	MNT 25	Mulheran, Richard	NYK 45	Mungar, Sheldon	DUT 90
Moyer, Danl	SUF 64	Mulherren, Jacob	MNT 115	Mungar, William	DUT 39
Moyer, David	MNT 22	Mulhinch, Peter	ALB 126	Munger, Amasa	CHN 960
Moyer, Garret	COL 244	Mulinox see Molineaux		Munger, Benj:	ONN 160
Moyer, Henry	MNT 26	Mulinox, Jesse	WST 119	Munger, Calvin	SRA 46
Moyer, Heny	SUF 64	Mulkin, Henry	DUT 52	Munger, Daniel B,	WSH 213
Moyer, Herdwix	MNT 55	Mulkin, John	DUT 20	Munger, Elijah	OND 193
Moyer, Jacob G.	MNT 27	Mulkins, Allen	WSH 256	Munger, Jonathan	ALB 77
Moyer, Jacob H.	MNT 27	Mulkins, Henry	ONT 316	Munger, Jonathan	CHN 950
Moye_, John D.	MNT 52	Mulkins, James	WSH 189	Munger, Nathan	OND 192
Moyer, John H.	MNT 26	Mulkins, Joseph	OTS 33	Munger, Oliver	CHN 952
Moyer, Peter	COL 235	Mulks, Benoni	ULS 200	Munger, Perley	OND 193
Moyer, Peter	MNT 26	Mull, Isaac	RNS 61	Munger, Philip	SRA 46
Moyston, John H.	ALB 11	Mull, James	ALB 122	Munger, Reuben	OND 189
Mozier, Ira	CHN 978	Mull, James	RNS 59	Munger, Salmon	SRA 42
Mozier, Josiah	COL 266	Mull, John	ALB 122	Munger, Samuel	SRA 46
Mozier, Lemuel	COL 179	M(ull)?, Thomas	MNT 116	Munger, Thomas	SRA 46
Mucelroy, John	NYK 18	Mull, Walter	RNS 61	Munger, Timothy	SRA 44
Mucklehone, William	ULS 211	Mullekin, Amos	SRA 47	Muning, John	SRA 5
Mucklehony, John	ORN 309	Mullen, James	NYK 94	Munn, Abel	HRK 558
Muckleraith, Gilbert	ULS 268	Mullen, John	ULS 209	Munn, Abner	ALB 99
Muckleroy, Alexander	ORN 385	Mullen, Michael	ULS 249	Munn, Asa	HRK 599
Muckleroy, Charles	RCK 100	Mullen, Phillip	ULS 209	Munn, David	HRK 466
Muckleroy, Daniel	ORN 287	Mullen, Thomas	NYK 24	Munn, Israel	ONN 143
Muckleroy, James	ORN 379	Mullender, Isaac	ONT 506	Munn, Jedediah	HRK 558
Muckleroy, John	ORN 287	Muller, Isaac	NYK 96	Munn, Nathan	HRK 557
Mucklevee, Henry	STB 198	Muller, John J.	COL 220	Munn, Patrick	NYK 45
Mud see Meed		Mullet, James P. A.	ONN 151	Munn, Reuben	DEL 283
Mudge, Aaron	OTS 24	Mullhullen, Daniel	ONN 172	Munn, Stephen B.	NYK 38
Mudge, Abrm	OTS 12	Mulligan, Elizabeth	NYK 61	Munn, Thomas	CAY 576
Mudge, Amasa	OTS 11	Mulligan, John	NYK 147	Munro, Abraham	OND 202
Mudge, Charles	OTS 19	Mulligan, John W.	NYK 34	Munro, David	ALB 21
Mudge, Daniel	OTS 24	Mulligan, Stephe. H.	MNT 43	Munro, Jacob	OND 205
Mudge, Daniel	QNS 70	Mullineaux, Israel	DEL 272	Munro, John	ESS 295
Mudge, David	ALB 115	Mulliner, James	NYK 74	Munro, John	NYK 23
Mudge, David Senr	ALB 115	Mullison, Timothy	ALB 112	Munro, John	SRA 29
Mudge, Ebeneser	MNT 113	Mullmine, John	ALB 40	Munro, Jonas	OND 202
Mudge, Ira	OTS 33	Mullock, Jesse	ORN 320	Munro, Joseph	WST 152
Mudge, Jacob & Wm		Mullock, William	ORN 312	Munro, Joseph Junr	WST 152
Mudge	QNS 83	Muls, Noah	SRA 46	Munro, Justice	WST 114
Mudge, James	OTS 24	Multer, Jacob	HRK 456	Munro, Lemuel	DUT 143
Mudge, Jared	OTS 24	Mulwaine, Thomas	ALB 107	Munro, Peter Jay	NYK 19
Mudge, John	CHN 802	Mum, Noah	CHN 802	Munro, Samuel	OND 180
Mudge, Joshua	OTS 24	Mumford, Antony	GRN 325	Munro, Thomas	NYK 140
Mudge, Joshua	OTS 33	Mumford, Geo.	OTS 27	Munroe, Abel A.	WST 115
Mudge, Luther	ORN 311	Mumford, George	QNS 81	Munroe, Daniel	COL 238
Mudge, Michael	ULS 186	Mumford, Gurdon S.	NYK 26	Munroe, David	HRK 530
Mudge, Rosel	OTS 24	Mumford, John	OTS 27	Munroe, David	OTS 34
Mudge, Samuel	OTS 10	Mumford, John	SUF 107	Munroe, David	WSH 267
Mudge, Wm & Jacob		Mumford, John P.	NYK 27	Munroe, Esquire	ONN 189
Mudge	QNS 83	Mumford, Joseph	OTS 27	Munroe, James	CLN 168
Muggs, John	ONT 462	Mumford, Peleg	HRK 586	Munroe, Joel	HRK 561
Muhan, Patrick	NYK 69	Mumford, Thomas	CAY 628	Munroe, John	ALB 146
Muier, John	CHN 850	Mumford, Ths	OTS 27	Munroe, John	WSH 282
Muir, James	WSH 197	Mumford, Thos G.	OTS 27	Munroe, Joshua	OTS 11
Muir, John	ALB 12	Mummy, Samuel	ONT 340	Munroe, Nathan	HRK 457
Muir, Peter	ALB 45	Mumois, Charles	SUF 90	Munroe, Noah	COL 207
Muir, William	ALB 45	Mumpford, Edward	SUF 108	Munroe, Robert	NYK 85
Muir, William	NYK 17	Mumpford, Elias	SUF 89	Munroe, Samuel	HRK 457
Muldebaugh, John	HRK 418	Mumpford, Elisha	SUF 106	Munroe, William	OTS 34

Munrow, Amos	WSH 234	Muroe, Justus	TIO 231	Murray, John	RNS 67		
Munrow, Daniel	MNT 32	Murphey, Benjamin	COL 221	Murray, John	SUF 94		
Munrow, George	SRA 33	Murphey, Gerret	QNS 67	Murray, John Junr	NYK 62		
Munrow, Jacob	MNT 50	Murphey, John	COL 228	Murray, John B.	NYK 98		
Munrow, John	MNT 77	Murphey, John	SRA 24	Murray, John K.	NYK 27		
Munrow, John	SRA 13	Murphey, John	WSH 306	Murray, John T.(?)	RCH 87		
Munrow, Reuben	WSH 210	Murphey, John Junr	COL 197	Murray, Joseph	NYK 99		
Munrow, Wm	MNT 50	Murphey, Morris	COL 216	Murray, Nancy a mulatto			
Munrow, Wm	MNT 82	Murphey, Morris	COL 222		NYK 117		
Munrow, Wm Junr	MNT 50	Murphey, Peter	ALB 141	Murray, Neil	WSH 255		
Munsel, Alaxr	SUF 64	Murphey, Philip	ALB 53	Murray, Partrick	NYK 16		
Munsel, John	SUF 64	Murphey, Samuel	COL 191	Murray, Peter	WSH 286		
Munsel, Nathl	SUF 65	Murphy, Elizabeth	NYK 108	Murray, Philo	HRK 520		
Munsel, Saml	SUF 66	Murphy, Ellenor	NYK 86	Murray, Reyer	ALB 19		
Munsell, Samuel	SUF 80	Murphy, Francis	MNT 2	Murray, Robert	NYK 85		
Munsell, Silas	SUF 81	Murphy, Henry	MNT 36	Murray, Samuel	ALB 19		
Munsell, Wm W.	ALB 105	Murphy, Isabella	NYK 27	Murray, Stephen	SUF 93		
Munsey, Daniel	HRK 415	Murphy, James	MNT 35	Murray, Thomas	NYK 103		
Munsey, Hendrick	QNS 75	Murphy, James	NYK 75	Murray, William	ORN 332		
Munsey, Isaac	SUF 94	Murphy, James	NYK 152	Murray, William	ORN 375		
Munsey, John	HRK 457	Murphy, James	OTS 6	Murray, William	WSH 204		
Munsey, Silas Junr	SUF 81	Murphy, James	QNS 66	Murrey, Alexander	ALB 40		
Munson, Anson(?)	ONT 404	Murphy, Jemima	NYK 33	Murrey, John	ALB 40		
Munson, Benjamin	OND 189	Murphy, John	NYK 54	Murrey, John	ALB 55		
Munson, Caleb	DEL 279	Murphy, John	NYK 113	Murrey, Richard	SUF 93		
Munson, Daniel	NYK 82	Murphy, John	RNS 109	Murrin, Daniel	GRN 333		
Munson, Ebenezer	DUT 136	Murphy, Joseph	NYK 62	Murrin, Daniel	GRN 341		
Munson, Edward	ONT 400	Murphy, Partrick	NYK 121	Murrin, Daniel Jun	GRN 341		
Munson, Ezra	OND 189	Murphy, Robert	HRK 465	Murrin, Nathan	GRN 343		
Munson, Hiram	ONN 144	Murphy, Robert	NYK 97	Murrin, Samuel	GRN 333		
Munson, Jacob	ORN 356	Murphy, Samuel	RNS 94	Murrin, Thomas	GRN 333		
Munson, Jacob	OTS 43	Murphy, Thomas	NYK 117	Murrow see Morrow &			
Munson, Jared	CLN 166	Murphy, Thomas	OND 158	Muro			
Munson, John	DEL 272	Murphy, Timothy	SCH 131	Murrow, Michael	ORN 306		
Munson, John	WSH 297	Murphy, William	CAY 556	Murry, Daniel	COL 203		
Munson, John Junr	WSH 297	Murphy, William	NYK 71	Murry, David	CAY 698		
Munson, John 3d	WSH 297	Murphy, William	NYK 95	Murry, Elihue	CHN 762		
Munson, Joseph	ULS 247	Murphy, William	WST 135	Murry, Elijah	ONT 448		
Munson, Leve	NYK 35	Murrain, Daniel	TIO 230	Murry, Gilbert	SRA 4		
Munson, Nathaniel	WSH 297	Murrain, Isaac	CAY 718	Murry, James	COL 249		
Munson, Samuel	OND 162	Murran see Muraan		Murry, James	MNT 109		
Munson, Silas	NYK 90	Murran, James D.	DEL 278	Murry, James	SRA 3		
Munson, Simeon	OND 174	Murray, Alexander	MNT 87	Murry, James	SCH 121		
Munson, Solomon	WSH 294	Murray, Alexander	ORN 278	Murry, John	COL 245		
Munson, Stephen	OND 174	Murray, Alexander	ORN 332	Murry, John	NYK 69		
Munson, Thadeus	ONT 426	Murray, Alexander	WSH 204	Murry, John	OND 184		
Munson, William	NYK 77	Murray, Angus	RNS 81	Murry, John	SCH 121		
Munster, Jacob	MNT 123	Murray, Anthony	MNT 113	Murry, Luther	ONT 480		
Munster, James	NYK 96	Murray, Archibald	SRA 25	Murry, Michael	COL 262		
Muraan, Micheal	CAY 636	Murray, Benjamin	DUT 67	Murry, Samuel	STB 207		
Murch, George	DUT 175	Murray, Daniel	ESS 303	Murry, Solomon	COL 196		
Murch, Richard	WSH 187	Murray, Daniel	GRN 356	Murry, Wm	MNT 122		
Murch, William	WSH 187	Murray, Daniel	HRK551½	Musgrove, Thomas	NYK 56		
Murday, James	ALB 142	Murray, Daniel	QNS 72	Mushet, John	WSH 194		
Murdoch, James	OND 199	Murray, David	RNS 81	Mushet, William	WSH 194		
Murdoch, James	ORN 338	Murray, Derick	WSH 204	Musier, George	GRN 328		
Murdock, Amos	ALB 86	Murray, George	ORN 312	Musier, John	ALB 148		
Murdock, Eliphalet	ALB 87	Murray, Hannah a mulatto		Musier, Thomas	GRN 326		
Murdock, Elisha	ALB 87		NYK 88	Musselman, Michael	ONT 378		
Murdock, Jas	ALB 12	Murray, Henry	ALB 20	Musson, Richard	OTS 22		
Murdock, James	ULS 199	Murray, Henry	QNS 72	Musson, Samuel S.	RNS 53		
Murdock, John	DEL 288	Murray, Hugh R.	NYK 77	Musson, William	OTS 22		
Murdock, Jonth	COL 207	Murray, Ichabod	HRK551½	Mustee, Mary	NYK 103		
Murdock, Lackey	ULS 253	Murray, Isaac	WSH 195	Mustic, Mathew	NYK 114		
Murdock, Marshall	NYK 125	Murray, James	NYK 95	Muston, John	NYK 62		
Murdock, Rial	ALB 84	Murray, James	ORN 333	Mute, John	SCH 164		
Murdock, Samuel	NYK 86	Murray, James	QNS 73	Mute, Peter	SCH 136		
Murdock, Samuel	WSH 224	Murray, Jasper	SRA 36	Mute, William	SCH 136		
Murdock, William	ALB 87	Murray, Jeremiah	NYK 118	Mutty, Peter	QNS 82		
Murdock, William	NYK 31	Murray, John	NYK 43	Muzey, Amos	CHN 898		
Murdock, Zerah	ALB 121	Murray, John	NYK 45	Muzey, Thadeus	CHN 856		
Murenbelt, Peter	KNG 5	Murray, John	NYK 90	Myer, Abraham	DUT 29		
Murfey, Archable	CHN 938	Murray, John	NYK 97	Myer, Abraham	ULS 224		
Murgatroy, Joseph	COL 199	Murray, John	NYK 121	Myer, Abraham	ULS 240		
Murig Not, Jacob	GRN 349	Murray, John	NYK 153	Myer, Adolph	DUT 22		
Murney, Eliza	NYK 69	Murray, John	ORN 280	Myer, Adolphus	DUT 61		
Muro, Alexander	NYK 41	Murray, John	ORN 343	Myer, Andrew	NYK 94		

Name	Loc.
Myer, Anne	ULS 223
Myer, Benjamin	DUT 157
Myer, Benjamin	ULS 224
Myer, Catherine	NYK 145
Myer, Christian	ULS 224
Myer, Chrystopher	OND 213
Myer, Cornelius	NYK 94
Myer, Cornelius C.	NYK 94
Myer, Daniel	NYK 146
Myer, Daniel	ORN 322
Myer, David	DUT 29
Myer, David	DUT 158
Myer, Ephraim	ULS 224
Myer, Esaias	ULS 219
Myer, Frederick	COL 224
Myer, Garret	DUT 155
Myer, Hendrick	DUT 155
Myer, Henry	NYK 89
Myer, Henry	ULS 219
Myer, Henry F.	MNT 40
Myer, Henry P.	DUT 159
Myer, Isaac	NYK 94
Myer, Isaac	ULS 224
Myer, Jacob	DUT 104
Myer, Jacob	NYK 153
Myer, Jacob	ORN 307
Myer, James	NYK 149
Myer, James	ORN 355
Myer, James	ULS 237
Myer, James J.	NYK 113
Myer, Johannis	ULS 223
Myer, John	DUT 33
Myer, John	NYK 94
Myer, John	NYK 153
Myer, John	ORN 322
Myer, John	ORN 347
Myer, John Junr	ORN 322
Myer, John H.	ULS 237
Myer, John J.	DUT 155
Myer, Jonas	DUT 142
Myer, Jonas Junr	DUT 142
Myer, Jonathan	ULS 222
Myer, Jonathan Junr	ULS 219
Myer, Laurence	NYK 20
Myer, Mary	ORN 322
Myer, Mathan	DUT 64
Myer, Nelly	ULS 223
Myer, Peter	DUT 34
Myer, Peter	DUT 62
Myer, Peter	DUT 131
Myer, Peter	ULS 219
Myer, Peter	ULS 224
Myer, Peter Ten Broeck	DUT 153
Myer, Phebe	DUT 33
Myer, Reuben	DUT 33
Myer, Samuel	DUT 68
Myer, Samuel	NYK 153
Myer, Simon I.	DUT 162
Myer, Stephen	SCH 128
Myer, Teunis	ULS 224
Myer, Tobias	ULS 224
Myer, Walter	COL 196
Myer, William	NYK 147
Myer, William	ULS 221
Myers see Meyers, Miers, Mirers & Myres	
Myers, Aaron	CHN 756
Myers, Abraham	NYK 31
Myers, Andrew	CAY 588
Myers, Andrew	CHN 756
Myers, Andrew	HRK 482
Myers, Anthony a mulatto	NYK 26
Myers, Charles	NYK 123
Myers, Chitlion	GRN 326
Myers, Cornelius	GRN 326
Myers, Cornelius	RNS 81
Myers, Danl	RCK 108
Myers, David	ALB 81
Myers, Dolphus	SRA 43
Myers, Frederick	HRK 437
Myers, Frederick	RNS 87
Myers, Frederck J.	SUF 101
Myers, Gabriel	CLN 157
Myers, George	MNT 98
Myers, Hazel	NYK 59
Myers, Henry	HRK 432
Myers, Henry	HRK 577
Myers, Henry	OTS 13
Myers, Henry	RNS 84
Myers, Henry Junr	RNS 84
Myers, Henry J.	HRK 435
Myers, Jacob	HRK 482
Myers, Jacob	MNT 98
Myers, Jacob S.	NYK 146
Myers, John	CAY 708
Myers, John	DEL 283
Myers, John	HRK 417
Myers, John	NYK 39
Myers, John a Black	NYK 78
Myers, John	OTS 30
Myers, John	RCK 106
Myers, John	RCK 110
Myers, John	SRA 45
Myers, John Junr	RNS 86
Myers, John Junr	RCK 110
Myers, John J.	OTS 15
Myers, Joseph	CAY 588
Myers, Joseph	HRK 439
Myers, Joseph	HRK 482
Myers, Judah A.	NYK 42
Myers, Judah H.	NYK 76
Myers, Leonard	RNS 89
Myers, Lydia	NYK 87
Myers, Maria	RCK 106
Myers, Martin	NYK 133
Myers, Mary	NYK 38
Myers, Michael	HRK 437
Myers, Michl Jr	HRK 418
Myers, Michael J.	HRK 420
Myers, Moses	COL 184
Myers, Nancy a Black	NYK 95
Myers, Nathan	OTS 30
Myers, Nicholas	HRK 463
Myers, Oliver	OTS 30
Myers, Peter	HRK 437
Myers, Peter L.	RNS 29
Myers, Richard	RCH 87
Myers, Sarah	NYK 111
Myers, Solomon	NYK 72
Myers, Thomas	NYK 106
Myers, Wm	MNT 98
Myers, Wm	RNS 30
Myers, Zebulon	NYK 131
Mygatt, Joseph	DUT 134
Mygatt, Mathew	NYK 83
Mygatt, Presson	DUT 134
Myler, Betsey	NYK 110
Myler, William	NYK 64
Mynderse, Barent	ALB 59
Mynderse, Frederick	ALB 130
Mynderse, Wilhelmus	CAY 516
Mynderts, Peter	ULS 225
Myndertse, Myndert	ULS 223
Myner, Timothy	GRN 325
Myors, Benjamin	NYK 39
Myre, John	NYK 150
Myres, George	RCK 102
Myres, Hendrick	GRN 348
Myres, Lomiche	RCK 102
Myrick, David	DUT 89
Myrick, David Junr	DUT 87
Myrick, Deborah	DUT 100
Myrick, Isaac	DUT 89
Myrick, John	DUT 89
Myrick, John	DUT 101
Myrick, Joshua	DUT 85
Mytier, Charles	ALB 21

N

Name	Loc.
N____, Joshua	CHN 758
N....., Phebe	SUF 64
Na__, Zineas	SCH 123
Nacrose, Abraham	WSH 241
Nafes, George	QNS 64
Nagel, John	DUT 69
Naillor, Peter	NYK 107
Nales, Wallis a mulatto	NYK 117
Nall, John	ULS 238
Nan a free wench	ALB 131
Nangle, James	ALB 69
Nanne, George	CAY 654
Nanney, David	ORN 367
Nanny, Jony	QNS 63
Nap, Amos	GRN 352
Nap, Ezrael	SCH 155
Nap, Gilbert	WSH 212
Nap, Milon	GRN 337
Nap, Silvenus	GRN 353
Naphy, Garret	NYK 100
Naphy, John Junr	NYK 100
Napp, Benjamin	CLN 162
Napp, Elihu K.	CHN 756
Napp, Joseph	ESS 318
Nappin, Asaph	RNS 111
Narsise, Francis a Negro	NYK 128
Narrowmer, Nathaniel	ONT 378
Nase, Cornelius	DUT 138
Nase, Johannis	ULS 218
Nase, John	DUT 138
Nase, John	ULS 235
Nase, Lawrence	ULS 232
Nase, Phillip	DUT 138
Nase, Phillip Junr	DUT 138
Nase, William	DUT 138
Nash, Aaron	SRA 13
Nash, Abner	CHN 850
Nash, Alexander	ALB 138
Nash, Alexander	HRK 553
Nash, Asor	OTS 23
Nash, Azor Junr	OTS 23
Nash, Daniel	DUT 62
Nash, Daniel	OTS 23
Nash, Danl	OTS 49
Nash, Ephraim	OND 189
Nash, Erra	SRA 21
Nash, Howell	NYK 68
Nash, Isaac	OTS 32
Nash, Jacob P.	OND 187
Nash, James	CHN 812
Nash, James	HRK 471
Nash, Jessee	SUF 90
Nash, John	CHN 768
Nash, John	CHN 808
Nash, John	NYK 131
Nash, John	SRA 13
Nash, John	SRA 34
Nash, Johnson	DEL 285
Nash, Jonathan	SRA 21
Nash, Joseph	WST 154
Nash, Josiah	COL 189
Nash, Justin	DEL 279
Nash, Marton	WSH 230
Nash, Nathanl	CHN 812
Nash, Oliver	OND 189
Nash, Ozias	WST 154
Nash, Samuel	DEL 274
Nash, Samll	SRA 13

Nash, Samuel	ULS 224	
Nash, Samuel	WST 141	
Nash, Silas	OTS 22	
Nash, Thomas	NYK 50	
Nash, Zenus	CHN 852	
Nashon, John	NYK 141	
Nathan] Negroes	CHN 932	
Gilbert]		
Nathan, Jane	NYK 16	
Nathan, Simon	NYK 24	
Nathaniel a Black	NYK 68	
Nathaniel Negro	QNS 73	
Nathaniel	SRA 33	
Nattaway, Billet	SCH 125	
Nattaway, Thomas	SCH 125	
Naught, Adam	MNT 34	
Naught, John	ONT 456	
Naught[on?], Duncan	MNT 107	
Naugle, Abrm	RCK 98	
Naugle, William	NYK 153	
Naugton, Daniel	MNT 107	
Navarro, Isaac	NYK 87	
Navarro, Isarel	NYK 121	
Navell, John	COL 262	
Navin, Robert	QNS 63	
Naw, Rene	NYK 111	
Nawlin, Samuel	SCH 144	
Naylor, Charles	NYK 64	
Ne_, Asel	ONT 502	
Neafie, John	NYK 100	
Neal see Neil, Niel &		
O. Neil		
Neal, Captn Anthy	RCH 87	
Neal, Henry	WST 115	
Neal, Ira	CHN 928	
Neal, James	NYK 71	
Neal, Joab	ALB 73	
Neal, Joseph	NYK 67	
Neal, Noah	CHN 886	
Neal, Philo	CHN 886	
Neal, Simmeon	CHN 740	
Neal, Thomas	WST 169	
Neal, Titus	RNS 103	
Neal, William	OND 194	
Neal, Zebulon	RNS 80	
Nealand, Jesse	RNS 48	
Nealand, Oliver	CHN 754	
Neally, Matthew	CHN 758	
Near, Charles	OTS 41	
Near, Conradt	MNT 20	
Near, George	MNT 34	
Near, Jacob	MNT 6	
Near, Jacob	RNS 39	
Near, Zachereas	MNT 14	
Nearing, Henry	OTS 32	
Nearing, Joseph	OTS 32	
Nearing, Zar	OTS 32	
Nearon, Sophia	NYK 62	
Neaves, Samuel	KNG 9	
Needham, Adriana	DUT 34	
Needham, Elias	DEL 282	
Needham, Ester	WSH 273	
Needham, Frances	WSH 272	
Needham, John	CHN 956	
Needham, John	NYK 43	
Needham, John a Black	NYK 132	
Needham, John	WSH 301	
Needham, William	WSH 273	
Neeland, Samuel	DEL 281	
Neeland, Timothy	DEL 282	
Neel_y, James	CAY 562	
Neelly, Edward	ORN 292	
Neelly, Edward Junr	ORN 293	
Neelly, Isaac	ORN 294	
Neelly, John	ORN 292	
Neelly, John	ORN 293	
Neelly, John	ORN 326	
Neelly, Reuben	ORN 295	
Neelly, William	ORN 293	
Neely, Abraham	HRK 447	
Neely, Abraham Junr	HRK 551	
Neely, Alexander	DUT 135	
Neely, Henry	HRK 579	
Neely, James	ORN 324	
Neely, John Junr	ORN 324	
Neely, Robert	CAY 642	
Neely, Thomas	ORN 324	
Neer, Charles	COL 243	
Neer, Frederick	COL 263	
Neer, Henry	COL 201	
Neet, Augustus	OND 199	
Nefas, William	RNS 96	
Neff, Joseph	OTS 39	
Neffen see Kniffen		
Neffen, John	SRA 50	
Neft, Adam	MNT 103	
Neft, Henry	MNT 103	
Neft, Isaac	MNT 103	
Neft, Jacob	MNT 103	
Nefus, Elijah	CHN 946	
Nefus, Peter	KNG 2	
Nefus, Rufus	KNG 4	
Negle_, DAvid	ONT 510	
Negro	QNS 65	
Negro	QNS 65	
Negro Jack	QNS 82	
Neg[rus?], Isaac	ONN 179	
Negus, Joseph	WSH 217	
Negus, Nathaniel	RNS 94	
Nehr, Charles	DUT 164	
Nehr, Francis	DUT 161	
Nehr, Frederick	DUT 158	
Nehr, George	DUT 151	
Nehr, Hannah	DUT 153	
Nehr, Henry	DUT 156	
Nehr, Henry	DUT 165	
Nehr, Jeremiah	DUT 159	
Nehr, John	DUT 156	
Nehr, John	DUT 164	
Nehr, Jost	DUT 158	
Neil see Neal		
Neil, Dennis	NYK 121	
Neil, Henry	NYK 83	
Neil, John	NYK 105	
Neillson, George	COL 244	
Neillson, Theophilas	COL 239	
Neilson, Cornelius	DUT 73	
Neilson, David	DUT 120	
Neilson, Elijah	DUT 82	
Neilson, Francis	DUT 109	
Neilson, Francis R.	DUT 109	
Neilson, Gilbert	DUT 38	
Neilson, Henry	ORN 287	
Neilson, Isaac	DUT 19	
Neilson, Jacob	DUT 73	
Neilson, James	DUT 76	
Neilson, John	DUT 65	
Neilson, John	DUT 73	
Neilson, John	WSH 290	
Neilson, Joseph	DUT 25	
Neilson, Joseph	WSH 247	
Neilson, Joseph Junr	WSH 247	
Neilson, Justus	DUT 72	
Neilson, Mephibosheth	DUT 74	
Neilson, Moses	WSH 285	
Neilson, Pheenas	DUT 72	
Neilson Reuben	DUT 41	
Neilson, Robert	NYK 57	
Neilson, Robert	WSH 249	
Neilson, Simeon	WSH 293	
Neilson, Stephen	DUT 73	
Neilson, Stephen	DUT 109	
Neilson, Thomas	DUT 65	
Neilson, William	ORN 301	
Nellis, Adam A.	MNT 3	
Nellis, David	MNT 105	
Nellis, George	HRK 454	
Nellis, George	MNT 37	
Nellis, Henry W.	MNT 18	
Nellis, Isaa	MNT 100	
Nellis, Jesse	MNT 116	
Nellis, John	MNT 4	
Nellis, John D.	MNT 25	
Nellis, John L.	MNT 16	
Nellis, John N.(?)	MNT 20	
Nellis, John W.	MNT 4	
Nellis, Joseph	MNT 2	
Nellis, Joseph	MNT 44	
Nellis, Joseph Junr	MNT 2	
Nellis, Ludwig	MNT 16	
Nellis, Peter	MNT 2	
Nellis, Peter H.	MNT 11	
Nellis, Peter M.	MNT 19	
Nellis, Philip Junr	MNT 17	
Nellis, Robert	OTS 56	
Nellis, Wm	MNT 2	
Nellis, Wm Junr	MNT 17	
Nellson, Allen	MNT 61	
Nellson, John	COL 261	
Nellson, Thomas	QNS 66	
Nelson, Ann	ALB 73	
Nelson, Bloman	GRN 353	
Nelson, Ely	GRN 352	
Nelson, Ethelanah	SRA 43	
Nelson, James	NYK 84	
Nelson, James	NYK 103	
Nelson, John	ALB 85	
Nelson, John	HRK 466	
Nelson, John	ONT 328	
Nelson, John	SRA 46	
Nelson, Jonathan	SCH 145	
Nelson, Joshua	SRA 47	
Nelson, Joshua	WST 156	
Nelson, Josiah	OTS 6	
Nelson, Levi	GRN 341	
Nelson, Paul	HRK 576	
Nelson, Partrick	NYK 135	
Nelson, Roger	ALB 73	
Nelson, Samuel	ONT 340	
Nelson, Thomas	MNT 59	
Nelson, William	NYK 68	
Nelson, William	NYK 131	
Nelson, William	NYK 149	
Nema, John	ALB 143	
Nemiah, Henry	ALB 143	
Nemmo_, Alexander	NYK 52	
Neptune	QNS 83	
Ner...g	MNT 67	
Nerman, William	GRN 341	
Nesbit, Archabald	NYK 89	
Nesbit, Samuel	NYK 72	
Nesbit, William	QNS 66	
Nesbitt, James	NYK 68	
Nesbitt, John	KNG 10	
Nesler, John	SRA 10	
Nessler, Barent	SRA 6	
Nestel, Michael	NYK 69	
Nestell, Adam	NYK 121	
Nestells, Christian	NYK 52	
Nestle, Christian	ALB 62	
Nestle, Gotleib	MNT 6	
Nestle, Henry	MNT 16	
Nestler, John	ONT 424	
Nestler, Michael	NYK 134	
Neth_ton, effeny	MNT 81	
Netherway, Ebenezar	SUF 86	
Netherway, James	SUF 86	
Netherway, William	SUF 86	
Netting, Joseph	NYK 63	
Nettleton, Abel	ONT 314	
Nettleton, Philemon	ONT 314	

Name	Ref	Name	Ref	Name	Ref
Nicherson, Mercy	DUT 116	Nichols, Eleazer	WSH 267	Nichols, Wm	MNT 14
Nicherson, Thomas	DUT 116	Nichols, Eleazer	WSH 267	Nichols, William	NYK 71
Nichol, Augustus	NYK 34	Nichols, Elezer	CLN 155	Nichols, William	NYK 91
Nichol, Cade	SUF 105	Nichols, Elijah	DUT 56	Nichols, William	NYK 127
Nichol, George	WST 115	Nichols, Elisha	WSH 305	Nichols, William	QNS 74
Nichol, Mary	NYK 106	Nichols, Enos	OND 191	Nichols, William	WSH 183
Nichol, Richard a Black	NYK 101	Nichols, Ezra	DEL 287	Nichols, Wright	QNS 71
Nichol, Selva a Black	NYK 111	Nichols, Ezra	OTS 24	Nichols, Zopher	NYK 124
Nicholas	QNS 82	Nichols, George	NYK 28	Nicholson, Andrew	ORN 291
Nicholas A Free Negro	WST 112	Nichols, George	ONT 466	Nicholson, Benjamin	NYK 152
Nicholas, Ezepheniah	GRN 333	Nichols, George B.	RNS 21	Nicholson, Daniel	ONT 502
Nicholas, John	MNT 21	Nichols, Gershem	WSH 219	Nicholson, James	NYK 150
Nicholas, John	SCH 164	Nichols, Henry	DUT 88	Nicholson, Jared	OND 174
Nicholas, John	TIO 231	Nichols, Henry	NYK 91	Nicholson, John	ORN 294
Nicholas, Joseph	NYK 54	Nichols, How	OND 183	Nicholson, Jonathan	OND 179
Nicholas, Thomas	MNT 92	Nichols, Isaac	CHN 976	Nicholson, Mary	ORN 285
Nicholds, James	CAY 704	Nichols, Isaac	GRN 330	Nicholson, Nicholas	DEL 271
Nicholds, Nathan	RNS 51	Nichols, Isaac	KNG 9	Nicholson, Thomas	ORN 288
Nichole, Jessee	SUF 90	Nichols, Isaac	ONT 466	Nicker, Thomas	NYK 18
Nicholes, Caleb	OND 207	Nichols, James	CHN 750	Nickerson, Abijah	CHN 758
Nicholes, Daniel	CHN 852	Nichols, James	WSH 219	Nickerson, Asael	GRN 346
Nicholes, John	OND 207	Nichols, James B.	CHN 750	Nickerson, Bassett	DUT 168
Nicholl, Deborah	SUF 93	Nichols, Jeremiah	QNS 70	Nickerson, Danl	OTS 39
Nicholl, Francis	ALB 97	Nichols, John	CHN 750	Nickerson, Edward	CHN 838
Nicholl, Henry	SUF 93	Nichols, John	CHN 798	Nickerson, Edward	DUT 177
Nicholl, Isaac	SUF 90	Nichols, John	DUT 56	Nickerson, Eliphaz	ALB 70
Nicholl, Jesse	ALB 88	Nichols, John	HRK 514	Nickerson, Isaac	WST 143
Nicholl, Joel	ALB 88	Nichols, John	ONT 502	Nickerson, Issachar	DUT 167
Nicholl, Paul	SUF 90	Nichols, John	ORN 281	Nickerson, Jabez	DUT 177
Nicholl, Robt	SUF 90	Nichols, John	QNS 80	Nickerson, Johnathan	GRN 343
Nicholl, Samuel B.	SUF 105	Nichols, John	RNS 33	Nickerson, Jonathan	DUT 52
Nicholl, William	ONT 430	Nichols, John	RNS 68	Nickerson, Joshua	DUT 171
Nichollas, John E.	NYK 91	Nichols, John	RNS 92	Nickerson, Levi	ALB 110
Nicholls, Benjm	COL 206	Nichols, John	TIO 260	Nickerson, Moltroup	DUT 171
Nicholls, Eliakim	ALB 88	Nichols, John	WSH 217	Nickerson, Nathan	DUT 174
Nicholls, Eliakim	COL 186	Nichols, John	WSH 305	Nickerson, Nathaniel	DUT 174
Nicholls, Elial	OTS 47	Nichols, Jonathan	CHN 836	Nickerson, Seth	ALB 110
Nicholls, Enoch	ALB 88	Nichols, Jonathan	ONN 139	Nickerson, Seth	DUT 171
Nicholls, Jonathan	ALB 88	Nichols, Jonathan	WSH 216	Nickerson, Sillick	WST 155
Nicholls, Jona	OTS 31	Nichols, Jonothan	CHN 780	Nickerson, Elihu	SRA 26
Nicholls, Nona	OTS 35	Nichols, Joseph	DUT 57	Nickeson, Joseph	CHN 756
Nicholls, Martin	OTS 35	Nichols, Joseph	NYK 149	Nickeson, Robert	SRA 26
Nicholls, Nicholas	COL 253	Nichols, Joseph	OND 179	Nickesson, James	SUF 102
Nicholls, Samuel	COL 246	Nichols, Joseph Junr	OND 179	Nickhales, Hesikiah	MNT 123
Nicholls, Saml	OTS 37	Nichols, Josiah	DUT 85	Nickinson, William	SRA 24
Nicholls, Samuel	SUF 92	Nichols, Lewis	OND 190	Nickle, Andries	DUT 163
Nicholls, Thaddeus	ALB 88	Nichols, Martin	CLN 168	Nickle, John	DUT 166
Nicholls, William	SUF 94	Nichols, Moses	ORN 284	Nickleson, Israel	OTS 54
Nichols, Abraham	DEL 270	Nichols, Nathan	HRK 408	Nicknels, John	CHN 750
Nichols, Abraham	ESS 318	Nichols, Nathaniel	OND 181	Nickoles, John	WST 142
Nichols, Abraham	WSH 286	Nichols, Perry G.	SRA 52	Nickolls, John	RNS 66
Nichols, Albert	DUT 72	Nichols, Philep	WSH 219	Nickols, Daniel	WST 159
Nichols, Allen	WSH 224	Nichols, Reuben	ULS 268	Nickols, Jesse	RNS112A
Nichols, Alexander	ONT 466	Nichols, Robert	NYK 46	Nickols, John	RNS 54
Nichols, Benjamin	CHN 750	Nichols, Robert	ULS 183	Nickols, John	RCH 92
Nichols, Benjamin	ESS 309	Nichols, Roswell	OND 189	Nickols, John Junr	RCH 89
Nichols, Benjamin	HRK 559	Nichols, Samuel	ALB 86	Nickols, Levi	RNS 25
Nichols, Benjamin	ONT 494	Nichols, Samuel	CHN 750	Nickson, Aaron	STB 200
Nichols, Benjamin Junr	RNS 43	Nichols, Samuel	MNT 122	Nickson, Ezra	CHN 756
Nichols, Caleb	CLN 165	Nichols, Samuel	OND 181	Niclsie, Ester	NYK 38
Nichols, Caleb	NYK 149	Nichols, Samuel	OND 182	Nicolas, Abel	RNS 54
Nichols, Caleb	TIO 245	Nichols, Samuel	ORN 284	Nicolds, Rowland	RNS 25
Nichols, Caleb	WSH 240	Nichols, Samuel	QNS 74	Nicoll, Jacob a mulatto	NYK 123
Nichols, Catherine	NYK 136	Nichols, Samuel Junr	OND 182	Nicoll, John D.	ORN 286
Nichols, Cyrus	OND 191	Nichols, Silas	GRN 355	Nicoll, Leonard	ORN 287
Nichols, Daniel	ALB 25	Nichols, Simeon	TIO 245	Nicolls, Benjamin	QNS 74
Nichols, Daniel	DEL 278	Nichols, Simon	MNT 6	Nicolls, Gideon	QNS 73
Nichols, Daniel	OND 180	Nichols, Thomas	CLN 155	Nicolls, John	OND 168
Nichols, Daniel	WSH 286	Nichols, Thomas	OND 197	Nicolls, Nathan	RNS 25
Nichols, David	CHN 836	Nichols, Thos	TIO 250	Nicolls, Samuel Junr	COL 248
Nichols, David	CHN 968	Nichols, Timothy	WSH 293	Nicolls, Sisson	RNS 100
Nichols, David	DUT 10	Nichols, Walter	NYK 46	Nicolls, William	QNS 73
Nichols, David	OND 182	Nichols, Wanton	HRK 559	Nicols, Benjamin	RNS 43
Nichols, David	OTS 47	Nichols, William	CHN 782	Nicols, Hagar a Black	NYK 41
Nichols, David	WSH 233	Nichols, William	DUT 26	Nicols, James	NYK 65
Nichols, Ebenezer	OND 196	Nichols, William	DUT 81	Niels, Hezekiah	SCH 166
		Nichols, William	HRK 449	Nielson, Ezekial	WSH 294

Norten, David Jur	CHN 912	Northrop, Nathan	WST 155	Norton, Henry	WST 125
Norten, William	CHN 902	Northrop, Thomas	HRK 587	Norton, Isaac	GRN 338
North, Aaron	ESS 303	Northrop, Thomas	WST 155	Norton, Isaac	GRN 338
North, Abijah	CLN 171	Northrop, Tibbets	WSH 271	Norton, Isaac	HRK 598
North, Asel	ONN 162	Northroup, Amos	DUT 22	Norton, Isaac	RNS 43
North, Benjamin	COL 221	Northroup, Daniel	DUT 102	Norton, Jacob	RNS 43
North, Benjamin	NYK 121	Northroup, Enos	DUT 102	Norton, Jacobus	SUF 66
North, Benjn	OTS 6	Northroup, John	DUT 102	Norton, James	HRK 560
North, Daniel	OTS 6	Northroup, Joseph	DUT 92	Norton, James	OTS 23
North, Daniel	QNS 60	Northroup, Joseph	DUT 166	Norton, James	ULS 239
North, Daniel	ULS 198	Northroup, Moses	DUT 90	Norton, Jeremiah	WSH 281
North, Gabriel	DEL 277	Northroup, Nathaniel	DUT 139	Norton, Joel	CAY 674
North, James	ORN 388	Northroup, Samuel	DUT 139	Norton, Joel	GRN 338
North, Joel	ONN 162	Northroup, Samuel Junr	DUT 139	Norton, Joel	WSH 276
North, John	MNT 83	Northroup, Stephen	DUT 91	Norton, John	HRK 552
North, John D.	ULS 197	Northroup, William	DUT 102	Norton, John	NYK 151
North, John S.	ULS 197	Northroup, William	DUT 139	Norton, John	ONN 175
North, Jno & Robt	COL 217	Northrup, Abraham	SRA 24	Norton, John	OTS 35
North, Margaret	NYK 47	Northrup, Asa	CHN 800	Norton, John	TIO 213
North, Noah	HRK 530	Northrup, Benjamin	CHN 810	Norton, John	WSH 233
North, Orsimus	ULS 197	Northrup, Benjamin	OND 200	Norton, John Junr	WSH 232
North, Robert	CHN 980	Northrup, Caleb	ONN 137	Norton, Jonathan	WSH 231
North, Robt & Jno	COL 217	Northrup, Caleb	SRA 28	Norton, Joseph	WSH 281
North, Robert	DEL 277	Northrup, Clark	WSH 272	Norton, Medad	CAY 704
North, Robert	DUT 67	Northrup, Daniel	SRA 26	Norton, Nathan	DEL 269
North, Robert	ULS 198	Northrup, Desire	DUT 169	Norton, Nathl	HRK 582
North, Saml	OTS 13	Northrup, Eli	SRA 23	Norton, Nathaniel	ONT 404
North, Samuel	ULS 197	Northrup, Isaac	DUT 169	Norton, Nathl	SUF 66
North, Sebastian	NYK 56	Northrup, Jabez	SRA 26	Norton, Noah	ONT 358
North, Semeon	ESS 294	Northrup, Joel	CHN 806	Norton, Oliver	CHN 906
North, Stephen	ESS 293	Northrup, John	OND 200	Norton, Oliver	WSH 249
North, Stephen	OTS 13	Northrup, Lewis	SRA 28	Norton, Peter	OND 194
North, Thomas	CAY 618	Northrup, Needham	RNS 99	Norton, Phinehas	ONN 168
North, Thomas	CHN 808	Northrup, Remington	OND 199	Norton, Richard	WSH 232
North, Thomas	ONN 163	Northrup, Stephen	CHN 810	Norton, Robert	HRK 546
North, Thomas	ONN 163	Northrup, Thaddeus	SRA 26	Norton, Robert B.	NYK 151
North, Thomas	ORN 392	Northrup, William	OND 199	Norton, Russel	GRN 340
North, William	ALB 35	Northrup, Wilson	SRA 23	Norton, Samuel	ALB 130
Northam, Assa	WSH 278	Northway, Gaus	ALB 84	Norton, Samuel	CAY 726
Northam, Ebenezer	WSH 305	Northway, Rufus	OND 178	Norton, Samuel	OND 182
Northaway, Zenus	ALB 70	Norton, Aaron	CLN 158	Norton, Samuel	SRA 42
North hu, John	MNT 53	Norton, Aaron	ONT 398	Norton, Samuel	SRA 60
Northop, Abrahan	ONN 130	Norton, Aaron	OTS 55	Norton, Sebe	CHN 792
Northop, Samuel	SRA 4	Norton, Aaron	WSH 265	Norton, Sinus	OND 176
Northorp, Joel	RNS 39	Norton, Aaron Ju.	ONT 398	Norton, Solomon	WSH 195
Northorp, Moses	NYK 130	Norton, Abel	COL 187	Norton, Stephen	OTS 24
Northorp, Unis	NYK 126	Norton, Abroes	GRN 338	Norton, Theodore	COL 208
Northrige, Eldrige	MNT 61	Norton, Ambroes	GRN 338	Norton, Thomas	OND 174
Northrip, Joseph	DEL 267	Norton, Andrew	COL 207	Norton, Timy	SUF 68
Northrip, Joseph	WSH 201	Norton, Asac	GRN 342	Norton, William	ALB 49
Northrip, Joseph P.	SCH 141	Norton, Asahel S.	OND 199	Norton, William	COL 207
Northrip, Nicholas	RNS 99	Norton, Asher	CAY 702	Norton, William	WSH 187
Northrop, Abraham	MNT 92	Norton, Benjamin	HRK 574	Norton, William	WSH 281
Northrop, Caleb	CLN 156	Norton, Benjn	OTS 24	Norton, William	WSH 285
Northrop, Christopher	SRA 5	Norton, Benjamin	SRA 53	Norton, Wm W.	COL 207
Northrop, Cornwell	ALB 74	Norton, Benjn	TIO 213	Norton, Winthroup	DUT 149
Northrop, David	COL 266	Norton, Briant	SUF 66	Norton, Zebulon	ONT 362
Northrop, David	WST 155	Norton, Caleb	DUT 148	Norton, Zenas	OND 177
Northrop, Elam	ALB 74	Norto., Christopher	MNT 31	Nortrip, Andrew	SCH 140
Northrop, Elijah	OND 207	Norton, Clarissa	ONT 384	Nortrip, William	WSH 199
Northrop, Emanl	OTS 28	Norton, Clark	WSH 199	Norvel, Jane	ORN 396
Northrop, Emanuel Junr	OTS 27	Norton, Dan	GRN 338	Norway, Anthony	NYK 142
Northrop, Enoch	GRN 358	Norton, David	DEL 269	Norwood, Andrew	NYK 25
Northrop, Gideon	OND 200	Norton, David	SRA 18	Norwood, Andrew S.	NYK 36
Northrop, Isaac	COL 246	Norton, Eber	ONT 404	Norwood, Benjamin	NYK 42
Northrop, Isaac	GRN 335	Norton, Edward	ALB 23	Norwood, David	COL 240
Northrop, Isaac	WST 153	Norton, El_an	GRN 345	Norwood, Francis	TIO 244
Northrop, Job	ONT 362	Norton, Elijah	ONN 171	Norwood, Jacob	COL 236
Northrop, Joel	ONT 356	Norton, Elijah	WSH 195	Norwood, Richard	NYK 42
Northrop, John	OTS 2	Norton, Elijah	WSH 279	Nostrand, Caty	QNS 68
Northrop, John	WST 155	Norton, Elizabeth	WST 111	Nostrand, Cornelius	KNG 7
Northrop, John H.	WSH 291	Norton, Elnathan	TIO 213	Nostrand, Elizabeth	QNS 68
Northrop, Lewis	SRA 19	Norton, Francis	CHN 962	Nostrand, Foster	NYK 145
Northrop, Lewis	SRA 22	Norton, Geo.	OTS 18	Nostrand, Jacobus	SUF 79
Northrop, Lewis	WST 153	Norton, George	SUF 68	Nostrand, James	SUF 82
Northrop, Lewis	WST 161	Norton, Gideon	OTS 15	Nostrand, Nathaniel	QNS 68
Northrop, Moses	ONN 130	Norton, Giles	CAY 704	Nostrand, Peter	QNS 68

Nostrand, Peter	SUF 80	Nugent, Minchen	NYK 79	Oakley, Jacob	SUF 94
Nostrand, Peter Junr	SUF 80	Nugent, Richard	NYK 119	Oakley, James	NYK 28
Nostrand, Ram	QNS 68	Nukerk see New Kirk		Oakley, James	RNS 35
Nostrand, Timothy	NYK 34	Nukerk, John	NYK 26	Oakley, James	SUF 82
Nostrandt, Daniel	NYK 130	Numans, Shubb	GRN 349	Oakley, Jared	HRK 464
Nostrandt, George	NYK 108	Numon, Israel	SRA 56	Oakley, Jeremiah	ORN 321
Nostrandt, Gerret	QNS 69	Nuoll, Alexander	NYK 22	Oakley, Jesse	DUT 7
Nostrandt, John	SUF 80	Nuron, Charles	MNT 124	Oakley, Jesse	NYK 135
Nostrant, Frederick	QNS 72	Nurse, Caleb	CHN 752	Oakley, Jesse	RCH 94
Nostrant, Garret	NYK 138	Nut, David	ALB 136	Oakley, John	NYK 71
Nostrant, George	QNS 65	Nute, Obid	CHN 896	Oakley, John	NYK 71
Nostrant, Jacob	QNS 72	Nutman, Isaac	ALB 9	Oakley, John	NYK 96
Nostrant, James	QNS 72	Nutmeg, Derck	MNT 67	Oakley, John	ORN 324
Nostrant, John	ALB 23	Nutt, David	OND 195	Oakley, John	SUF 79
Nostrant, John	QNS 68	Nutt, Eunice	DUT 147	Oakley, John	ULS 203
Nostrant, John	QNS 72	Nutt, Henry	OND 195	Oakley, John	WST 153
Nostrunt, Daniel	QNS 78	Nutt, Robert	OND 195	Oakley, John	WST 169
Nostrunt, Daniel	QNS 78	Nutter, Valentine	NYK 153	Oakley, John Junr	SUF 80
Nostrunt, Daniel	QNS 79	Nutting, Simeon	OND 179	Oakley, Joseph	WST 147
Nostrunt, David	QNS 81	Nutting, Simmeon	CHN 838	Oakley, Moses	NYK 152
Nostrunt, Garret	QNS 79	Nutting, Stephen	OND 192	Oakley, Nathaniel	QNS 69
Nostrunt, George	QNS 79	Nye, Benjamin	HRK 575	Oakley, Nathaniel	RCH 90
Nostrunt, Isaac	QNS 81	Nye, Benj:	ONN 164	Oakley, Nehemiah	COL 228
Nostrunt, Jacob	QNS 75	Nye, Caleb	ONT 360	Oakley, Nehemiah	DUT 5
Nostrunt, John	QNS 75	Nye, Ichabod	HRK 487	Oakley, Nehemiah	DUT 78
Nostrunt, John	QNS 75	Nye, Joshua	HRK 515	Oakley, Peleg	SUF 82
Nostrunt, John	QNS 81	Nye, Nathan	ONT 360	Oakley, Phoebe	SUF 91
Nostrunt, Peter	QNS 81	Nye, Silas	ONT 360	Oakley, Richard	SUF 79
Notch, William	NYK 93	Nye, Stephen	ULS 239	Oakley, Saml	SUF 79
Notrage	GRN 335	Nye, Sylvanus	DUT 133	Oakley, Samuel	WST 150
Nott see Naught		Nyhoff, John	MNT 9	Oakley, Solomon	DUT 121
Nott, Eliphalet	ALB 129	Nymham, Henry	WSH 306	Oakley, Solomon Junr	DUT 121
Nott, Epharous	ONT 426			Oakley, Stephen	SRA 35
Nott, John	NYK 57	O		Oakley, Stephen	WST 147
Nottingham, John	HRK 507			Oakley, Thomas	WST 148
Nottingham, Margaret	ULS 203	O..n., Parre.	MNT 21	Oakley, Thomas	WST 153
Nottingham, Stephen	ULS 254	O..w.ll, Ebenz	TIO 232	Oakley, Timothy	DUT 85
Nottingham, William	ULS 204	Oachley, James	HRK 549	Oakley, Timothy	ORN 336
Notts, Medad	CHN 974	Oak, Jesse	OTS 41	Oakley, Wm	RNS 30
Nought, Abraham	ONT 456	Oak, Saml	OTS 41	Oakley, William	WST 126
Nourse, Thomas	NYK 75	Oakden, Joseph	NYK 42	Oakley, Wm Junr	RNS 30
Novel, John	SRA 8	Oake, Charity	NYK 97	Oakley, Wilmot	QNS 75
Novell, John	SRA 12	Oakely, Andrew	QNS 69	Oaks, Abraham	OND 204
Nowell, Samuel	CLN 170	Oakely, Zedeah	WST 169	Oaks, Ebenr	OTS 57
Nower, Henry	MNT 110	Oakes, Ephiram	SUF 85	O ks, Jonathan	ONT 476
Nowles, Samuel	DEL 267	Oakes, Henry	NYK 95	Oaks, Stephen	RNS112A
Nowley, Joseph	ONT 402	Oakes, Job	RNS 61	Oaky, Martin	NYK 145
Nowlin, Mathew	NYK 118	Oakes, John,	SUF 67	Oals, Isaac	OND 202
Noxon, Barthw	ALB 53	[Oak?]es, Samuel	ONT 476	Oar, Adam	DEL 271
Noxon, Bartholomew	DUT 48	Oakes, Simon	SUF 82	Oarlop, Peter	MNT 47
Noxon, Bartholomew	RNS 63	Oakes, Thomas	NYK 30	Oates, Isaac	OTS 25
Noxon, Benjamin	DUT 13	Oakey, Abraham	ALB 133	Oates, James	SRA 60
Noxon, Gilbert	DUT 18	Oakey, Jacob	ALB 54	Oathout, Abraham	ALB 5
Noxon, Hannah	DUT 43	Oakey, John	ALB 131	Oathout, Andrew	ALB 145
Noxon, James	DUT 28	Oakhouse, Jere.	SUF 96	O.th.ut, Conrod	MNT 42
Noxon, Pasco	ALB 62	Oakley, Abraham	COL 228	Oathout, Evert	ALB 42
Noxon, Peter	DUT 53	Oakley, Amos	SUF 81	Oathout, Henry	ALB 49
Noxon, Robert	DUT 14	Oakley, Augustus	ORN 324	Oathout, Humphrey	ALB 42
Noxon, Robert	DUT 64	Oakley, Benjamin	NYK 71	Oathout, John	ALB 42
Noxon, Thomas	RNS 63	Oakley, Benjamin	NYK 88	Oathout, Myndert	ALB 98
Noyce, Asa	COL 262	Oakley, Benjamin	WST 117	Oathout, Volkert	ALB 49
Noyce, Samuel	COL 202	Oakley, Cornelius	WST 117	Oathout, Volkert D.	ALB 12
Noyce, William Junr	COL 191	Oakley, Daniel	SUF 81	Oatman, Benjamen Jur	WSH 265
Noyes, Amos B.	OND 213	Oakley, David	WST 146	Oatman, David	WSH 289
Noyes, Eunice	DUT 90	Oakley, Elephalet	SUF 80	Oats, John	CLN 173
Noyes, Hatch	DUT 94	Oakley, Elisha	COL 228	Obe	QNS 82
Noyes, John	COL 202	Oakley, George	NYK 116	Obediah	QNS 82
Noyes, John	OTS 39	Oakley, George P.	DUT 63	Obert, John	CAY 670
Noyes, Jonathan	ORN 276	Oakley, Gilbert	COL 228	Obils, Michael	MNT 105
Noyes, Moses	DUT 135	Oakley, Gilbert	DUT 22	O. Blane, Patrick	ALB 54
Noyes, Moses	OTS 51	Oakley, Gilbert	WST 116	Oblemus, Barnet	NYK 100
Noyes, Nehemh	OTS 26	Oakley, Henry	CAY 676	Oblenis, Garret	RCK 106
Noyes, Saml	OTS 26	Oakley, Henry	SUF 82	Oblenis, Hendrick	RCK 106
Nu___, Nathan	MNT 85	Oakley, Isaiah	ULS 198	Oblenis, Peter	RCK 106
Nucomb see Newcomb		Oakley, Israel	RCH 94	OBlenus, Albert	KNG 2
Nucomb, Eleazer	ONT 476	Oakley, Israel	SUF 84	Oblinus, Henry	WST 147
Nugent, Edmond	NYK 88	Oakley, Jacob	ORN 276	OBrian, Jeremiah	SCH 145

Name	Loc	No	Name	Loc	No	Name	Loc	No
Ogh, George	MNT	23	Olin, Daniel	CHN	956	Olmsted, David	COL	185
Ogh, Peter	MNT	23	Olin, James	OND	207	Olmsted, Elijah	SRA	26
Ogilvie, Gabriel	NYK	89	Olin, William	OTS	29	Olmsted, Elijah Jun	SRA	26
Ogilvie, Margaret	NYK	28	Olindorf, Daniel	MNT	37	Olmsted, Jabes	WSH	297
Ogle, John	NYK	121	Oliphant, Duncan	SRA	16	Olmsted, Jabis	GRN	345
Oglen, Abraham	MNT	108	Oliphant, James	SRA	11	Olmsted, James	RNS	49
Oglivel_, James	MNT	105	Oliphant, Peter	SRA	13	Olmsted, Jeddedeah	WSH	287
Ogsbury, Alexander	NYK	27	Olis, William	WSH	258	Olmsted, Jesse	OND	181
Ogsbury, Alexander	NYK	53	Olivant, Peter	HRK	486	Olmsted, John	WSH	286
Oham, Flora a Black	NYK	40	Olive, Mary	NYK	49	Olmsted, Joseph	SRA	35
OHara, Henry	NYK	30	Olive, Nicholas	NYK	145	Olmsted, Justus	SRA	35
OHara, John	CAY	640	Oliver	QNS	65	Olmsted, Mahittabel	ALB	95
OHare, Hugh	NYK	145	Oliver, Aaron	ALB	109	Olmsted, Mala	OND	181
OHarity, Partrick	NYK	114	Oliver, Aaron	RNS	54	Olmsted, Moses	COL	225
Oharrow, James	MNT	91	Oliver, David	CAY	568	Olmsted, Nathan	WST	158
Ohg, G.orge Junr	MNT	23	Oliver, Evert	ALB	109	Olmsted, Nathl	COL	205
OHonaghy, Patrick	ALB	13	Oliver, Edward	CAY	574	Olmsted, Nehemiah	GRN	345
Oisterbank, Adam	GRN	357	Oliver, Ellich	NYK	114	Olmsted, Richard	GRN	344
O Keefe, Daniel	COL	261	Oliver, Isaac	NYK	143	Olmsted, Samuel	WST	159
Okerman, John	NYK	60	Oliver, Jacob	ALB	99	Olmsted, Stephen	RNS	56
Okey, Hendrick	KNG	4	Oliver, Jacobus	ALB	99	Olmsted, Timothy	OND	157
Okey, Jane	KNG	4	Oliver, James	NYK	106	Olmsted, Willm Junr	COL	202
Okie, Abraham	NYK	21	Oliver, James	ULS	204	Olney, Benjn	TIO	239
Okley, Benjamin	SRA	7	Oliver, John	ALB	106	Olney, Daniel	ONN	179
Olcot, James	ONN	130	Oliver, John	ALB	147	Olney, John	CAY	644
Olcot(?), Joseph	OND	208	Oliver, John	NYK	109	Olney, Joseph	MNT	12
Olcot, Nathaniel	NYK	27	Oliver, John	SRA	17	Olney, Nathaniel	CAY	642
Olcott, Abel	ONN	147	Oliver, John Junr	ALB	109	Olney, Stephen	NYK	66
Olcott, Ezekiel	OND	176	Oliver, Mary	NYK	84	Olney, Thomas	OTS	31
Olcott, Hezikiah	ONN	148	Oliver, Richard	ALB	142	Olney, William	OND	207
Olcott, Nathaniel	CAY	596	Oliver, Richard	ULS	206	Olney, Zelotus	TIO	248
Olcott, Noadiah	ONN	147	Oliver, Richard N.	NYK	117	Olnie, Nicolas	NYK	152
Olcott, Phinehas	DUT	99	Oliver(?), Robert	CAY	542	Olshaver, Stephen	MNT	50
Olcott, Samuel	ALB	71	Oliver, Robert	WSH	195	Olts, Martin	ORN	271
Olcott, Thoms	ONN	147	Oliver, Thomas	NYK	119	Olvoord, Ira	CHN	940
Olcut, Thomas	WSH	279	Oliver, Thomas	ORN	337	Olvord, Benjaman	CHN	934
Olcutt, Josiah	COL	251	Oliver, William	NYK	102	Olvord, Elisha	COL	212
Oldboy, Sihy a Black	NYK	39	Oliver, William	NYK	134	Omick, Stephen	RCH	91
Older, Jonathan	WSH	248	Oliver, Willm	SCH	129	Ommerman, Aurt	RCK	104
Older, Thomas	WSH	234	Olivet, David	DUT	103	Ompsey, Thomas	MNT	71
Older, William	DUT	29	Olivie, Laurence	CLN	169	Omsbeaury, Isaac	CHN	900
Oldfield, Elias	ORN	321	Ollwood, Joseph	GRN	337	Omsted, David	WST	140
Oldfield, George	ORN	327	Olman, Benjamin	WSH	264	Omsted, Mary	NYK	89
Oldfield, Jane	QNS	68	Olmstead, Abraham	MNT	88	Onbesock, John	ALB	67
Oldfield, William	ORN	322	Olmstead, Ambrose	CAY	694	Onderdonk, ...t	QNS	71
Oldis, John	RCK	108	Olmstead, Benjamin	ALB	127	Onderdonk, ..orge	QNS	72
Oldman, Christoph	MNT	48	Olmstead, Benjamin	ULS	192	Onderdonk, Hendrick	QNS	70
Oldridge, Gersham	SUF	74	Olmstead, Coleman	CAY	586	Onderdonk, John	NYK	40
Oldridge, Jacob	SUF	74	Olmstead, Daniel	TIO	215	Onderdonk, Joseph	QNS	71
Oldridge, James	SUF	74	Olmstead, Daniel	ULS	233	Onderdonk, Mi	QNS	71
Oldridge, Joshua	SUF	74	Olmstead, David	ALB	43	Onderdonk, Roeliff	ORN	366
Oldridge, Mary	SUF	74	Olmstead, David	ONN	171	Onderdorsk, Andrw	NYK	114
Olds, Elijah	CAY	720	Olmstead, Ebenezer	DUT	172	Onderdunk, Abrm	RCK	109
Olds, James	CAY	718	Olmstead, Ebenezer Junr	DUT	172	Onderdunk, Adrian	RCK	102
Olds, James	ONN	188	Olmstead, Elijah	ULS	233	Onderdunk, Adrian	RCK	105
Olds, John	WSH	275	Olmstead, Gideon	CAY	716	Onderdunk, Adrian	RCK	107
Olds, Joseph	ONT	396	Olmstead, Henry	ULS	202	Onderdunk, Adrian Junr	RCK	102
Olds, Luke	GRN	334	Olmstead, Isaa	MNT	88	Onderdunk, Andrew	RCK	105
Olds, Mediam	SRA	47	Olmstead, Jeremiah	CAY	638	Onderdunk, Andrew	WST	169
Olds, Rufus	ONT	486	Olmstead, John	DUT	169	Onderdunk, Andries	RCK	107
Olds, Samuel	CAY	694	Olmst..d, Justice	MNT	83	Onderdunk, Andries	WST	169
Olds, Stephen	WSH	285	Olmstead, Mr	DEL	269	Onderdunk, Danl	RCK	97
Olds, Timothy	ONN	129	Olmstead, Nehemiah	ALB	89	Onderdunk, Garret	RCK	97
Olds, Zebulon	CAY	728	Olmstead, Noah	CAY	692	Onderdunk, Garret	RCK	105
O. Leary, Uncles	DUT	73	Olmstead, Noah	SRA	47	Onderdunk, Garret	RCK	107
Olebert, Ezra	SRA	60	Olmstead, Reuben	COL	205	Onderdunk, George	RCK	97
Olen, John	CHN	750	Olmstead, Richard	HRK	583	Onderdunk, Hendrick	RCK	105
Olen, Stephen	ONT	424	Olmstead, Richard	MNT	85	Onderdunk, Isaac	RCK	97
Oler, William	CHN	752	Olmstead, Samuel	COL	205	Onderdunk, James	RCK	109
Oles, Caleb	OTS	14	Olmstead, Silas	CAY	692	Onderdunk, John	WST	169
Oles, Danl	OTS	14	Olmstead, Stephen	COL	180	Onderdunk, Peter	WST	169
Oles, Ezekiel	CHN	770	Olmstead, Stephen Junr	COL	186	Onderdunk, Phebe	RCK	97
Oley, Benajah	WSH	209	Olmsted, Aaron	COL	205	Onderdunk, Ruliff	RCK	105
Oley, Christopher	ALB	137	Olmsted, Amaziah	WST	158	Onderdunk, Thos	RCK	106
Oley, Christopher	ALB	141	Olmsted, Daniel	OND	172	Onderkerk, Isaac	RNS	19
Olger, David	SCH	134	Olmsted, Daniel	SRA	21	Onderkerk, Jacob	RNS	24
Olger, Isaac	ALB	52				Onderkerke, Isaac	RNS	24

Name	Code	Name	Code	Name	Code
Osburn, Justin	RNS 56	Osterhout, Phillip	ULS 214	Ostrander, Peter Junr	ULS 254
Osburn, Lot	SRA 13	Osterhout, Samuel	ULS 214	Ostrander, Phillip	COL 257
Osburn, Nathan	WSH 241	Osterhout, Samuel	ULS 221	Ostrander, Phillip Junr	COL 257
Osburn, Nehemiah	ALB 55	Osterhout, Wilhelmus	ALB 102	Ostrander, Samuel	ULS 255
Osburn, Paul	CLN 154	Osterhout, William	ULS 218	Ostrander, Solomon	SCH 150
Osburn, Peter	ONT 362	Osterhout, William	ULS 223	Ostrander, Solomon	SCH 156
Osburn, Phenius	WSH 206	Osterman, Christion	MNT 109	Ostrander, Teunis	ALB 38
Osburn, Seth	ESS 309	Ostin, Phenius	WSH 211	Ostrander, Thomas	SRA 11
Osburn, Thomas	ALB 21	Ostraman, John	QNS 64	Ostrander, Thomas	SRA 42
Osburn, William	ALB 21	Ostrander, Aaron	COL 193	Ostrander, Wilhelmus	ULS 254
Osburn, William	SRA 52	Ostrander, Abbot	OND 165	Ostrander, William	ALB 139
Osburne, Hedges	SUF 64	Ostrander, Abm	RNS 62	Ostrander, William	COL 195
Osden, Isaac	MNT 13	Ostrander, Abraham	SRA 10	Ostrander, William	COL 225
Osgood, Aaron	WSH 281	Ostrander, Abraham	ULS 255	Ostrander, Wm	MNT 76
Osgood, Aaron	WSH 297	Ostrander, Abraham	WSH 301	Ostrander, William	ONT 488
Osgood, Caleb	WSH 298	Ostrander, Adam	RNS 5	Ostrander, William	ULS 251
Osgood, David	RNS 110	Ostrander, Andrew	MNT 30	Ostrander, Wm H.	GRN 358
Osgood, Jabez	WSH 298	Ostrander, Aron	MNT 30	Ostrandt, Charles	NYK 133
Osgood, John	ONN 154	Ostrander, Benjm	COL 227	Ostrandtder, Gidion	NYK 126
Osgood, Josiah	HRK 476	Ostrander, Benjamin	ULS 251	Ostrom, Anthony	MNT 106
Osgood, Lemuel Jun	DEL 274	Ostrander, Catherine	ALB 127	Ostrom, Cornelius	DUT 112
Osgood, Levy	WSH 297	Ostrander, Charles	RNS 5	Ostrom, Daniel	DUT 113
Osgood, Nathaniel	CAY 554	Ostrander, Christopher	ULS 254	Ostrom, David	DUT 164
Osgood, Samuel	NYK 70	Ostrander, Cornelius	DUT 29	Ostrom, David	OND 182
Osgood, Samuel	QNS 62	Ostrander, Cornelius	RNS 11	Ostrom, Henry	DUT 11
Osgood, Silas	CAY 552	Ostrander, Daniel	NYK 131	Ostrom, Jacob	DUT 117
Osgood, Thomas	WSH 281	Ostrander, David	ULS 254	Ostrom, Jacobus	DUT 63
Osier, John	WST 118	Ostrander, David Junr	ULS 258	Ostrom, James	DUT 19
Osman, Bartholemew	MNT 47	Ostrander, Edward	RNS 35	Ostrom, John	DUT 65
Osman, David	SUF 71	Ostrander, Elias	ULS 196	Ostrom, John	DUT 69
Osman, Gersham	SUF 71	Ostrander, Elias	ULS 255	Ostrom, John	DUT 113
Osman, John	ALB 95	Ostrander, Elisha	ULS 208	Ostrom, John	DUT 165
Osman, William	NYK 74	Ostrander, Evert	SRA 11	Ostrom, John	MNT 106
Osmer, Josiah	OND 195	Ostrander, Evert	ULS 248	Ostrom, Paulus	DUT 152
Osmer, Thomas	OND 192	Ostrander, Gideon	ULS 231	Ostrom, Peter	DUT 116
Osmond, John	MNT 8	Ostrander, Harbert	RNS 62	Ostrom, Peter	DUT 164
Osmore, Ashbel	OTS 37	Ostrander, Henderick	ALB 59	Ostrom, Roeliff	DUT 165
Ossner, Nathan	CAY 520	Ostrander, Hy	ALB 15	Ostrom, Roeliff B.	DUT 152
Osten, Edmund	OTS 16	Ostrander, Henry	CLN 161	Ostrom, Rudolph	CHN 766
Osterhoudt, Abm	SCH 164	Ostrander, Henry	COL 195	Ostronder, David	MNT 69
Psterhoudt, Samuel	SCH 144	Ostrander, Henry	RNS 13	Ostrorm, Derick	RNS 39
Osterhout, Abraham	ULS 225	Ostrander, Herman	SRA 41	Ostrum, Anthony	MNT 106
Osterhout, Abraham Junr	ULS 226	Ostrander, Hermanus	ULS 251	Ostrum, Benjn	RNS 53
Osterhout, Aldert	ORN 316	Ostrander, Isaac	ORN 316	Ostrum, Daniel	ALB 35
Osterhout, Benjamin	ULS 212	Ostrander, Jacob	CAY 676	Ostrum, Daniel	SRA 24
Osterhout, Benjamin	ULS 225	Ostrander, Jacob	ULS 251	Ostrum, Dirck	ALB 27
Osterhout, Benjamin P.	ULS 216	Ostrander, Jacobus	ALB 16	Ostrum, Isaac	ALB 142
Osterhout, Cornelius	ULS 212	Ostrander, Jacobus	GRN 358	Ostrum, John	ALB 28
Osterhout, Daniel	ULS 226	Ostrander, James	ALB 139	Ostrum, John	DEL 278
Osterhout, Elias	ULS 224	Ostrander, James	COL 193	Ostrum, Joshua	MNT 95
Osterhout, Francis	ALB 110	Ostrander, James	SRA 10	Ostrum, Simon	SRA 5
Osterhout, Frederick	MNT 16	Ostrander, James	ULS 255	Ostrum, Thomas	MNT 95
Osterhout, George	ALB 100	Ostrander, John	ALB 58	Ostsum, ...phen	MNT 92
Osterhout, Gertruyde	ULS 212	Ostrander, John	ALB 140	Oswald, Philip	NYK 73
Osterhout, Henderick	ALB 106	Ostrander, John	HRK 507	Oswell, George	WSH 221
Osterhout, Henry	CAY 678	Ostrander, John	MNT 24	Oswell, Thomas	WSH 193
Osterhout, Henry	ULS 185	Ostrander, John	SRA 48	Othercark, Minard	OTS 44
Osterhout, Henry Junr	ULS 196	Ostrander, John H.	ALB 16	Othercark, Mind Junr	OTS 44
Osterhout, Henry P.	ULS 201	Ostrander, John J.	ALB 127	Otis, Calvin	NYK 58
Osterhout, Henry T.	ULS 209	Ostrander, John J.	RNS 13	Otis, Chandler	OND 220
Osterhout, Herman	ULS 183	Ostrander, John W.	ALB 16	Otis, Charles	CHN 844
Osterhout, Jacobus	ULS 214	Ostrander, Johnathan	GRN 351	Otis, David	SRA 29
Osterhout, James	ULS 226	Ostrander, Jna	OTS 14	Otis, Ensign	MNT 97
Osterhout, John	ALB 89	Ostrander, Jonathan	RNS 13	Otis, Isaac	ONN 133
Osterhout, John	ALB 100	Ostrander, Levi	ULS 255	Otis, Joseph	NYK 37
Osterhout, John	ULS 214	Ostrander, Mary	RNS 53	Otis, Joseph	OND 212
Osterhout, John	ULS 226	Ostrander, Mary	ULS 206	Otis, Matson	WSH 305
Osterhout, John Junr	ULS 226	Ostrander, Moses	OND 219	Otis, Nicholas	ONN 158
Osterhout, John J.	ULS 226	Ostrander, Peter	ALB 41	Otis, Perez	SRA 29
Osterhout, John P.	ULS 226	Ostrander, Peter	COL 227	Otis, Richard	WSH 257
Osterhout, Jonathan	ULS 223	Ostrander, Peter	DUT 33	Otis, Richard	WSH 305
Osterhout, Joseph	ALB 20	Ostrander, Peter	RNS 13	Otis, Robert	ESS 321
Osterhout, Kryne	ULS 214	Ostrander, Peter	RNS 19	Otis, Thomas	SRA 38
Osterhout, Peter	COL 252	Ostrander, Peter	SRA 9	Otis, William	OND 166
Osterhout, Peter	GRN 328	Ostrander, Peter	ULS 191	Otley, Bened	OTS 31
Osterhout, Peter	ULS 219	Ostrander, Peter	ULS 231	Otman, Christian	SCH 164
Osterhout, Peter L.	ULS 226	Ostrander, Peter	ULS 255	Otman, Nichs	SCH 165

Otman, Peter	SCH 165	Oversant, Mathias	COL 243	Owen, Jonathan	ULS 183
Otman, Willm	SCH 163	Overton, Benjn	HRK 549	Owen, Joseph	ALB 70
Otman, Willm	SCH 165	Overton, Benjn	SUF 66	Owen, Joseph	WST 129
Ott, Cornelius	SRA 50	Overton, Colmon	SUF 75	Owen, Joseph	WST 135
Otter, Amos	WSH 273	Overton, Danl	SUF 65	Owen, Joshua	DUT 149
Otter, John	SCH 117	Overton, David	SUF 65	Owen, Joshua	ONN 141
Otter, John	WSH 266	Overton, Davis	SUF 65	Owen, Joshua	ORN 323
Otter, John Junr	SCH 117	Overton, Elizabeth	SUF 75	Owen, Josiah	OND 199
Otterson, Andrew	NYK 33	Overton, Elton	SUF 75	Owen, Lewis	ONN 184
Ottewell, Rebecca	NYK 114	Overton, Elzar	SUF 75	Owen, Mary	ORN 343
Otto, James	ONT 490	Overton, Ezra	RNS112B	Owen, Nathaniel	ALB 70
Otto, John	ONT 490	Overton, Isaac	ORN 318	Owen, Nathaniel	CAY 566
Oudeka.k, Isaac	HRK 525	Overton, Isaac	SUF 75	Owen, Nathaniel	COL 228
Oudenarde, Henry	OND 160	Overton, Isaac	SUF 94	Owen, Nathl Junr	ALB 70
Oudenarde, Marinus	OND 160	Overton, James	ORN 366	Owen, Nicholas	NYK 152
Ouderkirk, Abm	ALB 43	Overton, James	ULS 183	Owen, Rodrick	ONN 184
Ouderkirk, Andrew	MNT 95	Overton, Joel	QNS 75	Owen, Samuel	ALB 70
Ouderkirk, Aurant	ALB 16	Overton, John	SUF 65	Owen, Samuel	DUT 135
Ouderkirk, Frederick	ALB 40	Overton, John	SUF 65	Owen, Samuel	ORN 274
Ouderkirk, Isaac	ALB 7	Ov[erton?], John	SUF 69	Owen, Samuel	WST 156
Ouderkirk, Jacob	ALB 60	Overton, Jonathan	SUF 75	Owen, Solomon	TIO 220
Ouderkirk, John	ALB 7	Overton, Joseph	SUF 75	Owen, Stephen	MNT 58
Ouderkirk, John	ALB 57	Overton, Joshua	SUF 75	Owen, Terry	ORN 358
Ouderkirk, John	ALB 64	Overton, Justice	SUF 66	Owen, Thomas	NYK 86
Ouderkirk, Peter	ALB 16	Overton, Martha	SUF 74	Owen, Thomas	ULS 237
Ouderkirk, Peter	ALB 56	Overton, Meltia	SUF 76	Owen, Thomas	WST 134
Ouderkirk, Tackle	ALB 56	Overton, Moses	ORN 331	Owen, Thomas	WST 138
Ousterhoudt, John	HRK 492	Overton, Nathl	SUF 65	Owen, Timothy	ORN 379
Ousterhoudt, Nicholas	HRK 492	Overton, Nathl	SUF 75	Owen, Warren	ALB 70
Out, Benjamine	GRN 350	Overton, Nathl	SUF 75	Owen, William	ORN 303
Out, John	GRN 358	Overton, Nehemiah	SUF 65	Owen, William	ORN 346
Out(?), Martin	SCH 140	Overton, Parmer	SUF 65	Owen, William	ORN 353
Out, Mathias	GRN 350	Overton, Sten	SUF 69	Owen, William	SRA 17
Outerbridge, Joseph	NYK 75	Overton, Stephen	SUF 94	Owens, ..omion	ONN 177
Outhouse, Daniel	WST 132	Overton, Thos	SUF 73	Owens, Benjamen	WSH 288
Outhout, Henery	GRN 328	Overturn, Ensy	NYK 46	Owens, Charles	DEL 283
Outman, Isaac	WSH 201	Overturn, James	OND 209	Owens, Charles	ESS 322
Outman, Jacob	ORN 393	Overturn, Joel	OND 209	Owens, Daniel	ONT 440
Outman, James	ORN 393	Ovet, Isaac	WSH 191	Owens, Daniel	SRA 17
Outman, Stephen	ORN 393	Oviatt, Thomas	SRA 12	Owens, Daniel	SRA 19
Outterkeg, Nichs	ONN 192	Ovitt, John	DUT 83	Owens, David	ONN 179
Outwater, Daniel	DUT 31	Ovitt, John	ONT 398	Owens(?), David	TIO 226
Outwater, Jacob	RCK 98	Owans, George	WSH 257	Owens, Elijah	SRA 17
Outwater, Peter	DUT 23	Owen, Aaron	DEL 254	Owens, Elijah Junr	SRA 17
Outwater, Thos	RCK 98	Owen, Abel	ONN 186	Owens, Evan	OND 159
Ovaitt, Ebenezer	HRK 587	Owen, Abner	ULS 188	Owens, Henry	ALB 132
Ovalbaugh, Peter J.	ULS 222	Owen, Abraham	OND 175	Owens, Hugh	DUT 79
Ove_, Eliphalet	MNT 44	Owen, Adam	COL 265	Owens, Hugh	NYK 55
Ovelbaugh, Jeremiah	ULS 222	Owen, Alvin	OTS 24	Owens, Humphry	NYK 138
Ovelling, Paul	DUT 40	Owen, Alvin	ULS 188	Owens, Jane	DUT 78
Ovens, Ep.raim	MNT 92	Owen, Archibald	ORN 360	Owens, Jesse	DUT 79
Ovens, Michael	SUF 71	Owen, Benjaman	CHN 978	Owens, John	ALB 88
Overacker, Adam	MNT 85	Owen, Benjamin	ORN 344	Owens, John	ALB 131
Overacker, Emanuel	DUT 5	Owen, Charles	HRK 526	Owens, John	NYK 59
Overacker, Jacob	DUT 5	Owen, Daniel	WSH 269	Owens, John	NYK 122
Overacker, Jacob	RNS 30	Owen, Daniel	WST 122	Owens, John	SRA 56
Overacker, John	DUT 5	Owen, David	ONN 174	Owens, Leonard	ESS 322
Overacker, Martin	RNS 30	Owen, David	ORN 318	Owens, Levi	DUT 78
Overacker, Martinus	DUT 5	Owen, David	ORN 373	Owens, Maubry	CAY 578
Overacker, Michael	RNS 30	Owen, Eliphalet	ONN 142	Owens, Noah	ALB 118
Overacker, Wen	MNT 36	Owen, Enoch	ULS 182	Owens, Pheneus	CHN 898
Overaker, George_	MNT 28	Owen, Israel	ORN 368	Owens, Samuel	DUT 78
Overaker, Michael	RNS 45	Owen, James	ORN 273	Owens, Solomon	NYK 122
Overaker, Wm	MNT 31	Owen, James	ULS 259	Owens, Solomon	ONN 140
Overbergh, Benjamin	MNT 109	Owen, Jesse	ORN 340	Owens, Stephen	WST 117
Overheys_, Bernard	OTS 28	Owen, John	COL 198	Owens, Thaddeus	ESS 322
Over hiser, Conradd	MNT 36	Owen, John	DEL 278	Owes, Ambrose	SCH 152
O_erhiser, Mic.ael	MNT 85	Owen, John	DEL 278	Owings, Oliver	ONN 170
Overhizer, Abraham	DUT 14	Owen, John	ONN 184	Owins, Asse	WST 169
Overing, Henry	NYK 16	Owen, John	ORN 333	Ox, George	SCH 156
Overocker, Wandell	RNS 37	Owen, John	ORN 345	Ox, Meleth	SCH 156
Overpaw, Clament	GRN 327	Owen, Jonathan	COL 211	Oxborough, David	ALB 61
Overpaw, Isaac	SCH 144	Owen, Jonathan	DUT 114	Oxner, Christopher	HRK 484
Overpaw, John	GRN 327	Owen, Jonathan	ORN 318	Oxner, John	HRK 487
Overpaw, Mrss	GRN 327	Owen, Jonathan	ORN 341	Oxoss, John Junr	NYK 24
Overpaw, Peter	GRN 327	Owen, Jonathan	ORN 353	Oyer, Frederick	HRK 455
Overpaw, William	GRN 327	Owen, Jonathan	ORN 358	Oyer, Jacob	HRK 456

Name	Loc	Name	Loc	Name	Loc
Palmer, David	DUT 105	Palmer, John	NYK 28	Palmer, Robert	DUT 98
Palmer, David	DUT 139	Palmer, John	NYK 55	Palmer, Rogers	WSH 300
Palmer, David	DUT 173	Palmer, John	NYK 82	Palmer, Rowland	OTS 15
Palmer, David	OTS 37	Palmer, John	NYK 108	Palmer, Samuel	COL 187
Palmer, Dennison	CHN 830	Palmer, John	OND 191	Palmer, Samuel	COL 243
Palmer, Dyer	RNS 18	Palmer, John	OND 212	Palmer, Samuel	RNS112B
Palmer, Ebenezer	DUT 171	Palmer, John	ONT 310	Palmer, Samuel	ULS 260
Palmer, Eber	DUT 129	Palmer, John	RNS 18	Palmer, Samuel	WSH 188
Palmer, Edmund	ALB 73	Palmer, John	RNS 57	Palmer, Samuel	WSH 298
Palmer, Edward	CAY 604	Palmer, John	RCK 105	Palmer, Samuel	WST 135
Palmer, Edward	ESS 306	Palmer, John	WST 115	Palmer, Sarah	CHN 846
Palmer, Edward	NYK 81	Palmer, John	WST 119	Palmer, Sarah	CHN 872
Palmer, Eliakum	CHN 862	Palmer, John	WST 120	Palmer, Silas	ALB 110
Palmer, Elias	ESS 323	Palmer, John	WST 125	Palmer, Silas	NYK 136
Palmer, Elias	GRN 352	Palmer, Jesse	WST 126	Palmer, Silas B.	ULS 184
Palmer, Elias	HRK 502	Palmer, Johnathan	GRN 352	Palmer, Silence	CAY 698
Palmer, Elias	SRA 47	Palmer, Jonathan	CAY 606	Palmer, Simeon	SRA 31
Palmer, Elihu	WST 121	Palmer, Jonathan	OND 203	Palmer, Solomon	GRN 351
Palmer, Elijah	CHN 842	Palmer, Jonathan	ONN 192	Palmer, Solomon	DEL 270
Palmer, Eliphalet	CAY 612	Palmer, Jonathan	RCK 105	Palmer, Solomon	OND 188
Palmer, Elisabeth	WST 125	Palmer, Jonathan Junr	OND 203	Palmer, Solomon	WSH 195
Palmer, Enoch	COL 216	Palmer, Joseph	RCH 88	Palmer, Stephen	DEL 290
Palmer, Ephraim	ALB 79	Palmer, Joseph	RCK 105	Palmer, Stephen	NYK 148
Palmer, Ephraim	SRA 26	Palmer, Joseph	SRA 12	Palmer, Stephen	OTS 34
Palmer, Ethel	OND 203	Palmer, Joseph	SRA 50	Palmer, Stephen	TIO 209
Palmer, Ezekiel	ESS 306	Palmer, Joseph	WSH 277	Palmer, Stephen	WSH 212
Palmer, Ezekiel	OND 224	Palmer, Joseph	WSH 290	Palmer, Stephen	WST 125
Palmer, Fenner	RNS 58	Palmer, Joseph R.	ONT 310	Palmer, Stephen	WST 135
Palmer, Gamalael	ALB 87	Palmer, Joshua	COL 202	Palmer, Stephen	WST 169
Palmer, Gamaliel	COL 187	Palmer, Joshua	RNS 103	Palmer, Stutely	HRK 477
Palmer, George	CHN 780	Palmer, Joshua	SRA 51	Palmer, Sylvanus	CLN 154
Palmer, George	CHN 818	Palmer, Lancaster	NYK 148	Palmer, Sylvanus	WST 125
Palmer, Geo	OTS 50	Palmer, Lauther	CHN 828	Palmer, Sylvenus	SRA 26
Palmer, George	SRA 47	Palmer, Leonard	DUT 132	Palmer, Temperance	RNS 72
Palmer, George	WST 121	Palmer, Levi	DEL 270	Palmer, Thomas	CAY 588
Palmer, Gershom	OTS 2	Palmer, Levi	SRA 21	Palmer, Thomas	DUT 36
Palmer, Gershom	OTS 50	Palmer, March	WST 125	Palmer, Thomas	DUT 48
Palmer, Gideon	WST 152	Palmer, Mary	DUT 138	Palmer, Thomas	NYK 148
Palmer, Gilbert	COL 183	Palmer, Matthew	SRA 5	Palmer, Thoms	RNS 73
Palmer, Gilbert	OND 196	Palmer, Messenger	SRA 30	Palmer, Timothy	MNT 106
Palmer, Gilbert	WST 115	Palmer, Micah	DUT 97	Palmer, Titus	WSH 201
Palmer, Gilbert C.	COL 243	Palmer, Micah Junr	DUT 59	Palmer, Uriah	CLN 157
Palmer, Guidean	GRN 352	Palmer, Midad	WST 169	Palmer, Vinus	WST 113
Palmer, Harrison	WST 115	Palmer, Nancy a Black	NYK 65	Palmer, Vose	CHN 818
Palmer, Henry	RNS 108	Palmer, Nathan	DUT 166	Palmer, Vose	OTS 47
Palmer, Henry	RCK 106	Palmer, Nathan	OTS 34	Palmer, Vose Junr	CHN 818
Palmer, Henry	TIO 210	Palmer, Nathan	WST 120	Palmer, Wait	SRA 30
Palmer, Humphrey	OTS 49	Palmer, Nathaniel	NYK 128	Palmer, Willeam	WSH 294
Palmer, Hyatt	RNS 66	Palmer, Nathaniel	WSH 277	Palmer, William	ALB 111
Palmer, Ichabod B.	OTS 22	Palmer, Nathaniel	WST 152	Palmer, William	CHN 774
Palmer, Ira	GRN 352	Palmer, Nathaniel	WST 157	Palmer, William	CHN 818
Palmer, Isaac	DUT 130	Palmer, Nehemiah	CHN 834	Palmer, Willm	COL 222
Palmer, Jacob	QNS 62	Palmer, Nehemiah	CHN 842	Palmer, William	DUT 105
Palmer, Jame	QNS 61	Palmer, Nicholas	CLN 158	Palmer, William	DUT 166
Palmer, James	CHN 776	Palmer, Nicholas	RNS 4	Palmer, William	ESS 322
Palmer, James	DUT 24	Palmer, Nicholas	SRA 50	Palmer, William	NYK 21
Palmer, James	DUT 137	Palmer, Noah	ONN 143	Palmer, William	NYK 143
Palmer, James	GRN 349	Palmer, Noah	WSH 216	Palmer, William	OND 175
Palmer, James	GRN 352	Palmer, Noys	CHN 824	Palmer, William	QNS 61
Palmer, James	OND 204	Palmer, Obadiah	DUT 142	Palmer, William	ULS 186
Palmer, James	OND 207	Palmer, Obediah	DUT 24	Palmer, William	WST 111
Palmer, James	OTS 14	Palmer, Obediah	ULS 242	Palmer, William	WST 125
Palmer, Ja_es	SRA 31	Palmer, Orry	CHN 946	Palmer, Zacheus	CLN 154
Palmer, James	WST 149	Palmer, Ozias	OND 212	Palmer, Zephaniah	ESS 323
Palmer, Japeth	SRA 31	Palmer, Paul	RNS 105	Palmerter, Amos	ONN 141
Palmer, Jerad	CAY 612	Palmer, Pelug	CHN 818	Palmerter, Daniel	ONN 141
Palmer, Jerard	SRA 50	Palmer, Peter	COL 253	Palmerton, Jesse	CHN 832
Palmer, Jared	DUT 53	Palmer, Peter	NYK 25	Palmerton, John	DUT 106
Palmer, Jeremiah	DUT 28	Palmer, Peter	NYK 137	Palmerton, Thomas	ULS 200
Palmer, Jeremiah	RNS 53	Palmer, Phillip	SRA 8	Palmes, Richard	NYK 82
Palmer, Jeremiah	SRA 59	Palmer, Prentice	CAY 698	Palmeter, Josiah	HRK551½
Palmer, Jesse	CHN 834	Palmer, Reuben	DUT 101	Palmeter, Phinias	OTS 48
Palmer, Jesse	DEL 269	Palmer, Reuben	SRA 31	Palmeter, Sylvanus	HRK 597
Palmer, John	CHN 806	Palmer, Richard	WST 126	Palmetier, Abraham	ULS 236
Palmer, John	COL 181	Palmer, Robard G.	GRN 352	Palmetier, Adriana	DUT 65
Palmer, John	DEL 286	Palmer, Robbart	GRN 352	Palmetier, Damon	ULS 234
Palmer, John	DUT 11			Palmetier, Henry	DUT 121

Palmetier, Isaac H.	DUT 61	Parcells, Thomas	KNG 7	Parker, Abby	NYK 35		
Palmetier, Jacob	DUT 65	Parcels, Frederic	NYK 100	Parker, Abel	OTS 7		
Palmetier, Jacobus	DUT 65	Parcels, Hannah	NYK 128	Parker, Abel	SRA 38		
Palmetier, John	DUT 61	Parcels, Jacob	NYK 103	Parker, Able	CHN 908		
Palmetier, John	ULS 236	Parcels, John	NYK 81	Parker, Abraham	NYK 61		
Palmetier, Michael	ULS 235	Parcels, Mary	NYK 27	Parker, Abrm	SRA 20		
Palmetier, Peter	ULS 239	Parcels, Richard	NYK 126	Parker, Adam	NYK 32		
Palmetier, Stephen	DEL 285	Parcels, Sarah	NYK 39	Parker, Al[exander?]	OTS 37		
Palmetier, Thomas	DUT 120	Parcels, Susannah	NYK 41	Parker, Amasa	SRA 20		
Palmetier, William	DUT 67	Parcus, Joseph	CHN 808	Parker, Ambrose	WSH 274		
Palmetier, William	ULS 239	Parcus, William	CHN 806	Parker, Amelia	NYK 25		
Palminta, Isaac	SRA 35	Parcutt, James	WST 150	Parker, Amos	CHN 760		
Palmiteer, John	ALB 99	Pardee, Eli	ULS 239	Parker, Amos	DEL 273		
Palmitier, John Junr	ALB 102	Pardee, James	ULS 239	Parker, Amos	OND 168		
Palmitier, Michael	ALB 77	Pardee, James Junr	ULS 239	Parker, Andrew	WSH 286		
Palsner(?), Wm	GRN 357	Pardee, John	COL 214	Parker, Anna	WST 111		
Palton, Edward	NYK 148	Pardee, John	HRK 586	Parker, Asa	CHN 908		
Pamadore, Mary Ann	NYK 71	Pardee, Josiah	HRK 593	Parker, Asael	RNS 41		
Pamerley, Abraham	ALB 27	Pardee, Lemuel	ULS 238	Parker, Asaph	WSH 275		
Pamerly, Jared	COL 214	Pardee, Nathl	HRK 549	Parker, Benjn	OTS 39		
Pameter, Jonathan	RNS 72	Pardee, Thomas	DUT 138	Parker, Dr Benjamin	RCH 92		
Panar, John	MNT 65	Pardie, John	ONT 450	Parker, Bethiah	SUF 105		
Panburn, Richard	SCH 158	Pardy, Aaron	ONN 164	Parker, Charles	WSH 269		
Pancas, Joseph	NYK 123	Pardy, David	WST 155	Parker, Chauncey	CAY 716		
Pand, Samuel	GRN 334	Pardy, Eben....	ONN 164	Parker, Cornelius	ONT 482		
Pandall, James	NYK 54	Pardy, Ebenezer	WST 155	Parker, Dan	DEL 281		
Pane see Pain & Payne		Pardy, Elijah	ULS 215	Parker, Daniel	NYK 59		
Pane, Robart	GRN 354	Pardy, Ezra	WST 155	Parker, Daniel	RNS 82		
Pane, Smith	RNS 65	Pardy, Isaac	WST 155	Parker, Daniel	WST 146		
Pane, Stephen	RNS 82	Pardy, Jesse	COL 212	Parker, David	DEL 272		
Pane, Wheaton	RNS 12	Pardy, John	COL 212	Parker, David	OND 205		
Panel, Abraham	HRK 507	Pardy, John	WST 156	Parker, David	WSH 273		
Panel, Hugh	HRK 507	Pardy, Joseph	GRN 343	Parker, Ebenezer	HRK 454		
Pangborn, James	ESS 311	Pardy, Joshua	WST 155	Parker, Edward	ALB 41		
Pangborn, John Junr	ESS 310	Pardy, Levi	OND 212	Parker, Edward	QNS 68		
Pangborn, Samuel	ESS 310	Pardy, Rachel	RNS 101	Parker, Elephalet	WSH 275		
Pangborn, Abigal	NYK 76	Pardy, Robart	GRN 325	Parker, Eliada	OND 172		
Pangburn, Benjamin	ALB 16	Pardy, Samuel	DUT 178	Parker, Elias	RNS 109		
Pangburn, David	ESS 319	Pardy, Silas	COL 212	Parker, Elijah	ONT 418		
Pangburn, Edward	ALB 24	Pare, John	COL 262	Parker, Elijah	OTS 42		
Pangburn, Edwd Jn	ALB 96	Parent, Jacob	WST 131	Parker, Elijah	WSH 240		
Pangburn, John	ESS 311	Parent, Jemima	WST 128	Parker, Elisha	OTS 37		
Pangburn, John	ESS 319	Parent, Levi	WST 131	Parker, Elisha	WST 156		
Pangburn, John	SCH 125	Parent, Thomas	SRA 28	Parker, Elizabeth	NYK 98		
Pangburn, John E.	ALB 96	Pares, Augustus	NYK 56	Parker, Enos	DEL 281		
Pangburn, John R.	ALB 101	Parin.., Daniel	MNT 99	Parker, Ephraim	ONT 452		
Pangburn, Joseph	ESS 310	Paris, Daniel	MNT 43	Parker, Ezekiel	CAY 640		
Pangburn, Joseph	ESS 319	Paris, Daniel	MNT 58	Parker, Ezra	OND 205		
Pangburn, Libbeus	ESS 319	Parish, Daniel	QNS 80	Parker, Frederick	CHN 740		
Pangburn, Peter	MNT 89	Parish, Ebenezer	COL 253	Parker, Gabriel a			
Pangburn, Richard	ALB 36	Parish, Elkaner	OTS 25	Black	NYK 130		
Pangburn, Richard	CAY 574	Parish, Jacob	GRN 358	Parker, George	CAY 678		
Pangburn, Solomon	ALB 44	Parish, John	DEL 284	Parker, George	DUT 63		
Pangburn, Stephen	ALB 61	Parish, Joshua	OTS 15	Parker, George	ESS 309		
Pangburn, Timothy	ESS 311	Parish, Knolton	DEL 271	Parker, George	NYK 57		
Pangburn, Timothy	ESS 319	Parish, Solomon	ONT 476	Parker, George	NYK 137		
Pangburn, William	ALB 99	Parish, Stephen	WSH 186	Parker, Green	CAY 706		
Pangburn, Wm Junr	ALB 105	Parist, John	QNS 80	Parker, Henry	MNT 43		
Pangbuurn, William	ONT 310	Park, Amos	TIO 264	Parker, Henry	NYK 49		
Pangman, David	COL 218	Park, Benjamin	NYK 68	Parker, Herculas	HRK 591		
Pangman, Samuel	CLN 173	Park, Disborough	WST 115	Parker, Ira	WSH 275		
Pangmore, David	WSH 284	Park, Ebenezer	DUT 136	Parker, Isaac	ALB 91B		
Pannel, Archd	OTS 7	Park, Ephraim	GRN 336	Parker, Isaac	HRK 546		
Pannel, Jeremiah	ALB 143	Park, Ephraim	WSH 301	Parker, Isaac	NYK 117		
Panno, Laurence	CLN 163	Park, Gehe	MNT 81	Parker, Isaac	ORN 390		
Panton, Jane	NYK 53	Park, James	NYK 53	Parker, Isaac	RCK 102		
Panton, Rd a free		Park, Jesse	WST 112	Parker, Jacob	NYK 93		
Negro	ALB 121	Park, John	NYK 133	Parker, Jacob	RCK 104		
Pappison, Augustin	ALB 142	Park, John	NYK 142	Parker, Jacob	WSH 189		
Par.e, James	ONT 474	Park, Joseph	WST 111	Parker, James	CAY 522		
Parady, Emanuel	COL 251	Park, Peter	NYK 125	Parker, James	CHN 782		
Paramour, Joseph	NYK 139	Park, Reubin	GRN 336	Parker, James	COL 247		
Parce, James	GRN 327	Park, Roger	WST 112	Parker, James	MNT 15		
Parce, John	GRN 327	Park, Rufus	DUT 134	Parker, James	NYK 81		
Parcell, Henry	CAY 678	Park, Timothy	WST 112	Parker, James a			
Parcell, Nathaniel	CAY 678	Parkenson, Richard	NYK 141	mulatto	NYK 140		
Parcell, William	NYK 149	Parker see Packer		Parker, James	OND 189		

Name	Loc	Name	Loc	Name	Loc
Parker, James	ONT 410	Parker, Thadhius	GRN 348	Parks, John	SRA 15
Parker, James	OTS 42	Parker, Thomas	CAY 688	Parks, Jonas	DEL 278
Parker, James	WSH 204	Parker, Thoms	TIO 238	Parks, Jonas	GRN 349
Parker, Jared	OND 199	Parker, Timothy	OTS 42	Parks, Jonas	GRN 350
Parker, Jason	OND 159	Parker, William	CHN 942	Parks, Jonathan	COL 203
Parker, Jeremiah	SUF 100	Parker, William	DEL 285	Parks, Joseph	MNT 110
Parker, Jesse	CLN 163	Parker, Wm	GRN 335	Parks, Joseph	OND 207
Parker, Jesse	WSH 283	Parker, Wm	GRN 350	Parks, Joseph	WSH 211
Parker, Job	STB 203	Parker, William	HRK 441	Parks, Josiah	DEL 274
Parker, Joel	WSH 185	Parker, Wm	OTS 38	Parks, Mary	DUT 146
Parker, John	CHN 810	Parker, Wm	RCK 102	Parks, Nathan	COL 215
Parker, John	CLN 166	Parker, William	SUF 104	Parks, Oliver	COL 215
Parker, John	ESS 302	Parker, William W.	NYK 109	Parks, Richard Junr	DUT 49
Parker, John	NYK 15	Parker, Wyman	DEL 281	Parks, Richard Senr	DUT 49
Parker, John	NYK 102	Parkerson, John	RCK 101	Parks, Robert	CAY 632
Parker, John	ONT 354	Parkes, Benjamin	ORN 321	Parks, Robert	OND 200
Parker, John	TIO 230	Parkes, Dan	OND 207	Parks, Robert	SRA 39
Parker, John	WST 111	Parkes, Daniel	OND 208	Parks, Rufus	RNS 18
Parker, John C.	WSH 271	Parkes, Elisha	OND 207	Parks, Salomon	SRA 51
Parker, John E.	NYK 77	Parkhurst see Parkurst		Parks, Samuel	COL 202
Parker, John Fry	WST 115	Parkhurst, Abraham	WSH 306	Parks, Samuel	COL 205
Parker, Jonas	OTS 18	Parkhurst, Alpheus	HRK 450	Parks, Samuel	GRN 350
Parker, Jonathan	CAY 518	Parkhurst, Aureleus	WSH 303	Parks, Simeon	CAY 634
Parker, Jonathan	ONT 378	Parkhurst, David	WSH 306	Parks, Smith	GRN 336
Parker, Joseph	ALB 98	Parkhurst, Eliphalet	HRK 581	Parks, William	ULS 184
Parker, Joseph	DUT 93	Parkhurst, George	HRK 581	Parks, Whiting	RNS 54
Parker, Joseph	ONT 374	Parkhurst, George Junr	HRK 581	Parkurst, Abraham	ULS 183
Parker, Joseph	SUF 107	Parkhurst, Joel	HRK 551½	Parkus, Solomon	SRA 12
Parker, Joseph	WST 116	Parkhurst, John	CAY 516	Parky, Levy	WSH 274
Parker, Joseph	WST 140	Parkhurst, John	OND 164	Parlee, Abraham	RCH 94
Parker, Joseph P.	NYK 136	Parkhurst, Jonathan	OND 210	Parlee, Bornt	RCH 94
Parker, Joshua	CHN 936	Parkhurst, Josiah	OND 212	Parlee, Henry	RCH 89
Parker, Joshua	DUT 93	Parkhurst, Nathan	OND 172	Parlee, Isaac	RCH 89
Parker, Joshua	NYK 40	Parkhurst, Nathaniel	ORN 366	Parlemen, Edward	ULS 252
Parker, Joshua	RNS 81	Parkhurst, William	HRK 581	Parlemen, Edward Junr	ULS 252
Parker, Joshua	RNS 96	Parkins, James	NYK 15	Parlemen, Jacob	ULS 252
Parker, Josiah	NYK 71	Parkinson, Aaron	SCH 171	Parlemen, James	ORN 379
Parker, Jotham	CHN 746	Parkinson, Christopher	RCH 90	Parlemen, John	ULS 252
Parker, Jotham	OND 195	Parkinson, John	NYK 17	Parliment, James	RCK 105
Parker, Judiah	OTS 38	Parkinson, Reuben	SCH 165	Parlo, Joseph	COL 247
Parker, Levy	CHN 746	Parkinson, Silvenus	SCH 165	Parmalee, Elias	RNS 81
Parker, Lyman	ALB 126	Parkis, Nahum	HRK 574	Parmela, Camp	OND 182
Parker, Mary	NYK 116	Parkis, Nathan	HRK 574	Parmela, Ozias	OND 170
Parker, Michael	NYK 74	Parkis, William	HRK 573	Parmela, Shelden	OND 168
Parker, Michael	WSH 275	Parkiss, Daniel	ESS 298	Parmela, Sylvester	OND 170
Parker, Moses	WST 147	Parkley, Michael	ALB 59	Parmela, Thomas	OND 191
Parker, Nathan	CHN 796	Parkman, Alexander	CAY 722	Parmele, Roger	NYK 24
Parker, Nathaniel	DUT 95	Parkman, Alexander	OND 178	Parmenter, William	SRA 6
Parker, Nathaniel	ONT 324	Parkman, Thomas	COL 247	Parmer, Guidean	GRN 350
Parker, Nathaniel	WSH 274	Parks, Alexander	ALB 138	Parmer, John	GRN 341
Parker, Nehemiah	RNS 25	Parks, Arthur	ORN 295	Parmer, Oliver	GRN 350
Parker, Nicholas	WST 156	Parks, Benjamin	CAY 634	Parmerlee, Reuben	ONT 388
Parker, Oliver	ONT 492	Parks, Christopher	ONT 406	Parmerlee, Reuben	ONT 390
Parker, Pardon	OTS 37	Parks, Daniel	GRN 349	Parmerlee, Reuben	ONT 402
Parker, Peter	NYK 118	Parks, Daniel	RNS 104	Parmerly, Silvenus	CHN 874
Parker, Peter	RCK 102	Parks, Daniel	SRA 51	Parmerly, Sophia	WST 169
Parker, Peter	WSH 205	Parks, David	ALB 29	Parmerly, Stephen	CHN 874
Parker, Peter	WSH 271	Parks, David	DUT 126	Parmerton, Nathan	GRN 338
Parker, Pheneas	OTS 42	Parks, David Senr	DUT 126	Parmeter, Charles	OND 189
Parker, Pherinton	SRA 14	Parks, Elijah	COL 229	Parmeter, John	ONT 348
Parker, Phineas	OND 184	Parks, Elijah	MNT 38	Parminter, Joshua	SRA 6
Parker, Reuben	WSH 265	Parks, Elijah B.	COL 229	Parmirton, Elisha	GRN 337
Parker, Reuben Senr	OTS 21	Parks, Ezekiel	RNS 104	Parmot, Joshua	ESS 321
Parker, Richard	WSH 241	Parks, Ezra	COL 204	Parnell, Aaron	CAY 672
Parker, Richard	WSH 253	Parks, Isaac	CAY 648	Paroy, Elisha	GRN 353
Parker, Robert	WST 111	Parks, Jacob	DUT 53	Parr, James	WST 169
Parker, Samuel	OND 189	Parks, Jehial	SRA 48	Parr, John	OTS 29
Parker, Samuel	ONN 163	Parks, Jehiel	CAY 636	Parr, Josiah	ONT 358
Parker, Samuel	ONT 334	Parks, Jeremiah	TIO 229	Parr, Wm	RCK 101
Parker, Saml	OTS 36	Parks, Joel	CAY 634	Parras, ...	MNT 78
Parker, Samuel	RCH 89	Parks, Joel	ONT 408	Parree, Daniel	COL 234
Parker, Saml	RCK 102	Parks, John	ALB 39	Parrells, Michael	CAY 640
Parker, Silus	CHN 908	Parks, John	CAY 634	Parret, David	NYK 82
Parker, Simeon	CHN 760	Parks, John	CAY 634	Parret, Phillip	ULS 222
Parker, Stephen	CHN 806	Parks, John	NYK 141	Parrimore, Benjamin	NYK 113
Parker, Stephen	WSH 211	Parks, John	ONT 394	Pa[rris?], Joseph Junr	CAY 584
Parker, Stites	OTS 42			Parrisen, Phillip	NYK 67

Parrish, Abraham	ONT 432	Parsons, David	DUT 139	Passinger, Andrew	ALB 106

Patridge, Lanson	ALB	67	Patterson, John	ORN	382	Paul, William	SRA	31
Patridge, Pearl	COL	200	Patterson, John	TIO	220	Paulding, Damarus	QNS	78
Patridge, Thomas	CHN	750	Patterson, John	WSH	220	Paulding, James	WST	169
Patridge, William	CHN	754	Patterson, John W.	NYK	25	Paulding, John	WST	153
Patrie, Coenradt	COL	229	Patterson, Joseph	OND	195	Paulding, John & Peter	WST	164
Patrie, Maria	COL	229	Patterson, Joseph	ORN	385	Paulding, Jonathan	WST	169
Patrie, Nichs	SCH	172	Patterson, Josiah	COL	207	Paulding, Joseph	WST	153
Patry, John	COL	239	Patterson, Luther	COL	211	Paulding, Peter & John	WST	164
Patry, John C.	COL	239	Patterson, Mary	ORN	296	Paulding, Roger	WST	169
Patry, Leah	COL	239	Patterson, Matthew	DUT	169	Paulding, William	WST	164
Patten, Alexander	SRA	26	Patterson, Moses	ULS	199	Paulding, William	WST	169
Patten, Alexander	SCH	132	Patterson, Oliver	ALB	27	Paulin, Francis a
Patten, Benoni	HRK	413	Patterson, Phebe	ORN	342	Black	NYK	89
Patten, Daniel	WSH	194	Patterson, Reuben	ONN	150	Pauling, Cornelius	NYK	30
Patten, Eanes	WSH	257	Patterson, Robert	NYK	47	Paulis, Charles	NYK	126
Patten, Edward	WSH	257	Patterson, Robert	ONT	470	Paulis, Christian	NYK	89
Patten, James	NYK	76	Patterson, Robert	STB	200	Paulis, David	NYK	121
Patten, James	OTS	41	Patterson, Robert	WSH	251	Paulus, Peter	ORN	306
Patten, John	NYK	82	Patterson, Samuel	ULS	206	Pavie, John	NYK	22
Patten, John	ONT	476	Patterson, Stephen	WSH	266	Pawles, George	NYK	97
Patten, John	ONT	502	Patterson, Sunderland	ALB	81	Pawley, John	ORN	320
Patten, Johnson	NYK	43	Patterson, Susanna	DUT	40	Pawley, Uriah	CAY	592
Patten, Josiah	OND	163	Patterson, Thomas	ALB	27	Pawling, Abel	SRA	26
Patten, Mary	WSH	257	Patterson, Thomas	SRA	46	Pawling, Eleanor	ULS	206
Patten, Robert	MNT	52	Patterson, Thomas	WSH	202	Pawling, John	DUT	108
Patten, Thaddeus	ONN	168	Patterson, Thomas	WSH	243	Pawling, Levi	DUT	164
Patten, Willeam	WSH	244	Patterson, William	ALB	108	Pawling, Levi	SRA	14
Patten, William	NYK	58	Patterson, William	CAY	542	Pawlis, Cornelius	NYK	97
Patten, William	OND	174	Patterson, William	NYK	101	Pawlis, Jacob	NYK	98
Patten, William	ONT	340	Patterson, William	NYK	132	Pawly, John	ORN	306
Pattengall, Joseph	SCH	171	Patterson, Wm	ONN	175	Pawly, Moses	ORN	319
Pattent, Elisha	SCH	171	Patterson, William	ULS	187	Pawly, Samuel	ORN	317
Patterson see Paterson			Patterson, William	WSH	215	Paxton, Hanah	NYK	46
Patterson, Abejah	TIO	255	Patterson, William	WSH	301	Paxton, James	NYK	86
Patterson, Abijah Jur	TIO	255	Patterson, William J.F.	ONN	150	Paxton, John	NYK	32
Patterson, Alexander	COL	266	Patterson, Zacheus	CAY	720	Paxton, Samuel	NYK	88
Patterson, Amos	TIO	211	Pattin, Nathaniel	RNS	82	Paxton, William	SRA	14
Patterson, Andrew	DUT	138	Pattin, Robert	RNS	23	Payley, Gilbert	CLN	170
Patterson, Atta	COL	258	Pattison, Adam	ESS	307	Paylin, Hanna	CLN	170
Patterson, Azuba	ORN	316	Pattison, Andrew	HRK	510	Payn see Pain & Pane	
Patterson, Benjamin	CAY	664	Pattison, Jacob	DEL	268	Payn, Daniel	WSH	243
Patterson, Benjamin	STB	202	Pattison, Michael Junr	DEL	267	Payn, Daniel Jur	WSH	243
Patterson, Catharine	DUT	67	Patton, Alexander	SRA	23	Payn, Jacob	WSH	278
Patterson, Charles	ALB	27	Patton, John	DUT	102	Payn, Joanna	WSH	243
Patterson, David	MNT	123	Patton, John	NYK	122	Payn, Nathan	WSH	243
Patterson, David	WSH	229	Patton, John	ORN	351	Payn, Nathaniel	WSH	271
Patterson, David W.	COL	207	Patton, Samuel	OTS	7	Payn, Noah	WSH	243
Patterson, Eleazer	OTS	34	Patton, William	ORN	277	Payn, Noah Jur	WSH	243
Patterson, Ephraim	COL	208	Pattrick, Ebenezer	SRA	47	Payn, Reuben	WSH	243
Patterson, Ezra	ONT	358	Pau er, Joh.	MNT	40	Payn, Seth	HRK	478
Patterson, Ezra	ONT	506	Paul, Abigail	ALB	128	Payne, Abraham	CHN	846
Patterson, Frs	ALB	8	Paul, Bryster a Black	NYK	36	Payne, Benjamin	ESS	319
Patterson, Gaun	NYK	101	Paul, Catharine	RCK	102	Payne, Benjn	SUF	75
Patterson, George	OND	163	Paul, George	ALB	39	Payne, Brinton	TIO	259
Patterson, George	WSH	268	Paul, Hugh	COL	262	Payne, Daniel	HRK	599
Patterson, George	WSH	301	Paul, Hugh	WSH	303	Payne, Daniel	ONN	134
Patterson, Henry	ORN	342	Paul, Isaac	NYK	94	Payne, Daniel	SUF	102
Patterson, Hezekiah	DEL	291	Paul, James	NYK	67	Payne, Daniel Jun	HRK	599
Patterson, Hutchinson	ONT	360	Paul, James	RCK	101	Payne, David	SUF	73
Patterson, [Is?]iah L.	TIO	217	Paul, James	SRA	14	Payne, David	TIO	227
Patterson, Israiel	CHN	936	Paul, John	ALB	39	Payne, Eber	COL	213
Patterson, James	CHN	762	Paul, John	NYK	94	Payne, Elisha	CHN	846
Patterson, James	NYK	102	Paul, John a Black	NYK	111	Payne, Elisha	SUF	108
Patterson, James B.	NYK	30	Paul, John	RCK	106	Payne, Elnathan	SUF	98
Patterson, Jeremiah	ORN	315	Paul, John	SUF	71	Payne, Ezekiel	SUF	108
Patterson, John	ALB	92	Paul, Josiah	NYK	132	Payne, Ezra	OND	201
Patterson, John	ALB	101	Paul, Mary	SRA	30	Payne, Isaac	SUF	109
Patterson, John	ALB	130	Paul, Peter a mulatto	NYK	41	Payne, Isaac B.	SRA	50
Patterson, John	DUT	166	Paul, Rachael	NYK	88	Payne, James	NYK	36
Patterson, John	NYK	57	Paul, Richard	SRA	31	Payne, Jesse	HRK	599
Patterson, John	NYK	79	Paul, Robert	CLN	169	Payne, Joel	CHN	934
Patterson, John a			Paul, Sarah	NYK	33	Payne, John	OND	164
Black	NYK	91	Paul, Sarah	NYK	99	Payne, John	ORN	326
Patterson, John a			Paul, Simon a mulatto	NYK	38	Payne, John	SUF	76
Black	NYK	103	Paul, Simon	ORN	357	Payne, John	SUF	104
Patterson, John	NYK	123	Paul, Simon	WST	144	Payne, John Jr	SUF	76
Patterson, John	ORN	276	Paul, William	SRA	30	Payne, John Junr	SUF	104

Payne, Jonas	SUF 64	Pearce, Ezekiel	QNS 64	Pearse, Herekiah	OND 210
Payne, Jonathan	SUF 102	Pearce, Ezeriakam	OTS 28	Pearse, James	NYK 118
Payne, Joseph	ESS 308	Pearce, George	OTS 12	Pearse, Jeremiah	HRK 518
Payne, Joshua	HRK 503	Pearce, Henry	DUT 56	Pearse, Jonathan	NYK 36
Payne, Joshua	OND 165	Pearce, Isaac	DUT 177	Pearse, Richard	ALB 52
Payne, Lemuel	SUF 98	Pearce, Isaac	OTS 18	Pearse, Russel	GRN 344
Payne, Nathaniel	ONN 163	Pearce, James	DUT 173	Pearse, Solon	CHN 904
Payne, Nehemiah	ESS 305	Pearce, James	OTS 58	Pearse, Thomas	HRK 573
Payne, Oliver	CHN 850	Pearce, James	WST 169	Pears_, Theophelus	CHN 846
Payne, Paul	SUF 99	Pearce, Jobe	GRN 356	Pearsell, Thomas	NYK 50
Payne, Phenias	SUF 101	Pearce, John	GRN 331	Pearselock, David	NYK 75
Payne, Rufus	SUF 102	Pearce, John	GRN 356	Pearsevil, John	CHN 804
Payne, Ruggles	CHN 938	Pearce, John	WSH 265	Pearshall, John	OTS 7
Payne, Samuel	CHN 846	Pearce, John	WSH 291	Pearson see Peerson,	
Payne, Samuel	SRA 52	Pearce, Jona_	OTS 7	Peirson & Pierson	
Payne, Saml	SUF 75	Pearce, Jona_	OTS 40	Pearson, Abraham	SUF 101
Payne, Selden	OND 177	Pearce, Levi	OTS 16	Pearson, Benjamin	ONT 380
Payne, Seth	HRK 533	Pearce, Levy	WSH 264	Pearson, Benjamin	RCK 102
Payne, Silas	SUF 98	Pearce, Pardon	OTS 18	Pearson, Caleb	SUF 101
Payne, Silvenus	SUF 99	Pearce, Peter	SRA 38	Pearson, Catherine a	
Payne, Silvenus	SUF 102	Pearce, Pomp	OTS 25	mulatto	NYK 41
Payne, Stephen	SRA 50	Pearce, Robert	DUT 49	Pearson, Charles	SUF 101
Payne, Thomas	NYK 45	Pearce, Sheldon	OTS 44	Pearson, Daniel	QNS 76
Payne, Thomas	SUF 92	Pearce, Silvester	GRN 344	Pearson, Danl W.	SUF 101
Payne, William	COL 211	Pearce, Stephen	OTS 28	Pearson, David	ONT 380
Payne, William	HRK 549	Pearce, Thomas	DUT 36	Pearson, David	SUF 101
Payne, William	SUF 98	Pearce, Thomas	WSH 267	Pearson, Edward	OTS 47
Payne, Zachariah	SUF 99	Pearce, Thomas	WST 169	Pearson, Edward	RNS 102
Payne, Zachariah	SUF 104	Pearce, Timothy	DUT 58	Pearson, George	ALB 136
Pea_e, Henry	GRN 330	Pearce, William	CHN 862	Pearson, Henry	QNS 76
Peabody, Aaron	HRK 569	Pearce, William	DUT 57	Pearson, Jedediah	SUF 101
Peabody, Aoriel	CLN 164	Pearce, William	DUT 80	Pearson, Jessee	SUF 101
Peabody, Eliphalet	OND 174	Pearce, William	NYK 78	Pearson, Job	SUF 101
Peabody, Isaac	OND 179	Pearch, Co__fry	KNG 9	Pearson, John	ONT 380
Peabody, John N.	COL 207	Pearcy, Isaac	NYK 124	Pearson, John	SUF 101
Peabody, John P.	COL 205	Peares, James	WST 169	Pearson, John Junr	SUF 101
Peabody, Parker	COL 205	Pearl, John	OND 207	Pearson, Joseph	NYK 16
Peabody, Roswell	OTS 17	Pearley see Per Lee		Pearson, Lemuel	SUF 101
Peabody, Stephen	ONT 318	Pearley, Dudley	ONN 129	Pearson, Lemuel Junr	SUF 101
Peace, A_a	CHN 846	Pearren, Polly	NYK 110	Pearson, Mary	NYK 36
Peach, Jonathan	COL 215	Pearsall, Abner	HRK 422	Pearson, Mathew	SUF 101
Peacock see Pecock		Pearsall, Clark	OND 194	Pearson, Nathan	OTS 47
Peacock, Alexander	NYK 123	Pearsall, Daniel	SUF 80	Pearson, Nathan	SUF 101
Peacock, James	WSH 243	Pearsall, David	SUF 94	Pearson, Samuel	SUF 97
Peacock, Thomas	ONT 502	Pearsall, Edward	NYK 45	Pearson, Samuel	SUF 101
Peadack, Aaron	CHN 988	Pearsall, Elias	SUF 94	Pearson, Stephen	SUF 101
Peak see Peek		Pearsall, Elizabeth	DUT 125	Pearson, Theophilus	SUF 101
Peak, Roswell	DEL 291	Pearsall, George	DUT 123	Pearson, Uriah	QNS 73
Peak, Samuel	COL 260	Pearsall, George	SUF 73	Pearson, William	NYK 66
Peak, Samuel	COL 264	Pearsall, Henry	DUT 123	Pearson, William	SUF 101
Peake, Ephraim	OTS 7	Pearsall, Henry	DUT 152	Pearson, Zebulon	SUF 101
Peake, Oliver	DEL 291	Pearsall, Henry	QNS 76	Pearsons, James Junr	MNT 75
Peake, Reuben	HRK 589	Pearsall, James	DUT 152	Pearsons, Jehial	CHN 914
Peake, William	OND 197	Pearsall, John	NYK 131	Pearss, John B.	NYK 29
Pean, Catharine a		Pearsall, John	QNS 72	Peas see Pees	
mulatto	NYK 106	Pearsall, John	QNS 73	Peas, Ambroes	WSH 235
Pearall, Adam	QNS 72	Pearsall, Joseph	NYK 45	Peas, Daniel	OTS 47
Pearce see Peirce &		Pearsall, Joseph	QNS 76	Peas, Gideon	OTS 47
Pierce		Pearsall, Mary	NYK 148	Peas, Jahiel	RNS 20
Pearce, Aaron	OTS 44	Pearsall, Mary	QNS 70	Peas, Noah	OND 197
Pearce, Abizah	DUT 87	Pearsall, Mott	CHN 758	Peas, Oliver	WSH 231
Pearce, Abrm	OTS 18	Pearsall, Nathaniel	QNS 69	Pease, Abel	CAY 546
Pearce, Baker	OTS 6	Pearsall, Nehemiah	QNS 76	Pease, Abner	ONN 138
Pearce, Benjaman	CHN 846	Pearsall, Peter	DUT 118	Pease, Abner	OTS 40
Pearce, Benjamin	WSH 285	Pearsall, Robert	NYK 45	Pease, Abraham	WSH 235
Pearce, Benoni	DUT 57	Pearsall, Samuel	QNS 64	Pease, Amos	GRN 342
Pearce, Benoni	OTS 11	Pearsall, Samuel	QNS 72	Pease, Asa	CAY 546
Pearce, Benoni Junr	DUT 57	Pearsall, Silas	SUF 93	Pease, Barzilla	COL 252
Pearce, Caleb	WST 134	Pearsall, Thomas	CHN 758	Pease, Berzile	WSH 235
Pearce, Cromwell	WSH 271	Pearsall, Thomas	NYK 43	Pease, Daniel	COL 205
Pearce, Crumal	GRN 344	Pearsall, Thomas	QNS 63	Pease, Ebenezer	COL 205
Pearce, Daniel	DUT 57	Pearsall, Thomas	QNS 64	Pease, Elam	OND 207
Pearce, Daniel	DUT 82	Pearsall, Thomas	QNS 72	Pease, Elijah	ONT 398
Pearce, Daniel	WSH 267	Pearsall, Thomas C.	NYK 28	Pease, Elisha	TIO 223
Pearce, Dean	HRK 486	Pearsall, William	NYK 77	Pease, Ephraim	COL 205
Pearce, Ephraim	ORN 336	Pearsall, William	QNS 72	Pease, Jared	SRA 33
Pearce, Ephraim	OTS 6	Pearse, Elizabeth	NYK 42	Pease, Joel	CAY 546

Name	Code	No.	Name	Code	No.	Name	Code	No.
Peirce, Eliakem	WSH	184	Pells, Hendrake	SRA	9	Penfold, Mary Widow	QNS	61
Peirce, Elias	ONT	474	Pells, Hendrick	DUT	163	Penfold, William	QNS	62
Peirce, Job	ONT	378	Pells, Henry S.	DUT	41	Penier, Reuben	HRK	548
Peirce, Joel	COL	246	Pells, John	DUT	32	Peniman, John	OTS	49
Peirce, John	WSH	206	Pells, John	DUT	65	Pennear, David	WST	153
Peirce, John	WSH	215	Pells, John	DUT	112	Pennel, Robert	WSH	222
Peirce, Jonathan	WSH	206	Pells, John G.	DUT	66	Pennell, Hase	NYK	146
Peirce, Levi	RNS	25	Pells, Michael	DUT	61	Pennell, Mary	NYK	146
Peirce, Levy	COL	187	Pells, Michael	DUT	112	Penney, Benjn	SUF	75
Peirce, Luzerne	DUT	38	Pells, Simon	DUT	60	Penney, Edward	SUF	75
Peirce, Paletiah	WSH	206	Pellum, Elisha	WST	161	Penney, John	SUF	72
Peirce, Palmer	WSH	195	Pellum, John	WST	161	Penney, Joseph	SUF	96
Peirce, Perry	WSH	212	Pelor, George	NYK	136	Penney, Sara	NYK	21
Peirce, Phineas	ONT	430	Pelser, William	ORN	380	Pennil, John	WSH	209
Peirce, Ruth	DEL	278	Pelsue, Sarah	NYK	54	Penniman, Elias	RNS	53
Peirce, William	WSH	256	Pelt, .amuel	MNT	93	Penniman, Obadiah	ALB	130
Peire, Abraham	ONT	486	Pelting, Charles	MNT	65	Penniman, Obadiah	ALB	136
Peire, John	ONT	486	Peltit, Kiah	CHN	796	Pennington, William S.	DUT	64
Peire, Samuel	ONT	486	Pelton, Benjamin	DUT	81	Penno, Laurence	CLN	164
Peire, Thomas	ONT	486	Pelton, Daniel	WST	149	Pennock, Jeams	OND	223
Peirse, Caleb	ALB	91	Pelton, Ebenezer	ULS	238	Penny, Allen	ORN	274
Peirse, Levi	ALB	91	Pelton, Gideon	ORN	295	Penny, Amiel	OTS	46
Peirse, William	NYK	130	Pelton, James	WSH	267	Penny, Benjamin	DUT	57
Peirson see Pearson			Pelton, John	HRK	422	Penny, Christopher	DUT	57
Peirson, James	ORN	362	Pelton, John	ONN	190	Penny, Comfort	TIO	226
Peirson, Josiah	ORN	336	Pelton, John	WSH	267	Penny, Daniel D.	ORN	335
Peister, Barent	COL	230	Pelton, Joseph	SRA	42	Penny, David	ORN	336
Peister, Henry	COL	235	Pelton, Peleg	ORN	336	Penny, Ebenezer	CHN	970
Peister, Jacob	COL	230	Pelton, Richard	CAY	576	Penny, Edward	QNS	69
Peister, Phillip	COL	230	Pelton, Rowel	OND	200	Penny, Edward Junr	QNS	69
Pekam see Peckham			Pelton, William	HRK	422	Penny, George	OTS	46
Pekam, Allen	CHN	982	Pelton, William	NYK	145	Penny, Isaac	ORN	274
Pekam, Jiles	CHN	982	Pelton, William	OND	182	Penny, James	NYK	141
Peke, Abraham	NYK	144	Pelts, William	SRA	48	Penny, James	ORN	336
Pelcer(?), Anthony	ORN	384	Peltsen, Henry	NYK	78	Penny, John	DUT	20
Peles, Jenny	NYK	41	Pember, Andreis	CLN	172	Penny, John	DUT	176
Pelham, Ebenezer	WST	113	Pember, Asel	CLN	172	Penny, John	ORN	274
Pelham, Henry	GRN	326	Pember, Eli	WSH	287	Penny, John	ORN	361
Pelham, James	WST	112	Pemberton, Adam	ALB	101	Penny, John	ORN	372
Pelham, Robert	WST	112	Pemberton, John	ORN	389	Penny, Jonathan	NYK	16
Pelham, William	WST	113	Pemberton, Nathan	ORN	389	Penny, Joseph	ORN	285
Peling, Derik	SRA	5	Pemberton, Susanna	ALB	99	Penny, Joseph	ULS	257
Pelissier, Victor	NYK	36	Pembleton, Leonard	CHN	870	Penny, Joshua	DUT	56
Pell, Aaron	NYK	76	Pembroke, Enos	SCH	172	Penny, Richard	ORN	311
Pell, Anna	NYK	56	Pembrook, David	NYK	120	Penny, Robert	NYK	131
Pell, Benjamin	NYK	45	Pembrook, David	ORN	306	Penny, Robinson	ORN	274
Pell, Caleb	WST	150	Pembrook, John	ULS	248	Penny, Samuel	WSH	293
Pell, Caleb Junr	NYK	117	Pembrook, William	ULS	207	Penny, Seth	OTS	46
Pell, Catherine	NYK	72	Pemley, Hiel	RCK	107	Penny, Solomon	OTS	48
Pell, Christian	NYK	95	Pencoast, Solamon	NYK	77	Penny, Susanna	DUT	57
Pell, Coleb	NYK	111	Pendal, John	SRA	39	Penny, William	DUT	172
Pell, David	WST	119	Pendall, John	DUT	17	Penny, William	ORN	274
Pell, David J.	WST	148	Pendegast, Jediah	RNS	48	Penny, William	ORN	312
Pell, Gilbert	NYK	136	Pendegrast, Wm	RNS	48	Penny, William	ORN	336
Pell, Jemima	NYK	125	Pendel, Benjamin	WSH	204	Penny, William	OTS	48
Pell, John	NYK	150	Pendel, Elisha	WSH	204	Pennyhouse, John	NYK	69
Pell, John	WST	119	Pendel, Oliver	WSH	204	Penoch, Samuel	WSH	227
Pell, Jonathan A.	NYK	136	Pender, Natl	OTS	41	Penoyre, David	DUT	72
Pell, Joseph	WST	148	Pender, William	OTS	41	Penoyre, Jacob	ORN	302
Pell, Joshua	NYK	60	Pendergast, Martin	RNS	48	Penoyre, Jonathan	DUT	134
Pell, Philip	WST	119	Pendergast, Thomas	RNS	49	Penoyre, Joseph	DUT	134
Pell, Philip	WST	148	Pendergrass, Matthew	DUT	54	Penoyre, Thomas	DUT	72
Pell, Samuel	WST	150	Pendigrass, James	STB	199	Penoyre, Wright	ORN	302
Pell, Sarah	NYK	25	Pendil, John	WSH	206	Penrose, Jacob	MNT	96
Pell, Thomas	WST	149	Pendleton, Ethan	CHN	836	Penroy, Margaret	NYK	119
Pell, William	NYK	103	Pendleton, Nathaniel	NYK	29	Pentiele, Cornelius	MNT	109
Pellam, Abraham	DEL	272	Pendleton, William	ALB	42	Pentiele, Joseph	MNT	109
Pellam, Daniel	DEL	272	Pendox, Bennona	RNS	51	Pentiele, Martin	MNT	111
Pellet, Joseph	OTS	8	Penesot, John Glander	NYK	85	Pentiele, Peter	MNT	109
Pellet, Obadiah	ORN	331	Peney see Perry			Pentiele, Wm	MNT	111
Pellet, William	ORN	331	Penfield, Daniel	COL	193	Pentierass, Thomas	MNT	45
Pelletrain, Mary	NYK	38	Penfield, Ebenezer	DEL	287	Pentz, Frederick	NYK	31
Pells, Abraham	DUT	65	Penfield, Isaac	COL	254	Peoasall, Samuel	CHN	752
Pells, Esther	DUT	68	Penfield, Nathaniel	WST	114	Peoples, Hugh	MNT	111
Pells, Evert	DUT	61	Penfield, Peter	DEL	287	Pepen, Augustus Charles	NYK	56
Pells, Evert S.	DUT	110	Penfield, William	COL	180	Pepher, Christian	NYK	98
Pells, Francis	DUT	61	Penfold, Edmund	QNS	63	Pepper, Bill	ALB	139

Pepper, Elijah	DUT 31	Perrey, Absalom	SRA 53	Perry, Jacob	RCK 101
Pepper, Jacob	WST 123	Perrey, Artemus	SRA 53	Perry, Jacobus	RCK 101
Pepper, Stephen	DUT 52	Perrey, Benjamin	SRA 53	Perry, James	DUT 78
Pepper, William	ORN 329	Perrey, Cornelius	SRA 53	Perry, James	ESS 311
Pepper, Wm	OTS 40	Perrey, Edmund	SUF 102	Perry, James	SRA 34
Pepper, Wyant	MNT 54	Perrey, Eli	SRA 53	Perry, James	WST 123
Percel, Peter	NYK 82	Perrey, Henry	WSH 217	Perry, Jerimiah	WSH 197
Perdie see Purdee &		Perrey, James	WSH 264	Perry, Johanis	RCK 101
Purdy		Perrey, John	SRA 53	Perry, John	ALB 102
Perdie, John Jun.	CAY 538	Perrey, Josiah	SRA 53	Perry, John	DEL 269
Perdie, John Sen.	CAY 538	Perrey, Josiah Junr	SRA 53	Perry, John	ORN 305
Perdun, Cato	SRA 53	Perrey, Phinehas	CAY 594	Perry, John	RCK 99
Perdy, William	ONN 142	Perrey, Reuben	SRA 38	Perry, John	RCK 102
Pergason, Jonathan	SCH 156	Perrey, Roswell	SRA 53	Perry, John	SRA 34
Perguson, Caron	SCH 156	Perrey, Roswell	SRA 53	Perry, John	WSH 186
Perguson, Willm	SCH 156	Perrey, Samuel	SRA 39	Perry, John F.	SRA 3
Perham, John	ORN 382	Perrey, Samuel	SRA 53	Perry, Jonas	ESS 309
Periam, Dinah	NYK 48	Perrey, Samuel	WSH 190	Perry, Jonas	OTS 9
Perigaud, William	NYK 58	Perrey, Seth	SRA 53	Perry, Jonathan Junr	OTS 43
Perine, Abraham	NYK 130	Perrey, Seth Junr	SRA 53	Perry, Jona Senr	OTS 43
Perine, Abraham	RCH 89	Perrey, Seth W.	SRA 53	Perry, Joseph	OND 181
Perine, Edward	RCH 91	Perriam, John	NYK 146	Perry, Joseph	RCK 98
Perine, Edward	RCH 95	Perriga, Rufus	ESS 303	Perry, Joseph	WSH 227
Perine, John	ONT 340	Perrigo, Frederick	ESS 305	Perry, Joshua	CLN 171
Perine, Joseph	RCH 91	Perrigo, Robert	WSH 219	Perry, Joshua	ONN 151
Perine, Nancy	RCH 91	Perrigo, Robert	WSH 248	Perry, Lois	DUT 138
Perine, Capt Peter	RCH 91	Perrigo, Robert Junr	WSH 248	Perry, Mary	DUT 80
Perine, Robert	NYK 20	Perrill, James	SCH 158	Perry, Mary	NYK 101
Pe....., ...		Perrin, Daniel	ONT 354	Perry, Mathew	RNS 82
(possibly Perkins)	RNS 99	Perrin, Glo	ONT 358	Perry, Moses	ONT 408
Perkins see Pirkins		Perrin, Jacob	ONT 358	Perry, Nathan	ALB 114
Perkins, Archd	OTS 31	Perrin, Jesse	ONT 356	Perry, Nathan	ESS 311
Perkins, Chales	WST 134	Perrin, John	CAY 624	Perry, Nicholas	ALB 102
Perkins, Christopher	SRA 39	Perrin, Lemuel	CAY 624	Perry, Obadiah	DUT 138
Perkins, Daniel	CHN 892	Perrin, William	NYK 142	Perry, Obadiah	SRA 34
Perkins, Daniel	OND 182	Perrine, Peter	NYK 129	Perry, Paul	SRA 60
Perkins, Danl	OTS 31	Perrine, Susan	NYK 79	Perry, Peter	CHN 742
Perkins, Daniel B.	ALB 30	Perris, David	NYK 116	Perry, Richard	NYK 114
Perkins, Ebenezer	OTS 35	Perrise, Justus	SRA 25	Perry, Robert	NYK 111
Perkins, Elisha	ONT 402	Perrot, John	NYK 42	Perry, Rouse	ONT 452
Perkins, Elisha	WSH 204	Perry, Aaron	WSH 186	Perry, Samuel	CHN 884
Perkins, Henry	ULS 239	Perry, Abraham	COL 252	Perry, Samuel	GRN 355
Perkins, Ichabod	OTS 29	Perry, Almon	SRA 15	Perry, Silas	DUT 79
Perkins, James	ONN 160	Perry, Amos	OTS 32	Perry, Simeon	DUT 166
Perkins, Jenks	WSH 249	Perry, Andrew	SRA 60	Perry, Thomas	DUT 138
Perkins, John	CAY 702	Perry, Andrew	WST 132	Perry, Thomas	RNS 14
Perkins, John	OTS 35	Perry, Anthony	WSH 230	Perry, Uriah	RCK 106
Perkins, Joseph	ONT 400	Perry, Arbie	SRA 34	Perry, William	CHN 886
Perkins, Joseph	SRA 8	Perry, Arthur	OND 175	Perry, William	WSH 186
Perkins, Moses	WSH 287	Perry, Benjamin	CHN 786	Perry, Winsloe	CAY 670
Perkins, Nathaniel	MNT 88	Perry, Benjn	CHN 884	Persall, Elias	SUF 64
Perkins, Nathaniel	MNT 90	Perry, Benjamin	DUT 142	Persall, Paul	SUF 64
Perkins, Nathaniel J.	ULS 240	Perry, Brayton	WSH 189	Persans, James	SRA 45
Perkins, Oliver	SRA 38	Perry, Daniel	CHN 742	Persen, Cornelius	ULS 223
Perkins, Phineas	ONT 418	Perry, Daniel	CLN 171	Persen, John	DEL 267
Perkins, Richard	OND 182	Perry, David	CAY 560	Persen, Margaret	ULS 225
Perkins, Rosel	OND 212	Perry, David	CHN 800	Persen, Matthew	ULS 228
Perkins, Samuel	GRN 336	Perry, David	COL 218	Persen, Sarah	ULS 228
Perkins, Silas	OND 212	Perry, David	ORN 272	Persey, Samuel	SCH 165
Perkins, Solomon Junr	CHN 886	Perry, David	ORN 305	Persival, Elchany	GRN 343
Perkins, Sprague	CHN 888	Perry, Ebenezer	ULS 181	Persival, Paul	GRN 343
Perkins, Stephen	RNS 99	Perry, Edward	COL 206	Person, Garret	GRN 331
Perkins, Thomas	CAY 538	Perry, Edward	DUT 26	Person, Isaac	NYK 99
Perkins, Valentine	ULS 240	Perry, Edward Junr	COL 210	Person, J_eph	ONT 380
Perkins, William	NYK 147	Perry, Eli	ALB 94	Persons, Begordes	WSH 208
Perkins, William	NYK 151	Perry, Elijah	ULS 198	Persons, Benjn	CHN 932
Perkins, William	ULS 239	Perry, Elmon	SRA 12	Persons, Jeremiah	SRA 15
Perkins, Zophar	ULS 239	Perry, Ely	CLN 157	Persons, Joseah	CHN 922
Perkins, Zophar E.	ULS 239	Perry, Freeman	WSH 301	Persons, Levi	SRA 56
Perkley, Hannah	ALB 68	Perry, George T.	CHN 770	Persons, Moses	SRA 19
Per Lee, Edmund	DUT 140	Perry, Gilbert	ALB 41	Persons, Samuel	WSH 192
Peron, John B.	CLN 160	Perry, Hermanus	RCK 102	Perters, Samuel	GRN 345
Perree, Nichs	OTS 32	Perry, Icabod	CAY 708	Pertilow, Allen	WSH 256
Perrego, Joseph H.	WSH 244	Perry, Ichabod	OND 181	Peru, Eliphalet	OND 208
Perren, Thomas	WSH 278	Perry, Ichabot	GRN 352	Peru, Simeon	OND 207
Perrey, Abner	SRA 51	Perry, Isaac	CHN 742	Peru, William	SRA 58
Perrey, Abner	SRA 53	Perry, Isaac	RCK 101	Pesinger, John	NYK 123

Name	Loc	Pg
Pesor, Powel	QNS	72
Pesse_na, Luke	NYK	133
Pestana, Mannuel	NYK	22
Pestis, Philip	ONT	440
Petchard, Godfray	CHN	940
Petebone, Charls	CHN	946
Petengil, Oliver S.	OND	207
Peter a free Negro	ALB	3
Peter a Black	NYK	104
Peter a mulatto	NYK	130
Peter	QNS	63
Peter	QNS	64
Peter	QNS	74
Peter	QNS	82
Peter	QNS	83
Peter	QNS	85
Peter a Negro	SUF	67
Peter a Negro	SUF	72
Peter	SUF	86
Peter	SUF	96
Peter, Daniel	RNS	42
Peters,] Negroes James	CHN	932
Peters, Abijah	ONT	432
Peters, Amasa	OND	197
Peters, Barbary	NYK	58
Peters, Barnet	ONT	354
Peters, Benjamin	ONT	440
Peters, Benjamin	ULS	202
Peters, Charles	QNS	81
Peters, Charles	SUF	79
Peters, Cipio a Black	NYK	52
Peters, George	DUT	7
Peters, Harry	NYK	29
Peters, Henry	NYK	53
Peters, Henry	ORN	326
Peters, Herman	ALB	25
Peters, Hewlet	DUT	122
Peters, James	ALB	11
Peters, James	NYK	141
Peters, James a Black	NYK	146
Peters, James	QNS	72
Peters, John	NYK	20
Peters, John	NYK	28
Peters, John	QNS	69
Peters, John	QNS	81
Peters, Nicholas a Black	NYK	46
Peters, Peter	ALB	10
Peters, Peter	WSH	306
Peters, Richard	DEL	270
Peters, Richd	SUF	76
Peters, Salle	SUF	109
Peters, Samuel	DUT	16
Peters, Samuel	SRA	14
Peters, Sarah	DUT	120
Peters, Smith	DUT	120
Peters, Stephen	ONT	354
Peters, Volutine	ESS	304
Peters, Wm	ALB	12
Peters, William	NYK	37
Peters, William	ONT	348
Peters, William	ONT	356
Peters, William	ULS	202
Peterschen, Mary	NYK	30
Petersen, Francis	OTS	44
Peterson, Benjamin	COL	258
Peterson, Benjamin	ORN	341
Peterson, Cornelius	CAY	710
Peterson, Cornelius	NYK	122
Peterson, Cornelius Junr	CAY	710
Peterson, David	ORN	372
Peterson, David	SUF	69
Peterson, Garret	NYK	113
Peterson, Garret	NYK	115
Peterson, George	CAY	710
Peterson, Henry	ORN	374
Peterson, Isaac	ORN	332
Peterson, Isaac	SRA	4
Peterson, Isaac	ULS	180
Peterson, Jack Blackman	WST	154
Peterson, Jacob	NYK	114
Peterson, James	COL	215
Peterson, James	SRA	4
Peterson, John	NYK	122
Peterson, John a Black	NYK	127
Peterson, John	NYK	137
Peterson, John	ORN	374
Peterson, John	WSH	244
Peterson, Jonathan	NYK	49
Peterson, Lawrence	ONT	314
Peterson, Lemuel	WSH	210
Peterson, Nathan	WSH	246
Peterson, Paul a Black	NYK	60
Peterson, Peter a Black	NYK	118
Peterson, Peter	NYK	135
Peterson, Phillip	COL	215
Peterson, Ralph	CAY	710
Peterson, Richard	CAY	710
Peterson, Richard	SRA	4
Peterson, Robert	ORN	374
Peterson, Samuel	ORN	380
Peterson, Silvenus	CHN	838
Peterson, Solomon a mulatto	NYK	87
Peterson, Thomas a mulatto	NYK	97
Peterson, Willm	COL	215
Peterson, William	NYK	120
Peterson, William	NYK	122
Peterson, Wright	ORN	332
Petersoun, Zebulon	QNS	72
Petett, Fabes	MNT	73
Pethplace, David	CHN	794
Petingile, Elihu	OND	212
Petir, Timothy	ONN	153
Petit, Jaber	MNT	16
Petit, Michael	QNS	73
Petit, William	NYK	32
Petitt, Jonathan	COL	212
Petitt, Partrick	NYK	62
Petitt, Robert	NYK	70
Petitt, Samuel	COL	193
Petmore, Abraham	ULS	190
Petmore, Henry	ULS	190
Petmore, John	ORN	308
Petre, Amelia	NYK	98
Petre, Elias	COL	229
Petre, Jacob J.	COL	229
Petre, Richard	CHN	944
Petre, Richard	CHN	944
Petrie, Conrad	SCH	145
Petrie, Conrad	SCH	152
Petrie, Daniel	HRK	453
Petrie, Daniel	HRK	486
Petrie, Frederick	HRK	487
Petrie, Jacob	HRK	486
Petrie, Jacob Junr	HRK	486
Petrie, John	HRK	452
Petrie, John J.	HRK	452
Petrie, John M.	HRK	449
Petrie, Joseph	HRK	451
Petrie, Joseph J.	HRK	579
Petrie, Jost D.	HRK	449
Petrie, Marks	HRK	453
Petrie, Richd	HRK	452
Petrie, Richd Junr	HRK	452
Petrie, William	HRK	436
Petry, Hendrick	GRN	343
Petry, John D.	OND	162
Petry, Mark	HRK	448
Petry, Peter	ALB	81
Pettee, Benjn	SUF	65
Pettee, Benjn	SUF	71
Pettee, Danl	SUF	77
Pettee, David	SUF	77
Pettee, Elisha	SUF	68
Pettee, James	SUF	72
Pettee, Jonathan	SUF	77
Pettee, Joseph	SUF	77
Pettee, Penne	SUF	71
Pettee, Phineas	SUF	69
Pettee, Uriah	SUF	68
Pettee, Wm	SUF	65
Pettengale, Jacob	CHN	938
Pettengale, Thomas	CHN	822
Petter, Jacob	OND	207
Petter, Patience a Black	NYK	111
Pettery, Jacob	ALB	79
Pettery, John	ALB	79
Pettes, William	WSH	242
Pettet, Daniel	GRN	354
Pettet, Hesekia	GRN	335
Pettet, Hezekeah	WSH	298
Pettet, Josiah	GRN	335
Pettey, James	SUF	96
Pettey, James Junr	SUF	96
Pettey, Nathaniel	SUF	96
Petteys, Mathew Jur	WSH	244
Pettibone, Daniel	ULS	234
Pettibone, Jacob	MNT	61
Pettiger, Richard	NYK	66
Pettingal, Joseph	ORN	278
Pettingale, Samuel	WSH	299
Pettinger, Richard	SRA	26
Pettingil, Josiah	OTS	22
Pettingill, Edmund	OTS	21
Pettingill, Edmund Junr	OTS	21
Pettis, David	HRK	436
Pettis, Elizabeth	COL	249
Pettis, John	OTS	46
Pettis, Samuel	CAY	712
Pettis, William	OND	223
Pettit, Abigail	QNS	60
Pettit, Abraham	ORN	272
Pettit, Benjamin	QNS	78
Pettit, Carman	DUT	39
Pettit, Daniel	NYK	84
Pettit, Daniel	QNS	61
Pettit, Ebenezer	DUT	23
Pettit, Ebenezer	HRK	501
Pettit, Elijah	QNS	75
Pettit, Elisha	COL	197
Pettit, George	QNS	78
Pettit, Gilbert	DUT	114
Pettit, Isaac	KNG	9
Pettit, Isaac	QNS	70
Pettit, James	CHN	798
Pettit, James	COL	202
Pettit, James	QNS	77
Pettit, Jane	QNS	75
Pettit, John	KNG	3
Pettit, John	MNT	94
Pettit, John	QNS	77
Pettit, John	RNS	96
Pettit, John	SRA	30
Pettit, John	SRA	60
Pettit, Jonathan	CHN	798
Pettit, Joseph	NYK	60
Pettit, Joseph	QNS	78
Pettit, Joshua	QNS	75
Pettit, Macajah	WSH	216
Pettit, Obadiah	QNS	70
Pettit, Peter	DUT	106
Pettit, Peter	QNS	78
Pettit, Rebeca	SRA	8

Pettit, Richard	QNS 77	Phelps, Friend	CAY 628	Phero, Valentine	SCH 144
Pettit, Samuel	DUT 103	Phelps, George	RNS 107	Pherris see Ferris	
Pettit, Samuel	QNS 77	Phelps, Gerard	ONT 350	Pherris, Martin	MNT 51
Pettit, Sarah	QNS 75	Phelps, Giles	ESS 318	Pherrist, Gilbert	GRN 355
Pettit, Seth	COL 185	Phelps, Hanah	CHN 742	Pherrist, John	GRN 355
Pettit, Silas	ALB 27	Phelps, Hezekiah	ESS 318	Pheston, Thomas	ALB 5
Pettit, Silas	DUT 5	Phelps, Homer	COL 184	Phethplace, Phillup	CHN 794
Pettit, Simeon	QNS 74	Phelps, Ira	ESS 311	Phettiplace, John	WSH 298
Pettit, Stephen	QNS 74	Phelps, Isaac	WSH 275	Phiddens, Hugh	TIO 238
Pettit, Sylvanus	QNS 73	Phelps, Israel	COL 219	Phifer see Pifer	
Pettit, Thomas	SRA 29	Phelps, Israel	ONT 500	Phifer, Michael	CAY 588
Pettit, William	QNS 77	Phelps, Israel	SRA 30	Phifer, Peter	CAY 590
Pettit, William	QNS 77	Phelps, Jacob	CHN 946	Philan, James	NYK 45
Petti[tt?], Amos	SUF 81	Phelps, James	ALB 140	Phileps, Burdin	WSH 216
Pettitt, William	COL 204	Phelps, James	CHN 762	Phileps, Noah	WSH 195
Pettreau, Elias Junr	SUF 97	Phelps, Jedediah	OND 177	Phileps, Peter	WSH 215
Pettreau, John	SUF 97	Phelps, Jeremiah	HRK 516	Phileps, Samuel	WSH 217
Petts, Samuel	SRA 39	Phelps, Joel	WSH 214	Philip	QNS 63
Petty, Arthur	ORN 319	Phelps, John	OND 189	Philip	SUF 93
Petty(?), James	ESS 307	Phelps, John	ONN 178	Philip	SUF 108
Petty, James	ESS 320	Phelps, John	OTS 11	Philip, Jacob P.	COL 265
Petty, Truman(?)	ESS 305	Phelps, John	SRA 30	Philip, Joshua	OND 207
Petty, William	ESS 307	Phelps, John	SCH 146	Philips, Abraham	MNT 14
Pettyes, Mathew	WSH 244	Phelps, John	WSH 298	Philips, Amaziah	CAY 614
Pettys, David	WSH 231	Phelps, John B.	COL 203	Philips, Ann	ALB 17
Pettys, David	WSH 232	Phelps, John S.	RNS 94	Philips, Archibald	NYK 34
Pettys, Eli	WSH 232	Phelps, Jonah	COL 187	Philips, Conrad	ONN 167
Pettys, James	WSH 205	Phelps, Jonathan	ONT 428	Philips, Danl	RCK 100
Pettys, James	WSH 219	Phelps, Jonathan	ONT 430	Philips, Darius	OND 207
Pettys, Jesse	WSH 205	Phelps, Jonathan	WSH 192	Philips, David	MNT 98
Pettys, John	WSH 203	Phelps, Joseph	CHN 792	Philips, David	OND 207
Pettys, John	WSH 231	Phelps, Joseph	CHN 848	Philips, Eli	RCK 100
Pettys, Joseph	WSH 252	Phelps, Joseph	CHN 962	Philips, Elijah	ONN 172
Pettys, Oliver	WSH 210	Phelps, Joseph	COL 222	Philips, Elisha	OND 207
Pettys, Peleg	WSH 210	Phelps, Joseph	OND 178	Philips, Elisha	WSH 228
Pettyt, Heman	WSH 222	Phelps, Joseph	ONT 440	Philips, Francis	WSH 188
Petus, Joseph P.	CHN 960	Ph lps, Joseph	WSH 298	Philips, Frederick	SUF 68
Pew, Abraham	SRA 39	Phelps, Josiah	CAY 632	Philips, Gedieon	WSH 248
Pew, Jacob	WSH 222	Phelps, Luke	ONT 342	Philips, Gilbert	RCK 100
Peynoyer, John	COL 264	Phelps, Luman	ONT 468	Philips, Israel	SRA 38
Pezer, Martin	RNS 45	Phelps, Miriam	CAY 632	Philips, James	ALB 124
Pfieffer see Phifer &		Phelps, Moses	SRA 23	Philips, Jason	CAY 624
Pifer		Phelps, Moses	SRA 26	Philips, Jehial	ALB 22
Pfieffer, George H.	DUT 158	Phelps, Nathan	ONT 444	Philips, John	ALB 16
Pharo, Daniel a		Phelps, Niel	SCH 143	Philips, John	HRK 460
Black	NYK 135	Phelps, Noah	CHN 974	Philips, John	ONN 172
Pheatt, Benjamin	ONN 156	Phelps, Noah	HRK 457	Philips, John	ONT 372
Phelan, Denis	NYK 31	Phelps, Norman	WSH 298	Philips, John	ONT 374
Pheleppe, Harmanus	MNT 47	Phelps, Olever	CHN 974	Philips, John	ONT 424
Pheleps, Roswel	WSH 208	Phelps, Plinny	CHN 792	Philips, John	OTS 4
Phelips, Edmond	SCH 171	Phelps, Ralph R.	SCH 118	Philips, John	OTS 49
Phelpes, Benjaman	CHN 832	Phelps, Roger	OND 214	Philips, John	RNS 83
Phelps, Alexander	CHN 764	Phelps, Ruben	CHN 858	Philips, John	RCK 100
Phelps, Alvin	SCH 148	Phelps, Rubin	CLN 162	Philips, Jonathan	ONT 412
Phelps, Ambrose	ONT 426	Phelps, Rufus	OTS 22	Philips, Joseph	ALB 26
Phelps, Asa	ALB 88	Phelps, Samuel	ALB 42	Philips, Joseph	ALB 39
Phelps, Asa Junr	ALB 89	Phelps, Samuel	SRA 48	Philips, Joseph	SUF 68
Phelps, Authur	CAY 648	Phelps, Sarah	COL 184	Philips, Joseph	SUF 95
Phelps, Barney	SCH 171	Phelps, Seth	CAY 628	Philips, Josiah	SUF 95
Phelps, Bela	ALB 89	Phelps, Silas	OND 178	Philips, Levi	ONN 183
Phelps, Beriah	COL 181	Phelps, Siles	WSH 192	Philips, Luther	ONT 412
Phelps, Daniel	WSH 196	Phelps, Simeon	HRK 523	Philips, Martin	MNT 73
Phelps, Darius	SCH 143	Phelps, Simeon	SRA 33	Philips, Michael	GRN 327
Phelps, David	CLN 162	Phelps, Simri	CAY 632	Philips, Moses	SUF 96
Phelps, David	COL 184	Phelps, Stephen	ALB 106	Philips, Nathan	SUF 68
Phelps, David	DEL 275	Phelps, Stephen	ONT 350	Philips, Nicholas	ONN 167
Phelps, Ebenezar	CAY 688	Phelps, Syah	CHN 760	Philips, Perly	ONT 350
Phelps, Egabud	SCH 144	Phelps, Thomas	CHN 944	Philips, Peter	RNS 87
Phelps, Eli	HRK 457	Phelps, Timothy	SRA 24	Philips, Phebe	SRA 40
Phelps, Elijah	RNS 31	Phelps, Timothy Junr	SRA 24	Philips, Philetus	WST 126
Phelps, Elisha	CAY 520	Phelps, William	CHN 792	Philips, Rachael	HRK 519
Phelps, Elizabeth	CAY 520	Phelps, Zerah	CHN 902	Philips, Reuben	SRA 38
Phelps, Emon	ONN 181	Phenix, Daniel	NYK 31	Philips, Rewmea	SUF 64
Phelps, Enoch	DEL 278	Phenix, Philip	NYK 110	Philips, Richard	HRK 451
Phelps, Ezra	ONT 342	Pheppenny, Joseph	WSH 302	Philips, Ronald	WSH 254
Phelps, Felix	CAY 646	Phero, Christian	ALB 51	Philips, Roswell	ALB 22
Phelps, Flora	ALB 49	Phero, John	ALB 86	Philips, Samuel	ALB 85

Philips, Saml	SUF 68	Phillips, Jeremiah	ORN 287	Philmore, John	CAY 722
Philips, Solomon	SRA 53	Phillips, John	COL 237	Philpot, Richard	RCK 101
Philips, Somers	SRA 25	Phillips, John	DUT 150	Philps, Jonah	MNT 46
Philips, Thomas	ALB 34	Phillips, John	GRN 346	Philps, William	NYK 44
Philips, Thomas	HRK 427	Phillips, John	NYK 57	Philupson, John Junr	MNT 45
Philips, Thomas	QNS 64	Phillips, John	NYK 79	Phin_y, Ber___	ONT 504
Philips, Thos	RCK 101	Phillips, John	NYK 100	Phinemors, David	ALB 46
Philips, William	ALB 148	Phillips, John	RNS 65	Phinnett, Bennona	CHN 790
Philips, William	ONT 462	Phillips, John	RNS 74	Phinney, Elihu	OTS 19
Philips, Wm	SUF 68	Phillips, John Junr	RNS 74	Phinney, Joel	ESS 317
Philips, William	SUF 95	Phillips, John H.	DUT 37	Phinney, John	COL 214
Philips, William	WSH 235	Phillips, John R.	DUT 34	Phinney, Sylvanus	COL 249
Philips, Zebulon	WST 153	Phillips, Jonathan	OND 163	Phinney, Sylvester	OND 193
Philips, Zephaniah	HRK 518	Phillips, Joseph	DUT 94	Phinny, Heman	ESS 318
Phillemore, Cepta	CLN 172	Phillips, Joseph	RNS 12	Phino, Philander	SRA 30
Philleps, Elijah	WSH 195	Phillips, Joseph	STB 198	Phippany, Joseph	WSH 306
Philler, George	ALB 88	Phillips, Joseph P.	RNS 74	Phips, Joseph	OND 207
Phillip a Black	NYK 22	Phillips, Jued	CHN 764	Phoebus, William	NYK 124
Phillip, Abraham	COL 265	Phillips, Levina	DUT 37	Phoenix, James	DEL 273
Phillip, Beaty	COL 193	Phillips, Mary	NYK 96	Phoenix, John	STB 202
Phillip, George	COL 191	Phillips, Michael	RNS 87	Phoenix, William	DEL 271
Phillip, Henry	COL 195	Phillips, Mills	SUF 90	Phoenix, Wm	STB 202
Phillip, Isaac	GRN 343	Phillips, Moses	ORN 346	Phrasy, Eliphalet	SCH 139
Phillip, Jacob	COL 257	Phillips, Nicholas	DUT 150	Phricky, John	MNT 3
Phillip, Jacob Junr	COL 259	Phillips, Oliver	CHN 780	Phyfe, Duncan	NYK 53
Phillip, Jacob H.	COL 193	Phillips, Parley	OTS 47	Phyle, John	NYK 54
Phillip, Jeremiah	COL 213	Phillips, Peleg	SCH 171	Pibbots, Samuel	NYK 26
Phillip, John	COL 257	Phillips, Peter	RNS 74	Pick, George	NYK 76
Phillip, Patrus	COL 257	Phillips, Ralph	DUT 25	Pick, Noah	ULS 199
Phillip, Peter	COL 189	Phillips, Roeliff I.	DUT 34	Pick, Peter	WSH 210
Phillip, Peter	COL 259	Phillips, Samuel	HRK 556	Pickard, Adolps	OTS 58
Phillip, Peter Junr	COL 257	Phillips, Samuel	RNS 68	Pickard, Conradt	OTS 58
Phillip, Peter M.	COL 229	Phillips, Samuel	SUF 90	Pickard, Coonrod	CHN 940
Phillip, Wilhelmus	COL 189	Phillips, Samuel	WST 152	Pickard, George	MNT 35
Phillip, Wilhelmus	COL 195	Phillips, Sarah a		Pickard, Hack	CHN 942
Phillip, William	COL 193	Black	NYK 44	Pickard, Isaac	MNT 35
Phillips, Aaron	DUT 70	Phillips, Sophia	RNS 7	Pickard, John	CHN 940
Phillips, Abraham	DUT 40	Phillips, Suire	RNS 43	Pickard, John	MNT 27
Phillips, Abraham	NYK 139	Phillips, Sylvester	CHN 766	Pickard, John	OTS 58
Phillips, Alexan	MNT 42	Phillips, Thomas	DUT 148	Pickard, Joseph	CHN 940
Phillips, Allen	MNT 92	Phillips, Thomas	NYK 129	Pickard, Nicholas	CHN 940
Phillips, Anthony	NYK 83	Phillips, Thomas	RNS 68	Pickard, Nicholas	CHN 944
Phillips, Asahel	CAY 672	Phillips, Thomas 2d	RNS 74	Pickard, Nicholas	MNT 33
Phillips, Benjamin	CLN 155	Phillips, Timothy	RNS 56	Pickard, Wm	OTS 58
Phillips, Chandler	CLN 158	Phillips, Vespatian	CAY 670	Pickering, Nathanl	TIO 246
Phillips, Christian	HRK 471	Phillips, Volkert	SCH 171	Pickerns, John	MNT 37
Phillips, Cornelius	ULS 208	Phillips, Wadsworth	OND 169	Pickerton, James	WST 136
Phillips, David	DUT 95	Phillips, Welcome	WSH 287	Picket, Christian	HRK 577
Phillips, David	NYK 139	Phillips, William	DUT 39	Picket, Daniel	TIO 232
Phillips, David	RNS 12	Phillips, William	NYK 39	Picket, Eldad	GRN 351
Phillips, David	ULS 254	Phillips, William	NYK 116	Picket, Jonathan	SCH 135
Phillips, Gabriel N.	ORN 346	Phillips, William E.	RNS 106	Picket, Joseph	GRN 354
Phillips, George	NYK 121	Phillips, William I.	DUT 34	Picket, Lidea	WSH 271
Phillips, George	ORN 332	Phillips, Zachariah &		Picket, Philip	ALB 34
Phillips, Gilbert	OND 175	W.	DUT 150	Pickett, Barthole_w	MNT 53
Phillips, Henry	DUT 37	Phillips, Zachariah		Pickett, Elbert	NYK 88
Phillips, Henry	NYK 24	Junr	DUT 156	Pickett, Samuel	CHN 810
Phillips, Henry	NYK 98	Phillips, Zacheus	HRK 512	Pickett, Selah	CHN 802
Phillips, Henry	NYK 104	Phillis a Black	NYK 104	Picki_, Samuel	MNT 36
Phillips, Henry	ORN 358	Phillo, Adam	SRA 10	Pickle, Henry	RNS 96
Phillips, Henry Junr	DUT 39	Phillo, Azor	SRA 11	Pickle, John	MNT 9
Phillips, Henry C.	DUT 71	Phillo, Nathan	SRA 11	Picksley see Pixley	
Phillips, Henry H.	DUT 35	Phillo, Samuel	RNS 111	Picksley, Reuben	ONN 140
Phillips, Henry R.	DUT 38	Phillo, Samuel	SRA 10	Picksley, Welcome	OND 207
Phillips, Isaac	RNS 53	Phillops, Edward	GRN 336	Picktel, Catharine	COL 198
Phillips, Isaac	SRA 51	Phillops, Ezekiel	GRN 336	Picktel, Christopher	COL 235
Phillips, Jacob	DUT 142	Phillops, James	GRN 336	Pideon, William	QNS 76
Phillips, Jacob	GRN 325	Phillops, Jeremiah	GRN 336	Pier see Peer	
Phillips, Jacob	ORN 391	Phillops, Jesse	GRN 336	Pier, Abner	OTS 16
Phillips, James	DUT 37	Phillow, Enoch	DUT 44	Pier, David	OTS 16
Phillips, James	DUT 68	Phillps, Almon	ESS 321	Pier, Henry a Black	NYK 50
Phillips, James	DUT 170	Phillups, John A.	CHN 896	Pier, John E.	MNT 3
Phillips, James	NYK 143	Phillups, Michal	CHN 784	Pier, Silas	OTS 16
Phillips, James	ORN 273	Phillups, Parker	CHN 794	Pier, Solomon	OTS 17
Phillips, James	ULS 184	Philly, Reuben	DEL 268	Pier, Thomas	OTS 16
Phillips, James Senr	DUT 40	Philmon, Cyrus	ONN 169	Pierce see Pearce,	
Phillips, James C.	DUT 70	Philmon, Earle	OND 207	Peirce, & Pearse	

Name	Ref	Name	Ref	Name	Ref
Pitcher, John	RNS 87	Place, Sarah	QNS 78	Platt, George	CLN 166
Pitcher, John W.	DUT 156	Place, Smith	NYK 89	Platt, Gilbert	SUF 81
Pitcher, Jonath	SRA 51	Place, Solomon	WSH 252	Platt, Gilbert	SUF 85
Pitcher, Jonathan	WSH 208	Place, Thomas	NYK 121	Platt, Henry	RNS 108
Pitcher, Joseph	ALB 37	Place, Uriah	SRA 33	Platt, Isaac	SUF 86
Pitcher, Peter	ALB 76	Place, William	SUF 86	Platt, Israel	SUF 86
Pitcher, Peter	RNS 87	Place, William	ULS 264	Platt, James	CLN 157
Pitcher, Phillip	COL 228	Placer, Lawrence	HRK 430	Platt, James	COL 185
Pitcher, Phillip	DUT 156	Plangburn, Isaac	NYK 76	Platt, James	MNT 60
Pitcher, Samuel	WST 127	Plank, Cornelius	MNT 26	Platt, James	NYK 60
Pitcher, Wilhelmus	COL 196	Plank, Dudley	RNS 92	Platt, Janas	SUF 87
Pitcher, William	ALB 76	Plank, Elisha	CHN 898	Platt, Jared	COL 214
Pitcher, William	DUT 150	Plank, George	GEN 327	Platt, Jeremiah	SUF 89
Pitkin, Elisha	COL 247	Plank, George	GRN 328	Platt, Jessee	SUF 83
Pitman, Isiah	NYK 113	Plank, Henry	ALB 91	Platt, Joel	COL 183
Pitman, John	ORN 326	Plank, Henry	MNT 13	Platt, John	ALB 18
Pitman, John	WSH 298	Plank, Jeremiah	GRN 341	Platt, John	CLN 157
Pitman, Samuel	WSH 298	Plank, John	GRN 341	Platt, John	OND 214
Pitman, Samuel C.	NYK 67	Plank, John	MNT 71	Platt, John	RNS 13
Pitney, James	ONT 468	Plank, John Jun	GRN 341	Platt, Jonas	OND 157
Pits, Philip	WSH 187	Plank, Michael	GRN 327	Platt, Jonathan	TIO 234
Pitt, Abraham E.	DUT 68	Plank, Peter	ALB 91	Platt, Joseph	GRN 357
Pitt, John	NYK 40	Plank, Phelip	MNT 55	Platt, Joseph	OTS 44
Pitt, Nicholas	NYK 76	Plank, Ryn..a..	MNT 72	Platt, Levi	CLN 157
Pitt, Richard	RCK 99	Plank, William	GRN 327	Platt, Mary	NYK 74
Pitts, Amasa	COL 216	Plank, Wm	GRN 328	Platt, Moses	DUT 103
Pitts, David	HRK 484	Plank, Wm	MNT 49	Platt, Nathaniel	CLN 165
Pitts, Freeman	WSH 301	Plank, Zebediah	OND 193	Platt, Nathaniel S.	ONN 162
Pitts, Gideon	WSH 301	Plant, Benjamin	OND 175	Platt, Nehemiah	WSH 216
Pitts, Jacob	ORN 296	Plant, John	ONT 464	Platt, Nehemiah	WSH 216
Pitts, Jacob	ORN 361	Plant, Leonard	CAY 522	Platt, Obediah	SUF 86
Pitts, John	ORN 361	Plantain, John	NYK 96	Platt, Peleg	SUF 89
Pitts, Joseph	COL 221	Plants, Peter	MNT 69	Platt, Peter	SUF 82
Pitts, Levi	ONN 151	Planvelt, Jesse	NYK 102	Platt, Philetus	SUF 87
Pitts, Peter	ONT 332	Plapher, Christian	MNT 14	Platt, Philetus	SUF 87
Pitts, Peter	WSH 193	Plass, Catherine	COL 224	Platt, Philip a Negro	QNS 65
Pitts, Phillip	COL 217	Plass, Coenradt	COL 253	Platt, Richard	QNS 64
Pitts, Samuel	WSH 223	Plass, Hendrick	ULS 192	Platt, Richard	QNS 65
Pitts, Sylvester	ONT 416	Plass, Johannis	COL 197	Platt, Robert	CLN 158
Pitts, William	COL 246	Plass, Michael	ULS 192	Platt, Samuel	WSH 216
Pitts, Wm	GRN 355	Plass, Petrus	COL 224	Platt, Scudder	SUF 88
Pitts, William	ONT 332	Plass, Phillip	DUT 155	Platt, Selah	SUF 82
Pixley see Peckesly,		Plass, William	COL 224	Platt, Silas	SUF 86
Picksley, Pifsley &		Platner, Hannah	COL 230	Platt, Stephen	ALB 87
Pigsley		Platner, Jacob	COL 233	Platt, Stephen	GRN 346
Pixley, Cooper	CAY 590	Platner, Jacob	DUT 150	Platt, Stephen	NYK 134
Pixley, Enoch	CAY 590	Platner, Jacob C.	COL 198	Platt, Stephen	ONN 168
Pixley, Ephraim	COL 233	Platner, Jacob F.	DEL 290	Platt, Theodorus	CLN 164
Pixley, James	COL 178	Platner, Jacob M.	COL 231	Platt, Tredwell	SUF 89
Pixley, Job	CAY 566	Platner, Jonas	COL 230	Platt, Truman	CLN 157
Pixley, John	COL 180	Platner, Marcus	COL 230	Platt, Uriah	QNS 69
Pixley, Joseph	COL 180	Platner, Marcus Junr	COL 229	Platt, William	HRK 475
Pixley, Nelly	COL 178	Platner, Mathias	COL 231	Platt, William	NYK 145
Pixley, Obed	ONN 180	Platner, Thomas	COL 233	Platt, William	OND 189
Pixley, Planner	CHN 798	Plato Negro	QNS 66	Platt, William P.	CLN 160
Pixley, Samuel	CHN 798	Plato Negro	QNS 73	Platt, Zebulon	SUF 86
Pixley, Willm	COL 178	Plato	SUF 108	Platt, Zephaniah	CLN 164
Pixley, William	SRA 34	Plato, Isaac	SUF 108	Platt, Zephaniah	DUT 40
Pizer, Peter	RNS 45	Plato, James	ALB 56	Platt, Zopher	SUF 86
Place, Aaron	NYK 142	Plato, James	HRK 456	Plau, Jan G.	ULS 255
Place, Benjamin	WST 115	Platt	GRN 344	Pleas, Freeman	DUT 26
Place, Elijah	OTS 26	Platt, Abell	WSH 285	Pleas, Isaac	DUT 36
Place, Elkanah	SUF 86	Platt, Annanias	ALB 136	Plimpton, John	ONT 460
Place, Ephraim	NYK 104	Platt, Benjamin	WSH 221	Plooker, Samuel	NYK 17
Place, Jacob	COL 196	Platt, Benoni	WST 116	Ploss, Emerick	COL 255
Place, Jeremiah	WSH 252	Platt, Brewster	OTS 25	Ploss, Henry	COL 255
Place, John	NYK 22	Platt, Charles	CLN 164	Ploss, John	COL 255
Place, John	ONT 444	Platt, Charles	WST 143	Ploss, John	RNS 87
Place, John	QNS 76	Platt, Cipio a Black	NYK 36	Ploss, William	RNS 87
Place, John	SUF 86	Platt, Daniel	COL 262	Plough, Henry	SCH 121
Place, Joseph	NYK 96	Platt, Daniel	OTS 44	Plough, Jacob	ULS 226
Place, Mary	NYK 73	Platt, Ebenezar	GRN 338	Plough, Peter	ULS 267
Place, Morris	SUF 86	Platt, Ebenezar	SUF 86	Plough, Samuel	ULS 218
Place, Nathan	RNS 73	Platt, Epenetus	NYK 129	Plough, Teunis	ULS 205
Place, Nathan	WSH 299	Platt, Epinetus	SUF 83	Plough, William	DUT 41
Place, Pardon	RNS 67	Platt, Ethel	COL 183	Ploughman, William	ORN 347
Place, Pierce	NYK 131	Platt, Ezra	ONT 430	Plum, David	COL 246

Name	Loc	Name	Loc	Name	Loc
Plum, Elisha	COL 208	Pollock, James	CLN 160	Pool, Michal	CHN 794
Plum, Peter	COL 208	Pollock, John	DUT 35	Pool, Thomas	KNG 7
Plum, Samuel	COL 248	Pollock, John	GRN 328	Pool, Thomas	ONN 150
Plumb, Allen	GRN 357	Pollock, John	RNS 4	Pool, Thomas	ONN 152
Plumb, Amariah Junr	CHN 778	Pollock, Robert	DUT 35	Pool, Timothy	OND 221
Plumb, Ameriah	CHN 778	Pollock, William	DUT 35	Pool, Wm	RCK 103
Plumb, Bailey	OTS 13	Pollock, William W.	ONT 438	Pool, Zalmon	HRK 587
Plumb, David	NYK 125	Pollutro, Elias	NYK 76	Poolar, John	DEL 280
Plumb, Ebenezer	HRK 426	Polly(?), James	SUF 87	Poolar, Phineas	DEL 280
Plumb, Henry	DUT 68	Polly, John	DEL 269	Poole, Pierce	WST 145
Plumb, Isa	MNT 122	Polly, Jonathaniel	WSH 281	Poole, Solomon	WST 145
Plumb, James	GRN 357	Polock, Carlile	NYK 20	Poole, Townsend	WST 145
Plumb, John	GRN 357	Polock, Peter	RNS 84	Pooler, Jacob	DUT 21
Plumb, John	STB 199	Polock, Philip	RNS 87	Pooley, Thomas	WSH 224
Plumb, John	WSH 211	Pols, John B.	NYK 122	Poolman, Psalter	ALB 85
Plumb, John Jun	GRN 357	Poltzeroft, Peter	NYK 151	Pooly, George	HRK 416
Plumb, Joseph	OND 182	Pomeroy, ...	MNT 77	Pooly, Joseph	HRK 416
Plumb, Nathaniel	OND 185	Pomeroy, Abner	CLN 162	Poor, Benjamin	WSH 219
Plumer, Samuel	WSH 211	Pomeroy, Dan	COL 216	Poor, Goniot	MNT 101
Plumley, Calvin	OND 223	Pomeroy, Elijah	MNT 34	Poorman, John	ONT 384
Plummer, Enoch	QNS 74	Pomeroy, Heman	WSH 303	Pop, Aaron	HRK 479
Plummer, Ezra	NYK 147	Pomeroy, John S.	ULS 184	Pope, Barney	CAY 548
Plummer, John	WSH 242	Pomeroy, Noah	ALB 79	Pope, Benjn	OTS 5
Plumstead, John	ULS 257	Pomeroy, Oliver	OND 177	Pope, Benjn	OTS 16
Plumstead, Mary	ULS 266	Pomeroy, Phinehas	TIO 211	Pope, Edward	OTS 31
Plumstead, Robert	ORN 273	Pomeroy, Rufus	HRK 441	Pope, Gates	OTS 34
Plymets, Peter	NYK 27	Pomeroy, Silas	CLN 166	Pope, Gershom	OTS 34
Plymoth	CHN 940	Pomeroy, Thaddeus	ALB 124	Pope, Henry	NYK 34
Pobasco, John	QNS 84	Pomeroye, Ethan	OTS 52	Pope, Ichabod	OTS 16
Poff, John	NYK 50	Pomery, Ralph H.	RNS 93	Pope, Jedediah	OTS 34
Pohlman, Jacob	OND 224	Pomford, Danison	SRA 15	Pope, Job	OTS 5
Poillon, James	NYK 106	Pompey Negro	QNS 71	Pope, John	ORN 361
Poillon, John	NYK 15	Pompey a Negro	SUF 72	Pope, John	OTS 38
Poillon, John	RCH 89	Pompey	SUF 97	Pope, Jonathan	COL 227
Poillon, John Junr	RCH 90	Pompy a free Negro	ALB 131	Pope, Lathrop	SRA 50
Poillon, John Senr	RCH 91	Pomroy, Timothy	DUT 7	Pope, Lewis	OTS 31
Poillon, Peter	QNS 67	Pond, Barnabas	OND 202	Pope, Seth	OTS 13
Point, John	ORN 391	Pond, Bartholomew	OND 200	Pope, Seth	OTS 34
Poishus, Paul	NYK 93	Pond, Catalina	DUT 67	Pope, Squire	OTS 49
Polar, Simeon	SRA 44	Pond, David	CHN 780	Pope, Timo	OTS 48
Polar, Simeon Junr	SRA 44	Pond, Jesse	OND 200	Popham, William	WST 119
Poleman, Daniel	ALB 47	Pond, Phenias	OTS 46	Poppino, Anne	ORN 328
Poleman, Daniel	RNS 89	Pond, Philip	OND 166	Poppino, Daniel	ORN 346
Polhemey, Cornelius	NYK 138	Pond, Philip	OND 200	Poppino, Daniel	ORN 361
Polhemius, Abraham	NYK 63	Pond, Samuel	OND 208	Poppino, James	ORN 324
Polhemius, Dorus	NYK 63	Pond, Timothy	OND 202	Poppino, John	ORN 365
Polhemius, Francis	NYK 63	Pond, Timothy Junr	OND 202	Poppino, Richard	ORN 365
Polhemus, Abraham	QNS 61	Pond, Zebe	CHN 780	Poppino, William	ORN 377
Polhemus, Abrm	RCK 103	Pond, Zera	OND 165	Poppins see Poppino	
Polhemus, Aurt	RCK 103	Pontineer, Henry	ULS 244	Popple, Ebenezer	ESS 306
Polhemus, Cornelius	ULS 255	Pontineer, Magdalena	ULS 244	Popple, Ebenezer	HRK 416
Polhemus, Cornelius	ULS 266	Pontus	WST 144	Popple, William	CHN 776
Polhemus, Daniel	ULS 224	Pooble, Charles	ALB 55	Popple, William	HRK 555
Polhemus, Hendrick	QNS 60	Pool, _erron	MNT 48	Por___, Moses	MNT 84
Polhemus, Jacob	NYK 84	Pool, Aaron	RNS 103	Porri, Domenick	NYK 34
Polhemus, Jacob	RCK 110	Pool, Benjamin	HRK 587	Porsons, Stephen	OND 222
Polhemus, Johannis	QNS 67	Pool, Benjamin	OND 167	Port see Post	
Polhemus, John	ORN 270	Pool, Chester	TIO 231	Port, Israel	SRA 33
Polhemus, John	RCK 106	Pool, Daniel	ORN 296	Port, Nicholas	MNT 3
Polhemus, Jordan	ULS 243	Pool, Easter	RNS 105	Portagu, John (Blk)	QNS 73
Polhemus, Sarah	NYK 118	Pool, Garret	RNS 14	P[orter?], Abijah	CHN 888
Polhemus, Theodorus	KNG 7	Pool, Hannah	NYK 104	Po_ter, Alexander	ONT 338
Polhemus, Theodorus	RCK 102	Pool, Henry	RNS 64	Porter, Amos	SRA 8
Polhemus, Tobias	RCK 108	Pool, Hudson	OND 167	Porter, Amos	TIO 209
Polis, Cornelius	RCK 97	Pool, Isaac	ALB 96	Porter, Amos	TIO 225
Pollard, David	CHN 754	Pool, Isaac	NYK 20	Porter, Andrew	SRA 24
Pollard, Moses	COL 249	Pool, James	MNT 2	Porter, Anna	OTS 34
Pollard, Thomas	CHN 754	Pool, James	QNS 71	Porter, Asa	ONT 368
Pollard, Walter	OND 200	Pool, John	ALB 57	Porter, Asahel	OND 179
Polley, Lemuel	MNT 102	Pool, John	ALB 96	Porter, Asel	OND 218
Polley, Prosper	ONN 156	Pool, John	NYK 106	Porter, Augustus	ONT 430
Polley, Willm	COL 207	Pool, John	RNS 15	Porter, Benjn	CHN 902
Pollock, Elijah	CAY 594	Pool, Joseph	CHN 754	Porter, Daniel	MNT 45
Pollock, George	DUT 61	Pool, Joseph	NYK 42	Porter, Daniel	OND 222
Pollock, George	GRN 328	Pool, Joseph Junr	CHN 756	Porter, Daniel	ULS 187
Pollock, George	NYK 86	Pool, Malichi	COL 203	Porter, David	ALB 115
Pollock, Hugh	NYK 86	Pool, Malkert	RNS 60	Porter, David	CHN 986

Name	Ref	Name	Ref	Name	Ref
Porter, David	DEL 275	Post, Abraham	DUT 82	Post, John	RCK 107
Porter, David	ONN 178	Post, Abraham	GRN 339	Post, John	RCK 109
Porter, David	ONN 186	Post, Abraham	NYK 103	Post, John	ULS 223
Porter, David Junr	ALB 115	Post, Abraham	RCH 88	Post, John	WSH 189
Porter, Eldad	NYK 62	Post, Abrm	RCK 99	Post, John	WSH 199
Porter, Eleazer	CHN 866	Post, Abraham	SUF 95	Post, John H.	ULS 232
Porter, Elijah	MNT 118	Post, Abraham	ULS 230	Post, John J.	COL 190
Porter, Elijah	OTS 34	Post, Abraham Junr	COL 234	Post, John J.	NYK 46
Porter, Elijah	WSH 191	Post, Abraham Jun	GRN 339	Post, John J.	ULS 227
Porter, Ezekiel	OND 219	Post, Abraham A.	ULS 225	Post, Jordan	ESS 293
Porter, Francis	ULS 210	Post, Abraham P.	ULS 225	Post, Joseph	DUT 30
Porter, Gad	OND 177	Post, Absalom	DUT 76	Post, Joseph	RCK 107
Porter, Giles W.	ALB 136	Post, Anthony	NYK 51	Post, Joshua	WSH 255
Porter, Hezekiah	SRA 6	Post, Benjamin	ALB 59	Post, Jotham	DUT 107
Porter, Ichabud	SRA 30	Post, Benjamin	QNS 82	Post, Jotham	NYK 53
Porter, Israel	HRK 530	Post, Charles	COL 237	Post, Jotham	NYK 70
Porter, James	STB 207	Post, Charles J.	COL 237	Post, Lawrance	WST 147
Porter, Jeremiah	SRA 8	Post, Christepher	GRN 343	Post, .ewis	WST 146
Porter, John	ALB 90	Post, Christian	RCH 88	Post, Lodowick	SUF 100
Porter, John	NYK 55	Post, Christopher	CAY 710	Post, Lydia	ULS 225
Porter, John	OND 165	Post, Cornelius	MNT 38	Post, Martin	NYK 102
Porter, John	OND 166	Post, Cornelius	ULS 225	Post, Martin	ULS 225
Porter, John	OND 177	Post, Dan	HRK 523	P[ost?], Martin	WST 158
Porter, John	WSH 190	Post, Daniel	COL 237	Post, Michael	SUF 93
Porter, John	WSH 198	Post, Daniel	RCH 88	Post, Nathan	ESS 304
Porter, John	WST 133	Post, Darius	OND 190	Post, Nathan	SUF 65
Porter, Jonathan	NYK 91	Post, Darius Junr	OND 190	Post, Nathan	SUF 100
Porter, Jonathan	OND 205	Post, David	ORN 367	Post, Nathaniel	COL 237
Porter, Joseph	NYK 23	Post, Dennis	WST 147	Post, Nathaniel	HRK 563
Porter, Joseph	ONT 328	Post, Edmond	QNS 72	Post, Peter	NYK 98
Porter, Joseph	ONT 364	Post, Elisha	QNS 78	Post, Peter	ORN 363
Porter, Josiah	MNT 118	Post, Elizabeth	ULS 225	Post, Peter	RCH 88
Porter, Labeus	SUF 104	Post, Enoc	GRN 353	Post, Peter	RCK 109
Porter, Lemuel	OND 177	Post, Ezra	GRN 342	Post, Peter J.	ULS 225
Porter, Martin	OND 194	Post, Frances	NYK 92	Post, Peter P.	ULS 224
Porter, Medad	SRA 8	Post, Francis	RCH 89	Post, Richard	QNS 78
Porter, Moses	ONT 414	Post, Gabriel	ORN 370	Post, Richard	QNS 81
Porter, Moses	WSH 290	Post, Garret	ORN 374	Post, Richard	SRA 46
Porter, Nathan	OTS 34	Post, Garret	RCH 88	Post, Richard	SUF 79
Porter, Nathan	WSH 244	Post, George	CAY 710	Post, Robert	DUT 77
Porter, Nathaniel	COL 251	Post, Gertruyde	ULS 225	Post, Rossel	GRN 342
Porter, Nathaniel	ONN 129	Post, Henry	DUT 77	Post, Samuel	GRN 328
Porter, Nicholas	ORN 393	Post, Henry	MNT 13	Post, Saml	RNS 108
Porter, Noah	OND 168	Post, Henry	QNS 71	Post, Samuel	SUF 97
Porter, Noah	ONT 352	Post, Henry	SRA 38	Post, Samuel	ULS 225
Porter, Norton	OND 179	Post, Henry	ULS 218	Post, Sarah	SUF 97
Porter, Numan	SUF 65	Post, Howell	SUF 97	Post, Silas	QNS 65
Porter, Perry	SCH 117	Post, Isaac	DUT 82	Post, Stephen	ONT 348
Porter, Peter	NYK 92	Post, Isaac	ULS 223	Post, Stephen	ONT 450
Porter, Philip	SRA 32	Post, Isaac	WST 146	Post, Stephen	SUF 96
Porter, Phineas	OND 166	Post, Isaac Junr	ULS 224	Post, Thomas	NYK 80
Porter, Raphel	OND 220	Post, Isaiah	ONT 338	Post, Titus	OND 197
Porter, Reuben	COL 241	Post, Israel	NYK 84	Post, Valentine	DUT 157
Porter, Richard	STB 207	Post, Israel	WSH 255	Post, William	CAY 710
Porter, Robert	CAY 616	Post, Jackson	QNS 74	Post, William	DUT 159
Porter, Samuel	CHN 778	Post, Jacob	ALB 70	Post, William	NYK 113
Porter, Samuel	OND 165	Post, Jacob	ALB 72	Post, William Senior	NYK 34
Porter, Samuel	OTS 34	Post, Jacob	NYK 102	Post, William B.	NYK 88
Porter, Stephen	WSH 302	Post, Jacob	QNS 76	Post, Wright	NYK 27
Porter, Thomas	ALB 98	Post, Jacob	RCK 99	Pots, Abraham	NYK 102
Porter, Thomas	ORN 344	Post, Jacob	WST 146	Potte, Roderick	NYK 109
Porter, William	ALB 115	Post, Jacob Junr	ALB 71	Pottenburgh, John	DUT 161
Porter, William	DUT 10	Post, Jacobus	ORN 371	Potter, Aaron	DUT 51
Porter, Wm	GRN 353	Post, James	SUF 69	Potter, Aaron	HRK 476
Porter, William	ONT 354	Post, James	WST 144	Potter, Aaron	ORN 389
Porter, William	STB 207	Post, Joel	NYK 28	Potter, Abel	HRK 453
Porter, William	WSH 230	Post, John	ALB 90	Potter, Abigail	SRA 28
Porter, William	WSH 295	Post, John	CAY 586	Potter, Abner	WSH 189
Portland	QNS 62	Post, John	DUT 21	Potter, Allen	WSH 239
Portter, Christopher	SRA 60	Post, John	NYK 25	Potter, Amos	OND 172
Portter, Jesse	SRA 60	Post, John	NYK 56	Potter, Amos	OTS 37
Portter, John	SRA 60	Post, John	NYK 99	Potter, Amos	RNS 41
Posson, Peter	ALB 90	Post, John	OND 160	Potter, Amos Junr	RNS 41
Post see Port		Post, John	ORN 370	Potter, Angel	HRK 559
Post, Abraham	COL 191	Post, John	ORN 382	Potter, Anson	OND 181
Post, ...aham	COL 227	Post, John	QNS 72	Potter, Arnold	ONT 456
Post, Abraham	DUT 21	Post, John	QNS 73	Potter, Asa	DUT 161

Potter, Aseph	OTS 10	Potter, Lemuel	OND 182	Poules, Andrew	RCK 106
Potter, Augustus	OND 214	Potter, Levi	OND 181	Poules, Wm	RCK 106
Potter, Benjamin	SRA 35	Potter, Lyman	OTS 18	Poulin, Antoine	CLN 169
Potter, Benjamin	WSH 202	Potter, Nathl	ONN 177	Poulk, John	OND 184
Potter, Benjamin Junr	WSH 202	Potter, Nathaniel	SRA 29	Pound, Isaac	ORN 367
Potter, Borden	OND 181	Potter, Nathaniel	SUF 86	Pound, John	ORN 368
Potter, Charles	OTS 52	Potter, Nathaniel	ULS 239	Pound, Thos	RCK 110
Potter, Christopher	WSH 251	Potter, Nathaniel	WSH 189	Powel, Edward	GRN 352
Potter, Clark	RNS 70	Potter, Nathaniel	WSH 236	Powel, Elisha	GRN 351
Potter, Constant	MNT 82	Potter, Nathaniel G.	SRA 28	Powel, Elisha	SRA 19
Potter, Cornelius	WSH 234	Potter, Noah	SRA 35	Powel, Frederick	GRN 351
Potter, D....	MNT 67	Potter, Pardon	OTS 52	Powel, Isaac Junr	WSH 242
Potter, Daniel	CHN 818	Potter, Payn	WSH 237	Powel, James	DEL 270
Potter, Daniel	HRK 533	Potter, Pearce	OTS 26	Powel, John	GRN 352
Potter, Daniel	MNT 64	Potter, Peleg	HRK 587	Powel, Jonathan	SRA 5
Potter, Danl	OTS 18	Potter, Peleg	ULS 185	Powel, Joshua	QNS 72
Potter, Daniel	RNS 70	Potter, Perry	ALB 33	Powel, Moses	GRN 352
Potter, David	CLN 174	Potter, Restcome	SRA 29	Powel, Obadiah	SRA 43
Potter, David	OTS 18	Potter, Richard	DEL 270	Powel, Richard	NYK 112
Potter, David	RNS 42	Potter, Robert	DUT 82	Powel, Samuel	GRN 352
Potter, David	RNS 67	Potter, Robert	OTS 26	Powel, Sarah	QNS 72
Potter, David	RNS 106	Potter, Robert	RNS 70	Powel, Saviech	RNS 25
Potter, David	WSH 189	Potter, Rollinus	SRA 51	Powel, Solomon	QNS 76
Potter, David	WSH 202	Potter, Rowland	MNT 90	Powel, Stephen	GRN 328
Potter, Ebenezar	CAY 674	Potter, Rowland	OND 192	Powel, Stephen	WST 169
Potter, Ebenezer	COL 183	Potter, Rufus	OTS 39	Powel, Stephen Junr	QNS 75
Potter, Edward	NYK 59	Potter, Samuel	ALB 90	Powel, Thomas	GRN 352
Potter, Elisha	CHN 832	Potter, Samuel	COL 203	Powel, Thomas	WST 169
Potter, Elisha	OTS 47	Potter, Samuel	ORN 300	Powel, Thomas E.	GRN 351
Potter, Elisha	RNS 22	Potter, Samuel	SRA 33	Powel, William	OND 207
Potter, Emer	SRA 40	Potter, Samuel	WSH 245	Powel, William	SRA 4
Potter, Ephraem	WSH 243	Potter, Seth	SRA 33	Powell, Abraham	WST 135
Potter, Ephraim	OND 193	Potter, Shelden	OND 181	Powell, Amos	QNS 78
Potter, Ephraim	SRA 31	Potter, Silas	CAY 550	Powell, Amos	QNS 78
Potter, Ephraim	SRA 35	Potter, Silas	DUT 120	Powell, Anne	QNS 71
Potter, Ephraim	WSH 189	Potter, Simm	SRA 28	Powell, Archd	OTS 55
Potter, Ephriam	SCH 140	Potter, Stephen	OND 158	Powell, Benjamin	DUT 111
Potter, Esach	CAY 614	Potter, Stephen	SRA 31	Powell, Benjamin	NYK 50
Potter, Esake	RNS 33	Potter, Stephen	WSH 202	Powell, Benjamin	QNS 78
Potter, Gedion Junr	WSH 202	Potter, Stokes	WSH 202	Powell, Charles	DUT 113
Potter, George	SRA 33	Potter, Sylvester	DUT 14	Powell, Charles	MNT 41
Potter, George	WSH 232	Potter, Thomas	DUT 60	Powell, Cypreon	COL 203
Potter, Gilbert	OND 194	Potter, Thomas	WSH 300	Powell, Daniel	DUT 111
Potter, Godfry	WSH 232	Potter, Vine	WSH 218	Powell, Daniel	ONT 344
Potter, Hazard	ONT 456	Potter, William	DEL 282	Powell, Ebenezer	WSH 244
Potter, Henry	DUT 101	Potter, William	HRK 459	Powell, Elijah	CHN 802
Potter, Ichabod	OTS 52	Potter, Wm	OTS 26	Powell, Erastus	OND 188
Potter, James	MNT 101	Potter, William	OTS 26	Powell, Felix	ULS 231
Potter, James	ORN 338	Potter, Wm	RNS 31	Powell, Frost	DUT 109
Potter, James	RNS 77	Potter, William	WSH 300	Powell, Grone H.	MNT 71
Potter, James	SRA 41	Potter, Willis	OTS 37	Powell, Ira	CAY 544
Potter, James	ULS 188	Potter, Willis	OTS 38	Powell, Isaac	DUT 114
Potter, Jeremiah	COL 185	Potter, Zebadiah	SRA 33	Powell, Isaac	QNS 66
Potter, Jeremiah	HRK 559	Potts, Daniel	SRA 7	Powell, Isaac	QNS 78
Potter, Jeremiah	WSH 204	Potts, David	WST 157	Powell, Isaac	WSH 242
Potter, Jeremiah Jun	HRK 559	Potts, Frederick	RNS 56	Powell, Israel	DUT 120
Potter, Jesse	RNS 27	Potts, George	COL 237	Powell, Jacob	DUT 111
Potter, Job	OTS 29	Potts, Hendrick	COL 198	Powell, Jacob	ORN 283
Potter, John	HRK 502	Potts, Hendrick	COL 229	Powell, Jacob	SUF 79
Potter, John	HRK 533	Potts, Isaac	WST 157	Powell, Jacob	SUF 79
Potter, John	RNS 26	Potts, Jacob	CHN 942	Powell, James	DUT 113
Potter, John	RNS 99	Potts, Jacob	COL 229	Powell, James	NYK 18
Potter, John	RNS 109	Potts, Jesse	ALB 125	Powell, James	OND 201
Potter, John	SRA 28	Potts, John	NYK 94	Powell, Jeremiah	OND 185
Potter, John	WSH 249	Potts, John	RNS 58	Powell, John	COL 250
Potter, Jonathan	OND 179	Potts, Lodewic	COL 238	Powell, John	DUT 111
Potter, Jona	OTS 9	Potts, Sally a Black	NYK 110	Powell, John a mulatto	NYK 143
Potter, Jonathan	WSH 240	Potts, Thomas	WST 157	Powell, John	QNS 64
Potter, Joseph	DUT 14	Potts, William	COL 237	Powell, John	QNS 83
Potter, Joseph	DUT 95	Potts, Willm F.	COL 236	Powell, John	WST 132
Potter, Joseph	OND 214	Poty, Nicholas	MNT 30	Powell, Jonas	QNS 78
Potter, Joseph	RNS 24	Poucher, Casparus	DUT 150	Powell, Joseph	DUT 63
Potter, Joseph	SRA 31	Poucher, James	COL 190	Powell, Joseph	WSH 242
[Po?]tter, Joseph	SRA 33	Poucher, John	COL 197	Powell, Joshua	QNS 78
Potter, Joseph	ULS 253	Poucher, John	COL 202	Powell, Moses	DUT 113
Potter, Joseph	WSH 202	Poucher, Joseph	COL 197	Powell, Nathaniel	DUT 119
Potter, Lemuel	DEL 270	Poudre, Joseph	ONT 312	Powell, Richard	QNS 72

Powell, Richard Junr	QNS 78	Powers, William	WSH 304	Pratt, Stephen	DUT 98
Powell, Richard Senr	QNS 78	Powers, William Jur	WSH 304	Pratt, Stephen	MNT 123
Powell, Robert	QNS 76	Powes, Edward	GRN 358	Pratt, Stephen	ONT 510
Powell, Rowland	NYK 125	Poyer, Thomas	DUT 35	Pratt, Stephen	RNS 46
Powell, Samuel	QNS 78	Prady, Charles	NYK 84	Pratt, William	GRN 346
Powell, Samuel	ULS 265	Prall, Isaac	NYK 117	Pratt, William	OND 181
Powell, Silas	QNS 79	Prassaw, Jeremiah	WSH 232	Pratt, William	OND 188
Powell, Solomon	QNS 74	Prat, Daniel	WSH 251	Pratt, William	WSH 247
Powell, Stephen	DUT 129	Prater, Mary	NYK 119	Pratt, William	WSH 284
Powell, Stephen	QNS 75	Prath, David	WSH 258	Pratt, Zedock	SCH 132
Powell, Thomas	ALB 115	Pratt, Abel	ESS 308	Prattiway, Richard	SCH 158
Powell, Thomas	ONT 508	Pratt, Abijah	ALB 91	Praul, Abigail	RCH 88
Powell, Thomas	QNS 78	Pratt, Abrm	OTS 57	Praul, Abraham	RCH 90
Powell, Thomas	QNS 78	Pratt, Abraham	WSH 200	Praul, Benjamin	RCH 93
Powell, Thomas	SUF 80	Pratt, Anson	COL 215	Praul, Bornt	RCH 91
Powell, Thomas	WSH 265	Pratt, Asa	WSH 257	Praul, Daniel	RCH 91
Powell, Truman	COL 179	Pratt, Banoah	ONN 145	Praul, John	RCH 91
Powell, Vincent	ORN 369	Pratt, Calven	WSH 285	Praul, Lewis	RCH 90
Powell, Willet	QNS 78	Pratt, Chalker	MNT 68	Praul, Peter	RCH 91
Powell, Willet	QNS 78	Pratt, Coleb	ONN 169	Praul, Peter	RCH 93
Powell, Wm	MNT 74	Pratt, Daniel	OND 167	Praul, Sarah	RCH 91
Powell, William	NYK 134	Pratt, Daniel	OND 170	Prausey, Jonathan	WSH 232
Powell, William	NYK 145	Pratt, David	COL 179	Prawsaw, Benjamen	WSH 242
Powell, William	WST 131	Pratt, David	WSH 200	Prawty, John W.	TIO 241
Power, Abiather	ONT 436	Pratt, David Junr	COL 179	Pray, Andrew	DUT 47
Power, Arthur	ONT 436	Pratt, Doggery	OND 166	Pray, Ephraim	DUT 47
Power, James	DUT 86	Pratt, Ebenezer	ONT 444	Pray, John	HRK 516
Power, Joseph	COL 197	Pratt, Edmund	WSH 284	Pray, John	NYK 149
Power, Moses	ONT 438	Pratt, Edward	ONT 494	Pray, Jonathan	CAY 532
Power, Nicholas	DUT 62	Pratt, Edward	OTS 39	Pray, Joseph	DUT 47
Power, Samuel	ONN 190	Pratt, Eleazer	CHN 886	Pray, Richd	OTS 54
Power, William	CHN 922	Pratt, Elias	GRN 346	Pray, Thomas	ESS 303
Powers, Abel	CAY 696	Pratt, Enos	OND 182	Pray, Wm	OTS 54
Powers, Abigail	SRA 46	Pratt, Ezra	TIO 227	Prayls, Asa	MNT 117
Powers, Asa	OND 198	Pratt, Ezra	TIO 227	Preachard, Asahel	TIO 246
Powers, Avery	CHN 782	Pratt, Hiram	WSH 200	Preastly, Edward	WST 169
Powers, Benjamin	ORN 395	Pratt, Israel	MNT 124	Preham, Henry	RNS 96
Powers, Benjamin	WSH 186	Pratt, Jacob	COL 218	Preill, Christopher	NYK 141
Powers, Charles	CHN 880	Pratt, Jacob	OTS 6	Prendell, Liman	RNS 20
Powers, David	OND 180	Pratt, James	CHN 894	Prentes, Benjamen	WSH 273
Powers, Edward	NYK 80	Pratt, Jemima	COL 213	Prentice, Amos	SUF 104
Powers, Elijah	CHN 922	Pratt, Jerh	OTS 39	Prentice, Daniel	DEL 287
Powers, George	ESS 319	Pratt, Joel	ALB 81	Prentice, Daniel Jun	DEL 283
Powers, George	KNG 7	Pratt, John	ALB 36	Prentice, Elisha	CHN 914
Powers, George Junr	KNG 7	Pratt, John	ALB 80	Prentice, Gilbert	DEL 287
Powers, Jacob	DUT 104	Pratt, John	QNS 74	Prentice, Holday	SRA 24
Powers, Jacob	MNT 94	Pratt, Jonas	HRK 491	Prentice, John	NYK 96
Powers, Jacob	OND 207	Pratt, Jonathan	WSH 217	Prentice, John	NYK 143
Powers, James	NYK 138	Pratt, Joseph	WSH 207	Prentice, Jonas	DEL 272
Powers, James	OTS 55	Pratt, Joshua	COL 182	Prentice, Josiah	DUT 150
Powers, James	WST 128	Pratt, Laban	NYK 70	Prentice, Pierce	WSH 185
Powers, Jane	NYK 71	Pratt, Lemuel	CHN 756	Prentice, Russell	CAY 676
Powers, Joel	WSH 183	Pratt, Lemuel	MNT 99	Prentice, Saml	OTS 19
Powers, John	WSH 189	Pratt, Lemuel	WSH 243	Prentice, Timothy	CHN 914
Powers, John	WST 121	Pratt, Lucy	DUT 80	Prentice, Thomas	OND 162
Powers, John Junr	OTS 46	Pratt, Michael	WSH 200	Prentice, William	CHN 790
Powers, John Senr	OTS 46	Pratt, Nathaniel	SRA 28	Prentis, Daniel	OTS 22
Powers, John Snr	WSH 186	Pratt, Nathaniel Jur	SRA 28	Prentis, Jared	OTS 22
Powers, Joseph	COL 199	Pratt, Nathen	WSH 199	Prentis, Otis	OTS 27
Powers, Joseph	OTS 41	Pratt, Nathen	WSH 217	Prentis, Reuben	WSH 290
Powers, Josiah	OND 207	Pratt, Nehemiah	OND 170	Prepon, Stephen	CHN 902
Powers, Moses	TIO 264	Pratt, Noah	ONN 138	Prescot, Oliver	OND 180
Powers, Nathan	CHN 812	Pratt, Peabody	ALB 91B	Prescott, Fortunatus	RNS 94
Powers, Nicholas 2d	RNS 24	Pratt, Peter	NYK 126	Prescott, Joel	ONT 480
Powers, Oliver	HRK 570	Pratt, Peter	ONT 440	Presler, Abraham	ULS 235
Powers, Peter	ONT 504	Pratt, Philip	HRK 434	Presler, Anthony	ULS 257
Powers, Peter	WSH 189	Pratt, Reuben	WSH 284	Presler, George	ULS 257
Powers, Reuben	WSH 267	Pratt, Rufus	OND 176	Presler, Jacob	ULS 234
Powers, Rubin	CLN 156	Pratt, Rufus	WSH 199	Presler, Jeremiah	ULS 235
Powers, Rubin	CLN 157	Pratt, Samuel	CLN 167	Presler, John	ULS 235
Powers, Saml	OTS 46	Pratt, Samuel	COL 177	Presler, Jonathan	ULS 234
Powers, Samuel	SRA 8	Pratt, Samuel	OND 167	Presler, Matthew	ULS 257
Powers, Thomas	CHN 976	Pratt, Samuel	OND 176	Presler, Matthew Junr	ULS 257
Powers, Thomas	COL 250	Pratt, Samuel	WSH 266	Presler, Solomon	ULS 257
Powers, William	HRK 514	Pratt, Silas	COL 204	Presley, Joseph	RNS 74
Powers, William	ONN 143	Pratt, Silas	ESS 302	Preslow, Henry	ULS 228
Powers, William	WSH 186	Pratt, Silas	ESS 305	Preslow, Henry Junr	ULS 228

Purdy, Andrew	WST 114	Purdy, Nehemiah	WST 161
Purdy, Andrew	WST 118	Purdy, Obadiah	WST 129
Purdy, Andrew	WST 152	Purdy, Peter	RNS 50
Purdy, Augustus	NYK 147	Purdy, Rhoda	NYK 73
Purdy, Bartholemew	NYK 147	Purdy, Richard	CHN 822
Purdy, Benjamin	NYK 89	Purdy, Robert	ORN 285
Purdy, Benoni	RNS112B	Purdy, Roger	WST 114
Purdy, Budd	WST 117	Purdy, Roger Junr	WST 111
Purdy, Charity	WST 117	Purdy, Samuel	DUT 75
Purdy, Daniel	STB 205	Purdy, Samuel	ORN 270
Purdy, Daniel	STB 205	Purdy, Samuel	ORN 271
Purdy, Daniel	WST 111	Purdy, Samuel	WST 111
Purdy, Daniel	WST 124	Purdy, Samuel	WST 149
Purdy, Daniel Junr	WST 127	Purdy, Samuel H.	NYK 58
Purdy, David	QNS 62	Purdy, Seth	SUF 80
Purdy, David	WST 129	Purdy, Siah	CHN 802
Purdy, David Junr	DUT 20	Purdy, Silvanus	WST 111
Purdy, David Senr	DUT 20	Purdy, Solomon	ORN 270
Purdy, Deliverence		Purdy, Solomon	ULS 266
Junr	WST 134	Purdy, Stephen	CHN 800
Purdy, Delivrence	WST 133	Purdy, Thomas	WST 139
Purdy, Ebenezer	WST 125	Purdy, Thomas	WST 169
Purdy, Ebenezer	WST 130	Purdy, Timothy	WST 117
Purdy, Elias	WST 111	Purdy, Tyler	WST 124
Purdy, Elijah	WST 116	Purdy, William	NYK 100
Purdy, Elijah Junr	WST 117	Purdy, Wm	STB 205
Purdy, Elisha	WST 164	Purdy, William	WST 111
Purdy, Francis	DUT 37	Purdy, William	WST 117
Purdy, Francis	DUT 77	Purdy, William	WST 124
Purdy, Francis	RNS 47	Purdy, William	WST 128
Purdy, Gilbert	DUT 39	Purdy, William	WST 152
Purdy, Gilbert	WST 114	Purdy, William	WST 159
Purdy, Hachaliah	WST 133	Purington, Jonathan	COL 247
Purdy, Hakaliah	WST 114	Purkens see Perkins	
Purdy, Hannah	WST 123	Purkens, Solomon	CHN 886
Purdy, Henry	CLN 159	Purkins, John	GRN 325
Purdy, Henry	WST 112	Purple, Anson	OTS 34
Purdy, Henry	WST 128	Purple, David	OTS 56
Purdy, Isaac	CHN 820	Purple, Edward	OTS 34
Purdy, Isaac	ORN 338	Purple, Elias	WSH 272
Purdy, Isaac	WST 116	Purrington, Joseph	HRK 504
Purdy, Isaac	WST 124	Purrington, Selvenus	SCH 147
Purdy, Isaac	WST 156	Purviss, George Junr	ULS 183
Purdy, Isarel	NYK 68	Purviss, George Senr	ULS 183
Purdy, Ithael	WST 132	Purviss, William	ULS 183
Purdy, Jacob	WST 118	Pusham, Peter	SCH 153
Purdy, James	CHN 780	Pusher, Peter	MNT 35
Purdy, James	WST 111	Putman, Aaron L.	MNT 70
Purdy, James	WST 117	Putman, Adam	MNT 25
Purdy, James	WST 128	Putman, Anastus	ALB 10
Purdy, James	WST 155	Putman, Andrew	CHN 812
Purdy, Jeremiah	CHN 802	Putman, Arent	MNT 20
Purdy, Jesse	DEL 270	Putman, Aron D.	MNT 67
Purdy, John	DEL 274	Putman, Christiana	SRA 3
Purdy, John	DUT 77	Putman, Cornelius	ALB 21
Purdy, John	NYK 147	.utman, Cornelius	MNT 67
Purdy, John	ORN 270	Putman, David	ALB 46
Purdy, John	WST 114	Putman, David	MNT 21
Purdy, John	WST 169	Putman, David	MNT 67
Purdy, Jonathan	WST 116	Putman, Elisha	ALB 143
Purdy, Jonathan	WST 123	Putman, Frances	MNT 67
Purdy, Joseph	DUT 24	Putman, Frederick	MNT 42
Purdy, Joseph	STB 205	Putman, Gilbert	MNT 19
Purdy, Joseph	WST 123	Putman, John	ALB 21
Purdy, Joseph	WST 146	Putman, John	MNT 95
Purdy, Joseph	WST 169	Putman, John A.	MNT 67
Purdy, Joshua	DUT 74	Putman, Lewis	RNS 82
Purdy, Joshua	WST 115	Putman, Lodiwick	MNT 46
Purdy, Joshua	WST 152	Putman, T	MNT 70
Purdy, Josiah	WST 111	Putman, Thomas	NYK 114
Purdy, Mary	WST 114	Putman, Vector	MNT 71
Purdy, Micah	WST 132	Putnam, Victor	ALB 51
Purdy, Monmouth	DUT 144	Putnam, Abijah	OND 212
Purdy, Moses	WST 111	Putnam, Asa	ESS 308
Purdy, Munmuth	WST 132	Putnam, Asaph	ESS 308
Purdy, Nathaniel	WST 114	Putnam, Benajah	WSH 202
Purdy, Nehemiah	WST 111	Putnam, Caleb	OND 212

Putnam, Charles	OND 164
Putnam, Christopher	HRK 417
Putnam, Clark	OND 212
Putnam, David	OND 157
Putnam, Francis	OTS 32
Putnam, Frederick	OND 164
Putnam, Geo.	OTS 28
Putnam, Gideon	SRA 42
Putnam, John	CAY 634
Putnam, John	OND 218
Putnam, Jonas	CAY 634
Putnam, Lewis	WSH 297
Putnam, Peter	ONN 163
Putnam, Timothy	OND 185
Putnam, Uziel	OND 199
Putney, Isaac	OND 224
Putney, Joseph	CHN 862
Putney, Joseph	OND 191
Putney, John	WSH 288
Putney, Joseph	WSH 287
Putney, Joseph	WSH 288
Putney, Joseph	WST 130
Putney, Joshua	WST 122
Putnum, Asel	SRA 51
Putnum, Parks	SRA 51
Puttney, John	WST 130
Pya_, Nicholas	CHN 888
Pye, David	RCK 102
Pye, David Junr	RCK 106
Pye, John	ALB 126
Pye, John	RCK 102
Pye, Thomas	NYK 130
Pyke, Rebbecca	CHN 788
Pyncheon, Nanthaniel	ONN 162
Pynnes, Zenas	SCH 171
Pyor, Elijah	CHN 760
Pyors, Jonah	CHN 798
Pyors, Levy	CHN 760
Pyron, Verean	NYK 123

Q

Qaak, John	ORN 365
Qua, John	WSH 290
Qua, John Junr	WSH 292
Qua, Robert	WSH 289
Qua, Thomas	WSH 292
Quaak, Samuel	ORN 379
Quack, Jacob	ALB 66
Quackenboss, Abraham	ORN 395
Quackenboss, Benjamin	RNS 19
Quackenboss, John	WSH 198
Quackenboss, John G.	ALB 11
Quackenboss, John H.	WSH 199
Quackenboss, Rignier	ORN 351
Quackenbus, Abraham	SRA 11
Quackenbus, Goser	RNS 19
Quackenbus, Jacob	SRA 10
Quackenbush, Abraham	MNT 38
Quackenbush, Abraham	NYK 88
Quackenbush, Abrm	RCK 107
Quackenbush, Abraham D.	MNT 95
Quackenbush, Abraham T.	MNT 95
Quackenbush, Albert	MNT 44
Quackenbush, Benjamin	NYK 136
Quackenbush, Cornelius	RCK 106
Quackenbush, Daniel	SRA 41
Quackenbush, David H.	MNT 39
Q....enbush, David P.(?)	MNT 47
Quackenbush, Gerret	WSH 297
Qu...enbush, Hunter	MNT 25
Quackenbush, Isaac	NYK 21
Quackenbush, Isaac	RCK 106
Quackenbush, James	NYK 93
Quackenbush, Jeremeah	MNT 47
Quackenbush, John	MNT 111
Quackenbush, John	NYK 17

Quackenbush, John	NYK 73	Quick, James	DUT 119	Rab, William	GRN 329
Quackenbush, John	RCK 110	Quick, John	ULS 180	Rabine, Henry	COL 251
Quackenbush, John P.	MNT 39	Quick, John	ULS 260	Race see Rase
Quackenbush, Margaretta	MNT 95	Quick, John	WST 125	Race, Abraham	COL 253
Quackenbush, Peter	MNT 39	Quick, John Junr	WST 123	Race, Andrew	WSH 288
Quackenbush, Peter	SCH 118	Quick, Lewis	ORN 346	Race, Andrew A.	COL 230
Quackenbush, Vencent	MNT 94	Quick, Luke C.	NYK 85	Race, Benjamin	COL 266
Quackenbush, Wm	MNT 40	Quick, Peter	DUT 121	Race, Benjamin Junr	COL 266
Quackenbuss, Jas	OTS 45	Quick, Peter	ORN 320	Race, Coroline	COL 196
Quackinboss, Adrian	ALB 44	Quick, Phillip	ULS 216	Race, Derrick	CHN 740
Quackinboss, Frederick	ALB 56	Quick, Samuel	WST 125	Race, Hendrick	COL 201
Quackinboss, Gerrit	ALB 144	Quick, Sarah	ULS 267	Race, Henry	COL 254
Quackinboss, Hendk	ALB 139	Quick, Stephen	WST 169	Race, Jacob	CHN 808
Quackinboss, Henry	ALB 47	Quick, Tunis	NYK 24	R[ace?], Jacob	WSH 288
Quackinboss, Isaac A.	ALB 56	Quick, William	NYK 26	Race, John	COL 255
Quackinboss, John	ALB 56	Quickly, Martin	SCH 120	Race, John	WSH 288
Quackinboss, John	WSH 239	Quicman, Samuel	MNT 11	Race, Jonathan	COL 253
Quackinboss, John Junr	ALB 46	Quidore, Peter	RCK 98	Race, Jonathan Junr	COL 253
Quackinboss, John P.	ALB 47	Quidore, Peter	RCK 99	Race, Phillip	COL 228
Quackinboss, Nichs	ALB 47	Qu.g, John	TIO 233	Race, Stephen	COL 196
Quackinboss, Nichs N.	ALB 47	Quigley, James	CAY 520	Race, Teunis	COL 239
Quackinboss, Sybrandt	WSH 198	Quigley, James	ORN 274	Race, Thomas	COL 255
Quackinbus, Jesse	SRA 11	Quigley, Robert	CAY 600	Race, Thomas W.	COL 256
Quackinbush, James	NYK 60	Quigley, Thomas	TIO 212	Race, William	COL 261
Quackinbush, Richard	RCK 107	Quilthop, John	MNT 105	Racet, Peter	MNT 37
Quail, Michael	OTS 40	Quim, Andrew	NYK 119	Rachet, Havens	SUF 77
Quail, Wm	OTS 41	Quimbee, Josiah	WST 127	Rachet, Noah	SUF 77
Quain, John	NYK 132	Quimbee, Josiah	WST 133	Racket see Rachet
Quakenbush, John Isaac	MNT 39	Quimbee, Samuel	WST 133	Racket, Abm	SUF 77
Quakenbuss, Harman	RNS 34	Quimby, Basheba	WST 145	Racket, Jonathan	SUF 77
Quakinboss, Abm	ALB 124	Quimby, Hannah	WST 144	Racket, Mahatible	SUF 77
Quakinboss, Isaac	ALB 13	Quimby, Stephen	OTS 24	Racket, Phe	SUF 77
Quakinboss, Isaac	ALB 44	Quin, Robert	NYK 30	Racket, Saml a Negro
Quakinboss, Walter	ALB 46	Quinby, Daniel	DUT 125	man	ALB 44
Quan, Abraham	DEL 284	Quinby, Elnathan	RNS 54	Racket, Samuel	ORN 349
Quant, Frederick	ALB 17	Quinby, Enos	ULS 264	Rackles, Benjn	SUF 77
Quarl, James	NYK 139	Quinby, Francis	WST 113	Rackmire, John	GRN 327
Quarls, Abraham	MNT 111	Quinby, Isaac	ULS 263	Radcliff see Ratcliff
Quarry, John	NYK 126	Quinby, Isaiah	WST 113	Radcliff, Jacob	ALB 147
Quarterness, Richard	ESS 294	Quinby, James	ULS 264	Radcliff, James	ALB 131
Quarters, Josiah	ORN 362	Quinby, John	RNS 54	Radcliff, John	ALB 10
Quarters, Sylvanus	ORN 320	Quinby, Levi	ULS 263	Radcliff, John	ALB 107
Quash a free Negro	ALB 75	Quinby, Levi Junr	ULS 263	Radcliff, John	DUT 162
Quay, John A.	ALB 76	Quinby, Moses	ULS 263	Radcliff, John I.	DUT 162
Quenet, Bazel	NYK 147	Quinby, Moses	WST 115	Radcliff, Nicholas	ALB 125
Quenton, John	WSH 287	Quinby, Nathaniel	ULS 263	Radcliff, Rebecca	DUT 162
Quereau, Abigal	NYK 105	Quinby, Obadiah	WST 113	Radcliff, Thomas	NYK 81
Quereau, Elias	DUT 82	Quinby, William	DUT 52	Radclift, William	ALB 44
Quereau, Joshua	NYK 39	Quinion, Joseph	NYK 37	Radclift, Cornelius	ULS 227
Query, Samuel	NYK 85	Quink, Winney	NYK 17	Radclift, Peter	DUT 108
Quest, Thomas	NYK 62	Quinman, Thomas	DUT 16	Radclift, Peter W.	DUT 63
Qui t, Henry	MNT 67	Quintar, Peter	WST 114	Radclift, William Junr	DUT 155
Qui__th__, James	MNT 105	Quinter, Parr	ALB 63	Radell, Benjamin	RNS 68
Quibby, Nathan	ONT 310	Quir, Wm	STB 199	Radell, Benjamin Junr	RNS 68
Quick, Abraham	NYK 106	Quirck, Thomas	NYK 141	Radell, Nathaniel	RNS 68
Quick, Abraham	ULS 266	Quithel, Cole	ONT 510	Radickson, Peter	MNT 92
Quick, Andrew	ESS 308	Quitman, Frederick H.	DUT 158	Radley, Aurant	ALB 100
Quick, Andrew	WST 125	Quitterfield, Abner	SRA 47	Radley, Bernard	NYK 55
Quick, Benjamin	CAY 574	Quive, Amasa	SRA 6	Radley, Henry	ALB 128
Quick, Benjamin	ULS 180	Quive, James	SRA 5	Radley, John L.	ALB 130
Quick, Benjamin	ULS 216	Quive, John	SRA 5	Radley, Philip	ALB 135
Quick, Cornelius	ULS 216	Quive, Jonathan	SRA 6	Radley, Richard	ALB 106
Quick, Daniel	ULS 215	Quixsal, Samuel	RNS 90	Radley, William	ALB 101
Quick, Daniel	WST 133	Quony, Thomas	NYK 63	Radley, William	CAY 578
Quick, Dirck	ULS 214	Quough	SUF 108	Radley, William J.	ALB 105
Quick, Edward	NYK 26			Rae see Ray
Quick, Elijah	MNT 94			Rae, Hannah	WST 155
Quick, Elijah	WST 134	**R**		Raelmore, Cato a Black	NYK 51
Quick, Ephraim	ULS 214	R__, Mark	CAY 562	Ragan, John	NYK 131
Quick, George	ORN 316	R__y, Nathan	GRN 334	Ragan, Thomas	DUT 56
Quick, Grardus	DUT 123	R dley, James	MNT 2	Ragg, William	NYK 113
Quick, Henry	NYK 128	R sey, Ebeneser	MNT 61	Raggers, Green	SRA 60
Quick, Henry	ULS 180	R....d, James	MNT 83	Ragins, Nicholas	COL 233
Quick, Henry	ULS 262	R y, William	NYK 72	Raham, Joseph G.	NYK 114
Quick, Jacob	ULS 215	R son, Mathew	ONT 494	Raimond see Reymond &
Quick, Jacobus	ULS 213	R...., ...	WST 169	Reymond
Quick, Jacobus Junr	ULS 213	Ra__on, Jacob	MNT 74	Raimond, John B.	NYK 36

296

297

Raymond, Andrw	NYK 74	Rayner, Jacob	RNS 32	Readway, James	SRA 31
Raymond, Asa	WST 153	Rayner, Jesse	CAY 618	Ready, David Junr	MNT 109
Raymond, Caleb	COL 239	Rayner, John	KNG 9	Ready, Timothy	ORN 299
Raymond, Clapp	DUT 170	Rayner, John	SUF 65	Real, Adam	OND 198
Raymond, Daniel	RNS 32	Rayner, Joseph	QNS 77	Real, Frederick	OND 198
Raymond, David	DEL 277	Rayner, Lambert B.	NYK 18	Real, Frederick Junr	OND 198
Raymond, David	ORN 329	Rayner, Lester	QNS 76	Rease see Reese	
Raymond, Ebenezer	DUT 41	Rayner, Mary	QNS 77	Rease, Joab	CAY 544
Raymond, Ebenezer	ULS 256	Rayner, Mordecai	QNS 77	Reasoner, Jacob Junr	DUT 16
Raymond, Elikam	NYK 56	Rayner, Sarah	ORN 353	Reasoner, Jacob Senr	DUT 16
Raymond, Enoch	WST 137	Rayner, Thomas	QNS 77	Rea[v_?], James	WST 164
Raymond, Ephraim	WST 137	Rayner, Willet	QNS 76	Reave, Samuel	OND 197
Raymond, Francis	ORN 280	Rayner, Willett	QNS 63	Reaves, Asel	OND 220
Raymond, George	WST 124	Rayner, William	ORN 364	Reaves, Silus	CHN 928
Raymond, George	WST 137	Rayner, William	QNS 67	Reaves, William	SRA 5
Raymond, Henry	NYK 121	Raynes, John	NYK 58	Rebeck, William	NYK 90
Raymond, Henry	NYK 126	Raynor, Benjn	SUF 70	Rebelle, Stephen	CAY 562
Raymond, Isaac	CHN 800	Raynor, Benjamin	QNS 77	Reborg, Catherine	NYK 40
Raymond, Isaac	COL 217	Raynor, Benjamin	QNS 77	Rechmyer, Conrad	SCH 152
Raymond, Isaac	NYK 140	Raynor, Benjamin Junr	QNS 77	Rechmyer, Fredrick	SCH 137
Raymond, James	CHN 800	Raynor, David	SUF 69	Rechmyer, George	SCH 126
Raymond, James	QNS 67	Raynor, Ebenr	SUF 69	Rechmyer, Henry	SCH 138
Raymond, James	WST 137	Raynor, Elijah	QNS 77	Rechmyer, Jacob	SCH 145
Raymond, James	WST 160	Raynor, George	SUF 70	Rechmyer, John	SCH 145
Raymond, Jedediah	ORN 273	Raynor, Henry	QNS 77	Rechmyer, Peter	SCH 144
Raymond, Jesse	SRA 25	Raynor, Heny	SUF 69	Rechmyer, William	SCH 152
Raymond, Joel	SRA 28	Raynor, Heny	SUF 69	Rechmyre, Jacob	SCH 126
Raymond, Joel	SRA 33	Raynor, Heny	SUF 70	Reckert, George	SCH 126
Raymond, John	CHN 974	Raynor, Heny	SUF 70	Record, Comfort	RNS 71
Raymond, John	DUT 179	Raynor, Higby	SUF 64	Record, John	DUT 61
Raymond, John	HRK 465	Raynor, Isaac	QNS 78	Record, John Junr	DUT 130
Raymond, John	HRK 547	Raynor, Isaac	SUF 70	Records, Daniel	NYK 72
Raymond, John	OTS 36	Raynor, Jacob	QNS 77	Rector, Henry	ALB 34
Raymond, John	RNS 95	Raynor, Joel	QNS 77	Rector, Henry Junr	ALB 34
Raymond, John	WST 137	Raynor, John	QNS 77	Rector, Jacob	COL 244
Raymond, John Junr	DUT 175	Raynor, Jonathan	SUF 72	Rector, John	ALB 35
Raymond, Jonathan P.	DUT 175	Raynor, Joseph	QNS 77	Rector, John	COL 243
Raymond, Joshua	DUT 176	Raynor, Joseph	SUF 69	Red_cer, Wm	RNS 45
Raymond, Joshua	WST 137	Raynor, Joseph	SUF 70	Redabock, Henry	NYK 92
Raymond, Judd	DEL 277	Raynor, Joseph Senr	QNS 77	Redah, Samuel	TIO 257
Raymond, Lemuel	OND 170	Raynor, Lewis	HRK 524	Redault, George	MNT 78
Raymond, Mary	OND 160	Raynor, Pettee	SUF 69	Redaway, Samuel	CAY 712
Raymond, Nathan	WSH 280	Raynor, Stephen	HRK 524	Redaway, Samuel Junr	CAY 712
Raymond, Newcomb	CHN 800	Rays, John Senr	RNS 31	Redbon, Thos	OTS 53
Raymond, Peter	ALB 124	Read see Reed, Reid,		Redden, Moses	RNS 39
Raymond, Samuel	ORN 329	Rhead, Ried & Rud		Reddett, Mathew	NYK 89
Raymond, Samuel	ULS 256	Read, Aaron	WST 140	Redding, James	NYK 139
Raymond, Samuel	WST 161	Read, Andrew	NYK 120	Reddington, John	ALB 137
Raymond, Samuel Junr	WST 161	Read, Anthony a		Reddington, John	HRK 551½
Raymond, Sands	WST 153	Black	NYK 49	Redebauck, John	NYK 93
Raymond, Sands Junr	WST 153	Read, Archer	WST 169	Redfield, Bela	RNS 81
Raymond, Seth	WST 126	Read, Benjamin	DUT 166	Redfield, Daniel	HRK 575
Raymond, Stephen	DUT 176	Read, Daniel	DUT 166	Redfield, David	ORN 298
Raymond, Stephen	WST 137	Read, Eleazer	WST 126	Redfield, Eleazer	WST 140
Raymond, Thaddeus	DUT 41	Read, Eli	STB 197	Redfield, James	DEL 269
Raymond, Thomas	ALB 73	Read, George	ALB 101	Redfield, Jerred	CHN 758
Raymond, Thomas	DEL 277	Read, Isaac	DUT 176	Redfield, John	ORN 308
Raymond, Thomas	WST 137	Read, Jacob	DUT 176	Redfield, John	ULS 248
Raymond, Uriah	DUT 175	Read, James	NYK 59	Redfield, Petig	ONT 442
Raymond, Uriah	ULS 263	Read, James	NYK 137	Redfield, Richard	ESS 293
Raymond, Uriah	WST 136	Read, John	DUT 104	Redfield, Rossel	CHN 758
Raymond, Willeam	WSH 276	Read, John	ONT 502	Redfield, Theophilus	OND 199
Raymond, William	CAY 622	Read, Jonathan	ALB 100	Redford, John	ONT 320
Raymond, William	COL 204	Read, Matthew	WST 133	Redington, Jacob	OND 223
Raymond, William	DUT 90	Read, Robert	DUT 104	Redman, Abram	ONN 191
Raymond, William	RNS 95	Read, Samuel	NYK 137	Redman, David	ORN 275
Raymond, Zachariah	HRK 537	Read, Sarah	DUT 79	Redman, Henry	NYK 76
Raymond, Zamel	ONN 188	Read, Stephen	OTS 22	Redman, James	ONT 324
Rayner, Alaxr	SUF 64	Read, Taff	ONT 502	Redman, John	NYK 134
Rayner, Benjamin	QNS 77	Read, Thomas	OND 165	Redman, John	ORN 276
Rayner, David	QNS 77	Read, Timothy	DUT 173	Redman, Michael	ORN 275
Rayner, Elijah	QNS 77	Read, Wm	STB 197	Redner, Catharine	ORN 387
Rayner, Elizabeth	ORN 377	Reade, John	DUT 67	Redner, Henry	ULS 251
Rayner, Ezekiel	QNS 77	Reading, Sarah	NYK 24	Redner, John	ORN 308
Rayner, Gilbert	QNS 77	Reading, Thomas	NYK 134	Redner, John	ORN 381
Rayner, Isaac	QNS 77	Readly, John	SCH 172	Redner, Peter	ORN 337
Rayner, Jacob	DUT 28	Reads, Christion	CHN 940	Redway, James	ONN 133

Redway, Preserved	SRA 31	Reed, John	RNS 50	Reese, Adam	HRK 492
Ree__, Leonard	RNS 87	Reed, John	RNS 91	Reese, Andrew R.	COL 234
Reeber, Andrew	MNT 17	Reed, Jonathan	ONT 442	Reese, Andries A.	COL 238
Reed, Aaron	RNS 60	Reed, Jonathan	ONT 496	Reese, Benjamin	COL 239
Reed, Abner	HRK 571	Reed, Joseph	HRK 424	Reese, Christopher	COL 234
Reed, Abraham	COL 187	Reed, Joseph	ORN 329	Reese, Ephraim	COL 228
Reed, Abraham	ESS 319	Reed, Joseph	RNS 46	Reese, Frederick	ALB 25
Reed, Abraham	GRN 354	Reed, Joseph	SRA 58	Reese, Jeremiah	ALB 13
Reed, Abraham	WSH 286	Reed, Joshua	HRK 414	Reese, John	COL 234
Reed, Abraham Junr	WSH 286	Reed, Josiah	NYK 149	Reese, John	RNS 6
Reed, Amos	OND 178	Reed, Josiah	RNS 50	Reese, Turi Shaddar	NYK 98
Reed, Amos	RNS 64	Reed, Kitchell	WSH 286	Reese, William	COL 234
Reed, Asa	ONT 444	Reed, Lebbeus	DUT 54	Reese, William Junr	COL 233
Reed, Augustus	MNT 55	Reed, Lewis	CAY 702	Reeselbergh, George	COL 229
Reed, Augustus Junr	MNT 56	Reed, Mary	NYK 81	Reeve, Abigal	SUF 72
Reed, Benjn	RNS 42	Reed, Mathew	NYK 74	Reeve, Abm	SUF 69
Reed, Brister	RNS 64	Reed, Moses	ORN 347	Reeve, Benjn	SUF 71
Reed, Burch	SRA 52	Reed, Nathaniel	ORN 286	Reeve, Benjn	SUF 74
Reed, Calvin	CAY 666	Reed, Netus	GRN 356	Reeve, Benjamin S.	ORN 271
Reed, Cary	COL 187	Reed, Peter	RCK 108	Reeve, Daniel	ORN 333
Reed, Daniel	CAY 530	Reed, Philip	ONT 330	Reeve, Daniel	ORN 356
Reed, Daniel	COL 187	Reed, Phineas	COL 186	Reeve, Daniel	SUF 90
Reed, Daniel	DEL 290	Reed, Phineas	COL 220	Reeve, David	ORN 334
Reed, Daniel	DUT 176	Reed, Polly	SRA 28	Reeve, Elijah	ORN 311
Reed, Daniel	ONN 136	Reed, Reuben	DUT 138	Reeve, Elisha	ORN 340
Reed, Daniel	SRA 28	Reed, Reuben	RNS112B	Reeve, Elisha Junr	ORN 312
Reed, Daniel	WSH 290	Reed, Richard	ONT 328	Reeve, Elizabeth	SUF 74
Reed, Daniel	WST 147	Reed, Robert	WST 147	Reeve, Heny	SUF 70
Reed, David	DUT 177	Reed, Rogers	HRK 415	Reeve, Hezekiah	SUF 73
Reed, David	GRN 344	Reed, Rosel	GRN 356	Reeve, Hezekiah Jur	SUF 73
Reed, David	OND 164	Reed, Samuel	CAY 538	Reeve, Isaac	SUF 71
Reed, David	RNS112A	Reed, Samuel	GRN 356	Reeve, Isaac	SUF 72
Reed, Diah	HRK 415	Reed, Samuel	ORN 328	Reeve, Isaac	SUF 74
Reed, Ebenezer	ONT 350	Reed, Samuel	RNS 50	Reeve, Ishmeal	CAY 660
Reed, Ebenezer	ULS 183	Reed, Samuel	SRA 18	Reeve, Israel	SUF 75
Reed, Eliakim	DUT 133	Reed, Samuel	WST 145	Reeve, James	ORN 330
Reed, Elijah	MNT 23	Reed, Sebry	HRK 563	Reeve, James	RNS 93
Reed, Elijah	ONN 170	Reed, Silas	ONT 450	Reeve, James	SUF 74
Reed, Elijah Junr	DUT 133	Reed, Simon	HRK 415	Reeve, James	SUF 74
Reed, Eliphalet	RNS 110	Reed, Simon	ONT 328	Reeve, James	ULS 180
Reed, Ezra	COL 255	Reed, Squire	OND 200	Reeve, James Junr	ORN 325
Reed, Ezra	DUT 133	Reed, Stephen	OND 200	Reeve, Jesee	SUF 72
Reed, Garret	CHN 838	Reed, Stephen	WSH 284	Reeve, John	RNS 72
Reed, George	HRK 559	Reed, Thomas	MNT 58	Reeve, John	SUF 74
Reed, George	HRK 565	Reed, Thomas	SRA 39	Reeve, Jonathan	SUF 71
Reed, George	SRA 33	Reed, Tolcott	ONT 426	Reeve, Jonathan	SUF 72
Reed, Gershom	COL 220	Reed, Walter	NYK 152	Reeve, Jonathan	SUF 105
Reed, Gilbert	COL 260	Reed, Willeam	WSH 290	Reeve, Joseph	ORN 280
Reed, Henderson	NYK 118	Reed, William	HRK 589	Reeve, Joshua	SUF 75
Reed, Henry	DUT 44	Reed, William	NYK 80	Reeve, Josiah	SUF 72
Reed, Isaac	DUT 149	Reed, William	NYK 117	Reeve, Keturah	ORN 272
Reed, Isaac	RNS 42	Reed, Wm	RNS 22	Reeve, Mary	SUF 75
Reed, Isaac	RNS 64	Reed, William	SRA 44	Reeve, Moses	SUF 73
Reed, Israel	HRK 465	Reed, William	WST 158	Reeve, Nathaniel	ULS 180
Reed, Israel	ONT 408	Reeder, Frederick	DUT 154	Reeve, Paul Jun	SUF 73
Reed, Israiel	CHN 890	Reeder, Johannis	DUT 154	Reeve, Paul Sen	SUF 73
Reed, James	DUT 133	Reeder, John	ORN 351	Reeve, Robert	CLN 160
Reed, James	ORN 289	Reeder, Josiah	ORN 351	Reeve, Selah	ORN 282
Reed, James	ORN 323	Reeder, Josiah Junr	ORN 351	Reeve, Silas	CAY 586
Reed, James	QNS 61	Reeder, Peter	ULS 202	Reeve, Silas	SUF 69
Reed, James	SRA 42	Reeder, William	ORN 351	Reeve, Silas	ULS 185
Reed, James	WSH 290	Reef, Margaret	NYK 118	Reeve, Silvea	SUF 76
Reed, Jesse	CAY 708	Reef, Mary	NYK 139	Reeve, Thomas	ORN 338
Reed, John	CHN 804	Reeky, Peter	DUT 23	Reeve, Thos	SUF 64
Reed, John	CHN 856	Reel see Real		Reeve, Thos	SUF 74
Reed, John	DEL 276	Reel, Christian	ONN 165	Reeve, Walter	SUF 74
Reed, John	GRN 358	Reel, Christian Jur	ONN 165	Reeve, Wm	SUF 71
Reed, John	KNG 10	Reel, Margaret	NYK 125	Reeve, Zadock	SUF 71
Reed, John	NYK 152	Reelen, Jeremiah	ONT 366	Reeves see Reves	
Reed, John	ONT 432	Reelman, George	ALB 57	Reives & Wreeves	
Reed, John	ONT 472	Reer, Peter	NYK 73	Reeves, Abagail	CAY 532
Reed, John	ONT 504	Reerdolph, Abraham	NYK 134	Reeves, Abner	MNT 64
Reed, John	ORN 291	Rees see Rease, Rese &		Reeves, Daniel	DEL 276
Reed, John	ORN 311	Ries		Reeves, Daniel	SUF 95
Reed, John	OTS 32	Rees, James	ONT 508	Reeves, David	SUF 96
Reed, John	OTS 49	Rees, Nathan	MNT 103	Reeves, Edward	SUF 97
Reed, John	RNS 39	Rees, Nicholas	MNT 101	Reeves, Elias	SUF 89

Reeves, Hester	SUF	96	Remer, Adam	ALB	76	Renoud, Peter	WST	149
Reeves, James	ONT	344	Remer, Henry	ALB	76	Renoud, Stephen	WST	149
Reeves, Joel	SUF	98	Rem_r, __cob	ONT	490	Renowd, Andrew	WST	145
Reeves, John	GRN	329	Remer, Rulof	ALB	76	Rens_er, Johannis	DEL	282
Reeves, John	HRK	481	Remick, Simeon	SRA	41	Rent, Michael	SUF	83
Reeves, John	SRA	12	Remington, Benjamin	HRK	546	Rent, William	NYK	138
Reeves, John	SUF	96	Remington, Benjamin	RNS	108	Renvill, Joseph	NYK	128
Reeves, John	SUF	97	Remington, David	WSH	241	Renwick, George	NYK	92
Reeves, Joshua	CAY	536	Remington, Elephalet	HRK	526	Renwick, James	ORN	283
Reeves, Joshua	ONT	478	Remington, John	HRK	526	Renwick, James	WST	169
Reeves, Levi	ONT	348	Remington, John Junr	HRK	525	Renwick, John	WST	169
Reeves, Nathan	ONT	346	Remington, Joseph	OTS	55	Renwick, Robert	OTS	32
Reeves, Paul	ONT	348	Remington, Moses	CAY	596	Renwick, William	NYK	28
Reeves, Rufus	ONT	348	Remington, Shederick	ALB	20	Repose, John	NYK	71
Reeves, Selah	HRK	594	Remington, Stephen	HRK	546	Repsom, William	OTS	42
Reeves, Stephen	ONT	344	Remington, Uriah	DEL	289	Requa, Daniel	ULS	244
Reeves, Stephen	SUF	96	Remington, Wm	OND	206	Requa, Frederick	NYK	149
Reeves, Thomas	SUF	96	Remington, Wm	RNS	102	Requa, Gabrial	WST	164
Reghmire, Henry	MNT	23	Remmesnyder, Henry	MNT	53	Requa, Glods	WST	169
Reghtmire see Ryhtmeyer			Remmington, David	CAY	696	Requa, Isaac Esqr	WST	164
Reghtmire, John	MNT	23	Remmington, Jabez	CAY	694	Requa, James	WST	169
Reheman, Isaac	NYK	130	Remmington, Joseph	TIO	222	Requa, John	NYK	149
Rehern, Caleb	WSH	235	Remmington, Martin	CAY	694	Requa, John	ULS	244
Reid, Abigal	NYK	68	Remmins see Kemmins			Requa, John	WST	169
Reid, Alexander	WSH	247	Remney, John	NYK	108	Requa, William	WST	164
Reid, Daniel	WSH	257	Remny, Heny	NYK	92	Requart, Cornell	MNT	121
Reid, Jane	NYK	36	Rempler, Philip	SCH	144	Requaw, Abraham	WST	126
Reid, Joel	WSH	215	Remsen, Abraham	KNG	7	Resco, Nathaniel	RNS	34
Reid, John	NYK	30	Remsen, Abrm	RCK	106	Rese see Reese		
Reid, John	NYK	33	Remsen, Aurt	RCK	106	Rese, Henry	NYK	120
Reid, John	WSH	250	Remsen, Derick	KNG	3	Rese, Philip	ALB	4
Reid, John	WSH	286	Remsen, George	ORN	373	Resenbergh, Henderick	ALB	119
Reid, John	WST	148	Remsen, Henry	NYK	26	Reside, William	COL	194
Reid, Josi..	MNT	83	Remsen, Henry J.	NYK	17	Resler, Frederick	NYK	62
Reid, Nancy	WSH	187	Remsen, Isaac	NYK	117	Resque, John	MNT	82
Reid, Samuel	WSH	239	Remsen, Jeremiah	KNG	7	Ress, James a mulatto	NYK	73
Reid, Thomas	NYK	64	Remsen, Jeremiah	KNG	7	Resson, Elijah	WSH	219
Reid, William	NYK	51	Remsen, Johannas	KNG	3	Resue, George	SCH	138
Reid, William	WSH	250	Remsen, John	NYK	80	Retleman, George	NYK	150
Reid, William Junr	WSH	250	Remsen, Peter	NYK	24	Retleman, Valentine	NYK	150
Reideker, Henry	ORN	304	Remsen, Sophia	ULS	203	Retsley, John	TIO	242
Reighter see Ruyter			Remsen, William	QNS	70	Retter, Elizabeth	NYK	64
Reighter, Andrew	COL	235	Remsnider, John	MNT	54	Retter, Frederick	MNT	53
Reighwort, Edward	SRA	12	Remson, George	QNS	81	Retter, John P.	NYK	73
Reig ten burgh, Da(niel)	MNT	52	Remson, John	NYK	16	Reub..., Merril	MNT	71
Reil, Margarit	NYK	34	Remson, John	WST	169	Reupert, Francis	MNT	71
Reilly see Rieley &			Remson, Ruliff	WST	169	Revenbergh, George	COL	225
Ryley			Remson, Simeon	OND	160	Revenbergh, Jacobus	COL	225
Reilly, Terence	RCH	87	Remson, William	NYK	16	Reves see Reeves		
Reily, Barcley	NYK	108	Ren, Isaac	OTS	10	Reves, Eber	SRA	52
Reives, Catherine	NYK	15	Renaud, William	WST	149	Reves, Nathan	OTS	56
Relawran, Rebecca	COL	206	Renaud, William Junr	WST	149	Rew, Joseph a Black	NYK	112
Relay, Henry	DUT	63	Renauf, Edward	OTS	3	Rewbottum, John	WSH	240
Relay, Lewis	DUT	68	Renfield, Thomas	SCH	154	Rexford, Daniel	WSH	264
Relay, Robert	COL	252	Renier, Robert	MNT	41	Reyckman, Hester	ALB	127
R[eles?]son, Peleg	SRA	57	Renkins, William	NYK	144	Reyckman, Peter	ALB	129
Relly see Kelly			Rennals, Abner	SRA	39	Reyckman, Wilhelmus	ALB	127
Relly, Charles	NYK	152	Rennals, David	SRA	39	Reyhtmyer see Reghtmire		
Relly, William	NYK	135	Rennals, Elisha	SRA	50	& Ryhtmeyer		
Relyea, David	ULS	236	Rennals, James	SRA	39	Reyhtmyer, Peter	ALB	91
Relyea, Dennis	ULS	258	Rennals, Jerard	SRA	39	Reymond see Raymond		
Relyea, Henry	ULS	234	Rennals, John	SRA	41	Reymond, Silas	SUF	104
Relyea, Isaac	ULS	258	Renne a Black	NYK	103	Reymond, Stephen	SRA	61
Relyea, John	ULS	254	Rennels, Jonathon	NYK	98	Reynhart, John	ALB	72
Relyea, John D.	ULS	255	Renney, James	GRN	346	Reyno see Rhino		
Relyea, Simea	ULS	254	Renney, Jerremiah	CHN	910	Reyno, Simeon	RNS	64
Relyea, Simon	ULS	259	Renney, John	GRN	347	Reynold, Jedediah	CAY	616
Relyea, William	ULS	255	Rennolds see Reynolds			Reynolds see Rennolds		
Relyea, William Junr	ULS	252	Rennolds, Solomon	NYK	80	R..nolds, ...	RNS	77
Rema, Christian	HRK	579	Rennolds, William	NYK	78	Reynolds, Abraham	ESS	303
Rema, David	HRK	579	Rennols, Abraham	NYK	59	Reynolds, Allen	COL	248
Rema, George	HRK	439	Rennols, John	NYK	51	Reynolds, Andrew	WST	115
Rema, Peter	HRK	455	Renny, David	NYK	34	Reynolds, Andrew	WST	130
Remarfield, Solo	TIO	250	Renny, Dennis	NYK	139	Reynolds, Assahel	WSH	276
Remaw, John	MNT	37	Renny, Nathaniel	QNS	62	Reynolds, Benjan	MNT	47
Rembell, Enoch	MNT	42	Renny, Samuel	QNS	62	Reynolds, Benj	OND	206
Remble, Charles	NYK	144	Renoud, John	WST	149	Reynolds, Benjamin	WST	113

Ripple, Merry	MNT 116	Rivers, Henry	WST 169	Robbins, Timothy	CHN 840
Ripsom, Peter	SCH 156	Rivers, Isaac	WST 169	Robbins, Timothy	GRN 352
Ripsom, Peter	SCH 172	Rivers, Jacob	NYK 103	Robbins, Tracey	CHN 842
Ripsom, Willm	OTS 41	Rives, Mary Ann	NYK 16	Robbins, William	WST 114
Ripson, Peter	SCH 121	Rivier, Francis	NYK 123	Robbinson, Andrew	ONN 163
Ripsumner, John	MNT 51	Rivington, Josiah	WST 133	Robbinson, Benjn	ONN 153
Risbey, John	NYK 72	Rix, Thos	RNS 68	Robbinson, Ezra	SUF 64
Risden, Daniel	ONT 330	Rizeau, Peter	RCH 89	Robbinson, James	GRN 357
Risden, Josiah	SRA 18	Rizler, Christopher	DUT 161	Robbinson, Jespir	GRN 335
Risdorp, Peter	ULS 207	Ro.., John E.	ONN 183	Robbinson, Jonathan	ONN 162
Risdorph, John	RNS 12	Ro__, William	WST 156	Robbinson, Nathaniel	ONN 163
Rise, Oliver	MNT 69	Roach see Roch		Robbison, Edward	GRN 354
Risenberger, John	RNS 88	Roach, Charles	QNS 62	Robbison, Stephen	SRA 20
Risenbergh, John	RNS 39	Roach, Francis	NYK 79	Robelit, Peter	NYK 27
Risenbery, Henry	RNS 75	Roach, James	NYK 144	Robens, Joseph	SRA 10
Rishea see Richea		Roach, James	WSH 294	Robenson, Richard	ALB 98
Rishea, Thomas	DUT 83	Roach, John	ALB 66	Robersheaux, Jas	ALB 148
Rising, Abel	WSH 207	Roach, John	NYK 138	Roberson, Andrew	COL 232
Rising, Benjamin	OND 209	Roach, John	WSH 245	Roberson, Anna	SRA 17
Rising, Josiah	OND 206	Roach, John	WSH 294	Roberson, Daniel	SRA 34
Rising, Russle	WSH 198	Roach, Pheneas	WSH 285	Roberson, Daniel	SRA 46
Rising, Seth	WSH 191	Roach, Timothy	QNS 62	Roberson, Ebenezer	SRA 16
Risler, Andries	ULS 192	Roach, William	WSH 294	Roberson, Gabriel	COL 232
Risley, Allen	OND 178	Roades see Rhodes		Roberson, Isacher	SRA 35
Risley, Benajah	SUF 70	Roades, Henry	SUF 97	Roberson, Jabez	SRA 16
Risley, David	OND 181	Roades, Richard	SUF 90	Roberson, Levi	SRA 16
Risley, Elijah	CHN 930	Roads, Josiah	WST 169	Roberson, Nicholas	COL 232
Risley, Richard	OND 186	Roads, Richard	GRN 353	Roberson, Rachel	COL 232
Risley, Rusill	RNS 88	Roads, Samuel	WST 169	Robert a free Negro	ALB 98
Risley, William	OND 195	Roadt, Jacob	COL 233	Robert	QNS 80
Risley, Wm	SUF 70	Roadt, Nicholas	COL 233	Robert	SUF 85
Rislingburg, Jacob	GRN 338	Roadt, Peter	COL 239	Robert, Georg	NYK 85
Rissam, Jacob a Black	NYK 133	Roath, William	RNS 96	Robert, John	WST 147
Risselbrack see Kissel-		Roax, Thomas	WST 127	Robert, John J. Alexis	ULS 265
brack		Robards, Aron	GRN 350	Roberts, ... Junr	MNT 79
Risselbreck, George	COL 240	Robarge, Pierre	CLN 168	Roberts, Abel	SRA 19
Rissigue, John	SCH 172	Robart, Danl	SUF 65	Roberts, Abraham	CLN 161
Rist, Jonathan	ULS 219	Robart, David	MNT 104	Roberts, Abraham	OND 172
Risum, William	SUF 107	Robart, Harry a Black	NYK 98	Roberts, Amasa	CHN 954
Ritch see Rich		Robarts, Charles	MNT 106	Roberts, Amos	COL 210
Ritch, Ebenezer	WST 125	Robarts, Samuel	MNT 106	Roberts, Amos	DEL 284
Ritch, Henry	WST 126	Robasco, Abraham	QNS 84	Roberts, Benjamin	CLN 166
Ritch, Jacob	WST 125	Robb, John	NYK 17	Roberts, Benjamin	DUT 172
Ritch, Joseph	WST 126	Robb, William	WSH 229	Roberts, Benjamin	ONT 324
Ritchie, Gregory	QNS 70	Robbin	QNS 60	Roberts, Benjamin	ORN 336
Ritchie, Jacob	QNS 70	Robbin	QNS 68	Roberts, Benjn	OTS 38
Ritchie, Orphan	NYK 82	Robbin	QNS 75	Roberts, Benjamin	STB 199
Ritchie, Thomas	NYK 126	Robbin a Negro	SUF 68	Roberts, Caleb	OTS 37
Ritchie, Thomas	NYK 130	Robbins, Abemiel	ALB 118	Roberts, Christina	DUT 90
Rites, Frederick	ALB 55	Robbins, Asher	OND 116	Roberts, Christopher	OND 184
Rittan, John	NYK 91	Robbins, Benjamin	DUT 147	Roberts, Conrod	NYK 20
Rittenhouse, Maria	NYK 96	Robbins, Benjn	ONN 153	Roberts, Cornelius	ONT 500
Ritter see Bitter		Robbins, David	SUF 68	Roberts, Daniel	CAY 586
Ritter, Daniel	NYK 44	Robbins, Edward	CHN 768	Roberts, Daniel	DUT 44
Ritter, David	WSH 229	Robbins, Elijah	ALB 32	Roberts, Daniel	ORN 383
Ritter, Geo.	OTS 34	Robbins, Ephraim	OND 175	Roberts, Daniel	ORN 398
Ritter, Henry	GRN 332	Robbins, Ephraim	OND 191	Roberts, Danl	OTS 38
Ritter, John	NYK 37	Robbins, Ezekiel	NYK 34	Roberts, Danl	SUF 67
Ritter, John	NYK 150	Robbins, Evans	ALB 34	Roberts, Daniel	WSH 276
Ritter, John	SCH 172	Robbins, Gideon	CHN 776	Roberts, Daniel	WST 129
Ritter, Margaret	NYK 110	Robbins, Jacob	QNS 79	Roberts, David	CLN 171
Ritter, Nathew	MNT 54	Robbins, James	ALB 54	Roberts, David	CLN 172
Ritter, Michael	NYK 32	Robbins, Jane	NYK 131	Roberts, David	NYK 72
Ritter, Peter	NYK 48	Robbins, Job	ORN 341	Roberts, David	SRA 14
Ritt[_s?], James	MNT 74	Robbins, Job	WST 114	Roberts, David	WST 148
Ritt[es?], Peter	MNT 74	Robbins, John	GRN 349	Roberts, Ebenezer	WSH 211
Ritton, Abraham	NYK 58	Robbins, John	OND 191	Roberts, Edmond	NYK 108
Ritton, Harmon	NYK 147	Robbins, John	QNS 79	Roberts, Eleeazer	CHN 982
Ritton, Peter	DUT 44	Robbins, Joseph	COL 250	Roberts, Eli	ORN 313
Ritton, Peter	ORN 375	Robbins, Joseph	ESS 310	Roberts, Elijah	MNT 119
Ritts, Peter L.	MNT 7	Robbins, Joseph	ONT 398	Roberts, Elizabeth	NYK 53
Rivenbergh, Adam	COL 189	Robbins, Mary	NYK 114	Roberts, Ethan	CLN 161
Rivenbergh, Johans M.	COL 225	Robbins, Oliver	CHN 910	Roberts, Francis	NYK 136
Rivenbergh, Peter	ALB 92	Robbins, Robert	OND 177	Roberts, George	OTS 15
Rivers, Adam	COL 227	Robbins, Robert	RCH 89	Roberts, Gideon	SRA 36
Rivers, Cornelius	WST 169	Robbins, Samuel	WST 114	Roberts, Gilbert	ORN 343
Rivers, Cornelius	WST 169	Robbins, Stephen	QNS 80	Roberts, Gilbert	TIO 235

Name	Loc	Name	Loc	Name	Loc
Roberts, Giles	OND 172	Roberts, William	ORN 352	Robertson, Thomas	WST 121
Roberts, Hiram	CHN 968	Roberts, Wm	OTS 6	Robertson, Thomas Junr	WST 121
Roberts, Hugh	OND 214	Roberts, William	RNS 90	Robertson, Timothy	OND 205
Roberts, Ichabud	SRA 29	Roberts, William	WSH 210	Robertson, Watson	OND 189
Roberts, Ira	DUT 167	Roberts, William Junr	WSH 210	Robertson, Willeam	WSH 288
Roberts, Isaac	ONT 418	Roberts, Zopher	WSH 201	Robertson, William	OND 167
Roberts, Isaac	SCH 143	Robertson, Aaron	CHN 960	Robertson, William	WSH 195
Roberts, Isaac	WSH 278	Robertson, Andrew	NYK 130	Robertson, William	WSH 197
Roberts, Jacob	COL 216	Robertson, Archabald	WSH 196	Robertson, William	WSH 250
Roberts, James	OTS 37	Robertson, Azel	SUF 69	Robertson, William	WST 134
Roberts, James	ULS 207	Robertson, Charles	OND 163	Robertson, Willis	SUF 68
Roberts, James	WSH 214	Robertson, Christopher	SUF 71	Robertson J., Gilbert	WST 121
Roberts, Jedediah	WSH 237	Robertson, David	SUF 69	Robeson, Geo	OTS 38
Roberts, Jeremiah	ORN 387	Robertson, Edmond	WSH 233	Robler, Maria	NYK 92
Roberts, Jesse	SRA 15	Robertson, Eliakim	CHN 968	Robin a Negro	SUF 68
Roberts, Joel	ONT 368	Robertson, Elnathan	CHN 788	Robins, Andrew	KNG 10
Ro...ts, John	CAY 556	Robertson, Ezra	ALB 78	Robins, Beman	SCH 146
Roberts, John	CLN 161	Robertson, Frances	WSH 253	Robins, David	HRK 595
Roberts, John	COL 221	Robertson, Francis	WSH 248	Robins, Elisha Junr	SCH 143
Roberts, John	MNT 119	Robertson, George	NYK 30	Robins, Elisha Senr	SCH 143
Roberts, John	NYK 27	Robertson, George	NYK 32	Robins, Helena	SUF 87
Roberts, John	NYK 145	Robertson, Gilbert	NYK 16	Robins, Jacob	HRK 514
Roberts, John	ONN 167	Robertson, Gilbert		Robins, Jeremiah	QNS 70
Roberts, John	ONT 322	Junr	WST 120	Robins, Job	RNS 8
Roberts, John	ORN 324	Robertson, Griffith J.	NYK 129	Robins, John	RNS 93
Roberts, John	OTS 37	Robertson, Isaac a		Robins, Joseph	MNT 67
Roberts, John	SRA 18	Black	NYK 98	Robins, Joshua	RNS 107
Roberts, John 2d	CLN 159	Robertson, Jabus	WST 139	Robins, Nathaniel	RCH 91
Roberts, John 3d	CLN 159	Robertson, James	NYK 106	Robins, Reuben	HRK 593
Roberts, Jonathan	DUT 61	Robertson, James	NYK 107	Robins, Samuel	NYK 67
Roberts, Jonathan	DUT 134	Robertson, James	NYK 127	Robins, Scudder	SUF 80
Roberts, Joseph	CLN 161	Robertson, James	NYK 130	Robins, Selas	WSH 299
Roberts, Joseph	CLN 165	Robertson, James	NYK 136	Robins, Thomas	MNT 64
Roberts, Joseph	DUT 158	Robertson, James	SUF 70	Robins, Thomas	MNT 71
Roberts, Joseph	ONT 322	Robertson, James	WSH 191	Robins, Vanhacley	SUF 83
Roberts, Lemuel	DUT 175	Robertson, James	WSH 243	Robins, William	HRK 595
Roberts, Martin	CHN 878	Robertson, James	WSH 294	Robins, William	SRA 44
Roberts, Martin Junr	CHN 876	Robertson, James	WST 121	Robins, Zebulon	SUF 82
Roberts, Michael	CLN 161	Robertson, Jerre:h J.	COL 218	Robinson, Abel	CAY 646
Roberts, Miner	RNS 18	Robertson, John	NYK 88	Robinson, Amos	OTS 50
Roberts, Nathaniel	MNT 100	Robertson, John	NYK 121	Robinson, Andrew	DUT 92
Roberts, Nathaniel	WSH 201	Robertson, John	SUF 70	Robinson, Andrew	NYK 79
Roberts, Nathen	WSH 207	Robertson, John	SUF 90	Robinson, Anthony	ALB 57
Roberts, Nicholas	NYK 110	Robertson, John	WSH 194	Robinson, Archibald	NYK 51
Roberts, Noah	ONN 189	Robertson, John	WSH 233	Robinson, Augustus	ORN 282
Roberts, Noah	SRA 42	Robertson, John A.	NYK 116	Robinson, Baker	DEL 267
Roberts, Peter	CLN 162	Robertson, Jonathan	NYK 107	Robinson, Benedict	ONT 468
Roberts, Peter	COL 217	Robertson, Jonathan	SUF 70	Robinson, Benj:	ONN 171
Roberts, Peter	RNS112A	Robertson, Joseph	NYK 135	Robinson, Benjamin	ORN 355
Roberts, Peter Junr	RNS 111	Robertson, Joseph	QNS 66	Robinson, Betsey	NYK 80
Roberts, Phillip	COL 221	Robertson, Joseph	SUF 64	Robinson, Beverly	DUT 169
Roberts, Richard	ONT 404	Robertson, Joseph	WSH 203	Robinson, Brice	NYK 81
Roberts, Robert a		Robertson, Moses	SUF 70	Robinson, Calvin	DUT 66
mulatto	NYK 73	Robertson, Nathan	OND 183	Robinson, Cato a Black	NYK 40
Roberts, Robert	NYK 116	Robertson, Nathen	WSH 288	Robinson, Chappel	DUT 92
Roberts, Rulal	WSH 205	Robertson, Peter	WSH 191	Robinson, Cornelius	ULS 199
Roberts, Samuel	DUT 159	Robertson, Peter	WSH 236	Robinson, Cyrus	OTS 51
Roberts, Samuel	HRK 422	Robertson, Phineas	SUF 64	Robinson, Daniel	CAY 668
Roberts, Saml	OTS 55	Robertson, Richard	OND 178	Robinson, Daniel	DEL 267
Roberts, Seth	OND 167	Robertson, Richd	SUF 68	Robinson, Daniel	DEL 277
Roberts, Thaddeus	ESS 319	Robertson, Robert	NYK 119	Robinson, Daniel	MNT 66
Roberts, Thomas	DUT 128	Robertson, Robert	ORN 321	Robinson, Daniel	ONT 382
Roberts, Thomas	NYK 30	Robertson, Robert	WSH 256	Robinson, Darius	OTS 49
Roberts, Thomas	NYK 92	Robertson, Samuel	COL 205	Robinson, David	CAY 616
Roberts, Thomas	ULS 210	Robertson, Samuel	OND 195	Robinson, David	DEL 267
Roberts, Thomas	WSH 205	Robertson, Saml	SUF 70	Robinson, David	HRK 595
Roberts, William	ALB 129	Robertson, Sanford	WSH 235	Robinson, David	OTS 50
Roberts, William	CAY 556	Robertson, Sarah	NYK 147	Robinson, David	ULS 200
Roberts, William	CLN 159	Robertson, Seth	OND 195	Robinson, David Junr	OTS 50
Roberts, William	CLN 172	Robertson, Seth	WSH 201	Robinson, Deborah	ORN 384
Roberts, William	CLN 174	Robertson, Sten	SUF 70	Robinson, Ebenezer	DEL 267
Roberts, William	DUT 172	Robertson, Stephen	WSH 294	Robinson, Ebenezer	DUT 92
Roberts, William	NYK 21	Robertson, Suzon(?)	MNT 12	Robinson, Ebenezer	
Roberts, Eilliam	NYK 42	Robertson, Tarah	WSH 236	Junr	DEL 267
Roberts, William	NYK 46	Robertson, Thomas	NYK 76	Robinson, Ebenezer	
Roberts, William	NYK 100	Robertson, Thomas	NYK 122	Lewis	ULS 200
Roberts, William	ONT 366	Robertson, Thomas	WSH 248	Robinson, Elsey	NYK 17

Name	Loc	Name	Loc	Name	Loc
Robinson, Enoch	DUT 21	Robinson, Samuel	ORN 392	Rockwell, Abel	ORN 346
Robinson, Erastus	ONT 388	Robinson, Samuel ye 2d	DUT 38	Rockwell, Abner	SRA 55
Robinson, Francis	DEL 289	Robinson, Senca	CHN 950	Rockwell, Above	TIO 213
Robinson, Gain	ONT 352	Robinson, Siah	ULS 250	Rockwell, Benjamin	OTS 23
Robinson, George	CAY 578	Robinson, Silas	OTS 11	Rockwell, Benjamin	WST 112
Robinson, George	DUT 114	Robinson, Silvester	NYK 35	Rockwell, Daniel	HRK 501
Robinson, Geo	OTS 16	Robinson, Solomon	WST 149	Rockwell, Eber	OND 214
Robinson, George	RNS 75	Robinson, Stephen	DEL 267	Rockwell, Eli	OTS 23
Robinson, Hector	RNS 55	Robinson, Thomas	CAY 688	Rockwell, Elijah	DUT 124
Robinson, Henry	NYK 64	Robinson, Thomas	NYK 68	Rockwell, Elkanah	ALB 32
Robinson, Hopkin	NYK 110	Robinson, Thos	OTS 10	Rockwell, Ezra	ONN 188
Robinson, Hugh	OTS 2	Robinson, Thomas	SUF 83	Rockwell, James	ALB 27
Robinson, Isaac	HRK 581	Robinson, Thomas	WST 144	Rockwell, James	TIO 265
Robinson, Isaac	ORN 323	Robinson, Timothy	CAY 566	Rockwell, James Junr	ALB 32
Robinson, Isaac	OTS 49	Robinson, William	NYK 73	Rockwell, Jeremiah	SRA 17
Robinson, Isaac	SUF 82	Robinson, William	NYK 95	Rockwell, Job	WST 155
Robinson, Isaac	ULS 200	Robinson, William	ORN 276	Rockwell, John	ESS 305
Robinson, Jacob	ULS 236	Robinson, Wm	OTS 41	Rockwell, John	ONT 362
Robinson, James	CAY 680	Robinson, William	ULS 233	Rockwell, Jonathan	TIO 261
Robinson, James	COL 239	Robinson, Zebulon	ULS 256	Rockwell, Jonathan	TIO 265
Robinson, James	GRN 338	Robinson, Ziba	OTS 8	Rockwell, Joseph	SRA 48
Robinson, James	NYK 78	Robison, Abraham	RNS 85	Rockwell, Joshua	OND 221
Robinson, James	OTS 28	Robison, Adam	SRA 52	Rockwell, Joshua Junr	OND 221
Robinson, James	WST 148	Robison, Caleb	ALB 16	Rockwell, Levi	OTS 23
Robinson, Johannis	ORN 309	Robison, Daniel	CLN 165	Rockwell, Nathan	WST 151
Robinson, John	CAY 686	Robison, Danl	SCH 124	Rockwell, Nathaniel	ORN 347
Robinson, John	DUT 28	Robison, Ezra	RNS112B	Rockwell, Rufus	ALB 31
Robinson, John	DUT 66	Robison, George	RNS 66	Rockwell, Samuel	OND 188
Robinson, John	DUT 92	Robison, Henry	SRA 52	Rockwell, Simeon	OTS 27
Robinson, John	DUT 119	Robison, James	MNT 62	Rockwell, Stephen	SRA 13
Robinson, John	DUT 169	Robison, James	ONT 484	Rockwell, Stephen	SRA 35
Robinson, John	HRK 592	Robison, James	SCH 134	Rockwell, Stephen	WST 136
Robinson, John	NYK 43	Robison, John	ALB 16	Rockwell, Thaddeus	WST 155
Robinson, John	NYK 62	Robison, John	ALB 59	Rockwell, Thomas	GRN 355
Robinson, John	NYK 76	Robison, John	ALB 148	Rockwell, Thms	ONN 188
Robinson, John	NYK 76	Robison, John	SCH 125	Rockwell, Thos Jur	ONN 188
Robinson, John	ORN 375	Robison, John	SCH 147	Rockwell, Timothy	ESS 303
Robinson, John	OTS 49	Robison, Richard	STB 207	Rockwell, Timo	OTS 32
Robinson, John	OTS 50	Robison, William	ALB 144	Rockwell, Valentine	SRA 20
Robinson, John	OTS 51	Robisson, William T.	NYK 151	Rockwell, William	WST 126
Robinson, John	ULS 200	Roboen, Mary	NYK 81	Rockwell, Zebulon	OND 222
Robinson, John Junr	DUT 93	Roboson, Joseph	SRA 16	Rockwhell, Nathaniel H.	NYK 77
Robinson, John Junr	DUT 168	Robson, John	ONT 494	Rockwood, Elam	HRK 441
Robinson, John Deck..	ONT 478	Robson, John	ONT 494	Rockwood, Elias	OND 167
Robinson, Joseph	ALB 71	Roccow, John	WST 149	Rockwood, Joshua	CHN 938
Robinson, Joseph	NYK 24	Roch see Roach		Rockwood, Micah	HRK 522
Robinson, Joseph	RNS 39	Roch, Ann	WSH 248	Rockwood, Nathaniel	OND 212
Robinson, Joseph	WST 164	Roch, Peter	MNT 17	Rockwood, Reuben	OND 221
Robinson, Joshua	GRN 354	Roch, Richard	WSH 228	Rockwood, Silas	HRK 441
Robinson, Lewis	DUT 168	Roche, Fontaine	ORN 281	Rocky, Christian	NYK 58
Robinson, Margaret a Black	NYK 19	Rock, John	MNT 60	Rockyfeller, Christian	ORN 295
Robinson, Martha	CAY 688	Rock, Peter	MNT 60	Rockyfeller, Christian Junr	ORN 295
Robinson, Martin	DUT 169	Rock, Silvenus	QNS 80		
Robinson, Mary	NYK 32	Rockafellow, Willm	SCH 128	Rockyfeller, Henry	ORN 295
Robinson, Matthw	OTS 32	Rockefeller, Deal P.	COL 230	Rockyfeller, Jacob	ORN 295
Robinson, Micha	OTS 11	Rockefeller, Diell	COL 191	Rockyfeller, Peter	ORN 293
Robinson, Nathel	COL 178	Rockefeller, Diell	COL 236	Rockyfeller, Rachel	ORN 295
Robinson, Noah	DUT 92	Rockefeller, Fredk	COL 191	Rodden, Daniel	WSH 188
Robinson, Peter	CAY 646	Rockefeller, Hermanus	COL 190	Rodemon, John	NYK 35
Robinson, Peter	DUT 92	Rockefeller, Jacob	COL 190	Roderick, Hannah	NYK 109
Robinson, Peter	MNT 48	Rockefeller, Jacob P.	COL 230	Rodes see Roads & Rhodes	
Robinson, Reuben	ALB 70	Rockefeller, John	COL 190	Rodes, Aaron	WST 126
Robinson, Richard	NYK 58	Rockefeller, Peter Ph:	COL 189	Rodes, Charles	SRA 56
Robinson, Richard	ORN 277	Rockefeller, Peter W.	COL 235	Rodes, Iaac	NYK 78
Robinson, Robert	HRK 563	Rockefeller, Ph: D.	COL 224	Rodes, Jeremiah	WST 160
Robinson, Robert	MNT 74	Rockefeller, Phillip	COL 189	Rodes, John	SRA 56
Robinson, Robert	NYK 35	Rockefeller, Phillip	COL 236	Rodes, John	WSH 186
Robinson, Robert	NYK 128	Rockefeller, Phillip P.	COL 225	Rodes, Peleg	SRA 56
Robinson, Robert	NYK 132	Rockefeller, Phillip S.	COL 190	Rodes, Timothy	WST 156
Robinson, Rowland	OTS 50	Rockefeller, Simon	COL 190	Rodgers, Anthony	NYK 100
Robinson, Rowland	ULS 233	Rockefeller, Wm	COL 190	Rodgers, Barnett	SUF 75
Robinson, Sabin	DUT 92	Rocket, John a free Negro	ALB 137	Rodgers, David	CHN 834
Robinson, Samuel	DEL 291	Rockinstire, Joseph	RNS 87	Rodgers, Ebenezer	QNS 76
Robinson, Samuel	DUT 28	Rockow, Sarah	WST 144	Rodgers, Ezra	CHN 800
Robinson, Samuel	DUT 174	Rockwel, Simeon	SRA 42	Rodgers, George	NYK 114
Robinson, Samuel	MNT 31	Rockwell	GRN 349	Rodgers, Henry	NYK 117

Roney, Michael	ALB 140	Roosa, Wilhelmus	ULS 252	Root, Solomon	RNS 75
Roning, John	SCH 132	Roosa, Zachariah	ULS 199	Root, Solomon	WSH 296
Ronk, Cornelius	ULS 253	Roosboom, Barent	MNT 46	Root, Stephen	GRN 330
Ronk, Johannis	ULS 253	Roosboom, Garrit	MNT 46	Root, Stephen	OTS 58
Ronk, Lawrence	ULS 253	Roose, David	OND 224	Root, Stephen	SRA 43
Ronk, Phillip	ULS 253	R..savelt, George	MNT 81	Root, Thomas	CHN 760
Roo_, John	MNT 48	Roosevelt, Adam a		Root, Thomas	GRN 342
Roo_, Robert	MNT 48	Black NYK 69		Root, Thomas	SRA 52
Rood, Allen	CAY 646	Roosevelt, Cornelius C.NYK 48		Root, William	ALB 45
Rood, Anne	CAY 646	Roosevelt, Cornelius C.WST 148		Root, Willm	COL 214
Rood, Assa	WSH 276	Roosevelt, Elbert	NYK 24	Root, William	COL 233
Rood, Caleb	CAY 696	Roosevelt, James	NYK 62	Root, William	ONT 422
Rood, Eli	COL 185	Roosevelt, James C.	QNS 68	Root, William	WSH 295
Rood, John	DUT 49	Roosevelt, James J.	NYK 38	Root, Winthrop	RNS 110
Rood, John	SRA 35	Roosevelt, James N.	WST 149	Root, Zenos	ESS 321
Rood, Jonathan	COL 201	Roosevelt, Margaret	NYK 55	Root, Zufus	CHN 964
Rood, Jonathan	OND 186	Roosevelt, Oliver	NYK 66	Rooth see Ruth	
Rood, Lucy	OND 201	Roosevelt, Mings a		Rooth, Jonathan	SRA 21
Rood, Noah	ORN 387	Black NYK 112		Roots, John	ULS 194
Rood, Oliver	OND 193	Root, Addeniger Jun	GRN 354	Roper, Esther	OND 182
Rood, William	SRA 35	Root, Adderiger	GRN 354	Roppoo, Mathew	NYK 107
Roof, Samuel	WST 128	Root, Asa	SRA 43	Rorapough, Peter	CHN 772
Roof, Samuel Junr	WST 128	Root, Asahel	OND 193	Rorbock, George	RNS 62
Rook, Abner	MNT 122	Root, Ashbel	RNS 81	Rorbock, John	RNS 62
Rook, Christian	DUT 165	Root, Assahel	WSH 300	Roreback, Wido C.	COL 201
Rook, Eli	MNT 49	Root, Azeriah	CHN 760	Roreback, George	RNS 64
Rook, John	WST 169	Root, Basley	GRN 354	Roreback, Teunis	COL 196
Rooker, Joseph	WSH 283	Root, Billa	OND 167	Rorebaugh, Alexander	COL 240
Rookhart, Jacob	RCK 101	Root, Charles	OND 203	Rorebaugh, Coenradt	COL 240
Rooks, Amos	RCH 90	Root, Christian	ORN 296	Rorebaugh, George	COL 240
Rool, Daniel	DEL 280	Root, Daniel	OND 169	Rorebaugh, John	COL 240
Roolback, Frederick	RNS 61	Root, Daniel	OND 193	Rorick. Casper	SCH 122
Room, Jacob P.	NYK 107	Root, Danl	OTS 19	Rorington, James	NYK 85
Roome, Catherine	NYK 87	Root, Ebenezer	CHN 760	Rortridge, Eve	NYK 145
Roome, Jacob	NYK 52	Root, Edward	ONT 444	Rosa, Joshua	SCH 138
Roome, John P.	NYK 51	Root, Eleazer	COL 210	Rosaw, Jacob	ALB 71
Roome, Nicholas	NYK 51	Root, Eli	OND 163	Roscronch, Joseph	TIO 235
Roome, William	NYK 22	Root, Elias	OND 170	Rosdale, Ruth	NYK 121
Roomer, Andrew	RCH 93	Root, Elihu	OND 170	Rose	NYK 79
Rooney, Elizabeth	NYK 124	Root, Elijah	CAY 644	Rose a mulatto	NYK 104
Roorbach, Arthur H.	DUT 153	Root, Elijah	CLN 173	Rose, Abam	OND 212
Roorbach, Isaac	DUT 154	Root, Elijah	RNS 75	Rose, Abel	ALB 102
Roorbach, John	CAY 642	Root, Elisha	OND 167	Rose, Abraham	GRN 351
Roorbach, John	ORN 286	Root, Erastus	DEL 290	Rose, Abraham	SUF 100
Roorback, Abagael	NYK 38	Root, Frederick	ORN 308	Rose, Adam	ALB 142
Roorback, Francis	NYK 44	Root, George	CLN 172	Rose, Alexander	NYK 21
Roorback, John	RCK 110	Root, Hannah	NYK 66	Rose, Bashebe	RNS 104
Roorback, Thomas	RNS 62	Root, Israel	RNS 14	Rose, Benjamin	COL 245
Roosa, Aarea	ULS 252	Root, Isreal	CAY 712	Rose, Benjamin	COL 262
Roosa, Abraham	ULS 187	Root, Jared	RNS 110	Rose, Benjamin	ORN 391
Roosa, Abraham	ULS 213	Root, Jehial	OTS 46	Rose, Benjamin	SRA 58
Roosa, Abraham I.	ULS 215	Root, Jerard	ONT 422	Rose, Benjamin	ULS 220
Roosa, Aldert	ULS 187	Root, Joel	CHN 760	Rose, Charles	RNS 104
Roosa, Aldert	ULS 212	Root, John	RNS 14	Rose, Cornelius	RNS 35
Roosa, Aldert	ULS 244	Root, Jonathan	OND 163	Rose, Dan	ONT 318
Roosa, Andries	ULS 201	Root, Joseph	OND 167	Rose, Daniel	GRN 340
Roosa, Andries I.	ULS 199	Root, Joseph Junr	OND 164	Rose, Daniel	RNS 19
Roosa, Dirck	ULS 251	Root, Joshua	CHN 742	Rose, Daniel	SUF 94
Roosa, Evert	ULS 252	Root, Joshua	CHN 760	Rose, David	DUT 45
Roosa, Gideon	ULS 251	Root, Josiah	CAY 706	Rose, David	ORN 391
Roosa, Hyman	ULS 206	Root, Josiah	OTS 57	Rose, David	SUF 90
Roosa, Isaac	ULS 215	Root, Luther	ONT 478	Rose, David	SUF 98
Roosa, Jacob	ULS 187	Root, Malachi	ORN 300	Rose, Doctor a Black	NYK 36
Roosa, Jacob I.	ULS 216	Root, Mary	OTS 24	Rose, Edebert	QNS 67
Roosa, Jacobus	ULS 253	Root, Medad	OND 169	Ro_e, Edward	GRN 342
Roosa, Johannis G.	ULS 203	Root, Moses	CHN 922	Rose, Eleazer	ULS 250
Roosa, Johannis I.	ULS 198	Root, Moses	OTS 17	Rose, Elijah	ONT 398
Roosa, Johannis W.	ULS 199	Root, Moses	OTS 21	Rose, Elijah	ONT 422
Roosa, John Junr	ULS 251	Root, Moses Junr	OTS 21	Rose, Elisha	ONT 398
Roosa, John E.	ULS 206	Root, Nicholas	CHN 742	Rose, Elizth	OTS 18
Roosa, Jonas	ULS 255	Root, Noah	ONN 169	Rose, Epharim	SRA 59
Roosa, Magdalena	ULS 248	Root, Peter P.	CHN 846	Rose, Ezekiel	CAY 522
Roosa, Matthew	ULS 252	Root, Reuben	OTS 37	Rose, Ezekiel	SUF 98
Roosa, Peter	ULS 251	Root, Roswell	ONT 426	Rose, Hendrick	RCK 101
Roosa, Peter Junr	ULS 252	Root, Samuel	COL 265	Rose, Henry	GRN 329
Roosa, Peter P.	ULS 206	Root, Seth	OND 193	Rose, Henry	GRN 333
Roosa, Teunis	ULS 217	Root, Simeon	OND 194	Rose, Henry	RNS 63

Name	Loc	No.
Rose, Hermanus	ALB	90
Rose, Hugh	DEL	269
Rose, Hugh	NYK	141
Rose, Hugh Junr	DEL	269
Rose, Ichabod	DUT	17
Rose, Isaac	CHN	742
Rose, Isaac	ORN	299
Rose, Isaac	RCK	101
Rose, Isaac	SUF	98
Rose, Israel	SRA	59
Rose, Israel	SUF	98
Rose, Israel Junr	SRA	59
Rose, Jacob	ALB	53
Rose, Jacob	RCK	100
Rose, Jacob Junr	RCK	100
Rose, Jacobus	ULS	237
Rose, James	DEL	285
Rose, James	GRN	346
Rose, James	NYK	136
Rose, Jeremiah	DEL	284
Rose, Jeris	ONT	422
Rose, Jesee	SUF	65
Rose, Jessy (Possibly Tessy)	GRN	346
Rose, Joel	NYK	144
Rose, Johannis	ULS	250
Rose, John	ALB	53
Rose, John	COL	260
Rose, John	DEL	275
Rose, John	MNT	36
Rose, John	MNT	85
Rose, John	NYK	56
Rose, John	NYK	69
Rose, John	OND	178
Rose, John	ORN	298
Rose, John	ULS	234
Rose, John	ULS	247
Rose, John H.	NYK	140
Rose, John P.	COL	265
Rose, Joseph	NYK	16
Rose, Joseph	NYK	133
Rose, Joseph Junior	NYK	43
Rose, Joshua	OND	211
Rose, Justice	SUF	67
Rose, Lemuel	SUF	81
Rose, Leonard	TIO	216
Rose, Lewis a mulatto	NYK	76
Rose, Martin	RNS	60
Rose, Martinus	ULS	196
Rose, Moses	SUF	98
Rose, Mrss	GRN	341
Rose, Mulford B.	DUT	138
Rose, Nathan	HRK	432
Rose, Nathaniel	RNS	104
Rose, Peter	CAY	660
Rose, Phebe	ORN	391
Rose, Phillip B.	DUT	159
Rose, Phineas	SUF	65
Rose, Phinehas	HRK	425
Rose, Richard	ALB	8
Rose, Rufus	SUF	99
Rose, Russell	SCH	148
Rose, Samuel	ALB	89
Rose, Samuel	ALB	90
Rose, Samuel	WSH	295
Rose, Samuel H.	SUF	100
Rose, Sarah	SUF	65
Rose, Simon	ULS	237
Rose, Starme	GRN	351
Rose, Stephen	HRK	415
Rose, Stephen	SRA	53
Rose, Stephen	SUF	98
Rose, Thomas	NYK	150
Rose, Thomas	SUF	86
Rose, Timy	SUF	65
Rose, Urial	OTS	18
Rose, William	ALB	89
Rose, William	DEL	275
Rose, William	ORN	314
Rose, William	SUF	90
Rose, Wm	TIO	210
Rose, William	ULS	207
Rose, William L.	NYK	38
Rose, Wm L.	OTS	39
Rose, William W:	DEL	275
Rose, Zalmon	TIO	216
Rose, Zebulen	SRA	58
Roseboom, Eve	ALB	149
Roseboom, Hester	ALB	129
Roseboom, Robert	OTS	44
Rosebrough, James	ONT	322
Rosecranch, Abraham	ONN	183
Rosecrans, Cornelius	ORN	315
Rosecrans, Frederick	ALB	81
Rosecrans, Frederick	ULS	217
Rosecrans, Hendrick	ULS	217
Rosecrans, Henry	ALB	61
Rosecrans, Jacob	ULS	217
Rosecrans, Jacob	ULS	248
Rosecrans, Jacobus	ULS	201
Rosecrans, James	ULS	194
Rosecrans, Jane	ULS	248
Rosecrans, John	ALB	15
Rosecrans, John	ORN	323
Rosecrans, John Junr	DUT	33
Rosecrans, John Senr	DUT	29
Rosecrans, Josiah	ORN	326
Rosecrans, Matthew	DUT	29
Rosecrans, Phillip	DUT	22
Rosecrans, Thomas	ALB	96
Rosecrans, Warren	DUT	33
Rosecrans, William	ULS	248
Rosecrans, Zachariah	ULS	217
Rosecrantz, George	HRK	412
Rosecrantz, Herry	HRK	411
Rosecrantz, Stephen	CAY	590
Rosecrons, Peter	ALB	96
Rosegrant, Hannah	NYK	35
Rosekrance, Benjamin	SRA	9
Rosekrance, Depui	RNS	80
Rosel, Peter D.	COL	242
Rosell, Peter	NYK	135
Rosell, Thomas	CAY	562
Roseman, Jacob J.	ALB	80
Roseman, John	SUF	66
Roseman, Richard	NYK	31
Rosenback, William	CAY	532
Rosenbear, John	DUT	75
Rosenberg, George	RNS	77
Rosennah a Black	NYK	91
Rosenpaugh, Anthony	ULS	213
Rosett, David	NYK	73
Rosett, Maria Theresa	NYK	88
Roosevelt see Roosevelt		
Rosevelt, Cornelius C.	WST	120
Rosevelt, John	SRA	34
Rosevelt, Peter	QNS	62
Roshay, Thomas	NYK	122
Roshore, John	NYK	50
Rosier, Nathan	ONN	192
Rosinbergh, Johanis	ALB	99
Rosler, Henry	ALB	67
Ross, Alexander	NYK	40
Ross, Alexander	ORN	273
Ross, Alexander	SRA	22
Ross, Alexander	ULS	252
Ross, Amos	SRA	21
Ross, Andrw	NYK	112
Ross, Asher	HRK	552
Ross, Benjamin	RNS	40
Ross, Benjamin	WSH	253
Ross, Benjamin L.	NYK	147
Ross, Charles	QNS	70
Ross, Charles S.	RNS	73
Ross, Christian	MNT	7
Ross, Danial	WSH	252
Ross, Daniel	ALB	62
Ross, Daniel	ESS	304
Ross, Daniel	ONT	324
Ross, David	KNG	8
Ross, David	NYK	57
Ross, David	NYK	90
Ross, David	SRA	22
Ross, David	WSH	222
Ross, Davis	ONT	426
Ross, Edward	DEL	267
Ross, Epiphras	SRA	29
Ross, Hugh	SRA	29
Ross, Isarel	NYK	88
Ross, James	SRA	22
Ross, James	TIO	214
Ross, James	ULS	181
Ross, James	ULS	257
Ross, John	DUT	47
Ross, John	KNG	6
Ross, John	NYK	35
Ross, John	NYK	59
Roos, John	NYK	101
Ross, John	NYK	123
Ross, John	OTS	8
Ross, John	RNS	41
Ross, John	ULS	181
Ross, John	WSH	251
Ross, Joseph	COL	259
Ross, Joseph	DUT	47
Ross, Joseph	ULS	181
Ross, Lawrence	COL	259
Ross, Levi	CAY	550
Ross, Libbeus	ONT	408
Ross, Phineas	NYK	116
Ross, Robert a Black	NYK	114
Ross, Robert	WST	148
Ross, Royal	OTS	36
Ross, Samel	WSH	248
Ross, Samuel	WSH	203
Ross, Sarah	WSH	231
Ross, Sophia	TIO	214
Ross, Stephen	NYK	129
Ross, Theadonus	STB	202
Ross, Thomas	NYK	80
Ross-Widow	QNS	61
Ross, Wm	MNT	109
Ross, William	NYK	42
Ross, William	NYK	44
Ross, William	NYK	48
Ross, William	SRA	50
Ross, Wm Junr	RNS	73
Ross, William Junr	SRA	50
Ross, Wm Senr	RNS	73
Rosse, Nicholas	NYK	91
Rossel, Abraham	WST	169
Rossel, John	WST	169
Rossell, Benjamin	ULS	235
Rossell, Thomas	NYK	95
Rosseter, Bryan	NYK	59
Rossetter, Charles	ALB	104
Rossier, George	NYK	21
Rossin, Silas	OND	172
Rossman, Coenradt	COL	229
Rossman, Coenradt J.	COL	235
Rossman, Elias	COL	229
Rossman, Elias	OTS	14
Rossman, Fite	COL	195
Rossman, George	DEL	287
Rossman, Hendrick	COL	229
Rossman, Henry J.	COL	231
Rossman, John	COL	200
Rossman, John	COL	229
Rossman, John	OTS	44

Name	Ref	Name	Ref	Name	Ref
Rossman, John J.	COL 238	Row, Jacob	CAY 554	Rowland, John	HRK 499
Rossman, Jonas	COL 198	Row, Jacob	COL 236	Rowland, John	RNS 44
Roswell, Fenton	MNT 90	Row, James	GRN 327	Rowland, John Jun	HRK 499
Rote, Henry	NYK 150	Row, John	ALB 90	Rowland, John R.	RNS 51
Roteroke, Peter	OND 208	Row, John	ALB 118	Rowland, Jonathan	NYK 109
Roth, Benjamin	SUF 82	Row, John	NYK 124	Rowland, Jonathan	QNS 63
Roth, Levi	CAY 616	Row, John	RNS 104	Rowland, Jonathan	RNS 46
Rothbern, Samuel	NYK 50	Row, John	SCH 172	Rowland, Marvil	DUT 26
Rothbon, Amos	CAY 646	Row, John	SRA 14	Rowland, Nancy	NYK 131
Rothbon, Joshua	CAY 660	Row, Joseph	ALB 90	Rowland, Nicholas	HRK 499
Rothbone, Josiah	CHN 838	Row, Joshua	ALB 118	Rowland, Oliver	RNS 46
Rothbone, Robert	CAY 624	Row, Lyman	ALB 37	Rowland, Robert	RNS 46
Rothbone, Solomon	CHN 824	Row, Nathan	ALB 119	Rowland, Salmon	SRA 15
Rothery, Matthew	DUT 67	Row, Nicholas	COL 244	Rowland, Samuel	RNS 46
Rothwell, Thomas	CAY 546	Row, Nicholas	GRN 325	Rowland, Samuel R.	RNS 47
Rotmour, George	MNT 39	Row, Noah	ALB 37	Rowland, Seth	COL 218
Rotmour, Henry	MNT 39	Row, Peter	OTS 25	Rowland, William	HRK 487
Rotmour, Jacob	MNT 39	Row, Peter	RNS 30	Rowland, Wm	RNS 42
Rottery, David	ALB 138	Row, Peter	SRA 14	Rowlandson, Reuben	TIO 230
Roualt, Theodore	NYK 142	Row, Samuel	ALB 118	Rowlen, Oliver	WSH 267
Rouan, James	WSH 291	Row, Wilhelmus	ALB 53	Rowlet, John Segwort	NYK 102
Rouan, Stephen	WSH 291	Row, Wilhelmus	ALB 100	Rowley, Abel	SRA 11
Rouen, Garret	COL 193	Row, Wilhelmus	ALB 119	Rowley, Abijah	ALB 22
Ro[ul?], Frederick	SCH 154	Row, William	ALB 17	Rowley, Alexander	ONT 346
Rouls, Aaron	ALB 102	Row, William	ALB 80	Rowley, Catharine	ULS 268
Round, Bartrem	OTS 54	Row, William	OTS 14	Rowley, Cornelius	SRA 47
Round, Joseph	HRK 512	Rowan, Abraham	WSH 225	Rowley, Daniel	COL 179
Round, Joseph	OTS 48	Rowan, Hugh	NYK 101	Rowley, Daniel	COL 204
Round, William	HRK 512	Rowan, James	WSH 221	Rowley, Daniel	DEL 280
Rounds, Calven	SRA 57	Rowan, John	WSH 229	Rowley, Daniel	MNT 120
Rounds, Charles	OTS 41	Rowan, John Esqr	WSH 229	Rowley, Daniel junr	COL 205
Rounds, Comfort	ONN 136	Rowan, Stephen	WSH 229	Rowley, David	ONT 366
Rounds, Daniel	ONN 136	Rowe, Abel	ONT 384	Rowley(?), D...d	RNS 109
Rounds, Jotham	RNS 100	Rowe, Andries	DUT 140	Rowley, David	RNS 109
Rounds, Jothem	WSH 234	Rowe, Ann	WSH 304	Rowley, Dudley	COL 216
Rounds, Moses	RNS 100	Rowe, Asa	ESS 317	Rowley, Eldrick	ALB 125
Rous, Rebeca	COL 220	Rowe, Bastian	DUT 149	Rowley, Erastus	WSH 299
Rouse	GRN 326	Rowe, Daniel	OND 186	Rowley, Gire	ONT 374
Rouse, Abraham	SRA 11	Rowe, David	ONN 169	Rowley, Griffeth	OND 214
Rouse, Andrew	MNT 20	Rowe, Frederick	DUT 143	Rowley, Heman	ORN 371
Rouse, Anthony	RNS 40	Rowe, Frederick	ULS 193	Rowley, Isacher	COL 210
Rouse, Benjn	OTS 29	Rowe, Garret	DUT 137	Rowley, Jabez	SRA 11
Rouse, Casper	SCH 156	Rowe, Henry	DUT 149	Rowley, Jacob	ULS 268
Rouse, Coenradt	COL 220	Rowe, John	DUT 149	Rowley, James	WSH 196
Rouse, Cosheram	CHN 784	Rowe, John	ESS 302	Rowley, Jemima	TIO 260
Rouse, Dumarnel	NYK 111	Rowe, John	ULS 193	Rowley, Jeremiah	ONT 364
Rouse, Elias	RNS 112	Rowe, John Junr	DUT 149	Rowley, Jesse	TIO 258
Rouse, Elizth	OTS 25	Rowe, John the 2d	DUT 151	Rowley, Joel	ALB 29
Rouse, George	WSH 203	Rowe, John H.	DUT 145	Rowley, John	ONT 424
Rouse, Harman	RNS 59	Rowe, Mark	DUT 149	Rowley, John	SRA 45
Rouse, Jacques	CLN 170	Rowe, Matthew	ORN 294	Rowley, Jonathan	MNT 116
Rouse, John	GRN 328	Rowe, Matthias	DUT 141	Rowley, Jonathan	ORN 370
Rouse, John	RNS 41	Rowe, Matthias	DUT 141	Rowley, Matthew	ORN 367
Rouse, John	SRA 11	Rowe, Matthias	DUT 159	Rowley, Moses	COL 235
Rouse, Jonathan	RNS 47	Rowe, Michael H.	DUT 145	Rowley, Moses	DEL 280
Rouse, Joseph	RNS 108	Rowe, Nathaniel	ONN 189	Rowley, Nathan	COL 236
Rouse, Michael	CLN 170	Rowe, Nicholas	DUT 134	Rowley, Nathan	ESS 287
Rouse, Nicholas	COL 224	Rowe, Phillip	DUT 131	Rowley, Nathan	OND 206
Rouse, Nicholas	GRN 332	Rowe, Phillip	DUT 151	Rowley, Nathaniel	COL 194
Rouse, Nicholas	QNS 62	Rowe, Roger	DUT 31	Rowley, Nathaniel	ONT 364
Rouse, Nichs	SCH 156	Rowe, Samuel	DUT 134	Rowley, Reuben	MNT 117
Rouse, Peter	GRN 328	R we, Thomas	ONT 492	Rowley, Reuben	RNS 109
Rouse, Simeon	DEL 283	Rowe, Wilhelmus	ULS 191	Rowley, Samuel	ULS 193
Rouse, Simon	ONN 142	Rowe, Wm	TIO 243	Rowley, Samuel N.	RNS 109
Rousseau, Charles	NYK 79	Rowe, Winthrop	TIO 218	Rowley, Seth	OTS 28
Rousseau, Peter	NYK 107	Rowell, Sampson	CHN 774	Rowley, Seth	RNS 9
Rover, Conrod	NYK 95	Rowen, Elephalet	WSH 187	Rowley, Simeon	COL 179
Row see Roe		Rowland, Amos	HRK 488	Rowley, Shubael	ORN 369
		Rowland, Benjn	OTS 34	Rowley, Sylvester	WSH 275
Row, Barlow	COL 204	Rowland, Benjamin	QNS 65	Rowley, Timothy	ALB 27
Row, Basell	ALB 118	Rowland, Cyrus	OTS 33	Rowley, Timothy Junr	RNS 109
Row, Charles	ONN 144	Rowland, David	QNS 63	Rowley, Walter	WSH 193
Row, Conrad	NYK 102	Rowland, David	ULS 184	Rowley, Warren	COL 210
Row, Frederick	QNS 80	Rowland, Henry	HRK 500	Rowley, William	CAY 564
Row, Henry	GRN 325	Rowland, Hezekiah	DUT 88	Rowley, William	SUF 97
Row, Henry	RNS 64	Rowland, Hezekiah	RNS 71	Rowley, Wix	COL 186
Row, Henry Junr	OTS 40	Rowland, Israel	RNS 45	Rowleys, .mos	TIO 258
Row, Henry Senr	OTS 40	Rowland, John	DUT 112		

Rowleys, E...	TIO 258	Rue see Rice & Ker		Rumsey, Jeremiah	ORN 389
Rowleys, Joel	TIO 258	R[ue?], Ephraim	ONT 404	Rumsey, Jerh	OTS 11
Rowlin, Gradus	SRA 57	Rue, Lott	ONT 406	Rumsey, Jesse	ORN 353
Rowlin, Joseph	SRA 57	Rue, Mark	SRA 25	Rumsey, John	CAY 524
Rowly, Elijah	SCH 160	Ruff, Chrisopher	DEL 274	Rumsey, Jonas	ORN 352
Rowly, Thomas	SCH 160	Ruff, Daniel	WSH 281	Rumsey, Jonathan	ORN 389
Rowse, Lothrop	OND 191	Ruff, Daniel	WSH 306	Rumsey, Joseph	HRK 549
Rowse, Thomas	COL 207	Ruff, Ebenezer	NYK 62	Rumsey, Lovel	SRA 7
Rowse, William	OND 203	Ruff, Henry	DEL 274	Rumsey, Moses	CAY 656
Rowson, Simon	TIO 220	Ruff, Philip	DEL 274	Rumsey, Nathan	ORN 389
Rox, Alexander	MNT 108	Ruffman, Henry	NYK 133	Rumsey, Noah	ESS 296
Roy, Cole	ONT 490	Rufun, Jacob	NYK 30	Rumsey, Phinehas	ORN 354
Roy, John	NYK 97	Rufus	SUF 108	Rumsey, Simon	ORN 389
Roy, John	ORN 379	Rugar, Francis	SRA 53	Rumstead see Bumstead	
Roya_, John	CAY 616	Rugen, John	DUT 41	Runals, George	SRA 52
Royce, Samuel	OND 208	Rugen, Mary	ULS 240	Rundall, Joseph	WST 142
Royley, Oliver	WSH 204	Rugen, Phillip	ULS 240	Rundals, Thomas W.	WST 169
Royley, Sylvaster	WSH 201	Ruger, Gideon	CLN 162	Rundel, Joseph	CHN 740
Rozel, Thomas	ONN 185	Rugg, David	ALB 91B	Rundel, Solomon	WST 116
Rozelle, Henry	DUT 8	Rugg, Isaac	WSH 206	Rundell, Shubael	DEL 268
Rozelle, Herman	DUT 12	Rugg, John	HRK 557	Rundell, Zedekiah	CAY 554
Rozelle, Jeremiah	DUT 27	Rugg, Levi	HRK 557	Rundells, Andrew	DEL 284
Rozelle, John	DUT 22	Rugg, Moses	ESS 303	Rundle, Abraham	ORN 318
Rozelle, Peter	DUT 143	Rugg, Samuel	ALB 104	Rundle, Abraham Junr	MNT 125
Rubard	GRN 349	Rugg, Samuel	OND 159	Rundle, David	DUT 138
Rubelee, Nathaniel	WSH 272	Ruggles, Comfort	OTS 32	Rundle, David	ULS 193
Rubelee, Philip	WSH 279	Ruggles, Denison	WSH 223	Rundle, Elnathan	ORN 318
Rubelee, Samuel	WSH 271	Ruggles, Isaac	TIO 232	Rundle, Ezra	DUT 88
Rubelee, Thomas	WSH 271	Ruggles, Nathl	SUF 68	Rundle, Ezra	WST 126
Ruben, Obadiah	ONT 366	Ruggles, Richard	WSH 282	Rundle, Isaac	WST 141
Rubidey, Charles	QNS 79	Ruggles, Timothy	WSH 200	Rundle, Jabez	SRA 48
Rubilee, Dorcas	ORN 374	Rugguls, John	TIO 226	Rundle, Jesse	CHN 788
Rubilee, Isaac	ORN 375	Ruland, Benjamin	ALB 94	Rundle, Joel	ORN 318
Rubilee, William	ORN 375	Ruland, Danl	SUF 64	Rundle, John	WST 126
Ruby, Christopher	ALB 46	Ruland, Danl	SUF 64	Rundle, Jonathan	ORN 318
Ruby, Christopher	HRK 409	Ruland, David	SUF 64	Rundle, Jonathan	WST 169
Ruby, John G.	ALB 48	Ruland, David	SUF 81	Rundle, Joshua	WST 141
Ruby, Robert	ALB 47	Ruland, James	SUF 81	Rundle, Reubin	GRN 351
Ruby, Sarah	ALB 141	Ruland, John	SUF 64	Rundle, Richard	GRN 352
Ruby, Thomas	WSH 291	Ruland, John	SUF 65	Rundle, Samuel	WST 123
Ruchel, Anna E.	NYK 101	Ruland, John	SUF 65	Rundle, Samuel Junr	WST 126
Ruchel, John Senior	NYK 47	Ruland, John	SUF 82	Rundles, David	GRN 355
Ruck, William	NYK 77	Ruland, John	SUF 83	Rundles, Joshua	GRN 355
Ruck, Zepheniah	NYK 127	Ruland, John Junr	SUF 83	Rundles, Richard	GRN 355
Ruckell, Philip	NYK 94	Ruland, Joseph	SUF 70	Runds, Hezekiah	SRA 48
Rud see Reed		Ruland, Joseph Jur	SUF 65	Runels, Andrew	GRN 340
Rud, Russel	TIO 242	Ruland, Luke	SUF 64	Runels, Benjamin	SRA 7
Rud, Stephen	NYK 151	Ruland, Luke	SUF 70	Runels, Isaac	SRA 57
Rud, William	NYK 119	Ruland, Mikel	SUF 70	Runels, Joel	SRA 57
Rudd, Bezaleel	DUT 143	Ruland, Peter	SUF 83	Runels, Joel	SRA 57
Rudd, John	OTS 53	Ruland, Richard	HRK 557	Runels, John	SRA 55
Rudd, John Junr	OTS 53	Ruland, Thomas	SUF 64	Runeons, Enos	ALB 11
Rudd, Levi	OTS 14	Ruland, Widow	SUF 84	Runia, John	CHN 778
Rudd, Stephen	NYK 119	Rule, Daniel	ONT 360	Runkle, Henderick	ALB 50
Rudder, Lewis D.	NYK 79	Ruleffson, Herman	SCH 139	Runkle, John	ALB 50
Ruddy, Barny	NYK 120	Ruleffson, Frederick	SCH 139	Runkle, John C.	MNT 46
Rude, Asa	TIO 228	Ruleppson see Ruleff-son		Runles, Darius	SRA 60
Rude, Charles	WSH 216	Ruler see Keeler		Runnells	GRN 357
Rude, Daniel	WSH 223	Riley, Abrahan	MNT 113	Runnells, Benjamin	CLN 164
Rude, Daniel	WSH 254	Rulin a Negro	SUF 76	Runnells, Erbin	ESS 320
Rude, Daniel Junr	WSH 223	Rull, Daniel	RNS 12	Runnells, Nuel	ESS 320
Rude, David	WSH 227	Rull, John	WST 131	Runnels, Amos	SRA 34
Rude, Ephraim	SRA 29	Rulleage, Patrick	MNT 71	Runnels, Cahoon	TIO 240
Rude, Ezra	SCH 149	Rumbout, Arnold	SUF 87	Runnels, David	SRA 4
Rude, Jonah	SRA 36	Rumer, David	NYK 124	Runnels, Fulleran	CHN 764
Rude, Rossel	GRN 343	Rummer, Elias	TIO 226	Runnels, George	SRA 51
Ruden, J_ques	NYK 20	Rummer, Peter	TIO 218	Runnels, Jacob	CHN 794
Ruder, Jacob	OND 212	Rump, Christian	ORN 301	Runnels, James	QNS 82
Ruder, Nathaniel	NYK 119	Rumsay, Joshua	DEL 274	Runnels, John	CHN 814
Rudes, Luther	SRA 53	Rumsey, Daniel	SRA 5	Runnels, John	SRA 51
Rudgers, Isaac	SUF 87	Rumsey, David	ORN 354	Runnels, Obediah	CHN 794
Rudgers, James	SUF 87	Rumsey, David	SRA 4	Runnels, Parker	ESS 319
Rudgers, John	SUF 87	Rumsey, David	SRA 6	Runnels, Richard	QNS 83
Rudley, John	NYK 69	Rumsey, David		Runnels, Samuel	GRN 355
Rudo, John	NYK 107	Rumsey, Isaac	ORN 305	Runnion, Stephen O.	CHN 770
Rudolph, Leonard	RNS 12	Rumsey, James	CAY 656	Runnolds, Benja.in	MNT 6
Rudyards, Daniel	ORN 270	Rumsey, James	ULS 247	Runols, Stephen	SRA 57

Rutzen, John	NYK	23	Ryhtmeyer, Abraham	ULS	222	Sabin, Elijah	DUT	56
Rutzer, Asa	ULS	265	Ryhtmeyer, Hermanus	ULS	222	Sabin, Hannah	DUT	57
Ruxer, Jacob	WST	129	Ryhtmyer, Coonradt	ULS	220	Sabin, Israel	ONN	160
Ruyter, Killian	SCH	156	Rykart, Barent	COL	196	Sabin, Jeremiah	ULS	264
Ryal, John	COL	182	Rykeman, Aaron	NYK	142	Sabin, Jeremiah Junr	ULS	264
Ryal, Peter	COL	182	Rykeman, John	MNT	70	Sabin, Mary	DUT	56
Ryan, Cornelius	NYK	120	Rykeman, John	NYK	144	Sabin, Wm H.	OTS	19
Ryan, Cornelius	NYK	139	Ryker, Abraham	QNS	63	Sabins, Abner	OND	200
Ryan, Edward	RNS	39	Ryker, Daniel	QNS	62	Sabins, Asa	ONT	458
Ryan, Elizabeth	NYK	55	Ryker, David	DUT	119	Sabins, Beckman	OND	221
Ryan, James	ALB	46	Ryker, Henry	DUT	119	Sabins, Bele	SRA	57
Ryan, John	DUT	65	Ryker, James	QNS	62	Sabins, Burch	ONT	458
Ryan, John	NYK	144	Ryker, John	NYK	93	Sabins, Isaac	CLN	168
Ryan, John	RNS	23	Ryker, John	ULS	234	Sabins, Israel	COL	243
Ryan, Lawrence	NYK	133	Ryker, Mathew	NYK	93	Sabins, John	ESS	302
Ryan, Michael	NYK	32	Ryker, Samuel	QNS	61	Sabins, Joseph	OTS	29
Ryan, Moses	NYK	144	Ryker, Susanna widow	QNS	61	Sabins, Josiah	OTS	30
Ryan, Phillip	NYK	105	Ryker, Thomas	ULS	236	Sabins, Stephen	RNS	76
Ryan, Ruth	WSH	264	Ryley, Abraham	MNT	112	Sabins, Timothy	OTS	12
Ryan, Thomas	NYK	45	Ryley, Adam	MNT	123	Sabins, Zeba	CHN	984
Ryans, John	TIO	262	Ryley, John	RNS	4	Sabriskie, John	ALB	147
Ryce, Allen	WST	169	Ryley, John	RNS	44	Sachaverell, Gustavus	ULS	220
Ryckman, Albert	NYK	65	Ryley, Neer	RNS	14	Sack, John	ULS	257
Ryckman, Robert	NYK	144	Rylyea, David	ALB	61	Sacket, Ananias	ULS	186
Ryckman, Tobias	ORN	552	Rylyea, David Jr	ALB	61	Sacket, Caleb	TIO	244
Ryckman, Tobias	ORN	385	Rylyea, Jacob	ALB	60	Sacket, Daniel	TIO	244
Rydenbergh, Henry	ALB	98	Rylyea, Peter	ALB	60	Sacket, Elijah	WSH	265
Ryder see Rider			Rylyea, Simeon	ALB	61	Sacket, Hezekiah	OTS	21
Ryder, Absolum	ALB	70	Rymph, George	HRK	561	Sacket, Isaac	COL	207
Ryder, Amos	KNG	3	Rynders, Reuben	SRA	11	Sacket, James	ALB	79
Ryder, Barnardus	KNG	4	Ryne see Rhine			Sacket, James	DUT	131
Ryder, Benjamin	RNS	87	Ryne, Andrew	SCH	172	Sacket, James	WST	143
Ryder, Catherine	KNG	4	Ryne, Andries	SCH	162	Sacket, Jehiel	DUT	130
Ryder, Charity	KNG	5	Ryne, Christian	SCH	172	Sacket, Joel	DUT	130
Ryder, Cornelius	WST	154	Ryne, Christopher	SCH	162	Sacket, John	ORN	396
Ryder, Isaac	KNG	4	Ryne, Peter	SCH	162	Sacket, Jonathan	QNS	62
Ryder, Jacob	QNS	67	Ryne, Timothy	DEL	274	Sacket, Joseph	HRK	574
Ryder, Jacob	WST	159	Ryneck, Wm	ALB	8	Sacket, King	OTS	22
Ryder, John	KNG	4	Rynehart, George	SCH	156	Sacket, Nathaniel	DUT	36
Ryder, John	QNS	67	Rynex, Andrew	ALB	9	Sacket, Nathaniel	WST	120
Ryder, Mitchel	NYK	46	Rynex, Ephraim	ALB	17	Sacket, Nathaniel Junr	DUT	38
Ryder, Reuben	WST	159	Rynex, John	ALB	17	Sacket, Richard	WST	142
Ryder, Robert	RCK	104	Rynex, Margaret	ALB	27	Sacket, Ruoben	SCH	120
Ryder, Samuel	ALB	91B	Rynex, Valentine	ALB	6	Sacket, Samuel	DUT	131
Ryder, Sten	SUF	70	Rynex, Wm	ALB	11	Sacket, Samuel Junr	DUT	131
Ryder, Sue a free			Rynex, William	ALB	17	Sacket, Skeen D.	OND	184
Negro	ALB	115	Rynold, John	SRA	11	Sacket, Wait	OTS	22
Ryder, Theodorus	QNS	68	Ryon, Amos	SUF	77	Sacket, William W.	ORN	284
Ryder, Urias	QNS	68	Rypenbergh, Abm	COL	195	Sackett, Augustus	NYK	30
Ryder, William	KNG	4	Rysdorph, George	COL	199	Sackett, Benjamin	RNS	101
Rye, David	MNT	75	Rysdorph, George Junr	COL	194	Sackett, Buell	COL	208
Ryer, Dennis	NYK	114	Rysdorph, Jacob	COL	194	S.ckett, Esehel	MNT	81
Ryer, Hendrick	WST	146	Rysdorph, Jacob	COL	258	Sackett, Hannah	NYK	52
Ryer, Henry	NYK	88	Rysdorph, Jacob	COL	262	Sackett, Jesse	COL	184
Ryer, John Senr	WST	145	Rysdorph, Jacobus	COL	261	Sackett, John	CAY	652
Ryer, Michael	NYK	92	Rysdorph, Lawrence	COL	260	Sackett, John	RNS	110
Ryer, Peter	DUT	35	Rysdorph, Phillip	COL	233	Sackett, John	STB	202
Ryer, Peter	DUT	77	Rysdyck, Garret	ORN	363	Sackett, Primus a		
Ryer, Tunes	NYK	153	Rysdyck, Harriet	DUT	41	Black	NYK	106
Ryer, William	NYK	100	Ryser, Andrew	NYK	15	Sackett, Rachael	NYK	59
Ryers, John	RCK	101	Ryvanck, Anna	NYK	44	Sackett, Samuel	NYK	52
Ryers, John	WST	146	Ryvenbergh, Peter M.	COL	224	Sackett, William	QNS	62
Ryerson, Cornelius	QNS	65				Sackman, Henry	ALB	48
Ryerson, Cornelius	QNS	74	S			Sackrider, Christian	SRA	11
Ryerson, Jacob	KNG	8				Sackrider, Moses	DEL	286
Ryerson, John	KNG	7	S___t_, Caleb	GRN	330	Sackrider, Solomon	DUT	96
Ryerson, Leffert	KNG	8	S___. Samuel	MNT	5	Sackrider, Solomon	SRA	9
Ryerson, Richard	NYK	96	S___man, Michael	MNT	46	Sackwell, Daniel	MNT	68
Ryerss, ...ah	RCH	90	S_ags, Nicholas	MNT	65	Sadlemier see Saidlemier		
Ryerss, Gozen	RCH	87	S_mons, Reuben	MNT	82	Sadlemier, Johannis	ALB	69
Ryerss, John P.	RCH	87	S__t, Sylvenus	MNT	83	Sadler see Saidler		
Ryerss, Lewis	RCH	87	S__ffield, John	ONT	454	Sadler, Peter	ALB	148
Ryfenbergh, David	COL	240	S___, Peter	WST	170	Sadler, Seth	SRA	42
Ryfenbergh, Johans	COL	226	Saar, John	ULS	185	Saffield, Lewis	NYK	59
Ryfenbergh, John	COL	245	Sabens, Josiah	CHN	976	Saffin, David	NYK	74
Ryhpart, Frederick	SCH	123	Saber, John W.	MNT	45	Saffin, Thomas	DUT	8
Ryhtmeyer see Reghtmire			Sabin, Anna	TIO	213	Saffon, Thomas	SRA	60

Saffor, Samuel	WSH 225	St. John, Hawley	SRA 52	Sallsbury, El_ha	GRN 328
Safford, Amos	WSH 225	St. John, James	SRA 21	Salm[an?], John	OND 221
Safford, Appleton	ALB 116	St. John, Joel	CAY 636	Salmon, Asahel	WSH 232
Safford, Benjamin	WSH 192	St. John, Joel	DUT 134	Salmon, Charles	DUT 56
Safford, David	WSH 192	St. John, John	CAY 706	Salmon, Ebenezer	DUT 21
Safford, David Junr	WSH 192	St. John, John	DEL 277	Salmon, Gershom	DUT 130
Safford, Gedion	WSH 225	St. John, John	MNT 49	Salmon, Gideon	ORN 356
Safford, John	CHN 908	St. John, John	RNS 58	Salmon, John	DUT 56
Safford, Joseph	OND 191	St, John, John	SRA 19	Salmon, John	ORN 281
Safford, Joseph	WSH 249	St. John, John	SRA 39	Salmon, John	OTS 21
Safford, Matthias	ALB 15	St. John, John	SRA 61	Salmon, John	OTS 36
Safford, Newton	WSH 287	St. John, John	ULS 187	Salmon, Ludlow J.	DUT 150
Safford, Samuel Junr	WSH 225	St. John, Joseph	WST 141	Salmon, Pheneas	OTS 38
Safford, Sandford	WSH 270	St. John, Josiah	SRA 39	Salmon, Samuel	ONN 133
Safford, Shubell	ONN 133	St. John, Josiah	WST 161	Salmond, Gilbert	MNT 52
Safford, Stephen	WSH 192	St. John, Justus	CHN 974	Salmons, Benjamin	ORN 368
Sagar, John	NYK 47	St. John, Lewis	DEL 281	Salmons, Stephen	ORN 324
Sage, Abraham	OND 181	St. John, Lodock	SRA 22	Salnave, Peter	SRA 26
Sage, Daniel	CHN 792	St. John, Mark	CHN 974	Salpagh, Jacob	COL 224
Sage, Daniel	COL 208	St. John, Mathew	SRA 30	Salsbeaury, John	CHN 848
Sage, David	SCH 145	St. John, Matthew	ALB 93	Salsbery, Amos	RNS 92
Sage, Elias	OND 221	St. John, Matthew	SRA 39	Salsbery, Bonet	RNS 23
Sage, Harley H.	CAY 692	St. John, Moses	WST 141	Salsbery, Harmanus	RNS 6
Sage, Hezekiah	OND 192	St. John, Nathan	ONN 129	Salsbery, Job	RNS 23
Sage, James	ONT 398	St. John, Noah	RNS 58	Salsbery, Joseph	RNS 23
Sage, Jeremiah	NYK 49	St. John, Samuel	NYK 30	Salsbery, Reuben	RNS 23
Sage, John	CAY 538	St. John, Samuel	SRA 59	Salsbugh, Jacob	SCH 124
Sage, Nathan	OND 209	St. John, Selick	DEL 277	Salsburgh, Jacob Jr	SCH 124
Sage, Seely	CAY 706	St. John, Thadeus	CHN 974	Salsburgh, John	SCH 124
Sage, Sela	ONT 404	St. John, William	ULS 262	Salsbury, Abraham	GRN 328
Sage, Simon	WSH 191	St. Oze, Jacob P.	ESS 318	Salsbury, Abraham Jur	GRN 328
Sagendoof, George	SCH 154	St. Paul, Peter	DUT 156	Salsbury, Barnet	OTS 43
Sagendorph, Eliza	COL 226	St. Victorbd	NYK 143	Salsbury, Benanuel	CAY 654
Sagendorph, George A.	COL 224	Sairs, Wm	MNT 101	Salsbury, Benjn	OTS 2
Sagendorph, George G.	COL 225	Saitor, Henry	CAY 566	Salsbury, Cornelius	OTS 2
Sagendorph, Harman	COL 194	Salbaugh, John Junr	COL 189	Salsbury, Edward	OTS 43
Sagendorph, Harman A.	COL 194	Salbaugh, Ph: Junr	COL 189	Salsbury, Elsy	NYK 24
Sagendorph, Nicholas	COL 224	Salbury, James	MNT 124	Salsbury, Frances	GRN 328
Sagendorph, Peter	COL 190	Sales, Benj:	RNS 31	Salsbury, Gideon	ONT 462
Saguez, John	DUT 59	Sales, Jerremiah	CHN 968	Salsbury, Henry	OTS 20
Sager, David	COL 196	Sales, Silvinus	CHN 970	Salsbury, James	OTS 36
Sager, George	CAY 574	Sales, Stukely	HRK 421	Salsbury, John	ONT 480
Sagsberry, Cors	OTS 28	Sales, Wm	ONN 171	Salsbury, Laurance	GRN 328
Sahler, Abraham	ULS 202	Salesbury, Marten	WSH 267	Salsbury, Oliver	SRA 43
Sahler, Daniel	ULS 217	Salesbury, Reserved	SRA 43	Salsbury, Peter	MNT 99
Sahler, Solomon	ULS 215	Salim, Assahel	WSH 301	Salsbury, Richard	OTS 57
Saidlemier see Sadlemier		Salisbury, _ial	OND 206	Salsbury, Samuel	RNS 18
Saidlemier, Fredk	ALB 64	Salisbury, Abraham	COL 257	Salsbury, Thomas	SRA 43
Saidlemier, George	ALB 64	Salisbury, Alexander	OND 206	Salsbury, Wm	GRN 328
Saidlemier, John	ALB 67	Salisbury, Corns	ALB 83	Salsbury, William	ONT 424
Saidler see Sadler		Salisbury, Daniel	WSH 300	Salter see Saulter	
Saidler, Henry	NYK 52	Salisbury, Edward	OND 206	Salter, Alexander	NYK 53
Saidler, James	NYK 31	Salisbury, Edward S.	OND 206	Salter, Catherine	NYK 52
Sailly, Charles L.	CLN 173	Salisbury, Enan	OND 211	Salter, John	NYK 22
Sailly, Peter	CLN 165	Salisbury, Harms	ALB 117	Salter, John a Black	NYK 110
St. Clair see Sanclair		Salisbury, Henry	ALB 42	Salter, John	RCH 89
St. Clair, Duncan	ONT 382	Salisbury, Henry	COL 185	Salter, Thomas	NYK 52
St. Clair, John	CHN 874	Salisbury, James	WSH 266	Saltmarsh, William	TIO 213
St. Clair, Samuel	CHN 872	Salisbury, Job	COL 208	S_ tanstall, Dudley	ONT 428
St. George, Peter	NYK 91	Salisbury, John	ALB 108	Saltonstall, Hariel	NYK 41
St. John, Abijah	SRA 30	Salisbury, John	COL 262	Salts, Benjamin	WST 153
St. John, Abijah	WST 136	Salisbury, Joseph	ALB 52	Salts, James	WST 158
St. John, Abner	CHN 974	Salisbury, Joseph Junr	ALB 108	Salts, John	RNS 57
St. John, Adam	ALB 93	Salisbury, Lodowick	OND 206	Salts, John	WST 156
St. John, Alexande	MNT 81	Salisbury, Nathan	GRN 336	Salts, William	QNS 71
St. John, Alvan	ONN 132	Salisbury, Nathl	HRK 586	Saltsma., Henry Junr	MNT 10
St. John, Azell	CHN 974	Salisbury, Nicholas	OND 211	Saltsman, John	MNT 10
St. John, Azra	WSH 239	Salisbury, Richd	HRK 586	Saltsman, William	MNT 10
St. John, Benjamin	SRA 28	Salisbury, Richard	OND 206	Saltus, John	GRN 352
St. John, Daniel	ORN 321	Salisbury, Samuel	GRN 331	Saltus, John a mulatto	NYK 49
St. John, Daniel	RNS 58	Salisbury, Sylvester	COL 257	Saltus, Solomon	NYK 24
St. John, David	DEL 277	Salisbury, Wessel	GRN 349	Salvage, John N.	ALB 127
St. John, Eanes	WSH 238	Sallenwert, Peter	KNG 6	Salvaster, Stephen	WSH 229
St. John, Ebenezer	ULS 262	Sallier, Zacehas	ORN 319	Salvester, Joseph	WSH 228
St. John, Elijah	ONN 178	Salliment, George E.	NYK 34	Salvester, Stephen Junr	WSH 229
St. John, Gamaliel	OND 172	Salls, Isaac	COL 208	Salyer, Edward	RCK 101
St. John, Gideon	OND 200	Salls, Samuel	COL 208	Salyer, Michael	RCK 101

317

Name	Loc	No.
Sam	QNS	80
Sam	QNS	81
Sam	QNS	83
Sam	QNS	84
Sam	QNS	84
Sam a Negro	RNS	92
Sam a Negro	SUF	67
Sam a Negro	SUF	67
Sam a Negro	SUF	67
Samburn, George	HRK	493
Samburn, Nathl	HRK	493
Sams, Augustus	NYK	78
Sams, Ebenezer	NYK	116
Sams, Scudder	NYK	116
Samler, Casper	NYK	151
Samler, John	NYK	110
Sammis, Alexander	SUF	87
Sammis, Benjamin	QNS	74
Sammis, Bethuel	SUF	85
Sammis, David	SUF	84
Sammis, David	SUF	85
Sammis, David	SUF	86
Sammis, Ebenezar	SUF	88
Sammis, Ebenezer	SUF	85
Sammis, Eliphalet	SUF	83
Sammis, Epinetus	SUF	87
Sammis, Gilbert	SUF	84
Sammis, Henry	SUF	86
Sammis, Jacob	SUF	85
Sammis, Jesse	ALB	86
Sammis, Jessee	SUF	86
Sammis, Jessee	SUF	87
Sammis, Joseph	SUF	86
Sammis, Nathaniel	SUF	86
Sammis, Philip	SUF	87
Sammis, Platt	SUF	87
Sammis, Rebecca	SUF	81
Sammis, Rebecca	SUF	87
Sammis, Ruben	SUF	81
Sammis, Salley	SUF	87
Sammis, Selah	SUF	88
Sammis, Silas	SUF	86
Sammis, Silas Junr	SUF	86
Sammis, Stephen	SUF	86
Sammis, Thomas	SUF	81
Sammis, Timothy	SUF	86
Sammon, Jacob	ULS	244
Sammon, John	ORN	315
Sammon, Teunis	ULS	245
Sammons, Benjamin	MNT	61
Sammons, Cornela	RNS	35
Sammons, Cornelius	ULS	204
Sammons, Cornelius	ULS	217
Sammons, Fredirick	MNT	61
Sammons, Michael	DEL	278
Sammons, Thomas	MNT	66
Sammson, Jacob	MNT	64
Samnis, David	QNS	79
Samond, Archd	OTS	7
Sample, David	ONN	174
Sample, James	NYK	119
Sample, Robert	OND	223
Sampsen, Sambo a Black	NYK	148
Sampson	SUF	94
Sampson, Abner	DUT	45
Sampson, Benjamin	MNT	56
Sampson, Enoch a Black	NYK	140
Sampson, Ezekel	WSH	195
Sampson, Ezekel Junr	WSH	195
Sampson, Ezra	COL	246
Sampson, George	DUT	154
Sampson, Isaac	TIO	230
Sampson, Levi	WSH	253
Sampson, Levi Junr	WSH	253
Sams(?), Isaac	NYK	54
Samson, Caleb	OND	193
Samson, Ezekiel	DEL	279
Samson, Ezekiel Jun	DEL	279
Samson, Henry	DEL	279
Samson, James	NYK	58
Samson, Samuel	DEL	279
Samsons, Thomas	MNT	71
Samuel	QNS	67
Samuel	QNS	80
Samuel	QNS	80
Samuel	SUF	93
Samuel, Cornelius A.	NYK	119
Samuels, Galty a Black	NYK	64
Samuels, Thomas	NYK	78
Sanaxy, James	NYK	139
Sanburn, Nathaniel	ONT	428
Sanclair see St. Clair		
Sanclair, George	NYK	65
Sand, Gristin	ALB	69
Sand, Jacob	ALB	69
Sander, Henry	MNT	25
Sander, Henry Junr	MNT	25
Sander, Solomon	MNT	25
Sanders, Athi_er	CAY	522
Sanders, Austin	WSH	211
Sanders, Benjn	OTS	26
Sanders, Charles	RNS	72
Sanders, Cyrus	OTS	26
Sanders, Edwd Clark	OTS	35
Sanders, Elisha	OTS	25
Sanders, Esic	OTS	54
Sanders, Francis	OND	211
Sanders, George	RNS	73
Sanders, George	WSH	300
Sanders, George Junr	RNS	104
Sanders, Henry	WSH	245
Sanders, Hezekiah	RNS	104
Sanders, Hezekiah Junr	RNS	98
Sanders, Isaac	COL	220
Sanders, Isaac	RNS	66
Sanders, James	RNS	100
Sanders, Jesse	OTS	54
Sanders, Jesse	RNS	113
Sanders, John	ALB	26
Sanders, John	ORN	284
Sanders, John	WSH	245
Sanders, Jona	OTS	17
Sanders, Joseph	OTS	9
Sanders, Joseph	OTS	26
Sanders, Oliver	ESS	306
Sanders, Peleg	RNS	66
Sanders, Peter	WSH	244
Sanders, Silas	SCH	165
Sanders, Theophelus	ESS	322
Sanders, Thomas	SRA	32
Sanders, Wait	WSH	243
Sanders, William	OTS	51
Sanders, William	OTS	54
Sanders, William	WSH	245
Sanderson, Elijah	ONT	442
Sanderson, Joseph	HRK	439
Sandford see Santford		
Sandford, Abraham	STB	204
Sandford, Abraham	SUF	100
Sandford, Benjamin	SUF	100
Sandford, Bethuel	SUF	98
Sandford, Charlotte	NYK	60
Sandford, Cyrenus	DEL	273
Sandford, Daniel	STB	204
Sandford, Daniel	SUF	98
Sandford, Darius	DEL	273
Sandford, David	STB	203
Sandford, Elias	SUF	100
Sandford, Elias	SUF	100
Sandford, Elias Junr	SUF	100
Sandford, Elisha	ONT	340
Sandford, Ephraem	STB	203
Sandford, Ephraem	STB	204
Sandford, Ezekiel	ONT	488
Sandford, Ezekiel	SUF	99
Sandford, Ezra	ONT	488
Sandford, Ezra	STB	204
Sandford, George	SUF	100
Sandford, Hezekiah	DEL	273
Sandford, Hezekiah	SUF	99
Sandford, Hugh	MNT	104
Sandford, Jeremiah	SUF	100
Sandford, Job	SUF	100
Sandford, Joel	NYK	21
Sandford, John	NYK	21
Sandford, John	NYK	100
Sandford, John	ORN	377
Sandford, John	SUF	100
Sandford, Lewis	SUF	101
Sandford, Luther	ONT	346
Sandford, Mathew	SUF	72
Sandford, Matthew	ORN	375
Sandford, Michael	NYK	91
Sandford, Peregine	NYK	47
Sandford, Rachael	NYK	42
Sandford, Samuel	SUF	98
Sandford, Simeon	WSH	275
Sandford, Widow	SUF	99
Sandford, William	DEL	273
Sandford, William	SUF	98
Sandford, William B.	NYK	103
Sandhovel, Herman	NYK	89
Sandie, Joseph	CAY	650
Sands, Abel	ULS	195
Sands, Andrew	ORN	381
Sands, Benjamin	DEL	278
Sands, Benjamin	NYK	51
Sands, Benjamin	ULS	267
Sands, Benjamin Junr	DEL	273
Sands, Caleb	WST	131
Sands, Charles a mulatto	NYK	75
Sands, Comfort	KNG	2
Sands, David	ORN	395
Sands, Ebenezer	MNT	42
Sands, Edmund	SUF	81
Sands, Edward	NYK	77
Sands, Edwin	ORN	395
Sands, George	DEL	271
Sands, George Junr	DEL	271
Sands, Griffen	QNS	72
Sands, James	QNS	79
Sands, James	ULS	256
Sands, Jessey	WST	155
Sands, John	QNS	71
Sands, John	QNS	84
Sands, John	ULS	259
Sands, John	ULS	267
Sands, John	WST	115
Sands, John	WST	121
Sands, John Junr	QNS	70
Sands, John W.	DEL	273
Sands, Joseph	WST	130
Sands, Joshua	KNG	8
Sands, Mary	NYK	117
Sands, Othneal	WST	115
Sands, Othniel	WST	155
Sands, Philip	NYK	29
Sands, Richard	QNS	71
Sands, Robert	DUT	164
Sands, Samuel	QNS	80
Sands, Samuel	WST	131
Sands, Samuel	WST	155
Sands, Samuel junr	WST	130
Sands, Sebe	WST	120
Sands, Thomas	WST	115
Sands, William	NYK	15
Sanford, Betsey	OND	171
Sanford, Caleb	ALB	83
Sanford, Cornelius	ALB	47

Saxon, Pliny	ONT 342
Saxton, Alanson	ALB 86
Saxton, Asher	ONT 396
Saxton, Chauncy	NYK 127
Saxton, Danl	SUF 66
Saxton, James	SUF 79
Saxton, Martha	ONT 396
Saxton, Noble	ESS 298
Saxton, Philander	ONT 396
Saxton, Rossel	SCH 160
Saxton, Samuel	SCH 160
Saxton, Wm	SUF 66
Saxton, Zepheniah	SRA 56
Sayer, Lucinda	HRK 415
Sayer, Paul	TIO 209
Sayes, Lewis a mulatto	NYK 57
Sayler, Eben	TIO 234
Sayler, Eben Jur	TIO 234
Sayler, Philip	TIO 234
Sayles, Abraham	CAY 676
Sayles, Darius	OND 175
Sayles, Ezekiel	CAY 676
Sayles, George	OND 175
Sayles, Thomas	OND 175
Sayls, Silvenus	SRA 44
Saylus, Augustus	CHN 958
Saymour see Seymour	
Saymour, Nathaniel	SRA 59
Sayre, Abraham	SUF 97
Sayre, Abraham Junr	SUF 98
Sayre, Benjamin	ORN 365
Sayre, Benjamin	SUF 100
Sayre, Daniel	CAY 532
Sayre, Daniel	ORN 376
Sayre, David	SUF 98
Sayre, David	SUF 101
Sayre, David	SUF 104
Sayre, James	ORN 350
Sayre, James	ORN 361
Sayre, James	SUF 100
Sayre, Job	ORN 349
Sayre, John	CAY 530
Sayre, John	DUT 63
Sayre(?), John	NYK 43
Sayre, John	ORN 373
Sayre, John	SUF 98
Sayre, Jonathan	ORN 355
Sayre, Joshua	ORN 323
Sayre, Joshua	SUF 97
Sayre, Lewis	ORN 370
Sayre, Mathew	SUF 97
Sayre, Nathan	SUF 104
Sayre, Paul	SUF 97
Sayre, Samuel	ORN 306
Sayre, Stephen	ORN 336
Sayre, Stephen	SUF 97
Sayres, Isaac	NYK 136
Sayres, Peter	HRK 537
Sayres, Stephen	HRK 538
Scaddin, Robert	CAY 708
Scallenger, David	ESS 322
Scansion, Unill	WST 124
Scantlin, Jeremiah	ORN 320
Scarles see Searles	
Scarret, James	RCH 92
Scarret, James	RCH 92
Scarret, John	RCH 92
Scarret, Richard	RCH 92
Scarret, Richard Junr	RCH 92
Scarret, William	RCH 92
Sceism, George	COL 244
Schafer See Shaffer	
Schafer, Coonradt	DUT 121
Schaffer, Daniel	ORN 296
Schaffer, David	DUT 7
Schaffer, David	DUT 159
Schaffer, Francis J.	DUT 159

Schaffer, Frederick	DUT 158
Schaffer, Frederick	ORN 321
Schaffer, George	DUT 158
Schaffer, Jacob	DUT 161
Schaffer, John	ULS 201
Schaffer, John D.	DUT 160
Schaffer, Phillip	
ye 1st	DUT 150
Schaffer, Phillip	
ye 2d	DUT 151
Schamerhorn, Cornelius	
Junr	RNS 53
Schanck, Wing	NYK 51
Schank, Ralph	MNT 74
Scharmahorn, Benjamine	GRN 335
Scharmahorn, John	GRN 326
Scharmahorn, Richard	GRN 335
Scharod, Hendrick	NYK 110
Schaver see Shaver	
Schaver, Dedrick	ULS 211
Schaver, Frederick	ORN 298
Schedle, John	WST 158
Schell see Shell	
Schell, Christian	HRK 446
Schell, John Junr	HRK 445
Schell, Mark	HRK 447
Schell, Peter	HRK 446
Schellenger, Abraham	SUF 108
Schellenger, Jacob	SUF 108
Schellenger, Jonathan	SUF 108
Schellenger, Jonathan	
Ju(?)	SUF 108
Schellenger, Samuel	SUF 108
Schemerhorn, John J.	ALB 15
Schemerhorn, Maus	ALB 10
Schemerhorn, Simon	NYK 17
Schemerhorn, Wm	ALB 3
Schemklin, John	NYK 89
Schemling, George	OTS 28
Schemiling, Hendk	OTS 28
Schenck, Abraham	DUT 33
Schenck, Abraham H.	DUT 36
Schenck, Hendrick	QNS 61
Schenck, Isaac	KNG 11
Schenck, John	DEL 286
Schenck, John	KNG 3
Schenck, John	KNG 10
Schenck, Lambert	KNG 8
Schenck, Martin	KNG 8
Schenck, Nicholas	KNG 3
Schenck, Nicholas	
Jun	KNG 3
Schenck, Paul	DUT 63
Schenck, Paul	SCH 153
Schenck, Peter T.	KNG 10
Schenck, Roeliff	DUT 33
Schenck, Rulef	QNS 71
Schenck, Santie	QNS 79
Schenck, William	SUF 86
Schenk, Abraham	QNS 70
Schenk, Jacob	CAY 682
Schenk, John	QNS 69
Schenk, John	QNS 80
Schenk, Minard	QNS 69
Schenk, Peter a	NYK 29
Schenk, Rulef	QNS 82
Schenk, Tanis	QNS 61
Schenk, William	HRK 479
Schenk, William P.	NYK 98
Schenmel, George	NYK 65
Schepmoes, Mary	ULS 218
Schepmoes, William	ULS 227
Schepmouse, Wm	COL 189
Scherer see Shearer &	
Sherer	
Scherer, Abraham	DUT 22
Scherer, Andrew	ULS 233

Scherer, Benjamin	DUT 122
Scherer, Israel	DUT 18
Scherer, John	DUT 18
Scherer, John	DUT 122
Scherer, John C.	DUT 18
Scherer, Manesseh	DUT 61
Scherer, Robert	ORN 338
Scherer, York	DUT 66
Schermahorn, Abraham	COL 254
Schermahorn, Frederick	COL 254
Schermahorn, Henry	COL 252
Schermahorn, Henry junr	COL 224
Schermahorn, Jacob L.	COL 220
Schermahorn, John	COL 225
Schermahorn, John	COL 238
Schermahorn, John	COL 252
Schermahorn, Peter	COL 265
Schermahorn, Willm	COL 222
Schermahorne, Henry	COL 224
Schermehorn, Aaron	SRA 24
Schermehorn, Corns	ALB 76
Schermehorn, Henry	ALB 76
Schermehorn, John	ALB 73
Schermehorn, Simon	ALB 10
Schermerhorn see Chem-	
erhorn, Searmehorn &	
Shermerhorn	
Schermerhorn, Abm	ALB 25
Schermerhorn, Abm Junr	ALB 25
Schermerhorn, Abm J.	RNS 18
Schermerhorn, Andw	ALB 17
Schermerhorn, Aurant	ALB 17
Schermerhorn, Barthw	ALB 15
Schermerhorn, Casparus	DEL 267
Schermerhorn Cornelius	COL 263
Schermerhorn, Cornls	HRK 411
Schermerhorn, Cornelius	RNS 63
Schermerhorn, Cornelius	
C.	RNS 56
Schermerhorn, Cornelius	
J.	RNS 61
Schermerhorn, Cornelius	
L.	RNS 59
Schermerhorn, Daniel	RNS 61
Schermerhorn, Dirck	RNS 61
Schermerhorn, Gerrit	ALB 17
Schermerhorn, Gertrude	RNS 7
Schermerhorn, Henry N.	ALB 56
Schermerhorn, Isaac	ALB 111
Schermerhorn(?), Isaac	RNS 56
Schermerhorn, Jacob	ALB 15
Schermerhorn, Jacob	OTS 43
Schermerhorn, Jacob	RNS 61
Schermerhorn, Jacob	RNS 83
Schermerhorn, Jacob	
Junr	RNS 60
Schermerhorn, Jacob C.	RNS 61
Schermerhorn, Jacob J.	RNS 61
Schermerhorn, Jacob J.	RNS 84
Schermerhorn, Jacob R.	RNS 61
Schermerhorn, Jacob S.	ALB 17
Schermerhorn, John	DUT 43
Schermerhorn, John	SCH 133
Schermerhorn, John C.	RNS 84
Schermerhorn, John J.	RNS 61
Schermerhorn, John Js	ALB 18
Schermerhorn, John W.	RNS 110
Schermerhorn, Leonard	RNS 88
Schermerhorn, Ns	ALB 18
Schermerhorn, Ns	ALB 18
Schermerhorn, Nichs	SCH 121
Schermerhorn, Peter	NYK 19
Schermerhorn, Philip	RNS 59
Schermerhorn, Reyer	ALB 118
Schermerhorn, Richd	ALB 15
Schermerhorn, Ryer	ALB 25
Schermerhorn, Ryer	RNS 61

s.ott, William	ONT 496	Scripture, Steven	WSH 202	Seacord, Eli	WST 111
Scott, William	ORN 290	Scriven, James	RNS 76	Seacord, Francis	WST 119
Scott, William	OTS 27	Scriv[en?], John	RNS 73	Seacord, James	WST 119
Scott, Wm	RNS 7	Scriven, Joseph	RNS 76	Seacord, James	WST 121
Scott, Wm	RNS 19	Scriven, Joshua	RNS 76	Seacord, James junr	WST 121
Scott, William	RNS 50	Scriven, Wm	RNS 76	Seacord, Joseph	WST 121
Scott, William	SRA 56	Scriven, Zebulon	RNS 76	Seacord, Sarah	WST 119
Scott, William	TIO 248	Scrivener, Andw	OTS 16	Seacord, William	WST 111
Scott, William	ULS 257	Scriver, Christian	COL 215	Seacraft, Jacob	OTS 27
Scott, William	WST 135	Scriver, Simeon	COL 201	Seagrave, Rachel	NYK 17
Scouten see Schouten		Scrivner, Henry	TIO 265	Seal, Hetty	NYK 32
Scouten, Abraham	DEL 284	Scromel, Patience a		Seal, Thomas	NYK 121
Scouten, Daniel	MNT 26	Black	NYK 72	Seales, Truman	ESS 306
Scouten, Jacob	SCH 137	Scrum, Clament	GRN 358	Sealey, Benjamin	WSH 227
Scouten, John	ALB 22	Scrum, Clement	GRN 329	Sealey, Benjamin	WST 158
Scoutin, Hugh	SRA 8	Scrum, Jeremiah	GRN 358	Sealey, Isaac	SUF 83
Scouton, Simon	MNT 8	Scudder, Assa	NYK 47	Sealey, James	WST 157
Scobel, Elisher	OND 220	Scudder, Edmund	SUF 84	Sealey, John	OTS 42
Scovel, Joseph B.	WSH 193	Scudder, Eliza	NYK 144	Sealey, Justice	WSH 211
Scovel, Josiah	GRN 326	Scudder, Ezekiel	ONT 402	Sealey, Reuben	WSH 211
Scovel, Lemuel	OND 220	Scudder, Gilbert	SUF 88	Sealey, Samuel	OTS 42
Scovel, Moses	GRN 326	Scudder, Henry	SUF 84	Sealey, Samuel	SRA 36
Scovel, Samuel	GRN 341	Scudder, Isaac	SUF 84	Sealey, Samuel	WST 158
Scovel, Samuel	WSH 184	Scudder, Jacob	WST 144	Sealey, Zedack	OTS 42
Scovel, Silvenus	GRN 349	Scudder, Jessee	SUF 84	Sealleck see Selleck	
Scovell, Eber	CHN 766	Scudder, Joel	ONT 362	Seallcck, Joseph	QNS 82
Scovell, Westers	RNS 19	Scudder, John	NYK 91	Sealy, Benjamin	WSH 218
Scovil, Benjamin	ONT 416	Scudder, John	ONT 402	Sealy, Eli	WST 137
Scovil, Casar	DUT 168	Scudder, John	SUF 84	Sealy, Isaac	WST 156
Scovil, David	WSH 245	Scudder, Jonah	SUF 84	Sealy, John	NYK 130
Scovil, Elijah	ONT 414	Scudder, Jonathan	DEL 268	Sealy, Joseph	NYK 72
Scovil, Ephraim	DUT 75	Scudder, Jonathan	SUF 88	Sealy, Joseph	NYK 139
Scovil, Ezra	DUT 94	Scudder, Moses	SUF 93	Sealy, Joshua	NYK 19
Scovil, Henry	DUT 55	Scudder, Nathaniel	SUF 86	Sealy, Nehemiah	WSH 218
Scovil, Lebbeus	DUT 76	Scudder, Samuel	NYK 116	Sealy, Robert	CHN 850
Scovil, Miles	DUT 75	Scudder, Thomas	SUF 86	Sealy, Robert	NYK 92
Scovil, Nathan	COL 214	Scudder, Thomas Junr	SUF 88	Sealy, Silas	WST 132
Scovil, Rufus	DUT 55	Scudder, Timothy	SUF 84	Sealy, Solomon	MNT 123
Scovil, Thomas	WSH 245	Scudder, Tredwell	SUF 94	Seaman see Seman &	
Scovill, Abner	OTS 43	Scudder, William S.	DEL 268	Seymon	
Scovill, David	ONN 138	Scudder, Youngs P.	SUF 84	Seaman, Abm	ALB 36
Scovill, Elijah	ALB 40	Scutt, Abraham H.	COL 238	Seaman, Albert	DUT 100
Scovill, Gideon	ALB 115	Scutt, Abraham W.	COL 229	Seaman, Albertus	RNS 86
Scovill, Gideon Junr	ALB 115	Scutt, Hendrick	COL 227	Seaman, Anna	RNS 94
Scovill, Israel	OND 183	Scutt, Hendrick	GRN 332	Seaman, Anthony	SCH 162
Scovill, James	ONN 132	Scutt, Hendrick Junr	COL 227	Seaman, Benjamin	QNS 69
Scovill, James	ONN 137	Scutt, Jeremiah	GRN 346	Seaman, Benjamin	WST 146
Scovill, John	ALB 129	Scutt, John	HRK 443	Seaman, Caleb	ULS 236
Scovill, John	OND 199	Scutt, John	SRA 8	Seaman, Daniel	QNS 70
Scovill, John	ORN 371	Scutt, Myndert	COL 229	Seaman, Daniel	RNS 86
Scovill, Michael	ALB 94	Scutt, Phillip	GRN 332	Seaman, David	RNS 97
Scovill, Nathan	RNS 110	Scutt, Solomon H.	COL 201	Seaman, Dorothy	QNS 76
Scovill, Silas	ONN 163	Scutt, Teunis	RNS 94	Seaman, Elias	RNS 83
Scovill, William	ONT 312	Scutt, Tunis	SRA 46	Seaman, Giles	WST 121
Scra_ling, John	ONT 362	Scutt, Wm	GRN 332	Seaman, Harmanus	RNS 83
Scramling, John	SCH 162	Scuyler see Schuyler		Seaman, Hendrick	RNS 83
Scramling, John	SCH 173	Scuyler, Jacob	CHN 940	Seaman, Henry	WST 132
Scranton, George	WSH 271	Scuyler, John	CHN 944	Seaman, Hentice	RNS 84
Scranton, Stephen	OTS 35	Se__e, Sanford	CAY 626	Seaman, Isaac	ALB 45
Scranton, William	GRN 346	Se..., P..._	HRK 541	Seaman, Isaac	WST 114
Scraper, George	ALB 57	Sea see See		Seaman, Isarel	NYK 53
Screeder, John	ORN 277	Sea, David	RNS 47	Seaman, Isarel	NYK 149
Scriba, George	NYK 27	Sea, David Junr	RNS 48	Seaman, Jacob	SUF 81
Scribner see Schribner		Seaberry, Benjamin	SRA 30	Seaman, _ames	NYK 42
Scribner, Able	MNT 81	Seabert, George	OTS 18	Seaman, James	NYK 126
Scribner, Daniel	CHN 790	Seabrery, Cornelius	SCH 123	Seaman, James	RNS 5
Scribner, Elias	ESS 320	Seabry, David	SCH 123	Seaman, Jesse	WST 113
Scribner, Enock	WST 143	Seabry, Oliver	CHN 898	Seaman, John	DUT 114
Scribner, Jared	DUT 141	Seabury, John	DUT 61	Seaman, John	NYK 37
Scribner, Job	NYK 149	Seabury, Samuel	QNS 76	Seaman, John	NYK 127
Scribner, John	RNS 22	Seabury, Tilman	DUT 68	Seaman, John	ULS 240
Scribner, Jonathan	CLN 163	SeaCar, David	GRN 354	Seaman, Jonas	RCK 104
Scribner, Samuel	ESS 320	Seacarl, John D.	SCH 139	Seaman, Jonathan	RCK 109
Scribner, Samuel	RNS 17	Seacock see Leacock		Seaman, Jones	RNS 97
Scribner, Zacheus	SRA 13	Seacomb, John	WSH 272	Seaman, Joseah	WSH 267
Scribnir, Elisha	SRA 6	Seacor, John	RCK 104	Seaman, Joseph	NYK 88
Scripture, Hiram	OND 173	Seacord see Secord		Seaman, Joseph	QNS 76

Seaman, Joseph	RCK 104	Searls, Daniel	GRN 353	Seasie, Philip	SCH 132		
Seaman, Joseph	ULS 238	Searls, Ebenezer	DEL 268	Seaton, Assa	WSH 280		
Seaman, Joshua	RNS 83	Searls, Eliphas	OND 222	Seaton, George	OND 176		
Seaman, Martin	SCH 162	Searls, John	GRN 353	Seaton, James	ESS 306		
Seaman, Mary	NYK 65	Searls, John	RNS 91	Seaton, James	WSH 292		
Seaman, Mary	WST 138	Searls, Lemuel	STB 201	Seaton, Willard	CAY 624		
Seaman, Moses	ORN 280	Searls, Moses	ESS 296	Seaver, Luther	NYK 125		
Seaman, Paul	RCK 105	Searls, Richard	TIO 249	Seaward, John	NYK 44		
Seaman, Peter	NYK 93	Searls, Samuel	ONT 446	Seaward, Noadiah	OTS 42		
Seaman, Peter	ORN 358	Searls, William	QNS 67	Seaymore see Seymore			
Seaman, Peter Junr	RNS 97	Searmehorn see Scherme-		Seaymore, Matthew	WST 152		
Seaman, Richard	NYK 151	horn		Seber, Jacob	CHN 944		
Seaman, [Ri?]chard	QNS 71	Searmehorn, Wm	GRN 331	Seberry, Nathaniel	SUF 104		
Seaman, Richard	RCH 95	S.ars, ...ard	RNS 18	Seborn, John	NYK 59		
Seaman, Robert	NYK 130	Sears see Seers		Seborough, Henry	ALB 99		
Seaman, Robert	QNS 78	Sears, Abijah	ALB 84	Sebra, Jacob	NYK 25		
Seaman, Samuel	ORN 396	Sears, Abraham	DEL 275	Sebree, John	SRA 42		
Seaman, Sarah	NYK 19	Sears, Annenias	SUF 104	Sebring, Corneleus	WSH 246		
Seaman, Silvanus	WST 113	Sears, Baldwin	DUT 175	Sebring, Cornelius	CAY 558		
Seaman, Stephen	KNG 8	Sears, Bartholomew	ULS 190	Sebring, Cornelius	RNS 47		
Seaman, Thomas	NYK 29	Sears, Benjamin	DEL 288	Sebring, Cornelius B.	NYK 36		
Seaman, Thomas	QNS 76	Sears, Benjamin	DUT 172	Sebring, Fulcert	CAY 556		
Seaman, Valentine	NYK 37	Sears, Benjamin	ORN 302	Sebring, Fuliart	CAY 544		
Seaman, Wandle	RNS 83	Sears, Benjamin	ULS 190	Sebring, Isaac	DUT 39		
Seaman, Willet	NYK 45	Sears, Benjamin Junr	ULS 190	Sebring, Isaac	NYK 26		
Seaman, William	NYK 24	Sears, Caleb	ALB 87	Sebring, Jacob	QNS 64		
Seaman, William	NYK 125	Sears, Charles	HRK 572	Sebring, Jacob	WSH 242		
Seamans, Andrew	COL 221	Sears, Daniel	ALB 85	Sebring, John	CAY 542		
Seamans, Isaac	SCH 173	Sears, David	COL 251	Sebring, John	WSH 250		
Seamen, Peleg	NYK 116	Sears, David	ONN 160	Sebring, Lafford	WSH 242		
Seamon, Edwmund	NYK 26	Sears, Ebenezer	TIO 259	Sebring, Peter	NYK 67		
Seamon, Nathaniel	QNS 73	Sears, Eleazer H.	DUT 172	Sebring, Ruloff	CAY 558		
Seamons, Simeon	SRA 44	Sears, Elizabeth	ORN 310	Sebring, Thomas	CAY 558		
Seamore see Semore &		Sears, Elnathan	ULS 190	Seburg, Abraham	WSH 244		
Seymore		Sears, Enoch	ALB 87	Seby Negro	QNS 74		
Seamore, Jona	OTS 18	Sears, Ezekiel	ESS 296	Secor see Seacor			
Seamore, Saml	OTS 13	Sears, Frank	SUF 96	Secor, Andrew	ALB 75		
Seamour, Drake	WST 113	Sears, Hannah	ULS 206	Secor, Benj.	RCK 109		
Seamour, Ebenezer	WST 159	Sears, Heman	DUT 173	Secor, Daniel	ALB 75		
Seamour, Itheal	WST 160	Sears, Henry	NYK 79	Secor, Daniel	NYK 150		
Seamour, Thaddeus	WST 158	Sears, Isaac	DUT 173	Secor, Eli	NYK 137		
Seamour, Thomas a		Sears, Isaac	ORN 297	Secor, Francis	NYK 139		
Black	NYK 127	Sears, Isaac	SUF 96	Secor, Gilbert	NYK 150		
Seamour, Thomas	WST 131	Sears, James	DEL 274	Secor, Isaac	ALB 75		
Sean, Joseph	NYK 16	Sears, James	DUT 128	Secor, Isaac	ORN 394		
Sear, John	CHN 944	Sears, James	ORN 295	Secor, Jacob	NYK 102		
Sear, William	SRA 9	Sears, James	TIO 259	Secor, James D.	ORN 390		
Seard, Joseph	NYK 25	Sears, Jasper P.	ONT 388	Secor, John	RCK 99		
Seare, Thomas	CHN 790	Sears, John	ALB 70	Secor, John	RCK 105		
Seares, Daniel	GRN 346	Sears, John	DUT 140	Secor, Jonas	RCK 110		
Searing, John	QNS 69	Sears, John	ORN 342	Secor, Moses	WST 148		
Searing, John 2d	QNS 69	Sears, John B.	ORN 299	Secor, Saml	RCK 109		
Searjant see Sergeant		Sears, Jonathan	HRK 422	Secord see Seacord			
Searjant, Caty	NYK 22	Sears, Joseth	WST 160	Secord, Alexander	DUT 76		
Searl, Edward	NYK 137	Sears, Joshua	ORN 286	Secord, Benjamin	DUT 81		
Searl, Elisha	STB 200	Sears, Judah	COL 250	Secord, Caleb	DUT 85		
Searl, Reuben	STB 201	Sears, Matthew	ULS 190	Secord, Daniel	WST 133		
Searl, Reuben Junior	STB 201	Sears, Merritt	SUF 97	Secord, Daniel	WST 149		
Searl, Timothy	STB 201	Sears, Moses	NYK 105	Secord, David	WST 149		
Searles see Serls		Sears, Nathan	COL 246	Secord, Elihu	DUT 91		
Searles, Abm	ALB 112	Sears, Nehemiah	STB 204	Secord, Isaac	DUT 84		
Searles, Daniel	WST 129	Sears, Obadiah	WSH 254	Secord, Isaac Junr	DUT 29		
Searles, Henry	WST 170	Sears, Obed	COL 250	Secord, Isaac Senr	DUT 24		
Searles, James	WST 158	Sears, Peter	NYK 99	Secord, James	ORN 275		
Searles, Jeremiah	ALB 112	Sears, Samuel	COL 194	Secord, James	WST 133		
Searles, Joel	WST 170	Sears, Samuel	NYK 90	Secord, John	DUT 84		
Searles, John	CAY 620	Sears, Samuel	ORN 383	Secord, John	WST 155		
Searles, John	WST 169	Sears, Samuel	ULS 190	Secord, Levi	WST 124		
Searles, Joseph	ESS 294	Sears, Sarah	NYK 23	Secord, Nehemiah	WST 112		
Searles, Joseph	WST 135	Sears, Seth	DUT 172	Secord, Oliver	WST 130		
Searles, Lott	WST 170	Sears, Seth Junr	DUT 172	Secord, Robert	DUT 84		
Searles, Marcus	WST 157	Sears, Sewell	ULS 190	Secord, Warner	DUT 106		
Searles, Samuel	WST 135	Sears, Silas	ALB 87	Secord, William	DEL 270		
Searles, Solomon	WST 133	Sears, Silas	SUF 102	Secore, Sarah	WST 148		
Searles, Willet	WST 170	Sears, Siles	WSH 254	Secoy, David	SRA 15		
Searles, William	WST 128	Sears, Sunderlands	SRA 13	Secoy, Elijah	NYK 106		
Searls, Boaz	DEL 273	Sears, Thomas	DUT 175	Secoy, John	CHN 764		

Name	Loc		Name	Loc		Name	Loc
Sergeant, Abel	ORN 351		Seward, Sylvanus	DEL 285		Seymour, Samuel	TIO 211
Sergeant, Isaac	ORN 331		Seward, William	DUT 40		Seymour, Selah	OND 194
Sergeant, Phins	ONN 188		Sewart, Swain	OTS 40		Seymour, Silas	SRA 18
Sergent, John	OND 162		Sewell, Daniel	ULS 195		Seymour, Silas	SRA 22
Sergent, Samuel	CHN 792		Sewell, Ebenezer	OTS 38		Seymour, Susanna	ULS 258
Serjeant, James	NYK 20		Sewell, Frederick	MNT 50		Seymour, Thomas	NYK 152
Serjeants, John	TIO 260		Sewell, Nicholas	ONT 444		Seymour, Thos	SRA 22
Serian, Daniel	WST 170		Sewell, Robert	OTS 38		Seymour, Uriah	OND 182
Sering, Samuel	SRA 60		Sexby, Abraham	ALB 17		Seymour, William	ORN 284
Serings, Abraham	SRA 60		Sexon, John	DUT 93		Seymour, William	SRA 46
Serivan, Benj:	ONN 174		Sexton, Gilbert	HRK 475		Seymour, William	ULS 258
Serivan, Thomas	ONN 174		Sexton, Amos	WSH 201		Seymour, Zaduck	CHN 810
Serley, John a Black	NYK 149		Sexton, Asel	CHN 848		Sh...., Adams	MNT 5
Serls see Searles			Sexton, David	CHN 848		Sh_e, Edward	MNT 87
Serls, Henry	RNS 14		Sexton, Elijah	CHN 804		Sh_ers, Joseph	ONT 490
Serrin, Daniel	WST 148		Sexton, Ezekiel	ALB 3		Sh_e, John	ONT 504
Serring, Coe	QNS 69		Sexton, Ezra	OND 167		Shace see Shall	
Serring, Jacob	QNS 69		Sexton, Gilbert	ULS 241		Shace, Daniel	SCH 125
Serring, James	QNS 69		Sexton, Henry	OTS 22		Shace, John	MNT 29
Serring, John Junr	QNS 69		Sexton, James	OTS 22		Shackerley, John H.	NYK 34
Serring, Moses	QNS 69		Sexton, Jehiel	OND 184		Shackerly, Mary	NYK 28
Serring, Richard	SRA 42		Sexton, Jesse	OND 206		Shacklock, George	NYK 48
Serring, Samuel	QNS 69		Sexton, John	WSH 192		Shad, Mary	NYK 42
Serring, William			Sexton, Lemuel	OTS 53		Shadbaat, Robt	SUF 83
Negro	QNS 71		Sexton, William	WSH 192		Shadbolt, Phebe	DUT 113
Serrur, Anthony	NYK 34		Seybolt, Frederick	ORN 313		Shadbolt, Thomas	DUT 114
Serus a Negro	SUF 75		Seybolt, Henry	ALB 89		Shadden, Daniel	WST 124
Servant, Anthony V.	NYK 69		Seybolt, Jacob	ORN 314		Shadden, Lawrence	WST 170
Serverence, Phillip	ESS 320		Seybolt, John	ORN 311		Shaddock, David	CHN 784
Service, Cornelius	ALB 59		Seymon see Seamon &			Shaddock, Isaac	CHN 894
Service, Frederick	ALB 59		Semon			Shaddock, John	CHN 782
Sessim, George	COL 264		Seymon, Lawrence	QNS 74		Shaddock, Thos	ALB 42
Seth	QNS 81		Seymore see Saymour,			Shaddock, Thomas	DEL 283
Seton, James	NYK 21		Seamore, Seaymore &			Shaddock, Thomas	NYK 105
Seton, James	WSH 183		Semour			Shaden, James	RCK 105
Seton, Wm	COL 207		Seymore, David	WSH 207		Shadock, Oliver	CHN 896
Seton, William M.	NYK 24		Sey.ore, Enos	MNT 65		Shadraack, Wm	MNT 96
Setterly, George	ALB 17		Seymore, Sherwood	MNT 93		Shadrick, Hellman	MNT 111
Settle, Peter	MNT 58		Seymore, Truman	ALB 127		Shadwell, David	ORN 304
Setts, Andrew	ALB 120		Seymour, Abner	OND 177		Shadwick, Coenradt	COL 238
Setts, David	ALB 72		Seymour, Abrm	SRA 22		Shadwick, Hendrick	COL 238
Setts, Matthew	GRN 357		Seymour, Andrew	SRA 47		Shadwick, Samuel	COL 238
Sevan, Charles	NYK 43		Seymour, Asa	CHN 982		Shadworth, Derias	SRA 43
Sevan, Jabez	ONT 480		Seymour, Billa	COL 181		Shafer, Henry	HRK 577
Seveed, Joseph	KNG 9		Seymour, Catherine	NYK 134		Shafer, Henry Junr	RNS 63
Sever, Ebenezar	RNS 82		Seymour, Constantine	OND 177		Shafer, John	RNS 12
Sever, John	OND 166		Seymour, Daniel	NYK 152		Shafer, Nicholas	RNS 88
Sever, Robert	OND 166		Seymour, Daniel	RNS 80		Shafer, Peter	ONT 316
Severanc_, Elisha	CHN 964		Seymour, Daniel	TIO 211		Shafer, Philip	RNS 12
Severince, Elisha	CHN 964		Seymour, Daniel	TIO 232		Shafer, Philip	RNS 63
Severly, George	CHN 758		Seymour, Daniel	ULS 258		Shafer, Thomas	RNS 63
Severns, Thomas	WSH 187		Seymour, David	ONN 165		Shafer, Wm	RNS 64
Severole, Jacob	CAY 580		Seymour, David	TIO 220		Shaff, John	HRK 456
Severs, Derrick	GRN 350		Seymour, Ebenezer	OND 206		Shaff, Henry	HRK 551½
Severs, James	CHN 802		Seymour, Elias	OND 181		Shaff, Wm	MNT 40
Severs, Jonathan	RNS 90		Seymour, Ephaim	ONN 133		Shaffer see Chaffer &	
Severs, Nathaniel	OND 198		Seymour, George	SRA 47		Schaffer	
Severse, Abraham	ALB 60		Seymour, Gideon	OND 194		Shaffer, Charles	ALB 57
Seversie, George	ALB 60		Seymour, Hezekiah	OND 178		Shaffer, Frederick	ALB 76
Seversie, Nicholas	ALB 60		Seymour, Hezekiah	OND 183		Shaffer, John	ALB 50
Severson, Derrick	GRN 357		Seymour, Hezekiah	SRA 58		Shaffer, John	ALB 72
Sevie, John a Black	NYK 103		Seymour, Hope	NYK 45		Shaffer, John H.	RNS 87
Sevill, Lewis	ALB 121		Seymour, Ira	ONT 402		Shaffer, John J.	ALB 72
Seviney, Barney	NYK 65		Seymour, Ira	TIO 220		Shaffer, Peter	ALB 50
Seward see Suard &			Seymour, Isaac	TIO 211		Shafferd, Willi..	RNS 90
Suward			Seymour, Jehiel	ULS 258		Shaffler, Henry	ALB 103
Seward, Aaron Junr	DEL 285		Seymour, Jesse	DUT 176		Shaft, Jasper	DUT 37
Seward, Abraham	COL 211		Seymour, Jesse	SRA 47		Shaise, Daniel	SCH 146
Seward, Christopher	NYK 42		Seymour, Joel	SRA 46		Shaise, Daniel Junr	SCH 146
Seward, Daniel	ORN 346		Seymour, John	CHN 914		Shakefast, William	GRN 343
Seward, Eliphalet	OTS 44		Seymour, John	COL 264		Shakelton, William	ONT 386
Seward, James	OTS 42		Seymour, John	TIO 220		Shakerly, Peter	NYK 123
Seward, Jedediah	ESS 302		Seymour, Joseph	OND 206		Shalenbergh, Casparus	HRK 460
Seward, Nathan	OND 174		Seymour, Josiah	OND 181		Shalion, Henry	MNT 94
Seward, Samuel	CAY 634		Seymour, Leverit	CHN 898		Shall see Shace	
Seward, Sirus	CHN 742		Seymour, Lyman	ONN 130		Shall, Bastian	MNT 29
Seward, Stephen	OTS 42		Seymour, Matthew	CHN 766		Shall, Georg	MNT 28

326

Name	Ref	Name	Ref	Name	Ref
Shall, Henry	MNT 30	Sharp, Harvey	HRK 491	Sharts, Teunis	COL 178
Shall, John	OND 222	Sharp, Hendrick	CHN 740	Shattuck, Daniel	ONT 424
Shall, Ma[ttice?]	MNT 29	Sharp, Henry	COL 264	Shattuck, Eliphater	CAY 534
Shalor, Nathaniel	NYK 57	Sharp, Isaac	DUT 177	Shattuck, Gideon	ESS 292
Shamard, John	NYK 96	Sharp, Jacob	COL 198	Shattuck, William	CAY 534
Shane, Martin	SRA 33	Sharp, Jacob	GRN 348	Shattuck, William	NYK 50
Shanewolfe, Frederick		Sharp, Jacob	GRN 350	Shatzel, Benjamin	NYK 82
H.	NYK 56	Sharp, Jacob	KNG 9	Shatzel, Jacob	NYK 18
Shange, Joseph	NYK 120	Sharp, Jacob	RNS 11	Shatzel, John M.	NYK 133
Shank, Jack Negro	QNS 71	Sharp, Jacob Junr	COL 198	Shatzel, John Michall	NYK 124
Shanklan, Robert	NYK 88	Sharp, Jacob Junr	GRN 348	Shatzel, William	NYK 44
Shankland, Alexr	OTS 4	Sharp, Jacob Jun	GRN 350	Shauber, David	SRA 6
Shankland, Catherine	NYK 58	Sharp, John	ALB 107	Shauber, David	SRA 12
Shanklin, Thomas	SRA 35	Sharp, John	COL 198	Shavelier, Hendrick	GRN 349
Shanklin, William	SRA 35	Sharp, John	KNG 8	Shavelier, John	GRN 349
Shankne..., John	MNT 18	Sharp, John	NYK 18	Shavelier, Jeremiah	GRN 349
Shankneble, Philip	MNT 12	Sharp, John	NYK 59	Shavelier, Peter	GRN 350
Shannan, James	NYK 98	Sharp, John	NYK 146	Shavelier, Peter Jun	GRN 350
Shannon, Alexr	ALB 38	Sharp, John	OND 223	Shaver see Schaver	
Shannon, Daniel	GRN 357	Sharp, John	WSH 254	Shaver	GRN 336
Shannon, George	DUT 49	Sharp, John J.	COL 262	Shaver, Abraham	DEL 271
Shannon, John	ALB 38	Sharp, Lawrence P.	COL 262	Shaver, Adam	DEL 271
Shannon, John	NYK 112	Sharp, Matthias	CAY 642	Shaver, Adam	OTS 15
Shannon, John	NYK 129	Sharp, Nicholas	NYK 120	Shaver, Adam	SCH 122
Shannon, Robert	ALB 16	Sharp, Nicholas	RNS 7	Shaver, Adam Junr	COL 232
Shannon, William	ALB 39	Sharp, Peter	ALB 146	Shaver, Adam Junr	DEL 276
Shants, Henry	RNS 56	Sharp, Peter	CAY 716	Shaver, Andrew	MNT 16
Shants, Jeremiah	RNS 56	Sharp, Peter	COL 189	Shaver, Bartholemew	MNT 10
Shantz, Christian	RNS 55	Sharp, Peter	COL 199	Shaver, Charles	COL 197
Shaper, Mary	TIO 265	Sharp, Peter	COL 262	Shaver, Christian	RNS 86
Shaperman, Christion	MNT 1	Sharp, Peter	MNT 124	Shaver, Christian	SCH 137
Shapley, David	CHN 760	Sharp, Peter	NYK 52	Shaver, Francis	ALB 75
Shapley, David	OTS 21	Sharp, Peter(?)	OND 224	Shaver, Frederick	ALB 94
Shapley, William	ESS 306	Sharp, Peter	ONN 193	Shaver, Frederick	SCH 124
Shapter, Thomas	NYK 24	Sharp, Peter	RNS 4	Shaver, George	CLN 154
Shapter, Thomas	NYK 142	Sharp, Peter	RNS 5	Shaver, George	SCH 138
Sharboum, Jethro	RNS 33	Sharp, Peter	SRA 32	Shaver, Gerrit	SCH 137
Share, Daniel	SRA 3	Sharp, Peter	SRA 41	Shaver, Harry	MNT 53
Sharer, Peter	HRK 446	Sharp, Philip	SRA 45	Shaver, Hendrick	COL 255
Shares, Jacob	GRN 342	Sharp, Robert	CHN 988	Shaver, Henry	DEL 271
Sharkey, Thomas	ULS 254	Sharp, Robert	NYK 27	Shaver, Henry	OTS 15
Sharks, Pearl	MNT 27	Sharp, Rufus	HRK 571	Shaver, Henry	RNS 59
Sharman, Caleb	RNS 44	Sharp, Samuel	CAY 642	Shaver, Henry	SCH 119
Sharman, Darias	RNS 61	Sharp, Solomon	COL 262	Shaver, Henry	SCH 150
Sharman, David	RNS 60	Sharp, Solomon	MNT 24	Shaver, Henry	SCH 152
Sharman, Elisha	RNS 44	Sharp, William	ALB 148	Shaver, Henry	SCH 153
Sharman, Giddeon	RNS 42	Sharp, William	CAY 716	Shaver, Henry J.	COL 240
Sharman, Levi	RNS 43	Sharp, William	COL 248	Shaver, Jacob	COL 234
Sharman, Levi	RNS 44	Sharp, William	KNG 9	Shaver, Jacob	DEL 271
Sharman, Michael	RNS 57	Sharp, William	NYK 86	Shaver, Jacob	MNT 23
Sharman, Rhodes	RNS 98	Sharp, William	RCH 93	Shaver, Jacob	SCH 137
Sharman, Stephen	RNS 56	Sharp, William Junr	CAY 716	Shaver, Jacob Junr	COL 232
Sharmon, Peleg	RNS 99	Sharpe, Coenrad	ALB 147	Shaver, Jacob F.	COL 231
Sharon, Chandler	WSH 246	Sharpe, Eliakim	CAY 592	Shaver, Jacob H.	COL 240
Sharp a Negro	SUF 67	Sharpe, Isaac	WST 124	Shaver, Jacob L. &	
Sharp, Abisha	RNS 24	Sharpe, James	ALB 136	Lucas L.	COL 263
Sharp, Andrew	CAY 716	Sharpe, Rachel	ORN 334	Shaver, Jeremiah	COL 227
Sharp, Andrew	OND 175	Sharpen, William	WST 170	Shaver, Johanes	MNT 23
Sharp, Andrew	WSH 188	Sharpless, Isaac	NYK 66	Shaver, John	COL 227
Sharp, Andrew J.	COL 262	Sharpless, James	NYK 93	Shaver, John	DEL 271
Sharp, Andrew L.	COL 262	Sharpston, John	COL 241	Shaver, John	MNT 56
Sharp, Andrew P.	COL 262	Sharpstone, Henry	DUT 105	Shaver, John	OTS 15
Sharp, Andrus	COL 262	Sharpstone, Jacob	DUT 105	Shaver, John	SCH 122
Sharp, Anna	COL 262	Sharpstone, John	DUT 105	Shaver, John	SCH 150
Sharp, Anna	NYK 90	Sharpstone, John H.	COL 236	Shaver, John Junr	COL 234
Sharp, Augustus	HRK 491	Sharpstone, Peter	DUT 105	Shaver, John Jr	MNT 36
Sharp, Bartholomew	RNS 83	Sharpstone, Peter	GRN 340	Shaver, John H.	SCH 154
Sharp, Coorod	CHN 740	Sharr, Randolph	ALB 67	Shaver, John J.	COL 197
Sharp, Cornelius	OND 175	Sharrack, James	WST 153	Shaver, John J.	COL 228
Sharp, Cornelius	WSH 188	Sharron, Richard	GRN 357	Shaver, John L.	COL 263
Sharp, David	GRN 358	Sharry, John	NYK 61	Shaver, John L.	COL 266
Sharp, David	HRK 490	Shartis see Sharks		Shaver, John M.	SCH 152
Sharp, Frederick	RNS 4	Sharts, Andries	COL 196	Shaver, Jonas	COL 235
Sharp, Garret	WSH 188	Sharts, Andries N.	COL 181	Shaver, Lambert	SCH 149
Sharp, George	RNS 11	Sharts, George	COL 178	Shaver, Lambert Jr	SCH 149
Sharp, Gisbert	ALB 56	Sharts, Nicholas	COL 185	Shaver, Lucas	COL 266
Sharp, Guy	ALB 117	Sharts, Nicholas Junr	COL 178	Shaver, Lucas L. & Jacob	COL 263

Name	Loc	Name	Loc	Name	Loc
Shaver, Peter	COL 233	Shaw, Joseph	ONT 420	Shear, James	ALB 17
Shaver, Peter	MNT 6	Shaw, Joseph	OTS 21	Shear, Jeremiah	SRA 10
Shaver, Peter	OTS 40	Shaw, Joseph	TIO 210	Shear, Matthias	SRA 8
Shaver, Peter	SCH 118	Shaw, Joshua	DUT 95	Shear, Peter	ALB 117
Shaver, Peter	SCH 154	Shaw, Lemuel	RNS 82	Shear, Peter	SRA 3
Shaver, Philip	DEL 271	Shaw, Mary	NYK 132	Shearer see Scherer &	
Shaver, Solomon	COL 242	Shaw, Michael	DUT 27	Sherer	
Shaver, Tawalt	SCH 153	Shaw, Moses	COL 189	Shearer, Luis	WSH 252
Shaver, Tunis	RNS 88	Shaw, Moses	ULS 188	Shearer, Uriah	WSH 252
Shaver, Tunis	SCH 119	Shaw, Nathan	COL 187	Shearer, Willeam	WSH 292
Shaver, Tunis	SCH 123	Shaw, Nathaniel	WSH 205	Shearman, Abraham	WSH 200
Shaver, Wm	RNS 62	Shaw, Nathen	WSH 198	Shearman, Abraham	WSH 217
Shavewood, Nathan	GRN 342	Shaw, Noah	DUT 147	Shearman, Adley	WSH 233
Shaw, Aaron	COL 189	Shaw, Peter	CHN 804	Shearman, Batchelor	WSH 197
Shaw, Abigail	OND 174	Shaw, Peter	DUT 108	Shearman, Benjamin	CLN 155
Shaw, Alexander	WSH 251	Shaw, Peter	WSH 271	Shearman, Christopher	WSH 226
Shaw, Amos	QNS 77	Shaw, Phebe	RNS 10	Shearman, David	WSH 200
Shaw, Anthony	RNS 100	Shaw, Pierre	CLN 168	Shearman, Ebenezer	WSH 210
Shaw, Barney	SRA 33	Shaw, Rebecca	DUT 152	Shearman, Elijah	WSH 197
Shaw, Benjamin	WSH 271	Shaw, Rebecca	RCK 104	Shearman, Elijah	WSH 240
Shaw, Benjamin	DUT 9	Shaw, Remeys	NYK 141	Shearman, Evert	KNG 4
Shaw, Benjn	OTS 42	Shaw, Robert	DUT 96	Shearman, Fortunatus	WSH 196
Shaw, Comfort	MNT 20	Shaw, Roswell	WSH 296	Shearman, Henry	WSH 197
Shaw, Comfort	RNS 104	Shaw, Samuel	CHN 802	Shearman, Jabaze	WSH 235
Shaw, Cons[ider?]	CAY 696	Shaw, Samuel	COL 178	Shearman, James	OND 211
Shaw, Crandell	WSH 296	Shaw, Samuel	OTS 23	Shearman, James	WSH 210
Shaw, Daniel	ONT 448	Shaw, Samuel	RNS 98	Shearman, Jedediah	OND 212
Shaw, Danl	OTS 14	Shaw, Samuel	WSH 246	Shearman, Jesse	WSH 265
Shaw, Daniel	RNS 37	Shaw, Samuel Junr	OTS 23	Shearman, Jobes	WSH 240
Shaw, Daniel	SRA 56	Shaw, Sarah	NYK 65	Shearman, Jonathan	WSH 236
Shaw, Danl	SUF 72	Shaw, Seth	ONN 181	Shearman, Joseph	OND 206
Shaw, Daniel	WSH 205	Shaw, Silas	QNS 77	Shearman, Lemuel	WSH 196
Shaw, Daniel	WSH 205	Shaw, Susanna	WSH 296	Shearman, Nathan	WSH 241
Shaw, David	OTS 23	Shaw, Thomas	ORN 291	Shearman, Nathan	WSH 300
Shaw, Deborah	DUT 87	Shaw, Thomas	WSH 188	Shearman, Nathen	WSH 202
Shaw, Duncan	WSH 256	Shaw, Thomas	WSH 296	Shearman, Oliver	WSH 200
Shaw, Ebenezer	DUT 77	Shaw, William	CHN 804	Shearman, Parker	WSH 233
Shaw, Eliz beth	ONT 432	Shaw, William	COL 254	Shearman, Philip	WSH 266
Shaw, Elizabeth	WSH 184	Shaw, William	DUT 9	Shearman, Samuel	WSH 238
Shaw, Enoch	DUT 26	Shaw, William	DUT 27	Shearman, Samuel	WSH 279
Shaw, Ephm	ONN 179	Shaw, William	DUT 51	Shearman, Subel	WSH 200
Shaw, Ezra	ALB 143	Shaw, William	DUT 127	Shears, George	ALB 116
Shaw, Ezra	OTS 40	Shaw, Wm	GRN 331	Shears, John	ALB 116
Shaw, Foster	ESS 294	Shaw, Wm	GRN 351	Shears, John B.	ALB 62
Shaw, Gidion	WSH 200	Shaw, William	NYK 36	Shears, Thomas	SCH 154
Shaw, Gilbert	DUT 75	Shaw, William	NYK 80	Shears, Venus	ALB 17
Shaw, Gilbert	DUT 96	Shaw, William	OND 223	Shears, Zachr	OTS 22
Shaw, Henry	QNS 73	Shaw, William	ORN 336	Sheather, John	STB 197
Shaw, Henry	RNS 98	Shaw, William	OTS 22	Shed, David	OND 177
Shaw, Isaac	DUT 77	Shaw, William	OTS 40	Sheddin, David	QNS 84
Shaw, Isaah	MNT 101	Shaw, William	ULS 183	Sheden, Robert	WST 147
Shaw, Jacob	WST 149	Shaw, William Junr	OTS 23	Shederly, Isaac	ALB 66
Shaw, James	ALB 57	Shaw, Wm Junr	OTS 41	Sheeke, John	DUT 113
Shaw, James	COL 217	Shay, Anson	ONT 444	Sheeke, Michael	DUT 119
Shaw, James	DUT 95	Shay, Dennis	ORN 304	Sheely, Coonradt	ULS 185
Shaw, James	NYK 36	Shay, George	NYK 123	Sheely, Jacob	ULS 209
Shaw, James	SRA 4	Shay, James	NYK 109	Sheely, Jacob C.	ULS 210
Shaw, James	STB 202	Shay, John	NYK 126	Sheep, Alexander	CAY 522
Shaw, James	WSH 251	Shay, Partrick	NYK 52	Sheer, Benjamin	ONT 488
Shaw, Jesse	WSH 296	Shay, Phillip	ORN 371	Sheer, John	COL 184
Shaw, John	ALB 7	Shay, Timothy	WST 127	Sheerer, John	CAY 594
Shaw, John	ALB 44	Shay, Timothy	WST 127	Sheerer, Joseph	SRA 21
Shaw, John	CAY 720	Shay, William	CAY 580	Sheerman, Abiel	RNS 57
Shaw, John	MNT 69	Shay, William	WSH 217	Sheerman, Anthony	SUF 101
Shaw, John	NYK 17	Shayler, Joseph	ORN 376	Sheerman, Hazael	RNS 6
Shaw, John	NYK 83	Shays, Benjamin	ALB 143	Sheerman, Howland	RNS 64
Shaw, John	ORN 281	Shays, George	ORN 276	Sheerman, Jedediah	RNS112B
Shaw, John	ORN 291	Sheack, Christian	RNS 31	Sheerman, John	SUF 104
Shaw, John	ORN 336	Shead, Daniel	OND 211	Sheerman, Josiah	RNS 81
Shaw, John	SRA 38	Shead, Isaih	WSH 199	Sheerman, Josiah	RNS 81
Shaw, John	ULS 201	Shead, John	OND 211	Sheerman, Lewis	RNS 57
Shaw, John	WSH 286	Shead, Oliver	WSH 199	Sheerman, Peleg	SUF 99
Shaw, John C.	NYK 25	Shead, Samuel	OND 170	Sheeter, Nathaniel	WSH 207
Shaw, Jonathan W.	OND 165	Sheader, George	DUT 162	Sheets, Jacob	ONT 322
Shaw, Joseph	COL 182	Shealds, James	WSH 205	Sheey, Partrick	NYK 153
Shaw, Joseph	MNT 89	Sheales, Thomas	RCH 91	Sheffernan, Mary	NYK 35
Shaw, Joseph	ONT 348	Shear, Andrew	SRA 3	Sheffield, Adam	ALB 102

Name	Code	Page
Sheffield, Caleb	RNS	58
Sheffield, Esther	WST	123
Sheffield, James	SRA	52
Sheffield, John	OND	199
Sheffield, John	ULS	268
Sheffield, Jonathan	TIO	245
Sheffield, Joseph	RNS	94
Sheffield, Joseph	WSH	231
Sheffield, Robert	NYK	136
Sheffield, Siles	WSH	202
Sheffield, Thomas	GRN	337
Sheffield, William	NYK	34
Shefield, Nathan	SRA	18
Shefley, Samuel	SRA	55
Shefman, William	SRA	41
Sheilds, Daniel	ALB	127
Sheilds, James	ULS	193
Sheilds, John	ULS	255
Sheirs, John	NYK	125
Shelburry, Joseph	NYK	98
Shelby, Jacob	MNT	50
Shelden, Archibald	DEL	285
Shelden, Asariah	WSH	187
Shelden, Benajah	WSH	253
Shelden, Benj	OND	206
Shelden, Benjamin	RNS	95
Shelden, Daniel	CAY	694
Shelden, Daniel	ESS	298
Shelden, Darias	WST	158
Shelden, Edmund	ESS	305
Shelden, Elisha	ALB	43
Shelden, Elisha	ALB	87
Shelden, Elisha	DEL	288
Shelden, Escek	OND	206
Shelden, Ezekiel	OND	181
Shelden, Ezekiel	OTS	38
Shelden, George	NYK	32
Shelden, George	NYK	109
Shelden, Jacob	CAY	696
Shelden, James	ALB	31
Shelden, James	OND	212
Shelden, Jeremiah	DEL	284
Shelden, John	OND	169
Shelden, John	ONT	392
Shelden, John	WSH	217
Shelden, Jonathan	CAY	550
Shelden, Jonathan	DEL	285
Shelden, Jonathan	OND	169
Shelden, Joseph	CAY	598
Shelden, Joseph	ESS	305
Shelden, Josiah	WSH	240
Shelden, Nathan	COL	225
Shelden, Nathaniel	CAY	578
Shelden, Reuben	OND	206
Shelden, Ruf..	CAY	696
Shelden, Samuel	OND	191
Shelden, Samuel	SRA	21
Shelden, Thomas	ESS	308
Shelden, Thomas	RNS	91
Shelden, Timothy	ESS	308
Shelden, William	ONT	406
Shelden, Winter	ESS	303
Sheldin, Anthony	CHN	920
Sheldin, Epifrass	CHN	740
Sheldin, Nathanl	CHN	962
Sheldon, Allen	COL	242
Sheldon, Amos	MNT	88
Sheldon, Asa	HRK	447
Sheldon, Augustus	RNS	71
Sheldon, Benjamin	ESS	303
Sheldon, Benjamin	RNS	103
Sheldon, Caleb	DUT	48
Sheldon, David	DUT	49
Sheldon, Ebenezer	DUT	47
Sheldon, Eleakem	OTS	55
Sheldon, Ezekiel	RNS	101
Sheldon, Frazer	ORN	348
Sheldon, Friend	DUT	145
Sheldon, George	DUT	144
Sheldon, Hannah	DUT	47
Sheldon, Isaac	ESS	303
Sheldon, Isaac	OTS	9
Sheldon, Isaa_ Junr	ESS	303
Sheldon, James	HRK	448
Sheldon, Jedediah	DUT	53
Sheldon, John	HRK	451
Sheldon, John	OTS	36
Sheldon, Jonathan	RNS	59
Sheldon, Joseph	ORN	390
Sheldon, Joseph	RNS	103
Sheldon, Lemuel	ORN	390
Sheldon, Luther	DUT	49
Sheldon, Mary	DUT	144
Sheldon, Nathan	WSH	298
Sheldon, Nathl	OTS	28
Sheldon, Paul	HRK	555
Sheldon, Samuel	WSH	241
Sheldon, Stephen	RNS	101
Sheldon, Sylvia	DUT	49
Sheldon, Thomas	DUT	49
Sheldon, Thomas	ORN	357
Sheldon, William	DUT	135
Sheldon, William	ONT	396
Sheldon, Wm	RNS	59
Sheldon, William	RNS	84
Sheldon, William	RNS	108
Sheleigh, Jane	NYK	129
Shell see Schell		
Shell, Elizabeth	NYK	109
Shell, Frederick	SCH	124
Shell, George	ALB	131
Shell, Joseph	SCH	126
Shell, Peter	SCH	124
Shell, Philip	ALB	56
Shelley, Ebenezer	SRA	53
Shelley, Roswell	WSH	270
Shellman, Francis	KNG	8
Shellman, Geo.	OTS	45
Shellman, Geo. Junr	OTS	45
Shellman, John	KNG	11
Shellman, William	OTS	44
Shellock, Nathaniel	CHN	742
Shelly, Aaron	WSH	269
Shelly, Abraham	WSH	232
Shelly, Alexander Junr	WSH	194
Shelly, Benjamin	WST	114
Shelly, .eorge	WST	111
Shelly, Gilbert	WST	112
Shelly, Ira	WSH	289
Shelly, Joseph	WST	111
She[ll?]y, Phinehas	ONT	314
Shelly, Samuel	ALB	22
Shelly, Samuel	CHN	926
Shelmantine, Barent	SCH	138
Shelmantine, Henry	SCH	138
Shelmantine, John	SCH	138
Shelmantine, Richard	SCH	138
Shelnir, Christoph_	OTS	4
Shelton, Abijah	ALB	142
Shelton, William J.	RNS	85
Shely, Martin	SCH	165
Shemeway see Shumway		
Shemeway, Reuben	RNS	46
Shenmcall, Valentine	NYK	66
Shenaham, Aaron	HRK	480
Shenewood, David	SUF	90
Sheno, Jacob	COL	236
Shep, George	NYK	143
Shepard, Asa	OND	182
Shepard, David	SRA	40
Shepard, David	SRA	52
Shepard, Ezra	COL	182
Shepard, Ezra	OND	169
Shepard, Henry	DEL	282
Shepard, Israel	HRK	585
Shepard, Israel Jun	HRK	585
Shepard, James	COL	180
Shepard, Jared	OND	177
Shepard, John	HRK	486
Shepard, Josiah	HRK	434
Shepard, Lemuel	OND	182
Shepard, Manning	HRK	538
Shepard, Moses	OND	188
Shepard, Nicholas	COL	248
Shepard, Nicholas	COL	251
Shepard, Samuel	OND	168
Shephard, Gideon	OND	221
Shephard, Jonathan	CLN	166
Shephard, Morris	ONT	470
Shephard, Winthrope	OND	221
Shepheard, David	OND	206
Shepherd, Abel	CAY	692
Shepherd, Abraham	ORN	367
Shepherd, Alford	GRN	345
Shepherd, Barzelell	WSH	273
Shepherd, Caleb	WSH	267
Shepherd, Catherine	ALB	140
Shepherd, Charles	DUT	104
Shepherd, Colvill	ORN	368
Shepherd, Daniel	CAY	630
Shepherd, Daniel	RNS	9
Shepherd, Daniel	SRA	3
Shepherd, David	SRA	20
Shepherd, David Junr	SRA	20
Shepherd, Edward	WSH	295
Shepherd, Eli	CAY	654
Shepherd, Hazael	RNS	49
Shepherd, Israel	RNS	49
Shepherd, Jacob	CAY	596
Shepherd, Jacob	WSH	267
Shepherd, Jacob Junr	CAY	654
Shepherd, Jacob Senr	CAY	652
Shepherd, James	RNS	108
Shepherd, Jesse	ORN	369
Shepherd, John	DUT	104
Shepherd, John	ONN	163
Shepherd, John	ORN	368
Shepherd, John	WSH	295
Shepherd, John	WSH	295
Shepherd, Jonathan	CAY	572
Shepherd, Jonathan	DUT	137
Shepherd, Jonathan	ORN	327
Shepherd, Jonathan	RNS	9
Shepherd, Joseph	GRN	349
Shepherd, Joseph	ONN	163
Shepherd, Josiah	SCH	151
Shepherd, Lemuel	ALB	36
Sh_ph___, Peter	MNT	68
Shepherd, Rachel	SRA	3
Shepherd, Ralph	CLN	166
Shepherd, Theodore	ALB	4
Shepherd, Thomas	ALB	125
Shepherd, Thomas	NYK	35
Shepherd, Thomas	RNS	41
Shepherd, Timothy	TIO	216
Shepherd, Wm	MNT	61
Shepherd, Wm	MNT	62
Shepherd, William	SRA	3
Shepherd, William	SRA	18
Shepherd, Zebulon R.	WSH	272
Sheppard, Benjn	OTS	28
Sheppard, Edward	NYK	18
Sheppard, Elisha	OTS	28
Sheppard, Jabe	CHN	742
Sheppard, James	NYK	128
Sheppard, John	NYK	27
Sheppard, John	NYK	58
Sheppard, John Senior	NYK	58
Sheppard, Jonas	CHN	832
Sheppard, Jonas Junr	CHN	832
Sheppard, Phelomon	OTS	17

Sheppard, Rufus	CHN 848	Sherman, John	ULS 250	Sherwood, Andrw	NYK 100
Sheppard, Stephen	NYK 21	Sherman, Joseph	GRN 357	Sherwood, Asa	DUT 52
Sheppard, Theron	CHN 846	Sherman, Joshua	OND 200	Sherwood, Asa	ONN 185
Sheppard, William	CHN 834	Sherman, Josiah	DUT 47	Sherwood, Asahel	DUT 137
Sheppard, Wm	GRN 349	Sherman, Lemuel	HRK 473	Sherwood, Benjamin	NYK 114
Sheppards, Ezekiel	GRN 347	Sherman, Levi	OND 198	Sherwood, Benjamin	ULS 257
Shepperd, John	GRN 342	Sherman, Mishael	DUT 49	Sherwood, Benjamin	WST 170
Sheppey, Nathan	OTS 11	Sherman, Moses	HRK 597	Sherwood, Cacob L.	SRA 25
Sheppey, Seth	OTS 11	Sherman, Nathan	ESS 303	Sherwood, Caleb	WST 146
Sherbrooke, Miles	NYK 17	Sherman, Nathaniel	NYK 66	Sherwood, Daniel	ALB 24
Sherburn, John	SCH 122	Sherman, Nicholas	NYK 153	Sherwood, Daniel	ORN 286
Sherburne, James	CHN 810	Sherman, Nicholas	OND 198	Sherwood, Daniel	ORN 392
Sherburne, William	ALB 64	Sherman, Pardon	ALB 35	Sherwood, Daniel	ULS 193
Sherdall, James	NYK 95	Sherman, Paul	GRN 357	Sherwood, Daniel	WST 139
Sherdink, John	ULS 187	Sherman, Paul	ORN 279	Sherwood, David	NYK 147
Shere, Lewis	RNS 44	Sherman, Peter	CAY 548	Sherwood, David	RNS 49
Shere, Lodewick	RNS 35	Sherman, Phineas	OND 198	Sherwood, David	SUF 90
Shereman, Teley	WSH 248	Sherman, Polly	NYK 135	Sherwood, David	ULS 256
Sherer see Scherer		Sherman, Rachael	NYK 51	Sherwood, Gershom	WST 170
Sherer, Chrissey	NYK 127	Sherman, Rebecca	OND 198	Sherwood, Gilbert	COL 179
Sherer, Henry	NYK 124	Sherman, Saml	ALB 35	Sherwood, Henry	HRK 585
Sherlock, Thomas	RNS 110	Sherman, Samuel	HRK 473	Sherwood, Hezekiah	CAY 708
Sherman see Schureman		Sherman, Samuel	HRK 598	Sherwood, Hosias	MNT 56
& Shurman		Sherman, Samuel	ONN 169	Sherwood, Hull	OTS 54
Sherman	GRN 343	Sherman, Shadrach	DUT 48	Sherwood, Isaac	CAY 688
Sherman, Abel	DUT 134	Sherman, Silas	SRA 26	Sherwood, Isaac	DUT 151
Sherman, Abel	HRK 434	Sherman, Solomon	CAY 548	Sherwood, Isaac	NYK 105
Sherman, Abel	OND 198	Sherman, Solomon	OND 169	Sherwood, Isaac	RNS 50
Sherman, Abijah	DEL 269	Sherman, Stephen	SCH 160	Sherwood, Isaac	RCK 110
Sherman, Abner	ULS 258	Sherman, Thomas	OND 200	Sherwood, Isaac	WST 164
Sherman, Abraham	ALB 71	Sherman, Tisdale	SRA 29	Sherwood, James	DUT 79
Sherman, Adderijah	GRN 330	Sherman, Uriel	DUT 49	Sherwood, James	HRK 520
Sherman, Amos	OND 199	Sherman, Watts	OND 160	Sherwood, James	ORN 320
Sherman, Benjamin	DUT 49	Sherman, William	ALB 113	Sherwood, James	SRA 24
Sherman, Bildad	OND 166	Sherman, Willm	COL 212	Sherwood, Jasper	DUT 130
Sherman, Briggs	CAY 678	Sherman, William	NYK 153	Sherwood, Jehiel	DUT 175
Sherman, Briggs	SRA 60	Sherman, William	OND 199	Sherwood, Jeremiah	HRK 520
Sherman, Daniel	ONN 158	Sherman, William	OND 200	Sherwood, Jeremiah	WST 146
Sherman, David	ALB 35	Sherman, William	ONT 342	Sherwood, Job	WST 170
Sherman, David	ALB 65	Sherman, Wm	OTS 35	Sherwood, Jobe Junr	WST 170
Sherman, David	ONT 344	Sherman, Andrew	SRA 60	Sherwood, John	CAY 580
Sherman, Ebenezer	HRK 597	Sheron, Elizabeth	NYK 108	Sherwood, John	DUT 126
Sherman, Eber	OTS 30	Sherrad, Nathan	CAY 598	Sherwood, John	NYK 135
Sherman, Elisha	DEL 270	Sherrad, Stephen	CAY 530	Sherwood, John	RNS 50
Sherman, Elisha	SRA 53	Sherrard, Daniel	COL 179	Sherwood, John	RNS 74
Sherman, Enoch	ONT 462	Sherrard, Elijah	NYK 149	Sherwood, John	RNS 74
Sherman, Ezekiel	ONT 458	Sherrard, John	WST 146	Sherwood, John	ULS 190
Sherman, Ezra	DUT 46	Sherrard, Joseph	NYK 84	Sherwood, John	WST 170
Sherman, Frederick	ESS 303	Sherrard, Nehemh	OTS 30	Sherwood, Jonathan	ALB 113
Sherman, George	DEL 273	Sherrard, Recompence	SUF 106	Sherwood, Jonathan	HRK 585
Sherman, George	DUT 56	Sherrard, Samuel	RNS 81	Sherwood, Jonathan	WST 112
Sherman, Gideon	ONT 342	Sherred, Henry	CHN 762	Sherwood, Jonathan	WST 147
Sherman, Gilbert	MNT 12	Sherred, Isaac	CHN 768	Sherwood, Joseph	COL 238
Sherman, Hazard	OND 199	Sherred, Jacob	NYK 26	Sherwood, Joseph	DUT 171
Sherman, Henry	CAY 516	Sherred, Levy	CHN 768	Sherwood, Joseph	ULS 253
Sherman, Henry	NYK 137	Sherreff, Maria	NYK 141	Sherwood, Joseph	ULS 257
Sherman, Henry	OTS 44	Sherrels, Jonathan	GRN 356	Sherwood, Joshua	OND 163
Sherman, Howland	COL 217	Sherrey, Jeremiah	SUF 108	Sherwood, Joshua	RNS 47
Sherman, Hugh	DUT 132	Sherril, Jeremiah		Sherwood, Levy	RCK 110
Sherman, Humphrey	ONT 346	Junr	DUT 125	Sherwood, Moses	WST 147
Sherman, Isaac	QNS 30	Sherrill, Abraham	SUF 106	Sherwood, Moses	WST 170
Sherman, Jacob	NYK 66	Sherrill, Abraham		Sherwood, Nathan	ONN 183
Sherman, Jacob	ONT 454	Junr	SUF 106	Sherwood, Nehemiah	WST 138
Sherman, James	ONN 140	Sherrill, Jacob	SUF 106	Sherwood, Nehemiah	WST 164
Sherman, Jenkins(?)	ONN 167	Sherrill, Jeremiah	DUT 127	Sherwood, Oliver	WST 138
Sherman, Jeremiah	COL 217	Sherrill, Joanna	SUF 106	Sherwood, Richard	WST 125
Sherman, Jeremiah	DUT 102	Sherry, David	NYK 74	Sherwood, Samuel	DEL 290
Sherman, Jesse	DUT 51	Sherry, Seth	CLN 162	Sherwood, Samuel	ONN 142
Sherman, Jethro	DUT 49	Sherry, William	NYK 138	Sherwood, Saml	RNS 49
Sherman, Job	ALB 80	Sherwan, Joshua	ONT 320	Sherwood, Samuel	WST 125
Sherman, Job	OND 194	Sherwin, Elizabeth	NYK 126	Sherwood, Seth	CAY 646
Sherman, John	ESS 311	Sherwod, Seth N.	WSH 201	Sherwood, Seth	WSH 247
Sherman, John	GRN 343	Sherwod, William	SRA 57	Sherwood, Seymour	DUT 130
Sherman, John	NYK 153	Sherwood, Aaron	WST 170	Sherwood, Seymour	NYK 71
Sherman, John	OND 200	Sherwood, Abraham	WST 139	Sherwood, Shubel	SRA 53
Sherman, John	ONT 346	Sherwood, Aial	WSH 219	Sherwood, Solomon	ULS 190
Sherman, John	ONT 480	Sherwood, Amos	SRA 25	Sherwood, Solomon	WST 170

Sherwood, Solomon	WST 170	Shirter see Shurter		Shook, Peter	COL 237		
Sherwood, Solomon		Shirter, Frederick	ORN 273	Shook, Peter	DUT 151		
Junr	WST 170	Shirter, James	ULS 200	Shook, Wm	OTS 13		
Sherwood, Squire	COL 180	Shirtliff see Shurtliff		Shoop, Lodowick	ULS 193		
Sherwood, Stephen	COL 238	Shirtliff, David	HRK 592	Shoot see Schut & Shute			
Sherwood, Stephen	RNS 49	Shirtliff, James	HRK 577	Shoot, William	CLN 171		
Sherwood, Stephen	WST 155	Shirts, Andrew S.	COL 195	Shoote, Joseph	NYK 135		
Sherwood, Stephen	WST 164	Shirts, David	COL 197	Shoots, Elvaser	MNT 122		
Sherwood, Thomas	NYK 135	Shirts, Peter	COL 233	Shop, Henry	DUT 160		
Sherwood, Thomas	RNS 47	Shirtwell, David	SRA 53	Shop, Peter	DUT 162		
Sherwood, Thomas	ULS 235	Shirtz, Daniel	CAY 692	Shophire, Benjamin	MNT 87		
Sherwood, Thomas	WST 146	Shittirly, John	MNT 7	Shoppy, Reuben	CHN 766		
Sherwood, Thomas	WST 164	Shlack, Coonrod	CHN 978	Short, Abel	ONT 334		
Sherwood, Warren	OND 199	Shlack, John	CHN 978	Short, Adam	ULS 224		
Sherwood, William	DUT 16	Shlack, Joseph	CHN 978	Short, Amasa	OTS 9		
Sherwood, William	HRK 585	Shoe, Mary Ann	NYK 126	Short, Asa	TIO 237		
Sherwood, William	ORN 394	Shoecraft, Jacob	MNT 71	Short, David	ULS 192		
Sherwood, William	WST 170	Shoecraft, John	MNT 81	Short, Edward	ULS 193		
Sherwood, William	WST 170	Shoemaker, Abraham	NYK 72	Short, John	ORN 321		
Sherwood, Zadock	MNT 85	Shoemaker, Abm	SCH 137	Short, Martin	NYK 132		
Sherwood W., Phebe	WST 155	Shoemaker, Benjn	TIO 241	Short, Peter Junr	ULS 191		
She[ur?]man, Palmer	OND 212	Shoemaker, Catherine	HRK 431	Short, Peter Senr	ULS 192		
Shew, Eronumus	SCH 145	Shoemaker, Christopher	HRK 410	Short, Philip	ONT 328		
Shew, Godfrey	MNT 81	Shoemaker, Christopher	HRK 474	Short, Samuel	OTS 9		
Shew, Jacob	MNT 75	Shoemaker, Christopher		Short, Sarah	OTS 9		
Shew, Stephen	MNT 69	Senr	HRK 475	Short, Theophilus	ONT 416		
Shewin, Chanler	SRA 50	Shoemaker, Edward	NYK 73	Short, Zachariah	ULS 192		
Sheyland, John	WSH 197	Shoemaker, Frederick	HRK 474	Shorter, John	ORN 299		
Sheyland, John Junr	WSH 197	Shoemaker, Garret	CAY 572	Shott, George P.	WST 146		
Sheurt, Adolphus	RCK 105	Shoemaker, George	DUT 155	Shott, Seth	NYK 136		
Shibley, Jacob	RNS 56	Shoemaker, George	MNT 44	Shottencock, George	MNT 60		
Shickle, Richard	ONT 476	Shoemaker, Isaac	TIO 234	Shottenkirk, Daniel	MNT 58		
Shields, Alexander	NYK 136	Shoemaker, Jacob	DUT 157	Shottenkirk, Ebeneser	MNT 73		
Shields, Edward	NYK 76	Shoemaker, Jacob G.	DUT 155	Shottle, Mr	OND 223		
Shields, Henry	NYK 64	Shoemaker, Johannis	COL 235	Shotts, Bernard	NYK 126		
Shields, James	NYK 95	Shoemaker, John	COL 232	Shotwald, Peter	NYK 84		
Shields, John	CHN 864	Shoemaker, John	HRK 475	Shotwell, Abraham	NYK 61		
Shields, Partrick	NYK 58	Shoemaker, John	ONT 398	Shoudler, Aandrew	WSH 192		
Shields, Patrick	CHN 852	Shoemaker, John	SCH 145	Shoulte, Jacob	ALB 50		
Shields, William	NYK 136	Shoemaker, John Jun	HRK 475	Shoulters, Jacob	ALB 68		
Shier, William	SRA 44	Shoemaker, Jno Peter	COL 233	Shoultis see Shultus			
Shiff, Christian	MNT 24	Shoemaker, Joseph	ONT 426	Shoultis, Jacob	ALB 82		
Shill, Jacob	MNT 6	Shoemaker, Lawrence	HRK 474	Shoultis, John	ALB 72		
Shilling, Alexander	ALB 28	Shoemaker, Lodowic	RCK 106	Shoultis, Matthias	ALB 70		
Shillingford, James	NYK 120	Shoemaker, Nicholas	HRK 410	Shoultis, Wm	ALB 69		
Shimel, Richard	MNT 31	Shoemaker, Penelope	ORN 372	Shoults, Matice	ALB 42		
Shimer, Jacob	ORN 316	Shoemaker, Peter	ALB 90	Shourman, Coenradt	ALB 92		
Shindle, John C.	NYK 135	Shoemaker, Rudolph	HRK 431	Shourt, Oliver	NYK 144		
Shiner, Henery	SRA 55	Shoemaker, Rudolph	HRK 474	Shout(?), Emanuel	DEL 267		
Shiner, Richard	SRA 55	Shoemaker, Rudolph		Shouters, John	ALB 82		
Shinere, Ramo	NYK 88	Jun	HRK 431	Shouters, Matts T. Junr	ALB 70		
Shinneman see Schinaman		Shoemaker, Samuel	TIO 263	Shouts, Stephen W.	GRN 332		
Shinneman, John	RNS 82	Shoemaker, Thomas	HRK 410	Shoutts, John G.	ALB 57		
Shipboy, John	OTS 6	Shoemaker, Thomas	HRK 475	Shouty, John	ALB 59		
Shipe, Enoch	OND 206	Shoemaker, Thomas	HRK 496	Shove, Benjamin	DUT 173		
Shipham, Daniel	WSH 210	Shoemaker, Widow	HRK 431	Shove, Benjamin	SRA 56		
Shipherd, Ruphes	WSH 214	Shoence, John	OTS 40	Shove, Danl	OTS 6		
Shipley, Ann	DUT 117	Sholdes, Barent	COL 191	Shove, Edward	DUT 50		
Shipley, George	NYK 35	Sholdes, William	DEL 286	Shove, Eli	OTS 6		
Shipley, Peter	ONT 488	Shole, Jost	MNT 20	Shove, Joseph	DUT 50		
Shipman, David	OTS 13	Sholes, Eli A.	WSH 256	Shove, Saml N.	OTS 19		
Shipman, Edmond	OTS 43	Sholt, Christian	TIO 264	Show, Prudy	COL 208		
Shipman, Edward	SRA 33	Sholt, John	MNT 9	Shower, John	COL 235		
Shipman, George	OND 176	Sholtes, Jacob	WSH 198	Showerman, John	COL 197		
Shipman, Jonathan	SRA 33	Shomaker, Godfre	RNS 58	Showerman, John P.	COL 233		
Shipman, Sa_	OTS 13	Shomburg, Mary	NYK 85	Showers, George	ALB 78		
Shipman, William	NYK 54	Shonce, Christian	ORN 334	Showers, Jacob	ALB 78		
Shippey, Josiah	NYK 24	Shonnard, Frederick	NYK 145	Showers, John Junr	ULS 180		
Shippey, Paul	ALB 79	Shonnard, George	NYK 77	Showers, John Senr	ULS 180		
Shippey, Randal	RNS 20	Shonnard, Peter	NYK 77	Showers, William	ALB 89		
Shippy, Jesse	SRA 55	Shoock, William	SRA 41	Showl, Johanis	MNT 2		
Shippy, Josiah	NYK 27	Shook, Christian	RNS 84	Showl, Joseph	MNT 2		
Shira, George	STB 207	Shook, George Adam	DUT 156	Showles, Mary	NYK 49		
Shirale, Samuel	MNT 123	Shook, Hendrick	COL 242	Shradry, John	NYK 110		
Shirclock, John	SRA 45	Shook, Hendrick	DUT 156	Shraker, George	MNT 46		
Shire, Julius	NYK 86	Shook, Jacob	OTS 13	Shreve, Caleb	NYK 30		
Shirley, Alexander	DUT 138	Shook, Jeremiah	DUT 157	Shrieves, John	CLN 162		

331

Name	Ref		Name	Ref		Name	Ref
Shrippen, Mary	COL 212		Shunk, Nicholas	MNT 51		Sibley, Timothy	RNS 55
Shrives, Christopher	RNS 33		Shunmaker see Schoon-			Sice, Boneventure	NYK 31
Shru_, Abraham	MNT 25		maker			Sickel, Harmonas	GRN 356
Shrum, Isaac	MNT 2		Shunmaker, Cherubub	SCH 172		Sickels, Anna	NYK 25
Shrumb, Samuel	MNT 97		Shurd, Jacob	NYK 143		Sickels, Henry	NYK 112
Shu_d, Jonas	MNT 124		Shurl_ff, Joseph	ALB 4		Sickels, James	COL 263
Shuart, Adolph	ORN 293		Shurlott, Mr	GRN 331		Sickels, John	NYK 35
Shuart, Coonradt	ULS 260		Shurman see Sherman			Sickels, William	NYK 39
Shuart, Henry	ULS 260		Shurman, Stephen	MNT 89		Sickels, Zachariah	COL 262
Shuart, John	ULS 260		Shurragar, Simeon	ULS 207		Sicker, William	NYK 20
Shuart, John Junr	ULS 260		Shurt, Susannah	NYK 89		Sickle, Jacob	GRN 358
Shuban, Hannah	CHN 756		Shurter see Shirter			Sickler, George	DUT 11
Shubray, Danford	SRA 48		Shurter, Felix	SRA 48		Sickler, George	SRA 9
Shufe_, William	ONT 504		Shurtliff see Shirtliff			Sickler, Phillip	DUT 12
Shufellt, Peter	SRA 11		Shurtliff, Clark	MNT 58		Sickles, Abm	ALB 141
Shufelt, Adam	DUT 161		Shurtliff, Hezekiah	ALB 130		Sickles, Abraham Junr	ALB 143
Shufelt, Frederick	COL 198		Shurtliff, Richard	WSH 184		Sickles, Christopher	ALB 117
Shufelt, Frederick 2d	COL 199		Shurtrel, Felix	SRA 48		Sickles, Daniel	ALB 47
Shufelt, Henry	COL 192		Shute see Schut &			Sickles, Elias	NYK 131
Shufelt, Jerremiah	COL 180		Shoot			Sickles, Garret	CAY 518
Shufelt, Johannis	COL 197		Shute, Aaron	DUT 34		Sickles, Garret	COL 263
Shufelt, John	COL 196		Shute, Benjamin	DUT 38		Sickles, Garret	NYK 55
Shufelt, John	COL 263		Shute, Elisha	WST 148		Sickles, Garrit	COL 266
Shufelt, Meeche	COL 259		Shute, Ezekiel	DUT 27		Sickles, Henry	ALB 141
Shufelt, Peter	COL 228		Shute, Gilbert	WST 148		Sickles, Jacob	COL 266
Shufelt, Phillip	COL 192		Shute, Henry	NYK 86		Sickles, James	ALB 48
Shufelt, Phillip Junr	COL 197		Shute, Henry	NYK 107		Sickles, Johanis	RCK 100
Shul, Thadeus	MNT 120		Shute, John	COL 218		Sickles, Revd John	COL 264
Shulds, Catherine	NYK 97		Shute, John	WST 149		Sickles, John	NYK 112
Shuley, Martin	MNT 31		Shute, John	WST 170		Sickles, John	NYK 153
Shulph, John	ORN 302		Shute, Michael	DUT 34		Sickles, Jonathan	MNT 45
Shuls, John Jb	MNT 10		Shute, Peter	WST 149		Sickles, Lodowick	ALB 51
Shult, Caspares	WSH 250		Shute, Richard	WST 170		Sickles, Robert	RCK 100
Shult, Caspares C.	WSH 250		Shute, Thomas	WST 149		Sickles, Thomas	RNS 93
Shult, Casparus J.	COL 195		Shuter, Jacob	ALB 76		Sickles, William	ALB 118
Shult, Hendrick	COL 195		Shuter, Jacob	NYK 151		Sickles, William	DUT 64
Shult, Hendrick Junr	COL 195		Shuter, James	ALB 11		Sickles, Wm Esqr.	RCK 100
Shult, John	COL 195		Shuter, James	NYK 53		Sickles, Wm Junr	RCK 100
Shult, William J.	COL 195		Shuter, William	NYK 93		Sickles, Zachariah	RNS 83
Shult, William J.	COL 201		Shutes, Frederick	MNT 113		Sickles, Zachariah W.	MNT 51
Shultch, Casper	DEL 267		Shutes, Frederick Junr	MNT 113		Sickles, Zax W.	OTS 12
Shulters, George	ULS 193		Shutes, John	NYK 35		Sickles, Zecheriah	ALB 148
Shulters, Henry	ULS 193		Shutes, John J.	MNT 7		Sickner, Conrad	HRK 472
Shulters, Peter	ULS 207		Shutes, John P.	MNT 2		Sickner, Henry	CLN 155
Shulters, Phillip	ULS 193		Shutlief, Amasa	NYK 152		Sickner, Jost	HRK 471
Shultes, Bastian	COL 225		Shutlif, Lotrip	WSH 207		Sicknir, Elizabeth	HRK 471
Shults, Christopher	COL 237		Shuts, Henry S.	MNT 7		Sidell, John	ORN 314
Shults, Jacob	MNT 10		Shutter, Abraham	ALB 98		Sidell, Magdalen	NYK 25
Shults, James	MNT 17		Shutter, Michael	ALB 98		Sidistine, John a	
Shults, John	MNT 8		Shutts, Abraham A.			Black	NYK 104
Shultus see Shoultis			Junr	COL 240		Sidman, Catharine	ULS 257
Shultus, Aaron	COL 190		Shutts, Andrew	COL 230		Sidman, John	RCK 105
Shultus, Barent	COL 190		Shutts, Andrus Junr	COL 187		Sidman, Samuel	SRA 10
Shultus, Bastian B.	COL 191		Shutts, Anna	COL 240		Sidney see Sydney	
Shultus, James	RNS 83		Shutts, Coenradt	COL 193		Sidney, Henry	SCH 120
Shultus, John	COL 190		Shutts, Christian	COL 193		Sidney, Jacob	SCH 120
Shultus, John	COL 237		Shutts, Frederick	MNT 37		Sidney, Joseph S.	CAY 576
Shultus, Keller	RNS 26		Shutts, Gabriel	CAY 628		Sidney, Jost	SCH 120
Shultus, Martin	COL 257		Shutts, Hendrick	COL 200		Sidney, Peter	SCH 120
Shultus, Martinus Junr	COL 265		Shutts, Ian (or Jan)	COL 195		Sidney, William	SCH 126
Shultz	NYK 97		Shutts, John	COL 194		Sidway, James	GRN 326
Shultz, Christian	NYK 126		Shutts, John Junr	COL 189		Siebe, Henry	NYK 49
Shultz, Christian Junr	NYK 126		Shutts, John P.	COL 234		Sieckler, Peter	SRA 41
Shultz, Frederick	NYK 150		Shutts, Nehemiah	COL 179		Sielie, Robert	SCH 147
Shultz, John	NYK 21		Shutts, Peter	COL 234		Siemon, Levy	QNS 74
Shultz, John	NYK 110		Siah	QNS 81		Siemon, William H.	COL 236
Shuly, Abraham	MNT 73		Sibbolt, Henry	CAY 726		Sifer, Peter	CAY 606
Shumings, John	ALB 121		Sibel, Michael	ALB 74		Siglar, David	COL 244
Shumway see Shemeway			Sibell, John	NYK 82		Siglar, John	COL 244
Shumway, Abner	COL 206		Sible, Abner	OTS 43		Signer, Jacob	ULS 235
Shumway, Assa	WSH 268		Sible, Adam	MNT 36		Signer, Jacob Junr	DUT 155
Shumway, Isaac	DUT 145		Sible, Geo	OTS 40		Sikes see Sykes	
Shumway, Jeremiah	DUT 145		Sible, Jacob	MNT 37		Sikes, Daniel	CHN 912
Shumway, Nehemiah	ALB 25		Sible, Robert	MNT 35		Sikes, Francis	OTS 56
Shumway, Rufus	COL 206		Sibley, Asa	ESS 302		Sikes, John	HRK 458
Shun_ls, Nicholas	MNT 48		Sibley, Mary	NYK 35		Sikes, Livi	OTS 45
Shundle, Abraham	MNT 125		Sibley, Saml	RNS 10		Sikes, Nathan	WSH 266

Sipperlee, Henry	RNS	8	Skam, Jevy Jur	MNT	47	Skilman, Joseph	SUF	72
Sipperlee, Jacob	RNS	30	Skatts, Bhynier	NYK	26	Skilman, Thos	SUF	71
Sipperlee, Michael	RNS	87	Skatts, Elizabeth	NYK	89	Skilman, Thos	SUF	72
Sipperlee, Philip	RNS	35	Skatts, Elizabeth	NYK	96	Skinkle, Henry	COL	250
Sipperley, Anna Mary	DUT	158	Skatts, Jacob	NYK	92	Skinkle, Henry Junr	COL	199
Sipperley, Frederick	DUT	158	Skatts, Thomas	NYK	103	Skinkle, Henry J.	COL	192
Sipperley, Frederick I.	DUT	154	Skeel, Elijah	SCH	172	Skinkle, Jacob	COL	199
Sipperley, John	DUT	158	Skeel, Jonathan	ALB	88	Skinkle, John	COL	199
Sipperley, John	DUT	160	Skeel, Miran	SCH	165	Skinkle, Jonas	COL	199
Sipperly, Barent	COL	190	Skeel, Niram	SCH	165	Skinner see Scinner		
Sipperly, John	COL	190	Skeel, Saml	ALB	13	Skinner, Abraham	NYK	21
Sire, Michael	NYK	41	Skeels, Amos	ALB	27	Skinner, Adonijah	WSH	190
Siren, William	QNS	74	Skeels, Simon	ONN	158	Skinner, Appollus	ESS	295
Sirus	SUF	101	Skeirman, Neirman	MNT	48	Skinner, Benajah	ULS	187
Sirus	SUF	108	Skeles, Joseph	ESS	310	Skinner, Benjamin	SUF	81
Sisco, Elizer	ESS	312	Skellenger, Chrisr	ONN	176	Skinner, Beriah	ONN	177
Sisco, Henry	WSH	281	Skelley, Hugh	WSH	196	Skinner, Bird	ONT	396
Sisco, John	WSH	306	Skellinger, Silas	COL	187	Skinner, Caty	SRA	45
Sisco, Joseph	WSH	283	Skellorn, George W.	NYK	70	Skinner, Chauncey R.	DUT	143
Sisco, Richard	ALB	33	Skelly, Alexander	WSH	196	Skinner, Cotton	CAY	670
Sisco, Solomon	ALB	66	Skelly, John	WSH	196	Skinner, Cyrus	ORN	313
Sisson see Cissen			Skelly, William	WSH	259	Skinner, Daniel	CHN	796
Sisson, Arnold	DEL	282	Skelton, Lydice	NYK	73	Skinner, Daniel	ORN	311
Sisson, Arnold	OTS	25	Sketchley, Thomas	DUT	68	Skinner, David	MNT	119
Sisson, Beriah	DUT	100	Skiddy, John R.	NYK	31	Skinner, Eleazer	TIO	209
Sisson, Daniel	NYK	74	Skidgel, John	RCK	102	Skinner, Eliazer	WSH	191
Sisson, George	ALB	84	Skidmoore, William	KNG	9	Skinner, Elijah	SRA	25
Sisson, George	ONT	466	Skidmore see Scidmore			Skinner, Elisha	WSH	216
Sisson, Gideon	SRA	38	Skidmore, Abner	SRA	39	Skinner, Elizabeth	NYK	136
Sisson, Giles	OTS	26	Skidmore, Ammon	ULS	210	Skinner, Ephraim	OTS	17
Sisson, Humphrey	WSH	204	Skidmore, Andrew	DUT	11	Skinner, Gersham	HRK	499
Sisson, Jabez	ALB	85	Skidmore, Andrew Junr	DUT	58	Skinner, Gideon	OND	180
Sisson, James	DUT	163	Skidmore, David	SRA	40	Skinner, Gideon Junr	OND	169
Sisson, Job	ALB	85	Skidmore, David	SUF	84	Skinner, Hannah	DEL	287
Sisson, Job	DUT	103	Skidmore, Hezekiah	SUF	73	Skinner, Henry	SRA	32
Sisson, John	ALB	85	Skidmore, Isaac	SCH	133	Skinner, Isaac	CHN	850
Sisson, John Junr	OTS	25	Skidmore, Isaac	SUF	84	Skinner, Isaac	NYK	59
Sisson, John nr	OTS	26	Skidmore, James	DUT	11	Skinner, Israil	WSH	252
Sisson, Lemuel	DUT	101	Skidmore, Jeremiah	QNS	68	Skinner, Jacob	CHN	782
Sisson, Nathaniel	WSH	210	Skidmore, Joel	SUF	84	Skinner, Jacob	CHN	784
Sisson, Peleg	COL	183	Skidmore, John	NYK	42	Skinner, Jacob	ORN	313
Sisson, Preserved	NYK	117	Skidmore, John	QNS	65	Skinner, James	NYK	39
Sisson, Richard	OND	194	Skidmore, John	QNS	68	Skinner, James	SUF	68
Sisson, Saml	OTS	27	Skidmore, John	QNS	75	Skinner, Jared	ALB	135
Sisson, Samuel Jur	TIO	228	Skidmore, John Junr	SRA	45	Skinner, Jared	OTS	41
Sisson, Stephen	ONT	414	Skidmore, Joseph	QNS	69	Skinner, Jerusha	ULS	187
Sisson, Thomas	OND	191	Skidmore, Joseph	QNS	72	Skinner, Jesse	OTS	25
Sisson, Thomas	WSH	204	Skidmore, Lemuel	NYK	53	Skinner, John	SRA	52
Sisson, Uriah	SRA	38	Skidmore, Luther M.	OTS	21	Skinner, John	WSH	197
Sisson, Wilson	OTS	26	Skidmore, Michael	QNS	67	Skinner, John E.	SRA	47
Sissum, John	COL	224	Skidmore, Nathaniel	SUF	84	Skinner, Jonathan	CHN	858
Sitterley, Jacob	ALB	57	Skidmore, Peter	QNS	64	Skinner, Jonathan	ONN	138
Sittle, Henry	ALB	57	Skidmore, Peter	SUF	68	Skinner, Joseph	CHN	796
Sittle, Jacob H.	ALB	58	Skidmore, Richard	ORN	312	Skinner, Joseph	HRK	596
Sitts, George	MNT	32	Skidmore, Saml	QNS	75	Skinner, Josiah	ALB	84
Sitts, Henry	MNT	32	Skidmore, Saml	SUF	71	Skinner, Luther	WSH	275
Sitts, Jacob	MNT	32	Skidmore, Saml	SUF	84	Skinner, Matthew	DUT	111
Sitts, Peter	MNT	32	Skidmore, Thomas	SUF	84	Skinner, Michael	WSH	276
Sitts, Wm	RNS	54	Skidmore, Timothy	ORN	347	Skinner, Nathl S.	ALB	149
Sitz, Roeliff	ULS	216	Skidmore, Timothy	SUF	84	Skinner, Nathen	WSH	197
Sitzer, Frederick	COL	262	Skidmore, Walter	DUT	107	Skinner, Otis	HRK	507
Sitzer, Jacob	DUT	160	Skidmore, Walter	QNS	72	Skinner, Reuben	WSH	275
Sitzer, Martin	DUT	161	Skidmore, Whitehead	QNS	75	Skinner, Richard	WSH	288
Sixby, Abraham	ALB	112	Skidmore, Willett	QNS	65	Skinner, Saml	ALB	121
Sixby, Evert	ALB	107	Skidmore, Wm	SUF	68	Skinner, Solomon	WSH	264
Sixby, Nicholas	ALB	107	Skidmore, Woolcot	DUT	170	Skinner, Thomas	CAY	638
Sixby, Nicholas A.	ALB	57	Skidmore, Zapha	SRA	40	Skinner, Thomas	NYK	16
Sixsmith, Michael	DEL	284	Skiff, James	WSH	188	Skinner, Timothy	SRA	52
Sixsmith, William	DEL	284	Skiff, Joseph	OTS	11	Skinner, Uriah	CHN	790
Sixton, Daniel	OTS	21	Skiff, Stephen	NYK	114	Skinner, Wright	ALB	73
Sizen, Elizabeth	NYK	121	Skiff, Stephen	OTS	11	Skinner, William	OND	167
Sizer, Eli	OND	214	Skiffen, John Junr	COL	234	Skinner, Zacharias	ONN	171
Sizer, Lemuel	DUT	139	Skillen, Simeon	NYK	79	Skranton, Daniel	DEL	279
Sizer, Samuel	OND	214	Skillinger, Jacob	RNS	20	Skudder, Stephen	NYK	59
Ska, Jevy	MNT	44	Skillman see Shellman			Skuddy, Sarah	NYK	15
Skaats, Bartholemew	NYK	21	Skillman, Joseph	NYK	106	Slack, Benajah Junr	COL	222
Skaggs, George	SCH	163	Skillman, Joseph	NYK	126	Slack, Frederick	ALB	118

335

Slack, Israel	OND	165	Slawson, John	WST	160	Slipman, Peter a		
Slack, Joel	ORN	392	Slawson, Mary	DUT	133	Black	NYK	87
Slack, Roswell	COL	222	Slawson, Nathan	WST	160	Sliter, Adam	WSH	220
Slade, Basum	SRA	28	Slawson, Samuel	WST	161	Sliter, Clement	RNS	9
Slade, Obedeah	WSH	264	Slawson, Stephen	ALB	92	Sliter, Clement	RNS	14
Slade, William	COL	247	Slaygel, Margaret	NYK	127	Sliter, Derick	RNS	70
Slagle, Koonrod	WST	114	Slayton, Amasa	OND	184	Sliter, Henry	RNS	14
Slaid, James	ALB	81	Slayton, David	OND	184	Sliter, John	RNS	58
Slaid, John	ALB	81	Slayton, Lucy	OND	184	Sliter, Jonas	OTS	25
Slaid, Joseph	RNS	85	Slayton, Reuben	OTS	55	Sliter, Nicholas	OTS	25
Slaid, Philip	RNS	26	Slayton, Roswell	OND	184	Sliter, Nicholas	RNS	14
Slaigh, John	NYK	133	Slayton, Ruben	CHN	852	Sliter, Peter	OTS	25
Slaight see Sleght			Slayton, Washington	OTS	55	Sliter, Walter	TIO	226
Slaight, Abraham	RCH	88	Slee, Samuel	DUT	63	Sliter, Wm	RNS	14
Slaight, Bornt	RCH	94	Sleele see Steele			Sliter, Wm	RNS	58
Slaight, Bornt	RCH	95	Sleeper, Benjn H.	OTS	29	Slites, James	HRK	440
Slaight, Elenor	RCH	94	Sleeper, James	OTS	29	Slitts, James	RNS	44
Slaight, Henry	RCH	94	Sleeper, Joseph H.	OTS	29	Slitts, John	RNS	30
Slaight, Henry	RCH	94	Sleeper, Joseph L.	OTS	29	Slitts, John	RNS	44
Slaight, Jacob	RCH	94	Sleeper, Nehemh	OTS	29	Slo...., Jacob	MNT	106
Slaight, John	RCH	94	Sleeper, Saml	OTS	28	Sloag, Phil[ip?]	MNT	94
Slarer, Corn	NYK	15	Sleght see Slaight			Sloag, Samuel	MNT	93
Slarrow, Joseph	WSH	226	Sleght, Abraham	DUT	26	Sloakum, Jesse	SRA	9
Slarter, Mrs	GRN	325	Sleght, Benajah	DUT	94	Sloan see Slone & Slown		
Slason, Abrahan	DUT	85	Sleght, Daniel	DUT	108	Sloan, Alexander	HRK	563
Slason, David	ORN	319	Sleght, Daniel	DUT	113	Sloan, Alexr	OTS	4
Slason, Deliverance	ALB	78	Sleght, Daniel H.	DUT	113	Sloan, Alexander	WSH	296
Slason, Ebenezer	ALB	77	Sleght, Frederick	DUT	159	Sloan, Hannah	WSH	266
Slason, Eliphalet	ALB	93	Sleght, Henry	DUT	113	Sloan, Hugh	DEL	284
Slason, Jonathan	ORN	356	Sleght, Henry	ULS	228	Sloan, James	HRK	563
Slason, Nathan	ORN	336	Sleght, Henry Junr	DUT	113	Sloan, James	WSH	301
Slassen, James	ALB	110	Sleght, Henry B.	ULS	228	Sloan, John	ALB	55
Slasson, Ebenezer	ALB	27	Sleght, Jacob	DUT	113	Sloan, John	HRK	563
Slasson, Henry	RNS	93	Sleght, James	DUT	41	Sloan, John	OTS	3
Slat, Henry	SCH	124	Sleght, John	DUT	6	Sloan, John	WSH	244
Slate, Ebenezer	SRA	30	Sleght, John	DUT	32	Sloan, Peter	OND	211
Slate, Thomas	ONN	175	Sleght, Nathan	DUT	94	Sloan, Philip	HRK	564
Slater see Sleighter			Sleght, Peter	ULS	231	Sloan, Robert	OND	178
Slater, Duncan	ULS	250	Sleght, Solomon	ORN	280	Sloan, Sturgeon	COL	237
Slater, Isaac	ORN	307	Sleght, Teunis	ULS	229	Sloan, William	OND	164
Slater, James	DUT	52	Sleght, Tjiertie	ULS	227	Sloan, Wm	OTS	13
Slater, James	DUT	68	Sleght, Walter	DUT	108	Sloan, William	OTS	23
Slater, James	ORN	307	Sleght, William	DUT	94	Sloan, William	SCH	165
Slater, John	DUT	57	Sleight, Peleg	CAY	676	Sloane, Gerard S.	DUT	63
Slater, John	DUT	141	Sleight, Richard	NYK	142	Sloane, Thomas	ORN	293
Slater, John	GRN	332	Sleighter see Slater &			Slocam, Mathew	WSH	236
Slater, John	ORN	309	Sluyter			Slocem, Eliazer	WSH	238
Slater, John	ULS	253	Sleighter, Benjamin	CAY	524	Slocomb, John	RNS	47
Slater, Levi	ULS	200	Sleith, Anne	ORN	305	Slocomb, Peleg	RNS	32
Slater, William	NYK	77	Slepper, Joseph	NYK	114	Slocum, Abigail	DUT	57
Slater, William	ORN	290	Sleter, Ns	ALB	6	Slocum, Abraham	DUT	54
Slater, William	ORN	304	Slette_, Peter	MNT	9	Slocum, Benjamin	DUT	53
Slatley, John	WSH	231	Slicer, John	SUF	86	Slocum, Ebenezer	DEL	289
Slator, James	COL	251	Slidel, John	NYK	148	Slocum, Ele..or	MNT	83
Slator, Robert	ALB	11	Sledell, Elizabeth	NYK	93	Slocum, Elijah	WSH	186
Slatt, Wm	MNT	96	Slidell, John H.	NYK	89	Slocum, Fitzgerald	HRK	485
Slatterry, John	MNT	94	Slighter, Richard	HRK	455	Slocum, Fortunatus	WSH	190
Slatts, David	NYK	96	Slilmon, Noah	MNT	99	Slocum, George	DUT	53
Slaughter, Abner	ESS	317	Slingelandt, Peter	SRA	11	Slocum, George	ONN	139
Slaughter, Demsey a			Slingerland, Abraham	COL	261	Slocum, Gideon	DUT	53
free Negro	ALB	17	Slingerland, Albert	ALB	99	Slocum, Giles	SRA	42
Slaughter, Jonathan	CLN	170	Slingerland, Aurant	ALB	102	Slocum, John	OTS	36
Slaughter, William	WST	113	Slingerland, Aurant	ALB	108	Slocum, Jonas	HRK	427
Slauson, Peter	OND	212	Slingerland, Henry	ALB	99	Slocum, Joseph	MNT	82
Slauter, Mrss	GRN	326	Slingerland, Isaa Junr	ALB	108	Slocum, Lyman	DUT	57
Slauter, Patrick	OND	179	Slingerland, John	ALB	99	Slocum, Pardon	DUT	58
Slawsen, Joseph	WSH	236	Slingerland, John A.	ALB	99	Slocum, Peleg	DEL	289
Slawson, _wels	MNT	14	Slingerland, Rachel	ALB	97	Slocum, Peleg	SRA	57
Slawson, Amos	WST	158	Slingerland, Storm	ALB	102	Slocum, Rescum	HRK	591
Slawson, Eleazer Junr	WST	160	Slingerland, Teunis	ALB	99	Slocum, Samuel	DUT	10
Slawson, Elijah	HRK	520	Slingerland, Teunis	ALB	149	Slocum, Thos Senr	OTS	36
Slawson, Eliphalet	WST	160	Slingerland, Teunis			Sloddart see Stoddart		
Slawson, Elsey	WST	138	Jr	ALB	102	Sloet, Budd	DUT	87
Slawson, Enoch	TIO	246	Slingerland, Walter	ALB	102	Sloet, Cornelius	ORN	308
Slawson, Esther	WST	160	Slingerland, Walter	CHN	802	Sloet, David	ORN	303
Slawson, Isban	TIO	246	Slingerland, Walter W.	ALB	108	Sloet, David	ORN	305
Slawson, Jesse	WST	154	Slipe, Nicholas	RCK	108	Sloet, Elias	DUT	88

Name			Name			Name		
Smith, Alexander	QNS	78	Smith, Benjamen	WSH	270	Smith, Charles	RNS	56
Smith, Alexander	SUF	92	Smith, Benjamin	DUT	31	Smith, Charles	RNS	80
Smith, Allen	CLN	163	Smith, Benjamin	ESS	318	Smith, Charles	SUF	91
Smith, Allen(?)	GRN	344	Smith, Benjamin	MNT	73	Smith, Charles	WSH	285
Smith, Allwood	CAY	640	Smith, Benjamin	NYK	20	Smith, Charles F.	ORN	280
Smith, Alpheus	COL	249	Smith, Benjamin	NYK	90	Smith, Christeen Free		
Smith, Alpheus	SRA	51	Smith, Benjamin	NYK	131	Black	COL	197
Smith, Alvertson	ORN	279	Smith, Benjamin	OND	171	Smith, Christian	COL	196
Smith, Amasa	WSH	185	Smith, Benjamin	OND	206	Smith, Christian	COL	220
Smith, Amos	CAY	726	Smith, Benjamin	ONT	362	Smith, Christian	NYK	98
Smith, Amos	CHN	750	Smith, Benjamin	ORN	276	Smith, Christian	SCH	119
Smith, Amos	CHN	790	Smith, Benjamin	ORN	284	Smith, Christian Junr	RCH	91
Smith, Amos	COL	194	Smith, Benjamin	ORN	311	Smith, Chr..tion	MNT	30
Smith, Amos	COL	202	Smith, Benjamin	ORN	317	Smith, Christopher	QNS	66
Smith, Amos	HRK	440	Smith, Benjamin	ORN	328	Smith, Christopher	SRA	7
Smith, Amos	OND	175	Smith, Benjamin	ORN	335	Smith, Clark	HRK	584
Smith, Amos	OTS	17	Smith, Benjamin	QNS	68	Smith, Clark	ORN	389
Smith, Amos	SRA	29	Smith, Benjamin	QNS	68	Smith, Clark	ULS	262
Smith, Amos	SUF	82	Smith, Benjamin	QNS	71	Smith, Clausy	RCK	109
Smith, Anche Widow	QNS	76	Smith, Benjamin	QNS	74	Smith, Coe	ORN	333
Smith, Andrew	ALB	103	Smith, Benjamin	QNS	77	Smith, Coenradt	COL	220
Smith, Andrew	CAY	532	Smith, Benjamin	RNS	42	Smith, Collins	QNS	73
Smith, Andrew	MNT	36	Smith, Benjn	SUF	66	Smith, Comfort	OND	173
Smith, Andrew	NYK	27	Smith, Benjamin	TIO	216	Smith, Comfort A.	COL	210
Smith, Andrew	NYK	31	Smith, Benjamin	ULS	200	Smith, Conklin	ORN	313
Smith, Andrew	NYK	41	Smith, Benjamin	ULS	246	Smith, Coonrad	TIO	262
Smith, Andrew	RCK	106	Smith, Benjamin	WSH	185	Smith, Coonrod A.	RNS	59
Smith, Andrew	SRA	26	Smith, Benjamin	WSH	188	Smith, Corey	ONN	135
Smith, Andrew	STB	198	Smith, Benjamin	WSH	207	Smith, Cornelius	HRK	551
Smith, Andrew	WST	121	Smith, Benjamin	WST	115	Smith, Cornelius	MNT	65
Smith, Ann	ORN	296	Smith, Benjamin Junr	ORN	328	Smith, Cornelius	MNT	73
Smith, Ann	SUF	91	Smith, Benjamin Junr	RNS	76	Smith, Cornelius	NYK	60
Smith, Anna	NYK	69	Smith, Benjn Rock	QNS	71	Smith, Cornelius	RCK	100
Smith, Anna	NYK	73	Smith, Benjamine	GRN	341	Smith, Cornelius	RCK	110
Smith, Anna	NYK	86	Smith, Bennet	DUT	17	Smith, Cornelius Junr	RCK	100
Smith, Annanias	SUF	65	Smith, Bernard	DUT	158	Smith, Cornelius A.	RCK	98
Smith, Annanias	SUF	70	Smith, Bethiah	NYK	26	Smith, ...elius R.	MNT	78
Smith, Anning	ULS	267	Smith, Bethuel	WSH	195	Smith, Cornell	DEL	287
Smith, Anthony	NYK	148	Smith, Betsey	NYK	90	Smith, Curstin	GRN	354
Smith, Anthony	NYK	152	Smith, Bill	OND	212	Smith, Curtiss	ESS	294
Smith, Anthony	RNS	83	Smith, Boorham	NYK	75	Smith, Dan	OTS	21
Smith, Archibald	NYK	144	Smith, Brown	OTS	34	Smith, Dan:	SCH	172
Smith, Arnold	OND	206	Smith, Bulus	CHN	968	Smith, Daniel	CAY	716
Smith, Arthur	NYK	96	Smith, Caleb	ALB	117	Smith, Daniel	CHN	844
Smith, Arthur	ORN	271	Smith, Caleb	CHN	922	Smith, Daniel	COL	202
Smith, Asa	CAY	534	Smith, Caleb	DEL	278	Smith, Daniel	COL	241
Smith, Asa	CHN	786	Smith, Caleb	ESS	305	Smith, Daniel	DEL	290
Smith, Asa	CHN	878	Smith, Caleb	OND	175	Smith, Daniel	DUT	103
Smith, Asa	ORN	360	Smith, Caleb	OND	176	Smith, Daniel	DUT	111
Smith, Asa	OTS	31	Smith, Caleb	OND	182	Smith, Daniel	GRN	353
Smith, Asa	RNS	78	Smith, Caleb	OND	206	Smith, Daniel	HRK	439
Smith, Asa	SRA	31	Smith, Caleb	ORN	318	Smith, Daniel	HRK	600
Smith, Asa	TIO	209	Smith, Caleb	ORN	340	Smith, Daniel	NYK	25
Smith, Asa	WSH	204	Smith, Caleb	ORN	367	Smith, Daniel	NYK	111
Smith, Asa	WSH	207	Smith, Caleb	SUF	90	Smith, Daniel	NYK	131
Smith, Asa Junr	WSH	207	Smith, Caleb	TIO	257	Smith, Daniel	OND	165
Smith, Asahel	ULS	187	Smith, Caleb	WST	127	Smith, Daniel	OND	176
Smith, Asahel	WSH	206	Smith, Caleb	WST	146	Smith, Daniel	ORN	272
Smith, Ashbil	DEL	282	Smith, Caleb	WST	170	Smith, Daniel	ORN	280
Smith, Aury	RCK	104	Smith, Caleb Junr	WST	127	Smith, Daniel	ORN	312
Smith, Aury	RCK	106	Smith, Carmon	QNS	66	Smith, Daniel	ORN	345
Smith, Authur	CAY	648	Smith, Casparus	COL	190	Smith, Daniel	ORN	347
Smith, Azel	OND	165	Smith, Caty	QNS	77	Smith, Daniel	ORN	375
Smith, B. & Nathan			Smith, Charles	CHN	852	Smith, Daniel	ORN	383
Betts	RNS	90	Smith, Charles	DUT	35	Smith, Daniel	QNS	66
Smith, Babzer	MNT	19	Smith, Charles	MNT	94	Smith, Daniel	QNS	68
Smith, Barent	ALB	43	Smith, Charles	NYK	30	Smith, Daniel	QNS	74
Smith, Barnabas	WSH	185	Smith, Charles	NYK	35	Smith, Daniel	RNS	63
Smith, Barnabus	SUF	64	Smith, Charles	NYK	53	Smith, Daniel	RNS	75
Smith, Bartholemew	NYK	106	Smith, Charles	NYK	56	Smith, Daniel	RNS	108
Smith, Bastian	ORN	301	Smith, Charles	NYK	68	Smith, Danl	RCK	108
Smith, Ben.	RCK	105	Smith, Charles	NYK	80	Smith, Daniel	SRA	26
Smith, Ben	RCK	108	Smith, Charles	NYK	92	Smith, Danl	SUF	70
Smith, Benajah	DUT	55	Smith, Charles	ONT	354	Smith, Daniel	SUF	91
Smith, Benajah	DUT	147	Smith, Charles	ORN	338	Smith, Daniel	SUF	92
Smith, Benajah	MNT	125	Smith, Charles	ORN	370	Smith, Daniel	WSH	237
Smith, Benjamen	WSH	270	Smith, Charles	OTS	21	Smith, Daniel	WST	112

Smith, Daniel	WST	127	Smith, Edmund	NYK	48	Smith, Enoch	HRK	489
Smith, Daniel Junr	QNS	68	Smith, Edward	DUT	91	Smith, E...h	TIO	234
Smith, Danl Jr	SUF	67	Smith, Edward	NYK	68	Smith, Enoch	ULS	196
Smith, Danl Sr	SUF	67	Smith, [Edw?]ard	ONT	444	Smith, Enos	DUT	13
Smith, Darius	CAY	716	Smith, Edward	ORN	333	Smith, Enos	ORN	343
Smith, Darius	HRK	477	Smith, Edward	OTS	53	Smith, Enos	OTS	21
Smith, David	ALB	36	Smith, Edward	RCK	105	Smith, Enos	SUF	84
Smith, David	ALB	77	Smith, Edward Junr	DUT	55	Smith, Epenetus	NYK	78
Smith, David	CAY	574	Smith, Edward Junr	RCK	108	Smith, Epharim	SRA	60
Smith, David	CAY	712	Smith, Eldad	OND	208	Smith, Ephraim	DUT	136
Smith, David	CAY	722	Smith, Elead	WSH	276	Smith, Ephraim	OND	178
Smith, David	CHN	838	Smith, Eleana	KNG	8	Smith, Ephraim	OND	184
Smith, David	CHN	920	Smith, Eleazar	TIO	247	Smith, Ephraim	RNS	112
Smith, David	COL	206	Smith, Eleazer	CHN	772	Smith, Ephraim	SRA	28
Smith, David	COL	229	Smith, Eleazer	OND	212	Smith, Ephraim	ULS	183
Smith, David	DEL	267	Smith, Eleazer	RNS	9	Smith, Ephraim	ULS	187
Smith, David	DEL	277	Smith, Eleazer	SRA	29	Smith, Ephraim	WSH	268
Smith, David	DEL	279	Smith, Eleazer	WSH	264	Smith, Ephram	CHN	852
Smith, David	DUT	88	Smith, Eleazer	WSH	303	Smith, Ephrim	SUF	65
Smith, David	DUT	102	Smith, Eleazer Junr	WSH	274	Smith, Epinetus	SUF	84
Smith, David	DUT	140	Smith, Elephalet	SUF	91	Smith, Epinetus	SUF	85
Smith, David	HRK	564	Smith, Elephlat	DEL	281	Smith, Epinetus	SUF	92
Smith, David	KNG	9	Smith, Eli	SRA	29	Smith, Excuse	WSH	295
Smith, David	NYK	20	Smith, Eliakim	SUF	88	Smith, Ezekiel	COL	177
Smith, David	NYK	75	Smith, Elias	ALB	51	Smith, Ezekiel	HRK	539
Smith, David	OND	206	Smith, Elias	COL	201	Smith, Ezekiel	NYK	59
Smith, David	ONT	498	Smith, Elias	SRA	25	Smith, Ezekiel	QNS	68
Smith, David	ORN	281	Smith, Elias	SUF	89	Smith, Ezekiel	RNS	25
Smith, David	ORN	309	Smith, Elias	WSH	269	Smith, Ezekiel	SRA	20
Smith, David	QNS	77	Smith, Elias P.	COL	230	Smith, Ezekiel	WSH	278
Smith, David	RCK	99	Smith, Elihu	RCK	109	Smith, Ezra	ALB	21
Smith, David	SUF	70	Smith, Elihu	SRA	30	Smith, Ezra	ALB	71
Smith, David	SUF	89	Smith, Elijah	DUT	135	Smith, Ezra	ORN	370
Smith, David	SUF	92	Smith, Elijah	DUT	136	Smith, Ezra	OTS	36
Smith, David	SUF	100	Smith, Elijah	ESS	296	Smith, Ezra	TIO	235
Smith, David	SUF	104	Smith, Elijah	GRN	344	Smith, Fanny	NYK	76
Smith, David	ULS	187	Smith, Elijah	HRK	439	Smith, Felter	ULS	203
Smith, David	WSH	207	Smith, Elijah	HRK	479	Smith, Fordham	SUF	91
Smith, David	WST	125	Smith, Elijah	MNT	39	Smith, Fortuno a Black	NYK	134
Smith, David	WST	126	Smith, Elijah	OTS	26			
Smith, David J.	COL	235	Smith, Elijah	SRA	20	Smith, Fraderick	RCK	108
Smith, David R.	QNS	78	Smith, Elijah	TIO	227	Smith, Francis	ORN	271
Smith, David V.	NYK	46	Smith, Elijah	WSH	201	Smith, Francis	RNS	40
Smith, David W.	ONT	496	Smith, Elijah	WSH	206	Smith, Frederick	COL	243
Smith, Davis	RNS	81	Smith, Elijah	WST	127	Smith, Frederick	DEL	287
Smith, Deliverance	COL	183	Smith, El_halb	WSH	186	Smith, Frederick	GRN	327
Smith, Deniston	ALB	91	Smith, Eliphalet	SUF	82	Smith, Frederick	HRK	436
Smith, Dennis	RNS	29	Smith, Eliphalet	SUF	85	Smith, Frederick	ORN	272
Smith, Denton	WST	127	Smith, Eliphalet	ULS	262	Smith, Frederick	ORN	310
Smith, Derick	COL	214	Smith, Elish	GRN	352	Smith, Frederick	QNS	76
Smith, Derick	WSH	272	Smith, Elisha	CAY	624	Smith, Frederick	RNS	64
Smith, Doctor	WST	154	Smith, Elisha	CHN	782	Smith, Frederick	SRA	52
Smith, Dolly	ALB	63	Smith, Elisha	CHN	788	Smith, Gabriel	SRA	20
Smith, Dudley	HRK	553	Smith, Elisha	CHN	884	Smith, Gabriel	WST	141
Smith, Dudley	SRA	24	Smith, Elisha	CHN	990	Smith, Gabriel Junr	DUT	31
Smith, Dunkin	WST	164	Smith, Elisha	DUT	88	Smith, Gabriel Junr	WST	138
Smith, Easther	WSH	222	Smith, Elisha	DUT	144	Smith, Gabriel 3rd	WST	136
Smith, Eaton	ORN	311	Smith, Elisha	ORN	325	Smith, Gager	OND	165
Smith, Ebenezar	CAY	678	Smith, Elisha	ORN	370	Smith, Gamalion	NYK	51
Smith, Ebenezar	CAY	712	Smith, Elisha	OTS	21	Smith, Gardener	NYK	18
Smith, Ebenezar	CAY	716	Smith, Elisha	SRA	38	Smith, Garret	RCK	97
Smith, Ebenezar	SUF	88	Smith, Elisha	SRA	57	Smith, Garret	RCK	98
Smith, Ebenezar H.	SUF	79	Smith, Elisha	ULS	186	Smith, Garret	RCK	106
Smith, Ebenezer	ALB	65	Smith, Elisha	WSH	220	Smith, Garret	RCK	107
Smith, Ebenezer	ALB	139	Smith, Elisha	WSH	224	Smith, Garret	RCK	107
Smith, Ebenezer	DEL	287	Smith, Elisha	WSH	286	Smith, George	HRK	435
Smith, Ebenezer	HRK	415	Smith, Elisha M.	CHN	788	Smith, George	HRK	444
Smith, Ebenezer	NYK	32	Smith, Elishua	SRA	60	Smith, George	NYK	41
Smith, Ebenezer	NYK	79	Smith, Eliza	RCK	103	Smith, George	NYK	84
Smith, Ebenezer	NYK	105	Smith, Elizabeth	QNS	77	Smith, George	NYK	128
Smith, Ebenezer	SRA	29	Smith, Elkanah	NYK	83	Smith, George	ONN	165
Smith, Ebenr	SUF	67	Smith, Elkanah Junr	RNS	74	Smith, George	ORN	346
Smith, Ebenr	TIO	229	Smith, Elknah	RNS	74	Smith, George	RCK	106
Smith, Ebenezer	WSH	293	Smith, Ellihu	GRN	339	Smith, George	SUF	64
Smith, Ebenezer	WSH	306	Smith, Ellis	COL	191	Smith, George	ULS	189
Smith, Edmond	QNS	76	Smith, Elnathan	SRA	29	Smith, George	ULS	246
Smith, Edmond Junr	QNS	76				Smith, George Junr	MNT	19

Name	Ref	No.
Smith, George Senr	HRK	444
Smith, George A.	COL	199
Smith, George B.	NYK	64
Smith, George C.	COL	199
Smith, George P.	COL	257
Smith, Gersham	SUF	91
Smith, Gershom	RCK	108
Smith, Gideon	DUT	102
Smith, Gideon	SUF	82
Smith, Gilbert	NYK	22
Smith, Gilbert	OTS	42
Smith, Gilbert	SUF	85
Smith, Gilbert	SUF	88
Smith, Gilbert Junr	ORN	383
Smith, Gilbirt H.	SUF	79
Smith, Gravill	NYK	135
Smith, Gergory	GRN	351
Smith, Griffin	CHN	764
Smith, Grover	CAY	564
Smith, Gurdon	OND	211
Smith, Gurdon	OTS	7
Smith, Gurdon	WSH	264
Smith, Guy	ORN	386
Smith, Hannah	NYK	90
Smith, Hannah	RCK	103
Smith, Han Tice	DUT	145
Smith, Haviland	NYK	80
Smith, Haviland	QNS	77
Smith, Hazael	DUT	101
Smith, Hazard	KNG	9
Smith, Helmas	RNS	85
Smith, Hendrick	COL	225
Smith, Hendrick	TIO	215
Smith, Hendrick	ULS	204
Smith, Hendrick J.	TIO	215
Smith, Henry	ALB	100
Smith, Henry	CAY	592
Smith, Henry	CAY	606
Smith, Henry & Jno	COL	190
Smith, Henry	COL	242
Smith, Henry	COL	257
Smith, Henry	DUT	15
Smith, Henry	DUT	63
Smith, Henry	DUT	163
Smith, Henry	DUT	173
Smith, Henry	HRK	575
Smith, Henry	MNT	2
Smith, Henry	MNT	3
Smith, Henry	MNT	18
Smith, Henry	MNT	25
Smith, Henry	MNT	106
Smith, Henry	NYK	60
Smith, Henry	NYK	75
Smith, Henry	NYK	100
Smith, Henry	NYK	124
Smith, Henry	ORN	301
Smith, Henry	ORN	310
Smith, Henry	ORN	346
Smith, Henry	RNS	87
Smith, Henry	SRA	3
Smith, Heny	SUF	66
Smith, Heny	SUF	67
Smith, Henry	SUF	85
Smith, Henry	SUF	88
Smith, Henry	SUF	92
Smith, Henry	SUF	93
Smith, Henry	SUF	97
Smith, Henry	ULS	190
Smith, Henry	WSH	185
Smith, Henry	WSH	250
Smith, Henry C.	COL	215
Smith, Henry J.	COL	265
Smith, Henry M.	MNT	24
Smith, Henry P.	COL	198
Smith, Henry P.	COL	230
Smith, Henry T.	RNS	58
Smith, Hertimus	ALB	55
Smith, Hester	NYK	71
Smith, Hezekh	OTS	10
Smith, Hezekiah	SUF	85
Smith, Hezekiah	ULS	254
Smith, Hezekiah	WSH	189
Smith, Holleab	WSH	270
Smith, Holmes	WSH	295
Smith, Hophni	ORN	386
Smith, Hosea	OND	192
Smith, Howel	WSH	275
Smith, Hubbard	DEL	287
Smith, Hugh	OTS	38
Smith, Humphrey	ONT	350
Smith, Humphrey	WSH	203
Smith, Humphrey Jun.	ONT	350
Smith, Icabod	SUF	88
Smith, Icabode	WSH	215
Smith, Ira	TIO	226
Smith, Isaac	ALB	23
Smith, Isaac	DUT	20
Smith, Isaac	DUT	40
Smith, Isaac	DUT	141
Smith, Isaac	DUT	146
Smith, Isaac	HRK	439
Smith, Isaac	OND	194
Smith, Isaac	ORN	364
Smith, Isaac	ORN	370
Smith, Isaac	OTS	53
Smith, Isaac	OTS	53
Smith, Isaac	QNS	72
Smith, Isaac	QNS	77
Smith, Isaac	RNS	41
Smith, Isaac	RCK	98
Smith, Isaac	RCK	105
Smith, Isaac	SRA	26
Smith, Isaac	SCH	135
Smith, Isaac	SUF	65
Smith, Isaac	SUF	66
Smith, Isaac	SUF	66
Smith, Isaac	SUF	67
Smith, Isaac	SUF	67
Smith, Isaac	SUF	70
Smith, Isaac	SUF	84
Smith, Isaac	SUF	90
Smith, Isaac	SUF	91
Smith, Isaac	WST	130
Smith, Isaac	WST	139
Smith, Isaac	WST	170
Smith, Isaac B.	COL	242
Smith, Isaac M.	DUT	118
Smith, Isaiah	ORN	355
Smith, Isaiah	ORN	392
Smith, Israel	CHN	758
Smith, Israel	COL	249
Smith, Israel	DUT	125
Smith, Israel	QNS	75
Smith, Israel	QNS	77
Smith, Israel	SUF	66
Smith, Israel	SUF	82
Smith, Israel	SUF	84
Smith, Israel Junr	CHN	758
Smith, Israiel	CHN	886
Smith, Isreal	CAY	702
Smith, J___	CAY	598
Smith, Ja___	CAY	560
Smith, Jabez	ALB	36
Smith, Jabez whiteman	SRA	29
Smith, Jabez	SCH	141
Smith, Jacob	CAY	636
Smith, Jacob	CLN	167
Smith, Jacob	COL	260
Smith, Jacob	DUT	55
Smith, Jacob	DUT	66
Smith, Jacob	DUT	121
Smith, Jacob	HRK	445
Smit., Jacob	MNT	94
Smith, Jacob	NYK	37
Smith, Jacob	NYK	39
Smith, Jacob	NYK	62
Smith, Jacob	NYK	117
Smith, Jacob	NYK	117
Smith, Jacob	NYK	141
Smith, Jacob	ONN	138
Smith, Jacob	ONT	436
Smith, Jacob	OTS	39
Smith, Jacob	OTS	52
Smith, Jacob	QNS	66
Smith, Jacob	QNS	72
Smith, Jacob	QNS	77
Smith, Jacob	QNS	80
Smith, Jacob	RNS	6
Smith, Jacob	RNS	7
Smith, Jacob	RNS	84
Smith, Jacob	RCK	103
Smith, Jacob	SRA	8
Smith, Jacob	SUF	79
Smith, Jacob	SUF	84
Smith, Jacob	SUF	84
Smith, Jacob	SUF	92
Smith, Jacob	ULS	246
Smith, Jacob	WST	122
Smith, Jacob Junior	NYK	37
Smith, Jacob Junr	WST	126
Smith, Jacob A.	COL	231
Smith, Jacob D.	ORN	302
Smith, Jacob H.	SUF	79
Smith, Jacob J.	COL	222
Smith, Jacob P.	COL	265
Smith, Jacobus	ORN	308
Smith, Jacobus	RCK	100
Smith, Jacobus	ULS	203
Smith, Jahael	RNS	32
Smith, James	ALB	71
Smith, James	CAY	606
Smith, James	CAY	626
Smith, James	CAY	654
Smith, James	CHN	784
Smith, James	CHN	788
Smith, James	CHN	964
Smith, James	CLN	163
Smith, James	COL	241
Smith, James	DEL	274
Smith, James	DEL	287
Smith, James	DEL	290
Smith, James	DUT	13
Smith, James	DUT	20
Smith, James	DUT	31
Smith, James	DUT	108
Smith, James	HRK	441
Smith, James	HRK	526
Smith, James	HRK	537
Smith, James	NYK	22
Smith, James a Black	NYK	43
Smith, James	NYK	51
Smith, James	NYK	57
Smith, James a mulatto	NYK	88
Smith, James	NYK	102
Smith, James	NYK	106
Smith, James(?)	NYK	116
Smith, James	NYK	129
Smith, James	NYK	131
Smith, James	OND	173
Smith, James	OND	181
Smith, James	OND	198
Smith, James	OND	206
Smith, James	OND	212
Smith, James	ORN	285
Smith, James	ORN	288
Smith, James	ORN	296
Smith, James	ORN	349
Smith, James	ORN	379
Smith, James	ORN	385
Smith, James	OTS	21

Name		Name		Name	
Smith, James	OTS 53	Smith, Job[e?]	GRN 332	Smith, John	ONT 460
Smith, James	QNS 65	Smith, Joel	DUT 102	Smith, John	ONT 490
Smith, James	QNS 66	Smith, Joel	ORN 357	Smith, John	ORN 273
Smith, James	QNS 67	Smith, Joel	SUF 88	Smith, John	ORN 295
Smith, James	QNS 69	.mith, Joel	TIO 234	Smith, John	ORN 311
Smith, James	RCK 109	Smith, Joel	ULS 182	Smith, John	ORN 320
Smith, James	SRA 8	Smith, Johannis	DUT 156	Smith, John	ORN 336
Smith, James	SCH 172	Smith, Johannis	ORN 297	Smith, John	ORN 339
Smith, James	SUF 66	Smith, Johannis	ULS 218	Smith, John	ORN 346
Smith, James	SUF 66	Smith, Johans H.	COL 225	Smith, John	ORN 361
Smith, James	SUF 67	Smith, John	ALB 17	Smith, John	ORN 386
Smith, James	SUF 67	Smith, John	ALB 55	Smith, John	OTS 6
Smith, James	SUF 70	Smith, John	ALB 104	Smith, John	OTS 26
Smith, James	SUF 88	Smith, John	ALB 116	Smith, John	OTS 52
Smith, James	SUF 89	Smith, John	ALB 128	Smith, John	QNS 66
Smith, James	SUF 92	Smith, John	ALB 133	Smith, John	QNS 67
Smith, James	TIO 240	Smith, John	CAY 562	Smith, John	QNS 67
Smith, James	TIO 242	Smith, John	CAY 584	Smith, John	QNS 68
Smith, James	WSH 200	Smith, John	CAY 588	Smith, John	RNS 13
Smith, James	WSH 208	Smith, John	CAY 596	Smith, John	RNS 34
Smith, James	WSH 239	Smith, John	CAY 636	Smith, John	RNS 60
Smith, James Jun	CHN 780	Smith, John	CHN 740	Smith, John	RNS 86
Smith, James Junr	DEL 287	Smith, John	CHN 944	Smith, John	RNS 111
.mith, James Junr	MNT 55	Smith, John	CLN 163	Smith, John	RCK 102
Smith, James Junr	OND 198	Smith, John	COL 194	Smith, John	RCK 106
Smith, James A.	NYK 65	Smith, John	COL 203	Smith, John	RCK 107
Smith, James M.	WST 128	Smith, John	COL 218	Smith, John	RCK 108
Smith, James P.	DUT 136	Smith, John	COL 225	Smith, John	RCK 108
Smith, James R.	NYK 38	Smith, John	COL 231	Smith, John	RCK 110
Smith, James R.	QNS 74	Smith, John	COL 259	Smith, John	SRA 6
Smith, James S. Esqr	RCK 103	Smith, John	DEL 269	Smith, John	SRA 20
Smith, Jane a free		Smith, John	DUT 28	Smith, John	SRA 20
wench	ALB 138	Smith, John	DUT 82	Smith, John	SRA 22
Smith, Jane	NYK 30	Smith, John	DUT 91	Smith, John	SRA 50
Smith, Jane	NYK 94	Smith, John	DUT 103	Smith, John	SRA 61
Smith, Jared	ALB 93	Smith, John	DUT 130	Smith, John	SCH 121
Smith, Jared	HRK 598	Smith, John	DUT 146	Smith, John	SCH 144
Smith, Jared	ONN 159	Smith, John	DUT 152	Smith, John	SCH 156
Smith, Jarvis	OTS 11	Smith, John	ESS 323	Smith, John	SCH 172
Smith, Jeddediah	SUF 91	Smith, John	GRN 352	Smith, John	SUF 65
Smith, Jedediah	CHN 758	Smith, John	HRK 516	Smith, John	SUF 66
Smith, Jedediah	OND 168	Smith, John	HRK 593	Smith, John	SUF 66
Smith, Jedidh	OTS 16	Smith, John	KNG 10	Smith, John	SUF 70
Smith, Jedh	OTS 17	Smith, John	MNT 27	Smith, John	SUF 91
Smith, Jeffery	QNS 67	Smith, John	MNT 34	Smith, John	SUF 97
Smith, Jeffery	SUF 89	Smith, John	MNT 39	Smith, John	TIO 236
Smith, Jeremiah	DEL 283	Smith, John	NYK 15	Smith, John	TIO 241
Smith, Jeremiah	DUT 109	Smith, John	NYK 39	Smith, John	TIO 245
Smith, Jeremiah	ESS 297	Smith, John	NYK 40	Smith, John	TIO 263
Smith, Jeremiah	GRN 326	Smith, John	NYK 41	Smith, John	ULS 200
Smith, Jeremiah	HRK 595	Smith, John	NYK 43	Smith, John	WSH 230
Smith, Jeremiah	MNT 106	Smith, John	NYK 58	Smith, John	WSH 238
Smith, Jeremiah	NYK 99	Smith, John	NYK 59	Smith, John	WSH 259
Smith, Jeremiah	ONT 354	Smith, John	NYK 74	Smith, John	WSH 268
Smith, Jeremiah	ORN 340	Smith, John	NYK 84	Smith, John	WSH 280
Smith, Jeremiah	RNS 84	Smith, John	NYK 87	Smith, John	WST 113
Smith, Jeremiah	SRA 23	Smith, John	NYK 113	Smith, John	WST 130
Smith, Jeremiah	WST 147	Smith, John	NYK 117	Smith, John	WST 131
Smith, Jeremiah N.	MNT 18	Smith, John	NYK 128	Smith, John	WST 158
Smith, Jeremy	HRK 594	Smith, John	NYK 130	Smith, John Junr	ALB 63
Smith, Jerod	GRN 342	Smith, John Junr	NYK 132	Smith, John Junr	CAY 636
Smith, Jerremiah	CHN 990	Smith, John Junr	NYK 133	Smith, John Junr	COL 203
Smith, Jesee	SUF 65	Smith, John Junr	NYK 133	Smith, John Junr	WSH 223
Smith, Jesse	DUT 112	Smith, John Senr	NYK 134	Smith, John Senr	ALB 63
Smith, Jesse	OND 205	Smith, John	NYK 139	Smith, John ye 2d	DUT 104
Smith, Jesse	ORN 357	Smith, John ye 2d	NYK 142	Smith, John ye 2d	SCH 148
Smith, Jesse	SRA 14	Smith, John ye 2d	NYK 142	Smith, John	CAY 556
Smith, Jesse	TIO 230	Smith, John	NYK 151	Smith, John A.	COL 239
Smith, Jesse	WST 141	Smith, John A.	OND 160	Smith, John A.	NYK 92
Smith, Jesse Junr	SRA 14	Smith, John A.	OND 206	Smith, John A.	RCK 105
Smith, Jessee	SUF 81	Smith, John C.	OND 211	Smith, John C.	SCH 172
Smith, Jessee	SUF 91	Smith, John C.(?)	OND 224	Smith, John C.(?)	TIO 264
Smith, Jessee H.	SUF 79	Smith, John F.	ONN 166	Smith, John F.	RCK 109
Smith, Jirah	CLN 159	Smith, John G.	ONT 310	Smith, John G.	RCK 104
Smith, Joab	OND 212	Smith, John G.	ONT 322	Smith, John G.	ULS 251
Smith, Job	COL 249	Smith, John H.	ONT 322	Smith, John H.	NYK 53
Smith, Job	WST 154	Smith, John H.	ONT 414	Smith, John H.	QNS 64

Name	Loc	No	Name	Loc	No	Name	Loc	No
Smith, John H.	SUF	79	Smith, Joseph	SRA	41	Smith, Margaret	MNT	31
Smith, John H.	SUF	79	Smith, Joseph	SUF	90	Smith, Margaret	NYK	73
Smith, John J.	COL	233	Smith, Joseph	ULS	200	Smith, Maria	NYK	58
Smith, John J.	OTS	38	Smith, Joseph	WSH	293	Smith, Martha	ORN	283
Smith, John J.	SRA	11	Smith, Joseph Junr	ORN	371	Smith, Martha	RCK	106
Smith, John K.	COL	233	Smith, Joseph Junr	ORN	394	Smith, Mar_in	ALB	63
Smith, John L.	WSH	205	Smith, Joseph B.	SRA	7	Smith, Martin	DUT	23
Smith, John M.	COL	200	Smith, Joseph J.	SRA	8	Smith, Martin	NYK	151
Smith, John M.	HRK	435	Smith, Joshua	CAY	612	Smith, Martinus	RNS	14
Smith, John M.	MNT	24	Smith, Joshua	CHN	846	Smith, Mary	DUT	66
Smith, John M.	NYK	32	Smith, Joshua	DUT	27	Smith, Mary	NYK	75
Smith, John M.	QNS	70	Smith, Joshua	GRN	354	Smith, Mary	NYK	103
Smith, John M.	ULS	262	Smith, Joshua	NYK	144	Smith, Mary	NYK	106
Smith, John P.	COL	198	Smith, Joshua	OND	192	Smith, Mary	NYK	110
Smith, John P.	COL	230	Smith, Joshua	QNS	71	Smith, Mary	ORN	355
Smith, John P.	NYK	18	Smith, Joshua	QNS	74	Smith, Mary	QNS	66
Smith, John P. 2d	COL	197	Smith, Joshua	QNS	77	Smith, Mary	QNS	68
Smith, John P. 2d	COL	199	Smith, Joshua	RNS	66	Smith, Mary	SRA	46
Smith, John R.	QNS	78	Smith, Joshua	STB	203	Smith, Mary	SUF	86
Smith, John R. Junr	QNS	78	Smith, Joshua	SUF	65	Smith, Mathew	COL	248
Smith, John S.	COL	199	Smith, Joshua	SUF	70	Smith, Mathew	SUF	91
Smith, John S.	RCK	97	Smith, Joshua	SUF	90	Smith, Matson	WST	149
Smith, John T.	NYK	77	Smith, Joshua	TIO	251	Smith, Matthew	DEL	286
Smith, John W.	DUT	135	Smith, Joshua	WSH	190	Smith, Matthew	WST	125
Smith, Johnti_	MNT	50	Smith, Joshua	WST	113	Smith, Matthew	WST	139
Smith, Jonas	ALB	60	Smith, Joshua Junr	SUF	90	Smith, Matthias	DUT	148
Smith, Jonas	DUT	132	Smith, Joshua H.	NYK	145	Smith, Maubray	SUF	94
Smith, Jonas	ORN	371	Smith, Josiah	CAY	652	Smith, Maurice	DUT	108
Smith, Jonas	SUF	91	Smith, Josiah	DUT	62	Smith, Melancton	SUF	82
Smith, Jonas	ULS	207	Smith, Josiah	HRK	553	Smith, Merrit	KNG	9
Smith, Jonas	WSH	245	Smith, Josiah	ONT	492	Smith, Merrit	QNS	70
Smith, Jno & Henry	COL	190	Smith, Josiah	SUF	65	Smith, Michael	ALB	23
Smith, Jonathan	DUT	176	Smith, Josiah	SUF	69	Smith, Michael	DUT	34
Smith, Jonathan	HRK	596	Smith, Josiah	SUF	88	Smith, Michael	GRN	328
Smith, Jonathan	NYK	59	Smith, Jost	HRK	444	Smith, Michael	HRK	441
Smith, Jonathan	ONT	436	Smith, Jotham	QNS	76	Smith, Michael	ORN	398
Smith, Jonathan	ORN	346	Smith, Justice	MNT	114	Smith, Michael	ULS	192
Smith, Jonathan	ORN	358	Smith, Justice	WSH	208	Smith, Micah	SUF	91
Smith, Jona	OTS	6	Smith, Justus B..	CHN	844	Smith, Milus	TIO	226
Smith, Jonathan	RNS	14	Smith, Kenner	DEL	274	Smith, Mordecai R.	QNS	76
Smith, Jonathan	SRA	13	Smith, Killian	COL	233	Smith, Moris	WST	113
Smith, Jonathan	SRA	34	Smith, Lambert	RCK	106	Smith, Morris	DEL	271
Smith, Jonathan	SRA	38	Smith, Lambert	RCK	106	Smith, Morris	NYK	87
Smith, Jonathan	ULS	197	Smith, Larkin	OTS	52	Smith, Moses	ALB	79
Smith, Jonathan	WST	130	Smith, Laurence	ALB	112	Smith, Moses	CAY	704
Smith, Jonathan B.	QNS	73	Smith, Lefford	QNS	75	Smith, Moses	CHN	970
Smith, Jonothan	CHN	920	Smith, Lemuel	DUT	80	Smith, Moses	DUT	11
Smith, Josep	MNT	69	Smith, Lemuel	OND	184	Smith, Moses	NYK	139
Smith, Joseph	CAY	550	Smith, Lemuel	SRA	39	Smith, Moses	ONT	360
Smith, Joseph	COL	177	Smith, Lemuel	WST	123	Smith, Moses	SRA	23
Smith, Joseph	COL	203	Smith, Lennington R.	QNS	73	Smith, Moses	WSH	252
Smith, Joseph	COL	218	Smith, Leonard	ONT	492	Smith, Moses	WST	139
Smith, Joseph	DEL	283	Smith, Leonard	ORN	270	Smith, Moses R.	NYK	83
Smith, Joseph	DUT	121	Smith, Leonard	RNS	86	Smith, Mosher	WSH	293
Smith, Joseph	DUT	135	Smith, Levi	DUT	154	Smith, Munson	RNS	34
Smith, Joseph	HRK	475	Smith, Levi	HRK	515	Smith, Nahum	OND	183
Smith, Joseph	MNT	44	Smith, Levi	OND	206	Smith, Nancy	WSH	257
Smith, Joseph a Black	NYK	43	Smith, Levi	OND	220	Smith, Nathan	ALB	91
Smith, Joseph	NYK	46	Smith, Levi	ONT	436	Smith, Nathan	COL	251
Smith, Joseph	NYK	61	Smith, Levi	ONT	436	Smith, Nathan	COL	254
Smith, Joseph	NYK	68	Smith, Levi	ORN	357	Smith, Nathan	DEL	279
Smith, Joseph	OND	190	Smith, Levi	WSH	230	Smith, Nathan	HRK	581
Smith, Joseph	ONN	139	Smith, Levy	CHN	784	Smith, Nathan	OND	157
Smith, Joseph	ONN	148	Smith, Lewis	NYK	128	Smith, Nathan	OND	223
Smith, Joseph	ONT	436	Smith, [Lew?]is	OND	219	Smith, Nathan	ORN	287
Smith, Joseph	ORN	279	Smith, Lewis	SUF	104	Smith, Nathan	OTS	31
Smith, Joseph	ORN	311	Smith, Locey	SUF	92	Smith, Nathan	RNS	103
Smith, Joseph	ORN	331	Smith, Lockwood	CAY	604	Smith, Nathan	SUF	64
Smith, Joseph	ORN	370	Smith, Lodowick	ULS	225	Smith, Nathan	SUF	86
Smith, Joseph	ORN	394	Smith, Loth[um?]	GRN	336	Smith, Nathan	SUF	93
Smith, Joseph	OTS	21	Smith, Lucius	SUF	89	Smith, Nathaniel	NYK	87
Smith, Joseph	OTS	34	Smith, Lucy Negress	QNS	71	Smith, Nathaniel	ONN	151
Smith, Joseph	QNS	75	Smith, Ludlum	ULS	262	Smith, Nathaniel	ORN	276
Smith, Joseph	QNS	76	Smith, Luff	NYK	96	Smith, Nathaniel	ORN	317
Smith, Joseph	QNS	76	Smith, Lydia a Black	NYK	110	Smith, Nathaniel	ORN	339
Smith, Joseph	SRA	4	Smith, Lydia	NYK	135	Smith, Nathaniel	ORN	375
Smith, Joseph	SRA	7	Smith, Major	ONT	438	Smith, Nathaniel	QNS	69

Name	Loc	Pg	Name	Loc	Pg	Name	Loc	Pg
Smith, Nathaniel	QNS	77	Smith, Peter	QNS	73	Smith, Ri...rd	ONT	460
Smith, Nathaniel	RCK	105	Smith, Peter	RNS	13	Smith, Richard	OTS	30
Smith, Nathl	SUF	66	Smith, Peter	RNS	83	Smith, Richd	OTS	38
Smith, Nathaniel	SUF	91	Smith, Peter	RCK	109	Smith, Richard	QNS	71
Smith, Nathaniel	ULS	255	Smith, Peter Junr	CAY	540	Smith, Richard	QNS	77
Smith, Nathaniel	WSH	207	Smith, Peter A.	COL	231	Smith, Richard	RNS	60
Smith, Nathaniel	WSH	306	Smith, Peter A.	MNT	23	Smith, Richard	SRA	4
Smith, Nathaniel	WST	154	Smith, Peter D. W.	RCK	102	Smith, Richard	SCH	144
Smith, Nedebiah	DUT	147	Smith, Peter H.	ALB	89	Smith, Richard	SUF	91
Smith, Nehemiah	CAY	692	Smith, Peter J.	DEL	283	Smith, Richard	WST	113
Smith, Nehemiah	DEL	287	Smith, Peter N.	MNT	19	Smith, Richd Junr	SUF	91
Smith, Nehemiah	DUT	174	Smith, Peter P.	COL	238	Smith, Richard R.	QNS	73
Smith, Nehemiah	ONN	178	Smith, Peter P.	DEL	283	Smith, Robert	ALB	110
Smith, Nehemiah	RNS	78	Smith, Peter P.	ULS	200	Smith, Robert	DUT	145
Smith, Nehemiah	ULS	267	Smith, Peter P. Junr	COL	198	Smith, Robert	NYK	120
Smith, Nehemiah Junr	DUT	173	Smith, Peter W.	DUT	135	Smith, Robt	ONN	189
Smith, Nicholas	ALB	20	Smith, Peter Z.	COL	230	Smith, Robert	ORN	282
Smith, Nicholas	HRK	478	Smith, Pettit	SRA	30	Smith, Robert	ORN	305
Smith, Nicholas	ONT	400	Smith, Phebe	ORN	311	Smith, Robert	RNS	7
Smith, Nichs	OTS	41	Smith, Phebe	ULS	267	Smith, Robert	WSH	218
Smith, Nicholas	QNS	67	Smith, Pheneas	SUF	83	Smith, Roderich	ONN	145
Smith, Nicholas	RNS	58	Smith, Philander	DEL	268	Smith, Roeliff	OTS	43
Smith, Nicholas	RCK	107	Smith, Philep	WSH	199	Smith, Roger	OND	212
Smith, Nichs	SCH	156	Smith, Philep	WSH	269	Smith, Roger	ONN	159
Smith, Nicholas	SUF	91	Smith, Philip	OND	206	Smith, Roliff	COL	220
Smith, Nichs	TIO	215	Smith, Philip	RNS	13	Smith, Romeo a Black	NYK	18
Smith, Nicholas Junr	ALB	105	Smith, Philip	SUF	88	Smith, Ruben	WST	170
Smith, Nicholas Junr	MNT	19	Smith, Philip	SUF	94	Smith, Rufus	ONT	494
Smith, Nichs Senr	ALB	105	Smith, Philip	WSH	297	Smith, Russel	OND	206
Smith, Nicholas T.	RNS	58	Smith, Phillip	COL	186	Smith, Sally	TIO	215
Smith, Noadiah	RNS	8	Smith, Phillip	COL	199	Smith, Salmon	CHN	970
Smith, Noah	HRK	597	Smith, Phillip	DUT	55	Smith, Samson	ESS	318
Smith, Noah	OND	165	Smith, Phillip	DUT	87	Smith, Samuel	CAY	532
Smith, Noah	ONT	372	Smith, Phillip	NYK	135	Smith, Samuel	CAY	654
Smith, Noah	ONT	372	Smith, Phillip H.	COL	253	Smith, Samuel	CHN	988
Smith, Noah	SRA	28	Smith, Phillis	NYK	73	Smith, Samuel	COL	187
Smith, Noah	SRA	51	Smith, Philo	HRK	598	Smith, Samuel	COL	202
Smith, Noah	WST	139	Smith, Phineas	QNS	78	Smith, Samuel	DUT	64
Smith, Norton	OND	168	Smith, Phinehas	HRK	515	Smith, Samuel	DUT	80
Smith, Obadiah	CAY	552	Smith, Phinehas	RNS	47	Smith, Samuel	DUT	99
Smith, Obadiah	DUT	125	Smith, Platt	CAY	552	Smith, Samuel	GRN	343
Smith, Obadiah	ORN	399	Smith, Platt	NYK	100	Smith, Samuel	KNG	7
Smith, Obadiah	OTS	2	Smith, Platt	QNS	67	Smith, Samuel	NYK	50
Smith, Obadiah R.	QNS	73	Smith, Platt	QNS	68	Smith, Samuel	NYK	70
Smith, Obadiah R.	QNS	78	Smith, Platt	SUF	90	Smith, Samuel a Black	NYK	70
Smith, Obediah	SUF	91	Smith, Policarpus	OND	165	Smith, Samuel	OND	177
Smith, Obediah	SUF	104	Smith, Polley	SUF	106	Smith, Samuel	ONN	156
Smith, Olied	NYK	74	Smith, Polly	NYK	18	Smith, Samuel	ONN	172
Smith, Oliver	HRK	483	Smith, Ralph	WSH	289	Smith, Samuel	ONT	360
Smith, Oliver	OND	211	Smith, Randel	SRA	56	Smith, Samuel	ONT	510
Smith, Oliver	ONN	157	Smith, Ransom	ONT	378	Smith, Samuel	ORN	368
Smith, Oliver	ORN	363	Smith, Reuben	ALB	92	Smith, Samuel	ORN	374
Smith, Oliver	OTS	56	Smith, Reuben	CAY	564	Smith, Samuel	ORN	378
Smith, Oliver	RNS	71	Smith, Reuben	DEL	280	Smith, Samuel	ORN	382
Smith, Oliver	SUF	69	Smith, Reuben	ONT	330	Smith, Samuel	OTS	27
Smith, Oliver Jun	ONN	158	Smith, Reuben	ONT	406	Smith, Samuel	OTS	28
Smith, Othey	QNS	68	Smith, Reuben	ORN	368	Smith, Samuel	OTS	33
Smith, Othniel D.	DUT	121	Smith, Reuben	WSH	206	Smith, Saml	OTS	45
Smith, Otis	HRK	478	Smith, Reuben	WSH	232	Smith, Samuel	QNS	74
Smith, Pall	WSH	238	Smith, Reuben S.	DEL	281	Smith, Samuel	RNS	91
Smith, Parker	ONN	156	Smith, Reynere	RCK	109	Smith, Samuel	RCH	93
Smith, Paschal N.	NYK	19	Smith, Rhoda	NYK	71	Smith, Saml Esqr	RCK	103
Smith, Paul	SUF	90	Smith, Richard	ALB	18	Smith, Samuel	SRA	5
Smith, Peleg	SUF	88	Smith, Richard	CAY	714	Smith, Samuel	SRA	16
Smith, Peter	ALB	86	Smith, Richard	DEL	271	Smith, Saml	SUF	66
Smith, Peter	CAY	540	Smith, Richard	DUT	76	Smith, Saml	SUF	81
Smith, Peter	CHN	962	Smith, Richard	DUT	108	Smith, Samuel	SUF	89
Smith, Peter	DEL	284	Smith, Richard	HRK	538	Smith, Samuel	SUF	89
Smith, Peter	DUT	9	Smith, Richard	HRK	584	Smith, Saml	SUF	90
Smith, Peter	DUT	145	Smith, Richard	HRK	595	Smith, Samuel	SUF	91
Smith, [Pet?]er	GRN	334	Smith, Richard	NYK	33	Smith, Samuel	ULS	240
Smith, Peter	MNT	52	Smith, Richard	NYK	55	Smith, Samuel	WSH	211
Smith, Peter	MNT	73	Smith, Richard	NYK	85	Smith, Samuel	WSH	298
Smith, Peter	NYK	78	Smith, Richard a Black	NYK	134	Smith, Samuel	WST	125
Smith, Peter	NYK	91	Smith, Richard	NYK	138	Smith, Samuel	WST	130
Smith, Peter	OND	161	Smith, Richard	OND	160	Smith, Samuel	WST	141
Smith, Peter	ONT	438				Smith, Samuel	WST	159

Name	Loc	Name	Loc	Name	Loc	Name	Loc
Smith, Samuel Junr	COL 184	Smith, Stephen	OTS 17	Smith, Thomas H.	NYK 46		
Smith, Samuel Junr	DUT 80	Smith, Stephen	QNS 75	Smith, Thomas J.	NYK 129		
Smith, Samuel Junr	WST 130	Smith, Stephen	QNS 77	Smith, Thomas N.	GRN 342		
Smith, Samuel A.	DUT 155	Smith, Stephen	WST 147	Smith, Thomas R.	NYK 40		
Smith, Samuel M.	DUT 122	Smith, Stephen Junr	ORN 358	Smith, Thomas U.	SRA 5		
Smith, Samuel T.	GRN 326	Smith, Stephen C.	NYK 126	Smith, Timothy	COL 194		
Smith, Sanders	CAY 584	Smith, Stephen G.	ORN 318	Smith, Timothy	DUT 71		
Smith, Sanford	WSH 189	Smith, Stoddard	GRN 354	Smith, Timothy	ESS 322		
Smith, Sarah	ALB 27	Smith, Susan	SUF 89	Smith, Timothy	OND 211		
Smith, Sarah	CAY 516	Smith, Susanna	ORN 280	Smith, Timothy	ONT 342		
Smith, Sarah	DUT 17	Smith, Sylvanus	CLN 164	Smith, Timothy	ORN 333		
Smith, Sarah	ORN 360	Smith, Sylvenus	QNS 69	Smith, Timothy	QNS 69		
Smith, Sarah	QNS 78	Smith, Tabitha	SUF 91	Smith, Timothy	SRA 28		
Smith, Sarah	WST 114	Smith, Teunis P.	COL 266	Smith, Timothy	SRA 52		
Smith, Saul	CHN 910	Smith, Thaddeus	NYK 37	Smith, Timothy	TIO 263		
Smith, Scudder	SUF 84	Smith, Thadeus	GRN 342	Smith, Titus	CAY 704		
Smith, Sebastian	ALB 89	Smith, Thadius	WSH 221	Smith, Tobias	ORN 381		
Smith, Selah	KNG 8	Smith, Theman	GRN 342	Smith, Tower a Black	COL 249		
Smith, Selah	ORN 361	Smith, Theodore	COL 211	Smith, T. Tredwell	ULS 229		
Smith, Selah	SUF 67	Smith, Theodore	RNS 80	Smith, Tunis	MNT 29		
Smith, Selah	SUF 91	Smith, Theophilus	SUF 69	Smith, Tunis	RCK 98		
Smith, Selah	ULS 186	Smith, Thomas	ALB 2A	Smith, Tunis	RCK 98		
Smith, Semion	SUF 66	Smith, Thomas	ALB 13	Smith, Uriah	DUT 115		
Smith, Semion	WSH 230	Smith, Thomas	CAY 516	Smith, Valentine	CAY 684		
Smith, Seth	COL 221	Smith, Thomas	CAY 704	Smith, Victorius	CHN 778		
Smith, Seth	HRK 553	Smith, Thomas	CHN 878	Smith, Vincent	SUF 67		
Smith, Seth	HRK 566	Smith, Thomas	CLN 167	Smith, Vinsent	SUF 66		
Smith, Seth	MNT 18	Smith, Thomas	COL 204	Smith, Wail	ORN 334		
Smith, Seth	NYK 30	Smith, Thomas	DUT 87	Smith, Wail	ORN 354		
Smith, Shadrach	OND 157	Smith, Thomas	DUT 153	Smith, Waitstill	OND 184		
Smith, Shubel	SUF 86	Smith, Thomas	GRN 343	Smith, Walter	MNT 53		
Smith, Silas	NYK 117	Smith, Thomas	GRN 354	Smith, Walter	QNS 67		
Smith, Silas	QNS 77	Smith, Thomas	HRK 451	Smith, Walter	SUF 94		
Smith, Silas	RNS 83	Smith, Thomas	MNT 102	Smith, Walter	WST 122		
Smith, Silas	SCH 165	Smith, Thomas	NYK 15	Smith, Ward	TIO 240		
Smith, Silas	SUF 82	Smith, Thomas	NYK 29	Smith, Warren	SRA 47		
Smith, Silas	SUF 85	Smith, Thomas a Black	NYK 37	Smith, Waters	NYK 40		
Smith, Silas	SUF 86	Smith, Thomas	NYK 59	Smith, Wecks	CHN 788		
Smith, Silas	WSH 304	Smith, Thomas	NYK 92	Smith, Wesell	SUF 90		
Smith, Silas	WST 129	Smith, Thomas	NYK 98	Smith, Wessels	ORN 365		
Smith, Silvenus	QNS 77	Smith, Thomas	NYK 100	Smith, Whealer	CHN 852		
Smith, Simeon	CHN 758	Smith, Thomas	NYK 107	Smith, Whitehead	ALB 91B		
Smith, Simeon	OND 180	Smith, Thomas	NYK 136	Smith, Widow	QNS 66		
Smith, Simeon	ONN 136	Smith, Thomas	NYK 150	Smith, Wilhelmus	COL 185		
Smith, Simeon	ONN 153	Smith, Thomas	ONT 456	Smith, Willet	NYK 137		
Smith, Simeon	ONT 494	Smith, Thomas	ORN 350	Smith, Willeam	WSH 241		
Smith, Simeon	QNS 67	Smith, Thomas	QNS 67	Smith, William	CAY 590		
Smith, Simeon	RNS 75	Smith, Thomas	QNS 68	Smith, William	CHN 782		
Smith, Simeon Jun	ONN 150	Smith, Thomas	QNS 70	Smith, William	COL 249		
Smith, Smith	QNS 67	Smith, Thomas	QNS 77	Smith, William	COL 257		
Smith, Solomon	ALB 128	Smith, Thomas	QNS 79	Smith, William	DEL 272		
Smith, Solomon	COL 193	Smith, Thomas	QNS 81	Smith, William	DUT 65		
Smith, Solomon	DEL 280	Smith, Thomas	RNS 31	Smith, William	DUT 75		
Smith, Solomon	HRK 490	Smith, Thomas	RNS 34	Smith, William	GRN 341		
Smith, Solomon	OND 206	Smith, Thomas	RCK 99	Smith, William	HRK 538		
Smith, Solomon	OND 211	Smith, Thomas	SRA 5	Smith, William	MNT 15		
Smith, Solomon	ORN 364	Smith, Thomas	SRA 5	Smt., Wm	MNT 55		
Smith, Solomon	ORN 381	Smith, Thomas	SRA 14	Smith, William	MNT 107		
Smith, Solomon	RNS 75	Smith, Thomas	SRA 38	Smith, Wm	MNT 123		
Smith, Solomon	SUF 89	Smith, Thos	SUF 67	Smith, William	NYK 24		
Smith, Solomon	WSH 256	Smith, Thomas	SUF 81	Smith, William	NYK 24		
Smith, Solomon	WST 122	Smith, Thomas	SUF 93	Smith, William	NYK 29		
Smith, Solomon	WST 153	Smith, Thomas	SUF 93	Smith, William	NYK 41		
Smith, Solomon Junr	ORN 357	Smith, Thomas	ULS 183	Smith, William	NYK 47		
Smith, Stephen	CHN 946	Smith, Thomas	ULS 191	Smith, William	NYK 79		
Smith, Stephen	COL 185	Smith, Thomas	ULS 200	Smith, William	NYK 80		
Smith, Stephen	DUT 76	Smith, Thomas	ULS 250	Smith, William	NYK 82		
Smith, Stephen	DUT 123	Smith, Thomas	WSH 189	Smith, William	NYK 102		
Smith, Stephen	DUT 125	Smith, Thomas	WSH 238	Smith, William	NYK 114		
Smith, Stephen	DUT 150	Smith, Thomas	WST 126	Smith, William	NYK 129		
Smith, Stephen	HRK 596	Smith, Thomas	WST 139	Smith, William	NYK 131		
Smith, Stephen	NYK 29	Smith, Thomas	WST 146	Smith, William	NYK 149		
Smith, Stephen	ORN 346	Smith, Thomas	WST 164	Smith, William	OND 158		
Smith, Stephen	ORN 357	Smith, Thomas	WST 170	Smith, William	OND 208		
Smith, Stephen	ORN 375	Smith, Thomas ye 2d	ULS 200	Smith, William	OND 212		
Smith, Stephen	OTS 8	Smith, Thomas G.	ULS 231	Smith, William	ONT 364		
Smith, Stephen	OTS 11			Smith, William	ONT 470		

Name	Loc	No.
Sm_h, William	CNT	492
Smith, William	CNT	492
Smith, William	ORN	270
Smith, William	ORN	304
Smith, William	ORN	321
Smith, William	ORN	361
Smith, William	ORN	384
Smith, Wm	OTS	8
Smith, Wm	OTS	34
Smith, Wm	QNS	65
Smith, William	QNS	68
Smith, William	QNS	69
Smith, William	QNS	70
Smith, William	QNS	75
Smith, William	RNS	19
Smith, William	RNS	71
Smith, William	RNS	86
Smith, Wm	RCK	99
Smith, William	SRA	7
Smith, William	SRA	9
Smith, William	SRA	29
Smith, William	SRA	41
Smith, William	SRA	44
Smith, William	SCH	156
Smith, Wm	SUF	64
Smith, Wm	SUF	68
Smith, Wm	SUF	70
Smith, William	SUF	89
Smith, William	SUF	90
Smith, William	SUF	92
Smith, William	ULS	181
Smith, William	ULS	195
Smith, William	ULS	205
Smith, William	ULS	208
Smith, William	ULS	234
Smith, William	ULS	247
Smith, William	WSH	220
Smith, William	WSH	282
Smith, William	WST	129
Smith, William	WST	142
Smith, William	WST	170
Smith, Wm Junr	RNS	71
Smith, William Junr	ULS	181
Smith, William Junr	WST	141
Smith, Wm A.	MNT	102
Smith, William Aaron	NYK	66
Smith, William H.	ORN	283
Smith, William Henry	NYK	42
Smith, William J.	COL	265
Smith, William L.	NYK	129
Smith, William M.	ORN	339
Smith, William P.	COL	199
Smith, Woodhull	SUF	66
Smith, Woodhull	SUF	91
Smith, Young	OTS	21
Smith, Zachariah	DUT	156
Smith, Zachariah	RNS	57
Smith, Zachariah	SUF	85
Smith, Zadock	SRA	25
Smith, Zebulin	SUF	65
Smith, Zebulon	QNS	74
Smith, Zebulon	SUF	82
Smith, Zecheriah	ALB	105
Smith, Zelack	CHN	970
Smith, Zelman	ONT	448
Smith, Zenus	GRN	356
Smith, Zephaniah	RNS	112
Smith, Zepher	COL	221
Smith, Zoeth	GRN	346
Smith, Zopha	QNS	78
Smithan, Robert	NYK	32
Smithins, Abraham	TIO	223
Smithman, Catherine	NYK	137
Smitzer, George M.	NYK	118
Smock, John	CAY	554
Smock, Mathias	MNT	74
Smuck, William	NYK	123
Smultz, Coonradt	ORN	383
Smyder, George	MNT	33
Smyth, Joseph	NYK	45
Sn_de(?), Is..c	TIO	251
Snacall, Joseph	CLN	160
Snapp, Henry	CAY	710
Sneckinbeger, Franc	TIO	253
Snedeca, Abraham	QNS	67
Snedeca, Abraham	QNS	81
Snedeca, Abraham	QNS	82
Snedeca, Bann	QNS	81
Snedeca, Garret	QNS	67
Snedeca, Halimus	QNS	81
Snedeca, Ram	QNS	67
Snedecar see Schnedecar		
Sneidicker, Snideker		
& Sniderker		
Snedecar, John	SUF	81
Snedecher, Uriah	OND	175
Snedecor, Isaac	KNG	3
Snedecor, Isaac Ju	KNG	3
Snedecor, Louis	KNG	8
Snedecor, Phelitus	KNG	8
Snedeka, Abraham	QNS	77
Snedeka, Isaac	QNS	77
Snedeka, Orrey	QNS	68
Snedekar, Isaac	RNS	95
Snedeker, Abraham	QNS	81
Snedeker, Albert	QNS	65
Snedeker, Eliza	RCK	101
Snedeker, Garret	QNS	81
Snedeker, Garret	RCK	102
Snedeker, Isaac J.	KNG	2
Snedeker, Jacob	DUT	9
Snedeker, James	DUT	40
Snedeker, John	DUT	28
Snedeker, John	SUF	80
Snedeker, Michael	RCK	101
Snedeker, Samuel	ORN	288
Snedeker, Sylvester	DUT	63
Snedeker, Theodorus	RCK	101
Sneden, Dennis	RCK	99
Sneden, John	RCK	99
Sneden, John Junr	RCK	97
Sneden, Mary	RCK	99
Sneden, Robert	NYK	88
Sneden, Susan	NYK	88
Sneder, Cabet	MNT	34
Sneder, Jacob	WSH	244
Snedgrass, George	NYK	116
Sneedecker, Garrit	TIO	229
Sneeden, Cobantihie	NYK	20
Sneeden, Elijah	NYK	75
Sneely, William	CLN	166
Sneidicker, Jacob	CAY	550
Snell see Snell		
Snell, Adam	MNT	45
Snell, Fredereck J.	MNT	8
Snell, Frederick N.	MNT	19
Snell, George	MNT	9
Snell, George	TIO	254
Snell, H. S.	MNT	56
Snell, Han yost P.	MNT	55
Snell, Isaac	WSH	236
Snell, Jacob	MNT	74
Snell, Jacob	OND	222
Snell, Job	OND	197
Snell, John	KNG	7
Snell, John	MNT	8
Snell, John	NYK	138
Snell, John J.	MNT	8
Snell, John Jb	MNT	9
Snell, Major	ALB	4
Snell, Nicholas	MNT	15
Snell, Peter J.	MNT	8
Snell, Peter N.	MNT	18
Snell, Robert	ALB	4
Snell, Thomas	NYK	64
Snelly, Edmond	OND	190
Snethen, Barrick	RCH	93
Snevill, Andrew	MNT	102
Sneyder see Snider & Snyder		
Sneyder, Christopher	ALB	112
Sneyder, Daniel	ALB	139
Sneyder, George	NYK	149
Sneyder, Henry	ALB	33
Sneyder, Isaac	ALB	103
Sneyder, Jeremiah	ALB	92
Sneyder, Martinus	ALB	118
Sneyder, Peter J.	ALB	69
Sneyder, Philip	ALB	35
Sneyder, William	ALB	149
Snideker, Garrett	SRA	8
Snider, Abraham	GRN	344
Snider, Andrew	GRN	326
Snider, Christopher	CAY	618
Snider, Christopher	CAY	642
Snider, Christopher	RNS	46
Snider, Coonrad	CAY	620
Snider, Frederick	CAY	594
Snider, Harmanus	RNS	11
Snider, Henry	OND	211
Snider, Jacob	CAY	708
Snider, Jacob	HRK	479
Snider, Jacob	WSH	303
Snider, John	CAY	696
Snider, John	HRK	508
Snider, John	MNT	93
Snider, Joh.	RNS	11
Snider, John	RNS	44
Snider, John Junr	CAY	696
Snider, Michael	MNT	37
Snider, Moses	WSH	253
Snider, Peter	MNT	39
Snider, Peter	ONT	334
Sniderker, James	GRN	339
Sniffen see Smiffen		
Sniffen, Amos	WST	113
Sniffen, Andrew	DEL	290
Sniffen, Andrew	WST	116
Sniffen, Anna	WST	114
Sniffen, Caleb	WST	113
Sniffen, Elisha	WST	114
Sniffen, Jacob	RCK	103
Sniffen, John	WST	114
Sniffen, Lewis	WST	170
Sniffen, Rachel	WST	113
Sniffen, Rachel Jr	WST	114
Sniffen, Thomas	WST	113
Sniffin, Amos	WST	161
Sniffin, Ebenezer	WST	151
Sniffin, Gilbert	WST	131
Sniffin, James	WST	164
Sniffin, Jeremiah	WST	128
Sniffin, Jeremiah	WST	152
Sniffin, John	WST	131
Sniffin, Joseph	WST	151
Sniffin, Nathan	WST	156
Sniffin, Nathan	WST	161
Sniffin, Robert	WST	131
Sniffin, Silvanus	WST	130
Sniffin, Thomas	WST	129
Sniffin, William	WST	156
Shipsoper, Conrod	MNT	50
Snirley, Francis	NYK	85
Snitakar, William	ONN	137
Snook, Cornelia	COL	192
Snook, Frederick	COL	229
Snook, James	DUT	30
Snook, John	DUT	154
Snook, John Tice	RNS	12
Snook, Martinus	COL	229
Snook, Matthew	DUT	72

Name	Code
Sonn, Thomas	COL 222
Sonnendyck, Marian	NYK 143
Soop, Conradt	ALB 98
Soop, Dyrick	ALB 98
Soper see Loper	
Soper, Amos	SUF 83
Soper, Augustus	OND 205
Soper, Benjamin	SUF 83
Soper, Burtis	SRA 41
Soper, Cornelius	CLN 157
Soper, Cornelius	DUT 61
Soper, David	ULS 241
Soper, Edmund	CLN 157
Soper, Edward	COL 213
Soper, Elemuel	SUF 89
Soper, Elias	SCH 148
Soper, Elkanus	SUF 83
Soper, James	ULS 241
Soper, Jesse	CLN 165
Soper, Joel	OND 205
Soper, Joel	SUF 93
Soper, John	CLN 157
Soper, John	SUF 83
Soper, Jonah	DEL 290
Soper, Josiah	SUF 92
Soper, Moses	CLN 160
Soper, Philo	OND 205
Soper, Platt	SUF 83
Soper, Thankful	SUF 83
Soper, Timothy	CLN 157
Soper, Timothy	DUT 60
Soper, Timothy	MNT 113
Soper, Whitson	SUF 83
Soper, William	ORN 309
Sopher, Joseph	QNS 77
Sor_im, Wm	MNT 2
Sorenberger, George	COL 179
Sorine, James	WST 123
Sorine, James	WST 126
Sorinierd, Louis	NYK 98
Sornborger, David	DUT 135
Sornborger, George	DUT 135
Sornborger, John	DUT 136
Sorrel, Abigal	WSH 229
Sorrenberger, Mathew	COL 179
Sorton, John	GRN 353
Sotherland see Souther-	
land	
Sotherland, John	RCK 109
Sottle, Asa	CAY 662
Sottle, Daniel	ONT 408
Sottle, Levi	CAY 662
Sotton, Daniel	SCH 153
Soul, Cornelius	WSH 207
Soul, Elijah	SRA 21
Soul, Felix	SRA 32
Soul, Jacob	SCH 139
Soul, John	WSH 201
Soul, Nathaniel	SRA 35
Soul, Recompence	SCH 139
Soul, Silas	SCH 139
Soule, Ebenezer	COL 178
Soule, Ebenezer Junr	COL 185
Soule, Stephen	COL 179
Soules, Titus	ALB 74
Souls, Isaac	MNT 38
Souls, Jacob Senr	SCH 140
Souls, Lamuel	SCH 140
Souls, Zealous	ALB 63
Souque, Michael	NYK 41
Sourbien, Francis	NYK 92
Sourerland, Joel	GRN 354
Sourtherland, Daniel	GRN 351
Sourtherland, Wm	GRN 351
Soutand, Vinis	GRN 357
South, John	SCH 162
South, Lewis	OTS 56
South, Zedekiah	OND 212
Southard, Amos	QNS 74
Southard, Amos	TIO 213
Southard, Caleb	QNS 76
Southard, Cole	QNS 74
Southard, David	QNS 76
Southard, Edward	CHN 986
Southard, George	DUT 34
Southard, Gilbert	DUT 36
Southard, Henny	ALB 34
Southard, Isaac	DUT 29
Southard, Isaac	QNS 74
Southard, James	QNS 77
Southard, James	QNS 84
Southard, John	ALB 34
Southard, John	DUT 29
Southard, John	SRA 48
Southard, Jonas	ALB 2A
Southard, Jonas	DUT 29
Southard, Joseph	OTS 36
Southard, Martha	DUT 29
Southard, Micajah	QNS 74
Southard, Richard	DUT 29
Southard, Richard	DUT 35
Southard, Richard	QNS 74
Southard, Samuel	CAY 658
Southard, Solomon	QNS 77
Southard, Stephen	SRA 43
Southard, Thomas	ALB 31
Southard, Thomas	QNS 76
Southard, Thomas	QNS 77
Southard, Wm	QNS 73
Southerlain, Smith	GRN 354
Southerland see Soth-	
erland, Southerland,	
Sutherland & Stuth_	
erland	
Southerland, Elisabeth	WST 155
Southerland, Israel	TIO 218
Southerland, Mary	TIO 217
Southerland, Moses	ONN 134
Southerland, Silus	WST 113
Southerland, Silus Jr	WST 113
Southerland, Simon	DEL 272
Southerland, William	CLN 155
Southerland, William	GRN 331
Southerland, Wm	OTS 15
Southmaid, John W.	ESS 321
Southmead, Daniel	OTS 55
Southmead, Daniel N.	OTS 55
Southward, John	NYK 139
Southward, Selvenus	OTS 39
Southward, Thomas	MNT 123
Southward, Wm	OTS 37
Southward, Wm	QNS 72
Southwark, Beriah	COL 182
Southwark, Thomas	COL 180
Southwell, F.	OND 259
Southwell, Jacob	ESS 311
Southwell, Joseph	HRK 413
Southwell, Semeon	ESS 318
Southwich, Lemuel	CHN 794
S..thwick, Benjamin	CAY 626
Southwick, Benjamin	RNS 66
Southwick, Caleb	CLN 154
Southwick, Edward	DUT 119
Southwick, George	WSH 209
Southwick, Henry	DUT 62
Southwick, Icabod	CAY 658
Southwick, Ichabod	TIO 218
Southwick, Moses	TIO 218
Southwick, Nathan	WSH 286
Southwick, William	ALB 96
Southwick, Zadoc	DUT 119
Southworth, Barent	DUT 165
Southworth, Benjamin	DUT 165
Southworth, Beriah	DUT 42
Southworth, Constant	ONT 352
Southworth, Elias	SRA 55
Southworth, Elias	WSH 219
Southworth, Elijah	NYK 50
Southworth, Ezekiel	ONT 356
Southworth, Fobes	DUT 15
Southworth, James	OND 211
Southworth, John	DUT 42
Southworth, Owen	WSH 219
Southworth, Sylvanus	ORN 324
Southworth, Willm	COL 185
Southworth, Wm	OTS 39
Southwoth, Samuel C.	WSH 249
Sovel, Daniel	GRN 336
Soverhill, Isaac	ONT 476
Soverhill, Isaac	ONT 512
Soverill, Samuel	ONT 344
Sovrine, Charles Junr	DUT 83
Sovrine, Charles Senr	DUT 85
Sovrine, Isaac	DUT 80
Sovrine, James	DUT 83
Sovrine, James	DUT 85
Sovrine, Nathaniel	DUT 80
Sovrine, Peter	DUT 77
Sovrine, William	DUT 76
Sovrine, William	DUT 85
Sowarby, James	NYK 127
Soweedow, Frances	NYK 120
Sowen, William	CLN 156
Sowers, Teunis	COL 218
Sowers, Uldrick	COL 194
Sowl, Thomas	RNS 31
Sowle, Jonathan	DUT 115
Sowle, Tibbits	SRA 38
Sowles, Joseph	HRK 419
Sowles, Lemuel	HRK 419
Sowles, Perry	HRK 419
Sox, Christian	GRN 327
Sox, John	GRN 327
Sox, Mrss	GRN 327
Sox, Mrss	GRN 327
Sox, Peter	GRN 327
Sox, Peter	GRN 328
Sox, Peter C.	GRN 327
Sox, Peter P.	GRN 327
Soyne, Israel Negro	QNS 71
Sp_en, John	WST 170
Spackman, James	NYK 118
Spade, Henry	COL 195
Spadeling, Mary	DUT 57
Spader, Daniel	NYK 147
Spader, Jonathan	NYK 147
Spader, William	KNG 7
Spafford, Jacob	CAY 672
Spafford, Jehial	WSH 213
Spafford, John	ALB 24
Spafford, John	COL 209
Spafford, Thomas	OND 165
Spag, David	SUF 81
Spag, Jacob	SUF 80
Spague, Dorus	OND 197
Spalden, Jotham	RNS 23
Spalden, Samuel	GRN 340
Spaldin, Asa	RNS 21
Spaldin, Elijah	RNS 21
Spalding, ...	DUT 49
Spalding, ...	MNT 86
Spalding, Abijah	DUT 49
Spalding, Abraham	DUT 49
Spalding, Amos	MNT 72
Spalding, Coit	ONN 157
Spalding, Daniel	ALB 112
Spalding, David	OND 201
Spalding, David	SRA 61
Spalding, Edward	CAY 528
Spalding, Edward	OTS 46
Spalding, Elnathan	ALB 93

Spalding, Ephraim	CAY 624	Speck, Peter a		Spencer, Jabes	WSH 281
Spalding, Erastus	CAY 630	Negro	ALB 45	Spencer, Jabez	COL 185
Spalding, Ezra	ALB 61	Speckerman, Peter		Spencer, Jabez	OTS 2
Spalding, Frederick	CAY 660	Free Black	COL 198	Spencer, James	DUT 14
Spalding, Herman	ALB 93	Speed, Henry	COL 197	Spencer, James	DUT 15
Spalding, Jacob	OTS 13	Speed, Paul	NYK 18	Spencer, James	DUT 26
Spalding, James	HRK 569	Speed, Simon	COL 195	Spencer, James	ONT 468
Spalding, James	OND 214	Speer, John	WSH 226	Spencer, James	RNS 93
Spalding, Jonathan	OND 170	Speerer, Robert	SRA 22	Spencer, James Ju.	ONT 470
Spalding, Levi	OTS 46	Speers, Christopher	QNS 63	Spencer, Jared	DUT 45
Spalding, Nathan	DUT 49	Speers, Elijah	ESS 294	Spencer, Jeremeah	WSH 276
Spalding, Nehemiah	CAY 630	Speers. Robert	SRA 15	Spencer, Jeremeah	WSH 276
Spalding, Oliver	COL 184	Spees. Treat	TIO 220	Spencer, Jeremeah	WSH 279
Spalding, Phenius	WSH 222	Speevy, Abel	RNS 21	Spencer, Jeremeah	WSH 280
Spalding, Philip	DEL 276	Spegerman, Philip	ALB 100	Spencer, Jeremiah	RNS 27
Spalding, Rebecca	CAY 654	Spier, James	NYK 52	Spencer, Jeremiah	WSH 279
Spalding, Rufus	DUT 162	Spelmam, Richard	GRN 332	Spencer, Jesse	COL 185
Spalding, Samuel	COL 180	Spe_man, John	ONT 484	Spencer, Jesse	DEL 283
Spalding, Samuel	DUT 49	Spence see Spince		Spencer, Job	CHN 800
Spalding, Silas	WSH 300	Spence, John	CAY 558	Spencer, Job	CHN 814
Spalding, Solomon	OTS 51	Spence, Nathan	ONN 171	Spencer, Joel	COL 187
Spalding, Timothy	ESS 309	Spencer see Spincer		Spencer, Joel	OTS 44
Spalding, Timothy	OND 191	Spencer, Aaron	ONT 448	Spencer, John	CHN 804
Spalding, William	ULS 198	Spencer, Aaron	OTS 44	Spencer, John	DUT 12
Spaldwin, Phinehas	TIO 233	Spencer, Abijah	ONT 416	Spencer, John	HRK551½
Spaltsburgh, Jacob	OTS 58	Spencer, Abner	COL 185	Spencer, John	HRK 561
Spaltsbury, John	OTS 58	Spencer, Abner	WSH 279	Spencer, John	OTS 44
Spaltsbury, John Junr	OTS 58	Spencer, Alexander	DUT 142	Spencer, John	RNS 13
Spangler, George	CAY 638	Spencer, Alpheus	CAY 664	Spencer, John Jun	HRK 561
Spangler, Henry	CAY 638	Spencer, Ambrose	COL 250	Spencer, Jonas	CLN 167
Spankneble see Shank-		Spencer, Amos	OTS 25	Spencer, Jonas	ONT 376
neble		Spencer, Amos	OTS 44	Spencer, Jonathan	OTS 25
Spankneble, John Junr	MNT 14	Spencer, Asa	COL 187	Spencer, Jonathan L.	CHN 742
Spann, Peter	ALB 97	Spencer, Benjamin	WSH 279	Spencer, Jonathan R.	SRA 23
Spannon, Thomas	ALB 18	Spencer, Caleb	ALB 92	Spencer, Joseph	OND 172
Sparbeck, Andries	ALB 57	Spencer, Caleb	DUT 20	Spencer, Jude	OND 165
Sparbeck, Coenradt	ALB 66	Spencer, Calvin	WSH 277	Spencer, Justiss	ONT 462
Sparbeck, Henry	ALB 67	Spencer, Cato a Black	NYK 42	Spencer, Levi	OND 208
Sparbeck, Martin	ALB 57	Spencer, Christopher	DUT 10	Spencer, Martin	COL 181
Sparbeck, Martin G.	ALB 67	Spencer, Christopher	HRK 561	Spencer, Mary	ALB 139
Sparbeck, Michael	ALB 66	Spencer, Cornelius	NYK 117	Spencer, Mary	WSH 238
Spark, Jonas	NYK 58	Spencer, Cyrus	RNS 103	Spencer, Mathias	COL 186
Sparkes, John	WSH 239	Spencer, Dan	HRK 415	Spencer, Matthias	DUT 120
Sparks, Abraham	ULS 249	Spencer, Daniel	MNT 50	Spencer, Micah	OTS 24
Sparkes, George	ULS 247	Spencer, Daniel	ORN 381	Spencer, Michael	MNT 118
Sparks, Hallet	ULS 250	Spencer, Daniel	SRA 31	Spencer, Miller	GRN 342
Sparks, Henry	WSH 267	Spencer, David	COL 186	Spencer, Nathan	ALB 92
Sparks, Jacob	ULS 259	Spencer, David	OND 163	Spencer, Nathaniel	MNT 55
Sparks, James	ALB 35	Spencer, David	OND 188	Spencer, Nathen	ONT 420
Sparks, John	NYK 105	Spencer, Ebenezar	CAY 724	Spencer, Nehemiah	COL 186
Sparks, John	WSH 221	Spencer, Ebenezer	CHN 750	Spencer, Nicholas	WSH 216
Sparks, Robert	ULS 246	Spencer, Eldad	CAY 636	Spencer, Obediah	CHN 804
Sparks, Robert Junr	ULS 247	Spencer, Eleazer	COL 182	Spencer, Oliver	ALB 93
Sparks, Thomas	OTS 51	Spencer, Elhue	CHN 740	Spencer, Oliver	RNS 78
Sparlin, John	GRN 328	Spencer, Elijah	WSH 254	Spencer, Orange	OTS 25
Sparlin, Richard	ONN 172	Spencer, Eliphaz	COL 185	Spencer, Peleg	COL 206
Sparling, George	ALB 137	Spencer, Eliphaz	RNS112A	Spencer, Peleg	SRA 44
Sparling, George	NYK 134	Spencer, Eliphaz		Spencer, Pheneas	OTS 44
Sparling, George	ONT 372	Junr	COL 189	Spencer, Philip	ALB 31
Sparling, Henry	ALB 77	Spencer, Elizabeth	DUT 55	Spencer, Philip	OTS 44
Sparling, Paul	ALB 77	Spencer, Ely	CHN 746	Spencer, Phillip Junr	DUT 135
Sparling, Peter	ULS 218	Spencer, Enos	OND 163	Spencer, Randall	RNS 72
Sparling Philip	ONT 372	Spencer, Enos	SRA 35	Spencer, Reuben	DUT 112
Sparling, Phillip	DUT 7	Spencer, Ezra	CAY 634	Spencer, Reuben	HRK 527
Sparman, Thomas	RNS 104	Spencer, Ezra	COL 186	Spencer, Reuben Jun	HRK 527
Sparrow, Benjn	TIO 246	Spencer, George	DEL 280	Spencer, Rial	OTS 26
Sparvie, Bennet	SRA 28	Spencer, George	HRK 549	Spencer, Robert	DUT 59
Spaulding, Philip	SRA 29	Spencer, Giles	ALB 125	Spencer, Robert	NYK 110
Spaun, Henry	ALB 82	Spencer, Goddard	GRN 331	Spencer, Robert	ONT 436
Spea, Lemuel	ONT 352	Spencer, Henry	ALB 130	Spencer, Robert	OTS 32
Speaker, Peter	ONT 442	Spencer, Henry	NYK 109	Spencer, Rodman	WSH 198
Speaker, Wyan	ONT 442	Spencer, Henry	WSH 208	Spencer, Roswell	COL 186
Spears, Allen	ONT 444	Spencer, Ichabod	GRN 341	Spencer, Rufus	HRK 462
Spease, Benjamine	GRN 340	Spencer, Ichabod SS.	GRN 341	Spencer, Russel	HRK 530
Specherman, John	COL 265	Spencer, Israel	OTS 44	Spencer, Saml	RNS 14
Speck, Abrm a free		Spencer, Israel B.	ALB 64	Spencer, Silas	RNS 72
Negro	ALB 48	Spencer, Ithamer	COL 181	Spencer, Stephen	ALB 72

Name	Loc		Name	Loc		Name	Loc
Spring, Zephaneah	WSH 266		Sprung, Folkert Jun	KNG 3		Squires, Stoddart	HRK 591
Springer, Andrew	DUT 81		Sprung, John	RNS 62		Squires, Zachariah	ONT 496
Springer, Benjm	ALB 17		Sprung, Mary	NYK 39		Squirrel, Daniel	ORN 297
Springer, Benjamin	RNS 68		Sprung, Stephen	KNG 4		Squirrel, Jacob	ORN 312
Springer, Daniel	ALB 56		Sprung, Volkert	MNT 94		Sreck, Abm a free	
Springer, Durfa	RNS 78		Spry, John	ONT 466		Negro	ALB 7
Springer, George	DUT 70		Spu__	CHN 842		Sriner, John	STB 204
Springer, George	RNS 67		Spuring, George	MNT 44		St__, Wm	MNT 82
Springer, Henry	OTS 57		Sp[urr?], Abraham	ONT 442		St____, Peter	TIO 255
Springer, Henry	QNS 82		Spurr, Cornelius	RNS 10		Sta__, Peter	MNT 59
Springer, Hezekiah	DUT 82		Spurr, Dick	CAY 518		Staats, Barent G.	ALB 144
Springer, Isaac	ONT 344		Spurr, Edmond	CHN 842		Staats, Daniel	OND 185
Springer, Isaac	ULS 266		Spurr, Isaac	COL 197		Staats, Gerrit	ALB 47
Springer, Jacob	ORN 305		Spurr, John	CHN 772		Staats, Henry	ALB 126
Springer, Jacob	RNS 87		Spurre, Robert	NYK 43		Staats, Henry G.	ALB 134
Springer, James	NYK 98		Spurs, Barjonas	CLN 167		Staats, Jacob	RNS 60
Springer, Moses	ALB 27		Spyser, Jacob	SCH 135		Staats, Joachim G.	SCH 118
Springer, Night	RNS 50		Squan, Augustus	OND 211		Staats, John	DUT 159
Springer, Noah	DUT 81		Square, John	SUF 93		Staats, John	RNS 5
Springer, Richard	WSH 232		Squiers, Jeremiah	SUF 66		Staats, Nicholas	RNS 60
Springer, Robert	ONT 344		Squiers, Nathan	SUF 66		Staats, Peter	SCH 165
Springer, Vincent	ALB 56		Squiers, Solomon	HRK 540		Staats, Philip	RNS 60
Springer, William	DUT 81		Squir, Zachaias	TIO 211		Staats, Rachel	ULS 223
Springfield, George	NYK 54		Squire	QNS 64		Staats, Thomas	SRA 5
Springfield, William	NYK 55		Squire, Ambros	GRN 342		Staats, William	ALB 58
Springstead, ...	QNS 60		Squire, Asa	COL 184		Stacey, Oliver	WSH 304
Springstead, Aaron	ORN 398		Squire, Asher	OND 174		Stack see Stark	
Springstead, Abraham	QNS 60		Squire, David	DEL 268		Stack, John	NYK 142
Springstead, Casper	QNS 60		Squire, David	DUT 49		Stackhouse, Margaret	NYK 39
Springstead, David	QNS 60		Squire, David	ONT 492		Stackhouse, Stacy	COL 192
Springstead, George	ORN 350		Squire, Ellis	SUF 96		Stacks see Starks	
Springstead, Henry	ORN 383		Squire, Ellis	SUF 99		Stacy, Isaac	OTS 9
Springstead, Jacob	ALB 119		Squire, Ellis Junr	SUF 96		Staddard, Israel	OND 208
Springstead, Jacob F.	ALB 121		Squire, Ezra	CLN 171		Stade, Richard	NYK 139
Springstead, Jacob S.	ALB 119		Squire, George	COL 250		Stafford, John	CLN 154
Springstead, James	ONT 458		Squire, James	ONT 512		Stafford see Statford	
Springstead, James	ONT 470		Squire, Jesse	COL 187		Stafford, Abraham	MNT 87
Springstead, Jeremiah	ALB 120		Squire, Joel	OTS 16		Stafford, Amos	ESS 302
Springstead, John	ORN 361		Squire, John	SUF 104		Stafford, Amos	SRA 42
Springstead, John	ORN 368		Squire, John	TIO 217		Stafford, Benjamin	ESS 298
Springstead, John	ORN 383		Squire, ..hn	TIO 223		Stafford, David	OND 162
Springstead, John Junr	ORN 383		Squire, John	TIO 255		Stafford, David	OND 188
Springstead, Joseph	ALB 120		Squire, John Jur	TIO 255		Stafford, Ichabod	OND 162
Springstead, Leonard	ALB 122		Squire, Jonathan	DUT 169		Stafford, James	OND 162
Springstead, Susanna	ORN 355		Squire, Jonathan	SUF 98		Stafford, Joab	OND 197
Springsted, Jacob	RCK 102		Squire, Justice	GRN 333		Stafford, John	ALB 75
Sprinsted, Jonathan	ONT 492		Squire, Justus	ESS 319		Stafford, John	DUT 133
Springsteel	NYK 96		Squire, Luthar	RNS 22		Stafford, John	OND 164
Springsteel, Christeen	DUT 15		Squire, Nathan	CHN 776		Stafford, Jonathan	CLN 155
Springsteel, Garret	DUT 39		Squire, Nathl	TIO 256		Stafford, Jonas	CLN 155
Springsteel, Jacob	TIO 231		Squire, Phoebe	SUF 99		Stafford, Levi	OND 162
Springsteel, John	RCK 105		Squire, Widow S.	DEL 268		Stafford, Martha	CLN 155
Springsteel, John	TIO 231		Squire, Seth	SUF 96		Stafford, Palmer	CLN 155
Springsteel, Samuel	WST 157		Squire, Silvenus	SUF 107		Stafford, Rowland	CLN 156
Springsteen, Bostian	RNS 61		Squire, Thomas	ESS 310		Stafford, Rowland	CLN 163
Springsteen, Cosper	RNS 59		Squire, Zachaiah	ONT 504		Stafford, Rowland Junr	CLN 163
Springsteen, David	RCK 101		Squires, Amos	NYK 112		Stafford, Rufus	CLN 163
Springsteen, David	RCK 101		Squires, Andrew	WSH 245		Stafford, Spencer	ALB 162
Springsteen, Jacob	RCK 104		.quires, Benjamin	ONT 386		Stafford, Stukely	OND 162
Springsteen, John	RCK 101		Squires, Daniel	OND 173		Stafford, Thomas	CLN 155
Springsteen, John	RCK 104		Squires, Daniel	WSH 230		Stafford, Thomas	ESS 298
Springsteen, John	RCK 109		Squires, Ebenezer	WSH 206		Stafford, Tilor	WSH 197
Springsteen, Joseph	RCK 104		Squires, Ezra	CLN 173		Stafford, William	OND 162
Springsteen, Mary	RCK 104		Squires, Francis	MNT 123		Stag, Cornelius	RCK 101
Springsteen, Mary	RCK 104		Squires, Gedion	WSH 206		Stage, Abraham	NYK 87
Springsteen, Resolvert	RCK 101		Squires, James	ONT 496		Stage, Cornelius	ORN 275
Sprinsteel, Jasper	TIO 230		Squires, Jesse	CAY 712		Stage, David	ULS 191
Sprong, Bernard	RCH 91		Squires, Jesse	ONT 496		Stage, John	NYK 88
Sproul, William	NYK 66		Squires, John	WSH 206		Stage, John Junr	ULS 191
Sprout, Hugh	ALB 46		Squires, Jonathan	CAY 700		Stage, John Senr	ULS 191
Sprout, Jenet	NYK 57		Squires, Joseph a			Stage, Silas	ULS 191
Sprout, John	ORN 341		Black	NYK 79		Stage, Thomas	ONN 191
Sprout, Nathanl	HRK 502		Squires, Josiah	STB 201		Stagg, Abraham	NYK 132
Sprowle, James	QNS 67		Squires, Salmon	ONN 143		Stagg, Cornelius	SUF 89
Sprowles, Thomas	NYK 35		Squires, Samuel	WSH 244		Stagg, Daniel	NYK 98
Sprowls, William	WSH 225		Sq...es, Sebo	ONT 496		Stagg, Isaac	NYK 55
Sprung, Christian	RNS 56		Squires, Stephen	RCH 92		Stagg, Isaac	NYK 98

Starkweather, Asa	SRA 24	Stawback, Frederick	SCH 165	Steel, Reuben	WSH 212
Starkweather, Billings	OTS 47	Stawson, Nathaniel	NYK 133	Steel, Richard	ONT 382
Starkweather, Every	SRA 30	Stead, Benjamin	ORN 334	Steel, Robert	NYK 22
Starkweather, Ezra	ALB 65	Stead, Benjamin Junr	ORN 334	Steel, Samuel	WSH 306
Starkweather, Jeremiah	OTS 46	Stead, Jacob	ORN 910	Steel, Thomas	WSH 228
Starkweather, Joel	CHN 782	Steadman, John	GRN 341	Steel, William	SRA 52
Starkweather, Nathan	HRK 514	Stear, William	WST 170	Steel, Wolcott	OND 204
Starkweather, Nathan		Steat, John	ORN 338	Steele, Aaron	TIO 220
Junr	HRK 545	Steat, William	ORN 309	Steele, Catherine	NYK 21
Starkweather, Pearly	HRK 545	Steats, Peter	ORN 342	Steele, George	HRK 407
Starkweather, Rufus	HRK 514	Stebbings, David	NYK 76	Steele, George Junr	HRK 407
Starkweather, Seth	SRA 30	Stebbings, Simon	NYK 29	Steele, Henry	DUT 89
Starkweather, Thos	OTS 47	Stebbins, Abiel	ONN 178	Steele, John	HRK 407
Starkweather, Widow	HRK 593	Stebbins, Abraham	CHN 910	Steele, Nicholas	HRK 407
Starkwell, Daniel	SRA 24	Stebbins, Abraham Jr	CHN 910	Steele, Richard	HRK 407
Starkwether, Amos	COL 203	Stebbins, Asel	CHN 810	Steele, Richard	HRK 410
Starkwether, Shubel	GRN 332	Stebbins, Elijah	OND 167	Steele, Rudolph	HRK 431
Starling, Jasper	CHN 984	Stebbins, Jabez	OND 162	Steele, Seth	OND 167
Starling, Nicholas	OND 162	Stebbins, James	CHN 910	Steele(?), Solomon G.	ONN 163
Starns, Isaac	OTS 27	Stebbins, Jerry	WST 155	Steele, Solomon G.	ONN 163
Starns, Moses	WSH 287	Stebbins, Jesse	OTS 22	Steeley, Matthias	ALB 28
Starns, Shadreck	WSH 287	Stebbins, John	OND 205	Steen, Georg	MNT 110
Starr see Stam & Star		Stebbins, Joseph	OND 198	Steen, John Junr	MNT 109
Starr, Abijah	DUT 168	Stebbins, Judah	OND 198	Steenback, Anthony	NYK 105
Starr, Daniel	SRA 15	Stebbins, Judah Junr	OND 197	Steenbank, John	DUT 80
Starr, David	OND 214	Stebbins, Lewis	DUT 54	Steenbank, Phillip	DUT 80
Starr, David	OND 221	Stebbins, Nehemiah	WST 155	Steenbarugh, Jeremiah	MNT 3
Starr, Eleazer	DEL 287	Stebbins, Samuel	DUT 54	Steenbergh, Corns	ALB 51
Starr, Elijah	ONT 320	Stebbins, Thomas	OND 165	Steenbergh, Elias	ALB 121
Starr, Epenetus	CAY 686	Stebbins, Titus	ONN 185	Steenbergh, Henry	ULS 198
Starr, Ethel	OTS 6	Stebbins, Walter	HRK 496	Steenbergh, Jacob	COL 234
Starr, Ezra	SRA 19	Stebbins, William	ONN 140	Steenbergh, John	ALB 29
Starr, Giles	NYK 34	Stebbs, Henry	NYK 39	Steenbergh, John	DEL 271
Starr, John	CAY 710	Stebens, Solomon	WSH 245	Steenbergh, Jonathan	ALB 29
Starr, John	DUT 66	Stebins, Gaius	COL 180	Steenbergh, Peter	ALB 29
Starr, Jonah	SRA 48	Steddeford, Gerrard	NYK 89	Steenbergh, Richard F.V.	DUT 70
Starr, Joseph	CAY 590	Stedeford, Nehemia	CHN 762	Steenberhg, Wm	MNT 32
Starr, Joshua	OTS 19	Stediran, Lany	NYK 21	Steenburugh, Elias Junr	SRA 3
Starr, Orange	DUT 172	Stedman, Isaac	OND 181	Steenburgh, Elias	SRA 10
Starr, Roswell	OTS 51	Stedman, James	NYK 152	Steenburgh, James	SRA 10
Starr, Ruler	OND 196	Stedman, John B.	OTS 31	Steenburgh, John	SRA 4
Starr, Samuel	OND 212	Stedwell, David	WST 112	Steenburgh, Richard	SRA 6
Starr, Samuel	OND 221	Stedwell, James Junr	DUT 52	Steenrod, Ebenezer	DEL 273
Starr, Thomas	CAY 686	Stedwell, James Senr	DUT 52	Steenrod, Ebenezer Jun	DEL 273
Starr, Thomas	OND 211	Stedwell, John	WST 129	Steenrod, Solomon	DEL 276
Starr, Truman	COL 218	Steeber, Jacob	COL 235	Steer, Christopher	COL 245
Starr, Vine	OTS 54	Steel, Adam	NYK 127	Steer, George	WST 169
Start, Henry	COL 182	Steel, Benjamin	WST 164	Steer, John	ALB 7
Start, Nathan	HRK 424	Steel, Bethel G.	CAY 706	Steer, Nichs	OTS 12
Startens, Thomas	QNS 64	Steel, Daniel	ALB 129	Steer, Rufus	OTS 12
Startin, Sarah	NYK 56	Steel, Daniel	ONT 434	Steer, Stephen	CHN 794
State see Slate		Steel, Eldad	CAY 706	Steers, Danl	RCK 101
Stater, Nicholas	RCK 102	Steel, Elijah	WSH 202	Steers, John	ALB 7
States, Elizah	NYK 75	Steel, Eliphelet	OND 193	Steever, John	SCH 156
Statford, Stanyash	CHN 952	Steel, Elisha	OND 204	Steeves, Jeremiah	OND 211
Statte[ne?], John	MNT 58	Steel, Elisha	ONT 400	Steger, Cornelius	ORN 394
Statts, Abraham	COL 258	Steel, Frederick	MNT 64	Steiford, Letitia	NYK 56
Statts, Abraham J.	COL 262	Steel, Frederick	NYK 106	Steinback, Susannah	NYK 59
Statts, Benjamin	COL 209	Steel, Henry	NYK 77	Steinbergh see Stine-	
Statts, Daniel	COL 258	Steel, He_y	ONT 434	bergh	
Statts, Isaac	COL 261	Steel, Hesekiah	MNT 64	Ste_nbergh, Nicholas	MNT 22
Statts, Jacob	COL 257	Steel, James	OND 176	Steinbergh, Peter	MNT 22
Statts, John	COL 189	Steel, James	OND 177	Steinbrach, John	NYK 137
Statts, John	COL 257	Steel, James	OTS 44	Stelley, George	ALB 40
Statts, John A.	COL 261	Steel, Job	CAY 706	Stelman, Benjamin	CHN 834
Statts, Peter	COL 224	Steel, Joel	ONT 404	Stemets, Peter	NYK 128
Statts, Phillip	COL 189	Steel, John	MNT 88	Stemmels, George	NYK 143
Statts, Phillip	COL 191	Steel, John	WSH 225	Stephen	QNS 67
Stauncey, William	DEL 275	Steel, Jonathan	WSH 274	Stephen	QNS 74
Staunton, Amos	CHN 834	Steel, Jshua	WSH 228	Stephen	QNS 82
Staunton, John	CHN 832	Steel, Justin	WSH 245	Sten	SUF 71
Staunton, John	CLN 159	Steel, Michael	NYK 145	Stephen	SUF 90
Staus	GRN 336	Steel, Nancy	SRA 17	Stephen	SUF 95
Staus, Luther	GRN 336	Steel, Nathaniel	DEL 277	Stephens	GRN 330
Staus, Widdow	GRN 336	Steel, Patrick	NYK 65	Stephens, Aaron	ALB 120
Staver, Daniel	SCH 119	Steel, Perey	CAY 564	Stephens, Abel 2d	RNS 108
Staves, John	GRN 339	Steel, Peris	GRN 329	Stephens, Abigal	CHN 770

Stephens, Abijah	CHN 754	Stephens, Thomas	WST 133
Stephens, Albert	WST 170	Stephens, Uriah	CHN 898
Stephens, Ansill	RNS 103	Stephens, Waterman	CHN 922
Stephens, Archibald	ALB 116	Stephens, William	ALB 35
Stephens, Caleb	SRA 24	Stephens, William	ALB 67
Stephens, Charles	ALB 57	Stephens, William	CAY 696
Stephens, Charles	SUF 95	Stephens, William	CHN 882
Stephens, Edward	SUF 95	Stephens, Wm	MNT 91
Stephens, Ehud	OND 222	Stephens, Wm	ONN 190
Stephens, Elias	STB 206	Stephens, Wm	OTS 27
Stephens, Elija	STB 206	Stephens, William	RCK 103
Stephens, Elisher	OND 222	Stephens, Wm	STB 206
Stephens, Elizer	OND 221	Stephens, William	SUF 95
Stephens, Elnathan	ESS 306	Stephenson, John	ALB 124
Stephens, Elnathan	MNT 109	Stephenson, Sherman	DEL 274
Stephens, Ezra	CHN 982	Stephenson, Stephen	NYK 101
Stephens, George	ALB 34	Sterling, Jacob	ALB 148
Stephens, Gersham	ALB 91B	Sterling, James	NYK 25
Stephens, Gertrude	ALB 20	Sterling, James	ONT 374
Stephens, Gideon	ALB 116	Sterling, John	MNT 113
Stephens, Gillard	CHN 868	Sterling, Samuel	ONT 362
Stephens, Henry	GRN 355	Sterling, William	NYK 25
Stephens, Henry	ONN 188	Sterlitz, Joseph	NYK 38
Stephens, Henry	RCK 107	Stern, Oliver	NYK 152
Stephens, Isaac	STB 201	Sternberg, David	SCH 119
Stephens, Jabez	ALB 64	Sternbergh, Abm	SCH 119
Stephens, Jacob	CHN 762	Sternbergh, Abraham	SCH 165
Stephens, James	ALB 146	Sternbergh, Adam	HRK 478
Stephens, James	GRN 355	Sternbergh, Lambert	SCH 122
Stephens, James	OTS 13	Sternbergh, Lambert	SCH 142
Stephens, James	RNS 74	Sternes, Abraham	WST 170
Stephens, James	SRA 24	Sterns, Cyrus	OTS 3
Stephens, Jarah	OTS 16	Sterns, John	SRA 6
Stephens, Jared	ALB 67	Sterns, Lemuel	RNS 40
Stephens, Jedediah	ALB 67	Sterns, Mrs	CHN 780
Stephens, John	ALB 35	Sterns, Nathaniel	WSH 225
Stephans, John	CHN 896	Sterns, Stephen	RNS 47
Stephens, John	CHN 906	Sterrett, Henry	TIO 258
Stephens, John	NYK 74	Sterrett, Robert	TIO 263
Stephens, John	STB 206	Sterry, Joseph	NYK 26
Stephens, Jonathan	ALB 20	Steuart, Lemmuel	CHN 870
Stephens, Jonathan	CHN 852	Stevar, Samuel	SCH 165
Stephens, Joseph	CHN 896	Steven, William a Black	NYK 94
Stephens, Josiah	CHN 770	Stevendoff, George	NYK 148
Stephens, Leonard	ONT 446	Stevens, ___les	CAY 516
Stephens, Levi	CAY 648	Stevens, Abel	COL 206
Stephens, Lodiwick	MNT 75	Stevens, Alexander	NYK 105
Stephens, Lucy	ALB 67	Stevens, Benjamin	HRK 583
Stephens, Matthew	CAY 662	Stevins, Benjamin	WSH 286
Stephens, Moses	ONN 183	Stevens, Chester	NYK 69
Stephens, Moses Junr	WST 160	Stevens, Cyrus	OTS 17
Stephens, Noah	CHN 896	Stevens, Dan	OND 176
Stephens, Oboidiah	GRN 344	Stevens, Daniel	HRK 434
Stephens, Oliver	CHN 896	Stevens, Daniel	ORN 386
Stephens, Oliver	OND 211	Stevens, Daniel	WSH 302
Stephens, Orange	RNS 103	Stevens, Daniel	WST 159
Stephens, Peleg	ONT 332	Stevens, Daniel Junr	WST 159
Stephens, Peter	RCK 103	Stevens, David	ORN 378
Stephens, Philo	OTS 47	Stevens, Ebenezar	RNS 31
Stephens, Phineas	ONT 502	Stevens, Ebenezer	NYK 41
Stephens, Phinehas	CAY 608	Stevens, Ebenezer	OND 176
Stephens, Phinehas	ONN 169	Stevens, Ebenezer	QNS 63
Stephens, Putman	MNT 60	Stevens, Eber	HRK 583
Stephens, Resolvert	RCK 103	Stevens, Eber	HRK 594
Stephens, Reuben	CAY 632	Stevens, Eden	OTS 47
Stephens, Richard	WST 124	Stevens, Edmond	HRK 583
Stephens, Samuel	CHN 896	Stevens, Edward	DUT 81
Stephens, Samuel	QNS 76	Stevens, Eliakem	OTS 17
Stephens, Silas	HRK 546	Stevens, Elias	WSH 287
Stephens, Silus	CHN 754	Stevens, Elijah	CLN 167
Stephens, Silvanus	WST 161	Stevens, Elijah	ULS 197
Stephens, Siperon	CHN 764	Stevens, Elisha	ORN 382
Stephens, Stephen	NYK 99	Stevens, Ephraim	CLN 162
Stephens, Stephen	RCK 103	Stevens, Ephraim	DUT 58
Stephens, Thomas	ALB 20	Stevens, Esther	HRK 581
Stephens, Thomas	CHN 896	Stevens, Francis	ONT 374
Stephens, Thomas	SUF 97		

Stevens, Frederick	WST 149
Stevens, Hallaway	ORN 329
Stevens, Henry	DUT 92
Stevens, Henry a Black	NYK 95
Stevens, Henry	SUF 95
Stevens, Hipsebe	SRA 14
Stevens, Horace a Black	NYK 71
Stevens, James	DUT 29
Stevens, James	OTS 17
Stevens, James	RNS 76
Stevens, James Junr	DUT 78
Stevens, James Senr	DUT 78
Stevens, Jehiel	DUT 168
Stevens, John	COL 205
Stevens, John	DUT 168
Stevens, John	NYK 29
Stevens, John a Black	NYK 49
Stevens, John	NYK 58
Stevens, John	NYK 90
Stevens, John	NYK 92
Stevens, John	NYK 99
Stevens, John	NYK 108
Stevens, John	NYK 152
Stevens, John	ONN 146
Stevens, John	ORN 314
Stevens, John	RNS 9
Stevens, John	SCH 119
Stevens, John	ULS 259
Stevens, John	WST 160
Stevens, John T.	WST 149
Stevens, Jonathan	ORN 382
Stevens, Joseph	DUT 145
Stevens, Joseph	NYK 122
Stevens, Joseph	ORN 382
Stevens, Joseph	SRA 46
Stevens, Joshua	WSH 276
Stevens, Laurence	NYK 145
Stevens, Leader	HRK 551
Stevens, Luther	HRK 568
Stevens, Matia	ORN 293
Stevens, Matthias	ORN 352
Stevens, Nathan	DEL 291
Stevens, Nehemiah	SRA 51
Stevens, Nicholas	ORN 276
Stevens, Obediah	STB 206
Stevens, Oliser	WST 159
Stevens, Oliver	OTS 17
Stevens, Peter	DUT 112
Stevens, Peter	WSH 292
Stevens, Resolvert	RCK 108
Stevens, Reubin a Black	NYK 108
Stevens, Roelef	NYK 102
Stevens, Russell	DUT 92
Stevens, Samuel	DEL 288
Stevens, Samuel	DUT 47
Stevens, Samuel	HRK 464
Stevens, Samuel	HRK 520
Stevens, Samuel	HRK 583
Stevens, Samuel	ONT 366
Stevens, Sarah	DUT 38
Stevens, Simeon	HRK 525
Stevens, Simion	WSH 252
Stevens, Simon 3d	WSH 252
Stevens, Stephen	DUT 67
Stevens, Susanna	ULS 238
Stevens, Thadius	WSH 223
Stevens, Thomas	DUT 54
Stevens, Thomas	DUT 133
Stevens, Thomas	ULS 221
Stevens, Thomas	WSH 184
Stevens, Thomas	WSH 295
Stevens, Thomas	WSH 302
Stevens, Thomas	WST 115
Stevens, Timothy	DUT 139

Stevens, Uriah	STB 206	Steward, Ezra	OND 164	Stewart, Gilbert	ALB 129
Stevens, Willm	COL 204	Steward, Gamaliel	DEL 270	Stewart, Henry	TIO 248
Stevens, William	OND 157	Steward, Henry	WSH 218	Stewart, Henry W.	DUT 151
Stevens, William	ONT 324	Steward, Isaac	COL 207	Stewart, Hugh	ONN 187
Stevens, William	OTS 16	Steward, Jabez	OND 198	Stewart, Isaac	RCH 94
Stevens, William	WST 160	Steward, James	DEL 268	Stewart, Isabella	NYK 80
Stevens, William Junr	WSH 184	Steward, James	MNT 123	Stewart, James	ALB 10
Stevens, Williams	WSH 184	Steward, James	WSH 198	Stewart, James	ALB 15
Stevenson, Alexander	DUT 68	Steward, James	WSH 217	Stewart, James	COL 263
Stevenson, Alexander	DUT 146	Steward, James B.	WSH 217	Stewart, James	NYK 28
Stevenson, Alexander	NYK 82	Steward, Jesse	DEL 285	Stewart, James	NYK 151
Stevenson, Amasa	CLN 163	Steward, John	DEL 270	Stewart, James	ONT 450
Stevenson, Andrew	WSH 281	Steward, John	MNT 78	Stewart, James	ORN 324
Stevenson, Andrew	WSH 303	Steward, John	WSH 195	Stewart, James	OTS 42
Stevenson, Caleb	MNT 125	Steward, John	WSH 195	Stewart, James	RNS 32
Stevenson, Cornelius	NYK 24	Steward, John	WSH 218	Stewart, James	RCK 102
Stevenson, David	NYK 107	Steward, John	WSH 256	Stewart, James	ULS 223
Stevenson, David	WSH 227	Steward, Joseph	WSH 185	Stewart, Jane	NYK 83
Stevenson, Ebenezer	NYK 124	Steward, Mathew	MNT 103	Stewart, Janus (possibly	
Stevenson, Ezekiel	CLN 162	Steward, Nathan	CHN 816	James)	
Stevenson, James	CAY 666	Steward, Nathan	HRK 513	Stewart, Jehiel	ULS 182
Stevenson, James	NYK 139	Steward, Nathaniel	DEL 289	Stewart, Joel	RNS 68
Stevenson, James	ORN 347	Steward, Obediah	MNT 20	Stewart, John	CAY 558
Stevenson, James	RCK 105	Steward, Oliver	OND 164	Stewart, John	COL 209
Stevenson, James	WSH 195	Steward, Robert	SCH 149	Stewart, John	DUT 73
Stevenson, James	WSH 210	Steward, Robert	WSH 222	Stewart, John	DUT 170
Stevenson, John	CLN 162	Steward, Simmeon	CHN 894	Stewart, John	GRN 328
Ste...son, John	MNT 84	Steward, Stephen	HRK 506	Stewart, John	KNG 10
Stevenson, John	NYK 73	Steward, Thomas	MNT 75	Stewart, John	NYK 124
Stevenson, John	NYK 109	Steward, Thomas	MNT 118	Stewart, John	ONT 338
Stevenson, John	NYK 138	Steward, William	WSH 232	Stewart, John	ORN 326
Stevenson, John	SCH 121	Steward, Wm Junr	MNT 75	Stewart, John	ORN 359
Stevenson, John	SCH 136	Stewart see Steuart,		Stewart, John	OTS 8
Stevenson, John	WSH 227	Stuart, Stwart &		Stewart, John	OTS 32
Stevenson, John	WSH 255	Stuwart		Stewart, John	OTS 38
Stevenson, John L.	ALB 11	Stewart, Abraham	NYK 84	Stewart, John	OTS 48
Stevenson, Joseph	NYK 30	Stewart, Alexander	NYK 31	Stewart, John H.	ONT 390
Stevenson, Matthias	RCH 93	Stewart, Alexander	NYK 77	Stewart, Jonathan	HRK 506
Stevenson, Nathaniel	DUT 52	Stewart, Alexander	ORN 289	Stewart, Joseph	CAY 666
Stevenson, Nathaniel	DUT 145	Stewart, Alexander	SRA 13	Stewart, Joseph	HRK 422
Stevenson, Peter	SRA 52	Stewart, Alexander	SRA 55	Stewart, Joseph	ORN 327
Stevenson, Peters a		Stewart, Alexander	WSH 269	Stewart, Lemuel	RNS 76
Black	NYK 151	Stewart, Allen	SRA 55	Stewart, Lemuel	SRA 16
Stevenson, Phebe a		Stewart, Amasa	OTS 53	Stewart, Luther	ORN 328
Black	NYK 109	Stewart, Ambrose	WSH 185	Stewart, Luther	ULS 182
Stevenson, Robert	NYK 84	Stewart, Andrew	DUT 127	Stewart, Mary	DUT 151
Stevenson, Samuel	WSH 226	Stewart, Andrew	SRA 41	Stewart, Mathew	RNS 110
Stevenson, Steven	WSH 210	Stewart, Archibald	DUT 62	Stewart, Nathaniel	SUF 101
Stevenson, Thomas	NYK 38	Stewart, Archibald	WSH 242	Stewart, Nathaniel	WST 134
Stevenson, William	WSH 193	Stewart, Asa	ORN 304	Stewart, Oliver	WST 151
Stever, David	COL 181	Stewart, Benjm	ALB 119	Stewart, Peter	DUT 87
Stever, David	SCH 136	Stewart, Benjamin	NYK 135	Stewart, Phebe	NYK 35
Stever, David P.	COL 177	Stewart, Benjamin	OND 223	Stewart, Phineas	RNS 68
Stever, George	COL 194	Stewart, Catharine	DUT 151	Stewart, Robert	NYK 112
Stever, Henry	OTS 42	Stewart, Charles	NYK 40	Stewart, Robert	OTS 4
Stever, Henry	OTS 42	Stewart, Charles	NYK 85	Stewart, Samuel	RNS 101
Stever, Jacob	COL 218	Stewart, Charles	NYK 114	Stewart, Samuel	SRA 7
Stever, Jacob	COL 244	Stewart, Charles	ONN 176	Stewart, Sarah	DUT 68
Stever, John	COL 230	Stewart, Charles	SRA 46	Stewart, Senica	WST 131
Stever, Samuel	SCH 161	Stewart, Colvin	ORN 293	Stewart, Silas	ORN 328
Steverson, Antoney	GRN 351	Stewart, Daniel	NYK 16	Stewart, Silas	SUF 102
Steves, Abijah	RNS 60	Stewart, Daniel	NYK 152	Stewart, Simon	WST 125
Steves, John	WSH 300	Stewart, Daniel S.	ULS 182	Stewart, Solomon	CAY 610
Steves, Richard	WSH 299	Stewart, David	KNG 9	Stewart, Solomon W.	DUT 47
Stevins, John	NYK 19	Stewart, David	WSH 290	Stewart, Thomas	DUT 122
Stevins, Joseph	NYK 21	Stewart, Duncan	ALB 32	Stewart, Thomas	NYK 113
Stevis, Conradt	MNT 47	Stewart, Eliphalet	OTS 46	Stewart, Walter	ALB 124
Stevnsbergh, Marks	MNT 21	Stewart, Eliphalet	RNS 78	Stewart, Walter	WSH 247
Steward, Aaron	DEL 285	Stewart, Eliphalet Junr	RNS 78	Stewart, William	ALB 115
Steward, Abram	COL 207	Stewart, Elisha	RNS 108	Stewart, William	HRK 548
Steward, Alexander	WSH 224	Stewart, Eluster	ONN 142	Stewart, Willm	KNG 9
Steward, Anthony	MNT 73	Stewart, Etheal	RNS 68	Stewart, William	NYK 18
Steward, Besili	WSH 208	Stewart, Finley	RNS 6	Stewart, William	OTS 4
Steward, Charles	SCH 149	Stewart, Fraderick	SRA 47	Stewart, William	WSH 281
Steward, Daniel	SCH 141	Stewart, George	ALB 4	Stewell, Elizabeth	NYK 80
Steward, Duncon	MNT 104	Stewart, George a		Stias, Stephen	DUT 53
Steward, Ebenezer	OND 198	Black	NYK 20	Stibbens, Ebenezer	ALB 25

Name	Loc	No.	Name	Loc	No.	Name	Loc	No.
Stick, Godfree	RNS	24	Stillman, Jesse	RNS	70	Stilwill, Barnet	SRA	29
Stickel, Nicholas N.	COL	193	Stillman, John	OND	174	Stilwill, David	SRA	29
Stickel, Peter F.	COL	239	Stillman, Josiah	OND	179	Stimbell, Mathias	NYK	116
Stickels, Catharine	COL	191	Stillman, Justus	OND	174	Stimes, John	OTS	14
Stickels, Nicholas	COL	200	Stillman, Samuel	OND	168	Stimets, John	NYK	84
Stickels, Nicholas Junr	COL	200	Stillman, Samuel	RNS	72	Stimpson, Enos	ONN	182
Stickels, William	COL	191	Stillman, Wait	RNS	72	Stimpson, John	ONT	394
Stickle, Andries	DUT	144	Stillman, Willet	OND	174	Stimpson, Leonard	ONT	310
Stickle, Edward	CLN	163	Stills, Richard	ONT	426	Stimpson, Robert	ONT	390
Stickle, Frederick	DUT	147	Stillson, Amos	RNS	106	Stimson, Ephraim	GRN	338
Stickle, Jacob	CLN	163	Stillson, Cyrenus	DEL	289	Stinard, Austin	WST	119
Stickle, John	DUT	157	Stillson, Jeremiah	DEL	273	Stine, Henry	NYK	52
Stickle, John I.	DUT	157	Stillson, Nathan	DEL	289	Stine, Nicholas	QNS	68
Stickle, Nicholas	DUT	142	Stillson, Treuman	DEL	289	Stinebergh see Stein-		
Stickle, Nicholas ye			Stillwell, Absolom	ORN	331	bergh		
2d	DUT	148	Stillwell, Barnet	DEL	284	Stinebergh, John	COL	191
Stickle, Nicholas I.	DUT	159	Stillwell, Benjamin	ONT	406	Stinehart, William	COL	220
Stickles, Adam	COL	193	Stillwell, Cornelius	ULS	215	Stiner, Casper	ALB	70
Stickles, John	CLN	164	Stillwell, Daniel	ALB	28	Stiner, Jacob	ALB	70
Stickles, John	COL	193	Stillwell, Daniel	ORN	369	Stiner, John	ALB	70
Stickles, Peter	ALB	34	Stillwell, Elias	ONN	171	Stinnard, Oglesbery D.	DUT	42
Stickles, Wilhelmus	COL	191	Stillwell, James	ULS	197	Stinor, Michael	MNT	69
Sticklin, Jonathan	QNS	65	Stillwell, John	DUT	5	Stinson, James	MNT	102
Sticklin, Oliver	QNS	65	Stillwell, John	OND	184	Stinson, John	CAY	702
Sticklin, William	SRA	50	Stillwell, Samuel	ONT	382	Stinson, Samuel	SRA	34
Stickney, Elipht	OTS	17	Stillwell, Thomas	DUT	145	Stinson, William	SRA	48
Stickney, James	ORN	338	Stillwell, William	ALB	44	Stiol, Caleb	TIO	229
Stickney, Jonathan	ORN	310	Stillwell, William	SRA	16	Stirling, James	OTS	46
Stickney, Marshall	ORN	311	Stillwill, Anthony	RNS	35	Stirney, John	WST	170
Stickney, Moses	HRK	530	Stillwill, Jeremiah	WSH	190	Stiv_s, Robert	ONT	508
Stickney, Reuben	OND	180	Stillwill, Samuel	NYK	123	Stiver, Peter	HRK	500
Stickney, Samuel B.	ORN	310	Stillwill, [W?]ill...	RNS	95	Stivers, Elisha	COL	220
Stidell, John Junr	NYK	19	Stillwill, Wm	SUF	64	Stivers, Jesse	COL	222
Stidman, Samuel	CHN	762	Stilman, Nath_	CHN	836	Stivers, Joshua	CAY	602
Stienback, Lawrence	NYK	128	Stilmon see Stimon			Stivers, Richard	COL	220
Sti[le_?], Janas	ONN	187	Stilson, Ezra	WSH	199	Stivers, Thomas	QNS	84
Stiler, James	MNT	66	Stilson, Gideon	ULS	235	Stivers, William	COL	221
Stiles, Aaron	DEL	278	Stiltson, Ebenezer	OND	208	Stiverson, Casparus	HRK	461
Stiles, Amos	CAY	670	Stilwell, Abraham	RCH	88	Stiverson, Jasper	HRK	456
Stiles, Arol	STB	201	Stilwell, Abraham	RCH	90	Stiverson, John	OND	200
Stiles, Avery	CLN	168	Stilwell, Abraham	WSH	278	Stiverson, Samuel	HRK	456
Stiles, Beriah	SCH	121	Stilwell, Barent	ESS	304	Stivus, Thomas	QNS	83
Stiles, David	OND	193	Stilwell, Christopher	KNG	6	S[to___?], George	CAY	538
Stiles, Frances	CHN	750	Stilwell, Daniel	NYK	33	Sto__, John	CHN	898
Stiles, Gold	WSH	188	Stilwell, Daniel	QNS	75	Sto_er, James	RNS	80
Stiles, Henry	NYK	127	Stilwell, Daniel	QNS	78	Stocher, Alexr	ALB	103
Stiles, Isaac	QNS	63	Stilwell, Daniel Junr	QNS	75	_tockbridge, Benjamin	NYK	135
Stiles, Isaiah	TIO	225	Stilwell, David	QNS	70	Stocker, Henry	ALB	74
Stiles, James	ULS	229	Stilwell, Diana	NYK	89	Stocker, Hugh	NYK	19
Stiles, John	MNT	125	Stilwell, Elias	NYK	89	Stocker, John	ALB	103
Stiles, Lewis	GRN	330	Stilwell, Elizabeth	NYK	33	Stocker, Stephen	DUT	54
Stiles, Loton	WSH	200	Stilwell, Jaques	KNG	5	Stocker, Wm	OTS	58
Stiles, Martin	CAY	702	Stilwell, Jeoicham	RCH	92	Stockham, John	ONN	179
Stiles, Mary	NYK	124	Stilwell, John	NYK	97	Stockholm, Aaron	DUT	25
Stiles, Nathan	OTS	15	Stilwell, John	NYK	113	Stockholm, Andrew	KNG	10
Stiles, Reuben	SRA	48	Stilwell, John	QNS	62	Stockholm, Harmonus	KNG	10
Stiles, Reuben	SRA	53	Stilwell, John	QNS	79	Stockhouse, Statea	RNS	53
Stiles, Robert	SCH	120	Stilwell, Joseph	KNG	5	Stocking, Alvin	DEL	281
Stiles, Robert	WSH	200	Stilwell, Lucritia	KNG	6	Stocking, Josiah	DEL	281
Stiles, Rowland	HRK	537	Stilwell, Mary	RCH	92	Stockings, Billious	WSH	289
Stiles, Samuel	CAY	658	Stilwell, Nicholas	KNG	4	Stockings, Hezekiah	OTS	55
Stiles, Samuel	ONT	426	Stilwell, Nicholas	RCH	90	Stockings, Timothy	TIO	214
Stiles, Timothy	STB	200	Stilwell, Nicholas	RCH	95	Stockman, John C.	ALB	124
Stiles, Widow	SRA	53	Stilwell, Peter	RCH	90	Stockton, Charles W.	DEL	277
Stiles, William	NYK	97	Stilwell, Richard	KNG	4	Stockwell, Aaron	CHN	756
Stiles, William	ULS	232	Stilwell, Richard	QNS	76	Stockwell, Abraham	WSH	270
Stilese, Nicholas	GRN	329	Stilwell, Richard R.	KNG	4	Stockwell, Asa	CHN	912
Still, Ebenezer	ONT	356	Stilwell, Rogers	WSH	300	Stockwell, David	CAY	696
Still, Elizabeth	NYK	50	Stilwell, Rutgert	KNG	4	Stockwell, Eleazar	CAY	696
Still, James	SUF	64	Stilwell, Sally	KNG	6	Stockwell, Eleazar B.	CAY	712
Still, Leonard	SUF	64	Stilwell, Samuel	QNS	73	Stockwell, John	WSH	270
Still, Leonard	SUF	65	Stilwell, Stephen	QNS	66	Stockwell, Levi	ESS	306
Still, Peter S.	NYK	125	Stilwell, Stephens	ESS	294	Stockwell, Levy	WSH	283
Still, Wm	SUF	66	Stilwell, Thomas	RCH	90	Stockwell, Moses	CHN	756
Stille, Henry	ORN	287	Stilwell, Thomas	WST	156	Stockwell, Samuel	NYK	35
Stillman, Elijah	OND	174	Stilwell, Wilkie	DUT	59	Stockwell, Timothy	OND	174
Stillman, George	RNS	71	Stilwell, William	NYK	34	Stockwell, Widow	CHN	912

Storms, John	WST 170	Stove, Martin	WSH 185	Strait, John	DUT 8
Storms, Matthias	WST 129	Stovell, William	CHN 802	Strait, John	MNT 113
Storms, Nicholas	WST 164	Stover, Adam	ALB 74	Strait, Joshua	CHN 740
Storms, Peter	MNT 16	Stover, Adam	DUT 13	Stranahan, James	COL 213
Storms, Peter	WST 164	Stover, Frederick	ALB 79	Stranahan, John	COL 213
Storms, Thomas	WST 164	Stover, Jacob	RNS 30	Stranahan, Lucy	COL 213
Storrs, John	OND 186	Stover, Martin	RNS 46	Stranahan, Wm	COL 203
Storrs, Joseph	ESS 317	Stover, Michael	ALB 80	Stranahan, Wm	OTS 21
Storrs, Joseph	ESS 323	Stover, Peter	ALB 74	Strang, Daniel	NYK 71
Storrs, Nathl	OTS 41	Stow see Stoe		Strang, Daniel	ORN 391
Story, Amos	DUT 148	Stow, Amos	WSH 302	Strang, Daniel	WSH 216
Story, Benjn	OTS 39	Stow, Cyrus	WSH 272	Strang, Daniel	WST 114
Story, Charles	RCH 88	Stow, Daniel	HRK 595	Strang, Daniel	WST 122
Story, Daniel	RCH 94	Stow, Daniel B.	COL 196	Strang, Ebenezer	WST 126
Story, Enoch	OND 164	Stow, David	TIO 231	Strang, Francis	WST 122
Story, James	DUT 121	Stow, David	TIO 231	Strang, Gilbert	WST 128
Story, Jonathan	ORN 318	Stow, Jacob	NYK 138	Strang, Henry	WST 122
Story, Oliver	OTS 13	Stow, John	WSH 272	Strang, James	WST 122
Story, Rowland	QNS 77	Stow, Josiah	TIO 231	Strang, John	NYK 113
Story, Saml	OTS 17	Stow, Lemuel	TIO 231	Strang, John	WSH 298
Story, States	HRK 447	Stow, Pitman	DUT 43	Strang, Joseph	WST 154
Story, Thomas	RCH 94	Stow, Silas	OND 222	Strang, Nathaniel	WST 123
Story, William W.	NYK 71	Stow, Simeon	WSH 281	Strang, Samuel	WST 157
Story, Zachariah	DUT 148	Stow, Timothy	WSH 201	Strang, Solomon	QNS 63
Story, Zachariah Junr	DUT 148	Stow, William	DUT 171	Strang, Thomas	WST 123
Story, Zebediah	QNS 67	Stow, William Junr	DUT 171	Strang, Underhill	WST 126
Stotesbury, Sarah	DUT 65	Stowe, Abi ah	CLN 160	Strangmen, Thomas	NYK 26
Stothoff, Wilhallimus	KNG 7	Stowe, Abijah	CLN 165	Strank, Philip	RNS 15
Stott, Alexander	NYK 71	Stowel, Samuel Jur	TIO 231	Strat, Dirck	RCK 107
Stott, Elizabeth	NYK 82	Stowell, Abijah	OTS 51	Straton, John	WSH 191
Stottle, Peter	CAY 538	Stowell, Asa	CHN 752	Strator, John	COL 246
Stottle, William	CAY 532	Stowell, Calvin	CHN 752	Stratten, David	ULS 231
Stoughton, John	ONT 430	Stowell, Daniel	CHN 876	Stratten, Eliza	NYK 22
Stoughton, John	RNS 93	Stowell, David	CHN 870	Stratten, Lotham	NYK 46
Stoughton, Samuel	CLN 168	Stowell, Elijah	CHN 752	Stratten, Samuel	ORN 271
Stoughton, Thomas		Stowell, Elisha	CHN 752	Stratten, Seth	COL 252
Spanish Consul	NYK 20	Stowell, Enoch	CHN 844	Stratton, Benjamin	NYK 45
Stoughton, William	HRK 451	Stowell, Hesekiah	CHN 752	Stratton, Benjamin Junr	NYK 45
Stouks, William	WSH 246	Stowell, Israel	CHN 752	Stratton, Daniel	COL 186
Stout, Andrew	NYK 21	Stowell, Israel	COL 202	Stratton, John	CLN 161
Stout, David	DEL 285	Stowell, Jacob	OTS 51	Stratton, John	CLN 165
Stout, Epemima	NYK 52	Stowell, Jesse	CHN 876	Stratton, John	SUF 106
Stout, George	DEL 285	Stowell, Jonathan	WSH 293	Stratton, John Junr	SUF 106
Stout, Jacob	WST 147	Stowell, Josiah	CHN 752	Stratton, Jonathan	SUF 81
Stout, James	DEL 285	Stowell, Solomon	CHN 876	Stratton, Jonathan	SUF 106
Stout, Jemima	NYK 38	Stowell, Wm	OTS 9	Stratton, Joseph	DEL 268
Stout, Johnson	CAY 726	Stower, Thomas	ESS 298	Stratton, Joseph Jun	DEL 268
Stout, Peter	NYK 150	Stowers, Joshua	CHN 856	Stratton, Samuel	DEL 268
Stout, Seymour	NYK 45	Stowers, Zebecka	CHN 856	Stratton, Stephen	SUF 81
Stout, Voluntine	WSH 236	Stoyell, James	CAY 672	Stratton, Stephen	SUF 107
Stout, William	HRK 466	Stoyell, John	CAY 670	Stratton, William	COL 191
Stout, William	WSH 251	Str___, Baullis	MNT 56	Stratton, William	COL 234
Stout, Zebedee	CAY 538	Strader, Nicholas	MNT 19	Stratton, William	NYK 64
Stouten, Amaziah	ONT 314	Straff, John	SRA 6	Straud, Jacob	MNT 31
Stoutenburgh, Luke P.	DEL 286	Strahan, James	ORN 291	St ause, Augustus	GRN 342
Stoutenburgh, Abraham	DUT 124	Straher, John	MNT 10	Straut, Jacob	RCK 110
Stoutenburgh, Benjamin	DUT 124	Straight, Calvin	OTS 30	Strawback, Adam J o Jr	SCH 172
Stoutenburgh, Ellen	NYK 53	Straight, Elijah	WSH 280	Strawback, Cornelius	SCH 165
Stoutenburgh, Henry	NYK 53	Straight, Franklin	OTS 28	Strayder, Nicholas	MNT 3
Stoutenburgh, Isaac	DUT 110	Straight, Henry	DUT 125	Strayton, Daniel	WSH 203
Stoutenburgh, Isaac	DUT 157	Straight, Henry	RNS 34	Strebeck, George	NYK 63
Stoutenburgh, James	DUT 107	Straight, Job	RNS 71	Street, Greenleaf	DUT 30
Stoutenburgh, James L.	DUT 124	Straight, John	OTS 30	Street, John	HRK 550
Stoutenburgh, James P.	GRN 351	Straight, John	WSH 264	Street, Levi	HRK 543
Stoutenburgh, James W.	DUT 114	Straight, John Jur	WSH 264	Street, Louisa	NYK 80
Stoutenburgh, John	DUT 110	Straight, Jonathan	ONT 410	Street, William	WST 170
Stoutenburgh, John	NYK 53	Straight, Nehemiah	WSH 280	Streeter, Amos	HRK 442
Stoutenburgh, John		Straight, Ruth	OTS 36	Streeter, Elias	ONT 484
ye 2d	DUT 107	Straight, Samuel	RNS 110	Streeter, James	HRK 413
Stoutenburgh, Peter		Straight, Thomas	ONT 438	Streeter, Joab	WSH 274
Junr	DUT 112	Straight, Thomas	WSH 188	Streeter, John	ONN 190
Stoutenburgh, Tobias	DUT 110	Strain, James Junr	OTS 40	Streeter, John	SRA 23
Stoutenburgh, Tobias	DUT 124	Strain, James Senr	OTS 40	Streeter, John	WSH 221
Stoutenburgh, Tobias L.	DUT 107	Strainho___, Frederick	MNT 30	Streeter, Joseph	OND 203
Stoutenburgh, William	DUT 114	Strait, Anthony	DUT 155	Streeter, Joshua	WSH 222
Stouter see Slouter		Strait, Catharine	DUT 163	Streeter, Nathan	WSH 288
Stouts, Henry	ALB 33	Strait, Jacob	DUT 159	Streeter, Stephen	ONT 484

357

Streeter, Thomas	ONT 484	Stronder, Mathew	WSH 184	Strong, Wm		ALB 11
Streight, Aspenwall	WSH 255	Stronder, Peter	WSH 184	Strong, Wm		MNT 42
Stretter, Eliab	ONT 484	Strong, Adonijah	OND 175	Strong, William		SRA 44
Streval, Benjamin	COL 243	Strong, Amos	CAY 608	Strong, William Junr		SRA 44
Streval, John	COL 243	Strong, Asa	ESS 293	Strong, Zodok		ONN 185
Strevel, Adam	COL 243	Strong, Asel	ESS 309	Strope, Fradrick		RNS 55
Strever, Adam	COL 241	Strong, Asher	OTS 16	Strope, John		RNS 10
Strever, Benjamin	COL 241	Strong, Assa	WSH 294	Strope, Wessles		ALB 93
Strever, Jacob	COL 242	Strong, Baley	GRN 345	Strope, William		RNS 12
Strever, Jacob	COL 243	Strong, Belly Junr	GRN 345	Stroud, James		NYK 31
Strever, John	DUT 145	Strong, Benajah	CAY 588	Stroud, Jasper		ONN 173
Strewbridge, James	WST 170	Strong, Benajah Junr	CAY 588	Stroud, Thomas		ONN 173
Stricker, Abraham	CAY 678	Strong, Benjamin	NYK 31	Stroud, Thomas		ONN 173
Stricker, Barney	CAY 548	Strong, Benjamin	ORN 362	Stroudger, John		ONT 362
Stricker, Jacob	CAY 548	Strong, Caleb	DEL 289	Strouh, Henry		MNT 19
Strickhoff, George	NYK 151	Strong, Charles	COL 203	Stroup, Wm		MNT 23
Strickland, Abraham	ULS 256	Strong, Danl	OTS 4	Strouse see Strause		
Strickland, Benjm	OTS 3	Strong, Eleazer	SRA 52	Strouse, Adam		ONT 310
Strickland, Ebenezer	ULS 255	Strong, Eli	OND 209	Stroveyer, John		SRA 39
Strickland, Ebenezer	WSH 233	Strong, Elias	ULS 186	Strowbridge, George		ONN 188
Strickland, Jacob	ULS 255	Strong, Elijah	GRN 333	Strum, David		MNT 49
Strickland, John	OTS 56	Strong, Elijah	HRK 429	Strunk, Henry		ONT 378
Strickland, Noah	OTS 56	Strong, Elisha	GRN 333	Strunk, John		RNS 97
Strickland, Roger	OTS 8	Strong, Elisha	ONN 191	Struss, John		COL 191
Strickland, Saml	OTS 3	Strong, Epaphroditus	CAY 644	Strut___, Jacob a		
Strickland, William	ORN 383	Strong, Ezra	CAY 644	Black		NYK 88
Strickler, John	NYK 19	Strong, Francis	ONN 185	Strutt, Soloman		RNS 62
Striker, Abraham	ULS 251	Strong, Gabril	SRA 44	Stryker, Burdet		KNG 8
Striker, Barent	SCH 145	Strong, George	SUF 107	Stryker, Cornelius		KNG 5
Striker, Daniel	NYK 18	Strong, Gilbert	CHN 838	Stryker, John		KNG 2
Striker, Dennis	NYK 17	Strong, Hannah	NYK 15	Stryker, Michael		KNG 2
Striker, Garret	OTS 54	Strong, Isaac	CAY 688	Stryker, Peter		KNG 2
Striker, Henry	NYK 124	Strong, Isaac	OTS 16	Stryker, Samuel		KNG 4
Striker, James	NYK 152	Strong, Jedediah	ALB 52	Stuard, Charles		SRA 14
Striker, John	NYK 52	Strong, Jeremag	GRN 333	Stuard, James H.		GRN 325
Striker, Peter	OTS 51	Strong, Jeremiah	COL 224	Stuard, [W?]m		GRN 357
Striker, Peter	SCH 137	Strong, Joel	MNT 110	Stuart see Stewart &		
Striker, Peter	SCH 145	Strong, John	NYK 151	Stuart		
Striker, Peter Junr	SCH 145	Strong, John	OND 194	Stuart, Angus		NYK 95
Striker, Valentine	ONT 470	Strong, John	RNS 53	Stuart, Benjamin		ONT 434
Strile, John	ALB 28	Strong, John	SRA 20	Stuart, Bern B.		WST 132
Stringer, Jeremiah	CAY 580	Strong, John	SUF 107	Stuart, Dennis		SRA 21
Stringer, Samuel	ALB 147	Strong, Joseph	NYK 42	Stuart, Enoch		CAY 560
Stringham, Daniel	ORN 337	Strong, Joseph	ONN 178	Stuart, Hugh		NYK 30
Stringham, Daniel	WST 149	Strong, Joseph	OTS 19	Stuart, James		CAY 656
Stringham, Henry	CAY 632	Strong, Josiah	ALB 30	Stuart, James		CAY 664
Stringham, Henry	WST 119	Strong, Josiah	GRN 345	Stuart, James		NYK 79
Stringham, Henry	WST 148	Strong, Luther	WSH 275	Stuart, John		NYK 88
Stringham, Jacob	WST 149	Strong, Mary	COL 197	Stuart, John		NYK 137
Stringham, James	DUT 123	Strong, Nathan	OND 180	Stuart, John		TIO 226
Stringham, James	NYK 72	Strong, Oliver	SRA 50	Stuart, Joseph		SRA 21
Stringham, James	ORN 343	Strong, Othniel	OND 187	Stuart, Mary		NYK 109
Stringham, James	QNS 71	Strong, Ozias	ONN 185	Stuart, Nathan		ONT 344
Stringham, John	ESS 318	Strong, Peter B.	OND 191	Stuart, Robart		CAY 656
Stringham, John	QNS 79	Strong, Philip	CAY 644	Stuart, Robert		CAY 666
Stringham, Owen	DUT 105	Strong, Philo	ESS 309	Stuart, Thomas		CAY 542
Stringham, Peter	DUT 116	Strong, Phinehas	SRA 53	Stuart, William		ESS 295
Stringham, Samuel	DUT 9	Strong, Return	NYK 19	Stuart, William		NYK 88
Stringham, Samuel	QNS 75	Strong, Roger	SRA 40	Stuart, William		NYK 88
Stringham, Samuel	QNS 76	Strong, Salmon	CAY 588	Stuart, William		ONT 510
Stringham, Stephen	DUT 121	Strong, Samuel	ORN 353	Stubbs, Charles		NYK 128
Stringham, Thomas	DUT 112	Strong, Saml	OTS 16	Stubbs, William		ORN 340
Stringham, William	DUT 105	Strong, Samuel	SUF 93	Stubrach, Barent		SCH 120
Stringham, William	ORN 337	Strong, Samuel Junr	ORN 354	Stubrach, Christian		SCH 120
Stringham, William	ULS 256	Strong, Selah	NYK 44	Stubs, Wm		MNT 93
Stringom, Peter	GRN 342	Strong, Selah	ORN 353	Studdevan, John		NYK 140
Stripple, Henry	NYK 67	Strong, Selah	SUF 66	Studley, Joseph		OTS 2
Stritch, Samuel	NYK 21	Strong, Sim..n	CAY 588	Studley, Warren		OTS 2
Strite, John	NYK 126	Strong, Solomon	CAY 608	Studson, Benjaman		CHN 912
Strit[ur?], Daniel	STB 199	Strong, Solomon	CAY 608	Studwell, Gabriel		CAY 612
Strock, Eliza	RCK 105	Strong, Stephen	GRN 343	Studwell, Henry		CAY 612
Stroeback, Jacob	SCH 173	Strong, Talmage	SUF 107	Studwell, Peter		CAY 614
Stroecker, Frederick	MNT 14	Strong, Thomas	OND 181	Stuffenbeam, Volentine		TIO 260
Stroecker, Philip	MNT 14	Strong, Thomas	SRA 29	Stufflebeam, John		CAY 572
Stronder, Alexander	WSH 184	Strong, Thos	SUF 68	Stufflebeam, Michael		CAY 572
Stronder, John	WSH 184	Strong, Thomas	SUF 99	Stufflebeen, Henry		COL 199
Stronder, John Tice	WSH 183	Strong, Timothy	OTS 16	Stufflebeen, Jacob		COL 196

Stufflebeen, Martin	COL 198	Suett, Abraham	SRA 5	Susa, Emanuel	RNS 83
Stuheven, Anna	NYK 36	Sufelt, George Junr	COL 193	Susan a Black	NYK 91
Stuiles, Daniel	QNS 63	Sufelt, Zacheriah	COL 238	Susan a mulatto	NYK 99
Stuine, Elizabeth	QNS 68	Suffern, Andrew	RCK 100	Susanna a free wench	ALB 8
Stulls, Jacob	TIO 262	Suffern, John	RCK 105	Susanna a wench of	
Stultz, Charles	ORN 386	Suffren, George	NYK 32	Arent Veeder	ALB 9
Stump, John	ULS 189	Suffren, John	NYK 96	Susanna a free wench	ALB 146
Stump, John	ULS 247	Sugars, George	ALB 143	Susannah a Black	NYK 18
Sturdevant see Surtivent		Sugner, Henry	NYK 151	Susannah	NYK 82
& Sturtevant		Suise, Nicholas	GRN 330	Suser, Lewis	GRN 352
Sturdevant, Asher	ULS 240	Suit_, Adam	MNT 62	Suta, John	NYK 19
Sturdevant, Charles	DUT 93	Suitt, James	SRA 5	Suter, Robert	ORN 294
Sturdevant, Elijah	DUT 93	Sukels, John H.	NYK 19	Sutfern, Derick	SRA 40
Sturdevant, Ephr	OTS 7	Sukels, Phoebe	NYK 47	Sutfield, Clion	QNS 69
Sturdevant, John	DUT 95	Sukels, Sarah	NYK 19	Sutfin, John	WSH 253
Sturdevant, John	ORN 272	Sukely, George	NYK 52	Sutfin, Peter	CAY 680
Sturdevant, Jonathan	DUT 94	Sukerson, William	NYK 15	Sutherland see Souther-	
Sturg, Hillsdale	GRN 355	Sullard, Barney	SRA 13	land	
Sturge, Aaron	SRA 45	Sullard, David	ALB 132	Sutherland, Adam	SCH 134
Sturge, Augustus	RNS 107	Sulliman, Isaac	DEL 269	Sutherland, Alexander	ORN 296
Sturges, Aaron	SRA 16	Sullivan see Sylliven		Sutherland, Amos	COL 219
Sturges, Aquila	CLN 157	Sullivan, Benjamin	NYK 129	Sutherland, Andrew	ORN 396
Sturges, Daniel	ULS 186	Sullivan, Betsey	NYK 75	Sutherland, Angus	NYK 109
Sturges, David	GRN 343	Sullivan, Charles	ALB 40	Sutherland, Charles	ORN 396
Sturges, Ebenezer	DEL 269	Sullivan, David	ALB 111	Sutherland, David	ONT 454
Sturges, Isaac	ALB 141	Sullivan, George	ORN 319	Sutherland, David	ORN 395
Sturges, John	NYK 16	Sullivan, James	WST 148	Sutherland, David J.	DUT 125
Sturges, Nathaniel	SRA 20	Sullivan, John	ALB 28	Sutherland, Eliza	KNG 9
Sturges, Nathaniel L.	NYK 42	Sullivan, John	NYK 31	Sutherland, George	COL 262
Sturges, Perry	DEL 269	Sullivan, John	NYK 72	Sutherland, James	COL 220
Sturges, Peter	COL 181	Sullivan, John	NYK 78	Sutherland, James	NYK 44
Sturges, Samuel	DEL 269	Sullivan, Sarah	NYK 15	Sutherland, James	ORN 388
Sturges, Simion	SRA 6	Sults, John P.	MNT 20	Sutherland, James	ORN 396
Sturges, Strong	NYK 77	Sults, Peter	MNT 17	Sutherland, Jane	NYK 17
Sturges, William	DEL 288	Sulvary, Emanuel	COL 249	Sutherland, Joel D.	DUT 127
Sturgis, Mary	DUT 166	Sumervil, Elizabeth	WSH 203	Sutherland, John	COL 219
Sturman, Edward	NYK 76	Sumervill, Thomas	WSH 203	Sutherland, John	ONT 422
Sturtevant, Eliphalet	NYK 101	Sumey, John	NYK 18	Sutherland, Joseph	DUT 102
Sturtevelt, Zadock	HRK 479	Summer, John	SCH 163	Sutherland, Joseph	DUT 119
Sturtivent, Consider	WSH 220	Summer, Nichs	SCH 163	Sutherland, Joseph	ORN 396
Sturversant, Peter	NYK 28	Summer, Nichs W.	SCH 163	Sutherland, Josiah	DUT 124
Stutherland, John	NYK 147	Summers, Elijah	ALB 84	Sutherland, Leonard	COL 220
Stutlief, Gad	CHN 816	Summers, Joel	ALB 23	Sutherland, Patrick	ORN 396
Stutson, Eli	OTS 32	Summers, Joel	ALB 24	Sutherland, Reuben	ONT 422
Stutson, Robert	CLN 171	Summers, Samuel S.	ALB 45	Sutherland, Roger	DUT 102
Stutson, Rubin	CLN 171	Sum[mers?], Syllick	TIO 251	Sutherland, Roger Junr	DUT 130
Stutson, Saml	OTS 32	Summers, Waldrop	NYK 69	Sutherland, Roger B.	DUT 132
Stutson, Timo	OTS 32	Summers, William Munk	NYK 84	Sutherland, Rowland	DUT 124
Stuwart see Stewart		Summerton, John	CAY 676	Sutherland, Smith	COL 219
Stuwart, Torry	RNS 68	Summerton, Phinehas	CAY 676	Sutherland, Solomon	DUT 59
Stuyersant, Peter	NYK 142	Summerton, Thomas	CAY 676	Sutherland, Thomas	DUT 102
Stuymets, Garret	NYK 84	Summerux, Peter	WST 127	Sutherland, Wm	ALB 13
Stuyversant, Nicholas W.	NYK 142	Summons, Thomas	STB 204	Sutherland, Willm	COL 220
Stuyversant, Peter	NYK 36	Summons, Widow	STB 204	Sutherland, William	ORN 396
Stwart, Daniel	WSH 276	Summur, Wilhelmus	SCH 163	Sutherland, William R.	DUT 125
Stwart, George a Black	NYK 102	Sumner, Amasy	SRA 34	Sutherland, William T.	DUT 102
Styles, Daniel	HRK 565	Sumner, Benjamin	SRA 34	Suthpon, Richard	MNT 50
Styles, James	DUT 162	Sumner, Caleb	WSH 304	Sutlif, John	NYK 122
Stymeson, Auchy	QNS 78	Sumner, Jacob B.	DEL 282	Sutliff, Samuel	HRK 547
Stymets, George	NYK 55	Sumner, John	SRA 34	Sutphin, Gilbert	OTS 2
Stymets, Isaac	NYK 149	Sumner, Jonathan	DEL 282	Sutphin, John	OTS 2
Stymets, Jonas	NYK 151	Sumner, Robert	SRA 34	Sutphin, Peter	OTS 2
Stymets, Sarah	DUT 30	Sumner, Samuel	ESS 303	Suts, Catharine	MNT 13
Stymets, William	NYK 22	Sumner, Thomas	OTS 43	Suts, Nicholas	MNT 10
Stymets, William	ULS 234	Sumpsom, Joseph	SCH 160	Suts, Peter P.	MNT 7
Stymits, Jasper	WST 164	Sunderland, Daniel	DUT 91	Suts, Peter R.	MNT 10
Suard see Seward &		Sunderland, John	DUT 168	Suts, Richard	MNT 10
Suward		Sunderland, John	WSH 267	Sutten, Mercy	ONT 312
Suard, Daniel	WST 151	Sunderland, Joseph	WST 129	Suttenfield, Margret	ONT 310
Suard, Stephen	WST 151	Sunderlin, Jeremiah	WSH 300	Suttle, David	ALB 103
Subel, Smith	ALB 79	Sunn, John	COL 215	Suttle, Peter	MNT 66
Suckels, Daniel	NYK 75	Supplie, John	ONT 466	Sutton, Benjamin	CAY 534
Suckels, Zacharius	NYK 75	Surdivent see Sturdevant		Sutton, Benjamin	NYK 128
Suckler, James	MNT 97	Surdivent, James	WSH 206	Sutton, Benjamin	ONN 131
Suddert, Daniel	SRA 35	Surmandyke, William	NYK 97	Sutton, Caleb(?)	DEL 274
Sude_, J[acob?]	MNT 44	Surrie, Aaron	NYK 26	Sutton, Caleb	DUT 20
Suel, Jonathan	WSH 252	Surtivent, Peirce	WSH 216	Sutton, Caleb	ORN 399

Name	Loc	Pg	Name	Loc	Pg	Name	Loc	Pg
Sutton, Daniel	NYK	128	Swade, Dirck	DUT	18	Swart, Lawrance	DEL	288
Sutton, Daniel	WST	132	Swaen, John	WSH	269	Swart, Lodiwick	MNT	11
Sutton, David	ULS	243	Swaim, Ellenor	NYK	58	Swart, Nelles	SRA	39
Sutton, Edward	DUT	26	Swaim, Isaac	RCH	89	Swart, Nicholas	ALB	24
Sutton, Elihu	ONT	324	Swain, Azre	WSH	220	Swart, Peter	ALB	72
Sutton, Elisha	HRK	567	Swain, Benjamin	RCH	94	S[wart?], Peter	DEL	282
Sutton, Elisha	ONT	454	Swain, Christopher	NYK	67	Swart, Peter	SCH	118
Sutton, George	NYK	86	Swain, Daniel	WSH	265	Swart, Peter	ULS	228
Sutton, Giles	COL	238	Swain, Isaiah	COL	248	Swart, Peter Junr	SCH	127
Sutton, Henry	DEL	274	Swain, John	RCH	91	Swart, Phillip	ULS	227
Sutton, Isaac	ORN	275	Swain, John	WSH	234	Swart, Samuel	ULS	232
Sutton, Jacob	CAY	540	Swain, Jonathan	WSH	220	Swart, Sebastian	DEL	283
Sutton, James	NYK	35	Swain, Mary	WSH	235	Swart, Thomas	COL	234
Sutton, James	WST	132	Swain, Mortinus	RCH	92	Swart, Thomas	SRA	12
Sutton, James	WST	133	Swain, Sarah	NYK	96	Swart, Thomas Junr	ULS	226
Sutton, Jeremiah	CAY	694	Swain, Simon	RCH	89	Swart, Tobias	ULS	230
Sutton, Jesse	WST	112	Swain, Thos	OTS	41	Swart, Tunis	SRA	24
Sutton, John	ORN	276	Swain, Willeam	WSH	264	Swart, Walter J.	MNT	115
Sutton, John	ORN	371	Swaine, Abner	OTS	57	Swart, William	DEL	283
Sutton, John P.	WST	129	Swaine, Calvin	OTS	14	Swart, Wm	MNT	108
Sutton, John P. Junr	WST	129	Swale, Matthias	SRA	8	Swart, William	ULS	227
Sutton, Joseph	NYK	15	Swales, Henry	NYK	87	Swarthout see Swortwout		
Sutton, Joseph	NYK	130	Swalm, Godfrey	ORN	296	Swarthout, Adolphus	ALB	79
Sutton, Joseph	ONT	326	Swan, Adam	SRA	28	Swarthout, Jesse	SCH	172
Sutton, Joseph	WST	132	Swan, Adin	RNS	102	Swartout, Anthony	CAY	536
Sutton, Joshua	ULS	267	Swan, David	SRA	20	Swartout, Anthony	CAY	540
Sutton, Moses	CAY	618	Swan, Dyer	ALB	67	Swartout, Anthony Jun	CAY	536
Sutton, Moses	WST	132	Swan, Edward	ULS	217	Swartout, Barney	CAY	536
Sutton, Nathaniel	CAY	556	Swan, George	ALB	105	Swartout, Cornelius	RNS	84
Sutton, Nehemiah	WST	155	Swan, Isaac	ULS	198	Swartout, Cornelius	SRA	43
Sutton, Noah	WST	159	Swan, Jesse	ALB	67	Swartout, James	SRA	9
Sutton, Robert	ONN	131	Swan, Jesse	SCH	133	Swartout, James	SRA	43
Sutton, Robert	QNS	70	Swan, John	CAY	646	Swartout, John	RNS	85
Sutton, Robert	WST	124	Swan, John	NYK	142	Swartout, Nathaniel	CAY	536
Sutton, Rozel	ONN	131	Swan, Jonathan	OND	206	Swartout, Ralph	CAY	542
Sutton, Samuel	WST	132	Swan, Joseph	RNS	105	Swartout, Joseph	GRN	351
Sutton, Solomon	ALB	9	Swan, Joshua	SRA	20	Sw[arts?], John	CAY	536
Sutton, Stephen	ULS	267	Swan, Joshua Junr	SRA	22	Swarts, Philip J.	HRK	420
Sutton, Thomas	DUT	72	Swan, Nathaniel	ALB	64	Swartscoap, Valentine	KNG	10
Sutton, William	DUT	73	Swan, Peleg	SRA	58	Swartwood, Daniel	TIO	241
Sutton, William	HRK	435	Swan, Sarah	NYK	113	Swartwood, Isaac	TIO	233
Sutton, Zachariah	CAY	560	Swan, Timo	OTS	52	Swartwood, Jacob	TIO	233
Suward see Seward			Swan, Wheeler	OTS	53	Swartwood, James	TIO	241
Suward, Samuel S.	ORN	366	Swan, William	ORN	368	Swartwood, Peter	TIO	233
Suweny, Hamiah	NYK	131	Swan, Ziba	ALB	139	Swartwout, Aaron	ULS	181
Suydam see Sydam			Swant, John Reed	DEL	278	Swartwout, Bernardus	DUT	62
Suydam, Andrew	KNG	2	Swantan, William	NYK	65	Swartwout, Bernardus	NYK	50
Suydam, Cornelius	KNG	8	Swap, Andrew	WSH	290	Swartwout, Cornelius	DUT	69
Suydam, Cornelius	QNS	79	Swap, Frederick	ALB	114	Swartwout, Cornelius	ORN	315
Suydam, Garret	QNS	79	Swart, Abraham	ULS	254	Swartwout, Isaac	DUT	29
Suydam, George	KNG	4	Swart, Adam	SRA	24	Swartwout, Jacob	OTS	4
Suydam, Hendrick	KNG	2	Swart, Adam	ULS	228	Swartwout, Jacobus	DUT	31
Suydam, Hendrick	KNG	7	Swart, Bartho	SCH	118	Swartwout, Jacobus	ORN	315
Suydam, Hendrick	KNG	7	Swart, Bartho Junr	SCH	118	Swartwout, James	DUT	124
Suydam, Hendrick	KNG	10	Swart, Benjamin	ULS	226	Swartwout, James R.	DUT	26
Suydam, Hendrick	QNS	63	Swart, Catharine	COL	232	Swartwout, John	MNT	15
Suydam, Hendrick H.	KNG	2	Swart, Coenradt	ALB	72	Swartwout, John	NYK	31
Suydam, Henry	QNS	79	Swart, Cornelius	ULS	218	Swartwout, Mary	DUT	66
Suydam, Jacob	QNS	65	Swart, Cornelius Junr	DUT	157	Swartwout, Moses	OTS	4
Suydam, Jacobus	QNS	79	Swart, Cornelius L.	ULS	225	Swartwout, Myndert	DUT	62
Suydam, James	QNS	61	Swart, Daniel	MNT	108	Swartwout, Peter	ORN	315
Suydam, James	WST	145	Swart, David	SCH	118	Swartwout, Richard	RCK	101
Suydam, John	KNG	9	Swart, Dirk	SRA	47	Swartwout, Robert	ULS	227
Suydam, John	NYK	20	Swart, Isaac	ULS	249	Swartwout, Samuel	DUT	119
Suydam, Lambert	KNG	7	Swart, Jacob	ALB	71	Swartwout, Simon	DUT	38
Suydam, Maria	KNG	5	Swart, Jacob	SRA	24	Swartwout, Thomas	ULS	195
Suydam, Minney	QNS	79	Swart, Jacobus	ALB	24	Swartwout, William	ULS	195
Suydam, Oke	ULS	228	Swart, James	ULS	226	Swartz, Daniel	CAY	584
Suydam, Peter	CAY	708	Swart, Jeremiah	ALB	19	Swartz, Jacob	NYK	68
Suydam, Ram	QNS	60	Swart, John	ALB	69	Swarwout, Elizabeth	NYK	23
Suydam, Ryneer	NYK	17	Swart, John	COL	232	Swating, Nathaniel	OND	164
Suydam, Tunis	KNG	5	Swart, John	DUT	30	Sweat, Eleazer	CHN	816
Suyland, Johannis	ULS	206	Swart, John	MNT	108	Sweat, Elijah	CHN	792
Suyren, Rowland	QNS	81	Swart, John	ULS	248	Sweat, Elijah Junr	CHN	792
Suzan a Black	NYK	65	Swart, John	ULS	254	Sweat, Jarvis	CHN	812
Sw__	GRN	336	Swart, Josiah	ALB	3	Sweat, Ruscom	QNS	65
Swabee, George	ULS	212	Swart, Josiah	MNT	114	Sweat, Stephen	CHN	906

Sweatland, Caleb	CHN 932	Sweet, Perseus	DUT 12	Swesey, Hannah	SUF 64
Sweatman, Abraham	MNT 47	Sweet, Philip	OTS 30	Swesey, Isaac	SUF 69
Sweeney see Suweny &		Sweet, Philip	RNS 113	Swesey, James	SUF 69
Sweney		Sweet, Reuben	OND 189	Swesey, Joseph	SUF 65
Sweeney, James	NYK 117	Sweet, Richard	WSH 302	Swesey, Joseph	SUF 71
Sweeney, Thomas	NYK 66	Sweet, Robert	DUT 58	Swesey, Joshua	SUF 69
Sweeny, John	DUT 85	Sweet, Rogers	RNS 100	Swesey, Richd	SUF 69
Sweep, Jacob	DEL 278	Sweet, Rowland	ALB 84	Swesey, Richd	SUF 71
Sweet, Abel	MNT 104	Sweet, Rowland	COL 243	Swesey, Sten	SUF 69
Sweet, Abner	RNS 83	Sweet, Rowland	SRA 52	Swesey, Wm	SUF 67
Sweet, Amos	CAY 578	Sweet, Rufus	DUT 13	Sweting see Sweeting	
Sweet, Amos	DUT 13	Sweet, Samuel	ALB 82	Sweting, Lewis Jur	ONN 167
Sweet, Amos	OTS 38	Sweet, Samuel	CAY 642	Swetzer, Peter	NYK 43
Sweet, Amos	SRA 60	Sweet, Samuel	DUT 12	Swezey, David	SUF 95
Sweet, Asa	HRK 531	Sweet, Samuel	MNT 113	Swezey, Joseph	SRA 3
Sweet, Asa	RNS 76	Sweet, Samuel	OTS 38	Swicks, Benjamin	CAY 540
Sweet, Benjamin	ALB 119	Sweet, Samuel	RNS 72	Swicks, John	CAY 542
Sweet, Benjamin	CAY 690	Sweet, Samuel	SRA 28	Swicks, Martin	CAY 550
Sweet, Benjamin	DUT 8	Sweet, Samuel	SRA 50	Swift, Abraham	DUT 104
Sweet, Benjamin	HRK 503	Sweet, Samuel T.	RNS 98	Swift, Alpheus	RNS 9
Sweet, Benjamin	HRK 562	Sweet, Silas	ALB 82	Swift, Ambrose	HRK 469
Sweet, Benjn	OTS 33	Sweet, Silas	RNS 72	Swift, Charles	CHN 938
Sweet, Benoni	WSH 209	Sweet, Simeon	RNS 20	Swift, Daniel	COL 182
Sweet, Benoni	WSH 209	Sweet, Simon	RNS 76	Swift, Elisha	ONT 484
Sweet, Benoni	WSH 210	Sweet, Stephen	DUT 42	Swift, Herman	ONT 480
Sweet, Caleb	OTS 47	Sweet, Stephen	OTS 47	Swift, Ichabod	ULS 183
Sweet, Caleb	SRA 26	Sweet, Stephen the 2d	DUT 47	Swift, Isaiah	DUT 90
Sweet, Daniel	ALB 119	Sweet, Stephen W.	ONN 130	Swift, Jesse	CAY 650
Sweet, Daniel	NYK 109	Sweet, Sylvester	DUT 98	Swift, John	COL 207
Sweet, David	DUT 13	Sweet, Thaddeus	RNS 23	Swift, John	DUT 178
Sweet, David	OTS 47	Sweet, Theophilus	DUT 58	Swift, John	ONT 352
Sweet, David	RNS 101	Sweet, Thomas	RNS 98	Swift, Jonathan	CAY 650
Sweet, David	SRA 17	Sweet, Thomas C.	SRA 26	Swift, Judah	DUT 133
Sweet, Dodge	WSH 209	Sweet, Timothy	ONN 145	Swift, Nathaniel	COL 184
Sweet, Eber	ALB 82	Sweet, Waltor	MNT 124	Swift, Nehemiah	CAY 706
Sweet, Edmond	HRK 562	Sweet, Widow	HRK 523	Swift, Perez	COL 187
Sweet, Eleazer	OTS 38	Sweet, Wilber	CAY 686	Swift, Philetus	ONT 478
Sweet, Elnathan	DUT 12	Sweet, Willeam	WSH 264	Swift, Pompey	DUT 100
Sweet, Elnathan	RNS 100	Sweet, William	RNS 17	Swift, Samuel	CHN 934
Sweet, Ethan	DUT 132	Sweet, Wm	RNS 72	Swift, Samuel	DUT 132
Sweet, Ezekiel	WSH 300	Sweet, William	WSH 298	Swift, Seth	COL 182
Sweet, Ezra	WSH 294	Sweeten, Ambrous	SRA 41	Swift, ons	CHN 930
Sweet, Francis	OTS 32	Sweeting see Sweting		Swift, Thomas	COL 184
Sweet, Francis	OTS 38	Sweeting, John	ONN 167	Swift, Thomas C.	HRK 478
Sweet, Freeborn	RNS 20	Sweeting, Lewis	ONN 167	Swift, William	ALB 31
Sweet, George	RNS 72	Sweeting, Mason	OND 167	Swift, Zaccheus	MNT 21
Sweet, Griffen	OTS 47	Sweetland, Aaron	WSH 275	Swim, Cornelius	ORN 392
Sweet, Henry	DUT 10	Sweetland, Abner	WSH 279	Swim, Cornelius Junr	ORN 392
Sweet, Henry	HRK 425	Sweetland, David	RNS 14	Swim, Henry	ORN 394
Sweet, Henry	OTS 32	Sweetland, Ebenezer	WSH 279	Swim, John	ORN 392
Sweet, Isaac	HRK 571	Sweetland, Joseph	ONN 178	Swin, Henry William	NYK 56
Sweet, James	OND 189	Sweetland, Samuel	SRA 5	Swinburn, Anna	NYK 70
Sweet, Jesse	MNT 122	Sweetman, Henderson	MNT 6	Swinburn, Peter	HRK 599
Sweet, Job	ALB 111	Sweetman, John	SCH 156	Swinell, Francis	NYK 93
Sweet, Job	WSH 298	Sweetman, Michael	NYK 81	Swingle, Jacob S.	TIO 248
Sweet, John	GRN 352	Sweetman, Thomas	SRA 23	Switcher, Henry	RCK 106
Sweet, John	MNT 125	Sweeton, Michael	OTS 4	Switeser, Peter	WSH 228
Sweet, John	RNS 72	Sweets, James	CAY 522	Switser, Christopher	WSH 183
Sweet, John	SRA 26	Sweett, Charles	SRA 56	Switser, John	WSH 228
Sweet, John	WSH 294	Sweezey see Swezey		Switts, Schuyler	RNS 6
Sweet, Jonathan	OTS 38	Sweezey, David	ONT 344	Switz, Abm	ALB 9
Sweet, Jonathan	RNS 20	Sweezy, Daniel	HRK 588	Switz, Andrew	ALB 8
Sweet, Jonathan	RNS 101	Sweezy, Daniel	SUF 92	Switz, Henry	ALB 8
Sweet, Jonathan Junr	RNS 101	Sweezy, David	ORN 318	Switz, Jacob	ALB 4
Sweet, Jonathan J.	RNS 100	Sweezy, David	ORN 362	Switz, Walter	ALB 4
Sweet, Joseph	OTS 38	Sweezy, Jonathan	ORN 356	Swobe, Michael	ONT 338
Sweet, Joseph	SCH 173	Sweezy, Joseph	ORN 338	Sword, Thomas	SCH 121
Sweet, Joshua	ALB 78	Sweezy, Moses	SUF 92	Swords, James	NYK 25
Sweet, Lebbeus	DUT 139	Sweezy, Richard	HRK 600	Swortwout, Josep.	TIO 237
Sweet, Levius	RNS 111	Sweigle, Matthew	ORN 323	Sybert, John	WST 145
Sweet, Nathan	DUT 42	Swells, John	NYK 133	Syckman, Hendrick	ULS 222
Sweet, Nathaniel	DUT 10	Sweny see Sweeney		Sydam see Suydam	
Sweet, Nathaniel	RNS 111	Sweney, Archibald	ONT 502	Sydam, Andrew	RNS 20
Sweet, Oliver	HRK 561	Sweney, Cornelius	NYK 144	Sydam, Anthony	RNS 20
Sweet, Oliver	ONN 135	Swesey, Aeneas	SUF 69	Sydam, Cornelius	QNS 81
Sweet, Peleg	RNS 20	Swesey, Asey	SUF 65	Sydam, Peter	RNS 20
Sweet, Peleg	RNS 111	Swesey, Elihue	SUF 72	Sydam, Saml	RNS 20

Name	Loc	Name	Loc	Name	Loc
Syde_, John	MNT 33	Tabour, Phelix	SRA 33	Tallman, William	ALB 18
Sydney see Sidney		Tack, Cornelius	ULS 215	Tallow, Tobias	WST 170
Sydney, Joseph a		Tack, Sarah	ULS 203	Tallow, Vincent	NYK 26
mulatto	NYK 22	Tackles, Alexander	OND 203	Talmadge, Joseph	CAY 660
Syes, John	WST 145	Tadwell, Joseph	NYK 103	Talmadge, Josiah Junr	RNS 33
Syfer, William	DUT 69	Taff, Asa	ONT 364	Talmage, David	SUF 109
Syfer, William	ORN 384	Taff, Caleb	ONT 364	Talmage, David Junr	SUF 106
Syker, Jeremiah	NYK 88	Taff, Otes	NYK 103	Talmage, David Junr	SUF 109
Sykes, John J.	DEL 273	Tafft, David	OTS 51	Talmage, Enos	DUT 130
Sykes, Philip	NYK 36	Tafft, James	OND 164	Talmage, Enos Junr	SRA 21
Sykes, Willard	OND 198	Ta Foe, John	COL 266	Talmage, Ezra	SRA 48
Sylas, Thomas	MNT 124	Taft see Faft		Talmage, James	DUT 62
Sylliven see Sullivan		Taft, Asa	SCH 161	Talmage, Jemima	SUF 107
Sylliven, Michael	WST 155	Taft, Daniel	OTS 54	Talmage, Jeremiah	SUF 107
Sylvester see Silvester		Taft, Daniel	OTS 58	Talmage, John	COL 200
Sylvester, Cornelius	COL 260	Taft, Gideon	WSH 282	Talmage, John	NYK 139
Sylvester, John	ONT 342	Taft, Grindal	RNS 51	Talmage, Jonathan	DUT 5
Sylvester, Peter	COL 260	Taft, Mathew	WSH 267	Talmage, Joseph	DUT 20
Sylya, Adam	HRK 420	Ta[ft?], Robert	ONT 392	Talmage, Josiah	RNS 33
Sylya, Henry Junr	HRK 407	Taft, Samuel	COL 261	Talmage, Luther	CHN 774
Symes, Robert	COL 222	Taft, Silas	SCH 161	Talmage, Margarett	SUF 99
Sympson see Simpson		Taft, William	OND 206	Talmage, Martin	ALB 80
Sympson, John	ONN 190	Tager, Henry	NYK 57	Talmage, Moses	DUT 130
Sympson, Joseph	ONN 180	Taghert, Nathl	TIO 228	Talmage, Stephen	SUF 98
Syms, Tobias	NYK 148	Taint_, Benjamin	ONT 410	Talmage, Thomas	SRA 21
Synott, Patrick	CHN 778	Tainter, Benjn	OTS 42	Talman, Briton	DUT 8
Syper, Peter	ORN 270	Tainter, Joseph	OTS 42	Talman, Darius	DUT 42
Syphar, John	MNT 56	Talbers, Catherine	NYK 91	Talman, David	DUT 98
Sypher see Cypher		Talbert, William	ALB 141	Talman, Hermanius	NYK 55
Sypher, John	DUT 18	Talbot, Amasa	SRA 57	Talman, Isaac J.	HRK 592
Sypher, John	WST 170	Talbot, Elizabeth	DUT 112	Talman, Jedediah	DUT 42
Sypher, Samuel	DUT 18	Talbot, Frederick	NYK 114	Talman, John	DUT 59
Sypher, William	NYK 105	Talbot, George W.	NYK 28	Talman, John	NYK 95
Sypher, William	WST 170	Talbot, Jacob	OTS 36	Talman, Jonathan	DUT 98
Syrus	QNS 81	Talbot, Silas	NYK 54	Talman, Joseph	ALB 95
Syvrendth, Rip Van Dam	WSH 255	Talcott, Daniel	HRK 435	Talman, Louis	DUT 57
		Talcott, Daniel	HRK 489	Talman, Peter	NYK 53
T		Talcott, Daniel	OND 219	Talman, Restcomb	SRA 61
		Talcott, Hezekiah	HRK 435	Talman, Samuel	NYK 36
T...rs, Gideon	CAY 546	Talcott, Hezekiah	OND 219	Talman, Stephen	DUT 58
T_n, Charles	CHN 978	Talcott, John	HRK 586	Talman, Timothy	DUT 30
T_mble, Alexander	ESS 296	Talcott, Joseph	DUT 105	Talman, William	DUT 30
T_t_, John	WST 164	Tales, Samuel	GRN 341	Talman, William	NYK 141
Tabconer, Samuel	NYK 101	Talk, Cornelius Junr	ULS 200	Talman, William	ORN 284
Tabeley, John	NYK 113	Talket, Samuel	SRA 35	Talman, William	QNS 64
Tabely, Jacob	NYK 36	Talkutt, Joshua	CHN 800	Talor, William	CHN 836
Tabely, Jacob Junior	NYK 36	Talkutt, Joshua Jun	CHN 800	Taluley, William	NYK 110
Taber, Abraham	WSH 213	Taller, Solomon	WST 161	Taluus(?), Ellenor	NYK 108
Taber, Amos	SUF 77	Tallet, John	CHN 834	Talvande, Cossee	NYK 111
Taber, Augustes	WSH 244	Talliday, Sarah	DUT 9	Tamage, Henry	GRN 340
Taber, Fredk	SUF 77	Tallmage, Joel	COL 219	Tamage, Jonah	GRN 352
Taber, Gidion	WSH 202	Tallman see Taulman		Tamage, Joseph	RCK 105
Taber, Jeremiah	DUT 50	Tallman, Abrm	RCK 102	Tamney, John	NYK 73
Taber, Jethro	SRA 38	Tallman, Briton	ONN 162	Tankard, George	NYK 85
Taber, Job	DUT 42	Tallman, Catharine	RCK 97	Tankard, Mary	ORN 290
Taber, John	WSH 236	Tallman, Dowh D.	RCK 103	Tanner, Abel	RNS 104
Taber, Judith	DUT 105	Tallman, Dowh T.	RCK 103	Tanner, Benjamin	OND 168
Taber, Lolowick	CAY 660	Tallman, Garret	RCK 107	Tanner, Benjamin	OTS 22
Taber, Luis	WSH 236	Tallman, Herman	RCK 104	Tanner, Benjamin	QNS 81
Taber, Nathaniel	DUT 10	Tallman, Herman	RCK 106	Tanner, Benjamin	SRA 60
Taber, Pardon	ALB 71	Tallman, Hermanus	RCK 104	Tanner, Daniel	ALB 86
Taber, Peleg	RNS 54	Tallman, Isaac	RCK 99	Tanner, Francis	RNS 113
Taber, Records	RNS 103	Tallman, Isaac	RCK 100	Tanner, Ira	OTS 16
Taber, Thomas	DUT 45	Tallman, Jacob	NYK 116	Tanner, Isaac	HRK 465
Taber, Tucker	GRN 349	Tallman, Jacob	RCK 101	Tanner, Isaac	OTS 16
Taber, William	DUT 42	Tallman, Jeremiah	ALB 71	Tanner, Isaac Junr	HRK 465
Tabor, Benjamin	COL 182	Tallman, John	COL 248	Tanner, Jacob	MNT 94
Tabor, Benjamin	COL 194	Tallman, John	RCK 106	Tanner, James	DUT 43
Tabor, Benjamin	ONN 134	Tallman, John Junr	RCK 106	Tanner, James	WSH 207
Tabor, Gideon	ALB 68	Tallman, John G.	RCK 107	Tanner, James	WSH 238
Tabor, Humphrey	CAY 654	Tallman, John H.	RCK 103	Tanner, Job	DUT 146
Tabor, Jonah	SUF 98	Tallman, John J.	RCK 107	Tanner, John	HRK 465
Tabor, Philip	ALB 87	Tallman, Nathl	ALB 34	Tanner, John	RNS 110
Tabor, William	ALB 80	Tallman, Thomas	OTS 44	Tanner, John	WSH 255
Tabor, William	SUF 98	Tallman, Tunis	RCK 97	Tanner, John	WSH 279
Tabot, Joseph	ESS 295	Tallman, Tunis	RCK 106	Tanner, Joseph	WSH 238
Tabour, Gideon	SRA 32	Tallman, Tunis Junr	RCK 97		

Tanner, Joseph	WSH 280	Tarbill, Sylvanus	DUT 120	Taylor, Abraham	NYK 19

Taylor, Gilbert	OND 208	Taylor, John Senr	WSH 242	Taylor, Samuel	CLN 156
Taylor, Gilbert	SCH 165	Taylor, John N.	COL 189	Taylor, Samuel	COL 262
Taylor, Gilbert	WST 147	Taylor, Jonas	RCK 110	Taylor, Samuel	OND 178
Taylor, Giles	RNS 99	Taylor, Jonathan	COL 182	Taylor, Samuel	ONT 500
Taylor, Giles Junr	RNS 105	Taylor, Jonathan	ORN 390	Taylor, Samuel	RNS 96
Taylor, Gurden	SUF 81	Taylor, Jonathan	COL 262	Taylor, Saml	RCK 110
Taylor, Harman	COL 227	Taylor, Jno Junr	OTS 28	Taylor, Samuel	SRA 55
Taylor, Henry	WST 170	Taylor, Joseph	NYK 32	Taylor, Samuel	WSH 269
Taylor, Hezekiah	ORN 324	Taylor, Joseph	NYK 49	Taylor, Samuel D.	ALB 146
Taylor, Isaac &		Taylor, Joseph	ONT 338	Taylor, Sarah	NYK 95
C. Ackles	ORN 340	Taylor, Joseph	ONT 340	Taylor, Shadrack	WST 147
Taylor, Israel	OND 172	Taylor, Joseph	ONT 414	Taylor, Silas	DUT 114
Taylor, Israel	SRA 44	Taylor, Joseph	ONT 420	Taylor, Solomon	ALB 17
Taylor, Jacob	COL 239	Taylor, J___h	ONT 434	Taylor, Solomon	DUT 23
Taylor, Jacob	RCK 110	Taylor, Joseph	RNS 88	Taylor, Solomon	NYK 130
Taylor, Jacob	SUF 90	Taylor, Joseph	RCH 91	Taylor, Spencer	ESS 295
Taylor, Jacob	WST 147	Taylor, Joseph	WSH 269	Taylor, Stephen	CLN 154
Taylor, James	ALB 16	Taylor, Joshua	DEL 272	Taylor, Stephen	ESS 303
Taylor, James	NYK 19	Taylor, Joshua	RCK 99	Taylor, Stephen	NYK 67
Taylor, James	NYK 29	Taylor, Joshua	SRA 11	Taylor, Stephen	NYK 97
Taylor, James	NYK 73	Taylor, Josiah	CAY 716	Taylor, Stephen	ONT 500
Taylor, James	NYK 94	Taylor, Josiah	SRA 13	Taylor, Stephen	RCK 106
Taylor, James	OND 163	Taylor, Lewis	WST 157	Taylor, Thaddeus	DEL 281
Taylor, James	ORN 288	Taylor, Luke	ALB 107	Taylor, Theodore	OND 208
Taylor, James	ORN 397	Taylor, Luke	CAY 666	Taylor, Thomas	ALB 82
Taylor, James	OTS 35	Taylor, Luthar	RNS 91	Taylor, Thomas	DEL 269
Taylor, James	SRA 26	Taylor, Lydia	NYK 112	Taylor, Thomas	DUT 56
Taylor, James	WST 158	Taylor, Manning	DUT 110	Taylor, Thomas	GRN 339
Taylor, Jane	NYK 130	Taylor, Martha	WST 115	Taylor, Thomas	NYK 58
Taylor, Jasper	TIO 238	Taylor, Martin	CHN 796	Taylor, Thomas a	
Taylor, Jemma	NYK 53	Taylor, Mary	NYK 18	mulatto	NYK 113
Taylor, Jeremiah	ALB 45	Taylor, Mary	NYK 29	Taylor, Thomas	OTS 17
Taylor, Jeremiah	CAY 622	Taylor, Mary	NYK 94	Taylor, Thomas	OTS 35
Taylor, Jeremiah	NYK 96	Taylor, Medad	WSH 274	Taylor, Thomas	OTS 46
Taylor, Jesse	GRN 351	Taylor, Michael	WST 124	Taylor, Thomas	SRA 48
Taylor, Job	RNS 66	Taylor, Minord	CAY 692	Taylor, Thomas	WST 113
Taylor, John	ALB 5	Taylor, Morris	RCH 92	Taylor, Thomas	WST 170
Taylor, John	ALB 46	Taylor, Moses	NYK 19	Taylor, Thos Junr	OTS 17
Taylor, John	ALB 90	Taylor, Moses	NYK 71	Taylor, Thomas H.	NYK 48
Taylor, John	ALB 91	Taylor, Moses	OND 165	Taylor, Timothy	OTS 35
Taylor, John	ALB 136	Taylor, Moses	ONT 408	Taylor, Timothy	SUF 83
Taylor, John	ALB 148	Taylor, Moses	WST 144	Taylor, Violletta R.	NYK 36
Taylor, John	CAY 522	Taylor, Nathan	ESS 292	Taylor, Walter	ALB 17
Taylor, John	COL 182	Taylor, Nathan	ONT 474	Taylor, Widow	SRA 35
Taylor, John	DUT 70	Taylor, Nathan	WSH 299	Taylor, William	CHN 968
Taylor, John	DUT 85	Taylor, Nathaniel	ORN 390	Taylor, William	CLN 154
Taylor, John	NYK 23	Taylor, Nathen	WSH 269	Taylor, William	COL 178
Taylor, John	NYK 29	Taylor, Neri(?)	CAY 676	Taylor, William	COL 227
Taylor, John	NYK 29	Taylor, Noah	CAY 604	Taylor, William	DUT 41
Taylor, John	NYK 99	Taylor, No_h	CHN 962	Taylor, William	DUT 57
Taylor, John	NYK 116	Taylor, Noah	SRA 6	Taylor, William	NYK 32
Taylor, John	NYK 121	Taylor, Noah	WSH 229	Taylor, William	NYK 135
Taylor, John	ONN 129	Taylor, Obediah	OND 208	Taylor, William	ORN 274
Taylor, John	ONT 416	Taylor, Oliver	CAY 692	Taylor, Wm	OTS 35
Taylor, John	ONT 426	Taylor, Oliver	NYK 43	Taylor, William	RNS 83
Taylor, John	ONT 500	Taylor, Oliver	OTS 4	Taylor, Willm	SCH 166
Taylor, John	ORN 297	Taylor, Othniel	ONT 430	Taylor, William	SUF 102
Taylor, John	ORN 346	Taylor, Peter	COL 253	Taylor, Wm	TIO 236
Taylor, John	OTS 28	Taylor, Peter	KNG 6	Taylor, William	WSH 193
Taylor, John	QNS 79	Taylor, Peter	NYK 36	Taylor, William	WST 164
Taylor, John	RCH 95	Taylor, Peter	TIO 241	Taylor, Zebe	CAY 666
Taylor, John	RCK 103	Taylor, Phebe	ONT 398	Taylor, Zebedee	SRA 4
Taylor, John	SRA 9	Taylor, Phillup	CHN 914	Taylor, Zebulon	OND 202
Taylor, John	SRA 18	Taylor, Philo	SCH 165	Taylor, Zebe	SRA 42
Taylor, John	SRA 23	Taylor, Ph..as	ONT 438	Teabon, Sarah	NYK 92
Taylor, John	SRA 25	Taylor, Rayment	SRA 13	Teabout, Corneius	SCH 131
Taylor, John	SRA 29	Taylor, Reuben	CHN 796	Teach, George	NYK 147
Taylor, John	SRA 42	Taylor, Reuben	SRA 9	Teachout, Abraham	SRA 8
Taylor, John	SRA 53	Taylor, Reuben	SRA 10	Teachout, Gideon	HRK 442
Taylor, John	STB 200	Taylor, Richard	NYK 118	Teachout, Isaac	HRK 443
Taylor, John	SUF 67	Taylor, Richard	RNS 86	Teachout, Isaac	SRA 8
Taylor, John	SUF 86	Taylor, Richard	RCH 92	Teachout, Jacob	HRK 443
Taylor, John	ULS 246	Taylor, Richard	SRA 23	Teachout, Jacob	SRA 7
Taylor, John	WSH 259	Taylor, Robert	ALB 105	Teachout, Jacob	SRA 10
Taylor, John	WSH 278	Taylor, Robert	COL 240	Teachout, Jacob	WSH 302
Taylor, John	WST 170	Taylor, Robert	NYK 84	Teachout, John	HRK 443
Taylor, John Jur	WSH 242	Taylor, Robert	OTS 29	Teachout, Nicholass	SRA 8

Tennant, John	OTS 56	Terrey, James	SUF 98	Terry, Joseph Ser	SUF 69
Tennant, John Junr	OTS 56	Terrey, James	SUF 102	Terry, Joseph Ser	SUF 69
Tennarit, Owen	CLN 172	Terrey, Jeremiah	SUF 93	Terry, Joseph Sen	SUF 77
Tennent, John	WSH 212	Terrey, John	SUF 109	Terry, Joshu	ONT 346
Tennery, Joseph	RNS 80	Terrey, Joseph	SUF 91	Terry, Joshua	SUF 73
Tenney, Joseph	CHN 908	Terrey, Ketchum	SUF 93	Terry, Josiah	CLN 156
Tenny, Asa	CHN 846	Terrey, Shadrick	SUF 93	Terry, Josiah	WST 130
Tenure, Woodhull	MNT 118	Terrey, Thomas	SUF 90	Terry, Luther	ORN 332
Tenyck see Ten Eyck		Terrey, William	SUF 92	Terry, Mary	SUF 75
Tenyck, Abraham	NYK 109	Terrey, William	SUF 96	Terry, Joses	SUF 72
Tenyck, Hendrick	RCK 101	Terril, Jerad	ONT 434	Terry, Moses	SUF 73
Tenyck, Hendrick	RCK 102	Terril, Joel	ONT 434	Terry, Nathan	ONT 346
Tenyck, Jacob	NYK 60	Terril, John	WSH 227	Terry, Nathaniel	COL 197
Tenyck, John	RCK 102	Terril, Richd	SUF 67	Terry, Nathaniel	ONT 346
Tenycke, Jacob	RCK 108	Terrill, Amos	WSH 296	Terry, Noah	HRK 529
Terboon, Andrew	ALB 37	Terrill, Arad	DUT 99	Terry, Noah	ORN 326
Ter Bos, Abraham	DUT 35	Terrill, Bennajah	RNS 20	Terry, Peter	DUT 52
Ter Bos, Christian	DUT 39	Terrill, Israiel	CHN 824	Terry, Peter	DUT 167
Ter Bos, Henry	DUT 35	Terrill, Joseph	CLN 173	Terry, Phinehas	ORN 324
Ter Bos, Henry	ULS 265	Terrill, Nathan	QNS 73	Terry, Richard	ORN 271
Ter Bos, Henry Junr	ULS 265	Terrill, Nicholas	SUF 69	Terry, Richd	SUF 75
Ter Bos, Isaac	DUT 38	Terrill, Richard	ALB 131	Terry, Samuel	DUT 90
Ter Bos, Isaac	ULS 265	Terrill, Samuel	WSH 296	Terry, Saml	SUF 73
Ter Bos, John	ORN 275	Terrwillger see Ter-		Terry, Samuel Junr	DUT 90
Ter Bos, Joseph	DUT 35	willeger		Terry, Sarah	NYK 70
Ter Bos, Levi	DUT 120	Terrwillger, Isaac	TIO 251	Terry, Seth	ORN 326
Ter Bos, Peter	DUT 152	Terry see Ferry		Terry, Shubal	WSH 266
Ter Bos, Richard	DUT 124	Terry, Abner	OTS 25	Terry, Silas	DUT 129
Ter Bos, William	ORN 342	Terry, Amos	ALB 64	Terry, Thomas	DUT 168
Terbus, William	NYK 94	Terry, Benjn	ALB 119	Terry, Thomas	OTS 35
Ter Bush, Cornelia	ALB 127	Terry, Constant	ORN 338	Terry, Thos	SUF 76
Terce, Archiball	WSH 245	Terry, Danl	SUF 65	Terry, Thos	SUF 77
Terce, Peter B.	WSH 245	Terry, Danl	SUF 65	Terry, Uriah	ORN 331
Tercot, Francis	ULS 186	Terry, Danl	SUF 70	Terry, William	DUT 101
Terhuen, David	ULS 205	Terry, Danl	SUF 72	Terry, William	NYK 113
Terhune, Abraham	KNG 4	Terry, Danl	SUF 73	Terry, Wm	SUF 64
Terhune, Albert	KNG 4	Terry, Danl Jur	SUF 73	Terry, Wm	SUF 72
Terims, Timothy	GRN 332	Terry, Danl T.	SUF 77	Terry, Zeno	CHN 914
Terne, Laurence	NYK 97	Terry, David	SUF 75	Terul, Richd	SUF 71
Ternum, Nathl	OTS 51	Terry, Ebenezer	WSH 273	Terwilger, Peter	CAY 684
Ternure see Turner		Terry, Edward	DUT 14	Terwilger, Josiah	ULS 211
Ternure, Cornelius	RCK 110	Terry, Eli	WSH 284	Terwilleger see Der-	
Ternure, Danl	RCK 98	Terry, Elijah	SUF 75	willeger, Terrwillger,	
Ternure, Henry	RCK 106	Terry, Elijah	WSH 281	Trewilleger & Tuwill	
Ternure, Henry	RCK 107	Terry, Elijah Jr	SUF 75	eger	
Ternure, James	RCK 107	Terry, Elizabeth	SUF 65	Terwilleger, Clafas	TIO 250
Ternure, Maria	RCK 97	Terry, George	WST 170	Terwilleger, Matthew	TIO 250
Ternure, Michael	RCK 110	Terry, Gersham Ju	SUF 75	Terwilliger, Aaron	ORN 302
Terone, Simon	NYK 57	Terry, Gersham Sen	SUF 75	Terwilliger, Aaron	ULS 242
Terpanning, Abraham	ULS 232	Terry, Gilbert	ORN 331	Terwilliger, Abraham	ULS 244
Terpanning, Abraham	ULS 252	Terry, Heny	SUF 73	Terwilliger, Abraham J.	ULS 247
Terpanning, Benjamin	ULS 208	Terry, Isaac	CHN 916	Terwilliger, Abraham P.	ULS 246
Terpanning, Bowdoine	ULS 218	Terry, Is..c	OTS 24	Terwilliger, Abraham T.	ULS 246
Terpanning, Bowdoine		Terry, Isaac	SUF 72	Terwilliger, Benjamin	ULS 241
Junr	ULS 232	Terry, Isaac Jur	CHN 908	Terwilliger, Benjamin T.	ULS 211
Terpanning, Dirck	ULS 232	Terry, Isaac Jur	CHN 914	Terwilliger, Benjamin T.	ULS 245
Terpanning, Elias	ULS 232	Terry, Isaac Junr	CHN 916	Terwilliger, Benjamin U.	ULS 241
Terpanning, Henry	ULS 231	Terry, Isaiah	SUF 71	Terwilliger, Cornelius	ULS 247
Terpanning, James	ULS 231	Terry, James	SUF 71	Terwilliger, Daniel	ULS 249
Terpanning, John	DUT 42	Terry, James	SUF 72	Terwilliger, Daniel	ULS 252
Terpanning, John	ULS 233	Terry, Jeremiah	SUF 75	Terwilliger, David	ULS 241
Terpanning, John Junr	DUT 42	Terry, Jesee	SUF 77	Terwilliger, Elisha	ULS 253
Terpanning, Jonathan	ULS 232	Terry, John	ALB 65	Terwilliger, Evert	ULS 186
Terpanning, Levi	ULS 252	Terry, John	HRK 451	Terwilliger, Evert J.	COL 264
Terpanning, Marinus	ULS 255	Terry, John	SUF 64	Terwilliger, Evert J.	ULS 249
Terpanning, Peter	ULS 232	Terry, John	SUF 72	Terwilliger, Henricus	ORN 308
Terpanning, Simeon	DUT 42	Terry, John C.	SUF 72	Terwilliger, Henry	ULS 246
Terpanning, Simeon	ULS 232	Terry, Jonathan	SUF 74	Terwilliger, Hermanus	ULS 255
Terpanning, William	ULS 231	Terry, Jonathan Jur	SUF 77	Terwilliger, Hezekiah	ORN 308
Terpen, Seth	SRA 47	Terry, Jonathan Sen	SUF 77	Terwilliger, Hugo	ULS 248
Terrel, Cathrine	SUF 68	Terry, Jonothan	CHN 920	Terwilliger, Hugo Junr	ULS 248
Terrel, John	SRA 53	Terry, Joseph	HRK 588	Terwilliger, Isaac	ULS 246
Terrel, Widow	SUF 68	Terry, Joseph	SUF 65	Terwilliger, Isaac P.	ULS 253
Terrell, Jacob	ONN 167	Terry, Joseph	SUF 75	Terwilliger, Jacob	ULS 236
Terrell, William	HRK 528	Terry, Joseph Jr	SUF 69	Terwilliger, Jacobus	ULS 250
Terrey, Gamiel	CAY 610	Terry, Joseph Jr	SUF 69	Terwilliger, James	ORN 317
Terrey, Gersham	SUF 93	Terry, Joseph Jur	SUF 77	Terwilliger, James S.	ULS 249

366

Name	Loc	No.	Name	Loc	No.	Name	Loc	No.
Thompson, John	COL	250	Thompson, Robert	NYK	36	Thomson, James	CHN	898
Thompson, John	DEL	270	Thompson, Robert	NYK	50	Thomson, James	QNS	62
Thompson, John	DEL	270	Thompson, Robert	NYK	121	Thomson, James	QNS	78
Thompson, John	DUT	10	Thompson, Robert	ONT	498	Thomson, John	CHN	904
Thompson, John	DUT	58	Thompson, Robert	OTS	2	Thomson, John	SRA	52
Thompson, John	DUT	131	Thompson, Robert	SRA	51	Thomson, Joseph	CHN	834
Thompson, John	MNT	53	Thompson, Robert	WSH	194	Thomson, Judah	WSH	299
Thompson, John	NYK	27	Thompson, Robert ye 1st	ORN	300	Thomson, Robert	QNS	63
Thompson, John	NYK	38	Thompson, Robert ye 2d	ORN	300	Thomson, Samuel	CHN	988
Thompson, John	NYK	47	Thompson, Robert ye 3d	ORN	301	Thomson, Samuel	WSH	187
Thompson, John	NYK	106	Thompson, Samuel	CHN	798	Thomson, Samuel	WSH	298
Thompson, John	NYK	107	Thompson, Samuel	CHN	810	Thomson, Thomas A.	ORN	360
Thompson, John	NYK	132	Thompson, Samuel	COL	215	Thomson, William	CHN	836
Thompson, John	ONN	161	Thompson, Samuel	NYK	30	Thonpson, James	MNT	69
Thompson, John	ONT	380	Thompson, Samuel	NYK	36	Thorburn, James	NYK	47
Thompson, John	ONT	496	Thompson, Samuel	NYK	106	Thorburns, Grant	NYK	47
Thompson, John	OTS	2	Thompson, Samuel	OND	166	Thorington see Thorr-		
Thompson, John	OTS	44	Thompson, Samuel	ORN	284	ington		
Thompson, John	RNS	93	Thompson, Saml	OTS	41	Thorington, Able	CHN	980
Thompson, John	RCH	87	Thompson, Samuel	SRA	46	Thorington, J.	SUF	96
Thompson, John	SRA	7	Thompson, Sarah	DUT	141	Thorn, .ill..	QNS	72
Thompson, John	SRA	47	Thompson, Seth	DUT	131	Thorn, Amos	DUT	32
Thompson, John	ULS	183	Thompson, Seth	WSH	206	Thorn, Benjamin	DUT	151
Thompson, John	WSH	194	Thompson, Silas	SCH	117	Thorn, Charity	WST	115
Thompson, John	WSH	214	Thompson, Siles	WSH	223	Thorn, Charles	QNS	83
Thompson, John	WSH	222	Thompson, Smith	DUT	63	Thorn, Christopher	DUT	147
Thompson, John	WSH	227	Thompson, Solomon	OND	188	Thorn, Daniel	DUT	85
Thompson, John	WSH	232	Thompson, Stanley	DUT	163	Thorn, Daniel	NYK	130
Thompson, John	WST	146	Thompson, Stephen	CHN	882	Thorn, Daniel	ORN	399
Thompson, John ye 2d	ULS	184	Thompson, Stephen	RCK	102	Thorn, Edward	ALB	112
Thompson, John A.	CAY	644	Thompson, Susanna	ORN	332	Thorn, Gilbert	ULS	265
Thompson, John H.	NYK	28	Thompson, Thomas	GRN	330	Thorn, Isaac	DUT	101
Thompson, Jonathan	DEL	280	Thompson, Thomas	NYK	33	Thorn, Isaac	ORN	274
Thompson, Jonathan	DUT	157	Thompson, Thomas a			Thorn, Isaac Junr	DUT	101
Thompson, Jonathan	DUT	166	Black	NYK	117	Thorn, Jacob	ORN	329
Thompson, Jonathan	NYK	74	Thompson, Thomas	ORN	290	Thorn, Jacob	QNS	83
Thompson, Jonathan	ORN	349	Thompson, Thomas	ORN	378	Thorn, James	DUT	64
Thompson, Jonathan	SRA	44	Thompson, Thos	OTS	2	Thorn, James	GRN	357
Thompson, Jonathan	SUF	94	Thompson, Thomas	RNS	8	Thorn, James	QNS	82
Thompson, Joseph	ALB	33	Thompson, Thomas	SCH	166	Thorn, James	QNS	82
Thompson, Joseph	CHN	890	Thompson, Thomas	WSH	210	Thorn, James	WSH	303
Thompson, Joseph	NYK	37	Thompson, Wells	WSH	283	Thorn, James	WST	113
Thompson, Joseph	OND	164	Thompson, William	DUT	163	Thorn, James	WST	132
Thompson, Joseph	ONT	400	Thompson, William	KNG	10	Thorn, Jeffry Free		
Thompson, Joseph	OTS	8	Thompson, William	NYK	54	Black	COL	198
Thompson, Joseph	OTS	15	Thompson, William	NYK	72	Thorn, Jesse	SCH	134
Thompson, Joseph	RNS	57	Thompson, William	NYK	80	Thorn, John	DUT	148
Thompson, Joshua	ALB	91	Thompson, William	NYK	136	Thorn, John	ORN	276
Thompson, Joshua	ESS	295	Thompson, William	ORN	294	Thorn, John	ORN	287
Thompson, Joshua	ORN	350	Thompson, William	ORN	361	Thorn, John	QNS	69
Thompson, Joshua	ULS	202	Thompson, William	ORN	365	Thorn, John	SRA	40
Thompson, Josiah	HRK	457	Thompson, Wm	OTS	32	Thorn, John	WST	130
Thompson, Judah	ALB	34	Thompson, Wm	OTS	56	Thorn, John Senr	QNS	70
Thompson, Levi	ESS	293	Thompson, Wm	RNS	75	Thorn, Joseph	DUT	60
Thompson, Levi	ESS	320	Thompson, William	RNS	81	Thorn, Joseph	DUT	98
Thompson, Levi	ULS	219	Thompson, William	SCH	135	Thorn, Jotham	ULS	265
Thompson, Matthew E.	ULS	226	Thompson, Willm	SCH	166	Thorn, Justus	WST	153
Thompson, Michael	COL	222	Thompson, William	ULS	185	Thorn, Lucretia	ULS	265
Thompson, Moses	OTS	8	Thompson, William	ULS	208	Thorn, Mary	DUT	30
Thompson, Moses	TIO	244	Thompson, William	WSH	214	Thorn, Michael	COL	257
Thompson, Nathan	OND	190	Thompson, William	WSH	227	Thorn, Nathaniel	RNS	83
Thompson, Nathaniel	DEL	277	Thompson, William	WSH	234	Thorn, Nicholas	ALB	110
Thompson, Nathaniel	MNT	71	Thompson, William	WST	120	Thorn, Obadiah	DUT	98
Thompson, Nathaniel	OND	194	Thompson, William			Thorn, Obediah	DUT	37
Thompson, Nathen	WSH	223	Junr	ORN	354	Thorn, Oliver	ONN	154
Thompson, Nathen	WSH	253	Thompson, William			Thorn, Peleg	ALB	112
Thompson, Nehemiah	CHN	882	Junr	WSH	227	Thorn, Richard Junr	QNS	70
Thompson, Peter	DUT	48	Thompson, William A.	NYK	30	Thorn, Richard Senr	QNS	70
Thompson, Peter	MNT	64	Thompson, Wm C.	RCK	104	Thorn, Samuel	ALB	5
Thompson, Peter	NYK	59	Thompson, William W.	ORN	359	Thorn, Samuel	DUT	41
Thompson, Peter	WSH	241	Thomson		GRN 329	Thorn, Samuel	DUT	101
Thompson, Phillip	NYK	132	Thomson, Abijah	CHN	892	Thorn, Samuel	GRN	353
Thompson, Ralph	ALB	126	Thomson, Able	CHN	904	Thorn, Samuel	KNG	9
Thompson, Ralph	NYK	121	Thomson, Andrew	WSH	188	Thorn, Samuel	ORN	285
Thompson, Reuben	OND	214	Thomson, Andrew Junr	WSH	188	Thorn, Samuel	SCH	134
Thompson, Richard	ORN	370	Thomson, Culvern	WSH	187	Thorn, Sherwood	WST	132
Thompson, Robert	ESS	317	Thomson, Elisha	GRN	333	Thorn, Stephen	DUT	105

Name	Loc.	Name	Loc.	Name	Loc.
Thorn, Stephen	QNS 84	Thorp, Joseph	RNS 95	Thurstin, David	RNS 33
Thorn, Stephen	RNS 59	Thorp, Nathan	DEL 286	Thurstin, Joab	ALB 116
Thorn, Thomas	ORN 359	Thorp, Thos	RCK 110	Thurstin, William	SRA 30
Thorn, Thomas	WST 127	Thorp, Wheeler	DEL 286	Thurston, Adam	OTS 14
Thorn, Thomas	WST 128	Thorrington see Thor-		Thurston, Benjamin	DUT 36
Thorn, Thomas	WST 130	ington		Thurston, Benjamin	NYK 123
Thorn, Thomas	WST 156	Thorrington, Ezra	DEL 289	Thruston, Chas Free	
Thorn, Thomas C.	QNS 69	Thorrington, James	CHN 980	Black	COL 252
Thorn, Timothy Negro	QNS 69	Thort, Glover	HRK 551½	Thurston, Charles	NYK 127
Thorn, Willeam	WSH 296	Thornton, William	NYK 141	Thurston, Daniel	CAY 600
Thorn, William	DUT 106	Thouire, Benjamin	ALB 142	Thurston, Daniel	QNS 77
Thorn, Wm	GRN 349	Thousand, Jacob	ALB 67	Thurston, Dinah	ORN 270
Thorn, William	ORN 390	Thousand, John	ALB 67	Thurston, Ebenezer	ALB 118
Thorn, William	QNS 69	Thrall, Aaron	OTS 33	Thurston, Edward	OTS 15
Thorn, William	WSH 219	Thrall, Benjamin	OND 210	Thurston, Edward Junr	OTS 15
Thorn, William	WST 154	Thrall, Charles	ALB 52	Thurston, George	CAY 538
Thorn, Wright,	WST 123	Thrall, William	OND 181	Thurston, Jacob	ALB 4
Thorne, Daniel	NYK 17	Thrall, Willm	SCH 160	Thurston, Jacob	NYK 58
Thorne, Daniel	QNS 64	Thrall, Willm Junr	SCH 165	Thurston, James	ORN 352
Thorne, Elizabeth	NYK 89	Thralt, Isaac	MNT 71	Thurston, Job Junr	ALB 118
Thorne, Gilbert	DUT 149	Thrasher, Asahel	DUT 20	Thurston, John	ALB 68
Thorne, Hannah	NYK 76	Thrasher, Francis	OND 206	Thurston, John	NYK 62
Thorne, Henry	NYK 82	Thra_her, George	CHN 922	Thurston, John	NYK 137
Thorne, Isaac	NYK 74	Thrasher, Joseph	HRK 449	Thurston, John	NYK 146
Thorne, Jacob	NYK 129	Thrasher, Joseph	HRK 587	Thurston, John	QNS 73
Thorne, James	QNS 64	Thrasher, Stephen	OND 206	Thurston, John	QNS 76
Thorne, James J.	OTS 30	Thrasher, Wm	OTS 31	Thurston, John	WSH 267
Thorne, Joseph	NYK 90	Throab, George	MNT 72	Thurston, John B.	MNT 118
Thorne, Langford	ORN 395	Throap, Jacob	MNT 69	Thurston, John M.	DUT 116
Thorne, Mary	QNS 64	Throap, Joseah	MNT 76	Thurston, Joseph	QNS 75
Thorne, Robert	NYK 29	Throap, Wm	MNT 74	Thurston, Joshua	OTS 15
Thorne, Robert	NYK 118	Throop, Benjamin	COL 261	Thurston, Luther	CHN 756
Thorne, Samuel	NYK 80	Throop, Dan	COL 215	Thurston, Nathan	MNT 101
Thorne, Samuel	QNS 64	Throop, Joseph	MNT 116	Thurston, Seth	CHN 778
Thorne, Stephen	NYK 45	Thumb, Adam	MNT 102	Thurston, Seth	CHN 780
Thorne, Stephen	NYK 138	Thumb, Joseph	MNT 124	Thurston, Thomas	DUT 33
Thorne, William	NYK 20	Thumb, Melcher	HRK 446	Thurston, William	NYK 123
Thorne, William	NYK 82	Thumb, Nicholas	HRK 446	Thurston, William	NYK 126
Thornton, Abraham	ALB 2A	Thurbee, Benjamin	RNS 68	Thurston, William	QNS 73
Thornton, Charles	OTS 12	Thurbee, Joseph	RNS 68	Thurston, William R.	NYK 45
Thornton, Constant	WSH 304	Thurber, Abner	OTS 19	Thurton, Peter	NYK 53
Thornton, Ezra	WSH 197	Thurber, Cromwell	CLN 170	Thus, Samuel	WSH 233
Thornton, James	ALB 18	Thurber, Darias	RNS 43	Thusten, Daniel G.	WSH 235
Thornton, James	OTS 31	Thurber, David	ONT 436	Thuston, Joel	WSH 235
Thornton, Jerh	OTS 24	Thurber, Eddy	CLN 170	Thuston, John	WSH 202
Thornton, Jerimiah	WSH 304	Thurber, Edward	CHN 922	Thuston, John	WSH 236
Thornton, Jesse	OTS 40	Thurber, Edward	CLN 169	Thuston, Norton	WSH 234
Thornton, Job	DUT 58	Thurber, Edward Junr	CLN 170	Thuston, Solomon	WSH 212
Thornton, John	ALB 137	Thurber, Ezra	CLN 170	Tibbalds, Solomon	CAY 694
Thornton, Martha	WSH 230	Thurber, Ichabod	WSH 298	Tibbes, Ebenesar	GRN 341
Thornton, Remember	OND 190	Thurber, Isaiah	OTS 19	Tibbets, James	ALB 85
Thornton, Saml	OTS 31	Thurber, James	OTS 19	Tibbets, Job:	SCH 143
Thornton, Stephen	OTS 38	Thurber, John	CLN 170	Tibbets, Henry	SCH 143
Thornton, Thomas	ALB 33	Thurber, Jonathan	NYK 81	Tibbets, John	OND 211
Thornton, Thomas	WSH 244	Thurber, Jona	OTS 11	Tibbets, John	OND 224
Thornton, Thomas	WSH 304	Thurber, Joseph	OND 224	Tibbets, John Junr	OND 224
Thorp	GRN 345	Thurber, Kelcy	OND 224	Tibbets, Jonathan	OND 166
Thorp, Abigail	OTS 21	Thurbot, Amos	STB 203	Tibbets, Jonathan	OND 211
Thorp, Andres	GRN 351	Thurbot, Hesekiah	STB 203	Tibbets, Joseph	COL 179
Thorp, Archible	GRN 329	Thurbur, Caleb	OTS 26	Tibbets, Joseph	OND 164
Thorp, Aron	GRN 343	Thurby, Benjamin	SUF 94	Tibbets, Stephen	OND 166
Thorp, Arron	NYK 59	Thurington, John	SRA 58	Tibbetts, Benjamin	RNS 93
Thorp, Asa	SRA 30	Thurman, John	MNT 119	Tibbetts, George	ONN 138
Thorp, Benj:	ONN 174	Thurman, John	WSH 203	Tibbetts, John	COL 183
Thorp, Daniel	DEL 288	Thurman, Richardson	WSH 204	.ibbins, Nathan	CAY 690
Thorp, David	COL 194	Thurman, William M.	NYK 80	Tibbins, Nathaniel	CAY 644
Thorp, David	HRK 557	Thurst, Julius	DUT 152	Tibbit, Edward	ESS 310
Thorp, David	NYK 85	Thursten, Amos	OTS 33	Tibbit, Martin	ESS 311
Thorp, Ebenezer	GRN 330	Thursten, Amos Junr	OTS 33	Tibbit, John	ESS 309
Thorp, Edward	OTS 21	Thursten, Amos 3d	OTS 33	Tibbits, Benjamin	WSH 208
Thorp, Epraim	GRN 354	Thursten, Cleveland	RNS 9	Tibbits, Isaac	SCH 143
Thorp, George	CHN 978	Thursten, David	OTS 33	Tibbits, John	DUT 13
Thorp, Increase	NYK 93	Thursten, Increase	OTS 33	Tibbitts, George	RNS 91
Thorp, James	SRA 30	Thursten, Moses	OTS 33	Tibbitts, Henry	RNS 99
Thorp, John	GRN 325	Thurstin, Daniel	OND 167	Tibbitts, Oliver	ONT 434
Thorp, John	WST 141	Thurstin, Daniel Junr	OND 167	Tibbles, Stephen	GRN 346
Thorp, Joseph	NYK 104	Thurstin, David	OND 175	Tibols, David	SRA 28

Name	Loc	Name	Loc	Name	Loc
Tice, Christopher	ULS 191	Tiffs, Joseph	RNS 112	Tillinghast, Henry	HRK 553
Tice, David	ORN 295	Tifft, Ammon	OND 172	Tillinghast, Jeremiah	NYK 20
Tice, Henry	ORN 342	Tifft, Jesse	OTS 17	Tillinghast, John	SUF 106
Tice, Henry	ULS 191	Tifft, Robert	ULS 260	Tillinghast, Phoebe	SUF 106
Tice, Henry	WST 156	Tift, Arnold	RNS 77	Tillinghast, Thomas	SUF 106
Tice, Jacob	ALB 133	Tift, Asa	WSH 254	Tillingherst, Thomas	WSH 189
Tice, Jacob	SCH 142	Tift, Benjamin	WSH 253	Tillitson, Eleazer	WST 133
Tice, Jacob	WST 155	Tift, Dan:	SCH 165	Tillitson, Elisha	WST 129
Tice, James	NYK 129	Tift, David	WSH 253	Tillitson, James	WST 129
Tice, John	NYK 36	Tift, Edmond	HRK 591	Tillman, Christopher	ALB 33
Tice, John	OTS 28	Tift, George	RNS 98	Tillman, John	ALB 48
Tice, John	RCK 107	Tift, James	DEL 289	Tillman, Richard	ALB 44
Tice, John	SCH 142	Tift, John	CLN 166	Tillon, Francis	NYK 24
Tice, John	ULS 191	Tift, John	ESS 306	Tillot, Josephus	DUT 178
Tice, John Crist	ORN 307	Tift, John	HRK 591	Tillotson, Adonijah	CAY 598
Tice, Joseph	ORN 315	Tift, John	RNS 104	Tillotson, Daniel	DUT 88
Tice, Jost Hendrick	ULS 191	Tift, John	WSH 231	Tillotson, Daniel	ULS 264
Tice, Matthias	DUT 129	Tift, John	WSH 249	Tillotson, Eleazer	OTS 19
Tice, Peter	ORN 307	Tift, John 2d	RNS 112	Tillotson, Elijah	ONT 422
Tice, William	WST 155	Tift, Johnston	WSH 205	Tillotson, Ezra	OTS 22
Tichenor, Israel	DUT 59	Tift, Joseph	WSH 231	Tillotson, Isaac	SUF 90
Tickles, James	WSH 223	Tift, Obediah	SCH 160	Tillotson, Isaac	ULS 180
Ti[ckner?], Asahel	DEL 286	Tift, Pardon	WSH 251	Tillotson, Jacob	SCH 166
Tickner, Elias	OND 201	Tift, Reuben	RNS 105	Tillotson, Jeffry	KNG 8
Tickner, Elijah	COL 183	Tift, Stanton	WSH 231	Tillotson, Joel	OTS 43
Tickner, Hezh	COL 186	Tift, Taber	WSH 254	Tillotson, John	CAY 598
Tickner, Joseph	COL 180	Tift, Thomas	WSH 250	Tillotson, John	SCH 166
Tickner, Willm	COL 186	Tift, William	WSH 231	Tillotson, John	WST 129
Tickney, Royal	OTS 29	Tift, William	WSH 252	Tillotson, John Junior	SCH 166
Ticknor, Joshua	SCH 166	Tift, William	WSH 253	Tillotson, Joseph	DEL 282
Tickrey, Jonah	CHN 974	Tigeet, Joseph	SRA 60	Tillotson, Joseph	OND 163
Tidd, Joseph	ONT 390	Tigner, William	DEL 283	Tillotson, Joseph	OND 173
Tidd, Samuel	SCH 141	Tilden, Israel	SUF 85	Tillotson, Lemuel	OND 173
Tidd, Solomon	CAY 612	Tilden, Joel	OND 178	Tillotson, Matthew N.	CAY 598
Tideebach, Margaret	ORN 380	Tilden, John	COL 206	Tillotson, Nat:	SCH 166
Tidell, Andrew	CAY 612	Tilden, John	OND 177	Tillotson, Nicholas	SUF 92
Tiebout, John	NYK 44	Tiler see Tyler		Tillotson, Pheneus	SCH 166
Tier see Teer		Tiler, Eli	WST 142	Tillotson, Samuel	ULS 246
Tier, Daniel	NYK 123	Tiler, Jabus	WST 123	Tillotson, Stephen	SCH 166
Tier, Jacob	NYK 146	Tiler, John	WST 134	Tillotson, Thomas	DUT 163
Tier, Margaret	NYK 72	Tiles, Phinehas	GRN 344	Tillotson, William	SUF 83
Tier, Valentine	NYK 146	Tiles, Wareem	GRN 344	Tillott, John	DUT 36
Tiers see Tears		Tiletson, Nathaniel	WSH 229	Tillou, James	ULS 239
Tiers, John T.	NYK 143	Tiletson, Richard	WSH 229	Tillou, Joseph	DUT 113
Tiers, Mathew	NYK 146	Tiley, James	WST 140	Tillou, Peter	DUT 42
Tieubout, Anthony	NYK 97	Tiley, Jonathan	WST 140	Tillou, Peter	NYK 39
Tieubout, Elbert	NYK 97	Tilford, Charity	WST 114	Tillou, William	DUT 122
Tieubout, George	NYK 87	Tilford, Charles	WST 113	Tillou, William Junr	DUT 122
Tieubout, Grace a		Tilford, Cornelius	WST 111	Tillow, John	NYK 81
Black	NYK 98	Tilford, Elizabeth	WST 115	Tillson, Isaiah &	
Tieubout, James	NYK 102	Tilford, George	WST 129	John	ULS 207
Tieubout, Tunis	NYK 8	Tilford, William	NYK 131	Tillson, Job	ULS 207
Tifany, Calvin	OND 211	Till, Abraham	WSH 241	Tillson, John &	
Tifany, Henry	SRA 35	Till, Abraham J.	WSH 241	Isaiah	ULS 207
Tiffany, Benjm	COL 178	Till, John	WSH 241	Tilly, Jona	NYK 80
Tiffany, Benjn	OTS 33	Till, Willeam J.	WSH 241	Tilman, Elizabeth	DUT 160
Tiffany, Clark	COL 220	Tillbury, James	TIO 214	Tilness, Joseph	SUF 77
Tiffany, Daniel	CAY 594	Tillbury, John	TIO 214	Tilson, Cephas	OTS 23
Tiffany, Ebenezer	HRK 511	Tillbury, Richard	TIO 214	Tilson, Jonah	OTS 54
Tiffany, Ebenr	OTS 2	Tillen, Salmon	GRN 356	Tilt, Thomas	RCK 98
Tiffany, Ezekiel	ALB 127	Tiller a Black	NYK 94	Tilt, Thos	RCK 99
Tiffany, Ezra	ALB 92	Tillery, James	NYK 19	Tilton, Elijah	WSH 231
Tiffany, George	DEL 276	Tilleson, Joseph	CHN 770	Tilton, Ephriam	WSH 233
Tiffany, George	OTS 39	Tilletson, Abraham	CHN 972	Tilton, Icabode	WSH 233
Tiffany, Hezh	OTS 11	Tilletson, Benjamin	WST 152	Tilton, John	MNT 107
Tiffany, Humphrey	OND 194	Tilletson, Daniel	COL 202	Tilton, John	NYK 127
Tiffany, Isaiah	RNS 5	Tilletson, David	COL 184	Tilton, John	WSH 197
Tiffany, Jacob	ONN 135	Tilletson, Eleanor	WST 128	Tilton, Joseph	ORN 285
Tiffany, Joel	OTS 40	Tillett, Joseth	SUF 79	Tilton, Siles	WSH 233
Tiffany, Nathan	ULS 190	Tilley, Daniel	QNS 82	Tilton, Warren	WSH 233
Tiffany, Nathaniel	DEL 267	Tilley, David	QNS 82	Tilyou, Peter	ALB 79
Tiffany, Nathaniel C.	DEL 276	Tilley, David Junr	QNS 82	Tilyow, Peter	NYK 49
Tiffany, Samuel	SRA 42	Tilley, George	QNS 82	Timas, Gerret	OTS 4
Tiffany, Seth	OTS 2	Tilley, George Junr	QNS 82	Timberman, Jacob	GRN 325
Tiffany, a hariah	ONT 436	Tilley, John	NYK 122	Timberman, Widdow	GRN 325
Tiffeny, Simon	CHN 920	Tilley, John	QNS 84	Timbner, Silus	GRN 343
Tiffing, Benjamin	WSH 189	Tillinghast, Amos	OTS 53	Timerson, Christopher	GRN 339

Timmerman see Temmerman		Tipple, Adam	COL 199	Titus, Peter	QNS 71
		Tipple, Jacob	COL 257	Titus, Platt	SUF 85
Timmerman, A. H.	MNT 56	Tipple, Marthias	SCH 152	Titus, Rhode	CAY 676
Timmerman(?), Adam	MNT 27	Tipple, Martin	SCH 165	Titus, Richard	DUT 97
Timmerman, Conrod	MNT 55	Tipple, Peter	COL 257	Titus, Richard	SUF 87
Timmerman, Conrod	MNT 56	Tippt, Stephen	SRA 14	Titus, Robard	GRN 356
Timmerman, Cornelius	MNT 50	Tirrell, William	NYK 24	Titus, Robert & Jacob	QNS 70
Timmerman, George	MNT 56	Tisdale, Abijah	OND 195	Titus, Ruth	GRN 339
Timmerman, Hendrick	ULS 210	Tisdale, George	OND 196	Titus, Samuel	ALB 37
Timmerman, Henry	MNT 4	Tisdall, Benjamin	HRK 419	Titus, Samuel	CAY 698
Timmerman, Henry H.	MNT 56	Tisdall, Ephraim	HRK 495	Titus, Samuel	CHN 788
Timmerman, Henry S.	MNT 56	Tisdall, Lemuel	HRK 420	Titus, Samuel	DUT 98
Timmerman, Jacob	MNT 4	Tisdell, Paris A.	ONT 440	Titus, Samuel	GRN 353
Timmerman, Jacob H.	MNT 55	Tishball, Jacob	MNT 99	Titus, Samuel	ORN 383
Timmerman, John	MNT 56	Titch, Nathan	SRA 58	Titus, Samuel	QNS 61
Timmerman, Wm	MNT 56	Titchwith, Henry	NYK 106	Titus, Samuel	QNS 71
Timothy Negro	QNS 71	Titesort, Gideon	RCK 105	Titus, Samuel	QNS 72
Timothy	QNS 80	Titford, Isaac	NYK 37	Titus, Samuel	WST 149
Timothy	SUF 93	Tithean, David	SUF 107	Titus, Samuel Junr	DUT 97
Timpson, Cornelius	NYK 84	Tittemar, Hendrick	DUT 162	Titus, Silas	DEL 282
Timpson, Thomas	NYK 36	Titter, George	NYK 130	Titus, Silas	QNS 65
Timpson, Thomas	NYK 93	Tittles, George	WST 126	Titus, Silas	SRA 38
Tims, Michael	ALB 3	Titus a free Negro	ALB 97	Titus, Silas Junr	DEL 281
Tims, Mrs	GRN 338	Titus Free Black	COL 252	Titus, Stephen	DEL 282
Timsen, Benjamin	NYK 98	Titus Negro	TIO 218	Titus, Timothy	KNG 5
Timsom, Obigal	GRN 338	Titus, Abial	KNG 8	Titus, Timothy	QNS 81
Timson, George	GRN 338	Titus, Augustine	DUT 123	Titus, Timothy Junr	QNS 81
Timson, Nathaniel	GRN 338	Titus, Benjamin	DUT 6	Titus, Willett	QNS 64
Timson, Peter	GRN 350	Titus, Benjamin	DUT 130	Titus, William	ORN 380
Timson, Peter	GRN 350	Titus, Benjamin	NYK 113	Titus, William	ORN 395
Timson, Robart	GRN 350	Titus, Chales	GRN 353	Titus, William	QNS 64
Tinch, Jerard	SRA 18	Titus, Charles	KNG 11	Titus, Zebulon	SUF 87
Tincker, Anna	NYK 64	Titus, Charles	NYK 147	Tobby, Warden	SUF 64
T nckum, Samuel	TIO 236	Titus, Daniel	QNS 72	Tobee, Henry	RNS112A
Tindall, Samuel	NYK 127	Titus, Daniel	WST 147	Toben, Frances	NYK 151
Tindell, John	CAY 532	Titus, David	QNS 60	Tobey, Phylander	WSH 234
Tinderick, John	NYK 145	Titus, Ebenezer	COL 252	Tobey, Seth	COL 253
Tiness, Andrew	MNT 101	Titus, Edmond	QNS 81	Tobey, Stephen	OTS 24
Tinglebach, Hendrick	COL 244	Titus, Epharim	SRA 5	Tobey, Zacheus	OTS 22
Tinglebach, Jacob	COL 244	Titus, Francis	QNS 62	Tobey, Zacheus Junr	OTS 22
Tinglebach, John	COL 243	Titus, Francis	QNS 81	Tobey, Zoeth	OTS 22
Tinglebach, John Junr	COL 243	Titus, Frederick	WST 145	Tobias, Alida	COL 214
Tinglepough, Apalus	ALB 86	Titus, Gilbert	DUT 5	Tobias, Ally	COL 222
Tingley, Jonathan	SRA 25	Titus, Gilbert	DUT 97	Tobias, Daniel	ORN 394
Tink, Nathan	MNT 104	Titus, Gilbert	KNG 9	Tobias, Frederick	COL 218
Tink_, John	ONN 177	Titus, Henry	NYK 70	Tobias, Henry	ALB 29
Tinker, Stephen	ONT 368	Titus, Henry	QNS 81	Tobias, Isaac	ORN 397
Tinkery, John	ALB 66	Titus, Henry	SUF 86	Tobias, James	OND 206
Tinkery, William	ALB 66	Titus, Henry	SUF 87	Tobias, John	CAY 636
Tinkery, William	ALB 73	Titus, Hollet	GRN 351	Tobias, John	MNT 51
Tinkey, Andrew	RCK 107	Titus, Isarel	NYK 60	Tobias, Joseph	DUT 134
Tinkey, Henry	WSH 250	Titus, Israel	DUT 6	Tobias, Thomas	RNS 53
Tinkey, Jacob	RCK 108	Titus, Israel	WST 132	Tobias, Warren	ULS 234
Tinkham, Abijah	ONN 163	Titus, Jacob & Robert	QNS 70	Tobine, Samuel	CLN 164
Tinkham, Elias	SCH 166	Titus, Jacob	QNS 81	Tobour, Earl	SRA 33
Tinklebaugh, Jno Junr	COL 192	Titus, Jacob	SUF 87	Toby, Benjamin	COL 204
Tinklepaugh, Margaret	DUT 150	Titus, James	CHN 780	Toby, Cornelius	COL 246
Tinkley, John	ONT 428	Titus, James	ORN 346	Toby, David	OTS 2
Tinkum, Daniel	SRA 57	Titus, James	OTS 53	Toby, Jesse	ESS 321
Tinkum, Samuel	SRA 57	Titus, James	SRA 15	Toby, Joseph	CHN 802
Tinky, Conrod	RCK 110	Titus, John	CAY 672	Toby, Joshua	COL 246
Tinky, Garret	RCK 108	Titus, John	DUT 101	Toby, Josiah	SRA 35
Tinky, John	RCK 108	Titus, John	ESS 318	Toby, Noah	SRA 15
Tinland, James	NYK 153	Titus, John	NYK 44	Toby, Posthumus	MNT 97
Tinney see Jinney		Titus, John	QNS 64	Tod, David	NYK 38
Tinney, Is_	ONT 458	Titus, John	QNS 72	Tod, Margaret	NYK 70
Tinney, John	WSH 215	Titus, John	WST 126	Tod, Samuel	NYK 16
Tinney, Silus	CHN 874	Titus, Jonathan	DEL 282	Tod, Sarah	NYK 70
Tinsdall, Thomas	NYK 134	Titus, Jonathan	KNG 9	Tod, William	NYK 137
Tinseler, John	WSH 251	Titus, Jonathan	QNS 81	Todd, Abram	WST 154
Tinslar, James	HRK 489	Titus, Jonathan	SUF 86	Todd, Adam	ALB 132
Tintz, John	ORN 350	Titus, Jonathan	WSH 300	Todd, Amos	ONN 185
Tippet, Abrm	OTS 11	Titus, Joseph	NYK 118	Todd, Archibald	SRA 23
Tippets see Tibbets		Titus, Joseph Negro	QNS 71	Todd, Asa	OND 183
Tippets, Gilbert	SRA 14	Titus, Joshua	QNS 72	Todd, Caleb	HRK 573
Tippets, James	SRA 14	Titus, Leanard	MNT 100	Todd, Caleb	ONN 159
Tippets, John	SRA 15	Titus, Obidiah	GRN 353	Todd, Dan	ONN 185

Todd, David	WST 155	To..kins, ...	WST 170	Tompkins, Nehemiah	ALB 89
Todd, James	KNG 6	Tompkins, Aaron	DUT 153	Tompkins, Nehemiah	WST 122
Todd, John	ALB 146	Tompkins, Absalom	WST 130	Tompkins, Nehemiah	WST 125
Todd, John	DUT 110	Tompkins, Amos	DUT 79	Tompkins, Nehemiah Junr	WST 125
Todd, John	NYK 33	Tompkins, Amos	WST 152	Tompkins, Noah	WST 121
Todd, John	WSH 251	Tompkins, Aristides	DUT 153	Tompkins, Obadiah	SRA 45
Todd, John	WSH 256	Tompkins, Bartholomew	DUT 81	Tompkins, Oliver	ULS 209
Todd, Jonah	COL 217	Tompkins, Brundage	WST 129	Tompkins, Phillip	DUT 81
Todd, Joseph	ORN 379	Tompkins, Caleb	ALB 111	Tompkins, Phinehas	ORN 366
Todd, Mrs	QNS 73	Tompkins, Caleb	WST 119	Tompkins, Phinehas Junr	ORN 366
Todd, Nathl	OTS 42	Tompkins, Charles	MNT 62	Tompkins, Richard	WST 129
Todd, Oliver	WST 154	Tompkins, Cornelius	DUT 79	Tompkins, Richard	WST 164
Todd, Paul	ALB 68	Tompkins, Daniel	DUT 9	Tompkins, Robert	DUT 79
Todd, Robert	DUT 31	Tompkins, Daniel	ORN 365	Tompkins, Samuel	SRA 43
Todd, Robert	WSH 247	Tompkins, Daniel D.	NYK 19	Tompkins, Silvanus	WST 160
Todd, Samuel	HRK 573	Tompkins, Dorothy	ORN 391	Tompkins, Solomon	ULS 260
Todd, William	DUT 115	Tompkins, Elijah	ALB 81	Tompkins, Stephen	ALB 118
Todd, William	WSH 256	Tompkins, Elijah	ORN 352	Tompkins, Stephen	DUT 25
Toery, Zeerah	GRN 341	Tompkins, Elijah	WST 164	Tompkins, Thaddeus	DUT 94
Toffey, Daniel	QNS 69	Tompkins, Enoch	DUT 82	Tompkins, Thomas	ALB 111
Toffy, John	DUT 52	Tompkins, Enoch	DUT 99	Tompkins, Thomas	DUT 116
Tofts, Winchey	NYK 22	Tompkins, Enoch	WST 119	Tompkins, Thomas	ULS 239
Toland, Edward	ORN 300	Tompkins, Fanny	DUT 81	Tompkins, Thomas	WST 159
Tolburt, Ephraim	ESS 307	Tompkins, Gabriel	DUT 26	Tompkins, Thomas	WST 164
Tole, Charles	MNT 82	Tompkins, George	NYK 91	Tompkins, Thomas	WST 170
Tolin, Moses	NYK 64	Tompkins, George W.	WST 119	Tompkins, Thomas Jnr	WST 164
Toll, Charles	ALB 25	Tompkins, Gilbert	DUT 26	Tompkins, Thomas Jnr	WST 164
Toll, Charles	OND 164	Tompkins, Gilbert	DUT 110	Tompkins, William	ALB 113
Toll, Daniel	ALB 139	Tompkins, Gilbert	WST 164	Tompkins, William	DUT 27
Toll, Ebenezer	OTS 36	Tompkins, Hannah	RCK 109	Tompkins, Wm	MNT 101
Toll, Jesse	SRA 39	Tompkins, Haywood	DUT 118	Tompkins, Wm	MNT 102
Toll, John	ALB 25	Tompkins, Ichabod	ORN 277	Tompkins, William	NYK 79
Toll, Simon	ALB 25	Tompkins, Isaac	DUT 128	Tompkins, William	ULS 239
Toll, Simon	SRA 39	Tompkins, Isaac	ULS 236	Tompkins, William	WST 122
Tollehamer, Peter	SRA 3	Tompkins, Isaac	WST 130	Tompkins, William	WST 125
Tollepee, Robert	NYK 78	Tompkins, Isaac	WST 164	Tompkins, William	WST 170
Toller(?), Daniel	WST 122	Tompkins, Jacob	DUT 96	Tompson, James	WST 164
Tolman, Cornelius	WSH 239	Tompkins, James	DUT 21	Tompson, Robert	WST 131
Tolman, Darius	WSH 189	Tompkins, James	DUT 79	Tompson, Saml	SUF 67
Tolman, Ebenezer	WSH 202	Tompkins, James	DUT 110	Tompson, William	WST 156
Tolman, Elizabeth	WSH 203	Tompkins, James	OND 174	Toms, Benjamin	DUT 131
Tolman, Isaac	WSH 238	Tompkins, James	WST 164	Toms, Phebe	DUT 54
Tolman, Peter	WSH 218	Tompkins, James Junr	DUT 20	Tomson, Archabal	WST 154
Tolmie, Colin	NYK 59	Tompkins, John	DUT 81	Tomson, Asac	GRN 352
Tom a free Negro	ALB 4	Tompkins, John	DUT 99	Tomson, James	GRN 342
Tom a free Negro	ALB 141	Tompkins, John	GRN 353	Tomson, Solomon	RNS 42
Tom. Negro	ONN 168	Tompkins, John	RCK 109	Tone a free Negro	WST 117
Tom, John	NYK 44	Tompkins, John	WST 125	Tone, Henry	RNS 99
Tom, Jonathan	NYK 99	Tompkins, John	WST 153	Tone, John	CAY 656
Tom, Peter	NYK 84	Tompkins, John	WST 164	Toney	QNS 66
Tomb, David	WSH 225	Tompkins, John	WST 164	Toney	QNS 83
Tomb, George	ORN 282	Tompkins, John Junr	WST 125	Toney	SUF 93
Tomb, James	ORN 271	Tompkins, John 3rd	WST 125	Toney	SUF 93
Tomb, James	WSH 224	Tompkins, Jonas	NYK 58	Toney, Jethro free	
Tomb, John	WSH 225	Tompkins, Jonathan	ULS 236	Black	COL 251
Tombs, Andrew	NYK 29	Tompkins, Jonathan	ULS 240	Tonica Blackman and	
Tombs, Benjamin	SRA 44	Tompkins, Jonathan G.	WST 119	family	SRA 14
Tombs, Stephen	OND 195	Tompkins, Joseph	DUT 41	Tonkins, Lidia	RCK 103
Tomlson, David	ALB 12	Tompkins, Joseph	WST 164	Tonkray, David	COL 230
Tomkins, Caleb	GRN 352	Tompkins, Joshua	ALB 120	Tonnecree, Nicholas	DUT 143
Tomkins, Edmond	CHN 756	Tompkins, Joshua	DEL 272	Tonnele, John	NYK 81
Tomkins, Jacob	CAY 694	Tompkins, Joshua	DUT 81	Tonsend, Wm	QNS 84
Tomkins, John	COL 255	Tompkins, Joshua	WST 125	Tony, Tony	QNS 63
Tomkins, Joseph	KNG 7	Tompkins, Laurance	ALB 94	Tooffe, Catharine	DUT 156
Tomkins, Joseph	RNS 31	Tompkins, Margaret	WST 130	Tooker, Charles	ORN 313
Tomkins, Moses	HRK 556	Tompkins, Mary	WST 130	Tooker, Daniel	NYK 35
Tomkins, Rebeckah	RNS 83	Tompkins, Michael	DUT 115	Tooker, Daniel	ORN 357
Tomkins, Richard	CAY 548	Tompkins, Moses	DUT 119	Tooker, Enos	ORN 338
Tomkins, Richard	NYK 58	Tompkins, Moses	WST 130	Tooker, Isaac	ORN 289
Tomkins, Saml	TIO 253	Tompkins, Nathan	ORN 320	Tooker, John	ORN 273
Tomkins, Uriah	HRK 558	Tompkins, Nathanel	WST 164	Tooker, Jonah	CAY 586
Tomkins, William	CAY 650	Tompkins, Nathaniel	DUT 122	Tooker, Reuben	ORN 270
Tomlinson, Lemuel	COL 183	Tompkins, Nathaniel	OND 189	Tooker, Reuben	ORN 286
Tomlinson, Noah	ESS 296	Tompkins, Nathaniel		Tooker, Samuel	ORN 329
Tompkin, Elijah		Junr	DUT 79	Tooker, Selah	ORN 351
B. Smith	WST 164	Tompkins, Nathaniel		Tool, Francis	OND 165
Tompkin, Enos	NYK 102	Senr	DUT 79	Tooley, Jeremiah	OND 192

373

Tooley, Job	DEL 280	Totten, Thomas	NYK 72	Towner, Abm	COL 211
Tooley, Joseph	COL 209	Totten, Uriah	QNS 72	Towner, Ephraim	ONT 398
Tools, David	ONN 180	Totten, William	NYK 138	Towner, Gershom	COL 211
Toothackre, Roger	OTS 5	Totten, William	ORN 366	Towner, Harvy	GRN 331
Toper, Levi	GRN 342	Totten, Zebediah	RCH 88	Towner, Samuel	DUT 167
Toper, William	ALB 53	Totton, James	WST 122	Towner, Samuel	OND 183
Topin, John	CHN 974	Totton, James Junr	WST 124	Towner, Truman	ESS 304
Topin, Stephen	CHN 974	Totton, Peter	WST 123	Townley, Charles	CAY 586
Topliff, Luther	HRK 413	Totton, Samuel	WST 112	Townley, John	NYK 103
Toppan, Abraham	SUF 99	Tough, Isaac	ALB 32	Townley, Mary	NYK 21
Toppan, Henry	SUF 100	Tounsan, Jesse	GRN 342	Townley, Richard	CAY 586
Toppan, Stephen	SUF 100	Tounsand	GRN 345	Towns, Benjamin	OND 204
Toppan, Stephen Junr	SUF 100	Tounsand	GRN 355	Towns, Peter	OND 204
Toppan, Zephaniah	SUF 101	Tounsand, Christopher	GRN 355	Towns, Phineton	CHN 956
Toppen, Jered	OND 222	Tounsen, Caleb	GRN 326	Towns, William	CHN 962
Toppen, William	OND 219	Tounsen, Darius	GRN 336	Townsand, Jesse	SRA 21
Toppin, Coles	QNS 81	Tounsen, John	GRN 340	Townsand, Nathaniel	SRA 4
Toppin, George	QNS 81	Tounsend, Absalom	HRK 584	Townsand, Riderick	WST 164
Toppin, George	QNS 81	Tounsend, Absolem	RNS 6	Townsen, Henry A.	STB 199
Toppin, Silas	SUF 69	Tounsend, Benjamin	RNS 93	Townsend, Aaron	ESS 293
Topping, Daniel	ORN 306	Tounsend, C e er	RNS 106	Townsend, Abijah	DUT 90
Topping, Hezekiah	DUT 152	Tounsend, Charles	RNS 55	Townsend, Abraham	DUT 90
Topping, Job	ORN 347	Tounsend, Daniel	RNS 9	Townsend, Abraham	QNS 80
Torbet, Samuel	NYK 121	Tounsend, George		Townsend, Amasa	WSH 265
Tordham see Fordham		Senior	NYK 63	Townsend, Amasa Jur	WSH 266
Tormg, Thomas	NYK 66	Tounsend, Henry	RNS 91	Townsend, Benjamin	ALB 58
Torpeny, Lawrance	SRA 5	Tounsend, Isaac	HRK 539	Townsend, Benjamin	ALB 117
Torqua, Noal	NYK 56	Tounsend, James	RNS 41	Townsend, Benjamin	DUT 87
Torrance, Hugh	NYK 26	Tounsend, James	RNS 107	Townsend, Benjamin	ULS 268
Torrence, John	NYK 105	T..nsend, Rober.	RNS 6	Townsend, Calven	WSH 265
Torrence, Samuel	ONT 414	Tounson, Jonathan	SRA 34	Townsend, Charles	ALB 112
Torrey Negro	QNS 70	Tounson, Moses	GRN 336	Townsend, Charles	ULS 184
Torrey Negro	QNS 73	Tounson, Robard	GRN 336	Townsend, Christopher	DUT 177
Torrey, John	CAY 706	Tounson, Uriah	GRN 336	Townsend, Daniel	ALB 117
Torrey, John	NYK 73	Tounson, Zebediah	GRN 336	Townsend, Daniel	QNS 79
Torrey, William	NYK 106	Tousey, Grant	WSH 214	Townsend, Daniel Junr	ALB 117
Torry, Daniel	RNS 92	Tousey, Moses	GRN 344	Townsend, Eber	DUT 93
Torry, Enos	OND 164	Tousey, Thomas	GRN 344	Townsend, Elihu	ALB 70
Torry, James	ORN 310	Touz, Frances	NYK 78	Townsend, Elihu	DUT 178
Torry, James	OTS 21	Tower, Cornelus	OND 182	Townsend, Elijah	CAY 554
Torry, James	RNS 23	Tower, Ezra	ALB 38	Townsend, Elijah	DUT 18
Torry, Jesse	COL 206	Tower, Ezra	SCH 121	Townsend, Elijah	NYK 76
Torry, Job	SRA 14	Tower, Henry	ONT 462	Townsend, Elijah	ONT 460
Torry, Luthar	RNS 33	Tower, Isaiah	ALB 35	Townsend, Elijah	ORN 375
Torry, Martin	RNS 112	Tower, Jeduthan	OND 185	Townsend, Elijah	ULS 240
Torry, Solomon	RNS 112	Tower, Jothum	CHN 912	Townsend, Elizabeth	WST 149
Torum, Samuel	DUT 25	Tower, Justus	OND 197	Townsend, Enoch Negro	QNS 71
Toser, Thomas	WSH 284	Tower, Nehemiah	OTS 9	Townsend, Euriah	ONT 460
Tosh, William	WSH 251	Tower, Reuben	RNS 32	Townsend, Francis	QNS 84
Tosmpson, Alexander	SCH 166	Towers, Hannah	NYK 70	Townsend, Frederick	DUT 91
Toster see Foster		Towers, Luke	RNS 33	Townsend, Gamaliel	TIO 261
Totman, Asa	WST 113	Towers, Roger	NYK 42	Townsend, George	QNS 81
Tottan, Nathan	SUF 83	Town, Absalom	OND 185	Townsend, George	QNS 84
Tottan, Paul	SUF 84	Town, Asa	OTS 53	Townsend, Gideon	DUT 178
Tottan, Thomas	SUF 82	Town, Benjamin	WSH 271	Townsend, Gilbul	DEL 291
Tottan, Simeon	SUF 89	Town, Danl	OTS 45	Townsend, Hannah	ORN 363
Totten, Abraham	SCH 153	Town, David	HRK 548	Townsend, Hannah	QNS 84
Totten, Daniel	SCH 165	Town, Edward	WSH 257	Townsend, Helibel	OTS 21
Totten, Gilbert	KNG 7	Town, Elijah	SRA 55	Townsend, Henry	NYK 126
Totten, Gilbert	RCH 94	Town, Ephraim	HRK 416	Townsend, Henry	ORN 398
Totten, Israel	DUT 137	Town, Ephraim	OND 197	Townsend, Hezekiah	DUT 179
Totten, Jacob	QNS 79	Town, Frances	WSH 289	Townsend, Hezekiah	ONT 468
Totten, James	RCH 94	Town, Isaac	HRK 414	Townsend, Hulett	QNS 82
Totten, John	NYK 56	Town, John	OTS 45	Townsend, Isaac	CHN 902
Totten, John	NYK 83	Town, John	RCK 102	Townsend, Isaac	DEL 277
Totten, John	ORN 320	Town, John Junr	OTS 45	Townsend, Isaac	DUT 176
Totten, John	RCH 94	Town, Jonathan	SRA 30	Townsend, Israel	WST 115
Totten, Joseph	ALB 33	Town, Joseph	WSH 270	Townsend, Jacob	NYK 63
Totten, Joseph	ORN 365	Town, Polly	NYK 129	Townsend, Jacob Negro	QNS 71
Totten, Joseph	QNS 63	Town, Robert	HRK 570	Townsend, Jacob	SUF 85
Totten, Joseph	RCH 88	Town, Rubin	ONT 352	Townsend, James	DUT 90
Totten, Peter	ORN 364	Town, Ruphes	WSH 223	Townsend, James	ONT 504
Totten, Phebe	ORN 275	Town, Salmon	WSH 271	Townsend, James	ORN 385
Totten, Richard	QNS 78	Town, Stephen	HRK 548	Townsend, James	WST 127
Totten, Richard	QNS 79	Town, Stephen	WSH 271	Townsend, Jeremiah	OTS 22
Totten, Silas	NYK 112	Town, Willeam	WSH 271	Townsend, John	ALB 85
Totten, Silas	ORN 373	Town, Willeam	WSH 289	Townsend, John	CHN 900

Townsend, John	DUT 37	Tracey, Theophelus		Traver, Henry	DUT 164
Townsend, John	DUT 178	Jur		Traver, Henry J.	COL 179
Townsend, John	NYK 116	Tracey, Thomas	NYK 75	Traver, Henry P.	DUT 112
Townsend, John	OND 179	Tracey, Ury	CHN 768	Traver, Isaac	DUT 111
Townsend, John	ORN 385	Tracry, Henry	STB 201	Traver, Jacob F.	DUT 119
Townsend, John	QNS 71	Tracy, Charles	MNT 68	Traver, Jacob P.	DUT 112
Townsend, John	ULS 256	Tracy, Christopher	TIO 210	Traver, Jacobus	DUT 165
Townsend, John	WST 118	Tracy, Ebenezer	DEL 281	Traver, John	ALB 119
Townsend, John	WST 148	Tracy, Edmund	CAY 644	Traver, John	DUT 111
Townsend, John Junr	DUT 178	Tracy, Elijah	OTS 48	Traver, John	RNS 61
Townsend, Joseph	COL 223	Tracy, Enos	OTS 48	Traver, John H.	DUT 164
Townsend, Joseph	COL 237	Tracy, Ephraim	OTS 48	Traver, John J.	DUT 151
Townsend, Joseph	DUT 170	Tracy, Gashum	GRN 356	Traver, John N.	DUT 164
Townsend, Joseph	QNS 80	Tracy, Hestus	OND 224	Traver, Jonathan	COL 266
Townsend, Jotham	QNS 82	Tracy, Hezekiah	ALB 138	Traver, Joseph	ALB 118
Townsend, Kezia	ORN 360	Tracy, Isaac	STB 206	Traver, Joseph	COL 232
Townsend, Laurence	ONT 460	Tracy, Israel	CLN 173	Traver, Jost	DUT 160
Townsend, Mary	NYK 51	Tracy, Jabez	SCH 147	Traver, Lawrence	DUT 109
Townsend, Melancton	NYK 77	Tracy, James	CHN 768	Traver, Martin	DUT 163
Townsend, Nathaniel	KNG 9	Tracy, John	NYK 44	Traver, Peter	ALB 56
Townsend, Nathaniel	OND 179	Tracy, Jonas	ONN 163	Traver, Peter	DUT 161
Townsend, Narhaniel	QNS 83	Tracy, Jonathan	CLN 174	Traver, Peter N.	COL 261
Townsend, Nicholas	ORN 397	Tracy, Jonathan	STB 200	Traver, Peter P.	DUT 112
Townsend, Joah	ORN 288	Tracy, Levi	ALB 91B	Traver, Phillip	DUT 165
Townsend, Obadiah	QNS 71	Tracy, Lycenus	OND 211	Traver, Sebastian	DUT 165
Townsend, Peter	ORN 363	Tracy, Sanford	ALB 91B	Traver, Solomon	DUT 108
Townsend, Platt	DEL 277	Tracy, Stephen	WSH 280	Traver, Thomas	COL 231
Townsend, Pryor	QNS 84	Tracy, Theophelus	WSH 280	Traver, William	DUT 122
Townsend, Richard	COL 224	Tracy, Thomas	CHN 802	Traver, Zachariah	DUT 161
Townsend, Richard	COL 228	Tracy, William C.	SCH 147	Travers, Elisha	QNS 68
Townsend, Richard	QNS 71	Tracy, William G.	OND 157	Travers, George	NYK 118
Townsend, Richard	QNS 81	Trafford, John	COL 179	Travers, James	NYK 97
Townsend, Richard 2d	QNS 70	Trafford, Thomas	COL 235	Traverse, Amos	ORN 287
Townsend, Robert	QNS 78	Trail, John	ORN 303	Traverse, Amy	DUT 126
Townsend, Samuel	DUT 177	Train, Asel	ESS 321	Traverse, Daniel	QNS 79
Townsend, Samuel	QNS 80	Train, Daniel N.	NYK 74	Traverse, David	DUT 88
Townsend, Samuel	WST 127	Train, David	RNS 107	Traverse, Ezekiel	ORN 334
Townsend, Sarah	QNS 82	Trainer, John	ORN 398	Traverse, George	DUT 82
Townsend, Sarah	QNS 84	Trale, William	NYK 57	Traverse, Gilbert	DUT 86
Townsend, Silvanus	WST 127	Trall, Roger	OTS 18	Traverse, Gilbert	DUT 88
Townsend, Silvanus Junr	WST 127	Trall, Silas	OTS 18	Traverse, Gilbert	DUT 177
Townsend, Solomon	NYK 38	Trambla, Babtiest	CLN 168	Traverse, Gilbert	QNS 84
Townsend, Stephen	DUT 18	Trambla, P[runo?]	CLN 168	Traverse, Isaac	DUT 115
Townsend, Stephen	WST 125	Trambless, Joseph	ALB 141	Traverse, Isaac	DUT 126
Townsend, Susannah	WST 148	Trances see Frances		Traverse, Isaac	ULS 192
Townsend, Sylvenus	QNS 83	Trankline see Frank-		Traverse, Jacob	ORN 334
Townsend, Thomas	DUT 41	line		Traverse, Jacob	QNS 84
Townsend, Thomas	DUT 93	Transon, Benjamin	SRA 33	Traverse, James	QNS 84
Townsend, Thomas S.	NYK 32	Trapp, James	ULS 248	Traverse, John	ALB 103
Townsend, Timothy	COL 205	Trapp, William	ULS 190	Traverse, John	DUT 81
Townsend, Uriah	DUT 173	Trappel, Michael	NYK 65	Traverse, John	DUT 115
Townsend, William	ORN 381	Trash, George	COL 221	Traverse, John	ORN 312
Townsend, William	ORN 398	Trask, Ebenezer	OND 173	Traverse, Jonathan	DUT 88
Townsend, William	WST 127	Trask, John	OND 186	Traverse, Joseph	CLN 169
Townsend, Zebulon	ORN 398	Trava, Philabut	NYK 31	Traverse, Joseph	DUT 26
Townsend, Zepheniah	DUT 90	Travase, James	GRN 357	Traverse, Joseph	DUT 88
Townsley, Abner	CHN 898	Traver, Abraham	COL 197	Traverse, Joshua	DUT 125
Townsley, Samuel	WSH 252	Traver, Abraham	DUT 112	Traverse, Joshua	ULS 221
Townson, Samuel	QNS 69	Traver, Adam	DUT 160	Traverse, Marcus B.	ORN 334
Towsend, William	NYK 97	Traver, Adam P.	DUT 112	Traverse, Nathaniel	ORN 312
Towser, Lewis	HRK 417	Traver, Bastian	COL 197	Traverse, Nehemiah	DUT 73
Towser, Richd	OTS 14	Traver, Bastian	ORN 338	Traverse, Phillip	DUT 92
Towsey, John	ULS 195	Traver, Bastian J.	DUT 109	Traverse, Titus	DUT 82
Towsley, Amos	TIO 208	Traver, Charles	ALB 117	Traversee, Andrew	CLN 169
Towsley, Samuel	DEL 277	Traver, Charles	DUT 112	Travice, Abraham	SRA 10
Towt, Robert H.	NYK 49	Traver, Charles	RNS 35	Travis, Abel	WST 152
Towt, Sarah	NYK 37	Traver, Christian	ONT 460	Travis, Abel	WST 152
Tozer, John	DUT 55	Traver, Coonradt	DUT 111	Travis, Abraham	CLN 164
Tr_ton, James	MNT 77	Traver, Daniel	COL 232	Travis, Abraham	CLN 165
Tracey, Alanson	CAY 646	Traver, David	COL 245	Travis, Abm	RNS 49
Tracey, Avery	CAY 648	Traver, David Junr	DUT 112	Travis, Absalom	WST 159
Tracey, Benjamin	CAY 648	Traver, David Senr	DUT 112	Travis, Annanias	WST 122
Tracey, Gilbert	CAY 644	Traver, David P.	DUT 112	Travis, Bartholamew	WST 130
Tracey, John	QNS 82	Traver, Frederick	ORN 342	Travis, David	WST 129
Tracey, John	QNS 82	Traver, Georg H.	DUT 160	Travis, David	WST 154
Tracey, Mary	CAY 646	Traver, George F.	DUT 112	Travis, Elijah	WST 155
Tracey, Robert L.	CAY 646	Traver, George J.	DUT 161	Travis, Elisha	WST 129

Travis, Ira	ONT 326	Tremain, Augustus	COL 186	Tripler, Thomas	NYK 25
Travis, Jacob	WST 157	Tremain, Julius	OTS 22	Tripley, Christian	NYK 149
Travis, Jacob	WST 159	Treman, Jared	COL 184	Tripp, Anthony	DEL 289
Travis, James	CAY 624	Tremble, Edwd A.	ALB 103	Tripp, Benjamin	COL 194
Travis, Jesse	SRA 28	Tremble, John	ESS 294	Tripp, Benjamin	SRA 52
Travis, Jesse	SRA 28	Tremper, Adam	COL 192	Tripp, Caleb	WSH 202
Travis, Jesse	WST 122	Tremper, Catharine	DUT 161	Tripp, Daniel	DUT 142
Travis, John	RNS 34	Tremper, Daniel	ULS 229	Tripp, David	ONN 137
Travis, John	RNS 89	Tremper, George	DUT 161	Tripp, David	RNS 112
Travis, John	SRA 39	Tremper, George	ORN 305	Tripp, David	WSH 202
Travis, John	WST 126	Tremper, Jacob	NYK 136	Tripp, Ebenezer	SRA 52
Travis, Jonathan	WST 131	Tremper, Jacob	ORN 274	Tripp, Everet	WSH 202
Travis, Joseph	WST 153	Tremper, Jacob	ULS 227	Tripp, Gideon	COL 213
Travis, Joseph Carpt.	WST 156	Tremper, Jacob Junr	ORN 274	Tripp, Gideon	RNS 112
Travis, Joshua	WST 122	Tremper, John	ULS 229	Tripp, Israel	COL 182
Travis, Joshua Junr	WST 131	Tremper, Margaret	ORN 282	Tripp, Israel	COL 200
Travis, Levina	ONT 472	Tremper, William	DUT 164	Tripp, James	DUT 97
Travis, Nathaniel	ALB 9	Tremper, William	ORN 274	Tripp, James	OND 192
Travis, Phebe	WST 126	Tremper, William	ULS 219	Tripp, James	WSH 209
Travis, Robert	WST 123	Trempo, Jacob	GRN 327	Tripp, John	DUT 104
Travis, Sylvanus	CAY 554	Trempo, Nicholas	GRN 327	Tripp, John	DUT 129
Travis, Uriah	WST 114	Trempo, Zachariah	GRN 328	Tripp, John	WSH 239
Travis, Willes	WST 130	Trempour, Jacob	ULS 222	Tripp, John Junr	DUT 142
Travis, Zebulon	WST 137	Trempour, John	ORN 279	Tripp, Jonathan	ALB 32
Traviss, David	NYK 39	Trempour, Nicholas	ORN 296	Tripp, Jonathan	WSH 211
Traviss, Stephen	NYK 99	Trempour, Valentine F.	ULS 222	Tripp, Joseph	COL 198
Travus, Sylvanus	SRA 11	Trempour, William	ORN 279	Tripp, Levi	ALB 33
Tray Negro	QNS 63	Trempter, Jacob	ORN 387	Tripp, Lott	SRA 52
Trays, George	NYK 150	Trenchard, Henry	WST 147	Tripp, Mary	SRA 31
Treadway, Benjamin	MNT 102	Trenton, Stephen	MNT 90	Tripp, Pardon	ALB 22
Treadway, Benjamin	MNT 102	Trepan, Anthony	NYK 59	Tripp, Peleg	WSH 202
Treadway, David	HRK 514	Trephagen, Jonathan	ULS 241	Tripp, Reynolds	DUT 18
Treadway, David	OTS 57	Trescot, Joseph	CHN 774	Tripp, Samuel	DUT 104
Treadway, Ezra	OTS 57	Treter, Abraham	SCH 151	Tripp, Samuel	DUT 105
Treadwell, Daniel	OND 179	Trewilligar see Ter-		Tripp, Sarah	WST 135
Treadwell, James	DUT 97	williger		Tripp, Silas	DUT 9
Treadwell, Reuben	ALB 91	Trewilligar, Dirick	ALB 104	Tripp, Stephen	RNS 54
Treadwell, Squire	DUT 32	Trewilligar, Simon	ALB 104	Tripp, Stokes	SRA 31
Treat, Aaron	CAY 698	Tribers, Elisha	NYK 148	Tripp, Timothy	CAY 628
Treat, Ashbel	CAY 698	Trickey, Jeremiah	ORN 382	Tripp, Timothy	DUT 105
Treat, Charles	HRK 456	Trickey, William	ORN 382	Tripp, William	DUT 105
Treat, Dan	HRK 443	Trimble, Eliphalet	ALB 132	Tripp, William	ESS 306
Treat, John	ALB 113	Trimble, Mary	ORN 293	Tripp, William	OND 192
Treat, John	OTS 42	Trimble, Richard	ORN 285	Tripp, William	WSH 209
Treat, John	SRA 34	Trimble, William	ORN 293	Trison, William	NYK 52
Treat, Moses	CAY 698	Trimell, Andres	NYK 55	Trist, Andries	DUT 151
Treat, Richd S.	ALB 147	Trimmer, Anthony	ONT 500	Trithene	SUF 97
Treat, Thos	OTS 8	Trimmon, Daniel	CHN 742	Trivet, Samuel	NYK 34
Treat, Timothy	ONN 185	Trimmon, John	ONT 426	Troat, Grove	MNT 67
Treat, Willeam	WSH 277	Trimpley, Alexander	NYK 94	Troat, Jess	MNT 67
Treats, Peter	OTS 8	Trion, Asac	GRN 345	Trobridge, Samuel	WST 141
Tredway, Asa	CHN 832	Trip, Abial	SCH 156	Troll, Levi	DEL 274
Tredway, Ezekel	CHN 832	Trip, Anthony	WST 116	Troop, Daniel H.	SCH 133
Tredwell, Benjamin	QNS 71	Trip, Benjamin	ALB 36	Troop, Horice	SCH 133
Tredwell, Benjamin	QNS 71	Trip, Benjamin	SRA 28	Troop, John	RNS 105
Tredwell, Benjamin	QNS 77	Trip, Benjamin	WST 113	Troop, William	SCH 133
Tredwell, Gilbert a		Trip, Billy.	SCH 123	Tropp, Job	RNS 72
Black	NYK 81	Trip, Calvin	ALB 69	Trotter, James	CAY 520
Tredwell, Humphry	DEL 287	Trip, Daniel	WST 116	Trotter, Matthew	ALB 134
Tredwell, James a		Trip, Ezekiel	ALB 36	Trottman, Andrew	KNG 9
mulatto	NYK 75	Trip, Gideon	SRA 4	Troup, George	WSH 300
Tredwell, John	QNS 72	Trip, Job	ALB 35	Troup, Henry	NYK 40
Tredwell, John	QNS 77	Trip, John	SRA 60	Troup, John	QNS 68
Tredwell, John	WST 148	Trip, Jonathan E.	ALB 37	Troup, Robert	NYK 19
Tredwell, Niram	WST 164	Trip, Joseph	ALB 36	Troup, William	NYK 73
Tredwell, Richard	QNS 83	Trip, Lot	NYK 45	Trouss, John(?)	NYK 116
Tredwell, Samuel	WST 112	Trip, Obediah	SCH 157	Trout, Adam	CAY 708
Tredwell, Samuel	WST 148	Trip, Othenial	ALB 39	Trout, Michael	RCK 103
Tredwell, Thomas	CLN 161	Trip, Philip	SCH 156	Troutt, Robert	RCK 105
Tredwell, Thomas	CLN 165	Trip, Richard	ALB 80	Trover, John	ONT 472
Tredwell, Thomas	QNS 70	Trip, Robert	CLN 172	Trowbridge, Alvah	DUT 85
Tredwell, William	NYK 109	Trip, Thomas	ALB 39	Trowbridge, Caleb	CAY 568
Tredwell, William	QNS 70	Trip, Thomas	SRA 9	Trowbridge, Caleb	WSH 283
Tree, Margaret	NYK 30	Triphagen, Garret	ULS 253	Trowbridge, Daniel	OND 173
Treeman, Israel	COL 263	Triphagen, Henry	ULS 251	Trowbridge, David	ALB 135
Treet, Cornelius	ONT 394	Triphagen, Jacobus	ULS 251	Trowbridge, Eli	DUT 131
Treland, Daniel	QNS 71	Triphagen, Jonathan	ULS 251	Trowbridge, Isaac	NYK 145

Name	Loc	Pg
Tucker, Rodes	SRA	18
Tucker, Rufus Senr	OTS	22
Tucker, Sally	OND	198
Tucker, Samuel	HRK	591
Tucker, Samuel	ONN	132
Tucker, Sarah	NYK	146
Tucker, Thomas	NYK	143
Tucker, Timothy	NYK	75
Tucker, Walter	NYK	104
Tucker, William	GRN	342
Tucker, William	HRK	446
Tucker, Wm	SUF	66
Tucker, Wm	SUF	66
Tucker, William	SUF	80
Tucker, William	WST	113
Tucker, Zebah	OTS	30
Tucker, Zepheniah	OND	157
Tucker, Zepheniah	OND	206
Tucker, Zeth	WSH	201
Tucker, Zopher	SUF	65
Tuckerman, Benjn	OTS	53
Tuckerman, Frederick	ULS	196
Tuckerman, Isaac	NYK	76
Tuckness, John	NYK	24
Tudder, Soloman	NYK	108
Tuesler, John J.	MNT	4
Tuft, John	RNS	105
Tuft, Nathan	WSH	249
Tuft, Wm	ONN	168
Tufts, Joshua B.	NYK	60
Tugood see Tewgood		
Tugood, Daniel	RNS	43
Tugood, James	RNS	40
Tugood, John	RNS	75
Tuleron, Edward	MNT	47
Tuley	GRN	328
Tulhenson, John	NYK	139
Tull, Daniel	WSH	231
Tuller, Israel	OND	171
Tuller, James	OND	163
Tuller, Moses	OND	183
Tully, Hendrick	GRN	358
Tully, Jeremiah	GRN	358
Tully, John	CAY	644
Tully, John	GRN	358
Tully, Samuel	SCH	165
Tulor, Benjamin	SUF	93
Tune, Nathan	CAY	656
Tunessin, Jacob E.	NYK	152
Tunier, Laurence	NYK	93
Tunis, Ephraim	MNT	113
Tunis, Gosher	MNT	102
Tunisson, John	CAY	554
Tunnecliff, John	HRK	509
Tunnecliff, John Jun	HRK	509
Tunnecliff, Willm	HRK	509
Tunnicliff, Joseph	OTS	13
Tunnicliff, Willm	OTS	51
Tunnikil, John	ALB	12
Tupper, Charles	CAY	670
Tupper, Phebe	ORN	281
Tupper, Rufus	ORN	348
Tupper, William	CHN	922
Tur, Princeton a Black	NYK	89
Turce, John	NYK	149
Turce, Nancy	NYK	123
Turk, Aaron	RNS	63
Turk, Abraham	ALB	56
Turk, Abraham	ALB	74
Turk, Abraham	GRN	330
Turk, Abm	RNS	63
Turk, Ahasuerus	NYK	47
Turk, Benjamin	ULS	226
Turk, Henry	RNS	17
Turk, Henry	ULS	226
Turk, Jacob	ULS	219
Turk, Jacob Junr	ULS	226
Turk, Johannis	ULS	226
Turk, John	ALB	78
Turk, John	RNS	59
Turk, John A.	DUT	145
Turk, Thomas	ALB	114
Turk, Urone	SRA	55
Turkey, Peter	NYK	25
Turnbull, Andrew	NYK	89
Turnbull, George	ALB	27
Turnbull, George	MNT	113
Turnbull, George	NYK	20
Turnbull, George	NYK	150
Turnbull, John	ALB	39
Turnbull, John	NYK	38
Turnbull, John	NYK	99
Turnbull, Thomas	KNG	5
Turnbull, Walter	ALB	30
Turnbull, William	ALB	27
Turner see Ternure & Turnner		
Turner, Abner	TIO	236
Turner, Abner	TIO	239
Turner, Alexander	NYK	139
Turner, Alexander	WSH	221
Turner, Allen	OND	163
Turner, Andrew	ALB	55
Turner, Archabald	WSH	221
Turner, Asa	OND	204
Turner, Benjamin	SRA	26
Turner, Benjamin	WSH	203
Turner, Caleb	OTS	46
Turner, Caleb	WSH	196
Turner, Cathrine	SUF	64
Turner, Charles	MNT	85
Turner, Cornelius	ALB	111
Turner, Cornelius	ORN	278
Turner, Cornelius	ULS	185
Turner, Cornelius	ULS	213
Turner, Daniel	ALB	111
Turner, Danl	OTS	34
Turner, Danl	SUF	70
Turner, David	RNS	56
Turner, Denison	OND	212
Turner, Edmund	ULS	231
Turner, Edmund	ULS	258
Turner, Edward	RNS	56
Turner, Elijah	OTS	34
Turner, Elisha	DEL	276
Turner, Elisha	DUT	55
Turner, Enoch	ALB	102
Turner, Ezra	CLN	159
Turner, Frederick	COL	177
Turner, Gilbert	COL	240
Turner, Gilbert	DUT	168
Turner, Gilbert G.	COL	240
Turner, Heny	SUF	70
Turner, Hezekiah	OND	219
Turner, Hezekiah	ONN	157
Turner, Hezekiah	ULS	212
Turner, Hugh	ORN	386
Turner, Isaac	OND	208
Turner, Isaac	WSH	267
Turner, Jacob	OND	214
Turner, Jacob	ONT	328
Turner, Jacob	ULS	213
Turner, James	DUT	148
Turner, James	HRK	534
Turner, James	MNT	107
Turner, James	STB	201
Turner, Jeddediah	CHN	956
Turner, Jedit. F.	CHN	956
Turner, Jeremiah	GRN	352
Turner, Jesse	TIO	213
Turner, Johannis	ULS	212
Turner, John	CHN	956
Turner, John	DEL	284
Turner, John	DUT	56
Turner, John	NYK	34
Turner, John	NYK	37
Turner, John	NYK	63
Turner, John	NYK	140
Turner, John	OND	206
Turner, John	ONN	168
Turner, John	ORN	270
Turner, John	RNS	111
Turner, John	SRA	60
Turner, John	SUF	69
Turner, John	WSH	285
Turner, John	ULS	258
Turner, John Junr	NYK	30
Turner, John Junr	OND	206
Turner, John L.	NYK	49
Turner, Jonathan	RNS	111
Turner, Joseph	ORN	278
Turner, Joseph	SCH	136
Turner, Joseph	SUF	70
Turner, Joseph	SUF	70
Turner, Joseph	WST	120
Turner, Joseph	WST	121
Turner, Joshua	WST	131
Turner, Lebeus	RNS	24
Turner, Lemuel	OTS	55
Turner, Mary	ALB	46
Turner, Mathew	CHN	988
Turner, Nathan	DEL	275
Turner, Nathan	DUT	55
Turner, Nathan	DUT	73
Turner, Nathan	SRA	29
Turner, Nathan Junr	DUT	55
Turner, Nathaniel	OND	194
Turner, Nathaniel	ONT	400
Turner, Noah	ONT	352
Turner, Paul	DEL	284
Turner, Reuben	ORN	301
Turner, Reuben	WSH	225
Turner, Richard	OND	201
Turner, Roger	WSH	275
Turner, Roswell	ONT	332
Turner, Salah	KNG	7
Turner, Samuel	CLN	167
Turner, Samuel	OND	193
Turner, Saml	SUF	69
Turner, Samuel	ULS	197
Turner, Samuel Junr	OND	194
Turner, Sarah	NYK	25
Turner, Sarah	NYK	40
Turner, Seth	GRN	332
Turner, Simeon	ULS	214
Turner, Stephen	DUT	55
Turner, Stephen	OND	193
Turner, Stephen	OTS	22
Turner, Stephen	ULS	187
Turner, Stephen	WST	152
Turner, Thomas	CHN	956
Turner, Thomas	ORN	298
Turner, Thomas	RNS	83
Turner, Thos Junr	OTS	16
Turner, Tice	COL	233
Turner, Wilhelmus	COL	200
Turner, Wilhelmus	COL	236
Turner, William	DUT	77
Turner, William	NYK	32
Turner, William	NYK	79
Turner, William	RNS	88
Turner, Wm	SUF	65
Turner, William	ULS	190
Turner, William	ULS	212
Turney, Luke	NYK	90
Turney, Matthew	ORN	348
Turnner, Alexr J.	OND	224
Turnner, Jeams	OND	223
Turnner, Reubin	OND	223
Turpan, Richard	COL	243

Name	Loc	Name	Loc	Name	Loc
Turpin see Terpen		Tuttle, Abraham	WST 170	Tuttle, Timothy	MNT 83
Turpin, Henry	ULS 206	Tuttle, Andrew	OND 208	Tuttle, Uzal	NYK 87
Turpin, Michael	COL 241	Tuttle, Anna	GRN 355	Tuttle, Wm	ONN 189
Turrell, Ebenezer	NYK 68	Tuttle, Benjamin	ALB 114	Tuttle, William	ULS 180
Turrell, Isaac	TIO 226	Tuttle, Charles	GRN 337	Tuttle, William	ULS 232
Turrey	GRN 349	Tuttle, Daniel	HRK 354	Tuttle, William Y.	HRK 453
Turrey, William	GRN 341	Tuttle, Daniel	MNT 122	Tuttle, Zeptimus	HRK 469
Turril, Zalmon	ONN 163	Tuttle, Daniel	QNS 66	Tuttle W., Catharine	WST 154
Turtle, Abner	STB 207	Tuttle, Danl	SUF 74	Tuwilleger see Terwilli-	
Turville, John B.	CLN 165	Tuttle, Daniel	SUF 95	ger	
Turzer, Daniel	NYK 44	Tuttle, David	ALB 126	Tuwilleger, James	TIO 225
Tusler, Marcus	MNT 4	Tuttle, David	SUF 71	Tuwilliger, Thomas	SRA 11
Tusten, James	ORN 355	Tuttle, David	SUF 74	Tweed, Anna	NYK 136
Tutel, Daniel	NYK 70	Tuttle, David	WST 154	Tweedy, John	DUT 171
Tutfin, William	CAY 680	Tuttle, Elijah	SRA 43	Twills, Mary	NYK 132
Tuthill, Abm	SUF 77	Tuttle, Elisha	SUF 74	Twist, Alphius	CHN 958
Tuthill, Ann	ORN 350	Tuttle, Enoch	ORN 311	Twist, Benjamin	COL 201
Tuthill, Ann	SUF 77	Tuttle, Ezekiel	ULS 180	Twist, David	WSH 199
Tuthill, Anna	ORN 353	Tuttle, Ezra	SUF 64	Twist, Elias	WSH 199
Tuthill, Barnabas	SUF 72	Tuttle, Gershom	OND 187	Twist, Elijah	WSH 199
Tuthill, Benjamin	ORN 353	Tuttle, Gershom Junr	OND 187	Twist, Joseph	WSH 199
Tuthill, Benjamin	ULS 245	Tuttle, Israel	KNG 8	Twitchel, _seph	WSH 204
Tuthill, Christifer	SUF 77	Tuttle, James	DUT 57	Twitchel, Joshua	WSH 204
Tuthill, Daniel	NYK 129	Tuttle, James	DUT 67	Twitchins, Henry	NYK 63
Tuthill, Daniel	ORN 347	Tuttle, James	MNT 122	Twoo, John	COL 259
Tuthill, Daniel	ORN 353	Tuttle, James	WSH 206	Tydgat, Margaret	NYK 74
Tuthill, Danl	SUF 73	Tuttle, James	WST 155	Tygart, Nicholas	MNT 26
Tuthill, Danl	SUF 77	Tuttle, Jehial	GRN 337	Tyger, William	ALB 64
Tuthill, David	SUF 72	Tuttle, Jehiel	OND 192	Tygert, Henry	ONN 166
Tuthill, David	SUF 77	Tuttle, Jered	ONT 418	Tygert, Peter	ONN 153
Tuthill, Elizabeth	SUF 75	Tuttle, Jesee	SUF 74	Tyger_, Peter S.	MNT 22
Tuthill, Fanny	ORN 353	Tuttle, Jesse	CHN 928	Tygert, Sephrenus	MNT 38
Tuthill, Freegift	ORN 356	Tuttle, Joel	GRN 337	Tygert, Sephrenus S.	MNT 38
Tuthill, Isaac	SUF 72	Tuttle, Johial	GRN 329	Tyggert, Abraham W.	MNT 51
Tuthill, Israel	NYK 133	Tuttle, John	GRN 334	Tyggert, Peter	MNT 73
Tuthill, James	SUF 75	Tuttle, John	OND 185	Tylar, Ephraim	STB 204
Tuthill, Jane	ORN 347	Tuttle, John	OND 198	Tylee, ..man 2d	RNS 108
Tuthill, Jeremiah	SUF 76	Tuttle, John	OND 206	Tyler see Tiler	
Tuthill, Jeremiah Y.	SUF 77	Tuttle, John	OTS 43	Tyler, Abisha	OND 173
Tuthill, John	ORN 327	Tuttle, John	SRA 43	Tyler, Amos	CAY 692
Tuthill, John	ORN 340	Tuttle, John	SUF 71	Tyler, Amos	ULS 181
Tuthill, John	ORN 353	Tuttle, John	SUF 74	Tyler, Asa	OND 211
Tuthill, John	SUF 95	Tuttle, John	WST 161	Tyler, Asa	SCH 139
Tuthill, John Junr	ORN 323	Tuttle, Jonathan	OND 223	Tyler, Ashbel	OND 183
Tuthill, John W.	ORN 351	Tuttle, Joseph	OTS 52	Tyler, Benajah	CAY 706
Tuthill, Jonathan	ORN 329	Tuttle, Joseph	QNS 67	Tyler, Benjamin	CAY 626
Tuthill, Jonathan	SUF 76	Tuttle, Joshua	CAY 534	Tyler, Benjn	SUF 67
Tuthill, Jonathan	SUF 76	Tuttle, Joshua	SUF 74	Tyler, Bezaleel	ULS 182
Tuthill, Jonathan	SUF 95	Tuttle, Josiah	SUF 65	Tyler, Charles	NYK 65
Tuthill, Jonathan	SUF 106	Tuttle, Lewis	ORN 311	Tyler, Charles	ULS 181
Tuthill, Joshua	ORN 355	Tuttle, Mary	MNT 122	Tyler, Comfort	ONN 153
Tuthill, Josiah	SUF 95	Tuttle, Nathan	ALB 90	Tyler, Daniel	WST 151
Tuthill, Leonard	ORN 326	Tuttle, Nathl	SUF 68	Tyler, Ebenezar	RNS 108
Tuthill, Luther	SUF 72	Tuttle, Nathl	SUF 71	Tyler, Edward	RNS 93
Tuthill, Nathan	SUF 73	Tuttle, Noah	OND 208	Tyler, Eli	OTS 43
Tuthill, Nathan Jur	SUF 73	Tuttle, Noah	ORN 311	Tyler, Elisha	GRN 342
Tuthill, Nathaniel	ORN 326	Tuttle, Oliver	OND 157	Tyler, Ezra	ONN 190
Tuthill, Nathaniel	ORN 355	Tuttle, Oliver	OND 187	Tyler, Gideon	CAY 692
Tuthill, Nathl	SUF 77	Tuttle, Philemon	OND 177	Tyler, Henry	OTS 31
Tuthill, Patience	SUF 72	Tuttle, Phinehas	CAY 534	Tyler, Heny	SUF 67
Tuthill, Rufus Jur	SUF 77	Tuttle, Phinehas	OND 208	Tyler, Hezekiah	HRK 554
Tuthill, Rufus Ser	SUF 77	Tuttle, Salman	MNT 122	Tyler, Isaiah	OTS 26
Tuthill, Samuel	ORN 349	Tuttle, Samuel	OND 199	Tyler, Jacob	NYK 43
Tuthill, Samuel	ORN 353	Tuttle, Samuel	QNS 66	Tyler, James	DEL 274
Tuthill, Saml	SUF 73	Tuttle, Saml	SUF 74	Tyler, James	MNT 60
Tuthill, Selah	ULS 244	Tuttle, Saml	SUF 74	Tyler, James	NYK 69
Tuthill, Temperance	SUF 72	Tuttle, Samuel	TIO 263	Tyler, Jared	DEL 274
Tuthill, Thomas	SUF 105	Tuttle, Seth	NYK 132	Tyler, Jehiel	DEL 274
Tuthill, William	ORN 332	Tuttle, Silas	CAY 654	Tyler, Job	COL 234
Tuthill, William	ORN 353	Tuttle, Solomon	OND 198	Tyler, Job	OND 205
Tutle, Elijah	CHN 982	Tuttle, Solomon	SRA 43	Tyler, Joel	CAY 712
Tutle, Jonathan	GRN 355	Tuttle, Stephen	DEL 281	Tyler, John	OTS 31
Tutle, Mellicha	CHN 838	Tuttle, Stephen	HRK 469	Tyler, John	SUF 66
Tutle, Thomas	GRN 355	Tuttle, Stephen	OND 214	Tyler, Joseph	HRK 436
Tuttell, John F.	KNG 8	Tuttle, Thomas	CAY 578	Tyler, Joseph	NYK 149
Tuttle, Aaron	SRA 43	Tuttle, Thomas	OND 185	Tyler, Joseph	OND 199
Tuttle, Abner	SRA 43	Tuttle, Thomas	ORN 323	Tyler, Major	COL 180

Name	Loc	Name	Loc	Name	Loc
Tyler, Mary	SUF 66	Underhill, Abel	WST 133	Underhill, Samuel	WST 151
Tyler, Nathan	RNS 102	Underhill, Adonijah	QNS 81	Underhill, Sarah	WST 132
Tyler, Nathl	HRK 436	Underhill, Amos	QNS 65	Underhill, Solomn	QNS 72
Tyler, Nathaniel	NYK 71	Underhill, Amos	WST 111	Underhill, Stephen	QNS 82
Tyler, Nathaniel	ULS 181	Underhill, Anthony L.	NYK 53	Underhill, Thomas	WST 133
Tyler, Paul	ULS 181	Underhill, Augustine	WSH 268	Underhill, Thomas	WST 149
Tyler, Samuel	NYK 15	Underhill, Barrick	QNS 81	Underhill, William	WSH 237
Tyler, Samuel	ONN 160	Underhill, Benjamin	WST 119	Underhill, William	WST 164
Tyler, Saml	OTS 31	Underhill, Benjamin	WST 131	Underwood, Artemus	ONN 155
Tyler, Shubael	DUT 126	Underhill, Benjamin	WST 133	Underwood, Asa	CHN 740
Tyler, Silas	ULS 182	Underhill, Bishop	WST 148	Underwood, Eliab	CHN 840
Tyler, Silvanus	NYK 33	Underhill, Caleb	WST 124	Underwood, Elias	CHN 838
Tyler, Silvanus	WST 154	Underhill, Caleb	WST 132	Underwood, Elisha	CHN 920
Tyler, Simeon	MNT 81	Underhill, Charles	QNS 83	Underwood, Enos	WST 158
Tyler, Simeon	WST 111	Underhill, Cuffey	QNS 71	Underwood, Esther	WST 158
Tyler, Sylvester	COL 263	Underhill, Daniel	DUT 111	Underwood, Isaac	CAY 600
Tyler, Timothy	DEL 267	Underhill, Daniel	QNS 80	Underwood, James	NYK 59
Tyler, Timothy	ULS 181	Underhill, Daniel	QNS 81	Underwood, John	HRK 533
Tyler, Truman	OND 193	Underhill, Daniel	QNS 82	Underwood, John	NYK 116
Tyler, William	CAY 690	Underhill, Daniel	QNS 83	Underwood, Jonas	COL 251
Tyler, William	ULS 181	Underhill, Daniel	WST 132	Underwood, Jonas	DEL 279
Tylor, Fradrick	OND 221	Underhill, Daniel		Underwood, Joseph	DUT 129
Tylor, Joseph	CHN 786	Junr	QNS 80	Underwood, Joseph	OTS 13
Tylor, Noah	CHN 882	Underhill, David	HRK 552	Underwood, Marvin	CHN 926
Tylor, Peter	CHN 962	Underhill, David	NYK 44	Underwood, Nathan	HRK 532
Tylor, Rossel	CHN 856	Underhill, Edmund	QNS 63	Underwood, Parker	HRK 527
Tylor, Samuel	CHN 920	Underhill, Elizabeth	NYK 46	Underwood, Phineas	NYK 143
Tylor, William	CHN 856	Underhill, Frederick	WST 147	Underwood, Robinson	DUT 129
Tymeson, Corns P.	ALB 51	Underhill, George	QNS 83	Underwood, Russel	
Tymeson, Eldert C.	ALB 51	Underhill, Gilbert	WST 148	Waterworks Company	ALB 48
Tymeson, Eldred	ALB 52	Underhill, Gilbert	WST 164	Underwood, Stephen	MNT 41
Tymeson, Peter C.	ALB 51	Underhill, Henry	ALB 73	Underwood, Timothy	OND 221
Tyoll, Michael	CLN 170	Underhill, Isaac	CLN 159	Underwood, Widow	OTS 36
Tyrrell, Joseph	COL 258	Underhill, Isaac	DUT 102	Underwood, Willm	HRK 527
Tyrrell, Lewis	COL 211	Underhill, Isaac	QNS 63	Underwood, William	WST 157
Tyson, Barnt	RCH 92	Underhill, Isaac	QNS 83	Unger, Fredk	OTS 44
Tyson, Cornelius	NYK 116	Underhill, Isaac	WST 123	Upam, Wright	ALB 78
Tyson, Jacob	RCH 92	Underhill, Isarel	NYK 71	Upham, Ebenezer	SRA 5
Tyson, John	RCH 92	Underhill, Israel	QNS 83	Upham, Ezekiel	HRK 439
Tyson, John Junr	RCH 93	Underhill, Israel	ULS 207	Upham, John	MNT 104
Tyson, Richard	RCH 93	Underhill, Israel	WST 144	Upham, Joseph	OTS 26
		Underhill, Jacob	QNS 83	Upham, Joseph	WSH 277
U		Underhill, Jacob	QNS 84	Upham, Ketump	CHN 768
		Underhill, Jacob	WST 124	Upham, M ss Marry	GRN 343
Udall, Daniel	KNG 9	Underhill, Jacob	WST 130	Upham, Thomas	RNS 107
Udall, Nathaniel	SUF 85	Underhill, James	DUT 110	Upham, Wintia	COL 250
Udall, Oliver	ONT 462	Underhill, James	QNS 83	Upmorehouse, Jacob	ONN 141
Udall, Richard	SUF 93	Underhill, James	WSH 237	Upright, Benjamin	ULS 249
Udell, John	RNS 108	Underhill, James	WST 131	Upright, George	ULS 248
Udell, Leonell	ALB 81	Underhill, Jesse	WST 153	Upright, Michael	ULS 249
Udell, Samuel	RNS 108	Underhill, John	DUT 103	Upright, Nathan	ORN 308
Udell, William	ALB 81	Underhill, John	QNS 64	Upright, William	ULS 250
Ufford, Charles	OND 206	Underhill, John	QNS 83	Upsam, Bazzel	COL 209
Uhl, Daniel	DUT 11	Underhill, John	ULS 222	Upsom, Joseph	DUT 100
Uhl, Frederick	DUT 108	Underhill, John	ULS 260	Upson, Ahab	GRN 329
Uhl, Henry	DUT 123	Underhill, John	WSH 268	Upson, Daniel	STB 205
Uhle, Henry	HRK 411	Underhill, John	WST 149	Upson, Daniel	STB 206
Uline, Adam	RNS 8	Underhill, John	WST 150	Upson, Mary	CHN 766
Uline, Barnet	RNS 8	Underhill, John Junr	ULS 223	Upson, Ryer	STB 205
Ulman, Barney	MNT 67	Underhill, Joseph	QNS 82	Upson, Trueman	NYK 67
Ulman, Peter	MNT 67	Underhill, Joshua	NYK 71	Upson, Uriah	STB 206
Ulshaver, Bastian	MNT 41	Underhill, Lancaster	WST 146	Upton, Anna a Black	NYK 112
Ulshaver, Steph..	MNT 40	Underhill, Lewis	ONT 380	Upton, Daniel	DUT 128
Ulshoeffer, George	NYK 48	Underhill, Moses	WST 144	Upton, Edward	COL 220
Ultermark, Stephen	MNT 39	Underhill, Nathanel	WST 164	Upton, James	ONT 404
Umber, James	CLN 159	Underhill, Nathaniel	DUT 105	Upton, John	WSH 253
Umphrey, Abner	CHN 754	Underhill, Nathaniel	DUT 123	Upton, Paul	DUT 125
Umphrey, John	OTS 42	Underhill, Peter	NYK 74	Upton, Samuel	DUT 130
Umphrey, Thomas	CHN 756	Underhill, Peter	QNS 84	Upton, William	NYK 122
Umpstead, James	WST 153	Underhill, Phebee	WST 129	Upton, William	SRA 41
Umpstead, Jonathan	CHN 846	Underhill, Richard	WST 117	Uquarhart, John	MNT 110
Umstead, Darius	OTS 14	Underhill, Richardson	NYK 74	Uran, John	ALB 47
U stead, Jeremiah	ONT 318	Underhill, Robert	WST 159	Uriah	QNS 74
Umstead, Joseph	SCH 147	Underhill, Samuel	ORN 275	Urik, David	MNT 95
Umsted, Eliphalet	SUF 66	Underhill, Samuel	QNS 80	Usele, William	MNT 69
Umsted, James	QNS 83	Underhill, Samuel	WSH 268	Usher, Bloomfield	OTS 4
Undax, Nicholas	NYK 119	Underhill, Samuel	WST 124	Usher, John	CHN 870

Name	Loc	
Usher, John Jun	CHN	870
Usher, Lee	CHN	830
Usher, Robert	CHN	866
Ustage, James	NYK	41
Ustick, William	NYK	21
Ustick, William	NYK	45
Ustick, William	ORN	310
Ustick, William	QNS	65
Utler, Sarah	COL	183
Utley, David	OND	206
Utley, David Junr	OND	206
Utley, Elijah	OTS	46
Utley, Hancock	OND	205
Utley, Jonathan	OND	203
Utley, Jonathan Junr	OND	203
Utley, Rufus	OTS	39
Utley, Samuel	COL	179
Utley, Sanford	CAY	660
Utley, William	SRA	39
Utt, John	NYK	53
Utt, John Henry	ULS	182
Utt, Jonas	NYK	85
Utt, Jonas	NYK	101
Utter, Abraham	CAY	694
Utter, Caleb	WST	124
Utter, Caleb	WST	156
Utter, Ebenezer	ONT	386
Utter, Elijah	RNS	36
Utter, Ephraim	ULS	181
Utter, Gilbert	DUT	55
Utter, Henry	DEL	279
Utter, Jabez	DUT	166
Utter, James	DUT	132
Utter, Jesse	ALB	120
Utter, Joel	WST	137
Utter, John	ALB	118
Utter, Josiah	DEL	279
Utter, Moses	ORN	355
Utter, Samuel	ONT	384
Utter, Samuel Junr	ONT	386
Utter, Solomon	ULS	266
Utter, Thomas	RNS	42
Utter, William	DUT	169
Utter, Zebulon	RNS	8
Utterbergh, Mary	NYK	37
Uttey, Asa	ONT	316
Uttey, Timothy	SRA	53

V

Name	Loc	
V..ory, Henry	ONN	192
V...nt, J ...	MNT	23
Vache, John	NYK	27
Vacter, Sarah	NYK	129
Vader, Peter V.	MNT	44
Vador, Aaron	ONN	187
Vador, John	ONN	187
Vador, Nichs	ONN	187
Vaelluncourt, Peter	CLN	160
Vaelluncourt, Peter Jur	CLN	160
Vaghn see Vaughan & Von		
Vaghn, Titus	RNS	100
Vail, Aaron	WSH	190
Vail, Abraham	ORN	362
Vail, Absalom	ORN	364
Vail, Alsop	ORN	335
Vail, Asa	ORN	362
Vail, Barnabas	NYK	135
Vail, Benjn	SUF	76
Vail, Benjn Jun	SUF	76
Vail, Calup	CHN	792
Vail, Daniel	DUT	110
Vail, David	ORN	339
Vail, Gamaliel	SRA	50
Vail, Gilum	SUF	76

Name	Loc	
Vail, Isaac	DUT	7
Vail, Isaac	DUT	38
Vail, Isaac	DUT	128
Vail, Isaiah	ORN	344
Vail, Isaiah Junr	ORN	333
Vail, Israel	DUT	9
Vail, Israel	DUT	120
Vail, Jacob	WSH	183
Vail, James	DEL	278
Vail, James	DUT	177
Vail, Jeremiah	ORN	392
Vail, Jesse	DUT	38
Vail, Job	CHN	792
Vail, John	CHN	792
Vail, John	DUT	87
Vail, John	DUT	118
Vail, John	DUT	138
Vail, John	ORN	333
Vail, John	ORN	362
Vail, John	SUF	76
Vail, John	WST	122
Vail, John	WST	123
Vail, John	WST	129
Vail, John ye 2d	ORN	335
Vail, Jonathan	SUF	77
Vail, Joseph	COL	220
Vail, Joseph	DEL	271
Vail, Joseph	DEL	280
Vail, Joseph	DUT	9
Vail, Joseph	NYK	133
Vail, Joseph	ORN	331
Vail, Joshua	NYK	146
Vail, Joshua	SUF	76
Vail, Joshua	SUF	77
Vail, Josiah	ORN	330
Vail, Lewis	WST	150
Vail, Mary	DUT	38
Vail, Michael	ORN	336
Vail, Moses	DUT	7
Vail, Moses	RNS	93
Vail, Moses	SUF	90
Vail, Nathan	DUT	113
Vail, Nathaniel	ONN	161
Vail, Nathaniel	OTS	31
Vail, Nathl	SUF	76
Vail, Obediah	ORN	339
Vail, Peter	SUF	76
Vail, Platt	DUT	8
Vail, Samuel	ORN	332
Vail, Samuel	ORN	358
Vail, Samuel	SRA	5
Vail, Saml	SUF	76
Vail, Silus	SUF	77
Vail, Solomon	DUT	128
Vail, Sten	SUF	77
Vail, Thankfull	SUF	72
Vail, Thomas	DUT	7
Vail, Thomas	NYK	140
Vail, Thos	SUF	77
Vail, William	NYK	139
Vail, William	NYK	140
Vail, William	ORN	354
Vail, William	WST	111
Vail, William	WST	127
Vain, Farmer	MNT	72
Vain, Peter	MNT	72
Vaincouer, Peter	ESS	295
Valadon, Martha	NYK	85
Valance, John	NYK	130
Val De Reen, Michael	ORN	376
Vale, Abijah	OTS	54
Vale, Daniel	ONN	191
Vale, Isaac	SRA	9
Vale, Thomas	WST	133
Valentin a Black	NYK	95
Valentine see Volentine & Vollintine		

Name	Loc	
Valentine, Abraham	NYK	33
Valentine, Absalom	QNS	79
Valentine, Alexander	RNS	21
Valentine, Ananias	ORN	357
Valentine, Ann	QNS	64
Valentine, Benjamin	DEL	283
Valentine, Benjamin	DUT	29
Valentine, Benjamin	QNS	70
Valentine, Benjamin	WST	145
Valentine, Benjamin Jr	WST	146
Valentine, Caleb	NYK	53
Valentine, Charles	NYK	73
Valentine, Charles	QNS	83
Valentine, Cornelius	DUT	21
Valentine, Crooker	QNS	71
Valentine, Daniel	WST	148
Valentine, David	NYK	28
Valentine, David	QNS	83
Valentine, Dennis	WST	145
Valentine, Elijah	WST	147
Valentine, Evert	NYK	106
Valentine, Frederic	SRA	24
Valentine, Frederick	WST	146
Valentine, Gabriel	KNG	7
Valentine, George	QNS	75
Valentine, Gilbert	WST	146
Valentine, Henry	NYK	97
Valentine, Isaac	DUT	151
Valentine, Isaac	NYK	113
Valentine, Isaac	NYK	141
Valentine, Isaac	QNS	79
Valentine, Isaac	WST	118
Valentine, Jacob	NYK	79
Valentine, Jacob	QNS	68
Valentine, Jacob	QNS	70
Valentine, Jacob	QNS	78
Valentine, Jacob	WST	148
Valentine, James	DUT	14
Valentine, James	DUT	65
Valentine, James	SRA	25
Valentine, James	WST	146
Valentine, Jeremiah	QNS	63
Valentine, Joel	RNS	53
Valentine, John	DUT	78
Valentine, John	DUT	163
Valentine, John	NYK	102
Valentine, John	NYK	123
Valentine, John	QNS	65
Valentine, John	QNS	70
Valentine, John	RNS	53
Valentine, John	RCK	108
Valentine, John	WST	144
Valentine, Joseph	WST	146
Valentine, Lewis	QNS	83
Valentine, Lewis	WST	148
Valentine, Matthew	DUT	19
Valentine, Obadiah	QNS	71
Valentine, Obadiah	QNS	79
Valentine, Oliver	QNS	71
Valentine, Peter	WST	145
Valentine, Peter	WST	148
Valentine, Philip	QNS	70
Valentine, Pompey a Black		
Valentine, Richard	COL	202
Valentine, Richard	QNS	71
Valentine, Richard	QNS	83
Valentine, Richard	RNS	54
Valentine, Robert	NYK	87
Valentine, Sarah	ULS	265
Valentine, Stephen	HRK	439
Valentine, Thomas	DUT	30
Valentine, Thomas	WST	147
Valentine, Titus Negro	QNS	70
Valentine, Willet	NYK	135
Valentine, William	DUT	97
Valentine, William	NYK	122

Name	Loc	No	Name	Loc	No	Name	Loc	No
Valentine, William	QNS	70	V. Denbergh, Silvanus	SRA	6	V. Henry, John	ALB	133
Valentine, William	QNS	77	V. Denburgh, Catherine	SRA	3	V. Heyder, Abraham D.	RNS	92
Valentine, William	SRA	29	V. Denburgh, Gysebert	SRA	11	V. Hoose, Rynard	SRA	13
Valentine, Zebulon	QNS	71	V. Denburgh, John	SRA	8	V. Horne, James	ALB	12
Vales	NYK	54	V. Denburgh, Maus	SRA	3	V. Housen, Rufus	ALB	13
Valkenburgh, Abraham	GRN	328	V. Denburgh, Nicholas	SRA	3	V. Hyden, Catherin_	SRA	11
Valkineer, John	COL	200	V. Denburgh, Phillip	SRA	6	V. Hynhing, Abraham	SRA	53
Vall, Thomas	NYK	106	V. Denburgh, Stephen	SRA	9	V. Hyning, Henry	SRA	7
Vallack, Peter	COL	259	V. Derbergh, Math_	RNS	5	V. Hyning, John	SRA	7
Vallan, William	NYK	63	V. Derbergh, Volkert			V. Hyning, Sara	SRA	6
Vallaw, Peter	NYK	112		W.	RNS	5	V. Ingen, Abm	ALB	12
Valleau, Fauthner	NYK	113	V. Derbergh, Wynant			V. Ingen, Derick	ALB	4
Valleau, Isaih	NYK	110		Junr	RNS	36	V. Inwagen, Hermanus	ORN	315
Valleau, John	DUT	61	V. Derburgh, Garret J.	RNS	5	V. Kirk, John V.	SRA	23
Valleau, Samuel	NYK	110	V. Der Bogart, Chad-			V. Kirk, Joseph	SRA	23
Valleau, Theodorus	DUT	32		wick	ALB	22	V. Kleck, Battus	SRA	50
Valleau, William	NYK	63	V. Der Bogart, Jeremh	ALB	109	V. Looven, Andrew	ALB	83
Vallence, Richard	GRN	339	V. Der Bogart, Joseph	ALB	3	V. Luven, Peter P.	ALB	96
Vallentine, Gilbert	SUF	79	V. Der Bogart, Joseph	ALB	101	V. Natta, Abm	ALB	23
Vallentine, Israel	SUF	88	V. Der Bogart, Peter	ALB	101	V. Natta, Benjm	ALB	99
Vallentine, Nathan	SUF	79	V. Der Bogart, Ns	ALB	2A	V. Natta, David	ALB	23
Vallentine, Richard	SUF	82	V. Derburgh, Nicholas	SRA	50	V. Ness, Antee	SRA	11
Vallentine, Scudder	SUF	79	V. Der Heyden, Danl	ALB	24	V. Orden, Sarah	ALB	11
Vallow, Lewis	NYK	121	V. Der Heyden, David	ALB	6	V. Patten, Aaron	ALB	60
Valten Car, Thomas	GRN	356	V. Der Heydon, Gersham	ALB	5	V. Patten, Andries	ALB	16
Vam Beuren, Wm	MNT	116	V. Derhuel, Abraham	SRA	19	V. Patten, Corns P.	ALB	25
Vamwermer, Peter	WST	165	V. Der Kuth, Jacob	ALB	70	V. Patten, Dirick, D.	ALB	15
Van, Eward	GRN	343	V. Der Volgen, Myndert	ALB	38	V. Patten, Dyrick	ALB	16
Van, Jacob	SRA	5	V. Der Waters, Henry	ALB	27	V. Patten, Frederick	ALB	25
V. Allen, John	ALB	5	V. Der Waters, Michael	ALB	26	V. Patten, Henry	ALB	25
V. Allen, John	ALB	97	V. Derwerker, Winant	SRA	50	V. Patten, Jacob	ALB	60
V. Allen, Peter	ALB	5	V. Der Zee, Albert	ALB	98	V. Patten, John	ALB	23
V. Allen, Peter	SRA	5	V. Der Zee, Albm	ALB	97	V. Patten, John B. T.	ALB	3
V. Allstine, Daniel	SRA	11	V. Deusen, James	WSH	265	V. Patten, Ns	ALB	6
V. Alstine, Andries	ALB	98	V. Deusen, Martin	WSH	282	V. Patten, Nicholas	ALB	25
V. Alstine, Matthew	ALB	61	V. Dewarken, Christ-			V. Patten, Nichs N.	ALB	59
V. Antwerp, Aurant	ALB	21		iana	SRA	3	V. Patten, Peter	ALB	60
V. Antwerp, Gerrit	ALB	6	V. Dewarken, F_	SRA	11	V. Patten, Philip	ALB	25
V. Antwerp, Hannah	ALB	24	V. Dewarken, Francis	SRA	6	V. Patten, Simon	ALB	18
V. Antwerp, Jacob	ALB	6	V. Dewarken, Hendrake	SRA	11	V. Patten, Simon	ALB	25
V. Antwerp, Simon	ALB	9	V. Dewarken, Henry	SRA	10	V. Patten, Simon J.	ALB	22
V. Antwerp, Simon	ALB	18	V. Dewarken, ..ria	SRA	8	V. Peeck, James	ALB	22
V. Arnor, John	SRA	5	V. Dewarker, Meritia	SRA	11	V. Rensselaer, James	ALB	96
V. Bayard, Samuel	WST	144	V. Dewarker, Tunis	RNS	32	V. Rensselaer, John J.	RNS	5
V. Belsher, William	ALB	100	V. Dewerkin, John J.	SRA	8	V. Rensselaer, Killian	ALB	124
V. Benthiusen, Obadiah	ALB	125	V. Dewerkin, John R.	SRA	8	V. Rensselaer, Maria	ALB	96
V. Benthuisen, Benjm	ALB	137	V. Dumond, William	ALB	138	V. Rensselaer, Solomon	ALB	144
V. Bogart, John	OND	191	V. Dusen, John	ALB	97	V. Rensselaer, Stephen	ALB	45
V. Bronk, Nichs	ALB	27	V. Dyck, Abm	ALB	24	V. Schaick, Albert A.	ALB	103
V. Brunt, Rulof	ALB	26	V. Dyck, Henry	ALB	6	V. Schaick, Egbert	ALB	96
V. Bueren, Beekman	WST	144	V. Dyck, John	ALB	89	V. Schaick, Gerrit	ALB	7
V. Buran, Peter	ALB	13	V. Dyck, John	ALB	96	V. Schaick, Gerrit W.	ALB	135
V. Buren, Benjm	ALB	96	V. Dyck, Lidia	ALB	7	V. Schaick, Hosea	SRA	8
V. Buren, Cortland	NYK	17	V. Dyck, Peter	ALB	18	V. Schaick, Nichs A.	ALB	103
V. Buren, Fryenmot	ALB	26	V. Dyck, Senaca	ALB	7	V. Schaick, Stephen	ALB	134
V. Buren, Harry Free			V. Epps, Alexander	ALB	21	V. Schaick, Sybrant	ALB	7
Negro	RNS	96	V. Epps, Alexr Junr	ALB	21	V. Schoohoven, Guertt	SRA	8
V. Buren, Henry	ALB	97	V. Epps, Gerrit	ALB	21	V. Schoonhoven, Grandus	SRA	8
V. Buskirk, Laurance	ALB	10	V. Epps, Hermanus	ALB	21	V. Schoonhoven, Jacobus	SRA	8
V. Buskirk, Laurance	ALB	103	V. Epps, Herms J.	ALB	18	V. Servant, Anthony	NYK	69
V. Buskirk, Martinus	ALB	26	V. Epps, Jacobus J.	ALB	17	V. Sise, ...id	SRA	8
V. Camp, Cornelius	MNT	27	V. Epps, James	ALB	21	V. Sise, Cornelius	ALB	19
V. Camp, Peter	SRA	7	V. Epps, James	ALB	21	V. Sise, Gilbert	ALB	10
V. Camp, Simon	SRA	7	V. Epps, John	ALB	21	V. Sise, John	ALB	25
V. Cortlandt, Augustus	WST	146	V. Epps, John B. T.	ALB	24	V. Sise, Simon	ALB	3
V. Cortlandt, Freder-			V. Epps, John E.	ALB	23	V. Slack, Corns	ALB	11
ick	WST	146	V. Epps, John J.	ALB	21	V. Slack, Herms	ALB	6
V. Curen, Casperus	SRA	10	V. Epps, Laurance	ALB	21	V. Slack, Jesse	ALB	6
V. Curen, Matthew	SRA	10	V. Epps, Laurance J.	ALB	21	V. Slaick, Adam	ALB	2A
V. Decarr, Nicholas	SRA	10	V. Eps, Abraham	SRA	24	V. Slaick, Adrian	ALB	7
V. Decor, Abraham	SRA	11	V. Eps, John B.	ALB	3	V. Slaick, Anthy	ALB	18
V. Decor, Daniel	SRA	11	V. Fredenbergh, Peter	SRA	11	V. Slaick, Elizth	ALB	5
V. Decorr, Jonitice(?)	SRA	11	V. Guelder, Reuben	WSH	279	V. Slaick, Herms H.	ALB	13
V. De[cur?], Abraham	SRA	11	V. Guelder, Stephen	WSH	279	V. Slaick, Martin	ALB	2A
V. DeKarr, John	SRA	8	V. Guysling, Elias	ALB	16	V. Slyck, Corns P.	ALB	20
V. Den Bergh, Gerrit	ALB	96	V. Guysling, Jacob	ALB	16	V. Slyck, Martin	ALB	23
V. Den Bergh, Matthias	ALB	38	V. Guysling, Peter	ALB	4	V. Slyck, Peter	ALB	23

Name		
Van Amy, Wm	RNS	43
Van Anden, John	DUT	38
Vanander, James	SRA	38
Vanander, Matthew	SRA	38
Van Anthwerp, Herbert	NYK	98
Van Anthwerp, James	NYK	98
V.. Antwerp, Abraham	ALB	51
Van Antwerp, Daniel	NYK	55
Van Antwerp, Danl G.	ALB	121
Vanantwerp, Daniel L.	SRA	48
Van Antwerp, Douw	HRK	489
Van Antwerp, Garret	RNS	36
Van Antwerp, Herman	ALB	51
Van Antwerp, James	NYK	35
Van Antwerp, James N.	NYK	29
Van Antwerp, John	MNT	76
Van Antwerp, John	MNT	83
Van Antwerp, Lewis	HRK	493
Van Antwerp, Maria	ALB	141
Van Antwerp, Nicholas	NYK	24
Van Antwerp, Samuel	MNT	69
Van Antwerp, Simon	NYK	55
Van Antwerp, Simon	RNS	36
Van Antwerp, Vandal	RCK	100
Van Apes, Evert	COL	259
Van Arnam, Avert	ALB	58
Van Arnam, Henry	ALB	60
Van Arnam, Isaac	ALB	144
Van Arnam, Isaac	WSH	249
Van Arnam, Isaac J.	ALB	57
Van Arnam, Jacob	ALB	60
Van Arnam, John	ALB	60
Van Arnam, Wm	ALB	60
Van Arnum, Abraham	ESS	305
Van Arnum, Hendrick	ESS	308
Van Arnum, Henry	RNS	85
Van Arnum, Isaac	ESS	305
Van Arnum, John	MNT	36
Van Arnum, John	RNS	86
Van Arnum, John	RNS	89
Van Arnum, Laurane	RNS	82
Van Arnum, Luke	ESS	308
Van Arnum, Miles	ESS	305
Van Arnum, Peter	ESS	307
Van Asdale, Abraham	ORN	287
Van Asdale, Christopher	ORN	289
Van Asdale, Dirck	DUT	24
Van Asdale, James	ORN	287
Van Asdale, Richard	ORN	295
Van Asdale, Teunis	ORN	294
Van Aster, James	TIO	258
Van Atten, Albert	ALB	74
Van Atten, Benjn	RNS	11
Van Atten, Matthew	DUT	163
Van Aucker, Henry	ALB	58
Van Aucker, Peter	ALB	61
Van Auger, Gideon	CHN	986
Van Augur, John	CHN	986
Van Auker, David	ALB	64
Van Auker, John	ALB	65
Van Auker, Levi	ALB	58
Van Auker, Peter	ALB	63
Van Auker, Peter	ALB	66
Van Aukor, Cornelius	CAY	684
Van Aulen, Aaron	NYK	117
Vanaulet, Lear	NYK	150
Van Aulin, Charles	NYK	90
Van Ausdoll, Orris	QNS	68
Van Ausvall, John	CAY	682
Vanawlen, Hannah	NYK	151
Van Banel, James	TIO	230
Van Bemer, Abraham	NYK	153
Van Benschoten, Aaron	ULS	185
Van Benschoten, Egenus	DUT	125
Van Benschoten, Elias	DUT	69
Van Benschoten, Garret	ULS	185
Van Benschoten, Herman	DUT	114
Van Benschoten, Jacob	ULS	185
Van Benschoten, John	DUT	70
Van Benschoten, John	ULS	192
Van Benschoten, John E.	DUT	69
Van Benschoten, Matt-hew	DUT	40
Van Benschoten, Peter	ULS	191
Van Benschoten, Solomon	ULS	191
Van Benschoten, Teunis	DUT	31
Van Benscotin, Jeremiah	CAY	678
Van Benthiusen, Jas	ALB	55
Van Benthousen, Henry	ALB	129
Van Benthuisen, Jas P.	ALB	130
Van Benthuisen, Thos	ALB	43
V.. Benthurson, James	RNS	90
Van, Benthuysen, Anna	DUT	155
Van Benthuysen, Baltus	DUT	112
Van Benthuysen Garret	WSH	213
Van Benthuysen, Jacob	DUT	155
Van Bergan, Garet	GRN	328
Van Bergan, Mathew	GRN	356
Van Bergan, Peter	GRN	356
Van Bergan, Peter H.	GRN	357
Van Bergan, William G.	GRN	329
Van Bergen, David	ALB	148
Van Bergen, Martin	COL	265
Van Bergen, Peter	ALB	144
Van Bergen, Peter	COL	246
Van Bergen, William	COL	265
Van Beu___, Cornelius	MNT	58
Van Beuren see Vam Beu-ren & Van Bueren		
Van Beuren, Abraham	COL	257
Van Beuren, Barent	COL	259
Vanbeuren, Baurnt	MNT	116
Van Beuren, Beekman M.	NYK	142
Van Beuren, Christina	ULS	193
Van Beuren, Derick J.	COL	261
Vanbeuren, Francis	MNT	116
Vanbeuren, Francis	MNT	119
Van Beuren, James	KNG	2
Van Beuren, James	NYK	90
Vanbeuren, John H.	KNG	2
Va. Beuren, Martin	MNT	49
Van Beuren, Martin	MNT	94
Van Beuren, Michael	NYK	68
Van Beuren, Peter	COL	263
Van Beuren, Peter M.	COL	258
Van Beuren, Tobias	ULS	229
Van Beuren, Tobias P.	COL	262
Vanbeuren, William	KNG	2
Van Beuren, Wm	MNT	3
Van Beuren, William	NYK	85
Van Blarcom see Van Plarcom		
Van Blarcom, Abraham	NYK	100
Van Blarcom, John	NYK	97
Van Blarcon, Byrn	NYK	152
Van Blarcum, David	NYK	97
Van Blarcun, James	RNS	90
Van Bleck, Abm	OND	206
Van Blokel, John	NYK	54
Van Bohlen, Labertus	NYK	114
Van Bomel, Garnet	NYK	138
Van Bommel, Christo-pher	DUT	59
Van Bommel, Marcus	DUT	61
Van Bommel, Peter	DUT	63
Van Braemer, Peter	DUT	40
Van Bramer, Jacob	COL	258
Van Bramer, Jacob Junr	COL	260
Van Bramer, Thomas	COL	260
Van Branan, John A.	COL	259
Van Brocklin, Simon	MNT	114
Vanbrunt, Abraham	KNG	5
Vanbrunt, Albert	KNG	6
Vanbrunt, Albert	KNG	6
Vanbrunt, Coert	KNG	3
Vanbrunt, Cornelius	KNG	7
Vanbrunt, George	KNG	6
Vanbrunt, Isaac	KNG	6
Vanbrunt, Jacob	KNG	7
Vanbrunt, Jaques	KNG	6
Vanbrunt, John	KNG	8
Van brunt, John	SUF	67
Vanbrunt, Nicholas	KNG	6
Van Brunt, Ralph	ORN	366
Van Brunt, Roeliff	ORN	361
Vanbrunt, Rulef	KNG	6
Vanbrunt, Rutgert	KNG	5
Vanbrunt, Rutgert	KNG	6
Vanbrunt, Rutgert A.	KNG	6
Vanbrunt, Rutgert W.	KNG	6
Van Brunt, Teunis	ULS	251
Van Brunt, Yoost	QNS	67
Van Bryck, Ruliff	RCK	99
Vanbryck, Saml G.	RCK	99
Van Bueren, Tobias T.	COL	266
Van Buren see Van Beuren		
Van Buren, Garret	WSH	235
Van Buren, George	RNS	95
Van Buren, Henry a free Negro	RNS	94
Van Buren, Henry	WSH	235
Van Buren, Henry	WSH	235
Van Buren, Henry	WSH	235
Van Buren, Martin	RNS	60
Van Buren, Martyr	WSH	235
Van Buren, Mary	RNS	19
Van Buren, Sarah	RNS	84
Vanbury, Tom	SRA	45
Van Bushark, John L.	GRN	348
Van Bushark, Laurence	GRN	348
Van Busker, Abraham	NYK	55
Van Buskerick, Corneli-ius	WSH	198
Van Buskerick, John	WSH	198
Van Buskerick, John D.	WSH	198
Van Buskerick, Martin	WSH	199
Van Buskerick, Richard	WSH	198
Van Buskerk, Andrew	NYK	56
Van Buskirk, Abraham Junr	NYK	53
Van Buskirk, David	ORN	377
Van Buskirk, John	ALB	75
Van Buskirk, John	NYK	150
Van Camp, Abraham	STB	200
Van Camp, Danl	TIO	256
Van Camp, Donas	SCH	157
Van Camp, John	DUT	124
Van Camp, John	STB	197
Van Camp, Moses	QNT	472
Van Camp, Moses	STB	205
Van Camp, Samuel	STB	205
Van Campen, John	STB	201
Vance, David	ORN	291
Vance, George	ORN	374
Vance, James	ORN	374
Vance, John	ORN	374
Vance, Samuel	ORN	374
Van Cleaf, William	NYK	91
Van Cleck, Baltus P.	COL	251
Van Cleeck, Jeremiah	NYK	138
Van Cleeck, Leonard	NYK	138
Vancleef, John	KNG	5
Vancleef, Michael	KNG	2
Van Clench, Benjn	ALB	124
Van Clief, Daniel	RCH	88
Van Clief, Lawrence	CAY	516
Van Clief, Mrs	RCH	87
Van Clief, Patty	RCH	91
Van Clift, Benjamin	ORN	357
Van Clift, Jesse	ORN	311
Van Cluef, Isaac	NYK	94

Name	Loc	Pg	Name	Loc	Pg	Name	Loc	Pg
Van Dyck, David	ALB	100	Van Gaasbeck, John	ULS	192	Van hooser, Albart	GRN	331
Van Dyck, Henry	ALB	89	Van Gaasbeck, John	ULS	229	Vanhooser, John	GRN	331
Van Dyck, Jacob	SCH	132	Van Gaasbeck, Sarah	ULS	228	Vanhooser, John C.	GRN	332
Van Dyck, John C.	COL	261	Van Gaasbeck, Thomas	ULS	228	Van Horne, Thomas	MNT	29
Vandyck, Mathias	KNG	8	Van Gaasbeck, Thomas C.	ULS	218	Van Horn, Abraham	MNT	29
Vandyck, Nicholas	KNG	8	Van Galden, Andrew	SCH	136	Vanhorn, Adam	KNG	11
Van Dyck, Richard	QNS	62	Van Garden, Abraham	ULS	253	Van Horn, Mills	RCK	103
Vandyck, William	KNG	4	Van Garden, Isaac	ULS	250	Van Horne, Aaron	COL	180
Van Dycke, James	NYK	34	Van Garden, John	ULS	244	Van Horne, Abraham	DUT	70
Van dycks, Aron	GRN	350	Van Garden, Laurence	ULS	209	Vanhorne, Andrew	NYK	123
Van Dyke, Abraham	DUT	109	Van Garden, William V.	ULS	190	Vanhorne, Augustus V.	NYK	51
Van Dyke, Cornelius	SCH	131	Van Gelder, Abraham	GRN	326	Vanhorne, Barnet	NYK	140
Vandyke, David	GRN	335	Van Gelder, Abraham	NYK	50	Vanhorne, Cornelius	NYK	112
Van Dyke, Eady	COL	259	Van Gelder, Abraham	NYK	104	Van horne, Cornelius	NYK	144
Van Dyke, Francis	NYK	43	Vangelder, Abraham	NYK	133	Van Horne, David	ALB	146
Van Dyke, George	COL	258	Van Gelder, David	NYK	147	Van horne, David	NYK	112
Van Dyke, Henry	QNS	62	Van Gelder, Henry	DUT	97	Van Horne, Frederick	ORN	304
Van Dyke, Henry E.	COL	259	Van Gelder, Isaac	ORN	383	Van Horne, Garrit	NYK	20
Van Dyke, Henry L.	COL	258	Van Gelder, Jacob	GRN	326	Van Horne, Jack a		
Van Dyke, Henry L.	COL	262	Vangelder, James	NYK	146	Black	NYK	84
Van Dyke, Isaac	NYK	39	Van Gelder, Jeremiah	CAY	678	Van Horne, James	CAY	542
Van Dyke, Israel	DUT	111	Van Gelder, John	ULS	181	Van Horne, Magdalen	NYK	28
Van Dyke, John	COL	258	Van Gelder, Matthew	CAY	516	Van Horne, Mary	NYK	63
Van Dyke, John	RCH	88	Van Gelder, Peter	GRN	326	Van Horne, Peter	ORN	379
Vandyke, Jonathan	GRN	354	Van Gerder, Isaac	ONT	410	Van hosen, Jacob	GRN	329
Van Dyke, Lawrence	COL	258	Van Gilder, John	NYK	21	Van Hosen, John	COL	183
Van Dyke, Mary	COL	258	Van Gorden, Isaac	TIO	210	Van Hosen, John J.	COL	192
Van Dyke, Peter	COL	259	Van Gorder, Gilbert	TIO	255	Van Hosen, Nancy Free		
Van Dyke, Peter	DUT	109	Van Gorder, Henry	GRN	329	Black	COL	251
Van Dyke, Peter Junr	DUT	109	Vangorder, Henry	TIO	252	Vanhoser, Garret	GRN	329
Van Dyke, Peter C.	COL	261	Van Gorder, Isaac	GRN	329	Vanhoser, Garret Junr	GRN	329
Van Dyke, Tobias	ULS	193	Van Gorder, Peter	GRN	330	Vanhoser, Jacob	GRN	338
Van Dyke, Willm	SCH	166	Van Gorder, Saml	TIO	255	Vanhoter, Peter	NYK	102
Van Dyne, James	NYK	62	.an Gorder, Wm	TIO	254	Van Housen, Herms	ALB	109
Van Dyne, John	QNS	69	Van Guelder, Elijah	WSH	279	Van Houten, Abrm	RCK	103
Van Elton, Samuel	MNT	8	Van Hagen, John J.	RNS	7	Van Houten, Claus	RCK	106
Vanemburgh, Abraham	KNG	5	Van Hagen, Martin	RNS	6	Van Houten, Claus Esqr	RCK	109
Van Epps, John J.	ALB	16	Van Harley, Peter S.	CAY	682	Van Houten, Dirck	RCK	107
Van Eps, Abraham	OND	173	Van Heusen, Francis	SCH	132	Van Houten, Hendrick	RCK	110
Van Ess, Corns	OTS	55	Van Hoesen, Abraham	COL	260	Van Houten, James	ORN	369
Vaness, David	MNT	102	Van Hoesen, Abm G.	COL	257	Van Houten, John	NYK	91
Vaness, William P.	NYK	18	Van Hoesen, Albert	COL	249	Van Houten, John	RCK	106
Vanest, Abraham	NYK	27	Van Hoesen, Caspar	ULS	233	Van Houten, John	RCK	109
Van Etten, Anthony	ORN	317	Van Hoesen, Catharine	COL	249	Vanhouten, John G.	NYK	103
Van Etten, Benjamin	ULS	215	Van Hoesen, Cornelius	COL	255	Van Houten, Mary	ORN	372
Van Etten, Elias	ULS	224	Van Hoesen, Elizabeth	COL	261	Van houten, Peter	CAY	574
Van Etten, Gilbert	ULS	218	Van Hoesen, George	COL	264	Van houten, Peter	NYK	99
Van Etten, Henry	ORN	317	Van Hoesen, Isacc	COL	266	Van Houten, Peter	RCK	108
Van Etten, Hermanus	ORN	384	Van Hoesen, Jacob	COL	220	Van Houten, Peter	RCK	110
Van Etten, Isaac	DUT	110	Van Hoesen, Jacob	COL	254	Van Houten, Peter R.	RCK	108
Van Etten, Jacob	ORN	314	Van Hoesen, Jennet	COL	255	Van Houten, Resolvert	RCK	105
Van Etten, Jacob W.	ORN	317	Van Hoesen, John	COL	253	Van Houten, Rulliff	RCK	105
Van Etten, Jacobus	DUT	108	Van Hoesen, John	COL	263	Van Houten, Tunis	RCK	109
Van Etten, Jacobus	ULS	212	Van Hoesen, John C.	COL	255	Van Houter, Gerrit	ALB	47
Van Etten, Jacobus	ULS	220	Van Hoesen, John J.			Van Houter, John	CAY	572
Van Etten, Jacobus	ULS	237	Junr	COL	194	Van houter, John	KNG	4
Van Etten, Jacobus Junr	ULS	214	Van Hoesen, Justus	COL	215	Van houter, Ruleff	WST	164
Van Etten, John	DUT	165	Van Hoesen, Mathew	COL	261	Van Huzen, Vubiar	NYK	15
Van Etten, John	ULS	212	Van Hoesen, Peter	COL	192	Van Imburg, John	ALB	121
Van Etten, John	ULS	218	Van Hoesen, Peter			Van Imburg, John	ALB	130
Van Etten, John Junr	ULS	220	Free Black	COL	252	Van Imburgh, Adanah	ALB	120
Van Etten, Levi	ORN	317	Van Hoesen, Peter	COL	255	Van Ingen, James	ALB	145
Van Etten, Peter	ULS	191	Van Hoesen, Peter J.	COL	255	Van Ingen, John V.	ALB	11
Van Etten, Peter	ULS	214	Van Hoesen, Solomon	COL	255	Van Ingen, Joseph	ALB	24
Van Etten, Richard	ULS	180	Van Hoesen, William	COL	265	Van Inwagen, Cornelius	ORN	315
Van Etten, Simon	DUT	165	Van Hoevenbergh, Eigho	DUT	108	Van Inwagen, Cornelius		
Van Every, Jacob	RNS	6	Van Hoevenbergh, Henry	ULS	234	Junr	ORN	314
Van Every, Martin	RNS	4	Van Hoevenbergh, Rud-			Van Inwagen, David	ORN	315
Van Every, Mary	DUT	41	olph	DUT	113	Van Ist, John	SRA	20
Van Eys, Philip L.	NYK	93	Van Holsen, Nichs	COL	219	Van Iter, John	GRN	350
Vanffouter, Garret	CAY	536	Van Hook, Abigail	NYK	42	Van Iter, Petter	GRN	350
Van Fleet, Joshua	ONT	442	Van Hook, Isaac	NYK	51	Van Iverin, Rynier	ALB	149
Van Fler, James	GRN	327	Vanhoosen, Albert(?)	GRN	329	Van Keuren see Van		
Van fosen, Levi	ONT	380	Van Hoosen, Albert	MNT	113	Curen		
Van Gaasbeck, Abraham	ULS	193	Vanho-sen, Jacob	GRN	328	Van Keuren, Abraham	DUT	70
Van Gaasbeck, Abraham	ULS	218	Van Hoosen, Jacob	MNT	110	Van Keuren, Abraham	DUT	161
Van Gaasbeck, Jacobus	ULS	218	Van hoosen, John C.	GRN	348	Van Keuren, Abraham G.	ULS	229

Van Keuren, Benjamin	NYK	61	Van Leuven, John	ULS	225	Van Ness, Henry	RNS	45
Van Keuren, Benjamin	NYK	126	Van Leuven, Martin	ULS	225	Van Ness, Isaac	COL	221
Van Keuren, Benjamin	NYK	139	Van Leuven, Peter	ULS	185	Van Ness, James	COL	214
Van Keuren, Benjamin	ORN	291	Van Lew, James	QNS	67	Van Ness, James	MNT	83
Van Keuren, Casparus	DUT	70	Van Lew, John	QNS	67	Van Ness, John	ALB	43
Van Keuren, Cornelius			Van Lew, John	QNS	69	Van Ness, John	ALB	143
E.	ULS	193	Van Loan, Albart	GRN	350	Van Ness, John	COL	221
Van Keuren, Cornelius			Van Loan, Jeremiah	GRN	350	Van Ness, Joremiah	MNT	75
M.	ULS	226	Van loan, John C.	GRN	348	Van Ness, Lanah	WSH	199
Van Keuren, Ephraim	ULS	193	Van Loan, Polly	GRN	348	Van Ness, Mary	ONT	310
Van Keuren, Hazael	ULS	247	Van Looen, Jacob J.F.	GRN	350	Van Ness, Peter	COL	262
Van Keuren, Hendrick	ORN	295	Van Looen, Mary	GRN	331	Van Ness, Philip	RNS	45
Van Keuren, Jacob	ULS	254	Van Looen, Mathias	GRN	331	Van Ness, William	COL	196
Van Keuren, Jacobus	NYK	138	Van Looen, Nicholas W.	GRN	350	Van Ness, Willm	COL	216
Van Keuren, Jacobus	ULS	247	Van loon, Albart	GRN	348	Van Ness, William W.	COL	192
Van Keuren, Jacobus			Van loon, Albart			Van Nest, Rynier	SCH	127
Junr	ULS	247	Junior	GRN	348	Van Nettee, Benjamin	SRA	15
Van Keuren, James	DUT	70	Van Loon, Isaac	GRN	329	Vannevour, Alexander	NYK	72
Van Keuren, James	NYK	134	Van loon, Jacob	ALB	138	Van New Kirk, Gospert	NYK	66
Van Keuren, Johannis	ULS	229	Van loon, Jacob	GRN	344	Vanneys, George	KNG	5
Van Keuren, John	DUT	160	Van Loon, Jacob	GRN	348	Vanneys, James	KNG	5
Van Keuren, John	ULS	233	Van Loon, Jacob	GRN	348	Vanneys, John V.	KNG	5
Van Keuren, Jonathan	ULS	253	Van Loon, Jacob	GRN	348	Vanneys, Ruluf	KNG	5
Van Keuren, Levi	ULS	217	Van Loon, Jeremiah	GRN	348	Vanneys, William	KNG	3
Van Keuren, Levi	ULS	247	Van Loon, John	GRN	331	Vanneys, Willim	KNG	5
Van Keuren, Matthew	DUT	70	Van Loon, John	GRN	334	Van Nocker, Anthony	CAY	526
Van Keuren, Matthew	ULS	231	Van Loon, John	GRN	344	Van Noorstrant, Isaac	DUT	29
Van Keuren, Matthew			Van loon, John	GRN	348	Van Norden, David	NYK	70
Junr	DUT	70	Van loon, John P.	GRN	328	Van Norden, Gabriel	NYK	60
Van Keuren, Matthew			Van loon, Nicholas	GRN	348	Van Norden, Henry	NYK	57
ye 3d	DUT	65	Van loon, Nicholas J.	GRN	348	Van Norden, John	NYK	60
Van Keuren, Phillip	ULS	226	Van Loon, Nicholas W.	GRN	348	Van Norden, John	NYK	63
Van Keuren, Phillip			Van Loon, Peter	ALB	136	Van Norden, Peter		60
Junr	ULS	230	Van Loover, Peter	ALB	79	Van Norden, Sophia	NYK	57
Van Keuren, Reuben	ULS	247	Van Loover, William	ALB	79	Van Norden, Theodorus		
Van Keuren, Robert	NYK	25	Van Lorne, John B.	NYK	97	W.	NYK	32
Van Keuren, Tjierck	DUT	31	Van Louten, Anthony	NYK	97	Van Norden, Thomas	NYK	89
Van Keuren, Tjierck	ULS	247	Van Luc, John	QNS	67	Van Norest, Philip	NYK	49
Van Keuren, Tjierck	ULS	250	Van Lue see Van Leu &			Van Norman, Daniel	ONT	422
Van Keuren, Tobias	DUT	161	Van Lew			Van Norman, Isaac	ONT	424
Van Keuren, William	NYK	139	Van Lue, Frederick	CAY	560	Van Norman, Jesse	ONT	424
Van Kiper, Harman	NYK	92	Van Lue, Frederick	CAY	640	Van Norman, Joseph	CAY	574
Van Kiper, John	NYK	60	Van Lue, Peter	CAY	640	Van Norman, Joseph	ONT	420
Van Kirk, John	SRA	17	Van Luvan, Nicholas	GRN	327	Van Norman, William	CAY	574
Van Kirk, Joseph	SRA	17	Vanmater, Gilbert	KNG	8	Van Nort, Isaac	GRN	348
Van Kirk, Joseph	WSH	184	Van Middleswarth, And-			Van Nort, Jacob	GRN	348
Van Kleck, John L.	NYK	59	rew	CAY	708	Van North, Cornelius	DUT	88
Van Kleeck, Barent	DUT	41	Van Middleswarth, Ja-			Vannortwick, Alexander	KNG	6
Van Kleeck, Barent B.	DUT	32	cob	CAY	708	Van Nostrand, Aaron	QNS	71
Van Kleeck, Barent P.	DUT	32	Van Mitchel, William	NYK	92	Van Nostrand, George	RCK	107
Van Kleeck, Charity	DUT	66	Van Nactor, Abraham	ALB	121	Van Nostrand, Jacob	NYK	83
Van Kleeck, Henry	DUT	40	Van Nalst, George	NYK	66	Van Nostrandt, Daniel	QNS	70
Van Kleeck, Isaac	DUT	66	Van Namber, Joseph	CAY	594	Van Nostrandt, Garret	NYK	124
Van Kleeck, James	DUT	61	Van Name, Aaron	RCH	88	Van Nostrandt, John	KNG	9
Van Kleeck, Jane	DUT	63	Van Name, Aaron Junr	RCH	88	Van Nostrant, Aaron	QNS	67
Van Kleeck, John	ALB	93	Van Name, Moses	RCH	88	Van Nostrant, Caspar	ULS	243
Van Kleeck, John	DUT	64	Van Name, Simon	RCH	88	Van Nostrant, George	DUT	18
Van Kleeck, John	DUT	115	Van Name, Thomas	RCH	88	Van Nostrant, John	ULS	207
Van Kleeck, Peter Junr	DUT	41	Van Natta, Isaac	ALB	101	Van Nostrunt, Albert	QNS	82
Van Kleeck, Peter B.	DUT	62	Van Natta, James	ALB	100	Van Nostrunt, Isaac	QNS	82
Van Kleeck, Peter P.	DUT	41	Van Natta, John	ALB	100	Van Nostrunt, Samuel	QNS	76
Van Kleeck, Teunis	DUT	46	Van Natta, Peter	ALB	100	Van O Linder, Abm	ALB	50
Van Kleek, Henry	CLN	161	Vannatta, Samuel	OND	222	Van Olinder, Daniel	SRA	11
Van Leu see Van Lue			Van Naul, John	NYK	86	Van O Linder, Jacob	ALB	50
Van Leu, James	CAY	556	Vanne see Nanne			Van O Linder, Jacobus	ALB	52
Van Leusen, Abraham	MNT	70	Vanne, William	CAY	658	Van O Linder, John	ALB	51
Van Leuson, Basfurt	MNT	70	Vannermir, Cornelius	GRN	329	Van Olinder, John	SRA	11
Van Leuven, Andrew	ULS	225	Van Ness see Van Ess			Van O Linder, Peter	ALB	50
Van Leuven, Christopher	ULS	198	Van Ness, Abraham	CAY	710	Vanon, John	GRN	351
Van Leuven, Daniel	ULS	201	Van Ness, Cherrick	ALB	55	Van Orchins, David	TIO	258
Van Leuven, David	ULS	216	Van Ness, Cornelius	COL	215	Van Orden, Abraham	NYK	99
Van Leuven, Elias	ULS	200	Van Ness, Cornelius	MNT	75	Van Orden, Andrew	RCK	97
Van Leuven, Isaac	DUT	144	Van Ness, David	DUT	159	Van Orden, Charles	NYK	93
Van Leuven, Johannis	ULS	200	Van Ness, David Junr	COL	263	Van Orden, Hendrick	RCK	102
Van Leuven, Johannis			Vanness, Deborah	NYK	63	Van Orden, Jacob	RCK	110
Junr	ULS	203	Van Ness, Garret B.	DUT	64	Van rden, Jacobus	RCK	108
Van Leuven, John	ULS	202	Van Ness, Henry	ALB	43	Van Orden, James	RCK	108

Van Orden, John	NYK 93	Van Rensselaer, Jerh	ALB 145
Van Orden, John	RCK 110	Van Rensselaer, John	ALB 55
Van Orden, John	RCK 110	Van Rensselaer, John	
Van Orden, Mathew	NYK 100	H.	COL 194
Van Orden, Peter	GRN 338	Van Rensselaer, John	
Van Orden, Peter	RCK 106	R.	COL 194
Van Orden, Peter	RCK 108	Van Rensselaer, Kill-	
Van Orden, Rachel	RCK 103	ian	COL 255
Van Orden, Stephen	RCK 107	Van Rensselaer, Peter	COL 194
Van Order, Benjamin	GRN 330	Van Rensselaer, Philip	ALB 134
Van Order, Mrs Eliza-		Van Riper, Caleb	SRA 30
beth	GRN 327	Van Riper, Cornelius	NYK 60
Van Order, John	GRN 327	Van Riper, Garret	CAY 520
Van Order, John Junr	GRN 327	Van Riper, Jeremiah	CAY 520
Van Order, Major	GRN 327	Vanrizer, Caleb	CHN 974
Van Order, Mrs	GRN 328	Van Rusdall, Abraham	QNS 68
Van Order, William	GRN 330	Van Ryper, James	CAY 518
Van Osdall, Garret	CAY 728	Van Ryper, John	SCH 161
Van Osdall, Jacob	CAY 710	Vans, Robert	WSH 295
Van Osdall, Jacobus	CAY 712	Van S___, Tobias	MNT 24
Van Osdall, James	CAY 680	Van Saligen, Henry	NYK 48
Van Osdall, John	CAY 672	Van Salsbery, Cosper	RNS 60
Van Osdall, John	QNS 72	Van Saun, Albert	RCK 108
Van Osdall, Peter	CAY 712	Van Schaack, Catharine	COL 264
Van Osman, Wm	TIO 223	Van Schaack, Cornelius	COL 258
VAn Ostrand, Sarah	QNS 71	Van Schaack, Peter	COL 262
Van Ostrand, Stephen	QNS 72	Van Schaick, Abraham	ULS 217
Van Ostrum, Aaron	SRA 20	Van Schaick, Anthony	ULS 225
V.. Ostrum, Isaac	SRA 11	Van Schaick, Christi-	
Van Otwick, Isaac	CAY 550	ana	ALB 49
Van Patten, Frederick	SCH 166	Van Schaick, Corns	ALB 147
Van Patten, Nicholas	ALB 59	Van Schaick, Garret	RNS 83
Vanpelt, Aaron	KNG 5	Van Schaick, John	ALB 56
Van Pelt, Anthony	RCH 89	Van Schaick, John	RNS 7
Vanpelt, Christopher	KNG 7	Van Schaick, John G.	ALB 49
Van Pelt, Daniel	RNS 89	Van Schaick, Levi	DUT 159
Van Pelt, David	RCH 88	Van Schaick, Mary	ALB 135
Van Pelt, George	RCH 89	Van Schaick, Michael	ALB 55
Van Pelt, George	RCH 89	Van Scheuyck, Henry	WSH 240
Van Pelt, Hannah	RCH 88	Van Schoonhoven, Jas	ALB 43
Van Pelt, Henry	NYK 75	Van Schoonhoven, James	ULS 247
Van Pelt, Jacob	RCH 88	Van Schuyck, Aaron	WSH 238
Van Pelt, John	NYK 65	Van Schuyck, Garret	WSH 240
Van Pelt, John	RCH 87	Van Schuyck, Jacob	WSH 240
Van Pelt, John	RCH 89	Van Schuyck, Philes	WSH 240
Van Pelt, Mrs	RCH 87	Van Scoick, Hose	GRN 328
Vanpelt, Peter	KNG 5	Van Scoit, Rachel	ORN 330
Van Pelt, Peter	RCH 94	Van Scoit, Samuel	DUT 95
Van Pelt, Peter	SRA 33	Van Scoit, Samuel	ORN 319
Vanpelt, Rem	KNG 5	Vanscoy, Abraham	WST 127
Van Pelt, Sarah	RCH 93	Vanscoy, Abraham Junr	WST 126
Vanpel_, Th[omas?]	KNG 9	Van Scoy, David	SUF 109
Van Pelt, Tunis	NYK 84	Van Scoy, Isaac	SUF 109
Van Pelt, Tunis	NYK 99	Van Scoy, Isaac Junr	SUF 109
Van Pelt, Walter	RNS 89	Vanscoy, Timothy Junr	WST 127
Van Pelt, William	RCH 92	Van Secklen, Abraham	KNG 2
Vanpelt, Wynant	KNG 5	Vansendren, Ulpianus	KNG 4
Vanpelt, Wynant	KNG 7	Van Shaack, Maria	COL 264
Van Pett_, Adam	MNT 46	Van Shaick, Robert	SCH 166
Van Pette, John	SRA 24	Van Sherline, Cornelius	
Van Pette, John	SRA 24	A.	MNT 45
Van Pickley(?)	GRN 346	Van Shoyk, Cornelius	GRN 348
Vanplank, David	SRA 52	Van Sice, Abm	SRA 3
Van Plank, David J.	ALB 109	Van Sice, John	NYK 73
Van Plank, Isaac D.	ALB 117	Van Sickle, Garit	ONT 488
Vanplank, Philip	WST 158	Van Sickle, Peter	TIO 240
Van Plarcom, John	NYK 53	Vansicklen, Catharine	KNG 5
Vanrance, John R.	KNG 10	Van Sicklen, Coonradt	DUT 56
Van Ranst, Abraham	NYK 77	Van Sicklen, Cornelius	DUT 71
Van Ranst, Cornelius	DUT 146	Van Sicklen, Cornelius	DUT 117
Van Ranst, John	ORN 278	Vansicklen, Faresner	KNG 2
Van Rantz, Peter	NYK 124	Van Sicklen, Ferdinand	DUT 38
Van Rensalaer, Jeremiah	OND 160	Van Sicklen, Johannas	KNG 2
Van Rensselaer, Henry		Van Sicklen, John	DUT 33
J.	COL 253	Van Sicklen, John	ULS 209
Van Rensselaer, Jacob		Van Sickler, David	MNT 58
R.	COL 192	Vansinderen, Adrian	NYK 38

Van Sise, Hazarus	ALB 10		
Van Sise, James	ALB 10		
Van Sise, Joseph	OND 161		
Vansite, John	CHN 978		
Van Sitz, Henry	a		
Black	NYK 22		
Van Size, Charles	QNS 79		
Van Size, Cornelius	QNS 79		
Van Skiver, Abraham	MNT 19		
Van Skoyk, Nicholas	GRN 348		
Van Slack, Martin	CHN 940		
Van Slei___, Peter	MNT 5		
Van Sleigh, Nicholas	MNT 5		
Vanslewer, Peter	NYK 94		
Van Slicke, James	ONN 165		
Van Sliek, Jo.ep	MNT 53		
Vansloyke, Cornelius	GRN 354		
Van Sluyck, Jno J.	COL 218		
Van Sluyck, Peter J.	COL 259		
Van Sluyck, Peter J.	COL 265		
Van Sluyck, William	COL 260		
Van Slyck, Adam H.	MNT 6		
Van Slyck, Jacobus	HRK 578		
Van Slyck, Jacobus	MNT 55		
Van Slyck, Jo..	MNT 41		
Van Slyck, Martinus	SCH 131		
Van Slyck, Peter	SCH 151		
Van Slyck, Peter P.	COL 222		
Van Slyke, Adam	SCH 163		
Van Slyke, Barent	COL 260		
Van Slyke, James	SCH 166		
Van Slyke, John	SCH 166		
Van Slyke, Peter Junr	SCH 157		
Van Slyke, Samuel	COL 260		
Van Slyke, Samuel	SCH 163		
Van Slyke, Tunis A.	GRN 357		
Van Slyke, Willm	SCH 166		
Van Steenbargh, Samuel	NYK 21		
Van Steenbergh, Abraham	ULS 221		
Van Steenbergh, Abraham	ULS 252		
Van Steenbergh, Anne	ULS 229		
Van Steenbergh, Barent	DUT 24		
Van Steenbergh, Benjam-			
in	ULS 227		
Van Steenbergh, Cornel-			
ius	ULS 222		
Van Steenbergh, Dirck	ULS 221		
Van Steenbergh, Girar-			
dus	DUT 164		
Van Steenbergh, John	DUT 155		
Van Steenbergh, John	ULS 222		
Van Steenbergh, John	ULS 227		
Van Steenbergh, John	ULS 228		
Van Steenbergh, Matthew	DUT 165		
Van Steenbergh, Matthew	ULS 229		
Van Steenbergh, Matthew	ULS 252		
Van Steenbergh, Peter	DUT 161		
Van Steenbergh, Sarah	DUT 160		
Van Steenbergh, Solomon	DUT 161		
Van Steenbergh, Teunis	ULS 252		
Van Steenbergh, Thomas	ULS 227		
Van Stenburgh, Cornelus	GRN 358		
Van Stike, Garret	CHN 942		
Van Swalts, Jacob	ALB 140		
Vantassel, Abraham	WST 170		
Vantassel, Benjamin	WST 170		
Vantassel, Frederick	COL 228		
Van Tassel, Henry	ALB 36		
Van Tassel, Henry	DUT 23		
Van Tassel, Isaac	DUT 78		
Van Tassel, Jacob	DUT 34		
Van Tassel, John	DUT 27		
Van Tassel, John	NYK 97		
Vantassel, John	WST 128		
Vantassel, John	WST 159		
Vantassel, John Junr	WST 165		
Van Tassel, Peter	NYK 87		

Name	Loc
Van Tassel, Phillip	COL 237
Vantassel, Robert	WST 131
Vantassel, Thomas	WST 127
Van Tassell, Charity	NYK 99
Van Tassell, Henry	MNT 56
Van Tassell, Henry	NYK 144
Van Tassell, Isaac	NYK 98
Van Tassell, Jacob	NYK 93
Van Tassell, Jacob	OND 189
Van Tassell, Jacob	SCH 153
Van Tassell, John	NYK 91
Van Tassell, John	NYK 114
Van Tassell, John	NYK 127
Van Tassell, John	OND 189
Van Tassell, John	WSH 241
Van Tassell, Joshua	NYK 94
Van Tassell, Nicholas	ORN 332
Van Tassell, Richard	ORN 332
Van Tassell, Tunis	SCH 152
Vantassle, Abraham	WST 171
Vantassle, Betsey	WST 165
Vantassle, Cornelias	WST 164
Vantassle, Cornelias	WST 171
Van Tassle, Cornelius	SRA 44
Vantassle, Jacob	WST 164
Vantassle, John	WST 164
Vantassle, John	WST 170
Vantassle, John	WST 171
Van Tassle, Matthias	CHN 804
Vantassle, William	WST 164
Vantassle, William (J? J?)	WST 164
Vantassle, William	WST 165
Vantassle, William	WST 171
Vanthuysen, John	DUT 159
Van Tile, John	ALB 80
Van Tile, John	CAY 542
Van, Tine, Abraham	RNS 93
Van Tine, Charles	CAY 680
Vantine, Charles	CAY 710
Van Tine, Charles Junr	CAY 680
Van Tine, Cornelius Junr	DUT 34
Van Tine, Cornelius Senr	DUT 35
Van Tine, Isaac	DUT 36
Van Tine, Jacob	CAY 680
Vantine, James	CAY 710
Van Tine, James	DUT 37
Van Tine, Matthais	CAY 680
Vantine, Robert	RNS 40
Van Tine, Samuel	DUT 23
Van Tine, William	DUT 33
Vantrap, Wm	RNS 9
Van Tuyl, Andrew	NYK 151
Van Tuyl, John	ORN 320
Van Tuyl, Jonathan	ORN 320
Van Tuyl, Walter	ORN 317
Van Tuyl, William	ORN 320
Van Tuyle, Abraham	WSH 190
Van Tuyle, John	WSH 227
Vantwarp, Heron	CHN 942
Van Tyle, Isaac	SCH 132
Van Tyne, Abraham	ALB 91B
Van Utter, Joseph	CAY 580
Van V..., John(?)	MNT 63
Van Vactor, Jacob	GRN 327
Van Vailing, Abraham	SCH 157
Van Vailing, Moses	SCH 157
Van Vaj, Jonas	STB 203
Van Valchenburgh, Der-rick	GRN 351
Van Valchenburgh, James	GRN 320
Van Valen, Abrm	RCK 97
Van Valen, Cornelius	NYK 103
Van Valen, Danl	RCK 98
Van Valen, Saml	RCK 97
Van Valer, Abraham	GRN 358
Van Valhenburgh	GRN 335
Van Valhenburgh, Jacob	GRN 335
Van Valhenburgh, Jacob Jun	GRN 335
Van Valkenbergh, And-rew	COL 266
Van Valkenbergh, Daniel	COL 266
Van Valkenburgh, Abraham	GRN 329
Van Valkenburgh, Abraham	ULS 207
Van Valkenburgh, Adam	DEL 283
Van Valkenburgh, James	MNT 13
Van Valkenburgh, James	RNS 63
Van Valkenburgh, Johannis	ULS 224
Van Valkenburgh, John	RNS 64
Van Valkenburgh, John	SCH 131
Van Valkenburgh, John Jost	SCH 166
Van Valkenburgh, Mary	RNS 59
Van Valkenburgh, Tunis	RNS 64
Vanvare, Jacob	WST 129
Van Varick, James	NYK 16
Van Vart, Wm	RCK 103
Van Vaugenburgh, John	MNT 1
Van Vaulkenburgh, Henry	MNT 119
Van Vechten see Venve-chten	
Van Vechten, Abm	ALB 146
Van Vechten, Anthony	MNT 75
Van Vechten, Cornelius	SRA 40
Van Vechten, Harman	RNS 90
Van Vechten, Herman	SRA 39
Van Vechten, Lucas	ALB 45
Van Vechten, Walter	WSH 198
Van Vechten, Samuel	GRN 329
Van Veeling, Moses(?)	SRA 3
Van Velser, James	NYK 126
Van Velzer, Peter	DEL 274
Van Verest, Aaron	NYK 129
Van Vicker, David	QNS 61
Van Vickle, Tunis	QNS 67
Van Vickler, Evert	QNS 68
Van Visher, Benjamin	MNT 102
Van Vleck, Aaron	CHN 802
Van Vleck, Abraham	COL 258
Van Vleck, Abraham	DUT 18
Van Vleck, Abraham J.	COL 258
Van Vleck, Alexander	DUT 25
Van Vleck, Garret	ONN 168
Van Vleck, George	DUT 25
Van Vleck, Hendrick	DUT 23
Van Vleck, Isaac	NYK 107
Van Vleck, Isaac	ONN 153
Van Vleck, Isaac A.	COL 258
Van Vleck, Ja[cob?]	MNT 70
Van Vleck, John	ULS 196
Van Vleck, John H.	DUT 23
Van Vleck, Marinus J.	DUT 25
Van Vleck, Orrey	OND 214
Van Vleck, Peter	COL 202
Van Vleet, George	CAY 558
Van Vleet, John	ALB 38
Van Vleet, Peter	CAY 558
Van Vlick, Benjam	MNT 59
Van Vlick, Ellenor	NYK 57
Van Vlieck, Garrot	MNT 60
Van Vlierden, Peter	ULS 222
Van Vliet, Abraham	ULS 231
Van Vliet, Arie	ULS 232
Van Vliet, Cornelius	DUT 112
Van Vliet, Daniel	ORN 315
Van Vliet, Daniel	ORN 318
Van Vliet, David	ORN 340
Van Vliet, Dirck	DUT 165
Van Vliet, Garret	DUT 156
Van Vliet, George	ULS 206
Van Vliet, Henry	DUT 111
Van Vliet, Jacobus	ORN 317
Van Vliet, Jacobus Junr	ORN 316
Van Vliet, Jan	ULS 232
Van Vliet, John	DUT 36
Van Vliet, John	ULS 209
Van Vliet, John	ULS 232
Van Vliet, John Junr	ORN 315
Van Vliet, Peter	DUT 62
Van Vliet, Peter	ORN 308
Van Vliet, Samuel	ORN 319
Van Vliet, William	ORN 319
Van Voit, Jacob	GRN 339
Van Volkenbergh, Abm J.	COL 264
Van Volkenbergh, Barent	COL 257
Van Volkenbergh, Barth-ow	COL 258
Van Volkenbergh, Barth-ow J.	COL 263
Van Volkenbergh, Barw L.	COL 219
Van Volkenbergh, Barw P.	COL 259
Van Volkenbergh, Chris-tian	COL 224
Van Volkenbergh, Corns J.	COL 265
Van Volkenbergh, Ephm	COL 186
Van Volkenbergh, Hannah	COL 265
Van Volkenbergh, Hend-rick J.	COL 266
Van Volkenbergh, Henry	COL 264
Van Volkenbergh, Jacob	COL 257
Van Volkenbergh, Jacob	WSH 186
Van Volkenbergh, Jacob J.	COL 265
Van Volkenbergh, James	COL 219
Van Volkenbergh, Jane	COL 200
Van Volkenbergh, John	COL 263
Van Volkenbergh, Jno H.	COL 261
Van Volkenbergh, Lam-bert P.	COL 261
Van Volkenbergh, Peter	COL 259
Van Volkenbergh, Peter R.	COL 259
Van Volkenbergh, Solom	COL 219
Van Volkenbergh, Sophia	COL 224
Van Volkenbergh, Willm	COL 258
Van Volkenbergh, Will: J.	COL 265
Van Volkenburgh, Joam J.	COL 260
Van Volkenburgh, John	ALB 56
Van Volkenburgh, Lucas	COL 266
Van Volunberg, Abraham	OND 211
Van Voohis, Daniel	NYK 51
Van Voorhis, Abraham	DUT 39
Van Voorhis, Abraham	DUT 108
Van Voorhis, Daniel	DUT 6
Van Voorhis, David	NYK 84
Van Voorhis, Garret	ULS 183
Van Voorhis, Henry	DUT 37
Van Voorhis, Henry	DUT 118
Van Voorhis, Isaac	DUT 60
Van Voorhis, John	DUT 35
Van Voorhis, John	DUT 39
Van Voorhis, John	DUT 111
Van Voorhis, John & Koert	DUT 118
Van Voorhis, Koert	DUT 11

Name	Ref
Vicory, Timothy	ONN 193
Victor, Jonas	MNT 98
Victor, Joseph	NYK 84
Victory, John	ALB 29
Victory, Mamre	OND 223
Vidalot, James	NYK 56
Videll, Paul	NYK 71
Vider, Isaac	MNT 106
Vieley see Veiley	
Vieley, Benjamin	SRA 50
Vieley, Garret	SRA 50
Vieley, Jesse	SRA 41
Vieley, John	SRA 40
Vieley, Lodawicus	SRA 40
Vieley, Stephen	SRA 40
Vielie, Lewis	RNS 35
Vielie, Hendrick	DUT 18
Vielie, Jacobus	ULS 248
Vielie, John	ULS 231
Vielie, Myndert	DUT 6
Vielie, Myndert	ULS 243
Vielie, Byndert B.	DUT 14
Vielie, Peter	DUT 62
Vielie, Sarah	ULS 231
Vielie, Stephen	RNS 35
Vielie, Sybrant	RNS 35
Vielie, Tunis	RNS 36
Vieliee, Sally	RNS 34
Viely, John R.	SRA 40
Viesse, Benvit	NYK 54
Vile, John	SCH 173
Vilie, Jesse	RNS 47
Villaber, John	OTS 40
Villee, Cornelius	NYK 17
Villier, John a Black	NYK 116
Vinal, Cologies	ONN 139
Vinal, Cologies Jur	ONN 139
Vinan, Mrs	GRN 350
Vincent, Abraham	MNT 23
Vincent, Allen	DUT 123
Vincent, Benjamin	HRK 555
Vincent, Caleb	HRK 596
Vincent, Charles	MNT 23
Vincent, Charles Junr	DUT 6
Vincent, Charles Senr	DUT 9
Vincent, Ester	NYK 96
Vincent, Gilbert	COL 196
Vincent, Gilbert	DUT 7
Vincent, Henry	OND 188
Vincent, Isaac	WST 147
Vincent, Jacob(?)	SRA 9
Vincent, Jacob	WST 147
Vincent, Jacob	WST 165
Vincent, James	ONN 177
Vincent, Jeremiah	RNS 71
Vincent, Jeremiah	SRA 9
Vincent, John	RNS 103
Vincent, John	SRA 12
Vincent, John	SRA 12
Vincent, John	WST 171
Vincent, John the 1st	DUT 16
Vincent, John ye 2d	DUT 7
Vincent, John H.	DUT 12
Vincent, Jonathan	DUT 97
Vincent, Joseph	NYK 149
Vincent, Joshua	ALB 73
Vincent, Joshua	RNS 71
Vincent, Leonard	DUT 97
Vincent, Levi	COL 187
Vincent, Mary Francis Fontoun	NYK 141
Vincent, Mary	WST 147
Vincent, Michael	COL 189
Vincent, Michael	DUT 15
Vincent, Nicholas	HRK 597
Vincent, Noel	HRK 589
Vincent, Peter	NYK 88
Vincent, Peter	NYK 126
Vincent, Philip	SRA 45
Vincent, Rachel	DUT 9
Vincent, Reuben	DUT 8
Vincent, Reynolds	DUT 10
Vincent, Richard	SRA 40
Vincent, Samuel	DUT 7
Vincent, Schadrach	HRK 596
Vincent, Sharp a Black	NYK 111
Vincent, Solomon free Negro	RNS 44
Vincent, Thomas	ONT 416
Vincent, William	NYK 141
Vincint, Shubael	TIO 235
Vine, Ebenezer	WSH 284
Vine, John	ALB 57
Vine, Solomon	WSH 283
Vines, Margaret	NYK 138
Vinigar, Jacob	MNT 109
Vining, Abijah	CHN 984
Vining, John	ONN 188
Vining, Jonas	ONN 188
Vining, Saml	ONN 188
Vinings, John	WST 124
Vinten, Benoni	HRK 426
Vinton see Venton	
Virgil	SUF 108
Virgil see Vergil	
Virgil, Asa	COL 187
Virgil, Benjn	CHN 920
Virgil, Henry	ONN 179
Virgil, Jacob	CAY 626
Virgil, Wm	ONN 179
Virtue see Vartue	
Virtue, David	NYK 109
Visage, James	MNT 55
Visher, Eldert	SRA 4
Visher, Elihu	COL 218
Visher, George	RNS 88
Visher, Jacob	RNS 89
Visher, Nanning	SRA 4
Visher, Nanning H.	SRA 17
Visscher, Gerrit	ALB 145
Visscher, Henry	ALB 137
Visscher, Jane	ALB 74
Visscher, Johannis	ALB 69
Visscher, John	RNS 5
Visscher, John T.	ALB 52
Visscher, Lydia	ALB 144
Visscher, Sebastian	ALB 136
Visscher, Teunis	ALB 52
Visscher, Teunis T.	ALB 52
Visscher, Tunis	SRA 12
Vitchie, John	NYK 18
Vithake, Frederick A.	NYK 50
Vixon, Solomon	STB 204
Vo__, John C.	WST 153
Voce, John	TIO 253
Vocher, William	NYK 97
Vocht, Henry	NYK 86
Vogle, Frederick	NYK 142
Vogle, Mathew	NYK 147
Voke, Akatias C.	DUT 73
Volant, Jacob	DUT 160
Volant, Jacob	ULS 226
Volant, Wilhelmus	ULS 218
Volentine see Valentine & Vallentine	
Volentine, Isaac	SRA 24
Volin, Martenus	WST 111
Volk, Christopher	MNT 40
Voll, Mary	WST 115
Vollintine, Henry	WST 165
Voluntine, Ezekel	WSH 213
Voluntine, Jacob	WSH 220
Voluntine, Joseph	WSH 191
Volwiser, Abram	SRA 3
Volwiser, Derick	SRA 3
Volwiser, Jacob	SRA 3
Von see Vaughan	
Von, Eliza	SUF 104
Vonch, Peter	NYK 146
Vonk, Peter J.	COL 200
Voogd, John G.	GRN 332
Voohis, Peter	NYK 60
Voorheis, Jacob	QNS 79
Voorheis, John	QNS 79
Voorheis, Stephen	QNS 68
Voorheis, Stephen	QNS 78
Voorhes, Abraham	KNG 3
Voorhes, Albert	KNG 5
Voorhes, Daniel	KNG 7
Voorhes, Henry	DEL 268
Voorhes, Jacob	KNG 3
Voorhes, Jacobus	KNG 4
Voorhes, John	KNG 3
Voorhes, John	KNG 4
Voorhes, Lawrence	KNG 3
Voorhes, Ralph	KNG 2
Voorhes, Stephen	KNG 4
Voorhies, James	CAY 668
Voorhis, Abraham	CAY 710
Voorhis, Henry	CAY 556
Voorhis, James	NYK 98
Voorhis, John	NYK 91
Voorhis, John	NYK 140
Voorhis, Paul	NYK 145
Voorhis, Peter	SCH 145
Voorhis, Ralph	SCH 138
Vooris, .eorge	MNT 78
Vooris, James	MNT 111
Vooris, Jeremiah	MNT 108
Vooris, John	MNT 94
Vooris, Wm	MNT 102
Voorse, Charles	ALB 82
Voosenbarrer, Abraham	STB 204
Vorce, Benjamin	WSH 233
Vorce, David	WSH 233
Vorce, Isaac	SRA 42
Vorce, Mathew	WSH 234
Vorce, William	SRA 42
Vores, Bejamin	WSH 232
Vores, Simon	KNG 3
Vorheis, Margaret	RCK 110
Voris, Jacob	WST 112
Voris, John	WST 114
Vorse, Thomas	CHN 802
Vorse, Timothy	COL 186
Vorse, Timothy	COL 200
Vorst, Stephen	GRN 354
Vort, Henry C.	WST 155
Vort, Joseph C.	WST 153
Vosburg, Abraham	COL 233
Vosburg, Isaac	SRA 24
Vosburg, Jacob	SCH 121
Vosburg, Martin	COL 262
Vosburgh, Abeel	MNT 64
Vosburgh, Abm	ALB 45
Vosburgh, Abraham	ALB 66
Vosburgh, Abraham	COL 215
Vosburgh, Abraham	COL 263
Vosburgh, Abraham	ULS 230
Vosburgh, Abraham Junr	COL 266
Vosburgh, Abm J.	COL 191
Vosburgh, Abm L.	COL 200
Vosburgh, Abraham L.	COL 265
Vosburgh, Adam	COL 239
Vosburgh, Adam	SCH 138
Vosburgh, Bartho:w	COL 257
Vosburgh, Barthomew	MNT 45
Vosburgh, Cornelius	COL 258
Vosburgh, Cornelius Junr	COL 231

Name	Loc	Pg
Vosburgh, Cornelius C.	COL	245
Vosburgh, Cornelius M.	COL	262
Vos burgh, David	RNS	60
Vosburgh, David	WSH	302
Vosburgh, Derick	COL	200
Vosburgh, Dirck	COL	266
Vosburgh, Evert	DUT	154
Vosburgh, Evert	MNT	29
Vosburgh, Gerrit	ALB	48
Vosburgh, Gilbert	COL	264
Vosburgh, Hannah	COL	259
Vosburgh, Harman	COL	260
Vosburgh, Henry	MNT	77
Vosburgh, Hermas	NYK	69
Vosburgh, Isaac	ALB	45
Vosburgh, Isaac	COL	191
Vosburgh, Jacob	ALB	47
Vosburgh, Jacob	COL	200
Vosburgh, Jacob	COL	231
Vosburgh, Jacob	MNT	29
Vosburgh, Jacob A.	COL	230
Vosburgh, Jacob C.	COL	245
Vosburgh, Jacobus	ALB	142
Vosburgh, James	COL	259
Vosburgh, Joachim	COL	257
Vosburgh, John	ALB	49
Vosburgh, John	COL	260
Vosburgh, John Junr	COL	240
Vosburgh, John A.	COL	260
Vosburgh, John J.	COL	198
Vosburgh, Lawrence	COL	244
Vosburgh, Martin	DUT	154
Vosburgh, Martin Junr	DUT	125
Vosburgh, Mathew	COL	259
Vosburgh, Myndert P.	COL	258
Vosburgh, Peter	COL	200
Vosburgh, Peter	COL	242
Vosburgh, Peter	COL	264
Vosburgh, Peter Junr	COL	266
Vosburgh, Peter J.	COL	263
Vosburgh, Peter L.	COL	200
Vosburgh, Peter L.	COL	265
Vosburgh, Richd	ALB	48
Vosburgh, Richard	MNT	36
Vosburgh, Richard	MNT	45
Vosburgh, Richard E.	COL	259
Vosburgh, Robert	COL	196
Vosburgh, Rue	COL	240
Vosburgh, Samuel	COL	242
Vosburgh, Samuel	COL	245
Vosburgh, Samuel	COL	259
Vosburgh, Samuel L.	COL	261
Vosburgh, Theo:s	COL	215
Vosburgh, William	COL	262
Vosburgh, Wm	MNT	108
Vose, James	NYK	133
Vose, Oliver	OTS	47
Voser, Wm	RNS	78
Vosmire, John	COL	266
Vosmire, John Junr	COL	266
Voss, Catherine	NYK	19
Votey, James	NYK	95
Vottee, John	NYK	92
Voucht, Peter	SCH	153
Vough, John	ALB	35
Vought see Nought		
Vouks, Samuel	QNS	67
Vowers, Andrew	WSH	201
Vowers, Jonathan	WSH	201
Vradenberg, Abraham	COL	215
Vradenberg, Elias	COL	234
Vradenbergh, Benjamin	COL	261
Vradenbergh, Elias	COL	245
Vradenburgh, John	COL	266
Vrandenbergh, James	COL	257
Vrandenburgh, John	ALB	23
Vredenbergh, Benjamin	DUT	163
Vredenbergh, Benjamin		
Vredenbergh, D.	ULS	207
Vredenbergh, Benjamin		
Vredenbergh, P.	ULS	208
Vredenbergh, David	ULS	207
Vredenbergh, Hezekiah	ORN	316
Vredenbergh, Isaac	ULS	234
Vredenbergh, Jacob	DUT	99
Vredenbergh, Jacob	DUT	163
Vredenbergh, John	ULS	207
Vredenbergh, John	ULS	259
Vredenbergh, Peter	DUT	155
Vredenbergh, William	DUT	43
Vredenbergh, William	DUT	156
Vredenbergh, William	ULS	259
Vredenburgh, A	CAY	516
Vredenburgh, Abraham	WSH	301
Vredenburgh, Benjamin	NYK	153
Vredenburgh, Benjamin	WST	129
Vredenburgh, Benjamin	WST	133
Vredenburgh, Daniel	WST	152
Vredenburgh, Evert	DUT	161
Vredenburgh, Isaac	DUT	74
Vredenburgh, Isaac	NYK	52
Vredenburgh, James	WST	157
Vredenburgh, John	DUT	74
Vredenburgh, Joseph	WST	146
Vredenburgh, Mary	RCK	104
Vredenburgh, Nicholas	WST	152
Vredenburgh, Peter	DEL	271
Vredinburgh, Abraham	WST	117
Vredinburgh, William	WST	117
Vreedenbergh, Wm	ALB	54
Vreedenburgh, John	ALB	54
Vreedenburgh, William		
Vreedenburgh, J.	QNS	62
Vreedonburgh, Cornelius	NYK	113
Vreeland, Eder	RCH	93
Vreeland, Jacob	RCH	93
Vreeland, Jane	RCH	93
Vreeland, Michael	RCH	93
Vreeland, William	RCH	93
Vreevauck, George	MNT	70
Vritenburgh, Jacob	WST	171
Vritenburgh, John	WST	171
Vroman, John	SRA	3
Vroom, George	NYK	145
Vroom, Gilbert Bogert	NYK	53
Vrooman, Abraham	ALB	15
Vrooman, Abraham	MNT	78
Vrooman, Abrm	OTS	4
Vrooman, Adam	ALB	22
Vrooman, Adam	ALB	60
Vrooman, Adam	SCH	130
Vrooman, Adam B.	SCH	119
Vrooman, Adam P.	SCH	131
Vrooman, Adam S.	ALB	3
Vrooman, Adam S.	SCH	130
Vrooman, Alleda	ALB	12
Vrooman, Andries	ALB	119
Vrooman, Aurant S.	ALB	25
Vrooman, Barent	MNT	71
Vrooman, Barent	SCH	127
Vrooman, Barent	SCH	162
Vro man, .arrant	MNT	75
Vrooman, Bartho: E.	SCH	130
Vrooman, Bartho: S.	SCH	130
Vrooman, Corns	ALB	12
Vrooman, Cornelius	ALB	119
Vrooman, Cornelius	SCH	131
Vrooman, David	SCH	130
Vrooman, Henry	ALB	15
Vrooman, Henry H.	HRK	412
Vrooman, Henry J.	HRK	469
Vrooman, Isaac	ALB	13
Vrooman, Isaac	ALB	22
Vrooman, Jacob	ALB	15
Vrooman, Jacob	ALB	22
Vrooman, Jacob	SCH	119
Vrooman, Jacob S.	OTS	28
Vrooman, Jacobus	ALB	119
Vrooman, Jacobus Junr	ALB	120
Vrooman, John	ALB	9
Vrooman, John	ALB	15
Vrooman, John Junior	SCH	166
Vrooman, John B.	ALB	9
Vrooman, Jonas	SCH	130
Vrooman, Josiah	SCH	163
Vrooman, Josias B.	SCH	127
Vrooman, Josias E.	SCH	130
Vrooman, Laurance	ALB	11
Vrooman, Martin Junr	MNT	76
Vrooman, Martinus	SCH	162
Vrooman, Martinus J.	SCH	131
Vrooman, Nicholas	ALB	57
Vrooman, Peter Jr	SCH	119
Vrooman, Peter C.	SCH	131
Vrooman, Simon	ALB	11
Vrooman, Simon	HRK	508
Vroo.an, Simon J.	MNT	13
Vrooman, Susanna	SCH	131
Vrooman, Tunis	SCH	162
Vrooman, Walter	ALB	58
Vrooman, Walter B.	ALB	12
Vrooman, Wyncha	ALB	16
Vunch, Henry	MNT	102
Vuske, David	SRA	18

W

Name	Loc	Pg
W..ple, Dow	MNT	61
W....an, Elisha	MNT	84
W.afre, Gidion	MNT	87
W khart, Ge ge	NYK	133
W...., Samuel	ONN	182
W...man, Jonathan	ONN	186
W oding, John	ONT	474
W...t.., Israel	ONT	504
W...on, John	RCK	97
W ight, Joseph	SRA	38
W , Archibald	SRA	45
W , John	TIO	251
Wa.d, C..rles	MNT	55
Wa.., Sa 1	MNT	90
Wackman, Henry	DUT	10
Wackman, Henry	ULS	243
Wackman, Marcus	ULS	244
Wadams, John	SCH	157
Waddell, Robert	NYK	28
Waddin, Stephen Negro	QNS	71
Waddington, Joshua	NYK	30
Waddle, Burdon	WSH	273
Waddle, Elijah	WSH	266
Waddle, Mary	DUT	66
Wade	GRN	341
Wade, Abner	NYK	112
Wade, Abraham	SRA	57
Wade, Alverson	OND	192
Wade, Amasa	OTS	10
Wade, Anna	NYK	30
Wade, Asahel	OTS	12
Wade, Benjamin	NYK	147
Wade, Caleb	NYK	15
Wade, Charles	NYK	78
Wade, Charles	NYK	145
Wade, Edward	NYK	75
Wade, Edward	NYK	78
Wade, Edward	OTS	14
Wade, Jacob	CHN	912
Wade, Jacob	CHN	916
Wade, James	NYK	99
Wade, James	NYK	137
Wade, Job	NYK	137
Wade, John	NYK	108

Wade, John	NYK 129	Waggoner, Mathias	COL 233	Wait, Olver	SRA 6
Wade, Jonathan	NYK 111	Waggoner, Peter	COL 231	Wait, Patience	SRA 31
Wade, Obidiah	NYK 111	Waggoner, Peter	RNS 82	Wait, Peleg	RNS 68
Wade, Robert	NYK 142	Waggoner, Rachael	MNT 56	Wait, Reuben	RNS 78
Wade, Seth	ONT 412	Waggoner, William	COL 218	Wait, Reuben	SRA 31
Wade, Stephen	NYK 65	Waggoner, William	COL 259	Wait, Rufus	RNS 78
Wader, Cornelius	NYK 87	Waggons, Andrew	RCK 101	Wait, Shadock	SRA 33
Waderwax see Wetherwax		Waggons, John	RCK 101	Wait, Stephen	SRA 33
Waderwax, Thomas	COL 266	Wagner, John	NYK 37	Wait, Stephen	SRA 33
Wadham, Alexr	COL 206	Wagner, Mathias	RNS 55	Wait, Thaddeus	HRK 457
Wadham, Enos	COL 206	Wagoner, Elsie	ALB 119	Wait, Thomas	WSH 279
Wadhams, John	COL 214	Wagoner, George	ALB 21	Wait, William	DEL 279
Wadkins, Dorothy	ORN 356	Wagoner, George	ALB 58	Wait, William	SRA 41
Wadkins, Hezekieh	ORN 355	Wagoner, George	ALB 77	Wait, William	SRA 44
Wadkins, Martha	ORN 355	Wagoner, Hontice	ALB 97	Wait, William	WSH 197
Wadley, John	OND 195	Wagoner, Isaac	COL 190	Wait, William	WSH 197
Wadley, Joseph	OND 195	Wagoner, John	ALB 38	Waite, Ezra	ONT 388
Wadley, Joseph	OND 220	Wagoner, John	ALB 57	Waite, Loring	ONT 388
Wadsworth, Ebenezer	OND 220	Wagoner, John	MNT 2	Waite, Richard	ONT 388
Wadsworth, Elijah	OND 220	Wagoner, John H.	ALB 98	Waite, Robert	NYK 119
Wadsworth, Gad	ONT 378	Wagoner, Jos	MNT 38	Wakefield, Oliver	OTS 45
Wadsworth, Jamima	OTS 34	Wagoner, Philip	ALB 128	Wakefield, Thomas	OTS 22
Wadsworth, John	CHN 962	Wagoner, William	ALB 98	Wakeley, John	OTS 8
Wadsworth, Joseph	ORN 321	Wagoner, William	ALB 119	Wakeley, Robert	WSH 291
Wadsworth, Josias	ALB 15	Wagoner, William	SRA 30	Wakelin, Ebenzr	CHN 984
Wadsworth, Silas	OND 211	Wagstaff, David	NYK 27	Wakely, Abel	GRN 340
Wadsworth, Thomas	OND 183	Wagstaff, Robert	NYK 25	Wakely, Joseph	DEL 270
Wadsworth, Timothy	OND 182	Wahous, Edward A.	SRA 12	Wakeman	SRA 13
Wadsworth, Timothy	OND 220	Wai___, Alfred	CAY 550	Wakeman, Adams	WST 140
Wadsworth, William	ONT 384	Waight see Wait, Wei-		Wakeman, Daniel	HRK 453
Wadsworth, John	COL 237	ght & Wates		Wakeman, David	WST 140
Wady, John	RNS 46	Waight, Ase	CHN 782	Wakeman, Hezekiah	WST 140
Waffle, Jo..	TIO 211	Waight, Benjamin	WST 133	Wakeman, James	DEL 278
Waffle, Sephrenus	OTS 58	Waight, Benjamin Junr	WST 133	Wakeman, Jonathan S.	KNG 10
Waffle, Wm	OTS 58	Waight, Edward	CHN 782	Wakeman, Loyd	SRA 12
Wagans, Michael	SUF 71	Waight, John	CHN 784	Wakeman, Moses	DEL 278
Wagant, Tobias	ALB 101	Waight, John Jun	CHN 782	Wakeman, Sabra	ORN 330
Wagener, Abraham	ONT 458	Waight, John Junr	CHN 784	Wakeman, Stephen	DEL 278
Wagener, Anne	ONT 464	Waight, Samuel	QNS 77	Wakeman, Stephen	SRA 13
Wagener, George	CAY 596	Waight, Solomon	CHN 784	Wakeman, Walker	WST 153
Wagener, Jacob	ONT 466	Waight, Thomas	GRN 330	Waklee, William	HRK 564
Wagener, John G.	CHN 868	Wail, Ebenr	OTS 25	Walace see Wallace
Wagener, Rebecca	ONT 458	Wailing, James	COL 231	Walace, Robert	WSH 196
Wager, Barent	COL 182	Wain see Wayne		Walbridge, Elias	DUT 126
Wager, Barent	COL 194	Wain, John	OTS 44	Walbridge, Gustavus	OTS 37
Wager, Coonrodt	RNS 29	Wainright, Daniel	GRN 357	Walbridge, Henry	OTS 37
Wager, Cornelius	DEL 283	Wainright, David C.	DEL 268	Walbridge, Zebulon	DUT 148
Wager, Daniel	RNS 89	Wainwright, Abijah	DUT 97	Walch see Walsh
Wager, David	COL 182	Wainwright, Francis	QNS 62	Walch, Alexander	RNS 81
Wager, David	COL 194	Wainwright, John	DUT 138	Walch, John	RNS 80
Wager, David	RNS 88	Wainwright, Joseph	RNS 30	Walden, John	CAY 606
Wager, Ephraim	RNS 29	Wait see Waight		Walden, John	NYK 87
Wager, George	OND 194	Wait, Abner	SRA 33	Walden, Nathan	ONT 404
Wager, Henry	RNS 87	Wait, Adin	DEL 279	Walden, Robert	COL 255
Wager, Jacob	COL 182	Wait, Benjamin	WSH 269	Walder, Henry	COL 232
Wager, Jacob	COL 193	Wait, Benjamin	HRK 425	Walderhiden, Cornelius	MNT 76
Wager, Jacob	RNS 88	Wait, Briggs	DUT 119	Walderoff, Abraham	CAY 526
Wager, Jacob	RNS 89	Wait, Catharine	DUT 10	Walderoff, George	CAY 526
Wager, John	COL 182	Wait, Christopher	DUT 15	Waldin, Thomas	QNS 74
Wager, John	RNS 88	Wait, Daniel	DEL 287	Walding, Jeremiah	DEL 283
Wager, Joseph	CAY 586	Wait, Daniel	SRA 33	Walding, Simeon	DEL 283
Wager, Margaret	RNS 88	Wait, Daniel	SRA 38	Waldo, Calvin	OTS 22
Wager, Peter	MNT 116	Wait, George	ALB 89	Waldo, David	COL 247
Wager, Peter	RNS 89	Wait, Gideon	SRA 31	Waldo, David	OND 211
Wager, Philip	RNS 88	Wait, Henery	SRA 9	Waldo, Ephraim	OND 205
Wagganer, George	MNT 17	Wait, Henry	COL 213	Waldo, Gershom	OND 177
Waggenen, Christian	NYK 152	Wait, Jeremiah	SRA 33	Waldo, Jerim	OTS 22
Waggenen, Henry	DEL 290	Wait, John	CLN 164	Waldo, Jesse	OND 205
Waggon, Tobias	WST 152	Wait, John	GRN 333	Waldo, Jonathan	OND 206
Waggoner, Abraham	MNT 39	Wait, John	WSH 307	Waldo, Jonathan Ju	OND 206
Waggoner, Adam	COL 198	Wait, Jonathan	CLN 159	Waldo, Joseph	HRK 523
Waggoner, Andrew	MNT 39	Wait, Jonathan	COL 213	Waldo, Nathan	OND 203
Waggoner, Geo...	MNT 39	Wait, Jonathan	GRN 355	Waldo, Nicholas	COL 232
Waggoner, Isaac	MNT 27	Wait, Jonathon	CLN 156	Waldo, Ozias	OTS 2
Waggoner, Jacob	COL 193	Wait, ...eph	ONT 392	Waldo, Steven	SRA 52
Waggoner, Jacob	MNT 26	Wait, Joseph	WSH 277	Waldo, William	SRA 4
Waggoner, John	COL 233	Wait, Mary	RNS 54	Waldon, Nathaniel	MNT 22

Waldorf, Hendrick	DUT 159	Waldrum, Jacob	QNS 62	Walker, John	RNS 83
Waldorf, Hendrick Junr	DUT 159	Waldrum, Samuel	QNS 61	Walker, John	SRA 46
Waldorf, John	DUT 159	Waleing, Edward	COL 235	Walker, John	WSH 185
Waldorf, Nicholas	COL 235	Walen, Valentine	NYK 54	Walker, John Junr	SRA 46
Waldorf, William	DUT 159	Walers, Samuel	MNT 34	Walker, Joseph	HRK 569
Waldorph, Henry	COL 242	Wales, Eisha	SCH 157	Walker, Joseph	OND 212
Waldow, Daniel	WSH 295	Wales, Elisha	SCH 152	Walker, Joshua	OTS 48
Wal_ow, Horatio	MNT 70	Wales, Jonathan	OND 168	Walker, Josiah	WSH 279
Waldow, Dr John	TIO 217	Wales, Nathan	CHN 778	Walker, Justice	MNT 82
Waldrach, Jacob H.	MNT 27	Waley, David	QNS 76	Walker, Justice	NYK 76
Waldract, George	MNT 34	Waley, James	QNS 77	Walker, Levi	SRA 55
Waldrat, Adam	MNT 4	Waley, John	NYK 59	Walker, Matthew	DUT 24
Waldrat, Adolphus	MNT 18	Walf, Andrew	GRN 347	Walker, Nathaniel	CAY 598
Waldrat, Casper	MNT 38	Walfo_, John	ONT 452	Walker, Nathaniel	CAY 662
Waldrat, Cosporus	MNT 53	Walgrove, Garret	NYK 17	Walker, Nathaniel	SRA 35
Waldrat, George	MNT 56	Walgrove, Samuel	NYK 150	Walker, Peter	NYK 47
Waldrat, Henry B.	MNT 38	Walk_, Samuel	CAY 568	Walker, Peter	ORN 327
Waldrat, Jacob	MNT 38	Walker see Wolker		Walker, Phineas	OND 198
Waldrat, Jacob H.	MNT 38	Walker, Abner	HRK 540	Walker, Richard W.	NYK 16
Waldrat, Margaret	MNT 51	Walker, Abraham	ALB 41	Walker, Robert	ESS 294
Waldrat, Peter	MNT 43	Walker, Abraham	NYK 127	Walker, Robert	NYK 98
Waldrath, Henry	MNT 27	Walker, Abraham	WSH 246	Walker, Samuel	MNT 54
Waldrath, Jacob A.	MNT 27	Walker, Adam	NYK 16	Walker, Samuel	ULS 180
Waldrath, John H.	MNT 29	Walker, Alanson	CLN 171	Walker, Sarah	NYK 106
Waldrom, Isaac	NYK 90	Walker, Andrew	ORN 303	Walker, Solomon	WSH 252
Waldron, ...	CAY 540	Walker, Anthony	NYK 76	Walker, Stephen	MNT 82
Waldron, Abraham	NYK 97	Walker, Archibald	COL 216	Walker, Stephen	SRA 34
Waldron, Abrm	RNS 36	Walker, Benjm	ALB 110	Walker, Stephen	SRA 47
Waldron, Abrm	RCK 102	Walker, Benjamin	OND 161	Walker, Stephen	WSH 303
Waldron, Barney	NYK 97	Walker, Benjamin	SRA 35	Walker, Thomas	CAY 582
Waldron, Benjamin	DUT 29	Walker, Bosworth	ESS 319	Walker, Thomas	NYK 143
Waldron, Benjamin	NYK 142	Walker, Charles	NYK 82	Walker, Thomas	WST 114
Waldron, Christiana	NYK 134	Walker, Charles P.	SRA 22	Walker, Timothy	HRK 568
Waldron, Corns	ALB 104	Walker, Daniel	MNT 71	Walker, Timothy	ONN 174
Waldron, Cornelius	RNS 36	Walker, David	SRA 55	Walker, William	DEL 278
Waldron, Cornelius	RCK 102	Walker, Ebenezer	OND 191	Walker, William	DEL 284
Waldron, ..rnelius H.	MNT 22	Walker, Ebenezer	WSH 274	Walker, William	NYK 85
Waldron, Daniel	WST 171	Walker, Edward	CAY 624	Walker, Wiram	WSH 274
Waldron, David	NYK 147	Walker, Edward	DUT 37	Walkoop, Aaron	WSH 207
Waldron, David	NYK 152	Walker, Edward	OTS 48	Wall, Bartlet	WSH 305
Waldron, Edward	RCK 101	Walker, Eli	OND 184	Wall, Coggswell	CHN 780
Waldron, Elizabeth	NYK 153	Walker, Elijah	CHN 746	Wall, Ezra	SUF 88
Waldron, Evert	SRA 50	Walker, Ephraim	OND 186	Wall, Frederick	GRN 326
Waldron, Garret	SRA 11	Walker, Ephraim	OND 191	Wall, Frederick Jun	GRN 326
Waldron, Henry	ALB 3	Walker, Ephraim	OTS 2	Wall, Henry	WSH 305
Waldron, Isaac	RCK 103	Walker, Ezra	WSH 274	Wall, James	NYK 16
Waldron, Jacob	RCK 103	Walker, Ezra	WSH 276	Wall, Joby Free Black	COL 250
Waldron, James	ALB 119	Walker, George	SCH 163	Wall, John	CAY 662
Waldron, James	ALB 120	Walker, George	SCH 172	Wall, John W.	COL 183
Waldron, James	DUT 76	Walker, George	TIO 241	Wall, Pompey a Black	NYK 151
Waldron, James	RCK 106	Walker, Henry	SRA 55	Wall, Rachael	NYK 90
Waldro_, Johanis	MNT 1	Walker, Hezekiah	OTS 48	Wall, William	MNT 14
Waldron, John	CAY 672	Walker, Hinckley	OTS 7	Wallace see Woll_ce,
Waldron, John	NYK 152	Walker, Hiram	DUT 107	Walace, Wallice &
Waldron, John	RCK 101	Walker, Hugh	NYK 72	Wallis
Waldron, John	RCK 103	Walker, Isaac	CAY 574	Wallace, Abijah	WST 125
Waldron, John	SRA 10	Walker, Isaac	CHN 778	Wallace, Benjamin	ALB 47
Waldron, John	ULS 237	Walker, Israel	ALB 113	Wallace, Benjamin	RNS 50
Waldron, Joseph	NYK 96	Walker, Jacob	CHN 954	Wallace, Cornelius	ONN 135
Waldron, Joseph	RCK 101	Walker, Jacob	ORN 312	Wallace, Daniel	RNS 18
Waldron, Oliver	NYK 150	Walker, James	ALB 51	Wallace, David	NYK 141
Waldron, Peter	ALB 49	Walker, James	COL 216	Wallace, David	ORN 301
Waldron, Peter	DUT 31	Walker, James	NYK 35	Wallace, David	WSH 266
Waldron, Peter	NYK 96	Walker, James	RNS 70	Wallace, Elijah	RNS 18
Waldron, Peter	RNS 36	Walker, James	WSH 200	Wallace, Elizabeth	ORN 281
Waldron, Peter	SRA 50	Walker, James	WSH 203	Wallace, Henery	CHN 750
Waldron, Samuel	CAY 538	Walker, James Junr	COL 214	Wallace, Hugh	ORN 285
Waldron, Samuel	NYK 152	Walker, John	ALB 27	Wallace, Hugh	ORN 296
Waldron, Samuel B.	NYK 152	Walker, John	ALB 90	Wallace, James	DUT 106
Waldron, Thomas	NYK 80	Walker, John	CLN 159	Wallace, James	WSH 297
Waldron, William	NYK 152	Walker, John	COL 216	Wallace, Jean	NYK 22
Waldron, Wm	RNS 36	Walker, John	MNT 106	Wallace, John	NYK 109
Waldron, William J.	NYK 49	Walker, John	NYK 51	Wallace, John	OND 163
Waldron, Winant	RNS 36	Walker, John	NYK 83	Wallace, John	ONN 135
Waldrot, Adam J.	MNT 4	Walker, John	NYK 101	Wallace, John	ORN 307
Waldrot, John A.	MNT 4	Walker, John	NYK 151	Wallace, John	RNS 18
Waldrum, Isaac	QNS 81	Walker, John	RNS 21	Wallace, John	WST 125

Name	Ref	Name	Ref	Name	Ref
Wallace, John Junr	RNS 21	Walsh, Joseph	ALB 140	Wamsley, William	NYK 27
Wallace, John 2d	ONN 180	Walsh, Nathaniel	WSH 305	Wandel, Ahasuerus	SRA 23
Wallace, Mary	ALB 136	Walsh, Patrick	ALB 144	Wandel, John	RCH 88
Wallace, Michael	ONN 187	Walsh, Patrick	WSH 304	Wands, Ebenezer	ALB 105
Wallace, Moses	CHN 752	Walsh, Robert	ALB 132	Wands, James	ALB 107
Wallace, Nathl	OTS 38	Walsh, Thomas	ALB 9	Wands, James 2nd	ALB 105
Wallace, Nathaniel	SRA 42	Walsh, Willeam	WSH 264	Wands, John Junr	ALB 105
Wallace, Nehemiah	RNS 50	Walson, Titus	SRA 13	Wands, John Senr	ALB 105
Wallace, Peter	DUT 113	Walsworth, Elisha	OND 210	Wangh, John	NYK 123
Wallace, Robert	NYK 137	Walsworth, Gilbert	DEL 274	Wanmaker, Adolphus	RCK 106
Wallace, Rosannah a		Walsworth, Griswold	RNS 23	Wannamaker, Abrm	RCK 106
mulatto	NYK 22	Walsworth, Jesse	OND 211	Wannamaker, Dirck	RCK 107
Wallace, Rozel	ONN 180	Walsworth, Marey	RNS 23	Wannamaker, Eliza	RCK 106
Wallace, Sally	SUF 104	Walsworth, William(?)	CAY 550	Wannamaker, James	RCK 106
Wallace, Samuel	WST 125	Walsworth, William	OND 211	Wannamaker, Peter	RCK 106
Wallace, Samuel A.	SRA 45	Walsworth, Zacheus	OND 211	Wanser, Abraham	SUF 80
Wallace, Wm	MNT 62	Walt, Henry	DUT 163	Wanser, Daniel	QNS 78
Wallace, William	NYK 51	Walt, Henry Junr	DUT 163	Wanser, David	QNS 72
Wallace, William	ULS 188	Waltemeyer, David	DUT 124	Wanser, Garret	SUF 80
Wallace, William	WST 134	Waltemeyer, George		Wanser, Henry	SUF 80
Wallace, William Peter	DUT 164	the 2d	DUT 124	Wanser, Isaac	DEL 274
Wallan see Wallace		Waltemire, Jacob	COL 198	Wanser, Isaac	MNT 15
		Waltemire, Michael	COL 198	Wanser, Joseph	QNS 66
Wallen, Elisha	CAY 620	Walten, Henry	SRA 15	Wanser, Joseph	QNS 70
Wallen, John	CAY 620	Walter, Charles	NYK 97	Wanser, Mary	QNS 72
Wallen, Sarah	NYK 130	Walter, Ch...ls	ONT 312	Wanser, Sarah	QNS 72
Waller, George	ORN 278	Walter, Christion	MNT 33	Wanser, Thomas	MNT 15
Waller, Joseph	WSH 270	Walter, Daniel	NYK 74	Wanser, Thomas	WST 124
Waller, Samuel	WSH 269	Walter, David	WSH 273	Wansor, Jared	DUT 93
Wallers, Benjamin	SUF 79	Walter, Henry	COL 224	Wanzer, Jacob	QNS 83
Wallett, Nathan	MNT 20	Walter, Henry	DUT 155	Wanzer, .ohn	QNS 84
Walley, Francis	ALB 108	Walter, Hires	COL 202	Wanzer, John	QNS 84
Walley, Garritt	OTS 45	Walter, John	MNT 36	Wanzer, Rebecca	QNS 84
Walley, John	ALB 107	Walter, John G.	ALB 49	Wanzer, Sarah	NYK 132
Walley, John	ORN 359	Walter, Joseph	MNT 119	War..., A__le	MNT 101
Walley, Joseph	ONT 384	Walter, Moses	CHN 906	Warcham, Joseph	COL 187
Wallgrove see Walgrove		Wal.er, S. V.	MNT 102	Ward, Aaron	HRK 545
Wallgrove, George	NYK 96	Walters, Hendrickson	SUF 79	Ward, Abijah	NYK 128
Wallice, Daniel	RNS 50	Walters, James	ONT 338	Ward, Abijah	SCH 130
Wallier, Elijah	RNS 24	Walters, John	QNS 79	Ward, Abraham	DUT 114
Walling, Inman	ORN 327	Walters, John	SUF 79	Ward, Abraham	ORN 281
Walling, James	COL 182	Walters, Peter	QNS 79	Ward, Adams	ESS 306
Walling, James	ORN 324	Walters, Richard		Ward, Alexander	NYK 90
Walling, James Junr	COL 182	Negro	QNS 65	Ward, Alexander	ONN 185
Walling, John	CAY 598	Walters, Seth	SRA 20	Ward, Andrew	MNT 31
Walling, Oliver	ORN 327	Walters, Simeon	QNS 79	Ward, Anthony	DUT 117
Walling, Phillip	NYK 129	Walters, Stephen	QNS 79	Ward, Anthony	SCH 162
Wallingback, John	WST 155	Walton see Watton &		Ward, Barnard	KNG 8
Wallis, Jacob	SRA 25	Wallon		Ward, Bartholomew	WST 118
Wallis, James	SRA 31	Walton, Aaron	CHN 836	Ward, Bela	HRK 572
Wallis, John	SRA 26	Walton, Abraham M.	NYK 28	Ward, Benjamen	WSH 289
Wallis, Joseph	NYK 25	Walton, Andw	OTS 40	Ward, Benjamin	SCH 150
Wallon, Archillus	WSH 266	Walton, Anthony	NYK 153	Ward, Benjamin	WST 158
Walls, James	NYK 89	Walton, Elisha	CAY 714	Ward, Caleb	RNS 41
Walls, John	TIO 248	Walton, Elisha	OTS 42	Ward, Caleb	RCH 94
Walls, Rosel	CHN 958	Walton, Eliza	NYK 91	Ward, Caleb	WST 158
Wallsworth, James	ONT 342	Walton, Gerard	NYK 80	Ward, Caleb Junr	WST 158
Wallsworth, William	OND 196	Walton, Grace	NYK 82	Ward, Catherine	NYK 22
Wallus see Walters		Walton, James	NYK 120	Ward, Chloe	CAY 700
Waln, George	NYK 98	Walton, John	ESS 310	Ward, Chrs	ALB 3
Walradt, Adophs J. B.	OTS 58	Walton, John	OTS 2	Ward, Cumfort	OND 221
Walradt, Jacob	OTS 46	Walton, John	ULS 257	Ward, Daniel	ALB 122
Walradt, Nichs	OTS 58	Walton, Jonathan	ALB 6	Ward, Daniel	DUT 114
Walradt, Peter	OTS 58	Walton, Samuel	RNS 90	Ward, Daniel & Owen	DUT 117
Walrath see Warlrath		Walton, Silas	SUF 74	Ward, Daniel	NYK 128
Walrath, Isaac	MNT 17	Walton, William	NYK 80	Ward, Daniel	NYK 148
Walrath, John A.	MNT 15	Walts, Conrad	MNT 35	Ward, Daniel	OND 214
Walrodt, Henry	HRK 411	Walts, Frederick	ALB 42	Ward, Daniel	ORN 330
Walroth, Peter H.	MNT 9	Walts, Jacob	MNT 35	Ward, Daniel	WSH 279
Walsh see Walch		Waltz, John	ALB 12	Ward, Daniel Junr	DUT 117
Walsh, Dudley	ALB 150	Walutt, Jonathan	MNT 124	Ward, David	CAY 642
Walsh, Hazelton	WSH 265	Walworth, Benjamn	RNS 22	Ward, David	CHN 912
Walsh, Hugh	ORN 283	Waly, Timothy	ONT 438	Ward, Ebenezer	ALB 100
Walsh, James	NYK 131	Wampole, Frederick	ONT 324	Ward, Edward	ALB 59
Walsh, John	CAY 682	Wampough, Coenrad	WST 144	Ward, Elihu	OTS 28
Walsh, John	HRK 418	Wamsley, Alexr	ALB 10	Ward, Elijah	HRK 419
Walsh, John	ULS 251	Wamsley, James	CHN 818	Ward, Elijah	WST 149

Name	Ref
Ward, Elisha	SCH 131
Ward, Ellis	ORN 354
Ward, Ethamore	OND 221
Ward, Ezekiel	ORN 329
Ward, Ezekiel Junr	ORN 330
Ward, George	NYK 106
Ward, Gilbert	WST 165
Ward, Hezekiah	WST 146
Ward, Hosea	WSH 294
Ward, Ichabod Junr	DUT 47
Ward, Ichabod Senr	DUT 48
Ward, Isaac	WST 148
Ward, Israel	WSH 302
Ward, Jacob	DUT 114
Ward, Jacob	OND 206
Ward, Jacob	OND 214
Ward, Jasper	NYK 82
Wa.d, Jeremiah	MNT 89
Ward, Jesse	NYK 57
Ward, John	ALB 58
Ward, John	DUT 110
Ward, John	DUT 114
Ward, John	HRK 505
Ward, John	HRK 545
Ward, John	KNG 9
Ward, John	NYK 81
Ward, John	NYK 108
Ward, John	OND 222
Ward, John	ORN 270
Ward, John	ORN 376
Ward, John	RNS 77
Ward, John	SCH 157
Ward, John	WSH 280
Ward, John Junr	DUT 122
Ward, Jonas	OTS 51
Ward, Jonathan	SRA 24
Ward, Jonathan	SRA 30
Ward, Jonathan	WST 147
Ward, Joseph	HRK 545
Ward, Joseph	MNT 89
Ward, Joseph	SCH 172
Ward, Joshua	ALB 17
Ward, Joshua	DUT 121
Ward, Joshua	NYK 98
Ward, Josiah	DUT 117
Ward, Levi	ONN 171
Ward, Levy	RNS 82
Ward, Lewis	ALB 32
Ward, Margaret	DUT 33
Ward, Mary	NYK 92
Ward, Mary	NYK 104
Ward, Mary	NYK 131
Ward, Mary	SUF 90
Ward, Moses	CHN 818
Ward, Moses	NYK 74
Ward, Moses	WST 171
Ward, Naham	WSH 229
Ward, Nathan	RNS 47
Ward, Nathaniel	NYK 118
Ward, Nichs	TIO 213
Ward, Owen & Daniel	DUT 117
Ward, Peletiah	DUT 48
Ward, Peter	DUT 117
Ward, Peter	HRK 576
Ward, Philip	WST 132
Ward, Rachael	NYK 112
Ward, Reuben	DEL 290
Ward, Richard	ALB 56
Ward, Richard	ORN 273
Ward, Richard	WST 148
Ward, Salman	OND 220
Ward, Samuel	CAY 646
Ward, Samuel	NYK 34
Ward, Samuel	NYK 44
Ward, Samuel	OTS 10
Ward, Saml	SUF 104
Ward, Samuel	WST 171
Ward, Silas	WSH 306
Ward, Simeon	ALB 81
Ward, Solomon	DUT 117
Ward, Stephen	ALB 32
Ward, Stephen	CAY 700
Ward, Stephen	GRN 349
Ward, S...hen	ONT 422
Ward, Thadeus	ONT 368
Ward, Thomas	ALB 96
Ward, Thomas	CAY 520
Ward, Thomas	NYK 40
Ward, Thomas	NYK 136
Ward, Thomas	ORN 270
Ward, Thomas Junr	WST 171
Ward, Uriah	ALB 125
Ward, William	ALB 58
Ward, William	ALB 81
Ward, William	ALB 113
Ward, William	CHN 890
Ward, William	DUT 34
Ward, Wm	MNT 31
Ward, Wm	MNT 66
Ward, William	NYK 66
Ward, William	ORN 270
Ward, William	SCH 136
Ward, William	WST 171
Ward, Zachariah	ONT 460
Ward, Zedok	SCH 129
Wardell, Isaac	CAY 632
Wardell, John	NYK 93
Wardell, Robert	NYK 34
Wardell, Samuel	STB 206
Warden, David	SRA 5
Warden, Gilbert	OTS 4
Warden, Nathaniel	NYK 92
Warden, Solomon	ONT 450
Wardon, Samuel	STB 206
Wards, Mary	NYK 36
Wardwell, Allen	DUT 137
Wardwell, David	ALB 68
Wardwell, Eliakim	DUT 79
Wardwell, Isaac	CAY 684
Wardwell, James	DUT 134
Wardwell, Palmer	DEL 289
Wardwell, William	DEL 285
Ware, James	WSH 206
Wareen, James	SRA 31
Warehouse, John	DUT 147
War_ing, Dennis	NYK 57
Wareing, James	COL 234
Waren see Warren	
Waren, Anson	SRA 42
Waren, Daniel	WST 153
Waren, Gilbert	SRA 42
Waren, Jeremiah Junr	WST 133
Waren, John	SRA 30
Waren, Jonathan	WST 119
Waren, Nelle	SRA 39
Wares, James	RCH 94
Warford, John	WSH 221
Waring see Warring	
Waring, Abraham	ULS 186
Waring, Annenias	WST 136
Waring, Cadwallader	DUT 54
Waring, Danl	RCK 103
Waring, David	WST 136
Waring, Ephraim	DEL 277
Waring, James	ORN 273
Waring, John	DUT 176
Waring, John	NYK 90
Waring, Jonathan	WST 158
Waring, Joshua	WST 136
Waring, Linus	DEL 277
Waring, Samuel	DUT 176
Waring, Silvenus	NYK 140
Waring, Solomon	ULS 234
Waring, Solomon Junr	ULS 260
Waring, Stephen	ULS 218
Warington, James	SRA 11
Wark, John	NYK 82
Warlow, William	NYK 137
Warlrath see Walrath	
Warlrath, Garrat	MNT 33
Warmer, Peter	MNT 37
Warmsley, Christopher	SRA 25
Warne, Benoni	CAY 706
Warne, Cornelius	NYK 57
Warne, Elbert P.	NYK 38
Warne, Jeremiah	NYK 63
Warne, John	CAY 706
Warne, Joseph a mulatto	NYK 75
Warne, Richard	CHN 770
Warne, Thomas	NYK 96
Warner see Worner	
Warner	NYK 127
Warner, Aaaron	WST 146
Warner, Abigail	COL 210
Warner, Abm	ALB 76
Warner, Abm	COL 212
Warner, Amese	CHN 792
Warner, Andrew	HRK 430
Warner, Andrew	OND 180
Warner, Arnold	OND 211
Warner, Asa	DEL 288
Warner, Asel	ONT 368
Warner, Asher	ONT 506
Warner, Austin	ALB 137
Warner, Benajah	MNT 81
Warner, Benjn	SUF 73
Warner, Benjamine	GRN 341
Warner, Buel	RNS 106
Warner, Caleb	HRK 479
Warner, Carman	SCH 157
Warner, Catherine	NYK 107
Warner, Charles	NYK 56
Warner, Charles	SRA 30
Warner, Chris	ALB 75
Warner, Chris Junr	ALB 75
Warner, Christian	NYK 131
Warner, Cyrus	DEL 283
Warner, Daniel	CAY 596
Warner, Daniel	CHN 888
Warner, Daniel	COL 209
Warner, Daniel	ONT 330
Warner, David	ESS 307
Warner, David	OND 206
Warner, David	ONN 130
Warner, David	ONT 352
Warner, David	SCH 150
Warner, David	SCH 152
Warner, David	SCH 172
Warner, David	SUF 73
Warner, Eleazer	OND 180
Warner, Eleazer	OTS 34
Warner, Elihu	OTS 57
Warner, Elihu C.	OTS 57
Warner, Elijah	GRN 341
Warner, Elijah	ONT 482
Warner, Eliphalet	ORN 341
Warner, Elisha	ONT 372
Warner, Enos	DEL 288
Warner, Everar	NYK 21
Warner, Ezra	COL 208
Warner, Gad	OND 172
Warner, Gad	SRA 21
Warner, George	NYK 27
Warner, George	RNS 11
Warner, George Junr	SCH 152
Warner, George J.	NYK 148
Warner, Gideon	DUT 44
Warner, Godfrey	NYK 111
Warner, Hannel	DEL 288
Warner, Henry	ALB 74

Warner, Henry HRK 430
Warner, Hezekia MNT 119
Warner, Jacob COL 245
Warner, Jacob NYK 114
Warner, James CAY 724
Warner, James COL 202
Warner, James NYK 56
Warner, James SUF 71
Warner, James WST 145
Warner, Jane NYK 40
Warner, Jason COL 210
Warner, Jesse CHN 774
Warner, Jesse ONT 482
Warner, Jesse WSH 246
Warner, John ALB 74
Warner, John CHN 888
Warner, John HRK 438
Warner, John NYK 58
Warner, John NYK 90
Warner, John RNS 10
Warner, John RNS 11
Warner, John SRA 53
Warner, John WST 146
Warner, John C. ALB 75
Warner, John J. ALB 75
Warner, Johnathan ONT 354
Warner, Jonathan COL 209
Warner, Joseph NYK 75
Warner, Joseph a Black NYK 120
Warner, Joseph ONN 151
Warner, Joseph SRA 16
Warner, Josiah GRN 331
Warner, Justice GRN 358
Warner, Leonard NYK 107
Warner, Lewis ONT 482
Warner, Lewis QNS 62
Warner, Lupton COL 212
Warner, Martillo MNT 81
Warner, Mathew ONT 368
Warner, Mathias NYK 128
Warner, Mathias Junr ALB 74
Warner, Matthias ALB 74
Warner, Mattice SCH 124
Warner, Moses WST 146
Warner, Nathaniel HRK 542
Warner, Nathl Jun HRK 542
Warner, Nichs SCH 152
Warner, Oliver HRK 514
Warner, Peter ALB 75
Warner, Philip ALB 75
Warner, Philip WSH 187
Warner, Phillip NYK 82
Warner, Rufus ONT 480
Warner, Samuel ALB 21
Warner, Samuel HRK 542
Warner, Samuel OND 214
Warner, Samuel ONT 506
Warner, Samuel OTS 32
Warner, Samuel WSH 247
Warner, Samuel WSH 270
Warner, Seth GRN 340
Warner, Seth GRN 347
Warner, Seth HRK 598
Warner, Seth ONN 130
War[ner?], Seth WSH 285
Warner, Solomon ONT 506
Warner, Stephen HRK 429
Warner, Stephen HRK 480
Warner, Sylvaster WSH 191
Warner, Thomas COL 208
Warner, Thomas DUT 64
Warner, Thomas NYK 57
Warner, Thomas NYK 128
Warner, Thomas OTS 32
Warner, Timothy DUT 134
Warner, Whiting ALB 130

Warner, Willard COL 209
Warner, Willeam WSH 270
Warner, William ONT 330
Warner, William QNS 62
Warner, William WST 147
Warner, Wm J. GRN 331
Warner, William S. ALB 127
Warner, Zebulon ESS 307
Warnerkneese, John NYK 56
Warran, William WSH 265
Warren see Waren
Warren, Aaron CHN 900
Warren, Abner HRK551½
Warren, Abraham CLN 173
Warren, Adam ORN 373
Warren, Adriel HRK 586
Warren, Amor ONT 356
Warren, Anna NYK 41
Warren, Benjm COL 211
Warren, Benjamin ESS 312
Warren, Benjamin OND 166
Warren, Beverly DUT 72
Warren, Caleb WSH 280
Warren, Charles DUT 126
Warren, Daniel DUT 29
Warren, Daniel DUT 74
War[ren?], Daniel ONT 446
Warren, Darius OTS 16
Warren, Ebenezer WSH 287
Warren, Elijah HRK 525
Warren, Elisha HRK 546
Warren, Enock TIO 254
Warren, Enock Jur TIO 254
Warren, Ephraim OND 180
Warren, Francis DUT 113
Warren, Francis WST 150
Warren, Giddeon WSH 287
Warren, Henry RNS 41
Warren, Isaac WSH 265
Warren, Isaiah RNS 93
Warren, Israel WSH 285
Warren, James ALB 149
Warren, James DUT 73
Warren, James DUT 127
Warren, James OTS 48
Warren, James SRA 56
Warren, James WST 158
Warren, Jason COL 186
Warren, Jeremiah WST 133
Warren, Joanna DUT 133
Warren, Joel TIO 218
Warren, John COL 250
Warren, John DEL 285
Warren, John DUT 74
Warren, John OND 198
Warren, John ONT 446
Warren, John RNS 91
Warren, John WSH 208
Warren, John G. NYK 26
Warren, Jonathan RNS 95
Warren, Joshua OND 163
Warren, Lazarus OND 166
Warren, Lemuel ALB 65
Warren, Levi HRK 525
Warren, Levi HRK 532
Warren, Luke HRK 483
Warren, Lyman CLN 173
Warren, Mark NYK 59
Warren, N than ESS 321
Warren, Nathel COL 210
Warren, Nehemiah RNS 70
Warren, Newman ONT 450
Warren, Oliver WSH 241
Warren, Peleg DUT 71
Warren, Perry RNS 42
Warren, Peter DEL 288
Warren, Peter DUT 74

Warren, Peter ULS 257
Warren, Peter WST 133
Warren, Richard a Black NYK 100
Warren, Richard SRA 14
Warren, Samuel DUT 75
Warren, Samuel WSH 265
Warren, Samuel WST 124
Warren, Seth OTS 48
Warren, Stephen DEL 286
Warren, Thomas DEL 271
Warren, Thomas NYK 35
Warren, William ALB 107
Warren, William DEL 267
Warren, William a Black NYK 110
Warren, Zephaniah SRA 18
Warrick, Henry ALB 28
Warrin, Obid WSH 223
Warriner, Israel OND 199
Warriner, Jacob OND 199
Warriner, Nathaniel WSH 279
Warring see Waring
Warring, Albert ALB 70
Warring, Anson OND 210
Warring, Burrel GRN 342
Warring, Johnathan GRN 332
Warring, Stephen GRN 358
Warring, Thaddeus ALB 70
Warring, Wells GRN 332
Warrington, William NYK 75
Warron, Elijah ONT 430
Warshburn see Washburn
Warshburn, Caleb CLN 168
Warterberry, John SUF 92
Warters, Amesa MNT 75
Wartman, Abraham CAY 556
Warts, Henry NYK 95
Wartus, Richard GRN 350
Wartz, George ULS 242
Warvell, George HRK 485
Warvell, George Junr HRK 485
Warvell, William HRK 431
Warwout, John NYK 100
Washball, Joseph NYK 96
Wash an, Zephanh HRK 443
Washben, Zebeck OTS 23
Washbern, Noah SRA 52
Washbern, Robert SRA 52
Washbon, Gale OTS 42
Washbon, Rufus OTS 48
Washbun, Martin WSH 188
Washbun, Nathan WSH 188
Washburn see Warshburn & Woshburn
Washburn, ... WST 171
Washburn, Caleb WST 131
Washburn, Daniel SRA 34
Washburn, Danl SCH 141
Washburn, Daniel WST 171
Washburn, Darius DUT 72
Washburn, David DEL 271
Washburn, Ebenezer DEL 271
Washburn, Ebenezer DEL 271
Washburn, Gertrude ALB 129
Washburn, Isaa RNS 58
Washburn, James DUT 173
Washburn, Jesse WST 171
Washburn, Joel SRA 56
Washburn, John COL 230
Washburn, John WST 129
Washburn, Jonathan DEL 271
Washburn, Jonathan DUT 90
Washburn, Joseph SCH 141
Washburn, Joseph ULS 209
Washburn, Joseph WST 171
Washburn, Joseph WST 171

Name	Ref	Name	Ref	Name	Ref
Washburn, Luther	COL 202	Waterman, John	RNS 92	Waters, Samuel	COL 189
Washburn, Luther	OND 206	Waterman, John	TIO 235	Waters, Samuel	DUT 144
Washburn, Martin	COL 230	Waterman, Leman	ALB 55	Waters, Samuel	MNT 18
Washburn, Miles	MNT 15	Waterman, Luther	CHN 848	Waters, Samuel	WSH 229
Washburn, Miles	SRA 55	Waterman, Oliver	ALB 65	Waters, Sarah	OND 211
Washburn, Nehemiah	DUT 124	Waterman, Peter	OND 211	Waters, Smith	OND 203
Washburn, Ozias	SRA 55	Waterman, Roswell	OTS 51	Waters, Starling	WSH 206
Washburn, Ozias	WST 158	Waterman, Samuel	ALB 53	Waters, Stephen	DUT 129
Washburn, Rachel	COL 202	Waterman, Samuel	OTS 43	Waters, Thomas	NYK 55
Washburn, Reuben	DUT 34	Waterman, Simeon	ALB 140	Waters, Thomas a mulatto	NYK 117
Washburn, Richard	WST 165	Waterman, Simeon	OTS 16	Waters, Thomas	ORN 359
Washburn, Samuel	DUT 168	Waterman, Thoms	TIO 235	Waters, Walter	CAY 534
Washburn, Samuel	SRA 55	Waterman, Uriah	CLN 154	Waters, Walter	TIO 262
Washburn, Samuel	WST 171	Waterman, Walter	OTS 14	Waters, William	CHN 794
Washburn, Seth	COL 193	Waterman, Wm	TIO 235	Waters, William	NYK 118
Washburn, Silas	WST 128	Waterman, Zeb	OTS 53	Waters, William	QNS 64
Washbur., Stephen	RNS 15	Waterman, Zepheniah	ALB 53	Waterson, John	NYK 91
Washburn, Thomas	DEL 271	Waterou, Edward	ONT 380	Waterson, John	SRA 29
Washburn, Timothy	DEL 288	Waters see Watters,		Waterson, Robert	ALB 55
Washburn, William	DEL 272	Warters & Woters		Wates, Thomas	CHN 812
Washburn, William	WST 129	Waters, Aaron	CLN 165	Watham, Caleb	CAY 640
Washburn, Zebulon	DUT 168	Waters, Abner	COL 189	Watkeys, Edward	NYK 47
Washer, Solomon	SRA 48	Waters, Adam	RNS 24	Watkeys, Henry	NYK 27
Washford, Thankford	NYK 112	Waters, Anthony	DUT 119	Watkins, Aaron	ONT 366
Wason, James	ALB 18	Waters, Anthony	WST 122	Watkins, Abel	DEL 269
Wasson, George	ALB 33	Waters, Austen	WSH 276	Watkins, Abel	ORN 347
Wasson, John	ALB 39	Waters, Austin	WSH 305	Watkins, Abel B.	ORN 347
Wasson, John	CHN 768	Waters, Barnabas	ALB 111	Watkins, Abner	ALB 131
Wasson, Thomas	ALB 40	Waters, Benjamin	OND 174	Watkins, Charles	NYK 24
Wasson, Thomas	CHN 768	Waters, Benjamin	ONT 468	Watkins, David	CAY 608
Wa[stcoa?]t, Marvil	WST 171	Waters, Bigelow	CHN 798	Watkins, David	MNT 108
Wat, Samuel	NYK 79	Waters, Ca_sar a Black	NYK 22	Watkins, Ebenezer	HRK 466
Wat__s, Josiah	ONT 380	Waters, Da___	MNT 14	Watkins, Edmund	ALB 71
Water, John	NYK 104	Waters, David	ALB 148	Watkins, Henry	CAY 646
Waterberry see Warter-		Waters, Dick Negro	QNS 63	Watkins, Henry Junr	CAY 648
berry		Waters, Dolly	NYK 118	Watkins, Hezekiah	SRA 25
Waterberry, Mary(?)	ESS 303	Waters, Elijah	OND 174	Watkins, Isaac	ONT 336
Waterbery, David	RNS112A	Waters, Elisha	WSH 247	Watkins, Jedediah	ONT 370
Waterbery, David Junr	RNS 54	Waters, Gerret	NYK 78	Watkins, Jo..	TIO 251
Waterbery, Ezra	RNS112A	Waters, Gideon	OTS 39	Watkins, Joel	ONT 336
Waterbery, John	RNS 112	Waters, Henry	HRK 543	Watkins, John	WSH 300
Waterbery, Jonathan	RNS 57	Waters, Henry	QNS 74	Watkins, Joseph	NYK 149
Waterbery, Joseph	RNS 57	Waters, Henry	WST 132	Watkins(?), Josiah	CAY 650
Waterbery, Saml	RNS 112	Waters, Hial	CHN 852	Watkins, Lydia	NYK 153
Waterburry, Gideon	NYK 77	Waters, Isaac	DUT 148	Watkins, Mark	HRK 580
Waterburry, Israel	NYK 58	Waters, Isaac	WSH 191	Watkins, Nathan	ONT 336
Waterburry, John	WST 159	Waters, Israel	RNS 82	Watkins, Nathan Junr	ONT 334
Waterburry, Josiah	WST 157	Waters, Jacob	DUT 144	Watkins, Robert	DEL 287
Waterburry, Samuel		Waters, James	CAY 534	Watkins, Roger	ONT 448
Junr	WST 159	Waters, James a Black	NYK 150	Watkins, Samuel	NYK 80
Waterburry, Squire	WST 158	Waters, James	QNS 67	Watkins, Samuel	ORN 311
Waterbury, Enos	OND 214	Waters, James	QNS 74	Watkins, Sarah	ALB 132
Waterbury, Henry	NYK 130	Waters, Jane	NYK 36	Watkins, Stephen	ONT 336
Waterbury, Holly	NYK 130	Waters, John	COL 216	Watkins, Thomas	ORN 344
Waterbury, Jona	OTS 13	Waters, John	DUT 144	Watkins, Widow	HRK 587
Waterbury, Peter C.	NYK 31	Waters, John	KNG 7	Watkins, William	ALB 113
Waterbury, William	SRA 42	Waters, John	OND 178	Watkins, William	COL 219
Waterhouse, Eleazer	OTS 22	Waters, John	ONN 183	Watkins, William	ONT 336
Waterman, Anson	CLN 160	Waters, John	QNS 61	Watley, John	OND 160
Waterman, Asa	SRA 14	Waters, John	QNS 63	Watrous, Elisha	SRA 10
Waterman, Asa Junr	SRA 14	Waters, John	QNS 79	Watrous, John	SRA 44
Waterman, Basset B.	DEL 282	Waters, John	RNS 49	Wats, Aaron	NYK 145
Waterman, Calvin	CAY 644	Waters, John	SUF 68	Watson see Wotson	
Waterman, Charles	COL 263	Waters, John Junr	QNS 79	Watson, Aaron	CAY 638
Waterman, Chester	ONN 137	Waters, Joseph	CHN 868	Watson, Abraham	NYK 93
Waterman, Darius	COL 263	Waters, Joseph	DEL 280	Watson, Alexr	ALB 6
Waterman, Darius Junr	COL 263	Waters, Leonard	OND 174	Watson, Alexander	HRK 426
Waterman, David	OTS 15	Waters, Mary	DUT 27	Watson, Archabald	WSH 194
Waterman, David	OTS 16	Waters, Moses	OND 222	Watson, Benjamin	ALB 83
Waterman, Ebenezer	RNS 109	Waters, Moses	TIO 218	Watson(?), Benjamin	ESS 310
Waterman, Elijah	COL 193	Waters, Nathaniel	HRK 593	Watson, Benjamin	NYK 77
Waterman, Elijah	OTS 51	Waters, Nathaniel	MNT 75	Watson, Betsey	NYK 44
Waterman, Henry	MNT 113	Waters, Peter	ULS 252	Watson, Caleb	SRA 41
Waterman, Jedediah	NYK 81	Waters, Robert	DUT 138	Watson, Catherine	NYK 90
Waterman, Jesse	COL 203	Waters, Samuel	CHN 794	Watson, Christopher	WSH 193
Waterman, John	NYK 63			Watson, Danl	OTS 32
Waterman, John	OTS 16				

Watson, Ebenezer	OND 194	
Watson, Elizabeth	NYK 72	
Watson, Elkanah	ALB 133	
Watson, Ephraim	SRA 46	
Watson, George	SCH 152	
Watson, George	SCH 157	
Watson, George	ULS 267	
Watson, George Jun	SCH 152	
Watson, George Jr	SCH 157	
Watson, Hezekiah	ALB 85	
Watson, James	NYK 16	
Watson, James	NYK 45	
Watson, James	ONN 162	
Watson, James	SCH 157	
Watson, James Junr	NYK 18	
Watson, Jesse	ESS 308	
Watson, John	CAY 638	
Watson, John	NYK 15	
Watson, John	NYK 68	
Watson, John	NYK 78	
Watson, John	ONN 161	
Watson, John	WSH 187	
Watson, John	WSH 224	
Watson, Joseph	WSH 251	
Watson, Josiah	ALB 84	
Watson, Jude	HRK 566	
Watson, Margaret	NYK 47	
Watson, Nancy	NYK 22	
Watson, Nancy	OND 171	
Watson, Nathan	HRK 565	
Watson, Phillip	NYK 117	
Watson, Reubin	GRN 341	
Watson, Robert	NYK 82	
Watson, Royal	OTS 32	
Watson, Samuel	HRK 580	
Watson, Stephen	ALB 86	
Watson, Susanna	ORN 292	
Watson, Thomas	ALB 84	
Watson, Thomas	ALB 131	
Watson, Thomas	COL 179	
Watson, Thomas	ONT 468	
Watson, Titus	SRA 13	
Watson, Wheelar	ALB 84	
Watson, William	DEL 267	
Watson, William	NYK 37	
Watson, William	ONN 135	
Watt, Joseph	CAY 620	
Watt, Robert	NYK 107	
Watters see Waters		
Watters, Joseph	OTS 49	
Wattles, Belcher	HRK 427	
Wattles, Belcher	HRK 476	
Wattles, Charles	OTS 25	
Wattles, Dan	DEL 280	
Wattles, David	OTS 16	
Wattles, Fitch	STB 202	
Wattles, George	NYK 35	
Wattles, James	OTS 25	
Wattles, Jehial	CHN 844	
Wattles, John	DEL 281	
Wattles, Mason	WST 158	
Wattles, Roger	DEL 281	
Wattles, Mrs Ruth	DEL 280	
Wattles, Samuel	WST 160	
Wattles, Sluman	DEL 280	
Wattles, Sluman Junr	DEL 280	
Wattles, William	CAY 674	
Watton, George	NYK 119	
Watts see Wats		
Watts, Ann	QNS 72	
Watts, Clemmons	QNS 76	
Watts, David	QNS 76	
Watts, Elizabeth	DUT 168	
W_tts, Francis	MNT 35	
Watts, George	ORN 284	
Watts, George	QNS 73	
Watts, Hannah	QNS 72	
Watts, Isaac	RNS 111	
Watts, James	NYK 29	
Watts, Janet	ORN 283	
Watts, John (possibly Jehu)	DUT 169	
Watts, John	ONT 320	
Watts, John	QNS 72	
Watts, John	QNS 76	
Watts, Nicholas	MNT 107	
Watts, Robert	NYK 17	
Watts, Robert	NYK 146	
Watts, Robert	ORN 288	
Watts, Robert	WST 147	
Watts, Simeon	QNS 65	
Watts, Thos	OTS 2	
Watts, William	NYK 74	
Watts, William	NYK 77	
Watts, William	ORN 354	
Waugh, Alexander	OND 209	
Waugh, Dan	OND 209	
Waugh, Elijah	OND 213	
Waugh, Normon	OND 209	
Waugh, Robert	ORN 277	
Waugh, Thomas	ALB 64	
Waught, Asa	NYK 66	
Waught, James	NYK 130	
Wawford, Thomas	SRA 15	
Way see Wey		
Way, Abel	HRK 592	
Way, Amelia	NYK 70	
Way, Asa	ONN 164	
Way, Barick	OTS 56	
Way, Benjamin J.	DUT 29	
Way, David	DEL 279	
Way, David	GRN 333	
Way, David	SRA 11	
Way, Francis	RNS 84	
Way, George	RNS 85	
Way, Hilleche	RNS 89	
Way, James	DUT 104	
Way, James	NYK 70	
Way, James Junr	DUT 103	
Way, Joanna	DUT 27	
Way, John	NYK 129	
Way, John	NYK 137	
Way, John	OND 179	
Way, John	RNS 10	
Way, Joshua	ONT 460	
Way, Josiah	ESS 321	
Way, Laurence	DUT 93	
Way, Nathl	SUF 77	
Way, Philemon	ORN 312	
Way, Rufus	COL 194	
Way, Samuel	NYK 138	
Way, Saml	OTS 55	
Way, Selah	OND 179	
Way, Sterling	OTS 56	
Way, Thadeus	OND 209	
Way, Thomas	DUT 27	
Way, Thomas	QNS 62	
Way, William Junr	DUT 23	
Way, William Senr	DUT 22	
Waydell, John	NYK 124	
Wayland, Francis	NYK 66	
Wayley, Alexander	KNG 10	
Wayley, Benjamin	QNS 82	
Wayman	GRN 330	
Waymon, Horris	CHN 874	
Wayne see Wain		
Wayne, Anthony	ALB 105	
Wead see Weed		
Wead, Asa	ALB 23	
Wead, David	SRA 59	
Wead, Eli	SRA 59	
Wead, Jonathan	SRA 59	
Wead, Noah	SRA 59	
Wead, William	OND 206	
Wead, [Z?]eadad_ach	GRN 344	
Weager, Henry	OND 206	
Weakman see Weekman		
Weakman, Hiel	CHN 750	
Weaks see Weekes		
Weaks, William	SRA 41	
Wealthy, Jacob	ORN 301	
Wealy, Robert	QNS 74	
Wear see Were		
Wear, William	ORN 275	
Weares, George	ULS 217	
Wearing, John	NYK 112	
Wearing, Solomon	OND 211	
Wearing, Thomas	NYK 21	
Wearing, .alantine	MNT 56	
Wearly, Peter	ALB 66	
Weast, Abrm	OTS 11	
Weatherax see Wether-wax		
Weatherax, William	DEL 279	
Weatherby see Wetherby & Wheatherly		
Weatherby, Hezekiah	WSH 214	
Weatherby, John	CHN 910	
Weatherby, John	RNS 106	
Weatherby, John Junr	WSH 218	
Weatherby, Lucius	HRK 505	
Weatherby, Oliver	WSH 217	
Weatherby, Richard	WSH 218	
Weatherhead, Edmund	SRA 47	
Weatherill, William	NYK 19	
Weatherington, Samuel	WSH 226	
Weathersine, John N.	NYK 108	
Weatherstone, John	HRK 446	
Weatherwicks, Andries Jr	ALB 106	
Weaver see Weever, Wever & Whever		
Weaver, Aandrew	WSH 203	
Weaver, Adam	COL 231	
Weaver, Asa	CHN 776	
Weaver, Benjamin	ALB 15	
Weaver, Benjn	OTS 20	
Weaver, Caleb	SRA 59	
Weaver, Christian	SCH 119	
Weaver, Christopher	DUT 153	
Weaver, Daniel	MNT 3	
Weaver, David	DUT 67	
Weaver, Edward	SRA 8	
Weaver, Elijah	CHN 776	
Weaver, Elizabeth	ALB 46	
Weaver, Frederick	NYK 138	
Weaver, George	RNS 78	
Weaver, Harris	RNS 19	
Weaver, Harry	DUT 144	
Weaver, Henderick	ALB 49	
Weaver, Hendrick	COL 243	
Weaver, Hendrick Junr	COL 242	
Weaver, Henry	ALB 26	
Weaver, Henry	ALB 49	
Weaver, Henry	DUT 152	
Weaver, Henry	SCH 119	
Weaver, Henry A.	COL 237	
Weaver, Hercules	ALB 49	
Weaver, Jacob	ALB 52	
Weaver, Jacob	COL 243	
Weaver, Jacob	NYK 79	
Weaver, Jacob	SCH 126	
Weaver, Jacob G.	MNT 12	
Weaver, Jane	NYK 44	
Weaver, Johannis	ULS 218	
Weaver, John	ALB 56	
Weaver, John	ALB 80	
Weaver, John	COL 223	
Weaver, John	COL 241	
Weaver, John	DUT 15	
Weaver, John	DUT 34	

Name	Loc	Name	Loc	Name	Loc
Wedden, Jonathan	NYK 112	Weekes, Amos	GRN 349	Weeks, Jacob	HRK 493
Weddle, William	DUT 140	Weekes, Ebenezar	SUF 90	Weeks, Jacob	NYK 114
Wedell, John	NYK 40	Weekes, Henry	GRN 350	Weeks, Jacob	QNS 70
Weden, Richard	RNS 40	Weekes, George	DUT 120	Weeks, Jacob	RNS 91
Weder, Peter	RNS 11	Weekes, Holly	ULS 223	Weeks, Jacob	SRA 38
Weder, Peter	RNS 90	Weekes, Jacob	DUT 120	Weeks, James	DUT 36
Wederwax see Wetherwax		Weekes, Jonas	SUF 94	Weeks, James	NYK 45
Wederwax, Abraham	DUT 157	Weekes, Jonus	SUF 76	Weeks, James	NYK 116
Wedfell, Christian	SRA 21	Weekes, Levi	MNT 28	Weeks, James	RNS 35
Wedge, David	HRK 538	Weekes, Moses	SUF 70	Weeks, James	WST 129
Wedge, Joseph	COL 219	Weekes, Peter	SUF 80	Weeks, James	WST 131
Wedge, Oliver	HRK 539	Weekes, Richard	SUF 94	Weeks, James Junr	WST 128
Wedge, Thomas	COL 209	Weekes, Silas	DUT 147	Weeks, Jemima	DUT 75
Wedger, John	ALB 30	Weekman see Weakman		Weeks, Jesine	QNS 83
Wedger, Samuel	ALB 30	Weekman, Abraham	MNT 94	Weeks, Jessee	SUF 81
Wedger, Samuel Junr	ALB 30	Weeks, Abel	WST 151	Weeks, Job	RNS 30
Wedman, Andrew	NYK 40	Weeks, Abel Junr	WST 151	Weeks, John	CAY 602
Weech, Abraham	ULS 236	Weeks, Abraham	NYK 138	Weeks, John	HRK 543
Weed see Meed & Wead		Weeks, Abraham	WST 132	Weeks, John	NYK 116
Weed	GRN 344	Weeks, Andrew	COL 229	Weeks, John	NYK 133
Weed, Abraham	SRA 51	Weeks, Ann	QNS 82	Weeks, John	QNS 74
Weed, Alanson	CAY 724	Weeks, Ann	QNS 82	Weeks, John	QNS 79
Weed, Alexander	CAY 642	Weeks, Anthony	NYK 139	Weeks, John	QNS 83
Weed, Asa	DUT 50	Weeks, Artemus	RNS 80	Weeks, John	SUF 86
Weed, Azariah	OTS 6	Weeks, Benjamin	ONT 316	Weeks, John	SUF 92
Weed, Charles	OND 214	Weeks, Benjamin	WST 113	Weeks, John	WST 130
Weed, Daniel	WST 159	Weeks, Benjamin	WST 122	Weeks, John	WST 131
Weed, David	ULS 262	Weeks, Benjamin	WST 124	Weeks, John	WST 171
Weed, Elijah	ONN 131	Weeks, Caleb	WST 127	Weeks, John Junior	WST 131
Weed, Elnathan	WST 159	Weeks, Charles	QNS 83	Weeks, Jonas	SUF 81
Weed, Enos	WST 124	Weeks, Chauncy	DUT 29	Weeks, Jonas	SUF 85
We_d, Ezra	ONT 410	Weeks, Daniel	QNS 71	Weeks, Joseph	SRA 51
Weed, Ezra	SRA 59	Weeks, Daniel	QNS 79	Weeks, Joseph	WST 151
Weed, Frederick	SRA 60	Weeks, Daniel	QNS 79	Weeks, Joshua	WST 151
Weed, Gilbert	CAY 724	Weeks, Daniel	SRA 48	Weeks, Jotham	QNS 80
Weed, Gilbert	SRA 18	Weeks, Daniel	SUF 93	Weeks, Jotham Junr	QNS 80
Weed, Gilbert Junr	CAY 724	Weeks, Daniel	WST 127	Weeks, Lemuel	SUF 85
Weed, Ichabod	SRA 18	Weeks, David	DUT 25	Weeks, Lewis	SUF 92
Weed, Ithamar	DUT 172	Weeks, David	SRA 36	Weeks, Mallica	WST 171
Weed, Jacob	SRA 19	Weeks, David	SUF 83	Weeks, Micajah	ORN 274
Weed, James	CAY 724	Weeks, David	WST 129	Weeks, Moses	SUF 89
Weed, James	DEL 277	Weeks, Ebenezer	OND 214	Weeks, Nathaniel a Black	NYK 111
Weed, James	NYK 130	Weeks, Edmond	QNS 79		
Weed, James Junr	DEL 277	Weeks, Edward	OND 194	Weeks, Nathaniel	SUF 85
Weed, Jared	SRA 19	Weeks, Elijah	ALB 87	Weeks, Nathaniel	WST 141
Weed, Jeremiah	GRN 338	Weeks, Elijah Junr	ALB 87	Weeks, Obadiah	RNS 95
Weed, Joel	GRN 329	Weeks, Eliphalet	QNS 66	Weeks, Oliver	QNS 80
Weed, John	DUT 172	Weeks, Elizabeth	QNS 84	Weeks, Peen	QNS 63
Weed, John	ORN 339	Weeks, Enoch	QNS 78	Weeks, Penn	SUF 81
Weed, John	SRA 38	Weeks, Enoch	SUF 82	Weeks, Peter	COL 236
Weed, John	SRA 58	Weeks, Ezekiel	SUF 83	Weeks, Peter	SUF 81
Weed, Jonas	DEL 268	Weeks, Ezra	NYK 100	Weeks, Phebe	NYK 135
Weed, Jonas	OND 188	Weeks, Ezra	SUF 93	Weeks, Reuben	NYK 125
Weed, Jonathan	DEL 281	Weeks, Francis	WST 129	Weeks, Richard	DUT 30
Weed, Jonathan	SRA 18	Weeks, George	DUT 75	Weeks, Richard	QNS 71
Weed, Joseph	ALB 43	Weeks, George	KNG 10	Weeks, Richard	QNS 82
Weed, Joseph	GRN 329	Weeks, George	NYK 79	Weeks, Richard	SUF 93
Weed, Josiah S.	SRA 56	Weeks, George	QNS 78	Weeks, Richard	WST 132
Weed, Justis	ALB 115	Weeks, George	QNS 81	Weeks, Richard	WST 151
Weed, Justus	DUT 170	Weeks, George	SUF 81	Weeks, Robert	DUT 89
Weed, Nathan	GRN 343	Weeks, Gideon	RNS 35	Weeks, Robert	NYK 134
Weed, Nathl	OTS 44	Weeks, Gilbert	DUT 35	Weeks, Ruth	NYK 62
Weed, Peter	SRA 19	Weeks, Gilbert	DUT 39	Weeks, Samuel	QNS 81
Weed, Phenias	SRA 12	Weeks, Gilbert	DUT 79	Weeks, Samuel	QNS 82
Weed, Reuben	SRA 58	Weeks, Gilbert	SUF 85	Weeks, Samuel	SUF 85
Weed, Reuben Junr	SRA 19	Weeks, Gilbert	SUF 89	Weeks, Samuel	SUF 94
Weed, Samuel	NYK 104	Weeks, Gilbert	WST 153	Weeks, Samuel Junr	SUF 85
Weed, Samuel	ORN 277	Weeks, Henry	GRN 350	Weeks, Seth	SUF 91
Weed, William	CAY 660	Weeks, Henry	WST 154	Weeks, Shubael	DUT 133
Weed, William	WSH 214	Weeks, Hezekiah	DUT 71	Weeks, Silas	OND 214
Weed, Youngs	NYK 126	Weeks, Ichabod	SUF 82	Weeks, Silas	RNS 95
Weeden, Francis	CHN 878	Weeks, Isaac	NYK 88	Weeks, Silas	SUF 85
Weeden, Thomas	ORN 378	Weeks, Isaac	QNS 79	Weeks, Simeon(?)	SRA 28
Weeden, William J.	ORN 378	Weeks, Isaac Junr	QNS 79	Weeks, Simon	WST 165
Weeker, Phillip	NYK 124	Weeks, Israel	WST 129	Weeks, Smith	WST 130
Weekes see Weaks		Weeks, Israel	WST 131	Weeks, Solomon	DUT 36
Weekes, Alexander	SUF 82	Weeks, Israel P.	ALB 87	Weeks, Stephen	CHN 762

Name	Loc	Name	Loc	Name	Loc
Weeks, Stephen	NYK 126	Welch, Ebenezer	CHN 780	Weller, Henry	ORN 302
Weeks, Stephen	NYK 133	Welch, Ebenr	OTS 36	Weller, Henry P.	ORN 297
Weeks, Stephen	SRA 23	Welch, Elizabeth	NYK 132	Weller, Hieronimus	ORN 307
Weeks, Stephen	ULS 182	Welch, Ellenor	NYK 144	Weller, Hiram	ORN 294
Weeks, Stephen	WST 130	Welch, Ezekiel	OTS 38	Weller, Jacob	ORN 298
Weeks, Stephen	WST 156	Welch, George	MNT 82	Weller, Jacob Junr	ORN 298
Weeks, Stephen C.	ONN 186	Welch, George	NYK 64	Weller, James	ORN 305
Weeks, Sussanah	RNS 91	Welch, George	NYK 80	Weller, Joel	DUT 132
Weeks, Thomas	ONN 186	Welch, Jabin	MNT 49	Weller, John	ORN 307
Weeks, Thomas	ORN 389	Welch, Jacob	STB 207	Weller, John	ULS 253
Weeks, Thomas	QNS 73	Welch, James	CLN 166	Weller, John Junr	ULS 253
Weeks, Townsend	QNS 84	Welch, James	COL 222	Weller, Jonathan	DUT 99
Weeks, Townsend	QNS 84	Welch, James	NYK 113	Weller, Peter	ULS 245
Weeks, Tunis	KNG 7	Welch, Jeremiah	COL 261	Weller, Robert	ALB 38
Weeks, Webb	QNS 84	Welch, Job	CHN 824	Weller, William	ALB 38
Weeks, Willett	QNS 84	Welch, John	CHN 784	Weller, William W.	ORN 295
Weeks, William	DUT 140	Welch, John	NYK 55	Welles, Benjamin	ORN 364
Weeks, William	NYK 132	Welch, John	NYK 67	Welles, Cornelius	ULS 221
Weeks, William	QNS 73	Welch, John	OND 194	Welles, David	COL 207
Weeks, William	QNS 81	Welch, John	OTS 14	Welles, Eleazer	COL 194
Weeks, William	WST 128	Welch, John	RNS 23	Welles, Elijah	COL 177
Weeks, William	WST 130	Welch, John	SRA 45	Welles, Elijah	COL 204
Weeks, William	WST 158	Welch, Joseph	SRA 39	Welles, Elijah	ORN 328
Weeks, Zadoc	CAY 602	Welch, Mary	NYK 29	Welles, Elisha	COL 254
Weeks, Zebulon	SUF 96	Welch, Mathew	NYK 64	Welles, Gershom	ORN 378
Weeks, Zeno	NYK 153	Welch, Nathaniel	OND 178	Welles, Henry	ULS 221
Weeks, Zophar	ULS 233	Welch, Patty	NYK 77	Welles, Hezekiah	COL 177
Weekwire see Wickwire		Welch, Richard	ONT 358	Welles, John	COL 177
Weekwire, Jerret	CHN 888	Welch, Samuel	CHN 784	Welles, John Junr	COL 179
Weeler see Wheeler		Welch, Vine	OTS 12	Welles, Joseph	COL 177
Weeler, George	SUF 90	Welch, Walter	OTS 36	Welles, Joshua	ORN 358
Weells, Caleb	SUF 96	Welch, Wm	MNT 82	Welles, Joshua	ORN 371
Weells, Cleaves	SUF 71	Welch, William	NYK 129	Welles, Joshua Junr	ORN 317
Weesmer, William	COL 237	Welch, William	NYK 138	Welles, Levi	COL 177
Weever see Weaver		Welch, William	WST 122	Welles, Nathaniel	ORN 333
Weever, Christr	OTS 28	Welcher, Aaron	ONT 486	Welles, Nathaniel G.	ORN 330
Weever, John	CHN 776	Welcher, John	ONT 486	Welles, Noah	ULS 228
Weever, Thos	OTS 28	Welcox see Wilcocks &		Welles, Peter	ULS 240
Weible, Coonradt	ORN 383	Willcox		Welles, Richard	ORN 328
Weidman, Jacob Junr	ALB 69	Welcox, Benjamin	MNT 22	Welles, Samuel	ORN 336
Weigher, Johannis	ULS 200	Weld, Isaac	OND 197	Welles, William	ORN 321
Weigher, John	DUT 165	Weld, William	CHN 862	Wellestone, Consider	OND 221
Weigher, Michael	DUT 165	Welden, Abraham	SRA 4	Wellett, Martinus	MNT 101
Weight see Waight & Wait		Welden, Abraham	SRA 7	Wellett, Taylor	NYK 130
Weight, Derastus	WSH 187	Welden, Benjamin	CLN 158	Wellham, Catherine	NYK 53
Weight, Stephen	WSH 197	Welden, David	CLN 171	Welling, Ezekiel	DUT 121
Weilds, George	MNT 3	Welden, David	SUF 7	Welling, Frederick	ORN 289
Weir see Were, Wear & Wier		Welden, Edmond	RNS 53	Welling, John	ORN 376
Weir, George	NYK 54	Welden, James	SRA 7	Welling, John	QNS 67
Weir, Jesse	ONT 310	Welden, Jonathan	DEL 268	Welling, Josiah	DUT 129
Weir, Thomas	WSH 183	Welden, Peter	SRA 7	Welling, Peter	ORN 290
Weisenfels, Rhoda	NYK 50	Welden, William	NYK 94	Welling, Richard	ORN 376
Weiser see Wiser & Wizer		Weldier, David	ALB 96	Welling, Thomas	DUT 121
Weiser, George	SUF 89	Weldin, James	SRA 4	Welling, William	ORN 352
Weismer, Peter	COL 196	Weldin, Simon	RNS 53	Welling, Thomas	ORN 374
Weist, Conradt	ALB 26	Welding, Isaac	ULS 193	Wellis, Asa	RNS 66
Weist, Gideon	DEL 278	Welding, James	CLN 158	Wellman see Welman	
Wejet, John	SRA 40	Weldon, Francis	OTS 57	Wellman, Joel	OND 164
Welb, Peter	GRN 344	Weldon, Jonathan	ONT 338	Wellman, John	DEL 280
Welch see Welsh		Weldon, Obed	ALB 129	Wellman, Josiah	ONN 186
Welch, Aaron	CHN 782	Weldon, William	OTS 58	Wellmarth, Isaac	OND 196
Welch, Abraham	COL 186	Weley, Abraham	MNT 48	Wells see Welles & Wels	
Welch, Abm	RNS 59	Weley, James	MNT 93	Wells, Abner	CHN 740
Welch, Ann	OTS 36	Weley, James	RNS 46	Wells, Abner	TIO 261
Welch, Anna	NYK 144	Welhelmer, Fero	MNT 99	Wells, Aleijah	NYK 93
Welch, Beldad	CHN 784	Welkie, Lydia	ALB 11	Wells, Arnold	OND 158
Welch, Benjamin	SRA 39	Well, Ebunezer	RNS 94	Wells, Azan	OND 210
Welch, Bildad	OTS 22	Well, John a milatto	NYK 49	Wells, Bak.man	SRA 22
Welch, Caleb	NYK 18	Wellar, Elijah	ONT 404	Wells, Barker	CHN 818
Welch, Charles	CHN 826	Wellcox, Isaac	MNT 50	Wells, Benajah	WSH 204
Welch, Charles Jur	CHN 826	Weller, Abel	WSH 283	Wells, Benjamen	WSH 268
Welch, Cornelius	NYK 144	Weller, Absalom	ORN 338	Wells, Benjamen	WSH 291
Welch, David	CHN 754	Weller, Andrew	ORN 297	Wells, Benjamin	CLN 158
Welch, David	CHN 784	Weller, Daniel	WSH 303	Wells, Benjamin	ONT 430
		Weller, Eleanor	ORN 296	Wells, Benjn	OTS 30
		Weller, Frederick	MNT 44	Wells, Benjn	RNS 112
		Weller, Frederick	ORN 294	Wells, Benjamin	SRA 39

Wendell, John J.	ALB 125	Wesson, William	ONT 392	West, Samuel	WSH 287
Wendell, John W.	ALB 134	West, Aaron	DEL 289	West, Samuel	WSH 302
Wendell, Mary	ALB 135	West, Abiel	ONT 496	West, Seabury	HRK 586
Wendell, Philip	ALB 124	West, Abraham	CHN 802	West, Seth	WSH 191
Wendell, Philip	RNS 5	West, Agnes	NYK 29	West, Simon	HRK 522
Wendell, Rhoda	COL 227	West, Alderman	DUT 57	West, Stephen	HRK 522
Wendell, Samuel	ORN 271	West, Amos	WSH 279	West, Stephen	SRA 28
Wendell, William	ORN 272	West, Anthony	TIO 222	West, Stephen	SRA 38
Wendicker see Wendecker		West, Antony	GRN 357	West, Stephen	SCH 141
Wendicker, John	MNT 53	West, Asa	DEL 283	West, Temperance	DUT 48
Wendicker, Thomas	MNT 53	West, Asor	SRA 29	West, Thomas	CHN 858
Wendol, Abraham E.	CHN 956	West, Barret	OND 194	West, Thomas	OND 167
Wendoll, John	NYK 55	West, Benajah	COL 210	West, Thomas	QNS 79
Wendover see Windover		West, Benjamin	ALB 31	West, Thomas	RNS 76
& Vendover		West, Benjamin	CHN 770	West, Timothy	CAY 672
Wendover, Elizabeth	NYK 103	West, Benjamin	RNS 76	West, Timothy	CAY 676
Wendover, John	ALB 79	West, Besael Junr	WSH 208	West, Tobias	DUT 104
Wendover, Stephen	COL 257	West, Caleb	WSH 279	West, Whitney	SUF 69
Wendover, Thomas	ALB 119	West, Charles	DUT 57	West, William	ALB 85
Wendover, William	WST 144	West, Christopher	WSH 279	West, William	ALB 91
Wendowman, Nichs	ALB 80	West, Corns	ALB 91	West, William	CHN 788
Wenman, Bernard	NYK 54	West, Daniel	WSH 287	West, William	OND 211
Wenman, Evert	NYK 54	West, David	COL 180	West, Wm	RNS 66
Wenman, Richard	NYK 100	West, David	DUT 106	West, William	SRA 44
Wennow, Daniel	WSH 241	West, David	NYK 114	West, William B.	WSH 208
Wenshel see Winchel		West, Ebenezer	WSH 287	West, Williston	OND 193
Wenshel, Job	WSH 209	West, Edward a		Westall, George	RNS 30
Wenshell, Justus	WSH 244	mulatto	NYK 49	Westar, John a Black	NYK 132
Wensor, Abraham	WST 151	West, Elisha	ALB 84	Westbrook, Abraham	ONT 488
Went, Christopher	NYK 111	West, Elisha	DUT 128	Westbrook, James	ONT 450
Went, Court	NYK 69	West, Eni	SCH 157	Westbrook, John	TIO 254
Wenton, James	NYK 139	West, Francis	RNS 66	Westbrook, Sam	TIO 254
Wentworth, Joseph	NYK 55	West, Francis	SRA 44	Westbrouck, Abraham	ULS 187
Wentworth, Alphs	OTS 10	West, Francis	SRA 44	Westbrouck, Dirck	ULS 215
Wentworth, Ezekiel	DUT 89	West, Francis Junr	RNS 66	Westbrouck, Frederick	ULS 214
Wentworth, Frederick	ULS 192	West, George	NYK 79	Westbrouck, Gideon	ORN 315
Wentworth, Isaac	COL 227	West, George	SRA 28	Westbrouck, Jonathan	ULS 214
Wentworth, James	WSH 282	West, Heman	WSH 279	Westcoat see Wastcoat
Wentworth, Jonah W.	SUF 102	West, Ichabod	RNS 25	& Wescoat
Wentworth, Lydia	NYK 32	West, Jabez	COL 217	Westcoat, Danl	OTS 16
Wenworth, John	MNT 14	West, James	DUT 34	Westcoat, Ezekiel	OTS 51
Were see Weir		West, James	DUT 104	Westcoat, James	OTS 27
Were, John	WSH 196	West, James	NYK 54	Westcoat, Oliver	OTS 51
Werter, Nerman	MNT 123	West, James	NYK 125	Westcoat, Warner	OTS 15
Werth see Worth		West, James	SUF 87	Westcot see Wescot	NYK 91
Werth, Jacob	SCH 118	West, James [1st?]	RNS 74	Westcot, Annaias	NYK 91
Werth, John	SCH 118	West, James 2nd	RNS 66	Westcot, Anthony	DUT 176
Werth, John Jacob	NYK 17	West, John	CAY 690	Westcot, Benedict	COL 219
Werts, Joshua	NYK 144	West, John	CHN 770	Westcot, Benjn	OTS 45
Werts, William	NYK 146	West, John	NYK 20	Westcot, Caleb	DUT 36
Wescoat see Westcoat		West, John	NYK 61	Westcot, David M.	ORN 356
Wescoat, Abraham	WST 139	West, John	NYK 112	Westcot, Elenor	NYK 39
Wescoat, Elisabeth	WST 139	West, John	NYK 112	Westcot, John	OND 211
Wescoat, Israel	WST 125	West, John	NYK 112	Westcot, Nathan	ORN 293
Wescoat, Stephen	OTS 54	West, John	OND 206	Westcot, Anias	WST 139
Wescot see Westcot		West, John	WSH 279	Westcott, Arnold	RNS 71
Wescot, Mary	SRA 18	West, John Junr	CHN 770	Westcott, Gardner	OND 196
Wescott, Caleb	OND 197	West, John L.	NYK 134	Westcott, Gardner	OND 197
Wescott, John	SRA 16	West, Jonathan	SRA 28	Westcott, Nathan	ONT 438
Wescott, Jonathan	SRA 35	West, Joseph	NYK 92	Westcott, Stutely	HRK 566
Wescutt, Sarah	SRA 29	West, Joseph	SRA 28	Westcott, Ziba	ESS 309
Wesener, James	ONN 190	West, Joseph	WSH 266	Westell, Daniel	RNS 30
Weslake see Westlake		West, Josiah	NYK 81	Westell, George Junr	RNS 30
Weslake, Benjamin	ORN 285	West, Levi	DEL 279	Westen, Jona	OTS 44
Wessell, Richard B.	NYK 46	West, Levi	OND 206	Westerfield, Andrw	NYK 85
Wessells, Evert	NYK 54	West, Mathew	NYK 96	Westerlo, Catherine	ALB 145
Wessells, Isaac	NYK 129	West, Minor	CAY 728	Westerman, Elisabeth	
Wessells, Mary	NYK 53	West, Minor	SRA 17	Mary	MNT 38
Wessells, Susan	NYK 110	West, Moses	WSH 191	Western, Mary	OTS 24
Wessels, Aurant	ALB 2A	West, Peter	ALB 91	Western, Thomas	NYK 110
Wessels, Herman	ALB 13	West, Prince	WSH 279	Westervaldt, John	WST 146
Wessels, Samuel	WST 159	West, Richard	ORN 314	Westervelt, Abraham	NYK 103
Wessely, Andrew	MNT 38	West, Richard	ULS 211	Westervelt, Albert	ALB 96
Wessely, Isaac	MNT 38	West, Rusmeyer	RNS 66	Westervelt, Albert	RCK 108
Wesser, Rosanna	NYK 64	West, Samuel	ALB 80	Westervelt, Benjamin	DUT 69
Wessett, Cownover	MNT 51	West, Samuel	CLN 155	Westervelt, Benjamin	NYK 99
Wesson, Nathaniel	ONT 452	West, Samuel	COL 195	Westervelt, Benjamin	NYK 135

Whedon, Augustus	DUT 139	Wheeler, Henry	STB 197	Wheeler, Thomas E.	OND 180
Whedon, Benjamen	WSH 297	Wheeler, Ichabud	COL 213	Wheeler, Thomas N.	DUT 135
Whedon, Calvin	DUT 26	Wheeler, Ira	DUT 130	Wheeler, Timothy	CAY 632
Whedon, Jehoida	DUT 85	Wheeler, Jacob	ALB 32	Wheeler, Timothy	DUT 132
Wheelar, Eliplet	GRN 334	Wheeler, Jacob	ONN 133	Wheeler, Timothy	HRK 427
Wheelar, Ephraim	GRN 332	Wheeler, Jacob	SUF 92	Wheeler, Timothy	SUF 92
Wheelar, Luther	GRN 345	Wheeler, Jason	HRK 426	Wheeler, Timothy	ULS 243
Wheelar, Noah	GRN 352	Wheeler, Jerh	OTS 35	Wheeler, Washington	RNS 41
Wheelar, Samuel	GRN 342	Wheeler, Joel	ORN 376	Wheeler, William	COL 238
Wheelar, Samuel Jun	GRN 342	Wheeler, Johannis	COL 235	Wheeler, William	DUT 157
Wheelarr, Ely	GRN 343	Wheeler, John	CHN 850	Wheeler, William	ONN 158
Wheelback, Lewis	OND 200	Wheeler, John	DEL 280	Wheeler, Wm	ONN 160
Wheelden, Jabes	WSH 231	Wheeler, John	NYK 83	Wheeler, Wm	OTS 25
Wheelden, Jabes Junr	WSH 231	Wheeler, John	NYK 93	Wheeler, William	SUF 92
Wheelden, John	WSH 195	Wheeler, John	ONN 133	Wheeler, William	WSH 256
Wheeler see Weeler,		Wheeler, John	ORN 372	Wheeler, York	DUT 133
Whealor & Wheler		Wheeler, John	OTS 10	Wheeler, Zachariah	WSH 201
Wheeler, Aaron	ONT 414	Wheeler, John	RNS 15	Wheeler, Zadock	WSH 282
Wheeler, Abel	OND 180	Wheeler, John	RNS 85	Wheeler, Zebulon	ORN 366
Wheeler, Abner	ONN 153	Wheeler, John	SCH 124	Wheeler, Zephe...h S,	SRA 59
Wheeler, Abraham	ORN 396	Wheeler, John	SUF 81	Wheelock, Alvin	HRK 546
Wheeler, Albert	DUT 45	Wheeler, John B.	DUT 45	Wheelock, Ariel	ONT 392
Wheeler, Amherst	WSH 222	Wheeler, John J.	COL 238	Wheelock, Levi	COL 207
Wheeler, Amos	DUT 104	Wheeler, John V.	DUT 43	Wheelock, Obadiah	COL 205
Wheeler, Andries	COL 235	Wheeler, Jonas	SRA 30	Wheelock, Samuel	HRK 527
Wheeler, Andries J.	COL 236	Wheeler, Jonas	SRA 31	Wheelon, Elias	COL 217
Wheeler, Anthony	DUT 135	Wheeler, Jonas	SUF 90	Wheemar, Paul	NYK 135
Wheeler, Ashbel	DUT 136	Wheeler, Jonathan	COL 208	Wheeton see Wheaton	
Wheeler, Ashbel	HRK 504	Wheeler, Jonathan	NYK 78	Wheeton, Benjn	OTS 26
Wheeler, Baltus	COL 239	Wheeler, Jonathan A.	COL 209	Wheeton, John	OTS 34
Wheeler, Barney	SUF 89	Wheeler, Joseph	RNS 41	Whelden, Samuel	WSH 195
Wheeler, Benjamin	MNT 96	Wheeler, Joseph	RNS 51	Wheler see Wheeler	
Wheeler, Charles	SUF 91	Wheeler, Joseph	WST 160	Wheler, Mathew	NYK 87
Wheeler, Christopher	COL 235	Wheeler, Joshua	OND 200	Whelker, John	NYK 118
Wheeler, Coenradt	COL 235	Wheeler, Joshua	ONT 416	Whelock, Alpheus	OND 206
Wheeler, Curtis	SRA 53	Wheeler, Josiah	DUT 43	Whelor, Jiremiah	SUF 66
Wheeler, Daniel	CHN 846	Wheeler, Josiah	ONT 394	Whelp, Peter	NYK 57
Wheeler, Daniel	NYK 95	Wheeler, Justice	WST 157	Whelpley, Amos	ULS 186
Wheeler, Daniel	SUF 90	Wheeler, Lemuel	OTS 49	Whelpley, Ebenezer	WST 154
Wheeler, Daniel	SUF 92	Wheeler, Levi	CAY 702	Whelpley, Henry	TIO 238
Wheeler, Daniel	TIO 220	Wheeler, Margaret	ORN 396	Whelpley, Isaac	CLN 167
Wheeler, Daniele	MNT 123	Wheeler, Mark	DUT 7	Whelpley, Isaac Junr	ULS 186
Wheeler, David	HRK 463	Wheeler, Mary	NYK 108	Whelpley, Isaac Senr	ULS 186
Wheeler, David	RNS 69	Wheeler, Melancton	WSH 282	Whelpley, Jerremiah	COL 242
Wheeler, David	SRA 30	Wheeler, Michael	COL 235	Whelpley, Samuel	DUT 7
Wheeler, David	ULS 186	Wheeler, Mordecai	ORN 321	Whelply, Daniel	WST 130
Wheeler, David	WSH 189	Wheeler, Moses	HRK 483	Whemster, David	NYK 78
Wheeler, Ebenezer	DEL 274	Wheeler, Moses	OTS 10	Wherry, Benjan	MNT 109
Wheeler, Ebenezer	NYK 118	Wheeler, Nathan	COL 213	Whetely, Frederick	TIO 238
Wheeler, Edmond	RNS 69	Wheeler, Nathan	DUT 52	Wheteman, John	NYK 142
Wheeler, Edward	CAY 716	Wheeler, Nathaniel	ORN 366	Whetford, Stukely	OTS 26
Wheeler, Edward	COL 213	Wheeler, Nicholas	NYK 152	Whetman see Witman	
Wheeler, Edward	DUT 45	Wheeler, Nicholas	RNS 85	Whetman, Eliphalet	SUF 90
Wheeler, Eli R.	WST 157	Wheeler, Noah	DUT 136	Whetmore see Witmore	
Wheeler, Elias	DUT 91	Wheeler, Obediah	SUF 83	Whetmore, Robert G.	ALB 32
Wheeler, Elijah	DUT 97	Wheeler, Peter	ULS 219	Whetstone, Increase	OND 196
Wheeler, Elijah	DUT 168	Wheeler, Peter	WSH 201	Whetten, John	NYK 44
Wheeler, Elijah	ONN 186	Wheeler, Platt	SUF 89	Whetten, Samuel	NYK 77
Wheeler, Elijah	ORN 370	Wheeler, Richard	NYK 121	Whever see Weaver	
Wheeler, Eliphalet	NYK 117	Wheeler, Robert	TIO 215	Whever, Peter	CHN 952
Wheeler, Elisha	COL 213	Wheeler, Roeliff	DUT 45	Whi__, James	MNT 68
Wheeler, Elkanah	SUF 90	Wheeler, Samuel	CHN 742	Whigham, Robert	ORN 351
Wheeler, Ephraim	COL 237	Wheeler, Samuel	COL 213	Whigham, Robert Junr	ORN 292
Wheeler, Ephraim	DUT 132	Wheeler, Samuel	DEL 271	Whigham, William	ORN 294
Wheeler, Ephriam	WSH 222	Wheeler, Samuel	NYK 70	While, Eliakim	WSH 258
Wheeler, Ephriam	WSH 230	Wheeler, Samuel	SUF 92	Whiling, Levy	WSH 244
Wheeler, Ephriam Junr	WSH 222	Wheeler, Samuel	WSH 300	Whilttesey, Ezra	TIO 216
Wheeler, Ezekiel	CHN 764	Wheeler, Samuel	WST 153	Whilttesey, Samuel Jur	TIO 216
Wheeler, Ezra	CAY 548	Wheeler, Samel Junr	COL 213	Whiple, Samuel	WSH 188
Wheeler, George	ONT 470	Wheeler, Sarah	DUT 135	Whiple, Thomas	CHN 780
Wheeler, George	ONT 472	Wheeler, Seth	DUT 136	Whipple see Wipple	
Wheeler, Gilbert	ORN 373	Wheeler, Seth	WSH 274	Whipple, Andrew	RNS 17
Wheeler, Gilbert	WSH 282	Wheeler, Sinon	CAY 546	Whipple, Asahel	OTS 18
Wheeler, Heman	CLN 162	Wheeler, Solomon	DUT 135	Whipple, Barnard	OTS 18
Wheeler, Henry	COL 264	Wheeler, Solomon	NYK 127	Whipple, Benajah	OTS 17
Wheeler, Henry	DUT 101	Wheeler, Thomas	DUT 97	Whipple, Benajah Jun	OTS 17
Wheeler, Henry	QNS 80	Wheeler, Thomas	SUF 92	Whipple, Benjamin	ALB 138

Whipple, Benjamin	CAY 650	Whitcomb, Josiah	DEL 276	White, Elias	RCK 100
Whipple, Calvin	ONT 346	Whitcomb, Oliver	OTS 40	White, Elias	SUF 95
Whipple, Daniel	CHN 756	Whitcomb, Peter	DUT 138	White, Elias	SUF 96
Whipple, Daniel	ONN 162	Whitcomb, Plenne	WSH 279	White, Elihu	ONT 492
Whipple, Elijah	CAY 688	Whitcomb, Samuel	HRK 563	White, Elijah	GRN 352
Whipple, Ephm	ALB 6	Whitcomb, Simeon	ALB 83	White, Elijah	WSH 273
Whipple, Eseck	SRA 56	Whitcomb, Thomas	HRK 423	White, Elijah Junr	WSH 273
Whipple, Esick	OTS 17	Whitcome, Esra	GRN 335	White, Eliza	NYK 69
Whipple, Innman	WSH 200	Whitcome, Isaac	GRN 335	White, Elizth	OTS 36
Whipple, Isaiah	ULS 182	Whitcome, Isreal	GRN 335	White, Elizer	WSH 280
Whipple, Isreal	SRA 59	Whitcome, Jesse	GRN 335	White, Ellinor	NYK 31
Whipple, James	OTS 17	White see Wight		White, Enoch	SCH 133
Whipple, Jerremiah	CHN 966	White, Abal	STB 200	White, Epenetus	SRA 13
Whipple, Job	WSH 249	White, Abel	CAY 590	White, Ephram	CHN 746
Whipple, John	CAY 722	White, Abel	RNS 85	White, Ephriam	SUF 96
Whipple, John	DUT 134	White, Abigail	OTS 42	White, Eve	RCH 89
Whipple, John F.	RNS 90	White, Abner	DUT 100	White, Ezra	CHN 754
Whipple, Jonathan	DEL 271	White, Abner	OND 202	White, Francis	NYK 55
Whipple, Lucretia	DUT 97	White, Abner	ONT 356	White, Frederick	ALB 77
Whipple, Luther	DEL 268	White, Abner	WSH 243	White, Gelbert	MNT 89
Whipple, Malichai	ALB 63	White, Alexanr	CHN 890	White, George	ALB 68
Whipple, Marmaduke	WSH 249	White, Alexander	SRA 21	White, George	NYK 62
Whipple, Marshal	WSH 197	Whit., Alwood	CAY 590	White, George a Black	NYK 64
Whipple, Nathan	CHN 980	White, Amariah	DUT 17	White, George	OND 187
Whipple, Nathan	RNS 77	White, Amos G.	ORN 386	White, Geo.	OTS 16
Whipple, Nicholas	HRK 574	White, Andrew	CLN 154	White, George	OTS 42
Whipple, Oliver	CHN 980	White, Andrew	NYK 61	White, George	SUF 97
Whipple, Otis	OND 197	White, Anna	NYK 28	White, Geo. C.	OTS 42
Whipple, Robert	OND 157	White, Ansel	OND 170	White, Giles	SCH 173
Whipple, Robert	RNS 72	White, Archabald	WSH 250	White, Green	OTS 41
Whipple, Samuel	DUT 8	White, Archibald	NYK 103	White, Hannah	SUF 98
Whipple, Thomas	COL 246	White, Arguilus	GRN 334	White, Havens	CHN 970
Whipple, William	ALB 33	White, Asa	CHN 798	White, Henry	GRN 332
Whipple, William	CHN 966	White, Asa	DUT 57	White, Henry	NYK 16
Whipple, Wm	OTS 17	White, Asa	ONN 181	White, Henry	NYK 19
Whipple, William	RNS 80	White, Benjn	CHN 898	White, Henry	NYK 128
Whipple, Wm R.	HRK 571	White, Benjamin	DEL 275	White, Henry	ONN 186
Whippo, John	NYK 141	White, Benjamin	DEL 282	White, Henry	ORN 352
Whipps, Frances	CAY 652	White, Benjamin	DUT 101	White, Henry	SUF 97
Whitacre, Ebenezer	HRK 444	White, Benjamin	OND 191	White, Hezekiah	NYK 135
Whitaker see Whitecur,		White, Benjamin	OND 206	White, Hugh	OND 157
Whiteker, Whitiker,		White, Benjamin	WST 146	White, Hugh Junr	OND 171
Whittteger & Witaker		White, Caleb	HRK 583	White, Icabode	WSH 254
		White, Caleb	OTS 47	White, Ichabod	ALB 33
Whitaker, Abraham	ULS 226	White, Charles	DUT 10	White, Ichabod	COL 209
Whitaker, Benjamin	ORN 398	White, Charles	NYK 40	White, Isaac	OND 198
Whitaker, Benjamin	ULS 225	White, Charles	NYK 82	White, rsael	COL 189
Whitaker, Benjamin		White, Charles	ONT 386	White, Isaac	HRK 419
Junr	ULS 226	White, Charles	ULS 253	White, Isaac	WSH 249
Whitaker, Edward	ULS 226	White, Charles	WSH 277	White, Isaeah	CHN 836
Whitaker, Ephraim	COL 252	White, Charles	WST 129	White, Isaiah	MNT 87
Whitaker, James	ULS 225	White, Charles Junr	DUT 12	White, Israel	COL 254
Whitaker, Jesse	OND 180	White, Christopher	ALB 35	White, Jacob	ORN 397
Whitaker, John	DEL 279	White, Christopher	NYK 77	White, James	ALB 5
Whitaker, John	ULS 220	White, Cornelius	COL 178	White, James	ALB 86
Whitaker, John	ULS 226	White, Cornelius	NYK 76	White, James	ALB 104
Whitaker, Joseph	RNS 9	White, Dan	NYK 31	White, James	CHN 890
Whitaker, Nell	ALB 91	White, Daniel	CAY 590	White, James	CLN 157
Whitaker, Oliver	COL 252	White, Daniel	GRN 346	White, James	COL 238
Whitaker, Peter	ULS 218	White, Danl	OTS 31	White, James	DUT 150
Whitaker, Peter	ULS 225	White, Daniel	SRA 53	White, James	MNT 59
Whitaker, Richard	ORN 323	White, Daniel C.	OND 157	White, James	MNT 75
Whitaker, Squire	DEL 279	White, Daniel H.	WSH 275	White, James	NYK 22
Whitaker, Wm	RNS 74	White, David	DEL 267	White, James	NYK 132
Whitaker, William	ULS 226	White, David	DUT 9	White, James	ONN 181
Whitaker, William Junr	ULS 225	White, David	OTS 57	White, James	ORN 297
Whitaker, Zacharias	RNS 78	White, David	WSH 187	White, James	OTS 19
Whitbeck see Witbeck		White, Deborah	NYK 63	White, James	SRA 10
Whitbeck, Andrew Junr	COL 263	White, Ebenezar	CAY 648	White, James	SRA 40
Whitbeck, Herman	DUT 154	White, Ebenezar	SUF 101	White, James	SUF 98
Whitbeck, Volkert	DUT 154	White, Ebenezer	DEL 267	White, James	WST 114
Whitchurch, John	NYK 62	White, Ebenezer	ULS 184	White, James Junr	ORN 344
Whitcklock, James	NYK 68	White, Ebenezer	WST 124	White, James J.	DEL 290
Whitcomb see Witcum		White, Ebenezer	WST 129	White, Jane	ORN 270
Whitcomb, David	HRK 551	White, Edward	ONT 442	White, Jared	ONN 146
Whitcomb, David	ONT 334	White, Edward	ONT 508	White, Jebson	NYK 62
Whitcomb, Edward	SCH 148	Whit., Edward	ONT 508	White, Jedediah	OND 192
Whitcomb, John	ALB 72	White, Elias	ONT 508		

INDEX TO THE 1800 CENSUS OF NEW YORK

Name	Loc	Name	Loc	Name	Loc
White, Jenkins	WSH 303	White, Peter	ALB 19	Whitecur see Whitaker	
White, Jeremiah	GRN 339	White, Peter	CLN 155	Whitecur, Stephen	STB 204
White, Jeremiah	TIO 236	White, Peter	COL 249	Whitefield, George	NYK 78
White, Jesse	WSH 214	White, Peter	NYK 75	Whitefield, Hannah	NYK 70
White, John	CAY 660	White, Phebe	QNS 84	Whitefield, Thomas	NYK 74
White, John	CHN 886	White, Phillip	COL 228	Whitehand, John	NYK 123
White, John	COL 198	White, Philo	OND 171	Whitehead, Aaron	NYK 55
White, John	COL 211	White, Rachel	COL 254	Whitehead, Amos	OTS 11
White, John	DUT 17	White, Reuben	ALB 112	Whitehead, Benjamin	QNS 74
White, John	DUT 149	White, Richard	SRA 39	Whitehead, Davia	NYK 101
White, John	GRN 329	White, Robert	CAY 530	Whitehead, Elisha	NYK 43
White, John	HRK 584	White, Robert	DUT 129	Whitehead, Isaac	CAY 528
White, John	NYK 89	White, Robert	NYK 84	Whitehead, Jas	ALB 74
White, John	NYK 114	White, Robert	WSH 255	Whitehead, Jesse	ALB 53
White, John	NYK 129	White, Rufus	COL 184	Whitehead, John	ALB 85
White, John	OND 210	White, Samuel	CHN 786	Whitehead, John	SRA 18
White, John	ONT 342	White, Saml	CHN 890	Whitehead, Joseph	ALB 53
White, John	ORN 343	White, Samuel	COL 247	Whitehead, Reuben	SRA 14
White, John	RCH 87	White, Samuel	ONN 184	Whitehead, Samuel	ORN 328
White, John	RCK 97	White, Samuel	ORN 343	Whitehead, Samuel	RNS 54
White, John	SRA 28	White, Samuel	RNS 83	Whitehead, Stephen	ALB 53
White, John	SRA 40	White, Sanford	SRA 32	Whitehead, Stephen	CAY 526
White, John	SUF 69	White, Sarah	NYK 116	Whitehead, Ward	ORN 282
White, John	SUF 96	White, Sarah	SUF 79	Whitehead, William	NYK 17
White, John	SUF 101	White, Sarah	WST 119	Whitehead, William	ORN 271
White, John	TIO 236	White, Silas	NYK 127	Whitehouse, John	QNS 78
White, John	TIO 239	White, Silas	SUF 101	Whiteing, Henry	COL 192
White, John	WSH 255	White, Silas Junr	SUF 101	Whiteing, Nathan	COL 210
White, John	WSH 256	White, Solomon	COL 246	Whiteing, William	COL 246
White, John	WSH 281	White, Stephen	NYK 79	Whiteker see Whitaker	
White, John	WST 144	White, Stephen	OND 211	Whiteker, Robert	ONT 448
White, John	WST 146	White, Stephen	SRA 16	Whitelaw see Whytlaw	
White, John 2d	WSH 282	White, Sylvanus	ORN 352	Whitelaw, James	NYK 120
White, Johnathan	GRN 342	White, Theophales	WSH 237	Whiteleg, William	NYK 144
White, Jonas	MNT 102	White, Thomas	CHN 886	Whiteley, Joseph	DUT 50
White, Jonas	SRA 13	White, Thomas	CLN 157	Whitely, Pardon	DUT 50
White, Jonathan	DUT 20	White, Thomas	COL 207	Whitely, William	DEL 269
White, Jonathan	OTS 35	White, Thomas	COL 211	Whiteman see Wheteman,	
White, Joseph	CHN 934	White, Thomas	DUT 101	Whetman, Whitman, Wit-	
White, Joseph	COL 213	White, Thomas	NYK 16	man & Wightman	
White, Joseph	DUT 55	White, Thomas	NYK 85	Whiteman, Aaron	NYK 50
White, Joseph	KNG 4	White, Thomas	NYK 146	Whiteman, Adam	ALB 72
White, Joseph	NYK 97	White, Thomas	NYK 146	Whiteman, Benjamin	WSH 199
White, Joseph	NYK 118	White, Thomas	OND 168	Whiteman, Hendrick	ALB 38
White, Joseph	NYK 141	White, Thomas	ONT 386	Whiteman, Henry	ALB 35
White, Joseph	OND 157	White, Thomas	ORN 336	Whiteman, Henry	NYK 50
White, Joseph	OND 206	White, Thomas	WST 114	Whiteman, Mary	COL 224
White, Joseph	ORN 316	White, Timothy	OTS 56	Whitemarsh see Whitmarsh,	
White, Joseph	OTS 3	White, Tully a mula-		& Witmarsh	
White, Joseph	OTS 49		tto	Whitemarsh, Acke	ALB 113
White, Joseph	SRA 36	White, Uriah	DEL 282	Whitemash see Whitmash	
White, Joseph	WSH 275	White, Ward	OND 185	& Whitmush	
White, Joseph	WSH 280	White, William	ALB 3	Whitemash, Abiatha	ALB 113
White, Joshua	ALB 32	White, William	ALB 98	WiteMire, Abraham	MNT 42
White, Joshua	DEL 267	White, William	CAY 636	Whiteneck, Peter	CAY 682
White, Joshua	OND 185	White, William	CHN 754	Whiter_, Jacob	CHN 798
White, Laurence	NYK 79	White, William	CHN 794	Whites, Archibal	NYK 148
White, Lephs	ONN 177	White, William	CLN 154	Whiteside, Edward	WSH 197
White, Levi	HRK 584	White, William	COL 205	Whiteside, John	WSH 197
White, Levi	OND 206	White, William	DEL 273	Whiteside, Oliver	WSH 197
White, Levi	ONN 187	White, William	DEL 277	Whiteside, Peter	WSH 197
White, Lewis	NYK 124	White, William	DUT 101	Whiteside, Thomas	WSH 197
White, Lewis	WSH 184	White, Wm	MNT 77	Whiteside, William	WSH 197
White, Lity	NYK 26	White, William	NYK 36	Whitesides, James	ORN 292
White, Mary	NYK 78	White, William	NYK 90	Whitesides, William	ORN 307
White, Mary	SUF 98	White, William	ONT 340	Whiteur, Seth	WSH 232
White, Mary	WST 116	White, William	OTS 36	Whiteur, Seth Junr	WSH 232
White, Michael	NYK 54	White, William	SUF 98	Whitford see Witford	
White, Michael	QNS 62	White, William	ULS 181	Whitford, Caleb	RNS 25
White, Nathaniel	DUT 49	White, William	WST 149	Whitford, Christopher	OND 184
White, Nathl	HRK 444	White, Willm Junr	COL 185	Whitford, David	CHN 816
White, Nathl	HRK 449	White, William Junr	DUT 101	Whitford, Dennis	SRA 43
White, Nathl	OTS 4	White, William A.	DUT 101	Whitford, Edward	RNS 70
White, Nathl	OTS 6	White, Wilson	WSH 273	Whitford, Ezekiel	WSH 266
White, Nathaniel	QNS 73	White, Wiris	GRN 345	Whitford, Foster	SRA 44
White, Noah	ONN 139	White, Zephoniah	CHN 850	Whitford, Green	WSH 287
White, Oliver	SRA 34	White__, Colup	CHN 892	Whitford, Jesse	CHN 816

411

Name	Loc		Name	Loc		Name	Loc
Whitford, Jesse	WSH 304		Whitman, Jarvis	SUF 82		Whitney, Aaron	DUT 178
Whitford, John	RNS 70		Whitman, Jessee Senr	SUF 79		Whitney, Aaron	OND 210
Whitford, John	SRA 41		Whitman, John	CHN 950		Whitney, Aaron	TIO 265
Whitford, Joseph	OTS 32		Whitman, John	CHN 980		Whitney, Abijah	ORN 376
Whitford, Joshua	CHN 828		Whitman, John	HRK 477		Whitney, Abijah	WST 126
Whitford, Joshua	RNS 71		Whitman, John	HRK 551½		Whitney, Amasiah	OTS 44
Whitford, Nathan	ALB 78		Whitman, John	ONN 190		Whitney, Amos	WST 123
Whitford, Orrisan	SRA 44		Whitman, John	SUF 94		Whitney, Asa	NYK 72
Whitford, Pascho	HRK 560		Whitman, Joseph	SUF 80		Whitney, Bascum	ONT 446
Whitford, Rufus	WSH 287		Whitman, Joshua	ORN 342		Whitney, Bela	ONN 187
Whitford, Wm	RNS 74		Whitman, Lemuel	COL 261		Whitney, Benjamin	ORN 379
Whitham, James	ORN 392		Whitman, Nathaniel	SUF 79		Whitney, Benjn	OTS 14
Whitherell see Witherell			Whitman, Nathl Junr	SUF 79		Whitney, Benjamin	WSH 301
Whitherell, John	NYK 128		Whitman, Nehemiah	OTS 48		Whitney, Betsey	NYK 37
Whithey, Ephraim	CAY 700		Whitman, Phoebe	SUF 79		Whitney, Corneleus	WSH 278
Whitieng, Augustus	COL 263		Whitman, Samuel	COL 218		Whitney, Cornelius	WSH 276
Whitiker see Whitaker			Whitman, Saml	OTS 34		Whitn.., Cristopher	ONN 187
Whitiker, John	GRN 327		Whitman, Samuel Junr	COL 218		Whitney, Daniel	DUT 54
Whitiker(?), John	ONT 462		Whitman, Stephen	OTS 48		Whitney, Darlin	QNS 79
Whiting see Whitting &			Whitman, Stephen	SUF 83		Whitney, David	ULS 240
Witing			Whitman, Timothy	SUF 87		Whitney, David	WSH 267
Whiting, Abel	OTS 51		Whitman, Valentine	HRK 589		Whitney, Elias	DUT 23
Whiting, Abisha	OTS 28		Whitman, William	ALB 70		Whitney, Elijah	CAY 596
Whiting, Alexander	RNS 111		Whitman, William	CHN 792		Whitney, Elisha	CHN 806
Whiting, Ebenezar	GRN 348		Whitman, William	HRK 589		Whitney, Ephraim	DUT 96
Whiting, Ebenezar	KNG 9		Whitmarsh see Witmarsh			Whitney, Ephrm	OTS 17
Whiting, Elihu	WSH 216		& Whitemarsh			Whitney, Ephrain	MNT 123
Whiting, Elijah	ORN 393		Whitmarsh, Amos	ONN 177		Whitney, Ezekel	WSH 212
Whiting, Henry	OND 188		Whitmarsh, Gideon	RNS 81		Whitney, Ezekiel	GRN 326
Whiting, James	WSH 288		Whitmarsh, Gideon	RNS 95		Whitney, Fisher	ONT 338
Whiting, Job	SCH 140		Whitmarsh, Nicholas	OTS 27		Whitney, Heman	SRA 47
Whiting, John	COL 210		Whitmarsh, Saml	OTS 27		Whitney, Henry	WSH 221
Whiting, Melzar	ONN 170		Whitmarsh, Saml Junr	OTS 27		Whitney, Isaac	ONT 456
Whiting, Nathan	SCH 147		Whitmarsh, Thomas B.	DEL 277		Whitney, Isaac	WSH 306
Whiting, Thomas	ALB 113		Whitmarsh, William	RNS 81		Whitney, Jacob	ULS 240
Whiting, Thomas	WSH 245		Whitmash, Samuel	RNS 90		Whitney, James	DUT 27
Whiting, William	WSH 288		Whitmire see WhiteMire			Whitney, James	SRA 26
Whiting, William B.	ALB 134		Whitmire, Ebeneser	MNT 123		Whitney, James	WSH 287
Whitley, Joseph	NYK 55		Whitmir_, George	MNT 1		Whitney, Jeremiah	DUT 94
Whitlock see Witlock &			Whitmire, Jonathan	MNT 97		Whitney, Jeremiah	ORN 395
Whitcklock			Whitmon, Stephen	CHN 896		Whitney, Jeremiah Junr	DUT 95
Whitlock, Abrm	SRA 20		Whitmore see Witmore			Whitney, Joel	ONT 506
Whitlock, Agnes	NYK 105		Whitmore, Appolos	SUF 69		Whitney, Jonas	ONT 482
Whitlock, Joel	ORN 317		Whitmore, Benjm	ALB 77		Whitney, Jonathan	CAY 722
Whitlock, Nathan	ORN 317		Whitmore, Benjamin	CAY 698		Whitney, Joseph	WSH 278
Whitlock, Samuel	WSH 275		Whitmore, Catherine	NYK 43		Whitney, Jo.hua	TIO 210
Whitlock, Samuel	NYK 60		Whitmore, Charity	NYK 125		Whitney, Joshua	WSH 245
Whitlock, Thaddeus	WST 156		Whitmore, Christopher	COL 194		Whitney, Joshua	WSH 276
Whitlock, Thomas	COL 254		Whitmore, Clark	OTS 6		Whitney, Joshua	WSH 306
Whitlock, William	NYK 64		Whitmore, David	SRA 48		Whitney, Josiah	OND 196
Whitlock, William	NYK 116		Whitmore, Gideon	CHN 786		Whitney, Josias	ULS 213
Whitlox, George	WST 129		Whitmore, Isaac	CHN 786		Whitney, Martha	TIO 259
Whitman see Whiteman,			Whitmore, Izrahiah	ALB 135		Whitney, Mason	HRK 441
Witman & Wheteman,			Whitmore, James	OTS 44		Whitney, Matthias	WSH 278
Whitman, Abraham	HRK 494		Whitmore, James	QNS 73		Whitney, Nathan	OND 196
Whitman, Amos	COL 187		Whitmore, John	CHN 840		Whitney, Nathan	ONT 506
Whitman, Amos	SUF 79		Whitmore, John	HRK 529		Whitney, Nathan	WST 133
Whitman, Asa	ALB 20		Whitmore, John	WSH 191		Whitney, Nathaniel	OND 175
Whitman, Begar	ONT 428		Whitmore, John Junr	CHN 842		Whitney, Robart	MNT 103
Whitman, Benjamin	CHN 792		Whitmore, Joseph	CAY 654		Whitney, Roswell	ULS 240
Whitman, Benjn	HRK 431		Whitmore, Joseph	CAY 698		Whitney, Ruth	CHN 924
Whitman, Benjamin	ORN 393		Whitmore, Joseph	OTS 6		Whitney, Sally	WSH 277
Whitman, Benjamin	RNS 108		Whitmore, Moses	COL 183		Whitney, Samuel	DEL 269
Whitman, Benony	RNS 108		Whitmore, Noah	QNS 66		Whitney, Samuel	OND 172
Whitman, Daniel	ALB 76		Whitmore, Oliver	ONT 506		Whitney, Samuel	OND 199
Whitman, Elijah	ALB 20		Whitmore, Oliver Ju.	ONT 506		Whitney, Saml	OTS 40
Whitman, George	HRK 494		Whitmore, Palelise	GRN 357		Whitney, Samuel	SRA 25
Whitman, George	ORN 361		Whitmore, Reuben	ALB 31		Whitney, Sarah	WSH 277
Whitman, George	RNS 108		Whitmore, Richard	NYK 136		Whitney, Seth	WST 123
Whitman, George	RCK 108		Wh_tmore, Samuel	CHN 842		Whitney, Seth Junr	WST 123
Whitman, Gideon	HRK 595		Whitmore, Saml	SUF 69		Whitney, Silas	DUT 178
Whitman, Isaac	SUF 83		Whitmore, Samuel	WSH 187		Whitney, Silas	ONT 332
Whitman, Isacah	MNT 85		Whitmore, Wells	ONT 480		Whitney, Thomas	TIO 259
Whitman, Israel	COL 187		Whitmore, William	ONT 480		Whitney, Walter	ALB 103
Whitman, Jacob	RCK 104		Whitmush see Whitemash			Whitney, William	ALB 54
Whitman, Jacob	RCK 108		Whitmush, Abiltha	ALB 77		Whitney, William	RNS 18
Whitman, James	HRK 477		Whitney, _____	DEL 289		Whitney, Wm	TIO 210

Wilkie, Edward NYK 32
Wilkie, James NYK 64
Wilkie, Jeremiah NYK 134
Wilkie, Thomas ALB 11
Wilkin, Henry RCK 99
Wilkin, James W. ORN 356
Wilkins, Cody CHN 850
Wilkins, Daniel ORN 309
Wilkins, Daniel WST 146
Wilkins, George CAY 572
Wilkins, Isaac WST 150
Wilkins, Jason ORN 307
Wilkins, Jason ORN 346
Wilkins, John CAY 562
Wilkins, John a Black NYK 138
Wilkins, John NYK 153
Wilkins, John ORN 345
Wilkins, Joseph CAY 690
Wilkins, Leonard CAY 562
Wilkins, Mary NYK 153
Wilkins, Nancy QNS 64
Wilkins, Othaniel DEL 279
Wilkins, Robert ORN 345
Wilkins, William ORN 345
Wilkinson, Allen CAY 556
Wilkinson, Amos CAY 716
Wilkinson, Asahel CAY 714
Wilkinson, Benjn HRK 504
Wilkinson, Berzabath OND 183
Wilkinson, Catherine NYK 52
Wilkinson, David DUT 109
Wilkinson, Duncan DUT 144
Wilkinson, Esther DUT 57
Wilkinson, Icabod CAY 716
Wilkinson, Isaac CAY 716
Wilkinson, Jacob HRK 504
Wilkinson, Jacob SRA 32
Wilkinson, James C. NYK 121
Wilkinson, John DUT 9
Wilkinson, John NYK 112
Wilkinson, John ORN 384
Wilkinson, John RNS 67
Wilkinson, John WSH 203
Wilkinson, Jonathan CAY 716
Wilkinson, Jonathan ORN 337
Wilkinson, Josiah OND 184
Wilkinson, Levi HRK 534
Wilkinson, Miles ONT 384
Wilkinson, Nathan NYK 143
Wilkinson, Orange CAY 728
Wilkinson, Peter CAY 716
Wilkinson, Richard NYK 88
Wilkinson, Robert ALB 4
Wilkinson, Robert DUT 127
Wilkinson, Samuel WSH 254
Wilkinson, Thankful CAY 716
Wilkinson, William HRK 554
Wilkison, Thomas WSH 270
Wilkison, Thomas WSH 282
Wilkley, William NYK 117
Wilklow, Daniel ULS 240
Wilklow, Jacob ULS 236
Wilklow, John ULS 236
Wilks, John NYK 26
Wilks, Nathan TIO 221
Wilks, Squires TIO 221
Will, Henry NYK 73
Will, Henry SCH 172
Will, Joseph SCH 163
Will, Laurence NYK 80
Willard, Abiather WSH 287
Willard, Andrew OTS 43
Willard, David OTS 18
Willard, Elias SRA 47
Willard, Ephraim OND 188
Willard, John ONN 148
Willard, John SRA 41
Willard, Jonathan ONT 310
Willard, Joseah WSH 304
Willard, Joseph HRK 521
Willard, Joseph Jun HRK 599
Willard, Levi ALB 9
Willard, Lewis OND 197
Willard, Matthew SRA 21
Willard, Moses RNS 80
Willard, Nathl HRK 438
Willard, Oliver WSH 222
Willard, Reuben RNS 80
Willard, Rufus OND 188
Willard, Simon OND 188
Willard, Simon Junr OND 188
Willbeaury, Benjn CHN 820
Willber see Wilber
Willber, David RNS112A
Willber, Gideon RNS 94
Willber, Joseph SRA 41
Willber, Saml RNS 107
Willber, Solomon RNS 91
Willber, Thomas 2d RNS 107
Willbor, Thomas RNS 97
Willborough, Joseph CHN 840
Willbur, Ichabod ALB 29
Willbur, Record CHN 746
Willcocks see Wilcocks & Welcox
Willcocks, Adam OND 222
Willcocks, Benjaman CHN 840
Willcocks, Ephraim SRA 6
Willcocks, Isaiah CHN 840
Willcocks, Lemuel SRA 17
Willcocks, Martin SRA 6
Willcocks, Stephen SRA 56
Willcooks, Elisher OND 219
Willcox, Aaron CHN 878
Willcox, Aaron Junr CHN 878
Willcox, Abraham OND 211
Willcox, Asa OND 173
Willcox, Benona RNS 4
Willcox, Daniel ALB 75
Willcox, Daniel OND 210
Willcox, Daniel WSH 215
Willcox, David ESS 296
Willcox, David RNS 67
Willcox, Easter WSH 221
Willcox, Elias ESS 311
Willcox, Elijah RNS 4
Willcox, Frederick CHN 876
Willcox, Isaac WSH 209
Willcox, John RNS 76
Willcox, Joseph ORN 369
Willcox, Joseph WSH 203
Willcox, Josiah WSH 237
Willcox, Moses CLN 166
Willcox, Nathan RNS 73
Willcox, Pliney OND 210
Willcox, Reynolds ONT 382
Willcox, Robert WSH 185
Willcox, Roger WSH 212
Willcox, Roger Junr WSH 212
Willcox, Samuel HRK 557
Willcox, Semion WSH 253
Willcox, Simeon RNS 78
Willcox, Stephen RNS 4
Willcox, Stephen RNS 78
Willcox, Thomas MNT 78
Willcox, Thomas ORN 369
Willcox, Wm RNS 9
Willeby, Ebenezer WSH 219
Willegee, William OND 220
Willeger, Benjamin MNT 36
Willen, John ALB 86
Willer, Burden CHN 872
Willer, John NYK 19
Willes, Azariah DEL 281
Willes, Caleb WSH 288
Willes, Charles WST 165
Willes, Hezekiah SRA 53
Willes, Stoton Jur WSH 288
Willet, Cornelius WSH 258
Willet, Ebert ALB 148
Willet, Edward ALB 146
Willet, Gilbert DUT 132
Willet, Gilbert C. NYK 151
Willet, Hannah NYK 40
Willet, James NYK 44
Willet, John NYK 44
Willet, Marinus NYK 141
Willet, Samuel ALB 128
Willet, Samuel CLN 172
Willet, Samuel WSH 200
Willet, Thomas DUT 24
Willet, William WSH 249
Willets, Amos QNS 80
Willets, Charles QNS 80
Willets, James DUT 103
Willets, Thomas NYK 32
Willett, Benjamin ONT 438
Willett, Edward S. ALB 126
Willett, Elbert RNS 92
Willett, Isaac ALB 44
Willett, James QNS 64
Willett, Lawrence QNS 63
Willett, Robert QNS 71
Willett, Samuel QNS 63
Willett, Samuel QNS 75
Willett, Thomas NYK 117
Willett, Thomas QNS 64
Willey, Ahijah ULS 185
Willey, Alfred OND 175
Willey, Ann ALB 11
Willey, Ansel HRK 564
Willey, Barzilla OND 174
Willey, Barzilla Junr OND 157
Willey, Eleazer OND 174
Willey, John DUT 142
Willey, Nathaneel OND 219
Willgus, Samuel RNS 82
William Negro QNS 70
William Negro QNS 71
William QNS 81
Wm Negro SUF 65
Wm a Negro SUF 68
Wm a Negro SUF 69
William SUF 100
William a free Negro WST 112
William, Williams ALB 35
Wil.iams, ...a. MNT 79
Williams, Aaron COL 228
Williams, Aaron HRK 587
Williams, Aaron Junr COL 228
Williams, Abener SRA 57
Williams, Abigail RCK 99
Williams, Abijah ONT 402
Williams, Abner ONT 372
Williams, Abraham DUT 82
Williams, Abraham DUT 96
Williams, Abm RNS 33
Williams, Abraham WSH 188
Williams, Abraham WST 154
Williams, Abram WST 152
Williams, Absolem COL 209
Williams, Adam CAY 586
Williams, After WST 129
Williams, Andrew MNT 110
Williams, Andrw NYK 114
Williams, Ann ALB 146
Williams, Ansel HRK 494
Williams, Asa RNS 112
Williams, Asahel OTS 49
Williams, Asher SCH 140

Williams, Augustin	QNS	69	Williams, Elisha	DEL	291	Williams, Jesse	WST	134
Williams, Bartholomew	COL	185	Williams, Elizth	ALB	121	Williams, Job	ONN	169
Williams, Bastian	CAY	532	Williams, Elizabeth	NYK	60	Williams, Job	ONT	332
Williams, Bela	OTS	9	Williams, Elizabeth	NYK	128	Williams, John	ALB	43
Williams, Bella a			Williams, Enos	RNS	96	Williams, John	ALB	68
Black	NYK	49	Williams, Ephraim	COL	209	Williams, John	ALB	86
Williams, Benjamin	NYK	82	Williams, Ephraim	SRA	31	Williams, John	ALB	146
Williams, Benjamin	NYK	130	Williams, Eseck	SRA	57	Williams, John	CAY	530
Williams, Benjamin	NYK	142	Williams, Ezekiel	OND	176	Williams, John	CAY	680
Williams, Benjamin	ORN	361	Williams, Ezekiel	OTS	16	Williams, John	CHN	906
Williams, Benjamin	ULS	268	Williams, Ezekiel	TIO	241	Williams, John	COL	228
Williams, Benjamin	WSH	277	Williams, Festus	HRK	497	Williams, John	COL	262
Williams, Benjamin	WST	144	Williams, Francis	DUT	111	Williams, John	DEL	273
Williams, Casparus	COL	230	Williams, Freeman	CHN	876	Williams, John	DUT	97
Williams, Catharine	NYK	110	Williams, Garet	WST	159	Williams, John	DUT	98
Williams, Charles	SRA	53	Williams, Garret	WST	141	Williams, John	DUT	115
Williams, Christopher	NYK	67	Williams, Garrett	WST	154	Williams, John	DUT	147
Williams, Cornelias	WST	171	Williams, George	MNT	123	Williams, John	HRK	567
Williams, Cornelius	COL	244	Williams, George a			Williams, John	MNT	91
Williams, Cornelius	COL	245	Black	NYK	41	Williams, John	MNT	109
Williams, Cornelius	MNT	94	Williams, George	NYK	143	Williams, John	NYK	34
Williams, Cornelius			Williams, George	QNS	71	Williams, John a		
a mulatto	NYK	89	Williams, George	WSH	225	Black	NYK	36
Williams, Cornelius	NYK	122	Williams, Gershem	WSH	191	Williams, John	NYK	55
Williams, Cornielus	NYK	137	Williams, Gilbart	GRN	325	Williams, John a		
Williams, Dan	ONT	392	Williams, Gilbert	DUT	109	Black	NYK	84
Williams, Daniel	NYK	31	Williams, Gilbert	RNS	43	Williams, John a		
Williams, Daniel	ONT	372	Williams, Gilbert	SUF	87	mulatto	NYK	88
Williams, Daniel	OTS	13	Williams, Gilbert	ULS	260	Williams, John a		
Williams, Danl	OTS	17	Williams, Gurden	CHN	776	Black	NYK	107
Williams, Daniel	OTS	21	Williams, Helmus	ONN	167	Williams, John	NYK	114
Williams, Darling	WSH	217	Williams, Hendrick	WST	152	Williams, John	NYK	117
Williams, Davenport	OND	183	Williams, Henery	CHN	786	Williams, John	NYK	150
Williams, Daves	OTS	14	Williams, Henry	COL	228	Williams, John	OND	163
Williams, David	ALB	15	Williams, Henry	NYK	124	Williams, John	OND	175
Williams, David	CHN	850	Williams, Henry	OND	209	Williams, John	OND	189
Williams, David	COL	209	Williams, Hiram	TIO	240	Williams, John	OND	211
Williams, David	COL	228	Williams, Ichabod	DUT	12	Williams, John	ONN	153
Williams, David	NYK	143	Williams, Ichabod	ULS	258	Williams, John	ONT	332
Williams, David	OND	165	Williams, Ira	DUT	47	Williams, John	ORN	309
Williams, David	OND	187	Williams, Isaac	NYK	137	Williams, John	ORN	339
Williams, David	OND	211	Williams, Isaac	ORN	311	Williams, John	ORN	381
Williams, David	ONN	146	Williams, Isaac	ORN	385	Williams, John	ORN	395
Williams, David	ORN	348	Williams, Isaac	OTS	17	Williams, John	OTS	5
Williams, David	RNS	12	Williams, Isaac	OTA	48	Williams, John	OTS	16
Williams, David	RNS	92	Williams, Isaac	SRA	57	Williams, John	OTS	16
Williams, David	SRA	9	Williams, Isaac	WSH	217	Williams, John	OTS	25
Williams, David	SRA	38	Williams, Isaac	WST	119	Williams, John	QNS	70
Williams, D..ld	TIO	235	Williams, Isaac	WST	148	Williams, John	QNS	71
Williams, David	TIO	248	Williams, Isaac	WST	152	Williams, John	RNS	47
Williams, David	WST	129	Williams, Isaiah	DUT	44	Williams, John	SRA	9
Williams, David	WST	156	Williams, Israel	NYK	47	Williams, John	SRA	26
Williams, David	WST	171	Williams, Israel	OTS	37	Williams, John	SRA	53
Williams, David Junr	COL	230	Williams, Israel	WSH	194	Williams, John	SCH	138
Williams, Deborah	QNS	69	Williams, Jabez	OTS	8	Williams, John	SUF	96
Williams, Durell	DUT	66	Williams, Jacob	COL	209	Williams, John	ULS	219
Williams, Ebenezer	ALB	68	Williams, Jacob	QNS	81	Williams, John	ULS	267
Williams, Ebenezer	OND	157	Williams, Jacob	RNS	31	Williams, John	WSH	241
Williams, Ebenr	OTS	25	Williams, Jacob	ULS	254	Williams, John	WSH	278
Williams, Ebenezer	ULS	195	Williams, James	CAY	682	Williams, John	WST	119
Williams, Edward	CHN	838	Williams, James	CHN	786	Williams, John	WST	125
Williams, Edward	NYK	143	Williams, James	CHN	852	Williams, John	WST	125
Williams, Edward	ORN	282	Williams, James	CHN	966	Williams, John	WST	130
Williams, Edward	OTS	5	Williams, James	DUT	97	Williams, John	WST	147
Williams, Edwd	OTS	5	Williams, James	MNT	13	Williams, John	WST	148
Williams, Elam	NYK	37	Williams, James	MNT	78	Williams, John	WST	152
Williams, Elezar	ONT	422	Williams, James a			Williams, John	WST	165
Williams, Eliakim	ALB	68	Black	NYK	47	Williams, John	WST	165
Williams, Elias	COL	212	Williams, James	OTS	15	Williams, John Jun	CHN	906
Williams, Elias	STB	201	Williams, James	TIO	212	Williams, John Junr	DUT	96
Williams, Elias	TIO	240	Williams, James	WSH	218	Williams, John Jun	WST	147
Williams, Elijah	ALB	32	Williams, James	WSH	277	Williams, John F.	SRA	53
Williams, Elijah	SRA	51	Williams, James	WST	160	Williams, John Mooney	ULS	201
Williams, Elijah	WSH	244	Williams, Jared	OND	182	Williams, Jonas	CAY	620
Williams, Elijah	WST	144	Williams, Jerimiah	NYK	141	Williams, Jonas	ORN	287
Williams, Eliphalet	OTS	12	Williams, Jesse	CLN	169	Williams, Jonas	SUF	87
Williams, Elisha	COL	246	Williams, Jesse	COL	252	Williams, Jonathan	KNG	10

Name	Loc	Pg
Williams, Jonathan	RNS	112
Williams, Josep	WSH	217
Williams, Joseph	CHN	898
Williams, Joseph	CHN	964
Williams, Joseph	DUT	95
Williams, Joseph	NYK	65
Williams, Joseph	NYK	96
Williams, Joseph	OND	196
Williams, Joseph	ONN	146
Williams, Joseph	ONN	171
Williams, Joseph	ORN	270
Williams, Joseph	SRA	45
Williams, Joseph	WSH	233
Williams, Joseph Junr	CHN	964
Williams, Josiah	ORN	279
Williams, Judah	RNS	92
Williams, Lemuel	ONN	133
Williams, Lemuel	WSH	277
Williams, Leonard	DUT	50
Williams, Levi	OND	166
Williams, Levi	TIO	240
Williams, Lewis	MNT	7
Williams, Liman	SRA	50
Williams, Luke	SRA	58
Williams, Luke	SRA	58
Williams, Mando	NYK	93
Williams, Marcus	RNS	50
Williams, Marcus	WST	142
Williams, Margaret	DUT	96
Williams, Mary	NYK	37
Williams, Mary	NYK	75
Williams, Mary	QNS	79
Williams, Mary	SUF	86
Williams, Mary	WST	149
Williams, Michael	ALB	135
Williams, Michael	QNS	74
Williams, Miles	GRN	345
Williams, Mingo a Black	NYK	36
Williams, Morgan	NYK	129
Williams, Moses	DUT	115
Williams, Moses	MNT	70
Williams, Moses	ORN	330
Williams, Nathan	OND	160
Williams, Nathan	OND	206
Williams, Nathan	RNS	105
Williams, Nathan	ULS	194
Williams, Nathaniel	CAY	694
Williams, Nathaniel	HRK	427
Williams, Nathl	HRK	476
Williams, Nathaniel	ONT	392
Williams, Nathaniel	ORN	333
Williams, Nathaniel	RNS	80
Williams, Nichodemus	MNT	96
Williams, Nicholas	RNS	40
Williams, Nicholas	SUF	88
Williams, Obadiah	RNS	46
Williams, Paul a Black	NYK	111
Williams, Peirmelia	GRN	329
Williams, Peter	ALB	7
Williams, Peter	COL	193
Williams, Peter	COL	228
Williams, Peter Black	NYK	26
Williams, Peter	SRA	15
Williams, Peter	WST	151
Williams, Peter	ULS	183
Williams, Philip	OND	209
Williams, Phinehas	SRA	51
Williams, Prentice	ALB	68
Williams, Prince	OTS	16
Williams, Ralph	OTS	12
Williams, Renssr	OTS	19
Williams, Richard	CHN	908
Williams, Richard	DUT	97
Williams, Richard	ORN	287
Williams, Richard	ORN	392
Williams, Richd	OTS	19
Williams, Richard	RCH	95
Williams, Richard	STB	204
Williams, Richard	WST	158
Williams, Richard Junr	DUT	81
Williams, Richard Junr	DUT	96
Williams, Richbill	DUT	109
Williams, Richbill Junr	DUT	115
Williams, Robert	CAY	598
Williams, Robert	CAY	618
Williams, Robert	DUT	64
Williams, Robert	NYK	107
Williams, Robert	RNS	37
Williams, Robert	RNS	109
Williams, Robert	WST	114
Williams, Robert	WST	171
Williams, Roger	OND	187
Williams, Salvinus	WST	165
Williams, Samuel	CAY	598
Williams, Samuel	DUT	78
Williams, Samuel	HRK	493
Williams, Samuel	MNT	102
Williams, Samuel	OND	204
Williams, Saml	OTS	46
Williams, Samuel	SRA	10
Williams, Samuel	WST	124
Williams, Samuel	WST	129
Williams, Sandford	ONT	504
Williams, Sebra	OND	200
Williams, Selden	ONT	452
Williams, Serrin	WST	146
Williams, Silas	OTS	17
Williams, Simeon	OND	166
Williams, Simeon	OND	166
Williams, Simon	MNT	102
Williams, Solomon	CHN	906
Williams, Solomon	OND	211
Williams, Solomon	RNS	55
Williams, Solomon	TIO	246
Williams, Solomon	WSH	272
Williams, Squire a Black	NYK	64
Williams, States	WST	159
Williams, Stephen	ALB	77
Williams, Stephen	CHN	844
Williams, Stephen	DEL	275
Williams, Stephen	DUT	96
Williams, Stephen a Black	NYK	126
Williams, Stephen	OND	183
Williams, Stephen	ONN	172
Williams, Stephen	WST	144
Williams, Stephen	WST	171
Williams, Susan	NYK	90
Williams, Sylvester	WSH	277
Williams, Thomas	ALB	111
Williams, Thomas	CHN	774
Williams, Thomas	CHN	980
Williams, Thomas	COL	200
Williams, Thomas	COL	210
Williams, Thomas	COL	217
Williams, Thomas	DUT	81
Williams, Thomas a Black	NYK	51
Williams, Thomas	NYK	69
Williams, Thomas	NYK	72
Williams, Thomas	NYK	82
Williams, Thomas	NYK	84
Williams, Thomas a Black	NYK	126
Williams, Thomas	OND	163
Williams, Thomas	OND	176
Williams, Thomas	OND	176
Williams, Thomas	ORN	348
Williams, Thomas	OTS	15
Williams, Thomas	OTS	46
Williams, Thomas	QNS	70
Williams, Thomas	SRA	48
Williams, Thomas	SRA	50
Williams, Thomas	ULS	180
Williams, Thomas Junr	COL	215
Williams, Thomas P.	RNS	40
Williams, Timothy	SUF	86
Williams, Timothy	TIO	240
Williams, Timothy	WST	155
Williams, Titus	DEL	274
Williams, Uri-- --	COL	209
Williams, Valentine	QNS	70
Williams, Warren	OND	196
Williams, Weiram	ONT	452
Williams, Wheaton H.	CHN	774
Williams, William	ALB	43
Williams, William	ALB	102
Williams, William	ALB	127
Williams, William	DEL	276
Williams, William	GRN	342
Willimas, Wm	MNT	81
Williams, William a Black	NYK	24
Williams, William	NYK	60
Williams, William a Black	NYK	93
Williams, William a Black	NYK	106
Williams, William	NYK	110
Williams, William	NYK	131
Williams, William	OND	166
Williams, William	OND	214
Williams, William	ONN	166
Williams, William	ONT	370
Williams, William	ORN	313
Williams, William	QNS	69
Williams, Wm	RNS	32
Williams, William	RCH	88
Williams, William	WSH	229
Williams, William	WST	114
Williams, William	WST	141
Williams, William A.	ONT	428
Williams, William D.	DUT	12
Williams, Williams	MNT	118
Williams, Wilson	QNS	70
Williams, Woodward	MNT	118
Williams, Zebulon	ONT	350
Williams, Zophor	TIO	240
Williamson, Alexander	WSH	289
Williamson, Charles	STB	197
Williamson, Christopher	HRK	509
Williamson, David	NYK	150
Williamson, David	SUF	74
Williamson, Elizabeth	KNG	8
Williamson, Garrat	OTS	54
Williamson, George	STB	203
Williamson, Henry	MNT	8
Williamson, Henry C.	NYK	47
Williamson, James	MNT	29
Williamson, James	WST	142
Williamson, Jedediah	SUF	66
Williamson, Jeremiah	RCK	106
Williamson, John	ALB	66
Williamson, John	ALB	148
Williamson, John	KNG	2
Williamson, John	NYK	72
Williamson, John	QNS	67
Williamson, John	SUF	98
Williamson, John	WST	142
Williamson, John Junr	WST	142
Williamson, Joseph	CAY	548
Williamson, Joseph	MNT	118
Williamson, Josiah	MNT	113
Williamson, Michl	ALB	23
Williamson, Nicholas	KNG	3
Williamson, Nicholas	RCK	106
Williamson, Peter	KNG	5

Wilson, Daniel	CAY 592	Wilson, John	WSH 279	Wilson, Thomas	WSH 294

Winans, Isaac R.	NYK 43	Winds, John	ALB 87	Winn, Isaac	COL 258
Winans, Jemima	NYK 26	Windship see Winship		Winn, James	MNT 45
Winans, Lewis	ALB 68	Windship, Joseph	TIO 214	Winn, Jesse	DEL 272
Winant see Wynant		Wine, Elizabeth	QNS 66	Winn, John	DEL 272
Winant, Daniel	RCH 94	Winecoop, William	GRN 328	Winn, John	MNT 34
Winant, George	RCH 94	Winegar, Ashbel	RNS 58	Winn, John	MNT 34
Winant, Peter	RCH 94	Winegar, Carance	WSH 300	Winn, John Jr	MNT 34
Winants see Wynants		Winegar, Coonradt	DUT 133	Winn, Peter	MNT 105
Winants, Abraham	ONT 468	Winegar, Gideon	HRK 458	Winn, Robert E.	OTS 28
Winants, Christian	RCH 94	Winegar, Hans	ALB 84	Winnck, John	NYK 87
Winants, Daniel	RCH 89	Winegar, Lois	DUT 133	Winne, Aaron	ALB 91
Winants, Daniel	RCH 94	Winegar, Reuben	ALB 83	Winne, Adam F.	ALB 97
Winants, David	COL 224	Winegar, Samuel	HRK 458	Winne, Anthony	ALB 58
Winants, George	RCH 94	Winegar, Samuel	WSH 300	Winne, Benjamin	ALB 48
Winants, Girardus	DUT 145	Winegott, Nicholas	GRN 348	Winne, Benjamin	ALB 101
Winants, Ira	DUT 145	Winerod, James a		Winne, Casparus	ALB 100
Winants, Isaac	RCH 94	mulatto	NYK 41	Winne, Cornelius	ALB 97
Winants, Jacob	RCH 94	Wines, Barnabas	SUF 74	Winne, Daniel	ALB 97
Winants, Jacob	RCH 95	Wines, Barnabus	SUF 70	Winne, Daniel J.	ALB 146
Winants, James	DUT 67	Wines, Saml	SUF 70	Winne, David	ALB 54
Winants, John	DUT 67	Wines, Wm	SUF 74	Winne, David	ALB 96
Winants, John	RCH 89	Winfield, Abraham	ULS 249	Winne, Jacob	ALB 58
Winants, Mary	RCH 94	Winfield, Benjamin	ULS 208	Winne, Jacob F.	ALB 49
Winants, Peter	RCH 89	Winfield, Daniel	ORN 327	Winne, Jellis	ALB 146
Winants, Peter	RCH 94	Winfield, Daniel	ULS 203	Winne, John	ALB 58
Winants, Seymour	COL 224	Winfield, Daniel	ULS 250	Winne, John	ORN 273
Winants, Cap. Winant	RCH 94	Winfield, David	ULS 249	Winne, John D.	ALB 97
Winants, Zadock	RCH 94	Winfield, Elias	ORN 282	Winne, John L.	ALB 43
Winas, Silas	GRN 349	Winfield, Jacob	ULS 231	Winne, Killian J.	ALB 45
Winas, William Junr	ALB 91	Winfield, John	ORN 342	Winne, Laurance	ALB 102
Winch, Benjamin	OND 211	Winfield, John	ULS 231	Winne, Levinus	ALB 54
Winch, Samuel	OND 184	Winfield, William	ORN 369	Winne, Mary	ALB 97
Winchel see Wenshel		Winford, John	COL 240	Winne, Peter	ALB 97
Winchel, Chauncey	OND 194	Wing, Abner	DUT 103	Winne, Peter	HRK551½
Winchel, Daniel	COL 180	Wing, Abraham	DUT 52	Winne, Peter D.	ALB 106
Winchel, Danil	WSH 245	Wing, Abraham T.	DUT 131	Winne, William	ALB 97
Winchel, John	CHN 920	Wing, Anstis	WSH 208	Winne, William B.	ALB 143
Winchel, John	DEL 274	Wing, Benjn	OTS 37	Winnecker, Catharine	MNT 24
Winchel, L[uke?]	OND 210	Wing, Benjamin	SRA 44	Winnee, Garret	RNS 36
Winchel, Martin	OND 206	Wing, Benjamin	WSH 208	Winnee, Garret J.	RNS 36
Winchel, Willm F.	CHN 904	Wing, Brice	DUT 46	Winnee, Hette	RNS 85
Winchell, Amasa	CAY 612	Wing, Danl	OTS 37	Winnee, John L.	RNS 36
Winchell, Amasa	CAY 612	Wing, David	RNS 23	Winnee, John R.	RNS 84
Winchell, Daniel	COL 201	Wing, Edward	WSH 208	Winnee, Lavinus	RNS 85
Winchell, David	CHN 740	Wing, Elisha	RNS 49	Winnee, Martin P.	RNS 36
Winchell, Eli	HRK 521	Wing, George	DUT 119	Winnee, Moses	RNS 85
Winchell, Jacob	COL 201	Wing, Isaac	SRA 44	Winnee, Peter P.	RNS 36
Winchell, James	DUT 142	Wing, Jackson	DUT 49	Winnee, Philip	RNS 36
Winchell, James	NYK 66	Wing, John	DUT 46	Winnee, Richard	RNS 85
Winchell, James	NYK 136	Wing, John	SRA 41	Winnenburg, Francis	NYK 40
Winchell, James	ULS 197	Wing, Jonathan	DUT 125	Winner, Dot	GRN 345
Winchell, James Jun	CAY 612	Wing, Jonathan	OND 190	Winner, John	GRN 328
Winchell, Jeddedeah	WSH 279	Wing, Josephus	SCH 157	Winner, Simon	DUT 164
Winchell, Joel	WSH 279	Wing, Mary	OTS 37	Winney, Levinus	SRA 50
Winchell, John	RNS 81	Wing, Mary	WSH 208	Winney, Mary	SRA 39
Winchell, Joseph	COL 204	Wing, Nehemiah	WSH 208	Winnison, James	GRN 330
Winchell, Lemuel	ULS 198	Wing, Prince	SRA 59	Winnow, John	WSH 256
Winchell, Martin	CLN 164	Wing, Russel	WSH 208	Winny, Jonathan	SCH 142
Winchell, Martin E.	DUT 142	Wing, Samuel	DUT 91	Winship see Windship	
Winchell, Peter	ULS 196	Wing, Shubil	SRA 38	Winship, Catherine	NYK 111
Winchell, Philo M.	DUT 142	Wing, Shubil	SRA 44	Winship, Daniel	NYK 141
Winchell, Robert	RNS 31	Wing, Sowery	OTS 32	Winship, Jabez	TIO 214
Winchell, Ruggles	TIO 212	Wing, Thomas	DUT 45	Winship, John	NYK 148
Wincher, Richard	MNT 37	Wing, Thurston	DUT 46	Winship, Joseph	NYK 120
Winchester see Wenchest-		Wing, Wm	MNT 94	Winship, Nehemiah	DUT 164
er		Wing, Wm	MNT 95	Winship, Samuel	NYK 147
Winchester, Amariah	DUT 134	Wing, William	WSH 208	Winship, Samuel	OND 182
Winchester, Jabez	HRK 530	Wingard, James	COL 261	Winship, Thomas	NYK 141
Wincoop see Wynkoop		Wingassen, Abraham	NYK 153	Winship, William M.	OND 182
Wincoop, Peter	GRN 326	Winis, Lewis	GRN 354	Winsloe, Stephen	ONT 406
Windcomb, James	MNT 99	Winis, Wm	GRN 354	Winslor, Seth	ONT 334
Windecker see Wendecker		Winkfield, John	NYK 110	Winslow, Asa	COL 251
Windecker, Frederick	MNT 57	Winklar, John	TIO 259	Winslow, Azariah	OTS 19
Windecker, Jacob	HRK 578	Winm, Simeon	SCH 134	Winslow, Calvin	OND 185
Windecker, John	HRK 578	Winn see Win & Wynn		Winslow, Dennah a	
Windover see Wendover		Winn, Henry	DEL 272	Black	NYK 55
Windover, Peter	DUT 115	Winn, Hugh	MNT 105	Winslow, George	ULS 263
				Winslow, Jared	COL 181

Winslow, Jellis	COL	252	Wire see Wier			Witbeck, John	COL	230
Winslow, Job	COL	211	Wire, Robert	WSH	230	Witbeck, John	COL	239
Winslow, John	OND	185	Wires, Amos	ULS	180	Witbeck, John	RNS	15
Winslow, John	WSH	189	Wirth see Worth			Witbeck, John Junr	ALB	118
Winslow, John	WSH	211	Wirth, James	OND	210	Witbeck, John Junr	COL	193
Winslow, Joseph	ALB	118	Wisdom, Peggy	NYK	18	Witbeck, John Junr	COL	230
Winslow, Joseph	ULS	263	Wise, Benjamin Junr	ULS	247	Witbeck, John B.	COL	236
Winslow, Luther	HRK	441	Wise, Benjamin Senr	ULS	247	Witbeck, John J.	COL	233
Winslow, Nathaniel	WSH	228	Wise, Israel	HRK	477	Witbeck, John L.	ALB	118
Winslow, Samuel	ULS	266	Wise, John	COL	183	Witbeck, John P.	RNS	15
Winslow, Thomas	NYK	32	Wise, Samuel	COL	183	Witbeck, Jonathan	RNS	56
Winslow, Thomas	OND	185	Wise, Stephen	NYK	130	Witbeck, Jonathan	RNS	62
Winson, John	RNS	87	Wiseburn, Daniel	NYK	142	Witbeck, Lucas	ALB	50
Winsor, Amos	OTS	10	Wiseman, Christopher			Witbeck, Lucas G.	ALB	42
Winsor, Anon	CHN	794	a Black	NYK	70	Witbeck, Peter	ALB	117
Winsor, Ezer	OTS	29	Wiseman, Jonathan	MNT	98	Witbeck, Peter	COL	193
Wins[or?], Joseph	OTS	12	Wiseman, Thomas	WSH	223	Witbeck, Peter	COL	245
Winsor, Joshua	CHN	794	Wiser see Weiser &			Witbeck, Peter J.	RNS	15
Winsor, Olney	CHN	794	Wizer			Witbeck, Sine	RNS	83
Winston, Abm Junr	RNS	102	Wiser, Catherine	NYK	144	Witbeck, Thomas	ALB	118
Winston, Isaac	ALB	78	Wiser, Herman	OTS	27	Witbeck, Thos	RNS	15
Winston, Isaac Junr	ALB	79	Wiser, Isaac	OTS	27	Witbeck, Tobias J.	RNS	62
Winston, Nathl C.	OTS	21	Wiser, John	MNT	107	Witbeck, Volkert	COL	261
Winston, Stephen	SRA	48	Wishart, Hugh	NYK	29	Witbeck, Walter	ALB	111
Winstone, Abm	RNS	102	Wishingham, Abraham			Witbeck, Walter Junr	ALB	109
Winstone, Jacob	RNS	102	a Black	NYK	110	Witbeck, William	OND	179
Winstone, Joel	RNS	108	Wismiller, Abraham	ULS	242	Witbeck, Wm	RNS	15
Winter, Abijah	DUT	86	Wismiller, Henry	ULS	242	Witber, Jacobus	COL	233
Winter, Andrew	ALB	25	Wismiller, Jeremiah	ULS	242	Witber, William	COL	233
Winter, Andrew	WSH	303	Wismiller, Peter	ULS	243	Witchibee, John	ALB	15
Winter, Asa	HRK	589	Wisner, Asa	TIO	264	Witcum see Whitcomb		
Winter, Christopher	ALB	81	Wisner, Daniel	CAY	724	Witcum, Robert	CLN	154
Winter, David	DEL	285	Wisner, David	CAY	536	Witford see Whitford		
Winter, David	SCH	144	Wisner, Henry	ORN	377	Witford, Constant	ESS	296
Winter, Elizabeth	NYK	75	Wisner, Henry Junr	ORN	377	Withenberry, Benjamin	NYK	104
Winter, Ezra	ORN	330	Wisner, Henry B.	ORN	333	Witherby see Wetherby		
Winter, Isaac	OTS	57	Wisner, Jahil	CAY	540	Witherby, Jacob	WSH	300
Winter, Jacob	COL	232	Wisner, Jeffry	ORN	373	Witherby, Jonathan	MNT	77
Winter, Jesse	OTS	52	Wisner, John	ORN	327	Witherwax see Wetherwax		
Winter, Josee	DUT	21	Wisner, John	ORN	366	Witherwax, Andrew	COL	220
Winter, Joseph	NYK	47	Wisner, Moses	CAY	722	Witherwax, Andrew	RNS	12
Winter, Joseph	QNS	72	Wisner, Moses	ORN	369	Witherwax, Andrew	RNS	29
Winter, Juvenal	OTS	58	Wisner, Nathan	CAY	724	Witherwax, Andrew G.	RNS	44
Winter, Levi	ORN	320	Wisner, Nehemiah	CAY	724	Witherwax, Barbara	RNS	29
Winter, Matthew	DUT	21	Wisner, Smith	CAY	520	Witherwax, Bostian	RNS	12
Winter, Matthew	DUT	151	Wisner, Stephen	CAY	724	Witherwax, Bostion	RNS	39
Winter, Peter	COL	232	Wisner, William	ORN	377	Witherwax, Henry	RNS	45
Winterenham, Isaac	DUT	104	Wisner, William	ONT	476	Witherwax, Jacob	RNS	45
Winterenham, John	DUT	106	Wissel, David	HRK	462	Witherwax, John	RNS	29
Wintermoot, Christopher	ULS	220	Wissmer, George	DEL	290	Witherwax, John	RNS	29
Winters, David	SCH	147	Wisson, John	QNS	78	Witherwax, Laurence	RNS	11
Winters, Elijah	ONT	498	Wisson, Silas	QNS	79	Witherwax, Leonard	RNS	12
Winters, Gideon	SRA	20	Wisson, Thomas	QNS	78	Withins, Jacob Junr	NYK	86
Winters, John	SRA	36	Wisson, Thomas	QNS	82	Withrell see Whitherell		
Winters, Jonas	SUF	96	Wist, John Junr	ULS	231	Withrell, David	WSH	271
Winters, Mathew	SCH	147	Wist, John Senr	ULS	232	Withrill, Zebedee	RNS	18
Winters, Moses	SCH	147	Wiswall, Samuel	COL	250	Withy, Mary	NYK	118
Winters, Roger	SCH	147	Wit_cair, David	MNT	42	Witing see Whiting		
Winters, Silas	DEL	278	Witaker see Whitaker			Witing, Jonathan	ESS	296
Winters, William	CAY	534	Witaker, James	OTS	2	Witlock see Whitlock &		
Winters, William	ESS	322	Witaker, Jas Junr	OTS	2	Whitcklock		
Winterton, William	ORN	289	Witaker, Thos	OTS	2	Witlock, Henry	SRA	18
Winthrop, Benjamin	NYK	142	Witbeck see Whitbeck			Witman see Whitman		
Winthrop, Francis B.	NYK	27	Witbeck, Abm	ALB	50	Witman, George	ESS	318
Winthrop, Peter	NYK	66	Witbeck, Abraham P.	COL	234	Witmarsh see Whitmarsh		
Winthrop, Wm	MNT	101	Witbeck, Andrew	COL	257	Witmarsh, Samuel	ALB	42
Winton, Abel	OTS	23	Witbeck, Andrew Junr	COL	257	Witmore see Whitmore		
Wintworth see Wentworth			Witbeck, Bruer	COL	239	Witmore, Etha	OND	219
Wintworth, Benjamin Junr	CHN	850	Witbeck, Casparus	ALB	109	Witmore, Ezrahiah	WST	114
Wintworth, Burrell	CHN	850	Witbeck, Cosporus	RNS	62	Witsel, John	GRN	328
Wintworth, David	GRN	340	Witbeck, Elizabeth	COL	199	Witsell, Jacob	GRN	329
Wintworth, David	SCH	146	Witbeck, Gabriel	HRK	471	Witscher, Asa	NYK	122
Wintworth, Edward	CHN	850	Witbeck, Gerrit	ALB	50	Witten, Jacob	ULS	249
Wintworth, Elisha	CHN	850	Witbeck, Jacob	COL	233	Witter, Ebenezar	CAY	662
Wintworth, Henry	ONN	157	Witbeck, Jacobus	ALB	59	Witter, Elijah	ONT	500
Wipple see Whipple			Witbeck, John	ALB	109	Witter, Isaac	ORN	341
Wipple, John	CHN	958	Witbeck, John	COL	193	Witter, Samuel	CHN	818

Witter, Saml	CHN 820	Wolgemuth, Widow	MNT 7
Witter, Samuel Junr	CHN 820	Wolgemuth, Wm	MNT 6
Witter, Wheaton	CHN 820	Wolker, Nathan	OND 224
Wittingham see Whittin-		Woll_ce, Peter	MNT 56
ham		Wollcott, Abraham	COL 231
Wittingham, Isaac	NYK 128	Wollcott, Charles	STB 202
Wittsey, Abel	ONT 324	Wollcott, Frances	COL 234
Wittsey, Jacob	CAY 708	Wollcott, Francis Junr	COL 228
Wixsom, Daniel	DUT 96	Wollcott, Joseph	STB 202
Wixsom, Ebenezer	DUT 173	Wollcott, Norman	STB 202
Wixsom, Elijah	DUT 86	Wollcott, Rebecca	COL 231
Wixsom, Elijah	DUT 92	Wollcott, Roger	STB 202
Wixsom, Elijah	DUT 167	Wollcott, Thomas	COL 230
Wixsom, Isaac	DUT 91	Wolle[g?], Jacob	STB 199
Wixsom, James	DUT 86	Wolley, Benjamin	QNS 70
Wixsom, John	DUT 95	Wollsey, Richard	COL 180
Wixsom, Joseph	DUT 20	Wolsay, Johnahan	GRN 349
Wixsom, Peleg	DUT 86	Wolsey, Andrew	MNT 41
Wixsom, Shubael	DUT 86	Wolsey, Zephaniah	GRN 349
Wixsom, Shubael Junr	DUT 86	Wolsworth see Wool-	
Wixon, Joshua	STB 203	worth	
Wixson, Barnabas	TIO 222	Wolsworth, William	WSH 238
Wiyley see Wylee		Wolver(?), Jeremiah	GRN 327
Wiyley, James	WST 156	Wolver, Michl	ALB 80
Wizer see Wiser		Wolverton, Stephen	SRA 25
Wizer, Benjn	CHN 960	Wolvier, John	CHN 950
Woddel, Robert	WSH 203	Wombough, William	DEL 273
Woddell, Silas	DUT 101	Womple, Cornelius	MNT 109
Woddle, James	WSH 191	Womsor, Ephraem	STB 204
Wodford, Solomon	GRN 354	Wood, Aaron	NYK 152
Woglom, Abraham	RCH 94	Wood, Aaron	ONN 172
Woglom, Abraham	RCH 94	Wood, Abel	SUF 81
Woglom, Cornelius	RCH 94	Wood, Abner	NYK 84
Woglom, John	RCH 94	Wood, Abner	RNS 46
Woglom, Joshua	RCH 94	Wood, Abm	ALB 76
Woglom, Peter	RCH 94	Wood, Abraham	DUT 116
Woglom, Simmons	RCH 94	Wood, Abraham	ORN 305
Wolberton, Isreal	CAY 696	Wood, Abraham	SRA 59
Wolcot, Benijah	NYK 82	Wood, Abraham	ULS 242
Wolcot, Francis	OTS 55	Wood, Abraham	WST 154
Wolcot, Nathl	OTS 39	Wood, Adriana	ORN 378
Wolcot, Timo	OTS 39	Wood, Alexander	ORN 283
Wolcot, Wm	OTS 55	Wood, Amasa	ESS 308
Wolcott, ...	CAY 576	Wood, Amasa	ESS 310
Wolcott, Elisha	ONT 472	Wood, Amos	RNS 108
Wolcott, James	COL 185	Wood, Amos	WSH 210
Wolcott, John	COL 183	Wood, Amos	WSH 270
.olcott, Luke	MNT 81	Wood, Amos	WSH 305
Wolcott, Nathaniel	DEL 280	Wood, Anthony	ORN 366
Wolcott, Thomas	MNT 81	Wood, Archabald	WSH 224
Wolcott, Thomas Junr	MNT 81	Wood, Arvin	RNS 100
Wolcott, Wheller	MNT 81	Wood, Asa	NYK 91
Wolcott, Wyatt	COL 184	Wood, Barnabus	ALB 35
Wole, Partrick	NYK 85	Wood, Benjamin	HRK 529
Wolf see Woolf		Wood, Benjamin	ONT 398
Wolf, Bithuel	WSH 286	Wood, Benjamin	ORN 305
Wolf, Christion	GRN 354	Wood, Benjamin	SRA 19
Wolf, Frederic	RNS 92	Wood, Benjamin	SRA 59
Wolf, George	GRN 357	Wood, Benjamin	SCH 123
Wolf, Henry	RCK 102	Wood, Benjamin	ULS 244
Wolf, Jacob	DEL 282	Wood, Benjamin	WST 113
Wolf, Jacob	RNS 30	Wood, Benjamin	WST 170
Wolf, John	RNS 30	Wood, Benjn L.	RNS 59
Wolf, John	WST 114	Wood, Bersheba	SUF 86
Wolf, Martin	COL 196	Wood, Brazella	CLN 162
Wolf, Michael	DEL 275	Wood, Caleb	COL 218
Wolf, Peter	GRN 353	Wood, Caleb	NYK 34
Wolf, Peter	RNS 90	Wood, Caleb	OTS 47
Wolf, Tunis	GRN 357	Wood, Catherine	NYK 32
Wolf, Valantine	MNT 17	Wood, Cezar a free	
Wolf, Willm D.	COL 219	Negro	ALB 96
Wolfcamp, John	ALB 54	Wood, Charles	NYK 49
Wolfe, Anthony	WST 145	Wood, Charles	NYK 80
Wolfe, David	NYK 36	Wood, Charles	WST 124
Wolfred, Danl	ALB 64	Wood, Clement	RCK 103
Wolfred, Henry	ALB 64	Wood, Consider	DUT 127
Wolfrom, Mathias	COL 192	Wood, Cornelius	ORN 277

Wood, Cornelius	WSH 198
Wood, Daniel	CAY 674
Wood, Daniel	CAY 674
Wood, Daniel	DEL 287
Wood, Daniel	DUT 120
Wood, Daniel	ORN 393
Wood, Danl	OTS 55
Wood, Daniel	QNS 83
Wood, Daniel	SRA 57
Wood, Daniel	ULS 214
Wood, Daniel	WSH 259
Wood(?), Daniel	WST 161
Wood, Danil	SRA 57
Wood, David	OND 175
Wood, David	OND 189
Wood, David	OTS 4
Wood, David	OTS 46
Wood, David	SRA 21
Wood, David	SRA 39
Wood, David	SRA 59
Wood, Dudley	NYK 112
Wood, Easther	WSH 218
Wood, Ebener	NYK 102
Wood, Ebenezar	CAY 668
Wood, Ebenezer	WST 155
Wood, Edmond	RCH 88
Wood, Edward	CAY 690
Wood, Edward	ULS 217
Wood, Edward W.	ULS 217
Wood, Eli	RNS 14
Wood, Elijah	DUT 137
Wood, Elijah	QNS 75
Wood, Elijah	QNS 76
Wood, Elijah	SRA 40
Wood, Elisha	MNT 122
Wood, Elisha	SRA 45
Wood, Elisha	TIO 245
Wood, Elisha	WSH 204
Wood, Enoch	SRA 39
Wood, Epenetus	QNS 72
Wood, Ephraim	RNS 17
Wood, Epinetus	SUF 89
Wood, Eseck	WSH 198
Wood, Ezra	ALB 91
Wood, Frederick	ULS 202
Wood, Furbush	OND 186
Wood, Gardner	RNS 26
Wood, George	ORN 321
Wood, George	RNS 49
Wood, George	WST 154
Wood, Gideon	CAY 682
Wood, Gideon	SRA 34
Wood, Gideon	SRA 41
Wood, Halsted	SRA 13
Wood, Hannah	SRA 23
Wood, Hannah	WST 114
Wood, Henry	DUT 25
Wood, Henry	ORN 388
Wood, Henry	WST 130
Wood, Hezekiah	WST 159
Wood, Isaac	ALB 79
Wood, Isaac	DUT 26
Wood, Isaac	DUT 115
Wood, Isaac	NYK 144
Wood, Isaac	OND 205
Wood, Isaac	RCH 88
Wood, Isaac	WSH 186
Wood, Isaac B.	DUT 121
Wood, Ishmael	DUT 26
Wood, Israel	DUT 177
Wood, Israel	NYK 60
Wood, Israel	ORN 360
Wood, Israel	ORN 378
Wood, Israel	SUF 81
Wood, Israel Junr	ORN 377
Wood, Isreal	CAY 602

Name	Loc
Wood, Jacob	DUT 98
Wood, Jacob	GRN 336
Wood, Jacob	ORN 287
Wood, Jacob	RNS 57
Wood, Jacob	RCH 90
Wood, Jacob	TIO 260
Wood, Jacob	ULS 234
Wood, Jacob	ULS 268
Wood, Jacob Junr	ORN 285
Wood, Jacobus	ULS 212
Wood, James	ALB 3
Wood, Ja_es	CAY 578
Wood, James	CAY 652
Wood, James	DUT 33
Wood, James	NYK 133
Wood, James	ONN 156
Wood, James	ONT 450
Wood, James	ORN 331
Wood, James	ORN 365
Wood, James	QNS 75
Wood, James	QNS 76
Wood, James	QNS 83
Wood, James	QNS 84
Wood, James	RCH 91
Wood, James	ULS 212
Wood, James	WST 127
Wood, James Junr	RCH 91
Wood, Jarvis	SUF 79
Wood, Jedediah	DUT 178
Wood, Jediah	RNS 51
Wood, Jehiah	WSH 188
Wood, Jered	WST 151
Wood, Jeremiah	COL 250
Wood, Jeremiah	NYK 66
Wood, Jeremiah	SUF 87
Wood, Jesse	ALB 76
Wood, Jesse	DUT 34
Wood, Jesse	GRN 347
Wood, Jesse	GRN 356
Wood, Jesse	ORN 319
Wood, Jesse	ORN 365
Wood, Job	OTS 4
Wood, Jobe	WSH 203
Wood, Johia	ALB 139
Wood, John	ALB 18
Wood, John	ALB 112
Wood, John	CAY 652
Wood, John	COL 244
Wood, John	DEL 284
Wood, John	DUT 13
Wood, John	DUT 27
Wood, John	DUT 52
Wood, John	HRK 575
Wood, John	MNT 43
Wood, John	MNT 125
Wood, John	NYK 22
Wood, John	NYK 43
Wood, John	NYK 56
Wood, John	NYK 126
Wood, John	ONT 320
Wood, John	ONT 432
Wood, John	ORN 278
Wood, John	ORN 314
Wood, John	ORN 331
Wood, John	ORN 360
Wood, John	ORN 393
Wood, John	OTS 8
Wood, John	OTS 34
Wood, John	OTS 52
Wood, John	QNS 75
Wood, John	RCH 89
Wood, John	RCH 92
Wood, John	RCK 109
Wood, John	SRA 16
Wood, John	SCH 135
Wood, John	SCH 146
Wood, John	SUF 79
Wood, John	SUF 81
Wood, John	ULS 212
Wood, John	ULS 268
Wood, John Junr	RCH 89
Wood, John Albert	NYK 34
Wood, John T.	ORN 330
Wood, John W.	HRK 575
Wood, Jonah	SRA 15
Wood, Jonah	SRA 19
Wood, Jonah	SUF 82
Wood, Jonas	CAY 644
Wood, Jonas	ESS 322
Wood, Jonas	ORN 325
Wood, Jonas	OTS 53
Wood, Jonas	SUF 84
Wood, Jonas	ULS 235
Wood, Jonas	WST 111
Wood, Jonas Junr	CAY 644
Wood, Jonathan	ALB 79
Wood, Jonathan	ALB 81
Wood, Jonathan	CLN 155
Wood, Jonathan	DUT 98
Wood, Jonathan	ESS 308
Wood, Jonathan	HRK 422
Wood, Jonathan	OND 172
Wood, Jonathan	OND 193
Wood, Jonathan	ORN 317
Wood, Jonathan	WSH 268
Wood, Jos:	SCH 121
Wood, Josep	MNT 43
Wood, Joseph	ALB 65
Wood, Joseph	DEL 274
Wood, Joseph	DEL 281
Wood, Joseph	DUT 29
Wood, Joseph	DUT 112
Wood, Joseph	DUT 118
Wood, Joseph	NYK 91
Wood, Joseph	NYK 98
Wood, Joseph	OND 166
Wood, Joseph	ONT 340
Wood, Joseph	ORN 310
Wood, Joseph	ORN 358
Wood, Joseph	OTS 2
Wood, Joseph	OTS 46
Wood, Joseph	OTS 47
Wood, Joseph	QNS 64
Wood, Joseph	QNS 83
Wood, Joseph	RNS 21
Wood, Joseph	RCH 92
Wood, Joseph	RCK 104
Wood, Joseph	SRA 13
Wood, Joseph	SRA 59
Wood, Joseph B.	DUT 54
Wood, Joshua	CHN 766
W[ood?], Lemuel	CAY 602
Wood, Levi	DUT 109
Wood, Levi	ESS 308
Wood, Levi	OTS 46
Wood, Luther	ONN 156
Wood, Luther	WSH 200
Wood, Lydia	ORN 284
Wood, Martha	SRA 16
Wood, Martin	QNS 75
Wood, Melancton	SUF 83
Wood, Michael	SRA 21
Wood, Michael	SRA 22
Wood, Miles	QNS 76
Wood, Mordica	ALB 37
Wood, Moses	RNS 55
Wood, Moses	ULS 180
Wood, Nancy	RCK 103
Wood, Nathan	OTS 36
Wood, Nathan	SRA 19
Wood, Nathan	SCH 147
Wood, Nathan	WST 160
Wood, Nathl	COL 204
Wood, Nathaniel	WSH 285
Wood, Nathaniel	WST 137
Wood, Nehemiah	DUT 176
Wood, Nehemiah	DUT 178
Wood, Noah	CHN 806
Wood, Noah S.	ALB 59
Wood, Oliver	DUT 161
Wood, Oliver	NYK 112
Wood, Palmer	DEL 287
Wood, Peleg	SUF 87
Wood, Peter	NYK 28
Wood, Peter	ULS 217
Wood, Phebe	ORN 394
Wood, Ralph T.	ONT 508
Wood, Reuben	SRA 4
Wood, Richard	ORN 329
Wood, Richard	ORN 359
Wood, Richard	RCH 90
Wood, Richard	RCH 93
Wood, Richd	SUF 68
Wood, Robert	WSH 276
Wood, Ruth	RCH 91
Wood, Salmon	OTS 24
Wood, Samson (free Negro)	RNS 59
Wood, Samuel	CLN 160
Wood, Samuel	DUT 106
Wood, Samuel	HRK 422
Wood, Samuel	MNT 93
Wood, Samuel	NYK 63
Wood, Samuel	NYK 86
Wood, Samuel	OND 218
Wood, Samuel	ORN 294
Wood, Samuel	QNS 76
Wood, Samuel	QNS 78
Wood, Samuel	QNS 83
Wood, Samuel	RCH 89
Wood, Samuel	SRA 19
Wood, Saml	SUF 79
Wood, Samuel	ULS 256
Wood, Samuel	WST 150
Wood, Saml D.	OTS 34
Wood, Sanford	SRA 20
Wood, Sarah	NYK 31
Wood, Selah	SUF 79
Wood, Semeon	CLN 159
Wood, Silas	ORN 284
Wood, Silas	OTS 18
Wood, Silas	RNS 101
Wood, Silas	SUF 100
Wood, Silas Junr	ORN 284
Wood, Silas Junr	RNS 110
Wood, Siles	WSH 203
Wood, Simeon	OND 205
Wood, Simeon	ORN 286
Wood, Solomon	CLN 168
Wood, Solomon	OND 190
Wood, Squire	WSH 301
Wood, Squire	WST 140
Wood, Stephen	DUT 105
Wood, Stephen	NYK 125
Wood, Stephen	ONN 157
Wood, Stephen	ORN 275
Wood, Stephen	ORN 396
Wood, Stephen	OTS 23
Wood, Stephen	OTS 45
Wood, Stephen	QNS 72
Wood, Stephen	QNS 75
Wood, Stephen	QNS 76
Wood, Stephen	QNS 76
Wood, Stephen	QNS 83
Wood, Stephen	RCH 93
Wood, Stephen	SRA 22
Wood, Stephen	SRA 45
Wood, Stephen	WSH 259
Wood, Stephen	WST 155
Wood, Stephen	WST 158
Wood, Stephen Junr	SRA 45

Name	Loc	No.
Wright, Eleazer F.	OND	181
Wright, Eli	CAY	676
Wright, Elias	HRK	473
Wright, Elias	OTS	47
Wright, Elihu	DUT	61
Wright, Elijah	CHN	778
Wright, Elijah	CHN	780
Wright, Elijah	CHN	870
Wright, Elijah	COL	196
Wright, Elijah	DUT	84
Wright, Elijah	DUT	92
Wright, Elijah	DUT	118
Wright, Elijah	WSH	253
Wright, Elisha	ALB	73
Wright, Elizabeth	OND	206
Wright, Enoch	WSH	285
Wright, Enos	ONN	135
Wright, Ephraim	OND	208
Wright, Ezra	OTS	35
Wright, Frost	QNS	60
Wright, Gabriel	OND	164
Wright, Gad	OND	206
Wright, Gardner	ESS	323
Wright, George	CHN	968
Wright, George	COL	202
Wright, George	GRN	345
Wright, George a Black	NYK	94
Wright, George	SCH	153
Wright, George Jun	GRN	345
Wright, Gideon	CAY	672
Wright, Gilbert	NYK	136
Wright, Gilbert	ONT	394
Wright, Gilbert	SRA	38
Wright, Hamilton freeman	SRA	25
Wright, Hannah	WSH	282
Wright, Hartshorne	NYK	144
Wright, Hendrick	GRN	338
Wright, Isaac	DUT	84
Wright, Isaac	DUT	156
Wright, Isaac	ESS	307
Wright, Isaac	NYK	45
Wright, Isaac	NYK	124
Wright, Isaac	QNS	77
Wright, Israel	OND	220
Wright, Jacob	DEL	289
Wright, Jacob	DUT	39
Wright, Jacob	DUT	109
Wright, Jacob	MNT	34
Wright, Jacob	NYK	51
Wright, Jacob	NYK	130
Wright, Jacob	ONT	376
Wright, Jacob	RNS	111
Wright, Jacob	SCH	149
Wright, Jacob	SCH	153
Wright, James	DEL	275
Wright, James	DUT	129
Wright, James	NYK	101
Wright, James	ONN	183
Wright, James	OTS	2
Wright, James	WSH	271
Wright, James	WST	128
Wright, James Junr	DUT	146
Wright, Jane	SUF	97
Wright, Jeremiah	ONN	147
Wright, Jeremiah	SCH	144
Wright, Jesse	DUT	54
Wright, Jesse	GRN	343
Wright, Jesse	OTS	43
Wright, Joab	HRK	557
Wright, Job	CAY	564
Wright, Job	NYK	60
Wright, Joel	OTS	7
Wright, John	ALB	15
Wright, John	ALB	73
Wright, John	ALB	144
Wright, John	CAY	658
Wright, John	COL	182
Wright, John	COL	212
Wright, John	DEL	281
Wright, John	DUT	21
Wright, John	ESS	304
Wright, John	HRK	559
Wright, John	NYK	85
Wright, John	OND	177
Wright, John	ONT	376
Wright, John	ORN	284
Wright, John	QNS	64
Wright, John	QNS	64
Wright, John	QNS	81
W.ight, John	QNS	83
Wright, John	RNS	83
Wright, John	RCH	93
Wright, John	SCH	172
Wright, John	TIO	215
Wright, John	WSH	192
Wright, John	WST	132
Wright, John Junr	COL	177
Wright, John Junr	RCH	90
Wright, John Junr	WST	132
Wright, John N.	SUF	65
Wright, Jonathan	DUT	170
Wright, Jonathan	HRK	562
Wright, Jonathan	NYK	128
Wright, Jonathan	QNS	64
Wright, Jonathan	QNS	82
Wright, Jonathan	ULS	266
Wright, Jonathan	WSH	276
Wright, Jordon	NYK	45
Wright, Joseph	DUT	20
Wright, Joseph	DUT	76
Wright, Joseph	GRN	347
Wright, Joseph	ONT	376
Wright, Joseph	QNS	84
Wright, Joseph	SCH	149
Wright, Joseph	ULS	184
Wright, Joseph	WSH	223
Wright, Joseph	WSH	297
Wright, Joshua	RCH	94
Wright, Josiah	RNS	92
Wright, Jotham	OND	168
Wright, Jotham	SRA	42
Wright, Justice	OTS	47
Wright, Justus	OND	204
Wright, Langdon	QNS	76
Wright, Lebeus	ONT	366
Wright, Lemuel	OTS	53
Wright, Lockland	WSH	190
Wright, Luther	OND	178
Wright, Luther	ONN	140
Wright, Luther	WSH	194
Wright, Luthur	CAY	672
Wright, Mary	WSH	199
Wright, Mathew	CHN	742
Wright, Mathew	WSH	187
Wright, Micajah	WST	128
Wright, Michael	GRN	338
Wright, Molly	QNS	72
Wright, Moses	OND	211
Wright, Moses	RNS	17
Wright, Nathan	OTS	35
Wright, Nathaniel	SRA	38
Wright, Nathaniel	WST	129
Wright, Nathaniel Junr	WST	129
Wright, Oliver	CHN	960
Wright, Oliver	HRK	479
Wright, Oliver	RNS	96
Wright, Orris	QNS	82
Wright, Paul	HRK	583
Wright, Phineas	NYK	88
Wright, Rachael	NYK	81
Wright, Reuben	NYK	134
Wright, Reuben	WSH	235
Wright, Reuben	WST	125
Wright, Reuben	WST	131
Wright, Richard	ORN	272
Wright, Robert	DUT	21
Wright, Robert	DUT	87
Wright, Robert	ORN	283
Wright, Robert Junr	DUT	88
Wright, Ruphes	WSH	239
Wright, Samuel	ALB	27
Wright, Samuel	ALB	73
Wright, Samuel	CAY	674
Wright, Samuel	HRK	593
Wright, Samuel	NYK	150
Wright, Samuel	OND	193
Wright, Samuel	OND	206
Wright, Samuel	ORN	281
Wright, Saml	OTS	7
Wright, Samuel	QNS	64
Wright, Samuel	QNS	72
Wright, Samuel	QNS	83
Wright, Samuel	WSH	227
Wright, Samuel	WSH	258
Wright, Samuel Junr	OND	194
Wright, Samuel B.	OND	210
Wright, Sarah	OTS	37
Wright, Sawyer	RNS	37
Wright, Silvanus	SRA	8
Wright, Simeon	SCH	149
Wright, Simeon Junr	SCH	149
Wright, Smith	HRK	504
Wright, Smith	WSH	276
Wright, Solomon	DUT	21
Wright, Stephen	ALB	73
Wright, Stephen	HRK	451
Wright, Stephen	NYK	139
Wright, Stephen	ORN	272
Wright, Thomas	CAY	694
Wright, Thomas	DUT	16
Wright, Thomas	DUT	21
Wright, Thomas	GRN	352
Wright, Thomas	GRN	355
Wright, Thomas	KNG	9
Wright, Thomas	NYK	111
Wright, Thomas	NYK	136
Wright, Thomas	OND	211
Wright, Thomas	QNS	84
Wright, Thoms	TIO	235
Wright, Thomas	WSH	250
Wright, Uriah	SRA	34
Wright, Uriel	HRK	429
Wright, Walter	WSH	194
Wright, William	DUT	75
Wright, William	GRN	352
Wright, Wm	GRN	356
Wright, William	NYK	120
Wright, William	NYK	137
Wright, William	NYK	144
Wright, William	ONT	382
Wright, Willm	OTS	47
Wright, William	QNS	64
Wright, Wm	QNS	80
Wright, Wm	QNS	84
Wright, William	SRA	34
Wright, William	WST	132
Wright, William Jun	GRN	352
Wright, Winess	GRN	343
Wright, Wise	GRN	340
Wright, York a Black	NYK	22
Wright, York a mulatto	NYK	152
Wright, Zebulon	ORN	319
Wright, Zebulon	QNS	84
Wright, Zenas	ONN	189
Wright, Zera	WSH	190
Wrightman, Noel	WSH	213

427

Yelverton, Bowdoine			York, Yearman	CHN 812	Young, Henry	CAY 610	
Le Count	DUT 110		Yorker, Jacob	SCH 136	Young, Henry	HRK 493	
Yelverton, Gale	DUT 67		Yos, Charles	NYK 112	Young, Henry	ORN 362	
Yelverton, John	DUT 110		Yost, George	RNS 19	Young, Henry	RNS 89	
Yelverton, John	ORN 363		Yost, Jacob	MNT 62	Young, Henry Junr	ORN 354	
Yelverton, Moses	DUT 62		Yost, John	MNT 62	Young, Isaac	ALB 76	
Yelverton, William	ULS 235		Yost, Peter	MNT 62	Young, Israel	OND 180	
Yendall, Joseph	ULS 245		Youkhout, George	SCH 123	Young, Jacob	MNT 29	
Yendes, George	DEL 290		Youl, John	NYK 140	Young, Jacob	NYK 66	
Yendes, Peter	DEL 290		Youlds, Nancy	MNT 45	Young, Jacob	RNS 68	
Yeoman see Youman &			Youle, George	NYK 81	Young, Jacob	SCH 151	
Yumans			Youle, Timothy	NYK 81	Young, James	ALB 20	
Yeoman, Thomas a			Youles, John	ALB 19	Young, James	ALB 34	
mulatto	NYK 151		Youman, Henry	NYK 149	Young, James	ALB 132	
Yeomans, Abrm	RCK 109		Youmans, Antoney	GRN 352	Young, James	HRK 502	
Yeomans, Asa	OTS 50		Youmans, Arter	GRN 352	Yo..g, James	MNT 42	
Yeomans, Ben	RCK 100		Youmans, Eliab	GRN 349	Young, James	NYK 92	
Yeomans, Benj	RCK 100		Youmans, Jeremiah	NYK 100	Young, James	NYK 107	
Yeomans, Danl	RCK 104		Youmans, Moses	GRN 354	Young, James	OND 206	
Yeomans, Francis	DEL 289		Youmans, Nathaniel	GRN 349	Young, James	ORN 338	
Yeomans, Isaac	CAY 578		Youmans, Samuel	GRN 352	Young, James	OTS 11	
Yeomans, Isaac	RCK 109		Youmans, Wm	GRN 355	Young, James	OTS 56	
Yeomans, James	ALB 116		Young, Abimel	ORN 348	Young, James	RCK 107	
Yeomans, James	DEL 289		Young, Abraham	ALB 77	Young, Jeremiah	ALB 90	
Yeomans, Jeremiah	RCK 109		Young, Adam	ORN 310	Young, Jeremiah	SCH 173	
Yeomans, John	OTS 26		Young, Alexander	RNS 83	Young, Jeremiah Junr	SCH 151	
Yeomans, John	RCK 105		Young, Alexander	ULS 267	Young, Job	WSH 242	
Yeomans, Jonas	DEL 275		Young, Andrew	MNT 67	Young, Johannis	ORN 343	
Yeomans, Jonathan	RCK 105		Young, Andrew	ONT 490	Young, John	ALB 34	
Yeomans, Richard	RCK 106		Young, Annariah	MNT 105	Young, John	ALB 76	
Yeomans, Saml	RCK 109		Young, Asa	OTS 54	Young, John	ALB 131	
Yeomans, Saml Junr	RCK 103		Young, Barent	HRK 453	Young, John	NYK 26	
Yeomans, William	DEL 289		Young, Benjamin	ALB 52	Young, John	NYK 65	
Yeranton, Wm	SUF 66		Young, Benjamin	ORN 325	Young, John	NYK 66	
Yerkis, Thomas	CAY 538		Young, Benjamin	SCH 149	Young, John a Black	NYK 110	
Yerks, Jacobus	WST 171		Young, Birdsey	ORN 354	Young, John	OTS 28	
Yerks, James	WST 171		Young, Catherine	NYK 94	Young, John	OTS 56	
Yerks, John	WST 165		Young, Charles	ORN 294	Young, John	RNS 82	
Y_rks, John	WST 171		Young, Christian	COL 233	Young, John	ULS 268	
Yerks, Peter	WST 171		Young, Christian	SCH 152	Young, John	WSH 231	
Yerks, William	WST 171		Young, Christian	ULS 247	Young, John	WSH 236	
Yerolawin, John	COL 264		Young, Christion	MNT 32	Young, John	WSH 242	
Yerrington, Ebenezer	DUT 135		Young, Clayton	WSH 231	Young, John	WST 148	
Yerrington, Waterman	DUT 135		Young, Clayton Jur	WSH 242	Young, John Junr	ONN 171	
Yerrington, Wm	MNT 15		Young, Colwin	MNT 118	Young, John D.	MNT 27	
Yerry, John	DUT 69		Young, Conrod	MNT 43	Young, Jonathan	SCH 149	
Yertmer, Henry	MNT 31		Young, Cornelia	NYK 62	Young, Joseph	COL 227	
Yesley, William	ALB 53		Young, Daniel	RNS 82	Young, Joseph	HRK 572	
Yewron, Jacob	MNT 54		Young, Daniel Cooper	RNS 94	Young, Joseph	NYK 37	
Yock, John	ULS 238		Young, David	ALB 114	Young, Joseph	ONN 172	
Yong, Daniel	SRA 48		Young, David	NYK 67	Young, Joseph	OTS 4	
Yong, William	SRA 50		Young, David	OTS 28	Young, Martin	CAY 610	
Yonkhans, Henry	COL 237		Young, David	SCH 151	Young, Martin	STB 201	
Yonkhans, Michael	COL 237		Young, Dyer	OTS 38	Young, Matthew	ALB 103	
Yonkhons, Mathew	RNS 8		Young, Ebenezar	CAY 672	Young, Mattice	SCH 152	
Yonkin, Gideon	SUF 77		Young, Ebenezer	COL 178	Young, Michael	MNT 41	
Yonkman, Adam	COL 190		Young, Ebenezer	MNT 110	Young, Nathl	ALB 85	
Yonks, Ephraim	COL 232		Young, Eli	RNS 105	Young, Nathaniel	NYK 54	
Yoper, Cosper	MNT 55		Young, Elias	SCH 151	Young, Peter	ALB 67	
Yorger, Christopher	COL 228		Young, Elizabeth	NYK 129	Young, Peter	ALB 143	
Yorger, Michael	COL 238		Young, Elizth	OTS 28	Young, Peter	CAY 560	
York a Black	NYK 154		Young, Elizabeth	RCH 93	Young, Peter	MNT 26	
York	OTS 38		Young, Elkanah	DUT 174	Young, Peter	SCH 151	
York, Daniel	OND 210		Young, Enoch	ALB 85	Young, Peter	ULS 220	
York, Jabez	ONN 172		Young, Ephriam	SCH 151	Young, Rebecca	NYK 81	
York, Jacob	ORN 341		Young, Francis	NYK 72	Young, Reuben	ORN 349	
York, James	QNS 80		Young, Georg	MNT 28	Young, Robert	NYK 78	
York, John	CHN 836		Young, George	ALB 11	Young, Robert	OTS 56	
York, John	ULS 227		Young, George	NYK 76	Young, Robert	SRA 25	
York, Moses	ULS 219		Young, George	RNS 94	Young, Seth	ALB 85	
York, Oliver	SRA 28		Young, George	SCH 172	Young, Shaw	ALB 85	
York, Peter	RNS 19		Young, Gideon	SCH 150	Young, Shaw	DUT 172	
York, Peter	ULS 208		Young, Godfrey	MNT 32	Young, Silas	ORN 349	
York, Stephen	CHN 812		Young, Grover	ALB 30	Young, Solomon	MNT 82	
York, Susannah	RNS 19		Young, Henderson	MNT 102	Young, Stephen	NYK 93	
York, Thomas	CHN 836		Young, Hendrick	ULS 220	Young, Thomas	CAY 672	
York, Thomas	SRA 36		Young, Henry	CAY 578			

Name	Loc	No.	Name	Loc	No.	Name	Loc	No.
Young, Thomas	MNT	25	Youngs, Newel	SUF	77	Zielie, David	SCH	127
Young, Thomas	ULS	187	Youngs, Oliver	SUF	81	Zielie, John	SCH	127
Young, Tunis	RCK	107	Youngs, Peter	ALB	63	Zielie, Martinus	SCH	127
Young, Uriah	ALB	76	Youngs, Peter	ONN	151	Zielie, Nehemiah	SCH	134
Young, William	ALB	69	Youngs, Philip	SUF	80	Zielie, Peter	SCH	127
Young, William	DUT	63	Youngs, Richd	SUF	74	Zielie, Peter P.	SCH	127
Young, William	DUT	133	Youngs, Richd	SUF	77	Ziely, David	MNT	7
Young, William	HRK	551½	Youngs, Richd Jr	SUF	77	Ziely, John	MNT	7
Young, William	NYK	25	Youngs, Rufus	SUF	72	Ziely, Thomas	MNT	6
Young, William	NYK	96	Youngs, Samuel	WST	171	Zillers, Samuel	NYK	65
Young, William	ORN	311	Youngs, Samuel	WST	171	Zimmer, Adam	SCH	125
Young, William	ORN	335	Youngs, Thomas	ALB	112	Zimmer, Elizabeth	SCH	124
Young, William	SCH	173	Youngs, Thomas	DUT	68	Zimmer, George	SCH	125
Young, William Junr	ORN	313	Youngs, Thomas	QNS	80	Zimmer, Jacob Jr	SCH	125
Young, Zachariah	ORN	329	Youngs, Thomas	SRA	4	Zimmer, Peter	SCH	125
Young, Zachariah	SCH	149	Youngs, Thos	SUF	74	Zimmer, Willm	SCH	129
Youngblood, Daniel	ORN	302	Youngs, Thos	SUF	76	Zimmer, Willm Jr	SCH	124
Youngblood, Johannis Wm			Youngs, Timothy	SUF	80	Zimmerman see Timmerman		
Younghans, John	ALB	64	Youngs, Warren	SUF	77	Zimmerman, Christeen	MNT	72
Younglove, Ann	WSH	223	Youngs, Warren	SUF	77	Zimmerman, Laurence	MNT	55
Younglove, Elihu	ONT	432	Youngs, William	SRA	22	Zimmermon, Andreo	NYK	85
Younglove, John	WSH	191	Youngs, William	WSH	211	Zion, Elias	GRN	357
Younglove, Joseph	WSH	187	Yourck, Hermanus	ULS	212	Zittle, Walkert	MNT	112
Younglove, Lucas	WSH	191	Yourks, Nicholas	ORN	300	Zoble, Wm	MNT	27
Younglove, Moses	COL	210	Yucker, George	MNT	16	Zoler, Henry A.	MNT	27
Younglove, Timothy	ONT	432	Yucker, Solomon	MNT	16	Zoles, Solomon	ONN	192
Youngs, Abm	ALB	91	Yule, James	HRK	428	Zoller, Henry J.	MNT	27
Youngs, Abraham	COL	242	Yumans, Benjamin	ORN	384	Zont, Henry	GRN	326
Youngs, Alexander	DUT	123	Yumans, Jacob	DUT	85	Zopher	SUF	90
Youngs, Alexander	ULS	233	Yumans, James	DUT	75	Zopher, Elizabeth	SUF	82
Youngs, Benjn	SUF	72	Yumans, John	ORN	384	Zowe, Samuel	CHN	884
Youngs, Calvin	OND	172	Yumans, John	ULS	196	Zufeld, Christopher	SCH	133
Youngs, Christian	CAY	608	Yumans, Johnson	DUT	89	Zufeld, John C.	SCH	133
Youngs, Christipher	SUF	72	Yumans, Moses	ULS	227	Zufeld, William	SCH	133
Youngs, Christopher	OTS	56	Yumans, Nathan	ORN	387	Zuntz, Alexander	NYK	24
Youngs, Clement	OTS	27	Yumans, Rachel	DUT	89			
Youngs, Daniel	QNS	80	Yumans, William	DUT	84	?		
Youngs, Danl	SUF	66	Yvonett, Francis	RNS	92			
Youngs, Danl	SUF	72				_____, ze	ALB	12
Youngs, Danl	SUF	77	Z			_ough, Charles	ALB	27
Youngs, Danl Jr	SUF	72	Zabriskie, Christian	CAY	618	_ckles, John	ALB	33
Youngs, David	ALB	79	Zabriskie, George	ORN	324	_illing, John	ALB	40
Youngs, Elenuel	SUF	77	Zagar, John	ALB	149	_lton, John	ALB	54
Youngs, Elizabeth	ULS	181	Zah, Jost	ALB	74	_nedy, Henderick	ALB	58
Youngs, Frederick	SRA	14	Zah, Peter	ALB	74	_is eran, Henry	ALB	69
Youngs, George	MNT	94	Zar, Parker	WST	138	_a na , Andrew	ALB	113
Youngs, Isaac	SRA	9	Zarissee, Laurence	NYK	113	_ison, James	ALB	120
Youngs, Isaac	SRA	53	Zea, Adam	SCH	172	_oper, Jeremiah	CAY	516
Youngs, Isaac	SUF	81	Zea, Christian	ALB	75	_oodruff, Charles	CAY	528
Youngs, Israel	SUF	74	Zea, David	SCH	152	[Se?]eley, Jonas	CAY	534
Youngs, Jacob	ONT	394	Zea, Henry	ALB	75	_adger, Elisha	CAY	536
You.gs, Jacob	WST	129	Zea, Jost	SCH	126	...burt, ...	CAY	540
Youngs, James	RNS	6	Zebra, Bristor a			.allock, ... Jun	CAY	540
Youngs, James	SRA	58	free Negro	ALB	88	....in(?), ...	CAY	540
Youngs, James	SUF	73	Zebulon	QNS	80	...w .., ...	CAY	540
Youngs, James	WST	129	Zebulon	SUF	81	[B?]aily, ...	CAY	540
Youngs, Jeremiah	SUF	73	Zedediah, Agnes	MNT	66	....y, Jacob	CAY	544
Youngs, Jeremiah	SUF	77	Zeeman, Dirck	ALB	128	....e, Tomkins	CAY	546
Youngs, Joel Y rks	WST	171	Zegar see Begar			[Smith?], Joseph	CAY	546
Youngs, John	COL	243	Zegar, Frederick	ALB	58	....in, Samuel	CAY	546
Youngs, John	GRN	353	Zegar, John	ALB	18	......, N(?)	CAY	546
Youngs, John	OND	168	Zegar, Peter	ALB	17	[Ho?]..., John	CAY	546
Youngs, John	QNS	83	Zegar, Peter	ALB	99	....ant, Nicholas	CAY	546
Youngs, John	SRA	6	Zeilie, David	SCH	130	....er, Rebecca	CAY	546
Youngs, John	SUF	76	Zeilie, Levi	SCH	134	....er, Abraham	CAY	546
Youngs, Jonathan	SUF	77	Zeilie, Martinus	SCH	130	..nlap, Robert	CAY	546
Youngs, Joseph	MNT	107	Zeilie, Robert	SCH	134	..nlap, John	CAY	546
Youngs, Joseph	OTS	42	Zeller, Casper	NYK	148	......, William	CAY	546
Youngs, Joseph	SUF	93	Zelmac, Johnson a			......, Jaune	CAY	546
Youngs, Luther	SUF	72	Black	NYK	127	_t, Joseph	CAY	554
Youngs, Luther	SUF	72	Zeluf, Peter	RCH	88	....., Daniel	CAY	556
Youngs, Margaret	ALB	29	Zeluf, Solomon	RCH	88	ert, Coonrad	CAY	564
Youngs, Margaret	DUT	25	Zenits, Philip	MNT	69	[Il?]let, Joel	CAY	568
Youngs, Margaret	ULS	187	Zenus, Franzer	MNT	67	___n, Samuel	CAY	572
Youngs, Naomi	SUF	87	Zenus, Fraser	MNT	69	_, John	CAY	576
Youngs, Necholas	MNT	105	Zider, Nathan	CHN	844	[Strong?], Amos	CAY	588